NEW TESTAMENT EPISTLES

1 CORINTHIANS

A CRITICAL AND EXEGETICAL COMMENTARY

_____ by _____

GARETH L. REESE

HEAD OF NEW TESTAMENT DEPARTMENT
CENTRAL CHRISTIAN COLLEGE OF THE BIBLE
MOBERLY, MISSOURI

Scripture Exposition Books, LLC
803 McKINSEY PLACE
MOBERLY, MISSOURI
65270

Copyright © 2004 by Scripture Exposition Books
Corrected edition printed in 2013

The information in this book is intended for personal study, for classroom and pulpit use by Bible students and teachers. Therefore, readers who wish to reproduce any of the comments or special studies in the form of free handouts to students or listeners or in sermon outlines as they are being preached are encouraged to do so with no need to seek prior permission. We ask that you simply include a line giving credit to the source you have copied. No other reproduction of this book in any form or by any means is allowed without prior written permission from the publisher.

Acknowledgments

The Scripture quotations contained herein, unless otherwise noted, are from the New American Standard Bible, copyrighted 1960, 1962, 1963, 1971, 1972, 1975, 1977, 1995 by the Lockman Foundation. Used by permission.

Suggested Cataloging Data

Reese, Gareth L., 1932-
    New Testament Epistles: 1 Corinthians, a critical and exegetical commentary / by Gareth L. Reese. Moberly, MO: Scripture Exposition Books, 2004, 2013.

    [xv], 32, 811 p. : ill., map. ; 26 cm. – (New Testament Epistles)
    Includes bibliographical references and index.
    ISBN 0-971-76525-1

  1. Bible. N.T. Corinthians, 1st – Commentaries. I. Title
  II. Series.

BS 2675.53.R259 2013

PREFACE

Interest in and attention to 1 Corinthians has ebbed and flowed through the ages of church history. When issues assail the church to which this letter speaks, interest revives. As the 21st century dawns, it is time to hear this timeless letter again. It is hoped that this volume will help arouse attention to 1 Corinthians so our generation will open it up and let it speak to us and direct our thoughts and lives.

What contemporary issues require its input? There are controversial matters that tend to polarize congregations into competing factions – worship styles, charismatic gifts, women's opportunities for ministry, the Lord's Supper relegated to a side room. There are lifestyles needing the corrective of the Word – homosexuality, litigiousness, sexual immorality, sky-rocketing divorce rates, the "right" to live my life the way I want to! Issues faced by missionaries in third-world cultures are still relevantly dealt with in 1 Corinthians – meats offered to idols, mixed marriages, importing old pagan ideas into new church settings.

Peter long ago noted that Paul's letters have some things in them that are difficult to understand (2 Peter 3:15ff). Peter's observation is certainly true of 1 Corinthians. Nevertheless, the study of this letter can be intensely rewarding. To help the reader better understand Paul's flow of thought, summaries giving an overview of each major section begin the comments on those units. To help modern readers apply the Scriptures to contemporary issues on which the Scriptures do not seemingly speak, special attention is given to the principles on which such issues may be decided.

A word about the text and the intended audience. The English Text chosen as the basis of this commentary is the NASB. There are two reasons for this choice: (1) it is one of the best translations available in English, and (2) it is the text used in classes at Central Christian College so that all of us, teachers and students alike, have the same text open as we read, study, discuss, and memorize. Three different groups comprise the intended audience for this work – college students, busy preachers, and serious Bible students. This book is a tool a Bible college student can use. This commentator has deliberately avoided trying to force the material into a social-science or rhetorical critical pattern, as though these modern methods of academic interpretation would enlighten. Commentaries that have done this recently have left the reader with little solid awareness of what Paul wrote. Effort has been made to avoid technical jargon (save for an occasional footnote) that academics delight to employ, and to use words in the body of the text the average reader can understand. Footnotes will direct the student who wishes to dig deeper to further resources. It is a tool the busy preacher can use to prepare for Bible Study classes, or to grasp the meaning of the text in preparation for preaching an expository sermon. It is a tool the layman can use to grasp what the letter says. Similar situations in the 21st century are to be solved just as those situations were solved in the 1st century. "Do you understand what you are reading?" Philip asked of the Ethiopian. Philip explained the passage and the Ethiopian's life was changed. It is the author's prayer that this book will help those who read 1 Corinthians to understand what God is saying in this wonderful letter.

The comments offered on 1 Corinthians are the result of years of study and teaching. Two separate college courses – one from George Mark Elliott and one from Merrill C. Tenney – covered the book, introduced its problem passages, and whetted a desire to know and understand more. I have taught a class on 1 Corinthians numerous times to college students who were preparing to become future church leaders, and I have preached from it in a variety of contexts. It is my custom to read one new commentary on the material each time I teach the course. At certain places in the study each year, sharp students tend to ask the same difficult questions. Over the years, teaching notes are added or revised, alternative interpretations considered, and students' insights recorded; if those teaching notations are not carefully documented at the time they are added to the teacher's notebook, it can become difficult to know what material derived from what source. This author certainly has endeavored in specific matters to cite credit where it is due. I am greatly indebted to those commentaries to which reference is made in the footnotes. While some of the undocumented comments are original, some of the sentences in this book are compositions made up of choice vocabulary words and insightful thoughts that have been gathered from numerous sources over nearly half-a-century of study of 1 Corinthians, and used so many times they have become a part of the author's thinking and speech patterns.

It is the author's hope and prayer that men and women will be blessed and nourished as they undertake a study of 1 Corinthians with the aid of this commentary. Much of what God said through Paul in this letter was ignored by the Corinthian church, to their loss. We ignore it to our loss, too! Perhaps each reader could memorize chapters 13 and 15 as well as certain other verses that are full of exhortation and guidance.

Moberly, Mo., June 30, 2004

Dedication

To KATHLEEN, my wife

*Who keeps pointing the way
to Jesus and Home, and while we
journey on together keeps
encouraging me to write.*

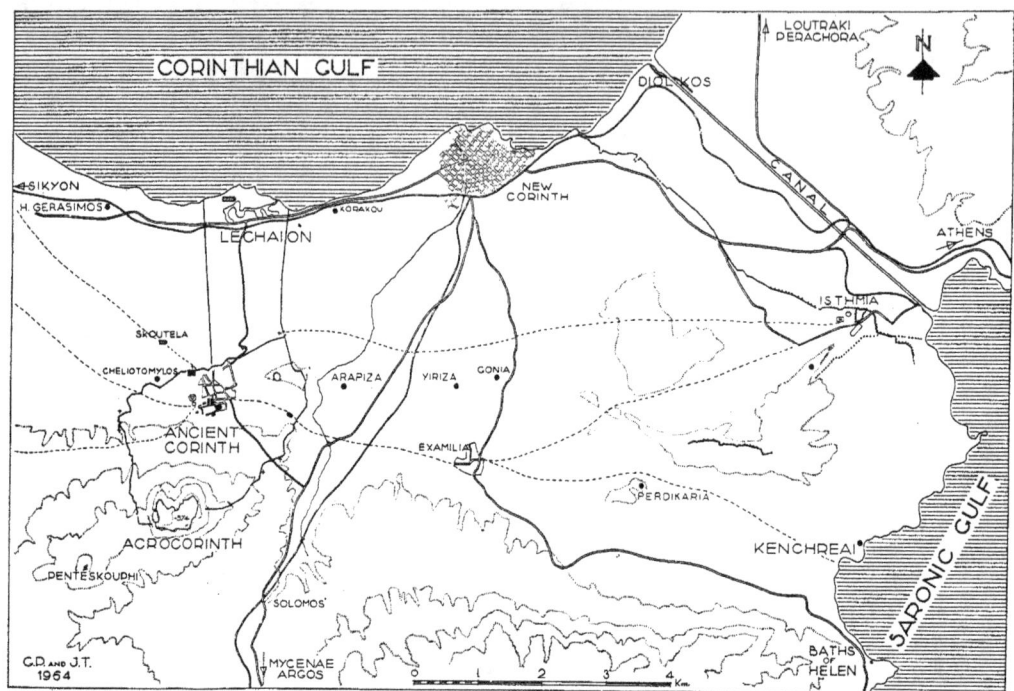

PLAN OF THE CORINTHIA

Courtesy of the American School of Classical Studies at Athens

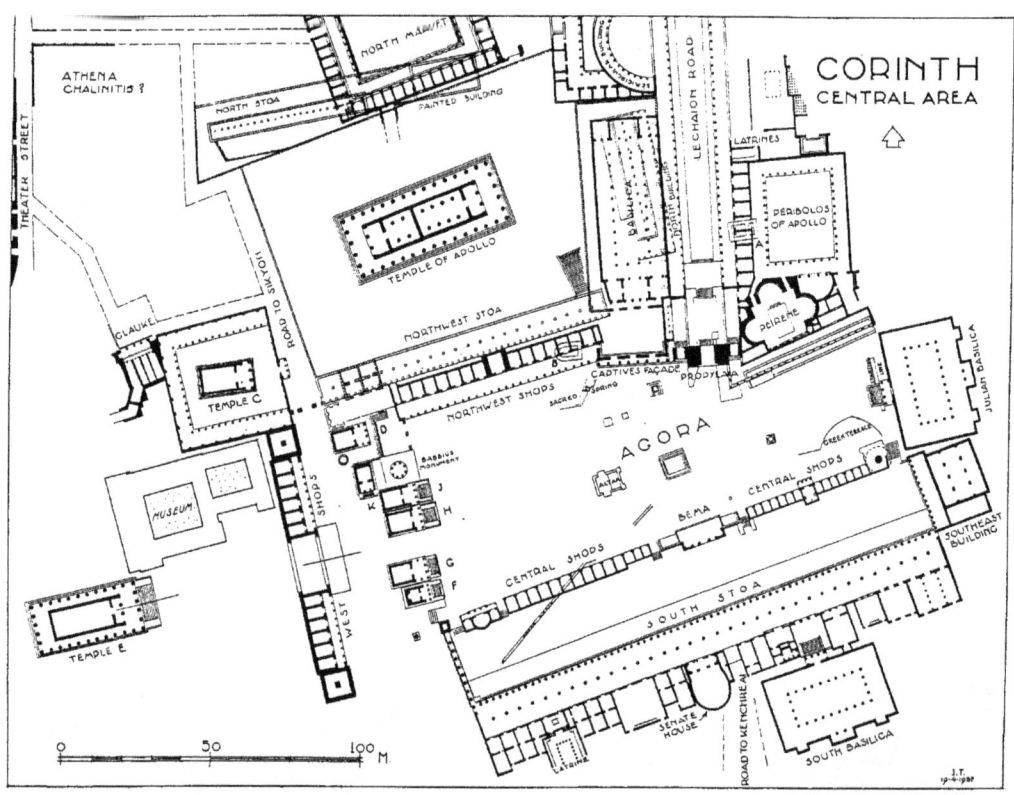

PLAN OF THE CENTRAL AREA OF CORINTH

Courtesy of the American School of Classical Studies at Athens

TABLE OF CONTENTS

Introductory Studies
                                                              Page

A. Historical Allusions 1
B. Information from the Book of Acts 3
C. Authorship and Attestation 6
D. The Integrity of 1 Corinthians 9
E. The Text of 1 Corinthians 9
F. The Inspiration of 1 Corinthians 10
G. The City of Corinth 10
H. The Church at Corinth 14
I. The Communication Between Paul and the Corinthian Christians 17
J. Paul's Visits to Corinth 22
K. Occasion of Writing 22
L. Purpose of Writing 22
M. Time and Place of Writing 23
N. The Placement of 1 Corinthians in the New Testament 23
O. History and Influence of this Letter 24
P. Range of Problems Embraced in 1 Corinthians 27
Q. Outline of 1 Corinthians 28

Commentary

Chapter 1 1
      Special Study #1: The Message of the Cross 58
Chapter 2 61
Chapter 3 91
Chapter 4 121
Chapter 5 151
      Special Study #2: Church Discipline at Corinth and Elsewhere 171
Chapter 6 175
      Special Study #3: Here I Stand, so Help Me God! 206
Chapter 7 220
      Special Study #4: Who Are the Virgins? 270
Chapter 8 272
      Special Study #5: "Who Do you say I Am?" The Deity of Jesus 291
Chapter 9 297
Chapter 10 329
Chapter 11 367
Chapter 12 419
Chapter 13 461

TABLE OF CONTENTS, cont.

	Page
Chapter 14	488
Special Study #6: Worship in the New Testament	547
Chapter 15	573
Special Study #7: He is Alive! You Had Better Believe It!	664
Special Study #8: Baptized for the Dead	684
Special Study #9: Is Man Immortal?	692
Chapter 16	697
Special Study #10: Do All Speak in Tongues and The Joy of the Holy Spirit	731
Bibliography	771
Index	789

THE PAULINE EPISTLES: GROUP TWO [1]

1 Corinthians

INTRODUCTORY STUDIES

A. HISTORICAL ALLUSIONS

As we study these historical allusions, we are looking for anything that will help us answer questions about the author, date, destination, and purpose of this letter.

1. Historical allusions in the beginning of the letter -- 1:1-16

a. 1:1,2 -- Paul signs the letter. Sosthenes is with Paul when Paul writes the letter. The letter is addressed to the church at Corinth. This gives us some help with the date of the letter. Who is Paul, and when did he live? When would he write a letter to Corinth? When did there come to be a church at Corinth? The letter is also addressed to all who call upon the name of the Lord. The letter is intended for other readers than just those who assembled on the Lord's Day in the city of Corinth.

b. 1:3 and 1:4-10 -- These verses contain the usual Pauline greeting and the usual Pauline thanksgiving. In these thanksgivings, Paul usually gives thanks to God for various spiritual advances and works done by those addressed. Compare 1 Thessalonians 1:3-8 and 2 Thessalonians 1:3,4. But in 1 Corinthians, there is no thanks for what is being done *at Corinth*. Paul is not thankful for the divisions, the disorder at the Lord's Table, the litigation, etc. But he does thank God that His grace has been given to the church.

c. 1:11 -- Information about the church at Corinth has come to Paul from Chloe's household, and Paul writes to correct what he has heard.

d. 1:12 -- Peter and Apollos apparently have been to Corinth since the church was established by Paul. This gives us help with the dating of the letter.

e. 1:14 -- Crispus and Gaius have been baptized by Paul.

2. Historical allusions at the close of the letter -- 16:1ff

a. 16:1 -- Instruction has been given to the Galatian churches about an offering being collected for the church at Jerusalem.

---

[1] Group Two of Paul's epistles includes 1 & 2 Corinthians, Galatians and Romans. While some emphasize the technical distinction between "epistle" and "letter," this commentator uses the terms interchangeably.

b. 16:1-4 -- Paul indicates he will come to Corinth on his way to Jerusalem, and he gives instructions to the Corinthians concerning their participation in the offering for Jerusalem. The Corinthians were to choose men from their own congregation to carry their offering; if done in this manner, none could accuse Paul of lining his own pocket. Verse 4 seems to indicate that if the offering is generous enough, Paul will accompany it to Jerusalem. (Or, it may be that if the Holy Spirit so led, he would go to Jerusalem with the offering.)

c. 16:5-9 -- Compare the subscription with what these verses say.[2] The subscription reads, "The first epistle to the Corinthians was written from Philippi by Stephanas, and Fortunatus, and Achaicus, and Timotheus." Verse 5 speaks of Paul's intentions to pass through Macedonia, and it is apparently from a misunderstanding of the verse that this subscription was taken. The King James Version translators evidently read the verse, "I am *now* passing through Macedonia," whereas Paul meant, "I *intend* to pass through Macedonia." Verse 6 gives Paul's intention of spending the winter with the brethren in Corinth (i.e., about three months). Verse 7 tells of Paul's wish to spend time with them, rather than making a hurried, passing visit. Verse 8 tells us that Paul is in Ephesus when he writes, and that he writes just some months before Pentecost. Verse 9 speaks of the good opportunity he has to preach and teach in Ephesus, but also of the adversaries to the work.

d. 16:10 -- Timothy had been sent to Corinth before the writing of the letter. Compare 1 Corinthians 4:17. We know of a time that Timothy had been at Corinth. Both 1 and 2 Thessalonians were written from Corinth, and Timothy was with Paul when these two letters were written in AD 51-52. This present letter to Corinth merely states that Timothy is expected to arrive in Corinth soon (i.e., Paul expected the letter to get there before Timothy did). While this 1 Corinthian letter is being written, Timothy is not with Paul, but Sosthenes is.

e. 16:11 -- Subsequent to his anticipated visit to Corinth, Timothy is expected to return to Paul and report what he has learned and been able to accomplish.

f. 16:12 -- Before 1 Corinthians was written, Paul has urged Apollos to go to Corinth, apparently to help straighten out the problems at Corinth. It may be the Corinthians had requested Paul to ask Apollos to come to Corinth again (cf. the formula, "Now as touching Apollos ..."). Since his earlier ministry in Corinth, Apollos appears to have left Corinth and joined Paul in or near Ephesus. He may have been preaching in one of the cities of Asia Minor, helping to carry on a province-wide evangelistic campaign, as was Paul's custom. It was Paul's wish that Apollos accompany the bearers of this letter back to Corinth, and use his endeavors to help heal the distractions that had arisen, but Apollos had refused to go. As to why Apollos refused, we can only guess. Perhaps it may have been that he feared his presence would only foment, rather than allay, the dissension. Perhaps it may have been that he was in the midst of a church planting venture, and was not able to

---

[2] In our English versions, subscriptions are regularly found in the KJV. The part that reads "by ..." refers to the ones who carried the epistle to its destination, rather than to the person or persons thought to have written the letter.

Introduction, page 3

leave without hurting that work. Paul goes on to indicate that in due time Apollos will come.

g. 16:17 -- Stephanas, Fortunatus, and Achaicus have just come to Paul and "supplied that which was lacking." Just what is intended by this is not certain. Perhaps Paul was longing for fellowship from Corinth, and these brethren from Corinth filled his desire. Perhaps it may be that these three carried the letter referred to in 7:1, and filled in the details for Paul (details not quite clear in the letter). In verse 15, Stephanas is characterized as "the first-fruits of Achaia."

h. 16:19 -- "The churches of Asia greet you," Paul writes. Paul is somewhere in the Roman province of Asia when the letter is written. If they were located in the major cities, the churches of Asia would be the seven churches of Revelation (Ephesus, Smyrna, Pergamos, Thyatira, Sardis, Philadelphia, Laodicea) plus Troas, Colossae, and Hierapolis. When this verse is compared with 16:8, it gives further evidence that Paul is in Ephesus when he writes. "Aquila and Priscilla greet you ..., [and so does] the church that is in their house." Acts 18:18ff likely places Aquila and Priscilla in Ephesus at this juncture.

i. 16:21 -- Paul signs this letter. Compare 2 Thessalonians 3:17. Paul puts a few words of benediction at the close of the letter in his own handwriting.

j. 16:22 -- Anathema ("Let him be accursed"). Maranatha ("the Lord has come," "O Lord come!" or "Let the Lord come").

3. Other historical allusions in the epistle

a. 5:6-8 -- Paul is perhaps writing right at the Passover season.

b. 5:9 -- Did Paul write a letter to Corinth previous to the one we now call 1 Corinthians?

c. 7:1 -- The Corinthians had written a letter to Paul. Here he begins to answer some questions they have asked of him.

d. 11:34 -- Paul is intending to come to Corinth shortly.

B. INFORMATION FROM THE BOOK OF ACTS

a. 18:1 -- On the Second Missionary Journey, Paul, leaving Athens, comes to Corinth.

b. 18:2 -- Aquila and Priscilla had recently been driven out of Rome. Whether these two were Christians before they met Paul at Corinth is not known, but it seems likely they were. When Claudius gave his edict, both Christians and Jews would have been included, for the

Romans made no distinction between Jews and Christians at this early time. Paul joined himself to this family, and worked at his trade of tent-making with them.

c. 18:4 -- Paul first went to the Jews, teaching them in the synagogues, as he attempted to evangelize them. After Silas and Timothy came from Macedonia to Corinth, Paul spent his whole time preaching. The unbelieving Jews took offense to Paul's message, and contradicted him and blasphemed.

d. 18:7 -- Paul than began to use the home of Titius Justus, located next to the synagogue, as his site for teaching. Crispus, the chief ruler of the synagogue, was converted (cp. 1 Corinthians 1:14). The church in Corinth grew. Many from the poorer classes were converted (1 Corinthians 1:26).

e. 18:11 -- Paul stayed in Corinth a year and six months.

f. 18:12 -- Unconverted Jews drag Paul to Gallio's judgment seat and accuse him. Gallio was proconsul in the year AD 51, according to an inscription found at Delphi in 1908 [SIG II^3.801]. See Jerome Murphy-O'Connor, *Corinth*, for wording of the inscription. July 1 was the time of year when newly appointed proconsuls took office. Mare thinks the Gallio inscription has Gallio in office in the first half of AD 52, and thus he must have begun his proconsulship on July 1, AD 51.[3] Mare also has Paul arriving in Corinth in the fall of AD 50, so that he can be there for a year and a half before his trial before Gallio. If Mare is correct, we'll have to change some of the dates on our accepted chronology of the Apostolic Age, which has the Jerusalem Conference in AD 51, and Paul's arrival in Corinth at a date later than that conference. Apparently Gallio had just become proconsul, and perhaps the Jews thought to take advantage of his inexperience as they dragged Paul before him. It didn't work. Gallio threw the case out of court.

g. 18:17 -- One "Sosthenes" is mentioned as being the ruler of the synagogue when Paul was tried before Gallio. We suppose he was elected ruler after Crispus converted to Christianity. When the trial went against the unbelieving Jews, some men grabbed Sosthenes and beat him. Now we have noted that a "Sosthenes" is with Paul when 1 Corinthians is written. Whether these two are the same man is not known with certainty, but it may well be that the beating started Sosthenes on the way to becoming a Christian.

h. 18:18ff -- Some days after the trial, Paul left Corinth, went to Jerusalem, and from thence to Antioch, thus ending his Second Missionary Journey. While on the way from Corinth to Jerusalem, he left Aquila and Priscilla at Ephesus as a sort of advance team to prepare for the coming Ephesian crusade. 1 Corinthians 16:19 includes a greeting to the Corinthian church from Aquila and Priscilla, likely from this location at Ephesus.

i. 18:24 -- Apollos comes to Ephesus. Apollos was from Alexandria, and was an eloquent

---

[3] W. Harold Mare, "1 Corinthians," in *Expositor's Bible Commentary* (Grand Rapids: Zondervan, 1976), Vol. 10, p.176.

preacher. He knew only the baptism of John. Priscilla and Aquila took him home and taught him the way of the Lord more perfectly. According to Acts 18:27, Apollos went from Ephesus to Corinth, and a church letter (i.e., a letter of introduction or recommendation) was sent with him. (On a different occasion, a similar letter of introduction was sent with Phoebe also, Romans 16:1.) After he arrived at Corinth, Apollos helped them much and the church was edified.

j. 19:1 -- At this juncture, Paul arrives in Ephesus in the midst of his Third Missionary Journey. Apollos at this time is in Corinth. Arriving at Ephesus, Paul taught some who knew only the baptism of John. Verse 8 -- He entered into the synagogue and taught there for three months. Verse 9 -- When he was no longer allowed to speak in the synagogue, he taught in the school of Tyrannus. He continued there in Ephesus for two years.

k. 19:21 -- Paul purposes to go through Macedonia to Jerusalem, then to Rome. Verse 22 -- Timothy is sent through Macedonia, while Paul stays longer at Ephesus. This fits with 1 Corinthians 16:10 and 4:17, where Paul indicates that before 1 Corinthians was written Timothy had been sent away on a missionary trip. Erastus accompanied Timothy, and it is most probable that it was the particular task of Timothy and Erastus to promote the collection being made for the relief of the Jerusalem church. Verse 23ff tells of the riot of Demetrius and the silversmiths at Ephesus. Could these men be some of the adversaries mentioned in 1 Corinthians 16:9? Paul expected to stay at Ephesus until Pentecost (1 Corinthians 16:8,19). Did the riot cut his stay short? When he first made his plans, Paul had not foreseen the riot. (To say Paul left Ephesus before Pentecost raises problems of chronology. This commentator has doubts that Paul's stay was cut short by the riot.)

A brief review of events between AD 56 and AD 60 may be helpful, though the calendar of months is only tentative at best. (a) **AD 56**, Sept. or Oct. (?) – Titus is sent to Corinth to start the offering for the poor saints at Jerusalem. 2 Corinthians 8:10 tells us that a year previous to the writing of 2 Corinthians, the Corinthian church desired to take up the offering. They were the first church to want to do so, and the first to actually begin to collect funds. With all their faults, there were still many good points about the church. At the same time (see Acts 19:22, 1 Corinthians 4:17, 16:10) Timothy and Erastus were sent to Macedonia, for the same purpose. (b) **AD 57**, April – Near Passover time, 1 Corinthians is written (cp. 16:8 and 5:7). In early May (?), Timothy arrives at Corinth, but is unable to deal with the situation, so Timothy goes from Corinth to Ephesus to report to Paul. In late May, Paul makes an "intermediate trip" to Corinth, and returns to Ephesus. Paul was "humbled" on this trip (2 Corinthians 12:21). In early June, Titus is sent to Corinth to deal with the crisis in the church, and eventually was successful (2 Corinthians 7:14-16). In June, about the day Pentecost was celebrated, the riot in Ephesus occurred (Acts 19:23-41), so Paul leaves Ephesus (Acts 20:1). In August and September (?), Paul waits for Titus at Troas (2 Corinthians 2:12,13). From October to December, prior to his arrival in Corinth, Paul had been working in Macedonia (Acts 20:1). During this period, 2 Corinthians and Galatians are written from Macedonia. (c) **AD 58**, January to March – Paul winters in Corinth (Acts 20:3). Romans is written from Corinth. Then about Passover time, Paul is in Philippi, just beginning his trip to Jerusalem, with the offering for the poor (Acts 20:6). By Pentecost, Paul arrives in Jerusalem (Acts 21:27ff). He had hoped to be in Jerusalem before Pentecost (Acts 20:16). At this time Paul is arrested, and a two-year imprisonment at Caesarea begins. (d) **AD 60** – Festus becomes governor in Felix's place (Acts 24:25).

Now, we can return to our brief overview of this period of Paul's life as given in the history book called Acts.

l. 20:1 -- Paul goes to Macedonia. As noted above, in 2 Corinthians we learn Paul waited at Troas for Titus to return from Corinth. Titus was to travel through Macedonia on his way to join and report to Paul. When Titus did not come as soon as expected, Paul passed over into Macedonia in order to cut down the length of time spent waiting. There Titus met him. Titus reported on how things at Corinth were going; in reply to this report, Paul wrote 2 Corinthians from Macedonia. Within a month of two of sending 2 Corinthians to Corinth, Paul himself goes to Greece (Corinth) where he stayed three months. Compare 1 Corinthians 16:6.

m. Acts 20:4 -- This records the start of the journey to Jerusalem with the offering for the church. The men listed are most probably carrying the offering (cp. 1 Corinthians 16:3,4).

n. *Conclusions.* (a) 1 Corinthians was written sometime between the founding of the church in Corinth (Acts 16:1 and 1 Corinthians 1:1) and the taking of the offering to Jerusalem (Acts 20:3, cp. 1 Corinthians 16:3,4). The offering was delivered at the close of Paul's Third Missionary Journey. The dates we have given to the journey are AD 54-58. (b) It was written while Paul was in Ephesus (1 Corinthians 16:8). If the above calendar is correct, the date for the writing of 1 Corinthians is AD 57, around Passover time, one year before the offering is delivered to Jerusalem.[4]

C. AUTHORSHIP AND ATTESTATION

Almost all Biblical scholars consider 1 Corinthians to be genuine. A book is "genuine" when it was written by the author named in it or when written by the author to whom it is attributed (i.e., 1 Corinthians is genuine only if Paul wrote it). Even the Tubingen school has not questioned the genuineness of 1 Corinthians, nor 2 Corinthians, nor Romans or Galatians, for that matter.

---

[4] Paul was twice in Ephesus between the founding of the Corinthian church and the end of the Third Missionary Journey in Jerusalem. The first time, Acts 18:19-21, was toward the close of the Second Missionary Journey, when Paul passed through Ephesus, leaving Aquila and Priscilla. The second time, Acts 19, Paul stayed in Ephesus for two or three years in the midst of his Third Missionary Journey. Which of these gives the events that fit with the information found in 1 Corinthians? We learn from 1 Corinthians that this letter was written after Timothy had been sent away from Paul and after Apollos had been to Corinth. Acts 19:22 tells of Timothy being sent away from Ephesus. Acts 18:24 tells of Apollos coming to Ephesus. From this, it becomes certain the letter was written during the Third Missionary Journey, during Paul's two or three year stay at Ephesus.

Internal evidence for authorship. Paul twice signs his name to the epistle, at 1:1 and 16:21. The style of Paul is also clearly evident. The mind of the great apostle is stamped on the composition with undeniable clearness.

External evidence for authorship. This is the first New Testament epistle cited by name in Early Christian Literature.

a. Allusions[5]

   1) Ignatius (AD 115)

"It is becoming, therefore, that in every way you should glorify Jesus Christ, who hath glorified you, that in one obedience ye may be perfectly joined together in the same mind and in the same judgment, and may all speak the same thing of the same thing." (*Ad. Ephes.* c.2) (1 Corinthians 1:10)

"The cross, which is a stumbling block to unbelievers, but to us salvation and eternal life. Where is the wise? Where is the disputer? Where is the boasting of them who are called prudent?" (*Ad. Ephes.* c.8) (1 Corinthians 1:18)

Ignatius also alludes to 1 Corinthians 4:4 (*Ep. ad Rome*), 5:7 (*Ep. ad Magnes.*), and 6:9,10 (*Ep. ad Eph.*).

   2) Justin Martyr (AD 150)

"For Christ was the passover who was afterwards sacrificed for us" (*Dial c. Tryph.* xxxv) (1 Corinthians 5:7).

   3) Epistle of Barnabas (AD 130)

There may be an allusion to 1 Corinthians 3:1,16 in chapter iv. "The habitation of our heart is an holy temple to the Lord."

   4) The Didache (AD 140)

The allusion here is to 1 Corinthians 16:22 (cf. ch. x).

   5) Shepherd of Hermas (AD 140)

"If therefore a man or woman perseveres in anything of this kind and repents not; depart from here, and live not with her; otherwise thou also shalt be partaker of her sin. But it is therefore commanded, that both the man and the woman should remain unmarried, because such persons may repent." (*Sim.* v.7) (1 Corinthians 7:11)

---

[5] An allusion is a reference that shows the passage or book being quoted exists. Ideas from the book are quoted, or paraphrased, without citing the author or the source.

b. Quotations[6]

1) Clement of Rome (AD 96)

"Take up the epistle of the blessed Paul the apostle. What did he first write to you in the beginning of the gospel? Of a truth, he wrote to you by the Spirit concerning himself, and Cephas, and Apollos, because you had even then formed parties." (*Ep. Ad. Corinth.* c.47)

There are also quotations and citations of 1 Corinthians 10:24, 12:12, 13:4, and 15:20. The very preservation of such a letter by the Corinthian church is strong evidence of authenticity. No church would accept, without careful scrutiny, so public a monument of its degradation.

2) Polycarp (AD 115)

"Do we not know that the saints shall judge the world, as Paul teaches?" (*Ad. Philippians.* c.11) (1 Corinthians 6:2)

Polycarp also cites 1 Corinthians 11:9.

3) Irenaeus (AD 180)

"This also the Apostle Paul manifestly shows in the epistle addressed to the Corinthians, saying 'Moreover, brethren, I would not that ye should be ignorant, how that all our fathers were under the cloud ...'" (*Adv. Haeres.* iv.27) (1 Corinthians 10:1)

4) Athenagoras

"It is manifest therefore that according to the apostle this corruptible must put on incorruption." (*De Resurrect. Mort.*)

5) Clement of Alexandria (AD 190)

"The blessed Paul, in the first epistle to the Corinthians, has solved the inquiry, when he writes thus. Brethren, be not children in understanding ...." (*Paedag.*)

6) Tertullian (AD 200)

"Paul, in the first epistle to the Corinthians, speaks of them who denied or doubted the resurrection." (*De Praescript.*)

---

[6] In quotations, unlike allusions, the author and/or the source is definitely named.

7) Cyprian (AD 245)

"In the first epistle of Paul to the Corinthians, 'Moreover, I would not that ye should be ignorant, how that all our fathers were under the cloud ....'" (*Testim*. lib. i.c 4) (1 Corinthians 10:1)

8) Epistle to Diognetus

"The apostle ... says, 'Knowledge puffeth up, but charity edifieth.'" (*Justini Opp.*)

The external evidence is abundant and continuous from the 1st century onward. None of Paul's other letters appears to have been quoted as widely and as early as 1 Corinthians. In the Muratorian Fragment, and in some other lists, it is the first of Paul's letters listed. No satisfactory reason has been given for this, but clearly it indicates something of the importance attached to 1 Corinthians.

Internal and external evidence both point to the conclusion that Paul is the author of 1 Corinthians. This conclusion is generally accepted by both liberals and conservatives.

D. THE INTEGRITY OF 1 CORINTHIANS

Integrity has to do with the question of whether all of a work was written by the same author at the same time. 1 Corinthians is generally held to enjoy integrity. Occasionally, critics have suspected interpolations, but not often, and then the reasons they have put forward have not commended themselves. J. Weiss, for example, suggested that a number of writings have been combined to form our epistle, but he has found few followers. We must not expect in a letter (and 1 Corinthians reads very much like an original letter) the same orderly classification of topics as in a theological treatise. As Moffatt says (quoted by Leon Morris, *Tyndale Commentaries* "The First Epistle of Paul to the Corinthians" (Grand Rapids, MI: Wm. B. Eerdmans Publishing, 1966, p.28), "If some editor really put together fragments from two or three letters, he has done his work so well that it is beyond our powers to recover their original shape and sequence." There is, then, no reason for doubting that this is a genuine writing of Paul's, and that it is free from any substantial interpolation. Robertson and Plummer say there may occasionally be doubt about a word, "but there is probably no verse or whole clause that is an interpolation" (A.T Robertson and Alfred Plummer, "1 Corinthians" in the *International Critical Commentary*, Edinburgh: T&T Clark, 1953, p.xviii).

E. THE TEXT OF 1 CORINTHIANS

Robertson and Plummer (*op. cit.*, p.54-66) provide an excellent reference for a discussion of the authorities from which the present text of 1 Corinthians has been determined. The complete letter is found in the following Uncial manuscripts: Aleph, A, B, L, and is found relatively complete in C, D, E, F, F^2, etc. It is also found complete in the following cursives: 17, 37, 47, 67. The papyri P^{46}, P^{51}, P^{65} also include 1 Corinthians.

F. THE INSPIRATION OF 1 CORINTHIANS

Paul claims to have the aid of the Holy Spirit as he speaks and writes. See 1 Corinthians 2:6ff, 7:40, and 14:37.

G. THE CITY OF CORINTH

1. Location[7]

Corinth is situated on the Isthmus (the narrow strip of land) connecting the mainland to the Peloponnesus. The city is situated on a tableland 200 feet above sea level. Behind it, on the south, rose the towering Acrocorinth ("hill of Corinth"), a rugged rock, nearly 2000 feet high. The summit was so extensive as to permit buildings to be erected on it. It was grander than the acropolis at Athens. Acrocorinth served as a lookout point for defenders of the city of Corinth.

Corinth had two harbors.[8] To the east, 8½ miles distant, on the Saronic Gulf, was the town of Cenchrea. To the northwest, 1½ miles distant, on the Corinthian Gulf, was Lechaeum. The Diolkos, or land road, connected the two towns of Cenchrea and Lechaeum. The present-day canal is 75' wide, the water is 26' deep, and its length is about 4 miles; the cut is 260' deep at its highest rise of the terrain of the Isthmus. The present-day canal was not there in Paul's day. Periander the tyrant (c.625-585 BC) planned to cut a canal across the Isthmus. Nero actually began the project. But the canal was not completed until 1893. Until the canal was completed, ships were dragged over the Diolkos on rollers in order to avoid the circumnavigation of Cape Melea. Sailors had a proverb. "If you sail around Cape Melea, have your will made." It was stormy and extremely dangerous sailing. The sailors stayed in Corinth while their ships and their cargoes were being transported across the Diolkos.

2. History

1400 BC -- The Phoenicians were the dominant people in this area of the world. They were sea merchants, importers and traders, importing raw materials such as wood, jewels, textiles, copper, metals, etc. They were manufacturers of things imported. They perhaps traveled as far as Britain, getting tin from the mines of Cornwall. They started a trading post at Corinth. The town became a crossroads for trade (a sort of "Chicago" of the ancient world – combining multiple forms of transport).

1200-600 BC -- *Middle period*, including city-states development. By the time of

---

[7] For ancient descriptions of the city, see Strabo, *Geography* 8.6.20-23 (written ca.7 BC), and Pausanias, *Description of Greece*, Book II: Corinth (written ca. AD 170).

[8] "Two-sea'd Corinth," Horace called the city in *Od.* I.7.

the city-states, trade from the interior was shipped through Corinth, as well as trade from east to west. According to Thucydides, ships of war were first built at Corinth in 664 BC.

600-450 BC -- *Glory*. Sparta was the military power, Corinth the center of world commerce. This is the period of the Persian wars, the battles of Thermopylae and Salamis.

450-350 BC -- *Decline*. Peloponnesian War, Sparta vs. Athens. Athens was defeated. Old Corinth had gained such a reputation for sexual vice that Aristophanes (ca. 450-385 BC) coined the verb *corinthiadzomai* (= to act like a Corinthian, i.e., to commit fornication).[9]

350-196 BC -- *Period of Foreign Domination*. After the battle of Chaeronea, 338 BC, Corinth fell into the hands of Philip of Macedon. In 243 BC, the town was freed from its Macedonian garrison by Aratus, who placed it in the Achaean League. Corinth soon rose to supreme political command of the league. Then the league ventured into foolhardy conflict with Rome. Rome won the war after a brief conflict. In 196 BC, Flamininus, after the Battle of Cynocephalae, proclaimed at Corinth the independence of Greece. Corinth was declared a "free city."

146 BC, L. Mummius defeated the combined forces of Achaia. Corinth, capital of Achaia, was leveled to the ground, her treasures rifled, her buildings burned, her inhabitants massacred. Of the Corinth which fell to the Romans, only 7 Doric columns of the Temple of Apollo, spared by the superstitious demolition squads, remained standing, high and prominent above the marketplace of the later town. For 100 years the city lay in ruins.

In 46 BC, Julius Caesar rebuilt the city from its foundations, gave it the name Julia Corinthus, and peopled it with a colony of Roman army veterans and freedmen from Italy, orientals (including large numbers of Jews), and local Arabs. In due time a new Corinth arose from the old ruins, and it vied in prosperity and political importance with the ancient city that Mummius had destroyed (Aristid. *Op*. 3, p.23). The reason for the rapid growth of new Corinth lay partially in its strategic location for commerce. All the natural ingredients for economic boom were available: the natural defense of the Acrocorinth, adequate water supply from springs, the relationship to Rome, being master of the two harbors for East-West commerce, and the control of the Isthmian games, which ranked just below the Olympian in importance.[10] According to Strabo (8.6.23c), Corinth was repopulated with freedmen from Rome. Since the status of a freedman was just above that of a slave, and since Rome often tended to be overpopulated with such, this was a convenient way for Rome to rid itself of potential trouble on the one hand, and for the freedman to seize an opportunity for socio-economic advancement on the other.[11] Strabo's description some

---

[9] Gordon H. Fee, "The First Epistle to the Corinthians" in *The New International Commentary on the New Testament* (Grand Rapids: Eerdmans, 1987), p.2.

[10] *Ibid.*

[11] *Ibid.*

50 years later makes abundantly clear that prosperity returned to the city almost immediately. Since money attracts people, Corinth quickly experienced a great influx of people from both West and East, along with all the attendant gains and ills of such growth.

The city became a favorite spot of the Roman emperors. Nero displayed his artistic prowess at the Isthmian games, and in a moment of exuberance declared the city free. He, Vespasian, and Hadrian were all patrons of the city, and made it the first city of Greece. It was Caesar's Corinth which Paul visited, almost a century after Julius Caesar had restored the city. So it was a new city – as far as cities in the ancient world were concerned – that Paul visited.

The Roman city of Corinth was ravaged by the Gothic hordes in the 3rd and 4th centuries AD. Alaric the Goth burned the city in AD 395. Its destruction by earthquake in AD 521 prompted Procopius to remark that God was abandoning the Roman Empire. It was refounded by the Emperor Justinian, and held in the Middle Ages by Normans, Venetians, and Turks. The city was sacked by Normans in AD 1147. The ancient site was abandoned in 1858 because of a severe earthquake. A new city was built near the gulf and further to the east.

3. Importance

Corinth was a shipping center.[12] The city was famous for trade and the arts. Corinthian brass – a mixture of gold, silver, and copper – became world famous, and Corinthian capitals and pillars are still known in architecture. There was also a flourishing ceramic industry, and Corinthian pottery was exported widely over the Mediterranean.[13] By AD 27, it had become the greatest city, the busiest city, and the capital of Achaia. It was thus a natural center for an evangelistic effort that would influence a great area. Corinth was the fourth largest city in the empire, with a population of 400,000 or more. It grew this large in about 100 years. Rome (government), Athens (education), and Alexandria (trade), were larger cities. Two-thirds of the population at Corinth was slave.

4. Metropolitan Character (as summed up by Davis-Greenlaw)

It was a center of commerce. It was a melting pot of the races. The bulk of the population was comprised of immigrants from all over the world: Jews, Egyptians, Greeks, Romans, Provincials (from the provinces of Asia Minor). Like Chicago, people of various nationalities settled in different sections of town, creating a sort of melting pot. This very mixed and volatile population would give rise to many differences of opinion about customs, attitudes, and values that would tend to surface in the church where hetero-

---

[12] Thucydides i.13. Cicero *Rep.* i.4.

[13] Pindar *Ol.* xiii.21. Herodotus ii. 167. Pliny xxxiv.3, xxxv.5.

geneous people were closely associated.

It was also a cesspool of immorality.[13] At night it was made hideous by the brawls and lewd songs of drunken revelry. In the daytime its markets and squares swarmed with Jewish peddlers, foreign traders, sailors, soldiers, athletes in training, boxers, wrestlers, charioteers, racing men, betting men, courtesans, slaves, idlers, and parasites of every description. To "behave as a Corinthian" was a proverbial synonym for "living an ungodly, immoral life." The verb "to Corinthianize" meant to have relations with a prostitute.

The population was transient. Sailors waiting for ships to be moved, or cargoes transported across the Diolkos, visited Corinth. Businessmen came, transacted their business, and left.

Nouveaux Riches -- The citizens of Corinth had newly and suddenly become rich, and didn't know what to do with the money.

5. Religions

The primary religion was the worship of Aphrodite, goddess of love and beauty. This was a "mystery religion," a sacramental drama which appealed primarily to the emotions and aimed primarily at producing psychic and mystic effects (sex appeal). The temple of Aphrodite was located on the Acrocorinth. In the old city, 1000 temple prostitutes were in service of the temple. One worshiped by having relations with one of the prostitutes in the temple. The descriptions of Corinth found in ancient writings indicate that there were temples to many other gods in this city, several of which were devoted to Egyptian deities. The fact that Egyptian deities were worshiped there is accounted for by the extensive trade carried on between Corinth and Alexandria. Roman historians said "Not every man should go to Corinth." You had to be of high character to be able to overcome the temptations to sin in that city.

Poseidon, god of the sea; Isis, god of religion; Aesclepius, the god of healing; the Roman emperor were other gods who were also worshiped. The religious expression of Corinth was as diverse as its population. Pausanius describes at least 26 sacred sites (not all were temples) devoted to the "gods many" (the Roman-Greek pantheon) and "lords many" (the mystery cults) mentioned by Paul in 1 Corinthians 8:5. Pausanius does not mention the Jewish synagogue, whose partial lintel with the inscription "synagogue of the Hebrews" has been discovered.[14]

---

[13] Athenaeus vii.281, xiii.543. Alciphron iii.60. Strabo viii.378. Eustath. *Iliad* b. p.220.

[14] Fee, *op. cit.*, p.3.

6. Morals of the people

Drunkenness was common. Roman comedians, in their plays, always represent the Corinthians as drunkards. It was a place of dissipation and debauchery. A visit to this town could have a depressing effect on any man. It was reputed to be the most sinful city in the world. The Aesclepius room in the present museum in Corinth provides mute evidence of the immorality at Corinth. On one wall are a large number of clay votives of human genitals that had been offered to the god for healing of that part of the body, apparently ravaged by venereal disease. Strabo's description of a thousand temple prostitutes who were alleged to have plied their trade at the temple of Aphrodite on the Acrocorinth is a reference to Old Corinth before it was destroyed by Mummius in 146 BC. Sexual sin undoubtedly was rampant in new Corinth, the same kind one would expect in any seaport where money flowed freely and women and men were available.

7. Names for the City

A variety of names was given to Corinth by contemporary writers. "Star of Hellas" and capital of Achaia. Bridge of the Sea. Gates of the Peloponnesus. The light and ornament of Greece. The city of two seas. "The palace of Neptune," Aristides called it. The capital and grace of Greece. The empire in miniature. The eye of Greece.

H. THE CHURCH AT CORINTH

Earlier in these introductory studies, the information from Acts concerning the beginning of the church in Corinth c. AD 52 was reviewed. By the time 1 Corinthians is written about AD 57, something has strained the relationship between Paul and the Christians at Corinth. What that "something" was is debated by modern scholars.

> The difficulty in determining the nature of that situation is intrinsic to the text. Paul addresses, in response to reports (1:11, 5:1, 11:18) or to their letter (cf. 7:1), at least eleven different, somewhat disparate concerns, ten of which are behavioral; only chapter 15 is theological as such, and even there he concludes both major sections with ethical warnings and imperatives (verses 33-34,58). But in every case his greater concern is the theological stance behind the behavior. Our difficulty at this distance is threefold: (1) to discover the relationship, if indeed there is one, of these various items to one another; (2) to determine the relationship of the community to Paul; and (3) to determine what influences/positions in the Corinthian 'theology' allowed them not only to adopt such behavior but also to argue for the right to do it.[15]

Certain decisions must be made by interpreters of 1 Corinthians. (a) Is Paul "informing" or "correcting" the Corinthians in areas where they were deficient or had gone astray?

---

[15] Fee, *op. cit.*, p.5.

> The language and style of 1 Corinthians are especially rhetorical and combative. Paul is taking them on at every turn. There is little to suggest that he is either informing or merely correcting; instead, he is attacking and challenging with all the weapons in his literary arsenal."[16]

(b) Is 1 Corinthians a response to their division into parties, wherein Paul takes one side over against the other(s)? Or are all the parties wrong? Or is one part of the Corinthian letter an answer to one party (say the Petrine), while other chapters answer another party (say the Pauline, or Christ-party)?

> The letter in its entirety is addressed to the whole church, with no suggestion that he is speaking now to one group, and then to another."[17]

What 1 Corinthians seems to imply about the church at Corinth includes these matters: (1) There was some form of internal dissension or division in the congregation. 1:10-12, 3:4-5, and 11:18-19 plainly indicate such dissension. Was the division merely along socio-economic lines (as 11:17-24 might indicate), or was the division also along theological lines? (2) There was some rejection of both Paul's apostleship and message, for Paul defends his apostolic ministry in 4:1-21 and chapter 9.

> The basic stance of [Fee's] commentary is that the *historical situation* in Corinth was *one of conflict between the church and its founder*. This is not to deny that the church was experiencing internal strife, but it is to argue that the greater problem of 'division' was between Paul and some in the community who were leading the church as a whole into an anti-Pauline view of things. For Paul this conflict presents a twofold crisis – over his authority and his gospel. Furthermore, the key issue between Paul and them, which created both these crises, has to do with the Corinthian understanding of what it means to be 'spiritual' (*pneumatikos*).[18]

Others suggest the rejection was the result of Paul changing his message. Though this suggestion rejects the chronology as given in Acts where the Jerusalem Conference *antedates* Paul's first preaching in Corinth, the suggestion is that as a result of the Jerusalem Conference Paul changed his preaching. There was a radical shift of positions from extreme freedom (earlier, original preaching at Corinth [*thesis*]) to restrictions (previous letter [*antithesis*]) to moderation (1 Corinthians [*synthesis*]). This shift confused the Corinthians and led to the conflict between Paul and the church.[19] (3) There was a failure to understand some of the practical implications of the Gospel, in terms of its application to everyday life situations. (4) How had such a situation developed? Had outsiders (say Judaizers) come and invaded the church, and poisoned the minds of the believers? By the

---

[16] Fee, *op. cit.*, p.6.

[17] *Ibid.*

[18] *Ibid.*

[19] See J.C. Hurd, *The Origin of I Corinthians*, 2nd ed., Macon, Ga., 1982.

time 2 Corinthians was written that is certainly true (2 Corinthians 10-13). Was some of the opposition led by insiders, who had brought some of their old worldly ideas into the church? "Some among you" might indicate this (see 4:18, 15:12). 6:9-11, 8:7, 12:1-3 make reference to how things were in their former pagan days. Had the exaltation of worldly "wisdom" infected their minds? Was it after Apollos had come as their "preacher" that worldly wisdom began to "cry up" one preacher against another? Or was it before he came? Was it this worldly "wisdom" that suggested to some that they had a right to sit in judgment of an apostle? Did they think of themselves as more "spiritual" (*pneumatikos*) than Paul (14:37)? Fee (*op. cit.*, p.10ff) suggests their idea of being "spiritual" derived from their over-emphasis on and experience of tongues. Was the error at Corinth somehow related to the wisdom speculation one finds in contemporary Hellenistic Judaism (Philo, Sirach, Qumran)? Fee contends the wisdom is more Hellenistic than it is an essential feature of Judaism; however, in this commentator's opinion, Fee does this to defend his thesis that the opponents at Corinth are in no way related to the Judaizers. Was one source of their misunderstanding to be found in "knowledge" (*gnosis*)[20] – i.e., was Greek philosophy influencing the thought of Paul's opponents? The Greek worldview was Hellenistic dualism, with its "spirit is good" v. "matter is evil" separation. It might not be anachronistic to call the opponents at Corinth *Jewish Gnostics* when we remember that Gnosticism started as a Jewish heresy. There is certainly something Jewish in the opponents' opposition to Paul's theology. Had the socio-economic division between the haves and the have-nots that was evident in Corinth also made itself felt in the congregation? Did this somehow contribute to the problem between the church and Paul?

1 Corinthians indicates several things about *what the church should be*. (1) The local church is God's temple in Corinth (3:16-17). As the temple of God they are expected to live as His alternative both to the pagan temples and to the way of life surrounding them. There is to be a recognizable difference in the way Christians live and the way unconverted Corinthian people live. What makes them God's temple is the presence of the Holy Spirit in their midst. So sacred to God is His temple that those who would destroy it (as they are doing by their quarrels, party strife and worldly wisdom) will themselves be destroyed by God (3:7). Church discipline is also necessary if His temple is to portray to the sinner, and to outsiders, what God wants His temple to be. (2) The church is the body of Christ (10:17, 11:29, 12:12-16). By one Spirit they were all baptized into one body, and all were made to drink of the one Spirit (12:13). Underlying this imagery is the necessity of unity, of harmony between the members. Underlying this imagery is the concomitant necessity of diversity; since not all have the same gifts, not all will exercise their liberty in the same rigidly uniform way. (3) There is little reference to church polity. There is no mention of "elders" or "deacons" as we find in Philippians 1:1. There have been apostles (Paul, Peter) and evangelists (Apollos, Titus) who have visited and worked at Corinth. (4) The

---

[20] Some scholars, such as Schmeidels, have claimed that Paul's opponents were Jewish Christian Gnostics, and hold to the theory that Gnosticism was already fully developed in Paul's day, or had been developed in pre-Christian times. It is this commentator's position that Gnosticism did not infiltrate the church until after it had caught hold in Jewish circles. Later books of the New Testament (Colossians, 1 and 2 Timothy, 2 Peter, Jude, and John's writings) all take on the new heresy, and contradict it, in an effort to keep the church from being influenced by this new religious/philosophical movement.

one body also met as "household churches." (5) "Worship services" occurred at the house churches assembled. 11:17-34 suggests they gathered regularly for a fellowship meal and the observance of the Lord's Supper. 14:1ff pictures the "order of worship," and certain instructions and limitations are given so that it may be an "orderly" service. The purpose of worship is twofold: on the one hand, singing, praying, and thanksgiving are directed toward God (11:13, 14:14-17); on the other hand, utterances of various kinds are directed toward the community that it may be built up.

I. THE COMMUNICATION BETWEEN PAUL AND THE CORINTHIAN CHRISTIANS

- **Someone from Chloe's household contacted Paul. 1:11**

a. *About factions (divisions)*, 1:10-4:21. (a) How many parties are condemned here? Some say two parties are all that were in Corinth and thus two parties are condemned. This was F.C. Baur's theory, that there were just a Pauline and a Petrine party at Corinth. The Pauline party ranged itself under the leaders Paul and Apollos, while the Petrine party ranged itself under Peter and Christ. (Some of Baur's students later showed that there is no basis for Baur's theory of antagonistic factions in the early church, some following Paul and others following Peter.) Others say three parties are condemned. Compare the way the passage is handled in the Living Bible, where the reading tends toward the three party position. According to this hypothesis, the Christ-party consisted of neutrals – those who ranged themselves under no human leader, but adhered to the simple doctrine of Christ, following Him alone as their master. However, this interpretation appears to be untenable. The other groups (Paul, Peter, Apollos) are mentioned by way of disapproval. And since the Christ-party is classed among them, it must be involved in the general condemnation. It is therefore best, we believe, to understand that four parties stand condemned by Paul in 1 Corinthians. (b) As to what the groups believed or emphasized, we have no sure information. Some try to describe the doctrine of the Petrine party as Judaism, and the Apollos party as using allegory (since he came from Alexandria, a town famous for allegorical interpretation), and the Christ-party as people who bigotedly and exclusively claimed to be the only Christians in Corinth. But we really know nothing of these factions, or what they taught or held. German scholars have spent much time trying to solve this problem, but their many conflicting theories only point to the fact that we just do not know the answer to the question.

b. *About gross immorality*, 5:1-13. A man was committing incest (with his step-mother). The congregation was condoning it, and Paul urges the Corinthian church to practice some church discipline. Concerning the church, the Scriptures give (1) the divine law of admission, (2) the divine law of organization, (3) the divine law of regulation, and (4) the divine law of exclusion. We have no right to ignore any of the four. When church discipline is not practiced, there is the tendency for the whole bushel to become rotten if one apple is bad.

c. *About litigation* (going to law before heathen judges and courts), 6:1-11. The Christians were airing their "dirty linen" in the pagan courts – one Christian against another. It is pretty nearly a rule that a Christian is never to be the plaintiff against another Christian. He may be the defendant if, say, an unbeliever drags him into court. The reason for Paul's instructions? The Christian, in a heathen court, would have to take an oath by a heathen god, and a Christian could not properly do this. Also, it betrays the love Christians are supposed to have, if they go to court and fight each other.

d. *About abuse of Christian liberty*, 6:12-20.

- **The Corinthian Christians had also written a letter to Paul. 7:1.** They asked:

a. *Concerning marriage*, 7:1-24. Apparently there were three questions: (i) Is mixed marriage a ground for divorce? (ii) What about widows and virgins entering into marriage? (iii) What is the father's responsibility to his unmarried daughter? Must he keep his promise to another family to whose son the daughter hás been pledged?

b. *Concerning things sacrificed to idols*, 8-10. Chapter 8 is an *ad hominem* argument. Chapter 10 shows it was improper to eat in the idol's temple. Christians had no business attending a feast in the idol's temple. What about the meat sold in the "shambles" (10:25, KJV)? A "shambles" was a marketplace, a butcher shop. Most of the meat sold in such markets had been part of an offering sacrificed to idols. In the case of some sacrifices, only the tail was burned; the rest of the animal was left. You invited all your friends to feast on what was left, the feast taking place in the idol's temple (and Paul says that Christians are not to go to this). After you and your friends ate all you could hold, the priests of the temple got the rest. They ate what they could, and took the rest to the shambles and sold it to the butcher; the butcher would sell it, in turn, to his customers. When a man became a Christian, he knew of the feasts and the source of most of the meat available in the marketplace. Paul indicates it was all right to purchase meat in the marketplace and eat it.

c. *Concerning disorder at the public services*, 11-14. In this section Paul writes about men's and women's dress while praying and prophesying; about the Lord's Supper and the love feast; and about the abuse of spiritual gifts.

d. *Concerning the resurrection of the dead*, 15.

e. *Concerning the collection for the Jerusalem saints*, 16:1-11

f. *Concerning Apollos*, 16:12.

- **Paul's correspondence with Corinth.**

How many letters did Paul write to Corinth? (It is important to note that the possible answers to this question do *not* cleave along conservative v. liberal lines.)

a. One theory is that Paul wrote *three letters* to Corinth[21] – a "Previous Letter" (now lost), 1 Corinthians, 2 Corinthians. The basis of the theory of a "previous letter" is found in 1 Corinthians 5:9, where Paul says, "I wrote." The particular tense of the verb in the Greek which is translated "I wrote" is aorist. It might be an *epistolary* aorist or an *historical* aorist. In the indicative mood, an aorist tense verb indicates action that is over and done in the past time, whether the immediate past or the remote past. The *epistolary* aorist would refer to this same letter, just as when we, in a letter, say "I wrote"; it may refer back to page one of the same letter. The *historical* aorist would refer to the some other letter, previously written, just as when we say "I wrote"; it may refer to a letter written some time previous to the one now being written. To illustrate, consider these examples of *epistolary* and *historical* aorists in the New Testament. 1 Corinthians 5:11 is epistolary; it refers to what he has already written in this very same letter. 1 Corinthians 9:15 contains an aorist verb in the Greek. The translators have put it in the present tense (ASV), indicating their opinion (which we believe to be correct) that the reference is to the present letter, and not to a previous one. At 2 Corinthians 2:3,4 the reference seems to be to a previous letter. 2 Corinthians 2:9 and 7:12 are the same; we think the reference is to 1 Corinthians. Galatians 6:11 is another epistolary aorist example. The ASV translators have rendered this by the present tense, "I write" where the KJV has "I have written." The obvious reference of 6:11 is to the very same Galatian letter; Paul makes reference to his own handwriting in this letter. At Philemon 19,21 the same letter is referred to. At 1 Peter 5:12 the same letter is referred to. At 1 John 2:12-14 verse 14 is aorist tense. It is not possible to tell exactly what verse 14 refers to, but it may be the same epistle, or to a previous writing, i.e., the Gospel of John (see also verses 21,26 and 5:13). 3 John 9 is another place the aorist appears.

Does 1 Corinthians 5:9 <u>prove</u> there was a "previous letter", a letter written by Paul to Corinth before the one we call First Corinthians? 1 Corinthians 5:9 might refer to a previous letter; the historical aorist is sometimes so used. However, 5:9 might be a reference to the same letter in which it appears; the epistolary aorist is sometimes so used. What Paul is doing in 5:9 seems to be this: The KJV uses "an epistle" at 5:9, and is not as satisfactory a translation as "my epistle" of the ASV. This commentator can see no objection to the supposition that 5:9 is an epistolary aorist referring to earlier portions of this 1 Corinthian letter itself. Some argue that Paul has not mentioned fornicators prior to 5:9 in the 1 Corinthians epistle. But at 5:1 and 5:5, Paul writes, "Deliver them to Satan," i.e., excommunicate them, disfellowship them. When Paul used "I wrote" in 5:9, he was clarifying what he had said in the previous verses and guarding against a possible misunderstanding of his instructions. 'I meant keep away from fornicators in the church. I didn't mean keep away from all such men, even those in the world – for to do that, you'd have to get entirely out of the world.' If the verses in the beginning of chapter 5 of 1 Corinthians satisfy the meaning of "I wrote" in 5:9, why theorize that there were other letters, perhaps now lost? We conclude that 5:9 is not <u>proof</u> that there was a "previous letter," written before our present 1 Corinthians.

---

[21] This is the view held by McGarvey, Elliott, Hayden (who wrote the Standard Sunday School Lessons in the fourth quarter of 1957), Hadjiantoniou, Lipscomb & Shepherd, Alford, Shore, Coffman, etc.

b. Another theory is that there were *four letters* written by Paul to Corinth, and that parts of each are preserved in our two letters[22] – a "previous letter" (2 Corinthians 6:14-7:1 is alleged to be part of this previous letter), 1 Corinthians, a "severe letter" (2 Corinthians 10-13 is said to be part of this severe letter), and 2 Corinthians (what is left with the above parts expunged). The alleged evidence for this theory is this: (a) A previous letter is referred to in 1 Corinthians 5:9 and since 2 Corinthians 6:14-7:1 speaks of having no company with "darkness," it is argued that 2 Corinthians 6:14ff fits what the "previous letter" might have been. (b) Evidence of the "severe letter" is said to be found in 2 Corinthians 7:8,9 and 2:1-9. It is argued that the "severe letter" references cannot be to 1 Corinthians, for would Paul be saying "I'm sorry I wrote you what the Holy Spirit told me to write"? (Answer: Paul might be lamenting the necessity of having to write such a letter.) Further, 2 Corinthians 10-13 are written in a tone of severity as Paul defends himself, and not like the "comforting" tone of reconciliation in chapters 1-9. Therefore, it is alleged, chapters 10-13 must be part of the severe letter.

Arguments against the idea that Paul wrote four letters to Corinth, that somehow have been put together to form the two letters in our present-day Bibles, include: (a) There is no proof of the writing of a "previous letter." (See the epistolary aorist discussion above.) (b) There is no real evidence of a "severe letter," but rather it seems the passages alleged to prove the existence of a "severe letter" are really references to the letter we know as 1 Corinthians. Paul spoke of being distressed and agitated after writing a letter (2:3,4,9 and 7:8). If we thoughtfully ponder the stern force with which he wrote 1 Corinthians 4:18-21, 5:1-8, 11:17-22, and 15:35, 36 we will find little difficulty in accounting for his uneasiness. Further, a comparison of 2 Corinthians would be evidence against the idea that a portion of a "previous letter" and a portion of a "severe letter" are to be found in our 2 Corinthians letter. We conclude this theory of four letters, with parts of each preserved, does not satisfactorily meet the information we have.

c. A third theory is that there were *four letters* written by Paul to Corinth, and that *two have been lost* completely[23] – a "previous letter" (now lost), 1 Corinthians, a "severe letter" (also lost in its entirety), and 2 Corinthians. Evidence for this theory is said to be found in 1 Corinthians 5:9 and 2 Corinthians 2 and 7. (See above.)

A key argument against this theory involves the question of possible lost canonical letters. Is it possible an inspired writing might be lost? This commentator thinks we must admit the *possibility*. We know some inspired spoken words were not preserved. For example, very little of Jesus' ministry is preserved. In Acts, many of the sermons are condensed; we are given only the bare outlines. No passage in the Bible says every inspired word would be preserved; only that which is necessary for our salvation was pre-

---

[22] This theory is defended by K. and S. Lake, Barclay, Holladay. Note the paragraphing in the RSV – with a space between 2 Corinthians 6:13, and 14, and another space after 7:1, and also between chapters 9 and 10 [so that chapters 10-13 make one block of material]. This is a subtle way of visually suggesting the fragmentary theory to the readers of that version.

[23] See Leon Morris in the *Tyndale Commentaries* "The First Epistle of Paul to the Corinthians (Grand Rapids, MI: Wm. B. Eerdmans Publishing, 1966), p.20ff, and the Wycliffe Bible Commentary.

served. Thus admitting the possibility some inspired writing might be lost, is there any *evidence* such has happened? It is striking that we do not have quotations either in the New Testament or in Early Christian Literature of the apostles from "unknown sources." When the early Christian writers quote the apostles, we can find the quoted words in the writings we have. For example, when Clement of Rome says Paul said "such and such" in an epistle to Corinth, we can find that quotation in one of the two letters we have. There are no quotations in Early Christian writings from letters (for example, from Paul's correspondence to the Corinthians) now supposedly lost. Continuing our search for evidence of "lost inspired writings," we turn to the New Testament itself. In Colossians 4:16, mention is made of "the epistle from Laodicea." Some say, "Here is a lost letter," or "Here is evidence that inspired writings were lost." However, upon examining the evidence, "the epistle from Laodicea" is in our Bibles under another name – it is Ephesians, which was a circular letter that started in Laodicea and ended up in Ephesus. 3 John 9 is also quoted as evidence of "lost inspired writings." But this could well be a reference to 2 John, or merely to a letter of commendation (i.e., a church letter). Some also appeal to 2 Peter 3:1 as evidence of an alleged lost letter, based upon an assertion that the reference in 3:1 is not to the letter we call 1 Peter. However, instead of evidence of a lost letter, most scholars find 3:1 to be a reference to the letter we call 1 Peter. Altogether, we are unable to discover positive and conclusive evidence that any inspired writing has been lost. In fact, whether or not a writing was considered to be inspired may very well have been the dividing point as to whether or not it was preserved. God brought together His Word, keeping it brief, but all-sufficient. It is brief – there is little redundant material, little overlapping, and little repetition. (Even in cases where repetition is necessary, viz., in the gospel accounts, new material is also given.) And it is all-sufficient – able to make a man wise unto salvation.

Having found no indisputable evidence that any inspired writing was lost, we conclude that it is *improbable* that any inspired writing is lost. We think it is possible, but not probable, that inspired writing has been lost. If any has been lost, it has been by the choice of the Holy Spirit. Paul wrote to both churches and to individuals. It is possible we do not have all his letters to individuals. But the letters to the churches are another matter. Would a church be so negligent as to lose the writings of an apostle? While theoretically it is possible some letters were lost, practically it is highly improbable. We conclude, under this point, that there is not sufficient evidence for the theory that Paul originally wrote four letters, two of which have been entirely lost.

d. A fourth theory concerning the number of letters written by Paul to Corinth is that he wrote *five letters* – a "previous letter, 1 Corinthians, 2 Corinthians 8-9 would be a portion of a third letter, 2 Corinthians 10-12:10 would be a part of the "severe letter," and 2 Corinthians 1-7 and 13:11-13 would be a portion of the last letter written by Paul to Corinth. The theory also posits that the fragments were put together in their present form by some other hand than Paul's, perhaps Timothy's, and possibly with the Apostle's own approbation and direction. But, like the above theories, this one will not bear a thorough investigation.

We are led, therefore, to the conclusion concerning Paul's letters to Corinth that he wrote two letters[24] – 1 Corinthians (just as we have it), and 2 Corinthians (just as we have it). This seems to best fit the evidence we have. There is no need to assert a "previous letter" since 1 Corinthians 5:9 is likely an epistolary aorist, and may well refer to earlier material in the same letter. Neither is there sufficient evidence for a "severe letter" between 1 and 2 Corinthians. The references in 2 Corinthians to a letter which made them sorry may well refer to 1 Corinthians.

J. PAUL'S VISITS TO CORINTH

For complete information, see the introductory notes to 2 Corinthians. It is convenient merely to summarize here the information given in detail there. 2 Corinthians 13:2 speaks of two trips having been made to Corinth, and a third one about to happen. The book of Acts records only two trips, the one when the church was established, and the one when the offering was collected for the Jerusalem Christians. Putting together the information gained from both Acts and 2 Corinthians, we arrive at these conclusions: Paul's first trip to Corinth was in AD 52 when the church was established. Paul's third trip was in AD 58 when the offering was collected. The "intermediate trip" evidently came somewhere between the writing of 1 Corinthians and 2 Corinthians.

K. THE OCCASION THAT LED TO THE WRITING OF 1 CORINTHIANS

During Paul's stay in Ephesus, on several occasions he had heard about the state of the church at Corinth. Members of Chloe's household had come to Paul (1:11). Perhaps Apollos, who appears to have taken up residence in Ephesus while Paul was there, gave Paul information concerning the situation at Corinth. The Corinthian church had sent a letter to Paul (7:1). Stephanas, Fortunatus, and Achaicus had come to Paul (16:17). Perhaps these men were members of Chloe's household, and eventually carried the letter from Corinth to Paul. The combination of these intelligences, culminated by the messages of 1:11 and 16:15, was the occasion that led Paul to sit down and compose this letter. Perhaps it was dictated to Sosthenes.

L. PURPOSE OF WRITING

The purpose unfolds in the epistle itself. Included are these points of emphasis:

- To counteract the party division and uphold his apostolic authority.
- To remove unchastity from the church at Corinth.
- To give instruction concerning the queries that had come to him.

---

[24] So hold L.A. Foster, G.L. Reese, and others.

M. TIME AND PLACE OF WRITING

Concerning the place of writing, it has been shown above that the letter was written at Ephesus.

Regarding the time of writing, Paul wrote the letter toward the end of his stay at Ephesus while on his Third Missionary Journey. In our study of New Testament Chronology[25] we have dated the Third Missionary Journey, AD 54-58. This letter was perhaps written near the time of Passover (1 Corinthians 5:6-8) and a short while before Pentecost (1 Corinthians 16:8). We shall date it in the spring of AD 57.

N. THE PLACEMENT OF 1 CORINTHIANS IN THE NEW TESTAMENT

The Pauline letters to churches are arranged in our English versions according to length, from longest to shortest. 1 Corinthians just happens to be shorter (in the number of lines of Greek Text) than Romans, etc.[26]

However, after examining the contents of each of the Pauline epistles, it is peculiarly fitting that 1 Corinthians should follow Romans in the New Testament.

   a. *Romans* is a grand exposition of the fundamental thesis set forth in Romans 1:16,17. It is a profound treatment of important anthropological and central soteriological principles, and of the Christian revelation and the corresponding Christian ethic. It contains little concerning the actual condition of the work in Rome.

   b. *Galatians* is a forceful polemic against those who would pervert the gospel of Christ. It provides some insight into the local situation, particularly concerning their tragic departure from the truth. But for the most part particulars are obscure as Paul's writing was "struck out at white-heat." Galatians is soteriological in character.

   c. *Ephesians* is a magnificent presentation of how God summed up all things in Christ, of how His eternal purpose is to be made known through the church, of the body of Christ. It contains no delineation of the local situation, which is not at all strange if it was a circular letter. It is Christological in character.

   d. *Philippians* is a gracious "thank you" letter – a letter of love, a letter of joy, a letter of thanksgiving. The classic *kenosis* passage arises out of practical considerations. The letter gives a glimpse of the affairs of the church as Paul

---

[25] See the introductory studies in the author's commentary on Acts, *New Testament History: Acts* (Moberly, Mo: Scripture Exposition Books, 2002), p. x-xxi.

[26] In the Chester Beatty Papyri, the order is Romans, Hebrews, 1 Corinthians, etc.

writes with deep appreciation and love to the brethren in this Roman outpost community. Philippians is Christological, pastoral, ethical in character.

e. *Colossians* offers a lofty Christology as Paul refutes Judaistic influence and also an influence of more local and heathen origin. Paul meets the main influences working for evil in the church by a direct presentation of the relevant Christian doctrine. We do not feel too intimate with the brethren at Colossae.

f. *Philemon* is Paul's outpouring of his great heart in Christian love as he pleads on behalf of the slave Onesimus, who is now a brother beloved in Christ. It provides "special reference to the *care of souls*".

g. *Thessalonians* are the first of the Pauline epistles, and share something of the severe trials through which the brethren at Thessalonica were passing. Paul exhorts them to continued steadfastness as they wait for the return of our Lord. These epistles give a closer look at the local life of a church, but not as in 1 Corinthians. The Thessalonian letters contain eschatological characteristics.

h. *1 & 2 Timothy and Titus* emphasize church polity. The office of evangelist, the office of bishop or elder, and the office of deacon are set forth in brief. The letters offer not much more than a glimpse of the affairs of the church. Rather, they are Christological, pastoral, ethical in character.

i. *Hebrews* - The Hebrew brethren are being tempted to apostasy, and are exhorted to remain faithful to Christ and His gospel. Detailed local problems are not discussed. Hebrews is a Christological-theological-practical polemic.

j. The *Corinthian* letters are unique in the Pauline group in revealing numerous precise problems which confronted Christians in the apostolic age. These letters offer an ecclesiastic polemic in regard to actual disturbances and corruptions in the life of the congregation. The letters also offer an apologetic for the ministerial office and Paul's apostolic status.

Preceding the Roman letter in order of time by nearly a year, the Corinthian letters rank next to it in importance and so fittingly appear second in Paul's signed epistles in the New Testament.

O. HISTORY AND INFLUENCE OF THE LETTER

1 Corinthians is the first New Testament writing to be cited by name in Early Christian Literature. Clement of Rome wrote, "Take up the letter of the blessed Paul the apostle. What was the first thing he wrote to you in the beginning of the Gospel? Of a truth he wrote to you in the Spirit touching himself and Cephas and Apollos, because even

then you had formed factions."[27] Other quotes of the letter in Christian Literature were noted above under the section on attestation and authorship.

The Gnostics used the letter with predilection (i.e., showing it favor). Perhaps this is because of the emphasis on "knowledge" found in the letter.

But the letter did not at first take a leading place among New Testament writings. Perhaps it was because it had little to say directly on the questions (except the resurrection) which chiefly interested the ante-Nicene Church.

In the 4th century, when controversies on church discipline and morals began to sway the minds of thoughtful men, the epistle came to the forefront. A number of church leaders of the time wrote commentaries on the epistle, including Theodoret (AD 420), Chrysostom (AD 407)[28], Oecumenius (AD 950), and Theophylact (AD 1078). The Latin commentaries of Pelagius and of Ambrosiaster testify to the wide use of this book in the West in the fourth and fifth centuries.

To Thomas Aquinas we owe the only interpretation of value bequeathed by the Middle Ages.

From the time of the Reformation come several lasting works. Colet's Oxford Lectures on this epistle (AD 1496) and the New Testament paraphrase by Erasmus (AD 1519) breathed the new spirit of the Reformation, which brought 1 Corinthians to the front again, along with Romans and Galatians. Reformation emphases regarding liberty and order, application of evangelical faith to secular life, and the reconstitution of the church with its sacraments and ministry raised a multitude of problems calling for the aid that this letter offers. Calvin's commentary on this letter was a masterpiece. Calvin's TULIP doctrine was based on his understanding of 1 Corinthians and then read back into other passages of the New Testament. Estius, a Roman Catholic, also produced a fine commentary. Among the German reformers, Melanchthon, W. Musculus, and Bullinger, all handled this epistle with effect. Beza's annotations, and especially his Latin translation, are always worth consulting. Grotius the Arminian also dealt with this book.

In the 17th century, 1 Corinthians suffered another eclipse. No commentary upon it of any mark appeared between the time of Grotius and Bengel.

In the 19th century, much attention was paid to 1 Corinthians. From Germany came the commentaries of DeWette, Meyer (rewritten in 1 & 2 Corinthians by Heinrici), von

---

[27] *I Clement* xlvii.

[28] *The Homilies of St. John Chrysostom on the First Epistle of Paul to the Corinthians*. Vol. 4,5 of the Library of the Fathers of the Holy Catholic Church, edited by Parker, 1839.

Hofmann, and Kling.[29] From England, Alford (Anglican, premillennial) and A.P. Stanley (*Ep. of Paul to the Corinthians*, 1855) illuminated the historical and picturesque aspects of the epistle. Beet (*Ep. to the Corinthians*, 1882) tracked the thought of the apostle with exceeding closeness, and presents it with concise force. It is full of doctrinal summaries, intended to contribute to systematic theology. Shore's interpretation (1887) is a model of exact and delicate verbal elucidation; no better book can be placed in the hands of a working Greek Testament scholar. Lightfoot's notes, posthumously published in 1895, cover chapters 1-7 and are typical of his conservative judgment. Hort (*Christian Ecclesia*) and Knowling (*Witness of the Epistles to Christ*) exhibited in the use they make of 1 Corinthians its decisive bearing on the questions of early church history and apologetics. William Kelly (*Notes on the First Epistle of Paul the Apostle to the Corinthians*, with a new translation from G. Morrish of London, reprint of 1882 edition) offered an independent, conservative exposition by a Plymouth Brethren scholar; his footnotes deal mostly with manuscript evidence for variant textual readings. From France came the work of Godet, 1880 (reprinted by Zondervan, 1957). Though not his most successful exposition, Godet's Corinthians is marked by his fine spiritual and literary qualities, and is full of instructive matter, though it is weak and out of date on matters of textual criticism. Two American scholars round out the list of 19th century commentaries. Charles Hodge (1857) illumined the epistle's theological side; it is Calvinistic in tone, and was reprinted by Eerdmans in 1965. Albert Barnes (1798-1870) has "1 Corinthians" in *Barnes Notes*, reprinted by Baker in 1953. Barnes was an American Presbyterian minister, a new school Presbyterian. He believed in unlimited atonement, i.e., he was not a strict Calvinist in his theology. He does teach faith-only (though not consistently in his "notes"), original sin and an inherited sinful nature, and unconditional eternal security (in the Calvinistic sense).

20th century commentaries on 1 Corinthians are also notable. Works from the first half of the 20th century include F.W. Farrar, "1 Corinthians," in *Pulpit Commentary*, c. 1900; it was reprinted many times by Eerdmans. Being amillennial, it is a very helpful exposition and is one of the sources from which this present commentator draws. Robertson and Plummer's "1 Corinthians" in *The International Critical Commentary* is a monumental work on the Greek text. It is good for every library, and is essential for the careful student who wishes to work on the original text. Published in 1914, it was reprinted by T&T Clark, 1953. G.G. Findlay wrote "The First Epistle of Paul to the Corinthians," in *The Expositors Greek Testament*, edited by W. Robertson Nicoll, 1900. It was reprinted by Eerdmans in 1967, and is a thorough commentary on the Greek text by an evangelical Methodist scholar of the past generation. It is characterized by a thorough grasp of Pauline thought in the epistle. It is for the advanced student. R.C.H. Lenski, *The Interpretation of St. Paul's First and Second Epistle to the Corinthians* (Columbus, OH. Lutheran Book Concern, 1935), was reprinted by Fortress Press (1946) and by Augs-

---

[29] Kling, Christian Friedrich, "The Epistles of Paul the Apostle to the Corinthians," in *Lange's Commentary on the Holy Scripture*. Translated from the German, with additions, by D.W. Poor (1808). Grand Rapids: Zondervan, reprint, nd. A voluminous conservative Lutheran exposition. The epistles are divided into convenient paragraphs, with the material under each section appearing in three parts, exegetical and critical, doctrinal and ethical, homiletical and practical. Contains much rich ore to be mined by those willing to dig into its closely printed pages.

burg (1963). This monumental work of 1383 pages includes the author's own literal translation and scholarly comments by this evangelical amillennial Lutheran scholar. It offers many significant word studies in unfolding the meaning of the epistles. Lenski strongly defends the unity of 2 Corinthians. This book is an indispensable tool for the serious student. David Lipscomb and J.W. Shepherd, "1 Corinthians" in *New Testament Commentaries* (Nashville, TN: Gospel Advocate, 1934) are Church of Christ scholars who produced this volume for the Sunday School teacher and Bible student. It gives conclusions on problem passages, without indicating other possible interpretations and usually without stating the reasons for the interpretations embraced and advanced.

Works from the second half of the 20th century include those by Gordon Fee and Anthony Thistleton. 1 Corinthians is receiving much attention because of the growing Charismatic movement and the controversy that group introduces into theological studies and everyday church life.

P. RANGE OF PROBLEMS EMBRACED IN 1 CORINTHIANS

1. The problem of parties, factions, and divisions in the local church
2. The teacher problem
3. The problem of self-satisfaction and worldly pride in the local church
4. The problem of spiritual babes and the carnal minded people
5. What is to be done when a member sins and will not repent?
6. To what extent is it permissible for Christians to have fellowship with sinners?
7. What about Christians going to law against one another?
8. What is the nature of the sin of fornication that makes it solitary among sins?
9. Is it better to marry or not to marry?
10. Should a Christian marry an unbeliever?
11. What if a Christian is married to an unbeliever? Should the Christian divorce?
12. Suppose the unbelieving party deserts his or her mate. Does the Christian have a right to marry another?
13. Can slaves, after they become Christians, continue to serve their masters?
14. What obligation does a Christian have toward a weak brother?
15. Who is a weak brother? Wherein does his weakness lie?
16. What about paying the preacher (evangelist)?
17. Can a Christian fall from grace?
18. Is it necessary for a Christian to study the Old Testament?
19. Suppose a Christian were invited to a friend's house for dinner. The host served milk to drink, but one of the guests thought it was wrong to drink milk. Now what should the Christian do? Drink his milk, or leave it alone?
20. How should the Lord's Supper be observed?
21. Who is the head of the house?
22. Who is the head of the head of the house?
23. What about women preaching?

24. There is the question of how women and men should dress when they come to the worship services.
25. There is the matter of the attitude members of the church should have toward each other and toward the various opportunities for service.
26. What is involved in Christian love?
27. What are the basic principles which should govern the nature and practices of a worship service?
28. "How are the dead raised? And with what manner of body do they come?"
29. What principles undergird the offering?
30. The nature of the gospel
31. The work of the cross
32. The headship of Christ
33. The apostolic office
34. The New Testament prophet, and the prophetic gift
35. Women and the prophetic gift
36. The nature of the church
37. The nature of the Christian ministry
38. The proper relation between the preacher and the congregation
39. The sectarian spirit
40. The doctrine of the Holy Spirit
41. Spiritual gifts
42. The marriage relationship
43. Formative church discipline
44. Corrective church discipline

It is instructive to see how Paul deals with each of the problems in the Corinthian church. For every aberration he has a word of censure. For every danger he has a word of warning. For every weakness he has a word of cheer and sympathy. For every returning offender he has a word of pardon and courage.

Q. OUTLINE

	Page
Superscription	1
INTRODUCTION. 1:1-9	1
A. Address and Greeting. 1:1-3	1
B. Paul's Thanksgiving for God's Work in Corinth. 1:4-9	9
SECTION ONE: CONCERNING PARTISAN STRIFE AND ITS CONSEQUENCES. 1:10-4:21	18
A. Party Spirit at Corinth. 1:18-25	18

	Page
B. The Nature of True Christian Preaching. 1:18-25	34
C. The Method of God in the Spread of the gospel. 1:26-31	47
Special Study #1: The Message of the Cross	58
D. Paul's Own Method of Preaching. 2:1-5	61
E. The Gospel, Which Disdains and Abjures Human Wisdom, has Nevertheless a Wisdom of its Own. 2:6-16	68
F. Reproof of the Corinthians for the Lack of Spiritual Wisdom as Evidenced by Their Carnal Divisions. 3:1-4	91
G. The Proper Estimate of the Position Held by Christian Workers (Apostles and Prophets). 3:5-4:5	96
H. Paul's Stirring Appeal for Unity in the Church at Corinth. 4:6-21	129
SECTION TWO: CONCERNING SEXUAL IMMORALITY AND THE CHURCH'S INDIFFERENCE TO IT. 5:1-13	151
A. Censure of the Deliberate Toleration of a Gross Case of Incest. 5:1-3	151
B. Instructions Concerning the Proper Discipline Procedure. 5:4-8	155
C. Correction of a Possible Misunderstanding of the Instructions Previously Given Concerning Association with Immoral People. 5:9-13	164
Special Study #2: Church Discipline at Corinth and Elsewhere.	171
SECTION THREE: CENSURE OF LITIGATION BEFORE OUTSIDE TRIBUNALS. 6:1-11	175
SECTION FOUR: REMONSTRANCE AGAINST ABUSE OF CHRISTIAN LIBERTY. 6:12-20	193
Special Study #3: Here I Stand, So Help Me God! *(A sermon about ethics)*	206
SECTION FIVE: CONCERNING MARRIAGE. 7:1-40	220
A. Rights and Obligations of Married Life. 7:1-16	220

Introduction, page 29

	Page
B. The General Principle ("Stay Where You Are!") Behind Paul's Instructions Applied to Other Civil Relations. 7:17-24	245
C. Inspired Advice Respecting the Unmarried in View of Circumstances Then in Existence. 7:25-40	253
Special Study #4: Who are the "Virgins"?	270

SECTION SIX: CONCERNING THINGS OFFERED TO IDOLS (and Christian Liberty) -- 3 QUESTIONS. 8:1-11:1 272

A. The Principles on Which Such Decisions are Made. 8:1-10:13	272
1. First, love (not just knowledge) must be the ethic that guides our behavior. 8:1-13	272
Special Study #5: "Whom Do You Say I Am?" The Deity of Jesus	291
2. Second, there are many times when a man should voluntarily restrict his own liberty because he loves. 9:1-27	297
3. Third, the history of Israel should serve as a warning about the danger of idolatry. 10:1-13	329
B. Paul's Answers (based on the above stated principles) to Their Three Questions. 10:14-11:1	345
1. The eating of sacrificial meat at an idol's table, or in an idolatrous feast, is prohibited. 10:14-22	346
2. The eating of sacrificial meat purchased at the meat market is permissible. 10:23-26	357
3. It is permissible for the Christian to eat at an unconverted friend's house (unless his eating gives offense to one sitting at the table). 10:27-30	360
C. Conclusion to the Questions about Meats Offered to Idols. 10:31-11:1	363

Introduction, page 31

	Page
SECTION SEVEN: CONCERNING DISORDERS IN PUBLIC WORSHIP IN THE CORINTHIAN CHURCH. 11:2-14:40	367
A. Disapproval of the Manner (heads covered or uncovered) in Which Men and Women Were Praying and Prophesying in the Public Assembly. 11:2-16	367
1. The principle stated (the doctrinal basis of these instructions). 11:3	369
2. The principle applied. 11:4-6	372
3. The principle defended. 11:7-10	381
4. The principle clarified. 11:11,12	386
5. The principle agreed to. 11:13-16	388
B. Correction of Abuses Regarding the Love-feasts and the Partaking of the Lord's Supper. 11:17-34	392
C. Correction of Abuses in the Exercise of Spiritual Gifts. 12:1-14:40	419
1. Principles by which to guide one's behavior in these matters. 12:1-13:13	419
a. Principle #1 -- Tests by which the Holy Spirit's leading may be discerned. 12:1-3	419
b. Principle #2 -- The need for a diversity of gifts in the church. 12:4-11	427
c. Principle #3 -- The need for a unity of purpose as the different gifts are used in the church. 12:12-31a	440
d. Principle #4 -- Love must be the motive that controls the use of our gifts. 12:31b-13:13	460
2. Applications of the principles to the abuses of spiritual gifts. 14:1-40	488
a. Application #1 -- Edification. 14:1-5	488
b. Application #2 -- Understanding. 14:6-25	496
c. Application #3 -- Orderliness. 14:26-40	527
Special Study #6: Worship in the New Testament	547
SECTION EIGHT: CONCERNING THE FINAL RESURRECTION OF DEAD BODIES. 15:1-58	573
A. Arguments for the Resurrection of the Body. 15:1-34	573
1. The historical argument. 15:1-11	573
2. The logical argument. 15:12-19	597
3. The theological argument. 15:20-28	605
4. *Ad hominem* arguments in favor of resurrection. 15:29-34	619

Introduction, page 32

	Page
B. Consideration of Objections to Bodily Resurrection. 15:35-49	627
1. First objection: How can the body be raised? 15:36-38	629
2. Second objection: What kind or manner of body is raised? 15:39-49	632
C. Explanation of What Becomes of those Who are Still Alive on Earth When Jesus Returns to raise the Dead. 15:50-58	646
Special Study #7: He Is Alive! You Had Better Believe It!	664
Special Study #8: Baptized For The Dead	684
Special Study #9: Is Man Immortal?	692
SECTION NINE: INSTRUCTIONS CONCERNING THE COLLECTION FOR THE POOR SAINTS IN JERUSALEM. 16:1-11	697
A. Directions Respecting the Collecting and Transmission of Alms for the Poor Saints at Jerusalem. 16:1-4	697
B. The Travel Plans of Paul and His Helpers are Somewhat Related to the Offering. 16:5-11	706
SECTION TEN: CONCERNING APOLLOS. 16:12	714
SECTION ELEVEN: CONCLUSION OF THE EPISTLE WITH VARIOUS EXHORTATIONS AND SALUTATIONS. 16:13-24	715
A. Summary Exhortations. 16:13,14	715
B. Special Entreaty Concerning Stephanas and Others. 16:15-18	718
C. Concluding Salutations. 16:19-21	723
D. Final Warning, Prayer, and Blessing. 16:22-24	726
Subscription	730
Special Study #10: Do All Speak in Tongues? and *The Joy of the Holy Spirit*	731
Bibliography	771
Index	789

COMMENTARY ON
1 CORINTHIANS

SUPERSCRIPTION

The oldest superscription was probably "to the Corinthians, the first (*pros korinthious a*)." This is found in a A, B, C, D.[1]

INTRODUCTION: 1:1-9

A. Address and Greeting. 1:1-3

A typical epistolary opening is found in all the epistles of Paul and in every epistle of the New Testament except the Epistle to the Hebrews and the First Epistle of John, both of which are more in the nature of treatises than letters.

The greeting follows the regular form used by Paul in most of his letters, the typical form found in letters from the Greco-Roman period: first, the writer's name in the nominative; second, the persons to whom he writes in the dative; and third, the words of greeting again in the nominative. Thus in this letter: "Paul ... and Sosthenes ... to the church, ... grace and peace." Each of the three parts of the greeting, as is frequently done by Paul, receives an amplification. In Paul's letters these amplifications invariably reflect the thought and the feeling that are in his heart as he sets out to write. Pauline greetings usually foreshadow the contents and the character of the letter to follow.

1:1 – *Paul, called as an apostle of Jesus Christ by the will of God, and Sosthenes our brother*

Paul -- After the beginning of the first missionary journey (AD 45), Paul seems to have finally abandoned his Hebrew name of Saul. Concerning his person and his history, his importance to the church and his labors, consult the general introduction to the Corinthian epistles in Lange's Commentary, or in any good Bible dictionary.

Called as an apostle ("who by the will of God was called to be an apostle of Jesus Christ,"

---

[1] *Pros korinthious a* is a subtitle, marking the epistle as part of a collection bearing the general name "The Apostle."

TEV) -- In this instance the addition (amplification) to the writer's name is compact and weighty as Paul asserts his apostolic authority. Paul stresses his special nearness to Jesus Christ as being one sent by Him, and at the same time points to the divine authority behind his words, an authority his readers are to acknowledge and to obey. All the instructions and the admonitions of this letter rest on this solid basis; the instructions are all important because they come from a called apostle of Jesus Christ. The ordinary rendering, "called to be an Apostle" (ASV), does not give sufficient prominence to the lead thought within the phrase, which per the order of the Greek words lies in "Apostle."[2] The sense is 'an *apostle* by the virtue of his calling.' The word "called" is absent from A, D, E, and other manuscripts, but it was probably in the autograph of 1 Corinthians. It is found in *Aleph*, B,C,F,L,P, etc.[3] Paul is emphasizing the fact that he became an apostle by an immediate call to that position from the Lord Jesus Christ Himself. He was as much sent by Jesus as were any of the original Twelve. "Called" reminds us of the Damascus Road experience (Acts 26:16) when Jesus appeared to Paul to call him to be the apostle to the Gentiles. Paul uses this title "apostle of Jesus" in every letter except the private one to Philemon, the peculiarly friendly and informal one to the Philippians, and the two to the Thessalonians, which were written before the Judaizers had challenged his claim to this title in its more special sense. He likely asserts his apostolic authority in this letter precisely because it had been questioned by some at Corinth.[4] Paul is asserting that the instructions he is about to give in this letter are in harmony with his commission as an apostle of Jesus Christ. He is expressing no less than the mind of Christ when he writes.

Of Jesus Christ by the will of God -- Paul's calling to be an apostle was given to him by Christ (Acts 26:16-18), having for its deeper ground the will of God (cp. Galatians 1:15ff). Jesus called Paul to be an apostle to the Gentiles when He appeared to him on the way to Damascus; and Jesus so appeared to Paul because God willed it to be that way. The name "Jesus" means "Jehovah Saves," or "Salvation of Jehovah" (cp. Matthew 1:21). "Christ"

---

[2] The word "apostle" speaks of "one who is sent on a mission." In the New Testament there are two kinds of apostles – apostles of Jesus (called and sent by Him), and apostles of churches (called and sent by a congregation on a special mission on behalf of the congregation, e.g., 2 Corinthians 8:23). Jesus, too, is called an "apostle" in Hebrews 3:1 because He was sent on a mission by the Father. To be an apostle of Jesus, a man had to meet certain qualifications (Acts 1:22) as well has have a personal invitation from Jesus to be one of His apostles.

[3] In classical Reformed theology, one often reads about an "effectual call." By such language is meant, not just an invitation through the Word and the work of the Holy Spirit to become a Christian, but through "the work of God's Spirit, whereby, convincing us of our sin and misery, enlightening our minds in the knowledge of Christ, and renewing our wills, He doth persuade and enable us to embrace Jesus Christ ... " (*Westminster Shorter Catechism*, Q. 31). According to Reformed theology, this act of effectual calling is wholly because of the grace of God, and its effectiveness is not in the slightest degree creditable to the one who is saved. We mention this only because commentaries in the Reformed tradition try to find another proof text for their doctrine in this verse. Paul's call to be an apostle was an effectual call, we are told. One of the great problems connected with this doctrine is that it seems to make God a respecter of persons – "effectually calling" some while only "inviting" others.

[4] Paul seems to have followed a pattern in his use or nonuse of the term "apostle" as he wrote his letters. When he wrote to churches where his apostolic authority was not in question, he did not use the title. But when he wrote to a congregation where his authority or doctrine was questioned, he did call attention to his apostolic office.

is the Greek equivalent of the Hebrew word "Messiah," which means "anointed." In the two names together our Lord is represented as "the Savior," and the anointed Prophet, Priest, and King – first to the chosen people, and then of all mankind. The words "by the will of God" ("through the will of God," ASV) are added by Paul probably because of the depreciation of Paul's apostolic authority at Corinth. In view of the parties at Corinth who refused to acknowledge Paul's apostleship, and sought to put him below the twelve who were personally called by Christ while He was on earth, it was exactly the needed point to bring prominently forward the fact that Paul's calling came through (*dia*) the Supreme will.[5]

And Sosthenes -- The association of one or more brethren with himself in the greeting of his letters is peculiar to Paul. The practice arose partly from Paul's courtesy and consideration toward his companions, and partly because he abjured mere personal prominence. Of Sosthenes nothing whatever is known for certain.[6] Some feel he is to be identified with the ruler of the synagogue in Acts 18:17.[7] One synagogue ruler (Crispus) had been converted at Corinth (Acts 18:8), so why not another (Sosthenes) afterward? Some have supposed Sosthenes' name occurs here because he was the penman (i.e., the amanuensis) of the epistle, writing it as Paul dictated it (cp. Romans 16:22). If Sosthenes served as Paul's secretary, then only the closing benediction (16:21) would have been in Paul's own handwriting. A different suggestion has Sosthenes mentioned here as an example of someone who sought Paul's direction. This hypothesis suggests Sosthenes was one of the members of Chloe's household (verse 11) through whom Paul received intelligence about matters at Corinth, and Paul holds him up as a good example of how to solve such matters; namely, by seeking the directions an apostle of Jesus can give. Another suggestion is that like Paul, Sosthenes, too, had been slighted by one or more of the factions in the church at Corinth, and for that reason Paul puts him forward. The association of Sosthenes with Paul in the composition and sending of this letter likely means much more than that Sosthenes was the amanuensis. In this commentator's opinion, it means Sosthenes and Paul had talked over the contents of this letter and had fully agreed on all that is here transmitted. In other words, Sosthenes subscribes to all that Paul has to say.

Our brother -- Literally, "the brother," i.e., one of 'the brethren,' one of our brothers in Christ. Until AD 42-44 when the apostles called the disciples "Christians" first at Antioch (Acts 11:26) there was no single recognized title for the followers of Christ. "Christian" is the family name of God's New Testament people. Christians are also described by other terms in the New Testament: brother, saint, children of God, citizens of the kingdom, members of the body, living stones, priests, soldiers, branches, and pilgrims.

---

[5] Paul's special call to apostleship is emphatically expanded in Galatians 1:1ff. It was not by human appointment, or authority, but in accordance with the will of God, that Paul served as an apostle.

[6] Later tradition – which may or may not be accurate – spoke of him as "one of the 70 disciples, and Bishop of Colophon" (Eusebius, *Hist. Eccl.*, i.12). Sosthenes is not further heard from as a companion or coworker of Paul either in this letter or elsewhere.

[7] So David Lipscomb, "First Corinthians," in the *New Testament Commentary* series (Nashville, TN: Gospel Advocate, 1960) p.19,20 and T. Teignmouth Shore, "The First Epistle to the Corinthians," in *The Layman's Handy Commentary* series (Grand Rapids: Zondervan Publishing House, 1957) p.11 say, but Henry Alford, *Alford's Greek Testament Vol. II* (London: Rivington's, 1871) p.473 thinks not.

1:2 -- *To the church of God which is at Corinth, to those who have been sanctified in Christ Jesus, saints by calling, with all who in every place call on the name of our Lord Jesus Christ, their* **Lord** *and ours:*

To the church of God which is at Corinth -- Verse 2 gives the address to which this letter is sent. It also gives a description of the church at Corinth. (1) It belonged to *God*! (2) It was "sanctified." (3) It was composed of "saints." The recipients of the letter are, first of all, designated collectively as a body, and then described by their Christian character and their associates.

- "*Church*" (*ekklēsia*) speaks of those who were 'called out' – in this case, called out of the world. (Any 'called out' assembly could be called an *ekklēsia*. See Acts 19:41.[8]) The term may be translated 'assembly,' or 'congregation,' or 'church' and is used in both a local and also in a universal sense in the Scriptures. In its universal sense, "church" embraces all the spirits in the universe that obey God as the ruler and lawgiver (Hebrews 12:22-29). In its local sense, "church" embraces all the people in a community who have been called out, separated from the world by the gospel, and who are bound together by a common faith in Jesus Christ. In verse 2 the term is used in a local sense, to designate the local congregation in Corinth.
- The members of the Corinthian church had fallen into many sinful habits, yet Paul speaks of the "church of God ... at Corinth." How far away from the Divine pattern can a people get, and still be recognized by God as a "church of God"? Or, could it be that when Paul speaks of the "church of God," he is thinking only of those in Corinth who have not disqualified themselves by sin from being members of Christ's church?
- The congregation of believers at Corinth was addressed as a "church of God"[9] to distinguish it from other groups which could also be called 'assemblies.' This is a theocratic designation. It denotes a chosen people, *called out* of heathen nations. The "congregation of God" or "church of God" is an Old Testament designation of Is-

---

[8] The Christians bypassed the regular 1st century Greek words in use for religious brotherhoods, and made this word (*ekklēsia*) their characteristic name for the believers. Perhaps they were influenced in their choice by the fact the LXX uses this word for the Old Testament assembly of Israelites. Its use points to the fact that the church is not merely one religious group among many. It is unique!

[9] The same expression can be found at Numbers 16:3, 20:4, 1 Corinthians 10:32, 11:16,22, 15:9, 2 Corinthians 1:1, Galatians 1:13, 1 Timothy 3:5. There are other Scriptural terms for the body of Christ. One familiar one is "Churches of Christ" - Romans 16:16 (or "Christian Churches" or "Christ's churches"). This designation emphasizes Christ's ownership of the church. Another title is "Church of the Lord" - Acts 20:28. This also speaks of Christ's ownership. "Church of the firstborn (ones)" - Hebrews 12:23 (the word is plural in the Greek). In ancient families, the "firstborn" had certain privileges and responsibilities. So it is with the men and women who have been born again and who make up the assembly of "firstborn ones." "Church of God" is the designation most used in the Scriptures for the Church, other than the word "church" itself. Some think this language points to the fact that God planned the church. Others think that since the New Testament epistles were written mostly to people who had come out of paganism, it is called "God's congregation" -- to distinguish it from Diana's congregation, or Astarte's or Apis' congregations. We possibly speak of it as the "church of Christ" more often than we do "church of God" in order that we may distinguish the church from anything that had its origin in the Old Testament (cp. Acts 7:38, KJV). It is a shame that because of factions in Christendom we have been forced to go looking for an appropriate name to tack above the door of the building so people can identify us.

rael as a divinely gathered people (Numbers 20:4 ASV). Many think in the New Testament that the church is often designated "church of God" because the church is a complement and expansion of the Old Testament Hebrew theocracy.

- In the Corinthian letter it is the "church *of God*," not the church of this or that party leader. This is a genitive of possession ("of God"). The Corinthian church is hereby emphatically declared to belong not to any human leader, but to God alone. This is a protest against the party spirit prevailing at Corinth.
- "At Corinth" reminds us that geographical divisions are the only divisions in the church recognized in the New Testament. The church in one place or city is always spoken of as a unit. Though consisting of one or more distinct congregations, it is regarded as an organic whole. The local church is the only divine organizational expression of the Kingdom of God on earth. These local churches were bodies distinct and separate, without any organic connection with one another; each was a distinct body within itself. The members of these local assemblies, under the direction of the Holy Spirit, chose their own overseers and workers.

To those who have been sanctified -- The ASV begins this phrase with "*even* them ..." with the "even" in italics. This is not another class of persons (in addition to the "church of God"), but is a description of those who comprise the church. The term "sanctified" is plural, whereas the term "church" just used is singular. Paul often loves to dwell on the multiple sides of a concept or an idea. The perfect participle *hagiasmenoi*[10] ("have been sanctified") tells of a past act and its present continuing result. The Corinthians, once made holy by the grace of God in Christ Jesus, by faith continue in this holiness. "Sanctified" here probably includes conversion, faith, justification, and the life of good works. In other words, "sanctified" in this place is a metaphor for conversion to Christ.[11] Paul calls the Corinthians "they that are sanctified" in spite of the fact that he has much fault to find with them. Those who overstrain the term to mean "total sanctification," or, if not that, a pietistic, puritanic, or other type of self-chosen holiness, are here corrected by Paul. He likewise corrects those who go to the other extreme and think holiness remains where grave faults are allowed to continue and become permanent in a congregation.

In Christ Jesus -- Those addressed in the letter are not only the "church of God ... in Corinth," but are those who are 'in Christ Jesus set apart to divine service.' Most commentators refer to the time the Corinthian church members had been baptized into Christ as the time when they were "sanctified in Christ Jesus." The phrase "in Christ Jesus" is to be understood as meaning "in union and communion with Christ" or "in connection with Him." Our entire Christian life became such and is such only in vital connection with Christ Jesus. If the connection signified by the preposition "in" (*en*) is canceled, we cease to be "sanctified" in any sense.

---

[10] The Greek form can be either a middle or passive voice. "Sanctify" is often found in the middle voice, since it is something one does for his own benefit.

[11] The student will find a Special Study concerning "Sanctification" in the author's *New Testament Epistles: Romans*.

Saints by calling ("called to be saints," ASV) -- This was Paul's and God's expectation for them. This is the intent of their calling. 'Saint' and 'sanctified' are translations of the same Greek root, a word meaning to be set apart to sacred service. In this context it is service to God, not service to this or that party. Their call or invitation to the Messianic kingdom,[12] like Paul's to his apostleship in Christ, came to them from God in Christ Jesus and through the preachers of the gospel. What is a 'saint' (*hagiois*)? Related to the word "sanctified", it means those who are separated from the world, set apart to God as holy. It does not mean the Corinthian believers were all they should have been, as Paul's letter shortly will make plain, and the term "saints" is never used by Paul in its restricted modern meaning (i.e., some exemplary saint, now dead and canonized by the church). Rather, Paul applies the term to the whole baptized, living church. Every Christian is a saint. Paul's repetition of the reference to the readers' holiness ("saints") recalls them to their vocation; low practice (such as found at Corinth) calls for the reassertion of high ideals.

With all who ... call upon the name of our Lord Jesus Christ -- The Greek verb "call" is here in the middle voice, meaning not 'who are called by the name' (cp. James 2:7, Amos 9:12 LXX), but rather, 'all who call upon the name for their own benefit.' The word "call upon" may imply conversion,[13] or prayer,[14] or worship.[15] Note that Paul uses various designations to characterize the readers. He calls the Corinthians "sanctified." He speaks of the "calling upon the name of our Lord" that Christians in other places are doing. Why does he thus vary the designations? It is a way of protesting against Corinthian party practice. As they look into their own hearts, do they find holiness? As they assemble together, is it the Lord Jesus who is uppermost in their minds, whose service and honor they are promoting? Does their behavior indicate they are God's church? Paul's emphasis that the church covers a large area, put forward in the very opening of the letter, at once directs the readers' minds from the narrow spirit of faction which was exhibiting itself at Corinth. The significance of the appellation "Lord" here given to Jesus is explained in comments on the following verse. We tend to think of this word as part of His name, as if it were "Lord Jesus Christ." But "Lord" is not His first name. When we remember the

---

[12] On the "calling" or "invitation" to become a Christian, see Ephesians 4:1,4; 2 Thessalonians 1:11; 2 Timothy 1:9; Hebrews 3:1; 2 Peter 1:10. All who accept the invitation offered in the gospel are the "called" of Jesus Christ. Cf. 2 Thessalonians 2:14, "called by the gospel."

[13] That it may speak of conversion ("belief" and "confession") is seen in Romans 10:9-13 where the "calling upon the name of the Lord" is explained in detail.

[14] At times the verb is used of prayer. Cf. Acts 7:59, 9:14, 2 Corinthians 12:8. "To call upon" is to invoke Christ's aid and help.

[15] That it has reference to worship in this Corinthian context is a very intriguing probability. *Worship* – While Jesus gave instructions concerning how the Father is to be worshiped (John 4:24), we note here (in 1 Corinthians 1:1ff) the very likely direct testimony to the divine worship of Jesus as being universal in the 1st century church. In similar fashion, we find reference in early Christian literature to the fact that the Christians "sang hymns unto Jesus as unto God." "Call" here is a present tense verb, referring to continuous worship. And note Who is the object of the worship – the Lord Jesus Christ. All this has a bearing on the letter's later content.

master of slaves in the 1st century was a "lord," and then think of Christians as being slaves of Jesus Christ, we begin to sense something of the meaning of "Lord."

In every place – This phrase may have two possible meanings.[16] Perhaps this may mean the same as 2 Corinthians 1:1, "With all the saints who are throughout Achaia." That is, Paul is reminding the Corinthians that they are part of a wider brotherhood. There were other brethren in other places called by the same gospel; the Corinthians are not the only saints. Or the words may imply Paul's exhortations are applicable to all Christians wherever they may be, and whatever may be their varying shades of individual opinion. Under this interpretation, Paul is writing to *all* the church, thus making this a "catholic epistle." This would make us duty bound to all the applicable principles set forth. It can be shown that Paul indeed expected his epistles to be read in all the churches (cp. 1 Thessalonians 5:27, Colossians 4:16).

Their *Lord* and ours -- "Lord" is in italics (in the ASV, NASB) to show there is no corresponding word in the original Greek, yet our translators felt the need to supply something to complete the meaning of a sentence. Have they supplied the right word here? The original simply reads, "both theirs and ours." To what does "theirs" refer? Some say that "place" is the proper word to supply. "In their country, wherever that may be ...."[17] It would then mean Paul's good wishes (for grace and peace, verse 3) are the same wishes that Christians in a number of places (wherever they may be) have for the Corinthians. Others say "Lord" is the best word to supply. It has been in all ages a fatal temptation of party Christians to claim a monopoly of Christ for themselves and their own sects, as though *they* only taught the gospel, and were the *only* Christians or the *only* 'evangelicals.' But Christ cannot be parceled into fragments (verses 12,13), nor has any party a right to boast exclusively, "I am of Christ." The word "our" (in the phrase "the name of *our* Lord Jesus") could not be regarded as superfluous in writing to a church of which one section wanted to assert an exclusive right in Christ. The Corinthians are to think of themselves as being joined together with all those who confess the Lord in every place over the entire world.

1:3 -- *Grace to you and peace from God our Father and the Lord Jesus Christ.*

Grace to you and peace -- This prayer for grace and peace is Paul's greeting in all his epistles (except the Pastoral Epistles, in which he adds the word "mercy"). It is a remarkable blending of the Greek and Jewish salutations. Greeks, when greeting someone, said "*chairein*;" to them, the word "grace" (*charis*) involved the notions of joy and brightness

---

[16] A recent, but unacceptable, third interpretation has been given to this expression. It is that at Corinth there were some folk who had not "transferred their membership" or become affiliated with the local congregation, and these are the ones identified by the words "in every place." The New Testament knows nothing of a concept of individual Christians who try to go it alone, without participation in a local congregation of believers.

[17] "To supply 'place' is far better than to join 'both theirs and ours' with Lord, thereby making the first 'our' superfluous." (Alford, *op. cit.*, p. 474)

and prosperity. Scripturally, it speaks of unmerited favor, lovingkindness, all the blessings bestowed on man by God. We do not deserve it, but we cannot get along without it. 'May the Lord give you an abundance of His undeserved gifts' is Paul's prayer. Grace, then peace. Tranquility can only come after grace. The usual Hebrew greeting was "*Peace* be to you" (Hebrew, *shalom l^{e}kha*), and it denotes much more than does "peace" in English. It includes the entire welfare of the individual, both spiritual and physical. It does not mean simply the absence of strife, but speaks of the presence of positive blessings. It encompasses the prosperity of the whole man, especially his spiritual prosperity (Morris, *op. cit.*, p.35), peace with God and peace with men. It has been remarked that "peace" here has a peculiar weight given the dissensions in the Corinthian church. The peace wished for them also includes rest, satisfaction, tranquility, and happiness of heart. The church unites both forms of greeting: "grace," the beginning of every blessing; and "peace," the end of all blessings.

From God our Father and the Lord Jesus Christ -- God and Jesus are the source of every good gift and every perfect gift, like grace and peace. That one of the members of the Godhead is described as "our Father" is a distinctive Christian designation for God. It goes back to the consciousness and teaching of Jesus.[18] This is the fourth time in three verses that the name of "Jesus Christ" has appeared.[19] Is there a significance to the repeated mention of the Savior? Should not the Corinthians be crying up the name of Jesus Christ, rather than the party names they are ranging themselves under?

What is the bearing of this salutation on the doctrine of "subordinationism" (i.e., the idea that Jesus is lower than God, and never was or will be equal with the Father)? Some have tried to show, since the Father is called "God" and Jesus is called "Lord," that Jesus is somehow a lesser deity than the Father. Several lines of thought show that whatever the reason for the different appellations given here, it is not because Jesus is somehow a lesser being than the Father. One line of thought results from a study of Hebrews 1 and John 5. Hebrews 1 gives several attributes that Jesus has which make him God. In fact, twice the Father calls Jesus "God" (Hebrews 1:8,9). John 5 gives five evidences of Jesus' equality with the Father. Jesus' deity is not somehow lesser than the deity of the Father! Another line of thought results from a study of the use of the term "Lord" in the Scriptures. The Hebrews were hesitant to pronounce the ineffable name YHWH ("Jehovah" or "Yahweh") lest they take it in vain, so they regularly substituted "Lord" (*Adonai*) for that term.[20] If Jesus is called "Lord," it is because He and the Father are equally 'self-existent

---

[18] See His cry from the cross, "Father, into thy hands ...." See also His prayers in Gethsemane (Matthew 26:39), or His reply to Joseph and Mary at the age of twelve, "I must be about my Father's business."

[19] Paul was an apostle of Christ Jesus. The Corinthians had become believers ("sanctified") in Christ Jesus. Christians universal are designated as those who call on the name of our Lord Jesus Christ. Now grace and peace are received from God the Father and the Lord Jesus Christ.

[20] When the Old Testament was translated into Greek, the LXX translators used *kurios* (Lord) to translate *Jehovah*. They used *theos* (God) to translate *Elohim*.

ones' (Jehovah). A third line of thought results from a study of the grammar of 1 Corinthians 1:3. By using the preposition "from" (*apo*) only once, Paul intends to show that the two objects (grace and peace) are governed by it. "God our Father" and "the Lord Jesus Christ" are regarded as a unit and are thus placed on a level of equality.

So, while insisting that Jesus is God (i.e., that Scripture presents Jehovah as being three co-equal and co-eternal persons in the Godhead), we at the same time recognize that Scripture presents Jesus, when He became incarnate, as being temporarily subordinate in function to the Father. (1) When the Father, Son, and Holy Spirit first conceived God's eternal plan (Romans 8:28-30), Jesus was the One who volunteered to become incarnate and be a sacrifice for sin, if one were needed by the men they were about to create. (He is the lamb slain from the foundation of the world.) (2) While Jesus was here on earth, He Himself affirmed that He did nothing on his own initiative (John 5:19,30; 12:49), and also said "The Father is greater than I" (John 14:28). While affirming His temporary subordination in order to effect redemption for man, Jesus at the same time claimed equality with the Father (John 5:17,18). He was subordinate in position or function, but not in the quality of deity! (3) We also suppose 1 Corinthians 15:22-28 indicates that at the time of His second coming, Jesus' temporary subordination to the Father will be ended. In the meantime, because He volunteered to become the Redeemer, Jesus is the "Lord" who is exercising all the authority that was given to Him before He ever came to Bethlehem (Mark 2:10; John 3:35, 5:27; Matthew 28:18).

It is misguided to attempt to prove Jesus is a created being, or a lesser deity than the Father, by appealing to the language Paul used in this greeting to the Corinthian church. The fact that one person is called "our Father" and the other "the Lord Jesus Christ" does not lower the second. It merely shows that in the Godhead all three persons were not fathers, all three were not incarnate, but each bears a distinct relation to us and our salvation which is unaffected by the identity of their essence. God is "our Father" because we are His children in Christ Jesus. Jesus is "our Lord" because He has redeemed, purchased, and won us; we are His own and live under Him in His kingdom. As long as this one preposition coordinates "our Father" and "our Lord," making them one fountain of saving grace and peace, no ingenuity of men will be able to sever them or use them to introduce a faulty theory of subordination (i.e., that Jesus is of lesser deity or essence than the Father).

B. Paul's Thanksgiving for God's Work in Corinth. 1:4-9

It was customary in 1st century letters to open with a word of thanksgiving. Such a word of thanksgiving is a regular feature in Paul's epistles – except the Epistle to the Galatians, in which he plunges at once into severe rebuke of his readers. Such thanksgivings were not a mere endeavor to flatter the readers. This thanksgiving is not designed to win their attention and acceptance of his subsequent exhortations. Compare

Romans 1:8; Philippians 1:3-5. Paul usually has a good word for something praiseworthy the people he was addressing were doing. But not in Corinthians! Paul's word of thanks speaks of what God has done for them through Christ, but there is no thanks for what the Corinthians themselves were doing.

1:4 -- *I thank my God always concerning you for the grace of God which was given you in Christ Jesus,*

I thank my God -- In this paragraph, Paul expresses his joyful thanks that the gospel has come to the readers of this letter, and that they have had an abundance of spiritual gifts bestowed by God. The use of the singular, "*I* thank *MY* God ...," in contrast with the plural in the previous verses, indicates Paul does not include Sosthenes with him as the author of this thanksgiving. It is written in Paul's name alone and expresses Paul's personal prayer, which he regularly offered to God. The verb "thank" is a present tense verb in the Greek, indicating habitual action on Paul's part. "My God" (as in Romans 1:8, Philippians 1:3-5, and elsewhere) is not used in an exclusive sense, but as an avowal of his own personal communion with God and direct interest in Him, a personal attestation of his religious position.

Always concerning you -- That is, constantly, on all occasions of special prayer. Paul made it a habit to thank God for them whenever he prayed. The Corinthians were but one of a number of churches included on Paul's regular prayer list.[21] This does not imply Paul was engaged all the time, day and night, in audible thanksgiving. But Paul did have this Corinthian church perpetually on his heart, with grateful emotions to God for what He had done for them.

For the grace of God -- The preposition is "for" (*epi*), and gives the occasion or cause of his thanksgiving to God. Sometimes "grace" is a reference is to the "unmerited favor" that God bestows upon us when we become Christians, forgiving our sins. However, in this context, "grace" is probably to be understood to be a reference to the "spiritual gifts" bestowed on them, as the following verses explain. It is not only because of verses 5-7 that we are inclined to so interpret. It is also because we regularly are accustomed to find in Paul's greeting and thanksgiving the ideas that will be unfolded and developed in the heart of the letter, and spiritual gifts certainly form a large part (chapters 12-14) of this letter. "Grace" then is an ellipsis for "gifts of God's grace." We find similar language in Romans 12:6, where spiritual gifts are called "grace."

Which was given you -- If the above reference to "grace" is to the grace given when one becomes a Christian, this aorist tense verb ("given") refers to the time of their baptism. This would then be one of Paul's baptismal aorists. If, as we believe, the word "grace" has specific reference to "spiritual gifts," then this word "given" would look back to the time when they received the gifts. Such reception of spiritual gifts usually resulted from the

---

[21] See also 1 Thessalonians 1:2, 2:13; 2 Thessalonians 1:3, 2:13; Colossians 1:3; Philippians 1:4; and Philemon 4 to get an idea of the churches who were on Paul's regular prayer list.

laying on of an apostle's hands (cp. Acts 8:17,18, 19:6; 2 Timothy 1:6). More will be said on the reception of spiritual gifts at 1 Corinthians 12-14. Paul ever bore his congregations on his heart and constantly prayed for them. He does not merely ask God to bestow additional grace and gifts upon them to supply their spiritual needs. He always remembers with a grateful heart the many gifts God has already granted to his people.

In Christ Jesus -- This "in" must not, as in the KJV, be rendered "by," for the grace had been given to those "in Christ," as members of Christ. It does not appear Paul is saying the grace was given "by" Christ. "In Christ" is the place where the grace of God is manifested (cp. 2 Corinthians 5:19). It is because of their relationship to Christ that they have received this "grace."

1:5 -- *that in everything you were enriched in Him, in all speech and all knowledge,*

That in everything -- Verse 5 extends the thought of verse 4, 'I give thanks for the grace given you, because (*hoti*) in everything ...!' *Hoti* stands as an explicative apposition. The "everything" for which Paul gives thanks is defined as "in every kind of speech [utterance] and all knowledge."

You were enriched in Him -- The Corinthians abounded (*ploutidzō*[22]) in the things he is about to mention. The spiritual gifts were abundantly bestowed upon them. "Enriched" is an aorist tense, and looks back to the same time implied in the word "given" used in the previous verse. The verb is *ploutidzesthai* instead of the more frequent *perisseuein*, 'to abound,' and suggests that formerly the Corinthians were poor spiritually, utterly destitute, but that this has now been wondrously changed; they have come into great spiritual wealth.

In all speech ("in all utterance," ASV) -- "All ... all." This English translates the Greek word *pas* which, when used in the singular as here and without the article, means "every kind of" (BAGD). "In" carries the meaning of 'in the sphere of.' "Speech" is one area where the enrichment took place. Those writers who think the reference in "speech" (*logos*) is to the spiritual gift of speaking in tongues are likely correct.[23] "The ability to speak the gospel in different tongues" (Lipscomb, *op. cit.*, p.23). "With the power of speaking various languages (*en panti logo*). That this power was conferred on the church at Corinth, and that it was highly valued by them is evident from chapter 14; compare 2 Corinthians 8:7."[24]

---

[22] The Greek word translated "enriched" is the basis of the English word *plutocrat*, indicating a wealthy person.

[23] Some have asserted that the reference is *not* to the gift of speaking in tongues. "*Logos* ought to be translated 'in all doctrine,' not 'utterance,' as though the reference were to powers of eloquence or the gift of tongues." So say Luther, Calvin, and Lenski. "Utterance, the telling forth of the truth" (Morris, *op. cit.*, p.36). However, this commentator can see no reason to doubt that the reference by Paul is to spiritual gifts.

[24] Albert Barnes, "1 Corinthians" in *Barnes Notes* (Grand Rapids: Baker, 1953), p.3.

And all knowledge -- From this word *gnōsis* ("knowledge") is derived the name Gnostic, which was applied to many forms of ancient heresy. It is doubtful that any reference to this ancient heresy here is to be imagined, for it seems 1 Corinthians was written 5 or 10 years before the incipient form of that heresy began to infiltrate the churches.[25] "Knowledge" (like the gift of tongues in the previous clause) was one of the spiritual gifts (see comments at 1 Corinthians 12:8, 13:8). What is the difference between "all speech [utterance]" and "all knowledge"? Considerable discussion has arisen concerning the precise meaning of these two expressions.[26] Some say the former represents *the truth spoken*; the latter, *the truth received*. Tongues were foreign languages used for evangelistic purposes (cp. Acts 2) to convey the Gospel to those of foreign tongue. God had granted this gift generously to the church at Corinth. Knowledge was one of the spiritual gifts, perhaps given so the early Christians could know God's will for the new dispensation. In this gift too, the Corinthians were rich. Paul thanks God that He had been so generous to the Corinthian church, as He made available to them an abundance of "spiritual gifts."

1:6 -- *even as the testimony concerning Christ was confirmed in you,*

Even as -- The idea in *kathōs* is "inasmuch as;" verse 6 is thus a continuation and an elaboration of what was said in the previous verse about the spiritual gifts. *Kathōs* suggests that the "enriching" and the "confirming" were simultaneous events.

The testimony concerning Christ ("testimony of Christ," ASV) -- "The testimony concerning Christ"[27] was spoken by the apostles Paul and Silas on the 2nd missionary journey, or perhaps by Paul in particular. Although not a common expression in Paul's writings (cp. 1 Corinthians 2:1, 2 Thessalonians 1:10, 2 Timothy 1:8), the term "testimony" refers to the gospel itself. We suppose Paul used this expression because he intended to use the verb "confirmed," and that verb better pairs with "testimony" than "gospel."

Was confirmed in you -- When the gospel was preached to the Corinthians, God "confirmed" the truth of the message by giving spiritual gifts. *Bebaioō* ("confirmed") means "guarantee, establish, make firm, prove reliable." It is a legal term from commercial law

---

[25] Nothing would be gained in our understanding of 1 Corinthians were we to suppose that *gnōsis* here should be construed to mean the Corinthians possessed some hidden mystical knowledge available only from Gnostics by which men could somehow reach God and be saved. In Gnosticism, that mystical knowledge was learned apart from the doctrine of Christ, whereas in this passage Paul explicitly affirms that what the Corinthians have received is "in Christ" (verse 4) and "in Him" (verse 5) – not apart from Him.

[26] Among the attempted explanations are these: (1) *Logos* refers to the gift of tongues and *gnōsis* refers to the gift of prophecy. (2) *Logos* refers to a lower and *gnōsis* refers to a higher kind of knowledge. (3) *Logos* refers to how the gospel came to them and *gnōsis* refers to their hearty acceptance of it. (4) *Logos* refers to the rational and *gnōsis* to the ecstatic gifts. (5) *Logos* refers to truth learned by rational means, while *gnōsis* refers to an inward awareness of cosmic relationships that supersede rational and conventional rules.

[27] Thus it is an objective genitive, and not a subjective genitive.

designating a properly guaranteed security. The verb is often used in the papyri in a legal sense of 'guarantee.'[28] The New Testament Scriptures everywhere indicate that the purpose of the miraculous spiritual gifts was to confirm the truthfulness of the gospel message. The things spoken about Christ were every bit true! "It was proved to be divine by the miraculous attestations of the Holy Spirit. The word translated 'confirmed' is used in the sense of establishing, confirming, or demonstrating by miracles – Mark 16:20; compare Hebrews 2:4, 13:9, Philippians 1:7."[29] B.B. Warfield has shown there were two signs by which a man could demonstrate beyond doubt that he was an apostle of Jesus – the ability to work miracles (2 Corinthians 12:12) and the ability to pass on spiritual gifts (Hebrews 2:3,4; 1 Corinthians 1:6; 2 Timothy 1:6; and Acts 8:16-18). The gifts the Corinthians received were evidence that Paul's testimony about Christ was a true message, and that God was even then generously at work among the Corinthians. For this activity of God, Paul is genuinely thankful.

1:7 -- *so that you are not lacking in any gift, awaiting eagerly the revelation of our Lord Jesus Christ,*

So that -- Beginning with "so that" (*hōste* and the infinitive speak of contemplated result, or the result tended to be produced), verse 7 describes the result of the 'gift of grace' and the 'enrichment' and the 'confirmation' spoken of in previous verses. Surely when we see how these verses tie together, there is no reason to explain "grace" in verse 5 as a reference to anything other than spiritual gifts!

You are not lacking in any gift ("Ye come behind in no gift," ASV) -- The 'gifts' are here the "spiritual gifts" (*charisma*), such as the powers of healing, miracles, and prophecy, which were the result of the outpouring of the Spirit (cp. 1 Corinthians 12:1ff).[30] Greek words ending in *-ma* emphasize the result of an action. A *charisma* is *charis* in some concrete result – a specific endowment of God's grace. "Not lacking" or "come behind" in the Greek may also mean 'causing you not to be conscious of inferiority.' The middle voice form *husteraisthai* ("not lacking") implies subjective reflection. Compare the case of the prodigal son (Luke 15:14) where he "began to feel his destitution." Among the Corinthian Christians there was to be no consciousness of lagging behind other churches or other individuals[31] in any of the gifts bestowed. The Corinthian church had as many or more gifts than any other church. God had done no less for them and in them than He had accomplished in others who are "in Christ."

---

[28] A. Deissmann, *Bible Studies*, p.104ff.

[29] Barnes, *op. cit.*, p.4.

[30] The word *charisma* is used, (1) of Christ's work for us (Romans 5:15); (2) of God's good gifts in general as He calls men to do a special task for Him (Romans 11:29), gifts such as enumerated in Romans 9:4,5; and (3) of special equipments of the Spirit, as enumerated in 1 Corinthians 12:4ff. Here the thought seems to be to #3, though a strong case could be made for #2.

[31] Later in 1 Corinthians, Paul will deal with the quest of some Corinthians for better gifts because they felt inferior to some of their brethren. Paul, anticipating what he will write later, says there is no need to feel impoverished in the area of gifts. God has not short-changed them!

Awaiting eagerly the revelation of our Lord Jesus ("waiting for the revelation," ASV) – "Waiting" is a word sometimes used of "waiting for the second coming of Christ" (cp. Philippian 3:20; Hebrews 9:28), but not always (cp. 1 Peter 3:20; Galatians 5:5). The word means to "wait diligently, persistently, devotedly." "Revelation" (*apokalupsis*) is also a word sometimes used to refer to the second coming (as 2 Thessalonians 1:7; 1 Peter 1:7,13), but again, not always. In fact, Thayer's first definition under the metaphorical use of the word is "a disclosure of truth, *instruction*, concerning divine things before unknown – especially those relating to the Christian salvation ...."[32] The KJV at this place reads "waiting for the coming[33] of the Lord Jesus Christ," and not a few commentaries on 1 Corinthians read "the reference (in this clause) is to the second coming of Christ." Such an interpretation results in the need to further explain what Paul did or did not imply. Some writers will affirm Paul mistakenly believed the second advent would occur during his own lifetime. (Since this impinges on the doctrine of inspiration, much is written to defend how Paul could be mistaken in what he writes, yet at the same time be inspired to write the very words he did.) Some eschatological views, which have the "revelation" occurring seven or more years after the "*parousia* and rapture of the church," will spend pages explaining how Paul could have suggested the raptured church will still be waiting the "revelation" (for such language would seem to require a post-tribulation rapture). Others will defend the view that "revelation" cannot refer to the destruction of Jerusalem (AD 70), which was still future when Paul wrote this letter. Still others will explain that even if the reference is to the second advent, Paul certainly did not imply that the gifts would last till then, any more than his statement would imply that the Corinthians would live till then.

It has already been observed that, in his thanksgiving paragraphs, Paul often alludes to topics he will discuss at length in the body of the letter. Could he be doing that here? If so, perhaps verses 5-7 anticipate the subject matter of chapters 12-14, and verse 7 may say the same thing 1 Corinthians 13:8-10 seems to say, that the gifts were intended to function only till "revelation" was completed. "Revelation" is used in 1 Corinthians 14:6, 26, 30, of a "revelation" of information concerning God's plans and purposes, rather than being a specific reference to the second advent. See also 1 Corinthians 2:10 where "revelation" speaks of a disclosure of truths about salvation, etc. (In fact, unless 1:7 is a reference to the second coming, the word "revelation" is not used in 1 Corinthians of the second advent of Jesus.) When people have been instructed about Jesus Christ and His mission or purpose in the world, they will have better opportunity to be "blameless" when the "day of the Lord" (verse 8) does finally come.

1:8 -- *who will also confirm you to the end, blameless in the day of our Lord Jesus Christ.*

Who -- To whom does the relative "who" refer? Alford (*op. cit.*, p.475) and Shore (*op.*

---

[32] J.H. Thayer, *A Greek-English Lexicon of the New Testament* (New York: American Book Co., 1886), p. 62.

[33] It is the only time the KJV *renders apokalupsis* as "coming." That version uses "appearing" or "manifestation" or "revelation" the other times this particular Greek word occurs.

cit., p.13) think "who" refers to "God," the One to whom Paul's prayer is addressed (verse 4). 2 Corinthians 1:21 and Romans 16:25 are adduced as evidence that "God" is the one who "confirms" or "establishes" Christians. However, others (e.g., F.W. Farrar, *The Pulpit Commentary Vol. 19*, Grand Rapids, MI: Eerdmans, 1962, p.4) think "who" refers to "Christ," and this indeed is likely the best choice. In 2 Thessalonians 3:3 we have likewise the work of confirming believers ascribed to Christ. Ephesians 5:27 has Christ presenting the church "unblemished and unimpeached" to Himself at the close of the church age. He confirms them and vindicates their character, just as God confirmed the gospel message about Him.

In verse 7, Paul used two present tense verbs, "you are not lacking in any gift" and "waiting for," and both point to the present state of the Corinthians. The "revelation of Jesus Christ" (i.e., the Corinthian's better understanding of the gospel message) will occur after this letter has been received by the Corinthians. In the interval until those future events occur (i.e., until they grow in their knowledge of Christ, and until the 'day of the Lord' dawns), Paul explains in this relative clause (verse 8) what Christ will continue to do for the Christians. Then in verse 9 Paul adds another sentence concerning what God will do in addition to what He has already done at Corinth.

Shall also confirm you -- The Greek means "to confirm, to establish, to guarantee." It is the same verb used in verse 6. The next phrase will explain the "how" of the confirmation done by Christ. As part of His work as intercessor and man's representative in heaven, Jesus will see to it that no indictment can be lodged successfully against the believer.

To the end -- Probably it speaks of the end of each Christian's present life.[34] Jesus will faithfully perform His mediatorial offices on behalf of each believer, so long as the person continues to be a believer (see Hebrews 3:6, 6:11). A reminder about theology is in order. It will be recalled that John Calvin found his major doctrinal emphases in Romans and 1 Corinthians, and then read those findings into all the rest of the Scriptures. We are now studying one of the verses Calvin used as the basis of his doctrine of unconditional eternal security – the perseverance of the saints.[35] While squaring Calvinistic dogma with Scripture is quite problematic, yet we must not ignore that this verse truly promises Christ's help in a believer's everyday life, until such time as the "end" comes. If a person ceases to be a believer, there is no promise of Christ's continuing help.

Blameless ("*that ye be* unreprovable," ASV) -- The KJV rendered it "blameless." The word may also be translated 'unimpeached.' The verb *anegklētous* (which also appears at

---

[34] Only if the "revelation of Jesus Christ" is made to refer to the second coming would the "end" be a reference to the end of the present age. While Jesus Himself will function in His high priestly role till the end of the present age, this verse certainly is not a promise that the Corinthian Christians to whom this letter is sent would themselves still be living on earth at the end of the age.

[35] On the "Perseverance of the Saints," see page 234ff in *Basic Christian Doctrines*, edited by Carl F.H. Henry (published in New York: Holt, Rinehart and Winston, 1962). See also Special Study #7 in the author's commentary on Romans, titled "Once in Grace, Am I Always in Grace?"

Colossians 1:22; 1 Timothy 3:10; Titus 1:6) means 'as not to be accused;' it is a forensic term. It says that no indictment may be successfully lodged before a judge. The word does not mean "perfect," but properly denotes those against whom there is no charge of crime, who are unaccused, and against whom there is no ground of accusation. A Christian is unreprovable, not in the sense of being sinless, but in the sense of having been forgiven, renewed, sanctified (1 Corinthians 6:11, Romans 8:30). The person who is 'unreprovable' when he is judged on the day of the Lord will appear at the judgment seat of Christ not indeed as sinless, but as a "new creature in Christ" (2 Corinthians 5:17), who having been previously restored (Ephesians 2:10) and progressively sanctified (1 Thessalonians 5:23), has worked out his own salvation in the moral power of a new life (Philippians 2:12). 'Unreproved,' yes, but by whom? During this life the devil, the "accuser of the brethren," makes accusation against them day and night (Revelation 12:10). But there is no evidence that the devil will accuse at the final judgment. Instead, compare Romans 8:33: being found holy in Christ and blameless before God, "who will bring any charge (impeachment) against God's elect? God is the one who justifies ...."

Is this promise of being "confirmed blameless" absolute or conditional? Some writers take it as absolute, saying we have to hold the doctrine of "eternal security" as being taught by Paul if this passage is to mean anything. If we treat it as conditional, we remove from the promise its blessedness and comfort, "for if this promise is to be of any value, it is the fact that it furnishes a guarantee against that greatest of dangers, the fickleness of the human will."[36] Other writers take the promise of "unimpeachableness" to be conditional. Conybeare and Howson add, "*He will do his part to* confirm you." Hammond (quoted by Kling, *op. cit.*, p.25), adds a qualification, "God will make good His promise if you yourselves do not fail." In light of what Scriptures elsewhere teach, this commentator treats this promise of unimpeachableness as conditional. Cf. Colossians 1:22,23 ("to present you holy and blameless and beyond reproach – if indeed you continue in the faith") and 1 Peter 1:5 (we "are protected by the power of God through faith, i.e., faithfulness ...."). If our sins have been forgiven, we are unaccusable, i.e., no one can accuse us. Note that Paul does not say the Corinthians are blameless *now* when he writes this letter to them; but with Christ's help that can be changed. Paul hopes they will redirect their thinking and attitudes so that when it comes time to stand in the judgment, Christ may Himself judge them blameless.

In the day of our Lord Jesus Christ -- This phraseology is regularly used to refer to the second coming of Christ and the judgment. We learn this truth by analogy of Scripture, appealing to 2 Peter 3:10-14, where the familiar Old Testament expression "day of the Lord" is synonymous with the second advent and the final judgment. In some verses, "day of the Lord" is called simply "the day" (cp. 3:13; Acts 1:20; Joel 3:4; 2 Thessalonians 1:10; Revelation 6:17). Both "unaccused" and "day of the Lord" show the character of the day. There is reference to the final judgment. In that day the Lord shall be revealed as Judge of the whole world. Several writers call attention to three distinct time periods alluded to

---

[36] C.F. Kling, "1 Corinthians" in *Lange's Commentary* (Grand Rapids: Zondervan, 1950 reprint), p.25.

in this paragraph of thanksgiving. *Past*: The time when the grace of God was given to them (verse 4). *Present*: The present time while they wait for the "revelation" of the Lord Jesus, endowed as they are with the gifts described in verses 5-7; it is the time when the glorified Christ ministers on their behalf ('confirms them') in the courts of heaven (verse 8). *Future*: the day of the Lord, the end of the age with its final judgment, when some will be accused, but not those who remained true to Jesus all their earthly lives.

1:9 -- *God is faithful, through whom you were called into fellowship with His Son, Jesus Christ our Lord.*

God is faithful -- The adjective *pistos* ("faithful") is placed emphatically forward in the Greek, and means trustworthy, reliable. God can be depended on! If He has been generous in His help to the Corinthians in days past (remember, this thanksgiving by Paul enumerates some things God has already done in Corinth), He can be counted on in the future. God will continue to do for faithful men everything He has promised He will do. He will not leave His promises unfulfilled or His work unfinished (10:13; 2 Thessalonians 3:3; Hebrews 10:23; Romans 8:28-30). He will not drop the work He has begun, after the fashion of weak, inconsistent men. But persevering in love, He will carry out that which was commenced in love, even to its goal. (Cp. Philippians 1:6; 1 Thessalonians 5:24; 2 Thessalonians 3:3; Romans 11:29.) If men continue steadfast in their obedience to God, God would persevere, and preserve them without blame through the power He exerts in Christ Jesus. The question that immediately comes to the reader's mind is, "Am I being faithful like my God is being faithful?"

Through whom -- We can speak of God as the mediating cause as well as the principal cause (Romans 11:36), as the moving cause and agent in salvation. It is His providence that, through a great variety of arrangements and cooperating circumstances, mediates the call, viz., the presentation of the gospel to them, and also its effect in their hearts.

You were called -- God calls men through the gospel (2 Thessalonians 2:14). The opening words of this letter reminded us that Paul's position as an apostle was due to a divine call. Now (as in 1 Corinthians 1:2) we see that there is likewise a "call" to every believer.

Into fellowship with His Son -- The genitive "son" (after *koinōnia*, "fellowship") can be subjective ("fellowship with") or objective ("fellowship in"). An example of the former is Philippians 1:5 (ASV), where "your fellowship" (literally, 'fellowship of you') means 'fellowship with you.' Objective genitives are like "the fellowship of His sufferings" (Philippians 3:10), which points to fellowship 'in' suffering. Since this is a genitive of a person, it is more likely to be a subjective genitive, though Ellicott thinks both ideas are included. Fellowship with Christ means a partnership with Him. Christians are partners with Christ (a) in His feelings and views, Romans 8:9; (b) in His trials and sufferings, being subjected to temptations and trials similar to His; (c) in His heirship to the inheritance and glory which awaits him; and (d) in His triumph in the resurrection and future glory. This participation in a common cause with Christ embraces our entire condition, from the time preachers were sent to share the gospel with us, through our baptism when we were buried with Christ and rose to walk in newness of life, on until we come into the inheritance of the glory which is to be revealed in Him and in us also. The content of this partnership – which the Corinthians share – is 'sonship to God,' since it is 'communion of [with] His Son,' with Christ the "firstborn among many brethren." Do we have here one of Paul's protests against party spirit at Corinth? The mention of fellowship may perhaps have been intended to prepare the way, as was done in verse 2, for the reproof which is coming, for "fellowship" is the direct antithesis to "divisions" in verse 10.

Jesus Christ our Lord -- Paul's whole desire was to rivet the mind of the Corinthian church to the name of Jesus Christ. Christ's name is repeated ten times in the first ten verses, while making no mention of any apostle or teacher. Nowhere in any other epistle is the name of Jesus Christ so oft repeated in such a short span of verses. The frequent mention of His name doubtless grew out of the desire of the apostle to draw them away from their party admiration of particular teachers to Christ alone (Lipscomb, *op. cit.*, p.25). Instead of treating Christianity as a matter of human choice and personal liking, the proper view is that in the church *CHRIST* is the one thing and everything! The title "Our Lord" (remember what was written at verse 3 on "Lord") added to "His Son, Jesus Christ" invests the Christian fellowship with present grandeur since it reminds us that Jesus is "God".

SECTION ONE: CONCERNING PARTISAN STRIFE & ITS CONSEQUENCES. 1:10-4:21

Summary: Beginning with 1:10, Paul introduces a topic which was one of the chief reasons he wrote this epistle -- viz., the divisive party spirit that existed in the hearts of many of the church members at Corinth. It is not until the close of chapter 4 that he will have finished with this topic.

A. PARTY SPIRIT AT CORINTH. 1:10-17

1:10 -- *Now I exhort you, brethren, by the name of our Lord Jesus Christ, that you all agree and that there be no divisions among you, but that you be made complete in the same mind and in the same judgment.*

Now -- The particle (*de* in the Greek) signals the transition from thanksgiving to reproof. *De*, often translated "but," introduces the transition from his exhibition of the bright side of the church to the reproof of its dark side. *De* is adversative. It sets what follows over against the preceding as a contrast to it. So far from "fellowship" (verse 9) being realized, there is division. Paul will state the problem, give his source of information (1:10-12), and then point out that such dissension violates a Christian's duty to complete and wholehearted devotion to Christ (1:13-17).

I exhort you, brethren ("I beseech you brethren," ASV) -- *Parakaleō* means 'I exhort you. I entreat you. I call upon you. I summon you. I plead with you.' ("Beseech" does not mean "beg;" that would not be the right idea.) He does not say, 'I order you,' or 'I command you.' The word Paul uses is tactful, yet Paul is not forgetting that he is writing as an apostle of Christ (verse 1). The authority he would exercise is the same whether he speaks softly or whether he finds himself compelled to speak sternly. Twice in two verses (10 and 11) Paul appeals to his readers as "brethren." He does this for several reasons: (1) It softens the rebuke. His language is not that of a schoolmaster with a rod; rather, he speaks from love. Both Paul and James (5:10) use the word to soften any harshness which might seem to exist in their language (cf. 7:29; 10:1; 14:20). (2) There is an appeal to them to aim at unity among themselves. After all, they are "brethren." (3) There were many troubles and faults among the Corinthians, and yet these do not sever the fraternal tie that binds them to Paul. (This reason is important and should not be minimized. However, this does not imply that congregations may settle permanently into evil conditions like those which existed at Corinth without eventually impairing their fraternal relations with Paul and with other Christians.) This entire letter is directed at one thing only: to remove the faults and evils that had begun to show themselves at Corinth, and which would, if unrepented, eventually lead to a rupture of the brotherhood.

By the name of our Lord Jesus Christ ("through the name ...," ASV) -- Here is the name of Jesus again. By it, Paul appeals to the strongest bond of union between true Christians – that of Christ's office and being. He is the Head of the church and thus is the source for unity. Paul's appeal to Christ would serve to remind the Corinthians (1) that into the name of Christ, and into none other, whether of Paul or of Apollos or of Cephas, had they been baptized; and (2) that the same Jesus Christ here designated "our Lord" was *their* Lord, and the "Lord of all," without an equal and without a rival, whether it be Paul or Apollos or Cephas. Paul urges them not to let any other name eclipse the name of Jesus Christ, by making it a rallying point around which to gather.

That you all agree ("that ye all speak the same thing," ASV) -- This is the subject of the first four chapters of this letter – that all may "agree" rather than permitting dissension and party spirit to continue. Compare Romans 15:6, "that with one accord you may with one voice glorify the God and Father of our lord Jesus Christ."[37] The Corinthians were doing the reverse – each one was glorifying himself and his party (verse 12). To "agree" or "speak the same thing" implies they were to have the same sentiments on the subjects which divided them (cp. Philippians 2:2). They were with one voice to avow their allegiance to the one Lord, to the exclusion of all divisive party watchwords. J.B. Lightfoot (*Notes on the Epistles of St. Paul*, Grand Rapids, MI: Zondervan, 1957, p.151) reminds us that "to speak the same thing" is strictly a classical expression used of political communities which are free from factions, or of different states which entertain friendly relations with each other. It is the regular word used of two hostile states or parties reaching agreement. To speak "the same thing" is to speak only as they were taught by the Holy Spirit. (Note that in verses 5-7 Paul has just mentioned the spiritual gifts with which they were endowed.)

---

[37] To speak "with one voice" does not rule out the Biblical truth that Christians may differ over matters of opinion (see Romans 14-15 and 1 Corinthians 8-10). Because we agree on matters of faith, it is entirely possible to have a loving, harmonious relationship while at the same time allowing our brothers to embrace their own convictions and practices in areas of Christian liberty. More will be said on this matter in the comments that follow.

And [that] there be no divisions among you -- The Greek is "schisms" (*schismata*). In Matthew 9:16 and Mark 2:21 the same Greek word is translated as "a rent (tear)" in a garment. The word is also used of ploughing a field. The Corinthian church is in danger of becoming as unsightly as a torn garment. In John 7:43, 9:16, and 10:19 we are told of a "division" of opinion about Jesus. It is the same word in the Greek, and those verses in John are an excellent illustration of the meaning here in 1 Corinthians. In John, they were arguing with one another about His significance. Reading this verse in light of verse 12, it is clear that these "divisions" were not denominations as we know them, but dissensions within the local church. The "divisions" at Corinth were not of the nature of hostile sects meeting in separate places and refusing communion with each other, but such as may exist in the bosom of the same congregation, consisting in alienation of feeling and party strifes (Charles Hodge, *An Exposition of the First Epistle to the Corinthians*, Grand Rapids, MI: Baker Book House, 1980, p.12). The dissension was still within the congregation at Corinth; it had not yet crystallized into split-off bodies, but it would have, if not attended to. Similar clashes occur in our congregations today.[38] Paul would not have us believe that differences of this kind are immaterial as long as no doctrine is directly involved. If they are allowed to continue, the result must eventually be a split in the congregation, and as such are both disturbing and destructive in their effect.

But you be made complete ("but that ye be perfected together," ASV) -- Literally, "to be repaired or reunited," it comes from the word *katartidzein*. It means to repair or to mend something that is torn (Matthew 4:21), to reunite and make perfect what has been broken, to knit together. A *katartister* was the acknowledged phrase in classical Greek for a reconciler of factions. William Barclay ("The Letters to the Corinthians" in *The Daily Study Bible Series*, Philadelphia: Westminster Press, 1956, p.15) has written: "The word he uses is a medical word which is used of knitting together bones that have been fractured, or joining together a joint that has been dislocated. The disunion is unnatural and must be cured for the sake of the health and efficiency of the body of the church."

In the same mind and the same judgment -- "Disposition" is the word Alford (*op. cit.*, p.476) picks to give the connotation he thinks one should get from the use of "mind" (*nous*). "What they think and believe" (on the topic of human leaders and the propriety of party spirit) is the idea of the word according to Farrar (*ibid.*). The word "embraces that peculiar mode of thought and of viewing life which lays the foundations for the moral judgments and for moral self-determination." "Opinion" is Alford's choice (*ibid.*) of an English word for "judgment" (*gnōmē*). "What they assert and do" is the comment by Farrar (*ibid.*). The word is used for "purpose, intention, opinion, declaration, resolve, design, aim, view expressed, counsel" (BAGD). "To be of the same mind and the same judgment must be practical among Christians, or else Paul would not have urged it. But it is only practical when all follow the things taught by the Lord. By deferring our judgment to His teaching and following the same we can be one. When we change things which God directs, or add

---

[38] Because of our own experience in congregations that have suffered dissension and division, and because we have experienced painfully destructive quarrels within our own congregations, we instinctively feel ourselves in touch with the life in the congregation at Corinth, and we read carefully to learn how to solve our own conflicts.

things not taught by the word, will we differ and divide."[39] Paul wants them to come to the same conclusions and practice on this subject of how they estimate the value of their preachers, and the following paragraphs through chapter 4 will help them see what that "same" mind and judgment is to be.[40] Paul desired for the Corinthian church members to have a spirit of love and harmony in Christ that would attract unsaved people to the gospel.

1:11 -- *For I have been informed concerning you, my brethren, by Chloe's* **people,** *that there are quarrels among you.*

For I have been informed concerning you, my brethren -- With "for" Paul begins his explanation of the area where the Corinthians need to be "knit together in the same mind and judgment." "For" means 'Let me explain what I'm talking about when I speak of divisions.' Here, Paul tells the Corinthians the source of his information about the dissension and bickering among the brethren at Corinth. "Informed" translates *edēlōthē*, and it speaks of definite information, the actual disclosure of facts. Paul did not learn about the sad situation from unsubstantiated rumors. The facts presented left no doubt as to what the situation was.

By Chloe's *people* ("by them *that are of the household* of Chloe," ASV) -- The Greek only has "by them of Chloe." Nothing is known of Chloe or her "people" with certainty. Was she a resident of Corinth? Have her "people" made a special trip to Ephesus? Was she a resident of Ephesus? She might have learned of the Corinthian church during a visit to Corinth.[41] Was she merely some Christian woman known to the Corinthians? It has been conjectured that Stephanas, Fortunatus, and Achaicus who were Corinthians now with Paul at Ephesus (16:16) may have been Chloe's slaves or freedmen.[42] Paul names the source

---

[39] David Lipscomb, "First Corinthians," in the *New Testament Commentary* series (Nashville, TN : Gospel Advocate, 1960), p.26.

[40] This passage has been lifted by a number of writers from its context (i.e., dissension over preachers) and used improperly to affirm that every church member must agree on every topic of belief and practice. To the contrary, this very letter (chapters 8-10), as well as Romans 14-15, allows for individual liberty in areas of opinion. And 1 Corinthians 12 speaks of the diversity in the congregational body. It is wrong to present 1 Corinthians 1:10 as teaching that in the congregation there must be dogmatic uniformity on all points, even points of opinion. (Of course, there must be agreement on the fundamental doctrines of the gospel. See 1 Corinthians 1:18, 3:23. See also Special Study #9, entitled "Faith, Opinion, and Love," in the author's commentary on Romans.) On many issues earnest and spiritual believers may have differences of opinion. These differences, however, should not lead to divisive attitudes and actions.

[41] T. Evans, writing comments on "1 Corinthians" in the *Bible Commentary* (New York: Scribners, 1886), says, "Chloe is usually considered a Corinthian Christian, whose people had come to Ephesus; but it is more in harmony with Paul's discretion to suppose that she was an Ephesian known to the Corinthians, whose people had come to Corinth and returned to Ephesus." Fisher and Fee (*op. cit.*, p.54) have similar comments.

[42] Stephanas is himself the head of a household (1 Corinthians 1:16). Perhaps the other two named are Chloe's people, who accompanied Stephanas to Ephesus, and together they were the source of Paul's intelligence about the situation at Corinth.

of his information. He is not entertaining idle rumors, which can do much damage in a church if their evil buzzing is not quieted. Nor is Paul secretive. The Corinthians need not ask, "Who told him?" Paul is quite open. Chloe's "people" certainly are not part of the group who called themselves "Paul's" people. For that matter, it would hardly have served to help the situation at Corinth to quote the words of one of the competing factions – whichever one they might have belonged to – as authorities on the situation there. Some suppose Chloe's "people" carried the letter written by the church to Paul (see notes at 7:1). Others suppose they arrived in Ephesus and are visiting Paul after the letter from Corinth had already been received by Paul. Whoever delivered the just-received Corinthian letter to Paul, one thing is rather noteworthy: in that letter, they asked him about a number of things that troubled them, but they had said nothing in their letter about the "contentions" that Chloe's people reported to him. We do not know why the Corinthians said nothing on this subject. We note only that Paul does not reprove them for this omission. Perhaps they did not realize the danger that threatened them through these bickerings. Was it ethically proper for those of Chloe to tell Paul what they knew about the conditions existing in Corinth? The question answers itself, for Paul accepted and acted on the information he thus received.

That there are quarrels among you ("that there are contentions ...," ASV) -- What was characterized as "divisions" in verse 10 are here called "quarrels." *Erides* denotes discords, strife, wrangling, argumentation, controversy, contention, which already had resulted in separations into competing cliques in the congregation. If not arrested, these quarrels could lead to a split in the church as first this and then that competing group separated itself from the others to form their own separate congregation. "Contentions" or "quarrels" are works of the flesh (2 Corinthians 12:20; Galatians 5:20; 1 Timothy 6:4).

1:12 -- *Now I mean this, that each one of you is saying, "I am of Paul," and "I of Apollos," and "I of Cephas," and "I of Christ."*

Now I mean this -- 'What I mean is this.' Their contentions are defined to be equivalent to "religious partisanships," antagonistic adoption of the names and views of special teachers. Paul now explains what he means by "divisions" (verse 10) and "contentions" (verse 11).

That each one of you is saying -- The party spirit ran so high that all were listed on one side or another. "None of them was wise enough and spiritual-minded enough to hold aloof from parties altogether," says Farrar (*op. cit.*, p.5). The party spirit had pervaded the whole community. Each one "has one or other of the following speeches in his mouth," says Kling (*op. cit.*, p.28). "'Each' does not mean everybody in the church at Corinth," said George Mark Elliott. "Each one of you" need not be pressed to indicate there were no exceptions at all, but it seems the trouble was widespread. Instead of all saying the same thing, each one had his own favorite saying, different from many of the others. "Is saying" seems to mean in a self-assertive way. It is a present tense verb, indicating a habitual action. "Saith boastfully," wrote Bengel (*Gnomon of the New Testament*, Edinburgh: T&T Clark, 1860, Vol. 3, p.203). We suppose that all four of the parties are criticized for their self-assertive partisanship.[43] The first three slogans implied that those who used them boasted of the excellence, the special gifts, and the grand results attained on the part of the man whose name they vauntingly proclaimed. Some of the party adherents had been converted by Paul, others by Apollos who followed Paul, and still others by Peter. The fact that these men were esteemed and that each had devoted personal admirers was not in itself wrong and dangerous. Rather, the danger came from the fact that these friends should exalt these teachers to an unwarranted degree, pitting the one against the other, and misusing their good names for the purpose of forming parties and wrong distinctions in the congregation.

---

[43] Several extensive notes are needed at this point. First, according to a fair exegesis, it must be maintained that the competing parties or factions were four in number. Kirsopp Lake has suggested that the fourth cry, "I am of Christ" is not a party cry, but is Paul's indignant corrective of the other party cries. Because it is rather difficult to explain how some would cry up Christ like they cried up preachers who had actually been to Corinth, and because it is not easy to see the fourth cry as being somehow as sectarian as the other three, Lake's suggestion has a certain attractiveness on the surface. But it has against it the clear listing intended in the Greek by the particles Paul used, *men, de, de, de*, with no signal that there is a break between the third and fourth member, or that the fourth member is somehow a correct cry when the other three are criticized as improper. Further, the first question asked in verse 13 seems to indicate that the fourth cry was made by the Corinthians, not by Paul himself.

Second, were these the actual party names used by protagonists at Corinth, or were the names used by Paul simply as symbolic designations for the actual parties at Corinth? (Paul is supposed to have refrained from naming the actual leaders lest his candid naming of men look like a personal attack against those men, and thereby drive their followers to embrace their position with a martyr-like fanaticism.) Many writers, as far back as Chrystostom, have affirmed that these designations are symbolic designations. And Henry Alford (*op. cit.*, p.476-477) wrote, "I have endeavored to substantiate (1) that these designations are not used as pointing to actual parties formed and subsisting among the Corinthians, but (2) as representing the *spirit with which they contended* against one another, being the sayings of individuals and not of parties ... (3) that these sayings, while they are not to be made the basis of any hypothesis respecting definite parties at Corinth, do nevertheless hint at matters of fact, and are not merely by way of example; and (4) that this view of the verse ... is borne out, and indeed necessitated by chapter 4:6." J.W. McGarvey and Philip Y. Pendleton ("Thessalonians, Corinthians, Galatians and Romans" in *The Standard Bible Commentary*, Cincinnati: Standard Publishing, 1916, p.68) likewise commented, "Though neither Paul nor Apollos had headed a faction in Corinth, Paul has spoken in this epistle as though they had done this, and that he might spare the feelings of the real leaders in the faction he had put himself and Apollos in their places, and had shown the heinousness of their supposed conduct as reproved by many passages of Scripture. He had done this that the Corinthians, seeing the evil of such a thing even in an apostle, might see it more plainly in their local party leaders, and might not boast themselves of any other leader to the disparagement of another." However, in this commentator's opinion, it puts too much weight on one word, and on but one interpretation of that word in 4:6, to follow the suggestion of Chrysostom and Alford that the names Paul uses are just symbolic. After all, the plain statements in 3:5-9 about his and Apollos' ministries are hardly "in disguise." This commentator agrees with other ancient expositors that the names we find in 1 Corinthians were the actual names claimed by the various antagonistic parties in Corinth.

Third, much ingenuity and labor has been spent in Germany trying to reconstruct the supposed doctrinal emphases of the four distinct parties at Corinth, and many eminent theologians have endeavored with very different results to allot to each party its definite tenets and practices. For a list of references see *Alford's Greek Testament*, V.2, pp. 48-50, and Davidson's *New Testament Introduction*, V.2, p. 224ff. We are not convinced by any of these efforts, most of which are but attempts to make the Bible fit the current popular philosophy at the time the commentator lived, rather than being an attempt to repeat what the Bible actually may imply. In our comments on each slogan, we shall list one or two of the major attempts, just to acquaint readers with what has been attempted.

Some of the members in Corinth sensed the wrong nature of this proceeding, and thus came to make their shibboleth "I am of Christ." But it will not do to place Christ into competition with man as the head of a party over against other parties. The fault of the Christ party is the fact that it allows itself to become only a party, and thus is also drawn into the party wranglings.

"I am of Paul" -- In the Greek there is emphasis on "I" – and the cry "I am a disciple of Paul," or "I follow Paul's way," was said in such a way as to reflect negatively on anyone who wasn't "of Paul." Paul shows his indignation at their partisanship by first rebuking those who had used his own name as a party watchword. That Paul himself was not the source of such partisanship is evidenced by the fact that at the very head of the argument, he condemns the Paulites. Commentators have offered conjectures about the beliefs of this party: (a) Those who follow Baur's hypothesis of Petrine vs. Pauline factions in the early church[44] have supposed the Paul-party consisted of those who adhered to his views about Gentile freedom.[45] (b) Still others suppose the members of the Pauline party liked the simplicity of his preaching,[46] and were perhaps converted under his ministry. (c) Yet others have observed that Judaizers had come among them and denied that Paul was an apostle. It is then supposed some in the congregation, in reaction to the Judaizers, became so zealous in his defense that they claimed to be his followers with greater enthusiasm than they claimed devotion to Jesus Christ. In reply to these conjectures, it is observed that Paul does not compare the doctrinal positions of each group, and apparently doctrine was not the real issue. Paul, Apollos, and Peter were in accord at the point of their commitment to Christ. Exactly what was behind these divisions is not stated, but the result was an attitude in each group of "us against them," instead of "all of us together for Christ."

And "I of Apollos" (Greek, 'I indeed am of Apollos') -- Apollos personally was absolutely loyal and honorable, but his visit to Corinth had done mischief. After Apollos' ministry was concluded and he left town, a section of the congregation unduly magnified the importance of his gifts and his ministry among them. On Apollos, see Acts 18:24-28, 19:1, and Titus 3:13. Apollos had come to Corinth after Paul had planted the church and left Corinth for new cities during his second missionary journey. Eloquent and mighty in

---

[44] See a fuller presentation of Baur's attempt to make the Bible match Hegel's dialectic philosophy in Reese, *New Testament History: Acts*, p.xxiii. Baur's theory has long ago been rejected by the scholarly community, but it is surprising how many comments are still read which reflect this long-rejected reconstruction of early church history. To make Corinthians match his "thesis/antithesis" philosophy, Baur actually condensed the four parties in 1 Corinthians 1:12 into two – a Paul-Apollos theological faction, and a Peter-Christ faction.

[45] Shore has suggested the Pauline party allowed his teaching on Christian liberty to develop in themselves an unchristian license (*op. cit.*, p.14). Another has offered an opposite opinion, that the Pauline party became legalistic in its treatment of others who viewed their liberty differently than the Pauline party did.

[46] The idea that Paul's preaching had a "simplicity" about it comes from higher criticism which unfavorably compares Paul's preaching with that of Apollos (who, supposedly was an eloquent orator).

the Scriptures, he attracted converts. Apollos, as we see by his refusal to return to Corinth under present circumstances (16:12), was as indignant as Paul himself at the perversion of his name into an engine of warfare. By his refusal to go to Corinth, he gave no opportunity of adding fuel to the fire. Scholars have likewise made conjectures about the tenets of this party: (a) His impassioned oratory, his Alexandrian refinements, his allegorizing exegesis,[47] and the culture and polish of his style, had charmed some Corinthians. Perhaps these were the ones who were contemptuous towards the weaker brethren, and who were sophistically condoning the vice in the church. (b) Others suppose 1 Corinthians 1:18-32 and chapter 2 are a reflection of the beliefs and positions held by Apollos' party members. In response to these guesses, from the general tone of Paul's references to Apollos, and from all that we know of the man from other passages, it is clear that there was no difference in the content of their teaching. The party choice must have been made on some other basis, perhaps on their methods of preaching.

And "I of Cephas" (Literally, 'I indeed am of Cephas') -- "Cephas" is the name Jesus gave to Peter (John 1:42). Paul usually refers to him by his Aramaic name *Kēphas* (cf. 3:22, 9:5, 15:5; Galatians 1:18, 2:9,11,14), although Galatians 2:7-8 plainly shows that for him the Greek and Aramaic are interchangeable, as they probably were in all the churches. Although Lenski says Peter had not been to Corinth,[48] this commentator believes Peter had in fact been to Corinth and taught there. Scholars have also attempted to ascertain the emphases championed by this party: (a) Those who have been influenced by Baur's elaborate theory of a "Petrine" vs. "Pauline" theological division in the early church will follow Baur's lead as they guess what the Peter-party at Corinth championed. For example,

> All we can say in possible explanation of this is that as Peter was the Apostle of the circumcision – and as we know from Galatians 2:11ff his course of action on one occasion was reprimanded by Paul, and as that course of action no doubt had influence and found followers it is very conceivable that some of those who in Corinth lightly esteemed Paul might take advantage of this honored name, and cite against the Christian liberty taught by their own spiritual founder, the stricter practice of Peter. If so, these persons would be mainly found among the Jewish converts or Judaizers, and the matters treated in chapters 8 and 9 may have been subjects of doubt mainly with these persons. (Alford, *op. cit.*, p.477)

(b) Another suggests that the use of the Aramaic name perhaps shows that these Petrinists

---

[47] An example of Alexandrian allegory can be found in the non-Biblical *Epistle of Barnabas*. In that work, it is argued from a comparison of Genesis 14:14 and 18:23 that Abraham had a household of 318 people whom he circumcised. Now it is that number 318 that is allegorized. In Greek it is written with three Greek letters, *iota*, *eta*, and *tau*. The Greek for 18 – since Greeks used letters as symbols for numbers -- is *iota* followed by *eta*, which just happen to be the first two letters of the name *Jesus*. The number for 300 is the letter *tau*, which is the shape of the Cross, the Alexandrian allegorists affirm. Therefore, the incident in the Old Testament is a foretelling of the crucifixion of Jesus on the cross! Alexandrian learning was full of this kind of thing.

[48] R.C.H. Lenski, *The Interpretation of St. Paul's First and Second Epistles to the Corinthians* (Minneapolis, MN: Augsburg Publishing, 1961), p.42. For the debate on the question, see O. Cullmann, *Peter* (London: SCM Press, 1953), p.53-55, especially the note on p.55.

were church members unduly influenced by the Judaizers who came to town.⁴⁹ They personally disliked Paul and questioned his apostolic authority. Perhaps the extravagances of the "speaking with tongues" arose in this party, who recalled the effects of the outpouring of the Spirit before Peter's great sermon on the day of Pentecost (Farrar, *op. cit.*, p.5).

And "I of Christ" (literally, 'I indeed am of Christ') -- Most commentaries express some hesitancy when it comes to explaining this phrase. A majority seem to think that it too is a party cry, but one made in the wrong spirit (just as the other three were). In footnote 43 above, we have called attention to a proposed rendering of this phrase which must be rejected; viz., that Paul – having mentioned the three parties – breaks off the party cries, and adds, speaking in his own person and position, "and I (I Paul) am of Christ!" However, this would make Paul guilty of the very self-assertiveness which he is rebuking. Against this proposed rendering is the fact that there is no change in the grammar or sentence structure that would support the idea of a change from what the Corinthians were saying to what Paul himself says. Further, such an idea does not match the following verse. Is the Christ party condemned? Yes. Not the Head, but the party. There is a certain attitude of exclusiveness about each of these parties, a haughty feeling that they were the only ones who were right, that the adherents of the other parties are not quite as good in God's sight as our party is! It is the privilege of every Christian to say, 'I am of Christ,' but if he says it in a haughty and loveless way, or while exhibiting an exclusive spirit, he forfeits his claim to that title. To ignore the teachers sent to them by Christ, and while doing this to claim to be of Christ, was as wrong a party spirit as any of the others. (See Luke 10:16.) Again, theologians have conjectured about the teaching of this party: (a) Alford (*ibid.*) offers this suggestion: "The words seem to apply to those who make a merit of not being attached to any human teacher, who therefore slighted the apostleship of Paul. To them frequent allusion seems to be made in this and in the second epistle, and more especially in 2 Corinthians 10:7-11." (b) "We trace the origin of this party to one man in particular (2 Corinthians 2:7), who was, or professed to be, an adherent of James, and therefore one of the more rigid Judaizers. He may have been one from the circle of Christ's earthly relatives – one of the *desposyni* ('the Lord's brethren,' cf. 9:5), and, like James, may have had views resembling those of the Essenes and Ebionites. If so, he was probably the author of the questions about celibacy and marriage ... This party at any rate, like some modern sects, was not ashamed to degrade into a party watchword even the sacred name of Christ, and to claim for a miserable clique an exclusive interest in the Lord of the church."⁵⁰

---

⁴⁹ Since Baur's day, commentators have seen "Judaizing influences" behind many of Paul's corrective assertions in 1 Corinthians. However, not all are convinced Judaizers have already been to Corinth and done their hurtful work before 1 Corinthians was written. Most admit that 2 Corinthians 10-13 reflects the fact that a Judaizing faction has been to Corinth and turned some against Paul. But perhaps those false brethren did not invade the church until after 1 Corinthians was written.

⁵⁰ F.W. Farrar, *The Pulpit Commentary Vol. 19*, Grand Rapids, MI: Eerdmans, 1962, p.5. If this explanation of the Christ party is correct, just how this clique then differed from the Judaizing party who supposedly claimed Cephas as their leader is hard to see.

1:13 -- *Has Christ been divided? Paul was not crucified for you, was he? Or were you baptized in the name of Paul?*

Has Christ been divided? ("Christ has been divided!" or "Christ is divided!" NASBmg.) -- Having stated the problem in the church, and having given his source of information (1:10-12), Paul now goes on to point out that such dissension violates a Christian's duty to complete and wholehearted devotion to Christ (1:13-17). Since there were no punctuation marks in the original manuscripts, it is not certain whether this phrase should be read as a question or as a simple declaration. Some think it is a declaration: 'Christ has been divided – torn into various pieces instead of being entirely and undividedly the Christ common to all!' Taken as a declaration, it asserts of the lamentable results of division, that the powers of Christ have been divided. If a declaration, it may also be a sudden denunciation of the Christ-party, after which he returns to expressing his indignation against the Paul party, and thus all the partyism at Corinth. However, most commentators regard this as a question. 'Is Christ dismembered?' Does one little portion go to one group, another little portion to another group, with one part of His teaching here, another there? (The Greek, *meridzō*, denotes "distribution," i.e., to assign, to proportion out, rather than actual dismemberment.) If P^{46} is correct at this place (it has the negative *mē* in the sentence), Paul intended it to be a question which expects a negative answer. 'No! Christ has not been divided!' And if Christ is not divided, neither should be any church of Christ! To participate in party dissension like the Corinthians were was, in effect, to divide Christ. This will never do. Even if antagonistic parties in a congregation were defensible, Christ is not the property of any one party in a church of Christ. Paul's general argument is that Christ alone ought to be regarded as their head and leader, and that His claims, arising from His crucifixion, and acknowledged by their baptism, were so preeminent they could not be divided; the honors due to Him should not be rendered to any other.

Paul was not crucified for you, was he? – Literally, the phrase could be rendered, 'Paul surely was not crucified for you, was he?' (*Mē* in the Greek introduces a question that expects a negative answer.) This tends to ask the question, 'Have you reduced the Christ in your estimation to the place of a co-savior with Paul and Apollos and Peter?' People, boasting of their connection to Paul, were assigning to him a position which belonged to Christ alone. If one were going to substitute a human leader for Christ, then it follows the human leader must also have been a redeemer like Jesus was. This line of argument soon shows the folly of elevating human leaders to a position equal to Christ's. Paul castigates the party that had been using his name and allows his readers to supply what is necessary for the rest. By repudiating for himself all possibility of being the head of the church, he does likewise *a fortiori* for Cephas and Apollos.

Or were you baptized in the name of Paul? ("...into the name of Paul," ASV) -- That is, 'Was the name of Paul called over you at your baptism, as though he were the person to whom you pledged yourselves, and in whom you believed and in whom you professed as your Lord and Savior?' For the meaning of "in the name" or "into the name" see Matthew 28:19.[51] To be baptized "into the name of" someone means that the one being baptized has turned over allegiance and has given himself/herself to the one named in the rite. In the Greek, this question also expects a negative answer. 'Did I ever,' Paul implies, 'baptize in my own name? Did I ever pretend to organize a sect, announcing myself as a leader? Did I ever direct you to some other Savior into whose name and service you have been baptized? Of course not!'

1:14 -- *I thank God that I baptized none of you except Crispus and Gaius,*

I thank God that I baptized none of you -- He is not saying, 'Thank God that there were not more folk baptized.' Rather, he is focusing on the human instrumentality. The person who administers the baptism is relatively unimportant.[52] Paul thanks God that in Corinth he had been kept, for the most part, from administering baptism, since he had thereby obviated all appearance of intention to bind the baptized to his own person. He thanked God,[53] not by way of any disparagement to baptism, but because he had thus given no excuse to the undue exaltation of his own name. Compare the practice of our Lord Himself, in leaving His disciples to perform the actual immersion of converts (John 4:2). Compare the practice of Peter (Acts 10:48). It is very likely that Paul brings up this matter of who baptized them precisely because that was one of the things the different groups were contending about.

Except Crispus -- Crispus was the one-time ruler of the synagogue (Acts 18:8) before he became a Christian. Crispus, it may be, was baptized before one of Paul's helpers arrived. Paul's practice, evidently, was to let his helpers do the actual immersing of the candidates.

And Gaius -- Gaius was one a very common Roman names (cf. Romans 16:23). From the home of Gaius of Corinth, Paul will write the epistle to the Romans in AD 58.[54] There

---

[51] This implies that words were spoken (called a "baptismal formula") when candidates were immersed, such as "in the name of Jesus," or "in the name of the Father, and the Son, and the Holy Spirit." Oneness Pentecostals insist any formula other than "in the name of Jesus" makes a person's baptism invalid. That insistence hardly matches what Jesus Himself said as He gave the Great Commission, nor should we find contradiction between Jesus' command and the practice of the early church when it came to the baptismal formula.

[52] For a useful discussion, see *Life of Luther* by Michelet, p. 262. Kling (*op. cit.*, p.30) wrote, "It will be seen that he baptized only the first converts; afterwards, when the converts multiplied, he transferred the business to helpers, possibly to the deacons, to whose functions this in course belonged." Barnes (*op. cit.*, p.10) gives another idea, when he writes, "The other persons at Corinth had been probably baptized by Silas and Timothy."

[53] It is not easy to decide which manuscript reading here represents what Paul originally wrote. "I am thankful" occurs in Sinaiticus*, B, 6, 1739, copt^{pt}. The Majority Text reads "I thank God."

[54] There is a strong likelihood that Gaius of Corinth is to be identified with the God-fearer Titus Justus of Acts 18:7. His whole Roman name would have been Gaius Titus Justus. His house was next door to the synagogue and was the place where the church gathered after it was excluded from the synagogue.

was also a Gaius of Derbe (Acts 20:4). A Gaius is known to John (3 John 1).[55]

1:15 -- *so that no one would say you were baptized in my name.*

So that no man should say ("Lest any man should say," ASV) -- *Hina* means 'so that, in order that.' "Lest" represents the purpose, not of the apostle's conduct at the time, but of the divine ordering of things: 'God so arranged it, that none might say ....' If Paul's converts from those early days of his labor in Corinth now made up the membership of the 'Paul party,' the members of the other parties or some other slanderous person might insinuate that those who constituted Paul's party had been baptized in Paul's name.

You were baptized in my name -- If Paul personally had baptized many of the converts,[56] his detractors could have said, 'he baptized in his own name,' and it might have carried a ring of plausibility. How glad Paul was that no one could claim he had taken unto himself honor that belonged to Christ alone.

1:16 -- *Now I did baptize also the household of Stephanas; beyond that, I do not know whether I baptized any other.*

Now I did baptize also the household of Stephanas -- The way this verse is worded, it appears to be a subsequent correction of the preceding statement. Three interpretations have been given: (a) After writing verse 14, Paul subsequently recollects having baptized Stephanas and his family – perhaps from information derived from Stephanas himself, who was with Paul in Corinth when this first letter to Corinth was written, or perhaps Paul was reminded of this by his amanuensis, Sosthenes. (b) It is possible that Stephanas did not reside at Corinth when he was baptized, but subsequently moved there.[57] Others also may have moved to Corinth after baptism, of whom Paul was not aware. (c) A third interpretation put on the verse is less than satisfactory. Barnes (*op. cit.*, p.10) supposed that the words mean "I baptized none of you who were *adult* members save Crispus and Gaius. I also baptized the *household* of Stephanas." This suggestion appears to this commentator to be a weak attempt to find support for infant baptism in the Bible.

Concerning "Stephanas," see 1 Corinthians 16:15,17. Stephanas and members of his house were the first converts in Achaia. Paul's first converts in Achaia were at Athens

---

[55] Barnes feels that this Gaius in Corinthians and the one in John are the same man (*op. cit.*, p.10). If so, then probably Diotrephes (3 John 9), who is mentioned as the one who loved "to have the preeminence," had been one cause of the difficulties at Corinth. Barnes is likely correct in this identification. If so, 3 John is addressed to Corinth.

[56] There is a manuscript variation here that accounts for the difference of reading found in the KJV ("that I had baptized in my own name"). The ASV/NASB readings are supported by Sinaiticus, B,C.

[57] Lenski has written, "The answer lies in 16:15. Stephanas was 'the first-fruits in Achaia' – note, not of Corinth – and while he was now a member of the congregation in Corinth, he had been baptized in Athens where he was the first person in all Achaia (Greece) to be converted. When Paul runs over in his mind the persons whom he had baptized in Corinth, he naturally did not at once remember this family whom he baptized before he even reached Corinth." (*op. cit.*, p.47)

(Acts 17:32-34), not Corinth. Has Stephanas subsequently moved from Athens to Corinth? Or are we to understand that when converts became more numerous, and helpers were present to do the immersing, Paul ceased to baptize them personally? Compare Acts 10:48, where Peter had the Jewish believers who accompanied him to Cornelius' house do the actual baptizing of the converts. Some have tried to identify Stephanas with the jailer of Philippi, who, it is supposed, afterwards moved to Corinth. But Philippi is not a city of Achaia; thus, this suggestion is contradictory to 16:15.

Proponents of the validity of infant sprinkling have to appeal to "household" baptisms to find alleged Scriptural evidence for the practice. It is difficult to find convincing proof that there were any infants in the "household" whom the Bible says were baptized. "Household" is used in the New Testament for (1) all the men of the house (Acts 7:10; 1 Timothy 3:4,5,12); (2) domestics, servants (Acts 10:2, 11:14, 16:15,31); and (3) a family in general (Luke 10:5, 16:27). Now, in fact, there are implications that the phrase cannot be used to justify infant sprinkling:

> We are told that the nobleman "believed, and his whole house" (John 4:53); that Crispus "believed in the Lord with all his house" (Acts 18:18); that the jailer "rejoiced greatly with all his house, having believed in God," (Acts 16:34); that Cornelius "feared God with all his house" (Acts 10:2); that "the house of Stephanas ... is the first fruits of Achaia, and that they have set themselves to minister unto the saints" (1 Corinthians 16:15).[58]

This by no means implies that in these five homes there were no infants. It merely tells us that those who obeyed the gospel were capable of understanding the gospel, believing it, and rejoicing because of forgiven sins.

Beyond that, I do not know whether I baptized any other -- Finding his memory had failed him once, Paul adds, 'I don't remember about any others ...' lest some super-critical opponents pick on this to deprecate Paul in the eyes of others. "I don't know if I baptized any others who are now (or yet) members of the church at Corinth." This clause argues against the absolute omniscience of the inspired writers on every topic which they handle. It also is important to our understanding of how inspiration worked. It did not supersede the writer himself using his own vocabulary, or relying on information learned by means other than a direct revelation from God. Inspiration, although it rendered his writing infallible, did not make Paul omniscient. The Spirit was given to the apostles to lead them into all the truth (John 16:13), but it was truth relative to man's salvation which was thus made known to them. Instant recall of the names of all the converts one has baptized, or even a statement of personal anticipation (such as when Paul says in Acts 20:38, "you will not see my face again") – which time will prove to be mistaken (i.e., according to the Pas-

---

[58] Lipscomb, *op. cit.*, p. 29. It is the nearly universal conclusion of New Testament scholarship that a biblical case for infant baptism cannot be decided on the basis of these "household" baptisms (and this is so, even without including evidence that "sprinkling" is not "baptism" in the New Testament). See Kurt Aland, *Did the Early Church Baptize Infants?* (Philadelphia: Westminster Press, 1963), and chapter 6 in G.R. Beasley-Murray, *Baptism in the New Testament* (Grand Rapids: Eerdmans, 1962).

toral Epistles, after some years had passed Paul did in fact return to Ephesus) – are not necessarily the kind of items where the inspiration of the Holy Spirit guarantees unerring facticity. In fact, "inspiration" can lead a Bible writer to record unerringly what someone said or did even when the content of the quoted speech was patently false; cp. the devil's "Has God said?" (Genesis 3:1), and the action was a sin.[59] The point to be noted and stressed is this, that Paul never personally baptized a sufficient number to constitute a party of any kind in the Corinthian congregation, and he is glad of that fact.

1:17 -- *For Christ did not send me to baptize, but to preach the gospel, not in cleverness of speech, so that the cross of Christ would not be made void.*

For Christ did not send me to baptize, but to preach -- Many denominationalists love to use this verse as a proof text that "immersion is not one of the conditions on which, when complied with, God grants justification (salvation)."[60] However, it is not baptism that is deprecated; rather, it is the person who administers baptism who is relatively unimportant! Behind at least some of the party pride at Corinth seems to have been a high esteem placed on the one who taught and baptized them when they first became converts. Paul affirms such pride in the administrator is out of place. There is no depreciation here of baptism, for Paul did indeed baptize upon occasion. An inspired man could not preach Jesus without preaching baptism (see Acts 8:35,36, where the Ethiopian asked to be immersed after hearing Philip's sermon about Jesus). Paul elsewhere indicates baptism completes our union with Christ (Romans 6:4). We are not Christians who are in union with Christ until we have been baptized, nor is it possible to walk in newness of life until one is immersed (Romans 6:5). Perhaps Lenski's explanation is satisfactory:

> The Lord's commission reads: "Disciple by baptizing," *matheteusate baptidzontes*, Matt. 28:19, and, thinking superficially, one might conclude that the apostles were to go on baptizing as many people as possible, but this is not the case. The duty of the apostles (the chosen men whom the Lord sent, *apesteile*) was to go from place to place and to spread the gospel (note *euaggelidzesthai*) as far as possible. Thus, the work assigned to them is really preaching and teaching. The work of administering baptism when the preaching and the teaching had produced faith and repentance was a matter that any assistant of an apostle could easily attend to, for it certainly required no immediate apostolic call. Nothing derogatory is thus implied in regard to baptism itself or to its vital importance. It

---

[59] See comments at 1 Corinthians 2:13 for more information about how "inspiration" worked.

[60] See for example, page 27 of W. Landon Miller, *Bible Studies of Difficult Doctrines* (Brookhaven, MS: Magee Printers, 1951). Miller attempts to answer standard Christian Church/Churches of Christ doctrinal matters that are at odds with Baptist beliefs. Care must be exercised here. When denominationalists hear us say baptism is necessary to salvation, they hear us saying we believe in 'baptismal regeneration' (i.e., that the mere administration of water causes the new birth). Christian preachers do not mean to imply anything like baptismal regeneration. What they are saying is baptism (immersion) is as much a part of the process of conversion/salvation as is repentance. Without either, a person's new birth is not complete.

is merely the slight task of administering baptism of which Paul speaks.[61]

For Christ did not send me -- "Send" translates *apesteilen*, a plain allusion to his office of apostle, *apostolos*. The appointment to the office of apostle did indeed include the work of baptizing (Matthew 28:19), but it was not the defining task of his ministry.

But to preach the gospel -- Some of the essential topics emphasized when the "gospel" is preached are listed in 1 Corinthians 15:3,4. The gospel includes not only facts to be believed, but commandments of Christ to be obeyed. One of those commandments is baptism. But there is more to the gospel than baptism. "Preach the gospel" translates *euaggelisdzesthai*, 'to evangelize, to announce the good news,' to proclaim the salvation that is available in Christ. Verse 17 is a transition verse. The first part continues the discussion on baptism. The second part introduces the thought which will occupy the rest of this section – namely, that the thing that is important is the content of the message, not the eloquence or cleverness with which it is presented. Fee paraphrases (*op. cit.*, p.63), "In any case, this discussion about who baptized whom is quite beside the point (verse 17a), so let us get on with the real issue, which has to do with the nature of the gospel itself (verse 17b)."

Not in cleverness of speech ("not in wisdom of words," ASV) -- It seems evident from this apology, and other hints in the two epistles (e.g., 2 Corinthians 10:10) that the plainness and simplicity of Paul's speech had been one cause among the Corinthians of alienation from him. Perhaps, as suggested above, the eloquence of Apollos was extolled to Paul's disadvantage (Alford, *op. cit.*, p.478). "Cleverness of speech" or "wisdom of words" (ASV) is an attempt by the translators to catch the idea in the original – of the flowery sounding words used by the professional rhetorician simply to impress the audience.[62] Paul is saying, 'I did not preach in a philosophic and oratorical style.' The simplicity of the style and teaching of the apostles awoke the sneers of philosophers like Celsus and Porphyry. This is the first use of the word "wisdom" in this letter.[63] The long discussion of "wisdom" that follows indicates this is one of the real issues causing dissension in the congregation at Corinth. Some at least of the Corinthians were setting too high a value on human wisdom and human eloquence in line with the typical Greek admiration for rhetor-

---

[61] Lenski, *op. cit.*, p.48.

[62] The Greek reads "wisdom of word" (singular), and the term is a bit unusual. In his translation, Moffatt rendered this phrase as "fine rhetoric" – where rhetoric was the affected or exaggerated display in the use of language. TEV suggests "the language of men's wisdom."

[63] Late 20th century scholars have been flirting with the idea that *sophia* ("wisdom") refers to content rather than manner of speech; that is, the Greeks at Corinth are unduly influenced with hypostatic (i.e., my own personal opinion) wisdom as the way of salvation. These contemporary scholars see the Corinthians as equating Sophia with the so-called heavenly redeemer of Gnosticism. This commentator is not convinced the current scholars have it right. At this early date when Corinthians was written, the incipient Gnosticism would have been a Jewish (not a Christian) heresy. Paul specifically says in this letter (1:22) that it is the Greeks, not Jews, who are pursuing wisdom. The traditional view, the one followed in this commentary, is that 'wisdom of word' reflects the Greek interest in philosophical or rhetorical flourish of speech, with its emphasis on the manner of delivery rather than on the content of what was being said.

ic and philosophical studies. In the face of this, Paul insists that preaching "in wisdom of words" was no part of his commission. That kind of preaching would draw men to the preacher, and it would nullify the cross of Christ. The danger was present that some would adore and desire to have the gospel preached to them, not as Christ proclaimed it (and as it was thus reproduced by the apostles), but as a wisdom-gospel, a philosophy-gospel, a gospel fitted to the proud Greek learning of the day. Similar danger exists today. Science is "king" in the educational sphere of the 21st century. There are some "intellectuals" among the Restoration Movement who plead that certain Scriptural categories of thought are worn out and must be replaced by modern categories of thought. (This is not to disparage education, but to remind that intellectualism is not an end in itself.) In the late 20th century, liberal theologians claimed we must make the gospel relevant to the 20th century mind by getting rid of all that was merely temporary in the early preaching. Such a plea is a species of deception that does away with the eternal, unchanging verities of God – in Paul's words, it "nullifies the cross of Christ." One other distinction needs to be made. What we are saying is that our original appeal to men must not be merely through a show of our intellectual abilities or mental acumen. While it is necessary to answer intelligently the objections that intelligent people raise to the truth of the gospel message, we must not try to win men by appealing to what the world thinks is wise and smart. We must rather allow God to use us as channels through which his Spirit may work. Otherwise, the cross of Christ will be made of none effect.

That the cross of Christ -- The cross of Christ was the great central emphasis of apostolic preaching; the cross exhibits man's guilt and God's love in their highest degrees and closest connection. In the next verse, Paul will begin an unfolding of the "word of the cross," and each of the Corinthian beliefs and practices is held up against this criteria. If a belief or practice matches the word of the cross, it is acceptable. If it reflects badly on the "word of the cross," there is something desperately wrong with the belief or the practice.

Should not be made void -- *Kenōthē* means 'to become empty' or 'to be divested of dignity.' Here, 'be robbed of its power and influence' catches the idea. The cross would be bereft of all efficiency for such results (i.e., its ability to deliver sinners from the power of tyranny and restore them to a new and divine life) were it set forth in the forms of philosophy. Set forth in the forms of philosophy, it would serve only to call out the assent of the intellect or awaken an aesthetic pleasure, while the will and the emotions would remain unaffected. But let the cross *only* be held up before the heart in all divine simplicity, and it would then display an energy destructive of the old sin-life and habits. Through it the flesh with its affections and lusts would be crucified (Galatians 5:24). That is, do not let the success which might attend the preaching of the gospel be attributed to the graces of eloquence, the charms of language, or the force of human argumentation, rather than its true cause, the preaching of Christ crucified. To attempt to dress up the story of Calvary in elaborate rhetoric, or wrap it up in fine-spun theorems, would have been tantamount to robbing the cross of any power and thus nullifying the gospel.

B. THE NATURE OF THE TRUE CHRISTIAN PREACHING. 1:18-25

1:18 -- *For the word of the cross is foolishness to those who are perishing, but to us who are being saved it is the power of God.*

For the word of the cross -- Note the word "for." Verse 18 is an explanation of how the cross of Christ would be nullified. People would consider it folly, and ignore the message of salvation. One reason for the internal dissension at Corinth was a misunderstanding of the nature of the gospel. Instead of their idea that it was dependent on human cleverness and wisdom, the correct view is that the gospel is dependent on divine power and divine wisdom. This topic covers 1:18-2:5. Paul's assessment of other reasons for the dissension at Corinth will be taken up in the verses following 2:5.

Paul's usual outline in his epistles is to present first doctrine, then the correct practice required by that correct doctrine. In Corinthians, this usual outline is not found. Instead, time and again, he returns to the emphasis on the "*word of the cross*."[64] In verse 17 Paul spoke of preaching the gospel. Now he uses the synonymous phrase "word of the cross." There is a contrast between "wisdom of *words*" and "the *word* of the cross." The message does not please the perishing any more than does the stark simplicity with which it was presented. Verse 18, beginning with "for," is an explanation of the foregoing clause. It assumes the mutual exclusiveness of the "preaching of the cross" and "wisdom of speech." It also assumes the identity of "they that are perishing" with the 'lovers of wisdom of speech.' It is as if it were said, 'Wisdom of speech would nullify the cross of Christ; for the doctrine of the cross is folly to the lovers of that wisdom.' The Corinthians might retort, 'The cross of Christ is rendered without effect by wisdom of speech?!? Why, your method of preaching is not half as compelling and effectual as the one you denounce.' This the apostle concedes, but limits its application only to a certain class, to those who are in the way of sin and are going to destruction. "These," he says, "are blind. They have no sense of sin, and therefore do not see the wisdom of the cross. To them it is folly. Yet to those who are in the way of salvation the cross is a thing of power. They see its meaning. They feel its disenthralling and life-giving influences" (Kling, *op. cit.*, p.34).

It is not the doctrine about the cross, but the word (message) which presents the cross itself in its concrete form and in its plain and direct application to human conditions. According to Romans 5:6-12, which best defines it, the "word of the cross" includes:

(1) Christ died as an atoning sacrifice for the sins of men.
(2) The cross as the expression of divine love was a voluntary sacrifice. Christ was not made an unwilling sacrifice to expiate the wrath of God. Instead, Christ exemplified the love of God.
(3) In the cross there is release from fear of the wrath of God.
(4) Men can be reconciled to God, pardoned, and saved only by the merits of this atoning sacrifice. We use the word 'reconciled' to speak of the restored relationship between

---

[64] See the Special Study on "The Message of the Cross" following chapter 1, pp.58-60.

lovers after a fight. After we have sinned and been at enmity with God, a restored relationship with God is provided through Christ's work.
(5) The prospect of future development when we are "saved through His life" (Romans 5:10). Salvation doesn't stop at reconciliation. God takes the life and reshapes it for His purpose.
(6) Redemption from servitude to sin, and delivered from the fear of death.

Is to those who are perishing -- The "perishing" are all those who are now walking in the paths that lead to destruction – all those who have not obeyed the gospel, those who are through unbelief on the way to everlasting perdition (2 Corinthians 2:15,16). This is a present participle, and the present tense gives the thought of a process which is going on at present.[65] The dative "to" means 'in their judgment.' In their judgment the word of the cross is foolishness.

Foolishness -- The Greek word is *moria*, which means "completely irrational, or nonsense, absurd, without learning or erudition." Jews and Greeks both held a low opinion of anyone involved with a "cross." To the Jews the cross was the tree of shame and horror, and a crucified person was accursed of God (Deuteronomy 21:23; Galatians 3:13). To the Greeks the cross was the gibbet of a slave's infamy or a murderer's punishment. There was not a single association connected with it except those of shame and agony. The thought of a 'crucified Messiah' seemed to the Jews a revolting folly; the worship of a crucified malefactor seemed to the Greeks "an execrable superstition" (Tacitus, *Ann*. 15:44; Pliny, *Epp*. 10:97). It seems absurd to have the fact of Christ's death nakedly held before them as the ground of all salvation – to hear a voice from the cross calling unto them, 'Look to me and be saved,' because they see no rational connection between cause and effect here.

But to us who are being saved -- The present participle pictures people who are on the way of salvation. Salvation is pictured as a process. By faith they have laid hold on Christ, and are by Him in the course of being saved. The appended personal pronoun "to us" speaks from and to experience: 'You and I know the cross is God's saving power.' The same present participle is used in Luke 13:23, Acts 2:27, 2 Corinthians 2:15, and Revelation 21:24 (KJV). They have not been saved once and for all at some moment in the past (that would require an aorist tense), rather, they are in the process of being saved. Salvation is viewed in the Scriptures as something that occurred to us in the past,[66] as a thing of the present,[67] and also a thing that has a future aspect.[68] The use of "lost ... saved" is not a place to introduce the idea of unconditional predestination, as some authors attempt

---

[65] The participles "perishing" and "being saved" are not to be taken as expressing "certain expectation" (as Heinrich A.W. Meyer, *Meyer's Commentary on the New Testament* Vol. 6, Winona Lake, IN: Alpha Publications, 1979, p.27), nor "fixed predestination" (as Beza), but simply as telling what course the rejecters and receivers of the word are presently on.

[66] An aorist tense is used in Romans 8:24; a perfect tense verb occurs in Ephesians 2:5.

[67] The present tense verb in this place speaks of continuous action in the present.

[68] A future tense occurs at Romans 5:10, while Romans 13:11 and 1 Peter 1:4,5 speak of future aspects to the salvation from sin the Christian already enjoys.

to do, taking the terms to denote the divinely appointed destiny of the two classes, for with Paul this idea never occurs in any such way as to exclude free self-determination in man's response to God's invitation (cp. 2 Thessalonians 2:10; Acts 13:46).

It is the power of God -- The gospel is the vehicle through which God's power to save is operative. The cross is the heart of that gospel which is the "power of God unto salvation to everyone who believes" (Romans 1:16, 8:3). Since "wisdom" is the opposite of "foolishness," we might have expected Paul to speak of the gospel as 'the wisdom of God.' Instead, he uses "power." Why does not Paul say that the word of the cross is 'God's wisdom'? Because "power" is the only proper correlative to "being saved." Power – nothing less – is required to save.

1:19 -- *For it is written, "I WILL DESTROY THE WISDOM OF THE WISE, AND THE CLEVERNESS OF THE CLEVER I WILL SET ASIDE."*

For -- Characteristically, Paul clinches his argument with a citation from Scripture. The principle Paul is expounding is not new. From of old, God's way had stood in marked contrast with that suggested by the wisdom of men. Verse 19 – a proof from the Old Testament – is given as proof of what was stated in verse 18 about the failure of worldly cleverness in dealing with things of God.

It is written -- This formula (see chapters 1:31, 2:9, 3:19, 9:9, 10:7, 15:45; 2 Corinthians 8:15) is used chiefly in letters to churches in which there were many Jews. It does not occur in Thessalonians, Ephesians, Colossians, or Philippians, where the churches were mostly Gentile. "It is written" is the customary way by which Paul introduces a reference found in the Old Testament Scriptures.[69] This is a continuation of the reason for not preaching in "wisdom of words"; namely, because it was prophesied in the Old Testament that such wisdom should be brought to nothing by God.[70] The perfect tense "it is written" indicates that what God promised through the prophet Isaiah continues to be true.

"I WILL DESTROY THE WISDOM OF THE WISE, AND THE CLEVERNESS OF THE CLEVER I WILL SET ASIDE" -- This is a free citation of Isaiah 29:14 (the same

---

[69] See E.E. Ellis, *Paul's Use of the Old Testament* (Grand Rapids: Eerdmans, 1957), p.22-25. For a discussion of how the Old Testament is quoted by Paul, see notes at 1 Corinthians 2:9.

[70] Some contemporary higher critics try to detect a Midrashic pattern to this section, and affirm Paul uses a *pesher* style of interpretation of the Old Testament passages he makes use of. Such "explanations" are part of redaction criticism's attempt to locate the genre of or to find the source of Paul's writings after any supernatural influence or inspiration has been *a priori* ruled out. Some of these critics even suggest this section had a prior existence and Paul only copied it or adapted it to his purposes. Other contemporary naturalistic critics allege a supposed similarity to 1st century rhetoric, and then expend great effort trying to identify intricate poetic patterns and chiasms in this section similar to what one would find in ancient rhetoric. This commentary rejects redaction criticism as a valid method of Scripture interpretation, just as it rejects rhetorical criticism as a legitimate method of interpretation of Scripture. In both Midrashic and *pesher* interpretations, the human interpreters often gave the passage a meaning directly in opposition to its authorial intent in order to make it fit the present-day situation (a situation where the old rules no longer seemed to be relevant). We deny vehemently that this is what Paul is doing as he applies Isaiah to the argument he is making to the Corinthians.

thought is found in Job 5:12,13; see also Matthew 11:25). The citation follows the Septuagint,[71] with the exception of "I will destroy," for "I will hide." (The Hebrew is "the wisdom of the wise shall perish, and the prudence of the prudent shall disappear.") The thrust of the Scripture passage is this – worldly men sometimes think their ways are better than God's ways, but in the end God strongly intervenes to show His ways (not men's) are the way things are going to be done. The passage quoted belongs to the cycle of Isaiah's prophecies against the worldly-wise politicians of Jerusalem in Assyrian times (Isaiah 28-32), who despised the Word of the Lord, relying instead on their own shallow and dishonest statecraft. Those worldly-wise politicians who advised alliance with Egypt were leading to a shameful overthrow, out of which God would so move history that His wisdom would be vindicated, and His salvation would be experienced by the city and the people. The prophecy of Isaiah culminates in an announcement of salvation through the Messiah (Isaiah 29:14, cf. verse 17), and as the result and penalty of the hypocritical conduct of the Jewish people, proclaims the downfall of the wisdom of their wise ones and the vanishing of the understanding of the prudent. Such wisdom and understanding would contribute nothing toward their deliverance in the day of evil.

The application of this to the subject at hand is this: the Old Testament and New Testament situations are analogous. Gentile and Jewish wisdom, united in rejection of the gospel, are coming to a like overthrow – and Paul draws a powerful warning from the sacred history. The Lord has been accustomed to punish the arrogance of those who, depending on their own judgments and thinking their wisdom is better than God's, put themselves forth as leaders of others. The coming forth of God is often such as to confound human prudence, in a manner which human wisdom would not have devised and in such a way as to show that He is not dependent on the wisdom of man. "Cleverness" ("discernment," ASV) refers to worldly common sense. In the days of King Hezekiah, God declared in regard to the political cunning and the secret, tricky plans of this king's advisers, by which they hoped to escape the Assyrian danger, that He would deal wondrously with his people by at last saving them by His own great deeds, so that the wisdom of the wise and their tricky plans would perish and be forced to hide itself. The quotation is very much to the point with its statement in regard to the wisdom of the wise at Corinth. This wisdom of Hezekiah's advisers was exactly like that which was trying to magnify itself in Corinth. It emanated, not from God, but from godless thinking.

1:20 -- *Where is the wise man? Where is the scribe? Where is the debater of this age? Has not God made foolish the wisdom of the world?*

Where is the wise man? -- Paul says we now see the prophecy fulfilled, for "where is ...?" In a triumphal tone, Paul declares that God's threat in regard to this spurious wisdom was actually carried out. The world's wisdom failed! As it failed in Old Testament times, it will at Corinth! Literally, where is a wise man? I.e., where is a wise man to be found? The designations here are all anarthrous in the Greek. Some translators insert the article,

---

[71] Versions may be trusted to be the word of God, if faithfully translated (cf. Christ's and the apostles' use of the Septuagint version of the Old Testament, and even loose paraphrases of the Old Testament).

others do not. The mere asking of the question implies that they are not to be found. There was nowhere in the world that a worldly-wise man could be found who had a solution for the predicament of men in sin! Those commentators who think the Greek philosopher is before Paul's mind say a "wise man" is one who is versed in a subject, here in philosophic ideas. It may be well perhaps to take the term "wise" in a general sense as denoting all those who would exalt human knowledge. The "scribe" and "debater" (following phrases) would be two examples of such "wise men." There is a question also as to whether these words likewise are cited from the Old Testament. There is something like them to be found in Isaiah 33:18 and 19:11ff.[72]

Where is the scribe? -- This question would come home to the Jews, who regarded their rabbis as exalted persons who could look down on ignorant persons (*amharatsim*, or 'people of the land'). With the Jews of that day "the scribe" was the theologian, the ideal of dignified learning and orthodoxy, though for the most part he mistook elaborate ignorance for profound knowledge. The "scribe" was the Jewish interpreter of the law, or one who is versed in literature. The term *grammateis* ("scribe") is related to the verb meaning "to write," and it sometimes refers to a secretary or clerk (Acts 19:13). But in 1st century AD Jewish circles it was a technical term for men expert in the Law. The word "scribe" ('expert in the Law') was not found among the Greeks for their scholars or teachers. It was the regular Jewish word for their rabbis or teachers of the Law, as can be seen from the Gospels where this word is traditionally translated "scribe." In Isaiah 33:18, the prophet describes the peace which shall follow after the terrors of the Assyrian danger are past, and Sennacherib's revenue clerks and army scouts have all disappeared (a sign of his defeat). Men will ask in astonishment, "What has become of the scribe who was to tabulate the tribute that had been forced from the Jews?" They will also ask what has become of the man who was to weigh the money, and of the man who was to count the towers of the walls which the Assyrians had planned to capture. Where are all of them? Isaiah says, 'All of them will be gone.' Out of the number of these significant questions, Paul selects only the one concerning "the scribe," and like Isaiah, asks, "Where is the scribe?" i.e., anyone that is a scribe.

Where is the debater -- The word "debater" ("disputer," ASV) would especially suit the disputatious Greeks, clever dialecticians, debaters. This is the regular word for the 'disputant' in the Greek philosophic schools, and in their general discussions and debates.[73]

---

[72] Some have advanced the theory that very early in the church, Christians made a collection of various Old Testament Scriptures that were particularly useful in evangelism and in the defense of Christian doctrine. This collection is sometimes called 'testimonies.' Such a collection (called a 'florilegium') for use by the Jewish people who lived at Qumran has been found among the Dead Sea Scrolls (4QFlor). But whether Christians had such a collection is still being debated by scholars. One can neither prove nor disprove that Paul had such a collection available to him, or that apostles who had heard the resurrected Jesus open and explain the Old Testament Scriptures pertaining to Himself would need such a man-made collection of Old Testament verses.

[73] In the comments we have treated "wise" as a reference to Jews, and "debater" as a reference to Greeks. Lightfoot (*op. cit.*, p.159-160) appeals to the Greek Fathers for evidence and argues that the usual way the terms are used is just backwards. "Debater" should be Jewish reference, and "wise" a Greek reference, he alleges. He appeals also to Acts 6:9 and 28:29 where "debater" is used of Jewish discussions and arguments.

This word would especially come home to the Greeks who regarded none but the philosophers as "wise." Mare (*op. cit.*, p.194) even suggests that we should render this passage "the philosopher of this age," and explains the person meant is the man who wanted to dispute every issue and solve it by human reason alone. The first two questions in verse 20 might come from Isaiah 33; to these Paul adds a question of his own. Since this word introduces the Greek idea of wisdom, Paul's three questions cover the entire domain of mere human or worldly wisdom. If the Corinthians sought some of this wisdom in the heralds of the gospel, whether in the Jewish form of legalistic teaching after the manner of a "scribe," or in the Hellenistic form after the manner of a Greek "disputer" or dialectician, they were surely wrong.

Of this age? -- "Of this age" is better than the KJV's "of this world." There is some dispute concerning with what this phrase is to be connected. The genitive "of this age" (says Lenski, *op. cit.*, p.57) is to be construed with only "disputer," and not with all three terms, for "the disputer of this age" is an expression that was coined by Paul himself, while the other two terms were borrowed from Isaiah. Shore thought "of this age" goes with all three questions, for he wrote, "The questions are rapid and abrupt, yet logically, apply to all three terms, and describes those mentioned as belonging to ... the age before the consummation."[74] The Hebrews divided time into two periods: (a) This age (Hebrew, *olam hazzeh*; Greek, *aiōn ekeinos*) is what we commonly call the Old Testament or Mosaic Age; (b) The age to come (Hebrew, *olam habba*; Greek, *aiōn mallon*) is what we commonly call the Messianic or Church Age. We use similar language. When we speak of "this age" (as also in the reference here), we speak of the church age. When we speak of the "age to come," we usually are thinking of heaven.

Has not God made foolish the wisdom of the world? -- As the Greek is written, this question expects an affirmative answer. This is Paul's own assessment of how things are! The time when God made foolish the wisdom of the world is given in the next verse, as well as how and why He did it. ('When' and 'why' are explained in verse 21a. 'How' is explained in verse 21b.) "Foolish ... wisdom" is an oxymoron – a combination of opposites. Paul was fond of using this figure, this sharp contrast of terms (see 1 Timothy 5:6; Romans 1:20). God, in His wisdom, delayed the coming of Christ that the world might see the barrenness of its own wisdom. That God would make foolish the wisdom of the world is a thought familiar to the Old Testament prophets (Isaiah 44:25) and to Paul (Romans 1:22). Even Horace saw that heathen philosophy was sometimes no better than "insaniens sapientia" (wise insanity) (Horace, *Od.*, 1:34,2). 'Did not God make foolish and futile the profane wisdom of the non-Christian world?' Carefully notice two things: (a) The knowledge of all the sciences is mere smoke where heavenly knowledge is lacking. (b) Without the aid of revelation from God, man – despite all his acuteness – is as likely to obtain for himself a knowledge of the mysteries of God, as a donkey is qualified to understand musical harmonies. Paul does not expressly condemn either man's natural perspicuity (i.e., wisdom acquired from practice and experience), or the cultivation of mind

---

[74] Shore, *op. cit.*, p. 18.

(obtained by learning). He merely declares all this is of no avail for acquiring spiritual wisdom. (John Calvin, "The First Epistle of Paul The Apostle to the Corinthians" in *Calvin's Commentaries*, John W. Fraser tr., Grand Rapids, MI: Eerdman's, 1960, p.38.) When properly used, rather than being a hindrance, learning is a great help in coming to a knowledge of the truth. But if a man is puffed up by it, so as to think himself wise and not dependent on God, it hinders. All that the wise, the scribe, and the disputer have to offer is here summarized in the phrase "wisdom of the world." Man's answers to man's problems are foolish, moronic; they don't work! God's answer does. Through the gospel, His power is at work saving men.

1:21 -- *For since in the wisdom of God the world through its wisdom did not* **come to** *know God, God was well-pleased through the foolishness of the message preached to save those who believe.*

For since -- We have in the first part of verse 21 the explanation of the *why* and *when* it was that God made foolish the wisdom of this world. After the world had learned by experience that men would never come by their own wisdom to the true knowledge of God, it pleased God to reveal the plan of salvation.

In the wisdom of God -- This phrase is susceptible of two interpretations: (1) It can speak of 'wisdom about God.'[75] Some see a reference to "the wisdom of God" as revealed to the Gentiles by the creation (Romans 1:18ff) and to the Jews by the Law. According to this interpretation Paul means to say that the world, by a survey of the works of God and by a keeping of the Law, 'did not know God.' Notwithstanding the creation and the Law, they were in deep darkness. This interpretation does not appear to be the best. "The order of words is against this interpretation," affirm Robertson & Plummer (*op. cit.*, p.21). (2) It could speak of God's attribute of "wisdom."[76] This interpretation makes it refer to the wise arrangement or government of God. Compare Romans 11:32ff, where God's providential arrangement is unfolded. "God, in his wise arrangement of things, delayed the coming of Christ, so that the world might see that the true knowledge of God could not be arrived at by man's unaided powers." This second is the sounder explanation, (a) being in accord with Paul's references elsewhere to the "wisdom" of God, (b) as presenting a pointed antithesis to the "wisdom of this world," and (c) harmonizing with Paul's theory of the education of mankind for Christ, expounded in Galatians 3:10-4:5 and Romans 5:20ff, 7:7-25, 11:1ff.

The world through its wisdom did not *come to* **know God** -- "World" here denotes the men of the world, particularly the philosophers and lawyers. The Jew as well as Gentile – the Pharisee as well as the Greek philosopher – had a "wisdom" of his own, which stood between his heart and a knowledge of God (Lightfoot, *op. cit.*, p.161). "Through its wisdom" speaks of men's wisdom, what they can know apart from special revelation. Indeed, much knowledge can be learned from a careful investigation of the works of the

---

[75] This interpretation is adopted by Meyer, Rosenmuller, Grotius, Calvin, Bengel, Beet, Ellicott.

[76] This interpretation is adopted by Alford, Findlay, Evans, Lightfoot, Robertson-Plummer, and Fisher.

universe, but as long as God's own special revelation is ignored, men will "not come to know God." "Knowing God," in this context, deals with salvation – misunderstanding the message of the cross. Paul's phrase does not deny the validity of natural theology to obtain a knowledge of what God is like.[77] 'Obtained not a true knowledge of Him' is the ultimate failure of human wisdom! Some denied His existence; some represented Him under the false and abominable forms of idol worship; some ascribed to Him horrid attributes. All showed they had no true acquaintance with a God of purity, with a God who could pardon sin, or whose worship conduced to holiness of life (Barnes, *op. cit.*, p.17). "Did not come to know God" might be written as an epitaph on the tomb of ancient philosophy, and of modern philosophy and science, so far as it assumes an anti-Christian form (Farrar, *op. cit.*, p.7). Human wisdom, when it relies solely on itself, may grope for God, but it will hardly find Him (Acts 17:26,27). The things suggested by human wisdom cannot save. The world, in spite of all its boasted intellect and philosophy, failed to obtain a real knowledge of God.

God was well pleased -- God 'concluded, determined, was disposed,' we would say. The verb signifies God's free determination, and it is a determination that is good and gracious toward those concerned. Our attention is drawn to the fact of God's free and sovereign choice. It was not in His plan at all that men by their exercise of wisdom should attain to the knowledge of Him. He determined to reveal Himself in quite a different way.

Through the foolishness of the message preached -- We are here being told *how* God made foolish the "wisdom of the world." This does not mean that the act of preaching is foolish (though the ASV reads "by the foolishness of preaching"). Preaching the gospel is not a waste of time, or foolishness. "By the foolishness of preaching," as in the KJV, is a mistranslation. That rendering would require *kēruxeos*, not *kērugmatos*. The word rendered "preaching" (*kērugmatos*) does not mean, as the English might suggest, the act of preaching. Rather, it directs attention to the content of the message. It is not merely the fact that men preach that is "foolish"; it is the content of gospel itself – contained in the message that God saves men through a crucified Savior – that is considered "foolish" by the worldly-wise men. It should read "by the foolishness (as men esteemed it) of the thing preached" (see ASV margin). It was the message of the cross (verse 18) that was the thing preached. It is a reference to the preaching of the cross, which was regarded as foolish and absurd by the men of the world. God's plan is wise, but it has been esteemed by most men of the world as ridiculous.

To save those who believe -- 'Through the foolishness of the thing preached' states the means; 'to those believing' defines the qualified objects of the salvation. "Those who be-

---

[77] Care must be exercised here that we define "wisdom" just as the context does. As one studies theistic arguments in an Evidences Class (causal, ontological, epistemological), he is often told in the books that these arguments do not prove the God of the Bible exists -- prove it, that is, to anyone but a believer. Such comments reflect Calvinistic presuppositions that because of inherited total depravity the unbeliever cannot think right. It is to be remembered that Calvin "found" many of his doctrines in Corinthians, and we must be careful lest this verse be used to prove total depravity, i.e., that the world cannot gain any true knowledge of God through the evidence given in nature.

lieve" are those who believe in the Lord Jesus Christ (see Mark 16:15,16). The participle is present tense, speaking of those who go on believing/obeying the good news.[78] "Believe" here stands opposed to Greek "knowledge," whereas in Romans 3:20,28 it stands opposed to man-made religious rules ("works") based on the Law. The world's wisdom failed. The divine "foolishness" succeeded. Deliverance from the guilt and penalty of sin is what God has provided in the gospel.

1:22 -- *For indeed Jews ask for signs and Greeks search for wisdom;*

For indeed Jews ask for signs -- We understand that verse 22 is an explanation of why the world failed to attain a saving knowledge of God.[79] "Signs" refer to miracles, miraculous signs. God regularly authenticated His messengers when they came bringing a message to the Jewish people. The Jews came to anticipate that Messiah would work stupendous miracles; this is what they asked of any one claiming to represent Messiah. Lipscomb (*op. cit.*, p.33) offered a listing of passages showing the constant seeking for signs by the Jews (cf. Matthew 12:38, 16:1, 27:42; Luke 11:16; John 2:18, 4:48, 6:30). This was characteristic of the Jewish people. God had manifested Himself to them by miracles and wonders in a remarkable manner in past times, and they greatly prided themselves on that fact, and always demanded it when any new messenger came to them, professing to be sent from God. "The Jews had been trained to accept the revelation of God attested by signs and miracles. It was the test of one claiming to be a teacher of the truth."[80] Jesus worked miracles. The Apostles, too, worked miracles (Acts 3:7, 6:8, 8:6; Romans 16:18; 2 Corinthians 12:12). Why then did not the Jews listen to the New Testament message when they had the numerous signs? Perhaps it was a stubborn refusal to be persuaded (cp. Luke 16:30,31). Perhaps it was because they were looking for a different kind of miracle.[81] If we remember that Jews thought of the Messiah as being One

---

[78] Note carefully, Scripture does not present the condition of salvation as being what is sometimes designated as "faith only." See James 2:14-26 and Galatians 3:26,27. Faithfulness (habitual doing what God says) is the condition of salvation everywhere presented in Scripture.

[79] Not all agree concerning the relationship of verse 22 to the rest of the passage. Both Meyer (*op. cit.*, p.31) and Alford (*op. cit.*, p.480) make verses 22-25 a new sentence, detached from verse 20ff, and complete in itself. They take verse 22 as a protasis, and verse 23 as an apodosis, of a conditional sentence. But this tends to lead us to the mistaken notion that the aims of the world supplied Paul's motive for preaching Christ. Instead, we believe verses 22-25 open out the thought introduced in verse 21. When they rely on the world's wisdom (and thus do not know God), Jews demand signs, and Greeks pursue wisdom. But the way to know God is through the preaching of the cross. (Another way of connecting to verse 21 is to suggest the reason for men's assessment that the thing preached is foolishness is because of their seeking signs and pursuing wisdom.)

[80] Lipscomb, *op. cit.*, p. 33.

[81] In AD 45, a man called Theudas had emerged. He had persuaded thousands of people to abandon their homes and follow him out to the Jordan River by promising that, at his word of command, the Jordan would divide and he would lead them across on dry land. In AD 54, a man from Egypt arrived in Jerusalem, claiming to be the Prophet. He persuaded 30,000 people to follow him out to the Mount of Olives by promising that at his word of command the walls of Jerusalem would fall down. This was the kind of thing the Jews were looking for. One wonders if they had searched the Scriptures and read about how the coming Messiah would make the deaf to hear, the lame made to walk, and the blind made to see, if they might not have better known what kind of credentials to look for.

attested by striking manifestations of power and majesty, then we can understand why to them a crucified Messiah was a contradiction of terms.

And Greeks search for wisdom -- The verbs in this verse, "ask" and "search," are *aiteō* and *dzeteō*. *Aiteō* expresses "the importunity of the Jews," and *dzeteō* speaks of "the curious, speculative turn of the Greeks," Lightfoot observed (*op. cit.*, p.162). *Aiteō* is present tense – the Jews keep asking for, keep on demanding signs. *Dzeteō* is also present tense – the Greeks too kept on seeking for wisdom. The Greeks asked for philosophy – wisdom of the world – before they would accept a message as being from Deity. The Greeks had been captivated by the outward show and glitter of their civilization. Whatever did not appear before them under the name of a new philosophy (Acts 17:19ff), or was not sustained by philosophic proof, or was not set forth with logical or rhetorical art, this they refused to accredit.[82] "The Greeks looked with philosophic indifference on the whole field of the supernatural, regarding even the resurrection of Christ, as adding but one more to the already plentiful childish fables, fit only for the simple-minded."[83] The Greeks were absorbed in speculative philosophy. No names were more honored among them than the names of their outstanding thinkers, Plato, Aristotle, and Socrates. From the lofty heights of their culture they looked down on and despised as barbarians all who failed to appreciate their "wisdom." That this wisdom often degenerated into meaningless sophistries, or the kind of pursuits mentioned in Acts 17:21, meant little to them. They still remained proud of their intellectual acuteness, and found no place for the gospel because of this.

1:23 -- *but we preach Christ crucified, to Jews a stumbling block and to Gentiles foolishness,*

But we preach Christ crucified -- "But we" is strongly contradictory to the foregoing. Because worldly wisdom (verse 22) has failed and will continue to fail to bring Jews and Greeks to a knowledge of God, Paul will continue to preach Christ crucified, which is, after all, real wisdom from God. "We" is the first appearance in this letter of a first person plural verb.[84] Paul naturally slips into use of "we" in such places as this, where he would be concerned to imply that such preaching is not unique to himself. Other inspired preachers preach the same message! We who are Christian preachers, Paul says, make Christ crucified the grand object of our instructions and our aims in contradistinction to what the Jew and Greek want. The present tense of the verb "preach" shows that the proclamation of the gospel is the one, constant business of the preachers. Instead of "Christ crucified," we might render it 'a crucified Messiah.' The power of God to save came from the death of Messiah on the cross, and this is what Paul preached. Instead of working great signs to satisfy the Jews, or propounding philosophy to entertain the Greeks, Christian preachers

---

[82] See Herodotus. iv.77; Aelianus *Var. Hist.* xii.25; Juvenal, *Satur.*, I, ii. 58ff.

[83] Lipscomb, *op. cit.*, p. 33.

[84] Compare notes at 1 Corinthians 1:1 and later at 2:6.

emphasized a crucified Messiah. The emphasis in this expression is on "crucified." It is a perfect tense participle, the tense signifying past completed action with present continuing results. The fact and result of His crucifixion has become something permanent and enduring from the very moment it happened. It was only by slow degrees that the title "the Christ," i.e., the Anointed, the Messiah, passed into the name of Christ.

To Jews a stumbling block -- "Messiah crucified" would have seemed like a contradiction of terms in the minds of earthly minded Jews. Messiah meant power, splendor, triumph. Crucifixion meant weakness, humiliation, defeat. From the standpoint of mere human understanding, it was difficult to see how the two could be put together. The Jews for centuries had been looking for a regal and victorious Messiah who should exalt their special privileges. The notion of a suffering and humiliated Messiah, who had reduced them to the level of God's other children, was to them a stone of stumbling and a rock of offense (Romans 9:33; cp. Isaiah 8:14). The word stumbling block (*skandalon*) means anything in the way over which one may trip and fall. The doctrine that the Messiah was to be put to death gave them great offense, excited, irritated, and exasperated them; they could not endure it. The Jew could even point to the Law (Deuteronomy 21:23) where it was unmistakably said, "He who is hanged is accursed of God." The message that emphasized crucifixion was an offense and a hindrance to faith, the occasion of a fall, something causing them to err. A person hanging on the accursed tree presented such a contrast to all their desires for some glorious exhibition of power (such as destruction to their enemies) that they rejected Him. The Jews demanded a victorious Christ, heralded by miracles, who would restore the glories of the Kingdom of David and Solomon. To the Jew, the cross was the sufficient and decisive refutation of the claim that Jesus was the Christ (Matthew 27:42, Luke 24:21).

And to Gentiles foolishness -- The term "Gentile"[85] denotes all who were not ethnically Jews; thus the phrase "Jews and Gentiles" encompassed the whole human family. That salvation could come to the world through a crucified Jew appeared to them absurd ("foolishness"). It was an instrumentality utterly inadequate to the end proposed. It wasn't reasonable to the Greek that there could be any power in the cross. After all, to Greeks and Romans, crucifixion branded a man throughout the empire as among the basest of criminals; it was outrageous and absurd that such a person could save them or help them know God. The Greeks, who thought that a man's moral and intellectual needs could be satisfied only by a system of philosophy, considered it an absurdity to announce a person, and that person as one who had been condemned to die the most ignoble of deaths. Barclay has suggested that if we understand a bit of the Greek idea of what a "god" is like it will help us to see why they thought the Christian message foolish.

> To the Greek, a chief characteristic of a "god" was *apatheia*. Now that word means more than "apathy" – it means total inability to feel. A god who suffered

---

[85] The KJV reads "Greeks" here, but the better manuscripts read "Gentiles" (see *Aleph*, A, B, C, D. etc.).

(like Christians taught that Jesus suffered) was to the Greek mind a contradiction of terms. Plutarch declared that it was an insult to a "god" to involve him in human affairs. A "god" was of necessity utterly detached and utterly removed. So, to Greek thinking, incarnation is a total impossibility. Not only was it unbelievable that God would become incarnate, it was even more difficult to swallow the idea that He would get involved in human affairs like Jesus was presented as having done.[86]

Profound contempt is discernible in all the early allusions of Greeks and Romans to Christianity. The only epithets which they could find for it were "execrable," "malefic," "depraved," "damnable" (Tacitus, Suetonius, Pliny). The milder term is "excessive superstition." The heroic constancy of martyrs appeared even to M. Aurelius only under the aspect of a "bare obstinacy." The word used to express the scorn of the Athenian philosophers for Paul's "strange doctrine" is one of the coarsest disdain (*exleuadzon*, "sneer," "scoff," Acts 17:32), and they called him an "idle babbler" (a 'seed-picker,' Acts 17:18), i.e., a mere picker-up of "learning's crumbs." There is also the well-known caricature found on the Palatine, of a slave boy bowing down to a crucified figure with an ass's head, inscribed "the worshiper is repelled by this god."

1:24 -- *but to those who are the called, both Jews and Greeks, Christ the power of God and the wisdom of God.*

But to those who are the called -- Literally, 'to the called themselves.' The called were those who believed in Jesus and who accepted the gospel invitation to come to Him. See 1:1,2. "Called" here designates those who are Christians.[87]

Both Jews and Greeks -- By the addition of these words, Paul gives us to understand that (in the purpose of grace denoted in their calling) the separation between Jew and Greek hitherto existing between these parties had been removed. Compare Romans 9:24 and 10:12. Henceforth the middle wall of partition between them is thrown down, and there is no difference (Romans 9:24). The call of God, through the gospel, is identical for all.

Christ the power of God and the wisdom of God -- It is necessary to supply a verb from the immediate context. "We preach" is the verb from verse 23, so that the expanded sentence reads, "*we preach* Christ *as* the power of God and wisdom of God." In "power" and

---

[86] William Barclay, "The Letters to the Corinthians" in the *Daily Study Bible* series (Philadelphia, PA: Westminster, 1956), p.20,21. Greek philosophy was not quite consistent on this point. A god becoming incarnate and getting involved in a god-man atonement for sin, they could not believe. Yet they could believe that the Olympian gods had human characteristics, including sin, and as somehow having the ability of begetting and being begotten by human kind. It is typical to often ignore some element of human philosophy, especially when it doesn't fit what we want to believe.

[87] "Called" in verse 24 may be the place where Calvin came up with his doctrine of "effectual call." In his system, those who are "being saved" (verse 18) and "those who believe" (verse 21) are so because of God's prior action – that action being an "effectual call" (they are those whom 'God has called'). See the author's Romans commentary and notes at 1 Corinthians 1:1,2,9 concerning how God calls through the gospel. The differing responses to the invitation do not depend on the efficacy of the invitation, but upon the soil into which the seed of the Word is sown.

"wisdom" we have the antithesis to "stumbling block" and "foolishness." It even carries us back to the thought of verses 18 and 21: power, fulfilling the requirement of those asking for a sign; wisdom, of those who sought wisdom.[88] What those "called" find Christ to be matches, in a way, what the foolish Jews and Greeks ask for and seek. The Jews ask for signs; but these could be wrought only by God's power. The most stupendous signs wrought by omnipotence in the skies could not save a single Jew – yet this same power of God, the power of His grace in Christ Jesus, did save both Jews and Greeks. The Greeks seek speculative, earthly wisdom. Yet all the philosophies and all the sciences from two millennia never saved a single Gentile. This the wisdom of God alone has done, actually and wondrously saved both Jews and Greeks.

1:25 -- *Because the foolishness of God is wiser than men, and the weakness of God is stronger than men.*

Because -- Verse 24 has used the subjective experience of the saved as evidence that the crucified Christ is both God's wisdom and God's power. Now, looking at the same crucifixion event objectively, it is explained why the "called" have the experience they do, why Christ crucified is the power and wisdom of God. It is because "the foolishness of God is wiser than men ...."

The foolishness of God -- "Foolishness" is not to be taken too abstractly, as if it meant there really is such a thing as Divine folly. The apostle is evidently here speaking from a human point of view and implies merely that which appears, from man's standpoint, to be foolishness in God. The "foolishness of God" is an act of God which men think foolish.

Is wiser than men -- The gospel is better adapted to accomplish important ends, and more certainly effectual than the schemes of human wisdom. This is especially true of the plan of salvation – a plan that appears foolish to the mass of men, yet indubitably accomplishes more for the renewing of men, and for their purity and happiness, than all the schemes contrived by humans. The gospel – with its message of a Messiah crucified – has proven stronger and wiser than anything human. It does what the world's wisdom fails to do.

And the weakness of God -- There is really no weakness in God, any more than there is folly. This phrase points to any act of God which men think weak. "Foolishness ... weakness" refers to *the method whereby God works*, and which men take to be foolish and weak, because with arrogant presumption they look upon themselves as the measure of all things. But God achieves the mightiest ends by the humblest means, and the gospel of

---

[88] "Two great evils consequent upon the Fall are weakness and ignorance. Nothing is more worthy, therefore, of divine benevolence and wisdom than to allow that one race (the Jews) should discover the helplessness of man, and another (the Greeks) his ignorance. The Jew went upon the first of these searches. He asked for a manifestation of power; he looked for the finger, the hand, the arm of the Almighty. The Greek went upon the second search. He endeavored to explain phenomena by philosophic theory. The intended result of the Mosaic Law was – 'the things which I would do I cannot do.' The result of Greek philosophy was 'the things which I would know, I cannot discover.' Christ satisfied both these wants." (T. Evans, "1 Corinthians" in *The Holy Bible Commentary* edited by F.C. Cook, New York: Charles Scribner's Sons, 1886, Vol. 3, p.250-251)

Christ allied itself from the first, not with the world's strength and splendor, but with all which the world despised as mean and feeble – with fishermen and tax-gatherers, with slaves and women.

Is stronger than men – God's workings were able to accomplish more than the utmost might of man. The feeblest agency God puts forth – so feeble as to be esteemed weakness – effects more than the utmost might of man. It exerts a mightier power than they with all their imagined strength and prowess. Lenski takes "foolishness" and "weakness" differently than we have. "God moved only a finger, as it were, in confounding the proud notions of wisdom and power which the world entertained. What might have happened if He had called on all the resources of his infinite wisdom and power?"[89]

> Before proceeding to the next paragraph, it seems useful to give a summary of the paragraph just concluded. Working backwards – "The Divine Power and Wisdom, at their seeming lowest, are far above man's highest (25). For this reason (22-24) our Gospel – a poor thing in the eyes of men – is, to those who know it, the Power and Wisdom of God. This exemplifies (21) the truth underlying the history of the world, that man's wisdom is convicted of failure by the simplicity of the truth proclaimed by God. This is how God, now as of old, turns to folly the wisdom of the wise (19,20), a principle which explains the opposite look which the 'word of the cross' has to 'those being lost' and 'those being saved' (18). That is why (17) my mission is to preach 'not in wisdom of words'." (Robertson and Plummer, *op. cit.*, p.24)

C. THE METHOD OF GOD IN THE SPREAD OF THE GOSPEL. 1:26-31

1:26 -- *For consider your calling, brethren, that there were not many wise according to the flesh, not many mighty, not many noble;*

For consider -- Paul begins with "for," as if he would say, 'What I have just told you about the wisdom of God's foolishness and the strength of God's weakness, you can actually see in your own selves.' *Blepete* is ambiguous, since it may be either in the indicative mood, as our translators have rendered it ('You do see'), or it may be in the imperative ('See, contemplate your condition!'). Perhaps the imperative is best. 'Look at your own ranks, my brothers!' Paul invites his readers to reflect on the type of person whom God has, in fact, chosen.[90] Paul is still discussing the Corinthians' misunderstanding of the nature of the gospel – how it was not dependent on human cleverness, but on divine power. The apostle here introduces a new argument in support of the general position taught in the previous section. In proof of what he said regarding the true method of preaching and the

---

[89] Lenski, *op. cit.*, p.70,71.

[90] Leon Morris, "The First Epistle of Paul to the Corinthians" in the *Tyndale New Testament Commentary* series (Grand Rapids, MI: Eerdmans, 1966), p.48.

utter vanity of the worldly wisdom they were tempted to prize, the Corinthians could plainly see for themselves what course the gospel had taken among those who were its converts. The whole history of the expansion of the church is in reality a progressive victory of men who were nobodies in the world's eyes, but through whom God's Spirit works.

> The thought of the contradiction that God's method offers to the wisdom of men is illustrated by the kind of people He has called to be His own. He might have chosen to put the gospel in a form which would have appealed primarily to the intelligentsia. Human wisdom would concentrate on outstanding men. But God has no need of human wisdom. Rather, He chooses those who have little to commend them from the worldly standpoint. These he transforms, and uses as instruments for the effecting of His purpose. His power works miracles in the most hopeless material. Thus the wisdom of God is shown to excel the best that men can produce.[91]

Your call, brethren – *Tēn klēsin* means "those who are called" (as 'the circumcision' means those who are circumcised, Romans 3:30). The sense is, 'Look upon the condition or social position of those who are now Christians.' "Your call" means "the principle God has followed in calling you" (Beza quoted by Farrar, *op. cit.*, p.8). 'Note the ranks from which one by one you were summoned into the society of God's people.' Paul emphasizes again the invitation God gave them to become Christians. (See notes at 1:1,2 on "calling" to become a Christian. The "calling" which they are requested to observe is not their secular vocation, though the word "calling" is sometimes used to signify secular vocation.) From Ephesians 4:1 and Hebrews 3:1, we understand "call" to be the Christian's call to serve Christ. The state of affairs Paul is describing did not come about because the only people who would interest themselves in Christianity were the depressed classes. Rather, it came about because God chose to work His marvels through people who were, from the human point of view, the most unpromising.

That there were not many wise according to the flesh -- In the light of the use of "wisdom" in verse 22 above, "wise" here places emphasis on the Greek intellectual or philosopher class, those who were "wise" according to human standards. Not many who were regarded as wise, or who ranked with philosophers, became Christians. There were not many from the educated class, from the intellectual class. In fact, there were not many educated men in general. "Not many" means there were some, but their numbers were few. The first of the terms in this verse must have a modifier, "after the flesh," to indicate what sort of "wise" Paul has in mind, for Scripture also speaks of those "wise unto salvation" (2 Timothy 2:15). "According to the flesh" equals "according to human standards."[92] Note that "not many wise" heads the list, perhaps because wisdom has been

---

[91] Morris, *op. cit.*, p.47

[92] This is the first use of the word "flesh" (*sarx*) in Paul's extant letters. (1 Corinthians was written about AD 57, the third of Paul's letters, after 1 & 2 Thessalonians, which were written in AD 51 or 52). In the years after the close of the New Testament canon, the word became a term over which much theological dispute has raged. The point that came to be debated is whether the word implies an inherited "sinful nature," inherited from Adam after he fell. (Cf. Galatians 5, Romans 5)

so much in mind throughout this discussion. The Corinthians had the typical Greek reverence for wisdom. Paul decisively rejects this as the criterion whereby God chooses His own.

Not many mighty -- "Mighty" (*dunatoi*) means persons of consequence in civil life, influential and powerful, whether it be by wealth or any other means. They are men of rank and political influence, men who were prominent, who carried clout in a sociological setting. That there were some of high rank and wealth at Corinth who converted to Christianity is well known:[93] (a) Crispus and Sosthenes, rulers of the synagogue (Acts 18:8,17; cp. 1 Corinthians 1:1); (b) Gaius, a rich and hospitable man (Romans 16:23); (c) Erastus, the chancellor of the city of Corinth (Romans 16:23). However, the fact that most Christians came from the lower class was the more noteworthy because the Jews won many rich and noble proselytes such as the Queen Helena, and the royal family of Adiabene, Poppaea the wife of Nero, and others. Unless their possessors are truly converted and submissive to the Lord, wealth and social power will be hindrances to Christian service and the growth of the kingdom.

Not many noble -- "Noble" (*eugeneis*) means of distinguished descent, well-born, aristocrats. In highly civilized, aristocratic Corinth, this was regarded as of great importance. In a Roman colony and capital like Corinth, the "noble" would be chiefly men of hereditary citizenship, men whose ancestors were virtuous and wealthy and the leading citizens of the town. The apostle does not say that there were no men of wealth or power or birth, but that the mass of Christians was not composed of such. The three terms in this verse – wise, mighty, noble – comprised the upper-class of the 1st century. There was no real middle class. Paul says God chose His "workers" for the most part from the lower classes. Again, for those who composed the church at Corinth, before their conversion, see at 6:9-11. Many of the early Christians[94] were slaves and men of low station. The whole history of the expansion of the church is in reality a progressive victory of the ignorant over the learned, the lowly over the lofty, until the emperor himself laid his crown before the cross of Christ.

Are called (ASV) -- These words are in italics in the ASV; the Greek has no verb, so we must supply one to form a complete sentence. Several verbs may be supplied: (a) "Are" is one possible verb we could supply. 'There are not many ....' 'Not many worldly great

---

[93] Several other illustrious converts in other parts of the ancient world included Nicodemus, Sergius Paulus, and Dionysius the Areopagite.

[94] Scholars in recent times have hotly debated the subject of the social status of the early church members. Some have defended the view that the majority were from the poorer classes and lower castes. Others have dismissed the words of Scripture as being mere rhetoric while defending the thesis that the early believers were by and large fairly well-to-do and from the upper-class of people rather than the very poor. The proper conclusion to this study seems to be that the early Christians were drawn from all across the sociological spectrum – the "brothers" were slave and free, Jew and Gentile, male and female. We must not think of the early church as composed entirely of slaves.

ones accept the divine call and become servants of God.'⁹⁵ (b) "Called" (as in the English Version) is another verb we could supply. Some of the early Church Fathers thought that "the called" here designates the persons who were chosen by God to preach the gospel. (So Lipscomb interprets, too. ⁹⁶) Others understand the verb supplied to be used in the same sense as "called" was used in verse 24 -- i.e., of those who had responded to the invitation and thus had become Christians.

1:27 -- *but God has chosen the foolish things of the world to shame the wise, and God has chosen the weak things of the world to shame the things which are strong,*

But -- Rather than choosing intellectuals and people from the political and social circles, God chose the "foolish things ...."

God has chosen the foolish things of the world -- The verb here is *exelexato*, a middle voice (the subject acts for His own benefit) aorist tense (implying completed action in the past time) verb form. God "selected" or "picked out" or "chose" for Himself.⁹⁷ This verb is used three times in verses 27 and 28. The repetition of this verb underlines the purpose of God.⁹⁸ God determined the plan He would follow before He ever created ("the eternal purpose of God," Romans 8:28) and also determined He would use the foolish and weak (verses 27,28) in order that no man should have any reason to boast (1 Corinthians 1:29). "Foolish things" translates *ta mōra*, 'the simpletons of the world did God choose' -- persons who were considered such by the world, because they were unphilosophical, uneducated. "Foolish things" are the things esteemed foolish among men.⁹⁹ The expression here may refer to people who were destitute of learning, rank, wealth, and power, and who were esteemed as fools, and were despised by the rich and the great. Or it may refer to things which the world thinks foolish. Some commentators take "of the world" to mean 'in the world's judgment.' Others (like Morris, *op. cit.*, p.48-49) say that not just in the world's judgment are they "weak" and "foolish" but they really are the ones who are weak and foolish in this world.

---

⁹⁵ Lipscomb, *op. cit.*, p.34.

⁹⁶ *Ibid.* Such an interpretation would be paralleled by Acts 4:13, where the Sanhedrin, too, was aware that the leaders of the Christian religion were "unlearned and ignorant men."

⁹⁷ We may strongly remark that there is no reason why the KJV translators of 1611 should use the same helpers ("have" and "has") to translate both aorist and perfect tense verbs. In this and many instances their lack of precision in translating the tense is unimportant, but sometimes it materially and injuriously affects the sense. One of the advantages of the NASB is its careful handling of Greek verb tenses.

⁹⁸ Nothing here suggests any idea of eternal unconditional election of certain individuals to salvation or damnation.

⁹⁹ In each case in verses 27 and 28, the "foolish," "weak," and "lowly" are neuter plural words in the Greek, while the first contrasting word "wise" is masculine, and the other two are neuter. Lightfoot (*op. cit.*, p.166) and Godet suppose the change in gender is important to the argument. Fee suggests (*op. cit.*, p.82), on the contrary, that Paul is here generalizing. Not only did he choose "foolish" people, but in all His ways He chose what the world deems foolish (including the cross). Likewise, Barrett translates "what the world counts foolish," which seems to clearly catch Paul's idea.

To shame the wise -- The word *kataischunē* ("put to shame") speaks of humbling them, and it was done by showing them how little He regarded their wisdom and how little their wisdom contributed to the success of His cause. The foolish things shame the "wise" of the world by succeeding where they failed. Not accidentally did God choose the foolish things, but purposely. He intended to heap shame on the "wise" of the world (beginning with *hina*, "to shame" is a purpose clause). Paul makes sure the Corinthians do not overlook God's plan in all this. "The wise" are the wise after the flesh. The term is masculine, 'the people who are wise' (wise in the eyes of the world).

And God has chosen the weak things of the world -- The weak of every kind, bodily, mentally, politically, holding no position of power and influence, those esteemed weak by the men of the world. James 2:5 is perhaps similar: "Did not God choose the poor of this world to be rich in faith?"

To shame the things which are strong -- The "strong" are the great, the noble, the learned. It says "things" (neuter). It may refer either to persons, or to the qualities and characteristics that make up those persons. "Shame" (the same *kataischunē* as before) is a present tense form which indicates continuous action. God continually brings to shame all those who think themselves strong, or that they are somehow special and superior to others. God, to show His power and presence, and to manifest the folly of man's wisdom, and the weakness of his greatest inventions, chose the things that to human wisdom appear foolish to confound or confuse the wisdom of the great ones.

1:28 -- *and the base things of the world and the despised God has chosen, the things that are not, so that He may nullify the things that are,*

And the base things of the world -- "Base things" (*agenē*) means of low origin, of lowly birth, illegitimate; it is the very opposite of *eugeneis* ("well-born," verse 26). "Base things" are those who are sprung from no one in particular, those who are not of noble or illustrious birth. Mare thinks "the slave class" is intended (*op. cit.*, p.196).

And the despised, God has chosen -- These whom the world regards as objects of contempt and treats as of no account. (Cp. Mark 9:12 and Acts 4:11.) The Knox Bible translates it "contemptible."

The things that are not -- Compare Hosea 1:10, 2:23; Romans 9:25; 1 Peter 2:10. In this designation "things that are not"[100] there is likely a reference to the Gentiles. The language is strongly expressive of the estimate which the Jews fixed on the Gentiles, as being a despised people, as being in fact no people; a people without laws, and organization, and religion, and privileges. Actually, Whitby discovers in the designations of verse 28 an

---

[100] *Ta mē onta* implies that the non-existence is not absolute but estimative (Alford, *op. cit.*, p.482). The classes to which Christianity appealed were nonentities for philosophers and statesmen; they were cyphers in their reckoning. Fisher suggests that "things that are not" is a reference to slaves, for slaves, he reminds us, had no independent existence in society apart from their masters.

allusion to both Jews and Gentiles. His observations are valuable.

> The Jews looked upon themselves as the only *eugeneis*, 'persons of true nobility,' as being of the stock of Abraham. 'Even the poorest Israelite,' saith R. Akibah, 'is to be looked upon as a gentleman, as being the son of Abraham'; but the Gentiles they horribly despised, as the base people of the earth, not fit to be conversed with, they being styled in their law, *oukethnos*, 'not a nation'; *laos ho techthesomenos*, 'a people that shall be born' (Psm. 22:31); *ho ktizomenos*, 'that should be created in the generation to come' (Psm. 102:19), and so yet had no being (Deut. 31:21). *Ou laos*, 'not a people,' (Hos. 1:10); and it being said by the prophet, that 'all the Heathen are as nothing, and were accounted as nothing' (Isa. 40:17), they still account them as such. Hence, Mordecai prays, 'Lord, give not thy sceptre' *tois me ousai*, 'to them that are not' (Esth. 4:11).[101]

As we have gone through these four categories in these last two verses, we have been heading toward an anticlimax. Each category causes us to descend in our estimation. We laugh at things foolish; we scorn or pity the weak; we despise things base and common; and we utterly disregard things rated as nothing. When we come to "the things that are not," we have come to the lowest step.

That He might nullify ("that He might bring to nought," ASV) -- *Kataergō* is not an easy word to translate. It occurs 27 different times in the Greek text of the New Testament, and is translated 17 different ways in the KJV, 13 different ways in the ERV (Morris, *op. cit.*, p.49). One suggestion is that here it means 'to humble and subdue,' to show them how vain and impotent they were. The word can also mean 'to render idle' or 'inoperative,' or 'render completely ineffective.' "In its scorned professors, the gospel has in fact displayed a power of action and endurance, which far transcends the measure of the natural man" (Neander, quoted by Kling, *op. cit.*, p.44). Here again, we have a purpose (*hina*) clause. God is showing that the power that produces Christianity's growth is in Him, not in the cleverness of the converts.

The things that are -- Those who on account of their noble birth, high attainments, wealth, and rank placed a high estimate on themselves and despised others. Here is a reference to any Jew or Gentile who, because of inordinate pride or human wisdom, looks down on others as being a lesser people.

1:29 -- *so that no man may boast before God.*

So that -- Literally, "That all flesh may have no ground of boasting before God." A final purpose clause[102] concludes all that Paul says regarding God's choosing. This verse (beginning with *hopōs* rather than *hina*) expresses God's ultimate aim in all His dealings with and through men.

---

[101] Quoted by Kling, *op. cit.*, p.44.

[102] Paul has used three *hina* clauses (expressing purpose) in verses 27-28, and now he uses the word *hopōs* (which also expresses purpose) to introduce this final clause of his long sentence.

No man ("no flesh," ASV) -- In the Greek, the negative "no" precedes "flesh." The usual word order in Greek for negative particles is that the negative stands immediately before the word (noun or verb) that is being negated. "*No* flesh is to boast" seems to be the emphasis. "No flesh" means that no men, no class of men (whether Jew or Gentile), indeed not even any faction in the church at Corinth, is to boast. The word "flesh" is often used to denote mankind (Matthew 24:22; Luke 3:6; John 17:2; Acts 2:17; 1 Peter 1:24).

Should boast ("should glory," ASV) -- "Boast" is the modern word that catches the idea, rather than "glory" (cp. Romans 3:27). The weak instruments of God's triumphs are so weak that it was impossible for them to ascribe any power or merit to themselves. In contemplating the victory of the cross the world could only exclaim, "This hath *God* wrought." "It is the Lord's doing ... and it is marvelous in our eyes." "Boasting" is exactly what the Corinthian factions have been doing when they kept saying "I am of Paul, I of Apollos, I of Cephas." God has now arranged things so that no man should boast. How out of harmony with God's plan and purpose the Corinthians are! No man should boast that he, out of his own endeavors or position or worth, had contributed anything to the great achievements of the gospel. No man should boast in other men, as though they were somebody great. God requires men to work through means unfitted to the end to be accomplished, to show them that the power is of God, not in man's cleverness, so that no man should boast in men or what men have done. God has taken away all occasion of boasting. How dare the Corinthians continue to boast as they have been.

Before God -- "Before God" seems to mean 'in His presence.' All men, especially the church members at Corinth, stand in the presence of God. In His presence, there is to be no boasting such as the Corinthians have been doing as they separated themselves into warring factions. God's selection of the foolish, the weak, the lowly, and the 'no peoples' should cause us and the Corinthians to be very slow to boast about ourselves or any human leaders.

1:30 -- *But by His doing you are in Christ Jesus, who became to us wisdom from God, and righteousness and sanctification, and redemption,*

But by His doing ("But of him," ASV) – This is the progression of thought: (a) Verse 17 introduced the topic of 'wisdom' ("cleverness of speech" is literally "wisdom of words"). (b) Verses 21 and 24 spoke about the "wisdom of God." (c) What is involved in that expression "wisdom" is now going to be explained. Whether we translate as the NASB or the ASV will depend largely on which of the two possible translations of this whole clause we adopt.

You are -- Two different translations are possible here: (a) "It comes from Him (God) that you are in Christ Jesus." That is, your being Christians is due to God's work. There is an emphasis on God's initiative, say Meyer, Edwards, Heinrici, Beet, Godet, Shore. To demonstrate that this is the translation to be preferred, Findlay affirmed "the whole passage

(1:17-29) is dominated by the divine initiative in salvation."[103]   Attention is also called to 1 Corinthians 3:6,9, 8:6, 10:12, 13:6; 2 Corinthians 4:6, 5:18. (b) "It is in Christ Jesus that you are of Him." That is, your new life is grounded in Christ. The emphasis is on Christ, on Christ's work, Christ's agency. Implied is the idea that the emphasis should not be on this or that human leader as the Corinthians had been doing. So interpret Grotius, the Greek Fathers, Calvin, Beza, Ruckert, Hoffmann, Lightfoot. To show that this is the preferable way to translate the Greek, appeal is made to the thrust of the whole passage about the wrong-headedness of the kind of party spirit that flourished in the Corinthian church. Certainly, this is one passage where the theology of the translator is likely to intrude, even in the translation of the Greek. Knowing this helps us better evaluate what we read in certain commentaries. Comments that say 'your being Christians is God's doing' often reflect a view that in salvation man is wholly passive, and God must do it all. The comment that says 'your existence as Christians is due to what God did in history through Christ Jesus' is in harmony with the idea that man is not wholly passive in salvation.

In Christ Jesus -- If we accept the second way of translating this phrase,[104] then "in Christ Jesus" means by the medium, or through the work of Christ, God's mercy has been conferred upon us. The rest of the verse is a wonderful description of how the work of Jesus makes it possible for God to confer His mercy on men.

Who became to us wisdom from God ("Who was made unto us wisdom from God," ASV) -- On the word "wisdom" the whole discussion from 1:17 onwards hinges. The wisdom that really matters is not the wisdom of the world, but God's wisdom. This verse will go on to explain that God's wisdom involves righteousness, sanctification, and redemption, all mediated in Christ. What a contrast to the false wisdom of men that the context has been condemning as worthless. Christ made God's "wisdom" visible and available for us by His coming into the world, and by what He accomplished for us. "Was made" (ASV, or "became," NASB) points back to the incarnation. When it is affirmed that "Christ was made to us wisdom" we are to understand that in Him, in His person, the fullness of which was unfolded in His history, the mystery of the divine plan of salvation has been disclosed. And with the disclosure of the plan of salvation, we have been afforded an insight into the dispensations and judgments of God; we are enabled to recognize and lay hold upon that which shall conduct us to the goal of our deepest longings

---

[103] Findlay, *op. cit.*, p.773. The language "divine initiative" is suspect and theologically loaded. All the context has spoken about is God's "choosing" certain foolish things, low things. That is hardly the same theological concept as is often being expressed when people speak of "divine initiative." That language about "divine initiative" often is based on the premise that man is wholly depraved (an inherited depravity from Adam), and that God must work a first work of grace, before a man can even want to believe.

[104] If we accept the first way of translating this phrase, the words 'in Christ Jesus' mean 'in union with Christ.' 'By God's work you are now in saving union with Christ Jesus.' Whether or not it is to be so interpreted in this verse, there is no doubt that at times the phrase "in Christ" is Paul's way of describing the relationship of believers to Christ. Whole books have been written in an attempt to unfold the meaning of this important phrase.   Christ is the atmosphere in which the believer lives. The believer stands in the very closest possible relationship to his Lord, and to all others who are also "in Christ."

(cp. 1 Corinthians 2:7ff; Colossians 1:9ff, 1:26ff, 3:2,10; Philippians 1:9ff; Ephesians 5:8ff). Are the Corinthians desiring "wisdom," actual wisdom? In Christ they have the very highest and most blessed wisdom that comes to them from God Himself. "Wisdom from God" (as the verse continues to explain) is to be understood as including righteousness, sanctification, and redemption.

And righteousness -- The NIV reads "that is" instead of "and." Commentaries following the KJV understand that Christ has been made *four* things for believers – wisdom, righteousness, sanctification, and redemption.[105] Perhaps it is better to understand that Christ was made to be *one* thing for believers – namely, "wisdom" – and that this wisdom then is then further defined or explained by the next *three* words "righteousness, sanctification, and redemption." When we contemplate what "righteousness" is, perhaps we should be reminded of 2 Corinthians 5:21, and of the Old Testament name, "*Jehovah-tsidkenu*" – the Lord our Righteousness (cf. Jeremiah 23:5). Perhaps we should think of God's way of saving man. While this is the first use of "justification" in Paul's letters,[106] we are already familiar with his use of the term "justification" or "righteousness" to express the saving work of Christ from his sermons recorded in Acts (cf. Acts 13:39). Christ is the source of our justification before God. This is the theme of Romans 3-8. The doctrine of justification is that God regards and treats those as righteous who believe on His Son, and who are pardoned on account of what He has done and suffered. The steps of the process may be thus stated: (a) All of us have sinned, and come short of the glory of God. We have violated a holy law, and that law condemns us. We have no power to make atonement or reparation. (b) Jesus Christ has taken the sinner's place and died in his stead. He has honored a broken law; He has rendered it consistent for God to pardon. By His dreadful sufferings, endured in the sinner's place, God has shown His hatred of sin and His willingness to forgive. God's truth will be vindicated and His law honored and His government secured, if now He shall pardon the offender when penitent. As Christ endured these sorrows for others, and not for Himself, they can be so reckoned, and are so judged by God. All the benefits or results of that atonement, since it was made for others, can be applied to those who have sinned. (c) God has been pleased to promise that these benefits may be conferred on anyone who believes and obeys the Savior. Example: I am in debt, with no way to pay the debt. Another pays my debt for me. My creditor now no longer threatens me. He considers it just as though I had paid the debt. Where does the world's wisdom have anything to compare with this?

And sanctification -- Perhaps the word speaks of our initial "sanctification."[107] God's

---

[105] Meyer, Alford, Godet, and others take the four words as co-ordinate.

[106] While "righteousness" or "justification" is a term much used in Romans, we say that this is the first use of the word in Paul's letters, for 1 Corinthians was written before Romans, even though it is included in our Bibles after Romans.

[107] See notes at 1:2 and 6:11 for an explanation of "sanctification." Also, see Special Study #5 on "Sanctification" in the author's commentary on Romans. Some of the key emphases in that study are: (1) The importance of sanctification (Hebrews 12:14); (2) How theological disputes through the ages have changed the church's presentation of what sanctification is; (3) A brief presentation of three views: the Wesleyan (sanctification is an instantaneous act following conversion by which the inherited sinful nature

wisdom has so ordered it that only through the work of Christ is it possible for man to be set apart or sanctified to the service of God. One will never find such an ennobling separation in the "wisdom of this age" or in "wisdom of words." Perhaps the word speaks of the spiritual growth that follows our initial justification. Christ dwells in us, and our thoughts, words, and deeds are to show it. Again, the world knows no such inner transforming power. The very idea of holiness is foreign to its mind, for the essence of holiness is separation from the world and devotion to God.

And redemption -- There are four main metaphors by which the atonement is described: (a) *Gaal* (Hebrew) - to free (by avenging or repaying). (b) *Padah* (Hebrew) - to free, redeem, buy back. (c) *Agoradzō* (Greek) - to purchase, acquire at the market. (d) *Lutroō* (Greek) - to ransom, to purchase with a price. The word here is *apolutrosis*. The meaning and the nature of the act, *as regards God,* lie in regions above our comprehension; all speculations as to the person to whom the ransom was paid, and the reason why it was indispensable, have only led to centuries of mistaken theology. But the meaning and the nature of it, *as regards man*, is our deliverance from the bondage of sin, and the payment of the debt which we had incurred (Titus 2:14; 1 Peter 1:18; Matthew 20:28; Romans 8:21-23). "It is by Christ that we are redeemed; by Him that an atonement is made; by Him that we are pardoned; by Him that we are delivered from the dominion of sin, and the power of our enemies; and by Him that we shall be rescued from the grave, and raised up to everlasting life" (Barnes, *op. cit.*, p.26). Because of its position after the preceding terms, "redemption" probably does not refer to the original "redemption" wrought by Christ on the cross, but must refer to our own final "redemption" (cp. Romans 8:23) of our bodies from death; i.e., what is elsewhere sometimes called 'resurrection and glorification.' And once more we ask, where does the world have anything like this to offer? The important thing in verse 30 is that Christ is God's wisdom. To have their thinking be in harmony with God's, the Corinthians will have to quit embracing the wisdom of this age, and embrace instead God's wisdom as mediated by Christ.

1:31 -- *that, just as it is written, "LET HIM WHO BOASTS, BOAST IN THE LORD."*

That -- Verses 29 and 30 have excluded all glorying based on human achievement or suggested by human wisdom. Yet men do like to boast. Well, there is room for a real expression of our delight, if we express our delight over what Christ has done for us. All glorying must be in what He has done, and not in the puny things that men, motivated by the wisdom of this world, can achieve.

---

is finally eradicated), Reformed (sanctification is a process of spiritual renewal that continues all through a believer's whole life), and Existential (when I begin to love my fellow man, I am sanctified); (4) A brief study of key verses dealing with the topic; (5) The observation that sanctification is not equivalent with sinless perfect. Also see what Paul writes at Ephesians 5:24-26.

Just as it is written -- This is evidently a quotation made from Jeremiah 9:23,24. It is not made literally, but the apostle has condensed the sense of the prophet into a few words, and has retained essentially his idea. All the blessings – righteousness, sanctification, and redemption – came to man, not because of man's wisdom or actions, but because of Christ. There is no room for man to be proud of himself. His own wisdom, his own ways, his own strength brought death, and still bring only ruin.

"LET HIM WHO BOASTS, BOAST IN THE LORD" -- Verse 29 has said, "No man should boast before God." Verse 31 tells us there must be some boasting and glorying – not however, in oneself before God, but in God as the author of all our blessings and advantages. Paul insists the only true object in which a Christian can glory is the cross (Galatians 6:14), not in himself, nor in other human leaders like the ones the Corinthians have been crying up. Paul's use of "Lord" here could only be understood by his readers as a reference to Jesus Christ. Already, five times in this letter, Jesus has been so titled. And manifestly in 2 Corinthians 10:17ff, where the same citation appears, the reference is patently to Jesus, not to the Father. Jesus is God! Characteristically Paul proves his point from Scripture. "We should not overlook the significance of the application to Christ of words which in Jeremiah 9:23ff refer to Jehovah. No higher view could be taken of the Person of Christ."[108] God would have no man exult in other men (no more "I of Paul, I of Peter,"). He would have men exult in the "Lord of Glory" (1 Corinthians 2:8; Philippians 2:9).

> Summing up what Paul writes, we may say that it is the gravest and the most dangerous error to introduce into the life of the church the wisdom of this world, whether that be the wisdom of our present or of any previous age. To introduce the wisdom of this world, a man must withdraw from Christ a part of the glory belonging only to Him, and transfer it instead to some "foolish, weak, lowly" person. The real issue at stake in the Corinthian wranglings about men is clearly brought out. With all the energy at his command, Paul determines to stop these disputes. All praise and glory of men must cease, and the praise and glory of "our great God and Savior, Christ Jesus" alone must prevail in Corinth and in the entire church.

This concludes Paul's general explanation of God's wisdom, and he now turns in chapter 2 to his own conduct, to show how entirely it was in harmony with God's plan, which he has just explained and vindicated.

---

[108] Morris, *op. cit.*, p.50,51.

Special Study #1

"THE MESSAGE OF THE CROSS"

This phrase, "the word of the cross" (NASB), "the preaching of the cross" (KJV), "the message of the cross" (TCNT) appears in 1 Corinthians 1:18, and it sets the tone for the doctrinal section (1:18 to perhaps 3:5) on which all the rest of the epistle is built. You can find appeals to the "preaching of the cross" and all of its implications in almost every section of the epistle. Right doctrine is the basis of right practice.

VERSES IN CORINTHIANS THAT HELP EXPLAIN THE EXPRESSION

In the closing verses of chapter 1 and in the early verses of chapter 2 are several expressions that help explain this expression that occurs in 1 Corinthians 1:18.

1:17 shows that the manner of presenting the message is involved: "Not in cleverness of speech." The same ideas appear in 2:1-5, where we learn that human wisdom – superiority of speech, persuasive words of wisdom, wisdom of men – was avoided deliberately.[1]

1:17 also shows the message ("the cross of Christ") brings together man's guilt and God's love at their highest degree and closest connection.

1:18 shows that power is involved. God exerts the same power to save a man that He used to raise Jesus from the dead (Ephesians 1:19ff). 2:5 speaks of "power" again, and in that connection may have reference to God's credentialing of the apostolic preaching by miracle. (See 2:4).

1:23 shows that Christ "crucified" is emphasized. Not a warrior Messiah, flashing His signs from the sky, breaking the heathen yoke, but a crucified Messiah – hanged on a cross – is what the apostles preach for their good news! It is a spiritual kingdom, not a political one.

1:24 and other verses show that God's wisdom is involved in the message of the cross. God's ways of doing things are marvelous. 1:30 shows that this "wisdom" includes righteousness (justification), sanctification (growth in the Christian life), and redemption (the ultimate glorification of the body). God's wise plan was not a new innovation; it was part of His eternal plan (2:7). It was revealed ever so dimly in the Old Testament (a "mystery," 2:7), and now through the apostles it was clearly explicated (2:7). "Our glory" at the resurrection and consummation is included (2:7). The message of the cross also includes a "call" (invitation, 1:26).

---

[1] The plea that our scientific age demands certain modifications of the Gospel captivates many today, and they do not decide as Paul did. And the ultimate result of the modern presentation is to void the cross – the very thing Paul was pleading that his readers should not let happen.

The message of the cross was not flashy, sensational, new; instead, it was different from what the world expected (1:20). It was not understood by wise men, nor can unaided men discover the truths of God (2:9). By revelation, inspiration, and illumination, God has gotten His message from His mind to the minds of men (2:10ff).

THE "MESSAGE OF THE CROSS" IS THE THEME RECURRING ALL THROUGH THE BOOK

All the questions asked by the Corinthians in their letter, and all the matters that were learned from Chloe's people, are answered in the light of the "message of the Cross" (i.e., the Christ-event – His death, burial, resurrection).

Party spirit – versus Christ (only) crucified for you.   1:23, 2:2, 4:5

Moral problems – You are a part of the body of Christ.   Christ our Passover was sacrificed for you.   The body must be disciplined so the soul is saved, or Christ's work was vain.

Legal problems – What happened when you became a Christian precludes any litigation, selfishness, etc.   Bodily members care for each other, even the judged ones.   6:11

Avoid prostitutes – If you do not, you void the reason for Christ's death.   Your body, all of it, is bought with a price.   Individual parts of it cannot live their own lives.   The God who raised Christ will raise us.

Concerning marriage – Paul's advice is based on the Lord's teaching.   7:23

Christian liberty – Don't hurt the brother for whom Christ died!   The Lord's Table v. the table of demons has a bearing on liberty.   Proper use of liberty can be seen in Paul's own example of forbearance as he follows the example of Christ.   Let love be the guiding principle.   10:16

Women in worship – Subordination of women, as Christ voluntarily submitted to the Father.

Love feast and Lord's Supper – Observance is to be just as Christ taught it at the time He was being betrayed, 11:23.   Observed correctly, you proclaim that the Lord has died for you, 11:26.   Improper partaking of the elements involves sin against the body and blood of the Lord, 11:27.

Spiritual gifts – Christians are all part of the same body, and the body of Christ needs all its members.   Self-discipline and edification of others is the important thing.   Substitute "Jesus" for "love" in chapter 13.   Follow Christ's example of "love."

Resurrection – Ours is tied to Christ's, 15:48, 49.   "Resurrection" is part of the original gospel message, 15:11. It is the heart of our message, 15:12. It is part of the final victory which was won for us by Christ, 15:50-58.

Offering – One part of the body helps another.

THE MESSAGE OF THE CROSS IS A UNIVERSAL MESSAGE.

It reaches those who otherwise would have been neglected or overlooked.

The Foolish – the inferior of mind.

> We tend to dismiss them as useless. Adam Clarke in grammar school was the dunce. He seemed unutterably stupid, hopelessly dull. One teacher told him, "You'll never learn anything!" A kindly superintendent of school laid a hand on him, one day, and said, "My boy, some day you'll be a great man!" That word of praise transformed him. Adam Clarke lived to master half-a-dozen languages, and became an outstanding scholar. His commentary on the Bible, printed first in the 18th century, has been reprinted and is still used. God often picks those who appear to be "foolish."

The Weak – the inferior in body.

> Fanny Crosby has been given as a modern example. She was blind, rather frail of body. She was the writer of 6000 hymns, among them, "Saved by Grace." She did a tremendous job; and once again, God used a "weak" one.

The Base – the inferior of birth.

> Merrill Tenney told about a Japanese man he met, a man who worked in a rural fishing community. He had won many of the community to Christ. He lived there practically on nothing. He wasn't of outstanding ability. As a baby, he had been cast out. His mother was a prostitute. His uncle took him home, but abused and hated him because he had to take care of him. This man had absolutely no start in life whatever. No money. No reputation. Not particularly good health. But he allowed God to use him, and he had a tremendous ministry there. God does that! He uses the base!

Those Who Are Not – inferior in everything.

> Men of no repute. God works with rejected material. Michelangelo and his students were passing the city dump. He spied a discarded marble piece there in the dump. He had his students carry it home. He said, "I must release the angel in it!" When he finished it, it was David and the harp, one of his most beautiful works. God, too, takes rejected material and does beautiful work with it!

D. Paul's Own Method of Preaching. 2:1-5

> *Summary:* To draw the Corinthians still farther away from their wranglings (1:11) and their glorification of men or glorying in men, Paul reminds them of the manner of his preaching among them when he founded their congregation (Lenski, *op. cit.*, p.86). In accordance with this principle of glorying only in the Lord, Paul did not use words of worldly wisdom, but preached Christ crucified only, in the power of the Spirit (Alford, *op. cit.*, p.483). Paul here affirms his own conduct to have been in strict accordance with the nature of his divine calling. The intent of this chapter is the same as the concluding part of chapter one (verses 17-31): to show that the gospel does not depend for its success on human wisdom, or the philosophy or intellectual abilities of men. This position he further confirms by two points: (1) Verses 1-5, by a reference to his own example, as having been successful among them, and yet not endowed with the graces of elocution; (2) Verses 6-16, lest it should be thought the gospel was real folly, and should be condemned, he shows that the gospel contained true wisdom, and that it was given by divine inspiration. It might be rejected by the man of the world, but it would be seen to be wise by those who were made acquainted with its real nature and value.

2:1 -- *And when I came to you, brethren, I did not come with superiority of speech or of wisdom, proclaiming to you the testimony of God.*

And when I came to you, brethren -- "Brethren" still keeps up the affectionate tone as Paul addresses the Corinthians. "I" is emphatic in the Greek, and this suggests a contrast. (a) Perhaps the contrast is to the attitude of the Corinthians. Unlike them, Paul's approach to preaching was in accordance with God's method for the spread of the gospel. Paul emphasizes the fact that he acted according to the principles laid down in 1:18-31. Just as his enemies charged (2 Corinthians 10:10), Paul was not a man of commanding appearance or an eloquent speaker. But Paul was a living example of the truth he was preaching. (b) Some have suggested further that the contrast is between Paul (and other true Christian preachers and teachers) on the one hand, and those who have introduced divisive tendencies into the Corinthian church. "When I came" is a reference to Paul's first visit to Corinth (Acts 18:1ff). The date of his first visit was in AD 52, and he had stayed a year and a half (Acts 18:11). The dative "to you" is merely incidental and lacks all emphasis. Hence, there is *not* a contrast as though Paul avoided these means only in the case of the Corinthians, as though he had employed them elsewhere.

I did not come with superiority of speech or of wisdom -- 'I did not speak to you oratorically (with overpowering oratory or flourish of rhetoric) or philosophically (trying to make the gospel match current popular philosophy).' Paul spoke in plain and simple language.[1]

---

[1] It is from this passage and 2 Corinthians 10:10 (where we are informed that certain of the Corinthians thought of Paul's speech as "contemptible") that certain Bible critics built the theory that Apollos' party was made up of those who were fond of brilliant rhetoric. In these early years of the 21st century, when critics are enamored with "Rhetorical Criticism," should not Paul's words be heard – that he did *not* come with superiority of speech (fine rhetoric)?

He did not pander to their (Greek) desires. He did not follow the fashion of the Greek orators. Paul could have used "excellency of speech" (ASV) since he was well educated. He had studied under Gamaliel. Elsewhere, his high-style Greek and his quotation of secular poets (Acts 17:28, 1 Corinthians 15:53, Titus 1:12) are perhaps evidence of education at the university in Tarsus.

Proclaiming to you the testimony of God -- "Proclaim" is *kataggellō*. The word used for "preach" in 1:23 was *kerusso*. Paul pictures himself as one through whom God was witnessing. *Kērussō*, denoting official declaration, gives place to *kataggellō*, signifying full and clear proclamation. Several manuscripts (as the marginal reading shows), instead of "testimony of God," here read "the mystery of God."[2] In Biblical language, a "mystery" is something that was not clearly revealed in the Old Testament but is now clearly revealed in the New Testament dispensation.[3] With this in mind, if "mystery" is what Paul originally wrote, he would be saying his own method of preaching had been dictated by the nature of the gospel – which depends on God's power and God's wisdom and on inspiration from God rather than on human cleverness. If the original reading was "testimony of God," two interpretations are possible: (a) Testimony about God – a reference to what Paul preached about the true character and plans of God, about what God has done in Christ to effect salvation (as verse 2 goes on to explain).[4] (b) Testimony from God – testimony of which God is the source.[5] In this case, the word "testimony" would be significant, for every testimony given unto us from God must be repeated simply as it is. It dare not be embellished with strange oratory or of wisdom that emanates from men. Whether we use "mystery" or "testimony" the content of the message hearkens back to 1:17 ("preach the gospel") or 1:18 ("word of the cross"). See also 1:6 and 2 Timothy 1:8.

2:2 -- *For I determined to know nothing among you except Jesus Christ, and Him crucified.*

For I determined -- The "for" that begins this verse shows that verse 2 is explanatory. Paul is offering a reason for his behavior outlined in verse 1. 'Before I ever arrived in Corinth, I made a resolution. This was my fixed, deliberate purpose, both before I came and when I arrived there.' This is Paul's reason for preaching as he did. 'The unadorned

---

[2] P[46], A*, C, 88, 436, Syr.P, and some early fathers read "mystery," and the NA[26] and UBS[3] texts treat it as the original reading. Metzger also argues that "mystery" was the original reading, arguing that it is preferred because it prepares the way for the usage of the word in verse 7.

B, D, G, 33, Old Lat., Vg. and some early fathers read "testimony." Those who prefer "testimony" at this place argue that "mystery" was substituted in verse 1 from its use in verse 7.

[3] Those who look for sources for Paul's theology are quick to observe that "mystery" was a word current in 1st century Greek mystery religions, wherein it meant "religious secrets known only to the initiated." Paul may have taken a 1st century word and poured new meaning into it, but it is hardly to be accepted that all he did was simply copy pagan religious ideas. That is a flat denial of the doctrines of both revelation and inspiration which Paul claims for himself later in this very chapter.

[4] So Barrett and Fee (*op. cit.*, p.92) interpret the verse.

[5] So Lightfoot, Godet, and Holladay interpret the phrase.

simplicity of my teaching was part of my fixed design.' Inspiration did not incapacitate a man's freedom. The inspired writers and speakers still had input into the delivery of the message. Paul could have chosen Corinthian words, had he wished. But Paul knew the negative result in the long-run of relying on human methods such as the Corinthians were now tending to do. It is from this passage that the idea has been advanced by some scholars that Paul was a failure in Athens, because there he attempted to use philosophical arguments.[6] However, there is no evidence for the supposition that at Athens (where he had been just before he came to Corinth) Paul had tried this "excellency of speech" approach when speaking to the philosophers, that he had accomplished little through its use, and that he now resolved to do something different when he came to Corinth, i.e., return to his old way of preaching. As we examine Paul's sermon on Mars' Hill (Acts 17), we see nothing but the simple gospel preaching. And with half a dozen converts, the sermon on Mars' Hill was not a failure. "I determined" does not imply a change of strategy after his visit to Athens, nor even a return to a former (temporarily abandoned) strategy. "I determined" means nothing more than that Paul purposed to continue his regular practice (cp. Galatians 3:1). Paul's words might imply rather that when he came to Corinth (and he might have had the same experience when he came to Athens) he felt a certain temptation, when speaking to these Greeks, to employ a manner of preaching that might have made a strong appeal to them; namely, fine dialectical oration or striking speculative thought. But nothing of the kind was ever uttered by him.

To know nothing among you -- 'I resolved not to give my time and attention while among you (a) to the laws and traditions of the Jews; (b) to your orators, philosophers, and poets; (c) to the beauty of your architecture or statuary; (d) to a contemplation of your laws and customs. I resolved to attend to this only, making known the cross of Christ.'[7] He did not mingle any sort of clever speech or oratorical flourish with the preaching of Christ.

Except Jesus Christ, and Him crucified -- "Jesus Christ, and Him crucified" is another way of saying "testimony of [about] God" or "mystery of God" (verse 1). "Jesus Christ" emphasizes His identity and His life and teachings on earth. Paul's sole aim was to portray before their eyes the information about Jesus Messiah that he had received by revelation (Galatians 1:12). We can get an approximation of Paul's presentation of Jesus as we read Luke's Gospel, for early Christian literature tells us that Luke's Gospel reflects how Paul preached Jesus. "Crucified" emphasizes Jesus' death for sinners (cp. Acts 10:37-43). You cannot separate the cross from the empty tomb. "Crucified" means blood, death, sacrifice, atonement, substitution, and reconciliation, as the Scriptures show in full detail.[8] "Crucified" is a perfect tense participle, signifying a past completed action, with present

---

[6] See Barclay, for example, p.36, who so handles this verse.

[7] "To know something" is equivalent to "playing the philosopher," says *Expositor's Greek Testament*, citing Plato, *Apol.* #6. Paraphrasing, Paul says, "I did not judge it fit to attempt to 'play the philosopher' while at the same time seeking to unfold the message about Jesus Christ and Him crucified."

[8] The cross is reduced to a merely human level when, through human statement and wisdom, it is made to mean only martyrdom for one's convictions, or is regarded as a mere symbol of love.

continuing results. It is important to note that this language is in no way restrictive, as though Paul presented only one portion of the gospel while he was in Corinth, and left the rest out. Paul offers no excuse for preachers who desire to eliminate certain teachings from the gospel (e.g., the need for repentance) on the plea that they can thus reach and attract more people than if they insisted also on these teachings. "Jesus Christ as the one crucified" is the perfect summary of the entire gospel. What Paul intended to omit was any addition to the gospel, any admixture, any sugarcoating of it by human, worldly wisdom. It might well be remarked here, with Barnes,

> This should be the resolution of every minister of the Gospel – to know nothing ... but Christ crucified. This is his business. It is not to be a politician; not to engage in the strifes and controversies of men; it is not to be a good farmer, or scholar merely; not to mingle with his people in festive circles and enjoyments; not to be a man of taste and philosophy, and distinguished mainly for his refinement of manners; not to be a profound philosopher or metaphysician, but to make Christ crucified the grand object of his attention. He is not to be ashamed anywhere of the humbling doctrine that Christ was crucified. It matters not what are the amusements of society around him, what fields of science, of gain, or ambition, are open before him, the minister of Christ is to know Christ and Him crucified alone. If he cultivates science, it is to be that he may the more successfully explain and vindicate the gospel. If he becomes in any manner familiar with the works of art, or of taste, it is that he may more successfully show to those who cultivate them, the superior beauty and excellency of the cross. The preaching of the cross is the only kind of preaching that will be attended with any kind of success.[9]

And Lenski adds a pertinent paragraph:

> In 2:2, Paul intimates that he knew well enough what would probably please and easily captivate the Corinthians, being what they were. He made his decision to use nothing whatever of this sort. He remained true to his Lord and to himself. Did he risk failure or meager results? He did not allow that to sway him. The plea that our age demands certain modifications of the gospel captivates many today, and they do not decide as Paul did. Of course, they intend to lose nothing of the gospel but only to aid it in finding more ready and widespread acceptance among men. But such good intentions on our part reflect on the Lord's intentions, who originally made the gospel what it is. His intentions always work out to the glory of His name; ours, even when they deviate only slightly from His, dim the glory of His name – may even darken that glory.[10]

2:3 -- *And I was with you in weakness and in fear and in much trembling.*

And I was with you -- He has given the negative side (verses 1,2). He now gives the positive side, reminding them in what fashion he did come (verses 3-5). Paul shows that

---

[9] Barnes, *op. cit.*, p.28,29.

[10] Lenski, *op. cit.*, p.88,89.

the real force of his preaching lay in its subject matter, not in any human power with which he may have proclaimed the gospel. "With you" (*pros humas*) could be 'before you' (i.e., when I preached to you). Paul continued at Corinth for at least a year and a half.

In weakness and in fear and in much trembling -- Is this a reference to his "manner of speech," or to his "physical condition"? Some say "manner of speech." It would thus refer to his feeling of utter inadequacy for the greatness of the work and the resistance he would have to encounter (Acts 18:9). "Physical condition" is a much better interpretation when compared with verse 4. In verse 3, Paul speaks of his physical condition; in verse 4, he speaks again of his manner of speech. A brief review of the record in Acts will call attention to Paul's physical weakness at this time in his life. During Paul's first missionary journey, when he arrives in Pamphylia, John Mark turns back (Acts 13:13). Shortly after this Paul travels northward to Galatia. In the Galatian letter, Paul writes that he came to Galatia the first time because he was sick (Galatians 4:13,14). Perhaps while he was still in the lowlands of Pamphylia, Paul contracted malaria. John Mark, fearing he would be stricken also, decided to leave the malaria country. Paul continued on to the high lands, where he could better recover. It can take several years to recover completely from malaria. The second missionary journey came along, and Paul was not completely recovered. He was liable to nervous weakness and depression (2 Corinthians 4:7-12, 10:1,10, 12:7,10). "Weakness" here in 1 Corinthians could well refer to either poor physical condition or sickness. We should rid ourselves of the idea that Paul was always in robust health and was always physically fit. (However, those who would make him an epileptic have yet to prove their supposition.) A man who labored as intensely as Paul did, who traveled under the hardship of those days and endured in mind and in body what Paul bore, may well report that at one very inconvenient time, just when he began work in an important place and wished he were quite fit, he found himself "in (bodily) weakness." He was conscious of a personal lack of resources for the task before him (2 Corinthians 2:6, 3:5). Paul's weakness served as a visible demonstration that his "message" was of divine, not human, origin. In fact, Paul came to glory in his weaknesses, not because he enjoyed ill health, but because the results of his ministry when weak were sure evidence that the power was of God, not himself. When Paul writes of "fear," that is probably literally true.[11] Paul had gone through troubled days (Acts 18:1-12). It was during this time that the Lord spoke to him by night in a vision, and said, "Stop being afraid, but go on speaking and do not be silent; for I am with you, and no man will attack you in order to harm you; for I have much people in this city" (Acts 18:9,10). Paul also confesses to "trembling," perhaps as a result of contemplating the nature of the task before him; namely, that the salvation of so many men depended on so weak an instrumentality. The same words are used elsewhere, and speak of a trembling anxiety to do a duty (2 Corinthians 7:15; Philippians 2:12,13; Ephesians 6:5). These last two words speak of a mental condition – not concern for his own person, but for the work and its success in Corinth. Run down as he was, he was a poor figure to come face to face with people who admired oratory and philosophic presentation. Paul feared and trembled that his condition might work a prejudice against the blessed message he had to bring.

---

[11] Some improperly (this commentator thinks) assert that it means, "fear lest he would be a failure like he was in Athens." For refutation of the idea that Paul was a failure at Athens, see above.

2:4 -- *And my message and my preaching were not in persuasive words of wisdom, but in demonstration of the Spirit and of power,*

And my message and my preaching -- It is not easy to see any substantive difference between "message (speech)" and "preaching," though attempts have been made to distinguish between them. "Message" – the word is *logos* – means word or "speech" (ASV). "Message" might refer to his private conversations. Some look back at 1:18 and think that "message" refers to the substance or content of the message. Fisher suggests "speech" refers to his manner of presentation, and "preaching" to the content of his message.[12] "Preaching" is *kērugma*. The reference might be to his public discourses. If "speech" refers to substance, "preaching" refers to the delivery of that message.

Were not in persuasive words of wisdom -- Some notes concerning text and grammar are needed. The NIV reads "not with wise and persuasive words," reflecting a manuscript variation.[13] In any case, the verb here has to be supplied. Either *egeneto* or *hen*, both of which can be translated "were," is satisfactory. The KJV reads, "with enticing words of man's wisdom"; but the word *anthrōpinēs*, "of man's" is a gloss. What Paul is saying is that the people expected "Corinthian words" from speakers who came to their town. "Corinthian words" was a proverb for choice, elaborate, and glittering phrases.[14] This is precisely the kind of speech Paul determined he would not use. Throughout the verses in this section, "wisdom" is synonymous with "philosophy." Paul used no philosophic terms, categories of thought, or reasonings that were calculated to captivate his hearers and to persuade their minds to assent.

But in demonstration of the Spirit and of power -- The word translated "demonstration" (*apodeixei*) signifies the most rigorous proof, convincing evidence. It is the word for the kind of proof against which there can be no argument. Some proofs indicate no more than that the conclusion follows from the premises. But with *apodeixis*, "the premises are known to be true, and therefore the conclusion is not only logical, but certainly true."[15] Paul is about to claim that his preaching had carried conviction, not because of his forceful and compelling personality, but because of the power of the Holy Spirit. The genitives

---

[12] Fred Fisher, *Commentary on 1 and 2 Corinthians* (Waco, TX : Word Books, 1975), p.36. Morris (*op. cit.*, p.52) opts for this definition, too.

[13] There are multiple problems with the text. (a) There are multiple manuscript readings. Some manuscripts read *peithois sophias logois* ['persuasive words of wisdom'], some read *peithois sophias* ['with the persuasion of wisdom'], and some read *peithoi sophias* ['with persuasion of wisdom']. (b) Another problem is with the word *peithois*, for this word is otherwise unknown in all of Greek literature. Is it a corruption by scribes, or was it a new word coined by Paul? (c) Lastly, not all manuscripts include the word *logois*. Was the word *logois* added from verse 13 to make sense of the dative plural *peithois*, or was the word *logois* omitted twice (at both verses 4 and 13) in the ancestors of P[46], F, G?

[14] See notes at 1 Corinthians 1:17 on "clever speech."

[15] Morris, *ibid*.

may be either objective or subjective.

- If objective, the meaning is, 'While preaching in Corinth, I gave the Holy Spirit and the power of God opportunity to work in your lives.' It was a demonstration about the Holy Spirit. The practical exhibition of the Spirit – as the source of spiritual life, renewing, enlightening, and sanctifying – cannot be replicated by "clever speech".
- If a subjective genitive, the meaning is, 'While I preached, the Holy Spirit himself furnished proof of the truth of my message.' The demonstration which the Spirit furnished was undoubtedly the miracles which were wrought. Paul would be saying that while he was at Corinth the Holy Spirit worked miracles to credential the message.

Based on 2 Corinthians 12:12, it is best to treat it as a subjective genitive. The apostle worked miracles through the Spirit and power of God.[16] He succeeded in spite of his poor condition for the very reason that he threw aside mere human aids and relied on the divine. And God once more showed He had chosen for himself "the things that are nothing."

2:5 -- *that your faith should not rest on the wisdom of men, but on the power of God.*

That your faith -- "That" introduces a purpose clause. Paul explains why he and God (cp. 1:27-31) did things the way they did. Although the purpose clause with which verse 5 begins technically refers to verse 4, it includes all that is stated in verses 1-4. To think Paul expresses merely his own purpose is only a small part of the truth. Back of Paul's purpose is God's purpose. It is God who wants our faith grounded on the true foundation, not on the "wisdom of men" but on the "power of God." Paul was God's mouthpiece in declaring the Gospel; he sought the same ends that God Himself sought – that God alone should be glorified in the faith of the hearers. What a sorry thing when any man's religious beliefs are based only on men's wisdom, because that wisdom changes ceaselessly with each new generation. Each new generation finds all manner of unreality, non-truth, and falseness in the wisdom of the generations that have preceded. With verse 5, the argument that began in 1:18 has come full circle. The message of the cross, which is looked on as folly by the "wise," is the saving power of God to those who believe. "Faith" here means not just the act of believing, but the substance of their belief. "Faith" here may stand for a "body of doctrine" or be synonymous with the Corinthian's experience of the Christian religion. When they looked back on their personal life in Christianity, Paul wanted them to be able to see that their religion was of divine origin, not human.

Should not rest on the wisdom of men -- The Greek reads, "should not be," i.e., it should not rest upon this, or be sustained by this. It should not be grounded on or owe its origin and stability to the wisdom of men. From the beginning, Paul wished to ground his converts in the divine power, to make them independent of human wisdom. That was why he made no attempt to employ rhetorical arts, but contented himself with the simplest approach.

---

[16] Hardly deserving mention are the following interpretations: One takes "spirit and power" as equivalent to "powerful spirit" (i.e., I really had my heart in the sermons). Another takes "demonstration of the Spirit" to refer to the proof afforded by the Old Testament prophecies, but what proof to a Gentile would appeal to the prophecies be?

But on the power of God -- How much better if one's faith is grounded on or sustained by the evidence of divine power accompanying the preaching of the gospel. Had Paul persuaded the Corinthians by clever and flowery speeches and by reasonings which grounded Christianity upon Greek philosophical arguments, his work would have perished with the wisdom of the age (1:19). Paul's message of the crucified Christ was credentialed by the Spirit of God (miracles), so the people would have evidence that their faith was well founded. The only safe foundation on which to base one's faith is God's wisdom and power – not man's.

E. The Gospel, Which Disdains and Abjures Human Wisdom, Has Nevertheless a Wisdom of Its Own. 2:6-16

> *Summary:* We have come to the second reason for the internal dissension at Corinth (see notes at 1:18). First, there was misunderstanding of the true nature of the gospel. Now (2:6-3:5), Paul emphasizes their misunderstanding of the source of true wisdom. Such wisdom does not come by unaided human research, but rather by revelation and inspiration. In this section of the letter, Paul will show that if human wisdom (philosophy and rhetoric) is absent from his preaching, his message is not therefore devoid of true, solid, and even divine wisdom. In view of Paul's repudiation (1:18ff) of human "wisdom," it might be inferred by the Corinthians that Christianity was a religion for the ignorant, a religion suited only to the uneducated. Paul therefore shows Christianity is not without a "wisdom" of its own.

2:6 -- Yet we do speak wisdom among those who are mature; a wisdom, however, not of this age, nor of the rulers of this age, who are passing away;

Yet we do speak wisdom – 'We do *not* admit that we utter foolishness. We have spoken of the foolishness of preaching (1:21), and of the estimate in which it is held by the world (1:22-28), and of our own manner among you as not laying claim to human learning or eloquence. But we do not admit that we in fact have been speaking folly! What we have been preaching is truly wise, but its wisdom is seen and understood to be such only by those who are qualified to judge – by those who are "full-grown."' In case some may think the gospel devoid of wisdom, Paul states that it involves a wisdom higher than any of the Greek wisdom which was simply of human origin. Before this (1:24,30), Paul has only spoken incidentally of the real wisdom found in the gospel. Now he develops the thought that the gospel is in reality the only genuine wisdom. Do the Corinthians want wisdom? Well, here it is – the one supreme wisdom in the whole universe. The word "wisdom" is placed emphatically forward in the Greek. It is the theme of this grand paragraph. The *content* of "wisdom," not its *form*, is now the emphasis. At he wrote verse 30 of chapter 1, Paul turned the idea of "wisdom" away from the Corinthian interest in philosophy and rhetoric, and transformed it into a soteriological term. Now he will develop that idea. "We speak" is present tense ('we continue to speak'), whereas verses 1 and 3 employ historical aorists, referring to the time past when Paul first preached in Corinth. This present tense mentions what Paul and his helpers ("we"[17]) do as a regular thing as they present the message of Christ.

Among those who are mature -- Where the NASB has "mature," the ASV choose "full-grown" to translate *teleios*, while the KJV chose "perfect." The English word "perfect" denotes an absoluteness not found in the Greek word, and which may not, therefore, be a good choice for an English translation. Because we have no exact English equivalent for this Greek word, which means 'those who have reached the goal,' it is difficult to find an English word that is not misleading, and whichever one we pick, be it "perfect" or "full-grown" or "mature", we will have to carefully define how we are using it. Importantly, the context always defines what is opposite of *teleios* ("full-grown, complete"), or wherein the lack of 'maturity, or reaching the goal' lies. Since that is true, several interpretations have been offered for this passage: (a) The first attempt at explaining this passage treats it as meaning "full-grown," or "mature." Some note that at 3:1 the word "babes" appears, and they suggest that in this verse there is a reference to the mature, or full-grown Christian as opposed to the babe in Christ. It is further argued that this is the right interpretation, for the whole following context shows it, especially at 3:1,2, where a difference is laid down between the milk administered to the babes and the strong meat to men. The "full-grown" are then said to be those who have advanced beyond the position of beginners in the Christian life, into the higher sphere of thorough and comprehensive insight into its duties, privileges, and blessings.[18] However, objection has been raised to the translation "mature" or "full- grown." It is asked, What point would it be to say Paul speaks wisdom to mature Christians, when he has been, and will be in 3:1ff, discussing his methods and message when he founded the church?[19] (b) A second attempt at explaining the use of *teleios* hinges on the possible meaning of "perfect." Some writers appeal to the heathen mystery religions for an explanation of this rather unusual term. In the mysteries, one who had been fully initiated was said to be "perfect," fully instructed in those rites and doctrines. If there is such an allusion here, this passage means that only those who have been fully instructed in the knowledge of the Christian religion will be qualified to see its beauty and

---

[17] There is a subtle rebuke of the dissensions at Corinth. The people might be divided, but their teachers were not!

[18] Lipscomb, *op. cit.*, p.40.

[19] Neo-liberalism has found in this verse an encouragement for their strange distinction between *kerygma* and *didache*. The neo-liberal school (and Barclay is one of them) makes a distinction between *kerygma* (a plain announcement of the basic facts of Christianity) and *didache* (teaching and explaining the meaning and the significance of the facts already announced). According to the theory (which was derived from Kant's philosophy) *kerygma* was addressed to the beginner in the faith, while *didache* was addressed to the advanced Christian. Barclay (*op. cit.*, p.28-29) uses this passage as proof that there was such a distinction in message in the early church. While we admit there may have been a gradation of teaching to the capacity of the students, and while we are aware that even Alexander Campbell made a distinction between "gospel" and "doctrine," we flatly and emphatically deny the further implications of the neo-liberal that *kerygma* is truth still good for us, but that *didache* (which were additions to the gospel message made by the church) is obsolete and inapplicable to our time! No one has yet sufficiently given a criteria by which to determine which verses in the New Testament are *kerygma* and which are *didache* – and we do not believe it can ever be given!

its wisdom. Objection has been raised to this proffered explanation for the fact that it does not seem to fit the context well.[20] (c) A third attempt at explaining the meaning of *teleios* appeals to the use of the word in early Christian literature. At one place in early Christian literature, *teleios* was used for those who "received the Spirit of God, and who through the Spirit of God do speak in all languages."[21] In contrast to this, 1 Corinthians 13:8-10 uses the word "perfect" (*teleios*) to speak of those among whom the spiritual gifts, including tongues, no longer continue to be exercised. (d) A fourth attempt at explaining "perfect" suggests it denotes those who have grown in their holiness so as to be "sinless perfect" (sanctified). The KJV uses "perfect", and many have misunderstood, thinking it means people who are "sinless perfect." The idea that Christians ever reach a stage of sinless perfection in this life is difficult to document in Scripture. The Bible does not seem to teach that any human, in this life, ever becomes so "sanctified" or "holy" as to be sinless perfect (see Philippians 3:12; 1 John 1:9). (e) As a fifth approach, it would appear Lenski's attempt (*op. cit.*, p.95-96) to explain *teleios* in this context comes nearest being correct. Lenski explains it in this fashion: The *teleios* is one who has reached the *telos*, or goal. The context invariably determines the goal referred to, and the sense in which the term is employed. The present context speaks of only two classes of people: the "mature" (i.e., these who recognize and appreciate the divine wisdom in the gospel), and the "immature" (i.e., those who still rely on human wisdom and think the gospel is foolishness). Lenski insists no reference should be made yet to the undeveloped Christians (the "babes" of 3:1). Lenski insists the "full-grown" are those who have seen in the Crucified Christ the power of God, and the wisdom of God (1:24).

A wisdom, however, not of this age -- The German word for 'wisdom of the age' is *zeitgeist*, the consciousness or spirit of the age.[22] Paul didn't appeal to the *zeitgeist* of the Greeks when he preached. Paul at once, and in a strong way, differentiates between the divine wisdom that was embodied in his message and the wisdom the world looked for (1:20). The gospel wisdom the Christian preachers presented is first described negatively ("not of this age, nor of the rulers of this age") and then positively (verse 7ff). James had something to say about the wisdom of this age. Sometimes the wisdom of this age has demonic sources – and it results in the very behavior Paul is criticizing at Corinth.

---

[20] Gnostics classified men into permanent groups according to their spiritual potential. They held that some were "perfect," while others could never attain that understanding. Paul is not dividing men into religious castes like this. Paul does recognize that there are "babes" in Christ, as well as those who are growing towards maturity. When men first believe, they do not all at once grasp the full implications of the faith. At first all are "babes." But the way to advance is open to all. There is no spiritual truth that is not available for even the humblest believer to appropriate.

[21] Irenaeus, *Ante-Nicene Fathers*, V.1, p.531.

[22] In the 1960s, the spirit of the age was rebellion to authority. Then came a time when ecology and the energy crisis were the hot topics. In the 80s and 90s, a resurgence of witchcraft seems to be a controlling idea in our culture. In a similar way, there were "ideas" that made up the "spirit of the age" in Paul's time.

> James 3:13ff -- Who among you is wise and understanding? ... If you have bitter jealousy and selfish ambition in your heart, do not ... lie against the truth. This wisdom is not that which comes down from above, but is earthly, natural, demonic.
>
> James 3:17 -- The wisdom from above is first pure, then peaceable, gentle, reasonable, full of mercy and good fruits, unwavering ....

Paul will show (verse 10ff) that the wisdom of this age is a result of a failure to include in one's thinking those truths that can be learned only from God's special revelation. The wisdom found in the gospel was not anything which sprang up in the natural progress of the race, either before or apart from Christ. The wisdom of the gospel was not a wisdom that the world had originated or loved.

Nor of the rulers of this age -- Special care must be exercised as we offer comments on the next several verses.

(1) We must keep in mind the general thrust of the passage, which includes these emphases: (a) The kind of "wisdom" (the "wisdom of men" verse 5; a "wisdom of this age," verse 6) the Corinthians have been following led to dissension between their "parties" rather than the unity God wants His people to exhibit. (b) The "wisdom" the Corinthians have been following has resulted from their failure to appreciate or apprehend God's wisdom, the kind of wisdom that comes by special revelation. (c) The "wisdom" the Corinthians have been following is the kind of wisdom that led to men crucifying Jesus. In contrast to these three emphases, God's wisdom – which deals with righteousness, sanctification, redemption (1:30) – can be known only by special revelation from God and by inspiration as God's mouthpieces progressively revealed it (2:10ff).

(2) There are a number of details in these verses that if paused upon, or if given a faulty explanation, can cause us to forget the main thrust of the passage. (a) Who are the "rulers of this age"? (b) What does the word "mystery" (verse 7) mean? (c) Wherein was the ruler's misunderstanding (verse 8) that resulted in their crucifying Jesus?

Who is it who are designated as "rulers of this age"? Either demonic rulers or human rulers are the two explanations usually offered for "rulers of this age." (1) If *Demonic rulers,* this passage would be similar to "the world rulers of this darkness" (i.e., evil spirits) of Ephesians 6:12 (ASV), and to the "princes" of Daniel 10-12 and Jewish angelology. Over the years, there seems to have been a growing acceptance of the idea that the "rulers" are demonic powers, or at least that by these words Paul wants the Corinthians to see demonic powers as lying behind the activity of human earthly rulers.[23] Ignatius seems to have understood it thus; for he adopted the strange notion that "the prince of this age" – Satan – had been deceived and frustrated by the incarnation from a virgin and

---

[23] At Revelation 12:6ff, the idea is presented in symbolic form that the devil tried to prevent the Messiah from coming into the world, and thus hinder or forestall the means of the redemption of man that the Messiah would provide. So to suggest that behind the actions of human governmental leaders may be demonic powers is not wholly foreign to the picture presented in Scripture. Nevertheless, it is difficult to see how we can say (as per 1 Corinthians 2:8) that the demons and their leader somehow didn't understand or they would not have crucified the Messiah.

the death on the cross.[24] There are several reasons why we believe the reference is not to demons here, even though Paul at times uses similar language (Romans 8:38ff; Colossians 2:15) to refer to demons. (a) Throughout this whole passage, Paul's contrast is between the wisdom and power of God as shown in the gospel, and the wisdom and power of men. To introduce now the thought of the wisdom of demonic powers is to bring in an extraneous thought. (b) In verse 8, it is the "rulers of this age" who crucified Christ. The most probable understanding of this is of the Jewish and Roman leaders, all the more so since in Acts 3:17 the same word "rulers" (*archontes*) is used of them. (c) The verse quoted from Isaiah at 2:9 talks about the "heart of man." Since Isaiah is quoted to corroborate what has been said, it would require that human rulers are here intended. (2) *Human rulers.* Paul, preaching at Antioch (Acts 13:27), said that the rulers at Jerusalem didn't recognize Jesus Messiah "nor the utterances of the prophets which are read every Sabbath, [and they] fulfilled *these* by condemning *Him* [to death]." Some have tried to limit the reference to the rulers of the Jews (see verse 8). Others say that the leaders intended are both political (Roman and Greek) and ecclesiastical (Jewish Sanhedrin).[25] Cf. 1:26ff. Perhaps Paul's use of *aiōn* ("age") is not without a glance at the transitory nature of their office.

Who are passing away -- "Passing away" is a present participle. "The rulers of this age" are in the process of passing even as Paul writes, in the sense that they are bereft of all authority and consideration in the kingdom of God.[26] We have had this verb *katargeō* at 1:28 ("nullify"). Their plans fail, their wisdom vanishes. They themselves, with all their pomp and splendor, come to nothing in the grave. Compare Isaiah 14:1ff.

2:7 -- but we speak God's wisdom in a mystery, the hidden* wisdom, *which God predestined before the ages to our glory;

But we speak -- The reference in "we" (as before) seems to be to the apostles (and other inspired men), who were engaged in preaching the gospel. The same is true each time the word "we" is used in this section. "But" is the strong adversative *alla*. The wisdom spoken by the apostles and other inspired men is utterly opposed to the wisdom mentioned in the previous verse. It is God's wisdom, and the word "God" is in an emphatic position.

God's wisdom -- Much effort has been expended in an attempt to delineate what in particular is meant by "God's wisdom." (1) Some have limited "wisdom" to those more difficult doctrines discussed and debated by long-time ("mature") Bible students and theologians: topics such as the doctrine of predestination in the divine plan of God, God's

---

[24] Ignatius, *Ad Eph.*, viii.19.

[25] This was the view of F.W. Farrar and George Mark Elliott, and is the view this commentator holds.

[26] Notice in passing that if we were to affirm that the "rulers" are demons, then this verse which affirms they are "passing away" (i.e., "a gradual nullification of their potency brought about by the Gospel" [Ellicott]) is one of the several in the New Testament which teaches that where the gospel goes, the power of the demons is greatly curtailed. See Revelation 20.

foreordination versus man's free will, what was involved in the penalty to the human race when Adam sinned, the problem of evil, and, among others,[27] which theory of eschatology is most in harmony with the predictions contained in Scripture. (2) Others think the reference in "God's wisdom" is to the gospel (i.e., the word of the cross, Christ crucified, 1:18,24,30, 2:7). This is the best understanding of this phrase since Paul himself has already written about God's "wisdom" in 1 Corinthians 1:30, which he told us involves "righteousness and sanctification and redemption." Two types of wisdom compete for men's souls. Some in Corinth have been pandering to human wisdom, the wisdom of this age. Paul and his co-laborers offer the divine. Which do the Corinthian believers want? Paul immediately qualifies his language ("*God's* wisdom") in four ways. The first three words he uses describe the nature of God's wisdom (i.e., mystery, hidden, for our glory), in order to distinguish it from the wisdom of this age. The fourth word describes how God's wisdom is attained (i.e., it comes by revelation and inspiration, rather than simply by unaided human investigation).

In a mystery -- The use of the term "mystery" is not to be interpreted to mean that when Paul preached, he spoke enigmas and riddles that people could not understand, or that the gospel was unintelligible. Nor is Paul saying Christianity is like the mystery religions with their secret doctrines that only the initiated can know. Nor is the use of "mystery" here to be taken as proof, as some have done, that one of the sources of Paul's religion was to be found in pagan mystery religious practices.[28] "Mystery," as used in Scripture, carries the idea of something that in Old Testament times was hidden (not clearly revealed) but is now revealed (in the gospel).[29] If one reads all of verse 7 without pause, this explanation of "mystery" becomes clear. The things now clearly revealed were only dimly foreshadowed in the Old Testament. Until their unfolding (their "revelation") by Jesus and the apostles, they were *concealed* from men, hidden under obscure types and shadows or prophecies. The word "mystery" is most commonly applied by Paul to the secret and long-concealed design of God to make known His gospel to the Gentiles; to break down the wall between them and the Jews, and to spread the blessings of the true religion everywhere (cp. Romans 11:25, 16:25; Ephesians 1:9, 3:9, 6:19).

---

[27] Some older writers have (improperly in our opinion) included in this list the differences between the Law and the Gospel (i.e., the preparatory dispensations before Christ and the church age), the manner in which the death and resurrection of Christ have promoted the salvation of mankind, and the great mystery of the call of the Gentiles and the rejection of unbelieving Israel. It seems to us that these issues were part of the everyday presentation of gospel truth, not something (as was true in the mystery religions) reserved only for the fully initiated.

[28] For a thorough refutation of Paul's use of pagan sources, see Machen, *The Origin of Paul's Religion* (Grand Rapids, MI: Eerdmans, 1925). The Hellenic "mysteries," which flourished at this time, were often practiced at night in an imposing dramatic form; and peculiar doctrines were taught in them, which the initiated were sworn to keep secret. This popular notion of "mystery," as a sacred knowledge disclosed to fit persons upon their subjecting themselves to prescribed conditions, has been alleged by some higher critics to be the source of Paul's doctrine. We flatly reject such suggestions concerning the origin of Paul's religion.

[29] Compare Romans 16:25; Ephesians 3:4,9; Colossians 1:26; Timothy 3:16.

The hidden *wisdom* -- The word "wisdom" has been supplied by the translators, and properly so, since we need some noun that agrees with the adjective "hidden." It was "hidden" in the sense that God did not fully reveal it in Old Testament ages. Now that the new covenant revelation has been given, it was no longer hidden. The gospel was hidden from mankind (it was a mystery) before it was proclaimed by Christ and the apostles. The wisdom of God had been hidden even from the prophets (Luke 10:24 and 1 Peter 1:12).

Which God predestined before the ages -- God predestined (or "foreordained" as the ASV reads) this wisdom. God made His plan before the beginning of the ages, before He ever laid down the foundation of the world. But it was not fully revealed until Jesus came to introduce the last in the series of ages in God's dispensation of time. Romans 8:28 speaks about God's eternal purpose (plan). This plan, so full of wisdom, God determined before the foundation of the world. It was a plan which from eternity He determined to execute. God determined on redemption before the creation. This verse will go on to say God "decided beforehand" upon "glory" for some. The gospel and the church are no afterthought or change of plan in the mind of God. "Before the ages" ("worlds," ASV) means "before time began." Perhaps we are to think of a series of ages in God's plan, such as patriarchal, Mosaic, and Christian. (Cp. Hebrews 1:2, "through [Jesus] also [God] made the worlds (i.e., ages)," and Ephesians 3:11 concerning God's plan for "ages.")

To our glory -- The ultimate aim of God's purposes and plans is that the saved, sanctified, and redeemed should ultimately share His "glory". Such "glory" is the result of the wisdom that comes from God. Where does the world's wisdom have anything like this to offer? "To our glory" means 'in order that we might be honored or glorified.' This "glory" is the final goal to which God determined to bring us. Included is more than the glory and honor God puts upon Christians in this life (cp. 2 Corinthians 3:8-18, "from glory to glory"). There is also reference to all the "glory" awaiting the Christian in heaven (cp. 2 Corinthians 4:17). The addition "to our glory" adds the thought of the tenderness of God. Even before time began, or a world had been created, God was concerned for our well-being, so He planned the gospel that we should enter into "our glory." What, pray tell, is all human wisdom compared with this wisdom of God's grace, which reaches from eternity to eternity, which is full of divine, spiritual power to lift us sinners from sin, corruption, and death to everlasting glory?

2:8 -- the wisdom *which none of the rulers of this age has understood; for if they had understood it, they would not have crucified the Lord of glory;*

***The wisdom* which** -- The words in italics show that in the Greek the only word we have is "which" – a feminine accusative relative pronoun. Pronouns have antecedents, and there are two possibilities for this one – "glory" or "wisdom", both of which are feminine in the Greek. Our translators have supposed it was not "glory" which the rulers did not understand. Rather, they suppose it was "wisdom" that the rulers did not grasp, and that Paul thus adds a second relative clause to describe God's wisdom. The first clause was in the latter part of verse 7. The marvelous "wisdom" (the plan of God formed before the creation), which was to issue in glory, none of the rulers of this world ever learned by their own efforts. God's "mystery" is not known by any other way than by revelation!

None of the rulers of this age has understood -- "Rulers of this age" has been explained in verse 6. Why did they fail to understand God's wisdom? Some have appealed to verse 7 for an answer to this question. Verse 7 told us that in Old Testament times the wisdom of God was a "mystery," and was "hidden." Others have appealed to Acts 13:27, which indicates the rulers didn't do well with the special revelation they had been given. That is why they failed to understand. *Egnōken* ("none ... understood"), a perfect tense, seems to imply (as *oida* does not) a process – 'has come to know, gain the knowledge of.' For all their eminence and perspicuity, the rulers of this age had not come to a knowledge of God's plans and purposes, since they are undiscoverable by unaided human research.[30]

For if they had understood it, they would not have crucified -- This verse adds information about the "rulers of this age." While they were acting as human wisdom prompted, they were involved in the crucifixion of the Messiah. A contrary-to-fact condition is given as proof the rulers did not know, did not comprehend, did not understand the wise plan of God. That Jesus should die was planned by God as essential to redemption from before the creation of the world, so that what the "rulers of this age"[31] did to Jesus was not something contrary to what God had planned. But had those men not been acting as human wisdom might dictate, they would have welcomed Jesus and made Him an earthly king – anything but kill Him. Is human wisdom (such as motivated the Corinthians to split up into competing factions) so contrary to God's wisdom that men who are motivated by it are led to act in ways that seem to be in direct opposition to God? What an indictment of human wisdom and its behavior!

The Lord of glory -- The title "Lord of glory" is applied in the Bible to both God and Christ (see Psalm 24:7-10, 29:3; Ephesians 1:17; Acts 7:2; James 2:1). This is one of those incidental verses which show how the Lord Jesus was estimated by the apostles, and how familiarly they applied to Him names and titles which belong only to God. Several options have been put forward in an attempt to explain just what is implied about Jesus in Paul's use of this title. (1) Some think there is an allusion to the deity of Jesus. Proponents of this view think it is likely that there is reference to the "glory" or Shekinah in which God revealed Himself from time to time. Some take the expression as a Hebraism meaning 'the glorious Lord' or 'the Messiah.' More than one scholar has thought this is the loftiest title Paul ever applies to Christ. Whether or not this is so, it certainly is

---

[30] Acts 3:17 records that Peter said that it was through ignorance the Jews had put Christ to death. That statement does not mean the same as what Paul here writes about the rulers' failure to understand. "In ignorance" means (in Peter's words), that what they did is a forgivable sin (cp. Numbers 15:30,31).

[31] In previous notes it has been discussed whether "rulers of this age" might be a reference to demonic beings. We are told the devil prompted Judas to betray Jesus into the hands of those men who were going to kill him (John 13:2,27; Luke 22:3). If we suppose "rulers" here in this verse means the devil and his hosts had something to do with Christ's crucifixion, are we to understand that Paul is saying, "the devil and his hosts suggested to Christ's enemies that they crucify Him because they did not understand the wisdom of God's plan"? Did those "rulers of darkness" somehow think if they could get Messiah Jesus killed that God's plan would be thwarted? Didn't they see opposition to Messiah and God's revealed way would be self-defeating?

an exalted title. It fitly stands alongside the application to Christ of a Scripture originally referring to Jehovah (1 Corinthians 1:31). Farrar (*op. cit.*, p.60) says, "This expression is not to be taken as equivalent to 'glorious Lord,' but, as in the analogous expressions, 'Father of Glory' [Ephesians 1:17] – showing Christ to be divine." (2) Some think "glory" in verse 8 picks up the idea introduced in verse 7. The "Lord of glory" is He in whom "our glory" (verse 7) has its manifestation and guarantee, first in His earthly and then in His heavenly state. This glory of the Son of God the disciples saw (John 1:14); of it believers now partake (Romans 8:29ff), and will partake in full hereafter (2 Corinthians 3:18; Philippians 3:21) when it culminates in a universal dominion.[32] (3) Some think the title brings out the indignity of the cross as compared to the majesty of the victim. The word "crucified" represents the deepest disgrace; the word "glory" the highest exaltation and majesty. There seems to be some irony in Paul's language. The kind of wisdom the Corinthians have been pursuing (the "wisdom" that led to their current dissension) is the same kind of "wisdom" that led men to crucify the Messiah. They thought they were crucifying a Messianic pretender, but they killed "the Lord of glory" Himself.

2:9 -- *but just as it is written*, "THINGS WHICH EYE HAS NOT SEEN AND EAR HAS NOT HEARD, AND which HAVE NOT ENTERED THE HEART OF MAN, ALL THAT GOD HAS PREPARED FOR THOSE WHO LOVE HIM."

But -- *Alla* is the strong adversative. Verse 9 is given as a contrast to something Paul has written in the text, and the contrast seems to be with "if they had understood, they would not have ...." Verse 9 says, '*But*, they didn't understand, just as one would expect given what is written' about how men cannot know of God's plans through unaided human research.[33]

Just as it is written -- Since the days of Clement of Rome, who lived 40 years after Paul wrote this letter to the Corinthians, the "written" source of Paul's quotation has been in dispute. A few things must be said by way of preparation if we are to identify the source. (1) *We must consider the manner by which New Testament writers cited Old Testament passages.* The Old Testament is quoted 175 to 600 times in the New Testament.[34] Are the quotes verbatim? The Hebrew version is quoted in some instances. The Septuagint is quoted in other instances. Sometimes neither is quoted directly; instead, there is a free rendering, such as a paraphrase of the Scripture or as a quotation of memorized passages.

---

[32] G.G. Findlay, "1 Corinthians" in *Expositor's Greek Testament*, edited by W. Robertson Nicoll (Grand Rapids, MI : Eerdmans, 1967), Vol.2, p. 779.

[33] Verse 9 is probably to be taken as a conclusion or climax to verses 6-8, rather than as an introduction to verse 10. What the Greek syntax does not seem to allow is an interpretation such as one finds in the RSV and NEB, which sees the quotation as the beginning of the next section of argument. RSV reads "But as it is written, 'What no eye has seen, nor ear heard, nor the heart of man conceived, what God has prepared for those who love him,' God has revealed to us through the Spirit." This destroys Paul's syntax altogether by missing the adversative force of *alla* ("but") in verse 9, and running roughshod over the explanatory *gar* (or *de*) that begins verse 10.

[34] The large spread between the smaller and larger numbers reflects the fact that sometimes whole verses are quoted, and sometimes just two or three words from an Old Testament passage are alluded to.

Perhaps the words may be a quotation of a version with which we are no longer acquainted since there was more than one Hebrew version available in New Testament times. Importantly, how do we *know* the New Testament writers are quoting the Old Testament (when there are no quotation marks in the original documents)? Who made the identification, and with what percent of accuracy? After AD 800, Bible manuscripts were written in small letters, but verses or phrases thought to be quotations of the Old Testament were written in capital letters. But before AD 800, how can you tell? Modern printed Greek texts put words identified as being from the Old Testament in bold print. But notice that UBS^2 has only the first half of verse 9 in bold type, whereas the NASB (which uses small caps to indicate words and phrases and verses thought to be taken from the Old Testament) has all of verse 9 in small caps. At times, New Testament writers introduced Old Testament quotations with "David said," or "Moses said," or "The Holy Spirit said," or "God said," or "it is written." But at times there is no indication in the passage that it is a quotation. (2) *At times writings other than the Old Testament are quoted in the New Testament.* Several times Paul quotes from the Greek poets.[35] At times other apostles are quoted (cf. Jude 17). (3) *Do the New Testament writers quote the Apocrypha or the Pseudepigrapha?* Old Testament Apocryphal books were written in the 400-plus year period between the close of the Old Testament and the writing of the last books of the New Testament.[36] The Old Testament Pseudepigrapha were also written in this period (between the 2nd century BC and the 1st century AD). But these are books of forged authorship, i.e., false writings, and such works are not quoted in the New Testament, even in the books of Peter and Jude. Lenski says, "As far as some known or some unknown apocryphal source is concerned, the fact is now established that no New Testament writer ever quotes from apocryphal sources."[37] (4) *From whence is this quotation (1 Corinthians 2:9) taken?* In the form which Paul writes, the text does not appear in the Old Testament. Because of this fact, differing answers have been given as to the origin of this quotation: (a) Chrysostom said the words are part of a lost prophecy. (b) Zacharias of Chrysopolis said that he read the words in the "Apocalypse of Elijah," an apocryphal book. In fact, as long ago as the time of Origen, some have thought Paul is quoting this apocryphal book, which is now lost. (c) The words are found in the "Ascension of Isaiah" in the same form as found in 1 Corinthians 2:9.[38] (d) The words occur in the Talmud (*Sanhedr.* 99a). (e) Another view is that this is a saying of our Lord which has not been recorded in the Gospels. That there were such sayings is indisputable (cf. Acts 20:35), but whether Paul would cite them in this way is another matter.

---

[35] "We also are his offspring" (Acts 17:28) is found in Aratus of Solensis, Cleanthes' "Hymn of Zeus," and several other poets. "Bad company corrupts good morals" (1 Corinthians 15:33) is found in Menander. "Cretans are always liars ..." (Titus 1:12) is found in Collimachus and Epimenides. "Against such things there is no law" (Galatians 5:23) is found in Aristotle, *Politics*, iii:8. Acts 14:17 and James 1:17 are said by some critics to sound like quotations, but no sources have been found.

[36] Probably none of the Apocrypha was written before 200 BC. A few of the books are dated AD 70-100; 1 and 2 Esdras, the additions to Esther, and the Wisdom of Solomon may be this late.

[37] Lenski, *op. cit.*, p.102.

[38] It is far from certain that either the *Ascension of Isaiah* or the *Apocalypse of Elijah* were in existence in Paul's day. Lightfoot (*op. cit.*, p.177) holds that these books were written later than Paul.

Where was this one written? This commentator has doubts that any of the above explanations is correct. In his other epistles, Paul uses the words, "It is written" only to introduce passages from the Old Testament, and this is in harmony with the practice of other New Testament writers. The passage most resembles Isaiah 64:4 and 65:17.[39] Paul often combines portions of several Old Testament passages because he wished to stress certain expressions. If the apostle were quoting from memory (not having a roll of Isaiah before him from which to copy), the 'quotation' here can readily be said to be from the Old Testament. *For what purpose was this quotation from the Old Testament made?* To show that it had been predicted that no human being unaided by divine revelation would ever discover God's ways of salvation, or the ways of God's wisdom. When he uses expressions from the Old Testament, Paul's evident object is to show the mystery character of the wisdom which he and the others are preaching.

THINGS WHICH EYE HAS NOT SEEN AND EAR HAS NOT HEARD, AND *which* **HAVE NOT ENTERED THE HEART OF MAN** -- Is this a reference to the *glory of heaven*,[40] or the *blessings of this present life*? Some immediately think of heaven. They say, the things which "God has prepared" include the whole work of redemption in all its essential particulars, from the foundation laid for it in Christ unto its final consummation. Remember that 1:30 spoke not only of righteousness and sanctification, but also redemption. However, the passage in Isaiah 64:4 had no reference to the future life. Why should it be given such a future explanation when it is quoted in the New Testament, and especially in this context? The object of the apostle is not to describe the future state of the redeemed, but to prove that the wisdom of this age will not let men understand God's wisdom, which was "hidden" during Old Testament times. In this present age, God's wisdom is proclaimed by the inspired apostles and prophets. The declaration in verse 10 is conclusive proof that Paul does not refer to the happiness of heaven, for he there says that God *has revealed* these things to Christians by his Spirit. If it is already revealed, assuredly it does not refer to that which is yet to come. The general thought is that God's revelations, the ones already made, help men know God's wisdom in a way that unaided human research (the "wisdom of this age") never can. The primary reference in this passage is to this present life.

The "heart of man" in the Bible includes intellect, affections, and will. Here it is man's reasoning process that is in Paul's mind as he writes "heart." Morris has this note about the "heart":

> Heart in the New Testament does not stand for the emotions, as with us. Among the Greeks the seat of the emotions was rather the intestines (cf. our "bowels of compassion"), while thought was located in the midriff, the diaphragm. Heart stood for the whole of a man's inner life, including thought and will as well as the

---

[39] Lines 1 and 2 are close to Isaiah 64:4 (64:3 in the LXX). Line 4 might be an adaptation of another phrase in this passage. Line 3 is closest to the LXX of Isaiah 65:16 (65:17 in our versions). The lines quoted in verse 9 do not form a complete sentence in the Greek, and this may be evidence that Paul is putting together more than one Old Testament passage.

[40] Verse 9 has often been used as a text for a funeral sermon which wishes to express what heaven will be like, and the point is made that the glory of heaven is beyond human description.

emotions, though sometimes it inclines to one or the other. Here the mind is, perhaps, most in view.[41]

ALL THAT GOD HAS PREPARED FOR THOSE WHO LOVE HIM -- The things God has prepared include the pardon of sin, the atonement, justification by faith, the peace and joy which Christianity imparts, and the complete and final redemption from sin and death – in short, the "wisdom of God." The verb "prepared" reinforces the thought of verse 7, that God in history is working out His plan which He made before the foundation of the world. The glories that come to believers are not haphazard, but are in accordance with God's plan from of old. "Those who love Him" affirms the moral precondition for God's full blessedness. Fisher suggests it means "those whose lives are dominated by their allegiance to God" (cp. Romans 8:28).[42] As Isaiah 64 and 65 show, God does things unlooked for by the world, to the confusion of its unbelief. In each case these things are done for fit persons – Isaiah's "the one who waits for Him," now being translated into Paul's "those who love Him."

2:10 -- *For to us God revealed them through the Spirit; for the Spirit searches all things, even the depths of God.*

For (ASV, "But") -- We have a manuscript variation at this place. (1) "But to us" (*hēmin de*) is found in a, A, C, D, G, L, P, Latt. Vulg. Syr, Origen, and was adopted by Tischendorf in his text, and in UBS². This reading makes verse 10 a contrast to the unaided human investigation spoken of in previous verses. Fisher suggests that verse 10 is the beginning of a new thought – namely, that a knowledge of divine wisdom comes by revelation and inspiration. (2) "For to us" (*hēmin gar*) is found in P⁴⁶, B, 69, Cop. Sah. and is the reading adopted in the WH text and Nestle's text. This reading seems to make verse 10 an illustration of the truth found in the quotation given in verse 9. The "rulers of this age" (verse 8) committed the frightful crime of crucifying the Lord of glory, because they in fact had only the 'spirit of the age.' This verse commences the part of this chapter in which the apostle shows *how* divine wisdom (which before this time was hidden) has been communicated to mankind.

To us God revealed *them* -- "Revealed" (*apokaluptō*) was used at 1 Corinthians 1:7 ("revelation"). The word signifies supernatural disclosure. Supernatural revelation is what Paul is talking about. Compare the use of the word at Matthew 16:17 and Luke 10:22. The "hidden wisdom" is no longer secret, but are "mysteries which now it is given us to know" (Matthew 13:11). When Paul says "us" he is speaking of himself and his fellow-apostles; he is not speaking of Christians in general.[43] Observe that throughout

---

[41] Morris, *op. cit.*, p.56,57.

[42] Fisher, *op. cit.*, p.40.

[43] Barnes feels that the reference is to all Christians and argues that the apostle's object is to show that all Christians had this knowledge and true wisdom (*op. cit.*, p.35). This commentator does not agree with Barnes. The context argues against this. Nor are we moved by the argument that "us" and "the mature" of verse 6 are synonymous.

verses 10-16, Paul speaks mostly in the first person plural ("we," not "you"), strengthening the interpretation that he is referring primarily to divine revelation given to New Testament apostles and prophets. Later, in 1 Corinthians 3:1-3, Paul returns to addressing the Christians at Corinth as "you." The emphatic *hēmin*, "to us," does not refer to Christians in general, but resumes the silent "we" of the verbs "we speak" occurring in verse 6 and verse 7. Who is intended by the "we"? The apostles, who were commissioned to speak this wisdom and make it known. As God originally hid this wisdom in mystery (2:7), so in due time He and He alone revealed it through the New Testament apostles and prophets.

Through the Spirit -- The reference is certainly to the Holy Spirit.[44] This shows that: (1) The apostles were guided by the Holy Spirit. If so, then the Scriptures were divinely revealed (John 16:13). (2) It is through the work of the Spirit as He reveals God that Paul and his co-laborers came to know about God's plans. (We Christians – as distinct from the apostles – come to know God's plans, not by direct revelation like the apostles received, but through their words as they wrote down by inspiration what they learned by revelation, John 17:20.)

For the Spirit searches all things -- "For" tells us that the Spirit is able to reveal things to the apostles because He first discovers what God is thinking. "Spirit" again is Holy Spirit, as earlier in the verse. The English word "searches" does not accurately express the force of the Greek. It does not mean the Spirit searches with a view to obtaining information, or acquiring knowledge, as though He were deficient in some areas of knowledge. Rather, it is a way of saying that there is nothing in God's mind that is beyond the Spirit's knowledge. The Spirit's knowledge of the things of God is complete and accurate. The Greek word literally means "to explore, to search through and through." But here and wherever else it is used of divine knowledge, it denotes the result of that exploring, i.e., a complete and thorough knowledge. (Cf. Psalms 139:1; Romans 8:27; Revelation 2:23.) "All subjects; all laws; all events; all beings," writes Barnes (*op. cit.*, p.36) as he comments on "all things," but his note is too general. The "all things" is limited or explained by the next phrase.

Even the depths of God – *Bathē tou theou*, 'deep things,' the 'in-most recesses' of God; the otherwise unexplorable depths where His thoughts and volitions have free play; the hidden mystery of His personality. The image is drawn from the sea, whose depths are supposed to be unfathomable and bottomless (Psalm 36:7, 92:6; Job 11:8). The "deep things of God" (ASV) are those inscrutable regions (where human eye cannot see, nor can it enter into the heart of men) where God's plans for mankind are developed. (Cf. Romans 11:33ff; Ephesians 1:9ff, 3:18.) The Holy Spirit has a thorough knowledge of the hidden counsels or purposes of God – of all His plans and purposes, some of which were formulated before creation. This passage proves concerning the Holy Spirit that the Spirit is in some respects distinct (a separate person) from the Father and the Son, that the Spirit

---

[44] Some manuscripts read "his (*autou*) Spirit" and some (P[46], *Aleph*, A, B, C) read "the (*tou*) Spirit." There are times the definite article *tou* may be translated as a personal pronoun. So the reference is to the Holy Spirit, rather than the human spirit – a reading which would make no sense here since the rulers of this age also had such 'spirits' and they were not helped thereby to understand the wisdom of God.

is omniscient, and that He shares certain attributes in common with the Father and Son.

2:11 -- *For who among men knows the* **thoughts** *of a man except the spirit of the man, which is in him? Even so the* **thoughts** *of God no one knows except the Spirit of God.*

For -- The design of this verse is to illustrate what Paul has just said. The searching and revealing work of the Spirit is brought out by the analogy of man's nature. No one can really know what is going on inside a man, nobody except the man's own spirit. From their position outside, other men can only guess. But the spirit of the man does not guess. He knows. In the same way, reasons Paul, no one outside God can know what takes place within God. No one, that is, but the Spirit. He knows what goes on inside God's mind.

Who among men knows the *thoughts* **of a man --** The "deep things" – the counsels thoughts, plans, intentions, motives, and volitions of a man.

Except the spirit of the man, which is in him -- "What was I just thinking?" I might ask you. Man does not have the ability to read other men's minds, so you cannot know what I was thinking, unless I tell you.[45] This diagnostic ability of the Holy Spirit, Who alone can search the heart of God, is further illustrated by an analogy from man's nature. For among men a man's thoughts are known only to the man's spirit that is in him; they are not known outside to the spirit of another man, unless the first man himself chooses to communicate and reveal them. Even so, the secret counsels or thoughts of God are known only to the Spirit of God, and to none else. The Spirit, however, may make them known by revelation. Since a man's own "spirit" is able to know or understand what is going on in that man's mind, the man's spirit seems to be separate from his mind.

Even so the *thoughts* **of God no one knows except the Spirit of God --** Man cannot search into the "thoughts of God" any more than one man can search the intentions of another man. "It is impossible to measure the arm of God with the finger of man."[46] Man could not know God's plans or His will without a revelation. "The Spirit of God alone knows the mind and purposes of God ...."[47] Note that the phrase, "which is in him" (used of man) is not repeated in reference to God. This shows a difference between God and the Holy Spirit. This passage is a classic text showing the deity of the Holy Spirit. The analogy is adequate only in regard to the one point stressed, for there is an obvious difference between man's spirit and the Spirit of God. Man's "spirit" is "in him"; it was

---

[45] Does this verse have any bearing on the question of "mind reading" and "extra-sensory perception"? The thrust of the passage before us is this – unaided man cannot know what another is thinking. A man, aided by the Holy Spirit (who is the heart-searcher of men, Acts 1:24), or by evil spirits, can know what another is thinking. Similarly, unaided man cannot discover or know true wisdom (the deep things of God). Man needs revelation and inspiration – activities of the Holy Spirit – to know the hidden things of God.

[46] Farrar, *op. cit.*, p.60.

[47] Lipscomb, *op. cit.*, p.42.

put there when God created man and breathed His breath into man and made him a "living soul." No counterpart to this exists in God, the essence of whose Spirit is identical (*homoousios*) with that of the Father and of the Son. There can be no question but that this passage ascribes full deity to the Holy Spirit.

2:12 -- *Now we have received, not the spirit of the world, but the Spirit who is from God, that we might know the things freely given to us by God,*

Now we have received -- Here is the application of the foregoing illustration. 'How did we apostles receive the divine revelation we proclaim to God's people? We received what we received by revelation from the Holy Spirit, who alone knows God's deep thoughts and can in turn make known those deep thoughts of God in the plan of redemption.' "We" is emphatic, and refers, as before (verses 6,7) to the New Testament apostles and prophets.[48]

Not the spirit of the world -- "Spirit of the world" is not an easy expression to explain. Various interpretations have been given to it. (1) "Spirit," some think, is a reference to the wisdom and knowledge which this age (cf. *zeitgeist*, 1 Corinthians 2:6) can give. In this case, it refers to the rhetoric and philosophy which were so much valued in Greece.[49] Such an explanation makes "spirit of the world" synonymous with "human wisdom" of verse 13ff. (2) "Spirit," others say, is "the spirit that is now working in the sons of disobedience" (Ephesians 2:2), i.e. the devil.[50] "The spirit of the world" is thought to be that person who controls the world in its thought and volition (elsewhere termed "the ruler of this world," John 12:31; and "the god of this world," 2 Corinthians 4:4). Such an interpretation yields an excellent sense. Paul would be saying that the wisdom of this world which he is opposing has its origin in something satanic. In passing we might note that the word used for "world" here is *kosmos*, "the ordered universe," and not *aiōn*, which was used in verse 7ff, and which means "age," the world in its temporal aspect.

But the Spirit who is from God -- 'We apostles and prophets are under the teachings and influence of the Holy Spirit.'[51] That is, Paul is here again stating that divine revelation is the source of his message. "From God" implies that just as the Son was sent out from God, so the Holy Spirit is sent – each to accomplish His proper function in God's eternal plan of redemption.

---

[48] Gordon Fee, *op. cit.*, in footnote 64, p.113, makes "received ... the Spirit" refer to the gift of the Spirit that every person receives at his or her immersion. In this commentator's opinion, this misses the point of the passage. In fact, Fee himself cannot so treat verse 13 as something true of all Christians. In his notes at that place, he has reference to *apostolic* "speaking."

[49] So say Barnes (*op. cit.*, p.37), Heinrici, Lightfoot (*op. cit.*, p.174,180).

[50] So say Meyer, Evans, Edwards.

[51] The small "s" for "spirit" in the modern editions of the KJV seems to be an error. The original rightly had a capital. It is the Spirit of God that is meant.

That we might know -- 'The purpose which God had in imparting His Spirit to us apostles is "that we might know ...," that we might fully understand and appreciate the favors which God has conferred on us through the gospel.' The apostles did not receive the Spirit's revelation in the way a computer hard drive receives information; those hard drives are inanimate and know nothing of that which is imprinted upon them. Rather, the apostles were to "know" these things. They were to possess these blessed things personally for themselves, and then in turn accomplish God's main purpose – i.e., having themselves apprehended these things, they might convey these things to others. The word translated "know" is *oida*. *Oida* is a knowledge that is simple and absolute. "Understand" might be a good rendering. Another word for "know," *ginōskō*, involves more or less the idea of a process of examination, of learning by experience. Paul's assertion here to "know" (understand) the things of God is rather bold.

The things freely given to us by God -- The "things freely given" are the things that collectively make up "God's wisdom" (see verse 7, "our glory"), the things before hidden (verse 7), the same "things" as those spoken of as having been "prepared" for us (see verse 9; cp. Romans 8:24, 6:23; Ephesians 2:8,9; 1 Corinthians 1:30). Included are the blessings of redemption, pardon of sin, justification, sanctification, divine favor and protection, and the hope of eternal life. "Freely given" translates *charisthenta*, "gifts of free grace" – bestowed by grace. The aorist tense participle points to the time these gifts were given to the apostles.[52] All God's gifts are "without money and without price" (Isaiah 55:1), and not to be obtained "with money" (Acts 8:20).

2:13 -- *which things we also speak, not in words taught by human wisdom, but in those taught by the Spirit, combining spiritual thoughts with spiritual words.*

Which things we also speak -- "We also speak" means the apostles spoke (i.e., they preached and explained) the things revealed to them. "Speak" (*laleō*) is the same verb used in verses 6 and 7, and is present tense – 'We continue to speak, we habitually speak.' Neither Paul nor the apostles had an esoteric doctrine, whispered only to a select circle. They spoke out forthrightly the "things" (verse 12) that had been revealed to them by God.

Not in words taught by human wisdom -- The very "words" which the apostles employ as they "speak" are now described, first by means of a negative, and then by means of a positive statement. Negatively, the Holy Spirit did not lead them to use philosophical arguments, or rhetorical forms, or "Corinthian words" (see 2:1-4), like men use. The Holy Spirit-led mouthpieces did not use words such as human philosophy or eloquence would dictate.[53] Here is Paul's answer to the modern commentators who make efforts to trace many of the terms and expressions found in Paul's letters to ancient apocalyptic or Hellenistic philosophical sources. No gospel thought wears a dress of pagan or pseudo-Jewish terms. Here is Paul's answer to the modernists of today who regard the Scriptures

---

[52] See the Special Study #3 in the author's Acts commentary, where the "baptism of the Holy Spirit" is shown to be the thing that empowered the apostles to do their special mission (cp. Acts 1:5 and 1:8).

[53] In 1:17 we had 'wisdom of word' ("cleverness of speech"). Now we have "not in *words* taught by human *wisdom*." We suppose the expressions are synonymous.

as wisdom of the world and then, because the Scriptures are old, proceed to do with them as they do with the old philosophies of the world, discarding such 'categories of thought' (as they call them) that are no longer modern in their opinion, categories which our age (they say) has outgrown.

But in those taught by the Spirit – 'The words we apostles speak are the ones which the Holy Spirit guides us to use.' The Holy Spirit helped the apostles to choose the words they used to pass on the message they had received by revelation.

Combining spiritual *thoughts* with spiritual *words* -- Note the different attempts at translating the Greek words *pneumatikois pneumatika sugkrinontes*: "Expressing spiritual truths in spiritual words" (NIV). "Interpreting spiritual truths to spiritual men" (NIV mg.). "Combining spiritual *thoughts* with spiritual *words*" (NASB). "Comparing spiritual things with spiritual" (KJV,[54] RSV mg.). "In language appropriate to the message (not with human wisdom)"[55] Two difficulties are found here: (1) The interpretation of this phrase depends partly on the explanation we give to *sugkrinontes*. The meaning of the word is 'to join together fitly, to combine, to compare, to compound, to interpret' or 'to combine by judicious selection.' It is pretty clear that the participle *sugkrinontes* should be rendered "comparing" or "combining." It is regularly rendered "combining," though "comparing" is used at 2 Corinthians 10:12 (twice).[56] A number of scholars have preferred "interpreting" (cf. RSV, Phillips, Fee). But the word has this meaning only in the Septuagint (Genesis 40:8,16,20; 41:12,13,15; Numbers 15:34; Daniel 5:7), and there it is never used of interpreting anything other than dreams, and in each case the context shows that such a meaning is required. That surely is not the case here. (2) The interpretation also depends partly on the answer to the question, Is "spiritual" (*pneumatikois*) masculine or neuter? (a) If masculine, it means "to spiritual men." 'For spiritual men you coordinate things that are spiritual – suiting spiritual matter to spiritual hearers.' 'You teach spiritual truths to spiritually minded men.' (b) If neuter, it means "to spiritual things" or "to spiritual words." If *things* be the meaning, it refers either to (i) the Old Testament types used to explain the New Testament, or (ii) the testimonies of the prophets, which, being inspired by the Spirit, are the fit illustrations of the things which Christ has revealed by His Spirit. If *words* be the meaning, it refers to 'uniting the spiritual matters which are the subjects of our discourses with words and forms that are taught by the Spirit.' This explanation fits the context best, where Paul is affirming that gospel preachers did not use the kinds of 'Corinthian *words*' the listeners loved to hear. *Pneumatika* ("spiritual," the second time "spiritual" appears in this phrase) is an adjective, and we must supply the noun. The con-

---

[54] The KJV translation gave rise to the use of this text at the popular level to support the analogy of Scripture – i.e., comparing one text with another so as to derive its meaning from within Scripture itself. Analogy of Scripture is a useful hermeneutical principle, based on the belief in the common inspiration by the Holy Spirit of all Scripture, but it is quite beside Paul's present point.

[55] Carl Holladay, *The First Letter of Paul to the Corinthians* (Austin, TX : Sweet Publishing Co., 1979), p.47.

[56] Paul is the only one to use the verb *sugkrinontes* in the New Testament, and it plainly means "compare" at 2 Corinthians 10:12. Some (MacArthur, Lightfoot, Goodspeed) have argued that the classical meaning of "combining" is to be preferred here in 1 Corinthians 2:13.

text has been talking about "words" used by the inspired preachers. It would be natural to supply "words" after the adjective *pneumatika*. So, from the context, the ASV and NASB translators have rightly supplied "words."

Given the answers to difficulties just listed, the proper interpretation of the verse is this:

- The grammar (a circumstantial participle) would seem to favor the view that Paul is giving further explanation about how it was the apostles could speak "in words taught by the Spirit."
- As the apostles went about 'explaining the things revealed to them by the Spirit,' they searched their vocabularies for the exact word that would express the truth learned by revelation. As they made this comparison, if they were going to choose a wrong word, somehow (though the somehow is nowhere explained) the Spirit kept them from using the wrong word, and instead encouraged them to use the exact right word that was fitted to convey in the most intelligible manner the truths learned by revelation.[57]
- Paul is engaging in the phenomenon being presented in verse 13 ('comparing spiritual things with spiritual words') as he writes this letter. He is being governed by the Holy Spirit. This verse is proof positive for verbal inspiration which is taught throughout the Scriptures, and is actually and factually apparent in the Scriptures. The Holy Spirit is the teacher of the "words" in regard to all that the apostles spoke, and hence also in regard to all of the gospel which they wrote, for the two are identical.

2:14 -- *But a natural man does not accept the things of the Spirit of God; for they are foolishness to him, and he cannot understand them, because they are spiritually appraised.*

But ("now," ASV) -- After speaking of the character of the divine wisdom and of its inspired transmission in words taught by the Spirit, Paul presents the reception which this divine wisdom received among men. Though what is taught is a revelation from God, and though it is taught in words given by the Holy Spirit, it is not received by all who hear it. Paul gives as the reason the fact that "a natural man" has limitations.

A natural man -- The word "natural" (*psuchikos*) here stands evidently opposed or contrasted to "spiritual" (in verse 15). Shore (*op. cit.*, p.25-26) has this useful note:

> To understand this and other passages in which Paul speaks of "natural" and "spiritual" men, it is important to recollect that our ordinary manner of speaking of man as consisting of "body and soul" – unless "soul" be taken in an untechnical sense to denote the whole immaterial portion – is altogether inaccurate. True psychology regards man as a trinity of natures. (See Matthew 10:28.) In accordance with this, Paul speaks of man as consisting of body (*soma*), soul (*psuche*), and spirit (*pneuma*); the *soma* is our physical nature; the *psuche* is our intellectual nature, embracing also our desires and human affections; the *pneuma* is our spiritual nature. Thus in each of us there is a somatical man, a psychical

---

[57] See the Special Study on "Inspiration" in the author's Acts commentary, pp. 127ff, for a further explanation of the doctrines of revelation, inspiration, and illumination which are here taught.

> man, and a pneumatical man; and according as any one of these parts of the nature dominates over the other, so is the character of the individual person. One in whom the *soma* is strongest is a "carnal" or "fleshly" man; one in whom the intellect or affections predominate is a "natural" or "psychic" man; and one in whom the spirit rules (which it can do only when enlightened and guided by the Spirit of God, which acts on it) is a "spiritual" man.

When a man (body, soul and spirit) commits his first sin, the "spirit" dies. Though the spirit can see the right, it is no longer able to control the man. Such a person whose "spirit" is suppressed or has "died" is designated in Scripture as "carnal" or "natural" ("soulical"). When a person becomes a Christian, it is the "spirit" part of the man that is reborn (John 3:6). God intended that the spirit, reborn, be the part of the man that gives directions to the body and soul. However, it is possible in a Christian for the soul or the flesh to be still giving directions, rather than the reborn spirit. Such a person would be a "natural man." So the "natural" man is the man whose "soul" dominates his behavior. It speaks of men who are governed or influenced by the natural (animal) instincts (the animal passions and desires), in contrast to those who are influenced by the "spirit."[58] The word "natural" does not mean anything like "sinful," but it does point to an absence of spiritual discernment. It refers to the man whose horizon is bounded by the things of this life – i.e., the worldly-wise man, the man who has been so much in Paul's thoughts throughout this passage. *The man who rejects special divine revelation is the natural man.*[59]

Does not accept -- This phrase helps explain what the "natural man" is. The verb translated "accept" is *dechomai*, a word that could be rendered "welcome." The natural man doesn't welcome the things of God; he does not accept them or embrace them willingly. This verse does not establish the doctrine of total inability, for it is not 'is incapable of receiving' but 'does not welcome,' i.e., he rejects, refuses.

---

[58] The word "natural" (*psuchikos*) was coined by Aristotle (*Eth. Nic.* III.X.2) to distinguish the pleasures of the soul, such as ambition and desire for knowledge, from those of the body. The epithet therefore describes a man who is commended in Greek philosophy for being actuated by the higher thoughts and aims of the natural life, as distinguished from the sensual man (the *anamalis* of the Vulgate) who is ruled by bodily impulse.

[59] G.M. Elliott gave this definition after working through the context in 1 Corinthians 2, where the wisdom that comes by revelation and inspiration is contrasted to the "wisdom of this age."

Attention needs to be called to several erroneous opinions about the "natural man." Calvin (*op. cit.*, p.61-62) offered the suggestion that the man who has not experienced a "first work of grace" is the natural man. But it is difficult to find in Scripture either the doctrine of an inherited sinful nature or the related idea that in salvation God must first do something to the man before he can even want to believe. Lipscomb's note (p.43), "The natural man, then, is the man who has never heard the will of God," is not correct. How could something never heard be esteemed "foolishness with him" (verse 14)? Likewise, Fee's attempted explanation of "natural man" as one who "never was a believer" (*op. cit.*, p.116) does not quite match the requirements of 1 Corinthians 1-3. Neither is it wholly proper to treat the words "natural" and "unregenerate" as synonyms. An unregenerate man may be unregenerate because he has never heard the Word of God, thus coming under the influence of the Holy Spirit. The natural man in this passage in Corinthians is one who does not accept (receive) the things of the Spirit – even after he has heard the Word, and come under the influence (to a certain extent) of the Spirit. The "natural man" of 1 Corinthians 2 and the "carnal man" of 1 Corinthians 3:3 would be the same. However, the "natural man" of 1 Corinthians 2 and the "inner man" of Romans 7 would not be equated. The "inner man" can see the righteous requirements of God's Law, but cannot make the man do them (Romans 7) whereas the "natural man" doesn't even welcome the things of God (1 Corinthians 2).

The things of the Spirit of God -- The "things of the Spirit of God" are the "deep things of God" (verse 10 ASV), also designated as "God's wisdom" (verse 7), those teachings from the mind of God which were revealed to the apostles and which were the subject of Holy Spirit-inspired preaching. See 1 Corinthians 2:12 where we had the same term. It is possible the words "of God" in this phrase are a copyist's addition, since a number of manuscripts omit the words. If we read simply "spirit", it might say that the natural man's "spirit" is struggling to control the man's behavior, and is not permitted to.

For they are foolishness to him -- This is the reason the natural man rejects the things of the Spirit. They seem foolish, because they conflict with his purely material and fleshly interests. He is seeking after the "wisdom of this age" and these things that constitute God's wisdom seem so foolish. The natural man is again using the wrong criteria for judging.

And he cannot understand them -- This clause may be joined to the previous one, thus assigning an additional reason why the natural man does not welcome the things of the Spirit.[60] Or the clause may be taken as parallel and explanatory to the phrase "he does not welcome them."[61] The natural man is not able to understand or comprehend the specially revealed wisdom of God. The next phrase will explain why the natural man does not understand God's revelation.

Because they are spiritually appraised -- "Spiritually" means either (1) once the "spirit of a man" is quickened, his own spirit can help a man to understand and appreciate the things of God, or (2) the indwelling Holy Spirit, received at conversion, helps men understand and appreciate special divine revelation.[62] "Appraised" is a translation of the verb *anakrinō*, a verb sometimes translated 'judged.'[63] *Anakrinō* must be distinguished from *krinō* ('to judge, deliver a verdict'), and from *diakrinō* ('to discern, distinguish different things'). *Anakrinō* signifies 'to examine, enquire into.' *Anakrisis* was an Athenian law term denoting a preliminary investigation. The gospel appears on trial before the "natural man." Like the Athenian philosophers, they give it a first hearing, but

---

[60] So it is treated by Meyer, Alford, Stanley, Tischendorf, and others.

[61] So the passage is explained by Calvin, Hodge, Barnes. Looking at the scholars on each side of the issue, one could almost say there is a Calvinistic and a non-Calvinistic position on the import of this phrase.

[62] In the Special Study on Inspiration in the author's book, *New Testament History: Acts*, three steps govern the process of getting information from the mind of God to the mind of man – revelation, inspiration, and illumination (i.e., the act of the Holy Spirit helping Christians understand the information given by revelation and spoken by inspiration). The first two steps were wrought on the apostles and prophets; the third step is accomplished in those who hear the inspired words of the apostles and prophets. This three-step process might be alluded to in this verse, if the words "spiritually appraised" have reference to the Holy Spirit.

[63] The word translated "appraised" (or 'discerned') occurs in Scripture only in the writings of Paul, and every time but one (1 Corinthians 14:24) it appears in a polemical or ironical context, making one think that it is a reflection of what the Corinthians are doing as a result of their party spirit. They are giving God's special revelation only a cursory, preliminary hearing before rejecting it as foolish.

they have no organon to test it by. The inquiry is thought ridiculous from the very beginning due to the incompetence of the jury. The "natural man" is out of court as a religious critic; he is like a deaf man trying to judge music. "It requires a spiritual eye to see the true value of spiritual things."[64]

2:15 -- *But he who is spiritual appraises all things, yet he himself is appraised by no man.*

But – This verse is in contrast to how the natural man does not welcome the things of God. In verse 14 Paul explained the rejection of the divine wisdom. In verse 15 he sets forth the reception of the divine wisdom.

He who is spiritual -- The man who is "spiritual" is contrasted with one who is a "natural man" (verse 14). He is one whose "spirit" (having been born again, John 3:6) now rules the man's life, and/or the one in whose life the indwelling Holy Spirit is allowed to lead.[65] Compare the use of "spiritual" and "carnal" in 3:1ff.

Appraises all things -- "Appraises" is the same Greek word used in verse 14 – the word for making a preliminary judgment (see notes there for the explanation of this term). The spiritual man has a discernment of those truths to which the natural man was unreceptive. "The Spiritual man has insight into the meaning of" God's wisdom. (Phillips version) We do not take "all things" as absolute. It does not say the Christian is omniscient, or that the Christian is the only one who can think correctly all the time.[66] As in this whole context, "all things" are the things related to divine wisdom, things which were the subjects of special divine revelation and apostolic inspiration. It is the "spiritual man" (the man who is willing to listen to what God says, rather than depend solely on human wisdom) who can appreciate and welcome God's things by their true standard and according to their true worth.

---

[64] Robertson and Plummer, *op. cit.*, p.48.

[65] The apostle ascribes to a man a natural "spirit" (5:5, 1 Thessalonians 5:23) which manifests itself in mind and conscience (Romans 2:15, 7:25), akin to and receptive of the "Spirit of God". But not till quickened by the latter is the "spirit of man" regnant in him, so that the man can be called "spiritual." Findlay, *op. cit.*, p. 782.

[66] In Calvinism, there is a belief called "presuppositionalism." It teaches that only Christians can think correctly. Non-Christians, we are told, cannot even do arithmetic correctly, let alone spiritual topics. Such a doctrine results from taking "all things" of verse 15 as broader than the context defines it (i.e., special divine revelation), making the topic to be 'all things that come within the sphere of man's judgment.' Then it is affirmed that only the spiritual man can pass a correct estimate by means of a judgment enlightened and controlled by the Holy Spirit. Paul, for example, is used to illustrate, having given a number of judgments passed by his enlightened judgment – marriage, slavery, whether or not to sail, etc. – and his advice was always characterized by a wonderful clearness, certainty, and impartiality. However, this confuses revelation and inspiration with 'appraisal.' Further, in accordance with the context (verse 14), the phrase "all things" should be understood to mean "the things of the Spirit of God" – not all things whatsoever a man may think about. The article that appears in some manuscripts before "things" in verse 15 (and it appears in P[46], A, C, D) points more distinctly to this limitation in "things."

Yet he himself is appraised by no man -- "Appraised" is 'judged, discerned.' the same word as earlier in this passage. The feelings, principles, views, hopes, fears, and joys of the spiritual man cannot be fully understood and appreciated by any natural or sensual man. Remember, this term was a legal term at Athens for a 'preliminary investigation,' preparatory to an actual trial. "No man" means no non-spiritual person, any natural man. This commentator thinks Paul says this with special allusion to such in the Corinthian church as were taking the liberty of criticizing him. These Corinthians were judging and comparing Paul and Apollos and Cephas, but *their* judgments were false and worthless. Paul, being guided by the Holy Spirit, is able to judge correctly and to write concerning all the problems at Corinth.[67] This does not mean each man is his own standard (that individual judgment is for each man the standard of truth), or that the spiritual man is immune from judgment (or is above criticism). Plummer's well-worded paraphrase of verse 15 is, "But the spiritual man sees the true value of spiritual things, yet his own true value is seen by no one who is not spiritual like himself" (*op. cit.*, p.48).

2:16 -- *For who has known the mind of the Lord, that he should instruct Him? But we have the mind of Christ.*

For who has known the mind of the Lord, that he should instruct Him? -- This verse seems to be intended as a proof of what was just said in verse 15, that the true value of spiritual things cannot be seen by the "natural man," or that the enlightened spiritual man cannot be judged by anyone who is not likewise enlightened by special divine revelation. The passage is apparently a quote from Isaiah 40:13. (It is not quoted verbatim. The words "or as His counselor has informed Him" are omitted between the words "Lord" and "that.") Paul also quoted Isaiah 40:13 at Romans 11:34. Since it is not easy, on the surface, to see the connection with the preceding, this verse has been interpreted in several ways.

(1) Adam Clarke (quoted by Lipscomb, p.44) translates it, "For who hath known the mind of the Lord, that he should teach *it*." This is a possible translation. "Mind" in the Greek is masculine, and "it" also is masculine, and so would agree with "mind." 'Which one of you people, unaided by the Holy Spirit, has the nerve to stand up and pretend to tell others what is the will of God?'
(2) Lipscomb goes to length to show the translators did not properly translate, and that it should read, "For who hath known the mind of the Lord, so as to be joined together with *him*." This is also a possible translation. The verb occurs several times in the New Testament in its classical sense of "join together" (Acts 9:22, 16:10; Ephesians 4:16; Colossians 2:2,19), but in Biblical Greek, though not in classical, it has also the

---

[67] The Roman Catholic Church uses this passage as a proof text that the hierarchy is to have the judicial office in settling doubtful questions. But this is manifestly perverting the sense of the passage, because the context must be ignored to put such an interpretation on the passage. The Roman Church must interpret the passage as though it is the church leaders to whom is given the job of judging. It is hardly correct to limit it to leaders. The principle in this verse is extended to every individual Christian. As long as the Christian is guided by divine revelation and submits to the will of God, he is able to judge matters of faith and matters of opinion. However, where a Christian is *sarkinos* ("of flesh," 3:1), his judgment is vitiated.

meaning of "instruct" (Acts 19:33, footnote). The meaning would be, 'Which of you uninspired men has known the mind of God, so as to be joined together with Him? But we inspired men so understand Him that we are united with Him in teaching His will.'[68]

(3) This commentator sees no objection to taking it as our translators have rendered it. The meaning then is, 'What man is there, on the basis of worldly wisdom, who can instruct God?' The Corinthians thought division and elevation of human wisdom and cleverness of speech was a better method than the unity and the wisdom that God has revealed. 'How is it that you think you have a better plan than God?'

But we have the mind of Christ -- "We" is again emphatic. The primary reference is again to the apostles; however, the spiritual people also have the mind of Christ. They had the Spirit of Christ (Romans 8:9), and therefore the mind of Christ. Paul substitutes "mind of Christ" where the Old Testament passage just quoted had "mind of the Lord."[69] By making this substitution, Paul makes sure there is no misunderstanding his point. The views of the apostles are the views, feelings, and temper of Christ. 'Since we apostles are influenced by His Spirit, you should listen to us as we try to help you understand again what God would have you to do in solving your problems at Corinth.'

---

[68] Lipscomb, *op. cit.*, p.44,45.

[69] By "mind" Paul probably means the thoughts of Christ as they are revealed by the Spirit. In fact, in the Greek Bible that Paul cites, the word "mind" translates the Hebrew *ruah,* which ordinarily means "spirit."

F. Reproof of the Corinthians for the Lack of Spiritual Wisdom as Evidenced by Their Carnal Divisions. 3:1-4

> *Summary:* Paul has shown that the dissension at Corinth was the result, first, of a misunderstanding of the nature of the gospel, and second, a misunderstanding of the nature of true wisdom. As he developed this second area of misunderstanding (chapter 2), Paul has shown that true wisdom comes by way of revelation and inspiration, rather than by depending on the wisdom of men, and that true wisdom can be understood only by spiritual men. Here in chapter 3, in an effort to take away any reason they might have to continue to nurse their pride (which was one of the reasons they tended to be involved in choosing sides), he will show that the Corinthians have gone backward since their conversion. When Paul first preached among them, he had confined his instructions to the rudiments of the gospel because the Corinthians were weak for the simple reason they were babes in Christ. Now they have gone backward and are weaker than when they were babes. They certainly have no reason to be proud of their current behavior.

3:1 -- *And I, brethren, could not speak to you as to spiritual men, but as to men of flesh, as to infants in Christ.*

And I, brethren -- Paul uses the word "brethren" here, as elsewhere in his epistles, to soften the reproof that was coming. "And" continues the thought of 2:16, where, speaking of himself and the other inspired mouthpieces for God, Paul said, 'We speak by inspiration, we have the mind (Spirit) of Christ.' While the inspired preachers speak God's wisdom when they preach, they still have to tailor their message to the audience.[1] In the Corinthians' case, when the church was first planted, they were not "spiritual men" but were "babes in Christ."

Could not speak to you as to spiritual men -- See the notes at 2:14,15 where "spiritual" has been explained.[2] The Corinthians had surrendered to the gospel invitation. They were "born again," and their spirits were alive because of righteousness (Romans 8:10), but they were still beginners, just "babes in Christ." Paul goes on in this verse to remind them that there were many times they behaved as their flesh prompted, rather than allowing their spirits (as guided and encouraged by the indwelling Holy Spirit) to control their lives. Ideally, all Christians are to be "spiritual" – but by no means do all measure up to the ideal. Many fail to grow as they should. This has happened to the Corinthians. Indeed, as we shall see, they have gone backward spiritually. What is the connection to Paul's main argument about partisan strife and its consequences? After their conversion, instead of growing into an understanding of God's wisdom, Paul compares their present state with their beginnings in the faith – a comparison that should fill them with chagrin, for they have gone backward in their spiritual lives.

---

[1] It is generally assumed that someone at Corinth has made an insulting comparison between Paul's simple preaching, and the preaching of some of the other party leaders claimed by the Corinthians.

[2] There is no reason to give the word a different meaning here than was given it in 2:14,15.

But as to men of flesh -- When Paul first preached the gospel in Corinth, and these readers were new converts, they were not "sensual" ("natural," 2:14), but they were "men of flesh" being still just "babes in Christ." The term used in 2:14 to describe the Corinthian's present state, and the one used here to describe an earlier state, are not quite synonymous.[3] The word here is *sarkinos* ('fleshen, fleshy'), a different word than the one used in verse 3, *sarkikos* ('fleshly'). *Sarkinos* (verse 1) evidently is not as strong a term of reproach as is *sarkikos* (verse 3).[4] "Of flesh" is a figure of speech borrowed apparently from the plumpness and chubbiness (fleshiness) of an infant. The KJV translators chose "carnal" to translate *sarkinos*; however, since this English word has come to have a negative connotation (like "carnal sin") it may no longer be a good choice. When the new converts on occasion behaved as their flesh prompted, not all the sins were sexual in nature. There are other ways to behave badly.[5] Paul clarifies in what sense he is using "of flesh" when he goes on rightly to characterize them as "babes in Christ."

As to babes in Christ -- Paul is saying that when he first came to Corinth and planted the church there, the Corinthian converts were only babies in Christ. The Corinthians were beginners in those early days, and as such could not be treated as "spiritual" (as people 'characterized by spirit'), but only as *sarkinoi*, people still fleshy in their way of thinking and acting, and not able, like a truly spiritual man, to judge aright (2:15) all things. They gave more attention to the promptings of the flesh (*sarx*) than they did to the promptings of the spirit. A babe in Christ is one recently born into the kingdom, one who has only recently become a Christian. The Jews called the novices in their schools 'suckling babes.' A recent proselyte also was regarded by the Jews as a 'newborn infant.' So new converts to Christianity may be called "babes." There is nothing wrong with being a babe in Christ. It becomes wrong only if unduly prolonged (1 Corinthians 14:20). Spiritual life is somewhat analogous to physical life. It begins with birth and comes to full maturity ("mature," 2:6) only slowly. It takes time and self-control to mature into a "spiritual" man.

3:2 -- *I gave you milk to drink, not solid food; for you were not yet able to receive it. Indeed, even now you are not yet able,*

I gave you milk to drink -- Paul is saying, "When I was in Corinth, I gave you nourish-

---

[3] The Greek words used in 2:14 and 3:1 are not the same words. Some English versions tend to erase the difference between the Greek words by using the same English word to translate both verses.

[4] A note about Greek word formation: The *-inos* termination signifies "made of ...." The *-ikos* ending means "characterized by ...."

[5] The careful reader will be aware that "flesh" (*sarx*) is sometimes thought to denote something inherently bad (like a 'sinful nature'). This whole matter is carefully explained in the author's comments in his Romans' commentary, chapter 5. It will hardly do to offer as an explanation for "of flesh" here at 1 Corinthians 3:1 a note like "the new-born Christians are still struggling with their old sinful nature." "Flesh" is not inherently evil. In the Incarnation, Jesus became flesh (His body was just like the body of other human being's), yet He was sinless. See Hebrews 2:17-18 and 7:26-27.

The careful reader is also aware there is a difference in Scripture between living "in the flesh" (Galatians 2:20) and living "according to the flesh" (Romans 8:12, 2 Corinthians 10:2,3).

ment suited to your spiritual age."⁶ In their spiritual infancy, they were not capable of digesting anything more substantial than what he gave them. To beginners in the Christian life, he gave instruction that was easy to be understood, the rudiments of Christian knowledge. Commentators have tried to identify what doctrines might be called "milk." Milk might include the basic good news about Jesus Messiah (Paul preached "Christ crucified" as he laid the foundation for their faith, 3:11; he did tell them about the resurrection, 15:1-4) and the proper response a man should make to the invitation offered in Christ (faith, repentance, confession, immersion, careful Christian living). Paul would have preached sermons to his unconverted audience similar to those we can read in Acts. He would have given basic instructions to the new converts in an effort to build their faith and life.

Not solid food -- Someone has apparently disparaged Paul and joined one of the other factions because Paul gave them no "solid food." Paul is saying, 'I couldn't give you solid food, for solid food is for the full-grown, for the spiritually mature.' Again, as commentators try to define what doctrines are "solid food," one reads about "solid food" including the doctrine of the trinity, the atonement, where are the dead, ontology, epistemology – the very things those of a philosophical turn of mind like the Corinthians would revel in. Most of these attempted identifications of "milk" and "solid food" are less than satisfactory, being at best educated guesses.⁷

For you were not yet able *to receive it* -- Paul is still speaking of the time when he came to Corinth, and laid the foundation of the church there. Paul is giving the reason he gave them milk and not solid food. The imperfect tense speaks of a continued state. They were not strong enough, not capable enough, not able to digest real solid food. They were not sufficiently advanced in Christian knowledge to comprehend the higher mysteries of the gospel, not sufficiently 'spiritually minded' to be able to understand the "solid food" of the gospel. According to 1 Peter 2:2 and 2 Peter 1:5ff, if we are going to develop, it will not be by the intervention of divine works. We ourselves must work to become learned.

Indeed, even now you are not yet able -- This phrase begins a rebuke by Paul and it must have deflated the Corinthians' ego. Five years before, when Paul was in Corinth, they were not able to digest solid food – and they still are not able even after this further interval of time. Paul will immediately go on to state the evidence that they are not yet grown up as Christians (verse 3). "Not even now" is an emphatic expression. They ought to have made progress by this time. It was all very well for the Corinthians to have been in the position of "babes" when they actually were "babes." But they should have outgrown that stage long ago.

---

⁶ Does Paul's defense of the content of his preaching reflect a reason why some in Corinth were now more interested in arranging themselves under other preachers ("I of Apollos, I of Cephas") than under Paul? Many commentators think that is precisely the case.

⁷ It is interesting to ponder whether the preachers of today impart milk or meat – and if no meat and all milk, if it is because the people are yet babes or if the problem is to be found in the training a preacher receives while he is in college, and in his own study habits since his college days.

3:3 -- *for you are still fleshly. For since there is jealousy and strife among you, are you not fleshly, and are you not walking like mere men?*

For you are still fleshly -- "For" indicates this verse is giving a reason why they still are not able to receive solid food. "Fleshly" (*sarkikos*) is language of rebuke. 'Spiritually you have gone backward, and your pride won't let you recognize it.' Paul is saying, 'You are being governed, not by your spirit, or by the Holy Spirit, but by the lusts and lower ideals of your body. You are men who are solely governed by the principles of this world when you act as you do. To the degree that you show a spirit of strife and contention, you show that Christ does not reign as He should in your lives. Instead, you are walking according to the flesh.' Paul makes a very fine distinction between the Corinthians' former and present state (note the change from *sarkinos* to *sarkikos*). At one time, in their early days, they were *sarkinoi*, beginners in the faith and still fleshy in their way of thinking and acting. (If they had listened to their newly reborn spirits, if they had allowed the indwelling Spirit to lead and guide, they would have grown till they were *pneumatikoi*, 'characterized by spirit.') But something had interfered with their development, and they have actually gone backward.[8] They are now *sarkikoi*, people who by a choice of their own obey the norm of the flesh, instead of being people who obey the true spiritual norm.

For since -- Paul goes on to prove that they were still "fleshly" by appealing to the strife and contention. It is as though Paul is anticipating a denial by the Corinthians of the allegation made in verse 3a.

There is jealousy -- "Jealousy" is a translation of *dzēlos*, from *dzēō*, meaning to boil over, to envy. The jealousy here referred to was that which arose from superior advantages and endowments which some claimed or possessed over others. Paul refers to that vice of heart which loves to lower another and to exalt self.

And strife among you[9] -- "Strife" translates *eris*, meaning verbal disputations, contentions or disputes – or as Phillips renders it, "squabbling." Compare notes at 1:10, where we already met this word. Strife is the outward result of envious feeling (jealousy). Both "jealousy" and "strife" point to self-assertion and unhealthy rivalries. Instead of these, the Christians should have been considerate of others.

Are you not fleshly -- *Sarkikos* means 'conformable to and governed by the flesh.' They

---

[8] Some writers defend the idea that the word in verse 1 is more a word of reproach than the one in verse 3 – just the opposite of the position taken in these notes. Were that view correct, and we doubt it, verse 3 would mean the Corinthians had made some spiritual progress since those early days, but not enough. And for this lack of progress Paul blames them. Our study of word derivation and formation leads us to believe the word in verse 3 is the more reproachful word.

[9] A number of manuscripts, including P^{46}, D, F, G, and 33 carry the additional words "and dissensions" (*kai dichostasiai*). Textual critics are divided as to whether the words were original in Corinthians and somehow omitted, or if they were an interpolation from the list of vices in Galatians 5:22 and Romans 16:17.

were actuated by low motives, above which they ought to have risen by this time. It is the same word used earlier in this verse.

And are you not walking like mere men? -- The question expects a "yes" answer. 'Yes, you are acting like mere men, and not as spiritual men. You are acting like mere men, and not as mature Christians. Your motivations are not much different from men who are irreligious.' The fault for their still being carnal – indeed having gone backwards – lies not in their teachers, nor in the message, but at their own door.

3:4 -- *For when one says, "I am of Paul," and another, "I am of Apollos," are you not* **mere men?**

For when one says -- "For," with which this verse begins, shows this verse is given as proof that there were the jealousies and contentions among them just as Paul affirmed in verse 3. Abbot translates, "In the very moment of saying, I am of Paul" – i.e., by uttering a party-cry – a man stamps himself as being jealous and envious. "When" is the indefinite pronoun *hotan*, 'whenever.' Each time such an affirmation is made, Paul's point is demonstrated over and over again.

"I am of Paul," and another, "I am of Apollos" -- I.e., 'I for my part stand by Paul.' In this commentator's opinion, the fact that only two men are named here has no bearing on the number of parties in Corinth (or the identity of the leaders). Meyer offers this attempt at explaining why only two men are named here. "Paul has been talking of two kinds of preaching in this section, and Paul and Apollos are the examples of such."[10] Meyer's explanation has not received wide endorsement. Why Paul selects only two of the party cries is not clear. But it may be significant that the two he selects are the one going by his name and the one attaching itself to Apollos, who might be thought to be close to Paul. These two factions – those of Paul and of Apollos – are mentioned as types of the rest.

Are you not *mere* men? (Moffatt's Translation reads, "What are you but men of the world?") -- 'Are you anything better than men who are uninfluenced by the Spirit of God? Are you not swayed by mere human passions? The Spirit which you received at baptism ought to have lifted you above these human rivalries.' Paul seems also to imply that the Corinthians ought to have been something more than mere men. Religious partisanship, in the eye of Paul, is simply irreligious. Those who indulge in such are men devoid of spiritual element. If we compare the Hebrew *'adam* ('mere man,' 'common man') as distinguished from *'ish* ('man of importance'), as at Isaiah 2:9, we begin to get the thrust of Paul's question. 'You Corinthians may think of yourselves as being men of importance, but you are not. You are just common. Does not your acting like them show that you are just like the unregenerate men in the world? Your outlook is that of worldly wisdom, not that of Spirit-filled men, is it not?'

---

[10] Meyer, *op. cit.*, p.67.

G. The Proper Estimate of the Position Held by Christian Workers (Apostles and Prophets). 3:5 - 4:5

> *Summary:* Paul has shown that the partisan strife at Corinth resulted, first, from a misconception of the nature of the gospel (1:18-25), and second, from a misconception of the nature and source of true wisdom because the Corinthians were thinking "like mere men" (2:1-3:4). Now, third, Paul is going to show that the strife resulted from a perverted view of the office and function of the Christian workers, wrongly elevated by them to the position of party leaders. In the remainder of chapter 3, Paul will develop the idea that workers such as he and Apollos are "ministers," not party leaders. Christian workers are "fellow workers" who must be careful how they build (verses 10-15); church members too must be careful how they view God's workers (verses 16-23). Then, in the opening verses of chapter 4, Paul will develop the idea that such workers are "servants (under-rowers) of Christ" and "stewards" who must be faithful to God.

3:5 -- *What then is Apollos? And what is Paul? Servants through whom you believed, even as the Lord gave* **opportunity** *to each one.*

What then is Apollos? And what is Paul? -- The neuter implies a great depreciation of the importance of human ministers when compared with God. The neuter "what," rather than "who,"[11] helps to take attention away from the preachers and concentrate it on their functions. McGarvey-Pendleton call this "the neuter of disparagement."[12] What are Paul and Apollos? Heads of different parties and theological schools? No! Nothing but ministers. Why should a party be formed which is named after Paul? What has he done or taught that should lead to this? What eminence has he that should induce any to call themselves by his name? What position do Apollos and Paul occupy that the Corinthians should divide over them? The Corinthians are making party heads of these men, and each party glorifies its man to the detriment of Christ and the gospel. 'Now just what are these men? Are they lords of some kind to whom you may attach yourselves?' The Corinthians ought to have known, and this knowledge should have prevented them from elevating men as they did. These men are only "servants" of God, and one is not a servant of higher rank than the other.

Servants through whom you believed -- *Diakonoi* ("servants," "ministers" ASV) is the same word sometimes translated elsewhere as "deacons." In this place, it is doubtful that it is intended to have a technical sense designating some who serve as church officers (as in Philippians 1:1 and 1 Timothy 3:8). There is no evidence that at this time *diakonoi* (or *diakonein*, a verb) had an exclusively official sense.[13] In post-apostolic times, the word

---

[11] The Majority Text reads "who" (masculine, *tis*) and so does the KJV. The better attested reading is the neuter "what" (*ti*).

[12] J.W. McGarvey and Philip Y. Pendleton, "Thessalonians, Corinthians, Galatians and Romans," in *The Standard Bible Commentary* series (Cincinnati, OH: Standard Publishing, 1916), p.67.

[13] See Hebrews 6:10, and see Westcott on Ephesians 4:12.

diakonoi came to be applied exclusively to the order of "deacons." The original word denotes properly "servants" in contradistinction from "masters" – i.e., those who are inferior in rank, those who are not in command. It is a word which stresses the lowly character of the service rendered. The word is applied to preachers of the gospel (Paul and Apollos in this case) because they are employed in the *service* of Christ.[14] Their work was beneficial to the Corinthians. "Through whom you believed" describes the kind of beneficial "service" the ministers wrought. The Greek is "*through* whom," not "*in* whom." Paul and Apollos were not leaders of parties, people to be believed *in*. Instead, they were people *through* whom someone else is believed in. "Believed" is aorist tense, and points back to the time of their conversion. Paul and Apollos were instruments in the conversion of some of the Corinthians but the preachers were not the source of faith; rather, they were the messengers (servants) who brought God's message. Christian workers like Paul and Apollos were simply Christ's *servants*. If we regard such workers like God does, then in our eyes they are servants of Christ, too – not leaders of church factions.

Even as the Lord gave *opportunity* to each one -- Commentators, for the most part, think "Lord" here is a reference to Christ.[15] The addition of the word "opportunity" in the NASB shows something must be added to complete the thought. Several suggestions have been proposed: (1) Perhaps it could be read "the Lord gave *believers* to each one." Though grammatically possible, it does not appear proper to make "believers" the object of the verb "gave," as though this passage were teaching that "belief" is something the Lord (Christ) gives to each potential convert. The Bible does not teach that each person's individual "faith" is a gift of God, not even at Ephesians 2:8. Instead, faith comes by hearing the word of Christ (Romans 10:17). (2) Perhaps it says "the Lord gave *abilities* and gifts to each preacher." The word "each" evidently refers to "servants" – i.e., Paul and Apollos. Later verses in this passage seem to teach that the gifts and abilities of the preachers differed according to the grace of God bestowed on each. If the word "abilities" or "gifts" is supplied, this statement is made to bring forward prominently the fact of the dependence of the ministers on the Lord – both for their gifts and their ministry. Each ministered as the Lord gave him ability and knowledge; so Christ, not one of His servants, is the leader to follow. (3) Perhaps it says that "the lord gave *converts* to each preacher." This idea would be supported by what is said in verse 6. Paul may have been an instrument to bring them to faith, and Apollos an instrument to further their development in the faith, but behind the responses to the invitation was the work of God. Since God had conferred these favors, it was improper for the Corinthians to divide themselves into sects and call themselves by the name of their teachers. All that the teachers had was to be traced to God

---

[14] In passing, note the force of this passage against the arguments of those who, advocating a mutual ministry, object to calling the preacher a "minister." Note also the force of this passage for those who object to calling the preacher "minister" because we should use Bible names for Bible things. It may be Biblical to use the term "minister" for the preacher since it is done in Ephesians 6:21 (Tychicus), Colossians 1:7 (Epaphras), and 1 Timothy 4:6 (Timothy). (The same term translated "minister" is translated "servant" in the last two passages cited.)

[15] A few writers, noting that the following verses all talk about "God," assert that "Lord" here is a reference to the Father, rather than to Jesus.

and God alone. (4) Perhaps it says "the Lord gave *opportunity* to each preacher." Implied would be the fact that behind whoever came to Corinth to preach was the providence of God, directing the man's path.

3:6 -- *I planted, Apollos watered, but God was causing the growth.*

I planted -- In verse 6 Paul explains how God chose to use these instruments (servants). God endowed one to plant, another to water. Paul's job was to *found* (plant, establish) new congregations. The apostle compares the establishment of the church at Corinth to the planting of a vine, a tree, or grain. He established the congregation at Corinth; he was the first preacher. Paul was the first to plant the seed of the kingdom (Luke 8:11) there.

Apollos watered -- This figure is taken from the practice of watering[16] a tender plant, or of watering a garden or a field. There is more to getting a harvest than just planting the field. Paul had labored to plant the congregation. Apollos had labored to increase it, to help it grow.

> This indication of Paul having been the founder, and Apollos the subsequent teacher, of the Corinthian church, is in complete harmony with what we read in the early history of that church in Acts 18:27 and 19:1ff. After Paul had been to Corinth (Acts 18:1), Apollos, who had been taught by Aquila and Priscilla at Ephesus, came there and "helped them much which had already believed."[17]

Augustine incorrectly made this a reference to baptism.[18] He also saw in "planted" a reference to the instruction of catechumens. The practice of long catechetical studies previous to conversion is something that began after the apostolic age was completed.[19] Paul's generous reference to Apollos here, as following up the work which he himself had begun, is a rebuke of the Corinthian party spirit, which set them up as rivals.

But God was causing the growth -- There is a change of verb tense in this verse that is significant. "Planted" and "watered" are both aorist – a work that was completed in the past. "Causing the growth" is an imperfect tense – God was working throughout, God was all along causing the growth.[20] God caused the seed sown to take root and spring up; God blessed the irrigation of the tender plants as they sprang up, and God caused them to grow.

---

[16] The same verb was rendered "fed" [ASV] and "drink" [NASB] in verse 2.

[17] Shore, *op. cit.*, p.28.

[18] Augustine, *Ep.* 148.

[19] Lightfoot (*op. cit.*, p.188) urges that what Augustine did with this verse "illustrates a general fault of patristic exegesis, the endeavor to attach a technical sense to words in the New Testament which had not yet acquired this [technical] meaning."

[20] The Latin and English Versions ignore this change of tense; and the difference between human activities, which come and go, and the divine action, which goes on forever, is lost.

(It would be vain for the farmer to sow his seed unless God should provide sunshine and rain to nurture the new life springing from the seed.) Paul and Apollos could do nothing to save men were it not that God was using them as instruments for saving men. The Word is adapted to save the soul, but someone has to plant it, and another has to cultivate it in the sinner's heart -- but all the time it is God who is bringing about the sowing, the cultivating, and working through the Word to produce new life and growth.

3:7 -- *So then neither the one who plants nor the one who waters is anything, but God who causes the growth.*

So then -- In verses 7-8, Paul draws some inferences from what he has just said in verses 5 and 6. First, he who plants and he who waters are nothing in comparison to God. Second, he who plants and he who waters are equal under God.

Neither the one who plants nor the one who waters is anything -- "Neither ... anything" is to be taken comparatively. They are nothing in comparison to God.

But God who causes the growth -- The sentence is unfinished. The sense is, "God, who causes the growth, *is everything*." This is the first inference drawn from verses 5 and 6. The human instruments are nothing. But God is everything, because, apart from Him, no result would follow. The labors of the farmer are indispensable in the ordinary operations of God's providence. If the farmer does not plant, God will not make the grain or tree grow. God blesses the labors of the farmer, but He does not work a miracle in lieu of the farmer's work.[21] God attends effort with success, but He does not interfere in a miraculous manner to accommodate the indolence of men. The argument is this: Neither Paul nor Apollos (or your other preachers) was a somebody, that you should make them leaders or heads of rival parties. But God is Somebody. He is the One Who is to be your leader. The attention of the Corinthians should have been fastened on God, who alone effects all spiritual work, and not on His unimportant instruments.

3:8 -- *Now he who plants and he who waters are one; but each will receive his own reward according to his own labor.*

Now he who plants and he who waters are one -- This is the second inference drawn from verses 5 and 6. There is an essential unity between planter and waterer. The work of neither can be successful without that of the other. So far from himself and Apollos being rivals, Paul maintains they are one. "One" in what respect, or in what sense? As contrasted with God, they are all of one value. They are all "servants." They are equal. They are not to be exalted above one another. They are instruments in the hands of God. They are not what the party factions tried to make them -- separate persons and rival heads

---

[21] Reformed theologians have "found" another of their doctrines in this passage (in the words "causes the growth"). It is one of the proof texts that in salvation God's work is monergistic. Man is wholly passive -- God does it all. However, to support the idea of monergism, all the passages that speak of man's part in salvation must be explained away. And it should be said that there is more to "growth" than causing the germinating process (which in Reformed theology, is something God alone initiates).

of opposing factions. They are united in reference to the same work. The work of one is as necessary as the work of the other. They are engaged in performing the same work; they are not doing different works. Paul reminds them that all these men whom they had made the heads of factions were unanimous in the message they preached.

But each shall receive his own reward according to his own labor -- We have a transition to a discussion of the recompense of teachers hereafter, according to the quality of their work done. When compared with God, teachers are of one value (verse 8a). But that does not mean that each, when compared with the other, is exactly equal in God's sight. The laborers are working under God. Their lines of labor, however, may be distinct, and each shall receive from God a specific recompense, measured by the quality of his specific work. There is an individuality as well as a unity in the work of the ministry. This is not a thing to be noticed by men, but it will be recognized by the great Master. "His own reward" suggests that there are degrees of service here, and degrees of glory (reward) hereafter.[22] The point being made is that only God (and not the Corinthians) is fit to judge between the teachers, to judge which one was better (more faithful) and therefore to be rewarded above his fellows. Paul and Apollos only do what God directs them to do, and each shall be rewarded according to his faithfulness in doing the will of God. The "wages" which each worker shall receive as his own are not the concern of men, but the supreme concern of God. What a mistake the Corinthians are guilty of when they usurp this function of God's, when one wretched party tries to exalt one man against another, and a second party exalts the other man. These rewards shall be given at the second coming of Christ (Daniel 12:3; Matthew 25:20ff; 1 Thessalonians 2:19; 2 Timothy 4:8; 1 Peter 5:4). In the phrase "according to his own labor," "labor, toil" (*kopon*) speaks of the exertion put forth.[23] God's criterion for giving "rewards" to Christian workers is not "their success," but "their labor." Workers are expected to serve God intently and intensely to the best of their ability. They are to "toil" for the Lord. For this toil they are rewarded. There is no reference here to a legalistic reward, or a reward on the basis of merit. The reward will be by the grace of God. Not that we earn it. "Reward" (*misthon*) denotes properly that which is given by contract for service rendered. It does not imply merit, or that they deserve the rewards. Rather, it means God will tender to them that which, according to the terms of the contract (i.e., the new covenant) He has promised. Compare the Parables of the Talents and Pounds, which show that each is rewarded "according to his own labor"; but in all cases the wonderful wages so exceed the labor, that each will be astonished at the reward he receives from his magnanimous Lord. In comparison with the wages and rewards God gives, the little glory which some misguided party in Corinth would bestow on this or that worker becomes a farce.

---

[22] See Luke 19:17ff – 10 cities, 5 cities, etc. Not all received the same "reward." See Matthew 5:12, "Great is your reward in heaven." See also Matthew 25:14ff, in the Parable of the Talents, the one to whom much was entrusted is given much (one ends up with ten talents, another four talents, etc.). See below, verse 14, for further discussion of rewards to teachers. See the special study in the author's Life of Christ III syllabus at Matthew 20:16 on "Degrees of Reward and Punishment."

[23] A different word, *ergon*, which denotes the "task achieved" or "work accomplished," will be used in verses 13-15.

3:9 -- *For we are God's fellow workers; you are God's field, God's building.*

For -- This verse now establishes the fact that the apportionment of reward is a matter that belongs wholly to God.

We are God's fellow-workers -- This phrase is capable of two interpretations: (1) "Fellow-workers *with* God" (KJV), or (2) "Fellow-workers *of* God" (ASV, NASB) or "laborers together *for* God" (RSV). Certainly, the KJV is possible in the Greek; the *sun* (of *theou sunergoi*) in such constructions often refers to the person in the genitive.[24] The meaning of the KJV is that God and the ministers were cooperating together to produce the effect. Throughout the Bible, we are taught that God requires the work of man, and that He will not help those who will do nothing for themselves or for Him. The world was to be evangelized, not by a sudden miracle, but by faithful human labor (Mark 16:20) – with God helping those who were ministering. However, the ASV-NASB-RSV treatment appears to be the better interpretation for the context. The sense is that the apostles were joint-laborers with each other, all in the service of God. The Corinthians acted as if these ministers were theirs, to be measured and weighed, to be exalted or to be lowered, to be rewarded with praise or to be chastised with criticism. Paul takes these ministers out of their hands. They are God's, doing His work under His special call and commission.

You are God's field, God's building -- It is fairly certain that the word "field" (*geōrgion*, "husbandry," ASV), speaks not of the ground that has been tilled, but to the process of the tilling itself. What is spoken of here – God's activity – Paul has been talking about in verses 1-8. Again, the word *oikodomē* appears to refer, not to the "edifice" (i.e., the completed building), but to the building process or construction process which results in an edifice. This building-process Paul will talk about in verses 10-15. God built the church: He planned it, He was fitting the living stones (1 Peter 2:5), and He was placing them into the building through His workmen. Both the words "field" and "building" refer to the church; the Corinthians are examples of God's operations in spiritual "husbandry" and the spiritual "building process." The term "*God's*" is emphatic in all three places in this verse. The Corinthians did not belong to Paul, Cephas, or Apollos. They belonged to God! It is *God* whose joint-laborers we are. It is *God* whose cultivated field you are. It is *God* whose building process you are. How then, can one party among you say, "I belong to Paul," or another, "I belong to Apollos," when we are only fellow-laborers in *God's* service, and you are actually *God's* husbandry and *God's* building? A double motive must then deter the Corinthians from their party cries and contentions: they are misusing God's ministers who because of their very office belong to God; and they are thereby untrue to themselves who as the very product of this ministry also belong to God.

3:10 -- *According to the grace of God which was given to me, like a wise master builder I laid a foundation, and another is building on it. But each man must be careful how he builds on it.*

According to the grace of God which was given to me -- The word "building" has intro-

---

[24] Robertson and Plummer, *op. cit.*, p.58, footnote.

duced a new figure of speech, and verses 10-15 will develop and elaborate its features. It is true that the image has suddenly been altered from agriculture to architecture, but this sudden change of metaphor is a characteristic of Paul's style. A similar instance is found in 2 Corinthians 10:4-8, where there is a change from a military to an architectural metaphor. See also 1 Corinthians 9:7, Ephesians 3:17, and Colossians 2:6,7, where there is the introduction of three distinct images in rapid succession.

Paul here emphasizes that his work was "according to" the grace that was given to him. In the light of the fact that God will judge each man's work and reward each worker accordingly, Paul himself was careful about his own conduct when he came to work at Corinth. "Paul, being about to speak of himself as a wise master-builder," takes care by commencing his statement with the words about "being given grace by God" to show that "he is not indulging in self-laudation, but merely pointing out what God had given him the grace to do."[25] "Grace" in this passage is a reference to the peculiar endowments which qualified Paul for laying the foundation.[26] Paul's gifts and spiritual blessings were bestowed on him by God. Paul disclaims any special credit for starting the work at Corinth. The fact that he was enabled to do so was due entirely to God. "Grace" (*charin*) means more than "commission" (as both Moffatt and the RSV under-translated the word). It includes the thought of God's enabling power, as well as a task to be done. When was this "grace" given to Paul? Some writers think the reference is to abilities and talents given to him at his birth. Farrar sees in this "another of Paul's baptismal aorists." He then adds, "He regarded his whole spiritual life as potentially summed up in this one crisis of conversion and baptism."[27] Others suppose this "grace" was given to Paul when he received the baptism of the Holy Spirit. Paul was empowered (1 Timothy 1:12) in the same way the original apostles were empowered (Acts 1:8). We suppose Paul received the baptism with the Holy Spirit during those three years in Arabia receiving revelations from Jesus Christ (Galatians 1:12ff).

As a wise master builder -- The "master builder" (*architektōn*) was the superintendent in the erection of buildings, the general supervisor of the day-to-day work of the other workmen.[28] God drew up the plans; Paul followed them wisely. As an expert supervisor (cf. Proverbs 8:30) and one who knew God's plans for building the church (Ephesians 3:7-10, 1 Corinthians 2:16), Paul had laid the doctrinal foundation of "Jesus Christ and Him crucified" (cf. 2:2 and "the word of the cross," 1:18). "Wise" equals 'skillful' or 'judicious.' Paul performed his task skillfully; He allowed Apollos and others to do their own work. Yet because he was an apostle, he felt responsible for the total work of the church (cf. 2

---

[25] Shore, *op. cit.*, p.29

[26] Kling, op. cit., p.75.

[27] Farrar, *op. cit.*, p.93.

[28] See Jay Shanor, "Paul as Master Builder: Construction Terms in First Corinthians," *New Testament Studies* 34, (1988), p.461-471. The Greek *architektōn* was not a designer of plans on paper; he was like the old cathedral builders, the *master-mason*, developing his ideas in the material.

Corinthians 11:28). The skillful builder secures first a firm foundation. Paul first laid the firm foundation on which the church could be raised. It is implied that recently some foolish builders at Corinth have not followed the plans (cp. Luke 6:49).

I laid a foundation -- Care must be taken lest the translation "a foundation" leave the impression that it was but one of many he could have laid. The Greek says Paul laid that which alone has the quality of being foundation (anarthrous "foundation"). Further, verse 11 indicates no other foundation was possible, and verse 11 specifies what the foundation was. Paul says the church at Corinth was first planted or begun by him. Of course, nobody builds without a foundation. The wisdom of Paul consisted, not in laying a foundation, but in laying the right one in the right way. Paul's meaning is plain: he first introduced the Corinthians to Christ and the true gospel.

And another is building upon it -- This reference in "another" is not limited to Apollos, but refers to all other teachers that came after Paul. The sequence of the work here is the same as in the planting and watering of the previous illustration. The use of the indefinite word "another" avoids the frequent repetition of the name of Apollos and also indicates there were others also who came after Paul, as is evident from 1 Corinthians 4:15.

But let each man be careful how he builds upon it -- "Each man" equals 'every man who is a teacher.' Let him be careful what instructions he shall give to the church. "Every man" (*ekastos*) brings out the thought of individual responsibility. Paul warns everyone to take heed and be careful how he builds on the foundation which Paul already laid.[29] God has given the blueprints, and they must be carefully and exactly followed. If the Corinthians will cease to be fleshly and will look upon their ministers as God's own ministers, if they will realize that God himself will reward each one rightly, they will never tolerate the party strife that tends to reward first this or that one, and they will even rightly view themselves as a product of God's ministry and thus as God's congregation. Behind this party strife in Corinth lies the unholy desire to introduce human wisdom (the wisdom of this age) and thus to corrupt the very gospel itself. No legitimate minister of God has as yet stressed this human wisdom in Corinth; at least Paul does not intimate such a state of affairs. But where this pseudo-wisdom is admired by the congregation, there is danger that ministers will be sought who will cater to this dangerous appetite. Then, instead of building with imperishable truth, they would be building with perishable material. This is a danger to be guarded against.

A foundation is laid but once; as Paul looks back on his work, he passes the verdict that he has acted wisely ("as a wise master builder"). The building operation is still in progress, but it is now in the hands of someone else. It will go on even after Paul is dead. Even now Paul has reason to fear that some of this present work is not being done right. Hence, this admonition and instruction regarding wise and unwise building.

---

[29] Apollos is not included in this warning since he is no longer working at Corinth. But many teachers (4:15) are busy there. Let these men beware that they build wisely!

3:11 -- *For no man can lay a foundation other than the one which is laid, which is Jesus Christ.*

For no man can lay a foundation other than the one which is laid -- The Greek emphasizes that the foundation is already laid. The work of the church planter is done. A congregation has been established. So long as the church there lasts, men will have to build on what Paul laid down. Paul is the one who laid the original foundation in the city of Corinth. He was the planter of the church of Christ in that town. However, it must be remembered that Paul is simply working as supervisor, erecting in the manner God wanted it done. Compare Isaiah 28:15-20, especially verse 16. God lays a well-founded foundation, one which a man could build on with security.

Which is Jesus Christ -- The foundation Paul laid is "Jesus Christ," i.e., His person and work. Not the words of Paul, or Apollos, but the message of Christ and Him crucified.[30] Not human wisdom, not clever words, not the philosophy of this age, not exalting human leaders. Paul has presented Jesus Christ in words directed by the Holy Spirit; this is the only foundation that could be built on with security and that would stand the ravages of time. When the Corinthians picked Paul or Apollos to be their party leader, they were acting like Jesus Christ was not the proper foundation on which to build their religious life! Jesus is the one God had planned (from eternity) to be the "foundation." Farrar reminds us that "The *doctrine* of Jesus Christ is the foundation of all theology; the *person* of Christ is the foundation of all life."[31] As was emphasized earlier, there must be no misconception as to the foundation. Paul does not wish to give the impression that a man can lay any foundation he chooses, and that it just happens that he had laid the foundation he did. There is only one foundation on which this spiritual edifice may be erected. That foundation is Jesus Christ. That is basic. No man may begin anywhere else. This is still worthy of emphasis in a day when so many build their 'Christianity' without Christ – on a foundation of good works, or humanism, or science. Modern theologians who belittle the significance of the historical Jesus for the church are in the position of men who would build without the only foundation possible! No true church can be raised which does not embrace and hold the true doctrines respecting Christ. If this foundation does not stand, there is no other. If the evidence that supports Christianity as being divinely given falls, then there is no valid world religion. The fundamental doctrines of the Christian religion must be embraced, or a church of Christ cannot exist; where those doctrines are denied, no association of men can be recognized as a church of God.

3:12 -- *Now if any man builds on the foundation with gold, silver, precious stones, wood, hay, straw,*

Now ("but," ASV) -- Paul now tells what he had in mind when he uttered the warning in verse 10 ("Let each one be careful how he builds upon it"); verse 12 continues the thought

---

[30] We are to understand that "Jesus Christ ... the foundation" is synonymous with "the word of the cross" (1:18). When Paul planted the church at Corinth, he preached the word of Christ, and that word and that preaching were unencumbered with human wisdom or worldly methods.

[31] Farrar, *op. cit.*, p.94.

of verse 10. Paul has paused in his argument to show that no other foundation could be laid than the one he had laid – yet the superstructure is a matter of separate and grave responsibility. In Paul's building metaphor, those teachers who have followed him and Apollos are directing their efforts at erecting the superstructure. The "but" (ASV) implies that there can be but one foundation, *but* there are many ways of building upon it. It is of vast importance to attend to the kind of structure which shall be built on the foundation – whether it shall be truly beautiful in itself, or whether it be mean, worthless, and such as shall at last be destroyed. The teacher must take heed of what sort of material he uses to build upon the one foundation; he is accountable, and he may win or he may lose a great recompense. The Corinthians must be careful that the superstructure they build on the foundation matches the foundation.

If any man -- "Any man" equals 'any teacher.' The indefinite "any man" does not intend to say that one individual builder uses all of these different materials as he works on the structure. Rather, it says that one builder uses one kind of material, and another builder uses a different material. In decidedly different ways, then, the architects may attempt to build on the "foundation ... Jesus Christ."

Builds upon the foundation – According to 2 Peter 3:16, Paul wrote "some things hard to understand." This phrase and the following verses here in Corinthians may be one of the passages to which Peter was alluding. As this passage is interpreted, we try to steer a course between such doctrines as: (1) eternal security – which Calvin found at verses 14,15; (2) purgatory – which the Roman Catholic Church finds at verse 13; and (3) the idea that teachers of false doctrine are saved – which some find at verse 12. What we *are* trying to emphasize is that preachers and teachers may indeed have different strong points as they serve among us, and each must constantly be aware that all of his work is to be judged (not by the church among whom they serve, but) by none less that God Himself!

Several interpretations have been advanced in an effort to explain this passage.[32] An overview of the different interpretations may be helpful toward understanding what Paul writes. (1) Some believe the building materials represent *doctrines*. According to the largest number of commentators, Paul here intends to denote by the building materials, not persons, but *doctrines*. So Clement, Alford (*op. cit.*, p.493), and most modern writers. Gold, silver, precious stones would be true doctrines. Wood, hay, straw, would be the vain speculations of men, the "wisdom of the world" which Paul has been deprecating all through this section.[33] (2) Some believe the building materials represent *persons*. McGarvey-Pendleton and Lipscomb refer this to persons. Lipscomb writes (*op. cit.*, p.51), "The members built into the church are compared to two classes of materials." So say Pelagius, Hofmann, Bengel, etc. (3) Some believe the building materials represent

---

[32] This commentator feels that it is nearly irrelevant to discuss whether the materials about to be enumerated (materials with which the builder builds) are 'doctrines which mold persons,' or whether they are 'persons molded by the doctrines taught,' though such a discussion fills pages in many commentaries.

[33] Paul singles out various materials which may be incorporated into the structure, and some commentators have used ingenuity in trying to find the precise doctrine or virtue in the spiritual world that each one stands for. Such labor is probably vain, for it seems Paul is concerned simply with two classes: the valuable, typified by the gold, silver, and precious stones, and the worthless, the wood, hay, and straw.

the moral fruits resulting from the labors of the various teachers – the character of the church members – this being the specific object of the final judgment (2 Corinthians 5:10; Romans 2:5-11). So Origen, Chrysostom, Augustine, Godet. (4) Some believe the building materials represent *methods* used by the different teachers. This way of explaining the passage is the one this commentator chooses to follow in these comments. Some methods the different teachers use cause the converts to be won by the power of God (gold, silver, precious stones); some methods cause the converts to be won by the wisdom of men (wood, hay, strew). Paul's whole thrust in this context is methods – like exalting human leaders instead of recognizing they are servants of the Lord. An emphasis on methods, like exalting the wisdom of this age and Corinthian words instead of emphasizing God's wisdom, seems to be what the context calls for.

With gold, silver, precious stones -- The Greek words "gold" and "silver" are diminutives and are commonly used of gold and silver made into something, such as money or utensils (though this is not a fixed rule). "Precious stones" are not gems such as diamonds or rubies, but beautiful and valuable marbles or granite. The ancients brought costly marble from Paros and Phrygia. The metaphor is not to be pressed too rigidly by seeking to identify each term with some detail in God's spiritual building. We believe the thing signified is the *method* of building which emphasizes God's wisdom and the Holy Spirit's revelation and inspiration.

Wood, hay, straw -- "Wood" would be used for heavy beams and pillars in many buildings. Either of the words "hay" and "straw" might mean straw or dried grass for mixing with clay (Exodus 5:12); or either might mean material for thatching. Dried grass was also used to fill up chinks in the walls. "Straw" is the stalks with the heads of grain cut off.[34] If our choice of interpretations is correct, the wood, hay, and stubble were designed in general to signify such *methods* teachers might use as they built on the one foundation, methods such as attempting to mingle the weak and disfiguring products of human wisdom, philosophy, Alexandrian rhetoric, and Jewish traditions with the truth of God.[35] The point Paul is making in the verse is that the teacher must be careful how he builds on that one and only possible foundation which Paul himself laid.

---

[34] Luther's contemptuous expression respecting the Epistle of James as a "right strawy epistle" was made in allusion to this passage.

[35] A point on which there is general agreement is that the "wood, hay, straw" do not represent teaching that is *intentionally* disloyal or false (for the one teaching such will be saved). While it is true that the Midrash Tehillin refers to the words of false teachers as "hay", that does not appear to be the meaning here. These words do not denote false, anti-Christian doctrines. (Milton S. Terry, *Biblical Hermeneutics*, Grand Rapids, MI: Zondervan Publishing, 1953 reprint, p.314.)

A point that is much disputed in the commentaries is whether there is one building or two in the apostle's mind. If there is but one building being erected on the one foundation, the meaning is that it would be absurd to try to work in, while raising the building, all six building materials, wood and hay and straw, along with gold and silver and precious stones: there would be a lack of beauty to this. If there are two buildings, the meaning seems to be that gold, silver, and costly stones are materials in palaces and finer buildings; wood, hay, straw are the materials in the poor dwellings and huts. If any man build upon the foundation already laid, let him look to the materials and the nature of his work. Is he building a stately and magnificent temple, or a mean hovel, consisting of nothing better than planks of wood roughly put together and thatched with hay and straw?

3:13 -- *each man's work will become evident; for the day will show it because it is* **to be** *revealed with fire, and the fire itself will test the quality of each man's work.*

Each man's work will become evident -- "Each" resumes the "each" of verse 10. Let each teacher take heed how he builds on the one foundation, for the time will come when each man's work will be inspected for quality.[36] "Work" speaks of each teacher's part in the erecting of the building of God (Alford, *ibid.*), of the teacher's methods as he tries building new "stones" into the superstructure being erected on the one foundation. "Will become evident" implies there will be a time of inspection for each man's work. The reference is likely to the final judgment. When ancient temples were built, the workmen did not receive their pay until their work had been inspected (by the commissioners or an approved inspector). When it comes to the work of building the congregation, the real worth or worthlessness of each leader's work will be made clear sooner or later.

For the day will show it -- Numerous are the interpretations offered for "the day."

(1) Some see a reference to "the day of the destruction of Jerusalem." This day would show the vanity of Judaizing doctrines. But this is out of context; it assumes nothing but Jewish errors are being spoken of in this section about party strife and divisions.
(2) Some think the word speaks merely of a "lapse of time" (time in general). "Time will tell if it be true or not." (Cf. Gamaliel's words, Acts 5:34ff). But the context seems to require a definite day. The New Testament writers seem never to use the term "day" of a "period of time in general," unless it be at this place.
(3) Some think it speaks of "the light of day." Day as compared to night, of clear knowledge as opposed to the present time of obscurity and night.[37] But the fire this verse goes on to talk about is not light-giving, but consuming.
(4) Augustine thought the "day of tribulation" was intended. But this is not definite enough, it seems to this commentator.
(5) "The day of judgment", the Day of the Lord, seems to be the proper answer. Many writers feel the day of testing (i.e., a day of judgment) speaks of a daily occurrence, which reaches a culmination in the final judgment day. So says Lipscomb, who writes, "A day of testing, whether in this world or the next" (*op. cit.*, p.51). However, in this commentator's opinion, we should limit "the day" to the final Day of Judgment. The article "the" before "day" shows that Paul had a specific day in mind – the final judgment when all Christians will stand before the "judgment seat of Christ" and give account for the deeds done in the body whether good or bad (2 Corinthians 5:10). The great Judgment Day shall reveal the secrets of all hearts. "The 'day' is not a day of calamity or hardship brought by man, but rather 'the day of the Lord' (1 Thessalonians 5:2-9), the day of the second coming of Christ (cf. 2 Thessalonians 2:2)."[38] "Show it" (*dēlōsei*) signifies 'to show its true character,' 'to reveal it for what is.'

---

[36] Verse 13 forms the conclusion to the "if clause" with which verse 12 began.

[37] This view, prevalent since the Reformation, was propounded by Calvin. He saw in it an allusion to the time when the pure knowledge of the gospel should spread over the earth.

[38] Mare, *op. cit.*, p.207.

Because it is *to be* revealed with fire -- This is a common use of the present tense, indicating that a coming event is so certain that it may be spoken of as already here. The predicted revelation is sure to take place. "It" refers to what? (1) The reference may be to Christ. It is possible to translate the Greek "because *He* shall be revealed in fire." A parallel passage would then be 2 Thessalonians 1:7, "the Lord Jesus shall be revealed from heaven ... in flaming fire." But such an ellipse of an unexpressed nominative is harsh (i.e., you must add "of Christ" after the word "day" in the previous clause.) This is quite a bit to be implied. (2) Some think "it" refers back to "work" mentioned in the first clause of this verse. Against this interpretation is the objection that this clause would then read "because each man's work is revealed in fire" – which creates an unnecessary repetition of the last clause ("the fire itself will test the quality of each man's work"). Those who hold this view see the next clause as elaboration, not repetition. (3) It seems best to understand that "it" refers back to its nearest antecedent, the word "day" of the previous clause (i.e., "the *day* is revealed in fire"). The next clause then expresses what the fire is, or does.

What is the "fire"? (1) Macknight speaks about "the fire of persecution," i.e., when persecutions come, those who are built into the church by speculative preaching (the "wood, hay, and straw") will not be able to stand. This explanation requires a different interpretation for "day" than the one we have chosen as most likely.

(2) The Roman Catholic Church sees reference to the "fires of purgatory." A 1950's publication by the Knights of Columbus in the *Cincinnati Enquirer* read this way:

CATHOLICS THANK GOD THERE IS A PURGATORY. You may not agree with this age-old Catholic belief.

You may contend, as many do, that Purgatory is not mentioned in the Bible. You may have heard that it is nothing more than a cunning fable, designed by the Catholic priesthood to frighten and deceive the faithful. You may have been told that the Apostles and the early Christians did not believe in Purgatory.

It is true that the Bible does not mention the word Purgatory, any more than it does numerous other words and terms commonly accepted by all Christians. But it DOES clearly indicate that there is such a place of satisfaction for sin and the temporal punishment due to it after death but before the general judgment.

"Fire shall try every man's work, of what sort it is," wrote Paul (1 Corinthians 3:13-15) ... and even though his work shall be "burned," the man himself "shall be saved, yet so as by fire." Paul himself observed the custom of praying for the dead: "The Lord grant unto [Onesiphorus] to find mercy of the Lord in that day" (2 Timothy 1:18). The "fires" that try a man's work are certainly not to be found on earth or in heaven, and the fires of hell do not save. Would Paul have prayed for Onesiphorus, then dead, if he believed the soul of his departed co-worker was beyond help?

Millions of people depart this life with no serious sins on their souls, and we know (Prov. 24:16) that even the just man has his small failings. God would not deny them heaven, nor would he condemn them to everlasting punishment. Therefore, as nothing defiled can enter heaven (Rev. 21:27) there must be a place where these lesser sins can be cleansed.

Proof of Purgatory is not limited to the Bible. The Fathers and doctors of the church speak repeatedly of the practice of the first Christians of praying for the dead. Tertullian admonished "the faithful wife to pray for the soul of her deceased husband." The fourth century historian Eusebius, St. Cyril of Jerusalem, St. Ephrem, St. Ambrose and St. John Chrysostom all spoke of the efficacy of prayers for the departed souls. The latter, in fact, said such supplication was "ordained by the Apostles."

The liturgies of the Church are replete with appeals for God's mercy upon the souls of the departed. Inscriptions on the walls of the catacombs of the first Christian era voice similar prayers. It would not be necessary to pray for those in heaven, futile to pray for those in hell. There must be a place in between, which Catholics call Purgatory.

And for Catholics, death would be a much more frightening prospect if there were no Purgatory. All who go there may be tried "as by fire,"' but all are assuredly saved.

The doctrine of Purgatory has been an article of Catholic faith since the Council of Florence, AD 1439. Arguments against verse 13 referring to Purgatory include: (a) Catholic commentators themselves are divided on the question of whether or not there is any allusion to Purgatory in this passage (Alford, *op. cit.*, p.494). (b) This fire is probatory, not purgatorial. It tests; it does not purge (Farrar, *op. cit.*, p.94). (c) See also Godet, *in loc.* for an extended refutation of the view that this passage teaches a doctrine of Purgatory.

(3) "Fire" in 3:13, contrary to some presentations, does not refer to "the fires of hell." Hell is to punish the wicked. There is no trace of wicked ones in verse 13, only unskillful builders. All build, although some unwisely, upon Christ, the one foundation.

(4) This is the "fire of judgment." The "day of the Lord" is often pictured as a bursting forth of fire (Malachi 3:1-3, 4:1; 2 Thessalonians 1:8, 2:8). Perhaps in back of Paul's imagery is past history of Corinth, when the Roman general Mummius desolated the city of Corinth. The stately palaces and temples, made out of incombustible materials were still standing after the conflagration. But the homes of the poor, made of wood, with cracks stuffed with dried grass, and roofs thatched with straw, were completely burned up. That, says Paul, is how it will be on the day of judgment. The fire of that day will prove and test the quality of each teacher's work.

And the fire itself will test the quality of each man's work -- As in this section generally, "each man" stands for each teacher who subsequently is working with the Corinthian congregation which Paul began by laying the one foundation. The point of the comparison is this: fire will not consume the gold and silver and precious stones, but it will burn up and consume the wood, hay, straw. So the day of testing will not affect the good work teachers have done as they built on the foundation, but it will leave the worker who used inferior methods with nothing to show for his work. "Fire" is figurative for 'judgment,' and the point of the comparison in "fire" is not its light, but its consuming power. It may not be seen in this life that using "wisdom of words" is not wise, but the final judgment will clearly show this. The NASB has a marginal note that instead of "quality" the Greek literally reads "of what sort it is." But the NASB rightly shows that Paul's point is that it is the quality of the work, not the quantity that counts.

3:14 -- *If any man's work which he has built on it remains, he will receive a reward.*

If any man's work which he has built upon it remains -- Paul is speaking primarily of teachers, and the way they build upon the one foundation. If the teacher has taught the true doctrines of Christianity, taught only Christ crucified, taught not in words which man's wisdom teaches, nor depended on the superiority of speech or on philosophical flourish, then he shall receive a reward.

He shall receive a reward -- Rewards may be received in this life, and in the life to come. *In this life*, when men who respond to your preaching remain loyal, faithful, and true, there is a satisfaction and a happiness that comes. *In the life to come*, if the rewards are received at the day of judgment, then we must suppose Paul has in view rewards in the heavenly age to follow the judgment. We are reminded of 1 Thessalonians 2:19, where we are told that one of the teacher's rewards will be to see his converts also enjoying heaven. There may also be a reference to degrees of reward in heaven.[39] (See also notes at verse 8 on degrees of reward.) The nature of the reward is not stated, but it is certainly not eternal salvation, which may be won even by those whose work perishes (verse 15). Something corresponding to the "ten cities" and "five cities" in Jesus' parable (Luke 19:11-27) may be meant.

3:15 -- *If any man's work is burned up, he will suffer loss; but he himself will be saved, yet so as through fire.*

If any man's work is burned up -- The wood, hay, and straw that he built out of his speculations, the followers he gained from such methods of teaching, do not stand the test. The teacher suffers loss.

He shall suffer loss -- *Dzemioō* means to 'forfeit' what is possessed or might be possessed. It does not much matter whether we regard this as indefinite 'He shall suffer loss,' or whether we understand it to mean 'He shall suffer loss of the reward' (verse 14). He shall lose the reward which would otherwise have been his. Bengel's illustration (*op. cit.*, p.219) of this "salvation through fire" is "as a shipwrecked merchant with loss of cargo and profit is through the breakers brought safe to land."

But he himself shall be saved -- The reward shall be lost (verse 14), but the worker himself will be saved. A preacher's salvation does not depend on the faithfulness of those whom he has converted. The word "saved" can hardly refer to anything else than eternal salvation, which he has not forfeited by his bad workmanship; he was building on the true foundation. Salvation is not the "reward," for salvation here talked about may be gained when all "reward" is lost. There is no reference here to a false teacher being saved, though

---

[39] Readers need to exercise caution here. Some who teach "unconditional eternal security" teach that while salvation may never be lost, a person's reward can be. This commentator has found in Scripture that one's 'security' is conditioned on faithfulness rather than being unconditional (see Colossians 1:23; 1 Peter 1:4,5). This commentator does not teach "unconditional eternal security;" he does teach "degrees of rewards."

perhaps there is a reference to a poor teacher being saved. It is presupposed that the individual has been building upon the true foundation; he is not a false teacher, but a faulty teacher. His failure is only in respect to the manner of building – carelessly, ignorantly.

Yet so as through fire -- This is a sort of proverbial expression, indicative of a narrow escape from great peril. Herein is expressed the narrowness of the person's escape. He will be snatched as a brand from the burning, saving nothing but his bare life (Zechariah 3:2; Amos 4:11; Jude 23). The image is of a man occupied with the building of a house, and he just escapes with great effort from the conflagration that has caught his work. He sees in sadness and anxiety the loss of all he has done.[40] Like Lot fleeing from Sodom, his salvation is reduced to a minimum; he rushes out through the flame, leaving behind the ruin of his work. For his work, which proved to be worthless, he receives no reward. Who wants to spend all his life in the ministry and end up this way? What an exhortation to avoid the wisdom of this world as we present the message of the cross! To explain "saved yet so as through fire" as meaning 'shall be kept alive in the midst of hell-fire' is an untenable translation and poor exegesis.

M.S. Terry has a paraphrase of Paul's preceding argument:

> The great thoughts in the passage, then, would be as follows: On the foundation of Jesus Christ, ministers, as fellow-workers with God, are engaged in building up God's house. But let each man take heed how he builds. On that foundation may be erected an edifice of sound and enduring substance, as if it were built of gold, silver, and precious stones: the kind of Christians thus "builded together for a habitation of God in the Spirit" (Ephesians 2:20) will constitute a noble and enduring structure, and such work will stand the fiery test of the last day.
>
> But on that same foundation a careless and unfaithful workman may build with unsafe material; he may tolerate and even foster jealousy and strife (v. 3) and pride (v. 18); he may keep fornicators in the Church without sorrow or compunction (5:1,2); he may allow brother to go to law against brother (6:1), and permit drunken persons to come to the Lord's supper (11:21) – all these, as well as heretics in doctrine (15:12), may be taken up and used as materials for building God's house. (In his parable of the tares and the wheat, Jesus himself taught that the good and the evil would be mixed together in the church.)
>
> In writing to the Corinthians the apostle had all these classes of persons in mind, and saw how they were becoming incorporated into that Church of his own planting. But he adds: The day of the Lord's judgment will bring everything to light, and put to the test every man's work. The fiery revelation will disclose what sort of work each one has been doing, and he that has builded wisely and soundly will obtain a glorious reward; but he that has brought, or sought to keep, the wood, hay, stubble, in the church – he who has not rebuked jealousy, nor put down strife, nor excommunicated fornicators, nor faithfully administered the discipline of the church – shall see his lifework all consumed, and he himself shall barely escape with his life, as one that is saved through the fire of a burning build-

---

[40] Kling, *op. cit.*, p.77.

ing. His labor will all have been in vain, though he assumed to build on Christ, and did in fact minister in the holy place of His temple.[41]

3:16 -- *Do you not know that you are a temple of God and* **that** *the Spirit of God dwells in you?*

Do you not know -- "You" is plural. The emphasis shifts slightly. From warning teachers to be careful how they attempt to build the superstructure (verses 5-15), Paul now turns to the church members, and warns them that they too must be careful. After all, they are supposed to be a holy temple, and they must be aware that they do not mar the beauty of the temple (verses 16-23). In the Greek the question expects an affirmative answer, "You do know, don't you ...?" The question is a rebuke to a people who were boasting in their "knowledge," for it introduces a matter which ought to have been common knowledge. Paul is likely appealing to a teaching which he had given them orally when he was preaching among them as he planted the church. Paul uses this device fairly often in this letter, at least ten times (3:16; 5:6; 6:2,3,9,15,16,19; 9:13,14). The question implies that their conduct was such as could only be pursued if they had forgotten, or were ignorant of, the truth of which he now reminds them.

That you are a temple of God -- "You" again is plural. Members of the congregation together are a temple of God.[42] There are two Greek words translated "temple" in the New Testament, *hieron* and *naos*. *Hieron* speaks of the whole temple area, all the courts and porches, etc. *Naos* on the other hand, speaks of the building that housed the holy place and the holy of holies. The *naos* (temple) is the place where the true God reveals His presence, bestows blessings and is worshiped. *Naos*, the word used in verse 16, is a place where a deity dwells. How shall we explain the expression "*a* temple"? Care must be taken lest it be inferred that there were other "temples" of God in Corinth besides the church of Christ. (1) Perhaps "*a* temple" points to the fact that a local congregation,[43] and not the church universal,[44] is in Paul's mind. The church in Ephesus,[45] or Antioch, or Jerusalem, likewise could be called "a temple" of God. There was more to the "temple of God" than just the church at Corinth. (2) Perhaps this passage is an illustration of Colwell's rule of grammar (that predicate nouns preceding the verb are usually definite, even though they

---

[41] Milton S. Terry, *Biblical Hermeneutics* (Grand Rapids: Zondervan, 1953 reprint), p.313. In a couple of places Terry misinterprets, but in the main his ideas are good.

[42] Here in chapter 3, since the "you" is plural, the temple refers to the church (i.e., the congregation of Christians). This passage does not refer to the human body; that reference comes in chapter 6:19 or 2 Corinthians 6:16.

[43] Paul was never guilty of the modern practice of calling a church building "a temple" of God. It was the people, the congregation, who together were pictured as being a "place where a deity dwells."

[44] On the scripturalness of the idea of a "church universal," see notes at Galatians 1:22 and Acts 9:31.

[45] At Ephesians 2:21, Paul also speaks of the church as a temple.

do not have the definite article in Greek). The Greek reads *naos theou este*. If Colwell's rule is applied here, Paul is saying, "Do you not know that you are *the* temple of God in Corinth?" (3) Perhaps there is a qualitative force to the expression, with emphasis on "temple." "*Temple* of God" is what you are. Never forget it!

And *that* the Spirit of God dwells in you? -- "Spirit of God" is but one of many names for the Holy Spirit, the third person of the Godhead. The Holy Spirit is the deity who dwells in God's New Testament temple. A visible symbol of God (e.g., the ark of the Covenant, or the Shekinah) dwelt in the *naos* in the Old Testament. What an improvement Christianity is! "You" is again plural in "Dwells in you." The congregation is in view. "Dwells" is present tense and indicates a continuous reality. The congregation is one sphere of Holy Spirit's operations, the field or abode in which He acts on earth. His influences are in the church, producing the appropriate effects of His agency. In the church, He sustains and guides His people. Are the Corinthians so carnal that they have never grasped, or have failed to retain, so fundamental a doctrine as that of the Holy Spirit in their midst, and of the corresponding responsibility to so live as to bring honor to Him?

3:17 -- *If any man destroys the temple of God, God will destroy him, for the temple of God is holy, and that is what you are.*

If any man destroys the temple of God -- In this context, "any man" seems to refer more to the members of the congregation than to the teachers (who were the point of emphasis in an earlier paragraph). The word *phtheirei* means 'destroy, corrupt, damage, defile.' 'Mar' or 'injure' might well convey the meaning of the word. In this context, it is the opposite of 'building up' which should be the interest of congregational members and teachers alike. The seriousness of the divisions at Corinth is seen in the light of this character of the church as God's temple. When men introduce dissension and strife and division into the fellowship of the congregation, they are destroying the temple of God. They make it impossible for the Spirit to operate. At the moment bitterness enters a congregation, love goes from it. They split up the congregation into little cliques. They literally cause the building of the church to stop. They reduce the congregation to a number of disconnected ruins. If the Corinthians are God's sanctuary because of the indwelling of the Holy Spirit, he who destroys this sanctuary, be he teacher or layman, by lies and deceptions and reliance on the wisdom of this world thereby drives the Spirit out of the hearts of the Corinthians, and instead fills them with the spirit of the world. What is more destructive than schism? Sectarianism is a moral issue. Compare Numbers 4:15ff. There is a reference here in the word "destroy" to rupturing the church by violent partisanship.

God will destroy him -- There was the penalty of death attached to anyone who desecrated the temple of Jerusalem (Leviticus 16:2; Exodus 28:43). Paul now shows that a penalty is attached to defiling God's New Testament "temple." A man who "defiles" the congregation (e.g., by introducing party strife and division[46]) is guilty of no light sin! "Destroys" (the word again is *phtheirei*) probably means 'exclude from salvation.' The exact meaning of the word "destroy" is nowhere revealed in Scripture, but terrible ruin and eternal loss of some kind seems to be meant. In verse 15 the 'bad' workman is saved, though he lost his reward. Here a greater crime than bad workmanship is in mind, and the punishment seems to be more than merely losing one's reward. In the Greek, "God" stands last in the phrase, thus being emphatic. The warning closes with an awful emphasis. Schism is a deadly sin! Whosoever disintegrates the church on earth, him will God destroy in hell. If any man, by his doctrines or precepts, shall pursue such a course as tends to destroy the church, God shall severely punish him. Proverbs 6:16 (KJV) tells us there are seven things God hates, and one is he who sows discord among brethren.

For the temple of God is holy -- It lies in the very idea of a temple that it is holy and inviolable, and that therefore all injury done to it is a crime! Both Jews and Gentiles regarded their temples as inviolable. God's temple is holy. Let no man lay his hands on the temple of God! God cannot allow part of His holy work to be damaged without bringing retribution on the one who does the damage. Every church member, and every church leader, should hear this warning!

And that is what you are -- The KJV reads, "of which *temple* ye are." "Temple" in italics has been added by the translators because they understood the meaning of the whole verse to be, 'The temple of God is holy: ye are the temple of God: therefore ye must guard against what violates your consecration.' But to repeat "temple" here makes unnecessary repetition, argues Alford (*op. cit.*, p.496). According to the ASV/NASB translators, the antecedent here is not "temple," but the adjective "holy." Meyer well remarks that "this clause is the minor proposition of a syllogism: Whoever mars the temple of God, him will God destroy, because His temple is *holy*: and ye also, as His ideal temple, are holy: therefore, whoever mars you, he shall be destroyed by God" (*op. cit.*, p.79).

3:18 -- *Let no man deceive himself. If any man among you thinks that he is wise in this age, he must become foolish, so that he may become wise.*

Let no man deceive himself -- Verses 18-23 are a warning to those who were choosing to align themselves under any of the party leaders.[47] The form of the prohibition in the Greek (*mē* with a present imperative verb) warns against the continuance of something already

---

[46] There are times when men must take a stand for the right, even if it results in hard feelings and polarization into sides. The one standing for the *right* is not the one who is troubling Israel! The one doing the wrong is the cause of the dissension. In this passage in 1 Corinthians 3, the one who is "destroying the church" is the man who is contending for the wrong things (wisdom of this age, party spirit, etc.). It is this kind of destroyer who is threatened with destruction, not the person who is contending for what is right.

[47] As we come to verse 18 we have a decision to make concerning the outline of 1 Corinthians. Some begin a new point in the outline with verse 18, supposing that the idea being developed since 3:5 is completed, and that a new argument begins at this place. We propose, rather, that Paul's instructions concerning the proper evaluation of their Christian leaders continues on through 4:5.

going on. 'Stop deceiving yourself!' is the idea. They had been deceiving themselves when they chose leaders for themselves. That must stop! "No man" appeals to each individual member personally. It is not the other fellow who must stop – it is you! The passage will go on to specify the area where the deceit was flourishing.[48] Let no man be puffed up any longer with a vain conceit about his own wisdom (the wisdom of this age), for this had been the real cause of all the evils which they had experienced. Let no man deceive himself into thinking worldly wisdom makes him wise enough to judge among leaders, thus crying one up and another down, as the Corinthians had been doing, and attaching themselves to one and not the other. Paul goes on once again to pin down the root cause of the dissension and the threatened destruction of the temple of God (the congregation) in Corinth. The root cause is the worship of intellectual, worldly wisdom.

If any man among you thinks that he is wise in this age -- This is where the form of self-deception that led to the rupture of the unity of the church is defined. "In this age" probably is to be taken with "wise" thus defining the wisdom that the party members at Corinth valued.[49] There is an obvious reference to those who thought themselves "wise" in attaching themselves to this or that teacher. What was not so wise is that they were using criteria learned from the "wisdom of this age" to decide with which teacher they would align themselves. Such criteria are faulty; Paul has already (2:6ff) shown the wisdom of this age to be contrary to God's wisdom.

Let him become foolish – How? By discarding all the worldly wisdom and the Corinthian words, which will cause him to be called "a fool" by the adherents of this wisdom. In this admonition Paul presents the very heart of all that he has discussed thus far. Each Corinthian is to examine his own heart. If he considers himself wise in this world's wisdom, or if he considers it wise to adhere to some teacher whom he foolishly rates as wise in the wisdom of this world, he is to change his thinking. He is to renounce dependence on the wisdom of this age so that he may be ready in heart and mind to welcome God's wisdom.[50]

That he may become wise -- By casting aside the spurious wisdom of the world, a person will not, after all, be a fool, for by so doing he will achieve the inner attitude necessary for really appropriating Christ, and will thereby actually attain the true wisdom, the wisdom that is from God.

---

[48] "Let no man deceive himself" looks forward, not backward. One may "deceive himself" about the value of the wisdom of this age, but scarcely about the truth of the threatening in verse 17.

[49] It is easier to follow the train of thought if we take "in this age" with "wise" than if we try to take it with the words which follow "Let him become foolish." If we were to construe "in this age" with "foolish" then that clause would read "Let him become foolish in the eyes of this age ...."

[50] Does this verse speak to 21st century scholars who tie their doctrine to the latest in higher critical scholarship – when the scholars themselves have a flawed philosophical base on which all their teaching is built?

3:19 -- *For the wisdom of this world is foolishness before God. For it is written, "He is THE ONE WHO CATCHES THE WISE IN THEIR CRAFTINESS";*

For the wisdom of this world is foolishness before God -- This verse, beginning with "for", gives a reason why one must become a 'fool if he would be really wise.' Paul shows this advice and instruction are in harmony with Scripture. "Before God" translates *para tō theō*. *Para* used with the dative expresses 'standing before a person as a judge, and submitting to his decision or sentence.' Hence, the expression "before God" carries a deeper meaning than simply 'in his sight.' God has passed judgment upon the "wisdom of this world" and condemned it; the proof is in the Scripture quoted next. "That which is esteemed to be wisdom by the men of this world on the subject of religion" is what is meant by "wisdom" here.[51] This same principle of the wide difference between God's wisdom and the wisdom of this world has already been established. What is written here, however, is the reverse of the argument in 1:18-25. There Paul demonstrated the wisdom of God (Christ crucified) is foolishness to the world. There, Paul emphasized man's judgment, man's perspective of things. Here Paul says, 'The wisdom of this world is foolishness in God's judgment.' In this paragraph God's perspective is emphasized, which is the perspective that ultimately counts.

For it is written -- "It is written" is Paul's usual way of introducing quotations from Scripture. Paul reminds his readers of two passages from Scripture to demonstrate the truth of what he has said (verse 19a) about how God views the wisdom of this world. The first passage quoted is Job 5:13. Paul's citation differs from the Septuagint, and may be his own translation from the Hebrew. It may be noticed that with the exception of the reference in James 5:11 to the "patience of Job," this is the only allusion to Job or the book of Job in the New Testament.

"*He is* THE ONE WHO CATCHES THE WISE IN THEIR CRAFTINESS" -- The word rendered "catches" here denotes to clench with the fist, to grip or grasp. It denotes: (1) however crafty, or cunning, or skillful they may be, however self-confident, they cannot deceive or impose upon God. He can thwart their plans, overthrow their schemes, defeat their counsels, and foil them in their enterprises. (2) He does it by their own cunning or craftiness. He allows them to involve themselves in difficulties, or to entangle each other. To be 'caught in craftiness' is like a criminal caught in the very act he thought would fool the authorities; he is arrested, exposed, and punished accordingly. "Craftiness" (*panourgia*) means 'slippery cleverness, versatile cleverness, ready to do anything in order to gain one's own end, cunning.' Paul does not minimize the capacity of the worldly wise within their own field. But he stoutly denies that their craftiness will avail against the might and wisdom of God. God has a good grasp on the slippery cleverness of the wicked. The fact that God catches them in the very act and exposes all their craftiness is factual evidence that His wisdom completely outranks theirs, and nothing is more convincing than the fact that he "catches" them at the moment they are at their slipperiest.

---

[51] See notes at 1:20 where this "wisdom" was explained.

3:20 -- *and again, "THE LORD KNOWS THE REASONINGS of the wise, THAT THEY ARE USELESS."*

And again -- The passage about to be quoted from Psalm 94:11 (the citation is freely taken from the LXX) is the second one used to demonstrate that the sentiment stated in verse 19a is God's sentiment. In the Psalm, these words are directed by God against proud men who acted as if there were no God above who observed and wrote down all their unrighteous deeds. The verse quoted will say that God knows the thoughts of the so-called wise men; nothing that enters their minds is beyond His understanding. And all that is not in tune with God's thoughts is vain!

"THE LORD KNOWS THE REASONINGS of the wise, THAT THEY ARE USELESS" -- Psalms has "man" where Paul writes "wise." This is another of Paul's free renderings of the Septuagint. "Reasonings" is from *dialogismoi*, and speaks of the plans that a man makes while thinking to himself. God knows these. He knows the thoughts of every man. Nothing can be hidden from Him. "Useless" (*mataioi*), means 'groundless, void of truth, hollow, foolish.' The reasonings are "useless" because, lacking real wisdom, they shall not accomplish what is expected. The worldly wise are unable to effect anything lasting. From the life of Jesus we have illustration after illustration of the ineffectiveness of the schemes, plots, and tricky questions that wise men hatch. Jesus' enemies often tried to entangle Him. But He always saw completely through their cunning and frustrated their designs with a word or two. So God's wisdom exposes the "reasonings" and worldly wisdom of the men of this age. Let the Corinthians keep Job 5:13 and Psalm 94:11 in mind when they are tempted to use worldly wisdom as they choose which party they will join and defend. God's perspective is that such wisdom is foolish!

3:21 -- *So then let no one boast in men. For all things belong to you,*

So then -- "So then" (*hōste*), as often in Paul's writings, introduces the imperative at the point where argument or explanation passes into exhortation. In light of all that has been said since verse 18 about not deceiving themselves any longer,[52] the command now comes, "Stop boasting in men!"

Let no one boast in men -- The form of the Greek prohibition prohibits the continuance of an action already going on. The Corinthians had been boasting in men. They were to stop it! In the light of what Scripture says about God's contempt for human worldly wisdom, let no one be still bold enough to say 'I belong to Paul' or 'I belong to Apollos.' Such "reasonings" are bound to be futile, out of harmony with God's wisdom. Remember what was written in 1:29 and 1:31. To "boast in men" is the opposite of "boast in the Lord" (1:31). 'Let the party-spirit cease! Quit calling yourselves after the names of any man.' It was common for the Jews to range themselves under different leaders, such as Hillel and Shammai; and for the Greeks, too, to boast of being the followers of Pythagoras,

---

[52] Some suppose the "so then" is based only on verse 19a. Some suppose all that has gone before since 1:31 is gathered up in the "so then." The notes offered above are based on the outline we've adopted for this section, with the current paragraph (about the proper way to view Christian leaders) covering 3:5 to 4:5.

Zeno, or Plato. The same thing began to be manifest in the Christian church. Paul here rebukes and opposes it. The caution is addressed to those who are inclined to make much of their teachers in consequence of their education or supposed wisdom, cleaving to them in partisan attachment, and disparaging other servants of Christ in comparison, to the overlooking of the unity of the church. To "boast in men" means to boast about them, their qualities, teachings, worldly wisdom, and in their 'Corinthian words.'

For all things belong to you -- "For" shows the words following are a reason why they should not range themselves in parties or factions under a single leader, and verses 22-23 will unfold what is meant by "all things." Paul shows the utter foolishness of what they were doing. They were cheating themselves by not laying hold of all the riches of God. It is always a tendency of Christians to underrate the grandeur of their privileges, by exaggerating their supposed monopoly of *some* of them while *many* rich advantages are at their disposal. Instead of becoming partisans of special teachers and champions of separate doctrines, they might enjoy all things. In Paul, in Apollos, in life, in death, they had a *common* interest, and no one should boast that he had any special proprietorship in any of these things. Yet Paul's aim is not merely to proclaim how wide their heritage is, but to show them that they have got the facts by the wrong end. They want to make him a chieftain when he is really their servant. Paul is saying, 'Why limit yourself to *one*, when you can have *all*? It is foolish to impoverish yourselves! Why do you limit yourselves by claiming that you belong to a particular teacher? Do you not realize that all teachers, yea, all things that are, belong to you in Christ?' So far from enriching themselves by staking their claim to exclusive rights to one teacher, the Corinthians were impoverishing themselves. They were cutting themselves off from the treasures that were really theirs.

3:22 -- *whether Paul or Apollos or Cephas or the world or life or death or things present or things to come; all things belong to you,*

Whether Paul or Apollos or Cephas -- This verse begins a list of the things which Paul had in mind when he said "all things" in verse 21. All these Christian leaders were their servants for Jesus' sake (2 Corinthians 3:5). Instead of becoming partisans of any one, they could enjoy the blessings of all. The sense is clear. Each teacher had something to share that would benefit the Corinthians. Why not take advantage of what each has to offer, rather than limiting yourselves to just one?

Or the world -- In this context, we must suppose that for reasons of human wisdom, one or more of the parties at Corinth were eschewing the "world" as being bad for them. Is there a reflection of dualism in Greek philosophy, where matter is evil, which led some of the Corinthians to avoid some of the "world" instead of being benefitted by what God has created? "World" (*kosmos*) can refer to the globe we live on, or the ordered universe, or the things which pertain to this life. Through the wisdom of Christ we see the universe as it actually is, as God's creation. We find His power, wisdom, and beneficence in all its creatures; we receive a thousand earthly blessings in this world from the hand of God, as many as our lives can hold. Upheld by His grace, we serve Him in this world and faithfully work for His glory. Thus, the world is intended to serve and benefit the Christian.

Or life -- "Life" translates *dzōē* rather than *bios*. "*Dzōē* is life in its *principle*, and is used for spiritual life and for immortal life; *bios* is life in its *manifestations*, denoting the manner of life [1 Timothy 2:2 speaks of a "tranquil and quiet life"]."[53] How was "life" looked on as inimical by the wisdom of this age? Was it then, as it is now, that the world thinks the spiritual life is a thing to be avoided because a "man can have no fun" and be a Christian at the same time? Contrary to the world's wisdom, believers can enjoy life because life in Christ is the only real life.

Or death -- Death is feared by sinners, and was looked on as the end of existence by Greek wisdom. Death is my servant if I am a Christian. If a man dies in Christ, he passes at once into a greater experience of eternal life with God. Death usually is regarded as a calamity and a curse. But it is not for the Christian: (1) Because they shall have peace and support in the dying hour; (2) Because it has no terrors for them; (3) Because it is the avenue which leads to their rest; (4) Because they shall triumph over it; it has been subdued by their Captain; (5) Because death is the means and occasion of introducing them to their reward.[54]

Or things present or things to come -- Compare Romans 8:28,38,39. See how the perspective learned from God is so different from the perspective gained by worldly wisdom? "Things present" are events which are now happening, happening in this present age. All the calamities, trials, persecutions, all the prosperity, advantages, and privileges of the present time, and all that shall yet take place, these all shall tend to promote our welfare and advance the interests of our souls, and promote our salvation.[55] Present things are ours because they bring us good.

> It is as if this multitude of servants surrounded us and on bended knees held out their precious offerings to us. Some of these servants like pain, injury, sickness, grief, and death may at first have a strange look to us who do not know our own royalty sufficiently. It is God who commissions them all and makes each one bring us some blessing so that as kings unto God we shall lack nothing.[56]

"Things to come" likely covers what we shall experience when this life is over – in the intermediate state, at the resurrection, and at the judgment.

All things belong to you -- Paul repeats triumphantly his "all things" of verse 22a. All shall tend to promote your comfort and salvation. And let it be noted that all these limit-

---

[53] George R. Berry, "New Testament Synonyms," in *A New Greek-English Lexicon to the New Testament* (Chicago, IL: Wilcox & Follett, 1948), p.19.

[54] Barnes, *op. cit.*, p.63.

[55] *Ibid.*

[56] R.C.H. Lenski, *Kings and Priests: The Priesthood of All Believers* (Burlington, IA: Lutheran Literary Board, 1927), p.26.

less blessings and benefits are theirs because they "are Christ's." They are possessors of these byproducts of the wisdom of God because they belong to Christ.

3:23 -- *and you belong to Christ; and Christ belongs to God.*

And you belong to Christ -- You belong to Him (and to no human leader). You should not, therefore, feel 'wise' or feel like 'boasting' when you are devoted to any earthly leader, whether Paul, Apollos, or Peter. The Corinthian Christians were redeemed by Christ. They were His property. They enjoy the benefits of all God has done and is doing, but they are to remember they belong to Christ, and are to use these benefits to serve Him, not some human leader they may elect to follow. By partaking in Christ's redemption, they once more attain unto a dignity which originally belonged to man (Genesis 1:26; Psalm 8:6). These words complete the rebuke of those who said they belonged to Paul. They belonged to no one but Christ, and they all alike belonged to Him. And men who belong to Christ ought not to live in a fleshly fashion. Their self-assertiveness was out of character for those who belonged to Christ!

And Christ belongs to God -- Christ, who expects our submission and allegiance, supplies in Himself a grand example for us to imitate. This statement should not be interpreted to assert an *eternal* subordination of Jesus to God, but rather that He was sent to do the will of God. It does indicate a *temporary* subordination in function in order to become our Redeemer, but not an *eternal* subordination.[57] Paul may be saying (in the context of 1 Corinthians 1-4) that Christ belongs, not to a party, but to God, the Father of us all. The argument here seems to be this: 'You belong to Christ, and He to God. You are bound therefore not to devote yourselves to a man, whoever he may be, but to Christ, and to the service of that one true God, in whose service even Christ was employed.'

> Perhaps these words were added, not only as being the great climax of the gradual ascent up which the apostle's thoughts and language have gone in the whole passage, but as avoiding any danger of the party who called themselves by the name of Christ, arrogating anything to themselves from the previous words, "Ye are Christ's," if the passage had concluded with them.[58]

---

[57] For Christ's filial submission to the Father, see 1 Corinthians 11:3, 15:22ff; Romans 6:10; John 8:29, 10:29; Hebrews 5:8. The statement that Christ belongs to God has nothing to do with Paul's concept of the deity of Jesus, or His equality with God before the incarnation. Paul makes it perfectly clear in other passages that Jesus is God. His subordination is for the function of redemption, not a subordination in the quality of divine being. In the redemptive program of God, His eternal plan being carried out in time, there is a system of subordination between the members of the Godhead. What this passage is saying, in context, is this: the apostles and teachers were the Corinthians' – theirs to use. The Corinthians were Christ's – Christ's to use. And Christ was God's – God's to use.

[58] Shore, *op. cit.*, p.33.

> *Summary:* The beginning of chapter 4 continues reason #3 (as Paul sees it) for the dissension in the church at Corinth. Reason #1 was a failure to remember the nature of the gospel, that it is the wisdom of God. Reason #2 was a failure to remember the source of true wisdom, that it comes by revelation and inspiration from God through God's chosen messengers. Reason #3, which covers 3:5 through 4:5, was a failure to properly evaluate the place of leaders (apostles and prophets). As Paul unfolds the proper evaluation Christians are to put on these leaders, he has emphasized they are to be thought of as "servants of the Lord," (3:5), as "fellow-workers" (3:9), as "under rowers" (4:1), and as "stewards" (4:1ff).

4:1 -- *Let a man regard us in this manner, as servants of Christ and stewards of the mysteries of God.*

Let a man regard us in this manner -- "Let a man" equals 'let all.' The word "regard" is *logidzesthō*, which implies a reasonable estimate: so think of us, so account of us. It is a present tense imperative verb, which says this is to be the habitual estimate. It is the duty of all the readers to so regard their leaders. "Us" is the apostles.[1] Paul has just named himself, Apollos, and Peter, in 3:22. "In this manner" points back to 3:23 – since all things are yours, and you are Christ's, and Christ is God's. Since it is inevitable that Christians should form some estimate of their Christian leaders, Paul proceeds to tell them what that estimate should be. If the Corinthians will think as Paul suggests, it will bring an end to the dissension over leaders in the church at Corinth. It is the Lord's prerogative at the final judgment to judge whether His servants have been faithful. In the meantime, the Corinthians should suspend their judgments for and against their leaders.

As servants of Christ -- "Servants" is not *diakonos* as in 3:5, but *hupēretas*, a word which Paul uses here only. The word *hupēretas* strongly expresses the idea of subordination. It is the same word used at Luke 1:2, "ministers of the word" (ASV). A "minister of the word" had an important function in the handing down of oral tradition. 'Under rower' is what the word *hupēretas* pictures; i.e., one who rowed in the lower bank of oars on a large ship.[2] From this word the picture has been drawn by some writers of the ministers (apostles) as pulling together in one galley where Christ sits at the helm, the vessel being the church, and the passengers the members of the church. Not only is disunion in the crew fatal to progress, but a thing tending to shipwreck.[3] This is the true estimate of the

---

[1] In trying to specify who is included in "us," George Mark Elliott said, "primarily the preacher." Alford (*op. cit.*, p.497) limits the "us" to Paul and Apollos. All who are charged with the ministry of the new covenant, says another commentator.

[2] Ancient ships were not like our steam driven, or diesel driven, or nuclear powered vessels. They had sails and oars. Those with oars were called galleys, and a reading of Lew Wallace's *Ben Hur* will give some idea of what the galleys and galley slaves were like. The rowers were chained to the seat, and pulled on the oars eight hours a day. There was a man at a desk, with a mallet. You pulled on the oar each time he struck the desk with the mallet. He could regulate the speed of the ship by the tempo of the mallet swings. These ships could sail into the wind; they were not at the mercy of the wind as sailing ships were. There were biremes and triremes as well as boats with a single deck of oarsmen. So, "under rowers" were galley slaves – under someone else's direction.

[3] George Mark Elliott insisted that such a complete picture does not come out of this text.

apostles and their office – they were not the heads of factions designing to form parties, they were just mere servants of Christ. The word speaks of an underling, a helper, an attendant.[4] Such a person's sole function was to take orders and unquestioningly execute them at once. His will is only that of his master. "Of Christ" is likely a genitive of possession; these "servants" belong to Christ.[5] He was their Master. Therefore, they were responsible to Him. The Corinthians have not only been *for* Apollos or *for* Peter, but they have also been *against* Paul (or Peter). They were rejecting the teaching *and* authority of an apostle. This presents Paul with a genuine dilemma. He must reassert the authority of an apostle without blunting the force of his argument that "all are yours!" *Servants* of Christ, they are His special mouthpieces since they are the special recipients of revelation and inspiration. Going one's own way, apart from where the apostles directed as they shared the Gospel, was not an option open to the Corinthians.

And stewards -- Here is a fourth term Paul uses to describe the proper standard by which to estimate the Christian leaders at Corinth. "Stewards" were those who presided over the affairs of a family and made provision for it (Luke 16:1). It was an office of much responsibility.[6] Stewards functioned as dispensers, subordinate distributors, managers. Though "stewards" in the everyday world were usually slaves, yet they were "free" to make decisions concerning the exercise of their stewardship, decisions for which they were accountable to their master. In both terms, "servants" and "stewards," the prominent idea is that of complete subordination to a master; but in the latter, there is also the idea of special accountability. In fact, this is the very point Paul will emphasize in the next verse. A "servant" merely takes his orders and at once carries them out without question. A "steward" also takes his orders and carries them out in due process, and then returns and renders his account. He works, as it were, by himself, in the absence of his lord, who trusts him to this extent. But he is always and fully accountable. He dare not deviate in the slightest from his orders, nor try to improve upon those orders with wisdom of his own in order to please others.

Of the mysteries of God -- See the explanation of the word "mysteries" given at 1 Corinthians 2:7. (See also Ephesians 1:9, 3:3,4; 1 Timothy 3:16.) The word speaks of divine truth which was once hidden but is now revealed, truths not discoverable by unaided

---

[4] Later in church history, this word became the technical term for 'sub-deacon.'

[5] In 3:5, "ministers through whom you believed," stressed the relation of the apostles to the Corinthians. Here Paul points out their relation to Christ. Jesus Christ is the One from whom they take orders.

[6] A steward was the *major domo*. He was in charge of the whole administration of the house or the estate; he controlled the staff; he issued the supplies and the rations; he ran the whole household. But however much he controlled the household staff of slaves, he himself was still a slave where the master was concerned. Whatever the apostles' or prophets' position in the church, and whatever power they might wield in that position, or whatever prestige they might enjoy, they still remained 'servants' of Christ. Joseph, the patriarch, would have been in such a position as "steward" (Genesis 39:4), though the actual term *oikonomos* is not used in the LXX of Genesis.

human reason. Here, "mysteries" has reference to the gospel and the plan of salvation.[7] No special difference is intended by making the servants belong to Christ and the stewards to God; and this differentiation does not indicate a subordination of Christ to God, for these servants and stewards are the same persons. One term speaks of their master, the other of the author of their message.

4:2 -- *In this case, moreover, it is required of stewards that one be found trustworthy.*

In this case, moreover -- The fidelity required of stewards is referred to here in order to show that the apostles acted from a higher principle than a desire to please men, or to be regarded as head of a party. The proper way to esteem the apostles was that they were bound, like all stewards, to be faithful to the master whom they served. The proper reading (*Aleph*, A, B, C, D, F) is *hōde loipon*, "here, moreover ..." (ASV) or "in this case" (NASB). "On this earth" is what Farrar thought "here" means (*op. cit.*, p.132). "Though in the case of stewards enquiry was necessarily made here below, yet he, God's steward, awaited no such enquiry from man's judgment, but one at the coming of the Lord," says Alford (*op. cit.*, p.498). But it is better to understand this as a reference 'to the case just mentioned,' namely, the judgment exercised by stewards. Paul is appealing to a well-known contemporary practice. "Moreover" means 'in addition to what is expected of servants.' In addition to subordination, a steward has further responsibility and accountability.

It is required of stewards -- "It is required"[8] means 'it is expected of them.' It is the main or leading thing about their office. The word also carries the sense of a reckoning being made in order to prove the steward faithful.

That one be found trustworthy -- "Found" implies there is an examination, a judgment, a reckoning that must be made in regard to the steward. Under the scrutiny of a careful examination they are proved to be faithful. Stewards, here on earth, all the time were called on to give an account of their stewardship by their earthly masters. Lest the Corinthians get the idea they were the masters who could call their teachers to account, Paul goes on in verse 3 to correct such an idea. "Trustworthy" ("faithful," ASV) says that fidelity was the great requisite for the office of a steward; there was to be fidelity to his master. Compare Luke 16:1ff for such a "judgment" as is here suggested. This is required particularly because being a steward is an office of trust – because the master's goods are at the steward's disposal, because there is so much opportunity for the steward

---

[7] Some try to make "mysteries" here a reference to the 'sacraments' (Lord's Supper and baptism). A 'sacrament' is a solemn religious rite, sometimes thought of as being a means of grace. An 'ordinance' is a command of Christ. Restoration Movement folk have tended to speak of ordinances rather than sacraments. The word "mystery" is never used for either baptism or the Lord's Supper in the New Testament. It is true that in later patristic usage, the word 'mystery' came to be used for the sacraments. (Compare patristic usage in notes at 3:6 on "plant" and "water.") But that was not the meaning of the term at the time Paul wrote, nor is this passage to be used as some are wont to do as a proof text that only ordained clergy should administer the sacraments.

[8] Some manuscripts have "you require," but *Aleph*, A, C, D have "it is required."

to appropriate those goods for his own use. What is sought in stewards like the apostles and prophets is not eloquence nor wisdom – nor even initiative nor success, which are our more modern standards – but faithfulness to the trust God gave them. For Paul, this means absolute fidelity to the gospel as he received it and spoke it.

4:3 -- *But to me it is a very small thing that I may be examined by you, or by* **any** *human court; in fact, I do not even examine myself.*

But -- Faithfulness is absolutely required of stewards. But, who is to judge whether there has been that faithfulness? 'Not you Corinthians, nor my own conscience, but the Lord only,' is Paul's reply. The Corinthians might have expected that the conclusion of Paul's remarks would be a recognition of their right to sit in judgment of his faithfulness. But Paul shatters such expectations. Since Christ and God alone are Paul's masters, they alone have the authority to examine and to judge him.

To me it is a very small thing -- "To me" means 'in my estimate, in regard to myself.' That is, 'I esteem it a matter of no concern. Since I am responsible as a steward to my Master only, it is a matter of small concern what *men* think of me, provided I have His approval.' "A very small thing" literally is "it amounts to the very least thing."[9]

That I should be examined by you -- Both those who favored Paul and those who preferred someone else to Paul are included in those who are "examining" or judging Paul. Neither one's decision is of any real estimate as far as Paul is concerned. It is his Master's opinion that counts, and it alone! "Examined" or "judged" (ASV) is *anakrinō*,[10] 'looked up and down.' Paul was perhaps being disparaged for his lack of elocution, or rhetoric, or a display of the wisdom of this age. Technically the word *anakrisis* means 'an examination preliminary to a trial.' The word does not so much refer to the verdict handed down at the end of the trial, but rather it speaks of the process of examining itself that leads to the verdict. It does not denote a final judgment, so it is a good word, for no human judgment could be final. Paul is not interested in any preliminary human sifting. He is content to await the Judge. The Corinthians dare not set up human standards of their own that are derived from some worldly wisdom of theirs, whereby to rate the various teachers who have labored among them. The teachers are ministers of Christ, and therefore answerable to Him. Paul is saying that an inquiry into his methods and conduct, if he is to be judged by human standards, is a small matter to him. And when men follow the example of the Corinthians, and set up their own standards by which to judge a minister, we can say with Paul that their judgment is a small matter to us. But when a congregation exercises its proper right and truly applies the Lord's Word to a preacher's teaching and to his conduct, he must not only recognize the validity of such an investigation, but also regard it as a matter of utmost gravity.

---

[9] Kling, *op. cit.*, p.88.

[10] See notes at 2:14 where this word was used before.

Or by *any* human court -- Literally, the Greek reads, 'of man's day' or 'by a human day.' Most interpreters think this is a proverbial expression or a figure of speech of some kind. Interpretations offered include: (1) It as a Cilicism (Jerome), an early expression due to Paul's training in Cilicia. (2) It is a Hebraism, and has reference to a day of trial. (3) It is a reference to "time in general", implying that the brief day of human life is bounded by too narrow an horizon for accurate judgments. The word "day" in all languages and idioms can signify "judgment" (Hammond, cited by Farrar, *op. cit.*, p.132). Our translators apparently properly interpreted "day" here since there seems to be a contrast to "day of the Lord" (3:13). 'I do not claim to be responsible to no one; inquiry will have to be made whether I am faithful. But the authority to which I bow is not yours, nor that of any human tribunal, but God's.' Is what men think of us ever important? There are times the court of public opinion is important and may not be ignored by Christians (see 1 Corinthians 9:20ff). The Corinthian use of tongues is judged by what others will think (1 Corinthians 14:23). One of the qualifications for elder is to be of good report from those outside the church (1 Timothy 3:7, KJV). Jesus grew in favor with men (Luke 2:52). The early church had "favor with all the people" (Acts 2:47). But as desirable as public opinion may be, it should always be courted within the strictest limits of absolute fidelity to Christ. Whether we are pleasing the Lord is the opinion that really matters; His is a higher court than public opinion.

In fact, I do not even examine myself -- "Examine" here again is the word is *anakrinō*. It seems that Paul is *not* saying that he did not examine himself, in the sense of seeing if he was doing his best to perform God's will (cp. 1 Corinthians 11:28, "Let each man examine himself ..."). It rather shows Paul is not arrogantly proclaiming himself superior to the opinion of the Corinthians. It was of great concern to Paul what men thought of him. He took careful forethought about his behavior so that he might not be misrepresented, lest the gospel should suffer. Paraphrased, he says, 'I don't boastfully place myself on a pedestal as the greatest preacher ever to come to Corinth. If I don't estimate highly my *own* opinion of myself, then it is not to be expected that I should set a high value on the opinions of others.' It is tremendously difficult to come to an accurate assessment of one's own achievement, and Paul points out that in any case it does not matter. "The Christian is to be judged by his Master. His own views on himself are as irrelevant as those of anyone else. This needs emphasis in a day when many are tempted to be introspective. Often they think that they themselves know just what their spiritual state is and just what their service for God has effected. The result may depress unduly or exalt above measure. But it is not our task to pass such judgments. We should get on with the job of serving the Lord. This does not mean that there is no place for times of heart-searching and rigid self-scrutiny with a view to more wholehearted and more efficient service. It is an attempt to anticipate the judgment of the Lord that Paul is condemning" (Morris, *op. cit.*, p.73).

4:4 -- *For I am conscious of nothing against myself, yet I am not by this acquitted; but the one who examines me is the Lord.*

For I am conscious of nothing against myself -- There is a *gar* ("for") in the Greek, showing that there is a reason why Paul does not use human standards of judgment to judge himself. Such self-evaluation can be very unreliable. *Sunoida* with a reflexive pronoun has the connotation of a guilty conscience.[11] 'I am not conscious of having been an unfaithful steward,' is the idea.[12] 'My own mind does not condemn me of unholy ambition or unfaithfulness. I didn't try to become a leader like some of you Corinthians are trying to make me; I was a good steward of my ministerial office.' Paul is saying he is not aware of any great matter where he has failed in his stewardship responsibilities. But that alone doesn't automatically bring Christ's acquittal.

Yet I am not by this acquitted -- 'Even though my conscience is clear, even though I am not conscious of a failure in my duty, that does not justify me.' God is the true Judge. A man may deceive himself into thinking he knows nothing against himself. So often the way of a man is right in his own eyes, but God ponders the heart. A man is not in a position to be saved just because his heart does not condemn him. A man's conscience may be thwarted and seared. *Dedikaiomai*, translated "justified" in the ASV, is a legal word meaning "acquitted of a charge, declared 'not guilty'." Paul delights to use this word of the believer standing before the Judge, and being pronounced not guilty.[13]

But the one who examines me is the Lord -- "Lord" is a reference to Jesus Christ.[14] Jesus Christ is the Judge, as verse 5 shows. Only He has all the information necessary to make a proper judgment as to which servant is to be honored above the other. There is a searching judgment to be passed through by all those who are stewards of the mysteries of God. But the judge is their Master, the Lord Jesus, and not any of the Corinthians. Further, this examination is something that happens, perhaps, every day.[15] "Examines" is a present tense verb – *anakrinō* (a preliminary judgment) again. Jesus checks to see if there is any ground for indictment. Jesus tests Paul's daily course of life to see if it is right. The Lord's present examination prepares for His final judgment (verse 5). There may be a gentle and tender reproof of the Corinthians who were so confident in their own integrity,

---

[11] The NASB's "I am conscious of nothing against myself" is better than the KJV's "I know nothing by myself." "By myself," the common usage in 1611, meant "against myself," but we do not so think of it, for the word "by" has changed connotations.

[12] To say he is "conscious of nothing against himself" is not a claim to sinless perfection. Elsewhere he calls himself the chief of sinners (cf. 9:27, 15:9; Ephesians 3:8; Philippians 3:3). They who claim the Bible teaches that sinless perfection is possible in this life cannot quote the sanction of Paul.

[13] Often in Scripture, the term speaks of the sentence ("not guilty") God pronounces when a sinner becomes an obedient believer. However, in this place, it is the Master's having judged the fidelity of the steward that is in Paul's mind.

[14] This is a clear case of Colwell's rule of grammar. There is no article ("the") before *kurios* ("Lord"), but it is a place where a definite predicate noun precedes the verb, and does not need the article in Greek to be translated as definite, as "*the* Lord." The next verse where we have the words, "the Lord comes," helps to determine which member of the Godhead is here designated by "Lord."

[15] The idea of present, everyday examination is the interpretation preferred also by Meyer, Heinrici, and Findlay (*Expositor's Greek Testament*). There are those expositors who take the present tense as a reference to the final, future judgment (Bengel, Alford, Godet, Calvin). There are other passages in the New Testament that refer to this daily scrutinizing by the Lord, including Romans 4:5, 1 Peter 1:17, and Revelation 2:23.

and a gentle admonition to them to be more cautious, as it was possible that the Lord would detect faults in them where they perceived none.

4:5 -- *Therefore do not go on passing judgment before the time,* **but wait** *until the Lord comes who will both bring to light the things hidden in the darkness and disclose the motives of* **men's** *hearts; and then each man's praise will come to him from God.*

Therefore -- *Hōste* ("therefore") introduces the practical conclusion to this paragraph regarding judging leaders like Paul and Apollos up or down, and who is the proper judge. In view of the danger of being deceived in your judgment and in the light of the Lord being the sole infallible judge, here is the proper course of behavior.

Do not go on passing judgment -- In the context, it has to do with passing judgment (for and against) on their Christian leaders. The use of *mē* with the present imperative is a construction that prohibits the continuance of an action already going on. The Corinthians had been engaging in this activity. 'Stop judging!' is the force of the construction. Specifically, the Corinthians are to stop pronouncing the phrase 'I am of Paul,' etc. The passage must not be wrested from its context, and made to mean 'There is to be no judging on *any topic* at all!' That this is true is seen from Paul's own example. In 5:12, in the context of flagrant immorality in their midst, they are commanded to "judge those who are within," and in 6:5, they are expected to be able to judge between petty disputes between brothers within the congregation. The kind of judging[16] which Paul forbids in regard to himself and concerning any teacher in the church is that kind indicated in verse 4, where human standards of judgment are made the basis of the examination and verdict.

Several thoughts need to be recalled concerning Christians and judging: (1) There is a judging which is forbidden (Matthew 7:1) – hypocritical condemnatory judging. (2) Eternal judgment is a prerogative of God. (3) In matters of church discipline, Christians are commanded to judge (see 5:5). (4) Like a doctor, there will be times when we must make a judgment (i.e., a diagnosis) to know the proper spiritual medicine to give. (5) Christians are to "test the spirits" to see whether they be of God (1 John 4:1). (6) Only when a teacher/leader teaches and practices contrary to the Word has the congregation the right both to make an examination (*anakrinein*) and pass a verdict (*krinein*). In that case such an investigation and such a judging in no wise usurp Christ's authority, but only vindicate the authority of Christ's Word against a man who is violating that Word.

Before the time -- "The time" is more fully explained below. It means "until the Lord comes," at which time the Lord shall "judge the secrets of men" (Romans 2:16). 'Do not pronounce verdicts, either favorable or unfavorable, on your faithful teachers, until you see how the Lord judges them.' If we may infer what lies back of Paul's words, it would be this: the Paul faction lauded Paul over against Apollos and against Peter, while the Apollos and the Peter factions found all manner of fault with Paul. Paul's admonition is directed against both proceedings. While he personally paid no attention to this kind of

---

[16] The Greek verb *krinein* that is used here is different from the word used in verse 3. This is the word for passing a verdict, whereas the one before dealt with preliminary examinations prior to sentencing.

praise or blame, the worst feature about it was that the Corinthians were acting in a way that was highly derogatory to Christ who gives His differing gifts and opportunities to His "stewards," Who knows what is in their minds and hearts as they do their work, and Who will apportion rewards to them in due time. Every verdict rendered before this time is both illegal and invalid; it could emanate only from some foolish person who is not a properly constituted judge although he pretends to be such a one.

***But wait* until the Lord comes** -- In the New Testament, the second advent of Jesus Christ is sometimes called the "epiphany," and sometimes the "parousia," and sometimes the "apocalypse" (or "revelation"). The phrase Paul uses here is indefinite, "until the Lord comes," *whenever* that might be. It points to a time entirely indefinite. Not the coming, but the time of the coming, is indefinite. (*Heōs an* with the subjunctive is the construction. It indicates the fact of the Lord's coming is certain. Its timing is unknown.[17])

Who will both bring to light the things hidden in the darkness -- "All things are open and laid bare to the eyes of Him with whom we have to do," Hebrews 4:13. If the expression "things hidden in the darkness" is to be distinguished from the next phrase, then it must refer to actions done in the darkness, things we think no one sees.

And disclose the motives of *men's* hearts -- "Motives" ("counsels," ASV) indicates the purposes, designs, and intentions of men that trigger their behavior. "Hearts" refers to men's thoughts. It is axiomatic in Scripture that the Lord knows and searches human hearts.[18] He does not refer to the deeds of the night, or those things which were wrought in secret places of idolatry, but the secret designs of the heart.[19] The apostle here speaks of the reason why judgment should be deferred until the coming of Christ. He alone can bring to light the secret acts and motives of men. Christ's judgment at the second advent will show what the teachers are at heart. Christ's judgment will also show the motives that led the Corinthians to praise one teacher and decry all the others. Two things are necessary to an unerring judgment of human actions: (1) a complete knowledge of the facts, and (2) full insight into the motives. An attempt to judge without these indispensable qualifications is futile arrogance. But Jesus, when He comes, will be perfectly competent to act as judge. Nothing is hidden from Him with whom we have to do. When Jesus judges, He will bring to light things men cannot see and consider when they presume to pass judgment.

And then each man's praise will come to him from God -- God, who sees in secret, will reward openly. Literally, 'each one shall then have his praise (i.e., such praise as he deserves) from God.' "Each man" says that unlike man, who selects only some*one* for praise, God – who alone can judge the worth of any man's work – will give to *every* worker his

---

[17] Morris, *op. cit.*, p.76.

[18] E.g., 1 Samuel 16:7; 1 Chronicles 28:9; Psalm 139:1,11-12; Jeremiah 17:10; Matthew 6:4,6,18; Hebrews 4:12,13.

[19] Barnes, *op. cit.*, p.70.

own proper approval. God will also give the Corinthian church members the praise they deserve.[20] "Praise" (*epainos*) means 'the reward which is due them.' (1) Some take the word in an intermediate sense, involving praise or blame. Every man will receive justice in the judgment of God, who judges fairly and impartially. Each man will be treated as he ought to be. The destiny of no one will be decided by the opinions of men.[21] (2) But Paul says "praise" for two reasons, says Farrar. (a) Partly because he is thinking of faithful teachers like Cephas, Apollos, and himself, who were depreciated by rival factions.[22] (b) Partly because he, like other apostles, shows an invariable tendency to allude to the bright side, rather than the dark side of judgment.[23] The praise "of God" (degree of reward), "Well done, thou good and faithful servant ..." (Matthew 25:21 KJV) is so infinitely precious that it reduces to insignificance the comparative value of human praise or blame.

H. Paul's Stirring Appeal For Unity in the Church at Corinth. 4:6-21

> *Summary:* Paul will drive home three things in this paragraph as he concludes his long section concerning partisan strife and its consequences: (1) Learn from your teachers not to go beyond what is written (verses 6-7). (2) Do not forget the sacrifices the apostles made to bring the Gospel to you (verses 8-13). (3) Understand the three practical steps Paul himself is taking to help them achieve unity (verses 14-21).

4:6 -- *Now these things, brethren, I have figuratively applied to myself and Apollos for your sakes, so that in us you may learn not to exceed what is written, so that no one of you will become arrogant in behalf of one against the other.*

Now these things, brethren -- Many expositors limit "these things" to what has been said since 3:5, but there is no need to. All that has been said since 1:10 concerning dissension can be included in "these things." The context and the emphatic position of "these things" demand a meaning wherein the figures, not the persons, are what have 'changed form' or 'been figuratively applied.' Paul has gone from metaphor to metaphor (i.e., from builders, to under rowers, to stewards, to servants), changing images as he went along, but always intending that at least most of them, as he now says, should be applied to leaders like him-

---

[20] The Scriptures everywhere present Christians as being present and being judged at the final judgment (whether we study the passage that talks about the Judgment Seat of Christ, or the Great White Throne, or the Sheep and Goats). See especially Matthew 16:27; 2 John 8; Hebrews 13:17; Revelation 22:12; James 3:1; Colossians 3:24,25; Romans 14-15; 1 Timothy 3:6 and 5:12.

[21] Barnes, *ibid*.

[22] Paul has not been speaking of those who might be worthy of blame. The subjects of this paragraph are the leaders like Paul, Cephas, and Apollos. Paul never implied by the slightest innuendo that any of these had been guilty of misconduct in the state of affairs at Corinth. However, he has already spoken of other teachers who might suffer loss, or even be destroyed (3:12-17).

[23] Farrar, *op. cit.*, p.133.

self and Apollos. He is now coming toward the conclusion of what he has to say regarding the Corinthians' party divisions.

I have figuratively applied to myself and Apollos -- The use of the verb translated "figuratively applied" or 'transferred' (*meteschēmatisa*) is unique. The word means 'to change the form of,' 'to transform.' It is used of such things as disguising oneself (2 Corinthians 11:15). Here the meaning is that Paul has done something like using a figure of speech (the corresponding noun, *schēma*, is often used of a rhetorical figure). As he has used the different metaphors to describe the function of ministers, he has *not* been addressing his remarks primarily to such preachers, laying down how they should think of themselves and their work. He has *not* been concerned to teach Apollos and himself; they perfectly understood their position in the church. His concern *has been* to teach the Corinthians. Paul has applied the metaphors to himself and Apollos so that his motive in rebuking the schismatic spirit may not be misunderstood, which possibly it might have been had he applied them strongly and directly regarding Cephas and his admirers. All the figures of speech that help the Corinthians correctly evaluate any of their Christian leaders are true of all, though he has spoken from time to time of himself and Apollos in particular. There are two interpretations that have been given to this phrase that to us seem to miss the point of the argument: (1) It has have been used to prove that neither Paul, nor Apollos, nor Peter were the actual men claimed as leaders of parties in Corinth.[24] In the light of 1:12, this commentator believes this interpretation is untenable. Paul's argument has been that there are divisions among the Corinthians. The proof of this? Some call yourselves "Paulites," others "Apollosites," etc. If these are mere designations and not the true party cries, there is little force to his argument. (2) It has been used to show that for reasons of tact, Paul used the names of himself and his beloved co-worker rather than publicly naming the ones responsible for initiating the party bickering into the congregation.[25]

For your sakes -- These metaphors, this whole discussion of the worldly causes of party spirit, have not been particularly for the benefit of teachers like Apollos, but for the benefit of the Corinthian church members.

That in us you might learn -- "In us" means by our example. 'You can learn by having our true office and standing set before you, and by seeing how we regard each other. If you abandon your pride and worldly standards of judging, and embrace the truths I have just written about the leaders and preachers whom God has sent to you, the causes and stain of divisiveness will soon be removed from your midst.'

---

[24] The idea that Paul substituted his and Apollos' names for the actual names of the leaders claimed at Corinth, goes back at least to Chrysostom. Meyer (*op. cit.*, p.92) modified Chrysostom's theory. For a defense of this interpretation, see David R. Hall, "A Disguise for the Wise: METASCHEMATISMOS in 1 Corinthians 4:6," in *New Testament Studies*, vol. 40 (1994), p.143-149.

[25] Our understanding of this verse will have some bearing on the use of 'names' as we preach and teach about error. Shall we name this group or that? Or shall we preach against the error, without actually naming the group who holds the error?

Not to exceed what is written -- The original reads, 'the not above the things which have been written.' An ellipse after the negative particle "not" is a common construction in Greek, and one which must be completed when the thought is rendered into English. Different versions insert different words in order to smooth the ellipse. The KJV has "to think." The ASV has "to go." NASB reads "to exceed." The five words in Greek translated "the not above what is written" have proven troublesome to scholars. Opinions differ greatly when it comes to explaining what Paul may have had in mind. (1) Some recent scholars opt for omitting altogether the five troublesome words from the text. However, the manuscript evidence for this text hardly permits this option. (2) Some think Paul is quoting a proverb or a well-known saying. It was a standard usage to have the neuter article "the" introduce a quotation (cp. 14:16). If this option were embraced, then the words of the proverb would follow the "the" – namely, "Do not go beyond what is written" (cp. NIV). However, such a proverb or saying as "Do not go beyond what is written" has never been found, either in Scripture or in extra-Biblical literature. So many scholars have been slow to embrace this option. (3) Some use the context to attempt a plausible explanation of Paul's meaning. It has been taken to mean something like, 'Keep yourselves to strict evidence,' i.e., say nothing which cannot be proved in black and white. Parry,[26] on the basis of the papyri, argues for the sense, "not to go beyond the terms," i.e., of their commission as teachers – namely, they are "servants, under rowers." (4) Likely, we should take our clue from the words "it is written" (Paul's usual way of citing Scripture[27]) and look for a verse somewhere in Scripture that Paul had in mind. Some suppose it refers generally to the Scriptural principle that requires the children of God to be modest and humble, and ever ascribe glory to God alone (cp. 1:19,21; 3:19). See Deuteronomy 17:20, where the sentiment about not being puffed up is expressed. Some see a reference to Matthew 23:8, "Do not be called Rabbi!" (or parallel references in Matthew 7:1,3 and Mark 10:43,44). Some think there is a reference to what Paul has just written at 1:19,31 and 3:19,20, 4:1.[28] In 3:19ff, and indirectly in 4:4ff, Paul has shown the Corinthians how to keep their thoughts about their teachers within the lines marked out in Scripture. We conclude that Paul is phrasing this admonition in his own words when he urges the Corinthians not to go beyond what all of them know is written in the Scriptures, which urge us in so many ways not to be proud or contentious.[29]

---

[26] Quoted by Morris, *op. cit.*, p.77.

[27] Remember, "It is written," when it appears in the New Testament, refers back to the Old Testament. See notes at 1 Corinthians 2:9.

[28] If we opt for either a reference to Matthew or to what Paul has just written, then "what is written" would imply Matthew's or Paul's writings were as much "Scripture" as any Old Testament passage. Since elsewhere (1 Timothy 5:18) Paul indicates that Luke's writings are Scripture, and Peter (2 Peter 3:16) indicates that Paul's writings were Scripture, we would not reject this possible implication out of hand. On the other hand, if the words following the neuter "the" are the actual quotation, then we cannot refer either to Matthew or to Paul's whole previous argument as we try to identify what is meant by 'that which is written.'

[29] This is one of several verses in the Scriptures which show Christians are to order their lives and service to God by the Scriptures. Avoid what the Scriptures prohibit, and practice what they enjoin.

In order that no one of you might become arrogant in behalf of one against the other -- The thing that is written, which Paul wants the Corinthians to observe in their conduct, is this: no one should use human wisdom or fleshly criteria to exalt one teacher to the disparagement of another.[30] The present tense (*phusiousthe*) points to a course of conduct which the Corinthians are to avoid: they are never at any time to act in this manner.[31] Some commentators picture the prohibition to be against thinking less of your Christian brother because he refuses to choose the same party leader as you do. Other commentators picture the prohibition to be against choosing one or another teacher as their party leader. To cry up a favorite leader of your own choosing is to betray an inflated self-conceit.[32] It must be said again that what Paul teaches is the fact that this exaltation of teachers was really a gratification of their own pride. It was not that they 'puffed up' the teacher; they were puffing up themselves.

4:7 -- *For who regards you as superior? What do you have that you did not receive? And if you did receive it, why do you boast as if you had not received it?*

For -- The *gar* introduces a reason why such "puffing up" is absurd. Even if one possesses some gift or power, he has not attained it by his own excellence or power; rather, it is the free gift of God.[33] Paul asks three very keen questions to puncture the bubble of Corinthian pride. This is done in order to bring these foolish people down to the level of proper Christian humility. With the change to the singular "you" (incidentally, in an emphatic position), Paul addresses an imaginary Corinthian who has become puffed up. He addresses them one-by-one.

Who regards you as superior? ("Who maketh thee to differ?" ASV) – 'Who has separated you from another; who gave you the right to consider yourself superior to others, so that they must look to you and admire you?' "Superior" means to distinguish between the various teachers. 'Who gives you the right to exalt one and debase the other?' is the idea of Paul's question. 'What warrant do you have for boasting, and for arranging yourself in this party or that?' Their glorification and deprecation of rival views and rival teachers in-

---

[30] This comment reflects a decision about the syntax at this place. What is not clear is whether this second *hina*-clause is coordinate with the previous one (and thus dependent on the verb 'transferred,' 'figuratively applied'), or whether it is subordinate to "learn" as an object clause, giving the content of what they should have learned. It is this latter view the notes above reflect.

[31] The very idea of puffing oneself up has a ludicrous touch – that is what a frog does when just before it lets out a "croak." From the size of the "puff up" you'd expect something important and earthshaking! And what do you get? "Ribbit!"

[32] A similar figure of speech from balloons, "filled with hot air," occurs in our language. "Puffed up" is a verb which Paul uses often in this letter (4:18,19; 5:2; 8:1; 13:4), but elsewhere only once. Evidently it was a problem particularly at Corinth; they more than others were addicted to the sin of pride, which is what party spirit actually is.

[33] Shore, *op. cit.*, p.35.

volved a claim to superiority and a right to sit in judgment which they did not possess. This question stigmatizes the partisan conceit at Corinth as presumptuous. The Corinthians would prefer to have better apostles than other Christians had – how they would then boast! But just as Paul and Apollos are not boasting, each one claiming that he is better and higher than the other, so the Corinthians should not imagine that they had an advantage when some of them followed Paul and others followed Apollos.

And what do you have that you did not receive? -- This question stigmatizes the partisan conceit at Corinth as a display of ingratitude. Commentators have differed concerning whom it was from whom the Corinthians had "received." (1) Some say "from me as your father in the faith." But this does not seem to be the proper interpretation. After 3:5-7 and 3:21, Paul would not be likely to make such a claim. (2) Lipscomb says "from the apostles" (*op. cit.*, p.62). (3) "From God" is likely the proper meaning. Whatever talent, or piety, or learning they have obtained, it was a gift from God. Whatever teachers have been sent to them have been a gift from God. "What do you have" is a reference to all the blessings of salvation. Where is the basis of our conceit? God has given us all the talents we have. "Let us grant that you have some superiority (and a right to exalt or debase). Is it inherent? You know you have nothing but what you have received. Your good things were all of them given you."[34]

But if you did receive it, why do you boast as if you had not received it? -- The receiver may boast of the Giver (1:31), but not of anything as his own. By using a third question, Paul here drives home the anticipated answer to his second question (which anticipates the answer, "Nothing!"). Why do you boast as if it were the result of your own toil, skill, or endeavor? Paul is not discouraging human exertion, but rather the spirit of vain-glory and boasting. Whether it be intellect, rank, health, wealth, food, clothing, liberty, peace – all come from God. Even those of us who imagine ourselves to be superior to others have everything as a gift from God. Why boast then about superior attainments? The Corinthians ought to praise and thank God in proper humility, instead of boasting as though what they have is due, not to a gracious gift from God, but to some superiority in themselves. It is certainly reprehensible to receive something and then to act as though one had not received it. Since they received everything as a gift, their boasting (as if their blessings were not gifts) is the height of ingratitude!

4:8 -- *You are already filled, you have already become rich, you have become kings without us; and would indeed that you had become kings so that we also might reign with you.*

You are already filled -- It is generally agreed that this is spoken in irony and sarcasm, as an attack on the self-esteem of his readers. They need rebuke beyond the three questions

---

[34] Robertson and Plummer, *op. cit.*, p.82.

(verse 7) which Paul asked, intending to puncture their bubble of pride. In his appeal for unity in the congregation, he has called attention to what was written, and insists they make that their guide. Now he is going to launch into a rehearsal of the sacrifices the apostles made to bring the gospel to them, lest forgetfulness of such sacrifices continues to leave room for inordinate pride. This rehearsal will cover verses 8-13. The verb "filled" (*kekoresmenoi este*) is used regularly of food (e.g., Acts 27:38). It denotes satiation, a feeling of satisfaction. 'You think you have enough. You are satisfied with your conviction of your own knowledge, and do not feel you need anything more. You behave as if the final judgment were past, and the goal gained; as if heaven were already begun.' It reminds us of Revelation 3:17, "You say, 'I am rich, and have become wealthy, and have need of nothing;' and you do not know that you are wretched, and miserable, and poor, and blind, and naked." The Corinthians think of themselves as perfected saints; their teachers are still very far indeed from any such perfection. There is emphasis on the word "already" in these phrases. 'You Corinthians – unlike us apostles – are already full, rich, kings,' is the idea.

You have already become rich -- 'You esteem yourselves to be rich in spiritual gifts, and graces, so that you do not feel the necessity of any more.' These type of phrases would be used with Messianic blessings (cf. Luke 22:29,30; 1 Thessalonians 2:12; 2 Timothy 2:12).

You have become kings without us -- The Scriptures seem to hold out the idea that in Heaven the redeemed will reign with Christ.[35] Paul ironically speaks of the Corinthians as having already arrived at that place. 'We poor apostles have become quite needless to you in your lordly independence and kingly position.' The Corinthians were "reigning" already – lording it over the other parties and individuals. It seems obvious that the three verbs (filled, become rich, become kings) form a climax, and the last gives the key to the allusion. These highly blessed Corinthians act as if they are already in the eternal kingdom of God, enjoying its banquets, its treasures, and its thrones. Full satiety, riches, and honor are blessings promised in the coming age to the redeemed. Do the Corinthians really think they are already in the great kingdom to come? "Without us" might mean without our counsel and instruction. 'You have taken the whole management of matters on yourselves without any regard to our advice or authority. You did not feel your need of our aid, and you did not regard our authority. You supposed you could get along as well without us as with us.' "Without us" might instead mean without our company. Paul is aware that he is not yet in heaven. If the Corinthians are, they got there before the apostles did!

And would indeed that you had become kings so that we also might reign with you -- The KJV reads "would to God" but the "to God" should be omitted. "Would to God" is too strong a rendering for *ophelon*. In later Greek, this verb simply expresses a wish. In

---

[35] See notes at Revelation 2:26ff and 21:24. The reigning with Christ in those verses seems to occur during the intermediate state.

the construction employed here, it is implied that the wish has not been fulfilled. 'Would that you did reign (though in fact you do not)' is the sense. The loving heart of Paul could never long keep up a strain of irony.[36] He drops the satire and passes on to impassioned and affectionate appeal. 'I wish that you had made such advances that you could be represented as full, and as rich, and as princes, needing nothing, that when I come I might have nothing to do but to partake of your joy.' Paul wishes for them that they should live in such a way that they should come to the consummation of the Messianic blessings. 'As far as my feelings are concerned, would that your imaginary royalty were real, for then our hard lot would be at an end.' The Corinthians are staging such a pitiful sham that Paul wishes they had the reality, that indeed they already reigned.

4:9 -- *For, I think, God has exhibited us apostles last of all, as men condemned to death; because we have become a spectacle to the world, both to angels and to men.*

For, I think -- "For" introduces the reason Paul expresses his devout wish that this life were over, and that he were reigning with Christ in the home of the blessed. 'It seems to me,' we would say. Paul states as opinion what is in truth an astounding fact – namely, the pitiful condition of the apostles. Some take this as still part of the irony, and believe Paul is saying, 'It seems then that God has designed that we, the apostles, should be subject to contempt and suffering, and be made poor and persecuted, while you are admitted to high honors and privileges. You seem to have arrived at the goal far in front of us poor teachers.' But it is better to take this as a simple yet serious declaration: 'There is abundant reason for wishing that both of us did now live in heaven – for we are in our present state afflicted ....' Verse 9 introduces the reason he may well express the devout wish which he has just uttered for the coming of the kingdom of his Lord.

God has exhibited us apostles last of all -- "Exhibited" (*apedeixen*) means to display as on a stage, or in an amphitheater, to place in public view before the eyes of the world. Paul used the plural "us apostles" to avoid claiming the position of hardship and suffering for himself alone. Some suppose "last of all"[37] is a reference to the lowest condition, the humblest estate. So it would be if the passage is ironical.[38] Instead, we believe Paul is alluding to the custom of bringing forth into the amphitheater at the conclusion of the spec-

---

[36] Some see the irony continued; his wish is pictured as being that they might give him some share in their kingdom. Some interpret this as if Paul had ironically expressed a wish that they were literal princes, that they might afford protection to him in his persecution and troubles. But it is better to take this as an earnest appeal.

[37] The ASV margin reads "the last apostles." If it be rendered this way, we have another passage that harmonizes with the idea that the function of an apostle of Christ was a temporary office in the early church, and by Paul's time the apostolic college had come to its last enrollees. If Paul does refer to the fact that he was the last of Jesus' apostles, the implication is, 'What will the Corinthians do for human leaders in the next generation when he and the other apostles are all dead?'

[38] So Farrar, Kling, Lange, Evans, Alford, and Barnes interpret. Lipscomb, on page 63, says, "The apostles are set forth as the lowest in the world. They fared worse than even the prophets, who, though grievously afflicted and tormented, were sometimes honored."

tacles those who were to fight with other men, and who had no chance of escape. They had to fight until they should die. George Mark Elliott saw a figurative picture of gladiators coming out into the amphitheater. This is the Grand Finale.

As men condemned to death -- 'Devoted to death' (*epithanatious*) is a rare word, and apparently refers to condemned criminals. Such were often paraded before the public gaze to be objects of derision. Tertullian explained it, "like criminals condemned to the wild beasts." The Corinthians in their blatant pride were like a conquering general who in the triumphal parade displayed the trophies of his prowess; the apostles were like the criminals at the end of the parade, on their way to the arena, doomed to die there, while the populace would be regaled with their sufferings. "This is a very strong expression, and denotes the continuance, the constancy, and the intensity of their sufferings for Christ."[39] "It implies that such were their continued conflicts, trials, and persecutions that it was certain that they would terminate in their death."[40]

Because we have become a spectacle -- The Greek is *theatron*, 'a theatre, what one sees at a theatre.' Here we have the same metaphor as Hebrews 10:33. Paul is here explaining more fully what he meant by 'exhibited.' The place of seeing easily comes to be substituted for what is seen there. The theatre (amphitheatre) of the ancients was composed of an arena, or level floor, on which the combatants fought, and which was surrounded by circular seats rising above one another to a great height, and capable of containing many thousand spectators. Paul represents himself as on this arena or stage, contending with foes, and destined to death. Around him and above him are an immense host of men and angels, looking on at the conflict and awaiting the issue. (Compare Hebrews 12:1,2, where the "great cloud of witnesses" may be pictured as spectators watching the struggle.)

To the world – 'The intelligent universe' is the idea in "world" (*kosmos*). The rest of the verse shows that angels and men make up the "world" to which the apostles are a spectacle.

Both to angels and to men -- These are the spectators, the "world" just spoken about. Which angels does Paul include among the spectators of the sufferings of the apostles? Some say only good angels and men are in Paul's mind. It is perhaps true to say that wherever angels are mentioned in the New Testament, good angels are always meant unless something is added in the context to intimate the contrary (Matthew 25:41; 2 Corinthians 12:7; Revelation 12:7,9). Some say good and bad alike watching. Robertson and Plummer (*op. cit.*, p.86) note that Atto of Vercelli supposes Paul means evil angels only.

4:10 – *We are fools for Christ's sake, but you are prudent in Christ; we are weak, but you are strong; you are distinguished, but we are without honor.*

We are fools for Christ's sake -- Again, Paul expresses irony: 'How different our lot from

---

[39] Barnes, *op. cit.*, p.74.

[40] Lipscomb, *op. cit.*, p.63.

yours. How you are to be envied – we, to be pitied!' "We are doubtless foolish men, but ye are wise in Christ. We apostles are to be regarded as fools, unworthy of confidence, and unfit to instruct; but you are full of wisdom."[41] Paul makes a series of contrasts between the proud Corinthians and the "dishonored" apostles – all from the warped viewpoint of the Corinthians, and all are withering blows to the proud Corinthians. The three contrasts refer respectively to teaching (wisdom), demeanor (power), and worldly position (honor). The apostles are "fools" in the eyes of the Corinthians because they didn't court and display the 'wisdom of this age' as they preached the gospel. Paul might have become as celebrated as Gamaliel had he gone along with worldly wisdom, but for Christ's sake he consented to pass as a fool. Behind the bitter irony is a feeling of deep hurt that some of the Corinthians should think so poorly of him and his fellow workers.

But you are prudent in Christ -- 'You are so proud of your attainments that you boast yourselves to be prudent. We apostles, on the other hand, who founded your church, are regarded as fools, and as unworthy of public confidence or esteem.' The design of the whole is to show the folly of their boasted wisdom. Paul's word for "prudent" ("wise," ASV) is different from that used up till now in this epistle. The word he now employs (*phronimos*) means 'a man of sense,' no fanatic, not rushing to extremes. The use of this word may be a means of putting a slightly different face on the Corinthians' behavior than the worldly wisdom which he has castigated earlier. In their proud self-satisfaction, they thought they already had treasures of wisdom. They had no need to rush to learn more from such as an apostle of Christ!

We are weak, but you are strong -- This second contrast refers to conduct or demeanor. Ironically, Paul puts it, 'We apostles are timid and feeble, but you are daring, bold, strong.' Paul has already indicated that when he came to Corinth, it was with "weakness and fear and much trembling" (1 Corinthians 2:3). Some see in the word "weak" a reference to Paul's own personal physical condition (2 Corinthians 10:10; 13:4). How different were the Corinthians from the apostles. The proud Corinthians would not admit to any weakness. As to conduct, they came before the public with the feeling of their strength. There is in them neither hesitation nor timidity. In their unholy self-estimation of themselves and their particular clique, there was no room for anything but putting on lordly airs. Paul's irony indicates the behavior of the Corinthians was anything but laudable.

You are distinguished, but we are without honor -- 'You are in glorious repute, party leaders and party men, highly honored and looked up to – whereas we apostles are disenfranchised, without honor, deprived of even common human respect, men who can be spoken of and treated with the lowest contempt.' "Distinguished" is *endoxoi*, enveloped in glory, already crowned, as it were, with a halo on your heads. "Without honor" is *atimoi*, a word often used of those deprived of citizenship. Paul is still trying to show the Corinthians how foolish was their self-confidence and self-flattery, and their attempt to exalt themselves by arranging themselves under various leaders.

---

[41] Barnes, *op. cit.*, p.75.

4:11 -- *To this present hour we are both hungry and thirsty, and are poorly clothed, and are roughly treated, and are homeless;*

To this present hour -- Paul here drops the irony and begins a serious recapitulation of the actual sufferings and trials experienced by apostles of Christ. Verses 11-13 show how intensely true is the word "dishonor" in the lives of the apostles. It is not only the condition Paul's life that is here pictured; it is true of the other apostles as well. "To this present hour" is a contrast to the imagined triumphs and bliss already enjoyed by the Corinthians. They may think themselves as reigning in heaven, but not the apostles. They were very much still in the midst of trouble. To set the record straight, Paul will describe in detail some of the hardships he and his fellow apostles suffered during their ministry. There were physical deprivations and abuse both physical and verbal.

We are both hungry and thirsty, and are poorly clothed -- "Hungry and thirsty" says the apostles, like their Master, were poor. As they traveled from place to place, it often happened that they scarcely found sustenance, nor had they money to purchase it. It is no dishonor to be poor, especially if that poverty is produced by doing good for others. Paul might have been rich, but he chose to be poor for the sake of the gospel. "Poorly clothed" ("in rags," NIV) speaks of lacking sufficient clothing (2 Corinthians 11:27). While traveling on various mission trips, the apostles' clothes become old and worn out, and they had no friends to replace them, and no money to purchase new. It is no discredit to be clad poorly if it is produced by self-denying toils on behalf of others. Paul was not ashamed to travel, to preach, and to appear before princes and kings in a soiled and worn out garment, for it was worn out in the service of the Master.[42]

And are roughly treated ("buffeted," ASV) -- The word *kolaphidzometha* means 'to strike with the fist' (2 Corinthians 12:7; Acts 23:2). The word speaks of physical violence and abuse. Perhaps harsh and injurious treatment in general is meant. The word was used for "beating a slave."[43] The apostles were treated like slaves, not like kings. For Christ's sake they submitted to being roughly treated.

And are homeless -- 'Vagrants' are always held in suspicion by the public. Apostles, like their Master, had no fixed or permanent home. They traveled to distant lands and threw themselves on the hospitality of strangers. They were driven from one place to another. Homelessness is one of the severest of all trials (Matthew 8:20, 10:23). Instead of being welcomed as they came to a new town, they were often met with hostility.

4:12 -- *and we toil, working with our own hands; when we are reviled, we bless; when we are persecuted, we endure;*

And we toil, working with our own hands -- This Paul often did (Acts 18:3, 20:34; 1

---

[42] How many professed Christians are ashamed to go to the house of God because they cannot dress well, or be in fashion, or outshine their neighbors?

[43] Plutarch tells how a man gave evidence that a slave belonged to another man, because he had seen that man beating the slave, and "beating" is *kolaphizesthai*.

Thessalonians 2:9; 2 Thessalonians 3:8). The word for "toil" is *kopiōmen*, which signifies extremely hard work, labor to the point of weariness. The same word was explained at 1 Corinthians 3:8. Paul supported himself by the dreary toil and scant earnings of a tentmaker while at Ephesus, the city from which this letter to Corinth was written -- and not only at Ephesus, but elsewhere. Such conduct was all the more noble because mechanical trades were looked down upon by the Greeks as a sort of low occupation. It was a disgrace to have to work in manual labor, according to Greek notions. Labor was fit only for slaves. It was most repellent to work all day long with the strong-scented black goat's hair used to make tents. Yet Paul did this to support not only himself, but his fellow missionaries (Acts 20:34). Paul seems to be speaking out of a disappointed and broken heart. Why should Paul endure all these privations for the sake of such thankless people as the Corinthians?

When we are reviled, we bless -- If we, today, are reviled, or persecuted, or defamed, we are tempted to get even by doing the same to our tormenters. But like Paul, we should do the opposite. Did Paul and the others allow these sufferings to affect them? Yes, but rather than stoop to seek revenge, they tried to use the opportunities to rise to greater heights of Christ-like spirit. In verses 12b and 13 we have the apostles' response to the ill-treatment they received. These men had learned the lesson Jesus taught (Luke 6:28, 23:34). The series of participles beginning here are all present tense, denoting habitual treatment and habitual response. "Reviled" means to be reproached, ridiculed, made fun of as followers of a foolish superstition, falsely accused of the most abominable crimes. "Bless" (*eulogeō*) means to 'speak a good word' for them, to offer a benediction. We return good for evil, following the directions of the Savior (Matthew 5:44). So little do the apostles resemble the proud Corinthians that they do not meet reviling by hurling back at their enemies their own wicked allegations; rather, they reply with the Christian meekness ordered by the Lord, "Bless those who curse you" (Luke 6:28).

When we are persecuted, we endure -- "Persecuted" (*diōkomenoi*) pictures being constantly pursued with persistent and active hostility. During this early portion of Paul's ministry, the persecutions would be the Jewish outbreaks of violence he suffered almost from city to city (as the record in Acts shows). To "endure" (*anechometha*) is to refrain from resistance or retaliation; the apostles let the mistreatment pass. Is this pacifism? No! Biblically, we do have the right to defend ourselves. But we do not have the right to be the aggressor.

4:13 -- *when we are slandered, we try to conciliate; we have become as the scum of the world, the dregs of all things,* **even** *until now.*

When we are slandered, we try to conciliate -- *Dusphēmoumenoi* means 'defamed, blasphemed, spoken of, and to, in a harsh, abusive, and reproachful manner.'[44] Perhaps "we try to conciliate" ("we entreat," ASV) means 'we entreat God on their behalf, praying Him to forgive them.' Perhaps it means 'We entreat them to turn from their sins, and become converted to God. We exhort them to save their souls by embracing the gospel

---

[44] Compare this word's use in 1 Maccabees 7:41.

instead of destroying themselves by rejecting it with contempt and scorn.' Perhaps it means, "We answer with mild and soothing words."⁴⁵ "The spirit of Paul was grand not to give them a piece of his mind," said George Mark Elliott.

We have become as the scum of the world -- "We have become" means this is how we are regarded or esteemed. The word "scum" (*perikatharmata,* "filth," ASV) has a technical sense, in which it means 'men devoted to death for purposes of expiation.' Compare the LXX at Proverbs 21:18, the only other place the word appears in the Greek Bible. Some exegetes attempt to use this technical meaning here. Wicked men and men of ignoble rank were sometimes kept as punishment for their offenses to be offered to the gods in time of pestilence to appease the anger of the gods. It cannot be proved that this practice was carried on in the apostles' time. It is doubtful such is the meaning of the word here.⁴⁶ The word also means 'filth,' or 'trash,' that which is collected by sweeping a house, or that which is collected and cast away by purifying or cleansing anything – hence, vile, worthless, and contemptible. "Of the world" says they were regarded as the most vile and worthless men which the whole world could furnish.

The dregs of all things, *even* until now -- "Dregs" (*peripsēma,* "offscouring," ASV) do not differ materially from "scum." This word denotes that which is rubbed off by scouring or cleansing anything, and hence vile or worthless. The term was also applied to vile and worthless men who were thrown into the sea as a sacrifice to the god Neptune. 'Look at us apostles,' says Paul. 'We're not rival idols. Look at us as servants and stewards of Christ, who pay dearly for the privilege of being servants and stewards.' Paul has reached the limits. Beyond these debasing terms even he cannot go. The Corinthians should be humbled and rebuked out of their pride when they compare their imagined inflated status with the real condition of God's true servants.

4:14 -- *I do not write these things to shame you, but to admonish you as my beloved children.*

I do not write these things to shame you -- Paul is coming to the conclusion of this appeal to be done with party strife. He now informs them about the three practical things he is doing to help them make the needed corrections. (1) He explains in what spirit he was writing this letter (verses 14-16). (2) He was to send Timothy to remind them of his ways of teaching (verse 17). (3) He was coming to Corinth himself, either to punish or to comfort, as the case might require (verses 18-21).

"These things" are the descriptions of the apostles' suffering (verses 8-13), and by comparison those descriptions show the Corinthians how little they were suffering. Paul's letters are real letters, not systematic theological treatises. They not infrequently contain the abrupt changes of tone and mood (as here) characteristic of letters. The apostle's sternness gives way to tenderness. "Shame" (*entrepōn*) means 'to cast down, to shatter, to shame.' Paul wants more of a response from them than a feeling of shame. 'I'm not in-

---

⁴⁵ Alford, *op. cit.*, p.502.

⁴⁶ The two genitives ["of the world" and "of all things"] cannot mean that the world and all men offer the apostles as sacrifices in order to ward off some calamities from themselves.

terested in simply making you feel ashamed, so as to appear that I have triumphed over you,' says Paul. The Corinthians may indeed feel ashamed under the lash of Paul's irony; they certainly have reason to feel thusly. Paul is, however, engaged in something far more important than merely making them feel ashamed. He goes on to say that he is offering them Christian admonition. Shame touches only the feelings; admonition reaches the heart.

But to admonish you -- *Nouthetōn* means 'to bring to mind, to warn, to admonish, to give counsel.' Ephesians 6:4 shows this to be one duty of a parent. Paul was writing in the same tone as a father would give warning instruction to his children. A father may use severe tones, but the severity is intended to bring back a child who has gone astray before greater harm comes to the child. Admonition corrects while not provoking or embittering the one being corrected. Superficially regarded, Paul's ironical expressions might sound like disciplinary castigation; understood in the proper way, they are full of appeals to the mind, full of meaning to reach the heart with earnest warning. The irony and reproach of the preceding verses here ceases, and the writer now turns to make a tender and touching appeal to their better nature and their sympathy. This abrupt and sudden change in style is characteristic of the writings of Paul, but are not often paralleled in the writings of the other apostles.

As my beloved children -- The church members at Corinth were like dear children to Paul. 'I speak as a father to his children whom he loves dearly, and I say these things for your own good.' He was their spiritual father, as verse 15 will remind them, and the things written were not written in a sour or morose or angry or bitter manner, but in a kind, tender, and affectionate manner. Here and in the following verse, Paul explicitly denies that his sharp words emanate from an unfatherly spirit or are lacking love (as is sometimes asserted). This language gives us a picture of Paul's attitude. His converts were not just "scalps hung on a belt"; they are beloved children.

4:15 -- *For if you were to have countless tutors in Christ, yet* **you** *would* **not** *have* **many** *fathers, for in Christ Jesus I became your father through the gospel.*

For -- Verse 15 is a justification of the expression "my beloved children." He has a right to address them as a father would his children.

If you were to have countless tutors in Christ -- "Countless" is literally "ten thousand" (*murious*) in the Greek; it is a hyperbole for the greatest possible number (cp. 14:19). It implies an indefinitely large number. Some see a sly reference to the false teachers at Corinth – as if Paul were saying, 'You've already had too many teachers.' This commentator, however, is not sure this idea can be drawn from the language. For the word translated 'tutor' or 'pedagogue' (*paidagōgous*, which also occurs in Galatians 3:24,25) we have no exact English equivalent. This word, among the Greeks, designated those 'slave-guides' employed to look after and train little children. They conducted the child to school and superintended his conduct during out-of-school hours. They looked after food and dress, speech and manners. Such a tutor might be more capable, and even more affectionate, than the father of the child, but he could never be the father. He looked after the child on behalf of the father. Paul applies this term to the teachers who followed him to Corinth (3:10ff), but without any negative implications (since a bad implication would not fit the likes of Apollos or Peter). "In Christ" likely means 'in the Christian system or doctrine.'

Yet *you would* not *have* many fathers -- The authority which Paul claims here is that which a *father* has in preference to a tutor or an instructor. Notice the figures which Paul has used of his relationship to the Corinthian church. Paul is the founder; his successors are the after-builders. Paul is the planter; they the waterers or gardeners. He is the father; they are the tutors. In days to come, the Corinthians might have many tutors and teachers, but none of them can do what Paul did for them – none of them can be the one who led them to Christ.[47] The Corinthians had but one spiritual father – Paul the apostle. He felt a yearning desire that his unique claim as the one who started ('fathered') the congregation in Corinth should not be so ungratefully overlooked, as though it were of no importance (cp. 3:6, 9:1,2; Acts 18:11). There is a sense in which we Christians are forbidden to call men our "father" (Matthew 23:9). What Jesus prohibited is not so much the titles themselves (cp. 1 Corinthians 4:15) as the spirit of pride and ambition which covets and abuses them, the haughty spirit which would domineer over inferiors and also the servile spirit which would basely cringe to superiors.[48] Spiritual paternity carries with it a high authority, a holy right to discipline, to rebuke, to exhort, to purify, with severity or mildness or both as circumstances may demand. Because the Corinthians were his own children, Paul is free to speak to them with sharp and stinging words; if they were strangers, his words might be resented.

For in Christ Jesus I became your father through the gospel -- "In Christ Jesus" may mean 'by the authority of Christ,' or it may mean 'in the realm of your Christian religion.'

---

[47] In the Greek, the construction is not a contrary-to-fact condition, as the wording in the NASB (note the words added in italics) makes it appear to be. It is a simple statement of a true fact.

[48] In the long struggle to defend the doctrine of the priesthood of all believers, as over against a special clergy, it has been an oft-heard appeal in the Restoration Movement, "Please Don't Call Me Reverend!" Perhaps the standard arguments should be revisited. "Reverend" harks back to a differentiation between clergy and laity, where a distinction is being made which is not in the New Testament. In the New Testament, we are all priests. A tract titled, "Please Don't Call Me Reverend!" made the argument that "the word 'reverend' is used only once in the Bible, and then it is used only of God." But this is not quite correct. It is true that in the KJV, the English word "reverend" appears only once, and that one time it is used of God. And He is the one to be "feared" above all others. However, the same Hebrew and Greek words translated "reverend" that one time occur many times, and are regularly translated "fear." Both men and God, and even inanimate things, are to be "feared." The Hebrew is *yareh*; the LXX translation of the same word is *phobiomai*. These words mean "fear, reverence, to be afraid." Some of the verses where these words appear are Psalm 89:7, 111:9, 139:14; Exodus 15:11; Deuteronomy 1:19, 8:15; Judges 13:6; Isaiah 18:2, 7, 21:1; Ezekiel 1:22; Leviticus 19:30, 26:2; Acts 9:26; Ephesians 5:33, and perhaps a hundred more references. Cf. Young's *Analytical Concordance to the Bible*. If the argument used in the tract is carried to its logical conclusion, we have no right to call Christians "holy." What names shall we use then? One of the mottoes of the Restoration Movement is "Call Bible things by Bible names." For Christians, saints, brethren, etc. are the Bible names. Ministers, preachers, evangelists, elders, etc. are the Bible names for church leaders.

The "I" in "I became your father"[49] is emphatic in the Greek. 'I alone' am your "father." 'I, and no other.' Paul had become these people's spiritual father by means of the gospel, by preaching it to them. The doctrine of the new birth was enunciated by Jesus during his conversation with Nicodemus (John 3:1-15). Jesus insisted that, in order to have a part in the Kingdom of God, men must be born of both the water and the spirit (John 3:5). Jesus explained that one is begotten by hearing the Word (John 3:8): "The Spirit breathes where He wills (inspires men, who then speak), and you hear His voice. In this way men are begotten (become believers)."[50] On another occasion, Jesus spoke of people who would become believers through the gospel the apostles preached (John 17:20). The Corinthians came to be believers in Jesus because Paul was the first to preach the gospel to them.[51] The seed being planted (as in the Parable of the Sower), the begetting of the spirit (John 3), and hearing the word (begetting by the gospel, 1 Corinthians 4:15) all speak of the same thing.

4:16 -- *Therefore I exhort you, be imitators of me.*

Therefore I exhort you -- "Therefore" equals 'since I am your spiritual father.' Since Paul can rightfully claim to be the first one to bring them the Gospel, as their spiritual father he feels he can also ask them to become imitators of him.

Be imitators of me -- Paul is not setting himself up as the perfect example, but asks the congregation to follow him as he imitates Christ.[52] 'Imitate me, copy my example, listen to my admonitions.' The word *mimētai* – from which we get the word "mimic" – is an apt description of how little children copy the actions and attitudes of their mothers and fathers. It is a present tense verb; it asks for continuous action. Right thinking is not enough. The gospel must result in appropriate behavior as well. In what particular should they be imitators of Paul? 'Be done with religious partisanship!' is the thrust of this context. 'You didn't hear from me, as I preached the gospel, that such behavior is acceptable with Jesus. The exact opposite. Return to the way of life in Jesus Christ which I always taught you!

---

[49] The NASB's "I became your father" is a rather free rendering of the Greek, and may be theologically incorrect. The Greek says simply "I begat you" ("I conceived you"). A man who believes Jesus is the Christ has been "begotten" (1 John 5:1 ASV). Faith (belief) comes by hearing the Gospel (Romans 10:17). Paul was the one who first preached the gospel among the Corinthians.

[50] Author's translation. See John 3:8 explained in detail in the author's notes on Gospels, and in his commentary on Acts, in the Special Study about the Holy Spirit's work in conversion. It is noted that, with one or two exceptions [1 in the KJV, 2 in the ASV], the Greek word *pneuma* is translated "spirit" or "Spirit" in our English Bibles. We see no reason why John 3:8 should be an exception. Translate it "Spirit" and Jesus' words to Nicodemus match what the New Testament says elsewhere (Romans 10:17; James 1:18; 1 Peter 1:23; 1 John 5:1) concerning how men come to believe.

[51] This passage thus is one of many that undermines the theory of miraculous conversion (prevenient grace and efficacious grace, where man is wholly passive and God does all the "work" to convert people).

[52] Compare 1 Corinthians 11:1; Galatians 4:12; Philippians 3:17; 1 Thessalonians 1:6; 2 Thessalonians 3:9.

Translate into your own lives what you have heard from me.'[53] "He had no disposition to form parties and sects, and entreats them in this to imitate his example.[54]

4:17 -- *For this reason I have sent to you Timothy, who is my beloved and faithful child in the Lord, and he will remind you of my ways which are in Christ, just as I teach everywhere in every church.*

For this reason -- As verse 17 explains, the second practical step Paul had taken to help the Corinthians correct their prideful divisiveness was to send Timothy to work and teach among them. At that moment in time Paul apparently was hindered from coming himself, so he sent his fellow-laborer as his messenger to them, in order that Timothy might do what Paul would do if he were with them. 'Since I, as a father, must insist on your imitating my example, I have sent to you Timothy ... and he will remind you of my ways which are in Christ.'

I have sent to you Timothy -- As explained in the Introductory Studies, Paul came to Ephesus at the beginning of his third missionary journey (Acts 19). This letter we call "1 Corinthians" was written from Ephesus. Timothy had started on a tour of churches before this letter was written (see 1 Corinthians 16:10 and Acts 19:22), and was to arrive in Corinth after this letter had been delivered there.[55] The instructions which Paul had given Timothy were general and not specific. He tells the Corinthians that Timothy can remind them of the truths which Paul taught constantly and everywhere so they, too, might adhere to them more closely.

Who is my beloved and faithful child in the Lord -- Meyer remarks that by the use of this word "child" (*teknon*, cp. 1 Timothy 1:2,18; 2 Timothy 1:2; and not "son"), we have

---

[53] That Paul wrote "be imitators of me!" rather than "be imitators of Jesus!" has been the source of much peculiar theology. Bultmann used this verse to prove that for all intents and purposes, the teaching of Jesus was irrelevant to Paul, and thus we too may treat it as irrelevant. But the historical evidence is against such speculation. Paul did not ignore what Jesus taught as he went about preaching the gospel. Paul did not shape Christianity into something totally different from what Jesus would have made of it. Don't forget that Paul specifies in 11:1 that they are to follow him as he follows Christ!

[54] Barnes, *op. cit.*, p.78.

[55] The comments treat "I have sent" as an example of what is called an 'historical aorist' – Timothy was sent before the letter was written. M.C. Tenney believed that "sent" is an 'epistolary aorist,' and that Timothy was actually carrying 1 Corinthians to Corinth. That Timothy was the courier is hard to square with 16:10, in this commentator's opinion. See more information about the constructions called 'historical' and 'epistolary aorists' in the Introductory Studies and in the comments at 1 Corinthians 5:9. It may be helpful to review what is said in the Introductory Studies about Timothy's travels as he and Erastus visited the churches at Paul's behest (Acts 19:22). Timothy did not reach Corinth until after this letter did, for he went by land through Macedonia, while the letter was delivered more quickly by someone crossing the sea from Ephesus to Corinth. We reconstruct the events on this supposition, that Timothy did arrive at Corinth, worked hard to correct the errors (especially the problem of immorality), but his efforts were rejected. So he journeyed on to Ephesus and reported to Paul. Paul thereupon himself made a hurried trip to Corinth, but he also failed to win the Corinthians to repentance. Upon Paul's return to Ephesus, Titus was sent to Corinth, and eventually under his encouragement and direction the Corinthians began to straighten out the problems that beset their congregation.

certain proof that Timothy was converted by Paul.[56] The events leading to Timothy's conversion can be reconstructed on this fashion: (1) During the first missionary journey, when Paul was at Lystra, the Jews instigated a persecution that resulted in Paul's being stoned (Acts 14:8,19-20). After a miraculous recovery, Paul continued on to evangelize other towns before the first journey ended. (2) Paul came back to Lystra on the second missionary journey, and we find Timothy living there, already a Christian (Acts 16:1). (3) We may assume that when Paul rose up (Acts 14:20) after the stoning, that one of the first people he saw was Timothy, standing over him (2 Timothy 1:4, "tears"). He was taken home by Timothy, who cleansed his wounds. Paul was allowed to refresh himself (and recover, if necessary) at Timothy's house. (4) If this attempted reconstruction is on target, we may conclude that Timothy then was converted on Paul's first missionary journey. "*Faithful* child in the Lord" means that Paul recognizes that Timothy is a true Christian, a faithful servant of Christ, and one who faithfully imitated and embodied what his spiritual father taught. The praise bestowed on Timothy appears also to have the incidental purpose of impressing upon the Corinthians, in a tender manner, the kind of conduct which they owed to their spiritual fathers.

And he will remind you of my ways which are in Christ -- The expression shows all of Paul's tact. He is not sending Timothy, who is a young man (he was about 30 years of age now[57]), as an authoritative teacher since the Corinthians, fond of high pretension and soaring oratory, might scorn to show any submission to someone so young. Paul is only sending him because, as Paul's closest companion, Timothy would be best able to explain to them his plans and wishes (i.e., the Lord's plans and wishes) for the organization and congregational life of the churches. Paul sweetly says he will "remind you." They had forgotten much of what Paul had taught them in person. "Remind you" is a very delicate touch. Paul does not accuse them of deliberate rebellion. He simply implies that they must have forgotten.[58] "My ways" speaks of 'my doctrine, my teaching, my mode of life.' The real apostle had been superseded in their imagination by an imaginary Paul, the leader of a party. Timothy, by being himself a close imitator of the Christian virtues and teaching of his and their spiritual father, would bring to their minds Paul's well-known character and way of teaching, which they seemed to have well-nigh forgotten (2 Timothy 3:10).[59] Paul's "ways" have been clearly indicated in 1:17, 2:1-5, 4:11-13, 9:15,22,27. Of course, they are not just Paul's ways; they are the ways the Lord has marked out for His followers

---

[56] Meyer, *op. cit.*, p.103.

[57] Several factors are taken into account in figuring Timothy's age. We suppose he was about 17 when he was converted during Paul's first missionary journey (AD 45 or 46). When Paul writes 1 Corinthians, it is some thirteen years later (about AD 57). In fact, when 1 Timothy is written (about AD 66), according to 1 Timothy 4:12, Timothy is still a "young man" (i.e., under 40 years of age). So at the time 1 Corinthians was written, he was about 30.

[58] Forgetting is so true of human nature, and it is not always deliberate. See how the Lord's Supper is needed regularly to help us remember.

[59] One writer calls Timothy's job as being a sort of director of Christian education.

to live.⁶⁰ The reason behind the instructions Timothy will give them is the fact that only right doctrine will produce right conduct.

Just as I teach everywhere in every church -- To show them the importance of his manner of teaching, he reminds them of his unvarying practice of it; Paul teaches the same divinely prescribed ways everywhere. Paul was not expecting something from the Corinthians that no other congregation was ever asked to do. This was designed to show them that he taught them no new or peculiar doctrines; rather, he wished them simply to conform to the common rules of the churches, and to be like Christian brethren everywhere. The Christian church is founded everywhere on the same doctrines; she is bound to obey the same laws; she is fitted to produce and cherish the same spirit.⁶¹ No more was required of them than is required of other Christians. The reference to this uniformity of his conduct was intended to strengthen the motive for their imitating him. Did they really wish to be peculiarly different from all other churches of Christ?

4:18 -- *Now some have become arrogant, as though I were not coming to you.*

Now some have become arrogant, as though I were not coming to you -- In the remainder of this chapter, Paul announces a third practical step he intends to take to help end the dissension and party spirit at Corinth. Who the "some" were, the Corinthians of course knew, for they had heard them talk. We can only surmise who they were. Perhaps the "some" were outside agitators who have infiltrated the congregation and stirred up the dissension. There have been other implications of the assertions of "false teachers" who have infiltrated the congregation at Corinth. (See notes at 1:12, 1:17, 2:11, 2:14, 3:1, 3:10.) Indeed, this third step may be intended as an attack on those ringleaders. Perhaps the "some" were members from within the church who, without any outside agitation, have on the basis of human wisdom and popular philosophy chosen sides and favorite leaders. If so, Paul's coming visit will be a challenge to them if they have not repented in the meantime. We've had the word "arrogant" at verse 6. Several views are plausible concerning Paul's next visit to Corinth. Perhaps Paul had communicated with them that he was going to come, only to have that coming delayed; then some used this delay against Paul, assuming (for whatever reason they wished to attribute to his behavior) that he really was not going to come. Perhaps it has been so long since Paul last visited Corinth, they were saying he was not coming back at all. After all, he did do so poorly among them the first time, it would be better not to return at all, rather than chance another poor showing.

---

⁶⁰ Paul's "ways" were not just his own personal emphases, which might or might not be right in God's sight. The Old Testament constantly uses the Hebrew equivalent for *hai hodoi* ("the ways") in the objective sense: the ways that God has marked out in his Word. These divinely prescribed ways Paul had made his own, and he calls them "mine" only in this sense.

⁶¹ Is there a pattern for the church that the Lord expects every congregation to conform to? Yes! What is included in that pattern? Well, one thing is the matter of unity and harmony. Another is that Paul taught the same truths he learned from Jesus in every place he preached. By implication, so should we. Harmony of doctrine will bring harmony of life.

What else may be involved in the assumptions[62] of the "some" is not easy to identify. Perhaps they were saying Paul would not dare come – that he would be afraid to appear among them, to administer discipline, to rebuke them, or to supersede their authority. Some might think that because he sent Timothy, he was afraid to come himself. Perhaps the "some" were arrogant because they were all the time thinking it was safe to talk about an absent person. We speak about another who is absent, but have that person walk into the room and see how quickly the disparaging remarks cease. Some spoke against Paul while he was absent. Will they be brave enough to keep speaking such remarks when he returns – for return he will. Paul announces the certainty of his coming, if the Lord wills.

4:19 -- *But I will come to you soon, if the Lord wills, and I shall find out, not the words of those who are arrogant but their power.*

But I will come to you soon -- 'It is from no fear of the "some" that I am kept away. To convince you all of this, be it known that I will visit Corinth soon!' Paul intended to remain at Ephesus until Pentecost (16:8) and then come.[63] He came to Corinth after writing this letter sooner than he expected. He wrote the second letter to Corinth just three or so months later, and he had been to Corinth between the times of writing of these two letters. His "intermediate trip" was probably an unsuccessful visit. After that unsuccessful visit, Titus was sent to straighten out the difficulties. Titus got results.[64] However, the intended 'coming' spoken of in verse 19 does *not* refer to that "intermediate trip." When he writes this letter, Paul is thinking of the visit he intends to make in connection with the offering for Jerusalem, the trip we now call the "third trip" to Corinth.[65] The sending of Timothy and the sending of this letter were only preliminary measures. He intends to go to Corinth in person shortly.

If the Lord wills -- The "Lord" is Christ. Christ determines the movements of His servants.[66] 'If the Lord permits; if by His providence He allows me to come.' Paul regarded the entering on a journey as dependent on the will of the Lord, and felt that the Lord had all in His hand. No purpose should be formed without a reference to the Lord's will; no plan should be formed without feeling that He can easily frustrate it and disappoint us (cp. James 4:15).

---

[62] The relative adverb *hōs* here denotes the idea of 'on the assumption that.'

[63] His plans during this time in his life, and the changes of plans, are discussed in the Introductory Studies.

[64] For details about the intermediate trip and Titus' involvement in helping solve some of the Corinthian church's problems, see the Introduction to 2 Corinthians.

[65] This commentator holds to the inerrancy of Scripture. The doctrine of inerrancy as taught in the Scriptures themselves includes room for using *different* Greek words to translate what Jesus spoke in Aramaic (for example, by way of illustration, see Jesus' statement about the "eye of a *needle*" as translated by Matthew and Luke). Inerrancy also must have room for Christ's providentially overruling plans that are made contingently yet announced, as are Paul's travel plans in this passage.

[66] 1 Thessalonians 3:11; Acts 16:7, 18:9.

And I shall find out -- "I shall find out" (*gnōsomai*) denotes a consciousness attained by experience. 'I will examine; I will put to the test; I will fully understand.'

Not the words of those who are arrogant, but their power -- "Not the words" (as the marginal reading in the NASB shows) is singular; it is "word" in the Greek. Not their vain and empty boasting. Not their confident assertions and their self-complacent views. We have a saying, "Talk is cheap!" See the notes in verse 18 for the identification of "those who are arrogant." The perfect participle expresses a now-settled state. Paul contrasts "their power" with "their word." Is the contrast between "word" and "power" here the same as seen in 1:17,18? Is "power" here like the "power of God" alluded to at 1:24.[67] (1) Some see "power" as a reference to 'mighty in the Spirit.' 'When I get to Corinth, I'll then see how they are working for God and the advancement of His kingdom.' The power to work for the furtherance of God's kingdom – a power conditioned on the possession of true inward spiritual energy – is what Lange thinks Paul means. (2) Some take it to mean "power in the church at Corinth." "I will put their power to the proof; I will see whether they are able to effect what they affirm; whether they have more real power than I have. I will enter fully into the work of discipline, and will ascertain whether they have such authority in the church, such a power of party and of combination, that they can resist me, and oppose my administration of the discipline which the church needs" (Barnes, *op. cit.*, p.79).

4:20 -- *For the kingdom of God does not consist in words but in power.*

For the kingdom of God -- This is one of the rare occurrences outside the Gospels[68] of the term that dominates the ministry and teaching of both John the Baptist and Jesus. In this place, as at Romans 14:17, Paul uses the term "kingdom" of the church here on earth. Before Pentecost (Acts 2), the "kingdom of God/kingdom of heaven" was preached as being in the future. After Pentecost the kingdom was preached as being in existence. Therefore, in the church one can see the present manifestation of the kingdom. It is in the church where one can see Christ's present reign over the hearts of God's children. This is not to say there is no future manifestation of the kingdom which people already in the church have not yet experienced (see Acts 14:22). Indeed, in most instances when Paul uses the term "kingdom" he is speaking of what occurs beginning with the second coming of Christ.

Does not consist in words -- Empty, boastful words do not build the church. 'Corinthian

---

[67] To explain "their power" as the power of the Corinthians to work miracles (Chrysostom, Grotius), or as of moral virtue (Theodosius, Pelagius), or as of the influences of doctrine upon life (Calvin, *op. cit.*, p.101), does not suit the context.

[68] Modern scholars have noted the regular usage of "kingdom" in the Gospels, and the relative lack of use of the term in Acts and the epistles. Paul uses it about a dozen times – 1 Corinthians 6:9,10, 15:24,40; 2 Thessalonians 1:5; Galatians 5:21; Romans 14:17; Colossians 1:13, 4:1; Ephesians 5:5; 2 Timothy 4:18. Modern scholars have also had a running debate about exactly what is denoted by the phrase "kingdom of God" or "kingdom of heaven." How are the church and the kingdom related, if at all? This passage bears on the question and suggests that in the church is one place where the 'reign' of God is visible to men here on earth.

words' do not build the church (1 Corinthians 2:4,5). The kingdom of God is not built up by "cleverness of speech" (1 Corinthians 1:17).

But in power -- Here in the close of this whole section, Paul repeats an emphasis he highlighted earlier (2:4,5). Some Bible students have attempted to define the particular area of church life where Paul threatens to demonstrate "power." (1) Some say "it refers to the manner in which the church is established and continues to make lasting growth." "It has not been set up by empty boasting or by pompous pretensions" (Barnes, *op. cit.*, p.79). It takes the power of the Word of the cross. (2) Others say "the meaning here is the power or authority which was to be exercised in the government and discipline of the church." 'The thing that makes the church grow and go is not rhetorical speech and Corinthian words, but the power of God working through humble and consecrated men.' True Spirit-filled preaching, not false boasting, is the power that makes the church go.

> Paul was conscious of his own apostolic power. Elymas had been stricken blind for opposing Paul's teaching at Paphos (Acts 13:11), and many other notable miracles had been wrought by Paul at Corinth (2 Corinthians 12:12); there could be no doubt that Paul fully counted upon the future confirmation of the Word of God which he proclaimed at Corinth by just such signs and wonders and mighty deeds as God had enabled previously.[69]

4:21 -- *What do you desire? Shall I come to you with a rod, or with love and a spirit of gentleness?*

What do you desire? -- 'It depends on yourselves how I shall come.' Whether or not they would receive apostolic discipline and experience apostolic power depended on them.[70] "The whole thing lies with you," says Chrysostom. Having expressed his determination to visit Corinth soon, Paul here leaves it for them to decide in what form his authority shall be exercised (2 Corinthians 10:6, 13:2ff.).

Shall I come to you with a rod -- To correct and punish. *Hrabdō* is the regular Greek word for 'armed with a rod.' The "rod" was an implement of paternal discipline, not a "club."[71] 'If you still continue your contentions, and do not remove the occasions of of-

---

[69] James B. Coffman, *Commentary on 1 and 2 Corinthians* (Austin, TX: Firm Foundation Publishing House, 1977), p.69,70.

[70] This comment reflects the paragraphing in our English Bibles which makes 4:21 to be the closing verse of the previous section. Some have argued that this verse actually is the introduction of the topic in the next chapter, thus opening a new topic for rebuke. Those who so outline the book argue in this fashion: The major thing in Paul's actions when he went to Corinth just after writing this letter (i.e., the intermediate trip) was to deal with the man living in incest (the topic of chapter 5). If this is so, it shows how much Paul was concerned with the problem of immorality, even more so than the others mentioned in 1 Corinthians.

[71] Some, perhaps in an attempt to justify the practice of inquisition, interpret this to refer to the lictor's rod. Paul is certainly threatening more than a 'switching' or a 'wrist slapping.' When apostles had to demonstrate God's power to bring about repentance, it was severe, but not the 'torture' the lictor's rod might imply.

fense, I will come with severity and the language of rebuke.'

Or with love and a spirit of gentleness? -- "With love" would be comforting and commending instead of chastising. He would come to them in love in any case; but if they now rejected his appeals, the love would be compelled to manifest itself in sharpness and stern deeds. 'If you administer discipline as you should, if you give yourselves heartily and entirely to the work of the Lord, I shall come, not to reprove or to punish, but as a father and a friend.' "Spirit" or "spirit" (i.e., Holy Spirit or human spirit), which is the correct translation for *pneuma* for verse 21? (1) Some contend the reference is to the Holy Spirit. Meyer has remarked that in every place in the New Testament where *pneuma* is joined with an abstract genitive, it means the Holy Spirit, and the abstract genitive refers to the specific working of the Spirit in the case at hand.[72] Alford, however, shows that Meyer is mistaken when he affirms this (*op. cit.*, p.504). Some references do refer to the Holy Spirit (e.g., John 15:26, 16:13; 1 John 4:6; Romans 8:15; 2 Corinthians 4:13; Ephesians 1:17; Romans 1:4). But some exceptions are Luke 13:11, 11:8; 2 Timothy 1:7; and 1 John 4:6. (2) Others assert that the human spirit is what Paul has in mind. It is best to treat this as a reference to his human spirit, for the following reasons: (a) Since "love" is a quality found in Paul's heart, this "spirit" must also be such a quality. (b) In Scripture analogy, the Holy Spirit is never a person through whom we operate. Rather, *He* operates through *us*. (c) It is quite impossible to draw a parallel between the Holy Spirit and a rod or a stick. "Gentleness" (*prautēs*) denotes sparing, forgiving, mildness. In this winning way Paul gives them to understand that he would much rather be spared the necessity of discipline.[73] Paul has answered the charge of some that he was afraid to come to Corinth again.

This verse concludes this first part of the letter, in which the party spirit and the evils resulting from it in Corinth are addressed, and at the same time it naturally introduces the second topic to be discussed, viz., the case of incest which had occurred. This second topic was one of the things which could compel the apostle to visit Corinth, not "with love and a spirit of gentleness," but "with a rod."

---

[72] Meyer, *op. cit.*, p.105.

[73] Kling, *op. cit.*, p.106.

SECTION TWO: CONCERNING SEXUAL IMMORALITY AND THE CHURCH'S INDIFFERENCE TO IT. 5:1-13

A. Censure of the Deliberate Toleration of a Gross Case of Incest. 5:1-3

> *Summary:* This chapter is entirely occupied with instructions concerning the proper action by a congregation in those cases where members are involved in unrepented-of habitual sin. In the first three verses he rebukes them for tolerating a kind of sin which even the heathen did not tolerate, and he reproves them for being puffed up with pride even while this scandal existed among them in their congregation.

5:1 -- *It is actually reported that there is immorality among you, and immorality of such a kind as does not exist even among the Gentiles, that someone has his father's wife.*

It is actually reported -- Paul does not name his informants, as he did in the first section of this letter (1:11). "Actually" translates the adverb *holōs*, 'everywhere.'[1] It wasn't just Paul's informants who were talking. Nor was the report just idle gossip or empty rumor. The facts were a common topic of discussion among the Corinthians and folk who knew them, and the report was true. The phrase implies, 'It is *notorious* that there is sexual immorality among you.' This indictment, following 4:21 without any connecting particle, bursts upon the readers like a thunder clap. Since the immorality was the topic talked about in their midst, the members hearing about it from one another, there is no way they could claim the reason for their inaction and failure to discipline was that they were unaware the sin was going on. When a report obtains such circulation as this one had, it is certainly time to investigate it and correct the evil!

That there is immorality among you -- The word *porneia* covers a number of sexual deviations and extramarital sexual relations including prostitution, unchastity, fornication, and adultery.[2] In this case, the exact behavior that is intended is explained in the last clause of this verse.

And immorality of such a kind as does not exist even among the Gentiles -- Such "immorality" (a form of incest in this circumstance), indeed, did "exist" and was 'named' among the Gentiles, for it forms the basis of the story of Hippolytus, the scene of which was in the neighborhood of Corinth. But the feelings even of pagans were so shocked by it that Cicero alludes to such a crime in the words, "Oh, incredible wickedness, and – except

---

[1] Since adverbs usually modify verbs, we have opted for the view that *holos* ("actually") modifies "it is reported," rather than the noun "immorality."

[2] See notes also at 5:9 on the possible meanings of this word.

in this woman's case – unheard of in all experience."³ Even Roman law forbade unions of this kind since they are naturally abhorrent. One does not need Christianity to repudiate them. Leviticus 18:8 and Deuteronomy 22:30 record the pertinent Jewish law.⁴ When the whole Gentile world regarded this immoral act as disgusting, how infinitely worse that the Corinthian church members were tolerating it. Their standards should have been much higher! Paul has a concern for the reputation of the church in its society. If even pagans of Paul's day found this sin offensive, then for Christians to tolerate it among themselves would seriously compromise the church's witness.

That someone has his father's wife -- The Greek language has a word for "step-mother" (*metruia*), but for some reason Paul chose not to use it. See Leviticus 18:6-19 for the Old Testament laws concerning incest. Paul's very wording was used in Leviticus 18:8 to forbid this kind of union. Some suppose this method of writing it (the periphrasis) might remind some of the heinousness of the sin, and to point out the disgrace more plainly. Another idea is offered by Shore, who asserts that "his father's wife" is the Hebrew form of expression for stepmother.⁵ The expression "to have a woman" means to have sexual relations with her (Matthew 14:4, 22:28 [Greek]; 1 Corinthians 7:2,29). The present tense verb used here describes a continuing relationship with the woman. The modern euphemism is 'sleeping together.' Commentators have disputed whether this was marriage or concubinage or seduction to habitual criminal intercourse or adultery. It is not possible, perhaps, to conclusively determine. The whole sordid matter was aggravated by the fact that the father in the case is still living, and is presumably still married to the woman involved. The father, too, is a Christian (2 Corinthians 7:12). The son also is a member of the church. We assume the illicit relationship started after the son had been a Christian for a while. That the woman is not a member of the church is implied by the fact she is not made the subject of censure.

Why had the church at Corinth failed to act in this case? Why did they tolerate it? In many towns, society's general immoral standards tend to infect the church and dull church member's moral sensitivities. But while morals were lax in Corinth, not even pagans condoned this behavior. Perhaps in the church at Corinth the members had been so busy boasting their party membership that they did not have time to be concerned with this case. Perhaps they were like many church members and leaders today – they just did

---

[3] *Pro Cluent* 5,6. There is no verb in this phrase in the Greek, so a verb must be supplied as we translate. The ellipsis can be filled up most readily by "is reported" or simply by "is" as the ASV translators did it. The KJV reading ("not so much as named among the Gentiles") is a "clumsy gloss taken from Ephesians 5:3," says Alford (*op. cit.*, p.505). The KJV translators used the word "named" in the sense of "named with approval, tolerated, allowed," reads Barnes (*op. cit.*, p.83).

[4] Mare suggests that rabbinic law may have allowed such a marriage when a proselyte married his stepmother, since his becoming a proselyte broke all bonds of relationship (*op. cit.*, p.217). He alludes to Strack-Billerbeck, *Kommentar zum N.T. aus Talmud und Midrasch* (Munich: Beck, 1922-1961), Vol. 3, p.343-358. If the rabbis did allow such a union, it would be another example of the facticity of Jesus' accusation when He said, "by your traditions you have voided the Law of Moses" (Mark 7:9).

[5] Shore, *op. cit.*, p.40.

not love the sinners enough to want to get involved in trying to help them overcome habitual sin in their lives. In any case, Paul expresses astonishment at their conduct.

5:2 -- *You have become arrogant and have not mourned instead, so that the one who had done this deed would be removed from your midst.*

And you have become arrogant -- As the marginal reading shows, this and the following clause could be read as questions, "And have you become arrogant?"[6] The "you" is emphatic. '*You* – the very persons whose horror ought to have been most intense.' It might seem inconceivable that any community calling itself Christian would fall so low as to be conceited and puffed up when there existed such an offense among them. In the word "arrogant" Paul again alludes to the pride of the Corinthians, which he has spoken of much in the first four chapters (see 4:6,18,19). This verse does not mean they were puffed up or proud *on account of* the wickedness (as if it were a fine assertion of Christian freedom), but they were filled with pride *notwithstanding*, or in spite of it.

And have not mourned instead -- Instead of being puffed up with pride one against another, in party rivalry, should they not have been united in one common grief about the flagrant and habitual sin in their midst? They ought to have been a humbled people. They should have mourned, and should have given first attention to the removal of the evil. They should have been so afflicted and troubled as to take the proper means of removing the offence. The word Paul uses for the "grief" they should have shown (*pentheō*, "mourned") is the word that is used for mourning the dead. "Mourning" is the feeling which the outrageous occurrence should have evoked in the hearts of the Corinthians. (The next clause will mention the action that should emanate from this sorrow, namely, the disciplinary removal of the sinner – he should have been expelled from the congregation.) Acts of discipline in the church should always commence with *mourning* that there is occasion for the discipline. It should not be anger, or pride, or revenge, or party feeling, which prompt to discipline.

In order that the one who had done this deed might be removed from your midst -- "In order that" is a *hina* clause. Such a clause, which can express either purpose or result, here indicates not the purpose of the mourning but the result of it. A proper Christian instinct would have led them to have expelled the guilty person in irrepressible horror at his conduct. "Removed from your midst" evidently means to excommunicate. The unrepentant sinner, while he continues in this state, should not be allowed to remain in their communion. The words imply the Corinthians should have already acted in this case – and not have had to wait for Paul's prompting. Three reasons for church discipline are seen from the context: (1) To maintain the authority of Christ, verse 4 ("in the name of our Lord Jesus"); (2) To maintain the purity of the congregation, verse 6; (3) To save the sinner, verse 5 ("for the destruction of his flesh"). Sometimes a congregation merely deplores open moral defections in its midst and, like Eli in 1 Samuel 2, contents itself with that. Such conduct means the feeling of sorrow is still too shallow. The congregation thus remains a partaker of the sin and the guilt.

---

[6] So Kling, Westcott and Hort, Tischendorf, Tregelles, and the English Revised Version translate it.

5:3 -- *For I, on my part, though absent in body but present in spirit, have already judged him who has so committed this, as though I were present.*

For I, on my part -- Verses 3-5 are one long and difficult sentence in the Greek. The broken structure of verse 3 shows the deep emotion with which it was penned – as if it were accompanied with sobs (Wordsworth cited by Farrar, *op. cit.*, p.166). Such sorrow, leading to such results, should have prevailed in the church. Rather than being filled with pride, Paul confirms by stating the decision which he, on his part, had reached in the case. 'Whatever it may cost me, whatever you may think about my getting involved, and whatever personal ill-will may result toward me, I have judged this case to be so flagrant as to demand the exercise of discipline. Since the church to whom such disciplinary action belongs has neglected it, I use the authority of an apostle, and of a spiritual father, in directing it to take place.' There is much emphasis on the pronoun "I" in contrast to the "you" in the preceding verse. 'My feelings about it are very different from yours.' The "on my part," or 'verily,' puts Paul in strong contrast with the Corinthians, who were so indifferent and remiss in the case. There was no uncertainty on Paul's part.

Though absent in body – 'I am not personally present with you.' Paul was in Ephesus several hundred miles away from Corinth as he penned this letter. Again we have a contrast: 'You, who are on the spot, do nothing; I, who am far away, and might excuse myself on that account, take very serious action.'

But present in spirit[7] -- By "in the spirit" we are not to understand the Holy Spirit (as Chrysostom and others took it). Many suppose that Paul by this refers to some gift of the Holy Spirit, some special power which was given to the apostles, though at a distance, to discern the real circumstances of a case. But the phrase does not demand this interpretation.[8] We still say, "I am with you in spirit," when in some important matter our mind and heart are united with distant friends. 'I have judged the case and would act the same, and say the same things as though I were present with you. My heart is with you. My feelings are with you. I have a deep and abiding interest in the case.'

Have already ... as though I were present -- This energetic and prompt conduct on the part of an absent person forms a contrast all the more striking with the slackness of those among whom the shameful scandal had occurred.

Judged him who has so committed this -- In 2:2 this same verb *kekrika* is translated "determined." The perfect tense conveys the idea that Paul determined what should be done in the case and that this judgment stands. 'I have made up my mind, and have decided

---

[7] The NASB has a small case "s" on "spirit." This decision of the translators, we believe, is correct.

[8] Barnes, *op. cit.*, p.84.

what *ought* to be done in the case.' Paul intends to say the case is so clear in every respect that he finds no reason to hesitate regarding the required action. The needed action is settled.

B. Instructions Concerning the Proper Discipline Procedure. 5:4-8

> *Summary:* Included in the disciplinary procedure should be action by the congregation to excommunicate the offending member, and action by the congregation to correct their own lax attitudes. Paul's authority as an apostle is the basis of these instructions. He expects his instructions to be carried out by the church.

5:4 -- *In the name of our Lord Jesus, when you are assembled, and I with you in spirit, with the power of our Lord Jesus,*

In the name of our Lord Jesus -- In Paul's view, the action required is obvious – "deliver such a one to Satan" (verse 5). Yet all the additions and the modifications attached to this verdict are of the utmost importance. Paul uses a sort of legal formula – (1) first, in the name of our Lord Jesus; (2) second, with the power of our Lord Jesus. Then he sets forth the proper action – "deliver such a one to Satan for the destruction of his flesh." This first legal formula can be taken with either with "I have determined" (verse 3),[9] or with "assembled" (verse 4), or with the verb "deliver" (verse 5).[10] Probably it is best taken with "assembled" in verse 4, thus "when ye are assembled in the name of the Lord Jesus Christ."[11] Behind this expression would be Jesus' own instructions about discipline recorded in Matthew 18:16-18. "By the authority, or in the behalf, or acting by His commission or power," is the idea involved in the words "in the name of."

When you are assembled -- A regular church service, such as a Sunday assembly for worship, might be intended. At such a meeting they could take care of the discipline. However, in this commentator's opinion, a special meeting of the congregation seems more likely to be the thing Paul suggests.

And I with you in spirit -- 'You should act in accordance with my declared opinion. You should act just as if I were with you, knowing what I would advise.' Why all this emphasis on Paul's presence (in spirit) in Corinth for this judgment? Why not say, here and now, 'I command you to do thus and so'? Because not even an apostle can of himself and by himself excommunicate a person from a Christian congregation. The attempt to do such a thing is papal arrogance. No preacher can expel a member, no matter what the member

---

[9] So TEV, NAB, and Moffatt, understand the construction.

[10] Alford is one who takes it with "deliver" in verse 5, considering all the intervening words to be parenthetical (*op. cit.*, p.506).

[11] So the NIV, JB, NEB, and NASB (apparently).

has done. Expulsion is an act that can be performed only in a duly called meeting of the congregation. If a wrong-minded congregation refuses to expel where it ought to, the person involved remains a member to the disgrace of the congregation. A preacher should use all proper efforts, as Paul does here, to persuade the congregation to take action. If it refuses, at least the preacher's hands are clean; and he has been faithful to Christ, whose servant and minister he is. In reality, Paul's presence, either in body or in spirit, is not an essential feature of this or of any other action of the congregation. This is not a proof text that there must be a properly ordained member of the clergy present in order for an action of a congregation to be considered proper. The presence or absence of a preacher is not in itself an essential feature of the action, as if without a preacher the congregation were either not complete or not competent.

With the power of our Lord Jesus -- Should this phrase be connected with the verb "being assembled" or the verb "deliver"? In this commentator's opinion, the first is the better way to construe the verse. But whichever way we interpret this phrase will in turn impact and influence our interpretation of "deliver to Satan" (verse 5). (1) If we take it with "being assembled," the meaning of the verse is that the gathering would be accompanied by the power of the Lord Jesus. That is, the action taken by the congregation would be to recognize what has already taken place in Heaven where Jesus exercises His power and rule. From the very position in the Greek sentence, it makes it probable this phrase is to be connected with "being assembled."[12] Paul would have in mind Christ's instructions on "discipline" as found in Matthew 18:15-18. First, the offended goes to the offender. Then several go. Then the church takes action. We have an obligation to help save the sinner from hell. Matthew 18:18 then teaches that when corrective discipline, such as we have in 1 Corinthians 5, is exercised, the action is recognized in heaven.[13] (2) If we take it with "deliver," Barnes (*op. cit.*, p.85) asserts that the meaning of the verse reflects that the word "power" (*dunamis*) is used commonly in the New Testament to denote some miraculous and extraordinary power. (However, see Romans 1:16,17 for one of many exceptions to Barnes' dictum.) In the cases of Ananias and Sapphira (Acts 5:5) and Elymas (Acts 13:9-11), we have notable examples of a special power reserved to the apostles themselves, of inflicting bodily sickness or death as a punishment for sin (Shore, *op. cit.*, p.41). When you have disciplined the impenitent sinner, miraculous power will be demonstrated in the case, proceeding from the Lord Jesus Christ.

It has been said that three parties are active in the work of excommunication: (1) The Corinthian congregation. (2) The directing influence of the apostle Paul. (3) The power of Jesus Christ. This passage is one of the many strong indications that discipline belongs to the congregation itself. The New Testament teaches that congregations enjoy local autonomy under the authority of Jesus and the apostles. The general doctrine of the

---

[12] Kling, *op. cit.*, p.109.

[13] The future perfect passive participle found in Matthew 18:18 is not easy to translate. The NASB does well – "whatever you bind on earth *shall have been bound* in heaven, and whatever you loose on earth *shall have been loosed* in heaven." It does not say that the church acts first, and then heaven goes along with the church; it rather says that heaven has acted first, and the church is recognizing heaven's authority and action.

New Testament is that the government of each congregation is invested in the local eldership. However, elders do not assume dictatorial powers. They rule, having been selected by the people, and as being responsible to the wishes of the Lord and of the people (as far as the people's wishes are in harmony with the Lord's will). So deep was Paul's conviction on this matter of the congregation's autonomy that even he would not administer the discipline without the concurrence and action of the congregation itself. George Mark Elliott used to give a warning to be heeded. "In the exercising of excommunication, those who do the excommunicating may be far more guilty (by practicing non-Scriptural excommunication) than the person who is being excommunicated. But on the other hand, if a man is excommunicated Scripturally, the action is recognized in heaven."

5:5 – I have decided *to deliver such a one to Satan for the destruction of his flesh, so that his spirit may be saved in the day of the Lord Jesus.*

I have decided **to deliver such a one to Satan** -- What we call excommunication or church discipline is intended by these words.[14] Individuals who are in Christ and in His church have a certain protection from the devil (Romans 8:1-3; Matthew 6:13; Revelation 20:1ff). Conversely, the world was looked upon as the domain of Satan (John 12:31, 16:11; Acts 26:18; Colossians 1:13). 'Send this man back to Satan's world, to which he really belongs,' is Paul's verdict. This man had already placed himself under the power of Satan by his actions (i.e., habitual, unrepented-of sin). Paul recommended that the church deliver him over publicly and formally so that all the world might know where he stood. Let us remember that the man, by his sin and his impenitence, had placed himself into Satan's power. He merely deceived himself and others by thinking that he was still a Christian because he was being wrongfully allowed to continue his outward connection with the congregation. This wrongful outward connection is to be severed by an act of the congregation. And after the action has been taken, he and all the Corinthians will know the fact that the man is under Satan and not under Christ. Such a formal action by the church would inform the pagan world that this man's behavior did not represent the actions of people who live under Christ's rule. We take it that this is an ordinary case of church discipline – an example for us to follow.[15] Even if this case in the Corinthian congregation is not an ordinary case, we still have Jesus' instructions in Matthew 18:15-18 which teach us to practice church discipline.

For the destruction of his flesh -- Various interpretations and uses have been based on these words. (1) These are the phrases which the Roman Catholic Church used to justify the "inquisition" during the Middle Ages. The Roman Church would deliver a heretic to

---

[14] The words in italics indicate that "deliver" is an infinitive, and we must supply the main verb. The usual procedure is to supply some verb from the context, and the only main verb we have had is the one in verse 3, "I have determined" ("I have judged," NASB). Of course, Paul expects his apostolically sanctioned action to be the action followed by the congregation.

[15] See the Special Study #2 on "Church Discipline" at the close of this chapter where the reasons are itemized by which we arrived at the conclusion that this is a case of ordinary discipline. See also the author's Special Study on "Church Discipline" in his Acts Commentary, p.230ff (1976 and later editions).

the government (Satan) to be beaten or tortured (for the destruction of the flesh) in order to get the heretic to recant (that the spirit might be saved). (2) Some writers, because of efforts to defend the dogma of unconditional eternal security, speak of premature death as being what the sinning man would suffer as a result of this "delivery to Satan." He would lose his reward, but not his salvation. This commentator has no Scriptural need to defend the Calvinistic doctrine of unconditional eternal security, so he is reluctant to accept the idea that "delivery to Satan" speaks of premature physical death. "Destruction of his flesh" is not Paul's usual expression to signify physical death. Furthermore, verse 11 (which prohibits association with the man after he is disciplined) implies that no immediate physical death is in view. It does not mean the man was to *die* under the infliction of this censure, for the object was to recover him. Also, it is evident that whatever he suffered as a consequence of this, he survived; Paul later instructed the Corinthians to admit him again to their fellowship (2 Corinthians 2:7).[16] (3) Not a few writers suggest that "destruction of his flesh" includes physical suffering as the result of disease or miraculous infliction. "Flesh" is taken to be a reference to the man's physical body. However, there is no agreement concerning who was the agent who would inflict the suffering. Chrysostom suggested "that Satan might afflict him with a malignant ulcer, or other disease." It is a Biblical doctrine that the devil can cause afflictions of the human body (2 Corinthians 12:7; 1 Thessalonians 2:18; Job 2:4-10). Others suppose God is the one who would afflict the unrepentant sinner, in an effort to lead him to repentance. Apostles certainly could inflict bodily harm in an effort to encourage a person to repent. When Paul blinded Elymas for a season, it was to lead him to repentance. Perhaps something similar occurred in the case of Hymenaeus and Alexander (1 Timothy 1:19,20), whose delivery to Satan was intended to result in a change of life for the good. Now, we are not certain that regular congregational discipline (as distinguished from the discipline an apostle could inflict) also results in physical harm coming on the person who is disciplined. For lack of verses to corroborate such an idea, Lenski, for one, cautions against treating "delivery to Satan" as being synonymous with inflicting suffering, disease, or injury in some physical sense (*op. cit.*, p.216). Paul certainly did not contemplate that the man delivered to Satan would resume a normal and peaceful life in pagan society, with no further consequences to result from his sin. (4) This commentator accepts the idea that "destruction of his flesh" would be equal to repentance; through the discipline received, the man would recognize his need to crucify his own flesh (i.e., the fleshly appetites and carnal affections). "Destruction of his flesh" certainly includes ending the incestuous relationship, stopping the gratification of the desires of the flesh.[17] Care must be exercised at this place concerning the word "flesh," for Calvinistic writers tend to speak of the 'old sinful nature' (which they suppose has been inherited from Adam after the Fall). Indeed, one of the faults of the New Interna-

---

[16] Defenders of unconditional eternal security are forced to insist that the man of 2 Corinthians 2 is not the same man as the one in 1 Corinthians 5. See this matter of the identity of the person to be restored discussed in notes on 2 Corinthians 2. This commentator has determined that it likely is the same man as was disciplined according to instructions in 1 Corinthians 5.

[17] Just how removing a man from the dominion of Christ and transferring him back into the devil's dominion would lead to repentance is not easy to explain. Perhaps the shock of being excommunicated would lead the person to realize the precarious spot his habitual sin puts him in. Perhaps the downward suction of the corruption of the world will eventually lead the person to wish for the better days he knew in the church, and this will result in his repentance.

tional Version is that it regularly uses "sinful nature" to translate *sarx* ("flesh") whenever it can – see especially in Romans and here.[18]

That his spirit may be saved -- The object or purpose of the discipline was that the *pneuma*, the spiritual life,[19] which was being crushed by the catering to the desires of the "flesh," might be rekindled and "saved." Thus the proposed punishment, severe as it might seem, would be in reality a merciful one, designed to bring eternal happiness to the offender. This ever expresses the true design of the discipline of the church; it ought never to be inflicted if the direct intention to benefit the offender and save him is not also present. This merciful intention of Paul is clearly developed in 2 Corinthians 2:6-11. An unwarranted interpretation is sometimes given to these last two phrases. By some, "flesh" is identified with the "body" and "spirit" is then identified with the immortal part of man. Then, comment is made about the body being "destroyed" (remember the discussion about 'premature death'), but the "spirit" is ultimately saved. Against this suggested interpretation is the fact that the Scriptures know nothing of the final salvation of a sinner's spirit apart from his body. Either both are saved, or neither is saved.

In the day of the Lord Jesus -- This refers to the day of judgment, when the Lord shall judge the living and the dead at the end of the age. On that day He will confirm publicly every true gospel judgment of his church, and will publicly accept also every sinner who has been saved through the gospel discipline which He has committed to His church.

5:6 -- *Your boasting is not good. Do you not know that a little leaven leavens the whole lump of dough?*

Your boasting is not good -- A short explanation of Greek word formation will be helpful. Words ending in *-ma* place emphasis on the result of the action. Words ending in *-sis* place emphasis on the action itself. The word here is *kauchēma*. Literally, the phrase reads, "Not good is the result of your boasting!" The Corinthians were proud of the state of their congregation when they had no right to be proud. They should have been mourning. When a revolting sin is bringing disgrace and peril to the community, there can be no place for boasting. This language probably shows the Corinthians did more than merely acquiesce in the situation. They were proud of their attitude. "Not good" is not *agathon* but *ou kalon* (*kalos* means beautiful, fair, noble). When Paul says it is not good, he uses a figure of speech called litotes (*litotes*, an understatement to increase the effect; i.e., 'a citizen of no mean city' means an illustrious city). "Not good" is a litotes, and means "bad." The clause is thus equivalent to 'the results of your boasting are detestable.' The

---

[18] "Flesh" is used several ways in the Bible. Ethically, it often speaks of the whole human nature turned away from God. Physiologically, it refers to the body alone (as contrasted to "spirit"), as made out of flesh.

[19] Remember the explanation about the tripartite nature of man (body, soul, and spirit) in 1 Corinthians 2:14. The "spirit" has come alive as a result of conversion. Now, as a result of habitual sin, it is in danger of being overcome and crushed. (It takes habitual sin to ruin the Christian's spirit – Romans 6:12ff.) If that should happen, the person will be lost for eternity. The discipline is intended to be remedial, lest the spirit (the whole man) be lost.

Corinthians may boast of their wisdom, their great spiritual advances, the particular party or clique to which they belong. This case of open immorality is evidence that they really did not have the thing of which they were boasting.

Do you not know -- See notes on the force of such a question at 3:16.

That a little leaven leavens the whole lump *of dough?* -- In Scripture, "leaven" can stand for either good (Matthew 13:33) or bad (Matthew 16:6-12). Here it stands for evil. Leaven was yeast[20] – a small quantity works its way through the whole mass of dough. In case the Corinthians tried to defend themselves by saying their tolerance of the immoral man, though bad, was just a little thing, Paul responds that "a little leaven" is all it takes to affect the whole lump. The sense here is plain. A single sin, indulged in, or allowed in the church would act like leaven – it would pervade and corrupt the whole church unless removed. The taint alluded to is not so much the continued presence in the congregation of the unpunished offender; rather, it is a reference to their attitude of laxity and toleration toward habitual sin in their midst. The "leaven" is not so much the presence of the unrepentant sinner that will lead to the ruin of the congregation. Rather, it is the presence of indifference concerning the habitual sin and the lack of disciplinary action on the part of the church members. This latter is the real "leaven" that is likely to affect the whole "lump." The unlovely result of their boasting is that they were admitting evil into their own lives. Indifference to evil creates an atmosphere in which more evil is bound to spring up, and that in their own personal lives.

5:7 -- *Clean out the old leaven so that you may be a new lump, just as you are in fact unleavened. For Christ our Passover also has been sacrificed.*

Clean out the old leaven[21] -- The aorist tense (*ekkatharate*) speaks of a summary act. The compound verb with *ek-* implies a complete removal, a complete cleansing of such wrong attitudes as indifference to sin in the lives of other members of the congregation. The "old leaven" is not a reference to the incestuous person; that would make this command only a repetition of verses 2, 5, 13. Rather, it refers to the moral laxity which was defiling the church,[22] the careless spirit in the church which tolerated the evil. It is that which has to be purged from their midst that they may become actually (i.e., a new lump) what they were by profession (i.e., unleavened). It is called "old" in the sense of belonging to their unregenerate and unconverted condition; a remnant of the days when they had been Gentiles and Jews who had not known Christ.[23]

---

[20] Leaven was dough which had been kept over from a previous baking, and which, in the keeping, had fermented. After fermenting, it would cause dough to rise, and then the loaf of bread could be baked.

[21] The "therefore" which the KJV has at the beginning of this verse is absent from the best manuscripts.

[22] Kling, *op. cit.*, p.114.

[23] Paul traces the Corinthian disinclination to take action against this one horrific case to its real source. They did not learn such disinclination from Christ. Rather it was another example of living according to the wisdom of this age, like they did in their former life.

Perhaps this metaphor about leaven was suggested by the fact that Paul was writing about the time of the Passover (1 Corinthians 16:8), a feast also known as "the feast of unleavened bread." It was the custom of the Jews to clean out the leaven before the celebration of the Passover (Exodus 12:39, 13:6-9). The Jews searched every part of their dwellings with candles (even the mouse holes), that they might remove every particle of leavened bread from their habitations. The putting away of leaven was intended to teach a lesson about the need for sanctification in people's lives. Paul is exhorting each individual member to search out and remove all sin (of which indifference to sin is one example) found in their own hearts and lives.

That you may be a new lump -- That you may be like a new mass of flour, or dough, before the leaven is put into it. The goal is to be as free from leaven as a new lump of dough, in order that we may be pure and free from the corrupting attitudes carried over from the old life.[24] The church is to be "holy and free from sin, evincing its early love and zeal" (Starke quoted by Kling, *op. cit.*, p.114).

Just as you are *in fact* unleavened -- This language is probably to be taken metaphorically. This would be a designation of the church, ideally considered.[25] 'Let there be no impurity, and no mixture inconsistent with that holiness which the gospel teaches and requires.' Some have taken these words to mean 'You are actually keeping the Passover,' but it is doubtful the words can bear this meaning. Paul considered the ordinances of the Old Law as things passed away in their literal acceptance, though they may picture spiritual truths in Christ. The phrase "you are unleavened" wards off a possible misunderstanding, as though Paul is now calling on the Corinthians for the first time to emerge from the old life and make a new start. "You are unleavened, having been baptized and become a new creature (2 Corinthians 5:17, Ephesians 4:24, Colossians 3:10), having been purified from the leaven of your old self, by virtue of the death of your Savior."[26] In fact, Paul could not have told the Corinthians to clean out the old leaven if they had still been an unconverted people, because spiritual powers are needed for this purging. So Paul now reminds the Corinthians of what they really are as Christians, "unleavened." It would be altogether abnormal for such people to allow old leaven to continue to work among them.

For Christ our Passover also has been sacrificed -- "Passover" probably speaks of 'pass-

---

[24] Barnes, *op. cit.*, p.87.

[25] Some translate *este* as "you ought to be unleavened," pointing to the ideal view of Christians expressed in the word "unleavened."

[26] Robertson and Plummer, *op. cit.*, p.102.

over sacrifice.'[27] The argument[28] is this: As the Jews, when their Paschal lamb was slain, gave great diligence to put away all leaven from their dwellings, so we Christians, since *our* Passover lamb has been slain, ought to give like diligence to remove all that is impure and corrupting from our hearts. In the previous phrase, by calling the Corinthians "unleavened," Paul appealed to a subjective motive, to the real character of the Corinthians as Christians. But there is more; namely, the greatest possible objective motive or reason for this cleansing that Paul enjoins. Christ has been sacrificed for us! There can be no doubt the Paschal lamb was a type of the Messiah. There are these parallels between type and antitype: both were without blemish, slain in the first month of the year, died between two evenings, no bones were broken, the dead bodies saw no corruption, the sacrifice was slain before deliverance was effected (Israel delivered from Egypt, Christ delivered us from sin), the blood of each causes a passing over (Israel from the "death angel,"[29] Christ passing over the sins of those people covered by the blood). Incidentally, Paul is teaching that Christ had taken the place of the Paschal lamb of the Old Testament. That lamb was designed to adumbrate or typify Him. Consequently, when Jesus was offered, the Paschal offering was designed to cease.

5:8 -- *Therefore let us celebrate the feast, not with old leaven, nor with the leaven of malice and wickedness, but with the unleavened bread of sincerity and truth.*

Let us therefore celebrate the feast -- *Heortadzō* means to keep a feast day, to celebrate a festival. The cognate noun *hortō* is used in the Gospels of celebrating the feast of Passover. Paul's exhortation could be taken literally. If so, Paul is exhorting the Christians to clean out the leaven in their lives before it is time to next observe the actual Passover. Some think there is a reference to Easter celebrations. Paul wrote this letter about the time of Passover. Passover (the Jewish celebration) and Easter (the Christian festival) fall at the same time on the calendar.[30] Thus, Paul is supposed to say, 'Before the day when Jesus' resurrection is next celebrated, have all the old leaven purged from your

---

[27] In passing, the language Paul uses here in 1 Corinthians is of no help in deciding the quartodeciman controversy (John vs. the Synoptics on the day of the month on which Jesus was crucified). See H. Montefiore, "When Did Jesus Die?" *Expository Times* 72 (1960-61), p.53,54. When John is harmonized with the Synoptics, it becomes obvious that Christ observed the Passover at the regular time (lamb killed on the 14th of Nisan, and eaten on the 15th), and that Jesus died the day following the one on which the lambs were killed.

[28] How is this phrase related to the rest of the context? Does it go with the preceding or the following? If taken with the preceding, the sense is, 'Let us purge out all old leaven since our Passover lamb has been sacrificed.' If taken with the following, the sense is, 'Since Christ has been sacrificed, let us keep the feast ....' Whenever a verse or phrase begins with "for" (*gar*) as this one does, it either gives a reason for something already said, or a further explanation of something already said. We therefore interpret it as going with the preceding and as giving a reason.

[29] The Old Testament does not speak of an "angel" passing over, but of God Himself passing over (Exodus 11-13). However, in the light of Hebrews 11:28 and Exodus 12:23, we believe that the language "death angel" is not unwarranted.

[30] It is probably correct that a special 'festival of Easter' commemorating the resurrection of Jesus had not become a part of church life this early in church history. Rather, we picture the early church celebrating the resurrection of Jesus every first day of the week.

lives.' Paul's exhortation could also be taken figuratively,[31] as a reference to the Lord's Supper. Early Christians observed the Lord's Supper weekly. Thus, this text would be especially applicable to a consideration of the privileges and duties connected with the keeping of the Lord's Supper. How can folk observe the Lord's Supper and not make some effort to be rid of known sin in their lives? 'Before the next observance of the Lord's Supper, be sure to have taken care of this problem of evil in your midst.' Others have supposed there is a figurative reference to the entire Christian life. Edwin Hayden wrote that "celebrate the feast" speaks of "a continuing life of worshipful service."[32] Lenski, too, says, "The feast we are to celebrate embraces the entire Christian life" (*op. cit.*, p.223). "Let us celebrate" in the Greek is present tense, suggesting continuous action. Mare's comment is "that is, let us live the Christian life in holy consecration to God (cf. Romans 12:2, 1 Peter 2:5)."[33]

Not with old leaven -- I.e., 'not with leaven from our old lives' (see notes at verse 7). "Old leaven" would be that which Paul had just told them to purge out. Christians are to "keep the feast" not under the influence of, or in the indulgence of, the feelings learned from the wisdom of this world. This is a general statement, and Paul next comes to the particulars.

Nor with the leaven of malice and wickedness -- These two genitives are appositional or definitive, explaining "old leaven." "Malice" (*kakias*) is a desire and effort to injure a neighbor; it is ill-will in the mind. "Wickedness" (*ponerias*) is the performance of evil with persistency and delight; it is ill-will expressed in action. Both terms pertain to the case of the man whom the Corinthians should have expelled, as well as to their evil way of taking no action whatever in the case.

But with the unleavened bread of sincerity and truth -- When we partake the feast, let us be sure our attitudes are in harmony with God's expectations of sincerity and truth. "Sincere" (*eilikrineias*) is 'judged in the light of the sun.' Its derived meanings include 'freedom from all admixture, unadulterated.' The word meant, when used of honey, free from the smallest particle of wax, pure, and transparent. This discourages the admitting of evil *with* the good. In this connection, the foreign substance to be kept out is the old leaven which adulterates the pure motives and actions of the Corinthians. Purity of motive is the root idea. "Truth" (*alētheias*) speaks of an attitude of straightforwardness, integrity of purpose. It discourages the admitting of evil *instead* of the good. Here it speaks of a moral quality, the inner desire for doing things in God's way, a holy desire that tolerates and accepts no shams. Purity of action is involved.

---

[31] Paul often explained things of the Old Covenant in a symbolic or typical sense. See Hebrews 13:10; Romans 11:17; Galatians 4:26, 6:16; and Philippians 3:3.

[32] *Standard Bible Teacher and Leader*, 1957, p.353.

[33] Mare, *op. cit.*, p.218.

C. Correction of a Possible Misunderstanding of the Instructions Previously Given Concerning Association with Immoral People. 5:9-13

> *Summary:* Paul has already dealt with two matters in his discussion of the case of incest: (1) The need to end fellowship with those who openly and unrepentedly practice sin. (2) The action the congregation needs to take in relation to their own lax attitudes toward sin in their fellow-members. Paul will now make it clear that his command about not associating with immoral people was limited to relationships between members within the congregation, lest the Corinthians get the idea they are to isolate themselves (like an ascetic) from every worldly person.

5:9 -- *I wrote you in my letter not to associate with immoral people;*

I wrote you in my letter -- "In my letter" is a possible translation of *en tē epistolē*, for it treats the article as a possessive pronoun. It is not indefinite, as the KJV implies with its rendering "in an epistle." In the Introductory Studies, we have indicated our belief that "I wrote" is an *epistolary aorist*, referring to verses 2 and 5 of this very chapter.[34] However, for the record, these are the arguments on the other side of the question, that this is an *historical aorist*: (1) It is the natural and obvious interpretation, one that would be the first conclusion of the typical reader. It is the wording Paul *would* have used if he *had* written a previous epistle. (It seems to this commentator there should have been the modifier "first" or "last" before "letter" if this were the case.) (2) "In the epistle" is the very expression used in 2 Corinthians 7:8 to refer to this first epistle as one which he had already sent to them. (3) It is true that Paul had not in any former part of 1 Corinthians given such direction. He had commanded them to remove an incestuous person, and such a command might seem to imply that they ought not to keep company with such a person. But there is no general command *not* to have close social fellowship with them. (4) It is altogether probable Paul wrote more letters than we have preserved in our New Testament canon. We have but fourteen of his remaining. Yet he labored many years, founded many churches, and had frequent occasion to write to those churches. (5) We know in Old Testament times that a number of books have been lost which were either inspired or which were regarded as of authority by inspired men (cp. 2 Chronicles 9:29). So it would not be impossible for a New Testament letter to have been lost. (6) In 5:11 he expressly makes a distinction between the epistle which he was then writing and the former one. "But now," i.e., in this epistle, "I have written" (*egrapsa*) to you" – an expression which he would not use if verse 9 referred to the *same* epistle.[35] If this is an historical aorist, the scenario pictured is this: it is surmised that Paul wrote a short letter (often called a "previ-

---

[34] The early church fathers, except Ambrosiaster, referred to this as an epistolary aorist.

[35] This summary of arguments for "I wrote" being an historical aorist are taken from Barnes, *op. cit.*, p.89. Among the commentators who take it as referring to a "previous letter" are Grotius, Doddridge, Rosenmuller, Alford, Barnes, Kling, Farrar, Evans, Lenski, Lipscomb, Fisher, Ellicott. In fact, modern expositors, from Calvin onward, usually find traces here of a lost epistle.

ous letter") to the Corinthians before he wrote the letter we call First Corinthians. Perhaps the letter contained little more than the instructions not to have company with fornicators. McGarvey believed the letter we call "First Corinthians" more completely and accurately covers what was in the "previous letter," so the Holy Spirit allowed the "previous letter" to be lost.[36] What we can be sure of is that we have all the canon God intended for us to have, even if we do not have all the Holy Spirit has spoken and written (2 Chronicles 9:29).

Not to associate with immoral people -- "Associate" (*sunanamignusthai*) describes social intimacy, fraternal, friendly activities together. The word indicates that we are not to be mingled up among; not to keep company with, or be intimate with; not to mix ourselves up together with; not associate with on intimate terms; not to have regular fellowship with.[37] Lest his injunction against association with immoral people be misinterpreted, Paul goes on in verse 10 to explain that he is speaking particularly with reference to unrepentant immoral people within the church. He is not talking about sinners in the world. On "immoral people" see notes at 5:1 on "immorality." The word here is *pornos*, the word for male prostitutes, ones who practice sexual immorality. The word speaks of improper sexual relations without specifying the marital status of the parties involved. The case of the man who had his father's wife is the case in point. He has already urged delivery of this man to Satan (5:5). He was to be "removed" from their number (5:2). Paul has urged a change of attitude toward sin in the church ("clean out the old leaven," 5:7).

5:10 -- *I did **not at all** mean with the immoral people of this world, or with the covetous and swindlers, or with idolaters, for then you would have to go out of the world.*

I *did* not at all *mean* with the immoral people of this world -- These words correct a possible false inference, and mean 'I did not intend absolutely to prohibit all social contact under all circumstances with Gentiles guilty of sin.' Many are the people of the world with whom we must deal. We treat them with civility; we observe the social proprieties. But we should not so associate with them as to be esteemed to belong to them, or so as to be corrupted by their example.[38] "Not at all meaning" (ASV) is careful and exact. *Ou pantos* equals, 'I do not altogether forbid your social or business dealings with the world.' It intends to say that even in the case of such outside immoral people, some contacts are to be avoided; we do not make such people our closest friends. It also intends to say that certain other contacts with immoral people in the world are unavoidable, for example, those of a business nature. Circumstances will arise in which Christians must meet and deal with unconverted and immoral people. "Of this world" denotes people who are outside the church, or who are not Christians. Since he is treating, in this paragraph, moral purification in general, Paul adds yet other sorts of persons who presented a decided contrast to the Christian character, and with whom Christians will have contact.

---

[36] Quoted by G.M. Elliott.

[37] See also 2 Thessalonians 3:14, Ephesians 5:11.

[38] Barnes, *op. cit.*, p.91.

Or with the covetous -- *Pleonektēs* denotes one who wants to have more than his neighbors. Such a person is greedy of gain, a grasper who seeks to get more than belongs to him. It is a person whose greediness may appear as dishonest actions so that the congregation is able to see it clearly.

And swindlers -- *Harpaxin* ("swindlers, extortioners") denotes one who pursues his greed of gain in robbery or fraud. He may even use violent measures to get the object of his greed. It is one who oppresses the poor, needy, and fatherless to obtain money. Note that "covetous" and "extortioners" are lumped together with "and" into one class while they are separated from the others (and the others are separated from each other) by "or."

Or with idolaters -- The Gentile Corinthians, before the gospel was preached to them, worshiped idols. Notice, first Paul has talked about those who violate the rights of neighbors. Now he talks about those who violate the rights of God. This is said to be the earliest known instance of the use of this word, *eidōlolatres*. It is never used in the Septuagint, although *eidōlon* is constantly employed in that version to denote "false gods." Paul probably coined the word he uses here. There is a question whether the term is to be taken literally or figuratively. Literally, it would indicate actual idol worship.[39] Metaphorically, it would indicate putting anything else ahead of Jehovah God.

For then you would have to go out of the world -- It would be necessary to leave the world if we were to avoid all such persons, for the world is full of them. We meet them everywhere. They cannot be avoided in the ordinary transactions of life. Though Paul taught that there *are* associations with the world that are not allowed to the Christian (e.g., 10:14-22), he also taught that it is not right for Christians to become hermits, or ascetics, or monastics.[40] How far are we to have dealings with the people of the world? Barnes offers these guidelines: (1) Only as far as is necessary for the purposes of good society, or to show kindness to them as neighbors and as members of the community. (2) We are to deal justly with them in all our transactions. (3) We may be connected with them in regard to the things we have in common – such as public improvements, the business of education, etc. (4) We are to endeavor to do them good, to win them to Christ. (5) But we are not to make them our constant companions (15:33), or to associate with them in their wickedness. (6) We are not so to associate with them as to be corrupted by their example, or so as to be led by that example to neglect prayer and worship and the deeds of charity, and the effort to do good in the souls of men.[41] The basic idea of verse 10 is "bad

---

[39] This commentator sees no reason why the word cannot be taken literally in this context.

[40] The ascetic movement in Christian circles, which still influences some of our thinking about Christian behavior, arose much later, after Greek dualistic philosophy became influential. Then, by the Middle Ages, men came to feel the only way to live a Christian life was to cut off all contact with sinful men, to withdraw into monasteries. In our age, some insist that believers should withdraw into communes to keep themselves unspotted from the world. Asceticism was not Paul's idea. He felt, as Jesus had taught, that men must live out their Christian lives in the midst of sinful society. Jesus and Paul did not teach "no contact," but rather "no conformity."

[41] Barnes, *ibid*.

company corrupts good morals" (1 Corinthians 15:33). That is why certain social association is restricted for the Christian.

5:11 -- *But actually, I wrote to you not to associate with any so-called brother if he is an immoral person, or covetous, or an idolater, or a reviler, or a drunkard, or a swindler – not even to eat with such a one.*

But actually, I wrote to you -- "Actually" ("now," ASV, *nun* in the Greek) can be either logical or temporal. If temporal, one would use it to support the idea of a previous letter that was misunderstood. In contrast to that previous letter, "*now* I write ...." If logical, one would use it to show Paul does not want his previous prohibition in this letter (verses 2 and 9) misunderstood.[42] The verb form "I wrote" is identical with *egrapsa* in verse 9. The sense is, 'But what I meant when I prohibited association with immoral men was not immoral men in general, but that you have no association in the church with such ....'

Not to associate with any so-called brother -- "Not to associate with" is the same verb as used in verse 9. "Brother" is one of the names given to Christians. It ideally speaks to the fact that people in Christ have the same spiritual Father and belong to the same family. He outwardly belongs to the congregation, but he really is not living the life that "brother" was intended to imply. By his repeated sin, he is in danger of forfeiting that title and relationship. "So-called" indicates the person is called a Christian but he really is a disgrace to the name; that is a reason for shunning him. He bears the name, but lacks what the name implies.

If he should be an immoral person -- See the notes at 1 Corinthians 5:9 for the meaning of this word "immoral." The clarification in verse 11 intends to forbid any kind of association with a man who calls himself a "brother" and at the same time is a *pornos* (an "immoral person"), which is precisely what verses 1-8 were all about.

Or covetous -- See the notes on the previous verse for the meaning of this word.

Or an idolater -- See the notes on the previous verse for the meaning of this word. When applied to Christians, this word must denote not only one who was still an open worshipper of idols, but also one who insisted on eating the heathen sacrifices and participating in heathenish customs connected therewith. This verse anticipates the whole discussion of 'things offered to idols' in chapters 8-10. Modern experience teaches that it is very difficult to extinguish idolatrous practices among converts from such religions.

Or a reviler -- This is a reproachful man, a man of coarse, harsh, bitter words, a man whose characteristic is to abuse others. It is one who is incorrigibly given to the vice of abusing the character of other people. Origen notes with what very evil people the "reviler" is classed. See also notes at 6:10.

---

[42] See the same term used in a logical sense at 1 Corinthians 12:18 and 15:20.

Or a drunkard -- *Methusos* was a term in classical Greek used of women only,[43] but it is doubtful that Paul has only women in mind here. Just as there were then some in the church who were addicted to this vice, so there are today. And very seldom are they disciplined in an effort to lead them to repentance. Drunkenness has been the source of incalculable evils to the church. The apostle, therefore, solemnly enjoins Christians to have no fellowship with a person who is habitually intemperate.

Or a swindler -- See this word commented upon in the previous verse. This list of vices committed by members of the 1st century church gives us some idea of the background out of which some of the early converts came. A man still has struggles with his old temptations after he becomes a Christian, and not all are able to consistently overcome their temptations. If they continue such practices, the brethren are to ostracize them. Paul is not advocating that only sinless perfect people can be members in the church. Rather, he is concerned about those who persist in the sinful activities from which they have been freed in their conversion. Members who habitually sin must be lovingly disciplined if they are to be helped to repent so that they stop their sinning.

Not even to eat with such a man -- This is not exclusively a reference to the Lord's Supper, or to the Agape (love) feast. The apostle is not thinking exclusively of communion, in which case the emphatic "not even" would be quite out of place. Rather, he is thinking of social meals.[44] Do not invite them to your house or accept their invitations. On the other hand, it is true that the prohibition could include the Lord's Table, and the exclusion of the offender from participation in the communion service as long as he remains unrepentant. The phrase seems to be a way of saying, 'Have no social dealings or close associations with a so-called brother who habitually displays such sinful characteristics as just listed.' We are not to do anything that would acknowledge to him that he is a "brother" – not even eat at the same table.[45] Compare 2 Thessalonians 3:14,15.[46] When we reflect that our Lord ate with publicans and sinners, and that Paul regards it as permissible to accept invitations to eat in heathen homes (10:27), the detailed application of this injunction is not easy. But the principle is plain. There is to be no close fellowship with anyone who claims to be a Christian, but whose life belies his profession.

5:12 -- *For what have I to do with judging outsiders? Do you not judge those who are within the church?*

For -- "For" tells us that verse 12 is intended to give the reason for the limitation just im-

---

[43] In earlier Greek, *methusos* had a comic sense, "tipsy." Later it came to have a more serious connotation.

[44] The present tense verb form indicates the eating that is prohibited is a practice, or a usage.

[45] One might think of the "ban" or the "shun" that is practiced by Mennonites towards their members who fail to repent.

[46] Great caution is required in applying this prohibition, especially verse 15 of 2 Thessalonians 3.

posed in verse 11. He here gives two reasons why his injunctions about "no fellowship" refer only to people in the church, and not to people in the world.

What have I to do with judging outsiders? – 'What business is it of mine to judge those who are outside the church?' The rhetorical question expects the answer, "Nothing!" 'I have no authority over them, and can exercise no jurisdiction over them.' All Paul's rules, therefore, must have reference only to those who are within the church. "Outsiders" originally was a Jewish term, referring to all men who were not Jews. Jesus applied it (Mark 4:11) to those who were not his disciples. 'Outside the church' is the idea here in Corinthians. We also find a description of these as aliens "excluded from the commonwealth of Israel, and strangers to the covenants of promise" (Ephesians 2:12).

Do you not judge those who are within *the church***?** – 'Is it not those who are within that you judge? Is not your jurisdiction as Christians confined to those who are within the church? Ought you not to exercise discipline there, and inflict punishment there on unworthy members?' This question expects a "yes" answer.[47] As the Corinthian church could sit in judgment only on its own members,[48] they should they have concluded that such similar limitations applied to Paul's instructions. 'Since you yourselves confine your jurisdiction to those within the church, you have no reason to ascribe to my advice a meaning which goes beyond this limit.' This verse also has bearing on the matter of discipline. Note that Paul says "you" (plural) – the Corinthians – not "I," when he gives instructions concerning who should judge cases within the local congregation. It was their responsibility to take action in connection with their own members.

5:13 -- *But those who are outside, God judges. Remove the wicked man from among yourselves.*

But those who are outside God judges -- Judging those outside the church is God's matter. "Judges" (*krinei*) can be present tense or future tense, depending on the punctuation in the Greek. If present, God is judging them continually, at the present time.[49] If future, God will judge them at the last Judgment. The latter is perhaps the best interpretation. As was true of the last verse of chapter 4, these remarks in chapter 5 (this time, about judging) form a transition to the subject of the next chapter. The argument would be this: (1) Those outside the church are indeed sinners (Romans 1:28,29,30), and deserving punishment for their crimes, (2) but it is not *ours* to pronounce sentence upon them, or to inflict punishment. (3) *Our* proper area of judgment is in regard to the church. We are to judge those within; (4) God will take care of sentencing those outside the church.

---

[47] P[46], Syr[P], and cop[boh] omit the *ouchi*, thus turning the sentence into an imperative, "You judge those on the inside!"

[48] That some denominations find evidence in this verse that it is proper to sit in judgment of a man's fitness when he would initially join a congregation (voting them in), is hard to see. Instead, it speaks of sitting in judgment over a man who is already a member, when that man continues to live in flagrant sin.

[49] Compare comments on 1 Corinthians 4:4 concerning God's present-day, continuous examination of people.

Remove the wicked man from among yourselves! -- The KJV has "therefore" at the beginning of this phrase, but the better texts omit it. Paul in this passage adopts the form of pronouncing sentence on great criminals, with which especially the Jewish converts would be familiar (Deuteronomy 13:5, 17:7, 24:7). The NASB 3rd edition puts this phrase in small caps, indicating the translator's belief it is a quotation of an Old Testament verse. Put out, eject, excommunicate, expel him from your society!

Three expressions in chapter 5 help us understand what was involved in church discipline. Verse 2 speaks of "removing (the man) from your midst." Verse 5 said, "deliver such a one to Satan." Verse 9 explained it to mean "do not associate with" such people. *Ton ponēron* ("the wicked") is an adjective without a noun expressed. Calvin (*op. cit.*, p.115) made this a reference to the devil ("the evil one"). That this might even be supposed to be a reference to the devil is disproved by the fact that this is likely a quotation of Deuteronomy 17:7, 24:7. This commentator thinks the reference is to the immoral man, the incestuous person in the church at Corinth (5:1ff). Robert Milligan has written (quoted by Morrison M. Davis, *The Eldership*, Cincinnati: Standard Publishing Co., 1912, p.74), "Nothing can be more plainly taught in the Scriptures than that it is a duty of the church to withdraw fellowship from every member who persists in a disorderly course of conduct." Alexander Campbell (also quoted by Davis, *ibid.*) added this word: "To cut off an offender is good; to cure him is better; but to prevent him from falling is best of all. The Christian spirit and the system alike inculcate all vigilance in preventing and all [speed] in healing offenses and all firmness in removing incorrigible offenders."[50]

---

[50] Quoted in the booklet *On the Eldership* by Davis, p.74.

Special Study #2

CHURCH DISCIPLINE AT CORINTH AND ELSEWHERE

I. THE KIND OF DISCIPLINE AT CORINTH[1]

A. Do the words "deliver such a one to Satan" involve more than just excommunication? The notes at 1 Corinthians 5:5 included the additional thought that those who were ejected from the church of God – i.e., from the realm in which a person is exempt from the domination of Satan – were given over again into Satan's power, and unto his destructive influences.[2] However, remember that the sinner's own actions are what put a person into the devil's kingdom and realm; the action of the church merely recognizes what has already happened to the impenitent one.

B. Is this an ordinary case of church discipline? Is it an example for us to follow?

(1) *Some would answer, "No, this is not an ordinary case. It is something only an apostle could do."* This interpretation is reached by construing the phrase "with the power of our Lord Jesus" as modifying the verb "deliver." This view has prevailed in the Roman Catholic Church from the earliest times.[3] Many Protestant commentators have also advocated this view, including Meyer, Alford, Barnes, Hodge, et al. The idea is that, although the apostle is physically in Ephesus, yet he was somehow miraculously present in Corinth when the congregation met so that he could miraculously deliver the offender to Satan. Hodge (*op. cit.*, p.85) succinctly summed up the arguments supporting this opinion that the delivery to Satan was something only an apostle could do: (a) Scripture clearly reveals that bodily evils are often inflicted by the agency of Satan. (*Reply*: Wouldn't this argument be just as forceful to substantiate the belief that this is an ordinary case of discipline?) (b) The apostles were invested with the power of miraculously inflicting such bodily evils (Acts 5:1-11, 13:9-11; 2 Corinthians 10:8, 13:10). (*Reply*: While true, is this germane to the case in point?) (c) In 1 Timothy 1:20, the same formula ("deliver to Satan") occurs, and it was something an apostle did. (*Reply*: This is perhaps the strongest of the arguments produced by Hodge. But is Hodge's interpretation of 1 Timothy 1:20 the only possible interpretation?) (d) There is no evidence the Jews of that age ever expressed excommunication by this phrase, and therefore it would not be likely

---

[1] The notes in this section are the result of a special study of the numerous problems involved in this passage, and show how the conclusions given in the commentary were reached.

[2] Robertson and Plummer (*op. cit.*, p.99) have said, "This means solemn expulsion from the church and a relegation of the culprit to the region outside the commonwealth and covenant (Ephesians 2:11,12; Colossians 1:13; 1 John 5:19), the region where Satan holds sway."

[3] The Rheims version says: "Though the act was done in the face of the church, yet the judgment and authority of giving sentence was in [Paul] himself, and not in the whole multitude."

that Paul's readers would understand the phrase in this sense. (*Reply*: Did Paul have to use only the vocabulary and ideas available in old Jewish, or pagan, thought forms?) (5) Finally, it is alleged that ordinary excommunication by a congregation would not have the effect of destroying the flesh – in the sense in which "destruction of the flesh" is used in the following clause. (*Reply*: This begs the question; it assumes the point to be proven, that "destruction of the flesh" means a bodily harm of some kind, such as disease, sickness, death.)

(2) *Others would answer, "Yes, this is a case of ordinary church discipline. It is something any congregation can and should do in similar circumstances."* This interpretation is reached by construing the phrase "With the power of our Lord Jesus" as modifying the verb "are assembled." This is the view maintained by Calvin, Beza, Owen, Poole, Lenski, G.M. Elliott, et al. The idea is that the words "deliver ... to Satan" are a solemn mode of stating the fact of excommunication (cp. Matthew 18:15-16), and are designed to exhibit the sad condition of the one who has continued in unrepented-of sin – he has presented himself to the devil, to be a servant of the devil. Arguments used to support this as the proper interpretation include: (a) The idea that an ordinary act of discipline "delivers a man to Satan" is precisely in accordance with the view of Paul. Outside the kingdom of God, Satan reigned over men and spirits as "the prince of the power of the air," as the one who had "the power of death," as the one who was the source of bodily inflictions (cp. Ephesians 2:2; 2 Corinthians 4:4). (b) Scripture also teaches that the power of Satan is subordinate to the power of God. It is not inconsistent to hold that physical evils are intended by the phrase "destruction of his flesh" and also hold that this is a case of ordinary church discipline. (c) The fact that this formula of excommunication was never used by the Jews is in keeping with the whole tenor of Paul's doctrine – he learned none of his doctrine from men. (d) Hymenaeus and Alexander (1 Timothy 1:20) were handed over to Satan, not for their ruin and damnation, but with a remedial purpose, "that they might learn not to blaspheme." Even if the apostle did the delivery in their case, we would not thus show that an apostle has to do the act of excommunicating in every case. (The 1 Timothy passage could perhaps be interpreted that Hymenaeus and Alexander were apprentice preachers, whom Paul expelled from his company, and that publicly, so people would know where they really stood.)

(3) *This commentator has concluded that in 1 Corinthians 5 Paul is urging the Corinthian congregation to practice a case of ordinary church discipline.* True, Scripture nowhere defines the character and limits of such a sentence as this ("deliver such a one to Satan for the destruction of his flesh"). But, by cutting off an offender from church communion (2 Thessalonians 3:14,15) – that is, from all the visible means of grace – he was for the time separated from spiritual influence, and was, therefore, handed over to Satan. It is very doubtful that to "deliver such a one to Satan for the destruction of his flesh" necessarily involved such physical afflictions as fell on Ananias, Sapphira, or Elymas. There is no evidence from either 1 or 2 Corinthians that this man ever suffered any bodily punishment. This commentator accepts the idea that "destruction of his flesh" would be equal to repentance. Through the discipline received, the man would recognize his need to crucify his own flesh (i.e., the fleshly appetites and carnal affections).

II. ELSEWHERE

Special Study #10 in the author's *New Testament History: Acts*, p.230ff, addresses the purposes and processes of congregational church discipline.[4]

The dominant question emerging from this chapter is the issue of how and when to practice church discipline in settings other than 1st century Corinth. Matthew 18:15-18 outlines the preliminary steps. 1 Corinthians 5 explains how "tell it to the church" works. The final action must not be taken unilaterally by a handful of church leaders, but in agreement with the congregation as a whole. When the offending member has been excommunicated, Jesus says to treat that person as you would a pagan or tax collector (Matthew 18:17). Jesus' remark clearly refers to ostracism. That does not mean you do not try to win them over to the Christian point of view. Jesus Himself tried to win such people. The Christian equivalent would seem to be to treat the excommunicated person as an unbeliever. In other words, such people should not be permitted to take the Lord's Supper or participate in any of the Christian gatherings that are reserved for believers only. But they presumably could be allowed to sit in a service in which unbelievers are welcome, so long as they are not treated as if nothing had happened. Friends and fellow church members should continue to reach out and urge repentance just as they do in evangelizing non-Christians. But intimate social assembling cannot continue unchanged. Interpersonal relationships will inevitably be strained as long as the individual refuses to acknowledge any wrongdoing. The whole point of disfellowshipping is to so shock the person involved by the severity of the church's disapproval that he is stimulated to change his behavior.

If the incestuous man were a leader in the church, then additional questions about the discipline and restoration of fallen preachers or elders are raised. Because of their prominent roles of influence, a good case can be made for saying that the discipline of such leaders should be more firm and that the period of testing prior to restoration more lengthy than for other church members. Earl and Sandy Wilson (et al.), *Restoring the Fallen: A Team Approach to Caring, Confronting and Reconciling* (Downers Grove, IL: InterVarsity, 1997) give some helpful guidelines when it is a leader who has fallen, who is disciplined, and who responds to that discipline with repentance. Tragically, even church leaders commit sexual sin, defraud their congregations, and ruin a church's reputation. Leaders sometimes get away with the sin with virtual impunity. Sometimes a period of discipline and restoration is established, and the sinners refuse to agree to their church's terms. In some cases the period of time seems woefully inadequate to demonstrate a genuine and lasting change of heart and behavior. Some even endorse a philosophy of restoring fallen leaders to ministry as soon as possible in the name of grace and forgive-

---

[4] Other particularly helpful studies are: J. Carl Laney, *A Guide to Church Discipline* (Minneapolis: Bethany, 1985), John White and Ken Blue, *Healing the Wounded: The Costly Love of Church Discipline* (Downers Grove, IL InterVarsity, 1985), and Roy Weece, "The Elders and Church Discipline," included in Daniel Camp's book, *God's Blueprint for Leadership* (Wabash, IN: C&S Printers, 1979), which documents the steps taken as discipline was successfully administered in one central Missouri church.

ness. But forgiveness and restoration to fellowship do not automatically carry with them the privilege of returning to positions of leadership.

Another problem with replicating the effect of Biblical disfellowshipping today lies with the element of ostracism originally involved. The few churches who do excommunicate the defiantly immoral usually watch those individuals go down the road, or move to a new town, and join another church that pays little or no attention to the reasons they left their previous congregation. Churches even hire pastoral staff who have been let go from other ministries for unethical or illegal behavior without ever asking enough questions of the right people to find out that such behavior had occurred.

In the late 20th and early 21st centuries, important legal questions immediately clamor for attention. Ours is an age of rampant litigation, and church members who have been excluded from congregations, or even disciplined to lesser degrees, often sue those churches, compounding their prior sin with flagrant defiance of 1 Corinthians 6:1-11. (And in an age when many social forces discriminate against evangelical Christians, judges and juries are all too eager to award substantial sums of money to individuals who sue their former churches, often leaving those congregations in financial straits.) Still, there are legal ways by which churches can and must practice Biblically mandated discipline.[5] Constitutions and bylaws must clearly state the procedures of discipline, potential members must read and agree to them, a condition for membership may include signing forms waiving the right to sue the church, and then the congregation must carefully and consistently implement its policies.

Many will continue to view the whole notion of church discipline, and certainly excommunication, as repulsive and unloving. Yet such people fail to grasp God's utter repugnance to sin and His infinitely perfect standards for holiness. There have been some horrible abuses of 1 Corinthians 5 in past eras: the Catholic Spanish Inquisition, Luther's and Zwingli's excommunication of Anabaptists, Fundamentalist legalism against all kinds of morally neutral practices. Yet we must be careful lest we overreact to abuses so wildly as to refuse to practice any discipline at all. Not surprisingly, the church has regularly grown the fastest and become the healthiest where loving but firm church discipline has been implemented.[6]

---

[5] See J. Carl Laney, "Church Discipline Without a Lawsuit," *Christianity Today* 28:16 (Nov, 9, 1984), p.76, and Jay A. Quine, "Court Involvement in Church Discipline," (2 parts), beginning in *Bibliotheca Sacra* (Jan-Mar 1992), p.60ff.

[6] Ron Sider asks some pointed questions, "Would your church excommunicate anybody? Why not?" in his article "Spare the Rod and Spoil the Church" printed in *Eternity* 27 (Oct 1976), p.18-20ff.

SECTION THREE: CENSURE OF LITIGATION BEFORE OUTSIDE TRIBUNALS. 6:1-11

> **Summary**: Going to civil court before heathen judges is scandalous, verse 1. Christian brothers are clearly qualified to settle such matters, verses 2-6. There is something sinful in your attitude of demanding your rights, verses 7-8. Remember what happens to brethren who practice unrighteousness, verses 9-11. This is a second example of how the discipline process (judicial process) should work within the congregation. Not only in matters of immorality, but also in minor matters of covetousness that became causes of litigation between Christian brothers, the church should act.

6:1 -- *Does any one of you, when he has a case against his neighbor, dare to go to law before the unrighteous and not before the saints?*

Does any one of you ... dare -- Is this irony or not? Yes, said George Mark Elliott. It is fiery irony, sarcastic satire. No, says Kling (*op. cit.*, p.121). This is not ironic, but it is the direct outburst of indignation. The word "dare" is *tolma*. 'Does any one of you have the heart to do this?' The word, placed first in the Greek sentence, carries an emphasis. Paul expresses outrage at the impropriety of the action by using this word and emphasizing it. The word implies that it was inconsistent with their Christianity, and improper. 'Don't you have any shame? Dare you presume to violate all the principles of Christianity to do it?' "Any of you" says the trouble in Corinth lay not only with the litigants who would run to pagan courts, but with the entire congregation who interposed no check upon such actions. Hence, Paul first addresses the litigants (verses 1-4), then turns to the church in general (verse 5ff).

When he has a case against his neighbor – *Pragma echōn* ("has a case") is a phrase denoting civil suits, especially in matters of money and possessions. (Such things as a fence over a property line, and other such minor civil questions, is what is alluded to in "have a case.") In the papyri, this expression, literally "having a matter against," is a regular technical term and is frequent in the sense of a civil lawsuit. "Against his neighbor" translates *pros ton heteron*, literally, "against the other." The context indicates another Christian is intended. Paul recognizes such civil disputes between brethren will occur. When such a dispute arises, it should be settled within the brotherhood. When one of the litigants was a non-Christian, Christians were allowed to go before heathen law courts, because no other remedy was possible.

To go to law before the unrighteous -- There is a play on words here between "go to law" and "unrighteous." It is absurd to seek justice among the unjust. And the verb is in the middle voice – they were going to law for their own benefit. They were self-seeking. "Unrighteous" is a term regularly used of the non-Christians. Here it speaks of judges who are not Christians, men who are devoid of that true righteousness which is found in God's kingdom. Not a few writers believe there is an intimation that decisions rendered by such judges are not always just.¹ See the case of Jesus, and the case of Paul before the Jewish and pagan judges, to learn how at least some of the "unrighteous" give justice. We must not insist that the term "unjust" necessarily indicates that the courts at Corinth were unremittingly corrupt. Paul applies the term to all outside the church. People outside the church did not regulate their thinking and living by the law of God. They were not 'justified,' therefore 'not just, not righteous.' Paul's complaint is not that the believers would not obtain justice in the heathen courts, but that they had no business to appear there at all, at least as plaintiffs.² The problem of going to court was not a new one. It was unlawful among the Jews for any Jew to bring a lawsuit against another Jew before a Gentile judge (Exodus 21:1). Rabbinical writings also prohibited such a practice. See Hodge (*op. cit.*, p.93) who quotes them to this effect. Jews settled things before the elders of the village or the elders of the synagogue; to them, justice was far more a thing to be settled in a family spirit than in a legal spirit. And this right of settling their own disputes was conceded to the Jews by the Romans. One can see this even in the speech of Gallio to the Jews who had accused Paul in his courtroom (Acts 18:14,15). The Beth-din (house of judgment) was as regular a part of the Israelite economy as was the Beth-keneseth (house of assembly, synagogue).³ However, when one of the parties was a heathen, then it was not unlawful for a Jew to prosecute before a heathen tribunal.

Under these circumstances, it was natural that the same controversy, which in a mixed society of Jewish and Gentile Christians ran through so many other departments of human life, should be felt here in the church also, and that the Gentile Christians should still wish to carry on their litigations in the same courts to which they had previously been accustomed, and to indulge the same litigious spirit which characterized the Greek nation from the time of Aristophanes downward. But in whatever way the tendency originated, Paul deals with the topic irrespective of any Jewish or Gentile custom. He condemns the practice solely on the ground of the low view it expresses regarding the greatness of the Christian's privileges, and the closeness of the bond of Christian brotherhood (Stanley cited by Kling, *op. cit.*, p.121). Is Paul consistent in his teaching? In Romans 13, he inculcates being a good citizen, which is not only obedience to the law, but the recognition that the magistrate is God's minister. Christians are to obey the laws as administered by the courts. Paul himself used the protection of the Roman courts and Roman justice (Acts 18:12ff, 25:16), and he himself appealed to Caesar. Is it not inconsistent then to tell the Corinthians not to use the Roman courts? Not at all, for to invoke the courts to decide disputes between Christians was quite another matter from what Paul invoked the courts for. (Remember, *pragma echōn* denotes civil suits. Criminal cases may be handled by the state, but simple civil matters are to be handled by the congregation.) Paul does not here condemn those who from necessity have a cause before unbelieving judges, as when a person is summoned to court. But he is condemning those who *of their own accord* bring their *brethren* into this

---

[1] The difficulty of getting a fair trial in 1st century civil courts is documented in Bruce W. Winter, "Civil Litigation in Secular Corinth and the Church," *New Testament Studies* 37 (1991), p.559-572.

[2] Morris, *op. cit.*, p.93.

[3] Because of the Jewish aversion to trials before the heathen, it has been proposed that the evil in the church at Corinth was to be found among the Greek majority, and not among the Jewish minority.

situation, and harass them, as it were, through the means of unbelievers, while it is in their power to employ another remedy (Calvin, *op. cit.*, p.118). This paragraph does not teach a passive attitude on the part of a person unjustly accused (George Mark Elliott). Various reasons have been advanced for not going to court before the heathen. Such a proceeding belies the profession of mutual love Christians are supposed to have. It exposes internal differences to the eyes of unbelievers. There were certain formulas to be gone through in the heathen law courts, such as adjuration by heathen deities, which would involve the Christian in idolatrous practices.

And not before the saints? -- "Saints" are living Christians, as was learned in comments at 1:2. 'Can you not settle your differences among yourselves as Christians, by leaving the cause to your brethren, as arbitrators, instead of going before heathen tribunals?' Jesus had already laid down the rule that "brothers" ought to settle their quarrels among themselves (Matthew 18:15-17). Paul regarded it as a daring sin for Christians to neglect the law of Christ and seek the tribunals of the state. He does not mean Christian courts ought to be instituted. (See also the notes on verse 4. Some have taken this passage as proof that churches ought to have courts for settling disputes among brethren. The *Apostolic Constitutions* II. 4,5,46,47, and the Clementine Homilies, in language evidently founded upon this text, imply the existence of such courts at the time when those works were compiled, ca. AD 150.) He does mean Christian disputants should submit to Christian arbitration by one of the other members of their congregation.

6:2 -- *Or do you not know that the saints will judge the world? If the world is judged by you, are you not competent* **to constitute** *the smallest law courts?*

Or[4] – Paul, in this verse and those following, shows still further what an entire disregard of the true dignity of the Christian state was evidenced by their conduct. While Paul has words for the one doing the wrong (verses 8-10), and the one who took him to court (verses 1,7) before civil magistrates, he saves his heaviest censure for the whole congregation for allowing such a thing to happen and doing nothing (verses 2-6). Instead of ignoring discipline by the church, the brothers should take the initiative, and this initiative has several main thrusts: (1) If a judge is needed to settle a dispute, ask the congregation for help. Do not go to outside adjudicators. (2) Let the disputants consider the truth that it is better to accept being wronged than to demand recompense from a brother.

Do you not know that the saints will judge the world? -- Paul's formula "do you not know?" is his way of *reminding* them of what they had already been taught at an earlier time (see notes at 3:16). Paul is affirming that, in the time he was with them, he had already taught them about what he here recalls to their attention. Our problem is that this is the only place in the New Testament that this instruction appears about congregational responsibilities in judging civil matters between brethren. Since Paul assumes they know these matters, his instructions are brief; we, at times, must read between the lines to guess exactly when and where such judging might be done.   He has just said disputes among

---

[4] There is a manuscript variation here, as can be seen by comparing the KJV and the ASV. The word "or" found in the ASV and NASB should be included, as *Aleph*, A, B, C, D, F show.

Christians should be settled by using one of the church members as a judge. Might someone object that you cannot just pick any church member and make him a judge in a dispute? 'Not every church member is qualified to be a judge, is he?' they would urge. This is the objection Paul addresses in this verse. The argument is from the major to the minor. Those who are worthy of sitting as judges in a 'supreme court' are certainly qualified to function in a 'local court.' 'Or, are you ignorant of your qualifications as saints to judge?'

"Saints will judge the world." "Saints" are shortly identified as "you (Christians)." Compare also notes at 1:2. "Judge" is *krinō*, meaning to deliver a verdict, to judge, and it is distinguished from *anakrinō* (see 2:14) which means 'to examine, to enquire into, like a preliminary investigation.' *Krinō* at times has the meaning of "condemn," and "rule." Further, the verb here is future tense. "World" is *kosmos*. Thayer gives seven or so meanings for this word, so each time one comes across it in the New Testament, he must decide which of the seven meanings is the one intended by the author at that place. Many commentators opine that here it refers to "wicked men." Others believe it refers to "the right and wrong of the world's doings" (i.e., Thayer's #7 meaning, "worldly affairs, the aggregate of things earthly").[5] Is this a reference to the last judgment, or to some judgment in time before the final judgment day comes? The fact that the verb tense in this phrase is future tense has led many to look for the fulfillment of this statement at the final judgment. Verse 3, which speaks of saints judging angels, is also taken to point to the future judgment. However, in verse 2b, the same verb "judge" appears, but there it is a *present tense* verb, and so it is argued that verse 2a does not refer to the final judgment at all. The argument is said to be this – 'Why are you people going to the world to let them pass their judgment on you, when you are supposed to be judging them?'

Because of the uncertainty involved in the etymology of the words and in the tenses of the verbs, numerous interpretations have been given to this verse.

(1) Some say it has reference to the fact saints will be associated with Christ at the judgment day (or, some say, at the millennium). This interpretation then says we will judge in the sense that we will be approving His judgment. Barnes (*op. cit.*, p.97) insisted there are a number of reasons why this must be the correct interpretation. (a) It is the obvious interpretation, he asserts. (b) It accords with Matthew 19:28[6] and Luke 22:30. (c) It is the only interpretation which gives a fair explanation to the declaration that saints should judge angels (verse 3). It has been asked, by way of argument against this suggested interpretation, where else the Scriptures teach that the saints are to be co-judges with Christ? Or is Christ alone the judge?

(2) McGarvey-Pendleton (*op. cit.*, p.75) suggested that Christians judge when Christ judges because we are the body of which He is the head. When the head judges, the body judges. A strong objection to this interpretation is the question, How would this bear on the Christian's ability to judge now?

---

[5] Thayer, *op. cit.*, p.356-357.

[6] We reply that the apostles are judging [ruling] now. Matthew 19:28 does not refer to the final judgment, but to the time when men are being born again.

(3) A third suggestion is that the saints are to judge by promulgating the gospel – a life and death message. It is said that the church is the perpetual judge of the world, insofar as she carries the Light which ever separates the darkness of the world from itself. (This is the usual Roman Catholic interpretation.)

(4) Some see a reference to the time when all the judges (magistrates) on earth will be Christians. Isaiah 49:23 and Daniel 7:18 are quoted as parallel teachings. An objection to this interpretation is that it is not easy to see how the fact that one day all judges will be Christians would satisfy the Corinthians' objection that the church members in their day were not qualified to judge. Nor is it easy, under this interpretation, to explain what it means when it says that saints shall judge the angels (verse 3).

(5) A popular interpretation of the verse among the Greek Early Church Fathers is that it has reference to the fact that the world will be judged (condemned) by the presence of the saints. By their lives and examples the saints will be the occasion of greater condemnation of the world. By his righteous living, one righteous man in a community will condemn the wicked and evil doings in that community. As attractive as this interpretation is, objections have been raised against it. (a) Its detractors argue it is an unusual meaning of the word "judge."[7] (b) It does not fit the case before us. The apostle is saying that Christians occupy so high and important a station in the work of judging the world that they ought to be qualified to exercise judgment on things pertaining to this life. How their example against the heathen in a given community proves their qualification to make judicial decisions is not easy to see. (c) Such an idea would not satisfy the future tense verb in the first part of the verse, even if it satisfies the present tense verb in the last part of the verse.

(6) Kling (*op. cit.*, p.179) suggested that this verse has reference to our reigning with Christ, which is elsewhere promised to the faithful (Romans 8:17; 2 Timothy 2:13; Revelation 20:6). In short, Paul here asserts the active participation by the saints in the reigning work of Christ. A strong objection to this interpretation is that, even though we admit the verb *krinō* can mean "rule," such an interpretation is out of place in a context that speaks of judging and lawsuits, rather than of government.

(7) George Mark Elliott believed it spoke of an indirect participation by the saints in the judgment of the world. He appealed to passages like Matthew 12:41-42 and Hebrews 11:7 as passages that would help explain the idea. When it is said that the men of Nineveh would rise up in the judgment against this generation and condemn it, that condemnation was by a contrast in conduct, or in faith exhibited by them, thus setting forth the guilt of others in clearer light. The Ninevites would be "Exhibit A" for the case against the unrepentant. In this way they judge the world – as exhibits, not as co-judges. The time when this judgment occurs is purposely left indefinite in the verse, Elliott believed. It could be present (as in Hebrews 11:7) or future (as in Matthew 12:41-42). Attention must be given to the Hebrews' passage: "By faith, Noah, being warned by God about things not yet seen, in reverence prepared an ark for the saving of his household; by which he condemned (*katakrinō*) the world." "Every man, in fact, who gives heed to God's warnings and admonitions, condemns by his faith and

---

[7] However, in John 3:17, *krinō* is used where it says (KJV), "God sent not his Son into the world to condemn the world." So there is Scriptural support for such a use of the word "judge."

practice, all who neglect to do so. Thus, Noah condemned his own disobedient contemporaries, and thus also he will, on the day of final reckoning, condemn millions of our own more highly favored generation."[8]

(8) Another commentator believes the phrase in question has reference to the fact that the Christian has the ability to distinguish between right and wrong of the world's doings. One of the fundamental teachings of Christianity is that the saints shall judge the world (Daniel 7:22; Psalm 49:14; Revelation 2:26, 3:21, 20:4). What helps the Christian to know the difference between right and wrong is the fact that his mind has been schooled and tutored by the Word of God. The Christian is reflecting God's standards of right and wrong. We judge the world *now*. Paul does it when he calls the world "unrighteous." Whoever has the Word of God and rightly uses that Word thereby judges the world and judges it truly. Christians will judge in the *future*. In the final judgment at the last day, the saints will be Christ's associate judges. This is part of their royal rule as crowned kings. The Corinthians thought themselves "wise men;" helping to adjudicate the petty matters the Corinthians were taking their brothers to court over is one place where they may use some real "wisdom."

And if the world is judged by you -- The ASV correctly translated this present tense verb "is being judged." This phrase seems to make the judging a matter of the here and now, as well as in the future (as the former phrase suggested).

Are you not competent *to constitute* the smallest law courts? – 'Are you not qualified? Are you not able to judge?' "Law courts" translates *kritērion*, which could refer either to "insignificant courts" or to "trivial cases."[9] The NASB chose the former idea; the ASV chose the latter, rendering the word as "smallest matters." It also has the meaning of the instrument or means of judging, the rules by which one judges. James 2:6 seems to speak of a "panel of judges." The sense of 'tribunal,' or 'court of justice' is common in the papyri. "Smallest" speaks of things that were of the most trifling sort, having to do simply with earthly, and therefore transient things – money, property, and the like, the kind of things settled in small claims court. They are "smallest" as compared with the great judgments they are to pronounce (on the world, and on angels).[10] The idea in the verse is this: If you are to judge (future tense) the world, you are certainly capable of judging (present tense) matters in the church. 'The heathen are to be judged by you; they are your jurisdiction. How incongruous that you should ask to be judged by them!' This seems to be some degree of sarcasm. Do these "wise" church members presume to think that the saints who judge the world are unworthy to adjudicate in some trivial affair between himself and a brother? Do they really think it would be ridiculous to have some saint for a judge? Do they really think themselves wise when they rush off to some pagan judge, who stoops before idol shrines, to have their cases tried? If they get a judge who is so foolish as to worship dumb idols, do they really have a wise judge?

---

[8] R. Milligan, *Commentary on Hebrews* (St. Louis, MO: Christian Board of Publication, 194[?]), p.307.

[9] Wm. F. Arndt and F. Wilbur Gingrich, *A Greek-English Lexicon of the New Testament and Other Early Christian Literature* (Chicago, IL: University of Chicago Press, 1957), p.454.

[10] Shore, *op. cit.*, p.46.

6:3 -- *Do you not know that we will judge angels? How much more matters of this life?*

Do you not know – 'Don't you remember?' See notes at verse 2 for the same expression. In verse 2 the contrast was between the Corinthians as world judges and as judges of petty courts. In verse 3 the contrast is between the cases judged – between the great affairs in which angels are involved and the trifling affairs about what is mine and what is yours, about what you said and what I said.

That we shall judge angels? -- To what does this refer? (1) Some see a reference to church officers in the word "angels." Appeal would be made to Revelation 2:1 ("to the angel of the church") where *aggelos* (i.e., angel or messenger) seems to have reference to some human leader in the church. (2) Others think it speaks of actual angels. Most commentators take it in this sense, arguing that the thought is climactic – 'You'll judge the men of the world; yea, you will even judge angels. Therefore, you can certainly judge the trivial matters that come up between you and your Christian brothers.' There are several places where Scripture intimates that in the world to come, redeemed humanity will be superior to, and judges of, the angelic world. Those who take it of actual angels also dispute the question as to whether it speaks of good angels, bad angels, or both. (a) Good angels? *Aggeloi*, without any qualifying adjective, always means good angels, according to general usage in the New Testament, assert the Greek scholars Alford, Meyer, Hodge. But in what sense can it be said that Christians *judge* good angels? "Judge" would have to be taken in a very loose sense. It would have to be interpreted, as Stuart did, to mean that saints will be given a more exalted place in heaven than the angels are accorded (see Hebrew 2 and Revelation 7). Again, it seems that such an interpretation has little to do with Christians being *qualified* as judges here and now. (b) Bad angels? It has been argued that since there is no Scriptural account that good angels will undergo a judgment, it must refer to bad angels. Jude 6 would explain this as being "angels who did not keep their own domain." Good angels are represented as furnishing a part of Christ's retinue when He comes, and as acting the part of witnesses in His judicial work (Matthew 13:39, 16:27, 24:31, 25:31; 2 Thessalonians 1:7; Revelation 20:1ff). So if angels are judged, it must be the evil angels that are judged.[11] (c) Angels in general? From the word of God, Christians have learned how to discern good from evil (Hebrews 5:14), so they are qualified to see the justice of the sentence pronounced on fallen angels as well as the propriety of a place in heaven being given to the good angels. The same word of God, which when followed, helps the saints judge the angels, also helps them judge the matters of this world. Paul is insisting on the competence of church members to judge the kinds of trivial civil cases the Corinthian church members were taking to civil courts. Osiander wrote, "Just as we find a law of mediation in the ministration of grace from man to man although the Lord remains supreme, so we find the same law of mediation in the final ministration of justice, the believers judge the world including the angels, yet the Lord is always supreme. In what this judging consists, in promulgating or confirming the verdict or in otherwise assisting, we must leave until the great act takes place."

---

[11] Kling, *op. cit.*, p.123.

How much more, matters of this life? -- This, too, is an argument from major to minor. If Christians can judge angels, surely they ought to be regarded as qualified to discern the nature of justice among men, to settle the matters that may arise in the church. It is the exalted nature of angels that is the apostle's point: 'You are to judge the world. Nay, you are to judge, not only men, but angels. Are you unable to settle petty disputes among yourselves?' "Of this life" (*biōtika*) denotes things serviceable for this life, things which belong to bodily sustenance, and therefore are earthly, temporal. The Latin translation of this word is *saecularia* – secular, worldly – as opposed to spiritual. All their lawsuits respecting property, debts, or inheritance would be worldly and temporal.

6:4 -- *If then you have law courts dealing with matters of this life, do you appoint them as judges who are of no account in the church?*

If then you have law courts -- The same comments on "law courts" found in verse 2 apply here. It seems preferable to think of "law suits" rather than "courts." The verse implies that small claims civil disputes might naturally occur among them (though verse 7 will indicate that there ought to be no such trials among Christians). The 'if-construction' (*ean* with the subjunctive; contrast *ei* with the indicative in verse 2) carries the delicate implication that such lawsuits should not arise.[12]

Dealing with matters of this life -- Here "matters" (*kritēria*, the same word as in verse 2) is modified by *biōtika*, which denotes the affairs related to everyday living, as compared to issues related to the spiritual life.

Do you appoint them as judges -- The Greek verb can be either imperative, interrogative, or indicative. (1) The KJV and NIV ("appoint as judges even men of little account in the church") have understood it to be *imperative*. Thus taken, this becomes a command to cease going before heathen tribunals. Under this supposition, those who are to be appointed as judges, who are described in the next clause as "of no account" or "least esteemed" (KJV), would refer to church members who are regarded as the lowest members of the church. 'Let the insignificant decide the insignificant.' The apostle is sarcastically telling them that, so far from there being any excuse for resorting to heathen tribunals, any selection of the simplest among themselves would be competent to settle their disputes about trifles. To take it as imperative, making it a command to seat as judges those least capable of judging (we believe) would result in the Corinthians losing confidence in Paul, and would drive them to resort to the pagan courts more than ever. (2) The ASV, NASB, RSV, NEB, and NIV margin have understood it to be *interrogative*. Thus taken, this becomes a sarcastic question: 'Is this the way you wise people deal with such a matter?' Under this interpretation the "least esteemed" would designate the heathen judges. The heathen magistrates could be, in general, corrupt, easily bribed, and silly enough to worship senseless idols. Is this the type of person the Corinthians want to settle their cases? 'Do you really want people for your judges who are of little repute for their wisdom and equity?' McGarvey, who takes it as interrogative and as very deep irony, has this interesting paraphrase: "If called on as a church to judge any matter, would you chose its simpletons

---

[12] Morris, *op. cit.*, p.94.

and numskulls as judges? I ask you this to make you ashamed, for you do even more foolishly when you submit your cases to worldlings, who are even less competent judges."[13]

Who are of no account in the church? -- "No account" (*exouthenēmenous*) is a strong expression, which in 1:28 was rendered "despised." The expression 'those held in disdain' or "who are of no account" (NASB) is difficult to explain satisfactorily. Is Paul talking about heathen judges? Does it seem probable Paul would call heathen magistrates "those who, as far as the church is concerned, are of no account"? Could Paul somehow be referring to the same people he described as "unrighteous" in verse 1? At the same time it is difficult to imagine Paul, even in irony, referring to fellow Christians as those "who are of no account," especially in the light of what he will say about looking down at other members of the body in 12:21-25. Yet he might be saying that even folk who belong to a clique you do not approve of are wise enough to act as judges in these small-claims matters. If Paul speaks of heathen judges as being "of no account," it must be remembered that he does not assail their legal standing in the state, or preach rebellion and lawlessness, or offer disrespect to the judiciary of the state (Romans 13:1-7). The judgment bar of the church deals with spiritual findings and not with secular matters. Spiritually considered, every pagan or unbeliever is "nothing," and this includes every official pagan personage. Yet every case that occurs among Christians, even the smallest dispute, turns essentially on points that are spiritual in their nature and thus are far above not only the common law of the state but also far removed from the mind and apprehension of a pagan judge. We have now been led to the point we are ready for the instructions to set up Christians as arbitrators when there is a dispute between brothers in the church.

6:5 -- *I say* **this** *to your shame.* **Is it** *so,* **that** *there is not among you one wise man who will be able to decide between his brethren,*

I say *this* **to your shame** -- He adds this phrase to account for the severe irony of the last remark. In 4:14 Paul writes that he does not intend to shame the Corinthians but to admonish them. Here he expressly tells them, 'I say this to move you to shame. I want you to feel ashamed!'

Is it **so,** *that* **there is not among you one wise man** -- Paul is still deflating the bubble of Corinthian pride. This question drips with irony, especially since the Corinthians have claimed to be so wise (4:10 ASV). 'Can this be the case – in a church that boasts so much of its wisdom, and that prides itself so much in the number and qualification of its intelligent members – that there is not a single member so wise, intelligent and prudent, sufficiently esteemed for his wisdom, that his brethren may have confidence in him to settle their disputes? Is there a total lack among you of any such person, that you are obliged to go to outsiders, to find a judge?' This phrase is evidence that in the previous verse, Paul has not meant to say that when you have trifling disputes, seek out the moron, the no-account, to be the judge.

---

[13] McGarvey-Pendleton, *op. cit.*, p.75.

Who will be able to decide between his brethren -- That is, able to act as arbitrator between one fellow-Christian and another. In the relative clause "between his brethren (and another)," there is an unusual construction in the Greek. If we were to translate it "between his brother" (it is singular in the Greek), we would fairly represent this to the English reader. If we will remember the construction is proper for the Greek – though we do not as yet understand the reason for it – and if we remember that the sense is plain, we shall have little trouble with this construction. In English we would write the plural "between his brethren," as our translators have done, to arrive at the idea represented in the singular Greek construction. Paul is very careful to write *diakrinai*, 'to adjudicate between,' 'to arbitrate,' or "to decide between" (not *krinai*, "to judge"). When a Christian brother or several Christian brethren act in a case of dispute between their brethren, they do not function as legal judges in a secular court, but instead render a Christian decision which involves an amicable settlement by means of arbitration. In this effective manner Paul concludes the first point of his discussion on litigations: those who were disposed to be litigants about petty matters surely were not wise in their choice of judges.

6:6 -- *but brother goes to law with brother, and that before unbelievers?*

But brother goes to law with brother -- The second point Paul makes about the litigation is a censure of the congregation since they interposed no check upon such actions. Going to law against a brother is a breach of Christian love, which is Jesus' new commandment (John 13:34, 15:12ff). And it is preposterous and outlandish that it should be before unbelievers.

And that before unbelievers? -- This is the third term applied to the pagan courts and their judges. This phrase forms the climax for this verse.[14] That there should be disputes between Christians about "matters of this life" is bad; that Christians should go to law against Christians is worse; that Christians should do this before unbelievers is worst of all. And the most scandalous thing is the Corinthian congregation stands by and lets these foolish litigations before unbelievers go on without even a word of protest.

6:7 -- *Actually, then, it is already a defeat for you, that you have lawsuits with one another. Why not rather be wronged? Why not rather be defrauded?*

Actually, then, it is already a defeat for you -- The third point Paul makes about litigations is this: the very fact that the Corinthians have difficulties that are pressed to the point of requiring adjudication is a reflection on their Christian character. "Actually" emphasizes that even if they do not go before unbelievers, there is still this defeat. "Already," no matter what the decision turns out to be, or what tribunal sits in judgment, it was still a defeat! "Defeat" ("defect," ASV), *hēttēma*, is one of the Greek synonyms for

---

[14] Verse 6 should probably end with an exclamation mark rather than as the NASB has it, with a question mark. This is the practice that exists at Corinth! Indeed! The KJV has a question mark at the close of verse 5, and treats the "but" as the strong adversative it is, which implies that the situation was far different than it should be. Instead of accepting arbitration, they were going to the civil courts! How sad!

"sin."[15] "Defeat" carries the idea of falling short of spiritual attainment. In the next verse Paul will remind his readers of what Jesus taught on this subject, and then it becomes evident why their actions, which are disobeying what Jesus taught, are sin. The idea suggested by *hēttēma*, a rare word, is that of defeat and loss; it is the opposite of *nikan*, to conquer, to win. "Defect" in the ASV is not strong enough, and "fault" in the KJV points in the wrong direction. *"Loss"* is what the Corinthians are suffering.[16] They were beaten (by the devil who stirred up their covetous motives that led to the lawsuit) before they entered the court, as evidenced by the mere fact such quarrels arise and reach this pitch. Paul's point is that to go to law with a brother is already to sin, to incur a loss or a defeat, whatever the result of the legal process.

That you have lawsuits with one another -- "Lawsuits" refers not only to lawsuits before heathen judges, but refers to any suits over "matters pertaining to this life." Matters ought never to arrive at the point where it is necessary to have litigations, no matter who adjudicates them. Long before they reach that stage, such things should be settled quietly; otherwise the loss is very great. "You" is plural. The entire passage is written in the second person plural, and the reference is likely to the whole congregation, not just the two litigants. In a sense, verse 7 is directed at the plaintiff (the one who took his brother to court), and verse 8 is directed to the one who did the defrauding that led to the suit, but the plurals seem to suggest this selfish behavior was more widespread in the church than just one case. "With one another" is literally, 'with your own selves.' So close is the relationship of the members of the body of Christ that bringing suit against a fellow-Christian is like hurting your own self. The injury is to the body of Christ, not outsiders. How can the occurrence of such disputes be prevented? In an exceedingly simple way which even makes their beginnings impossible. That simple way Paul now explains.

Why not rather be wronged? Why not rather be defrauded? -- 'Why not permit yourselves to be injured or defrauded rather than dishonor the cause of Christianity because of your litigations?' (Both verbs are probably middle voice and have the permissive sense.) Is it not better to be wronged than to be covetous (cp. verse 10)? Is this not what Jesus taught (Matthew 5:38-42; Luke 6:27ff)?[17] The Corinthians' actions were far from basic Christian principles. The instruction Paul gives is what Christians so often forget. When a fancied or a real wrong has been done, we think we must demand and secure redress. We at least feel that the brother who supposedly wronged us or who actually did us wrong must be humbled and made to ask for pardon. Or to take a more specific case, this is also true when one is defrauded, or thinks he is. The approach of simply suffering the wrong,

---

[15] See George Ricker Berry, *New Testament Synonyms*, #2. It is the same word translated "diminishing" (KJV) or "loss" (ASV) or "failure" (NASB) at Romans 11:12.

[16] Lenski, *op. cit.*, p.244.

[17] Does this passage help us understand Jesus' teaching? He was not teaching how a Christian must always react when an outsider threatens to injure the Christian. But when both parties are Christians, then among brethren there is to be a spiritual kinship (a family "give and take") that ought to make lawsuits needless. Peter also makes application of Jesus' teaching (1 Peter 3:8ff), and Peter explains that Jesus' teachings apply specially where both parties are Christians.

the injustice, or the injury does not occur to many Christians. We often instead set up a loud complaint and then continue complaining and showing ill will. To forgive at once and to forget so thoroughly as to make no complaint at any time tends to be an unknown ethical practice, even to brethren who think they are well-read in the Scriptures and rather advanced as Christians. Of course, when Paul asks the Corinthians why they do not rather suffer wrong, he in no way excuses those who actually do wrong, nor encourages them to continue their wrongdoing. The obligation they have is plain; it needs no elucidation here.

Is it ever lawful for Christians to appear before a civil tribunal? Christians should seldom, if ever, be the plaintiff. We still must answer subpoenas.[18] We have a right to see that the laws of the land – if those laws are just in God's sight – are upheld. If a man commits murder, he should receive the proper punishment (see Romans 13). This passage, in this commentator's opinion, does not prohibit Christians from being lawyers, judges, or jury members in civil courts.

6:8 -- *On the contrary, you yourselves wrong and defraud, and that* **your** *brethren.*

On the contrary, you yourselves wrong and defraud -- Instead of following the right course ("on the contrary") when they were wronged or defrauded, the Corinthians were doing the very opposite – either by wronging and defrauding the original wrongdoer in retaliation for supposed or real injuries, or by practicing such things just because everyone else was doing it. Not only were they not ready to suffer wrong (as Jesus taught), but Paul makes the accusation that they were actively doing wrong to others. The present tense verbs suggest these injustices were regularly occurring. If each of the brethren would look to his brother's interest instead of his own, the occasions of difference would be greatly lessened, and the loss that the congregation was suffering would be lessened in proportion. This third point in Paul's discussion has revealed the disgraceful condition existing among the Corinthians, a condition that should never have been allowed to make this much progress among them.

And that *your* **brethren** -- The addition of this phrase does not imply the sin was not serious when committed against unbelievers. The sin is castigated against whomsoever it is committed. But it is the consistent New Testament teaching that in addition to that Christian love which the believer should exercise toward all men, there is a special 'love of the brethren.' Those in Christ should have a special care for one another. It might be said that the Corinthians were committing a double sin. They were sinning against ethical standards, and they were sinning against brotherly love. When a man defrauds his brethren, he is in danger of punishment from God (1 Thessalonians 4:6). So Paul proceeds to warn them what will happen if they continue in the same wicked ways.

---

[18] This commentator does not think the churches who fought the Disciples in the courts in the 1960's – after the Disciples started the trouble – were in the wrong. Yet, the cause of Christ in those communities has been hurt for 50 years or more to come.

6:9 -- *Or do you not know that the unrighteous will not inherit the kingdom of God? Do not be deceived; neither fornicators, nor idolaters, nor adulterers, nor effeminate, nor homosexuals,*

Or do you not know -- As before in verses 2 and 3, "Do you not know?" is a reminder of what they already know. Paul had taught them this when he was among them planting the church. The two "why" questions from verse 7 are the basis of this logical "Or do you not know ...?" question. Paul's thought is, 'I cannot understand why you do not rather let yourselves be wronged, unless it be that you do not remember that the unrighteous shall not inherit the kingdom of God. Do you drag your brothers into court from a reckless determination to do as you please, regardless of the consequences? Or is it from forgetfulness of the consequences?' In either case, the Corinthians' error, if continued, will end in disaster.

That the unrighteous -- *Adikoi* denotes those who do injustice to others, as just mentioned in the previous verse.[19] Those habitually doing wrong (*adikeō*) to others should remember that the unrighteous ('wrong-doers,' *adikoi*) will be excluded from the kingdom of God. "Unrighteous" is a general term; it can include a number of sins against one's fellow men in addition to covetousness which leads to petty lawsuits. Habitual wrong doing of any kind (not just being unjust in your dealings with Christian brothers) is meant here. Paul is saying, 'Do not think that your sin is any more respectable than fornication or homosexuality.' "Unrighteous" has no article in the Greek, so the stress is on the character and actions of these individual people, and not on the unrighteous as a class.

Shall not inherit the kingdom of God? -- Elsewhere, Paul uses the shorter form, "God's kingdom" (*theou basileian*), just as he does in 1 Corinthians 6:10 and 15:50. At Galatians 5:21, he writes with *theou* following *basileia*.[20] Here, *theou* is placed first, in order to emphatically juxtapose "wrong doing" and "God": *wrongdoers* are manifestly out of place in *God's* kingdom. The "kingdom" in this context[21] speaks of that part of the kingdom that is still future – what we call heaven, following the return of Christ. "Shall not inherit" warns that there is a danger of going to hell if you keep up your defrauding and injuring of your Christian brethren. All Christians are heirs, yet heirs may lose their inheritance. They may be disinherited. They may disqualify themselves.[22] "Shall not

---

[19] The word is "unrighteous" (*adikos*), and not "unjustified" (*adikaiosune*). It speaks of a Christian (not the unsaved) whose habitual sin leads to missing the kingdom.

[20] The long form of the construction, *hē basileia tou theou*, is used at 1 Corinthians 4:20; Romans 14:17; 2 Thessalonians 1:5.

[21] "Kingdom" in 1 Corinthians 4:20 was used of the church now present. Some have tried to treat "kingdom" in 6:9 also as a reference to the church now present (wrongdoers are out of place in the church). Such an interpretation does not take careful notice of the future tense verb "shall not inherit" which follows.

[22] Just as in chapter 5, so here in chapter 6, those who hold to the Calvinistic doctrine of unconditional eternal security as axiomatic find themselves in great difficulty trying to interpret these verses. The passage is undoubtedly speaking of Christians ("brethren") who are now practicing wrong-doing, and who are warned that they are in danger of being excluded from the inheritance. A believer's security is conditional – it is conditioned on faithfulness.

inherit" should not be reduced to mean only 'shall no longer participate in [this life],' yet not affecting their inheritance in the eternal kingdom. The view that no process of inheritance is ever indicated in Scripture is refuted by Romans 8:16,17, "if children, then heirs." God makes those who are "righteous" (i.e., justified) His adopted children. Those who become His children have an obligation to cease living according to the flesh, for if one continues to live according to the flesh, he must die (Romans 8:12,13). Romans 6:12 tells Christians to stop letting sin reign in their mortal bodies, and Romans 6:23 warns the Christian that the wages of sin is death. Worded another way, God has made His last will and testament, duly sealed and attested, in which are His promises. In this will, He names Christians as His heirs. We do much more than merely participate here and now in the kingdom. There is a heaven, too, which can be inherited or missed. The "unrighteous" are not named as heirs in the will, nor are they God's adopted sons.

Do not be deceived -- The form of prohibition ($m\bar{e}$ and a present imperative) prohibits the continuance of an action already going on.[23] Further, in this place, the imperative is middle voice. A good translation then would be "Stop deceiving yourselves!" They were deceiving themselves that they could get away with their own sin. And there was great danger of the church members being led to think lightly of the sins of other Christians, which were daily being committed by those among whom they were living. Like Eve, even if a man is deceived and sins, he is still guilty. Origen expanded this phrase, "Let no one lead you astray with persuasive words, saying that God is merciful, kind, and loving, and ready to forgive [all these willful] sins." Christianity cannot be divorced from morality. Even though a man is baptized and comes to church regularly, he still has no license to be unrestrained in the indulgence of every evil passion. Some Jews held that the belief in one God sufficed regardless of the kind of life a man lived. Perhaps Judaizers have been teaching in Corinth that "faith" sufficed – do not worry about your everyday activities. Paul now repeats six sins already listed at 5:10,11, and adds a list of four more sins that are also examples of being "unrighteous," so the Corinthians will surely know what he means. Ten different acts of sin are listed, with 'sexual immorality' and 'greed' furnishing the prevailing categories.[24] One thing these sins all have in common is that when you do them, you are hurting someone else as well as yourself.

Neither fornicators -- See notes at 5:9, where the same word was translated "immoral people." (The same subject will be taken up again in 6:12ff.) Christians who relapse into this vice are warned they will miss heaven! The first four sins listed were especially prevalent in Corinth, where impurity and immorality were the main part of the recognized worship of Aphrodite.

Nor idolaters -- Do not be like the kind of people who worship Aphrodite. The greatest

---

[23] We've already met a similar construction in prohibitions at 4:5, and will have it again at 7:5.

[24] Efforts to detect a reason for the order of the designations in this and the next verse have resulted in finding no order or outline in particular. Perhaps, then, we must say Paul was following no definite order in presenting this list.

building in Corinth was the temple of Aphrodite, the goddess of love, where idolatry and immorality flourished side by side. Christians are warned that relapse into idolatry is a sin that can cost them their inheritance.

Nor adulterers -- Adultery is sexual intercourse with someone other than one's married spouse.[25] Christians are warned that habitual adultery will lead to loss of salvation.

Nor effeminate (i.e., "effeminate, by perversion," is the explanatory note in the NASB margin) -- *Malakoi* means "soft" or "effeminate," and most likely refers to the 'passive' partner in a pederasty relationship. Pederasty was the most common form of male homosexuality in the Roman world.[26] "Effeminate" here references those who allowed themselves to be used as women in a sexual relationship; those who are kept to be prostituted to others; men and boys who allow themselves to be misused homosexually.[27] Christians who are tempted to indulge in this sin should remember that such "shall not inherit the kingdom of God."

Nor homosexuals ("nor abusers of themselves with men," ASV) -- The Greek word here, *arsenokoitoi*, is a compound word made up of "male" and "intercourse." This word refers to sodomy, male homosexuals, those who had relations with the "effeminate," those who are the 'active' partner in a male homosexual relationship.[28] "Homosexuals" is rightly the translation in several modern versions. There is much being written in the last few decades in an attempt to show that "homosexuality" is a legitimate "alternative life style." It has been urged more than once that the two terms in verse 9 have no reference to homosexuality, but rather to male prostitution. Fee, p.243-244 gives a fair and balanced treatment of the question, as well as bibliographical references for further study. He cautiously adopts the conclusion that "homosexuality" *is* the topic here warned against.[29]

---

[25] Bible dictionaries note that the acts which constitute adultery differ between Old and New Testaments. See notes at Matthew 5:27,28,32, 19:9; Romans 2:22; Galatians 5:19.

[26] Barclay has a saddening historical summary of how the vice had swept like a cancer through Greek and Roman society (*op. cit.*, p.60). David E. Malick, "The Condemnation of Homosexuality in 1 Corinthians 6:9," *Bibliotheca Sacra* 150 (1993), p.479-492, shows that "effeminate" and "homosexuals" are best understood as referring to the more passive and more active partners, respectively, in any male homosexual act.

[27] BAGD, p.489.

[28] Romans 1:26 shows that homosexuality among women is just as wrong as it is among men.

[29] Craig Blomberg, "I Corinthians," in *The NIV Application Commentary* (Grand Rapids, MI: Zondervan, 1994) offers very helpful guidance to today's Christian who is trying to understand and live by what Paul wrote. Among the points he makes are these: (1) It is linguistically invalid to limit the type of homosexual behavior Paul describes either to pederasty (adult men with underage boys) or to homosexual prostitution (casual sex for profit between individuals not committed to a lasting relationship with each other). (2) Under no circumstances can the Bible be made to defend the often-heard allegation that God created homosexuals that way. (3) Verse 11 will recall another crucial point in this discussion: homosexuality can be abandoned with God's help. For a good anthology of approaches to helping the church "promote hope and healing for gays and lesbians," see J. Isamu Yamamoto, *The Crisis of Homosexuality* (Wheaton, IL: Victory, 1990).

Christians are warned in this passage that relapse into the old sinful ways (homosexuality) will result in a forfeiture of eternal life.

6:10 -- *nor thieves, nor* **the** *covetous, nor drunkards, nor revilers, nor swindlers, will inherit the kingdom of God.*

Nor thieves -- *Kleptai* speaks of petty pilferers, sneak thieves, rather than pirates, brigands or highwaymen. Barclay calls attention to the fact that the ancient world was cursed with thieves. Folk had homes broken into by robbers. One's clothing and money were in danger of being stolen at the public baths and gymnasiums. It was also common to kidnap (steal) slaves who had special gifts. He also tells us three kinds of theft were punishable by death. (1) Theft of anything worth more than 50 days wages. (2 Theft of anything from the baths or gymnasiums worth more than 10 days wages. (3) Theft of anything during the night. The Christians lived in the midst of a pilfering population.[30] Since 'everybody was doing it,' Christians here were warned that it is not proper Christian behavior, and that to relapse into their old behavior has eternal consequences.

Nor *the* covetous -- See this word explained at 5:11. Christians are warned to beware of covetousness.

Nor drunkards -- A drunkard is one who habitually drinks to intoxication. Christians should take warning about relapsing into this old behavior.

Nor revilers -- As was learned in notes at 5:11, this word means 'to be abusive in speech or act.' This, too, is a sin into which Christians may sink, to their eternal hurt.

Nor swindlers -- This word too was explained at 5:11. Deissmann tells us the word carried the idea of "swindler" more than "extortioner" (ASV). Here is another sin Christians should studiously avoid.

Shall inherit the kingdom of God -- "Inherit" is the language of the Old Testament theocracy. The Jewish theocracy was a type of the church, and was but preparatory for it.[31] See notes in verse 9 above, where we had the same phrase.[32] Paul repeats this phrase as

---

[30] Barclay, *op. cit.*, p.59.

[31] See this idea developed in C.F. Keil and F. Delitszch, *Biblical Commentary on the Old Testament, Pentateuch*, (Grand Rapids, MI: Eerdmans, 1949), Vol. I, p.226, and Kling, *op. cit.*, p.125-6. Cf. also Romans 4:11-14.

[32] The distinction made by some between the "kingdom of God" (as if it were a reference to what happens on earth, say during a future millennium) and the "kingdom of heaven" (taken as a reference to what happens in heaven after earth-life is consummated) is not a proper distinction. See the author's commentary on Acts at 1:3.

if he would hammer this elementary truth into the consciousness of the Corinthians. Habitual sins will cause a Christian to lose his salvation.[33]

6:11 -- *Such were some of you; but you were washed, but you were sanctified, but you were justified in the name of the Lord Jesus Christ and in the Spirit of our God.*

And such were some of you -- Literally, 'And these things you were, some of you.' The neuter 'these things' is contemptuous. 'Such abominations!' The "some" softens the aspersion. But even if the majority of Corinthian Christians had not been guilty of extreme vice before their conversions, they all were sinners. The design of this verse is to remind them of what they were, and, now because of a changed status, to show them that they were under obligation to lead better lives – by accessing all the mercy which God had shown in recovering them from sins so degrading, and from a condition so dreadful. "Unrighteousness" (verse 9) in all its forms is a remnant from a bad past, which the Corinthians ought to have left behind them. The tremendous revolution brought about by the early preaching of the gospel is alluded to in the words "and such were some of you." It was no promising material that confronted the early preachers, but people whose values were exactly opposite of those of Christ. It required the mighty power of the Spirit of God to turn people like that away from their sins, and to make them members of Christ's church. The good news is that old patterns of behavior can be broken, and a whole new life can begin when a person becomes a Christian.

But you were washed, but you were sanctified, but you were justified -- All three verbs are aorist tense, showing that all three events happened at the same time, at the time of their conversion. Because of their conversion, their old slavery to sin was broken; so these old sins ought to no longer be a part of their lives. Only if the Christians choose to give into them can these old sins reassert themselves in lives that have been converted (Romans 6:12ff). "Washed" refers to the change that occurred in their lives when they were immersed, and rose to walk in newness of life (Romans 6:1ff).[34] The compound form of this word occurs only twice in the New Testament. It is the same word as in Acts 22:16 (arise, ... be baptized, and wash away your sins) and the same thing is referred to.[35] Both here and in Acts 2:38 and 22:16, the verb is not passive, but middle voice: 'You allowed yourself to be baptized, you let yourselves be washed. You were washed for your own benefit.' The middle voice indicates their submission to baptism (the washing).[36] They

---

[33] Bible students should beware! Commentaries will likely reflect a bias favoring either the Calvinist or the Arminian view of "eternal security" as comments are made on this passage. Paul is likely portraying the Corinthian Christians as being involved still in these vices. Habitual participation in such sins (not the occasional lapse), with no repentance and no change, will cause one to forfeit "any part in the kingdom of God." (This does not encourage any Christian to be less vigilant, less self-controlled, or even morally or ethically careless. It does not say that it is "OK" to go ahead and sin once in a while.)

[34] Compare Titus 3:5, and also Ephesians 5:26; 1 Peter 3:21; Hebrews 10:22; John 3:5.

[35] Robertson and Plummer, *op. cit.*, p.119.

[36] Kling, Alford, Farrar, and Beasley-Murray, *Baptism*, p.163.

were free, voluntary agents. It was not forced upon them. Seeking baptism was their own act, and they entered the water voluntarily, just as Paul did. Therefore, they ought to no longer be unrighteous. They ought to quit the fighting and the greed. (In passing, the middle voice shows baptism cannot be for babies and infants.) Paul is, of course, speaking of baptism, but his use of the word "wash" once names the effect of baptism, the spiritual washing away of all sin and guilt. Baptism, in the case of the Corinthians, was more than a mere outward sign.

"Sanctified" is passive voice, "You were sanctified." God did this "setting apart." Compare Ephesians 5:26. It cannot mean the inward, progressive sanctification accomplished by the Spirit, but rather points to a *one-time act of consecration to God* and separation from the world. (In the New Testament, sanctification is presented both as an act and a process. See notes at 1:2.) The consecration was a single act in the past, at the time of their baptism. It does not mean they were now perfect or sinless – the present reasoning of the apostle within this passage shows this was far from being the case with the Corinthians.

"Justified" is an aorist passive verb, too. God considers them as "just." See Romans 3:24-26, 4:1-8, 1:17, and James 2:21ff, where this concept is explained. (Baptism is involved in what the Bible calls "justification by faith," Galatians 3:26,27.)[37] When a person has met the conditions for forgiveness and God has "justified" him, his sins are pardoned: God accepts that person as righteous, treated as such on account of the atoning death of the Lord Jesus Christ. Three times Paul uses the strong adversative *alla* ("but") to stress the contrast between the old life that they had left, and their experience in Christ.

In the name of the Lord Jesus Christ -- "In the name of" may mean 'because Jesus commands it.' This expression was often connected with the baptismal service, spoken as the candidate was being immersed. Paul may have had Matthew 28:19 in mind. All this – washing, sanctification, justification – had been accomplished through the Lord Jesus. That is, in His name remission of sins had been proclaimed by the apostles (Luke 24:47), and by His merits all these favors had been conferred on the Corinthian believers.[38]

And in the Spirit of our God -- This phrase and the one previous belong to all three of the words – washed, sanctified, justified. The "Spirit of our God," i.e., the Holy Spirit, is

---

[37] Roman Catholic interpreters use the word order here in verse 11 (sanctification, then justification) to substantiate their doctrine of "ethical *continuatio justificationis*." In modern terms, the Roman Catholic theologian tends to include "sanctification" in his concept of "justification." Catholics believe in infused or imparted righteousness – not imputed righteousness (as the Reformers taught).

[38] That this formula "in the name of the Lord Jesus Christ" is used with all three verbs (washed, sanctified, justified) makes this verse difficult for faith-only commentators to explain. Lenski (*op. cit.*, p.253) suggested it means "the revelation of Christ presented in the Word of God." Edwards suggests this is the source of the church's authority. Fisher, who believes a person is saved before baptism, suggests it is a circumlocution for "in union with Christ" – a frequently used Pauline expression. None of these is satisfactory, since the "faith that saves" is an obedient faith!

the divine person through whose agency alone the three acts are possible. Because of His influence in our lives, we come to the place where we submit to baptism, and are thus sanctified and justified. We note incidentally that the entire Godhead is named in connection with the three saving acts. With the solemn mention of all three members of the Godhead, this section of the letter comes to a fitting close.

SECTION FOUR: REMONSTRANCE AGAINST ABUSE OF CHRISTIAN LIBERTY. 6:12-20

> **Summary**: The connection of this paragraph with the preceding seems to be this: many of the things specified in the previous vice list (verses 9-10) had to do with sexual immorality. Perhaps those practicing these sins were defending their behavior by saying 'these are just normal, physical urges we are satisfying, like eating food when hungry. Nothing wrong in that.' Such an approach is an abuse of the doctrine of Christian freedom which must be corrected. Food may be in the realm of the indifferent, but sexual immorality is not (verses 12-17). The paragraph ends with a strong prohibition against this sin (verses 18-20).

6:12 -- *All things are lawful for me, but not all things are profitable. All things are lawful for me, but I will not be mastered by anything.*

All things are lawful for me -- Some modern English versions put several of this paragraph's phrases ("all things are lawful" and "food for the stomach and the stomach for food") in quotation marks, as if they were quotations of arguments used by the Corinthians in attempting to justify their behavior. Perhaps they were quotations. This statement about all things being lawful is offered as a principle or rule of life. The principle itself the Corinthians had learned from Paul; but instead of understanding and using it aright, they made it cover doubtful and evil actions and thus misused it. Indeed, the matter of Christian liberty, and this particular principle of Christian liberty, the Corinthians had learned from Paul. But the way he introduces the subject here makes it seem as though the Corinthians had used the maxim to justify their improper conduct. Paul had probably learned about this misuse from private sources, just as he had found out about the divisions and the case of incest and the litigations. "All things" cannot be taken as an absolute. What God forbids is never allowed. What God commands, no man may set aside. So "all things" must be limited to such things as were called adiaphoristic – that is, indifferent or permissive, since they are not specifically commanded or forbidden by God. These are the things left to the Christian's own judgment and thus lie in the domain of Christian liberty (Galatians 5:1). Paul himself shows there are limitations to the application of the slogan "all things are lawful." He introduces two of these limitations with "but ...."

But not all things are profitable -- This is one limitation to the things that fall in the realm of the permissive. If the thing is not "profitable" why would the Christian insist on going ahead and doing it? "Profitable" ("expedient," ASV) translates *sumpherei*, which means "profit, conducive to profit, advantageous, beneficial." Some things may in themselves be permissible, but at a given time may not be advantageous or beneficial. (1) They may be injurious to the person who uses them. To illustrate from common life: I may have a perfect right in Christ to eat a certain food, but if that particular food should make me ill, it is not beneficial to me. It would be silly to eat it just because I have the right to. (2) Some things may be injurious to others. They may lead others to sin or tempt them to sin. In this first limitation, Paul is possibly thinking chiefly of how other people may be influenced by my behavior (cp. Romans 14 and 1 Corinthians 10). Christians have no right to do something which falls within the realm of liberty if it is disadvantageous to the highest interests of ourselves or others. The thing may not be wrong, but the law of expediency enters in. We no longer have any right to do what in itself is innocent when our doing it will have a bad effect on others.[39]

But I will not be mastered by anything -- This is the second limitation to the liberty we have in Christ. It is a second important principle by which a Christian determines whether he may or may not do the thing that he has freedom in Christ to do. There is a play on words in the original: 'All things are in my power, but under the power of none will I be subdued.' "Mastered" (*exousiasthēsomai*, "brought under the power," ASV) pictures 'being subdued' or 'becoming a slave' or 'being addicted' to something. I will not let it become a habit, so that I just have to have it. It is an abuse of Christian liberty to so indulge in anything that it becomes a habit! We are to have Christ as our master. We are to be His servants, and not slaves of some earthly habit. If a permissive thing is expedient, and if we do not become a slave to it, but control the use of it, then it may be done (entered into). We have no right to do what in itself is innocent when experience has proven that our doing it has a bad effect on ourselves. Our liberty is abused when our use of it weakens our character or lessens our power of self-control. The idea of liberty in Christ is a fundamental principle of Christianity. But "liberty" is not a license to do anything we please at any time. Before permitting ourselves to act in an area where we are free in Christ to act, we should first test the action being contemplated via two questions – "Is it profitable?" and "Am I becoming a slave to habit?"

Someone has pictured Christian behavioral guidelines as being of two kinds – mandatory and permissive.

    MANDATORY -- "we are under law to Christ" (1 Corinthians 9:20,21)
      1) Precepts -- "Thou shalt's"
      2) Prohibitions -- "Thou shalt nots"

---

[39] A classic example was given by Merrill Tenney. A missionary to Western China was home on furlough. He was invited after Lord's Day services to a lady's home. She had a lovely pork roast dinner. He asked, "I dearly love pork, but would you allow me to abstain from this pork roast?" He went on to explain. "Please don't be offended if I do not eat any pork. The people among whom I work are Moslems, and the Koran forbids pork. One of the first questions they will ask me when I return is, 'Did you eat pork while you were in America?' If I do eat any pork, I cannot possibly witness to them. I want, when I go back to the field, to be able to say that when on furlough, 'No, I didn't eat any pork.' Thus I will be more able to witness to them, and they will more readily listen to the Gospel." The missionary did not say it was sinful for others at the table to eat pork. He did not say it was sinful for the hostess to serve it. But he did say it was expedient in his case not to eat.

PERMISSIVE -- The realm of "Christian liberty" -- but this has its limitations:
    1) Limited by the law of expediency, 6:12a
    2) Limited by the law of self-control, 6:12b
    3) Limited by the law of self-preservation, 6:19
    4) Limited by the law of duty to God, 6:20

"Liberty" means we are free to do what is spiritually best for ourselves and for others.[40] When Paul says "all things are lawful," he is speaking in the realm of the permissive – the realm of Christian liberty. He is not saying Christians are free to ignore the precepts and prohibitions propounded by Christ and his apostles. Remember, the Corinthians had been tolerating violations of the law of purity. And they were defending their actions by using Paul's own words, "all things are lawful for me," as a shield for their questionable and wrong actions. They were erroneously applying this fundamental principle of Christian liberty to something which was in the mandatory realm. This is not to be done! We are not to understand that Paul is admitting that fornication is in any case lawful; in fact, in the following verses, he intends to show the practice cannot possibly be defended in any way.

In case someone should feel that the few rules imposed by Christian teaching are oppressive and restrictive, consider how great is the freedom in Christ compared to other religions. Other religions (in Paul's day and earlier) prescribed rules which men must keep if they would be saved, and abstaining from all unlawful things was a necessary part of attaining salvation. For example, food laws were especially common. Not so with Christianity. The believer will avoid things God has prohibited, but not in order to earn his salvation. Salvation is a gift. The believer does what he does out of gratitude to God who has saved him. But even with the few rules Christ has ordained, the believer is not hedged around with a multitude of restrictions such as were found in the other religions of the day. He has freedom in Christ. As Paul taught it, "All things are lawful."

6:13 -- *Food is for the stomach and the stomach is for food, but God will do away with both of them. Yet the body is not for immorality, but for the Lord, and the Lord is for the body.*

Food is for the stomach, and the stomach is for food -- This apparently was one of the justifications the Corinthians advanced for their sensual behavior. They were arguing from the *natural* to the *sensual*. They were arguing that as the stomach is to be satisfied with food, so the body is to be satisfied by fornication (if necessary).[41] 'Just as God has made us with appetites for food, and he has made food adapted to such appetites, and it is right therefore to eat – so God has made us with sexual desires, and they ought to be satisfied, even by fornication, if necessary.' The Corinthians seemed to place on the same level the appetite for food and the appetite for sex, and applied the maxim equally to both,

---

[40] In other words, there is no Christian liberty apart from Christian love. See 1 Corinthians 10:23.

[41] In Greek philosophy, the distinction made by Paul between the stomach and the body, between fornication and hunger, had no place. The two physical desires concerned were treated on the same footing, simply as physical functions. The higher ethical considerations involved in sexual relations were ignored. Hence, the degradation of woman and the decay of family life, which brought Greek civilization to a shameful end.

"All things are lawful." They failed to see the great difference between the stomach and the body. Anything that comes under the title of "food"[42] is for the stomach, intended for it by God; and the reverse is true, the stomach is intended for all that is food. The food must profit us both as to selection and quality. And again, we must maintain our "power" (self-control) and not become slaves of our appetite as drunkards or gluttons do. Paul is espousing the profound teaching of Jesus on this matter of foods (Mark 7:15-23).

But God will do away with both of them -- Paul's corrective for the slogan the Corinthians have put forth in defense of their behavior is that the correlation just alluded to between the food and the stomach is temporary. This relation between food and the organ for its digestion continues during this life. God who made both will eventually put both out of commission. This would occur in the resurrection when the physical body becomes a spiritual body (1 Corinthians 15:44,51; Matthew 22:30). There will be no need for the stomach when men "shall hunger no more, neither thirst anymore" (Revelation 7:16). The organs which serve for the maintenance of the present natural body will not be necessary in the future, spiritual, resurrection body.

Yet the body is not for immorality, but for the Lord, and the Lord is for the body -- Paul could have shown that fornication is not in the realm of the permissive, but in the realm of the mandatory, for God has specifically forbidden it. But Paul chooses to take the words of the Corinthians, and show that the parallel they were drawing was not legitimate. His statement regarding the body and the Lord is composed exactly like the one regarding foods and the stomach. Paul writes "the body" and not, as in the previous statement, only one organ of the body. For, in this case, the fact is that the entire body is involved in the matter of sex – not just one organ as in the case of the stomach and food. Perhaps we could paraphrase the verse thus far on this fashion: 'Food for the body to nourish it, and the stomach for food to receive the nourishment. The body for Christ to obey and to honor him, and Christ for the body to bless and to save it.'

Beginning in this verse, Paul gives six arguments against indulgence in licentiousness. The *first argument* might be stated on this fashion: it is not legitimate to say that just as the body's desires for food are to be satisfied, so the urges of sex are to be indiscriminately satisfied. No such relation exists between the body and fornication as exists between the stomach and food. "The body is ... for the Lord." The Bible recognizes a sacredness and dignity for the body. If a man has a proper regard for his body, he will not do some of the things the non-Christian will do with his body (where the proper esteem is not present). Paul is teaching that the Christian is to use his body for the Lord Jesus Christ.[43] By eating whole some food we are not perverting the digestive organs

---

[42] The KJV reads "meats," which to us speaks of the flesh of animals. However, "meats" in AD 1600 meant food of any kind, as does the Greek word (*brōmata*) in this place. Shore's lengthy presentation (*op. cit.*, p.49-50) that "meats" here means "meats offered to idols," and that it is these meats that Paul here makes a matter of indifference, does not carry with it the weight of conviction, especially in the light of what will be written in chapters 8-10. There are times when eating food offered to idols is not in the realm of liberty, but in the realm of the prohibited.

[43] The Greeks, with their dualistic philosophy that spirit was good and matter was evil, always looked down on the physical body. They thought of the body as a prison house in which the important part of man,

of the body to a use not intended for them; rather, we are putting them to the use God meant for them to serve. Fornication, on the other hand, is putting the body to a use God never intended. It is a perverted use of the body. There is no such connection between the body and fornication as there is between the stomach and food. The stomach may be made for food, but the body is not made for fornication but for the Lord. God did not design the body for fornication as He did the stomach for food. "The Lord is for the body" says that the Lord acts, and plans, and provides for the body. Jesus even died to redeem the body (as well as the soul). The Lord dwells in, acts for, and provides for the body. The Lord, in this case, speaks of Christ. "The Lord is for the body" brings the thought that just as food is necessary if the stomach is to function, so the Lord necessary if the body is to function. It is only as the Lord enables that we can live the kind of bodily life for which we were meant. And when all this has been done for the body, it is not right to take the body and devote it to purposes of pollution.

6:14 -- *Now God has not only raised the Lord, but will also raise us up through His power.*

Now God has not only raised the Lord -- The reference is to the bodily resurrection of Jesus from the dead. The *second argument* against indulgence in fornication is that God will exert His mighty power in raising up the body, and will make it glorious. It ought not, therefore, to be prostituted to purposes of licentiousness. The Corinthians have argued that fornication is just as natural as eating. Paul repudiates this argument with vigor. The stomach and food are transient. In due time God will do away with both. But the body is not destined to be destroyed. It is to be transformed and glorified (Philippians 3:21).

But will also raise us up through His power -- "Raise us up" out of the grave, is the idea. The future for the physical body of the Christian is the same kind of resurrection that Jesus experienced.[44] The reference is to the final resurrection, at the second coming of Jesus.[45]

---

the soul, was shackled. Their low view of the body resulted in one of two life-styles. Some taught rigorous asceticism where everything was done to subject and humiliate the body. The other view was libertinism, which tended to say that it doesn't matter what one does with the body (indulge all its desires if you wish) since such behavior didn't affect the soul. Paul here indicates that Jesus offers a different view of the body than did Greek philosophy.

[44] Some have thought this is a reference to the spiritual resurrection (i.e., like the new birth, where one rises to walk in newness of life). A parallel passage would be Ephesians 2:6 or Colossians 2:12. However, the Corinthians have already been justified – they have already risen to walk in newness of life ("unleavened," 5:8). Therefore, to so interpret the last half of verse 14 as speaking of the new birth would make the reference to Christ's resurrection in the first part of this verse of no point to this verse.

[45] Some systems of eschatology have the righteous and wicked raised at different times. One evidence used to support this view is the fact that the word used of our resurrection is *exēgeiren*, "he will raise us out [of something]," from which it is inferred that the righteous will be raised from amidst all the dead bodies, the wicked temporarily being left behind to await their resurrection later. Further discussion of the resurrection will be found in notes on chapter 15. The alleged difference implied in the expressions "resurrection *of* the dead" (all being raised) and "resurrection *from* the dead" (some being left behind, not being raised at the same time) is also commented upon in the author's Gospel's notes at Luke 14:14.

God is going to raise our bodies, and so the body is not perishable. The body is not like the stomach, which shall be brought to nought. Paul always grounds man's resurrection on the resurrection and ascension of Christ.[46] If the appetites, passions, and lusts are held in proper restraint and used as is good, then the Spirit of God will dwell in and be with us; and God, who raised Jesus, will by His Spirit raise us up to reign with him. Not only does Jesus have an interest in our physical bodies (6:13), but God the Father also has an interest in our bodies. The point Paul is making is this: If the body is to be raised, that shows it is important. It must not, therefore, be disregarded as though it were going to be destroyed, like the stomach is. It should be noted, in passing, that this passage shows that although Paul believed in the return of Christ and the consequent resurrection of the dead, he did not believe the event would be during his lifetime. He speaks of himself as one who would be among those raised from the dead when that momentous event finally comes.

6:15 -- *Do you not know that your bodies are members of Christ? Shall I then take away the members of Christ and make them members of a prostitute? May it never be!*

Do you not know -- Paul here presses home the principle that the body is for the Lord, and not for fornication. The implication is that the Corinthians *do* know this fact that our bodies are "members of Christ." As he has already done three times in this chapter, Paul employs the formula "do you not know?" to appeal to a matter which he has taught them, and which should therefore be a matter of common knowledge. The *third argument* against licentiousness is that we as Christians are united to Christ, and therefore cannot let a "harlot" give orders to, or use, our bodies.[47]

That your bodies are members of Christ? -- Here, the bodies of Christians are spoken of as members, essential parts, of Christ's body. "Members" (*melē*) is the ordinary word for parts of the body.[48] Christians are His hands and His feet and His voice. (It reminds one of the poem by John Palmer, "Christ has no hands but our hands to do His work today. He has no feet but our feet to lead men in the way. He has no tongue but our tongue to tell men how He died ....") Just as we ourselves possess our own members and use them as our own for our own purposes, so my entire body and your entire body are members of Christ to be used by Him alone for His own purpose. This is necessarily involved in the giving of our lives to Christ.[49]

---

[46] See 1 Corinthians 15; 2 Corinthians 4:14; Romans 6:5,8, 8:10,11; and Ephesians 1:19,20.

[47] Verses 15-17 form a syllogism, with two premises followed by the conclusion. Premise #1, the bodies of Christians are members of Christ. Premise #2, sexual intercourse is more than just a physical act; it unites two people (as taught in Genesis 2:24). Conclusion: It is wholly improper to take away something that belongs to Christ and give it to a prostitute!

[48] Parallel Scriptures where individual Christians make up the body of Christ are 1 Corinthians 12:27; Ephesians 5:30; John 15:5; Ephesians 1:23; and Colossians 1:18, 2:19. The thought of the congregation of Christians as being the body of Christ is more fully developed at 1 Corinthians 12:12ff; Ephesians 5:23ff.

[49] In Greek philosophy, the body was the perishing envelope of the man. In the Biblical view, it is the abiding vehicle of man's spirit.

Shall I then take away the members of Christ, and make them members of a harlot?
-- "Take away" (*airō* is the verb from which the participle here comes) means to alienate from the proper owner. The aorist tense indicates the "taking away" of the members from Christ is something that is done before the actual union with the harlot, and is something that is just not right.[50] Paul's use of this unexpected word "harlot" ('prostitute') in this context has been explained variously. Perhaps they were using the priestesses of Aphrodite to satisfy their sexual desires. Perhaps Paul uses this word to show the abominableness of what the Corinthians were doing, any time they participated sexually in an unlawful union. Paul's argument is that sexual union with an unlawful mate, unlike union with a lawful mate, requires robbing Christ of members which belong to Him before the illicit union can occur. Just like "members of Christ" means that the body is at the disposal of Christ, so "members of a harlot" means that the person's body is used just as and how the harlot wishes – for the harlot's own purposes.

May it never be! ("God forbid!" ASV) – *Mē genoito* is a negative optative mood verb expressing a strong wish, resulting from an abhorrent idea. 'Perish the thought! By no means! Never!' The older English translations tried to catch the vehemence of the wish by rendering it "God forbid!" though technically there is no word for "God" in the Greek.

6:16 -- *Or do you not know that the one who joins himself to a prostitute is one body* **with her?** *For He says, "THE TWO SHALL BECOME ONE FLESH."*

Or -- In verse 16 we have an explanation and justification for the expression, "members of a harlot." In Paul's mind, it is as if someone had objected that what he has just written in verse 15 was not what happened when one visited a harlot. The Corinthians would not question the statement that their own bodies are the "members of Christ," for that would be to repudiate their own Christianity. But they might deny that by an act of fornication their bodies would assuredly become members of a harlot. That, they would say, is surely overstating the result of illicit sexual contact.

Do you not know that one who joins himself to a harlot is one body *with her* -- Once again Paul appeals to that which is common knowledge. The view he expounds of the nature of the sexual act was no private opinion, but one known and accepted by the Corinthians. We have to add several words to complete the idea that is implied in the original. One suggests 'that he which is joined to a harlot, and the harlot, are one body.' Another has 'that he which is joined to a harlot is one body with her.' Whereas before the act there are two separate and distinct bodies and personalities, the act of fornication makes one single body of the two and produces a 'bond' between the participants.

For He says, "THE TWO WILL BECOME ONE FLESH" -- "For" shows that Paul is giving a reason for something just affirmed. The fact that two sinners, by an act of forni-

---

[50] The Greek behind "make" is *poiēsō* and may be either aorist subjunctive or future indicative. If we accept the aorist as correct, the implication is 'Have I any right to make ...?'

cation, become one body is established by a quotation of Genesis 2:24. The words in Genesis 2:24 were originally spoken of a legitimate sexual union. Here in Corinthians, Paul is speaking of an illegitimate union. The point is that there is the physical union, the making of one body, whether or not the union is legitimate. The words "the two" are not found in the Hebrew, but are in the Septuagint and in the Samaritan Pentateuch. They are always so quoted in the New Testament.[51] Who spoke the words "He says"? In the Genesis passage it is Adam speaking. Paul seems to word it so that it is God who is speaking. In Matthew 19:5, Jesus says it was God speaking. Notes at the Matthew 19 passage show that Adam must have been repeating what he had learned by revelation from God. What did Adam know of a father and a mother to be left when one marries a wife? "Shall become one flesh" is literally, 'shall become into one flesh.' "Flesh" denotes merely the substance of which the "body" is composed.[52] Incidentally, "flesh," which applies to all of the body, excludes the evasion that in the sexual act only a small part of the body is involved, since it is just the sexual organs. This appeal to Genesis 2:24 (Matthew 19:5) is equivalent to the rule that *no intercourse between the sexes is free from sin except under the sanction of marriage.*[53] If a man has a proper respect for his body, he just will not go out and commit such sin.

6:17 -- *But the one who joins himself to the Lord is one spirit* with Him.

But -- "But" introduces the directly opposite union, and states the fact as such without again asking "Do you not know this fact?"

The one who joins himself to the Lord -- This parallels the previous statement ("the one who joins himself to a harlot ...") exactly. The two opposites clash in every word. In verse 13 Paul has said, "The body is for the Lord." That concept is here explained and defined. We join ourselves to the Lord by faith and obedience. The body as such could, of course, never belong to the Lord. It is always the person as such who belongs to Him, and thus also the body. The verb "joins himself" is probably to be understood as middle voice. This belonging of our body to the Lord is not a passive act on the part of the person, but is an active relationship – joining Him for our own benefit.

Is one spirit *with Him* -- The italics show something must be supplied to complete the sense: 'The one who joins himself to the Lord is one spirit with Him' is the idea. This is the opposite of the sad result obtained when one joins himself to a harlot. A Christian who

---

[51] See Matthew 19:5. Also see Mark 10:8 and Ephesians 5:31.

[52] Paul introduces this quotation by speaking about the "body." Then he quotes the LXX at Genesis 2:24 which reads *sarx* ("flesh"). The same idea is in mind whether we speak of "body" or "flesh." Paul is speaking of the physical/spiritual union of the individuals involved.

[53] Farrar, *op. cit.*, p.194.

would be joined with a harlot[54] must first take himself away from Christ (6:15) in order to consummate a union that is wholly unspiritual, utterly carnal, and base. What a difference when one joins himself to the Lord. He becomes one spirit with the Lord. For while our union with Christ involves also our bodies as a part of our person, it is really a union of the spirit and only as such includes our bodies. This mysterious union with Christ is abundantly attested in the Scriptures.[55] With no absorption of our spirit into Christ, with no mingling or fusion of the two, with no loss of the identity of either, our spirit is joined to Christ's so that one thought, one desire, one will animate and control both; namely, His thought, desire, and will. It is remarkable how these verses contain the germ of three weighty sections which follow in this epistle, and doubtless were on the apostle's mind when he wrote them: (1) the relation between the sexes, (2) the question of meats offered to idols, (3) the doctrine of the resurrection of the body.[56]

6:18 -- *Flee immorality! Every* **other** *sin that a man commits is outside the body, but the immoral man sins against his own body.*

Flee immorality! -- This is a solemn command from God, as explicit as any that thundered from Mt. Sinai. This is also the conclusion that has been reached as a result of the entire array of facts just enumerated. There is a force and emphasis on the word "flee" (*pheugete*). It is a present tense – 'make a practice of fleeing fornication,' 'flee and flee and keep on fleeing.' It is a present imperative, which indicates a habitual action; 'make it your habit to flee!' That is the only way to treat immorality. There are some sins a man can resist, some about which a man can reason without danger of pollution. "Resist the devil and he will flee from you." And there are some sins we must necessarily face, fight, and thus conquer. But fornication is a sin where a man is safe only when he flees, like Joseph fled from Potiphar's house. The only way to conquer this lust is to run away from it. It cannot be dealt with by any less drastic measures.

Every *other* **sin that a man commits is outside the body** -- The *fourth argument* against sexual immorality now follows. Fornication is a sin against the body; it is a sin striking at the very roots of a man's being. Immorality does something to the body that no other sin does. "Every other sin" certainly includes the non-sensual sins, such as falsehood, theft, malice, dishonesty, pride, ambition. Every sin can jeopardize the eternal destiny of the body, but immorality directly affects the body *now* in a way other sins do not.[57] We

---

[54] What is true when immorality is involved is not true where marriage is involved. A person involved in a normal marriage does not have to end that relationship to be joined to the Lord. Ephesians 5:21-32 shows that the human marriage union is valid and compatible with being joined to the Lord. It is an unholy union that requires a man to rob Christ of a bodily member that should be His.

[55] See Galatians 2:20, 3:27; Colossians 3:17; John 17:21, 15:1-7.

[56] Alford, *op. cit.*, p.516.

[57] Commentators are divided over whether or not "drunkenness" and "gluttony" should be included in "every other sin." Those sins certainly harm the body. Various conjectures are offered to explain this apparent discrepancy. One suggests Paul's statement should be read hypothetically, 'although all other sins were without the body, yet this ....' Another suggests 1st century readers would have automatically

err when we question or challenge Paul's statement regarding the exceptional character of fornication by referring to a sin like suicide or others that damage the body like drunkenness, gluttony, or addiction to drugs. Paul is far more profound: no sinful act desecrates the body like fornication and sexual abuse. In this sense fornication has a deadly eminence.

But the immoral man sins against his own body -- Fornication does something to the body that no other sin does. "In the case of no other sin is such grievous injury done to the body as in this case."[58] The body has an eternal destiny ("the body is ... for the Lord, and the Lord is for the body," 6:13). Fornication takes the body away from the Lord and robs it of its glorious future. He does not say this is the most serious of all sins, but he does say its relation to the body is unique. Other sins will occur to us which have their effects on the body. But this sin, and this sin only, means that a man takes that body which is 'a member of Christ' and puts it into a union which sins against his own body. No other vice will separate the body of the Christian from Christ as does fornication. No other sin (not even drunkenness or gluttony) affects the relationship of the body to Christ in such a direct way as fornication; the person who fornicates sins against his own body. Therefore, fornication is not in the realm of the permissive; it violates the law of self-preservation. Our body is for the Lord. It is to be surrendered to Him. In fornication a man instead must surrender himself to the harlot. A man cannot be surrendered both to a harlot and to Christ; there is no middle ground. A man who has indulged in fornication will tell you from experience that what Paul says is true. After spending time with a prostitute, he feels like he is dirty and needs to take a bath, save that the bath does not do any good. He's "hurt" his body and there is not any "bath" that can take away the feeling. "It's almost as if you'd killed a part of yourself," said one man who had experienced such feelings after so sinning. And such a feeling as this you get from no other sin. Someone has seen the following syllogism in verses 18 and 19. Major premise = Fornication, as does no other sin, violates the body. Minor premise = The Christian's body is the Spirit's sanctuary. Conclusion = Fornication, as does no other sin, desecrates the very temple of the Holy Spirit. Therefore, we not only flee fornication, but make a conscious effort to glorify God in our bodies.

6:19 -- *Or do you not know that your body is a temple of the Holy Spirit who is in you, whom you have from God, and that you are not your own?*

Or do you not know -- For the sixth time in this chapter, Paul drives home his appeal to what the Corinthians already know so well with his argumentative question, "Do you not know?" The Corinthians do know what Paul is about to state; but as in the case of so many

---

associated gluttony and drunkenness with visiting a prostitute. Another says fornication pollutes the *whole* body as no other vice does. Or again, to 'sin against the body' is another way of saying "take it away from Christ" (verse 15).

[58] Robertson and Plummer, *op. cit.*, p.121.

things that we indeed know, we fail to apply them to our lives. We let them lie unused in our intellect. The *fifth argument* against sexual immorality is that the human body of the Christian is the temple of the Holy Spirit.

That your body is a temple of the Holy Spirit who is in you -- In 3:16, the congregation as a whole was called the temple of the Spirit. Here, the Christian's body is the temple in which the Spirit dwells. People would not think of marring or disfiguring the temples in which their heathen gods 'lived.' Neither should they mar or disfigure their body – a temple of the Holy Spirit. "In the temple of Aphrodite at Corinth, fornication was regarded as a *consecration*. The Corinthians are here told that for the Christian, it is a monstrous *desecration*."[59] Christians' physical bodies are temples of the Holy Spirit. That is what "who is in you" means when spoken of the Holy Spirit. Our humble earthly body is nothing less than a "sanctuary in which the Spirit dwells." Acts teaches that we receive the indwelling Holy Spirit when baptized (2:38). Galatians 3:2 speaks of the same indwelling Spirit. So do numerous passages (Romans 8:9,11, 14ff, 8:26,27; James 4:5; 1 John 3:24; Ephesians 1:13,14; 2 Corinthians 5:5[60]). "Temple" is *naos*, the same word for temple that was used at 3:16, and refers to the inner sanctuary rather than the whole courtyard and precincts (*hieron*). That a Christian's body is a temple in which God lives gives a dignity to his whole life as nothing else could do. Wherever we go we are the bearers of the Holy Spirit, the temples in which it pleases God to dwell. This must rule out all such conduct as is not appropriate to the temple of God. Its application to the sin of fornication with which Paul has been dealing is obvious, but the principle is of far wider application. Nothing that would be amiss in God's temple is ever proper in the body of the child of God. Since a *naos* (temple) was a place where a deity dwelt, this verse sheds light on the way the Holy Spirit was regarded by Paul. Clearly he viewed the Spirit as deity in the fullest sense.

Whom you have from God -- The Holy Spirit proceeds both from the Father and the Son (see John 15:26). The Spirit dwelling in the body of a Christian is the gift of God received at baptism (Acts 2:38), not the result of some man-induced experience. Incidentally, verse 19 has clarified the third limitation on a Christian's behaviors and actions in the realm of Christian liberty – the law of self-preservation (see the chart on p.195 in notes on verse 12).

And that you are not your own? -- The *sixth argument* against sexual immorality is 'We are not our own.' We no longer give the orders in our lives; rather, God tells us what to do because He owns us; we belong to Him. The next verse tells us that we have been purchased with a price. We are bound therefore to devote ourselves – body, soul, and spirit – as *God* directs. Christians do not belong to themselves, even if it were possible to

---

[59] Robertson and Plummer, *op. cit.*, p.128.

[60] An interesting sermon is, "Who Lives at Your House?" in the *Christian Standard*, 1956, p.409. How the indwelling Spirit helps the Christian is detailed in Special Study #10, "The Joy of the Holy Spirit."

commit fornication without personal contamination or self-violation. The plea here is to Christians to be clean as members of Christ's body.[61] We have no right to do as we please, unless we please to do what is right in our Owner's sight.

6:20 -- *For you have been bought with a price: therefore glorify God in your body.*

For you have been bought with a price – With "for", Paul begins an explanation of why we are not our own any longer. We "have been bought and paid for" says Goodspeed's translation. Many places in the New Testament teach this doctrine, that a man is "bought" or purchased.[62] "Bought with a price" is not the same metaphor as 'paying a ransom.' The imagery here is that of redemption, probably of sacral manumission. By this process a slave would save the price of his freedom, pay it to the temple treasury, and then be purchased by the god. Technically he was the slave of the god; as far as men were concerned he was a free man. Paul applies this imagery to the dealings of Christ with men. Deissmann tells us that Paul's words here are "the very formula of the records."[63] The price paid to purchase us from slavery to sin was no pious fiction, but the very heavy price of the death of our Lord Jesus (Matthew 20:28, 1 Peter 1:18). The result is to bring us into a sphere where, as far as men are concerned, we are free (remember verse 12, "all things are lawful for me"). But still, we are God's slaves; we belong to Him. He has bought us to be His own. Our having been bought results in our no longer being our own. The obligation resting on believers as a consequence is that they should "glorify God." Again, the "word of the cross" (1:18) is brought to bear on this question of behavior. The aorist "bought" is historical and reports the fact: God bought us when on Calvary He paid the blood of His own Son as the price (Acts 20:28). God, indeed, bought all men with this price, even those who deny the Lord (2 Peter 2:1). Yet what is thus true of all men in a general way is true of Christians in a particular way, for they have actually come into God's possession, are "a people for God's own possession" (1 Peter 2:9) and the price paid for them is not in vain.[64]

Therefore glorify God in your body[65] -- This is the conclusion to which he draws his argument. This would be the fourth limitation to Christian liberty (see the chart on p. 195

---

[61] Lipscomb, *op. cit.*, p.94.

[62] Acts 20:28; 1 Corinthians 7:23; 1 Peter 1:18,19, 2:9; 2 Peter 2:1; Revelation 5:9.

[63] A. Deissmann, *Light from the Ancient East* (Grand Rapids, MI: Baker, 1965), p.324.

[64] In this metaphor of manumission, there may be in the background the teaching that when a man commits his first sin, he becomes a slave to sin (Romans 6:17,18) and is then under devil's dominion (Colossians 1:13). That is all rectified when the benefits of Calvary are applied to the penitent believer.

[65] One more phrase, "And in your spirit, which are God's," appears in the King James Version, but does not enjoy integrity. It is not found in the best manuscripts, nor is it necessary to Paul's argument regarding the Christian's chaste use of his body. Metzger, *A Textual Commentary on the Greek New Testament* (New York: United Bible Societies, 1971), p.553, thinks the phrase is a marginal gloss that crept into the text.

in notes on verse 12). The Christian is to do all to the glory of God (10:31; John 21:19, 12:28, 13:31). In this context, the glorification would be accomplished by living a chaste life, with no sexual immorality. We might expect Paul to close by saying, "by all means, then, consecrate your body as a sanctuary for the Spirit." But that would not be the real climax. So he at once reaches the climax that alone properly ends this discussion. The great fact of our purchase establishes that we, including our body, no longer belong to our own selves, no longer dare desecrate our body with fornication, but must ever glorify God in our body. There is an urgency expressed by the aorist tense, and the postpositive particle *de* for which we have no English equivalent. We attempt to reproduce its force by the cumbersome term, "by all means, then." Paul does not want the command to glorify God to be taken as something that does not matter. There is an urgency about it. 'Let there be no delay in obeying!' To glorify God in our body means to so use our earthly body that men may actually see that these bodies belong to God. We refuse to use them for sinful acts; we reserve them wholly for obedience to God. Someone has said it like this: To glorify God means "that after we have left someone's presence, he thinks, 'Thank God that man was just here!'"

Fornication is an all too common sin, and much has been said, preached, and written about its vicious character. Yet who can point to a treatment that in any way compares with this one paragraph dictated by Paul's inspired lips? Principle and facts are combined; and these facts reach to the profoundest depth and to the most sacred height, and are yet presented with a simplicity and lucidity that are unique.

Special Study #3

HERE I STAND, SO HELP ME GOD!

Scripture: A reminder of some things Jesus taught. (Matthew 5:20-48, Luke 12:15, Acts 20:35)

INTRODUCTION

A. This is a sermon about "ethics" – mine and yours.[1]

B. WHAT IS AN 'ETHIC'?
   Ethics are the rules or standards by which I govern my personal and social behavior.

C. MY THESIS
   We must still start from the presupposition of authoritative Scripture: God has spoken and told us what our ethical standards are to be. These ethical standards are not open to input from non-revelatory religions, or cultures that for millennia have been idolatrous.

I. **DO YOU HAVE A NAGGING FEELING THAT SOMETHING IS NOT QUITE RIGHT ABOUT THE ETHICS BY WHICH OUR SOCIETY DETERMINES ITS BEHAVIOR?**

Since the 1930's believers in and signers of the Humanist Manifesto (#1 & #2) have made a deliberate effort to use the educational system to change our culture – from a culture that hears the rules and standards of their creator God to one where autonomous man makes whatever rules he wishes. America is reaping the consequences of the destruction of traditional education by the John Dewey and William Kilpatrick experimentalist philosophy (e.g., a godless world view promulgated by the National Education Association – the controlling body of teachers and administrators of public schools).

Every time I turn on the news on TV, or read the paper, or one of the weekly news-magazines, I have the matter of "ethics" thrust right into my consciousness. E.g.:

   Anti-semitism (as spoken by Louis Farrakhan, and the Black Muslim stance).

   Cheating at the Naval Academy.

---

[1] The author has chosen to include one of his sermon outlines at this place in order to make application of some of the ethical ideas suggested in 1 Corinthians. To fill in details of some of the illustrations suggested, the reader may find it useful to use an internet search engine.

Cheating by students in high school and college. A recent survey by the *Boston Globe* found that 50% of all college students admit to cheating; for high-school students, the figure is 75%.

Two tow-truck operators in New Jersey were convicted (1986) for pouring oil on a freeway ramp to cause accidents and boost their business.

In business and in sports, players are encouraged to do anything to win (including intentionally injuring your chief rivals).

People unknowingly are used as human guinea pigs by government researchers.

Someone at Morton Thiokol, perhaps to make a little more profit, sent some poorly manufactured "O-rings" on to NASA, and the result was tragedy to the space shuttle *Challenger*. There were several engineers from the company who spent the night before the launch pleading with their own management and with NASA for a precautionary delay, but to no avail.

Killing and kidnaping and rape. A jogger in Central Park was attacked by a band of wilding youths. Drive-by, random shootings are common.

Looting and theft, including cheating on welfare system. (People who were not victims of the flood or earthquake are found lining up for handouts.)

People commit mayhem on a fellow human being (be it with a night stick, or a brick), and are acquitted by the courts.

A defense contractor with $11 billion in annual sales charges the Government over $1,100 for a plastic cap on a stool leg.

Income tax evasion, false advertising, check kiting, and boiler room operations that sell nonexistent gold.

The IRS has a new law dealing with receipts needed for charitable gifts over $250 because some were giving a huge check and asking for money back – but claiming the whole amount as a deduction on their tax returns.

Only about 1/3 of American families are two parent homes. The divorce rate remains, stubbornly, one out of two.

The out-of-wedlock birthrate in America has tripled since 1970 – it is among the highest in the "developed" world.

Politically correct language is expected (a matter that involves my attitudes and ethics towards others).

Third graders curse their teachers, strike and kick their teachers, and the teachers dare not lay a restraining hand on the offending child. The only thing the school can do is call the police – who come and take away the children.

Pro-life and pro-choice are decisions that are based on ethics.

As long as I have been alive, there have been scandals in government – where it becomes obvious that long-held ethical ideals were ignored or repudiated by those we have chosen to be our leaders.

> Americans want to believe that while lying to the people may be the practice in other countries, it never was acceptable for government officials in our land.

And how many times we have been disappointed in our own government!

Even famous religious leaders are shown to have acted unethically.

These transgressions – some grievous and some petty – run the gamut of human failings, from weakness of will to moral laxity to hypocrisy to uncontrolled avarice. But taken collectively, the heedless lack of restraint in their behavior reveals something disturbing about the national character.

All of us have a nagging sense that something is not quite right about how we are living, but it has been difficult to put a finger on exactly what it is that is wrong.

What's wrong lies in the area of ethics.

II. WHAT IS THE PREVAILING ETHIC IN AMERICA?

A. There was a time when Biblical ethics tended to define American culture and society.

> In a previous time, there was a traditional language of public discourse, based partly on Biblical sources and partly on republican (Greek philosophy) sources. But that language has fallen into disuse, leaving American society with no moral lingua franca.
>
> Houses on the frontier had few books, but nearly all had a family Bible.
>
> McGuffey's Readers, from which people learned to read and write, were filled with Scriptures and stories that praised the good and condemned the evil. These re-inforced the ethics learned from Scripture.
>
> Now, in my lifetime, that traditional set of values has been challenged and jettisoned, and now there do not seem to be any moral landmarks at all.

B. Now, on the threshold of the 21st century, the prevailing ethic in America is no longer Biblical. Instead, the prevailing ethic has been variously called greed, avarice, value-free self-indulgence, self-centered hedonism.

The prevailing ethic seems to be "Enrich thyself." Money is the measure of achievement.

Among other undesirable effects, the view that wealth is the measure of all men tends to exalt the individual at the expense of the community. (Somewhere along the way Jesus' words, that it is more blessed to give than to receive, have been lost.)

The contemporary prevailing ethic tends to promote the idea of value-free self-indulgence.

The 1980s have been called the "My" Decade – a time when by one's possessions thou shalt be known and judged. Someone has said that if "Do your own thing" was the cry of the 60s, and "You *can* have it all" was the cry of the 70s, then "Greed is good" was the cry of the 80s.

One fellow, used to the lifestyles of the rich and famous, lamented when leaving a prominent office, "I can't live on $60,000 a year!"

The present flood of avarice perhaps has its roots in the run-up of middle-class housing prices in the 70s, which broke the traditional connection between wealth and work.

The frenzy of getting and spending makes anyone living outside the money culture feel like suckers.

> Logic dictates that change in family structure alone is not the cause for the moral mess we find in our land. Economics plays a role. In most two-parent families, mother now works outside the home. Perhaps the reasons lie as much in the realm of values, as need.
>
> There is the allure of excess, the deluge of crass propaganda – buying is more important than giving! It often seems that the sterile ceremonies of consumerism are the most profound rituals Americans share as a people.

Somehow we have failed to hear Jesus when He said, "A man's life does not consist in the abundance of the things he possesses" (Luke 12:5).

C. There has come to be a do-your-own-thing attitude toward rules. It is very self-centered.

Marine guards at the Moscow embassy bristled at strictures forbidding fraternization with foreign nationals, particularly Soviet citizens.

For years, many on Wall Street have held a cavalier attitude toward insider-trading laws. No one is really hurt by such abuses, they claimed. But when the abuses finally became public, a world-wide recession was triggered.

For many of us, our actions betray our beliefs that some laws are little more than inconvenient pieces of paper.

> What is our attitude toward traffic laws?
> How do we relate to the laws against littering the highways?
> Dilemma ethics are taught in college. *Example*: 7 people are in a lifeboat, with food for only 4. Who gets food and who does not? *Example*: A man has a critically sick wife, and he is indigent. Is it OK to steal medicine or food for her?

D. Self-centered hedonism is rampant in today's society.

III. HAVE YOU AND I BEEN CONTRIBUTING TO THE ETHICAL MORASS IN WHICH WE LIVE?

Jimmy Carter was right. "We get in Washington the kind of person who reflects how we live at home every day."

A. How do we make ethical decisions?

"It is highly improbable that the Scriptures ever function as an absolute authority, over-riding all other motives." (Exp. Times)

"In practice, the way most of us arrive at ethical decisions involves a wide range of attitudes, values, and internalized norms, as well as conscious decision. At most, the Bible constitutes but one factor in the adoption of ethical positions. More often than not, the Bible is used to support attitudes which have been taken up on quite other grounds." (Exp. Times)

B. What Ethics do you hold that are unequivocal? Where did you get them?

One college teacher, on a radio talk show, was asked these two questions. She stammered for a moment, and then gave this list of rights and wrongs.

> "It is wrong to mistreat a child, to humiliate someone, to torment an animal, to think only of yourself, to steal, to lie, to break promises.

> "It is right to be considerate and respectful of others, to be charitable and generous."

What might you have said? Do your children know you hold these values? Do they know why? Do they see you consistently practicing what you preach?

C. Where do we get our ethics? How were they shaped?
- Home? Did we get our ethics there?
- School? This can be a bad place to learn ethics, since absolute standards of right and wrong, learned from God, are deliberately excised from the classrooms and playgrounds.
- TV? Folk spend a lot of time in front of the TV.
- Reading?

  Who of us who are older fail to remember reading stories and biographies about great men and women. The good was always held up as the example to copy, and the evil to be avoided.

  Unfortunately, today's primary-school teachers, many of whom are heavily influenced by what they were taught in trendy schools of education, make little use of the time-honored techniques of telling a story and driving home "the moral of the story."
- Our peers?
- Laws made up by our governing officials?
- Maybe Sunday School and Church?

  Sometimes institutional churches make rules as they try to apply the Scriptures to the present situation.

  But if our ethic is no different than America's "value-free self-indulgence," it is obvious we didn't learn much at Sunday School and church.

  How difficult it is to allow the Bible to challenge and change our attitudes.

  More than we may want to admit, we all have a dangerous power exerted on us by our own prejudices and values derived from sources other than the Word of God.

- Ethics courses in College -- have not been much help.

  In 19th century America, the ethics course was a high point of college life. It was taken in the senior year, and was usually taught by the president of the college, who would uninhibitedly urge the students to become morally better and stronger. It was the culmination of the students' college experience.

  But as social sciences began to flourish in the early 20th century, ethics courses gradually lost prominence until they became just one of several electives offered by the philosophy departments.

  There has been a sharp rise in applied-ethics courses – medical ethics, business ethics, ethics for lawyers, social workers, nurses, journalists. In the light of recent developments in government, there has been an increase of courses on political ethics and ethics for financiers. But what is learned in these courses?

On a recent course evaluation were these comments: "I learned there was no such thing as right or wrong, just good or bad arguments." "I learned there is no such thing as morality."

If the course takes up such moral issues as abortion, censorship, capital punishment, world hunger, or affirmative action, what the student hears is that each issue has two sides, and that pretty good arguments can be made for both. They leave class thinking that *all* moral questions have two sides, and that *all* ethics are relative.

D. The bottom line is this: most of us don't really know where our ethics came from, and many of us have never taken time to enunciate them clearly even to ourselves. And we do unethical things, the same way our neighbors do.

IV. WE CAN'T GO ON MUCH LONGER WITH THESE UNCONSCIOUS, UNBIBLICAL ETHICS, CAN WE?

Have you noticed how crime and violence are beginning to overwhelm even rural America?

Have you noticed all the local news reports of spouse abuse, and child abuse?

Have you noticed the rash of burglaries and break-ins?

WHATEVER HAPPENED TO ETHICS?

Assaulted by sleaze, scandals, and hypocrisy, America searches for its moral bearings.

Those value questions – about how we've chosen to live our lives, and how it has affected our children, about the nagging sense that unlimited personal freedom and rampaging materialism yield only greater hungers and lonelier nights – have begun to dawn in the consciousness of many of us.

V. WHAT ETHICS, WHOSE ETHICS, THEN?

A. Who decides what are "right" values?

Church groups have tried to fill the values vacuum by energetically preaching and lobbying for a return to conventional standards.

But let some Evangelicals in Alabama or Tennessee demand that certain books that teach creationism be used in the classroom, and what an outcry of hurt indignation. "They've appointed themselves to be guardians of public morality" is the cry of disdain.

Just let the Vatican issue a document calling for legal restraints on medical manipulation of human birth, including in vitro fertilization, surrogate motherhood, and termination of flawed fetuses, and see how quickly some lawyer cries "I think the Roman Church is a little out of touch with reality."

B. Where does ultimate moral authority lie?

Are our moral standards to be determined by some kind of majority consensus?

What happens is that each special interest group scrambles around to shore up their little niche, even if it is at the expense of others.

And more broadly, does ultimate moral authority lie with institutions such as church, or state, to codify and impose "standards"?

What happens when the government makes rules – e.g., to curb ethical abuses. People simply find loopholes, or just blatantly ignore the new rules. And the abuses continue.

What are we to think when a hospital has an ethical advisory group which meets regularly to deal with questions ranging from which patients should receive specific types of surgery to treatment choices for newborns with potentially lethal flaws?

My thesis again:

> We must still start from the presupposition of authoritative Scripture: God has spoken and told us what our standards are to be. And these standards are not open to input from non-revelatory religions, or cultures that for millennia have been idolatrous.

C. Remember the Bible covers three dispensations – Patriarchal, Mosaic, Christian. Mosaic Rules are not binding today!

Romans 2:14 (ASV) -- "Do by nature (long practice) the things of Law." God made revelations to the patriarchs who were to pass along these rules by word of mouth. This passing down of God's revelation was done (sometimes not well), and by these rules men are still expected to live. (E.g., God's intention for marriage – one man and one woman for life [Genesis 2] – is still the norm by which men will be judged.)

D. Basically, the answer to the question "Whose ethics?" is "God's ethics – that's whose!"

Jesus not only came to give His life a ransom for many. Jesus came to explain God's expectations to us in clear language, and demonstrated them in His own life.

VI. WHAT IS EXPECTED OF ME?   WHAT SHALL I DO?

TAKE MY NEW TESTAMENT AND MAKE A LIST OF MY OWN PERSONAL ETHICAL STANDARDS

(Something I can refer to from time to time, and refresh my memory and resolve!)

These rules come from God!   They are not relative!

Some "Do nots" in our list of ethics – learned from Jesus' Sermon on Mount.
Do not commit adultery – don't even think of splitting.
Marriage is honorable – bed undefiled. (No moving in with a person of opposite sex.) (No pre-marital sex.) (No extra-marital sex.)

Jesus regarded as fundamentally evil such things as fornication, adultery, and licentiousness (Mark 7:21-23).   And, in addition, so is lustful desire (Matthew 5:28).

Marriage and divorce – Jesus took men back to the creation, and showed them God's intention, one man and one woman for life (Matthew 19:1-9).

Jesus also taught about 3 categories of those who were exempt from the divine plan for men and women (Matthew 19:12).

Do not steal (Matthew 19:18).
Do not lie.
Theft and murder (including the angry thought or word, Matthew 5:22), and malicious acts of any kind are condemned, as also is slander or abusive speech (Mark 7:21,22).

Do not covet – a man's life does not consist in the abundance of things he possesses (Luke 12:15).
Do not use abusive language (Matthew 5:22).
No hypocrisy (Matthew 6:1-5).   See also Jesus' denunciation of Scribes and Pharisees (Matthew 23:13,15).

THERE IS STILL SUCH A THING AS SIN, and it is to be avoided!

Some "Do's" in our list of ethics – learned from Jesus and His apostles.
Deny self (Mark 8:34) and follow Jesus.
Do good (Galatians 6:10).   See also the parable of Good Samaritan – do good without counting the cost.
Do to others ... – The Golden Rule (Matthew 7:12).
Do take care of body (Ephesians 5:29).

- Love (duty) to God – absolute and unqualified – with all the heart, soul, and mind (Matthew 22:37).   A man cannot serve two masters (Matthew 6:24).
- Honor father and mother (Ephesians 6:1-3; Colossians 3:20).
- Positive behavior towards our mates and children (Ephesians 5:22-33; Colossians 3:18,19).
- Work at honest job (Ephesians 4:28).
- Work on holiness of life (Romans 6:19; Hebrews 12:14).
- Be ready to forgive others their trespasses (Matthew 6:12,14,15; 18:21-35; Mark 11:25; Luke 11:4; 17:3,4).
- Recognize our duty to the state – render to Caesar the things that are Caesar's (Matthew 22:15-22; Romans 13:1-7).
- Lay up treasures in heaven (Matthew 6:20)

Take your own New Testaments and finish the list of ethics Jesus and the apostles taught.

VII. NOW WE KNOW WHAT TO EXPECT OF OURSELVES, AND THE GOALS FOR WHICH TO WORK FOR OUR SOCIETY.

A. That the other guy is not ethical is not our real concern.   You and I must start at home with our own standards and values.

B. CERTAINLY, WE MUST DEMAND CONSISTENT BEHAVIOR OF OURSELVES – in line with the Bible we know!

I MUST NOT WAIT TILL I GET INTO A SITUATION before I decide what I ought to do.   I must plan ahead!

The notion that nice guys finish last is not only wrong but poisonous.   In fact, the contrary is true.   Unethical conduct is always self-destructive and generates more unethical conduct until you hit the bottom.

If Americans want to strike a truer ethical balance, they may need to re-examine the values that society so seductively parades before them: a top job, political power, sexual allure, a penthouse or lakefront spread, a killing on the stock market.   It is just as Jesus said, "A man's life does not consist in the abundance of things he possesses."

C. HOMES CANNOT BE VALUE-NEUTRAL!

They are not!   "Monkey see -- Monkey do." is still true.

Novelist Saul Bellow, for example, asserts that the survival of Jewish culture would be inconceivable without the stories that give point and meaning to the Jewish moral tradition.

One such story, included in a collection of traditional Jewish tales that Bellow edited, is called "If not Higher." I sketch it here to contrast the story approach with the dilemma approach.

> There was once a rabbi in a small Jewish village in Russia who vanished every Friday for several hours. The villagers boasted that during these hours the rabbi ascended to heaven to talk with God. A skeptical newcomer arrived in town, determined to discover where the rabbi really was.
>
> One Friday morning the newcomer hid near the rabbi's house, watched him rise, say his prayers, and put on the clothes of a peasant. He saw him take an ax and go into the forest, chop down a tree, and gather a large bundle of wood.
>
> The rabbi proceeded to a shack in the poorest section of the village in which lived an old woman. He left her the wood, which was enough for the week. The rabbi then quietly returned to his own house.
>
> The story concludes: The newcomer stayed on in the village and became a disciple of the rabbi. And whenever he hears one of his fellow villagers say, "On Friday morning our rabbi ascends all the way to heaven," the newcomer quietly adds, "If not higher!"

In the story of the rabbi and the skeptical outsider, it is not up to the listener to decide whether or not the rabbi did the right thing. The moral message is clear. "Here is a good man – merciful, compassionate, and actively helping someone weak and vulnerable. Be like that person."

The message is contagious. Even the skeptic gets the point.

D. SCHOOLS CANNOT BE VALUE-NEUTRAL!

Should we demand that values be a part of our children's education at school? YES!

> "We may be one of the few societies in the world that finds itself incapable of passing on its moral teachings to its young people." When it comes to character development and moral education, "it is as though we've forgotten several thousand years of civilization – the great moral, religious, and philosophical traditions." (Sommers)

Some educators have tried to insist that public education should be value neutral. But it hasn't worked.

The hands-off posture is not as neutral as it professes to be.

Author Samuel Blumenfeld is even firmer on this point. He says, "You have to be dead to be value neutral."

In tacitly or explicitly promoting the doctrine that there are no "plain moral facts," the teacher condones the students' lack of confidence in a moral life that could be grounded in something more than personal disposition or political fashion.

Other educators, for the past 20 years, have tried "Values Clarification," which maintains that the teacher should never directly tell students about right and wrong; instead, the students must be left to discover "values" on their own. (That's not "clarification." That's "obfuscation"!)

One values-clarification technique is to ask children questions about their likes and dislikes, to help them become acquainted with their own personal preferences. The students' reactions to these wide-ranging questions – from "What is your favorite color" to "How do you feel about hit-and-run drivers?" – are elicited from them in the same tone of voice, as if one's personal preferences in both instances are all that matter.

How about this anecdote concerning a teacher in Massachusetts, who after learning values clarification, applied the techniques in her class? The day came when her sixth-graders announced that they valued cheating and wanted to be free to do it on their tests. The teacher was very uncomfortable. Her solution? She told the children that since it was HER class and since she was opposed to cheating, they were not free to cheat.

She said, "I personally value honesty; although you may choose to be dishonest, I shall insist that we be honest on our tests here. In other areas of your life, you may have more freedom to be dishonest."

Now what this teacher was telling the children is that cheating is not wrong if you can get away with it. She was telling them that "good values" are "what one personally values." "Not cheating" was binding on her, and she had authority to enforce that in her classroom – others, including her students, were free to choose other values when they were in other places.

Some opponents of directive moral education (there are some *basic* morals) argue that it could be a form of brainwashing. That is pernicious confusion. To brainwash is to diminish someone's capacity for reasoned judgment. It is perversely misleading to say that helping children to develop habits of truth-telling or fair play threatens their ability to make reasoned choices. Quite the contrary: Good moral habits enhance one's capacity for rational judgments.

Parents want help reinforcing the values they teach at home.

> Some parents deliberately choose to enroll their children in private religious schools – even Jewish – where the teaching staff "is not afraid to teach ethics and kindness, where morality is woven into the daily lessons."

Others are trying home-schooling, and are passing on the values this way.

Tell our legislators we want basic values back in the school curriculum.

E. First I get my own ethics in harmony with God's revelation, and then I do what I can to get others to adopt the same values.

VIII. IT IS DISCONCERTING TO FIND I'M NOT ALWAYS CONSISTENT in my application of the rules I claim to live by.

To the extent I'm not consistent, I'm contributing to the moral and ethical decay of the society I live in.

HOW DO WE HANDLE PERSONAL ETHICAL AND MORAL FAILURE?

> Not many of us, when we see in the depths of our souls, that our actions have not matched our standards of honor and integrity, are willing to exude a sense of remorse, repentance, and shame. We know we've done wrong, and we are sorry. We even deserve punishment, we know.

This kind of guilt, this assuming of moral responsibility for one's actions, has all but vanished from public life.

Instead, the new American Gospel is "damage control," using the arts of public relations to deflect blame to some one else.

Repentance and prayer! Go out and do better!

CONCLUSION

A. We can do something about the ethical decline we see all around us.

B. First we start with our own life's standards.

> A clear call to return to the ethical standards that our Creator has revealed to us.

Take your New Testament and make your list of ethics as taught by Jesus and the apostles. And then resolve, "HERE I STAND, SO HELP ME GOD!"

C. Work on consistent behavior, in harmony with these values discerned from a study of the Word.

D. Go to God with your personal ethical and moral failures -- in repentance and prayer.

E. And when our lives have become attractive and winsome, we'll be able to convince our neighbors of the value and permanence of the ethics God has revealed.

SECTION FIVE: CONCERNING MARRIAGE. 7:1-40

A. Rights and Obligations of Married Life. 7:1-16

> *Summary:* Several questions asked of Paul in a letter sent to him by the Corinthians are answered in this chapter.[1] The first questions which are discussed deal with what is the proper thing for Christians to do concerning marriage. Paul will give a general principle on which such questions may be decided, and then apply the principle to several situations.

7:1 -- *Now concerning the things about which you wrote, it is good for a man not to touch a woman.*

Now concerning the things about which you wrote -- This chapter commences the part of the epistle which answers the questions that the Corinthians had asked Paul in a letter which that church had sent to him while he was in Ephesus.

The problems introduced by Chloe's household
1) Factions
2) Gross immorality
3) Litigation
4) Abuse of Christian liberty

The problems they had inquired about in the letter
1) Concerning marriage, 7:1-40
2) Concerning things sacrificed to idols, 8:1ff
3) Concerning disorder at the public services (men and women praying and prophesying in an improper manner, abuses of the love feast and Lord's Supper, and abuses of spiritual gifts), 11:2ff
4) Concerning the resurrection of the dead, 15:1ff
5) Concerning the collection for the poor at Jerusalem, 16:1ff
6) Concerning the possible return of Apollos to Corinth, 16:12

As can be seen from this brief outline, Paul's answers to their questions take up the remainder of this epistle, through 16:12. Paul may be answering their questions in the order he found them in their letter to him, or he may be deliberately discussing their question about marriage immediately after the sexual topics discussed in chapters 5 and 6. Shore has given us this note:

> In the consideration of each of these subjects various collateral matters are introduced, and the great principles which guided the Apostle, and which ever should

---

[1] Some offer to outline chapter 7 under 4 points, as though Paul were dealing with four separate questions. We suppose it is as suitable to use Paul's two "Now concerning" statements (verse 1, verse 25) to provide us with two topics covered in chapter 7.

guide the Church and individuals, are set forth. Many of the subjects were of purely local and temporary interest. The particular combination of circumstances which for the moment rendered them important has ceased to exist, and can never arise again; but the principles on which the Apostle based his arguments, and which he enunciates as the ground of his decisions, are eternal. To apply the injunctions of the Apostle in these chapters with a rigid and unyielding literalism to the Church in all ages is to violate those very principles which guided Paul in enunciating them, and to exalt the dead and death-bearing letter at the sacrifice of the living and life-giving spirit of the apostolic teaching. As we proceed with our examination of Paul's reply to the Corinthians' letter, we shall have little real difficulty in distinguishing between those practical injunctions which were of local and temporary application, and the wider and larger truths which are of universal and lasting obligation; for the Apostle himself is always careful to point out when a command is based upon some particular necessity of the day, and when it arises from some unchanging Christian principle.[2]

It is good for a man not to touch a woman -- Different views have been advanced as commentators have offered possible explanations for this statement: (1) Perhaps this is Paul's own statement about sexual abstinence in marriage.[3] (2) Perhaps Paul is simply quoting the Corinthian's language in their letter, and then proceeds to give his own directives or corrections.[4] (3) Perhaps verse 1 is Paul's statement to the unmarried and is equivalent to 'No pre-marital sexual relations!' Verse 2 then begins Paul's instructions to the married and urges fidelity to the marriage relationship.[5] (4) These notes will follow the view that these words were a question ('Is it good for a man not to touch a woman?') asked by the Corinthians,[6] in answer to which (beginning in verse 2) Paul first states the

---

[2] Shore, *op. cit.*, p.52.

[3] To this view it has been rightly objected that the same writer could hardly write "Let marriage be held in honor among all, and let the marriage bed be undefiled" (Hebrews 13:4) unless he had changed his views between the time he wrote 1 Corinthians and the time he wrote Hebrews. Such an alleged change of views would impinge greatly on the doctrine of inspiration.

[4] Some have supposed that Paul taught, when in Corinth, that "it is good for a man not to touch a woman." What the Corinthians have done is quote Paul's own words in their letter to him. This raises the whole question of the tone of the Corinthian letter to Paul. Were the Corinthians, in a friendly fashion, asking spiritual advice of the one who brought Christianity to them? Or, in light of the factions and favorite preachers, were they asking in a combative tone, a question over which they have been squabbling among their parties and cliques? We hope the questions were friendly, and were honestly seeking instruction concerning the proper lifestyle for Christians.

[5] This interpretation leaves us without any actual statement of the Corinthian's question – save the general topic of 'marriage' – as might be deduced from what Paul writes in chapter 7.

[6] If we had to choose between the view that verse 1b is Paul's own proposition and the view that the words express the position held by some at Corinth, we would choose the latter. Perhaps just as Greek philosophy led to error concerning the ministry (chapters 1-4), so Greek philosophy, with its dualistic distinction between spirit which was seen to be good, and matter which was seen to be evil, lurks in the background of this question. If this wisdom of men is true, then surely it is good for a man not to have sexual relations with a woman – a view that would lead logically to pressure on the married to end all sexual relations and perhaps even dissolve their marriages, and put pressure on the engaged and widows not to marry at all. This explanation is as old as Origen and has been popularized in F.W. Farrar's *The Life and Work of St. Paul* (NY: Dutton, 1879).

guiding principle, and then makes applications of the principle to specific issues.[7]

"Good" translates *kalon* ("beautiful"), something which attracts admiration when others see it. Much ingenuity has been employed by the advocates of celibacy in an attempt to make this word *kalon* mean 'lofty or noble.' The Roman church points to this verse as though it taught that the unmarried monk or priest or the unwedded nun is a holier person than the Christian husband or wife, father or mother just because of the priest's or nun's state and condition in regard to this matter. This verse does not imply, as Jerome taught (*ergo est malum tangere*), that marriage is morally wrong. On the opposite side of the issue, much energy has been spent by the advocates of marriage in an attempt to redefine the word *kalon* to mean 'convenient in the present circumstances' (verse 26). The word *kalon* means 'fit, suitable, beautiful, praiseworthy.' The phraseology "not to touch a woman" (which is a euphemism for sexual relations) is used in the Old Testament (Genesis 20:4,6, 26:11; Proverbs 6:29), where it carries the idea of 'leaving the other fellow's wife alone – or be in danger of being put to death.' Reflecting the different ways this statement has been interpreted (see notes *supra*), commentators have assigned widely divergent meanings to it. (1) Some who think these are Paul's words opt for the view that Paul is advocating asceticism (i.e., 'Have nothing to do with women at all – no dates, no courtship, no fraternization, no marriage, no nothing!'). However, we should be slow to adopt an interpretation that has Paul teaching that married people are less spiritual than single, celibate people.[8] (2) Some suppose Paul quotes the Corinthian's words with some degree of approval – that there is something to be said in favor of remaining unmarried. Under what circumstances and in what respect this is true, he will elucidate later.[9] (3) If these words quote a question asked by the Corinthians, likely they were asking about whether or not Christianity demanded sexual abstinence even for married persons. "Do not touch a woman!" is hardly to be treated as an absolute. It has to be modified by (a) the example of Christ, who beautified with His presence the marriage at Cana (John 2:1,2); (b) the primeval law which says, "It is not good for man to be alone" (Genesis 2:18); and

---

[7] The difficult thing with this way of understanding the text is the "but" with which verse 2 begins.

[8] Those who take 7:1b as Paul's proposition feel obligated to defend Paul against the charges sometimes made against him that he held low view of marriage or that Paul argued for the celibate life. Paul is not stating that he has a low regard for marriage. Certainly he cannot be supposed to contradict what he has said elsewhere about marriage. 1) Hebrews 13:4 - "Let marriage be held in honor among in all, and let the marriage bed be undefiled." 2) 1 Timothy 4:3 - It is apostasy from the faith to "forbid marriage." 3) 1 Timothy 5:14 - "I want younger widows to get married." 4) Ephesians 5:23-32 - Marriage was a type of the union between Christ and the church. Nor should what he writes in this very chapter about the mutuality of marriage – husbands and wives have equal privileges and equal responsibilities – be ignored.

[9] Protestants, especially, have been quick to point out that marriage is not a *moral* matter (as the Roman Catholic Church would make it), but a *prudential* matter. There are certain times when it is better for a man not to marry. a) Cp. verse 26, "at this time, this year." See also verses 28, 35, 38, and 40. b) Cp. Jeremiah 16:1-4, which is a parallel passage and idea. c) The apostle was writing to the church in a time of pending persecution or current emergency. He speaks of the "present distress" in verse 26; cp. verse 29ff. d) He wrote in a day when to become a Christian, to be publicly baptized and to confess Christ, meant to put one's very life in jeopardy. Under such conditions it might really be best that a man should not be married.

(c) Whether or not a man has the gift of continence (Matthew 19:10-12, 1 Corinthians 7:7). It was not Bible teaching that led 1st century Corinthians or some of the 2nd century church to embrace the ascetic and celibate life-style, but rather the inroads of Greek philosophy.

7:2 -- *But because of immoralities, each man is to have his own wife, and each woman is to have her own husband.*

But -- The "but" with which this verse begins is clearly adversative to verse 1b. Here begins Paul's extended answer to the question being asked by the Corinthians. There seems to be a principle ('Stay where you are!' – cf. 7:17) that is applied by Paul not only to marriage (verses 2-16) but also to other areas of every-day 1st century concern – e.g., circumcision (verses 18-20) and slavery (verses 21-24).

Because of immoralities -- "Immoralities" is plural in the Greek. The plural indicates the manifold and irregular sexual vices which prevailed at Corinth. Because temptations abounded at Corinth, Paul indicates that the right remedy was for each man and each woman to continue to "have" his or her own mate. Since the temptation to act immorally can affect either sex, the best way to avoid this sin is for every man to have his own wife, and every woman to have her own husband. One reason married people should continue their sexual relations with each other is because of the acts of fornication that would likely result if such marital acts should be prohibited or should cease.[10]

Let each man have his own wife, and let each woman have her own husband -- The saying is not concessive but imperative.[11] It is not '*may* have' but 'must have.' If the general principle is 'Stay where you are!' then this passage commands folk who are already married to continue the marriage relationship.[12] Continuing the marriage relationship is a command.[13] There will be exceptions (verse 7), but Paul leaves no doubt as to what is

---

[10] The acts of fornication that have resulted from the Roman Catholic efforts to establish a limited clerical and monastic celibacy more than justify Paul's phrase. So, too, do the acts of immorality that have become almost commonplace in the present century.

[11] It is not easy to render third person imperatives into English, since English does not have an exact equivalent. We must therefore use the auxiliary form "Let him ..." or "Let them ..." (an expression often used to denote mere "permission" in English) while recognizing it is translating a Greek imperative (a command).

[12] Those who outline chapter 7 differently will offer slightly different explanations for this imperative. Some, supposing it is a general directive even to folk not yet married, will offer the proviso, "If it is a command, then 'each man' must be limited to such as do not have the gift of continence (compare verses 3,7,36,37)." Others suggest it means that unmarried people are commanded to marry if they don't have the gift of continence.

[13] It is a present imperative, commanding continuing action. "Let each one have ..." does not mean each person must get married. Paul uses a different verb (*lambanō*, see verse 9) for that. "To have" equals 'to continue sexual relations with' a man or woman.

normal. "His own ... her own ...."[14] Polygamy or adultery are unlawful under the gospel as this passage so shows. The two accusatives ("his own wife" and "her own husband") clearly point to monogamy, and accord with the original divine institution of marriage (Matthew 19:3-9). It has often been voiced that Christianity raised the status of women. However, when church members are asked to point to verses that were instrumental in such a change of status, they are hard put to think of one. This is one such passage. Here, as in all of his correspondence, when Paul spoke of the duties of wife to husband, he also spoke of the duties of husband to wife. While this may seem ordinary in our society, it was revolutionary in Paul's day. It is with equal rules for both women and men that Christianity elevated the status of women to their God-given and rightful position.

7:3 -- *The husband must fulfill his duty to his wife, and likewise also the wife to her husband.*

Let the husband fulfill his duty to his wife, and likewise also the wife to her husband -- In order that the command given in verse 2 may attain its purpose, he goes on to clearly insist upon the full consummation of the marital relationship. Marital intercourse is here set forth as a matter of duty (*tēn opheilēn*). The older manuscripts read "duty"[15] and the word expresses Paul's view of the obligatory nature of mutual sexual satisfaction in marriage.[16] The verb "fulfill" is present imperative. 'Continually fulfill ...' is the idea. In a marriage, each partner is to satisfy the desires of the other, lest the other be tempted to do wrong with another man or with another woman. The principle ('Stay where you are!') applied to those who are already married includes the idea that normal sexual intercourse between man and wife has not been changed by the principles and the spirit of Christianity. How much may we read between the lines which Paul here writes? Were there some folks in Corinth advocating total sexual abstinence even in the married state? As we read on, especially verses 5 and 6, this seems a fair deduction.

---

[14] "His own" translates a reflexive pronoun. "Her own" translates a possessive adjective. We doubt Paul intended anything special by the change. It is doubtful, for example, that Paul looked on the wife as being owned by the husband (though the pagan world did so look on the wife).

[15] "Due benevolence" (KJV) is a translation of *opheilomenēn eunoian*, an inferior reading. The later Syriac versions, and the Textus Receptus (the 9th century manuscripts K and L being the earliest extant Greek manuscript evidence) may well reflect a variant influenced by the asceticism of the post-apostolic church. *Eunoia* denotes kindness, good will, affection of mind. *Opheilēn* denotes debt, that which is owed.

[16] It has been thoughtfully observed that verses 3-5 are crucial if one is to understand the role of sex in marriage. It would not be easily harmonized with the dogma that sexual intercourse within marriage must be restricted to the express purpose of procreating children. Paul calls it a "duty," something each partner 'owes' to the other. So it would be improper for one mate to attempt to use sex as a bribe, or a reward for good behavior, or as something to be withheld as a threat or punishment. Implied, too, is the truth that husband and wife alike must be sensitive to the emotional and physical states of each other and not insist on sex on demand. But neither should one partner constantly try to get out of satisfying his or her spouse's conjugal needs.

7:4 -- *The wife does not have authority over her own body, but the husband* **does**; *and likewise also the husband does not have authority over his own body, but the wife* **does.**

The wife does not have authority over her own body, but the husband *does*; **and likewise also the husband does not have authority over his own body, but the wife** *does* -- Marriage is not a capricious union, but a holy bond. "The two" become "one flesh." Verse 4 states a principle that is to guide husband and wife in their relationships to their mate. It is implied in the very nature of marriage that the granting or withholding not be at the caprice of either party, but that each possesses a legitimate claim upon the body of the other and has a right to its enjoyment.[17] Equality between the sexes is indicated by using the same expression respecting both, thus correcting Jewish and Gentile ideas about the relative servitude of women. Paul is at pains to word the two statements exactly alike and even writes out the two verbs, whereas in verse 3 he allows the second verb to be supplied by the reader. In other connections Paul upholds the headship of the husband, and requires the submission of the wife. But in regard to their sexual relation, both are on the same level; both have equally lost their right over their own body, and both have transferred that authority equally to the other. "Authority over" suggests married people no longer control their own bodies, but must surrender authority over them to their spouses. Neither partner has power over his own body to refuse the marriage privileges to the other.

7:5 -- *Stop depriving one another, except by agreement for a time, so that you may devote yourselves to prayer, and come together again so that Satan will not tempt you because of your lack of self-control.*

Stop depriving one another -- The Greek construction in this prohibition is the kind that prohibits the continuance of an action already going on. What Paul forbids is the arbitrary refusal of the marriage relation (i.e., intercourse) when the other party desires it. There may arise occasions when the partners to a marriage agree to abstain for a time from normal intercourse (for reasons to be stated in the following phrases), but this is clearly exceptional. Normally each belongs to the other so fully that Paul can call the withholding of the body an act of 'fraud.'[18] Three conditions are required for a lawful abstention within the marriage relationship: (1) It must be by mutual consent; (2) It must be for a good reason or cause; (3) It must be temporary only.

Except by agreement for a time -- This is the first condition to be met before a married couple practices sexual abstinence. "Except" equals 'except perhaps.' It is a very tentative exception.[19] The Greek for "agreement" is our word transliterated "symphony." Un-

---

[17] Mare commented (*op. cit.*, p.228), "The verb *exousiazō* literally means 'has rights over'; that is, 'has exclusive rights to,' which has already been shown in the teaching of 1 Corinthians 6:16, "the two will become one flesh."

[18] The verb translated "deprive" is the same word used in 6:7,8. The ASV translated it "defraud." It speaks of taking away what rightfully belongs to another.

[19] The word "except" represents four Greek particles. The first two equal the English "except." The third adds a note of uncertainty to the exception. The fourth tends to further limit the exception to a particular case that is considered possible. But not even is abstention from sex in marriage necessary.

less both husband and wife speak in symphony, abstention becomes involuntary on the part of one, and constitutes robbery on the part of the other.[20] "For a time" (*kairon*) denotes a specific period of time. Temporary separation for special reasons had been recognized from the earliest times (Exodus 19:15; 1 Samuel 21:4), but it was not to be a permanent thing, such as was practiced in the Middle Ages. People in the Middle Ages considered it a virtue to be married and living under one roof, but to live separate lives. What Paul contemplates are brief periods, not continuous years, of abstention from sex.

That you may devote yourselves to prayer -- This is the second condition to be met before couples practice temporary abstinence – that the man or woman may engage in the ordinary duties of religion. "That you may devote yourselves" is *hina scholasēte*. (We get our word 'school' from this verb.) It literally means 'that you may have leisure for.' Prayer must be unhurried! In the rush of life it may be necessary sometimes to take exceptional measures to secure a quiet, leisurely communion with God. But for married people the breaking off of normal relations even for such a holy purpose can be only by mutual consent. Care must be taken here. There is no suggestion that continuing normal sexual relations within marriage makes prayer impossible. Abstinence is not one of the conditions of effectual prayer. The word "fasting," added to this phrase in the KJV, is an interpolation not found in *Aleph*, A, B, C, D, F. In the ages after the New Testament was written, fasting was associated with the periods of special devotion; hence, this addition to the Received Text.[21] The "fasting and prayer" (KJV) language has been applied by many religious groups to periods like the Lenten observance. The Roman Catholic Church, based on the Old Testament (Exodus 19:15), assumed sexual intercourse ought to be abstained from during such periods. Even though in Greek Paul wrote "the prayer," no one has used this verse to try to prove the early church observed Lenten seasons or holy week. Abstinence from intercourse is not a necessary condition to a spirit of prayer in general (see verse 6). Yet there may be in our lives special times of meditation and devotion when we put aside all else – food, the time of day or night, all physical desires. Paul is speaking generally; hence, he makes no reference to sickness, to separation due to travel, and the like. He speaks only about voluntary abstinence while husband and wife are living together.

And come together again lest Satan tempt you because of your lack of self-control -- Here Paul states the third condition on which married couples may abstain from sex. It is to be temporary. Even by mutual consent, this abstinence from sexual relations was not to become perpetual, since that would expose them to many of the evils which the marriage relation was designed to avoid. At this place, the Greek text bears further traces of alteration, making it seem as if the apostle meant that the return to *matrimonial life* should

---

[20] Fisher, *op. cit.*, p.100.

[21] Kling, *op. cit.*, p.141. In passing, the comment by Shore (*op. cit.*, p.54) may be helpful: "The alteration of the Greek text of the word 'give' into the present tense, so as to make the word 'prayer' refer to daily devotions, and not to special and exceptional seasons, and the interpolation of the word 'fasting' – not found in the older MSS – are a striking example of how the ascetic tendencies of a particular ecclesiastical school of thought led to their 'amending' the sacred text so as to make it be in harmony with their own views, instead of reverently regarding it as that by which those very views should be corrected."

be only a temporary union, and not a continuous state of life. The proper reading implies the *separation* was not to be continual. After the agreed upon period of abstinence has passed, husband and wife must come together, resuming normal sexual relations, lest through inability to restrain their lusts Satan should tempt one or both of them to sin with others. "Lack of self-control" does not say the readers were especially lewd, but that they were human.[22] Satan (an enemy of Christians, 1 Peter 5:8) is here pictured as being constantly on the watch and ready to tempt Christ's followers to fall. The devil is the "prince of this age." He is the instigator and promoter of the moral standards of men who do not know God. It must be our purpose to thwart his nefarious attempts.

7:6 -- *But this I say by way of concession, not of command.*

But this I say -- What is the "this" which Paul here says is not a command which requires unquestioned obedience, but is a favor or concession that may be used or left unused? (1) One answer given is that "this" refers to the resumption of the marriage relationship after the period of devotions, that Paul does not command a resumption but only concedes it. We reject this proposed explanation (that the married might abstain permanently by mutual consent) since it contradicts all the imperatives in verses 2-5. (2) Another answer is that the antecedent of "this" is all of verses 2-5, that all of these imperatives about marriage are not really commandments at all.[23] This interpretation reflects the belief that some principle other than 'Stay where you are!' (written to folk already married) is the topic of verses 2-5. This interpretation occurs most often in those commentaries which suppose verse 7:1b is Paul's view, rather than the Corinthian's. We reject this approach. Why would anyone, least of all Paul, give commands, and then in the end say he does not intend them as commands? (3) Because of the difficulty of matching "concession" with the commands of verses 2-5, some have supposed verse 6 begins a new paragraph, and that "this" points to verses 7-9. This interpretation also requires that verse 7 begin with "for" instead of "yet." (4) The best solution is that abstinence from sexual relations for devotional purposes (verse 5)[24] is not a command from God (the word "command" is *epitagen*), but a concession.

By way of concession, not of command -- Paul left it up to the discretion of the wife and the husband whether or not to keep apart by mutual consent, and, if so, for how long. "Not of commandment" should not be pressed as though it were a denial by Paul of inspiration.

---

[22] Self-control must be exercised by married people. Paul recognizes that human nature is such that once sexual intercourse has been started, it is difficult to stop. Fisher *(op. cit.*, p.102) observes, "This thought has meaning, not only in the context in which Paul used it, but also in any discussion of the rightness or wrongness of premarital sexual experimentation."

[23] So says Farrar, *op. cit.*, p.224.

[24] *Touto*, "this," refers to what immediately precedes.

He is saying *God* has made no "command"[25] concerning sexual abstinence as a condition for prayer.

7:7 -- *Yet I wish that all men were even as I myself am. However, each man has his own gift from God, one in this manner, and another in that.*

Yet I wish that all men were even as I myself am -- The NASB opens this verse with "yet." In this place there is a variation between *de* ("now, but, yet" found in P^{46}, *Aleph**, A, C, D, F, G, 82, 326) and *gar* ("for" found in B, ψ, Textus Receptus, Vg^{cl} and Cyprian). This is likely another case in this context where the post-apostolic church's ascetic elements influenced the variation in the text. By the end of the 2nd century, much of the church was reading the text ascetically. "Yet" is the better attested reading, and should be included in the English translation.[26] Paul seems to be saying, 'I rather wish that all men might have the gift of perfect continence (i.e., self-control in sexual areas) as I have,' while at the same time realizing all men do not have such self-control. He is not saying he wishes that all men were unmarried. Paul was not an ascetic.

However -- Paul admits his own personal feeling is not decisive, indeed, not in accordance with conditions of society which have their source in God. We perhaps understand the apostle's wish better if we assume that it refers, not to the fact of remaining unmarried, but to the possession of the gift of continence without which it was disastrous to remain unmarried.

Each man has his own gift from God -- God has not given to every man alike the ability to practice continence. The force of the word "gift" (*charisma*) has been disputed.[27] Kling (*op. cit.*, p.142) asserts, "The uniform use of *charisma* in this Epistle, as well as in the New Testament, is a reference to a special gift of grace – a capacity granted by God within the church" (cp. 1 Peter 4:10)." Kling also alludes to other scholars who believe *charisma* "in this case means a natural endowment, not some special gift of the Holy Spirit. He is talking about 'all men,' many of whom would not be Christians." Paul looked upon his own self-control at this point in his life as a gift of grace from the Lord, and not as a human achievement on his own part.

One in this manner, and another in that -- Some men were born with a complete sexual self-mastery, and could thus remain without a wife. Some men had different gifts (i.e., they had a self-control different from Paul's) which did not make such complete self-mastery possible, but they too were used in the service of God. The self-control that makes

---

[25] See the previous note on the word *epitagēn*. This is a word that implies a command from God.

[26] The NIV and some other modern (dynamic equivalent) translations leave many of the Greek conjunctions and particles untranslated. In this commentator's opinion, this is a serious flaw, for it leaves the English reader with little awareness that the Greek text may say something other than what the translator has suggested it means.

[27] This is the word that was used at 1:7, and it reminds us that "spiritual gifts" are not limited to the representative lists found in chapters 12-14.

a life of celibacy possible and the desire for marriage are both abilities which God graciously bestows on us for the edification of the church. Compare Matthew 19:10-12 where Jesus himself speaks of the same thing when He said, "Not all men can accept this statement (it is better not to marry, 19:10), but only those to whom it has been given [by God]." He recognized some could remain unmarried and serve God, while others would serve God while married. Both are equally acceptable ways of serving God.

7:8 -- *But I say to the unmarried and to widows that it is good for them if they remain even as I.*

But -- If we understand that verse 7:1b is the Corinthian's own position, and that verse 2ff (which begins with "but") is Paul's reply or correction, then we could see verse 8 (another "but") as Paul's further reply or correction to their position. Having laid down the general principle ('Stay where you are!'), Paul now turns from those currently married to those previously married, but at the present time single.

I say to the unmarried and to widows -- The verb "I say" stands first in the Greek, so there is an emphasis on it. This emphatic position has led some to infer that Paul is giving only his own opinion and advice, and not inspired advice at that. This denial of possible inspiration is a flat contradiction of what Paul himself says about his inspiration at the close of this chapter (verse 40). "Unmarried" is masculine plural in the Greek. It likely refers to widowers since it is compared to widows in the next phrase.[28] Widowers are men whose wives have died. The explicit Greek word for "widower" was falling into disuse in the 1st century, so Paul uses another word to cover those men whose wives have died. "Widows" – literally, 'especially to widows' – are women who had lost their husbands through death. Perhaps the widows are singled out for special mention because of a particular vulnerability of their position, and the consequent pressure to remarry. The reference is to the unmarried *Christians*, and widowed *Christians*.

It is good for them -- See verse 1, where the same word is used. Again, it is from the standpoint of unhindered service to God that the single life is spoken of as "good."

If they remain -- Here is the general principle ('Stay where you are!') stated again. As before, it is not a hard and fast rule, with no possible exceptions. Verse 9 will delineate at least one exception.

Even as I -- Paul gives himself as an example of how a widow or widower should live. It is implied that he is unmarried when he writes 1 Corinthians. There is some evidence that Paul at one time was married. To be a member of the Sanhedrin, a man had to be married. This commentator inclines to the belief that Paul, just before his conversion to Christianity,

---

[28] In the age when asceticism was considered the spiritual way, commentators tried to make "unmarried" include all unmarried men – bachelors and widowers – but not unmarried girls, whose case is discussed later (verses 25-38).

though a young man, was already a Sanhedrin member,[29] and a voting member at that (Acts 26:10). How did he come to be "unmarried" at the time he writes 1 Corinthians? Some,[30] on the basis of what is implied here in verse 8, say Paul was a widower, that he is now unmarried because his wife had died. It is also very possible that when he became a Christian and "suffered the loss of all things for the excellency of knowing Christ Jesus as Lord" (Philippians 3:8), that loss included a divorce by his unconverted Jewish wife, and being treated as 'dead' by his unconverted Jewish family.[31] Whatever may have been his marital status earlier, when Paul writes 1 Corinthians he is unmarried.

7:9 -- *But if they do not have self-control, let them marry; for it is better to marry than to burn* with passion.

But if they do not have self-control, let them marry -- It is the widow or widower who is pictured as not having self-control in the matter of sexual desires. "If they do not have self-control" is literally 'if they have not power over themselves' (a middle voice verb). Paul does not say (as the NIV has it) "If they *cannot* control themselves." What he did write is, "If they *are not* controlling themselves." The verb is present tense, speaking of habitual self-control.[32] Whoever lacks the gift of continence Paul enjoyed needs to be married; let him or her enter into marriage. "Let them marry" is an imperative mood. Marriage is the only proper framework in which to have sexual intercourse. The Christian widow or widower who is not able to practice self-control over sexual desires should not relieve them in an immoral fashion (whether with a prostitute or with a mutually consenting [but unwed] partner). They should marry and satisfy the sexual desires with a lawful mate.[33]

For it is better to marry than to burn *with passion* -- "For" indicates this clause gives a reason for the command "Let them marry!" "Marry," in the aorist tense, means "marry once for all." "Burn" is present tense and speaks of continuous lust. Such a fire of desire, if deprived of marriage, might result in immoral or criminal satisfaction, or may in secret

---

[29] Paul, just before his conversion, may or may not have been a full member of the Sanhedrin. See notes at Acts 9:1, in the author's commentary on *Acts*, for further discussion. See also Barclay (*op. cit.*, p.68), who gives general grounds and particular grounds for believing that at one time Paul was married.

[30] Clement of Alexandria, Grotius, Luther, Ewald, Selden, Conybeare, and Howson.

[31] If Paul is "unmarried" as a result of a divorce by his Jewish wife then we have a verse where it is recognized that divorce ends a marriage. This is a topic that becomes an issue later in our study of 1 Corinthians 7 (as well as when we study Matthew 19:1-10 and parallel passages).

[32] How some commentators find proof in this passage that the suppression of sexual desire should be looked on as a meritorious work, is hard to understand.

[33] Blomberg has called attention to the fact that verses 8 and 9 are a crucial corrective to the attitude heard among Christian singles who have been previously married. "Sadly," he writes, "it is common to hear attitudes voiced these days, particularly among divorced people, which insist on sex as a right but refuse ever again to consider marriage." Those who are widows and widowers (and those divorced) need to hear Paul's insistence that marriage is the only proper framework for satisfaction of sexual desires.

devastate the inner spiritual life.³⁴ To marry once for all is better than continuous lust and desire. The alternatives offered to widows and widowers³⁵ ("marry," or "burn") are not two evils, the lesser of which is to be chosen; rather, there is good on the one hand and evil on the other. Paul states the facts unblushingly: one either has the gift of continence or he does not. If he has, he *may* remain unmarried, although he too may marry. If one lacks the gift, only one course is in order. He must marry, for moral danger is deadly.

7:10 -- *But to the married I give instructions, not I, but the Lord, that the wife should not leave her husband*

But to the married -- Verse 10 begins with "but," just as did verse 2 and verse 8. It seems proper, therefore, to treat this paragraph as another of Paul's responses or correctives to the Corinthian dictum, "It is good for a man not to touch a woman!" This directive also makes application of the principle ('Stay where you are!') to those who are married. Verse 2ff instructed the married not to reject sexual relations within marriage. Now the married are told not to dissolve their marriages through divorce. When we compare verses 10-11 with 12ff, we find the instructions of verses 10-11 deal with marriages where both of the mates are Christians.

I give instructions, not I, but the Lord -- "I issue orders," is the idea in the verb. Yet it is in reality not Paul, but the Lord Jesus, who has issued the orders. "The Lord gives instructions" means Jesus' orders have continuous, permanent force. The commands Jesus gave during His earthly ministry on this subject of marriage and divorce are found in Matthew 5:32, 19:3-10, Mark 10:11,12, Luke 16:18.³⁶ In this instance, Paul can use a word that was spoken by Jesus Himself in regard to the permanency of marriage, a word that has validity for all time. There are some other questions about which Jesus had no occasion to speak while He was here on earth. When Paul himself answers some of these questions, he does so as the Lord's apostle through whom the Lord now speaks. No matter how the divine command comes to us, whether from the Lord's own lips or from the pen of the Lord's apostle, the command has equal binding power. These instructions concerning the Christian husband and wife staying together are not merely advice, but a solemn,

---

³⁴ "Burn" is used figuratively of sexual desire. It should not be interpreted to mean that if folk have been committing immoral acts, they had better get married, else they will "burn in hell." Such an interpretation, too often, has been used to excuse immorality which the Bible clearly condemns.

³⁵ The present generation of young people is plagued with encouragement towards sexual experimentation and numerous sexual partners. Often, little is said about such immoral behavior, unless the girl becomes pregnant. Then the couple who have conceived the baby are encouraged to marry, for "it is better to marry than burn." The rather common and flippant way of using this verse, applying it as though it were the remedy for the sexual desire of "inflamed youth," is actually a misuse of the verse, for it lifts the verse from its context. Remember, the context is giving alternatives for widows and widowers.

³⁶ How did Paul know what Jesus taught on marriage and divorce? By his own affirmation, Paul got his gospel by "revelation" from Jesus (Galatians 1:11,12). (It was even affirmed in early Christian literature that Luke's Gospel reflected what Paul preached.) Paul got his information by direct revelation from Jesus. That is a better answer than Mare's suggestion (*op. cit.*, p.229) that Paul may have had access to notes of one of the gospel writers, or to one of the Gospels themselves. Further, we are dubious of the idea of some that Paul had to rely on "uncertain" oral traditions for his information about Jesus. That is a flat contradiction of Paul's own affirmation about the source of his gospel.

divine command, from which we are not at liberty to depart. Under the Law of Moses (Deuteronomy 24:1-4) Jewish men had been permitted to divorce (see the "bill of divorcement") when displeased with their wives. Jesus told the Pharisees that Moses permitted this because of their hardness of hearts, but it was not God's marriage law as ordained in the beginning. Jesus' teachings about marriage and divorce brought the standards back to God's original intention. The man must leave all others, and cleave to his wife, and "the two shall become one flesh" (Matthew 19:3-9). God created one man and one woman, thus showing it was His original intention that marriage be between one man and one woman for life.

That the wife should not leave her husband -- The burden of Jesus' teaching is that when two Christians are married to each other, neither is to look for a way to end the marriage. Instead, they are to look for ways to stay together. Paul simply summarizes Jesus' teaching, applying it to both wife and husband. The word "leave" (*chōristhēnai*) in other contexts can refer to either "separation" or "divorce." What it might mean in this passage is inextricably wound up in the thorny problem debated by Bible scholars, namely, whether or not divorce ends a marriage, or whether only death ends a marriage.[37] Moulton and Milligan say that in the papyri this verb "has almost become a technical term in connection with divorce."[38] The verb here is likely middle voice, 'not to separate herself,' 'not to start divorce proceedings.' Paul puts into his own words the Lord's order to all Christian couples: the wife is not to leave (verse 10), and the husband is not to leave the wife either (verse 11).[39] Under Roman and Greek law, the wife could start the divorce proceedings; this was different from Jewish law, which did not permit the wife to start the divorce proceedings. It is the consensus of opinion that this verse must be interpreted in the light of Jesus' teaching "except for immorality."[40] We may note that Paul is not dealing with a case in which a Christian wife or husband commits fornication and thereby gives legitimate grounds for ending the marriage tie.   (Even where there has been unfaithfulness, the in-

---

[37] It has proven very difficult to find a satisfactory way of harmonizing all the New Testament verses that touch on the question of marriage and divorce, and possibly remarriage. Some have tried to find the elusive answer to this question by insisting that in the New Testament the word *chōrizō* (the word here translated "leave") is the word for separation (the couple is still "married," just not living together), while *apoluō* ("divorce" in Matthew 19:9, and 5:32) and *aphiēmi* ("send away" in 1 Corinthians 7:11) are the words for divorce (the marriage is ended). Contrary to this assertion, it seems evident that even in this passage *chōrizō* can also mean "divorce," for in 7:11 a person who has "left" (*chōrizō*) is called "unmarried." The words translated "separate," "divorce," and "leave," are throughout verses 10-16 used interchangeably. We'll have to look elsewhere besides this verb *chōrizō* to find a way to harmonize the passages on marriage and divorce. Too, we must keep in mind that the topic here is different from what we had in verses 3-5 where we had instructions about 'temporary separations by mutual consent.' What is contemplated here in verses 10-11 is something more than the separation envisioned in verses 3-5.

[38] James Hope Moulton and George Milligan, *The Vocabulary of the Greek Testament* (London: Hodder & Stoughton, 1963), p.696.

[39] While the wording is different ("leave not" in verse 10 v. "send away" in verse 11), the substance of the commands is the same, for in verse 13 and 15 the verbs are reversed.

[40] See the Special Study, "The Problems of Divorce and Remarriage," at Matthew 19:9 in the author's Gospel's Class notes.

jured mate does not have to get a divorce, but is permitted to do so, in Jesus' teaching.) The principle ('Stay where you are!'), when applied to earlier cases, was not absolute. It allowed for exceptions. So, too, does this rule that the wife is not to leave her husband. Immorality on the husband's part does give the wife permission to depart (although it might be more God-like to forgive if the erring mate repents). Paul does not mention the exception allowed by Christ on the grounds of fornication, for he is not writing a systematic treatise on divorce.[41] He is answering specific questions asked of him by the Corinthians. They had asked about voluntary separation based on ascetic arguments, not separation because of unfaithfulness on the part of either husband or wife.

7:11 -- *(but if she does leave, she must remain unmarried, or else be reconciled to her husband), and that the husband should not divorce his wife.*

(But if she does leave, let her remain unmarried, or else be reconciled to her husband) -- The whole first half of verse 11 is in parentheses. This sentence, introduced by *ean*, is plainly a parenthesis since it is inserted between the two coordinate infinitive clauses, the one regarding the wife, the other regarding the husband. "If she does leave" (*chōristhē*) implies, 'If, in spite of Christ's command, she goes so far as to depart (get a divorce).' If we were correct in our earlier notes, where we suggested Paul speaks here in concert with Jesus, then the 'leaving' envisioned is one on grounds other than marital infidelity.[42] In the Greek, the verb *chōristhēnai* ("does leave") may be either middle or passive voice. The NASB takes it as middle, 'she leaves on her own accord.' If we translate *chōristhēnai* as "divorce," then this verse indicates that a divorced person was considered to be "unmarried." Divorce has ended the marriage. If the Christian wife has withdrawn by a rash and foolish act (i.e., there was no unfaithfulness on her husband's part), if she has dissolved the marriage vow, she is to remain unmarried, or be reconciled to her husband. Those are the only options open to her. She is not at liberty to marry another.[43] This is

---

[41] Why does Paul make no mention of Jesus' "exception clause" ("except for immorality," Matthew 19:9)? The idea that Mark's tradition (which omits any reference to the exception clause) was the earliest, and the only one circulating, and that therefore Paul was unaware of the "exception clause" will not do! See the author's study on the Synoptic Problem in his notes on the Gospels. There it is argued that the gospels containing the genealogies were the ones written first. Attention should also be given to Etta Linneman's writings on the Synoptic Problem, which show that only when one assumes there must have been *literary* dependence between the Gospel writers does one even have to suppose Mark was written first. Finally, just because Mark does not include the "exception clause" hardly is proof that Jesus never uttered it. Redaction criticism, which has the editors who compiled the Gospels redacting (editing, emending, deleting) materials in such a way that the actual record was forever changed according to some human editor's whims is hardly satisfactory handling of the Gospels.

[42] Augustine wrote *De Conjugii Adulterinis* in an attempt to prove that this 'leaving' was on the grounds of fornication, and thus this passage proves that adultery does not end a marriage, but rather that only death can do that. This has become the classic Roman Catholic interpretation of this passage. Augustine seems to have rather quickly passed over the word "unmarried" (verse 11) when he taught the marriage was not ended. He also seems to have not noticed that "reconciled" implies the separation is based on dissension more than on adultery.

[43] A preacher in the local church might struggle to help his parishioners put these teachings into practice. (1) In abusive situations, what about a short time of separation while counseling for the abusive mate takes place? This commentator's practice has been to suggest very hesitantly that separation may be advisable in some cases. He identifies a safe house where the woman may go while the men counsel

a rule that is still binding for the followers of Christ. The Christian wife who has divorced her husband (unless it is in the case of immorality on his part), ought not look for another husband nor seek a wedding ceremony in disobedience to Christ's express wishes. "Or else be reconciled to her husband": if the wife who has left (divorced) her husband finds that, after all, she cannot live a single life, the only course open to her is to be reconciled to the husband whom she has injured. Of course, the same limitation would be true of the husband, though it is not repeated in so many words in the next phrase.

And that the husband should not send his wife away -- Christ's command, being paraphrased by Paul, which was interrupted by the parenthetical note ("but if she does leave ... ") is here continued. Christ's command was "the wife should not leave her husband, and the husband should not send his wife away." The easy divorce granted under Jewish law, and practiced among the Gentiles, is to be no part of the lifestyle of those who follow the gospel. Where both mates are Christians, there was to be *no* divorce, except possibly on the grounds of fornication (sexual infidelity). "Not send away" translates *aphienai*, a word which appears three times in these verses, and has been variously rendered within our English versions: "leave" (ASV), "put away" (KJV), "send away" (NASB), and "divorce" (NIV) are the common renderings.[44] Jesus' words in Matthew 19:3-10 were intended to prevent adultery. Paul's application of Jesus' teaching, 'if you divorce, remain

---

the man involved. This commentator is hesitant to counsel separation since this verse seems to speak of something stronger than separation, something that leaves the woman "unmarried." Yet he has seen temporary abstinence from sexual relations in previous verses for devotional purposes. (2) What about performing weddings for folk who ended a previous marriage in defiance of or disobedience to what Jesus taught? If folk knew the options given by the Lord (remain unmarried or be reconciled to first mate) when they ended the first marriage, and now want to get married to a different partner, this commentator is hesitant to perform the ceremony. He does so recognizing that each of us will answer in the judgment for how we have helped or hindered people to obey the Lord. This commentator, on the other hand, does not absolutely refuse to perform wedding ceremonies for all divorced people. In some cases, since he believes the divorce ends the previous marriage, he will try to help people repent and pick up the pieces of their lives. He does this cautiously, again keeping the final judgment in view. (3) Since each of the previous imperatives were exceptions or limitations to the general rule, one wonders if this rule (remain unmarried, or be reconciled) is a hard and fast rule, or, is it, too, a 'Stay where you are!' that has some limitations and modifications and exceptions? Since none are stated, this commentator is slow to introduce any exceptions, while at the same time trying to be loving and forgiving and helpful to folk who have sinned, or who are thinking about entering into relationships that are ill advised. (4) In some congregations, legalistically minded Christians are prone to treat divorced people as if they had committed the unpardonable sin. This commentator does not think that either Jesus' words or Paul's discussion justify such an attitude. Divorced people, if they have repented, should be treated in the same manner as other Christians who have sinned some other sin and have repented and are attempting to live a Christian life. They should be forgiven, helped, and encouraged in their Christian walk. At the same time, Jesus' directions to married Christians must be taught and held up as the model to be attained by all.

[44] The KJV in verses 11 and 12 has "put away"; in verse 13 it reads "leave." The ASV and ERV read "leave" in all three places. The RSV has "divorce" in all three places. The Confraternity Edition (Roman Catholic translation) has "put away" in all three places. R.A. Knox (also Roman Catholic) has "put away" in verses 11 and 12, and "part with" in verse 13. We suppose these last two are deliberately so worded so as not to contradict Catholic dogma that permits separation of bed and board, but no divorce. This commentator leans to the idea that both *chōrizō* and *aphiēmi* speak of divorce, not just separation (see above at footnote #37 for more on the two Greek words).

unmarried, or be reconciled,' likewise are intended to prevent adultery. In regard to this double prohibition, we should note its effect on the people's thinking at Corinth and in the Roman world in general. We note its effect upon Jewish minds. Any Corinthian who formerly was a Jew would remember that the husband thought he could send away his wife for even the slightest reason by merely giving her a letter of divorcement. The Lord Himself (Matthew 19:2-10) forbade such a procedure. Paul now reinforces Jesus' teaching. Roman state law and custom, of which the Gentile Christian would live by, granted either party the right to take the initiative in dissolving a marriage. In addition it made distinctions between the marriages themselves. Marriages between slaves had no legal standing (and thus no permanence) whatever. There were not a few slaves (7:21) in the congregation at Corinth. Marriage between a freedman (one released from slavery) and a slave had a low legal standing. In general, during this period in Roman history, the permanency of marriage unions was exceedingly uncertain. The effect of the Lord's command on the complete permanency of Christian marriage may thus be estimated. Here is a case where Christians will render unto God what is God's, rather than living as Caesar might allow them to live. What Paul writes still leaves a number of questions unanswered for us who are living under different circumstances. The best we can do is to absorb fully what the Lord and His apostle say, and then answer such additional questions in the light of their words in their spirit.

7:12 -- *But to the rest I say, not the Lord, that if any brother has a wife who is an unbeliever, and she consents to live with him, he must not divorce her.*

But to the rest -- Just as in verses 2,8, and 10, this "but" introduces another of Paul's correctives to the ascetic statement the Corinthians were making which urged 'Do not touch a woman!' The general principle behind all Paul's directives is still, 'Stay where you are!' Verses 10-11 dealt solely with a marriage where both parties were Christian. Verses 12-16 deal with "the rest," namely, cases of mixed marriage where one of the married partners was a Christian and the other was not. Further, it is usually understood to mean that these two were both unconverted when they were married, and then one subsequently embraced the Christian faith. Was the Christian to continue to live with his or her non-Christian mate? The answer will be, 'Yes, if the non-Christian partner consents to the arrangement.'

I say, not the Lord -- The thrust of this language is just the opposite of what was said in verse 10. Unlike the case where both mates were Christians (concerning which Jesus did speak during His earthly ministry), Jesus never spoke on the topic of mixed marriages. The cases that came to the attention of Jesus were those of Jews, in which husband and wife both belonged to the Jewish faith (Matthew 5:32, 19:9). Jesus, therefore, had no occasion to pronounce on the sort of cases Paul had to address among the Corinthians. Hence, Paul cannot appeal to a statement of Jesus when he wanted to instruct the Corinthians regarding such cases. It is totally amiss to suppose that "I say" is an affirmation by Paul that what he is about to say is uninspired advice, just his own personal opinion. Paul is speaking on this subject as an apostle who has divine apostolic authority. It is equivalent to 'under the influence of the Holy Spirit I give these directions.' It is only by ignoring what Paul himself claims about his apostolic teaching in 1 Corinthians 7:40 and 14:37 that one would express the view that chapter 7's instructions about marriage are uninspired advice. In some passages (e.g., Romans 12:3; 1 Corinthians 14:34,37, 15:51,52; 2 Corinthians 6:13), "I say" (*legō*) is a word of authority. In 1 Thessalonians 4:15, Paul speaks of that knowledge into which he was guided by the Holy Spirit as given "by the word of the Lord." Paul must not therefore be regarded as here claiming for some of his instructions apostolic authority, and not claiming it for others. The real point of the contrast is between a subject on which our Lord Himself while on earth gave direct verbal instruction, and another subject on which He now gives His commands through His apostle Paul. Moffatt (cited by Tasker, p.109) has pointed out that Paul's careful discrimination between a saying of the Lord and his own injunction is a strong argument against those who maintain that the early church was in the habit of producing the sayings it needed and then ascribing them to Christ.

That if any brother -- "Brother" here is one of the terms by which Christians were identified. The form of the conditional sentence implies such cases did exist at Corinth. Paul is not dealing with a hypothetical question, but with things as they really are.

Has a wife who is an unbeliever -- "Unbeliever" equals 'unconverted.'[45] In both instances "unbeliever" would include unconverted Jews as well as unconverted pagans.[46] This seems to be a case of a Christian with a heathen wife whom he married when he himself was an unbeliever. The man has become a Christian after he and the woman have been married awhile. The intent of the Greek here, 'has *already* a wife,' is no countenance for

---

[45] An alternative view of "unfaithful" can be found in E. Christian, "1 Corinthians 7:10-16: Divorce of the Unbeliever or Reconciliation with the Unfaithful?" *Journal of the Adventist Theological Society* 10 (1-2, 1999), p.41-62. This article suggests that throughout the history of the English Bible, translators have erred in translating the word *apistos* (in its several forms) in 1 Corinthians 7:10-16 as "unbelieving" rather than "unfaithful." The article offers the view that it is the "unfaithful" mate talked about in an effort to harmonize 1 Corinthians with what Jesus says about divorce. It is not easy to see how it can be said "Jesus never spoke on this subject" (as Paul does) if the topic is unfaithfulness.

[46] In modern religious circles, people who are looking for an escape from an unsatisfactory marriage have used this passage (and 2 Corinthians 6:14) as if "unbeliever" might mean "a careless Christian," a Christian who was not a practicing Christian. It is affirmed that if they were really converted, they would not be living in such a way as to make the marriage unbearable. In this commentator's opinion, this is not a fair handling of the word "unbeliever." It is possible for a person to be an immersed penitent believer and then not live a consistent Christian life. That he or she is not now living as the Lord taught does not impinge on their original conversion. When professed Christians so live as to make a marriage intolerable, there is certainly need for intervention and counseling, and perhaps discipline, by church leaders.

In the Restoration Movement, where only immersed believers are recognized as being Christians, one of those immersed believers has sometimes married out of the faith – marrying one who was simply poured or sprinkled, but not immersed. Then when the marriage becomes difficult, the Christian thinks "Ah, the unbeliever (the unimmersed person) has left," and so feels justified in thinking he or she has a Scriptural reason for ending the marriage. This commentator wonders if such a person is not just compounding the difficulties. First he or she married outside the Lord, a course that is inadvisable and perhaps even disobedient to Christ, and then instead of trying to keep the marriage together, adds to the wrong by looking for an excuse to leave.

entering a mixed marriage.[47]

And she consents to live with him -- "To live with" means to dwell together as husband and wife. It is assumed that, if she did *not* consent, the Christian convert would have no protection of his rights; pagan courts would regard conversion as a sufficient reason for breaking off marriages. Paul mentions the consent of only the unbeliever; the consent of the believing partner is taken for granted. Mixed marriages are not ideal, yet they are as truly marriages as other marriages are. The Christian will not look for ways to be separated or divorced from the unbelieving party just because he has become a Christian.

Let him not send her away -- "Send away" (*aphiemi*) has been discussed in verse 11. In harmony with conclusions reached on the meaning of the word, more than separation is here spoken of. The word means "divorce." The Christian is not to divorce the non-Christian on the grounds of unbelief. The Christian party must certainly not start the proceedings that would dissolve the marriage if the unconverted mate does not desire to do so.

7:13 -- *And a woman who has an unbelieving husband, and he consents to live with her, she must not send her husband away.*

And a woman who has an unbelieving husband -- In this verse, the thing in Paul's mind is the marriage where the wife has become a Christian but the husband has not yet been converted. The conditional sentence implies there were actual cases of mixed marriages in the church in the Corinthian community.

And he consents to live with her -- See notes on similar language in verse 12.

Let her not send her husband away -- According to Greek as well as Roman law, the wife also had the legal right of obtaining a divorce. (The Law of Moses, Deuteronomy 24:1-5, indicated that the man was the only one who could start the divorce proceedings.) "Send away" again translates *aphiemi*,[48] and just as it spoke of divorce in verse 12, so it speaks of divorce here. Some commentators have said verse 13 is a reference only to separation. But in the light of Greek and Roman divorce practices, we do not see how this can be maintained. "At Athens, when the divorce originated with the wife, she was said to *leave* (*apoluein*) the house of her husband; when the divorce originated with the husband,

---

[47] This passage, of course, does not give the Christian any legitimate reason to voluntarily enter into a marriage with an unbeliever. On the contrary, see 2 Corinthians 6:14-18.

[48] Some have attempted to build a theology on the fact that Paul uses a stronger word (*aphiēmi*) in verse 13 than he did in the woman's action (*chōristhenai*) in verse 10. They have suggested that the reason Paul applies the stronger word to the action of the Christian woman (in the case of a mixed marriage) is because, for him, the fact that she is a Christian inverts the usual order, the wife in such a case being superior to the husband (since he is still unsaved). This opinion, we believe, is wholly inadmissible and quite contrary to Paul's view of that the husband is head of the wife; see 1 Corinthians 11:3, Ephesians 5:22, 1 Timothy 2:11. We see no significance to the use of the stronger word here at all. He has just used the same word of the men in verse 12, and we picture him as simply repeating – in the same language – the teaching of the woman too.

the wife was said to be *sent away* (*apopempein*)."⁴⁹ The word Paul uses (*aphiēmi*) for the actions of both husband and wife is a synonym; he is speaking of divorce. The Christian is not to seek a divorce, or separation, just because the mate in the marriage may continue to be an unbeliever. Although unbelief (and the consequent lifestyle) may make for a more difficult marriage, it is not suitable grounds for divorce for the Christian.

7:14 -- *For the unbelieving husband is sanctified through his wife, and the unbelieving wife is sanctified through her believing husband; for otherwise your children are unclean, but now they are holy.*

For -- "For" shows that this verse gives a reason why the believer does not initiate divorce proceedings. Instead of there being ethical reasons for disrupting such a mixed marriage, a proper view of this type of marriage discloses the spiritual reason for leaving it intact. Some of the Christians may have argued that they ought to separate and divorce the non-Christian mate lest they be contaminated through the intimate communion with the unbeliever. Paul's denial that they should divorce implies that though they are "one flesh," still there is no detriment to the believing partner in this union.

The unbelieving husband is sanctified through the wife, and the unbelieving wife is sanctified through her believing husband -- Some are surprised at Paul's use in this passage of the words "sanctified" of the unbelieving spouse, and "holy" of the children. The unexpectedness of the term has led to some unusual interpretations of the phrase.

(1) Some propose the idea that the unbelieving husband is considered a member of God's family simply because he is married to a Christian wife. Because the non-Christian partner is "one flesh" with the Christian, some say the non-Christian is connected by this link to the church. But salvation is not by proxy. A non-Christian will not be saved merely because he has a Christian mate. 7:16 indicates the unbeliever is not saved, even though he is "sanctified." He is still an unbeliever (verse 14) even though he is called "sanctified."
(2) Some suggest the "sanctification" is potential. No such "potential" sanctification was recognized in the Old Testament. In the Mosaic Law, Jews were forbidden to inter-marry with the pagans who lived in the promised land (Exodus 34:15,16; Deuteronomy 7:3). In Ezra, we find that many Jews after the exile had entered into marriage with women from among the heathen; it was said that many of the children spoke half in the language of Ashdod and half in the language of Israel. In Ezra's time, the heathen wives were sent away; the marriages were ended. However, this interpretation suggests things are different in New Testament times. In the New Testament, if the pagan is pleased to dwell with the Christian, then the Christian is to show all due kindness and consideration, and seek to be a blessing to the pagan partner. The Christian tries to win his or her unconverted mate, and this Christian influence is what makes the "sanctification" of the unbeliever potential. Of course, when the husband is a Christian and the wife is not, the children will generally speak half in the language of heaven, and half in the language of earth. It is difficult to bring up children in a

---

⁴⁹ Alford, *op. cit.*, p.524

mixed home. The heathen partner may be wicked, hating the very name of Jesus; but the non-Christian partner will come under the influence of this new relationship with God that the converted partner experiences. There is now someone in that home to pray, someone who loves the Word of God, someone to live the Christian life, someone to let others see what it means to be a Christian. The idea of a future conversion, a future sanctification, is appealing to many interpreters.

(3) Several of our English versions (KJV, ASV, NASB) translate this verb as present tense, "is sanctified." It is, however, a perfect passive indicative in the Greek. Literally translated, it reads, 'has been sanctified.' "The perfect tense denotes completed action with the effect of the action still continuing at the time of speaking or writing."[50] The usual meaning of a perfect tense verb is hard to square with the idea of a future sanctification being the thing Paul has in mind.

What then does "sanctified" mean in this place? The usual meaning of sanctify is 'to make holy, to set apart to a sacred use, to consecrate.' However, Thayer indicates the word is used in a special sense in this place.[51] Barnes agrees when he wrote, "It is a good rule of interpretation that the words which are used in any place are to be limited in their signification by the context. All that we are required to understand here is, that the unbelieving husband was sanctified *in regard to the subject under consideration.*"[52] The main question being discussed is whether or not it is proper for the Christian and the heathen to remain married, or whether they should get a divorce. By using "sanctified," Paul is saying that continuing such a marriage is proper. If the marriage were improper, the children would be unclean. But they are not unclean; therefore, your marriage must be proper. This is the view McGarvey takes when he says, "The unbelieving husband is not unclean. In the Jewish sense of the word, unclean meant untouchable."[53] There was a sexual union that was defiling (see 6:16), but the union of a believer and an unbeliever, since they were married before one partner was converted, is not defiling to the believer.

For otherwise your children are unclean, but now they are holy -- *Akatharta*, 'impure, defiled, unclean,' is the regular word used in the Old Testament of ceremonial uncleanness, that which must be abstained from lest impurity may be contacted.[54] Barnes (*op. cit.*, p.118) and Lipscomb (*op. cit.*, p.101) attempt to show "unclean" here means 'illegitimate.' But in the other half of the sentence, "holy" is the opposite of "unclean;" and "holy" does not mean "legitimate." Such a rendering is "contrary to all usage."[55] 'If continuing your

---

[50] Henry L. Crosby and John N. Schaeffer, *An Introduction to Greek* (Boston, MA: Allyn and Bacon, 1949), p.173.

[51] Thayer, *op. cit.*, p.6.

[52] Barnes, *op. cit.*, p.117.

[53] McGarvey and Pendleton, *op. cit.*, p.80.

[54] Thayer, *op. cit.*, p.21. McGarvey and Pendleton, *op. cit.*, p.80. The word is also used in contexts where something is "defiled by idolatry."

[55] Kling, *op. cit.*, p.149.

mixed marriage were not proper, your children would be unclean.' But such is not the case. The children of mixed marriages are "holy" (*hagia*), so the fact that one of the parents is unconverted is no reason to discontinue the union. *Expositor's Greek Testament* explains it this way: "Paul appeals to the instinct of the parents – especially the religious one (in this context he is obviating an anticipated objection which the Christian partner might raise to a continued union with an unbeliever). The Christian father or mother cannot look on children, given by God through marriage, as things unclean!"[56] Children are not automatically "defiled" simply because one of the birth-parents is not a Christian.

Advocates of infant baptism are so hard put to find Scriptural warrant for the practice that this passage has often been pressed into service as a proof text for infant baptism. Commenting on the word "holy," we read in one commentary, "The child of Christian parents should be treated as Christian, and therefore baptized."[57] This passage also has been adduced to prove that children are *federally holy*,[58] and that they are therefore entitled to the privilege of baptism on the ground of the faith of one of the parents. Against this, let it be seen: (1) There is not a single word about baptism in this passage; not one allusion to it. Nor does the argument in the remotest degree bear upon it. (2) The question is not whether the children should be baptized, but whether the Christian spouse should end the marriage to an unconverted mate. (3) There is not the slightest proof that infant baptism was practiced during the time the apostles were living. If it had existed, this would have been the place to appeal to it. "To prove your mixed marriage is proper – the church still allows you to baptize your offspring, doesn't it?" – would have been very much in order. The fact that Paul does not mention it here is proof the rite did not exist in the early church.[59] He is not assuming that the child of a Christian parent would be baptized: that would spoil rather than help his argument, for it would imply that the child was not "holy" till it was baptized. (4) Baptism and circumcision are not parallel. (a) Circumcision was administered to males only. (Is baptism to be for men only?) (b) Circumcision required no faith on the part of its subject. (A pre-requisite to baptism is faith.) (c) Circumcision was administered on the eighth day. (Why not baptize on the eighth day?) (d) Circumci-

---

[56] Findlay, *op. cit.*, p.827.

[57] There is something not quite right in this wording. The Bible never did teach baptism was an "outward sign of an inward grace" – that is, that a person is already a Christian (by faith alone) before they are ever immersed. Further, the proper candidates for immersion are penitent believers. Can an infant repent or believe? Why then should innocent infancy be rushed to the waters of baptism?

[58] "Federal theology," sometimes called "covenant theology," was one of the features in the development of Calvinism, and was especially popular among Puritans and the Reformed theologians of Germany and Holland in the latter 16th and during the 17th centuries. The doctrine teaches that ever since Adam sinned, there has been but one covenant between God and man – a covenant of grace. If there is but one covenant (something that the book of Hebrews flatly contradicts), then it is fair to assume that the initiatory rite of circumcision in the Old Testament has an exact correspondence with the initiatory rite of baptism in the New, it is claimed. If infants were to be included in the Old Covenant because of their parents inclusion, then it would follow that children are included among the "holy" in the New Covenant simply because one or both of their parents are included. (See the topic of "one-covenant theology" examined in detail in the author's commentary on *Hebrews*.)

[59] Kling, *op. cit.*, p.149.

sion was not a mark on the face of the subject. (Why baptize – i.e., sprinkle – the face?) (e) Circumcision had nothing to do with salvation. (Jews did not circumcise a child that was about to die, even though less than eight days old. If baptism came in the place of circumcision, why do so many seem so anxious to have their infants sprinkled before they die?) (f) Those who say baptism came in the place of circumcision still say baptism is not essential to salvation. (Yet every Jewish male had to be circumcised, or else they were cut off from the congregation.)[60] The holiness which Paul here discusses regarding the children of a mixed marriage has nothing to do with baptism. It is exactly like that holiness (sanctification) bestowed upon the unbelieving parent. This commentator takes "holy" in a broad sense, just as we took "sanctify" in a broad sense.[61] The topic being discussed is the propriety of the Christian continuing in a mixed marriage. The children resulting from mixed marriages were not considered as outcasts, or unclean, or contaminated. They are "holy." Therefore, the continuing marriage of a Christian and a heathen was not to be considered as improper, or as something resulting in contaminated children.

7:15 -- *Yet if the unbelieving one leaves, let him leave; the brother or the sister is not under bondage in such cases, but God has called us to peace.*

Yet if the unbelieving one leaves, let him leave -- We have noted that there is a principle ('Stay where you are!') behind Paul's instructions. So far, the Christian has been instructed to continue in the marriage relationship with the unconverted mate. The Christian does not initiate divorce proceedings simply because his or her mate remains unconverted. After conversion, the Christian stays in the marriage if the unconverted mate consents to continuing the marriage. But what if the unbeliever departs? The unbeliever may positively refuse to continue the marital union with a believer. When the unbeliever decides to leave, it will be impossible for the Christian to 'Stay where he is!' The unbeliever simply leaves (*chōridzei*, divorces) the Christian spouse; the union is ended. Instead of trying to 'Stay where he is!' the believer is instructed to "let him leave," a present imperative which equals 'let the separation (divorce) take its course.' Paul writes succinctly. Short and done with. What can, indeed, be done other than this by the Christian when an unbeliever takes such action? The marriage is ended; let it remain thus.

---

[60] Colossians 2:11,12 are often appealed to as "proof" that baptism does in fact correspond to the Old Testament rite of circumcision. However, a careful reading of the passage says that what the Old Testament was trying to teach in the act of circumcision is in fact a spiritual reality in the person who has been immersed into Christ. When a man is in Christ he has found the reality that was merely symbolized in Mosaic circumcision.

[61] The fact of the case is, however "unclean" was interpreted, "holy" is likewise interpreted to mean just the opposite. Those who spoke of "illegitimate" for the one, speak of "legitimate" for the other. Those who spoke of "sanctified" as being potential, speak of the Christian influence that potentially would lead the children to conversion. Of course, it is the teaching of Scripture that little children (before they reach the age of accountability) have a purity that qualifies them for the kingdom of heaven (Jesus said, "of such is the kingdom of heaven"), but it is doubtful that the word "holy" here refers to that "purity."

The brother or the sister is not under bondage in such *cases* -- What follows in this verse is a reason why the believer is not to contest the unbeliever's determination to leave (end) the marriage. The Greek clause (*en tois toioutois*) can either be masculine or neuter. If masculine, 'by such,' it refers to such as separate themselves. The Christian is not a slave to such as separate themselves. If we treat it as neuter, 'under such circumstances" or 'in such matters,' it refers to cases where the unbeliever has chosen to end the marriage, rather than continue to live with the Christian. The verb "not under bondage" (*dedoulōtai*) is perfect tense – a past act with present continuing results. The perfect reaches back to the day when the unbeliever separated himself, and it states that from that moment onward the believing spouse has not been held 'bound.' From that day onward, the union that was the marriage has been broken and remains so. The deserting spouse broke it. Desertion is exactly like adultery in its effect. Both disrupt the marriage union.[62] The essence of marriage is union (recall 6:16). When this is disrupted, the union which God intended to be a continuing and permanent one is destroyed.

A heated controversy concerning what the Bible teaches turns upon the meaning given to the words *ou dedoulōtai* ("is not bound"). Do the words mean the previous marriage to the unbeliever is ended? If the previous marriage is ended, is either party permitted to marry again? Or do the words simply give permission to the deserted party to live apart without feeling constrained to enforce cohabitation? Worded another way, does the Bible allow separation, but not divorce? (1) What is the meaning of this verb ("not under bondage"), in the light of other New Testament uses of the same word? The verb "bound" is used of "marriage" and "divorce" in verse 27ff. There is no reason, then, to say it means any less here. (See verse 39 where "bound" is used of marriage. See also Romans 7:2.) When it is a mixed marriage, and the unbeliever walks out on the Christian, thus rupturing the union, then the marriage is ended. The Christian is to recognize that "divorce" has occurred. The marriage rules and responsibilities are no longer binding. If the unconverted partner disrupts the marriage union by willful desertion, the Christian partner need not feel so bound by Christ's prohibition of divorce as to be afraid to allow the heathen partner to depart. Marriages between Christians ought never be dissolved (7:10-11). The Christian should never start the divorce proceedings. But mixed marriages stand on a different basis. They ought to be respected as long as possible. It goes without saying that a believing spouse will by Christian kindness and persuasion do all that can be done to prevent a rupture. But if the one who remains an unbeliever demands a divorce (perhaps even going to court to take action to make legal what has already taken place in fact, i.e., the disruption of the union), the Christian is not bound, either by Paul's 'Stay where you are!' or by Christ's teaching about God's intention for the permanence of marriage, to oppose the (separation or the) divorce.[63] (2) Everyday appli-

---

[62] There is only this difference in the case of adultery – the innocent spouse may forgive and continue the marriage, or may accept the dire result, the sundering of the marriage. In the case of desertion, the former is not possible – the deserted spouse can no longer continue the union, for none exists.

[63] It is a rather popular saying in church circles that there is but one Scriptural reason for divorce – infidelity. It is true that while Jesus was on earth, and speaking on the subject of marriage and divorce, he gave infidelity as the only possible reason two folk might end a marriage. Now in 1 Corinthians 7, Paul seems to give another ground for divorce – willful desertion by an unbeliever. (This is sometimes called

cations of the instructions herein given are fraught with problems and ramifications. (a) What does the believer do by way of obtaining the civil court action regarding his or her status in civil law in regard to property rights and the like? Court action may almost be necessary after a marriage is wrecked, but it should not be considered the all-important thing, nor should it be confused with what has actually destroyed the marriage. (b) In the case of desertion, when a spouse runs away, a special question arises: 'Will the one who has deserted perhaps change his (her) mind and return?' The courts (and some denominational hierarchies) have set time limits on how long the innocent party should wait until a formal pronouncement is made to the effect that the desertion is, indeed, permanent. In light of the fact that the unbeliever may later wish to be reunited with ex-husband or ex-wife, what about the remarriage of the believer who is thus deserted? How long should they wait? Should they enter another marriage at all? In a case of willful desertion on the part of the non-Christian mate, some have offered the advice that the Christian should not remarry as long as the unbeliever remains unmarried. Thus if they should wish to return, the Christian is free to be remarried to their ex-spouse. On the other hand, there may be young children who need a father-figure or mother-figure in their lives, and a remarriage would be entirely recommended. If "is not under bondage" means the previous marriage is ended, there is no moral reason the two who are now divorced should not become married to another spouse should they wish to do so. The new union would not be adultery, since the old union was ended. (3) It has not been unknown for Christians to act towards their unconverted mates in such an unchristian way that the unbeliever decides to end the marriage. Preachers may then be called upon to perform wedding ceremonies for the Christian who has been deserted (divorced) by the unbeliever. It may be a difficult question to decide whether the Christian was deserted, or whether he or she drove the unbeliever away. If the latter is in fact the case, most conscientious preachers would hesitate before giving God's blessing to a proposed new union.

But God has called us to peace -- Commentators are equally divided whether this phrase goes with verse 15, or with verse 16.[64] If we take this phrase with what precedes, it gives a second reason for the permission to allow the unbeliever to leave. The meaning is, 'If you insist on living with a heathen who was anxious for a divorce, there would be little peace. You need not feel bound to remain with a heathen partner who objects to your remaining. Instead there might be constant tension and strife arising from divergent loyalties that could increase the unbeliever's alienation from both spouse and God.' If we take this phrase with what follows, it gives further reason for staying with the unbeliever who consents to continue the marriage. The idea is that when a believer finds himself with an unbeliever, instead of seeking a divorce, the believer should live in peace, and seek by

---

"the Pauline privilege.") Since Paul plainly says Jesus never addressed the topic of mixed marriages during His earthly ministry, it is not to be expected that we would find "willful desertion by an unbeliever" in the Gospel records of Jesus' ministry and teaching. Of course, those who insist that only death ends a marriage will do everything in their power to somehow make 1 Corinthians 7 match that dogma. "Not under bondage" just cannot mean the marriage is ended; it must be speaking of separation of bed and board, but not divorce, they will assert. It is this commentator's conviction that such a handling of the passage is not correct. Speaking by inspiration, Paul does teach a second grounds for divorce for the Christian – willful desertion by an unbeliever.

[64] See Sakae Kubo, "I Corinthians 7;16: Optimistic or Pessimistic?" *NTS* 24 (1978), p.539-544.

godly behavior to win the unbelieving spouse to Christ.

7:16 -- *For how do you know, O wife, whether you will save your husband? Or how do you know, O husband, whether you will save your wife?*

For how do you know, O wife -- Paul is now talking to the Christian spouse again. But what is the point of the verse? Is it an argument for separation, or an argument for remaining united?

(1) Some think this is an argument for not contesting the unbeliever's leaving (getting a divorce). Lyra, Meyer, Alford, DeWette, Lenski, and Shore see a ground for not contesting the unbeliever's actions to end the marriage, and thus not marring the Christian's peace for so uncertain a prospect as that of converting the unbelieving party. When the phrases are put together this is the resulting idea: 'Do not contend against the divorce on the ground that, if you remain, you may convert your heathen partner; for how do you know that you will do that? Even if you mar your peace, and remain together, how do you know that you will save your heathen partner?' If the Christian cause is grieved over lost opportunity, Paul brushes that aside. The RSV takes it this way: "Wife, how do you know whether you will ...."

(2) Others think this verse is an argument for remaining united with the consenting unbeliever. See Wordsworth, Lightfoot, Findlay, Barnes, Hodge, and most ancient interpreters. The meaning is this: 'Avoid divorce – you never know, it is possible that perhaps you will convert your non-Christian partner.' This very idea of living together with the unconverted partner and trying to win him/her is taught elsewhere (see 1 Peter 3:1,2). Appeal may be made to verses 17-24 as evidence that this verse (7:16) is an argument for remaining united, since the principle which governs this case (i.e., don't seek a change, 'Stay where you are!') is there applied to other fields of life.

(3) As this commentator understands it, verse 16 is an argument for remaining united. The argument of the context is that the Christian partner must not do anything to bring about a dissolution of marriage.[65] The context similarly will speak of the prohibition of the Christian slave doing anything to force his master to free him. However, if the slave's master grants the Christian slave freedom, the slave may embrace it. Likewise, if the unbeliever insists on ending the marriage, the Christian may accept freedom from living with an unconverted mate. Stanley, on this passage, gives two instances from history on which this passage likely influenced the Christian mate to stay and win her husband. "This passage ... probably had direct influence on the marriage of Clotilda and Clovis [Clovis, c. AD 466-511, king of the Franks, was converted in AD 496 after his marriage to Clotilda the Christian], and Bertha and Ethelbert [Ethelbert, AD 552?-616, king of Kent, to Bertha, a Frankish princess of the Christian faith, whom he married, c. AD 595, and was himself converted and baptized in AD 597], and consequently on the subsequent conversion of the two great kingdoms of France and England to the Christian faith."

---

[65] The Corinthians, with their dictum "It is good for man not to touch a woman!" surely needed dissuasives from – rather than encouragements to – divorce. We see most of the verses teaching Christians to do all in their power to keep the marriage together.

Whether you will save your husband? -- We believe the idea in the verse is this: "When one of the partners is a Christian, the non-Christian comes under an influence that might possibly save him." C.S. Lovett's book, *Unequally Yoked Wives*,[66] gives some very practical suggestions to guide the wife as she lovingly gives the Holy Spirit opportunity to produce conviction that leads to conversion of the unbelieving mate.

Or how do you know, O husband, whether you will save your wife? -- We hardly can think of Paul as being pessimistic about the possibilities of conversion.[67] In speaking of "saving" one's spouse, Paul is referring to evangelizing or winning them to Christ, whether by word or deed (cp. 1 Peter 3:1ff).[68] This is not the only time the word "save" is used in the sense of 'winning someone to Christ' (see, for example, 1 Corinthians 9:22 and Romans 11:14)

B. The General Principle ('Stay Where You Are!') Behind Paul's Instructions Applied to Other Civil Relations. 7:17-24

> *Summary:* In this paragraph Paul gives examples of how the principle behind his teaching can be applied to other areas. The first example is that of circumcision, verses 18-20. The second example he uses is slavery, verses 21-24. These two were the great religious and social distinctions which divided the world in Paul's day. This excursus is typically Pauline, for it shows that what Paul posits for the specific case of marriage relations is really a general Christian principle applicable to many other relations, some of which are introduced as illustrations. The principle itself is restated three times. Christians have a duty to remain in the state wherein each was called.

7:17 -- Only, as the Lord has assigned to each one, as God has called each, in this manner let him walk. And so I direct in all the churches.

Only, as the Lord has assigned to each one -- "Only" is the ASV/NASB translation of *ei mē*, an unexpected conjunction. It often means 'save,' or 'except.' So rendered, it points up a contrast between what precedes and what follows the conjunction. Paul is about to

---

[66] C.S. Lovett, *Unequally Yoked Wives*, (Baldwin Park, CA: Personal Christianity, 1968).

[67] Those who believe verse 16 is an argument for separation insist the Greek word *ei* ("if") with which these phrases begin ("how do you know *if*...") cannot express hope; rather, it expresses doubt. It is further argued that to make this verse an argument for remaining united, we must understand *ei* as though it were *ei ... mē*, 'How do you know if (*ei*) you will NOT (*mē*) save ...?' Is it grammatically possible that *ei* alone can express hope, as is suggested in the comments above? BAGD do give the translation of "whether" for *ei* in indirect questions, and treats 7:16 as being two examples of indirect questions, but few if any of the examples they quote from the New Testament seem to express hope. However, see the LXX of Esther 4:14; Joel 2:14; Jonah 3:9; 2 Samuel 12:22. It is argued that in these passages *ei* is used to express hope rather than doubt.

[68] That the unbeliever is yet to be saved, though in some sense "sanctified" (7:14), indicates that "sanctified" in 7:14 is used in a different sense than in 6:11.

give an exception to something just said. Thayer says, "By the addition of *ei mē*, Paul strives to prevent anyone in applying to his own case what Paul has said a little while before about 'not being bound in such cases' from going too far."[69] Verse 16 is regarded as a kind of parenthesis, and these words are taken as an attempt to correct an idea that might have been believed to be taught in verse 15, that Christians have a great deal of freedom ("is not under bondage"). Paul clearly says the Christian is not to cause or promote a separation, for he is to be guided by the great principle that we are to continue to walk in those social and political relations in which we were when we heard the call of the gospel. "Assigned" (*memeriken*, also 'distributed,' 'given, imparted, apportioned') speaks of an assignment of circumstances and talents by Christ (the "Lord").[70] The Lord Jesus Christ does have a hand in the everyday lot of Christians, whether married, single, deserted by a spouse, etc.

As God has called each – Paul refers to the condition or circumstances in which any one is when he is called by God to be a Christian. "Each one" (previous phrase) and "each" (here) are both in emphatic positions. The duty of each individual is stressed. Here is the first of three times in this paragraph where the principle 'Stay where you are!' is enunciated.

> If the unbeliever wishes to depart from the Christian on the ground of religious differences and there is no prospect of peace and unity, in such cases I grant permission: I give no injunction, unless it be the general rule, LET EVERY MAN WALK IN THE LOT OF LIFE WHICH THE LORD HAS APPORTIONED TO HIM; let every one abide in that station within which the God has called him to the kingdom.[71]

The general principle behind his instructions to the married to 'Stay where you are!' is a rule that applies to other areas of a Christian's life. Since the circumstances of our lives are regulated by the providence of the Lord, Christians do not arbitrarily seek to alter those circumstances on a whim or a caprice. People who become Christians are not obligated to immediately seek to change the everyday circumstances of their lives. Old sinful habits and patterns are abandoned, yes, but not those things that are morally neutral. "Has called" reminds us of God's initiative in the salvation of men. By initiative, we mean that God sends preachers to those who need to hear, and provides the gospel for them to obey.[72] God calls men to become Christians through the gospel (2 Thessalonians 2:14).

---

[69] Thayer, *op. cit.*, p.171.

[70] The words "God" and "Lord" are transposed in some versions that follow manuscript readings in which the words had been transposed by copyists. It is important to preserve the accurate reading here, for it speaks of Christ – "the Lord" – as the one who allots to men their natural condition in life, while "God" calls them from heathenism to the Christian faith. (Shore, *op. cit.*, p.59.)

[71] Evans, *op. cit.*, p.289 (emphasis mine, GLR).

[72] Care must be exercised here. The Bible never did teach total hereditary depravity, so that God must accomplish a 'first work of grace' to soften the depraved heart before a man can even want to believe. Such a 'first work of grace' is the idea that immediately comes to some men's minds when they hear the language 'God takes the initiative in the salvation of men.'

In this manner let him walk -- Based on the same principle he has used in answering all their questions about marriage, Paul lays down one of the first rules of Christianity – 'Be a Christian where you are!' The present imperative means 'let him continue to walk,' or 'let him go on walking.' "Walk" is a favorite metaphor with Paul for the living out of the whole of life, particularly for the Christian. Its idea of steady progress is very applicable. Having stressed the Lord's sovereign and providential assignment of men's circumstances, it follows that the Christian may continue in those circumstances. Men should continue their lives according to the Lord's order for them. Nothing is here said against embracing an opportunity for the improvement of one's circumstances after becoming a Christian. What is laid down is that, unless one's external condition of life is a sinful one (in which case repentance would automatically involve a change), no violent change needs to be made in it simply because one has become a Christian. One should continue in the same course, glorifying God by a good use of one's opportunities. The slogan (7:1b) of some at Corinth implied that a radical change in social status was needed in order to promote true spirituality. Paul is indicating that one's social status (married or single, slave or free, etc.), as such, is ultimately irrelevant to genuine spirituality; they can live out their Christian lives in any of the various options.

And thus I direct in all the churches -- 'Stay where you are and be a Christian where you are' was not a peculiar rule for the Corinthians alone. It is the universal rule Paul taught wherever he preached, and he taught by virtue of his commission as an apostle with divine authority entrusted to him. (The "I" is emphatic, as the writer speaks with apostolic authority.) This general principle was so important to Paul that he states that he has established it in all the churches under his care.[73] He will, in the next verses, give two illustrations of the application of the principle.

1. The first example of the application of the principle to other situations – circumcision. 7:18-20

7:18 -- *Was any man called when he was already circumcised? He is not to become uncircumcised. Has anyone been called in uncircumcision? He is not to be circumcised.*

Was any man called -- 'Did any one respond to the invitation to become a Christian?' is the idea. See notes at 1:2 ("saints by calling") and 7:17 on "called."

When *he was already* **circumcised** -- This is the first application or example of the rule, 'Be a Christian where you are.' We think more is intended than the simple fact of physical circumcision. Perhaps it actually means 'Were you living in the Jewish community when you heard and obeyed the gospel?'

Let him not become uncircumcised -- If our comment earlier was correct, then this direc-

---

[73] This is one of four times in this letter where Paul appeals to what he expects of all the churches. See 4:17, 11:16, and 14:33. See also on 1:2 and 16:1. There certainly was some kind of a "pattern" one would expect all Christians to follow, wherever they lived and served.

tive means 'Keep on living in the Jewish community.' 'Stay where you are! Be a Christian where you are. Tell your neighbors about Jesus Messiah!' Those who take "circumcised" as a reference to the actual physical condition itself think reference is made to certain efforts which were attempted by those who for some reason were ashamed of having been circumcised. The Hellenizing Jews in the days of the priest Menelaus (1 Maccabees 1:15, Josephus *Ant.* xii, 5, 1) had discovered a surgical procedure by which they could obliterate the appearance of circumcision; such persons were known as *masōochim*.[74] In the rebellion of Barcocheba many obliterated the sign of circumcision, and were afterwards, at great danger to themselves, re-circumcised (*Yevamoth*, fol. 72:1). Jews did this sometimes to avoid being known as Jews in gymnastic exercises in the palaestra (the ancient school where wrestling and other sports were held). The reason some at Corinth desired the change is nowhere given. One can think of a variety of reasons that might prompt a Jewish Christian to desire to hide his origin from Gentile Christians and from pagans. A Gentile Christian might likewise imagine it to be to his advantage to appear as if he, too, had originally belonged to the chosen nation. Paul tells both: Stay where you are and be a Christian there.

Has anyone been called in uncircumcision? Let him not be circumcised -- Perhaps it means, as before, 'Keep on living in your Gentile neighborhood.' Possibly it has reference to the actual physical condition. If so, then this command implies that the Old Testament Jewish rite is not binding on Christians. If this is the actual intended meaning, then the epistle to the Galatians is a powerful commentary on this verse.

7:19 -- *Circumcision is nothing, and uncircumcision is nothing, but* **what matters is** *the keeping of the commandments of God.*

Circumcision is nothing -- Verse 19 states the basis of Paul's admonition given in verse 18. Circumcision is of no consequence in itself. It is not that which God requires now. This same saying is found in the Apocalypse of Moses, but there is no evidence that Paul copied the Apocalypse of Moses. Rather, the copying seems to be the other way.

And uncircumcision is nothing -- Perhaps it says the neighborhood you live in is not the determining factor. One can keep the commands of God wherever he lives. Perhaps it says the outward sign of circumcision, which the Judaizers (Pharisees who pretended to become Christians so they could control the church from within, Galatians 2:4) tried to force on the Gentile Christians, was nothing. Some suppose a number of passages in 1 Corinthians, including these verses in chapter 7, reflect the fact that the Judaizers are already present in Corinth and are disturbing the tranquility of the brethren with their man-made rules based on the old Law of Moses. No man is either better or worse spiritually for being either circumcised or uncircumcised. This, of course, was said with reference to standing before God in Christ Jesus. Before Jesus' coming, this could not have been said without contravening the express command of God (Genesis 17:9-14; Leviticus 12:3). The circumcision of Timothy and the refusal to circumcise Titus by Paul himself are illus-

---

[74] "Epispasm" is the name of the surgical procedure. See Robert G. Hall, "Epispasm: Circumcision in Reverse," *Bible Review* 8:4 (1992), p.52-57.

trations at once of the application of the truth here enforced, and of the apostle's scrupulous adherence to the principles of his own teaching. In Timothy's case, the accompanying circumstances showed that circumcision did not attach any special spiritual value to the rite. To have circumcised Titus, in the midst of the controversy over the validity of the Pharisees' rules, would have attached some value to circumcision that it actually no longer had. (See Acts 16:3 and Galatians 2:3.)

But *what matters is* the keeping of the commandments of God -- As the italics indicate, something must be added to complete the thought in this phrase. We could add 'is something,' or 'is the main thing,' or 'is everything,' or 'is what is really important.' Wherever you live, this is the important thing – keep God's commands! Note the things that are contrasted to "circumcision" as being important in the Christian age. Here, it is the "keeping of the commandments of God." In Galatians 5:6, it is "faith which works through love." In Galatians 6:15, it is "a new creation." "Keep" means to 'guard, hold, observe' – like a guard who is posted to protest against violation or removal. There was a time, between Abraham and Calvary, when keeping "the commands of God" included submission to circumcision. But no more. One regulation in the Law of Moses required every male child to be circumcised, but (even as it was being given at Mt. Sinai) the Law of Moses was never intended to be anything but temporary (see the argument of Galatians and Hebrews). The commands included in the Mosaic legislation are no longer a binding code on Christians. Instead, when Paul speaks of the "commandments of God," he is speaking of the commands for this new age as found in the teachings of Jesus and His apostles (as will be made abundantly plain in 9:20,21). John says, "And hereby we know that we know Him (Jesus), if we keep His commandments" (1 John 2:3 ASV). Keeping God's new covenant commandments can be done whether or not the man is circumcised. The great question concerning which the Christian should be solicitous above everything else is whether or not he brings his heart and life into conformity to the will of God as revealed in Jesus Christ.

7:20 – *Let each man remain in that condition in which he was called.*

Let each man remain in that condition in which he was called -- "Remain" is present imperative, with the thought of continuance being stressed. Whatever your place in life when you hear the invitation to become a Christian, stay in that place even after you become a Christian. As the margin indicates, the word translated "condition" is actually "calling." This is perhaps the only time in Scripture the word "calling" is used in its modern connotation of profession or vocation. The illustration in the following verse shows that "condition" equals 'state, circumstances, life's occupation.' This principle is not intended to be made an absolute rule, with no exceptions allowed. For instance, when a man is pursuing a wicked calling or course of life when he is called, even if it is lucrative, he should abandon it speedily. Continuing in wickedness is incompatible with repentance. Yet illustrations of the application of the principle can be found outside of Paul's writings, and so it is a pretty general principle. John the Baptist did not tell the publicans or the soldiers to abandon their jobs, but to do their duty in that state of life to which God had called them (Luke 3:12-14). This is the second time in this paragraph the principle has been stated. It is not absolute, however; see the next verse "rather do that" ('use the freedom'). The Christian is not to go around forcing a change of life's situation. But if opportunity is given for a change, he should not hesitate to go where the Lord leads!

2. The second example of application of the principle to other situations – slavery. 7:21-24

7:21 -- *Were you called while a slave? Do not worry about it; but if you are able also to become free, rather do that.*

Were you called while a slave? -- As it did in verse 17, "called" has reference to the invitation offered in the gospel to become a Christian. "Slave" is *doulos*. Slavery was a widespread institution in the world of New Testament times. There were far more slaves in the Roman Empire than free citizens. Slaves were obtained from many nations by the ceaseless wars fought by the Romans. Very wealthy Romans sometimes owned ten to twenty thousand slaves, who did all the menial work, as well as all the mental work in the families. Among the slave class were to be found not only the common class who performed menial tasks, but also the literary men, doctors, government officials, midwives, teachers, artists, scribes, doctors, and skilled workers, who were constantly employed in work suited to their ability and acquirements.[75] There are a number of New Testament passages addressed to slaves and to slave-masters (Galatians 3:28; Colossians 3:22ff, 4:1; Titus 2:9-10; 1 Timothy 6:1,2; Ephesians 6:5-9, the book of Philemon), all of which indicate that many in the early church were from the slave class of society.

Do not worry about it -- "Let it not be a care to you," the marginal reading has it. 'Do not be troubled by the fact that you are a slave, because in Christ "there is neither slave nor free man" (Galatians 3:28). Do not think it disgraceful. Do not let it affect your spirits. Do not let it be a subject of deep anxiety and distress. Were you a slave when you became a Christian? Do not mind that! A slave can be a good Christian.'[76] 'Stay where you are!' suggests the converted slave may continue to serve his or her earthly master, doing his service as though he were serving the Lord.

But if you are able also to become free -- 'Stay where you are!' is not a rule set in stone, with no exceptions allowed. In the 1st century world, slaves could become free men. Sometimes masters freed their slaves. Sometimes the law led to a slave being set free (e.g., slaves were automatically freed when their masters died). Relatives sometimes located kinsmen who had been deported and sold into slavery and purchased their freedom.

---

[75] American readers, aware of the nature of slavery in the United States in the 1800's, are liable to equate slavery in the Roman Empire to the slavery in the United States. To be sure, in Rome, there were cruel masters, and slaves were treated as things, with no rights under law. However, many held responsible positions. In Rome it was possible for a slave to buy his own freedom, but many who could have chose not to, preferring the security of their "owners" to the personal responsibilities freedom requires.

[76] As might be imagined, this passage has a long history of use by pro-slavery advocates. See Willard M. Swartley, *Slavery, Sabbath, War and Women* (Scottdale, PA: Herald, 1983), p.31-64.

We suppose Paul is speaking of becoming free in any manner that is not sinful. Doubtless, the apostle is not speaking of insurrection. Under the rule of Christ, there was to be no attempt to obtain freedom by force and violence.

Rather do that -- To what does the "that" refer? Is the Christian instructed to use the slavery or the freedom? It depends on how you read the Greek.

(1) The slavery? ("Even if you are able to become free, remain a slave" is how the Greek would be read.) The NAB, Meyer, and Shore, so interpret. Alford gives the following reasons for so interpreting: (a) Greek syntax. (b) The ancient commentators so held. (c) It is the view required by the context since the context is saying, "Let each man remain in the state in which he was called." (d) 1 Timothy 6:2 suggests it. In that passage, slaves who are now Christians are urged to serve their masters all the more zealously. See also Ephesians 6:5-8.[77]

(2) The freedom? ("But if you can, be made free" is how the Greek would be read.) The NASB, NIV, Calvin, Beza, Godet, Lightfoot, Fee, and others so interpret.[78] Farrar[79] and others offer several arguments: (a) It sounds unnatural to advise a Christian slave to remain a slave when he might gain his freedom. (b) "Do" or "use" (*chrēsai*) can be translated "choose" or "make use of," which seems to favor the freedom idea. And it is an aorist tense, which more naturally would signify the beginning of a new "use" rather than the continuing of an old. (c) Unless the apostle means to make an exception to the rule he has just given, why introduce this verse at all? (d) The nearest antecedent of "it" is "freedom." (e) Just as there was an exception to 'Stay where you are!' when the Christian spouse was deserted by an unbeliever, so it is likely that this verse introduces an exception to the rule into the slavery situation. (f) Fee (*op. cit.*, p.317) argues that it is doubtful a 1st century world a slave could *reject* manumission (being set free).

The early Christians were people from various walks of life, and the basic principle was that they were to remain in the same jobs. The gospel did not depend on calling men out of their occupations for its existence. The Christian slave is not to rebel against a non-Christian master any more than a Christian wife against a non-Christian husband. But if the non-Christian is ready to grant freedom, the Christian slave, like the Christian wife, may take it without scruple.

7:22 -- *For he who was called in the Lord while a slave, is the Lord's freedman; likewise he who was called while free, is Christ's slave.*

For -- Verse 22 is an illumination of the idea that whether a man is a slave or a freedman, his real task is "keeping the commandments of the God."

---

[77] Alford, *op. cit.*, p. 527,528.

[78] Generally, the theologians before the Reformation favored the "slavery" idea, and those since the Reformation have favored the "freedom" idea.

[79] Farrar, *op. cit.*, p.227.

He who was called in the Lord while a slave, is the Lord's freedman -- "Called in the Lord" means one is invited to and becomes a Christian. Again, remember that God calls men (invites them) through the gospel (2 Thessalonians 2:14). "Slave" is *doulos* again. "Freedman" translates *apeleutheros*. The ASV margin has "made free." Christ has freed him from the slavery to sin and Satan (Romans 6:22). Freedom from sin is the highest blessing that can be conferred on men. This is speaking of the spiritual freedom that a child of God has.

Likewise he who was called while free, is Christ's slave -- The word is *doulos* ('slave, bondslave') again.[80] He who names Christ as master is bound to obey His law, and to submit himself to His authority. The cases of the two men are thus in a strange manner "likewise" or similar. In both we see a slavery, and in both freedom. In the first bodily slavery and a spiritual freedom or release from sin, guilt, bondage of sin, death, and all evil. In the second, bodily freedom and the spiritual bondage which binds to heavenly obedience, service, good works, a slavery as sweet as any freedom that can be imagined.

7:23 -- *You were bought with a price; do not become slaves of men.*

You were bought with a price -- Here is why Paul can speak of individual Christians as being Christ's bond-servants. They have been purchased by Him, and so belong to Him. The price He paid was His own blood. (See notes at 6:20 and 1 Peter 1:18,19.) The social slave who has been set free by Christ, and the social freeman who has been enslaved to Christ, have alike been bought, and are now the property of God.

Do not become slaves of men -- There was the practice at Corinth of selling one's self at the slave markets. Some see this prohibition as a statement made to free Christians -- to not sell themselves -- but this does not seem to be the argument here. There is a change to the plural in the verb "Do not become slaves!" Paul is now addressing all his readers, the Corinthians at large. It does not seem to be a dissuasion from men-pleasing in general, nor even compliance with the immoral demands and pressures exerted by men of the world. Nor is it dissuasion from undue attachment to human guides and leaders (though that was a topic earlier in this letter). Nor is "slaves of men" a reference to marriage, this statement thus being a prohibition of marriage. What Paul writes is a directive to keep away from subservience to the popular opinion (remember the Greek philosophy which was behind a call to asceticism, 7:1b) which would cause them to seek a change in their external social position. The form of the prohibition in Greek (*mē* with a present imperative) prohibits the continuance of an action already going on. Some at Corinth have been giving way to the currently popular philosophy in that town, and their Christian lifestyles have been negatively influenced. This is to stop! This is Paul's answer to the question they had asked him in their letter to him (7:1).

---

[80] This passage, which speaks of each and every Christian being "Christ's slave" probably has a slightly different connotation than, say, Romans 1:1, where "slave" seems to be used in the special sense that only an apostle or prophet can be called a "servant of the Lord." (Compare the Old Testament expression, where God speaks of "My servants the prophets," e.g., Jeremiah 44:4.)

7:24 -- *Brethren, each one is to remain with God in that* condition *in which he was called.*

Brethren, let each man remain with God in that *condition* **in which he was called** -- Compare verses 17 and 20. This is the third time the principle has been repeated. "With God" carries the idea of 'in God's sight,' or 'doing service as to God.' Do all, so as not to disturb fellowship with God. He has just said, 'Let your attachments be heavenward, not earthward.' With that proviso, all secular conditions, whether of family life, or caste, or service, are capable of being made the expression of a Christian character. The concluding "with God" rounds off the whole passage. Paul is not counseling some passive resignation and acceptance of the established order at all costs. He is pointing his friends to that God who is willing to be with them whatever their circumstances. It is for them, then, to seek first and always to abide with Him.

C. Inspired Advice Respecting the Unmarried in View of Circumstances Then in Existence. 7:25-40

> *Summary:* In this paragraph, we have apostolic counsel in reference to remaining single: for the unmarried, generally, verses 25-35; for fathers and their unmarried daughters, verses 36-38; for widows, verses 39,40. The progress of thought in this whole section is this – (1) Paul takes up another question the Corinthians had asked of him in their letter to him, verse 25. (2) The first thing Paul does is to give the source of the advice he is about to give, verse 25. (3) Next he calls attention to the bearing the "present distress" will have on living the Christian life – reminding his readers how a Christian decides his priorities, verses 26-31. (4) Then he calls attention to several overriding principles that guide his instructions. He wants them free of anxiety, and able to give undistracted devotion to the Lord, verses 32-35. (5) Based on all these considerations, he is now able to answer the question concerning the fathers' actions when it comes to giving or not giving their daughters to be married, verses 36-38. (6) He ends his discussion of marriage by dealing with whether widows should remarry or not, verses 39,40.

7:25 -- *Now concerning virgins I have no command of the Lord, but I give an opinion as one who by the mercy of the Lord is trustworthy.*

Now concerning virgins -- This commences Paul's answer to another question which the church at Corinth had directed to Paul in their letter to him (7:1) – whether it was proper for those who were unmarried to get married.[81] "Now concerning" indicates this is another matter on which the Corinthians had asked a specific question. We suppose the Corinthians were asking their question about the unmarried from the same ascetic stance that we observed in 7:1b ("it is good for a man not to touch a woman"). Who are the "virgins"? The genitive plural "the virgins" in verse 25 can, in the Greek, be either mascu-

---

[81] The first question had as its thrust whether people already married should continue in the relationship. This one asks whether or not the unmarried should get married at all.

line or neuter. So we must study the remaining paragraph for clues as we try to answer the question. A quick comparison of several modern translations at verse 36 will show the predominating views about the identity of the "virgins."[82] The NEB speaks of "a partner in celibacy" at verse 36. The NIV speaks of a young man who is acting improperly towards the virgin he is engaged to. The NASB speaks of a father being overly protective towards "his virgin daughter." We doubt the NEB or NIV are correct in the "interpretation" given at verse 36, for it requires a change of topics at verse 36, whereas Paul has indicated he is still answering the question introduced at verse 25.[83]

I have no command of the Lord -- Jesus Christ Himself had never directly dealt with this subject when He was on earth (cp. the language at verses 10 and 12). Lenski believes the implication is that the Corinthians had asked if Christ had left any directions concerning maidens, and if not, weren't they free to do as they wished.[84]

But I give an opinion -- The contrast here is *not* between Paul inspired by the Lord and Paul not inspired. Rather, the contrast is between Paul quoting the actual words of Jesus and Paul the apostle giving inspired instructions. Remember, verse 40 is a claim to inspiration for this whole section. Where the NASB has "opinion," the ASV translators chose "judgment" to translate the Greek word *gnōmēn*. This passage has furnished the two words *gnōmēn* (judgment) and *epitagē* (commandment) which the Vulgate translated *consilium* and *preaceptum*, "advice" and "command" – the origin of the famous distinction of later times in the Roman Catholic Church between "counsels of perfection" and "precepts." A "counsel of perfection"[85] is an advisory declaration, held not to be absolutely binding, but rather given as an aid to attaining approximate moral perfection. A "precept (command)" on the other hand was held to be "absolutely binding" since it came from Lord Christ Himself. But contrary to Catholic teaching, the real distinction in this passage lies only in the fact that one was a command of Christ spoken by Him during His earthly ministry, and the other was Paul's own inspired "judgment" pronounced with apostolic authority. Paul is far from resorting to evasion or equivocation. When the Lord's earthly teaching settled a question, Paul says so (verses 10,11). When the Lord has made no pronouncement during His earthly ministry, Paul again says so (verses 12,25). There are commands from God, spoken by the apostles of Jesus, that have equal and parallel authority to the personally spoken word of Jesus. When the apostles were so speaking, their words are just as binding as the Lord's own (see Luke 10:16). Conscientious Christians would do well to heed the advice!

---

[82] Included at the close of comments on chapter 7 is a Special Study which contains extended discussion in answer to the question, "Who are these 'virgins'?"

[83] Since the subject matter, "virgins," is specifically mentioned in verses 25, 28, 34, 36-38, common sense dictates that unless there are overwhelming reasons to think otherwise, the entire passage is dealing with the same topic. Further, at verse 28, Paul uses the feminine article (four manuscripts, B,F,G,425 lack the article; the rest carry the feminine article) with "virgin," indicating female virgins are the topic particularly in view.

[84] Lenski, *op. cit.*, p.308.

[85] The wording "a counsel to be perfect" implies that it is likely to be an unrealized ideal.

As one who by the mercy of the Lord is trustworthy -- Paul here gives a reason why his judgment is to be taken seriously. He has been called to be an apostle. He has had mercy conferred on him by the Lord Jesus so that he is a trustworthy messenger. He is being faithful to God who has spoken in these last days through His Son. He is being faithful to the task of delivering God's will to man. His words are worthy of the Corinthians' confidence and obedience. The appeal to the Lord's mercy is the language of humility, but it is not the language of uncertainty. Paul is aware of who he is (an apostle of Jesus), of his being an inspired mouthpiece for God, and of the consequent certainty and authority of what he spoke. Jesus may not have spoken on this subject while He was on earth, but the words Paul is about to write are God's directions just as if Jesus had so spoken. The result is that men ignore Paul's judgment at their own peril (see verse 28).

7:26 -- *I think then that this is good in view of the present distress, that it is good for a man to remain as he is.*

I think then -- "Then" ("therefore," ASV) indicates that Paul's "judgment" or "opinion" rests on the mercy given to him; it is a clear claim to be speaking God's thoughts after Him. He does not mean he is not sure, or that these are just his own personal thoughts. He is saying, 'This is an excellent principle, a good fundamental rule, in view of the present distress.'

That this is good in view of the present distress -- "Good" likely means 'good in principle.'[86] Paul, as in 7:1, takes up the fundamental axiom or principle ('Stay where you are!') that underlies this whole chapter, and uses it as the starting point for his whole remaining discussion respecting the unmarried. "Distress" (*anagkēn*) could also be translated by any one of several other English words including 'necessity, calamity, persecution, trial, emergency, crisis.' Translators waver on how to render *enestōsan*. The NASB text has "present," but the margin has "impending." "Present" says there were some urgent and trying conditions at the very time Paul wrote which were surrounding the Christians' lives. "Impending" suggests the distress had not yet begun, but was about to. Various ideas have been offered as writers attempt to identify the "distress":

(1) The famine under Claudius has had lingering effects, say some, though it is hard to determine what the conditions in Corinth were in the mid-50's AD. They seem to be as prosperous as any in the Roman world.
(2) Marital cares and sufferings.
(3) Oppressions and persecutions on Christians. These are hard times economically, and Christians are facing greater temptations than ever in the past. It is ever more difficult to be a consistent Christian. (The Neronian persecution was about 7 years in the future, and Jewish instigated persecutions were regular in occurrence.)
(4) The destruction of Jerusalem (AD 70). The same word "distress" is used in Luke 21:23 of the destruction of Jerusalem. That destruction was preceded by a number of "woes" (Matthew 24:8ff) – e.g., famines, persecutions, epidemics – some of which were

---

[86] Some modern translations, like the RSV, do not translate "good" both times it appears in this verse, and that failure in translation can cause readers to miss the point Paul is making.

occurring at the time Paul wrote, and some which were about to occur.[87]

(5) Some writers suggest the Second Coming of Jesus. But in order to propound this view, these writers are willing to impute to Paul a mistaken belief about the time of the Second Coming. How they can have Paul claiming "trustworthiness" in one breath and making a mistake in the next is difficult to understand. Certainly, it is not necessary to explain "the time is short" (verse 29) as though it speaks of how long it is before the Second Coming.

(6) In view of Paul's usage elsewhere, where the term "present" (*enestōsan*) invariably means "what is already present" (in contrast to what is yet to come – see 3:22 and Romans 8:38), we suggest that the "crisis" is already being experienced by the Corinthian Christians. Perhaps the "crisis" is further explained in verses 29-31. The significant issues there raised keep us from relativizing Paul's instructions as though they dealt only with some unique historical problem in 1st century Corinth. If the "crisis" is further explained in 29-31, then Paul's judgment remains equally valid for any time and place throughout church history.

That it is good for a man to remain as he is -- Paul seems to use "man" much as we use 'person.' *Anthrōpos* here means both men and women, as the illustrations of verses 27 and 28 show. "Remain as he is" repeats the theme behind Paul's instructions in this whole chapter, namely, 'Stay where you are, and be a Christian there.' Christianity does not require a change of condition, like the ascetics at Corinth have been preaching. Instead, Paul counsels 'remain married if you are married; single if you are single.'

7:27 -- Are you bound to a wife? Do not seek to be released. Are you released from a wife? Do not seek a wife.

Are you bound to a wife? -- Already married (the verb *deō*, "to bind") is a perfect tense in the Greek, indicating a state that has been true for some time. This is Paul's usual word for the bond of marriage (see verse 39 and Romans 7:2). Paul addresses the man, but the same is true of the woman, as the next verse will make clear.

Do not seek to be released -- 'Stay where you are!' There is no reason to seek a dissolution of the marriage bond.[88] It is a present imperative with *mē*, 'Stop trying to be loosed!' Stop what you are doing!

Are you released from a wife? – 'Are you unmarried at the present time?' 'Loosed' or "released" might also imply the person had been married before, but now has been divorced

---

[87] Jesus spoke about signs heralding the coming destruction of Jerusalem in Matthew 24:4-28. Only after did He speak about the signless second coming (Matthew 24:29-25:46).

[88] The word translated "loosed" or "released" is not the ordinary word for divorce, so some have questioned whether that is the meaning here. But a person might be "released" from a marriage by death also (verse 39). It seems Paul has chosen a word here that will cover both divorce and death. Further, the Greek word for "released" is the same verb stem as the word rendered "divorces" at Matthew 19:9.

or separated by death.[89]

Do not seek a wife -- The general rule is 'Stay where you are!' It is a present imperative with *mē*, "Stop seeking a wife!" Remember this is not an absolute "command" the breaking of which is sin (see the next verse), but Paul's apostolic judgment concerning what is best for the "present distress."

7:28 -- *But if you marry, you have not sinned; and if a virgin marries, she has not sinned. Yet such will have trouble in this life, and I am trying to spare you.*

But -- Paul's judgment in regard to remaining unmarried "in view of the present distress" lies in the realm of expediency, and dare not be transferred to the domain of moral right or wrong. Paul is stating what is best and most expedient under given circumstances, not what is right or what is sin under any and all circumstances. Therefore he is compelled to add this explanation found in verse 28.

If you should marry, you have not sinned -- Ignoring Paul's stated advice ("Do not seek a wife!") is not sin, but outward trouble and anxiety will be incurred by contracting marriage. And to spare them this, he gives them his advice. The ascetics said that marriage is sinful. Paul says it is not sin to marry. Marriage is honorable and lawful; and though there may be circumstances where it is advisable not to get married, yet there is no law which prohibits it.

And if a virgin should marry, she has not sinned – Remember, the point being discussed is, chiefly, whether daughters should be given in marriage, or permitted to marry.[90] And even if they marry in the face of the present distress, there is no sin. Verse 28 takes the discussion out of the realm of right and wrong, and places it in the realm of expediency.

Yet such will have trouble in this life -- In verse 26 Paul spoke of "the present distress." Now he speaks of *thlupsis*, 'trouble, anxiety, care, solicitude, trials.' In the following verses he will enumerate some of the "trouble" that people will face, and the troubles are only made more troubling when one has to worry not only about himself but about how his or her mate is faring. "Such" is masculine, and so it embraces all cases, and is not confined to female "virgins." "In this life" (the Greek literally is 'in the flesh') refers to such troubles as are regularly found in the human sphere of things.

And I am trying to spare you -- This is the reason Paul gave his advice to remain unmarried for the present. He was concerned for their physical and mental welfare, trying to spare them anxiety and trials.

---

[89] If you take this as "release" from a previous marriage, then the following injunction would speak of a second marriage – "If you should marry, you have not sinned." See Olan Hicks, "Does a Divorced Person Sin When He Marries Again?" *Image* (Sep-Oct 1994), p.27-29.

[90] The language of verse 27 is so nearly like the language of verses 36-38 that it is difficult to believe the two passages are not the same piece of advice to the same people.

7:29 -- *But this I say, brethren, the time has been shortened, so that from now on those who have wives should be as though they had none;*

But this I say, brethren -- If we translate *de* as "but," the idea is, 'Though I counsel none to change their state ("Stay where you are!"), I do counsel all to change their attitude toward earthly things.' If we translate *de* as "and," then this and the next several verses identify some of the trials Paul has in mind that folk would face. In verses 29-31 Paul breaks off into one of his characteristic digressions, in which he applies the principle he is discussing to fields other than marriage – the principle being that external circumstances while we are here on earth matter but little. Earthly things are not as important as spiritual matters.

The time has been shortened -- "Shortened" (*sunestalmenos*) is used of the 'furling of a sail,' of a burial cloth being 'wrapped around' (Acts 5:6) the corpse, of the 'packing of luggage,' and the 'shortening of a syllable.' All these are uses of the word in the papyri. The word cannot mean 'disastrous.' It does mean 'contracted, limited, shortened, allotted.' "Time" here is *kairos*, the amount of time left for any Christian to do what they have to do.[91] The shortness of human life, the shortness of time we each have to prepare for eternity, is the thing in view (see verse 31b). One writer makes an analogy to the terminally ill. For those who have made peace with their imminent death, the amount of time left is less in the forefront of their thinking than is the change of perspective. They see, hear, and value each day in a new way. The Christian who has a proper view of time judges what is important by a redeemed set of standards.

So that from now on -- The punctuation and reading are here uncertain. The idea may be this, 'In consideration of the shortness of time, the following is true.' Or the idea may be that 'God has shortened the time in order that: *Christians* may keep themselves from the world; *married people* may not bind all their interests to their wedlock; *mourners* may not be consumed with their misfortunes; and the *joyous* may not be totally engrossed in their prosperity.' "So that" means 'this is what God's intention was in making the time short.' Paul regards everything as having its place and purpose in the Divine economy.

Those who have wives should be as though they had none -- They are, as it were, to hold loosely to the things of the world. It is an exhortation against being wholly absorbed with no thoughts except marriage. This does not mean that they are to treat their wives with unkindness or neglect, or fail in the duties of love and fidelity. There is no contradiction here to his instructions in verses 3 and 4. It rather means they are to live above the world; they are not to be unduly attached to the world, so as to interfere with any duty which they owe to God. For ascetic reasons, some at Corinth were advocating that

---

[91] Various other interpretations of this phrase have been suggested: (1) It refers to the second coming, some say. The time until the second coming is short, is what the writer intends, says Lenski (*op. cit.*, p.317). But the apostles were hardly mistaken about the time of the second advent, nor did they teach that Jesus was going to return quickly. (2) Paul shows that the period of "present distress" will be short, interpret others. (3) Still others interpret it to mean that the "distress" is nearly upon us – its beginning is not very far off. None of these seem to satisfy the context, which requires this verse be a reason for being hesitant about getting married, instead of 'Staying where you are!'

the married should end their marriages, and the unmarried should stay as they are.[92] Paul urges on them a wholly different worldview. Being married or single is not the crucial question. What is important is that we live without the world's activities controlling us, and wholly taking up our time.

7:30 -- *and those who weep, as though they did not weep; and those who rejoice, as though they did not rejoice; and those who buy, as though they did not possess;*

And those who weep, as though they did not weep -- They were to restrain and moderate their grief by the hope of the life to come. If life brings sadness, do not be controlled by the sadness. The general idea in all these expressions is that in whatever situation Christians are, they should be dead to the world, and not improperly affected by passing events. Those who weep should live as if no earthly sorrow could greatly disturb them.

And those who rejoice, as though they did not rejoice -- Those who are happy; those who prosper; those who have beloved families around them; those who are blessed with success, honor, esteem, and health – those are the ones who "rejoice." Yet they must not forget that all these things must soon be left. If things of this life bring joy, do not be engrossed in them. Those who are enjoying 'the good life' (as it is sometimes called) should not let the good things become their sole object and passion.

And those who buy, as though they did not possess -- Earthly sorrow and joy and wealth are things which are merely transient and unreal when compared with the awe inspiring, eternal, permanent realities which we shall all soon have to face. "Our lands and houses, our stocks and bonds and mortgages, our goods and chattels, shall soon pass into other hands. Other men will plough our fields, reap our harvests, work in our shops, stand at our counters, sit down at our firesides, eat at our tables, lie upon our beds. Others will occupy our places in society, have our offices, sit in our seats. Others will take possession of our gold and appropriate it to their own use; we shall have no more interest in it, or control over it" because we are dead and gone from the scene (Barnes, *op. cit.*, p.128). Earthly goods are a trust, not a permanent possession. Those who have an abundance of material possessions should not cling to them, or make them the only object of their living.

7:31 -- *and those who use the world, as though they did not make full use of it; for the form of this world is passing away.*

And those who use the world -- Paul has in mind those who make a necessary and proper use of their time in this world to furnish food, clothing, medicine, and protection.   It is

---

[92] W. Edward Glenny, "I Corinthians 7:29-31 and the Teaching of Continence in *The Acts of Paul and Thecla*," *Grace Theological Journal* 11:1 (1991), p.53-70, is a critique of Dennis R. MacDonald's theory that *The Acts of Paul* preserve aspects of Pauline teaching which should be considered on a level with the Pastoral Epistles. That is, MacDonald implies that *The Acts of Paul* are closer to the primitive Pauline teaching on the role of women than the Pastorals are. Glenny proposes that MacDonald's thesis does not carry conviction, and that the teaching of *The Acts of Paul and Thecla* concerning marriage is closer to the ascetic doctrine of Paul's opponents at Corinth, than to the teaching of Paul in either 1 Corinthians or the Pastorals.

right to so use the world, for it was made for these purposes. Paul does not write 'this world,' as though he were referring to worldly pleasures and vices. With these Christians are to have nothing to do, let alone "not using them to the full."

As though they did not make full use of it -- The word translated "full use" is *katachrōmenoi*. "Abuse" (the KJV translation) does not sustain the analogy of the verses preceding. This is probably because the English word "abuse" has changed its meaning in the centuries since the KJV was first translated. In the 17th century, the word "abuse" meant to 'use something over-much.' That is probably the right idea for this context. Three centuries later, the word "abuse" means 'to misuse something.' That mental connotation would cause us to miss the point of Paul's paragraph. All the things mentioned in these verses are right things (there is a place for marriage, for weeping, for rejoicing, for buying, for possessing, and for obtaining food, clothing, and shelter). Paul is giving a warning against being in bondage to these things which are in themselves right and good; his warning is not against some criminal use of them. It is better to take it as "not using it to the full" (as does the ASV), i.e., not draining dry the cup of earthly advantages (Farrar, *op. cit.*, p.228). The man who remembers that he is only a sojourner in the world is likely to remember also that worldly possessions are not everything, and that worldly surroundings cannot be made permanent.

For the form of this world is passing away -- "For" tells us this phrase introduces the reason for the immediately preceding admonitions against being absorbed wholly in the things of this world. "Form" translates *schēma*, the word denoting outward shape, form, appearance. The word is probably taken from the shifting scenes of the drama, where the stage is changed often. The scene that allured and enticed us passes away, and we pass to other scenes. The good and right material things just listed in these verses, which the Christian is to hold loosely, would all be covered by the word "form." The only question in "passing away" (*paragei*) is to the 'when' of its passing. Some have argued that the passing takes place at the time of the second coming of Christ, when the elements shall melt with fervent heat and pass away (2 Peter 3:7-10).[93] Others understand that the use of the present tense verb suggests the process of "passing away" is already underway. If the "present distress" is already upon the readers (verse 26) then Paul is here speaking of the daily shifting of the events of the present. As the old song says, "change and decay in all around I see." Perhaps it fits best with the argument of the "present distress" to take this "passing away" as already in the process of happening. The meaning of the illustrations is clear. Married men are apt to become absorbed in domestic cares, mourners in their sorrow, buyers in the preservation of what they have bought, etc. A Christian, with dangers all around him, and with the time short, ought not to be engrossed in any of his surroundings, knowing how temporary they are. Their present condition was not to last

---

[93] The decisive passage of Scripture regarding the question as to whether this present world will be annihilated or will be transformed at the second coming is Romans 8:19-23, which declares for the latter. Not the world as such, but its outward form is passing away, and will at last pass away completely.

long, and their participation in its joys and sorrows was to be short-lived. This is the reason why the apostle urges the Corinthians not to be wedded to earthly things. What does Paul really say? Marriage, tears, joys, purchases, the whole world of earthly things – we Christians may have all of them, use all of them, experience all of them. But in what manner? For what they are, as belonging to the "form" of this present world. As soon as we forget this limit, and begin to think of these things as being more than transient, we will permit them to interfere with our spiritual life and our relation to the life to come – and a false power reaches into our lives and begins to ruin them. Compare Luke 12:18-20. When we see that marriage, weeping, etc. are transient, forever moving on and away, why try to cling to them, or make them more than they are, or value them more than their real worth? If Christians are to have their desires and motives right, they will have to remember the sobering truth emphasized in verse 31b.

7:32 -- *But I want you to be free from concern. One who is unmarried is concerned about the things of the Lord, how he may please the Lord;*

But I want you to be free from concern -- Just as verse 29 began with "but" and gave an explanation for his "judgment" that it was best to remain unmarried "in view of the present distress," so we understand that verse 32 (which also begins with "but") continues that line of argument. Not only was Paul trying to "spare them" by reminding them to have their values right in light of the transience of earthly relations (verses 29-31), he was trying to prevent 'anxiety.' "Free from concern" means 'without anxiety, solicitude, care, distraction,'[94] free from an unnecessary attention on the things of this life so that one's thoughts and affections are taken away from heavenly objects. Verses 32-35 offer crucial guidance for people in any time and culture trying to decide whether or not to marry. Instead of being guided by the countless criteria any society may offer, Christians should make such decisions in light of which state, single or married, enables them to best serve the Lord.

One who is unmarried is concerned about the things of the Lord, how he may please the Lord -- His attention is not distracted by the cares of this life. He can give his main attention to the things of religion. The unmarried man, having no family to provide for and to protect in times of distress and persecution, is less encumbered with worldly cares than the married man who is compelled to take care of a spouse and dependent children. The married man might be thus kept back from that unswerving courage in those dark days when full loyalty to Christ is demanded.[95] It is true that a man can be "overcharged ... with the worries of this life" (Luke 21:34). As Moulton and Milligan have shown, the verb *areskō* ("please") includes the thought of service in the interests of another,[96] in this case, of Jesus ("Lord" is likely a reference to Jesus). How do we know we are "pleasing" someone? First we become concerned that such pleasing is needful. Then we begin to do what we know brings delight to that person.

---

[94] The same root word (*amerimnous*) is used at Matthew 28:14 and Matthew 6:25-34.

[95] Lipscomb, *op. cit.*, p.111.

[96] Moulton and Milligan, *op. cit.*, p.75.

7:33 -- *but one who is married is concerned about the things of the world, how he may please his wife,*

But one who is married is concerned about the things of the world, how he may please his wife -- Just as there was a difference between the unmarried and the married man in their service for the Lord, so it is with the woman also (verse 34). The unmarried man has only one set of real cares, namely, how to please the Lord. In all his thinking and his doing, he has really only the Lord to consider, and no other person. Quite otherwise is the case of the married man. He has cares about the things of the world that are necessary for his family. In addition to the question of how he may please the Lord, for him a second question arises, how at the same time to please his wife. It is important to remember that if Paul had sinful things in mind, he would have written 'things of *this* world.' Instead, he is talking about everyday issues and responsibilities which, though not evil in themselves, can distract a person from full-time service to the Lord.

7:34 -- *and his interests are divided. The woman who is unmarried, and the virgin, is concerned about the things of the Lord, that she may be holy both in body and spirit; but one who is married is concerned about the things of the world, how she may please her husband.*

And *his interests* are divided -- The reading and punctuation at this place are surrounded with uncertainty.[97] The general sense of the passage, however, is not unclear. The differences of reading and punctuation can be ascertained by comparing several English versions. The KJV has a period after verse 33, and starts a new sentence with verse 34 so that it reads, "There is a difference also between a wife and a virgin ...." The ASV/NASB have a comma after verse 33, and a period in the middle of verse 34, so that it reads, "He that is married is careful for the things of the world, how he may please his wife, [34] and is divided. So also the woman that is unmarried and the virgin is careful for the things of the Lord ...." However we read it, the meaning follows along these lines. *Memeristai* can be translated "divided" or "distracted." It speaks of divided interests. He is no longer single-hearted. Hence, the married man is "divided" in the matter of cares – some matters call him in one direction, some in another direction. We see a good illustration of what being thus "divided" means in the case of Martha: "You are worried (literally, divided) and troubled about many things," said Jesus, i.e., she was trying to do a number of things at the same time (Luke 10:41).

And the woman who is unmarried, and the virgin, is concerned about the things of the Lord -- "And" ("so also," ASV) indicates that just as the married man has divided interests while the unmarried man is not so divided, so it is with the woman. "Unmarried"

---

[97] Lachmann's text reads *kai memeristai kai*, and after this, though the text is based on lesser authority, it reads *hē gunē hē agamos*. Tischendorf decided the text should read, *memeristai kai hē gunē kai parthenos*. The Textus Receptus drops the *kai* after *memeristai*. The texts of Westcott & Hort and Nestle read as does the ASV/NASB. Heinrici made an interesting textual emendation (a conjecture as to the original reading) here. He proposed to insert a second *memeristai* after the first, so the passage reads " ... *kai memeristai: memeristai kai hē gunē. hē agamos* ..." ("He that is married is anxious in regard to the things of the world, how he may please his wife, and is divided. Divided also is the wife. The unmarried woman, with the virgin, is anxious as to the things of the Lord.") This would account for the double *kai* which embarrasses some authors' critical texts, and gives a fuller and more balanced sense.

perhaps refers to the "widow" or the "divorcee." "Virgin" is likely used with special reference to the topic of this whole section, verses 25-38. Women who are not involved with husbands have fewer distractions to cause them to neglect a service they might perform for God.

That she may be holy both in body and spirit -- The word "holy" means "set apart to sacred service."[98] Remember the context where the opposite of "holy" is being "divided" in one's service. It is not in purity and spirituality that the virgin is said to have advantage over the wife, but in *freedom from distracting cares*. It would impugn a divine ordinance, and to contradict all experience, to say married women, because they are married, are for that reason less *pure* than the unmarried. But the unmarried can be more completely 'set apart' to God's service – free from the distracting cares of the married. Two things are certain: (1) God intended marriage to be the normal lot, and (2) marriage is by no means incompatible with the most absolute saintliness. Holiness in "body" comes first – think of the marriage relation and its drives. "Spirit" (the human spirit) is added to make up the entire person. The "spirit" is that portion of a person that gives directions to the soul which animates the body. Concerning the unmarried man, it was said "how he might please the Lord." Of woman it is said "in order that she may be set apart both in body and in spirit." Both expressions are the opposite of 'being distracted' or 'divided' concerning where one's duty lies.

But one who is married is concerned about the things of the world, how she may please her husband -- The married woman's case is exactly like that of the married man. She not only has the Lord to please, but she also has a husband to please. If Paul did not write a second time, "and is divided," it matters little for his readers can supply this thought without effort.

7:35 -- *This I say for your own benefit; not to put a restraint upon you, but to promote what is appropriate and* **to secure** *undistracted devotion to the Lord.*

And this I say for your own benefit -- Paul now tells the Corinthians why he has written these things. Paul is not trying to encumber them with the idea that if they marry it is sin. Paul is not saying that they should not get married at all. Paul is not trying to enforce upon them the celibate state. What he has said was said only out of regard to their own advantages – whether to spare them trouble in this life (verse 28); or as the following context would indicate, to render the maintenance of their Christian profession during the "present distress" a little easier. 'I am saying all this simply for your own spiritual profit. The entire question is not one of sinning or of avoiding sin, but of spiritual advantage.'

Not to put a restraint upon you -- The word *brochon* rendered "restraint" ("snare," ASV) means a cord, a rope, a bond, a halter, a lasso. It does not mean "trap," as the word "snare" suggests. 'I'm not trying to throw a lasso around your neck' to deprive you of your liberty, like a lasso would bind a wild creature. Paul would not bind them with any rule that God

---

[98] Compare notes on "holy" at 1 Corinthians 3:17.

had not made. Paul means he was not trying to *capture* his readers and shut them up to asceticism, as though that were the only option God permitted. There is likely a direct rebuke of some at Corinth who were trying to "restrain" the Corinthians to asceticism. 'I have no wish to throw a halter over your head and check your Christian liberty.' He is not appealing to a law at all, but the very opposite – to the liberty of the gospel which enables us to freely choose what most enhances our spiritual advantage.

But to promote what is seemly -- Decorous, fit, proper, noble is the idea of "seemly" (*euschēmon*). It is that which is best fitted to your present condition. Instead of restricting his readers, Paul is trying to free them for whatever is appropriate in each individual case as each person expresses his or her devotion to the Lord.

And *to secure* undistracted devotion to the Lord -- When a man or woman marries, there is bound to be some distraction. (Cp. Luke 10:38ff.) Paul's ideal pictures women being able, during the present distress, like Mary, to wait upon the Lord without Martha's distractions.

*7:36 -- But if any man thinks that he is acting unbecomingly toward his virgin **daughter**, if she should be of full age, and if it must be so, let him do what he wishes, he does not sin; let her marry.*

But if any man -- Finally, verses 36-38 are the answer to the question which was introduced at verse 25, toward which Paul has been building since then. As noted at verse 25, there are three prominent interpretations offered for this passage. Agreeing with the ASV/NASB translators, this commentator sees the topic being whether or not fathers should give their daughters in marriage. In most oriental nations the marriage of the daughter rested entirely in the hands of the father; his will was law in the matter. Greek and Jewish law, and indeed Roman law, gave the father absolute control over the child.[99] The Corinthians have apparently asked Paul for instructions about such cases, whether they should keep their promises to give their daughter in marriage.

Thinks that he is acting unbecomingly towards his virgin *daughter* -- Is pressure being applied to congregational members by those of ascetic persuasion still in the background? We think so. Ascetics would have argued that marriage was inappropriate. One can even imagine the ascetics filling the father's mind with anxiety by their ascetic "restraint" (verse 35). Paul here addresses the father's anxieties and says they are groundless. In fact, Paul will say there may be cases where the father ought to give his daughter in marriage. The verb *nomidzei* ("thinks") is used as it was in verse 26 – "if any one has this conviction, that he is acting unbecomingly ...." If the father's action would be "unbecoming," if keeping the daughter from marrying may cause her to be tempted to sin or it would bring scandal, he is to let her marry. In the East, it is particularly dishonorable to remain unmarried. It was a shame and a disgrace for the woman not to be married. Note that "daughter" is sup-

---

[99] When we are considering this answer in regard to the marriage of virgin daughters, we must remember the control which a father had over the marriage of his daughter in ancient times, remnants of which exist today in the custom of an aspiring son-in-law asking the father for the hand of his daughter, and that of the wedding itself where the father gives the daughter away.

plied by the NASB translators. There is no such noun in the Greek. We simply have "virgin" in the feminine case.[100] "His virgin" is not the common way of writing 'his daughter,' but it does occur. Liddel and Scott cite Sophocles saying, "my virgins" for "my daughters."[101] It is easy to envision that Paul used the unusual language "his virgin" in direct opposition to the claims made by the ascetics that "virginity" (and the single life) is preferable to marriage.

If she should be of full age ("if she should be past the flower of her age," ASV, or "if she is past her youth," current NASB – *huperakmos*[102]) -- If she is more than 20 years old, which the ancients (see Plato, *Republic*, v. 460) regarded as the acme of the woman's life (*akmē*, the period of greatest development). It was 30 years old for a man. The idea is that she has long since reached a marriageable age, she has reached sexual maturity.

And if it must be so ("and if need so requireth," ASV) -- The need may be found in the temperament of the daughter, to promote her happiness, to keep her from sinning, since she has reached sexual maturity and does not have the gift of continence. The need may be a moral obligation or necessity in the given case (e.g., she was promised years before).[103] Necessity might also be present in the case of a slave, whose master forced him to contract

---

[100] The subtle implication should not be missed that Paul expects those coming to the altar for the first time to be virgins.

[101] Henry G. Liddell and Robert Scott, *A Greek-English Lexicon* (New York: Harper & Brothers, 1846), p.1124. Because of the uncommon expression "his virgin," some modern translators have pictured these verses as dealing not with a parent and his daughter, but with a man and his fiancée (RSV, "his betrothed"; or NIV, "toward the virgin he is engaged to"). (1) Some have supposed the engaged couple (influenced by ascetics at Corinth) have at first agreed to remain celibate. When Paul says "Let them marry," he is telling them there is no sin if they change their mind about perpetual celibacy, marry, and break their agreement to stay celibate. However, under this hypothesis, it is difficult to assign a meaning to "acting unbecomingly." If a man and his fiancée are envisioned, what is the 'unseemly behavior'? Mare (*op. cit.*, p.237) offers the unlikely scenario that the man (the only one to embrace the ascetic arguments) is treating his fiancée dishonorably by depriving her of the privilege of the marriage she desires. Again, it is difficult to explain "let him do what he wishes" alongside "let them marry." Furthermore, "his virgin" is a strange designation for a man's fiancée. (2) Entirely amiss is the interpretation modern readers sometimes put on the passage, that the couple has been engaging in premarital sex ("unseemly behavior"), the girl is pregnant ("need so requires"), and that Paul then says such premarital sexual acts are not sin, and, in fact, the couple should get married.

[102] Thayer gives "plump and ripe (and so in danger of defilement)" for *huperakmos*. Arndt and Gingrich indicate the word, when used of men, means "strong passions." The RSV translates "if his passions are strong," a possible translation, since the verb is third singular, and could be translated "he," "she," or "it." The adjective *huperakmos*, too, can be either masculine or feminine. The nearest antecedent is "virgin" (feminine), so the ASV/NASB translators took it as feminine. The farther antecedent is "any man" so the RSV takes it as masculine. Most recognized lexicons give the primary meaning of *huperakmos* as "past the bloom of youth," and the RSV ignores this primary meaning.

[103] A possible scenario has the young people promised to each other before Christianity ever entered the life of the father and his daughter. The daughter, now a Christian, is still pledged to the young man, who is not converted. Does the father keep his promise to give his daughter? If so, does this passage indicate the possibility that in some cases interfaith marriages, and even mixed-marriages, may be contracted and consummated? This scenario has enough plausibility to keep any of us from being dogmatic about the good rule that Christians should marry only Christians.

marriage for his daughter, as Fisher (p.124) has suggested. Or it may be that the girl desires to marry, and in fact, she ought to marry, and her father realizes he would be acting improperly to continue to forbid her to marry. To withhold marriage from a girl of marriageable age, and anxious to marry, would have been to court disaster, especially in 1st century Corinth.

Let him do what he wishes -- He is to go ahead and permit the daughter to marry. The NASB translation (which seems to imply that he may consent or not, and whichever course he adopts is OK) is a bit weak, as though the father still may refuse to consent to the marriage. After saying the father has a conviction that it is unseemly to further forbid the marriage, and after saying the girl is sexually mature and wants to marry, that he can withhold her if he wants, is to miss the point of the need. It also contradicts what the next verse says.

He does not sin -- He is not doing wrong in giving his daughter in marriage, contrary to what ascetics may have insisted.

Let them marry[104] -- "Them," namely, the young people involved; the subject of the plural is derived from the context. Not the father and the daughter, but the daughter and her betrothed are the ones permitted to be married. All throughout this passage the apostle takes for granted the absolute control of the parent over the child, in accordance with the principles of both Greek and Jewish jurisprudence. Hence, no advice is given to the young maiden herself, but only to her father.

7:37 -- *But he who stands firm in his heart, being under no constraint, but has authority over his own will, and has decided this in his own heart, to keep his own virgin* **daughter,** *he will do well.*

But he who stands firm in his heart -- When a father has settled convictions that a single life is best for his daughter, because of the present distress, the father has no misgivings about the fact that he was doing the right thing for his daughter.

Being under no constraint -- There are no outward pressures that put the father under an obligation. There was nothing in her disposition or inclination that would make marriage necessary. There was no prior engagement to be honored, or no pressure of a master on a slave. The objection that the daughter's will is left entirely out of consideration is not in accord with the fact. For in each case the father considers the physical make-up of his daughter, and that means her desires and wishes as well. Thus the fact is that what eventually influences the father to decide one way or another is not simply his own will, but the daughter's as well.

But has authority over his own will -- The father, under no external constraints, is free to do as he pleases.   Often daughters were espoused, or promised, when they were young,

---

[104] The first edition of the NASB has "let them marry." Later editions have "let her marry" (since a few manuscripts do have the singular -- D, F, G, 2495.)

and in such a case a man would be bound to adhere to the engagement; he would not have power over his own will. Paul is very careful in his instructions not to run roughshod over the conscience of the people involved in the case.

And has decided this in his own heart, to keep his own virgin *daughter*, he will do well -- The general meaning of the verse is that the father, who from high motives remained unshaken in his intent to dedicate his daughter (as Philip did, Acts 21:9) to the virgin life, did well, though neither Jews nor Gentiles thought so (cf. Sirach xlii.9).[105] This phrase "keep his daughter" does not mean that some were selling their virgin daughters as chattel, but that this father was not going to. 'Selling a daughter into slavery' is not the topic of the context. The father who 'kept his virgin daughter,' of course, would care for her and provide for her in his own house all her days. So, four conditions have been laid down for the father who would keep his daughter unmarried at home: (1) Unshaken firmness in his own mind (as against social pressure). (2) The absence of constraint (arising from previous engagement). (3) His full authority to act as he will. (4) A judgment deliberately and independently formed to this effect.

As an aside, it is also not to be supposed Paul is here referring to a kind of spiritual betrothal between unmarried persons sometimes found in the 2nd century church. In the 2nd century, Christian spinsters with ascetic tendencies, in order to avoid ordinary marriage, placed themselves formally under the protection of a man, who in some sense was responsible for the woman. She might or might not share the same house, but she was pledged to share his spiritual life. The meaning of verse 36 would then be that such an arrangement could be turned into real marriage without sin. However, verses 36 and 38 both provide an obstacle to such an interpretation. "He that giveth her in marriage" is the correct translation for verse 38; Paul is speaking of the father or guardian giving an unmarried daughter in marriage. Further, *huperakmos* from verse 36 would have to be rendered as "over passionate," which is a more than doubtful rendering.

7:38 -- *So then both he who gives his own virgin* **daughter** *in marriage does well, and he who does not give her in marriage will do better.*

So then -- Paul now sums up what he has been saying about a father giving or not giving his daughter in marriage. This verse will clearly show that Paul has *not* been contrasting something that is right with something that is wrong; he has instead been contrasting comparative degrees of what was expedient.

Both he who gives his own virgin *daughter* in marriage does well, and he who does not give her in marriage will do better -- The father who gives his daughter in marriage does well, and he who does not do so will be found to have done still better. The *-izo* termination on the verb *gamizō* ("give in marriage") points to a meaning like that given in the ASV/NASB; it does not accord with the idea that the passage refers to fiancées or to

---

[105] Farrar, *op. cit.*, p.229.

'partners in celibacy' or to 'spiritual brides.'[106] "His own virgin" is the way the better manuscripts read, a reading that is difficult for any interpretation one might wish to make of the passage (see notes at verse 36). Note that the contrast is not between good and bad, but between well and better. The one option was better not because celibacy is morally better than marriage. The "unmarried" option is better in the realm of expediency, so that individuals may be free to devote their whole lives to the Lord, without any distractions. When all is said, Paul leaves the whole problem of getting married an open question, to be settled on a case-by-case basis.

7:39 – *A wife is bound as long as her husband lives; but if her husband is dead, she is free to be married to whom she wishes, only in the Lord.*

A wife is bound as long as her husband lives -- Paul now gives instruction regarding second marriages for widows (verses 39,40). Verse 34 spoke of the woman who was unmarried, and the virgin, both of them being situations the ascetics would have denied any freedom to marry or marry again. Having dealt with the unmarried virgin, Paul now turns to the widow, and gives his advice on what her best future course might be. In the dictum with which verse 39 begins, Paul is repeating what Jesus Himself had said when He was on earth (see notes at 1 Corinthians 7:10,11).[107] God's original intention was one man and one woman married to each other for life. In the case envisioned, both the wife and husband are Christian. There is to be no divorce, and neither a husband nor wife who takes Jesus' teaching seriously will initiate divorce proceedings against his or her mate. The wife is "bound" (*dedetai*, the perfect tense form of the same verb used at verses 15 and 27). Given God's intents for marriage, the only thing that can rightfully end the marriage is the death of one of the spouses (though adultery may also lead to the end of the marriage).

But if her husband is dead, she is free to be married to whom she wishes -- Contrary to what ascetics might think or teach, Paul says the widow is free to marry again. The passive "to be married" (*gamēthēnai*) indicates someone else performs the marriage ceremony. "Is dead" literally reads "is fallen asleep," a euphemistic expression for death (cp. John 11:11-13). "Whom she wishes" indicates the woman's consent to the new marriage relationship. Perhaps there is a subtle indication that widows had more of a say in a proposed marriage than did a man's virgin daughter (who sometimes had a voice, and sometimes did not, see verses 36-37). Someone opposed a widow's remarrying, saying it brings dishonor on her first mate if she marries again. On the contrary, in many ways, a

---

[106] Commentators defending all three views of the possible meaning of this passage appeal to the possible different meanings (found in classical Greek) between *gamizō* ('give in marriage, cause to marry') and *gameō* ('to marry,' 'to enter into matrimony'). (Note, in Greek word formation, verbs ending in -*izo* are causative.) Complicating the determination of the meanings of the words is the fact that *gamizō* is not found much outside the New Testament; in classical times, *gameō* was used to mean both 'marry' and 'give in marriage' (see Liddell and Scott). Only if it can be shown that *gamizō* is equivalent to *gameō* in its New Testament usage could the views possibly be sustained that the topic is fiancées or 'spiritual brides' getting married.

[107] Some English versions read "A wife is bound *by the law* for so long ....," but the words "by the law" are not in the best manuscripts. Thus the statement about the abiding nature of the marriage is not something based on Old Testament teaching, but is something that is New Testament teaching.

second marriage pays a great compliment to the one who has died. For the one who survives, remarriage means that the first marriage was so happy that another marriage can be entered into without fear. So, in fact, a second marriage can be a mark of honor to the dead.

Only in the Lord -- If the Christian widow chooses to enter into a second marriage, the person she marries must be a Christian ("only in the Lord"[108]). She is not to marry an unbeliever.[109] A Christian widow must watch her motives and let spiritual considerations guide her in her decision about marrying again.

7:40 -- *But in my opinion she is happier if she remains as she is; and I think that I also have the Spirit of God.*

But in my opinion she is happier -- "Happier" is the same root word used in the beatitudes (Matthew 5:23-12). She will be "happier" because she will be freer from cares, distractions, and entanglements. Happier, partly by being free to attend to the things of the Lord undistracted. All that was said on the word "opinion" at verse 25 is still true here at verse 40. This is Paul's inspired 'judgment' on this matter. Right to the end, Paul refrains from saying anything to indicate that there is something morally higher about celibacy. He thinks that the widow will be "happier" if she refrains from remarriage.

If she remains as she is -- Again we hear the theme that has undergirded all the instructions in chapter 7, 'Stay where you are!' "If she remains as she is" means 'If she remains unmarried, even though she could rightly enter into a new marriage to a Christian.' He does not mean offer a restraint, but he indicates the circumstances should govern. Paul suggests that though widows are free to remarry in the Lord, the situation is better (in his judgment) if they do not remarry, but remain single to the end. There is no inconsistency between this and 1 Timothy 5:14. The "younger widows" come under the rule given at 1 Timothy 5:9.

And I think that I also have the Spirit of God -- This is a modest way of saying, 'You may not deem my judgment to be of much value, yet, I have been speaking under the guidance of the Holy Spirit.' This does not indicate any doubt in the apostle's mind about whether or not he was speaking as the Spirit directed, but implies full persuasion. This is one of Paul's *litotes* – deliberate but effective understatement.

---

[108] Many take "in the Lord" in a wider sense, namely, "in a Christian way" or "in the fear of the Lord," asking His blessing. We believe this misses the point. It would be tantamount to saying that it is all right in some cases for a Christian widow to marry a non-Christian.

[109] This commentator's definition of "Christian" is an immersed penitent believer. If that is what "in the Lord" means, the question may be raised, "What about a Christian marrying an unimmersed denominationalist?" Long ago, Plutarch said that "marriage cannot be happy unless husband and wife are of the same religion." The *Reader's Digest*, October, 1951, carried a thought provoking article, showing the difficulty people experience trying to make inter-denominational marriages work. If in most inter-denominational marriages there is going to be trouble, what chance would children born in such a home have? This commentator tries to discourage couples whose religious backgrounds differ from entering into marriage. Settle the religious issue before you marry, is his counsel.

Special Study #4

WHO ARE THE "VIRGINS"?

M. Black (*The Scrolls and Christian Origins*, NY, 1961) and J.F. Bound ("Who are the 'Virgins' Discussed in 1 Corinthians 7:25-38?" *Evangelical Journal* 2 [1984], p.6,7) both argue that the "virgins" are male celibates. This is an extremely unlikely option since the noun *parthenos* ("virgin") is feminine throughout this passage.

J. Massingberd Ford, "Levirate Marriage in St. Paul (1 Corinthians 7)," *NTS* 10 (1963-64), p.361-365, proposed that the virgins are young widows who have been married only once, and that the question has to do with whether or not Old Testament Levirate marriage rules still apply to the widow and her brother-in-law. Ford thought Paul's answer basically releases both from this obligation. This view is also unlikely. It forces us to give the term "virgin" a peculiar meaning ('married only once'?), and also assumes the Corinthian church was essentially Jewish, and that the questions asked about marriage are asked from a Judaizing standpoint.

A third idea is that the virgins are bachelors and maidens who have voluntarily vowed to remain celibate. They are even called *Amtsjungfrauen*, virgins who were officially recognized as such by the congregation. We might call them monks and nuns who have not as yet withdrawn to monasteries.

A fourth idea, one alluded to from time to time in the comments, is that the topic in this paragraph of chapter 7 is whether engaged couples should go ahead and get married. This is the view that has been adopted by most recent commentaries on 1 Corinthians (Fee, Conzlemann, Barrett, Holladay, Senft, and Elliott [*NTS* 19:2, 1973, p.219-225]). As shown in the comments previously and in the arguments below, this interpretation requires us to handle rather loosely certain Greek words. For example, it is not easy to show that "virgin" is synonymous with 'betrothed girl' or 'betrothed fellow.' In addition, only in verse 25 do we find the plural "virgins;" elsewhere, the term is singular and feminine. One must stretch a bit to make all the singular references refer to the engaged couple.

Another idea advanced is that these were so-called "Joseph Marriages," or "spiritual marriages," where men and women with a vow of virginity lived together as husband and wife but did not engage in sexual intercourse. These couples, bachelors and maidens, would become betrothed to each other, but not in order eventually to marry, but rather always to remain celibate. It has even been claimed that they lived together so that the maiden might have male protection, and the bachelor might enjoy the company and the house keeping of the maiden. This view also forces us to stretch the meaning of several words Paul uses as he describes the people involved, and gives his inspired judgment concerning them. Further, it is not possible to show that this practice, known in the 2nd to 5th centuries, actually prevailed in Corinth in the 1st century.

Some attempt to read certain ideas into the text, but with only with the least thread of support. In the 3rd century we hear of *sorores* (Latin, devoted virgins) who lived together with ascetics and clerics and even shared their beds in order to demonstrate their strength of will and their ability to retain chastity. The church strongly opposed these unions at the time, and they disappeared. Later on they were revived when so-called "Joseph Marriages," or angel marriages of the Roman Catholic system, originated. (Meusel, *Kirchliches Handlexicon*, article *Subintroductae*.) Yet prior to the 3rd century, no one appealed to this paragraph of Paul's letter in justification of such practices. These ideas are extremely unlikely interpretations of the passage since nowhere does Paul give the least hint that vows were taken, and nowhere is there a trace of official recognition of such relationships.

The nearly universal interpretation of this passage, up until the 20th century, has been that the Corinthians had consulted Paul about the advisability of fathers giving their daughters in marriage.

- The Greek term "virgin" signifies maiden or virgin, and Paul uses the feminine article and thereby excludes all reference to a bachelor.
- We have suggested in our comments at verse 25 that verses 25-38 form one section dealing with the same subject. If true, what is said in verses 36-38 on the subject of "virgins" would also be true of verse 25ff. Not all agree with this judgment. Those in favor of verses 36-38 being a different subject than verse 25 offer the following arguments: (1) *Huperakmos* in verse 36 ("past the flower of *her* age") can rightly be rendered as has the RSV, "if *his* passions are strong." (2) There is no known evidence that "his virgin" was a way of speaking of a father-daughter relationship. (3) The Greek verb *gameitōsan* in verse 36 may be rendered "let *them* marry" or "let *her* marry." (The RSV is forced to render it as "let him marry her.") Those who defend the idea of a single topic or subject in the whole paragraph offer these arguments in support of their position: (a) 1st century marriage customs, in which fathers arranged marriages. (b) The Greek for the word "virgin" is feminine in this context.
- The word "virgin" (*parthenos*) is used a total of 6 times in this paragraph. The RSV translation, which has "unmarried" (verse 25), "girl" (verses 28-34), and "betrothed" (verses 36-38) certainly obscures the fact that Paul has used the same word all through the paragraph. Any interpretation that requires a different translation for these six occurrences is surely suspect.

The view adopted in these notes is that the Corinthians had consulted Paul about the advisability of fathers giving their daughters in marriage. This view leaves us with the fewest difficulties when it comes to explaining certain problem words, and it is adopted even though the words father, guardian, or daughter never actually appear in the text.

SECTION SIX: CONCERNING THINGS OFFERED TO IDOLS (And Christian Liberty) – 3 QUESTIONS. 8:1-11:1

A. The Principles on Which Such Decisions Are Made. 8:1-10:13

> *Summary:* First, love (not just knowledge) must be the ethic that guides our behavior, 8:1-13. Second, there are many times when a man should voluntarily restrict his own liberty because he loves, 9:1-27. Third, by way of warning, Paul draws an illustration of the danger of idolatry from the history of Israel, 10:1-13.

1. First, love (not just knowledge) must be the ethic that guides our behavior. 8:1-13

8:1 -- *Now concerning things sacrificed to idols, we know that we all have knowledge. Knowledge makes arrogant, but love edifies.*

Now concerning -- By this expression, Paul shows he is referring to another question asked of him in the letter the Corinthians wrote to him (7:1).

Things sacrificed to idols -- 'Food offered to idols' translates a Greek word of Jewish origin, *eidōlothuton*. The pagan word for the same thing is found in 10:28, *hierothuton*. Festive meals in the idol's temples were a regular part of holiday celebrations and private celebrations such as birthday observances. Every kind of special occasion was celebrated in this fashion, and the gatherings were both intensely religious (in honor of the gods) and intensely social affairs. The description of such a meal in the cult of Aesclepius (a prominent temple to Aesclepius was located in Corinth) can be found in Aristides.[1] Most pagan temples had a banquet room in which feasts to the god could be celebrated. Papyri have been found which contain invitations, typical of which would be "Chaeremon requests your company at the table of the lord Serapis at the Serapaeum tomorrow, the 15th at 9 o'clock." The animal sacrificed at such a banquet was divided into three parts. A portion (often the eye brows and tail) was burned on the altar. A second portion was given to the priests of the idol's temple. The remainder was given to the worshiper and served as the main meat dish for a banquet to which the worshiper's friends and acquaintances were invit-

---

[1] Publius A. Aristides, *Sacred Discourses* 2.27. One of Petronius' characters (in *The Satyricon*, p. 64ff) helps us to get a feel for the fabulous nature of such a banquet. "Let's see, first off we had some roast pork garnished with loops of sausage and flanked with more sausages and some giblets done to a turn. And there were pickled beets and some whole-wheat bread made without bleach ... Then came a course of cold tart with a mixture of some wonderful Spanish wine and hot honey ... Then there were chickpeas and lupins, no end of filberts, and an apple apiece ... The main course was a roast of bear meat ... It reminds me of roast boar, so I put down about a pound of it. Besides, I'd like to know, if bears eat men, why shouldn't men eat bears? To wind up, we had some soft cheese steeped in fresh wine, a snail apiece, some tripe hash, liver in pastry boats and eggs topped with more pastry and turnips and mustard and beans boiled in the pod and – but enough is enough."

ed. If there were several banquets the same day, there was no way the priests could consume all of the portion dedicated to the priests. So the priests would consign what they could not use to the meat market next door to the temple,[2] where it was offered for sale to the public. Families needing meat for a day's meal could go to the market and purchase what they needed. Thus it was that a considerable amount of the meat consumed in an average day in Corinth was only the day before a portion of an animal sacrificed to an idol. Jews were absolutely forbidden to eat such food. See *M. Abodah Zarah* 2:3, "Flesh that is entering in unto an idol is permitted, but what comes forth is forbidden." In fact the Old Testament distinction between clean and unclean meats formed an insuperable barrier between Jews and Gentiles. Wherever they lived, Jews required a butcher of their own, who had been trained in the rules and ceremonies which enabled him to decide and to ensure that all the meat which they ate should be clean (*tahor*), not unclean (*tame*). Jews could touch no meat which was not certified as free from legal blemish or ceremonial pollution by the affixed leaden seal on which was engraved the word "lawful" (*kosher*). But Gentiles had always been accustomed to buy meat in the markets. Much of this meat now consisted of remnants of animals slain as sacrifices, after the pagan priests had had their share. Pagan butchers, while butchering an animal (which had not been connected with any temple sacrifice) for sale in the marketplace, would often take hairs off the brows of the animals and cast them into the sacred fires in the idol's temple.

Did such action make the meat unfit for Christian consumption? The market was stocked with meat which had been connected with idol sacrifices in one fashion or another. The Christian could never be sure whether or not *any* meat he bought had been part of a sacrifice. The Council at Jerusalem (Acts 15:29) had also ruled on the matter of "things sacrificed to idols." This is one of four things which were forbidden to Gentile converts to Christianity, and Paul and the Corinthians are expected to abide by this Holy Spirit-inspired directive. Paul will eventually (10:14ff) answer three specific questions concerning such meat offered to idols.[3] But before he offers specific answers, he will emphasize the principles on which such decisions are made.[4]

---

[2] Consult the map of ancient Corinth included in the introductory studies to see that there were a number of such markets in downtown Corinth. See also "The Macellum of Corinth near the Temple of Apollo," *JBL*, LXX 1934, p. 134ff. The Greek word "makellon" (1 Corinthians 10:25) went into Latin transliterated as *macellum* and from it we get the word macerate (to cut up into small pieces), and thus the description of what happens at a butcher market.

[3] The questions seem to have been, "Is it permissible to go to the idol's temple and participate in a feast there? What about going to a friend's house and eating meat bought in the market place adjacent to the pagan temple? What about a Christian himself going to the market place and buying meat and eating it, when he knows the meat sold in the market may well have been offered to an idol?"

[4] Bible readers in locations where few people any longer are involved in "banquets in honor of pagan gods" may think chapters 8-10 are irrelevant and the topic innocuous. But the matters discussed in these chapters are still keen issues on the mission field. Norval Campbell in the northern Philippines found their converts were constantly facing such questions, especially on national holidays when ceremonies to pagan gods were often part of the main program of celebration. And Mike and Dezi Worstell in Taiwan found that leftovers from the nearby idol's temple were brought to the orphanage the Christians were running. The missionaries would eat the leftovers if no one's conscience was bothered; they would abstain if any of the orphans' consciences were bothered.

We know that we all have knowledge -- Probably this is a semi-ironical use by Paul of the Corinthians' own words.[5] We may suppose that some at Corinth were resisting the decision of the Jerusalem Conference on this matter of meats offered to idols. Further, it appears that one of the arguments that they apparently were giving for the right to eat meats offered to idols in the idol's temple was their knowledge that the idol was nothing (verse 4). The Corinthians were stating that they had knowledge on this subject of meats offered to idols. 'We are acquainted with the true nature of idols, and of idol worship,' they argued. 'We all esteem an idol to be nothing. We are not in danger of being led into idolatry.' But some of the people at Corinth did not know as much as they thought they did. They may have had the knowledge of One God, but they were drawing false inferences from that knowledge, inferences that it was all right to eat anywhere and anything at any time. One may be too conscious of his knowledge, and that consciousness will lead him to pride in how much he knows. Paul makes two answers to this argument of the Corinthians. (1) The last clause of verse 1 plus verses 2 and 3 form sort of a parenthetical statement: it was not safe to rely on mere knowledge when deciding such questions, since the effect of mere knowledge was often to puff men up and make them proud. He argues they ought to act rather from a motive of love. (2) Verse 7ff will emphasize the fact that "all" did not have this knowledge which the opponents claimed, and these might be injured by the "wise" Corinthians' actions.

Knowledge makes arrogant -- This is the beginning of the parenthetical statement that runs through verse 3. The Greek reads "the knowledge" and is rather equal to 'the kind of knowledge the Corinthians are bragging about.' On the word "makes arrogant" or 'puffs up' (*phusioi*, 'to inflate') see notes at 4:6. It is the first reply of Paul to the statement made by the Corinthians, that all had knowledge. 'The knowledge you are boasting of tends to fill you with pride and self-sufficiency and to lead you astray.' Their "knowledge" was much the same as the "wisdom" on which they relied that had led to parties and factions, which Paul has spoken against in chapters 1-4. It was prideful, human knowledge, not God-given knowledge.

But love edifies -- The knowledge the Corinthians boasted of puffed up the man himself; it was a selfish thing. Love, however, is not selfish; it builds up other people in the congregation. There is no reason whatever for the rendering of *agapē* sometimes by "charity" and sometimes by "love," as was done in the KJV.[6] Love is deliberately doing what is spiritually best for the other person. Hear it – "love" (*agapē*) is a deliberate, planned, willed action! Such action "edifies" says Paul; that is, it helps to build us up as stones in the spiritual temple (3:9, Romans 14:19, Ephesians 4:12). "For if because of food your

---

[5] In verse 4, the opening words of verse 1 are repeated, and the line of thought which was for a moment interrupted is resumed.

[6] "This fondness for variation which led King James's translators to do so only obscures the identity of thought which prevails among the apostles respecting the absolute primacy of love as the chief sphere and test of the Christian life" (Farrar, *op. cit.*, p.264).

brother is hurt, you are no longer walking in love" (Romans 14:15). Whereas knowledge puffs up, love builds up. Compare Phillips, "While knowledge may make a man look big, it is only love that can make him grow to his full stature." The argument is this: 'Your conclusion to the question of eating meats offered to idols should not be formed from mere abstract knowledge, but you should ask what love to others would demand.' Love, not knowledge, is the real foundation of Christian behavior, and this is the thrust of Paul's answer to their claim. Although Paul will, in harmony with the decision of the Jerusalem Conference, forbid them from going to the idols' temples, his first concern is with the incorrect ethical basis of their argument. The real problem was primarily attitudinal. The Christian does not predicate his conduct simply on "knowledge," even if that knowledge is correct. Before a man has a right to act, he must take into account what "love" would require of him.

8:2 -- *If anyone supposes that he knows anything, he has not yet known as he ought to know;*

If any one supposes that he knows anything -- This is designed to condemn conceited knowledge. 'If anyone is so conceited in his knowledge that he is led to despise others, and to disregard their true interests, he has not yet learned the very first elements of true knowledge.' "Knows" translates a perfect tense verb, indicating that the supposition is one of enduring knowledge – something known from some time in the past right down to the present moment. Humility is a key test of true knowledge.

He has not yet known as he ought to know -- Paul's point is hardly the truism that here on earth, all knowledge is at best incomplete. Rather, his point is that if anyone thinks he knows it all, such that his behavior cannot possibly be in error, he is flatly mistaken. There are still some things he needs to learn!

8:3 -- *but if anyone loves God, he is known by Him.*

But if any one loves God -- The wording here is unexpected. Since Paul has been talking about love, we might have expected him to write something like, 'If any one loves his brother.' Yet love for the brother will follow when a man loves God. Loving God is the way of acquiring genuine "knowledge" about one's duties. There is no true and real knowledge which is not connected with love of God. A Christian's course, therefore, is not to be regulated by mere knowledge which leaves God out of the picture. His course is to be regulated by the grand principle of love for God, which will translate into love for one's fellow man, thereby resulting in proper knowledge of how to act to benefit that man.

He is known by Him -- God knows the man who loves Him.[7] "Known" probably is taken

---

[7] "By Him" is omitted in P[46], *Aleph**, 33, and Clement. Omitting the words, the verse reads, "If any one loves God, this one truly knows!" Some textual critics think this reading has all the marks of being the original text.

in the sense of 'is approved of God.' The word "know" is similarly used of "approval" at Matthew 7:23 and John 10:14. There is a typical Pauline turn of construction here, a rather surprising way of wording it. After "If anyone supposes that he knows anything, he knows nothing. But if anyone loves God," we would expect something like, 'he has real knowledge.' But such wording "would have fostered the already overgrown conceit of knowledge which was inflating the minds of the Corinthians" (Farrar, *op. cit.*, p.250). Paul purposely uses a passive construction. The sense is, 'If any man acts under the influence of love to God, and consequently loves his brother, he will meet with the approval of God.' Lenski (*op. cit.*, p.337) wrote, "In regard to the question at issue among the Corinthians, Paul would say, 'What is the use of mere knowledge in trying to solve these perplexing questions about idol meats? Mere know-ledge gets you nowhere with your brethren or with God. Only a knowledge permeated with love, a love that rises to God, will make Him acknowledge us and our knowledge as His own. With such a knowledge we can solve these questions about meats offered to idols.'" In these three verses Paul has given a very gentle rebuke to those who gave too high a place to knowledge. Love – doing what is spiritually best for the other person – rather than knowledge should be the Christian's determining consideration.

8:4 -- *Therefore concerning the eating of things sacrificed to idols, we know that there is no such thing as an idol in the world, and that there is no God but one.*

Therefore concerning the eating of things sacrificed to idols -- The parenthetical statement which began at 1b closed with the end of verse 3. The thrust of the opening of verse 4 is, 'Let us return to the subject of eating the flesh of animals that have been sacrificed to idols.' After the explanation that one does not decide such questions on the basis of "knowledge," the resumptive *oun* takes up the original question of idol meats.[8] The apostle now proceeds to give the principles by which the question in debate – whether or not it is right to eat the meat of animals that have been slain in sacrifice to idols in the idol's temple – may be answered. The general thrust of chapter 8 is that more than "knowledge" is needed in order to rightly direct one's behavior.

We know -- Verses 4-6 give a brief summary of the "knowledge" about idols that satisfied the Corinthians, the knowledge on which they based their actions. We might paraphrase it like this: 'We know there is no idol in the world, and that there is no God save one. Although our pagan neighbors have many so-called gods and lords, for us Christians, there is one God the Father, and one Lord Jesus Christ. Our involvement in meats offered to idols does not mean we acknowledge the actual existence of the gods and lords of our pagan neighbors.' It is the view of this commentator that Paul is arguing *ad hominem* in chapter 8.[9] Paul grants for the sake of argument that the readers have the liberty they sup-

---

[8] Since the topic concerns altar sacrifices, the meat market, and "meat" (1 Corinthians 8:13), the comments will tend in that direction, even though the word Paul sometimes uses (*brōma*) can include foods of all kinds, not just the flesh of animals.

[9] A number of commentators note what seems to be a contradiction or an inconsistency between what Paul writes in chapter 8 and what he writes in chapter 10. The *ad hominem* argument approach to chapter 8 was first learned in George Mark Elliott's classes. Elliott is almost the only one this commentator has found who offers this method of harmonizing what at first seems inconsistent in these chapters.

posed, but then shows them that even if their argument were true, they still have no right to eat meat offered to idols if they are eating it *in the idol's temple* (verse 10).

That there is no such thing as an idol -- There is no living being who corresponds to the image. There is no Zeus who rules the sky, nor any Poseidon who rules the sea, etc. Nor are we so stupid as to suppose the block of wood, or the carved image, or the chiseled marble is a real intelligence who is conscious and capable of receiving worship. 'We are quite aware that there is no such thing[10] in the world as the being for which the idol stands' is the idea in this phrase. With respect to idols, three views were possible for Christians: (1) They were images of "demons" in the old classical sense of the word – the spirits of deified dead men (ancestor worship). (2) They were images of "evil spirits" in the Biblical sense of the word – a view common among the Jews (see 1 Corinthians 10:20; Deuteronomy 23:17; 2 Chronicles 11:15; Psalm 106:37; Revelation 9:20). (3) They were merely dead images corresponding to nothing at all. See Isaiah 44. If there were no Zeus, an idol (or image) of Zeus is an impossibility. It does not necessarily follow that there were no beings connected to the idol (see 1 Corinthians 10:20). Paul is arguing *ad hominem* here in chapter 8.

In the world -- The idol is nothing at all; it has no power over the world, no real existence anywhere. The world, of course, contains many images that are called "idols," such as those of Jupiter, Mercury, Apollo, Venus, etc. But nowhere do beings exist that correspond to these images; such reputed beings are simply non-existent. What kind of beings are in fact connected with the worship of these images and idols Paul tells us later, namely, demons. So the idols are not totally innocuous.

And that there is no God but one -- This is a great cardinal truth of Christianity. This belief is the signature of Judaism, according to their daily and oft-repeated *shema* (Deuteronomy 6:4, Jehovah our Elohim is the only Jehovah.[11]) The Christian was no less sure

---

Other attempts at solving the problem verses include: (1) After chapter 8 was dictated and written, Paul was interrupted. When he returned to the letter (perhaps the next day) he had changed his mind, so what he writes in chapter 10 differs from chapter 8. (2) Certain neo-orthodox writers simply affirm there is a paradox between chapters 8 and 10, and do not worry about it, for paradox is perfectly acceptable to any neo-orthodox theologian. (This commentator has trouble accepting such supposed paradox, for he holds to a consistency test for truth. If we must hold conflicting views at the same time, looking for the truth somewhere halfway between the two opposites, all of a sudden we do not have any absolute truth any more. This is an unacceptable worldview.) (3) Another suggestion is that Paul ignores the decision of the Jerusalem Conference in order to maintain his own apostolic authority among the Corinthians (as if the decision of that conference and what he teaches here in 1 Corinthians conflict).

None of these attempts prove as satisfactory a handling of the problem verses as the hypothesis that chapter 8 is an *ad hominem* argument.

[10] Some suppose Paul reflects a teaching as old as the Old Testament in this verse. The Hebrew word *elilim* meaning vain, null, nothing-worth, weakness is one of the common words for idol in the Old Testament.

[11] The reader should recall the refutation of "monism" – the Jewish belief there was only one person in the Godhead – at Mark 12:28-37, where Jesus unfolded the meaning of the Shema. In the light of deity being attributed to three persons in the Godhead, and in the light that *Elohim* is plural, and in light of the fact that the Jew used *adonai* (a plural form) whenever he came to the four letter name of Jehovah, it can-

of this absolute fundamental (verse 6). In an ordered universe, there can be only one self-existent deity, viz., the deity who made it. If there were gods many and lords many, there would be no order, for the order would be destroyed as the gods fight for supremacy and control over all the other gods. The Corinthians supposed that this idea must be admitted by all. And even though they should partake of the meat that was offered in sacrifice to idols, yet they supposed it was not possible that any of them could forget the great cardinal truth that there was but one God.

8:5 -- *For even if there are so-called gods whether in heaven or on earth, as indeed there are many gods and many lords,*

For even if there are -- Verses 5 and 6 together form a single sentence. "Even if" admits the existence (in some sense) of the reputed deities.[12] The heathen have beings that are called gods by them. 'Very well,' Paul says, 'let us grant for the moment that they are gods, and let us include all of them, "whether in heaven," their major gods, Jupiter and his company, or "whether on earth," their minor gods such as dwell in forests, streams, fountains.'

So-called gods -- Paul is recalling the fact that the heathen people everywhere worshiped multitudes of things they called gods.

Whether in heaven -- Residing in heaven, as some of the gods were supposed to. Jupiter, Juno, Mercury were thought to reside in the heavens, and they were supposed to visit the earth occasionally (Acts 14:11). Some see an allusion to the sun, moon, and stars, which were worshipped.

Or on earth -- Some of the gods (e.g., Ceres, Neptune) the pagans revered were thought to live on the earth, or in the sea. Pluto, who resided in and presided over the inferior regions of the earth, is another.

As indeed there are many gods -- "As indeed" (*hōsper*) points to the astounding multitude of these gods and lords. This is not an admission on Paul's part that there were truly many gods in the world. He is not advocating polytheism. This is a declaration that these idols were esteemed by the heathen to be gods. "Gods" might reflect the fact that the pagan deities were often called *Elohim* (the plural word often translated "God" in the Old Testament). The word was also sometimes applied to men, men who were judges, or men in great positions. Thus, in "gods many" there may be a passing reference to the habitual

---

not by any stretch of the imagination be affirmed that Deuteronomy 6:4-6 teaches only one person in the Godhead. What it does say is that Jehovah our Elohim (the three we recognize as deity – Father, Son, and Holy Spirit) is the only Jehovah (the only self-existent deities there are).

[12] "Even if there are so-called gods" grants the supposition for the sake of argument, although "even if" regards the supposition as in reality not being true, and in the face of it holds to the opposite that only one God exists. (A.T. Robertson, *A Grammar of the Greek New Testament in the Light of Historical Research* [Nashville, TN: Broadman, 1934], p.1026.)

deification of the Roman emperors. (The title "Augustus" implied that they were objects of reverence.)

And many lords -- A lord is a person to whom we submit ourselves and whose laws we obey. The name "lord" was often given to the idols, because their worshipers assumed they had dominion of some kind over this or that part of creation. For instance, the Canaanites called their idols 'Baal' (i.e., lord). See *'adonim* ("lords") at Isaiah 26:13, Deuteronomy 10:17, Psalm 136:2ff. Recall, too, the invitation to the feast in the temple of "lord Serapis."

8:6 -- *yet for us there is* **but** *one God, the Father, from whom are all things and we* **exist** *for Him; and one Lord, Jesus Christ, by whom are all things, and we* **exist** *through Him.*

Yet for us -- "Us" is us Christians. 'We Christians acknowledge but one God.' "Yet" is *alla*, the strong adversative. Christians sharply contrast with idolaters. 'Whatever the heathen worship, we know there is but one Jehovah; He alone has a right to rule over us.' Paul is not saying, 'Heathen people think and say one thing, while we Christians think and say otherwise.' The contrast between verses 5 and 6 is not between two subjective perceptions of reality, (as "to us" is sometimes interpreted), but rather between a false perception and a true one. "But one," in verse 4, is objective fact, not subjective opinion. Jehovah God has revealed Himself. Therefore, before this one God, the entire polytheistic host disappears as being a big fable!

There is *but* **one God, the Father** -- The heathen may have a multitude of gods, but we Christians have one – and He is a Father to us. And He is the Father of the Lord Jesus Christ (and this is not saying that Christ is a created being). He is our Father, because He has redeemed us and has a tender care for us.[13] Our living Father in heaven has a personal interest in us, He is concerned about our affairs, and answers our prayers. How different from the pagan gods!

From whom are all things -- Note that there is a difference in the things said of God and of Christ. About God, it is said "from whom" (*ex ou*). About Christ, it is "through whom" (*di' ou*). The Greek used about God ("from whom") says He is the originative cause of all things. It was by the Father's counsel, plan, and purpose that the universe was created. "All things" is a reference to the universe. There is an article in the Greek, a way of designating the totality of all things as a unity.

Some have limited "all things" at this place to the 'new creation' (as if Paul had said 'all things pertaining to our salvation'). Several objections to this interpretation include: (1) We usually understand "all things" as a reference to the universe, John 1:3. (2) The scope of the passage requires us to understand this passage as a reference to the universe.

---

[13] Occasionally in pagan writings we find Zeus called "the father of gods and men." And occasionally in the Old Testament (e.g., Isaiah) we find Jehovah described as "Father." But the idea of Jehovah God being a father is really a Christian idea. Jesus was the one who taught us to pray "Our Father ... in Heaven." The title Jesus most often used for God is "Father." The concept Jesus taught has passed over into the language of the church through the apostles' preaching and writings.

Paul is not speaking of the new creature. He is dealing with the question of whether there is more than one God, one Creator, one Ruler over the wide universe. The heathen said there was more than one; the Christian affirmed that there was not. The heathen divided up creation between their many gods and goddesses, each of whom had his proper sphere. But the one God, says Paul, is responsible for *all things*.

And we *exist* for Him – *Eis auton* can be translated "for Him" or "into Him." We are formed for Him. We should live to His glory. We have been made what we are (i.e., Christians) that we might promote His honor and glory. We are His sons in Christ, destined for His use and glory. See Romans 11:36. The preposition *eis* indicates the set or direction of one's life. The Christian lives for God. He lives only to do Him service. Do the Corinthians, insisting on their "rights," have this truth clearly in mind?

And one Lord, Jesus Christ -- We Christians have one Lord, where the heathen have many lords. Jesus Christ is the one Lord, the ruler and sovereign of His people (see comments at 7:17). It must be remembered that while Jesus always existed (He is called Jehovah in a number of prophecies), He was not always "Lord." He was the member of the Godhead who volunteered to become the Savior if the Creation should need one. Because of this, Jesus has been made or appointed or designated as the Messiah and Lord because of Calvary (Acts 2:36). In fact He was already "Lord" before He went to Calvary ("You call me Teacher and Lord, and you say right, for so I am," John 13:13). Jesus was Lord ever since all authority was given to Him in order that He might carry out His historic function (Mark 1:27; John 3:35, 5:27, 17:2; Matthew 9:6, 28:18).

Because Jesus is designated as "Lord" some have thought that Jesus is somehow inferior to the Father. The Arians and Socinians have made use of this passage to prove the Son was inferior to God. Their argument is that the name "God" is not given to Jesus, but the name "Lord." This, it is alleged, implies inferiority. They even argue that the design of the apostle was to make a distinction between God and the Lord Jesus. Answers to the argument: (1) Those who hold to the deity of the Lord Jesus and to the pluralistic unity (trinity) of the Godhead do not deny that there is a *distinction* between Christ and the Father. To believe there is a distinction between Christ and God is merely to repeat what the Scripture everywhere predicates. For example, see John 1:1. Further, we believe that Christ is deity, equal with the Father. Philippians 2:6,7 assert that He never lost His "existence in the form (*morphē*) of God" even when He emptied Himself. (See also John 1:1 and 1:18 [NASB].) The minute you ascribe deity to Christ, you have at least two persons in the Godhead. Either you must grant this, or you have polytheism (an unthinkable alternative for it would be contrary to Deuteronomy 6:4 and 1 Corinthians 8:4). While at the same time we hold that Jesus is, was, and shall continue to be no less than God, we also assert that during His Incarnation, and during His Mediatorial Reign, He is subordinate to the Father in the sense that He temporarily relinquished the independent exercise of the prerogatives of deity. (Cp. Hebrews 2:8ff; 1 Corinthians 15:22ff; John 4:34, 5:19, where we are told Jesus did and said nothing "on his own initiative.") (2) The term "Lord" cannot imply of necessity any inferiority to God since it is a term which is frequently applied to God Himself. As earlier in our study (see notes at 1:3 on "God" and "Lord"), so here, we call attention to the Biblical doctrines of the equality of Jesus with the Father, and to the matter of His temporary subordination. If there is a subordination of Jesus affirmed in this verse (8:6), it is not to be found in the words "God" and "Lord," but in the prepositions. Of the Father, we have the prepositions "for," and "from." Of Jesus, we have the prepositions "through" and "through." This contrast points to God the Father as the ultimate source and reason for both the universe and man, and to Christ as the agent of God. In other words, Christ's subordination is in *function*, and not in personality or essence. The whole topic of Jesus' deity is becoming an issue over which the church is going to struggle increasingly in coming years.[14]

Through whom are all things -- The preposition *dia* translated "through whom" indicates 'agency' – intermediate agency. Christ is the intermediate agent Who is the cause of all things. The Father had the idea (previous clause in this verse), and Jesus carried the idea out into action (this clause). The doctrine that the Son of God was the great agent in the creation of the world, and in its recreation, is abundantly taught elsewhere in the Scriptures. John 1:3 is an example, and Hebrews 1:2. This statement is clear proof of Paul's belief in the pre-existence of Christ. See also Colossians 1:16-18.

And we *exist* through Him[15] -- We are Christians because of (*di' autou*, 'through, or on account of') Him. This expression will apply either to our original creation or to our hopes of heaven, as being by Him, and is equally true of both. He is our Creator and our Redeemer. "The idea of the passage is this: From God, the Father of all, we derive our existence, and all that we have. We acknowledge immediate and direct subjection to the Lord Jesus as our lawgiver and sovereign. From Him Christians receive their laws, and to Him they submit their lives. And this idea is so far from supposing inferiority in the Lord Jesus to God, that it rather supposes *equality*; since a right to give laws to men, to rule their consciences, to direct their religious opinions and their lives can appropriately appertain only to One who has equality with God" (Barnes, *op. cit.*, p.143).

8:7 -- *However not all men have this knowledge; but some, being accustomed to the idol until now, eat food as if it were sacrificed to an idol; and their conscience being weak is defiled.*

However -- In the previous verses Paul has stated the argument of the Corinthians – that they *all* knew that an idol was nothing. Here he points out that though this might be generally true, it was not universally true among Christians. This sentence is a correction of the somewhat haughty assertion of the Corinthians, as recorded in verse 1, that everybody knows this about God and idols.

---

[14] See Special Study #5 at the close of this chapter where some of the issues and personalities are introduced.

[15] A few later manuscripts add another clause to this verse, "and one Holy Spirit, in whom are all things, and we in him," thus making this passage (like some others) a trinitarian formula. This longer reading is perhaps as old as the 4th century (it was known by Gregory Nazianzus, though we are not sure it was actually in his Bible).

Not all men have this knowledge -- "This knowledge" is the confession of verses 4-6 that there is but one God, and that an idol is nothing. The knowledge on which the Corinthians proposed they were free to exercise their "rights" ('going to the idol's temple won't hurt us!') was a knowledge of the Living God, the source of all, and a knowledge of the Lordship of Jesus Christ. When Paul says "not all men have this knowledge," he seems to have in mind an inner assurance based on that knowledge.[16] There is a difference between having knowledge, and lovingly making use of that knowledge. The duty to love is the point (verses 7-10) as Paul now enunciates the view that love takes into account the beliefs and inner assurances of others; knowledge alone is not the ethic that should guide the Christian's behavior.

But some, being accustomed to the idol until now, eat *food* as if it were sacrificed to an idol -- There is a variation of readings, some having *sunētheia* ('by familiarity with' or 'long association with') for *suneidēsis* ('with conscience of' as the KJV reads).[17] The idea is this: unconverted men, when eating the meat offered to idols in the idol's temple, were worshiping that idol. Eating was part of the worshiping. Even though these men have become Christians and know that there is only one God, they still cannot dismiss from their minds the painful sense that, in eating the idol-sacrifice, they are participating in idol worship. They have been so accustomed to regard an idol as a reality, as representing a god that exists, that even now, in spite of their conversion, they cannot get rid of the haunting feeling that, by eating food which has been offered to an idol, they are taking part in the worship of heathen gods.[18]

And their conscience being weak is defiled -- This phrase introduces two key words ("conscience" and "weak") that have considerable bearing on the thread of argument which follows. "Conscience" can be defined as an innate faculty which prompts men to do what their minds think is right, and criticizes them when they do what their minds think is wrong.[19] Since 1 Corinthians was one of Paul's earlier epistles, this is one of the first times we meet the word in Paul's writings. (We did have the verb from the same root at 1 Corinthians 4:4). It may be one of the few terms in Paul's theological vocabulary to have come from his Greek rather than Jewish background. In each context where the word appears, the precise nuance of "conscience" is not easy to capture. There are passages (perhaps Romans 13:5 is one) where the word speaks of that innate faculty, a sort of moral

---

[16] Fisher, *op. cit.*, p.133.

[17] The NIV, "when they eat such meat, they think of it as a thing having [formerly] been sacrificed to an idol," treats the verse as if Paul were talking of "market-place food" rather than a banquet in the idol's temple. This in our view ignores the context, verse 10 especially.

[18] Robertson and Plummer, *op. cit.*, p.169.

[19] Not everyone accepts this definition (as the considerable literature on "conscience" will attest), nor will this definition work every time the Greek word translated "conscience" appears in our Bible. Scholarly articles on "conscience" include: H. Osborne, "*Suneidesis*," *JTS* 32 (1931), p.167-179; C. Maurer, *TDNT* VII, p.898-919; M. Thrall, "The Pauline Use of *Suneidesis*," *NTS* 14 (1967/68), p.118-125; H.C. Hahn and C. Brown, *NIDNTT* I, p.348-353.

referee, that pronounces on the rightness or wrongness of one's actions. (Cp. Romans 2:15; 1 Timothy 1:5,19; 1 Peter 3:16). There are passages when the word is closer to its root meaning of 'awareness' or 'consciousness' (perhaps Romans 9:1; 1 Corinthians 4:4; or 1 Peter 2:19's "conscience toward God"). Part of the debate has been whether or not "conscience" pronounces only on past actions, or whether it also gives guidance beforehand.[20] If the definition offered ("prompts you to do what your mind thinks is right") is correct, then the conscience does give guidance beforehand. This is not to say that the popular dictum 'Let your conscience be your guide' is a foolproof rule. It is very doubtful that the "conscience" functions for Gentiles in the same way the Law did for the Jews; this is not the thrust of Romans 2:15! It is in the mind, not the conscience, wherein the determination of what is right or wrong is made. The conscience is just a prompter, not the source of the judgment. Unless a man's mind is schooled and tutored in the Word of God, he will have little guidance toward what is really right, and little conscientious criticism of his actions, even though God has decreed the actions are wrong.

What does it mean to say the conscience is "weak"? What is it 'too feeble' or 'too sick' to do? It is too weak to forcefully control the man's conduct. It prompts to do the right, but only feebly. And whenever the conscience is ignored, or overrun, it is damaged. "Whatsoever is not of faith is sin" wrote Paul in Romans 14:23. When a man's conscience is disobeyed and he does what his mind thinks is wrong, Paul says it is sin. It is subjective faith in the context of Romans 14:23. A 'weak brother' is someone who does not have the courage to live by his convictions when he is in the presence of others who are urging him (either by words or action) to do something that would violate his conscience. Paul is still arguing *ad hominem*. We affirm this because here in chapter 8, the weak brother is doctrinally right: Christians *are* forbidden to go to the idol's temple! The so-called 'strong brother' at Corinth, with all his vaunted knowledge, was doctrinally wrong.[21]

As stated earlier, a man's conscience can be "defiled" whether his mind is embracing something doctrinally right or something doctrinally wrong. What does it mean to be "defiled"? Our conscience tells us to do a certain thing; if we do not do it, our conscience is stifled or defiled (*molunō*, 'soiled' or 'stained'). If a person ignores and defiles his conscience on a given matter long enough, the conscience will quit prompting and quit criticizing. How sad it is for the person whose conscience quits working! In the case envisioned by Paul, the conscience prompts the Corinthian brother to avoid the idol's temple, but he goes ahead and does what he thinks is wrong when encouraged to do so by the example of other Christians. Not only is his conscience ignored, there also results a conviction of guilt – the conscience being troubled by a sense of the pervading divine displeasure towards his actions.

---

[20] It is this debate that is reflected in the terminology 'moral consciousness' found in some of the scholarly articles on 'conscience.'

[21] "Strong" and "weak" in Corinthians is just the opposite from what we find in Romans 14-15. In Romans, the strong brother is doctrinally right, and the weak brother is doctrinally wrong. So it appears the "weakness" lies not in the development of the mind (i.e., not knowing what God says is right and wrong), but in the strength of the conscience to actually control our behavior.

8:8 -- *But food will not commend us to God; we are neither the worse if we do not eat, nor the better if we do eat.*

But food will not commend us to God -- Verse 8 seems to be part of the argument used by the Corinthians to defend their "freedom" to go to the idol's temple, rather than part of Paul's presentation of the truth that love (not just knowledge) must be the ethic that guides a Christian's behavior.[22] We suppose the Corinthians have picked up Paul's teaching (which had correctly reflected what Jesus taught on the subject of foods ingested into the human body, Mark 7:1-23) and have twisted it to justify their desired actions. 'What a man eats does not, of itself, make that man more holy or less holy,' they argued. "Commend" may not be a good translation of the verb *paristēmi*, which means 'present' or 'bring near to.' Some manuscripts have the present tense, yielding the meaning, 'the eating of meat does not bring a man near to God at the present time.' Others have the future, which may look to bringing a man before God for praise or blame at the day of judgment.

We are neither the worse if we do not eat, nor the better if we do eat -- This also seems to be part of the Corinthians' argument for freedom to eat in the idol's temple. They were insisting they were neither morally "better" nor "worse." "Worse" – i.e., if we abstain from eating of meat offered to idols, 'we have no lack' (*husteroumetha*), the Corinthians were insisting. "Better" – i.e., the eating of meat does not 'make us abound'; the Corinthians were also insisting it 'gives us no advantage' (the verb is *perisseuomen*). They seem to have been saying that the simple act of eating or not eating does nothing to harm or enhance one's spiritual relationship to God. A man is not worse off if he does not eat, nor is he better off in God's sight if he does eat.

8:9 -- *But take care that this liberty of yours does not somehow become a stumbling block to the weak.*

But take care -- "But" seems to show that verse 9 is the beginning of Paul's reply to the Corinthians' argument given in verse 8. Paul's reply is, in essence, 'While the simple act of eating does not make one better or worse, there is something that can accompany the eating that will make a person better or worse. That "something" is the influence he exerts on his brothers by his behavior.' Though it may be true that the man himself is neither better nor worse for eating or not eating, the grand principle must still be observed – so act as not to injure your brethren. "Take care" means to be alert to the whole situation. There is more involved than just your own personal satisfaction when eating. Perhaps the Corinthians have insisted that rules like the Jerusalem Conference (against meats offered to idols) are too restrictive for folk with "knowledge." Paul reinforces that prohibition by his reminder to them that if eating meat in the idol's temple could be the occasion of tempting a brother to sin, then whether or not one eats is a matter of supreme importance.

---

[22] Since it begins with "but," some have supposed that verse 8, either all of it or part of it, represents words used by Paul to reply to the Corinthians. If it is so interpreted, then what Paul is doing is teaching the same thing Jesus taught (Mark 7:19). Others reply that it is hard to see how the last half of verse 8 can be made to square with an argument being made by Paul. It says "if we don't eat, we are worse; if we eat, we are better." Would Paul claim this to be true of meat offered to idols eaten in the idol's temple? A better solution is to find the beginning of Paul's answer in verse 9.

Lest this liberty of yours -- It was a "liberty" which the Corinthians asserted. "Liberty" translates *exousia*, a word which means 'authority' or 'right.' Some of the Corinthians were insisting on their 'rights' to eat as they pleased. Paul reminds them that no Christian is at liberty to assert his 'rights' if that means doing harm to other people, or putting a stumbling-block in another's path. Did they really have the liberty they were asserting? How does one decide whether or not he or she has "liberty"? See the question discussed at 1 Corinthians 6:12 and at Acts 15:31 in the author's commentary on Acts, in the chart on "Law and Liberty." In things which are in the realm of the mandatory, right or wrong is the sole test of action. Where God has spoken, that settles the question of right or wrong. But in the realm of the permissive, we must look for some other guide; one general rule is that we regulate our conduct by the effect it may have on others. There is more to it than just eating meat in the idol's temple. Would it be all right to eat meat in the idol's temple, other things being equal, and no weak brother involved? No! See Acts 15:28ff and 1 Corinthians 10:20ff. Eating in the idol's temple is not something in the realm of the permissive; it is in the realm of the mandatory. It is something God has forbidden! Paul is still arguing *ad hominem*. Even if this were in the realm of the permissive as they were claiming, Paul is showing them that they have no right to eat meat in the idol's temple.

Somehow become a stumbling-block to the weak -- "The weak" is anyone whose conscience is weak, as in verses 6 and 10. A weak brother is a fellow Christian who doesn't have the moral courage to stand for his convictions when peer pressure is against him. It is not talking about those who are weak in objective (i.e., Christian) faith (those lacking faith), for in Corinth the "weak" brothers were doctrinally right![23] Even at Romans 14:1, "weak in the faith" means weak in subjective faith. One who is "weak" *is one who does not have the moral courage to stand for his convictions*. In Corinth, in the case under consideration, the weak brother is the man who knows that eating in the idol's temple is wrong, but he does not have the moral courage to stand for his conviction. He is caused to stumble by those who profess to be Christians and yet frequent the idol's temple. "Stumbling-block" and that which causes or tempts another to sin (verses 12,13) are synonymous; each term helps explain the other. Christians don't demand their 'rights' in ways that cause fellow Christians to be tempted to sin. A *proskomma* ("stumbling-block") is something that lies in a path, against which an unwary foot may strike and cause a person to stumble or to fall; metaphorically, it is anything that may encourage a person to sin and to suffer injury to his soul, and be left with a sense of guilt (an accusing conscience), verse 7.

8:10 -- *For if someone sees you, who have knowledge, dining in an idol's temple, will not his conscience, if he is weak, be strengthened to eat things sacrificed to idols?*

---

[23] It is shallow thinking to define "weak brother" simply as one who is weak or lacking in real understanding or knowledge of the faith, for here in Corinthians, the "weak brother" is doctrinally right! He is certainly not weak for lack of proper teaching, or for grasp of the meaning of that teaching. A comparison of 1 Corinthians with Romans shows that a weak brother may be right or wrong doctrinally. (Here he is right; in Romans 14 he is wrong.) Nor does simply believing something to be wrong (e.g., use of musical instruments or robes worn by the clergy) prove someone is a "weak" brother, for some who claim to be "weak" can be very vocal in their demands that others accommodate their beliefs. Paul's use of "strong" and "weak" involves both the knowledge of right doctrine and the moral courage to live according to one's convictions.

For if someone sees you -- The "someone" is a Christian whose conscience is weak. How could the 'weak brother' see the other at the idol's temple unless the weak were also present in the temple? In this verse and the next two, Paul will make an impassioned plea for the strong brother to be concerned more about the 'rights' of the weak brother than he is about his own 'rights.'

Who have knowledge -- Paul is puncturing their conceit. They thought they had knowledge. They asserted they had knowledge about food and about the non-existence of the "gods" and "lords" to whom the meals in the idol's temples were dedicated. 'Whether you are right or wrong in your assertion of liberty to eat in the idol's temple, you are being watched; you are looked up to as an example.' Alford says, "This seems to imply that the weak brother thinks the Christian has knowledge – he is looked up to as an example of how to live ...."[24] The man who in this case asserted he had knowledge was doctrinally wrong (at least as far as attendance in the idol's temple is concerned). The weak brother was right. Paul is arguing *ad hominem*. We doubt that eating in an idol's temple was morally neutral, nor was it something in the realm of liberty. (See notes above on how does one determine matters of liberty, and see notes on chapter 10.)

Dining in an idol's temple -- "Dining" translates *katakeimenon*, which literally means 'to recline' – the usual posture at meals, reclining on a couch according to the Oriental custom. To recline at a banquet in the temple of Poseidon or Aphrodite, especially in such a place as the city of Corinth, was certainly an extravagant assertion of the rights of Christian liberty. "Idol's temple" translates *eidōleion*. The word is used by the Jewish writers, apparently to avoid designating heathen temples by the word *naos*, the word designating a place where deity dwells; after all, there was no actual deity as was being honored in the idol's temple. The Greeks spoke of the Athena*eum*, or the Appolon*eum*, or the Posid*eum*. The Jews spoke of an idol*eum*. The word *eidōlon* means a shadowy, fleeting, unreal image. It was perhaps a taunt to the heathen forms of worship.

Will not his conscience, if he is weak, be strengthened to eat things sacrificed to idols? -- The word "strengthened" ("emboldened," ASV) is *oikodomēthēsetai*, 'to be built up.'[25] The form of the question in the Greek shows that it expects an affirmative answer. The idea is this. The weak brother, looking to the person whom he considers to be a Christian (strong brother), sees that Christian (the perceived strong brother) eating meat in the idol's temple. The weak brother does not have the moral courage to stand for his convictions; so while knowing such to be wrong he goes ahead and eats in the idol's temple also. The picture is this. Both have been invited to a certain celebration being held in the idol's temple. The weaker brother's conscience tells him it is wrong to go, but he has been encouraged to go against his conscience by the example of the individual Christian who is

---

[24] Alford, *op. cit.*, p.539.

[25] Morris has this note (*op. cit.*, p.129): "Emboldened. The word is same as that rendered 'edifies' in verse 1. Here it is ironical. Evidently the strong among the Corinthians had spoken of the necessity of 'building up' the weak by encouraging them to do such actions. Paul takes up their word, and with a rhetorical question points out the harm. 'By setting such an example will you not "build up" the weak brother? You will "build him up" only to destruction!'"

proud of having the proper "knowledge" and whose reclining in the idol's temple is a sort of bravado – a thing done to show his "knowledge" and complete freedom from any superstition about the idol. Here in chapter 8, the action of the man who set the bad example is censured because of the effect it has on others. In Chapter 10:18ff, the act will be condemned on its own account, because of the effects it has on the 'know-it-all' brother himself. It is not the harmless act he claims it is.

8:11 -- *For through your knowledge he who is weak is ruined, the brother for whose sake Christ died.*

For through your knowledge – 'Because you think you know so much, are you going to set a wrong example, and cause a man to go to hell? By a reckless and unloving use of knowledge, are you going to cause a man to lose his eternal salvation?'

He who is weak is ruined -- "Ruined" translates *apollumi* – 'to be put away, to destroy, to perish, to be ruined, lost.' The Greek word is used of eternal destruction (e.g., John 3:16). One cannot use passages in which the word "perish" occurs to prove that there is no after life for the wicked.[26] The better manuscripts have a present tense, not future. Paul sees the man as even now perishing, in the process of being ruined, making shipwreck of the Christian life, which, if continued, results in eternal damnation.[27] This is deep irony. 'A fine way of building up your brother. For instead of building him up, you cause him to perish.'

The brother for whose sake Christ died -- This is the most aggravating thing about the 'know-it-all' brother's action – 'your conduct frustrates the purposes of Christ's atoning death.' The word "brother" reminded the Corinthians of their responsibility for the spiritual welfare of the "weak" Christian, for that weak person was not just a stranger, he was a brother! This verse contrasts the 'know-it-all' brother's indifference for his brother's spiritual welfare with Christ's self-sacrificial love for them. Compared to Christ's love, the selfish behavior of the 'knowledgeable' brother is shown to be exactly what it is – sin (verse 12).

> A tragic apposition says still more. "The brother for whose sake Christ died."
> Two mighty obligations converge: the one toward the brother, and the other toward Christ. Your knowledge is so great that you do not love your brother

---

[26] The Jehovah's Witnesses, for example, attempting to build a case for the doctrine of the annihilation of the wicked, insist the translation of *apollumi* be 'cut off.' However, it must first be proved that the body (*soma*) and soul (*psuchē*) are the same before you can say such passages prove there is no after life for the wicked. Ecclesiastes 12:7 would keep one from making such an identification. 2 Peter 3:6 is a good place to see that *apollumi* does not mean annihilate.

[27] Commentators who feel compelled to defend the doctrine of unconditional eternal security struggle with this verse. They especially emphasize that the verb is present tense – something in this life, not ("assuredly," they tell us) something extending to the life to come. Whether the strong brother is pictured as jeopardizing the weak brother's eternal salvation in the future, or his sanctification now, the end result is about the same, for without sanctification, no man shall see God (Hebrews 12:14).

enough to abstain from an idol feast in order to save his soul. Your knowledge is so great that you do not see the price which Christ paid by His death to save your brother's soul. The fact of brotherhood should be enough to impel you to reflect with tenderness and concern upon anything that may drive a weak brother to destruction. Regard for Christ should keep you from at least helping to rob Him of the soul for which He paid so great a price.[28]

Paul may be urging the "strong brothers" to practice some self-denial. 'If Christ endured so much to save the soul, assuredly we should not pursue a course that would tend to destroy it. If He *denied* himself so much to redeem, we should assuredly not be so fond of self-gratification as to be unwilling to abandon anything that would tend to destroy.' "We are to do nothing that will lead others into sin; we are to do nothing that will defile the conscience of others; we are not to assert ourselves when to do so will injure others; and we must deny ourselves things that would please us, to profit and save others. This is an important principle, far-reaching in its results, and embodies the essential principle of the Christian religion."[29]

8:12 -- *And thus, by sinning against the brethren and wounding their conscience when it is weak, you sin against Christ.*

And thus, by sinning against the brethren -- After pointing to the result which this action has upon the weak brother (verse 11), Paul points out to the 'strong' brother exactly how God views their thoughtless, selfish behavior. It is sin! Paul shows them that this is not an indifferent matter being discussed. If they had such liberty in the first place, to use it as they were doing was positively sinful! The word "sin" is *hamartanō*, 'missing the mark.' They were falling short of their responsibility to their brethren by acting in such a way as to encourage the weak brothers to sin. They had been so concerned about their own rights, about their liberty to do as they pleased, that they failed to live up to the standard required in brotherhood. Hear it! It is sin to act in such a way as to wound another's conscience (encouraging him to do what causes his conscience to bother him).

And wounding their conscience when it is weak -- Or 'smite their conscience which is weak,' 'injure ....' We wound the other man's conscience when we give him an example to follow that encourages him to ignore what his conscience is prompting. 'Wound' translates the verb *tuptō*. This is the only place in the New Testament where it is used metaphorically. Its customary use is for striking vigorous blows, for beating. It stresses the harm done by the strong to the weak. What can be more ruthless than a man who strikes one who is sick? Was it not a cowardly act to strike the conscience of the defenseless?

You sin against Christ -- It is "sin" for several reasons:

- Because Christ commanded you to love and seek their good, and disobedience is sin.
- Because they are united to Christ, and to offend them is to offend Him.

---

[28] Lenski, *op. cit.*, p.346.

[29] Lipscomb, *op. cit.*, p.124.

- Because "In that you have done it unto the least of these who are My brethren, you have done it also unto Me" (Matthew 25:40), so treatment of fellow Christians equals treatment of their Lord (as in Matthew 10:40 and Luke 10:16). After Paul persecuted the Christians, Jesus asked him, "Why are you persecuting Me?" (Acts 9:4) So a sin against the brethren is very serious, because it is a sin against Christ.
- Because there is a high dignity in the Christian calling.

It can be easy to think of certain church members as unimportant. But they are not so. They are part of Christ's body. We should honor them as members of Christ, and beware of sinning against the Lord.

8:13 -- *Therefore, if food causes my brother to stumble, I will never eat meat again, so that I will not cause my brother to stumble.*

Therefore -- This is the conclusion of the whole matter. *Dioper* is a very strong expression in the Greek. Because such behavior as the 'knowledgeable' Corinthians were proposing is a violation of our obligations to our brothers and to Christ, Paul now instructs the Corinthians about the right action in such circumstances. Paul's conclusion is that he will do his utmost to see that he does not hinder the weak brother, nor sin against Christ. He proposes his own example as the one the readers should plan to imitate.

If food causes my brother to stumble -- "Food" is not a different topic than the whole chapter has dealt with; it is meat ("flesh," next phrase) offered to idols (8:10 spoke of dining in the idol's temple). "Stumble" means 'leads him to sin, causes him to err, causes him to fall.' "Stumble" ("offend," KJV) translates *skandalidzō*. The word here in verse 13 is a different word for "stumble" than was used in verse 9. This word speaks of the crooked stick to which the bait is affixed, and by which the trap is sprung. It speaks of the trigger that springs the trap and thus leads to the death of the victim. To lead a man to violate his conscience about what was right and wrong was a 'trap' as well as a "stumbling-block."

An explanation of when and where a Christian is bound to forego his rights in deference to a "weaker brother" is needed. Must the Christian abstain always, whether or not he is in the brother's presence? Or only when the weak brother is there and makes his convictions known? In 10:24 and 10:28,29 Paul gives the answer. From examples in his own life, Paul will illustrate the waiving of rights out of love in chapter 9. While he waived his rights to a salary from the Corinthians, Paul did not always refuse support money, as the letter to the Philippians shows. He did not *always* waive his rights. By parity of reasoning, neither must the Christian *always* waive his rights.

I will never eat meat again -- Guthrie writes, "Paul's decision is conditional, not absolute. He does not say he will henceforth always be a total abstainer, but only IF and WHEN such eating may cause a brother to fall."[30] 'Whether I get what I want to eat is a matter of com-

---

[30] *New Bible Commentary*, p.1062. We suppose Paul is still arguing *ad hominem*. Actually, he will not go to an idol's temple at all, since it was not in the realm of liberty, but something absolutely prohibited by God.

parative unimportance. The important thing is not my own rights, nor my own comforts, but the well-being of my brother.' Paul makes this statement in the first person, but he certainly means to express the Christian ideal which he expects all his readers to follow. The meat ('flesh,' *krea*), the particular kind of food in question, is meat sacrificed to idols and eaten in the idol's temple (verse 10). Eating meat at home, or in a friend's home, is a different topic that will be dealt with in chapter 10.

That I might not cause my brother to stumble -- The repetition of this phrase emphasizes the two points – the man is a "brother" and you don't trigger a death trap for ('entrap,' cause them to stumble) a brother! We who are strong in knowledge must be equally strong in love. Knowledge alone is nothing; knowledge combined with love is everything. We must protect the weak till they too become strong. Said negatively, we must not offend their conscience; said positively, we must bear with them and instruct them (if they are doctrinally wrong).

Three timeless principles have dominated chapter 8: (1) What is safe for one Christian in the realm of Christian liberty may not be safe for another. (2) True discernment always requires love for the brother as well as knowledge of what God has taught. (3) Believers have no right to demand certain 'rights' if those 'rights' in turn prove detrimental to those around them.

Special Study #5

"Who Do You Say I Am?"
THE DEITY OF JESUS

SCRIPTURE'S PRESENTATION

Several lines of evidence in Scripture point to the fact that Jesus is God. One could appeal to Jesus' own teaching on the great day of questions (Matthew 22:23ff, Mark 12:18ff). As the religious leaders questioned His authority, at one point Jesus pointedly told them, "You understand neither the Scriptures nor the power of God," and His answers to their questions were intended to illuminate both the Scriptures and God Himself for them. Jesus based His answer to their question, "Whose wife is she?" on the present tense verb "am." His answer regarding "Which is the greatest commandment?" was based in part on the *Shema* (Deuteronomy 6:4). As explained in footnote 11 on pages 277-278, the plural nouns in the *Shema* are intended to point us to the fact that while "The LORD our God is one," there is not simply one person in the Godhead. On that same question, Jesus then used the phrase "and another is just like it." That phrase is perhaps a springboard for the question He then posed to the religious leaders, "What do you think about the Christ? Whose Son is He?" Jesus was trying to help them understand that the Father can be in heaven, and 'one just like *Him*' could also be on earth. Jesus' question about Messiah being David's "Lord" also has overtones of deity. "Lord" is the word Jews regularly used when they came across the tetragrammaton that we often transliterate as "Jehovah." Jesus as the Christ is Jehovah Lord, as much as are the Father and Holy Spirit.

One could appeal to John 5, where there are five evidences given by Jesus Himself of his deity. One could appeal to John 17:5 where Jesus speaks of the glory that He ever had with the Father before the creation of the world. Jesus is an eternal being.

One could appeal to passages like Romans 9:5 where Jesus is spoken of both as descended from the patriarchs and also as being "over all, God blessed forever," or Titus 2:13 where Jesus is called "our great God and Savior." One could appeal to Hebrews 1, where there are seven qualities ascribed to Jesus that can be true only if He is co-equal and co-eternal with God the Father.

We could speak of Jehovahism (a better term than 'monotheism') to describe what the Scriptures teach about deity – deity of the Father, Son, and Holy Spirit.

MODERN SCHOLAR'S PRESENTATIONS

At Caesarea Philippi, Jesus Himself posed the question to his apostles, "Who do people say that the Son of Man is?" The disciples responded by giving numerous human views. Then Jesus asked the apostles, "Who do you say that I am?" Peter answered "You are the Messiah, the Son of the living God" (Matthew 16:13-16).

For 17 or 18 centuries, the view Peter expressed was also upheld as the church's standard of orthodoxy. The historical Jesus was fully deity and fully human – deity incarnate in human flesh. Since the late 18th century, however, the supernatural Christ has been more and more relegated to the dustbin and treated as superstition by Bible critics. With humanism and rationalism as the prevailing philosophy, men tried to remold Jesus into someone who would match those non-supernaturalistic world views.

There have been quests for the historical Jesus[1] – producing a Jesus who is a psychic, or a sage, or a cynic, or a magician, or a peasant reformer, or a simple carpenter, or a model humanitarian. Gone are any ideas of a pre-existent deity who became incarnate, overcame demons, rose from the dead, and who will return to earth to renovate it and judge mankind.

- John Macquarrie suggested the biblical writers sought to exalt the human Jesus into a god-like figure by transposing aspects of His history into the framework of Greek mythology.

- J.A.T. Robinson, emphasizing that each of us have personal experiences we struggle to find words to express to someone else, thinks the words of the New Testament are likewise attempts to express the writers' experiences to someone else. The myths surrounding the man Jesus must be expressed in terms with which today's readers can identify. The banality of the bishop can be seen when he demythologizes the *parousia* myth into "You ain't seen nothing yet."

- Tillich, Barth, Brunner, Bonhoeffer, and Vincent Taylor all make use of Hegel's dialectic to explain Jesus Christ. According to neo-orthodoxy, the Bible presents Him as the Jesus of history and the Christ of faith; these two conflicting ideas (paradox), neither of which is actually true, must both be held in mind, they say, if we are to understand who Jesus really is.

- Cullmann and Pittenger emphasize a functional approach to understanding Jesus. The Christ can be known only through the effects of His work. That is, peoples' perception of Jesus is different from what the human Jesus actually was. Hear within this Kant's philosophy with its difference between *historie* (what really happened) and *geschichte* (people's interpretations of what happened). So we should be more concerned with *events* in Jesus' life than with His *person*. Instead of "deity" referring to Jesus' "nature," the church later coined the phrase "deity of Christ" to express its belief that Jesus was the special vehicle of God's activity.   Neo-liberal theologians insist that

---

[1] Albert Schweitzer (1906) initiated the first quest for the historical Jesus. A second was conducted in the 1960s by the students of Bultmann. Now, we are reading the results of the "third quest." Like previous quests for the historical Jesus before it, this third quest is dominated by the presuppositions and methods of naturalism. The first quest was sparked by the scientific method whose base-line philosophy was rationalism. The Bultmannian quest was an attempt to find an "existential" Jesus. This third quest is the child of the social sciences, in particular the ideologies of liberation and cross-cultural anthropology.

functionally Jesus was divine, but essentially He was not. ("Divine" is not synonymous with "deity" when the term is used by these neo-liberal theologians.)

- Teilhard de Chardin, adopting evolution as the framework for his world view, has Jesus being simply the product of the cosmic evolutionary processes. His pre-existence, incarnation, and divinity are given a radical re-interpretation in harmony with a naturalistic, evolutionary view.

- Hans Kung (in two books, *On Being a Christian* and *Nothing But the Truth*) has followed the view of many modern scholars that Jesus did not proclaim himself as the eternal Son of God, nor did the early Christians. Kung is not the only Roman Catholic to question the deity of Jesus – so have Ansfried Hulsbosch, Edward Schille-beeckx, Jacques Pohier, Michel Pinchon [who wrote of his liberation from "idolatry" of Jesus], Jose-Ramon Guerrero, Jose Ignacio, Gonzales Faus, and Jon Sobrino.

- Seven university theologians in England put out a book contending that Jesus was not really God at all.

The reason for the changed view of Jesus has nothing to do with what the Scriptures actually say, but what the Scriptures are interpreted to say once the interpreter has first adopted a modern philosophy (e.g., idealism, or Hegel's dialectic, or existentialism, or post-modernism), and then tried to make the Bible match this philosophy.

At the close of the 20th century, we have a "designer" Jesus who can be made to match man's every whim.

- Elizabeth Schussler Fiorenza, *Jesus: Miriam's Child and Sophia's Prophet*, gives us a feminist, liberationist portrayal of a Jesus whose main enemy is "kyriarchy" and "male-stream" theology.

- Burton Mack, *A Myth of Innocence: Mark and Christian Origins*, casts Jesus as a Hellenistic sage. Mack regards the story of Jesus told in Mark's Gospel as a "sorry plot ... a remarkably pitiful moment of early Christian condemnation of the world."

- Barbara Thiering, *Jesus and the Riddle of the Dead Sea Scrolls: Unlocking the Secrets of His Life*, presents Jesus as the wicked priest of Qumran who eloped with Mary Magdalene, and who survived crucifixion by drinking snake poison.

- Marcus Borg, *Meeting Jesus Again for the First Time*, presents Jesus as a shaman-like charismatic.

- John Dominic Crossan, *Jesus: A Revolutionary Biography*, tries to prove that Jesus is a peasant Jewish cynic.

- Morton Smith, *Jesus the Magician*, presents Jesus as a sorcerer.

- Robert W. Funk, et al., *The Five Gospels. The Search for the Authentic Words of Jesus: A New Translation and Commentary*, presents the findings of the "Jesus Seminar." No longer does one search just the canonical books to learn about Jesus; one must also search the Pseudepigrapha. (E.g., the *Gospel of Thomas*, a Gnostic work, is said to be the "fifth gospel"). In the view of the modern critics, the four canonical gospels were all produced by redaction criticism, and contain hardly an authentic saying or deed of Jesus.

The third quest for the historical Jesus is concerned with the social world of Jesus and the social forces at work in it. The resulting picture of Jesus is a peasant Jew, who like Buddha or one of the Cynic philosophers, espoused a subversive view of traditional wisdom, and who both preached and practiced radical egalitarianism. This Jesus had no messianic or divine self-concept, though He may have induced some trancelike states in order to "heal" by using the powers inherent in him as a "spirit-person" (powers no different than any of us enlightened people possess and can exercise). The modern profile of Jesus omits a large body of New Testament testimony.

- Supernatural miracles are gone, though Jesus is granted certain psychic powers.
- Conspicuously absent is any sense of Jesus' self-consciousness as Messiah or Son of God (those verses were all added by the later redactors!), or as standing in a unique relationship to the Father, endowed with authority to speak and act for God.
- Jesus was likely executed by crucifixion, but absent is any saving significance to His death.
- Nor is there any resurrection. (The accounts of His resurrection and exaltation to the right hand of God are said to be all the result of wishful thinking by the early church.) Crossan insists that Jesus' body was eaten by dogs.

WHAT IS LEFT IS AN IMPOVERISHED GOSPEL

In his book *Miracles*, C.S. Lewis observed that "a naturalist Christianity leaves out all that is specifically Christian."

While it's true that Jesus was a peasant Jew, the founder of a movement, an overcomer of social barriers, a healer, a prophet who called for reform, any attempt to package this list as the complete sum total of the historical Jesus is clearly false.

The chief flaw to the quests for the historical Jesus is the lack of openness to, or even interest in, the possibility that Jesus was God incarnate, as the Old and New Testament Scriptures clearly indicate. That Jesus was a peasant, or teacher, or founder of a movement is secondary to the core claims of the New Testament that He was the unique incarnation of God by whose life and death salvation is freely offered to the world, and by whose exaltation history is being moved by Him towards the goal for which it was created. A purely social reconstruction of Jesus cannot account for the effect that Jesus has had on history. To assume that the earnest though bewildered Jesus of the Jesus Seminar could have affected the course of human history as Jesus Christ really has, is like stumbling upon the Sudbury crater in Canada and supposing it is the result of a firecracker.

The crucial error of the quests for the historical Jesus is the assumption that the New Testament writings are essentially the fiction of the early church, and that the picture of Jesus contained therein is discontinuous with the historical Jesus.[2]

Modern literary criticism, with its assumption that every work is the biased words of the author rather than an objective description of what actually happened, treats the Scriptures in the same way. The assumption is that the Gospels must be treated as biased distortions of the life of Jesus, not a record of what actually and objectively happened. The critics assume that each writer chose and shaped the material that came to him in order to serve some dominant theme.

THE EARLY CHURCH -- CREATOR OR CUSTODIAN?

What shall we say about the assumption of modern scholarship that the early church had little or no interest in transmitting information about Jesus *per se*, but that it conveniently "remembered" and even invented "Jesus" material to reflect its needs and experiences? There are a number of evidences that strongly argue that the church was a custodian, not a creator.

- The Gospel writers did not wildly invent material about Jesus. Paul, for example, carefully distinguished between what Jesus actually said and did, and what were his own inspired judgments (1 Corinthians 7:10,12,25). Surely Paul is not an exception in this matter, but is typical of the apostles and the church as a whole. Paul could scarcely have won acceptance and the "right hand of fellowship" from the Twelve and the Jerusalem leaders (Galatians 2:9) had he been known to be careless with the Jesus tradition.

- Many eyewitnesses of Jesus were still alive when the four Gospels were written. These witnesses could testify whether or not the Gospels were "the faith once for all delivered to the saints," or whether they were new fables and myths just created.

---

[2] Modern religious liberalism finds three levels of material in our New Testaments: (1) What Jesus actually said and did, of which we know very little. (Such theologians say that just because some word or act is attributed to Jesus in the Gospels does not mean He actually said or did it.) (2) The beliefs of the apostles, of which we know very little. (These same theologians say that just because some book has an apostle's name on it, does not mean it is the apostle's actual writing or beliefs). (3) The beliefs of the early church, which, it is alleged, actually account for the majority of our New Testament books in their present form. (Modern theologians allege the early church took the traditions as changed and edited by the apostles, and re-formulated those traditions to meet the needs of the church at the time the books were finally edited and published.)

- In the ages when history was passed on by oral tradition, there were folk in every community who had memorized their family or nation's history, and who served as "controls" when others presumed to tell the story. If others told it wrongly, the person who was recognized as the arbiter of the true account would correct the story teller. "Ministers of the word" (Luke 1:1-4) is the exact title for such functionaries.

- The presence of embarrassing and even problematic material in the Gospels (e.g., Mark 9:1, 14:71) speaks against the alleged inventiveness of the early church, even when the church might have profited by it.

- The absence of parables in Acts and the Epistles (and even in other early Christian literature) strongly suggests that the parables in the Gospels were not projected onto Jesus from the early church, but rather were spoken by Jesus Himself.

- A comparison of the Epistles with the Gospels reveals that neither Paul's words nor those of other New Testament writers have been projected back into the mouth of Jesus. No passage from Paul (or any of the other New Testament letters) can be found in the Gospels or on the lips of Jesus. No Pauline concept, such as the "body of Christ," "justification by faith," "under the law," or "flesh," is attributed to Jesus. This is a strong argument against the idea that the Gospels are the early church's stories projected onto Jesus. If the early church was avidly and indiscriminately putting words into the mouth of Jesus, why do we not find some of the material from the Epistles in the Gospels or on the lips of Jesus?

- The supposed inventiveness of the early church meets a final stumbling block in the Gentile question. According to Acts and the Epistles, the preaching of the gospel to the Gentiles and their admission into the church was the burning question of the early church. This issue, however, is virtually absent from the Gospels. Had the church actively been engaged in "framing" the "Jesus material" according to its needs and interests, surely it would have developed sayings on the Gentile question and put them in Jesus' own mouth. The fact that such sayings are virtually absent in the Gospels argues in favor of the historical reliability of the material that is there.

The most reasonable answer to the question of why the Gospels and other New Testament books present Jesus as they do is because that is essentially who Jesus is.

Confession (*homologeō*) means to "say the same thing." When we confess Jesus Christ, we are saying the same thing about Him that God has said. On several occasions, the Father spoke, saying, "This is My beloved Son, in whom I am well-pleased." When it comes time to answer the question, "Who do you say I am?" it would be well to speak God's thoughts after Him, just as they are revealed in the pages of the Scripture. "Jesus is one of the self-existent members of the Godhead who became incarnate in order to redeem creation. Jesus is God!" "Jesus is the long promised Messiah, the son of the living God."

2. Second, there are many times when a man should voluntarily restrict his own liberty because he loves. 9:1-27

> *Summary:* In these verses, with their illustrations of renunciation of his own rights and liberties for the good of others, Paul is still highlighting the principles which should underlie all men's actions. When he was in Corinth, Paul waived certain apostolic rights for the sake of the Corinthians (9:1-18). Both before he came to Corinth and after he left, one reason Paul habitually accommodated himself to the customs of others was because he wanted to save those people (9:19-22). Then Paul calls attention to a second reason why he continued to exercise careful self-control in those areas where he had 'rights' – he wants to share in the benefits of the gospel himself (9:23-27).
>
> At first sight, chapter 9 appears to be a different subject altogether. Accordingly, not a few have thought that this chapter is an insertion from another letter, or that it is a parenthesis in which Paul temporarily leaves his subject. There is no need for such hypotheses. Paul has been dealing with people who asserted their rights to the detriment of others, and he has told them this is wrong. Paul now proceeds to show that he himself has consistently applied this principle. He practices what he preaches.

9:1 -- *Am I not free? Am I not an apostle? Have I not seen Jesus our Lord? Are you not my work in the Lord?*

Am I not free? Am I not an apostle? -- Beginning with verse 1, there are 16 rhetorical questions. Each of the questions is so worded that it expects a "yes" answer. 'Of course I am ... of course I have ... of course you are.' "Free"? A free man expects wages; a slave cannot. Paul is free. Therefore, he is able to talk about wages. The *liberty* referred to here is probably the privilege or right either of supporting himself, or expecting support from the people to whom he ministers. 'Being free, I have rights I can waive out of love, just like you do.' "Apostle"? The apostle had at 8:13 mentioned his willingness to deny himself ("I will never eat meat again ...") if that denial might be the means of benefitting others. In case someone asks, 'When did Paul ever do anything like that?' he now lists some of the rights which he voluntarily waived because he was motivated by love for others. He had acted before on the principle of self-denial, and he proposed to continue acting in this way in the future. In this chapter, he will remind them how he practiced self-denial. But this personal illustration is not given in the way of boasting.

The following illustration seems to be given to meet an objection that had been urged against him at Corinth. Some were objecting against *his apostleship*, making derogatory remarks and insinuations. The objections seem to have been these: (1) He had not seen Jesus Christ, and therefore could not be qualified to be an apostle (verse 1, cp. Acts 1:21,22). (2) He did not live like the other apostles, because he was unmarried, he was a solitary man, a wanderer. He was unlike the other apostles in his mode of life (verses 4,5). (3) Paul and Barnabas were compelled to labor for their support because they were conscious that they were not apostles (verse 6, see also 2 Corinthians 12:13). (4) Perhaps there was also a charge that Paul did not behave consistently like an apostle would (verses

19ff). Sometimes he acted like a Jew (when among Jews), and sometimes he lived like the Gentiles (when among the Gentile Christians). Paul now proceeds to answer these objections. He does so by asking questions of his readers, all of which expect an affirmative answer.

Have I not seen Jesus our Lord? -- Doubtless he mainly refers to the event that occurred when he was on the road to Damascus (Acts 9:3-6,17; 1 Corinthians 15:8). He had probably not seen Jesus during His life or ministry on earth (2 Corinthians 5:16 notwithstanding). The experience Paul had on the Damascus road in which he was called to be an apostle (Acts 26:16ff) was more real and objective than simply a vision in his head. It was an objective appearance of Jesus, as actual as any of Jesus' other post-resurrection appearances. Here, as in other verses, it is implied that in order to be an apostle of Jesus, it was necessary to have seen the Savior (Acts 1:21,22, 22:14,15, 26:16). The reason for this was that the apostles were appointed to be *witnesses* of the life, doctrines, death, and resurrection of Christ. There was more to being an apostle (i.e., 'one sent on a mission') than merely seeing the risen Lord. Others saw the risen Lord and did not become apostles. From Galatians 1:12,16 and Acts 26:26, we learn that there was a revealed message to be shared by those who had been specially commissioned. Paul implies that his apostleship rested on the same foundation as that of the other apostles. Jesus appeared to Paul – not to save him, but to make him an apostle (Acts 26:16-18). Paul almost always uses the title "Christ" or "Lord" when he speaks of the Savior; and it is therefore impossible to separate the Christ of Paul from the Jesus of history.

Are you not my work in the Lord? -- 'Have you not been converted by my labors?' A worker like Paul certainly had a right to expect financial support. No one could say Paul hadn't worked, or that lack of work was the reason he had not expected support. The questions asked in verse 1 are all connected. If the answer to any one were to prove negative, then all of Paul's claims to have waived rights would be shown to be false. But he was free, he was an apostle, he had seen Jesus, and he had worked! The addition of the words "in the Lord" pertaining to Paul's work at Corinth perhaps arises from the consideration emphasized in 3:5-7. Church planting and church growth do not come just from the work of the preacher/apostle, but also depend on the Lord who "gave the increase."

9:2 -- *If to others I am not an apostle, at least I am to you; for you are the seal of my apostleship in the Lord.*

If to others I am not an apostle -- 'If I have not given evidence to others of my apostolic mission, or of my being sent by the Lord Jesus, I certainly have to you,' is what Paul is saying. Who the "others" are we cannot be sure. Perhaps they were men from Jerusalem (remember the Judaizers who pretended to be Christian brethren, Galatians 2:4) who had come into the church from abroad and who sought to mislead the Corinthians in regard to his apostleship. The allusion here likely means that these people had arrived in Corinth subsequent to Paul's departure, and who, not recognizing his apostleship in relation to themselves, stirred up some of the Corinthians to repudiate it also. The same people are likely alluded to in 2 Corinthians 10-12.

At least I am to you -- "At least" means 'assuredly.' 'Assuredly you, among whom I labored so long and so successfully, should not doubt that I am sent from the Lord.' 2 Corinthians 12:12 asserts that the "signs of a true apostle" were worked at Corinth by Paul.

For you are the seal of my apostleship in the Lord -- When Paul says "apostleship" (*tēs apostolēs*) he has in mind the office of apostle – an apostle of Jesus (see notes at 1:1). This is the first use of this term in Paul's writings. We find it also in Galatians 2:8 and Romans 1:5. A "seal" (*sphragis*) is that which is affixed to a deed or other instrument to make it firm, secure, and indisputable. Examples of the use of seals in the ancient world include: (1) When grain was shipped in sacks, the top of the sack was tied and a seal affixed to the cord. If the shipment arrived with the seal intact, the receiver knew the sack contained what it claimed to hold. (2) Wills, written on papyrus, were folded, tied, and sealed. The will was not legally valid unless it could be produced with the seal intact. The seal guaranteed the will had not been altered. Paul argues that 'Your conversion and the resulting existence of a church in Corinth is a clear demonstration that I am an apostle. There wouldn't be a church there for me to write to, if I hadn't been sent to you by the Lord.' "Preachers who were not apostles might convert many, but the remarkable spiritual gifts which the Corinthians received were a guarantee that one who was more than a mere preacher had been sent to them."[1]

9:3 -- *My defense to those who examine me is this:*

My defense -- The word translated defense might be transliterated 'apology,' a defense against a charge (a derogatory charge in this instance). Here it means his answer to those who sat in judgment on his claims to be an apostle.

To those who examine me -- Because Paul voluntarily placed certain restrictions on his rights (doing so out of love for the other fellow), there were some who were saying he did not act like a real apostle. "Examine" is *anakrinō*, the word for a legal inquiry.[2] They were calling him to defend himself as one would before magistrates at a court. It was not actually an official legal proceeding, but the language is used figuratively to describe the actions of his opponents who negatively judged Paul's position and authority.

Is this -- "This" (*hautē*) points to something aforesaid; it is not a reference to what follows.[3] 'My reply to those who examine me is this – the existence of a Christian Church at Corinth. This fact shows that I am an apostle!'[4]

---

[1] Robertson and Plummer, *op. cit.*, p.178.

[2] See notes at 2:15 on this word. There it was translated "appraises."

[3] A difference of opinion as to exactly what constitutes his "defense" can be seen by observing the punctuation of the ASV and NASB. The ASV has a period after verse 3, thus making verse 2 the defense. The NASB has a colon at the close of verse 3, thus making the questions in verse 4 and following the defense.

[4] If the punctuation of the NASB is correct, then Paul's defense is his explanation of why he had not exercised all the rights one might expect an apostle to exercise.

9:4 -- *Do we not have a right to eat and drink?*

Do we not have a right -- The Greek is *mē ouk echomen*, showing that the question expects a negative answer. 'You Corinthians do not want to say we do not have a right, do you?' The implied answer would be, 'Of course not!' The plural "we" is either an editorial "we," or includes both Paul and Barnabas (see verse 6). The apostle means to say that though they had not exercised this right by demanding a livelihood, yet it was not because they were conscious that they had no such right. Having verified his own divine call for his apostleship, Paul now substantiates his claims to certain rights and privileges.[5] The Sophists blamed Socrates and Plato for teaching gratis, thus confessing that their teaching was nothing. This kind of charge may have been made by the Paul's detractors at Corinth.[6]

To eat and drink? -- Food and drink, as the context shows, has reference to the physical necessities of life. In the light of the question in the next verse, what Paul is asking is this, 'Do we not have a right to have the necessities of life provided by the people to whom we preach?' Compare Jesus' instructions to the Seventy whom He sent out two-by-two (Luke 10:5ff). In this immediate context: (1) There is no reference to the Jewish dietary laws respecting food. This is remote from the context. (2) There is no reference to flesh offered in sacrifices (though this is in the section dealing with meats offered to idols).

9:5 -- *Do we not have a right to take along a believing wife, even as the rest of the apostles and the brothers of the Lord and Cephas?*

Do we not have a right -- This question is like the preceding one, written with a double negative. 'You Corinthians certainly do not intend to say anything like this, do you?' And the implied answer again is, 'Of course not!' The point of this verse is not to assert the right of an apostle to marry. No one in the apostolic age would have questioned an apostle's right to marry. Rather, the verse affirms their right to "take along a believing wife," and expect the church to help provide her physical necessities, too, just as they did the apostle's necessities.

To take along a believing wife – *Adelpheē gunaika* is, literally, 'sister, a wife.' The allusion here is not to a serving matron whose business it was to use her own funds to provide for the physical food and drink necessities of the apostle as he went from place to place. However, Augustine, Jerome, most of the early fathers, and most Catholic exegetes still interpret the verse in this manner,[7] and point to Luke 8:2,3 (which speaks of women during Jesus' earthly ministry who traveled with Jesus and the apostles and contributed to

---

[5] "Right" is *exousia*, the word used at 1 Corinthians 8:9. It means 'authority, right, power.'

[6] It has been observed how often Greek philosophy was at the root of the problems at Corinth. Paul has said, 'Do not get your standards for judging preachers from Greek philosophy (chapters 1-4).' He has said, 'Do not get our doctrine about marriage from Greek philosophy (chapter 7).' Now he is saying, 'Do not get your ideas about support of the preacher from Greek philosophy.'

[7] Such an interpretation is maintained in the interests of celibacy. One interpreter, Villa, adopts the willful invention that the apostles, though married, traveled with their wives as sisters.

their support out of their private means) as evidence for such a practice in the church. The idea that Paul would have claimed the right to take a woman – other than his wife – about the country, and ask for her support, is repugnant.[8] Rather, Paul is arguing this point: he had the right to take a wife on his missionary journeys, and he would have had the right to ask for the support of his wife if he did so. "Sister" is used in the sense that the wife is a "Christian." The illustration from Peter and the other apostles shows in what sense "sister" is used. By using the unusual term "sister," the readers would be reminded that they have a special interest in the apostle's wife; after all, she is a sister in Christ, and Christians have a direct command from the Lord to be interested in the physical welfare (as well as spiritual) of their brothers and sisters in Christ. The apostles certainly had a right to marry and to take their wives along on their travels from place to place while they were engaged in their work. It was accepted that an apostle ought to be maintained by those to whom he ministered. Paul here asserts the right of the apostle, if married, to take his wife with him, the implication being that she, too, would be supported by the church.

Even as the rest of the apostles -- More literally translated 'the remaining apostles.' Paul here classifies himself as one of them. While this phrase should not be pressed to prove that all of the original Twelve apostles were married, there is independent evidence and tradition to show that most of them were. What Paul says implies that the people at Corinth were familiar with many of the original Twelve, and knew that their wives accompanied them on their missionary journeys, and were regularly provided with support from the congregations whom their husbands served.[9]

And the brothers of the Lord -- Mare is correct when he says, "The phrase 'brothers of the Lord' should be taken at face value – physical brothers, that is, half-brothers, children of both Joseph and Mary after Jesus was born."[10] The brothers of the Lord were named James, Joses, Simon, and Judas (Matthew 13:55). None of them were among the original Twelve apostles whom Jesus chose, for during His lifetime they were unbelievers in Him. Even after their conversion, they are mentioned as distinct from the Twelve (Acts 1:14). However, James eventually became an apostle (Galatians 1:19) and is the author of the

---

[8] Such things did happen in history. The practice of traveling about with unmarried women, who went under the name of 'sisters,' 'beloved,' 'companions,' was distinctly forbidden by the third canon of the first Council of Nicea.

[9] This passage in Corinthians helps us to interpret what is meant when we are told the apostles 'forsook' all to follow Jesus (Mark 1:16-20; Luke 5:11, 18:28-30; Matthew 19:28ff; Mark 10:28). 1 Corinthians 9:5 tells us they certainly did not leave their wives in order to fulfill their apostolic calling.

[10] Mare, *op. cit.*, p. 242. The several theories as to whom these brothers of the Lord were have been detailed in a Special Study, "The Brothers of the Lord," in the author's *Acts* commentary. (1) Jerome, AD 385, said they were *cousins* of Jesus, being sons of Alphaeus and Mary, a sister of the Virgin. (This is untenable, and was dropped even by Jerome himself in his later life.) (2) Epiphanius, AD 380, said they were sons of Joseph by a previous marriage. (This is a possible interpretation, but incapable of proof. It comes from a tainted source, the Apocryphal Gospels.) (3) Helvidius, AD 380, said they were the sons of Joseph and Mary. (This is the plain teaching of the Gospels, e.g., Matthew 13:55. This is also the ancient view of Clement of Alexandria.)

letter in the New Testament that bears his name. (See further notes on James at 1 Corinthians 15:7.) It seems from Paul's allusion that although at first His brothers did not believe in Him (John 7:5) and regarded Him as disgraced (Mark 3:21), they subsequently became converted and were employed as ministers and evangelists. From this statement it appears that they were married, and were attended by their wives in their travels.

And Cephas? -- "Cephas" is the name by which Jesus said Peter would be called (John 1:42). That Peter had a wife is mentioned at Matthew 8:14 and inferred at Mark 1:30. The tradition of his wife's martyrdom is found in Clement of Alexandria, *Stromata* (Book 7, chap. 11, P. 541). Tradition has her name as Concordia or Perpetua. Roman Catholic commentators assume there is a climax here, and Peter is the greatest of the listing. But if our suggestion as to who repudiated Paul's apostleship is correct, then this also explains the reference to the brethren of the Lord and to Peter. These men are mentioned especially, not as distinct from the apostles (for Peter, of course, was one), but as examples which would have great weight among those who had been swayed by the particular Jewish faction against whose derogatory view of Paul this argument was directed. Peter, the apostle, was married. Paul is arguing that, were he (Paul) married, he would have had as much right to have his wife with him as did Peter.[11]

9:6 -- *Or do only Barnabas and I not have a right to refrain from working?*

Or do only Barnabas and I -- When Paul came to Corinth, he worked as a tent-maker in order to provide for himself the necessities of life (Acts 18:3). Barnabas had not come to Corinth with Paul. They had separated before the second missionary journey began that brought Paul to Corinth (Acts 15:39). When they separated, that is the last time the name of Barnabas occurs in Acts, but this reference in Corinthians shows us that – even after their separation – there was widespread knowledge about the career of Barnabas, and that Paul regarded him with love and esteem. Barnabas apparently continued in his separate mission work, and practiced self-denial also, if by that he could possibly win more people to Christ. Paul singles out Barnabas and himself as two apostles (Acts 14:14) who made it a practice of earning their own living while preaching. This makes it seem as though it was the custom of all the others to accept their support from the people to whom they preached. "Or" here does not introduce a question which implies a new right in addition to the rights already claimed, but it merely completes the argument. Granting the existence of the rights established by the previous questions, Paul now says – still preserving the rhetorical questioning – 'These things being so, the only way you can possibly do away with this right is by making exceptions of myself and Barnabas.' And the form in which the question is put shows the impossibility of any such arbitrary exception being made.[12]

---

[11] See arguments in chapter 1:12 that Peter had been to Corinth. It is conceivable that while in Corinth both Peter and his wife were supported by the Corinthian Christians. Paul argues, 'If you supported both of them, don't I have a right to support also, since I also am an apostle?'

[12] Shore, *op. cit.*, p.78.

Not have a right to refrain from working? -- The sense of this is, 'Are we alone, of all the apostles, under obligation to personally provide for our own livelihood while we preach?' (*Ergadzesthai* refers to manual labor to earn one's living.) Paul has now claimed three rights, all of which he voluntarily waived: (1) The right to have his physical needs for living (food and drink) supplied, verse 4. (2) The right to be married and be accompanied on evangelistic tours by his mate, and to have enough support to provide living necessities for his mate, too, verse 5. (3) The right to not have to work at a trade to make ends meet, verse 6.

9:7 -- *Who at any time serves as a soldier at his own expense? Who plants a vineyard and does not eat the fruit of it? Or who tends a flock and does not use the milk of the flock?*

Who at any time serves as a soldier at his own expense? -- In verses 7-14, we have six arguments to prove the right of a minister[13] to be supported with food and drink and other necessities of life by the congregation to whom he ministers: (1) From the ordinary laws of human justice, verse 7. (2) By analogy from the Law of Moses, verses 8-10. (3) *A fortiori* from the obligations of common gratitude, verse 11. (4) From their concession of the right to others who had inferior claims, verse 12. (5) From the Jewish provision for the maintenance of priests, verse 13. (6) From the rule laid down by Christ Himself, verse 14. He first calls attention to the fact that soldiers are paid. They do not have to provide their own rations, or their own uniforms. Neither should the minister, who is a soldier in the army of Christ, have to pay his own way. *Opsōniois* means "wages." The word originally signified "rations."

Who plants a vineyard, and does not eat of the fruit of it? -- It is reasonable to suppose that those who labor should have a fair compensation. A man who plants a vineyard does not expect to labor for nothing; he expects to be paid for his labor. In fact, he will be the first to taste the grapes, and the entire harvest belongs to him (Deuteronomy 20:6, cp. also Proverbs 27:18). The apostles spent their time, strength, and talent for the needs of the Corinthians. It was reasonable that they should be supported while they were thus laboring for the good of the Corinthians. The church is often compared to a vineyard (Isaiah 5:1-4 and Luke 20:9-16). The one who plants churches, which are like vineyards, should be supported from that vineyard.

Or who tends a flock and does not use the milk of the flock? -- The Greek word *poimainō* means not only to feed, but to guard, protect, defend, tend, as a shepherd does his flock. The wages of shepherds in the East do not consist of ready money, but in a part of the milk of the flocks they tend. The church is often compared to a flock (cp. John 10:1ff, 1 Peter 5:2). The minister, who helps shepherd the flock, should be supported by it. It is perhaps accidental that in each case the status of each worker is different, but this strengthens the argument. The soldier works for pay; the vine-planter is a proprietor; the shepherd is a slave. But to all, the principle is applicable that the laborer may claim some kind of return. There is an "of" in the Greek before "milk." It would be strange to speak

---

[13] 9:14 will justify the use of the term "minister." This argument has broader application than that just "apostles" had a right to be supported.

of "eating" milk, but it is not strange to "eat *of* the milk." The shepherd would really be sustained chiefly by the sale of the milk and the purchase of food with the money so obtained.

9:8 -- *I am not speaking these things according to human judgment, am I? Or does not the Law also say these things?*

I am not speaking these things according to human judgment, am I? -- 'Do I speak only on human authority? Do I speak without the sanction of God?' As before, the form of the question in the Greek implies the answer, "Of course not!"

Or does not the Law also say these things? -- This question expects an affirmative answer, 'Of course it does!' The "Law" is the Law of Moses.[14] Paul was accustomed, when arguing with the Jews, to derive his proofs from the Old Testament Scriptures. It may just be that the people who urged these objections against Paul's apostleship were Jews from Palestine. In the previous verse, Paul has shown it was equitable that ministers of the gospel should be supported. He now shows that this same principle was recognized and acted on under the Jewish dispensation.[15] 'I am not saying all this merely from a worldly point of view. The Divine Law assumes the same principle.'

9:9 -- *For it is written in the Law of Moses, "YOU SHALL NOT MUZZLE THE OX WHILE HE IS THRESHING." God is not concerned about oxen, is He?*

For it is written in the Law of Moses -- With an explanatory "for," Paul proceeds to cite what is written in the Law. Deuteronomy 25:4 is about to be quoted. Note that Paul attributes Deuteronomy to Moses.[16] So did Jesus (Matthew 19:7,8). A denial of the Mosaic authorship of Deuteronomy would also be tantamount to denying the truthfulness of both Paul and Jesus.

"YOU SHALL NOT MUZZLE THE OX WHILE HE IS THRESHING" -- To muzzle the mouth means to cover or fasten the mouth to prevent the animal from eating or biting. This was done either by passing straps around the mouth, or by placing a small basket over the mouth, fastened by straps to the horns of the animal, so as to prevent its eating, but not to impede its breathing freely. The Gentiles had the practice of muzzling the oxen when they were driven around and around, and perhaps drew rough sleds over the grain that had been spread out in a circle in order to thresh it. Since it was more humane, the Mosaic Law forbade such a practice and allowed the ox to eat his fill of grain while he was at work.

---

[14] "*The* Law," with an article, is a construction that does not occur often in Paul's writings. While the Scriptures at times (cf. 1 Corinthians 14:21) use "Law" to refer to the whole Old Testament (Law, Prophets, and Holy Writings), in this place the reference is probably to the Pentateuch.

[15] The Law of Moses has been abrogated by the New Covenant (Jeremiah 31:31ff; Hebrews 8-10). But the Law does contain examples from which Christians can learn (1 Corinthians 10:11).

[16] P46 omits "Moses" at this place, but the other old manuscripts have the name. We suppose Paul wrote "Law of Moses." Elsewhere, Paul asserts the Mosaic authorship of the Pentateuch. See Romans 10:5,6,19.

To "thresh" means to knock the heads of grain free from the husks and stalks. In the age before mechanization, people did use flails, but the most common method of threshing was to use animals to walk over the grain. Some of the older English versions translate the one Greek word for "threshing" as 'treading out the corn.' "Treading out" gave a correct mental picture of how threshing was done in ancient times. However, the word 'corn' gives modern readers a wrong impression. When the KJV was translated, "corn" meant grain of any kind – wheat, rye, barley. Maize, to which we apply the word 'corn,' was then unknown. This same Old Testament verse is alluded to in 1 Timothy 5:18, where Paul is urging that church elders be given double honor.

God is not concerned about oxen, is He? -- The sense is, 'Is God interested only for the oxen? You certainly do not think it is only for the animal that God cares, do you?' The answer expected is, 'Of course not.' The apostle does not mean to imply God has no interest in the welfare of animals, for Matthew 6:26-29 indicates He does care for the animals. So does the Old Testament. But Paul means to ask whether it is to be supposed that God would regard the comfort of the oxen, and not men also. This is a Semitic idiom meaning, 'If God cares for the oxen, how much more does He care for the men?'

9:10 -- *Or is He speaking altogether for our sake? Yes, for our sake it was written, because the plowman ought to plow in hope, and the thresher* **to thresh** *in hope of sharing* **the crops.**

Or is He speaking altogether for our sake? Yes, for our sake it was written -- This does not seem to be saying that the *sole* or *only* design of this part of the Law was to teach that ministers of the gospel were entitled to support. We read this law in Deuteronomy 25, and generally find no more in it than a kindly regulation concerning brute beasts. But Paul sees much more in it than a concern for such beasts. The rules in the Old Testament were not intended simply to make sacred cows, to be taken care of by men. Is it only for the animals that God is concerned? Or does the care and concern of God extend farther? Surely it extends farther! How far the principle extends, Paul points out in the rest of verse 10. The word translated "altogether" (*pantos*) is capable of several connotations. The word may be rendered "chiefly, mainly, principally, or no doubt" (Luke 4:23; Acts 18:21, 21:22, 28:4). The word here means that the *principle* stated in the law about the oxen was so broad and humane that it might *certainly, surely, particularly* be applicable to the case under consideration. We take it that Moses did not have Paul, or any other minister, particularly in mind when he wrote, but the principle was one that applied. Paul should not be charged with misusing Scripture at this point, as though he claimed that God says "oxen" but means "men." What Paul does is something we find him doing throughout his writings: he goes back to the underlying God-given principle.

Because the plowman -- The *hoti* clause is explicative. The KJV translation "that" is better than the ASV/NASB's "because." Paul is explaining that this law concerning cattle was written into the Bible on our account. Paul regards the plowman and the thresher as two workers on whose account this law was written into the sacred record. These two illustrate and show that this principle concerning oxen applies to all of us. As these ought to work at plowing and at threshing in the hope of partaking of the fruits of their labors, so all of us should work in the same hope.

Ought to plow in hope -- In hope of reaping a harvest, or of obtaining success in his labors. When a person is hoeing the garden, what keeps him working on, even when he is tired and his hands hurt? Hope! The anticipation of how good the fresh vegetables will taste. "Ought" (*opheilō*) speaks of the moral obligation involved.

And the thresher *to thresh* **in hope of sharing** *the crops* -- This sentence is very elliptical, but the sense seems to be 'He who threshes ought to partake of the fruits of his labor. It is fair and right that he should enjoy the fruits of his toil.'

9:11 -- *If we sowed spiritual things in you, is it too much if we reap material things from you?*

If we sowed spiritual things in you -- In verses 11 and 12, Paul drives home the point of the illustrations and analogy from Scripture. He had a right to being financially supported by those to whom he preached, but it was a right he voluntarily waived because he loved – the very point he has been driving home since early in chapter 8. The figure of sowing to denote the preaching of the gospel is frequently used in the Scripture (Matthew 13:3; John 4:36-38). "Spiritual things" (*ta pneumatika*) equals the entire priceless wealth of spiritual blessings. Paul was the one who first preached the gospel at Corinth. His work resulted in the planting of the church in that town. His work was directly responsible for the fact the Corinthians have experienced the spiritual blessings they have.

Is it too much – 'Is it to be regarded as unequal, unjust, or burdensome? Is it to be supposed that we are receiving that for which we have not rendered a worthy work?' What the apostle gave was incalculable in its richness; what he might have claimed, but never took, was a trivial matter. Was a little bodily sustenance to be compared with the blessings of the gospel?

If we should reap material things from you? -- "Material" translates *sarkika* ("fleshly things"). The word is not to be taken as something 'wrong' here, i.e., the word is not to be taken in the ethical sense. The word speaks of those things which support the body – food, raiment, lodging. The force of Paul's presentation will be felt if we notice that in Paul's illustrations, the worker received pay in the same kind as the quality of his labor. The preacher asks for something of less earthly value than he gives. If a man ministers to a congregation, is it not right for the congregation to give bread and butter in return?

9:12 -- *If others share the right over you, do we not more? Nevertheless, we did not use this right, but we endure all things so that we will cause no hindrance to the gospel of Christ.*

If others share the right over you -- 'Rights' is what this argument is all about, namely 'rights' claimed by the Corinthians concerning eating in an idol's temple. Paul insists that there are 'rights' which a person who loves his brother will waive because he loves. "Others" refers to other teachers living in their midst. It is not necessarily a reference to false teachers (the "others" of 9:2), but it could include them. It could include the "tutors" of 4:15. It seems to speak of teachers at Corinth who had a lesser claim to support than Paul did.

Do we not more? – 'Have not we apostles a better claim than they to support from you?' The "we" probably extends to include Paul, Silas, Barnabas, and Timothy.

Nevertheless, we did not use this right -- Here in verse 12b, Paul begins to show that love was the thing that motivated him to deliberately and voluntarily waive his rights. The reason why they had labored to support themselves, rather than ask for financial support from their converts,[17] he states in the latter part of this verse and in a latter part of this chapter. It was so the gospel of Christ would not be hindered. Paul voluntarily waived his rights to support out of love!

But we endure all things -- "We endure all things," namely, all privations involved in foregoing our right to be provided with food and drink by the congregation among whom we labor. The present tense says, "We do so right along, even now."[18] The words are simple and brief and yet full of meaning. It is no easy burden to preach and to teach, and at the same time to earn enough to live and to travel from place to place. Paul's was a life of privations and self-denial. Yet however hard this made his lot and that of his assistants, he held to his purpose "in order that we may furnish no hindrance to the gospel of Christ." 'We subject ourselves to poverty, want, hunger, thirst, nakedness, rather than urge a *claim* upon you, and thus leave the suspicion that we are motivated by *mercenary motives*.'

That we may cause no hindrance to the gospel of Christ -- The word "hindrance" (*enkopēn*) is a word used of "destroying bridges" or "tearing up roads" to slow or stop the advance of an army. The gospel of Christ is the good news of salvation available in Jesus the Messiah. Paul is anxious lest anyone have a ready-made opportunity to slow the advance of the gospel. He was not about to give anyone an opportunity to make their malicious misrepresentations even appear to be plausible. (It is common for people to avoid or reject the claims of the gospel by saying 'Such and such a preacher is only in it for the money.') Paul waived the support to which he was entitled, not because he was conscious that he was not an apostle, but so that the gospel would not be hindered. If it came to having to choose between his 'rights' and someone else's hearing the gospel, there was no difficulty or hesitation on his part which to choose. His rights would be easily and gladly waived. This verse is a very close parallel to 8:9ff – Paul had a right, and yet for love's sake he refrained from using that right.

---

[17] H. Lynn Gardner has pointed out that Paul did not take wages from any congregation to which he was currently preaching. He did welcome financial offerings from older, established congregations (Philippians 4:15,16). In notes at 1 Corinthians 8:13, it was indicated that the 'waiving of rights' is not as absolute as it first sounds. Paul exercised his liberty to receive support if someone else's conscience was not in the way.

[18] The word here, *stegō*, is not Paul's ordinary word for "endure." This word uniquely recalls the hardships and long weary hours that are part and parcel of a tent-making form of ministry, where the preacher not only preaches and evangelizes, but must work long hours to earn his own living.

9:13 -- *Do you not know that those who perform sacred services eat the **food** of the temple, and those who attend regularly to the altar have their share from the altar?*

Do you not know -- 'Don't you remember?' implies this topic had been taught to the Corinthians earlier. See the same expression at 5:6 and 6:2,3,9,15,19. 'Of course we know it.' From the list given at verse 7, we have come to the fifth of the arguments Paul uses to show he had a right to financial support. We are glad Paul did not stop halfway through his presentation of the right of gospel messengers to live off the gospel. It is helpful for those of us who depend on someone else to preach the good news to us to know what God expects of us regarding our financial responsibility for the preacher's everyday living needs.

That those who perform sacred services -- The participle translated "perform" is *ergadzomenoi* ('working'). The Old Testament priests are in view here, it seems.[19] The priests officiating 'worked' as they helped the worshipers to worship. Paul is reminding the Corinthians that there is a higher and closer analogy to the situation of the Christian minister than that of the soldier or the husbandman.[20]

Eat the *food* of the temple -- Deuteronomy 18:1ff; Leviticus 6:14-18,24-26, 7:1ff, 10:12-15; and Numbers 18:8-13 (the words of God to Aaron) indicate that religious leaders were to receive a part of the offerings the people brought to the Lord. The priests were supported in their work by the offerings of the people and by the provisions which were made for the temple service. God Himself arranged the temple and its services for the Jews. All of the arrangements, even to the support of the priests, was by God's sanction.

***And* those who attend regularly to the altar have their share with the altar?** -- Parts of the offerings brought to the altar were consumed by the altar fire, and parts of the offerings were reserved for use of the priests (Leviticus 10:12-15). The gift was not made to the priest, but to God. The priest then received a share with the altar of what was sacrificed.[21] In this phrase "attending the altar" (*thusiastērion*, a word used of both the altar of burnt offering and the altar of incense) Paul makes reference to one of the chief tasks of the priests, working at the altar. Paul quite properly refers to the great altar which stood in the court of the priests, on which certain portions of the sacrificed animal were burned, the

---

[19] However, the heathen priests also lived off the things brought to the temple. But Paul is certainly not thinking of pagan practices. See Lenski, *op. cit.*, p 366.

[20] The fact that Paul sees a similarity between how the Jewish priests' living needs were provided by the peoples' offerings to the Lord and the rightness of the Christian congregation supporting their preachers should not be used to infer an identity of function. The preacher is no more a "priest" than he is a "threshing ox" (in light of the previous analogy).

[21] Barclay (*op. cit.*, p.88-90) has a succinct note about the perquisites of Jewish priests who worked in the temple. He notes there were five main offerings – the burnt-offering, the sin-offering, the trespass-offering, the food-offering, the peace-offering – and he notes how much the priest received of each. He also calls attention to the fact that the priests received the first-fruits of seven kinds – wheat, barley, the vine, the fig-tree, the pomegranate, the olive, and honey – and portions of the *Terumah* (an offering of choice fruits), the tithe, and the *Challah* (kneaded dough).

remainder of the carcass being given to the priests. Of course, Christianity had superseded the old temple arrangement. Paul does not need to explain this change here. Paul is merely pointing out what has been God's arrangement all along.

9:14 -- *So also the Lord directed those who proclaim the gospel to get their living from the gospel.*

So also -- "So also" equals 'Let no one say that this matter of payment of religious leaders is Jewish and has no bearing on Christianity and on the preachers of the Gospel.' Like the Old Testament system of support of religious teachers was ordained by God, so the New Testament system of support of preachers of the gospel is divinely sanctioned. In verse 8, Paul has appealed to an argument which would have had weight with the Judaizers. Now he turns to appeal to an argument which would have weight with them as Christians. The rights of the ministry to be supported by the church have been established by appeals to a number of parallel cases. There is one higher step in the argument. Payment of the ministry was not only a principle of the Jewish law (which Christ might have abrogated), but it was a provision which Christ formally commanded.

The Lord directed ("even so did the Lord ordain," ASV) -- "Lord" is a reference to Jesus. *Dietaxen* means 'directed, ordained, commanded, appointed.' Jesus Christ made this law; He has required it. This command of the Lord should be obeyed as much as any other command is. The reference seems to be to Matthew 10:10 and Luke 10:7, "The laborer is worthy of his wages." Allusions like this to Jesus' ministry and message are of special interest. They show that Paul was at least orally familiar with the discourses of Christ. Indeed, there is nothing impossible or improbable in supposing that some of these were already being circulated in manuscript form. It may also be that we do not have recorded in the gospels the exact words of our Lord by which He set forth this command. Acts 20:35 records a saying Jesus often spoke which is nowhere recorded in the four Gospels. So, perhaps this saying about the support of the ministry is another unrecorded saying of Jesus that Paul has preserved for us. This allusion to what the Lord taught implies a detailed knowledge of the sayings of Jesus on the part of writer and readers. Compare 7:10 and 11:23ff.

Those who proclaim the gospel -- Some have argued that this discussion in 1 Corinthians 9 refers to only an apostle having the right to demand support. But this phrase shows that Paul has all preachers in mind. Just as God appointed that the priests and Levites should be supported out of what the people offered to Him, so did Christ also appoint that gospel preachers should be supported by the gifts given by those who respond to the gospel.

To get their living from the gospel -- It says "live" off the gospel. It does not say grow rich. Perhaps a good rule is that the preacher should be paid the same amount that the average man in the congregation is paid. An example is Harold Dunson, who was a missionary in the Kiamichi Mountains (1948-1958). People came to him and said, "We don't know much about religion, but we do know how to raise potatoes and butcher beef and hogs. You preach to us, and we'll give you as much of our food as you can use." Mr. Dunson answered, "That's fine. I don't know how to raise a garden, but I can preach." So the Nashoba Church became the strongest of all the mission churches. The New Testament teaches that God's workers are to be supported. The hearers of the gospel are to take care of the everyday physical needs of their preachers.[22]

9:15 -- *But I have used none of these things. And I am not writing these things so that it will be done so in my case; for it would be better for me to die than have any man make my boast an empty one.*

But -- "But" means 'in contrast to what has just been shown about the rights of preachers to be supported.' 'Even though I have a "right" based on the very words of Jesus Himself, I have not personally insisted on exercising these rights no matter what.'

I have used none of these things -- "I" is emphatic in the Greek, and there is an implied contrast. Paul was unlike the Corinthians who were insisting on their 'rights,' or unlike the opponents of Paul at Corinth who waived no rights or privileges. "Things" is best explained as being the different 'rights' he has just asserted on the highest authority as available to all preachers of the gospel. Paul had not urged or enforced his right to support. He had chosen to support himself. Paul was in no doubt about his rights, but he had not used them. He is appealing to his own abandonment of a right to encourage the Corinthians to waive, if necessary, their claims of rights and Christian liberties. The perfect tense, "I have used none," indicates a continuing practice based on a past decision. Included, too, is the thought that Paul still pursues this course. Out of love he has renounced making any claims on the Corinthians for food, drink, clothing, etc.

And I am not writing these things that it may be done so in my case -- The preceding argument (verses 4-14) was not an appeal for support. He was not now asking them to provide for him, or to give him back wages. *Egrapsa* is another use (cp. 1 Corinthians 5:9) of the epistolary aorist; it is not a reference to a previous letter. "I write" refers to verses 4-14 of this same letter. When the readers get this letter, the time of writing will be past; thus, the aorist tense. Paul is saying, 'Do not take my argument as a hint to you that you have neglected your duty of maintaining me, and that I am now asking for my back pay. Nor do you need think that if I come again to Corinth that I will expect you to furnish my support then.'

For it would be better for me to die -- Chrysostom has said that "die of hunger" is the idea (i.e., die because of not being supported), but 'dying' in general seems to be the thought in Paul's mind. There were certain advantages growing out of his not claiming the support to which he was entitled. Paul would die, if necessary, rather than lose his sense of satis-

---

[22] Even though the passage says "so also," thus comparing the support of preachers with the support of priests, this verse does not prove tithing (said George Mark Elliott). The case is thus often argued, that just as the priests were supported by the tithes of the people, so the Christian ministry ought to be supported by *tithing Christians*. Other passages in the New Testament alleged to prove Christians must tithe are Matthew 23:23 and Hebrews 7:8. It is this commentator's contention that the New Testament teaches stewardship, not just tithing. Tithing is concerned with 10%; stewardship is concerned with how a man manages all 100% of what God has entrusted to him. If all the preachers and evangelists and elders and members of the church that need supporting were supported, it is likely the church should need to more than tithe to support them.

faction. These advantages were of more importance than life to Paul. 'I'd rather die than be deprived of my independence.'

Than have any man make my boast an empty one -- There is a broken sentence in the original.[23] It is a case of what is called *aposiopesis* – a figure of speech in which the 'speaker breaks off suddenly, as if unwilling or unable to state what was in his mind.' So fiercely did Paul hold his convictions in this matter that he can say, 'better for me to die, than ....' He just breaks off his sentence and does not complete it. The phrase that follows is then believed to be a simple exclamation, 'No man will make this boast of mine an empty one!' The break in construction marks Paul's deep emotion, and his emotion indicates the importance he ascribed to his practice of self-denial of things that were actually his rights.

There is much difference of opinion as to how the broken sentence should be completed; it is difficult to get a smooth translation out of what seems to be the true text. One suggestion is this: "Good were it for me rather to die than (receive support from you); my cause for boasting no one shall make void."[24] Another attempt at translation, though one that seems forced, is this: 'On the one hand, rather than suffer myself to be supported, I will prefer to die; on the other hand, if such a thing need not occur (if I don't need to be supported), my boasting none shall make void.' Alford (*op. cit.*, p.546) adopts the reading that translates it, "Better to die than that any one should make void my (matter of) boasting." Perhaps another construction is this: 'It were better for *me* to die than that my basis for boasting should die; no one shall make it void.'

As we go through the next several verses, Paul's meaning will become clear. His "boast" was that he had never had to be supported. He had never demanded from his hearers his right to support. This is not sinful boasting or glorying. Rather, Paul's 'boasting' equals a sense of satisfaction that he never had to demand pay, a sense of satisfaction over a piece of work well done.

9:16 -- *For if I preach the gospel, I have nothing to boast of, for I am under compulsion; for woe is me if I do not preach the gospel.*

For if I preach the gospel -- "For" introduces an explanation of something just said. Paul is going to show how his being supported by the church would deprive him of his right to "boast" in his work. Paul preaches all the time; it is a present tense verb. The mere fact of preaching the gospel is no basis for him for boasting. Paul feels that he can claim no particular credit for preaching.

I have nothing to boast of, for I am under compulsion -- *Anagkē* is translated "necessity" (Romans 13:5; Hebrews 7:12, 9:16), "inevitable" (Matthew 18:7), "I need to" (Luke 14:18), and "compulsion" (here and Philemon 1:14). Here, in verse 16, there is reference to his

---

[23] Other examples of broken sentences in Paul's writings are found at Galatians 2:4ff, 4:19; Romans 5:12-15, 9:10; 1 Corinthians 7:37; 2 Corinthians 11:9ff.

[24] Kling, *op. cit.*, p.186.

call on the Damascus Road; in verse 17, Paul confirms he did not preach voluntarily. This was not his original choice of a life's work; preaching is something Paul must do, ever since Jesus called him to preach. Paul was not compelled against his will to preach (verse 18 will say that he did still exercise choice), but the matter was not optional. He had been entrusted with a stewardship. He says, 'I have nothing to boast of.' Since he had been called by Jesus to preach, he could not boast of the mere fact of preaching. If he were going to "boast," the basis for boasting must be found other than in the act of preaching.

This verse, with the following two, forms a very difficult passage, and has been variously understood. The general scope of the passage is to show what was the reason for, or basis of, his 'boasting.' In verse 15 he intimated that he had cause for 'boasting,' and that he was determined no one should take away the cause of that boasting. In verses 16-18 he states what that cause was. It was not simply that he preached, for there was a necessity laid upon him; he could not help it. There could be no glory in doing what he was forced to do. However, all idea of 'boasting' or 'reward' must be connected with some voluntary service. If a man is in a job because he has to be, and is paid because he puts in his time, what ground is there for boasting? If a man is compelled to be in a job, how can he show that his heart is in his work? The only thing Paul could boast in was something that he *voluntarily did*. Paul therefore submitted *voluntarily* to trials; he denied himself; he waived his 'rights' to support; he forewent comforts he might lawfully enjoy. Thus he had a ground for boasting, for a deep and satisfying feeling of satisfaction. Paul is saying that his joy or boasting did not consist in the simple fact that he *preached*, but that he preached the gospel without charge. He was not forced to preach the gospel *gratis*; yet he does preach *gratis*. In this there is great satisfaction and a generosity that calls for recognition.

For woe is me if I do not preach the gospel -- The English reader must beware not to take the expression "preach the gospel" as if it made a distinction between preaching "the gospel" and preaching something else. It is true that false teachers shall be condemned, but this is not the verse to use to prove it. "Preach the gospel" is a translation of the word "evangelize"; i.e., to perform the work of a Christian missionary. "Woe" refers to the divine judgments which would fall on him if he ventured to disobey the heavenly call. Paul is saying, 'I should be miserable and wretched if I did not preach. My conscience would reproach me. My judgment would condemn me. My heart would pain me. I should have no comfort in any other calling. And God would frown on me.' Calamity and dire punishment from God would overtake Paul if he does not preach. Such an astounding statement needs explanation, and verse 17 gives it.

9:17 -- *For if I do this voluntarily, I have a reward; but if against my will, I have a stewardship entrusted to me.*

For if I do this voluntarily, I have a reward -- There have been two ways suggested for understanding this phrase, the first of which appears to this commentator to be the best. (1) 'If I did this gospel preaching voluntarily, I could talk about wages (rewards).' "This" refers to the nearest antecedent – i.e., preaching the gospel, verse 16. Verse 18 seems to point to this interpretation. See also below in the discussion of the second half of verse 17 for further evidence that this is the correct interpretation. (2) 'If cheerfully I preach without support, a reward awaits me.' It is usually suggested that the reward comes from God.[25] "Voluntarily" (*hekōn*) means 'spontaneously, without compulsion' – of my own motion, of my own accord.

But if against my will, I have a stewardship entrusted to me -- If we interpret according to (1) above, the meaning of this phrase is: 'As a matter of fact, I do not preach voluntarily. I preach because I must. I have a stewardship entrusted to me.' If we interpret according to (2) above, what is the sense of this phrase? Lipscomb tries valiantly to make sense of it by saying, "And what a woe would have rested upon him had he failed in the discharge of his duty."[26] But to arrive at this language we must insert a phrase, viz., "if not of mine own will, *woe is me*, for I have a stewardship entrusted to me." It is unnecessary to make this addition, since interpretation (1) is so smooth and easy. Since we find it difficult to interpret this phrase in the light of (2), we reject it in favor of (1).

Look at each of the last two phrases of verse 17 individually. "If against my will" (i.e., 'I do not preach voluntarily') indicates Paul was under divine obligation to preach (Acts 9:15, 22:14,21, 26:16; Galatians 1:6). He did not enter the ministry under his own volition; he was specially called. He makes special reference to the commission he received on the Damascus Road (Acts 26:16-18). Having been called to the ministry by Christ, he dared not disobey. (Note, this is not saying that he was reluctant to preach.) "I have a stewardship entrusted to me" describes his present position as being that of a steward, who, when he has done all that he could, has no more than discharged his obligations, and so has no title to a reward (cf. Luke 17:10).[27] Lenski offers a good explanation of the "stewardship" entrusted to Paul:

> Paul did not first become a follower of Christ and then, like the other apostles, of his own volition accept the Lord's call and commission to the apostleship. Paul's case was just the reverse. In Paul's case, the Lord himself decided the whole matter without in any way first asking Paul's consent.

---

[25] It should be taken into account that this passage has served as one of the proof texts for 'works of supererogation' in the Roman Catholic church. The terms "reward" in this phrase and "stewardship" in the next were taken together as though by voluntarily preaching after the compulsion of the Damascus Road, Paul thereby had a reward he could dispense.

[26] Lipscomb, *op. cit.*, p.133.

[27] This verse must not to be permitted to be pressed into service to defend any dispensational theory. Dispensationalists have used this verse to give 'Scriptural verification' to their theory because the KJV translation of *oikonomian* at this point is "a dispensation of the gospel" (cp. notes at 4:1). Appealing to the KJV, some have argued that a special type of message had been given to Paul ("hidden-mystery kingdom") to preach during this church age while the kingdom is in postponement. (This commentator rejects modern pre-millennialism, *aka* modern dispensationalism, which has the church as an afterthought in the mind of God, unforeseen in the Old Testament Scriptures.) Nor does this passage prove there have been seven dispensations – i.e., seven different ages, marked by seven different ways that God has dealt with men. (For a listing of the seven supposed ages, see *Scofield Reference Bible*, page 5, at Genesis 1:28.) We have regularly divided Bible history into three dispensations, Patriarchal, Mosaic, and Christian.

In order to understand Paul's statement we should remember that "stewards" (4:1,2) were slaves, whose masters simply gave certain goods or property into their hands to be administered in trust. The entire matter rested on the decision of the master to whom the slave in question belonged. The master did not ask, "Will you take this stewardship?" He only gave the order, "Take it!" The slave took it – woe to him if he was obstinate and refused. And when a slave, who had nothing to say in the matter, was put in charge of such a trust, he had no claim to wages for administering his trust. Being only a slave and belonging bodily to his master, that master could and did use him as he saw fit. And that was the end of the matter.

All this throws light on the parable of the Talents and on that of the Pounds in which masters make their slaves stewards by simply issuing orders to that effect. We even have two examples of slaves who refused to act as stewards, and from the punishment meted out to them we may gather what Paul means when he says "Woe to me, if I refuse to act." The incident in the parables where the master rewards his faithful slaves when the accounting is finally made at the close of their stewardship is simply an astounding exception, an example of the magnificent generosity of this Master who far excels all other slave masters.

This is Paul's case exactly. When Jesus acquired him as a slave while he was on the road to Damascus, right then and there Jesus issued his order and told his slave for what work he had decided to use him. Paul received the order right there to act as a "steward" for his new Master – Jesus said, "I have appeared to you to make you a minister and a witness ... " Acts 26:16. Placed into the apostleship and the work of preaching in this fashion, Paul has no credit due him, no pay of any kind, no reward. When then, as in 2 Timothy 4:8, he speaks of the crown that is laid up for him, which already now makes his eyes shine, this reward must, as in the parables, be referred to the astounding magnanimity of his divine Master.

Yet Paul is determined to have credit, pay, and cause to glory after all, slave though he is and therefore debarred from earning pay. He has not been in the company of his heavenly Master in vain, from his Master's magnanimity he has learned also to be magnanimous.[28]

9:18 -- *What then is my reward? That, when I preach the gospel, I may offer the gospel without charge, so as not to make full use of my right in the gospel.*

What then is my reward? That, when I preach the gospel, I may offer the gospel without charge -- There are two ways of interpreting this verse. (1) According to one, the question mark is moved to the end of the verse. The sense of the verse then becomes, 'What is my reward for preaching the gospel without pay?' (With the question mark moved to the end of the verse, the verse reads, "What then is my reward, that in preaching the gospel, I may offer the gospel without charge, that I use not to the full my power in the gospel?") And the answer to the question comes in verse 19 – his reward was the winning

---

[28] Lenski, *op. cit.*, pp.371-72.

of a multitude of souls. By foregoing the pay to which he was entitled, by preaching without pay, he had a freer access to men. (2) According to the other interpretation, we punctuate as does the ASV, NASB, RSV. The question mark is placed at the end of the first phrase, "What then is my reward?" The sense of the verse (first phrase) is, 'What pay (reward) do I get, since I must preach (stewardship)?' And the answer appears in the latter part of verse 18, 'My reward is the pleasure and satisfaction of being a preacher who gives the gospel free of charge, not using to the full a preacher's right to maintenance.' Paul's "without charge" is aptly chosen. We might speak of pay or salary, but that implies payment for services rendered. Providing the preacher with funds for his livelihood is not precisely 'wages.' We prefer to speak of 'support,' for that word implies the church is involved in the preacher's ministry too, enabling him to be free from worldly concerns so that he may carry on his ministry.

So as not to make full use of my right in the gospel -- If Paul had used to the full his rights,[29] he would have demanded maintenance everywhere he preached.

> Even as a slave-steward, Paul has the right to be fed, clothed, etc., while he is administering his Master's trust: the Master himself so ordained. Paul could exercise that right in the course of his work. It would not be wrong for him to do so. Then, he would, however, be like every other slave-steward with no claim on credit whatever. By foregoing his right as a steward, by making the gospel available wholly without charge to the church, Paul establishes a claim. He thereby imitates his great Master in a small way. Freely He dispenses His magnificent gifts to His servants, ten cities to one, five cities to another, so that His glory shines forth forever. Paul dispenses the gospel by his ministry, founds and builds up one congregation after another, asks absolutely no return so that his generosity stands forth to his credit and calls for recognition, if not on the part of men, then at least on the part of the Lord.[30]

9:19 -- *For though I am free from all* **men***, I have made myself a slave to all, so that I may win more.*

For though I am free from all *men* -- As pointed out in verse 18, the interpretation of verse 19 depends on the punctuation of verse 18. If all of verse 18 is a question, then verse 19 is the answer to that question. If verse 18 is both the question ("What then is my reward?") and the answer to that question, then beginning in verse 19 Paul gives further examples (in addition to waiving his right to financial support) of how he waived rights and privileges in order to save others and help spread the gospel.[31] If verse 19 begins a

---

[29] On "make full use" (*katachraomai*) see note at 7:31. "Right" is *exousia*, and Paul is saying he did not make full use of his 'rights.' It is part of his presentation that he voluntarily waived some of his rights because he loved; his behavior thus is a model for the Corinthians to follow.

[30] Lenski, *op. cit.*, p. 373.

[31] In the summary of chapter 9 offered at the very first of the comments on this chapter, we have offered the suggestion that verses 19-22 speak to the topic of Paul's lifestyle – before he came to Corinth, a lifestyle he continued while there, and since he left their town. He constantly took into account what would be best for the other person, lest they be caused to stumble. He waived rights because he loved.

further list of rights waived, "I am free from all men"[32] means 'Though none had any claim on me because they provided my financial livelihood; yet I reduced myself to the condition of a servant. Not only did I serve all men without requiring even maintenance from them, I also complied with their prejudices and customs in all cases where I could without violating God's will.' Paul adds this explanation which reveals to us the full extent of his surrender of his rights. He goes far beyond merely yielding his right to support. He also tells us he yields in the interest of the gospel so as to win as many souls as possible to the salvation available in Jesus Christ.

I have made myself a slave to all -- He voluntarily relinquished his freedom,[33] and many of the 'rights' that freedom guaranteed. Remember, Paul has been urging the Corinthians not to abuse their liberty in Christ just because they had 'rights.' He continues to call attention to his own practice as an example. Paul had liberty, but there is no liberty apart from Christian love. Paul was not going to abuse his liberty if demanding his rights would cause another to stumble. In the verses following are additional examples of 'rights' he waived as he made himself "a slave to all."

That I might win the more -- "Win" would be equal to 'save' – to gain by conversion. The saving of a soul was ever considered by Paul to be part of his reward (1 Thessalonians 2:19,20). This purpose clause shows that Paul was moved by love. This is the thing he wants the Corinthians to put into their actions – to love, and not just act on cold knowledge. "The more" ('the greater number') might include the idea that Paul wanted to win a greater number of converts than was gained by any other apostle. But more likely it means he would gain a greater number than he could have gained had he used his rights as an apostle. There was an evangelistic principle behind his behavior. He took care to avoid putting any unnecessary obstacles in the way that might hinder men from becoming believers in Jesus in the first place, or that might hinder them from staying faithful to Jesus after they had embraced the gospel.

To recap this difficult section (verses 17-20):

> Verse 17 -- If I did preach the gospel voluntarily, I could talk about wages. But as a matter of fact, I do not preach voluntarily. I preach because I must. It is a stewardship entrusted to me.

> Verse 18 -- Since I must preach, and since I choose to preach without demanding maintenance, what is my reward (you ask)?

---

[32] Compare notes at 9:1, "Am I not free?"

[33] Some modern translations treat this as a present tense. But Paul is not stating simply his *modus operandi* in the present; rather, he is explaining his actions in the past when he evangelized in the city of Corinth.

Verse 19 -- My reward is in the winning of a multitude of souls.

Verse 20 -- In fact, I do much more than just deny my right to support if it will lead men to salvation. I become all things to all men, that I might gain them.

9:20 -- *To the Jews I became as a Jew, so that I might win Jews; to those who are under the Law, as under the Law though not being myself under the Law, so that I might win those who are under the Law;*

And to the Jews I became as a Jew, that I might win Jews -- Paul now gives concrete examples of places he voluntarily waived his 'rights' (thus, becoming "a slave to all"). He is the slave of Christ, and becomes a slave to others in order, like a faithful steward, to make gains for his Master. Paul shows how he "made himself a slave to all" by enumerating the various parties to whose weaknesses and customs he had conformed in order to win them to Christ. Included among the "more" (verse 19) he hopes to win are Jews (verse 20a), classic Hebrews (verse 20b), Gentiles (verse 21), and "weak" people (verse 22). When Paul was with Jewish people, he "became as a Jew." That is, he complied with the rites, customs, and prejudices of Pharisaic Judaism as far as he could with a good conscience. He did not needlessly offend them. He did not attack and oppose their views when there was no danger that his conduct should be mistaken. Some examples from the history given in Acts of 'becoming as a Jew' could include: (1) He circumcised Timothy, Acts 12:3. (2) He took a vow, during which he let his hair grow long, Acts 18:18. (3) He paid for the sacrifice Jewish folk offered in the temple, Acts 21:21-26. (4) He called himself "a Pharisee, the son of a Pharisee," Acts 23:6,7. To "win them" means to lead them to become Christians, to win them to Christ.

To those who are under the Law, as under the Law -- How shall we explain the distinction between "Jew" and "those who are under the Law"? Some suppose the phrase "those ... under the Law" distinguishes a proselyte (who would be living by the Law) from an ethnic descendant of Israel. Perhaps a better explanation would be that there was a distinction between classic Mosaism and Palestinian/Diaspora/Pharisaic Judaism. Beginning at the time of the Old Testament captivities, much of what Moses taught began to be 'interpreted' or ignored because of the new and changing situations the people faced. Sacrifice at the temple, especially, was hard during the times when no temple was standing and the people themselves were captives in a foreign land. The traditions of the elders came to be recognized as equally authoritative to the commands given by Moses, and these traditions often flatly contradicted what Moses wrote. (At least that is what is implied by Jesus at Matthew 15:6ff, "You have made the Law void by your traditions.") Matthew 23 is also an indictment of the Pharisees (who were the forefathers of Palestinian/Diaspora Judaism) because they had "neglected the weightier provisions of the Law" while scrupulously keeping their own traditions. If 1 Corinthians 9:20 reflects this distinction, Paul is saying, 'I can live like a Law-keeping Jew of the old school, or I can live like a Diaspora Jew if it means I might have a chance to win them to Christ.' "Law" (even though Paul uses anarthrous *nomos*) is a reference to the Law of Moses. "It should be carefully observed that Paul is here describing the *innocent* concessions and compliances which arise from the harmless and generous condescension of a loving spirit. He never sank into the fear of man, such as made Peter unfaithful to his real principles at Antioch. He did not allow men to form from his conduct any mistaken inference as to his essential beliefs" (Farrar, *op. cit.*, p.289). Paul's actions in Acts 21 would be an example of his conforming to the practices taught in the Law in order that he might be enabled to approach them under the Law with greater acceptability. Paul was willing to accommodate himself as far as possible to win someone to Christ (Galatians 1:10). He would deny himself rights and privileges which were legally his to enjoy, rather than cause someone to stumble.

Though not being myself under the Law[34] -- This is but one of numerous New Testament verses which indicate the temporary nature of the Mosaic Law, and the fact that the Old Covenant has been abrogated and replaced, since Calvary, with a better covenant (see Galatians 2:19, 3:13-19; Romans 7:1-3; 1 Timothy 1:9-11; Hebrews 7-10). Paul tells us he is not under the Law of Moses because no Christians are. The Law is a dead ordinance now that the gospel has come.

That I might win those who are under the Law -- As it did in verse 19, to "win them" means to lead them to become Christians, win them to Christ.

9:21 -- *to those who are without law, as without law, though not being without the law of God but under the law of Christ, so that I might win those who are without law.*

To those who are without law -- Those "without law" are the Gentiles (Romans 2:12). It does not mean 'lawless.' It speaks of people not bound by the Law of Moses referenced in the previous verse.[35] Of course, people who did not have the Law of Moses to guide them were not completely without any revelation from God. Even people living under patriarchal rules have "laws" revealed by God – revealed in the distant past and handed down from generation to generation by word of mouth.

As without law -- Paul voluntarily conformed to Gentile practices when he was among Gentiles. He disregarded Jewish customs and dietary rules when among the Gentiles. He carefully avoided anything that might needlessly arouse their antagonism or make them hostile to a hearing of the Gospel. By way of illustration, think of the changes from western customs a missionary to Japan must make, if he wishes a hearing for the Gospel from the Japanese. To Western eyes, Japan seems a topsy-turvy land, someone has said:

> Entering a house, you take off your shoes, not your hat.
> You scrub yourself outside the bathtub, not in it.

---

[34] In passing, it should be noted that the KJV does not have this phrase. That is because the phrase is not found in the Byzantine manuscripts which formed the text represented in the KJV. This phrase is omitted by D³, K, Copt., Eth., KJV. This phrase is included by *Aleph*, B, C, D, E, F, G, P, Vulg., Arm., ASV, NASB, and the manuscript evidence is in favor of its integrity. The omission has probably occurred due to a homoioleleuton, *nomon* to *nomon*. A scribe accidentally omitted one of the four occurrences of *hupo nomon* that occur in this verse.

[35] The translators of the NASB, in this commentator's opinion, made a mistake when they left "law" uncapitalized in this verse, after using capital "L" (Law) four times in the previous verse. (The NASB consistently uses "Law" when the translators thought the reference was to the Law of Moses.)

Japanese mourners wear white.
"Footnotes" are printed at the top of the page.
Few gardens have flowers.
Wine is heated, but fish is served raw.
Cats have no tails.
Women help men off with *their* coats.

The island-bound Japanese, insulated from the rest of the world for centuries, have developed a culture distinctly their own (see R.B. Peery, *The Gist of Japan*, 1897). The changes a Westerner deliberately and willingly makes lest he offend the Japanese host would be similar to the changes Paul made when visiting in a Gentile's house.

Though not being without the law of God, but under the law of Christ -- Paul was not a person who had no rules or laws by which to live. When working among the Gentiles, Paul did not observe the Law of Moses, but He did obey the laws of Christ. He did not regard himself as being freed from an obligation to obey God merely because he was no longer under the Law of Moses. We cannot understand what Paul is here affirming unless we recognize that with the death of Christ the age of the Law of Moses came to an end (Galatians 3:19-4:7). Mosaic Scriptures may still be profitable for followers of Jesus (2 Timothy 3:16), but only by way of example, and only when it is recognized that Christ is the 'goal' toward which the Law pointed (Romans 10:4). Paul is not leaving room to have it supposed for a moment that he disregarded all law, like a libertine.[36] Paul was under law to Christ: he obeyed all His commands, followed His instructions, sought His honor, yielded to His will. The law of God which Paul lived by was found in Jesus' explicit teachings. (God has spoken to these last days through His Son, Hebrews 1:1,2.[37])

That I might win those who are without law -- As it did in verses 19 and 20, to "win those" means to lead them to become Christians, win them to Christ.

9:22 -- *To the weak I became weak, that I might win the weak; I have become all things to all men, so that I may by all means save some.*

To the weak -- "Weak" might be used as it is in Romans 5:6, of people who are helpless to save themselves. "Weak" might be used as it was in 1 Corinthians 1:27, of people who were powerless in society. "Weak" might be used as it was in 8:9-12, of those who did

---

[36] Barnes, *op. cit.*, p.167. The language of Paul was later distorted. In the Clementine writings (in the spurious letter of Peter to James) Paul is labeled "the lawless one." But to the honest reader, common sense indicates there is no basis for a claim of antinomianism or libertinism in this verse.

[37] Care must be exercised here lest "law of Christ" be used to justify "legalism" in the Christian Churches and Churches of Christ. "Legalism," where men make up rules based on this or that verse of Scripture and demand all members of the congregation behave in a uniform way, is not taught in Scripture. Nor is it compatible with 1 Corinthians 8-10 or Romans 14-15, among other passages, which do teach that believers have a liberty in Christ, and do teach that there is a unity (harmony) expected in the church, but not absolute uniformity in all practices and convictions. There are things in the realm of liberty which each believer is free to embrace or not, as he understands Christ's will to teach.

not have the moral courage to stand for their convictions, and whose consciences might be caused to stumble. It must be remembered, however, that the "weak" in this verse seem not yet to be "brothers" (as they are in 8:9ff), for Paul hopes to "win" them (i.e., convert them). Nevertheless, it would be possible for unconverted people to be "weak," that is, not have the moral courage to stand for their convictions, just as it is possible for Christians to be "weak." It was in chapter 8:9-12 we last had the word "weak." This whole discussion since (which to some seems to be a long digression) has had this point – to underline the loving concern a man should have for the weak, and the need for the strong to practice self-control so that the weak will not be hurt by the example or behavior of the strong. It was the law of love, as Paul himself followed it, that he would enforce on the Corinthians with regard to eating idol-meats.

I became weak, that I might win the weak -- All of Paul's writings reflect this spirit of selflessness and a willingness to give up 'rights' that freedom in Christ granted to him. "We who are strong ought to bear the weaknesses of those who are without strength, and not to please ourselves," he said to the Romans (15:1). See also 1 Corinthians 8:7; Romans 14:1; 1 Thessalonians 5:14; Acts 20:35. When he had to deal with the over-scrupulous, he sympathized with their scruples, abstaining from things which seemed to them (but not to him) to be wrong. Though he had a freedom in Christ to choose several different courses of action (anyone of which, in itself, would be right) and to behave differently from the present company and what their customs or scruples called for, he refrained from just doing as he personally pleased. Rather, when in other people's presence, Paul waived his own freedom and attempted to act (in all areas of things indifferent) as they would expect men to act. 'I complied with their customs. I conformed to them in my dress, habits. I abstained from food which *they* deemed it their duty to abstain from,' Paul is saying. Once more he emphasizes the reason he was determined to so live as not to offend needlessly: it was "that I might win the weak." Paul wants these people to be won to Christ, to have Calvary cover their sins, and to see their lives begin to conform to Christ's standards and expectations. It is difficult to win people who have been offended by our behavior before we ever began to talk to them about a commitment of their lives to the Jesus we claim to serve. Paul's example should teach us not to make it the main business of life to gratify ourselves; it should teach us that loving men as we should means we do not needlessly offend the feelings of others. If truth offends men, we cannot help it. But in matters of ceremony, dress, habits, customs, we should be willing to conform to them, as far as can be done, that their souls may be saved.

I have become all things to all men -- He repeats the same principle in 10:33, "I also please all men in all things, not seeking my own profit, but the *profit* of the many, that they may be saved." "All things" have some implied limitations: (1) By truth as taught by Jesus. Paul did not disobey Jesus' express commands as he became all things to all men. A man is not "free" to disobey express commands or prohibitions from God. (2) "All things" are the morally indifferent things, where freedom (liberty) in Christ is the rule determining behavior.[38] "I have become" is a perfect tense verb. This change from an aorist tense verb to a perfect tense is significant; this is the permanent result of his past action. Ever since his conversion to Christ, this has been the rule by which Paul decided his behavior in the realm of Christian liberty. Instead of simply acting selfishly, Paul took into account what was spiritually best for the other person and then behaved accordingly. This does not mean Paul's conduct was unprincipled. On occasion he could be very stubborn in following courses of action, even despite strong opposition. But where no principle was at stake he was prepared to go to extreme lengths to meet people. Personal considerations are totally submerged in his great aim to "by all means save some."

That I may by all means save some -- This explanation of the motive of his self-denial was repeated, lest any should accuse him of men-pleasing, as some of his Galatian opponents had done (Galatians 1:10). There are two things to be carefully observed in all cases of concession to the opinions and practices of others: (1) The point conceded must be a matter of indifference, i.e., a matter in the realm of Christian liberty. Paul never yielded in the smallest measure to anything that was in itself wrong. In this his conduct was directly the opposite of those who accommodate themselves to the sins of men, or to the superstitious observances of false religions. His accommodation has no limit excepting the one just stated, that he is "under the law of Christ." (2) The concession must not involve the admission that what is really indifferent is a matter of moral obligation. Paul's conduct in relation to Timothy and Titus shows the principle on which he acted. The former he circumcised because it was regarded as a concession. But the latter he refused to circumcise because it was being demanded as a matter of necessity. Peter in Galatians 2:11ff is an example of the wrong application of the principle. He sacrificed a Christian principle to keep himself from Jewish criticism. "Save" means 'win them over to Christ' as in 1 Corinthians 7:16 and earlier in this chapter. Paul is not trying to win the potential converts to himself, as his enemies might suggest. He is trying to win them to Christ. Although he is not less than an apostle, he knows that he will be able to save only "some." This relieves some of the hurt when we find that we who are less than apostles can also save only "some."

---

[38] This passage has sometimes been pressed into service to enforce certain social taboos among Christians. That is not the thrust of this passage, for it deals with folk who are yet to be won to Christ.

The passage has also been pressed into service to prove Christians must 'accommodate' the *message* to the language and perspectives of the recipients. Let it be noted that however much need there is to put the gospel in terms listeners can understand, this passage does *not* directly speak to that issue. This passage has to do with how one *lives* or *behaves* among those whom he wishes to evangelize. Just underneath the surface of this whole issue is the matter missionaries and theologians call 'contextualization.' An earlier generation of missionaries followed the principle of forming indigenous churches. They recognized that general and special revelation have been given by God, and that men are not free to change the message. Contextualization may be neo-liberal or neo-orthodox, and may be enamored with social science criticism. It is perfectly willing to change the 'forms' of the message in order to preserve its 'content.' Yet Christianity is not simply a cultural religion – in its origins, it was divinely revealed. If it were simply cultural, modern missionaries might be free to change it to match whatever new culture they try to enter. Or, if Christianity is simply cultural, then likely the call of the Bangkok '73 World Missionary Conference for a moratorium on sending missionaries to other ethnic groups with their diverse cultures should be heeded. But is not all this poor contextualization if it requires us to ignore Jesus' Great Commission or expects Christians to embrace and participate in cultural activities that are anti-Christian (like going to a feast in the idol's temple)?

9:23 – *And I do all things for the sake of the gospel, so that I may become a fellow partaker of it.*

And I do all things -- Beginning here, Paul calls attention (verses 23-27) to a second reason why he continued to exercise careful self-control in those areas where he had 'rights.' Up to this point all the purpose clauses reveal only Paul's desire to gain and save others. Now we learn that he so acts that he may also save himself. 'True, my motive is that others may be saved. But I'm also vitally interested in my own salvation! That's why I carefully follow Christ's teaching on this matter.'

For the sake of the gospel -- That it may be advanced, and may be successful; or, because the gospel is so precious to him. There is a manuscript variation here. Perhaps the better reading is, "I do all things for ..." rather than "I do this for ..." (KJV). The *all things* does not refer to just the above examples of waiving his 'rights.' Rather, this is Paul's manner of life. 'All things which I do, I do for the sake of the gospel.' Paul's whole conduct was determined by the gospel. That was what mattered: the gospel, not the preacher.

That I may become a fellow partaker of it -- The KJV reads, "that I might be a fellow-partaker with you." The "you" (of the KJV) does not appear in the Greek. The original reads, "a fellow partaker of it." Paul became all things to all men, waiving his rights because he loved, that he might be a partaker of the blessings of the gospel himself. This is the new point he introduces. Up to this point, Paul has been speaking of his self-denial for the sake of others; here he begins to speak of self-denial for his own sake, that he might be saved. Yet even here he thinks of others, for his word ("fellow partaker") stresses the thought of partnership. 'All this variety (assuming all kinds of characters) I practice for one and the same reason, that I may not keep the gospel to myself but share its blessings with others.' Salvation is offered by the gospel to all, and Paul must strive to be one of those who receive it. To some, this thought will certainly seem strange – that Paul would lose his own part in the gospel if he did not follow this lifestyle which called for the voluntary waiving of his rights. Many Christians think that they may choose their own way, do individualistically as they please in these matters of Christian liberty, and care more for their own personal interests than for the spiritual interests of men. They are sure that *they* will be saved no matter how they decide to exercise their liberty. Paul explains (verses 24-27) that he might, indeed, preach the gospel and yet lose his own personal participation in the benefits of that gospel if he failed to practice careful self-control.

9:24 -- *Do you not know that those who run in a race all run, but **only** one receives the prize? Run in such a way that you may win.*

Do you not know -- Of course, the Corinthians know all about this. The question expects an affirmative answer.[39] Since the days of Alexander the Great, athletic contests held in the public stadia had become popular in the entire Hellenic world. Games were even held regularly at Corinth. Crowds of people came to these athletic fields and watched the contests, much as the crowds now throng to the great college or professional football games

---

[39] It is the same expression used at 9:13.

and to major league baseball games. Because people were familiar with the games, Paul often (as he does here) used imagery drawn from the games to illustrate spiritual points.

That those who run in a race all run -- Every runner who lines up at the starting blocks runs with an all-out effort to win. They have each given up 'rights' while in training, even though they know only one will win a prize. How much more should Christians, who can all win in the 'race of life,' be willing to give up their 'rights' if that is what it takes to win? Throughout the chapter, Paul's object had been to show that in waiving his right to support for preaching, he had done it, not because he was conscious that he had no claim to it, but because by waiving his right he could better advance the salvation of men and the furtherance of the gospel. Paul denied himself. He voluntarily submitted to great privations. Now he points out the fact that athletes in the games did the same thing; that is, they denied themselves. And if they have done it for objects so comparatively unimportant as the attainment of an *earthly* garland, assuredly it was proper for him (and for them) to give up their 'rights' in order to obtain a crown which should never fade away.

The thought of a possible failure (verse 23), where failure would be so disastrous, suggests an exhortation to great exertion, as illustrated by the practice of runners and boxers in the Isthmian games. "In a race" literally is 'in the stadium.' Greek racing tracks were about 606 feet per lap. Greece had four famous stadiums in which games were held. (1) *Pythian (Delphic).* These were celebrated every four years at Delphi, in Phocis, at the foot of Mt. Parnassus, where was also the site of the celebrated Delphic Oracle. These games attracted people from all over Greece and from distant lands. (2) *Isthmian (Corinthian).* These were celebrated in the narrow part of the Isthmus of Corinth, to the north of the city. There are still today traces of the stadium where the Isthmian games were held.[40] All kinds of sports – racing (foot, horse, chariot), wrestling, boxing, leaping, throwing the quoit (discus), throwing the javelin, etc. – were involved. These games were held every three years (Plummer, *op. cit.*, p.194). Thousands of competitors and visitors from all over the empire came to the games. They stayed in tents before permanent facilities were erected in the 2nd century AD to house them. (3) *Nemean.* These were celebrated at Nemaea, a town of Argolis just a few miles south of Corinth. They were instituted by the Argives (men from the Achean city of Argos) in honor of Archemorus, who died by the bite of a serpent. These games had died out, but were renewed by Hercules. They were celebrated every third (or some say every fifth) year. (4) *Olympic.* These were celebrated in Olympia every fourth year and attended by people from all of Greece and from distant countries. It thus happened that in one or more of these places there were games celebrated every year, to which no small part of the inhabitants of Greece were attracted. The apostle probably had reference to the Isthmian games, celebrated in the vicinity of Corinth. Yet his illustration could apply to any of them. A map showing the location of these places makes it easy to understand why the Corinthians were familiar with the games:

---

[40] Archaeology has helped fill in our knowledge about the Isthmian games, held about 14 kilometers from Corinth. See O. Broneer, "The Apostle Paul and the Isthmian Games," *Biblical Archaeologist* 25 (1962), p.2-31, and Jerome Murphy-O'Connor, *Corinth*, p.14-17.

But *only* one receives the prize? -- "Prize" translates *brabeion* (Latin *bravium*, from whence comes our 'Bravo!'). The prize consisted of a wreath, made of pine branches at the Isthmian games, apple branches at Delphi, olive branches at Olympia, parsley at Nemea. These prize-wreaths were coveted honors throughout the whole Greek world. The prize to Christians is not always the same. God gives to each according as He pleases.

Run in such a way that you may win -- In this context, "run" means "be ready to voluntarily waive rights because you love!" The idea is this: as the runners practice careful self-control to be in shape to win the race and to obtain the prize, so should we Christians. Every man who runs in the race is endeavoring to be the one who shall receive the winner's prize. Everyone faithfully running the race of life will attain the crown, but only if he runs according to the rules (which include waiving rights for others' benefit).

9:25 -- *Everyone who competes in the games exercises self-control in all things. They then do it to receive a perishable wreath, but we an imperishable.*

And everyone who competes in the games exercises self-control in all things -- "Competes in the games" is 'agonizes' (*ho agōnidzomenos*); that is, is engaged in the strenuous exercise of boxing, running, wrestling. The fact that we can see our word "agony" in the Greek word helps us understand that no half-hearted effort is meant. "Exercises self-control" (*egkrateuetai*) denotes temperance in a positive degree. Not merely 'abstinence,' but vigorous *control* of appetites and passions. While training (which could be a ten-month period of time), the athletes exercised self-control with reference to food, sleep, and hours for practice. They avoided everything that might hurt them and devoted themselves to everything that might help them in their contests. The contestant knew his chances of winning the prize were gone if at any point or on any occasion he relaxed the rigor of the discipline of training. "Self-control" is the point of the illustration. That is exactly what is required before one will be likely to waive his rights because he hopes to win the great prize. In 1 Corinthians 8-10, lack of "self-control" may be exactly what led some Corinthians to insist on their 'right' to eat in the pagan temples. The strenuous self-denial of the athlete in training for his fleeting reward is a rebuke to all half-hearted, flabby Christian attempts to exercise self-control. Notice that the athlete denies himself many lawful pleasures. The Christian must avoid not only definite sin, but anything that hinders his complete effectiveness, even some of his 'rights.'

They then *do it* to receive a perishable wreath -- The prize-wreaths given to the winners were fading garlands. The flowers and branches would soon lose their beauty, and the leaves would wither and fall off. The crown was fading, corruptible. It would soon retain little intrinsic value. Yet we see how eagerly the athletes sought it, how much self-denial they would practice to obtain it. The argument is from the lesser to the greater. If those athletes practice such self-control merely to obtain a slight and fading earthly crown, shall we do less for a heavenly crown of glory, a crown that lasts forever?

But we an imperishable -- Christians are striving for an incorruptible crown, one that is "unfading." Paul takes it for granted that Christians would be self-denying in all things, in order that they might receive an incorruptible crown. If athletes will undergo discipline to win, how much more should we undergo discipline to win the race of life. How foolish to do more self-denial in sports than we do in the Christian life. The difficulty lies in putting this into practice, not in understanding this teaching. It is necessary to make an effort to secure eternal life. The blessings of heaven that shall be bestowed on the righteous are often represented under the image of a crown or diadem (2 Timothy 4:8; James 1:12; 1 Peter 5:4; Revelation 2:10, 3:11, 4:4).[41]

9:26 -- *Therefore I run in such a way, as not without aim; I box in such a way, as not beating the air;*

Therefore I run in such a way, as not without aim -- Paul is now speaking of the Christian race. In his everyday life, both before he came to Corinth, while he was there, and since, Paul has the same goal in mind – winning the imperishable wreath. From the second person plural with which Paul bids the Corinthians run to win the prize, he advances to the first person singular by telling what he for his part determines to do. (*Egō toinun*

---

[41] On the question of degrees of reward in heaven, see notes at 3:8. George Mark Elliott thought the degree might be a different type of service, or a greater degree of enjoyment. He cautioned that care must be taken in presenting this idea of degrees of reward, since some will think more of what they get, rather than thinking about degrees of service for others and for the Lord. Still, it seems that degrees of reward are taught in the New Testament.

would better be translated, 'I, for my part, so run,' rather than "therefore.") The word *adēlōs*, "not without aim," appears nowhere else in the New Testament. (1) Some suppose it means 'no fixed goal or finish line,' that as he ran Paul did not know the goal to which he ran. (A man might be able to run 100 meters in ten seconds flat; but if he did not know in what direction to run, his ability would be of little value.) However, this interpretation seems incorrect; Paul did not run haphazardly. He knew where the finish line was. He knew where the goal was. (2) Others translate this, 'as not out of view,' i.e., Paul regarded himself as being watched, always in view of the Judge, the Lord Jesus Christ, or always in view of those he was trying to win to Christ. Hence, he adjusted his behavior when among those potential converts (verse 19-22). How does a person live who has an 'aim' or a 'fixed goal' or who knows he 'is being watched'? The application of Paul's teaching is that they would live differently than the Corinthians who insisted on their 'rights' to go to the idol's temple! The apostle has appealed to his own conduct as an illustration of the lesson he is teaching, and by it he reminds his readers that the whole of this chapter has been a vindication of his own self-denial. Although his enemies have made his conduct an argument against him, Paul has explained the real reason for his conduct.

I box in such a way, as not beating the air -- In his usual manner, Paul broadens the illustration by adding the figure of boxing to that of the foot race. The reference is to the boxers of the Grecian games, where boxing was one of the sports in the pentathlon. Ancient boxers did not used padded gloves as do today's boxers. They wore lead-studded leather bands on their knuckles. The winner of the match could claim the beaten man as his slave for life, if the beaten man survived the fight! Some have supposed the reference in "not beating the air" is to shadow boxing. Others see a reference to missing the opponent with the intended blow, and so just striking the air. Neither of these seem to quite catch the point, in this commentator's opinion. The point of the illustration seems to be to highlight the purposefulness of his behavior. Paul's life is purpose-oriented. He had a definite target in mind. Achieving this purpose required self-control. Paul has said he intends to be a "fellow-partaker" of the gospel. Knowing that receiving the imperishable prize requires self-control, Paul is going to practice self-control.

9:27 -- *but I buffet my body and make it my slave, so that, after I have preached to others, I myself will not be disqualified.*

But I buffet my body -- The word occurs only here and in Luke 18:5, "Lest by her continual coming she *wear* me out." The word means properly, 'to strike under the eye' to render that part black and blue. Paul says, 'I give myself a black eye.' Paul practiced rigid self-denial and self-control so that all the blessings of the gospel might be given to him. He did not want to miss the imperishable wreath. By implication, when Paul says he "buffets (controls) his body," he is driving home the truth that his readers should do likewise. This is the very opposite of insisting on one's rights because the body would like to have a little meat. We now learn who Paul's opponent is; namely, his own body, with its desires, which, when stirred up and excited by temptations from the devil, are so ready to militate against his high calling.[42] The verb is present tense. Every time the body needs a 'knock out' of self-control, Paul applies the 'punch.'[43] This is how he makes his body a "slave."

And make it my slave -- The word means to reduce to servitude, or slavery, to totally subdue, to conquer, to reduce to bondage. 'I bruise my body, and lead it about as a slave.' The verb is present tense: Paul makes and keeps his body a slave. Paul was determined to be master of his body, not to have his body master him. He brought all the desires of his body under subjection. Do the Corinthians, insisting on their rights, need to hear this very emphasis about self-control? We think so. The Corinthians seemed to forget their need to practice self-control when they followed their desires to sit at meat in the idol's temple.

The reason he buffets his "body" is because that is where the devil stirs up desires, which if indulged in would lead to self-centered behavior. It is difficult to control the thoughts and the passions. The devil knows this and that is exactly where he attacks the Christian. The devil has the ability to plant evil thoughts in the mind and to stir up the desires of the body. To bring our thoughts and behavior into subjection to the will of God is the triumph of the Spirit; by constant prayer and watchfulness it can be done. By devotion to the Lord and a thoughtful commitment to holiness, the thoughts that fill the heart can be brought into subjection to the will of Christ. The heart can be so trained that the thoughts that are permitted to remain there will be of God, of our duties and obligations to Him, and of the high and exalted privileges and blessings that are bestowed on us as His children. This state is gained only by the constant study of God's Word, a drinking into the Spirit, a cultivation of the devotional feelings, and a constant effort to conform the life to the will of God.[44]

Lest possibly, after I have preached to others, I myself should be disqualified -- It has long been emphasized that this verse is difficult to harmonize with the 'once saved, always saved' doctrine. Paul knew that if he was not faithful unto death, including the practice of careful self-control, there was no hope for him. His salvation could be forfeited. The

---

[42] Care must be exercised as this passage is explained. Some have supposed that men have inherited a sinful nature from Adam, and that the seat of that depravity is in the fleshly body. Flesh is not intrinsically evil. One would have to hold metaphysical dualism to teach this. The body and sin are never equated, even in Romans 7. The body may be a tool or instrument the devil uses, but the body is not innately evil. What men have inherited from Adam is a dying body, dying physically – not inherited total depravity in the moral realm. The body may be corrupted with sin and disease, but there is nothing inherently evil in the body.

[43] This is figurative language. Paul did not mean for men to bruise their bodies like the flagellants and ascetics of the Middle Ages did, who found justification for their practice in this very text. Colossians 2:23 should have guarded against taking the passage literally. How Paul bruised his body may be seen in 2 Corinthians 6:4,5; Colossians 3:5; and Romans 8:13.

[44] Some of the above thoughts are paraphrased from Lipscomb, *op. cit.*, p.141.

word for "preached" is "herald" (*kērux*), a term applied to, among others, those who announced the rules of the ancient athletic contest. The Christian preacher ('herald') not only announces the rules, but plays in the game as well. Paul understood that he must not only preach the gospel, he must live the gospel. "Disqualified" (*adokimos*) means "rejected" (ASV) or "castaway" (KJV). The word is a metaphor derived from the testing of metals, and the casting aside of those which are spurious. It is the same word translated "reprobate" at Romans 1:28 (KJV), "fail the test" at 2 Corinthians 13:5-7, "depraved" at 2 Timothy 3:8, and "worthless" at Titus 1:16.

A hidden agenda behind the comments offered on this word is often the commentator's orientation towards or against 'unconditional eternal security' as taught in Calvinism. (1) Of course, if one can never lose his salvation, then this verse must be translated in such a way as to not contradict that doctrine. So it is made to say that Paul is worried about being "disqualified" from further competition, but not that he would lose his salvation. *In reply*: Manifestly, a future exclusion or disqualification from the contest is not the meaning. Paul represents himself as running and fighting. It is exclusion from the prize that is meant. (2) Some feel the allusion of the Grecian games is carried on through this verse. An examination of the victorious combatants took place after the contest. If it could be proved that they had contended unlawfully or unfairly, they were deprived of the prize and driven with disgrace from the games. (3) Others suppose the allusion to the games continues, and that Paul pictures himself both as "herald" (preacher) and as himself a contestant at the same time (see "fellow partaker" in verse 23). How tragic, therefore, if one who had instructed others as to the rules to be observed for winning the prize should himself be rejected for having transgressed them.

Remember, we are still in the midst of Paul's answer concerning meats sacrificed to idols. In this chapter, he has shown that there are times when a Christian voluntarily waives his 'rights' or freedoms, both to help others and to ensure his own salvation. *Adokimos* is the opposite of verse 23, continuing to be a "fellow partaker" of the gospel. *Adokimos* is the opposite of verse 24, "receiving the prize." *Adokimos* is the opposite of verse 25, 'receiving an imperishable wreath.' Paul is implying, 'Be careful. Practice self-control. Waive some of your "rights" or you may be excluded from the heavenly prize!'

3. Third, the history of Israel should serve as a warning about the dangers of idolatry. 10:1-13.

> *Summary:* We are still in the section introduced at 8:1 concerning meats offered to idols. As chapter 10 begins, Paul is still emphasizing the principles on which questions about Christian liberty are answered. In chapter 8 he has shown that love, not just knowledge, is the ethic that guides a Christian's behavior. In chapter 9 he has shown that there are times when a Christian voluntarily waives his 'rights' or freedoms, both to help others and to ensure his own salvation. Now, in the first paragraph of chapter 10, he will show that the history of Israel is full of examples of the dangers of involvement with idolatry, especially for those who thought they could participate because 'it wouldn't hurt them.' He shows that early enjoyment of high privileges does not guarantee entry into final blessing.

10:1 -- *For I do not want you to be unaware, brethren, that our fathers were all under the cloud and all passed through the sea;*

For -- "For" attaches this paragraph (10:1-13) to chapter 9.[1] This new paragraph explains in more detail what is involved in *adokimos*, being "disqualified," "castaway" (KJV), or "rejected" (ASV).[2] "The fear expressed in 9:27 suggests the case of the Israelites, who, through lack of self-control, lost their promised prize. They presumed on their privileges, and fell into idolatry, which they might have resisted."[3] The Corinthians likewise should beware of misusing their privileges. The Old Testament Jews, at the time of the exodus and wilderness wanderings, had been highly favored by God. But they insisted on frequenting feasts given in honor of idols, and we see what happened to them. They indulged their inordinate desires, became idolaters, were guilty of licentiousness, tempted their leader, murmured, and as a consequence were destroyed by God (Barnes, *op. cit.*, p.177). Failure through lack of self-control is not an imaginary peril; if you lack it, your great spiritual gifts will not save you from disaster (Robertson & Plummer, *op. cit.*, p.199). The risk of being rejected is real, as the case of the Israelites demonstrates. The fact that one may partake of the abundance of divine grace and yet be lost in the end, as Paul feared in regard to himself at 9:27, is verified by clear examples from the Old Testament which exhibit the terrible experiences of the ancient Jews (Lenski, *op. cit.*, p.389).

---

[1] The RSV omits the "For," and Coffman (*op. cit.*, p.145) calls it "deplorable" to simply ignore it. It is suspected the omission of this authentic conjunction is related to the critical bias which would make chapter 10 a fragment from a previous epistle (*ibid.*). The Introductory Studies and notes at 5:9 explored the matter of an alleged "previous letter" and the unity of both 1 & 2 Corinthians. H. Merklein, "Die Einheitlichkeit des ersten Korintherbriefes," *ZeitNTWiss* 75 (3-4, 1984), p.153-183, argues for the unity of 1 Corinthians on the basis of a literary analysis and the coherence of the various "units" usually found in a letter.

[2] The connection of chapter 10 with the preceding is not agreed upon by commentators. Some suppose Paul's purpose here (like his appeal to the Grecian games) is to emphasize the necessity for earnest self-control in order to continue to participate in the benefits of the gospel. Some speak of chapter 9 as being a long digression, and after the long digression, Paul returns to the topic introduced in chapter 8, namely meats offered to idols. But is it right to simply call chapter 9 a digression? Instead of being a digression, does it not give principles by which such questions in the realm of liberty are decided?

[3] Robertson and Plummer, *op. cit.*, p.198.

I do not want you to be unaware, brethren -- "I do not want you to be unaware" is not the same phrase as "do you not know" which we had in 9:13,24. Paul uses this phrase to underline the importance and gravity of a truth he is about to teach (cp. Romans 1:13, 1 Thessalonians 4:13). The ignorance to which he refers is not ignorance of the mere historical facts (with which they were probably familiar), but of the *meaning of the facts*. He did not want them to be unaware of the spiritual significance of the Old Testament events. The sense is, 'I want you to recollect the case and permit their example to influence your conduct.'

That our fathers -- Paul's readers, for the most part, were Gentiles. How could the Old Testament Jews be called their "fathers"? Two answers have been given to this question. (1) Paul is talking as Jew to Jew. Some members of the Corinthian church were Jews, or (2) The patriarchs and the Israelites were the fathers of the Christian church spiritually. The second answer is the best choice. Galatians 3:7-9 and Romans 4:7-13 say that Abraham is the father of the faithful, so "our fathers" need not limit the reference to Jewish Christians only. It would include all Christians by right of spiritual descent.

Were all under the cloud -- Note the emphasis on "all." The word is used five times in the first four verses. This emphasizes the danger of apostasy. All had privileges, but all did not inherit life; some, in fact, apostatized. They all did not exercise self-control. The fact that only two of the 603,550 who departed from Egypt and passed through the Red Sea eventually entered the Promised Land should cause us to be sober. No privilege justifies a sense of security: privilege must be used with fear and trembling. The Greek behind "were under the cloud" implies they *went* under it, and remained under its shadow. The cloud is the "pillar of cloud" (Exodus 13:21,22; 14:19,24) called by later Jews "the Shekinah," and in the LXX the "glory." It was the visible symbol of the divine presence and protection that attended them out of Egypt and afterward. It was one of Israel's special prerogatives to be attended by this "glory" (Romans 9:4). The cloud first appeared to lead Moses and Israel out of Egypt, and went before them by day as a cloud to guide them and by night it became a pillar of fire to give them light. When the Israelites were closely pressed by the Egyptians, the cloud went behind them, and became dark to the Egyptians but light to the Israelites, thus constituting a defense (Exodus 14:20). It covered Mount Sinai (Exodus 24:15-18). It filled the tabernacle when that tent was built and dedicated (Exodus 40:34,35). It guided Israel during their wilderness march (Exodus 40:36-40). In the wilderness, when the Israelites were traveling through the burning desert, it seems to have been expanded over the camp as a covering and a shade (defense) from the intense rays of the burning sun (Numbers 10:34, 14:14). It was a symbol of the divine favor and protection (cp. Isaiah 4:5,6). It was a guide, a shelter, and a defense.[4] Jewish rabbis said "the cloud *encompassed* the camp of the Israelites as a wall encompasses a city, nor could

---

[4] Concerning later appearances of the "glory" – the pillar of cloud and fire – note several passages. In Eli's time, when his grandson was named Ichabod ("the glory has departed"), it was no longer visible over the tabernacle (1 Samuel 4:19ff). When Solomon's temple was dedicated, the glory of the Lord filled that building (2 Chronicles 7:1). It later also filled Ezra's temple (Zechariah 2:8). It was visible at Jesus' birth (Luke 2:8,9), at His transfiguration (Matthew 17:5), and perhaps at His ascension (Acts 1:9). Jesus was called "the Lord of glory," and John could say that during Jesus' earthly ministry the apostles had seen his "glory" (John 1:14). Perhaps it also appears in heaven as heaven now is (Revelation 4:3).

the enemy come near them." The probability is that the cloud extended over the whole camp of Israel, and that to those at a distance it appeared as a pillar.[5]

And all passed through the sea -- The "sea" is the Red Sea.[6] Under the guidance of Moses and by the miraculous intervention of God (Exodus 14:21,22) the Israelites passed through this body of water and escaped the pursuing Egyptians. This was also a proof of the divine protection and favor. The apostle is accumulating evidences of the divine favor to the Israelites, to show that they had many opportunities when they were first delivered from bondage, and yet they still fell into sin when they dallied with idolatry.

10:2 -- *and all were baptized into Moses in the cloud and in the sea;*

And all were baptized ... in the cloud and in the sea -- The sea was on each side, land was on the bottom, and a cloud overhead. Many have seen this "baptism" of Israelites as being somewhat typical of a believer's baptism (more will be said on types in verses 5,6). "The two phrases (in the previous verse), 'were under the cloud' and 'passed through the sea,' seem to pre-figure the double process of *submersion* and *emersion* in baptism. We are not to press the analogy too far in the details, for neither rain from the cloud, nor wave from the Sea wetted the marching sons of Israel" (Evans, *op. cit.*, p.308). However, "what happened in the case of the Israelites is analogous to what happens through baptism in our case ... In the type, the cloud and the sea separate the Israelites from the Egyptians. In baptism we are separated from the world. Secondly, the type shows a unification. Israel was henceforth a separate and sacred body, set apart for God alone. So baptism now unites all the baptized into one body that belongs wholly to God" (Lenski, *op. cit.*, p.391). The word "baptized" (*ebaptisano* in the better attested reading) is in the middle voice. This middle voice has been explained as suggesting that the Israelites accepted baptism for their

---

[5] 20th century liberal theology has tried to explain away the pillar of cloud. In the *Bethany Bible Student* for Oct-Dec. 1951, p.36, we find this naturalistic explanation: "As for the fire and the cloud, it is often noted that a custom of early times was the carrying of braziers of burning wood at the head of marching columns at night, so that the army could easily follow the line of march." How sad that men can with straight face explain away God's involvement with His people.

[6] McGarvey's identification of the site of the crossing of the Red Sea can be studied in *Lands of the Bible* [Cincinnati, OH: Standard Publishing, 1848 reprint], p.438. During his visit to the area, he found a spot that exactly matches the Biblical description. How different is reverent faith based on evidence, and what one reads in the *Bethany Bible Student*, p.34. "Exodus 14:6. THE SEA. Archaeologists have made no discoveries which indicate the spot where the Israelites crossed the water in the Red Sea area. Geological surveys indicate that at one time the Red Sea may have extended along the present route of the Suez Canal to Bardawil Lake. In the time of the Exodus this strip of water connecting the two larger bodies [of water] may have been shallow and swampy, a small edition of the Florida everglades. Many scholars believe the crossing was made over these marshes, and that is why the place of the crossing is called the 'sea of reeds' in the Bible." Or again, "Exodus 14:21. STRONG EAST WIND. The wind struck the [shallow] water at an angle and rolled it up in two directions, so that a path comparatively free of water was made. DRY LAND. Sufficiently cleared of water so a crossing could be made. Not necessarily a 'dry, hard path.' The meaning is that the storm made a channel through the water." It is a telling indictment that no naturalistic explanation is offered for how the Egyptian horses, chariots, and men were covered and drowned in such "shallow water."

own benefit. They voluntarily entered into that affair, and this fact aggravates their apostasy. So it is with us when we become Christians. Baptism is something that is entered into voluntarily. When immersed folk choose to get involved with idolatry, that makes the deviation from the right path even more serious.

We need not suppose, as some have, that "the cloud and the sea" represent the two supposed elements in Christian baptism – the cloud representing the heavenly or the *spiritual* element, and the sea representing the earthly or the *water* element. To make such a comparison would tend to confusion. With what consistency can the cloud and the sea in the same clause typify the one a natural, the other a spiritual element? Nor, in our opinion, is there any ground for saying, 'The baptism of Moses was a baptism of the Spirit (God in the cloud), not of the water (Sea).' The passing under the cloud and through the sea, constituting as it did their deliverance from bondage into freedom, their death to Egypt, and their birth to a new covenant, was a general type or dim shadow of baptism as it is found in the Great Commission (Matthew 28:18-20).

We should note that some use this passage to deny that baptism is necessarily by immersion. Barnes, for example, said, "This passage is a very important one to prove that the word baptism does not necessarily mean entire immersion in water. It is perfectly clear that neither the cloud nor the water touched them."[7] Such an assertion that the mode of "baptism" can be anything but immersion simply ignores what is clearly taught in many verses.

Into Moses -- "Into" (the Greek is *eis*) is the same preposition which is used with baptism in Matthew 28:19. It is the same preposition used in Romans 6:3ff and Galatians 3:27, which speak of being baptized "into" Christ. It means that by 'baptism' they were dedicated to Moses; they received and acknowledged him as their ruler and guide and teacher. In the act of baptism they were united to Moses, the Old Testament mediator. What happened to the Israelites after they were "baptized" (they eventually perished for lack of self-control) and what could happen to the Corinthians after they are "baptized" are similar – they will be "reprobate," "destroyed," if they demonstrate the same lack of self-control. The Israelites were delivered from bondage yet they perished. Why? It demonstrates the danger of idolatry resulting from lack of self-control.

10:3 -- *and all ate the same spiritual food;*

And all ate the same spiritual food -- What is it that is called "spiritual food"? We do not believe this a reference to the "spiritual food" provided in the words of the Law given through Moses. Rather, we think the reference is to the manna. While Israel was in the wilderness, the manna descended in the form of kernels of grain or corn (or like coriander seed). It was used in the place of bread during the forty years. It came like rain out of the air and was unquestionably, like the column of cloud and of fire, of supernatural origin. How can it be called spiritual? (1) Because of its heavenly origin (miraculous, divine, supernatural), say some. The people knew the food and water were from God (see John

---

[7] Barnes, *op. cit.*, p.180.

6:31). As they ate day by day, it should have been a sign of grace that would be a constant reminder of God's love, mercy, goodness, sufficiency – sufficient to keep them from apostasy. (2) Others say that "spiritual" denotes the food came from the Holy Spirit, i.e., it was produced by a divine miraculous power. (3) Others say it was "spiritual" because it was a type of Christ's body, i.e., the manna was a type of the Lord's Supper. Whichever explanation of "spiritual" we accept, the adjective does not mean Paul is calling into question the physical reality of the manna. The point is that after they were delivered from bondage, they were sustained by God. And in spite of His provision and sustenance, they perished. Why? Because of their own behavior, namely, dalliance with idolatry.

10:4 -- *and all drank the same spiritual drink, for they were drinking from a spiritual rock which followed them; and the rock was Christ.*

And all drank the same spiritual drink -- The idea is essentially the same as in the previous verse. They had been highly favored of God and enjoyed tokens of His divine care and guardianship, but these did not automatically result in their salvation. Their own negative response to God's commands cost them, and likewise similar negative response will cost Christians dearly. Why the water from the rock is called "spiritual" is the subject of much discussion. (1) Because of the peculiar nature of the water, say some. While we are aware of the different taste of well, cistern, and sulphur water, we wonder what is meant by "peculiar nature." Apparently it was real water, fitted to allay their thirst. (2) Some have supposed that there was here the same kind of drink that was used by Christ in instituting the Lord's Supper.[8] But this is difficult to accept, for Jesus was using "fruit of the vine." (3) It seems best to take it to mean that it was bestowed in a miraculous and supernatural manner.

For they were drinking from a spiritual rock which followed them -- "They were drinking" is an imperfect tense in the Greek, picturing continuous or repeated action. It denotes their continuous drinking all through the entire march in the wilderness. There are two recorded accounts of Moses striking a rock to get water: at Rephidim near Mt. Sinai (Exodus 17), and at Kadesh (Numbers 20). But this verse speaks, not of two drinks, but of continual, day-by-day drinking. The rock "followed them," or 'accompanied them,' is the idea. Commentators have rushed in to explain how Paul could give information not recorded in the Old Testament. (1) Some say Paul was here led away by Rabbinical tradition. Cited by Farrar (*op. cit.*, p.323), the tradition goes like this: The Rabbis said the rock was round, and rolled itself up like a swarm of bees, and that when the tabernacle was pitched, the rock came and settled in its vestibule, and began to flow when the princes came and sang, "Spring up, O well, Sing to it" (Numbers 21:17). When the camp moved, the rock rolled alongside them. We doubt Paul is mistakenly using an old Jewish tradition, even if only by way of illustration. (2) Some say the water flowing from that rock formed a river which flowed along the ground alongside the route of march through the wilderness.

---

[8] A number of commentaries find an allusion to the Lord's Supper in Paul's language "spiritual food" and "spiritual drink." This writer is not convinced that such an allusion was intended. "Put it this way," George Mark Elliott used to say. "After baptism, God does not leave the new babe to go it alone. Spiritual food is provided. The Lord's Supper may be part of that food."

This commentator does not think that "rock" stands for the "water" that flowed from the rock. (3) Evans writes (*op. cit.*, p.309), "Between these two recorded instances comprising an interval of nearly 40 years, during which time the first rebellious generation died out, many rocks and cliffs must have been hallowed by the presence and vivified by the power of the Spiritual Rock, accompanying the march of Israel." (4) Lenski (*op. cit.*, p.392-393) cites another Jewish legend. After the first water-miracle recorded in Exodus 17:1-7, the rock which Moses struck rolled along on the journey of the Israelites until at the time of the death of Moses it disappeared in the Sea of Galilee. The second miracle, recorded in Numbers 20:2-13, is connected with this same rolling rock. Legend has it that the rock had been lost when Miriam died, and did not return until it was time for this second miracle to be wrought. Let's suspend our judgment until we read the last part of the verse.

And the rock was Christ -- The language seems to affirm that the eternally pre-existent One,[9] the One who later became the incarnate One and was demonstrated to be the promised Messiah, is the One who provided the water for Israel to drink during their wilderness wanderings.[10] The word translated rock is *petra*, a rocky mass, a cliff of rock, and not *petros*, a single, detached boulder. Paul says a "rock" did accompany Israel throughout the desert wandering, a "rock" which continually provided them with drinking water. "But it was not the rolling boulder of Jewish legend ... [It was a great mass of rock. The One who] never allowed Israel to perish of thirst in the desert, as any other similar expedition would quickly have perished, was Christ, the Son of God, who later became incarnate for our salvation. From Him came the water when upon two occasions two natural rocks miraculously sent out streams of water. But He, and He alone, provided water for the Israelites day by day, although he performed no miracle to accomplish this. Let no one imagine that the Israelites just happened to find water whenever it was needed, save upon these two occasions when it had to be furnished out of the rock. A wondrous

---

[9] Paul here implies that the Messiah was pre-existent. How else could He have had anything to do with the Israelites, 1400 years before Bethlehem?

[10] Other verses have Jesus active in Old Testament times. He did the creating (John 1:3; Colossians 1:16). He was the "Lord, high and lifted up" that Isaiah saw in his memorable vision (Isaiah 6 and John 12:41). And Jesus likely was the fourth man in the fiery furnace (Daniel 3:25). Perhaps even the Shekinah was Jesus, the "Lord of glory" (Romans 9:4).

A question, much more difficult to answer satisfactorily, is whether or not the "angel of Jehovah" who is alluded to in a number of Old Testament passages is really a theophany (a time when the second member of the Godhead became visible to human eyes). Some explain the allusion to the "angel" in Acts 7:30,35,38 as being a reference to Jesus. Some Bible dictionary articles on the "angel of Jehovah" present the idea that the nearer one comes to the time when Jesus is born at Bethlehem, the more we see Christ. There are times when the angel (messenger) of Jehovah seems to be identified with Jehovah (Exodus 3:2,4; Genesis 31:11,13). There are times when the angel of Jehovah is distinguished from Jehovah (Numbers 22:22-35; Genesis 22:11,12,15,16; Joshua 5:13-15). Furthermore, the argument of Hebrews may be summarized thus: The new covenant is superior to and takes the place of the old because the Messenger who gave the new (Jesus, the son of God) is superior to the messengers who gave the old. So we would not deny that Jesus was active in Old Testament times, but we would agree with the article on the Angel of Jehovah in the *International Standard Bible Encyclopedia* that "the angel of Jehovah is not always Christ." We are therefore very hesitant about identifying appearances of the angel of Jehovah as being theophanies. More often they are simply angels who have been sent on a mission by Jehovah.

Provider accompanied them. Just as He gave them manna daily, so daily He also provided water for them" (Lenski, *op. cit.*, p.393). The point the apostle is driving home is apparent. The 'know-it-all' Corinthians thought themselves to be very secure. It would not hurt them to eat in the idol's temple, they supposed. Paul is pointing out that the Israelites had all sorts of privileges, had the highest tokens of divine favor and protection, even had Jesus working on their behalf, and yet they fell into apostasy by getting involved with idolatry. 'Can you suppose, you Christians, that if your behavior is the same, your fate will be different?'

10:5 -- *Nevertheless, with most of them God was not well-pleased; for they were laid low in the wilderness.*

Nevertheless, with most of them God was not well pleased -- "Nevertheless" says God's attitude toward them was in stark contrast with the blessings the Israelites enjoyed. These words form a powerful contrast to the lofty experiences of God's gracious manifestations, of which all were partakers. Although God had given them daily and overt manifestations of His power and goodness, the majority failed to enter the Promised Land. God was not well-pleased with them! God was displeased with their conduct. They rebelled and sinned. "Not well pleased" could be rendered 'He was altogether displeased.' Paul is using litotes. God was angry. See Hebrews 3:7-11,17-19. "Most of them" leaves room for a few exceptions – e.g., Joshua and Caleb (Numbers 14:30-32). All the rest, thousands in number, though they entered the lists, were disqualified by their misconduct.

For they were laid low in the wilderness -- The verb *katastrōnnumi* ("laid low") lends a picturesque touch. It really means 'to spread out, to prostrate.' Paul pictures the trail through the wilderness as strewn with corpses. And it was not simply because of natural deaths in old age. The deaths were the result of plague, war, and unusual diseases. Those deaths were God's sentence against the rebels. This is identical language with the Septuagint at Numbers 14:16. Their death was a judicial overthrow. They started out for the land of Canaan. They were baptized in the Red Sea, and had signal examples of God's provision. But they perished in the wilderness. The fact that they perished is given as proof that God was displeased with them. Verses 6-10 will remind the readers of the reason why God was angry with them. In the closing verses of chapter 9, Paul has painted a picture of self-distrust and the need for self-control as being the proper attitude, rather than acting out of presumptuous confidence. Verse 5 just studied drives home the point again – the Israelites are an illustration of the need for self-distrust, an illustration of what happens to a presumptuously confident people.

10:6 -- *Now these things happened as examples for us, so that we would not crave evil things as they also craved.*

Now these things -- "These things" refers to the judgments inflicted on them by God for their sins, the judgments implied in the word "overthrown." The God-provoking conduct which caused the Israelites to incur the judgment of God in the wilderness, conduct which Paul will now illustrate, are the very attitudes and actions the Corinthians are arguing they have a 'right' to.

Happened as examples for us -- The word translated "example" is *tupos*, 'type.' There are several kinds of types in the Bible. (1) Theological, wherein type and antitype foreshadow, by divine appointment, the heavenly reality. (2) Ethical, which are examples of warning, outlines for us to follow or avoid, depending on the case in point. (3) Technical, such as a pattern by which something is constructed. (An example is the tabernacle, which was a little model of what heaven looks like now, Acts 7:44 and Hebrews 8:5.) We think the word "type" is used here 10:6 in its ethical sense. The things that happened to the Israelites are for warnings to us (as they were warnings to the remaining Israelites also) that we Christians should not lust after evil things. "The Israelites and the facts of their history are examples to us. The same Lord directs our affairs that ordered theirs; and if we sin as they did, we also must expect to be punished and excluded from His favor and from heaven."[11] Shore is probably correct when he asserts that we are not to understand verse 6 as a warning that Christians will die physically if they are not careful about running headlong into sin. He sees a "contrast between the physical Israel and the spiritual Israel, between the physical death which befell the majority of the former, and the spiritual death which, if privileges be neglected or abused, must befall the latter."[12]

That we should not crave evil things -- The word translated "crave" (*epithumētas*) could be translated 'strong desire' or 'lust.' A man can "crave" good things (Philippians 1:23), or he can crave things God has forbidden (2 Timothy 2:22). *Epithumētas* means one is habitually governed by desire. So Paul infers that the Corinthian Christians should not constantly crave, or desire, the meat offered in sacrifice to idols, lest it should lead them to sin and ruin. What "evil things" does Paul have in mind? He goes on in the next verses to list four different examples of the kinds of "evil things" the Israelites craved, and how those things led to their ruin. Perhaps there is a glance at the 'craving' for the diet of Egypt that led the Israelites to go back to Egypt in their hearts. In this language, is the apostle hinting at the real attraction of the idol-feasts to the Corinthians? We may include here whatever is a violation of duty or a denial of love to God or to the brethren.

As they also craved -- "As they also" says that the 'knowledgeable strong brothers' at Corinth were doing the very same things which had led to the overthrow of the Israelites. The idolatry and eating and drinking and committing fornication all refer to kinds of sin which the Corinthians were liable to commit if they did not keep themselves perfectly distinct from the idolatrous practices of the heathen. Instead of rejoicing in the spiritual blessings which God extended to them, they constantly lusted after "evil things."

10:7 – *And do not be idolaters, as some of them were; as it is written, "THE PEOPLE SAT DOWN TO EAT AND DRINK, AND STOOD UP TO PLAY."*

And do not be idolaters, as some of them were -- Four specific prohibitions follow. Notice that all four sins prohibited were brought about by 'craving after evil things,' not

---

[11] Lipscomb, *op. cit.*, p.147.

[12] Shore, *op. cit.*, p.89.

apart from it. This first prohibition could well be translated, 'Stop being idolaters!' This caution is evidently given in view of the danger to which the Corinthians would be exposed if they partook of the feasts that were celebrated in honor of the idols in their temples. The same warning will be repeated at verse 14. The repetition of this warning shows its urgency. Paul seems to be glancing at the case in 8:10, of a Christian showing his superior knowledge by sitting at an idol-banquet in an idol-temple. Such conduct does amount to taking part in idolatrous rites. Paul intimates, more plainly than before, that the danger of actual idolatry is not so imaginary as the Corinthians pretended to suppose. There were several instances of idol worship during Israel's wilderness wanderings, but the one that seems to be in the apostle's mind ("as some of them were") is recorded in Exodus 32, the worship of the golden calf.

As it is written -- Exodus 32:6 is quoted from the Septuagint.

THE PEOPLE SAT DOWN TO EAT AND DRINK -- The Israelites participated in a feast in honor of the idol, the golden calf. They ate the food on that occasion, which had been offered in sacrifice to the animal. This instance is particularly fitting to the apostle's argument – almost an exact parallel. The Corinthians wanted to *eat* in the idol's temple.

AND STOOD UP TO PLAY -- The Hebrew word used in Exodus 32:6 (*tsachaq*) means to laugh, to sport, to jest, to mock, to insult: and then to engage in wild, naked dances that concluded the feasts in honor of the idol. The word "play" does not denote some innocent diversion or game as the word does in our language. It is rather a euphemistic way of speaking of all sorts of the most sensual and licentious acts which men commit in connection with idol worship. In this case Paul does not add that the Israelites were punished, since that was well known.

10:8 -- *Nor let us act immorally, as some of them did, and twenty-three thousand fell in one day.*

Nor let us act immorally -- This is the second prohibition. 'Let us not be led on to commit fornication ....' Paul reminds the Corinthians to what their participation in the idol feasts may lead. Paul is here using the moral dissuasion that we should avoid one activity because of what it may lead to. Eating in the idol's temple may be a stepping-stone to other sins, and therein lay greater peril. There is something about the worship of idols that is conducive to sexual immorality. Immorality is encouraged by the very atmosphere and indeed was often part of the worship of the idol.

As some of them did -- The case referred to here was that of the licentious sexual relations with the daughters of Moab, referred to in Numbers 25:1-9. Like Corinth, this was a case of idol worship followed by fornication.

And twenty-three thousand fell in one day -- The Old Testament says 24,000 (Numbers 25:9). The Hebrew, Septuagint, Philo, Josephus, and the rabbis all attest to 24,000. Paul wrote "23,000." Is this a contradiction? Is this an alleged mistake in the Bible? There have been a number of attempts made to reconcile[13] the numbers: (1) Alford (*op. cit.*, p.555) thinks Paul is putting down the figure from memory. Another thinks there has been a scribal error, someone substituting one letter for another (i.e., a Greek γ' for a Greek δ'). Another thinks Paul makes a deliberate understatement to be within the mark. (2) Macknight and Lenski (*op. cit.*, p.398) suppose that the number was between 23,000 and 24,000 and might therefore be expressed in round numbers by either. (3) Others have us note that this passage says "one day," whereas the Old Testament does not have the words "one day." A thousand were killed in previous action by the judges as described in Numbers 25:5, before the one day when 23,000 more fell. Twenty-four thousand were killed, yet not all in one day. This verse points to the serious danger to which indulgence in idolatry exposes men. Corinthians, are you listening?

10:9 -- *Nor let us try the Lord, as some of them did, and were destroyed by the serpents.*

Nor let us try the Lord -- This is the third prohibition. The verb *ekpeiradzō* means 'to put to the test.' That is, they were testing the Lord to see what He would do. It means to try his patience, to provoke his anger, to see how far we can go, or to act in such a way as to see how much He will bear, or how long He will endure the wickedness and perverseness of men. The Lord was put to the test as to whether He had the will and power to punish, or would let sinning people get away with their continued sin. Likely the word "Lord" says the Israelites in the wilderness were testing Jesus.[14] Jesus is now exalted as Lord, and all authority has been given into His hands. Therefore, He is the one who would

---

[13] The reason for the attempts at reconciliation is the whole matter of inspiration. God cannot lie, and if the Scriptures are really God speaking (inspired), then there can be no contradiction, for lack of consistency is evidence of an untruth. According to 1 Corinthians 2:13, the very words (not just the central message) were the result of inspiration. Satisfactory explanations have been advanced to explain all of the 'alleged contradictions' that men have discovered in the pages of their Bibles, leaving us free to hold on to the doctrine of verbal inspiration.

[14] There is a difference in manuscript readings here. Some manuscripts read Lord (*kurion*) – Aleph, B, C, P, 17, 46, 73, Syr[hmg], Eth., Arm. Some manuscripts read Christ (*christon*) – P[46], D, E, F, G, K, L, Old Lat., Syr.[p,h], Copt[sa,bo], Vulg. The church fathers Irenaeus, Clement, and Origen knew this reading. Some manuscripts read God (*theon*) – A and a few others of little textual importance. From these it can be seen that "God" is a very poorly supported reading, and that "Lord" or "Christ" are better supported readings, and one of these two is most likely the original reading.

Robertson and Plummer (*op. cit.*, p.205-206) have summarized some of the arguments utilized to determine which reading is correct. One attempt to explain the variation reads in this fashion, "No doubt *christon*, if original, might have been changed to *kurion* or *theon* because of the difficulty of supposing that the Israelites in the wilderness tempted Christ." Another gives the opinion that "either *christon* or *theon* might be a gloss to explain the meaning of *kurion*." Epiphanius said that Marcion substituted *christon* for *kurion*, that the apostle might not appear to assert the lordship of Christ.

The apostle Paul (Romans 10:12,13) certainly attributes the names Lord and Jehovah to Jesus Christ. So did Peter (1 Peter 2:3). In fact, Jesus Himself used and accepted the term "Lord" in its full theistic sense (Matthew 22:44,45). Since there seems to be no difference in usage in the LXX between *kurios* and *ho kurios*, therefore in the New Testament we can affirm that the terms *kurios* and *ho kurios* are used of both the Father and of the Lord Jesus Christ.

Since Paul could call Jesus "Lord" or "Christ," it seems that Paul had Jesus in view here in verse 9, rather than the Father. Whether Paul originally wrote "Christ" or "Lord" in this passage, the end result is that we have another verse that speaks of the pre-existent Christ's activities in Old Testament times. Jesus' pre-incarnate activities included shepherding of the chosen people through the wilderness.

punish the Corinthian Christians who presumed to follow a course of action known to be against His will. What were the Corinthians doing that can be designated as trying or tempting the Lord? In light of the fact the event about to be alluded to (when the people perished by serpents) resulted from the people complaining 'there is no food or water, and we loathe this miserable food (the manna),' we suppose the Corinthians were arguing that one cannot get good food if one is not permitted to go to the idol's feast in the idol's temple. Such a complaint shows considerable ingratitude to the Lord about what He has been supplying day after day. The situation at Corinth seems to be analogous to the Israelite loathing of "this light bread" (the manna). Instead of rejoicing in their deliverance through Christ, and His daily provision for their nourishment, the Corinthians were dissatisfied and longed for the old pagan celebrations, especially the food.

As some of them did -- For "did" the margin reads "made trial." Whom did the Israelites "try"? (1) You would naturally understand the same word as in the former clause. It spoke of trying the "Lord" (or "Christ"). If we supply the same word as in the previous clause where Paul had Jesus in view, then this is another verse that speaks of the pre-existent Christ's activities in Old Testament times.[15] Jesus' pre-incarnate activities not only included creation and providing manna and water to Israel (as verse 4 indicated), Jesus also was involved in shepherding the chosen people in the wilderness. And it was He that the Israelites complained against and were punished by. (2) Others have tried to show it was not the pre-incarnate Christ whom the Israelites tempted, but the Father. Some manuscripts read, "as they *also* tempted." We have noted in verse 6 that such language implies both the Corinthians and the Israelites did the same thing.

Whomever the Israelites tempted, the Corinthians also were tempting by their "know-it-all" behavior.[16] Whether it was the Father or the Son who was provoked, the real thrust of this passage is clearly obvious. There was no discernible difference between the behavior of the Israelites (longing after the things left behind in Egypt) and the behavior of the 'knowledgeable' Corinthians (longing for things supposedly abandoned when they confessed Christ). There likewise will be no discernible difference in how such hankering

---

[15] This passage, after noting the reference to Jesus, has been marshaled as another proof that the "angel of Jehovah" in the Old Testament is none other than the pre-existent Christ. For instance, Kling (*op. cit.*, p.199) says, "We have in this verse strong evidence of the fact that Paul regarded the angel of Jehovah of the Old Testament as none other than Christ Himself, the Eternal Word, who in various ways, in natural phenomena and in the form of an angel, manifested himself to the fathers of the ancient dispensations, and was the real Ruler and Guide of Israel." To re-affirm a conclusion stated before: it is possible that in some instances the angel of Jehovah was none other than the pre-existent Jesus. But it is hardly true that in every instance when one meets the angel, one is seeing Jesus.

[16] Not all are ready to accept the idea that it was Jesus whom the Israelites were tempting. Those who question this conclusion like to point to the absence of "also" from the text, insisting that its absence greatly weakens the argument that somehow the Israelites tempted Christ during their wilderness wanderings. Furthermore, they call attention to the fact that the second word translated "make trial" is not the same as the first. "Let us not make trial" in the first phrase of this verse is *ekpeiradzō*, an intensified form of the verb *peiradzō* which is used in its simple form in "as some of them made trial." This change of verbs is alleged to further weaken the case for asserting that the Israelites somehow tempted Christ during their wilderness wanderings. In reply, if Jesus was busy providing every-day blessings to the Israelites, why should it be thought incongruous if the behavior of the Israelites provoked Him?

after worldly and physical pleasures (from which Christ by His death has delivered them) will be treated by Him whom they were tempting.

And were destroyed by the serpents -- Numbers 21:5,6 (an event also alluded to in John 3:14) is the historic occasion Paul makes reference to. 'Destroyed day-by-day by the serpents' uses the imperfect tense to mark a continual process. Does *apōllumi* ('perish,' 'destroy') here refer simply to physical death, or does it (as is true of its use in John 3:16) imply eternal punishment, too? The answer we give to this question will determine just what punishment is threatened on the Corinthians who insist on their 'rights' to keep going to the idol's temple for the feasts in honor of the idol. This commentator thinks there is more than physical death threatened to the Corinthians. They were endangering their eternal salvation by their dalliance with idols!

10:10 -- *Nor grumble, as some of them did, and were destroyed by the destroyer.*

Nor grumble, as some of them did -- *Mē* and the present imperative mean 'Stop grumbling!' Paul is prohibiting the continuance of an action already going on. Rebellious discontent of any kind is forbidden. Grumbling (complaining, murmuring out of discontent) is a sin of which the Israelites were frequently guilty (Numbers 21:4; Exodus 16:8; Numbers 14:1ff, 36ff, 16:41). But as the context shows, Paul here alludes specifically to the rebellion of Korah and its punishment (Numbers 16).[17] The Corinthians were perhaps now murmuring against their teacher, the apostle Paul, like the Israelites murmured against Moses and Aaron.

And were destroyed by the destroyer -- The particular case in view is that of Korah's rebellion (Numbers 16), where 14,700 persons were snatched away by a sudden visitation (verse 49). The "destroyer" is probably not a reference to Satan,[18] but rather to the destroying angel sent by God to smite the people. The Old Testament account at Numbers 16 does not mention the agent. Paul, by inspiration, tells us that there was such an agent, as there was in the slaying of the first-born (Exodus 12:23), in the plague that punished David (2 Samuel 24:16; 1 Chronicles 21:12), and in the destruction of the Assyrians (2 Chronicles 32:21). See also Acts 12:23 and Hebrews 11:28. Rather than being allowed into the Promised Land, the Israelites died in the wilderness. Will Christians who behave like the Israelites did enter the heavenly Promised Land?

---

[17] The murmuring of the people against Moses and Aaron for the punishment of Korah and his company (Numbers 16:41) is apparently intended, for we know of no other case where the murmurers were immediately punished with death. The murmuring against the report of the spies at Kadesh-Barnea can hardly be meant, for that was punished by the murmurers dying off in the wilderness, not by any special destruction (Numbers 14:1,2,29). There was a plague (Numbers 14:37), but did the destroying angel bring that?

[18] Satan sometimes is called the "destroyer" (e.g., Revelation 9:11). By introducing sin he brought men under the power of death (Romans 5:12, John 8:44), and there was a time when the devil had the power of inflicting physical death (Hebrews 2:14). In light of these facts, some have insisted the destroyer used by God to punish the Israelites was none other than the devil himself.

10:11 -- *Now these things happened to them as an example, and they were written for our instruction, upon whom the ends of the ages have come.*

Now these things happened to them as an example -- Having cited four different instances when God punished people for their involvement in idol worship, Paul returns to the general admonition begun in verse 6. He repeats that admonition and extends it. Paul says those things "happened" (*sunebainen*). This is inspired testimony to the historicity of the Old Testament account, i.e., these were not myths or legends or fables, but what actually happened. The verb "happened" is an imperfect tense, and calls upon us to see "these things" one after the other, as they continued to happen to the Israelites. The word "example" is the same word used at verse 6, and it speaks of an ethical example, as it did there. The sense seems to be that God punished those sinning people so that others would learn that such rebellious behavior angers God and will bring His punishment to them, too.

And they were written for our instruction -- "Were written," a passive verb form in the original, points to God as the agent through whom these things were put into writing. As God inspired the Bible writers, certain things were included and certain things left out, so that the resulting writings would accomplish the purpose for which God gave the writings.[19] Paul tells Corinthian Christians that one way to learn what kind of behavior God expects of them is to read and study the Old Testament accounts. This verse, like 2 Timothy 3:16,17, Romans 15:4, etc., has a bearing on the legitimate use to which Christians may put the Old Covenant Scriptures. Though the Mosaic covenant is no longer a binding covenant by which men relate to God (Hebrews 8-10, 1 Timothy 1:9), those writings contain warnings and "examples" from which Christians may learn. These things are recorded in the Old Testament Scriptures in order that we and all others might be admonished not to confide in our own strength, or to insist on our 'rights' as we enter into activities we want to do, whether or not God has said anything about such behavior. What happened to the Israelites is not exceptional by any means; it will in its way happen to God's people every time they turn away from Him.

Upon whom the ends of the ages have come -- "Have come" is a perfect tense verb; it is past completed action with present continuing results. The "ends of the ages" have already begun when Paul writes. (Both "ends" and "ages" are plural in the Greek.) This Christian age is the last time, the latter days, the last dispensation, the last in the series of ages in God's management of time.[20] (See also 1 John 2:18's "It is the last hour;" Ephesians 1:10; 1 Peter 1:20; Hebrews 1:2; Galatians 4:4.) The word translated "ends" is *telos*, which can mean either 'conclusion' or 'goal.' This side of Calvary, men are living in the last age; this

---

[19] Hebrews 7 speaks of information deliberately omitted from the Old Testament record of Melchizedek. Hebrews 11:2 and 11:39 tell us that certain men are immortalized in Scripture so that others might learn from their lives what is pleasing to God. Here in Corinthians, Paul tells us that God included certain historical events in order to "warn" later generations of readers.

[20] The KJV's "ends of the world" could give the reader a wrong idea, for it could be interpreted to mean Paul thought he and the Corinthians were in the last few days before the Second Coming of Christ. It is a total misreading of New Testament verses to make the charge that Jesus and the apostles were mistaken about the time of the Second Coming, thinking it would occur in their own lifetimes.

last age began with Pentecost. All the preceding ages since time began focus on the age in which Paul and the Christians live. We Christians are the goal of all past history. All that the past ages have to tell us should bear its fruit in us. The church is the heir to the spiritual training God has been giving mankind through the ages.[21] All of these past events would have happened and would have been recorded in vain if at the apex of the ages their instruction, their admonition, and their warning were to go unheeded.

10:12 -- *Therefore let him who thinks he stands take heed lest he fall.*

Therefore -- With "therefore" Paul introduces his intended application of the previous "examples" to the situation at Corinth. In verses 12-13 Paul drives home two warnings: (1) one to those who are so self-confident they think they have no need to be watchful; and (2) one to those who think they are so strong they can run headlong into temptation with impunity.

Let him who thinks he stands -- This passage refers to the person who thinks a certain activity won't hurt him, that he can do it with no danger to himself. Perhaps there is special reference to feeling secure against contamination from idol-feasts, because of the fact that the Corinthians had "knowledge."

Take heed lest he fall -- Again and again in the pages of history, a fortress has been stormed because its defenders thought it could not be. Think of the Maginot Line in France, and the German victory there during World War II. Think of ancient Sardis.

> The Acropolis at Sardis was built on a jutting spur of rock that was held to be impregnable. When Cyrus was besieging it he offered a special reward to any who could find a way in. A certain soldier, Hyeroeades by name, was watching one day and saw a soldier in the Sardian garrison drop his helmet accidentally over the battlements. He saw him climb down after it and marked his path. That night he led a band up the cliffs by that very path and when they reached the top they found it quite unguarded, so they entered and captured the citadel.[22]

The Corinthians, thinking that they stood, asserting that they had all knowledge, proud of the insight which led them to declare that "the idol is nothing," were not only liable to wound the conscience of the weak brother, but were in danger themselves of being personally lost. "Fall" may involve several things: (1) To be betrayed into sin; (2) To forfeit salvation, or in the language of 9:27, "to become a castaway."[23] None is so liable

---

[21] See John 4:37ff; 2 Timothy 3:16ff; Galatians 3:29 and 4:1ff; Ephesians 1:9ff.

[22] Barclay, *op. cit.*, p.99-100.

[23] Once more attention is called to the bearing of this passage on the doctrine of unconditional eternal security. "Whether taken alone or in context, this verse may not be referred to anything else other than to the danger of apostasy, which is an ever-present *possibility* for all of the saved in Christ as long as they are under the probation of earthly existence. We shall not take occasion here to demonstrate the lengths to which scholars have gone in their vain efforts to edit such a thought out of it. Unless there is a real danger of falling away so as to be lost, the message of this whole chapter is meaningless. 'The history of

to fall as those who, thinking themselves strong, run into temptation. The application is clear. The Corinthians were cocksure of their position. But then, so were the Israelites, and they had reaped nothing but disaster. Let the self-confident take heed, lest he fall!

10:13 -- *No temptation has overtaken you but such as is common to man; and God is faithful, who will not allow you to be tempted beyond what you are able, but with the temptation will provide the way of escape also, that you may be able to endure it.*

No temptation has overtaken you -- While verse 12 was a warning, this verse is an encouragement. God is not pleased when we run headlong into temptation, but on the other hand He gives grace when we are enticed to sin. Verse 13 is one of the most helpful verses in the New Testament to those who would understand how temptations come, and how they may be successfully resisted. "Temptation" (*peirasmos*), depending on the context, can have several possible meanings: (a) ORDEAL – especially by means of suffering and persecution. It is reading too much into the verse to suppose the Corinthians had been pleading that they must go to idol-feasts, lest they be persecuted and thus tempted to apostatize. (b) TEMPTATION – enticement to sin. This perhaps fits this context best. Enticement to forsake their allegiance to their Lord, and to get involved again in idolatry and the sins that accompany that abominable practice.

The promise Paul here makes of divine help when tempted is limited to cases where the victim is "overtaken." It is not promised to those who deliberately put themselves in a place to be tempted. Now when a man is "overtaken" through no fault of his own, it is not a sin to be tempted (Jesus was tempted, yet without sin). But temptations are enticements to sin and are made very alluring. All the while, the danger involved in the sin is disguised and hidden from the one being tempted. The devil is the one who comes and plants evil thoughts in men's minds, or stirs up the wrongful desires of their bodies. The devil does this without invitation. It's bad enough to have to put up with this adversary and his schemes when he has not been invited, but it is infinitely worse to put oneself into a place where the devil is invited and welcomed to come tempt. This latter is precisely what one would do who participated in the feast in the idol's temple.

But such as is common to man -- The Greek reads *ei mē anthrōpinos*, "such as is human." The idea seems to be this: the temptations which the Corinthians were facing were not unique. Indeed, all converts from old religions will be tempted to go back to that from which they were converted to Christianity. Such temptations can be quite forceful, not only because it is one's old friends and acquaintances who are inviting the Christian to return, but also because of the fascinations surrounding the idolatrous way of life.

And God is faithful -- The devil may try to overwhelm us with temptations, but God has not gone off and forgotten His creation. He is right there to help us when the devil tempts

---

Israel not only showed the mere possibility of apostasy, but demonstrated its actual reality and the sad prevalence of it'." (Coffman, *op. cit.*, p.155)

us. God is absolute in His faithfulness. He is true to the covenant He has made. He is consistent with His love and purpose. He can be relied upon. The Corinthian Christians are to rely on Him for escape from the danger that always accompanies temptation, not on themselves or their own strength. God had called them (1:9), and since He knows "how to rescue the godly from temptation" (2 Peter 2:9), He will surely keep His side of the covenant. If the Corinthians do their parts, He would strengthen and protect them from evil (2 Thessalonians 3:3). Paul will go on to enumerate two things their faithful God could be counted on to do for them when they are tempted: (1) He will put limits on the devil, so the temptation is not too great to bear; (2) He will provide the way of escape.

Who will not allow you to be tempted beyond what you are able -- He would not be much of a God if He allowed temptations to befall His people that were beyond their powers to bear. This is but one of several verses which promise the Christian that God will help limit the pressure the devil is allowed to apply when he comes to tempt. Other verses include Matthew 6:13; Luke 22:31ff; and James 1:12ff. See also the case of Job in the Old Testament, where God put limits on the devil when he wanted to tempt Job. Meditate on the depths of this phrase. A man *can* be faithful to death! God knows the powers with which He has endowed us, and how much pressure we can withstand. We do not have to fall victim to circumstances which He Himself has permitted for us. It is also implied that there is no divine aid when one is "testing" Christ in the way the Corinthians are currently doing (verse 9).

Barnes calls attention to some things to be noted: (1) All the circumstances, causes, and agents that lead to temptation are under the control of God. These cannot operate unless God permits it. (2) When men are tempted, it is because God permits it. He does not Himself tempt men. Compare Job and James 1:13. (3) One positive result that comes from temptation is that the one who resists becomes stronger. (4) People have differing abilities to resist temptation. Some can handle very little temptation, while others can endure much. God knows what each man's capabilities are, and He controls the Tempter so that no man is tempted beyond the limit of his ability to resist if he wants to. (5) So, if men fall under the power of temptation, they only are to blame.[24] We have the strength to resist all the temptations; so if we sin, we only are at fault.

But with the temptation will provide the way of escape also -- "*A* way of escape" (KJV) ignores the definite article in the Greek. The thing spoken of is "the necessary way of escape," the one suitable for such a difficulty. Morris (*op. cit.*, p.142) writes, "The word translated 'escape' (*ekbasis*) may denote a mountain defile. The imagery would then be that of an army trapped in the mountains, which escapes from an otherwise impossible situation through a narrow mountain pass. The assurance of this verse, that God provides the way of escape when we are tempted, is a permanent comfort and source of strength to believers. Our trust is in the faithfulness of God!" Right at the moment the devil plants the tempting thought, God will simultaneously call to the Christian's mind *the* way to go to avoid sinning and be victorious over the temptation. Temptations and "the way of escape"

---

[24] Barnes, *op. cit.*, p.188.

always go in pairs. God so arranges it. He permits no unfairness or advantage to Satan, who must be permitted to tempt in the first place (Job's case is an example). When tempted, men are not forced to go either way, but they must make a choice between the two: (1) they have the choice of *sinning*, or (2) they have the choice of *escaping*. The way of escape may be different for each temptation. When it comes to the matter of idolatry (the matter in which the Corinthians were claiming certain 'rights') the way of escape was to "flee from idolatry" (verse 14).

That you may be able to endure it -- That you may be able to endure the temptation, that you not fall into sin because of the temptation. Temptation is a time of testing, a time of probation, and God controls the test in such a way "that you (Christians) may be able to endure it." Three things have been said about temptations in the life of a Christian: (1) Temptations will come. The devil will try to "overtake" the Christian. (2) Temptations the Christian faces are not unique. Others have been similarly tempted, endured those same temptations, and come through victorious. (3) The Christian (no such promise seems to be made to the non-Christian) may count on God to always be there to provide the way of escape. If the Christian looks for it, and takes advantage of it, the temptation will not lead to sin. What a comfort!

> We have now finished the long presentation (which began in 8:1) by Paul of the principles by which 'liberty' is regulated. (Review the summary of the principles given at the beginning of these comments on chapter 10.) As Paul spoke of the warning that should be learned from Israel's history, he made these points: (a) God delivered them, yet they subsequently perished. Why? Idolatry! (verse 2). (b) God sustained them, yet still they perished. Why? Idolatry! (verses 3,4). (c) There is a moral contagion connected with idolatry. See the four evil results of "craving evil things" in verses 7-10. Paul finished with his appeal to Israelite history by making application of what one can learn from a study of that ancient history (verses 11-13).

B. Paul's Answers (based on the above stated principles) to Their Three Questions. 10:14-11:1

> *Summary:* To their first question, Paul's answer is 'Do not go to the idol's temple to participate in banquets held there,' 10:14-22. To their second question about purchasing meat at the local meat market, Paul's answer is, 'It is permissible for the Christian to buy meat which is indiscriminately offered for sale at the meat market (even though some of it previously may have been sacrificed to idols), and take it home and consume it,' 10:23-26. Thirdly, concerning eating at a non-Christian's table, his answer is, 'It is permissible for the Christian to accept an invitation to a friend's house, and there to eat the meat set before him, even though it previously may have been sacrificed to an idol (unless his eating gives offense to one sitting at the table),' 10:27-11:1.

1. The eating of sacrificial meat at an idol's table, or in an idolatrous feast, is prohibited.   10:14-22

> *Summary:*   May a Christian go into the heathen temples, and there partake of the feasts which were there made in honor of the idol?   The answer is 'No!'   This paragraph is a dissuasion from partaking of idol feasts in the idol's temple, because such feasts involved a *fellowship* with demons, and were therefore hostile to all fellowship with Christ in His supper.   Idolatry is by all means to be shunned.

10:14 -- *Therefore, my beloved, flee from idolatry.*

Therefore -- *Dioper* ("therefore") is a stronger particle than that used in verse 12. It indicates a very close logical sequence. Because of the dangers of close contact with idolatry (dangers illustrated in 10:1-13 from the Old Testament record of Israel's history), the Corinthians were to act in such a way as to shun the dangers. Paul is now beginning to answer the questions about meats offered to idols that were introduced at 8:1. The "therefore" would thus include all that has been said in principle and example against such eating. Paul stated (in chapter 8 reasoning *ad hominem*), 'There is no Christian liberty apart from Christian love.' Here in chapter 10 he discusses the eating of meat in an idol's temple (not *ad hominem*, but) on the basis of its merits. 'The Lord's Supper and the Jewish sacrifices ought to convince you of the fact that to participate in a feast is to participate in worship. Therefore, avoid all idol-feasts, which are a worship of demons.'

My beloved -- The address "my beloved" is not a common one. It indicates something of Paul's deep emotion as he urges his dear friends to take the right course. Paul does not deliver this verdict as though he were an unfeeling judge. He delivers this instruction as one who had their welfare at heart.

Flee from idolatry -- Do not deliberately put yourself in a place where you will be tempted, and do not linger in any place where you find yourself being tempted. Especially in the matter of idolatry, run for your life. 'Continue to flee away from it (present imperative[25])!' "Keep on fleeing!" Whether strong or weak brother – whoever they are – they are to flee from idolatry! For the Christian, no going to the feasts in the idol's temple is permitted! God provides the way of escape from idolatry – "Flee from it!" Deliberately avoiding idolatry is the only way of escape God has provided for this particular temptation.

10:15 -- *I speak as to wise men; you judge what I say.*

I speak as to wise men -- The command in verse 14 prohibiting participation in feasts offered to idols might appear, at first sight, to be abrupt and absolute.   Now Paul seeks to

---

[25] As he had counseled them in 6:18 to "flee immorality," so now he says "flee from idolatry." Here, as there, the present imperative gives the thought of habitual practice. There is to be no leisurely contemplation of sin, thinking that one can go so far, and yet be safe from going farther. The only wise course is to have nothing to do with it.

show his beloved readers how sensible it is. Calling them "wise men" does not appear to be irony. Indeed, the Corinthians prided themselves on their wisdom. And one might think Paul is saying, 'If you are as wise as you claim, then you will listen to my instruction.' But "wise" is not the word (*sophoi*) regularly used[26] in the notable discussion in 1:20ff. The word here is *phronimos*, which signifies 'intelligent, sensible.' These words imply "the point of view from which the apostle is now regarding his readers, viz., competent to recognize the force of his argument."[27] Paul appeals to the Corinthians to use good sense as they evaluate the truth of what he has just written.

You judge what I say -- "You" is emphatic. Paul never asks mere blind obedience; he calls on them to "judge" and then to obey as a result of thorough conviction. Paul has already used several Old Testament examples to warn his readers about the dangers of idolatry. He has more to say on the subject in the following verses. The warning is no longer drawn from Old Testament history, but rather from Christian practice, namely, participation at the Lord's Table. The same realities which are true of the Lord's Table, and true of Old Testament sacred meals, carry over to the meals offered to idols. Such realities make it absolutely incompatible to think one can participate both in the Lord's Table and in the table of demons. To attempt to do both is inconsistent behavior that provokes Christ to jealousy.

10:16 -- *Is not the cup of blessing which we bless a sharing in the blood of Christ? Is not the bread which we break a sharing in the body of Christ?*

Is not the cup of blessing -- The design of this verse and the ones following seems to be to show the Corinthians why Paul's injunction to stay away from the idol's feast is the only right judgment they can draw from the principles and examples he has called to their attention. First, Paul has said, do not put yourself in a place where you can be easily tempted. If you do, you are just asking for trouble. Now, he says, you cannot participate in both the Lord's Supper and also participate in the idol's feast in the idol's temple and continue to be a consistent Christian.[28] "The cup of blessing" is a designation for the cup of the fruit

---

[26] *Phronomoi* is used with irony at 4:10, but the context there shows it is used ironically. Not so here.

[27] Shore, *op. cit.*, p.92.

[28] In a moment, Paul will use the verb "participate" or "share" as he speaks of what happens during the celebration at the Lord's Table or in the idol's temple. This particular verb, as well as other ideas in the context, have proven difficult for commentators to explain since each of us, if we are not careful, tends to allow our doctrinal positions to influence our comments. The main debate in church circles is over the way in which "participation" in the Lord's Supper affects the worshiper, or brings spiritual benefits to the worshiper. Roman Catholic commentators tend to think of the sacraments as being a miraculous (automatic, mechanical) means of grace, dependent not on the attitude of the worshiper, but on the administrator. Reformed churches who emphasize *sola gratia* (without a medium) tend to emphasize how God works directly on the hearts of men, no sacraments needed. Thus Reformed explanations of "participate" will differ markedly from Roman Catholic comments. Other Protestants teach that grace depends on Calvary and on our response. Thus, emphasis is on the heart of the participant more than on the validity of the administrator, and comments about 'participation' will reflect this doctrinal position. What does "participation in the blood and body of Christ" mean? What does "participation in the table of demons" mean? Are any of the views just listed anywhere near correct?

of the vine used in the celebration of the Lord's Supper. Why is this cup called the "cup of blessing"? (1) Some say it is because Jesus used the words "cup of blessing" when He instituted the Lord's Supper. Jesus instituted the Lord's Supper during the last Passover meal of His earthly ministry. There was a cup (the third cup) used during the Passover meal called the *cos haberecah*, "cup of blessing." This cup was drunk near the end of the celebration of the feast of the Passover. Before those partaking of the feast drank of this cup, they gave thanks to God over it for the feast.[29] (2) Some suggest it is because the cup brings a blessing to those who partake of it. (3) Because the cup had a blessing pronounced over it, say others. The context ("which we bless") may make it clear that this is the correct interpretation. Some have inferred from the use of the singular "cup" that the ancient custom was that only one cup was used at the Lord's Supper. The word is thought to picture the cup being passed around from person to person, and each sipped from it as they shared the meal in memory of Jesus.[30]

Which we bless -- What is meant by "bless"? It probably does not mean 'over which we bless God' or 'for which we bless God.' Instead, this is probably parallel to Matthew 26:27 and 1 Corinthians 11:24, 'giving thanks to God.' Among the Jews the usual prayer of thanksgiving was one that began with the words "Blessed art thou, O Lord." Then came the mention of the thing for which thanks was given. Grace before meals, for example, even began this way. So the reference may well be to the prayer of thanksgiving said over the cup. "Bless" is a present tense verb, pointing to a customary action among the Christians when it was time for the Lord's Supper to be observed. Who is the "we" who do the blessing? (1) Some say it is the apostles and their official successors. This passage then becomes a major proof text for the Roman doctrine of transubstantiation.[31] (2) Some think it is the one who presided at the Lord's Table who did the "blessing." It was not until nearer the time (c. AD 150) when Justin Martyr wrote that the function of presiding at the Lord's Table was reserved for the *proestos* (the 'president'), but even then it was with the understanding that he represented the congregation and acted in unison with them. On the plurals, "we bless" and "we break," Meyer observes (*op. cit.*, p.228), "Whose [responsibility] was it to officiate in this consecration? At this date [when Paul writes to Corinth], when the order of public worship in the Church was far from being settled, *any Christian man was competent* [to preside at the Lord's Table]." (3) Others say, the "we" denotes the whole congregation, which unitedly consecrated the cup by prayer and thanksgiving. Observe that the first person plural is the same throughout this context. The blessing of the cup and the blessing of the bread – acts of consecration – were not simply the acts of the "minister" or the person leading the 'celebration' at the table. Each

---

[29] See the Special Study on the Lord's Supper in the author's *Acts* commentary, where the institution of the Lord's Supper is explained. Note how the "cup of blessing" figured in that institution.

[30] This commentator has not been in the habit of making apostolic example binding on us today, so he has not insisted on using one cup at the Lord's Table as some in the Restoration Movement have done.

[31] Fee (p.467) has offered this comment against using this passage to prove the dogma of transubstantiation: "Though the deity is somehow present at the meal, it is not as if they were 'participating in the Lord' by actually eating of the food, as though the food were the Lord himself. Neither the language nor the grammar, nor the example of Israel, nor the examples from pagan meals allows such a meaning."

individual worshiper was involved in and participated in the act. Why do we have prayers of thanks before the Lord's Supper is served? Because of the Lord's example and command ("continue to do this!" [see notes at 11:24,25]), and because of Apostolic precedent.

[Is not the cup] a sharing in the blood of Christ? -- This question expects an affirmative answer, "Yes it is a sharing!" The word is *koinōnia*, 'to have a thing in common, to have a share of a thing,' from *koinos*, 'common.' Note the ASV margin, "a participation in." If no other passages hindered, we might suppose transubstantiation or consubstantiation to be correct. But the passages that say "Do this in remembrance of me" seem to militate against either of these views. Doctrines like transubstantiation or consubstantiation cannot be demonstrated from this passage. "All that the passage asserts is the fact of a participation. The nature of that participation must be determined from other sources."[32] Lenski calls attention to the fact that Paul "cannot write '*the* communion,' for such a statement might leave the impression that in the Lord's supper is 'the *only* means of participation' in the blood of Christ" (*op. cit.*, p.409). "Sharing in the blood of Christ" means more than 'this is the interpretation others put on our actions' (i.e., if we are at the Lord's Table, folk will think we are Christians). The interpretation others put on the act may be true, but there is more involved in "participation" than what others may think.

"Sharing in" looks at the Lord's Supper from two different directions. From one aspect, it is a way for the communicant to say 'I wish to continue to participate in the benefits of Christ's body and blood.' From another aspect, it is a way for the communicant to say 'I wish to invite Jesus to have a continuing relationship with me.' The first hardly needs documentation. It is the second that likely will need more explanation. The same phrase ("participation in") is used in verse 20 where we read about "participating with demons." Whatever "share/participation" means in that verse, it means in this verse. At verse 20, it is difficult to find that the phrase means less than 'inviting the demons to have a relationship with us.' Likewise, when we share in the Lord's Table, we are inviting Jesus to have a continuing relationship with us.[33] Through the cup we share the benefits of Christ's blood. When the Christian partakes of the cup in the proper manner – recognizing what the cup stands for, recognizing Christ's claims about Himself, and recognizing the need to submit to His Lordship – he or she shares in the benefits of Christ's shed blood.[34]

---

[32] Morris, *op. cit.*, p.146.

[33] In addition to inviting Jesus to have a relationship with the worshiper, is Jesus considered to be somehow present at the time the Lord's Supper is celebrated (though not in the Roman Catholic sense of transubstantiation)? Or does the discussion of "presence' add a foreign and extraneous note that causes us to miss what is here affirmed about what happens at the Lord's Table?

[34] See the Special Study on the Lord's Supper at Acts 20:7 in the author's *Acts* commentary. Church history has seen four generally recognizable positions developed down through the ages concerning how this 'fellowship' or 'participation' or 'sharing' actually takes place. (1) Some have embraced transubstantiation, the idea that the loaf and cup are transformed into the actual blood and body of the Lord, and that is how we share in the body and blood. (2) Some have embraced consubstantiation, the idea that the elements are not actually transformed, but that there is an real presence of Christ in and under the elements, so that eating and drinking constitutes an actual sharing in the body and blood of Christ. (3) Some affirm that we may speak of the real presence of Christ in the elements, but not an actual presence.

When He instituted the Lord's Supper, Jesus said the contents of the cup represent "the new covenant in my blood" (1 Corinthians 11:25), i.e., the blood that inaugurates or validates the new covenant. The language of 1 Corinthians 10 ("participating in the blood of Christ") certainly refers to the communicants' sharing in the provisions and benefits of that new covenant.

Is not the bread which we break a sharing in the body of Christ? -- The phrasing of this question is a parallel construction with the preceding one, and likely is parallel in meaning. It too expects an affirmative answer. 'Breaking' of the loaf was necessary for distribution. One loaf of bread was passed, and each communicant broke off a small piece as it was passed, and then ate the small piece. This verse should never be used as proof that the act of breaking during a communion celebration really is a new 'killing' or 'sacrificing' of Christ (as some have taught) since Hebrews argues that at Calvary Christ died once for all.

It is interesting to find the cup mentioned before the bread in this verse. Some, comparing this verse with Luke 22:17-20, suppose that in the early church the order of observance had not become fixed, and that in some places, the cup was shared before the loaf. But the first cup mentioned in Luke 22 is not a Lord's Supper element, but rather one of the cups of the Passover meal. Further, when we come to 1 Corinthians 11:23-30, where Paul deals with the institution of the Lord's Supper, the bread comes first. Nevertheless, since the usual order is reversed here in 1 Corinthians 10, commentators have speculated as to the reason. Perhaps Paul spoke of the cup first in order to stress the shedding of the blood of the Lord. Or, the order here may be due to the prominence of the cup and the insignificance of bread in pagan sacrifices to which Paul is leading up, says another. Perhaps Paul deliberately put the bread second at this place because he intends to dwell at greater length upon the bread.

That leads us to ask, what does Paul mean when he speaks of the "body of Christ"? Influenced by the fact that Jesus said, as He instituted the Lord's Supper, "This is my body which is given for you," some have supposed Paul is talking about the benefits that come to the Christian because Jesus became incarnate (took on a human 'body'). Fisher reminds us not to put our modern connotation on the word "body" as though it meant only the physical body. "Body" to a Hebrew referred to the totality of earthly life. To share in the body of Christ is to share in the benefits of His incarnation, crucifixion, and resurrection.[35] Others, influenced by what Paul writes in verse 17, have supposed that the word "body" is used figuratively for the church (as the body of Christ). The person who shares in the Lord's Supper is thereby part of the "one body" made up of worshipers gathered around the table. Opponents of this view call attention to the parallel construction of verse 16, insisting that the reference to "blood" in the previous clause argues against "body" being a reference to the "one body."

---

(4) Some affirm that the elements are purely symbolic of the body and blood of Christ. None of these seem to convey the whole thrust of Paul's language at this place.

[35] Fisher, *op. cit.*, p.161.

10:17 -- *Since there is one bread, we who are many are one body; for we all partake of the one bread.*

Since there is one bread, we who are many are one body -- For "one bread" the margin reads "one loaf." This verse is difficult to interpret in detail. From the following verses it seems clear that what Paul is stressing is the idea of the involvement of the worshipers. Participants in the Lord's Supper, or the Jewish sacrifices, or the pagan sacrifices, are not just uninvolved bystanders. People who share together in acts of worship, by that sharing become part of the group.

For we all partake of the one bread -- As explained earlier, as part of the Lord's Supper observance, one loaf was apparently passed from hand to hand that each might break off a piece. The fact that a person, in a company of other members of the congregation ("one body"), participated in the breaking and eating of the bread, by that act indicated to the world that he was a part of the group[36] and wished to participate in the benefits which the God being worshiped made available to the communicants.

10:18 -- *Look at the nation Israel; are not those who eat the sacrifices sharers in the altar?*

Look at the nation Israel -- The Greek reads 'Israel according to the flesh.' Israel in its merely human aspect, not spiritual Israel (Romans 2:28; Galatians 4:29, 6:16), is what Paul calls attention to. Christians are a new Israel, Israel after the Spirit. Therefore the reference is not to Christians.[37] Paul is producing another illustration of the sentiment which he is establishing, by a reference to the fact that among the Jews, those who partook of the same sacrifices were regarded as being one people, and as worshiping one God. The meaning is that, by sharing in the sacrifices, the Jews stood in direct association with the altar, the victims, and all that they symbolize. The sacrifices of the Jews furnish a similar argument to show that participation in sacrificial feasts is communion (sharing, participation) with the unseen.

Are not those who eat the sacrifices -- According to Deuteronomy 12:18,27, Leviticus 3:3, and Hosea 8:13, Jewish worshipers oftentimes ate part of the animals that were sacrificed. In fact, the parts to be offered and the parts to be eaten were even specified in Scripture. The application to the matter of eating in the idol's temple is obvious. What was true for the Old Testament worshipers' participation in the sacrifices is equally true for the participants at an idol's feast.

---

[36] Paul is not here suggesting (as some modern churchmen have erroneously stated) that unimmersed people who partake of the Supper are somehow by that act made members of the body of Christ. People do not *become* members of the one body by participation in the Lord's Supper. In 1 Corinthians 12:13, Paul shows that people *become* part of the body, in the first place, by their common immersion into the body.

[37] Paul's language here has been pressed into service in the discussion among dispensationalists and their opponents concerning how Paul uses the term "Israel" in his letters. The view Paul taught is today called "supersessionism." Briefly, the doctrine is that Israel was God's specially chosen instrument in Old Testament times. Now that Christ has come, only those Israelis and Gentiles who are immersed into Christ are his specially chosen instruments in New Testament times.

Sharers in the altar? -- This question, like those asked earlier, expects an affirmative answer. The "altar" likely stands for 'God.' The idea is not that the Jewish worshiper had fellowship with a physical altar made of stone, but rather they had a fellowship with the God to whom the altar was dedicated. To eat at an altar is far more than ordinary eating that merely fills the stomach with food. In the case of Old and New Testament worshipers, to eat is to have a part in all of the benefits of the altar and of the sacrifices laid upon it, i.e., to have the forgiveness which this altar mediates, the standing among God's people which it bestows, and thus the holiness with which it enfolds and surrounds. It was no small thing, no mere indifferent meaningless act, to eat of Israel's sacrifices that were brought to the altar of burnt offering. The sacrifice was divided, with a portion offered upon the altar and a portion taken and eaten. Whoever ate a portion of that same sacrifice was a partaker in common *with* (not "of," as some English translations have it) the altar.

We remember that Paul is insisting that Christians avoid banquets in the idol's temple, and is appealing to the common sense of the Corinthians (verse 15) as he pleads for their agreement in this matter. A simple summary of what he has written is this: (1) To partake of a Jewish sacrifice as a sacrifice, and in a holy place, was an act of Jewish worship. (2) To partake of the loaf and the cup in a communion service was an act of Christian worship. (3) By parity of reasoning, to partake of a heathen sacrifice as a sacrifice, in a holy place, was an act of heathen worship. Going to the idol's temple, and eating the food offered in sacrifice to the idol, is not just an innocent pastime. It involves you with the pagan god in the same way that Israel's sacrifices involved them with God.

10:19 -- *What do I mean then? That a thing sacrificed to idols is anything, or that an idol is anything?*

What do I mean then? -- Before making application to the participation in pagan sacrifices and pagan altars, Paul first cuts off a false deduction[38] which someone might make from his analogy of the Israelite altar. The inference from the preceding analogies would naturally be that Paul was representing the god worshiped in the idol's temple as being as real as is Jehovah or Jesus. But Paul corrects this false inference. He is not implying the validity of the 'gods' symbolized by the idols. No inference from these analogies should be drawn in contradiction to what has already been written at 1 Corinthians 8:4. An idol is a non-entity; indeed, there is no such being as that represented by the idol. But behind the idol are demons, and Christians have no business inviting a relationship with demons.

That a thing sacrificed to idols is anything -- Does the animal carcass or the loaves of bread become somehow 'holy' (or, for that matter, somehow contaminated) by being used in the idol's temple? The question expects a negative answer. 'No, the things sacrificed to idols are not affected one way or the other by the use to which they have been put.'

Or that an idol is anything? -- Paul has not forgotten what he has written in 8:4. Jesus is real. The God worshiped at the Jewish altar is real. Does it follow that the "god" worshiped at the feast in the idol's temple is real? No! On this Paul and the Corinthians are

---

[38] The Greek verb here is *phēmi*, 'I say.' 'What am I saying?' asks the readers to be careful how they hear what Paul writes, lest they draw some false inferences.

agreed. There is no actual being (no Zeus, Aphrodite, Apollo, or Aesclepius) such as is represented by the image in the idol's temple. An idol is nothing but an inanimate piece of wood or stone or precious metal. There is no such god at all, except, perhaps, in the imagination. But there is something 'real' back of the idol – there are demons. That is the point made in the next verse, as Paul continues to clarify what his analogy is teaching.

10:20 -- No, *but* I say *that the things which the Gentiles sacrifice, they sacrifice to demons and not to God; and I do not want you to become sharers in demons.*

No, but I say -- There is no Greek word for "no," and no verb in this verse. The negative comes from the adversative conjunction *alla*, and the verb "I say" is supplied from the first half of the sentence (verse 19). While there is no real god behind the idol's feast, Paul's analogy is still valid. There is an analogy between the Lord's Supper and the Jewish feasts on the one hand, and the pagan feasts on the other. The sense is, 'No, I do not say this, *but* I say that there are reasons why you should not participate in the heathen sacrificial feasts. One of those reasons is that such sacrifices are a means of inviting the demons to have a part in the worshiper's life. Demons are as real as Jesus or the Father.' Both in the Lord's Supper and in the Jewish temple services, participating in feasts is fellowship with an unseen power, a power that is divine. There is something analogous to this in the sacrificial feasts of the heathen, but in that case the unseen power is not divine. It is demonic.

That the things which the Gentiles sacrifice, they sacrifice to demons -- "Demons" (*daimonioi*), as the use of the term elsewhere in Scripture indicates,[39] are those beings called "evil spirits" or "unclean spirits" in the Gospels.[40] They are very likely fallen angels.[41] The Greeks themselves called their deities "demons." In Acts 17:18 the term seems to be used as a synonym for "gods" or "deities" ('he seems to be a preacher of foreign deities'). In pagan thought, some demons were helpful, while others were harmful. The inspired Scriptures, however, are not so generous towards demons. They are all evil and

---

[39] This is Paul's first use of the term. In fact, the term "demons" occurs only one other time in Paul's writings, where the "doctrines of demons" are warned against (1 Timothy 4:1). He uses a different term for demons at Ephesians 6:12. The word "demons," among the Jews, was employed only to designate evil beings. Thus, in the Septuagint, the word is used to translate *elilim* (idols, non-existent things, Psalm 96:5 ["all the gods of the nations are demons {idols}"], Isaiah 55:10) and *shaid* (devils [KJV], demons [NASB], Deuteronomy 32:17 [Israel in the wilderness had rejected God their Rock for beings that were "demons"]). Other Old Testament passages from which the terminology "demon" may be derived include Leviticus 17:7, Psalm 106:37, Isaiah 65:3 (LXX) and 65:11 (LXX). Perhaps Paul has quoted the passage from Deuteronomy 32 here in 1 Corinthians 10:20, contemporizing the language of the Song of Moses to the situation at Corinth.

[40] In the New Testament the word "demon" is uniformly used also to denote evil spirits, such as those who had taken possession of men in the time of Christ (Matthew 7:22, 9:33,34, 10:8, 11:18; Mark 1:34,39).

[41] In Revelation 9:20 we read of wicked men who "worshiped demons and idols of gold." In Matthew 25:41 and Revelation 12:9 we read of "the devil and his angels." Evidently when the devil rebelled, as many as 1/3 of the heavenly host joined in his rebellion and were "thrown down to the earth" (Revelation 12:4,9), and some were imprisoned in chains of darkness awaiting the final judgment (Jude 6). For a detailed study of demons and demon possession, see the Special Study in the author's *Acts* commentary.

unclean. Unless demons actually exist, and are a most dangerous threat to the Christian's spiritual growth and well-being, this warning by Paul makes no sense.[42] Heathendom being under the dominion of Satan (the ruler of this world), he and his angels are in fact the powers honored and worshiped by the heathen, however little they may be aware of it.

> It is a great mistake to imagine that back of their idolatry and their idol sacrifices there is nothing but an empty vacuity. True enough, as 8:4 makes plain, the gods of the idols have no existence whatever; no being by the name of Jupiter exists, and this is true with respect to all other gods. But something does exist, something that is far more terrible than these pseudo-gods, namely, an entire kingdom of darkness which is hostile to God, a host of demons or fallen angels who are ruled by the greatest of their number, namely, Satan, Ephesians 2:3, 6:12.[43]

Paul identified the idol feasts as one arena where demons are operative, attempting to destroy men's lives and souls. Christians refuse to believe this fact at their own peril.

And not to God -- The translation, "and not to God," introduces a thought which is quite superfluous; there is no need to declare that sacrifices to idols are not offered to God. Because the "not" does not modify the verb, but instead modifies "god," it would be better to translate this clause 'and to a no-god.' Compare Deuteronomy 32:21. "They have made me jealous with a no-god ... and I will make them jealous with a no-people." Evans gives the sense:

> Not only to what is no-god do they sacrifice, but to demons, who behind the screen and curtain of idol-worship are busy in their work of ruin to the souls and bodies of men who serve the images. While the worshippers offer to what they think is a god, they were really offering to a non-entity (i.e., the idols were no-gods at all), but at the same time they were laying their souls open to the enticement of demons and their bodies to their obsessions.[44]

And I do not want you to become sharers in demons -- This is tantamount to a command, 'Avoid meats offered to idols in the idol's temple!' – just as God Himself had commanded

---

[42] One of the great blind spots in modern thinking regards the very existence of Satan as a person, and the demons as his agents. Modern scholars are confident that in our enlightened age, we know better than to believe in the devil and the demons, and they 'exonerate' Paul at this point as being a man of his times, believing (erroneously) in demons as did all his contemporaries. Such a presentation is inimical to any doctrine of revelation guiding Paul's thinking or of inspiration guiding his writings so that they are infallible, and is to be rejected as being contrary to what Paul himself wrote in 1 Corinthians 2:6ff. How sad that scholars take neither biblical revelation nor spiritual reality seriously. How hollow their denials sound to folk who have grown up in the Third World where experience of the world of the occult is real, and it is on a daily basis evidenced to be real and dangerous to its participants.

[43] Lenski, *op. cit.*, p.415.

[44] Evans, *op. cit.*, p.315-316.

in Acts 15:29.[45] Now we understand the reason for the prohibition. Demons are the actual beings behind all pagan religions, a fact documented in both Testaments and by missionary experience. Idolatry is one medium through which Satanic and demonic power gets a foothold in men's lives. When a person participates in idolatry, that person is inviting the demons to have a major influence in the worshiper's life. Idolatry is dangerous! This is not an argument that there is always actual communion with demons when a man (e.g., a tourist) merely visits an idol's temple. But when a man eats of a banquet in the idol's honor at the idol's table, there is participation with demons. The connotations are all negative. (1) He has fellowship with demon worshipers. This "fellowship" is no different from what one finds also in Christianity. Paul has written in verse 17 how those at the Lord's Table are all one "body." (2) He tacitly acknowledges that the demon has the right to worship. (There is a moral connection with God in true communion of the Lord's Supper. Not only is there fellowship with Christian worshipers, there is also an acknowledgment that God and Christ have the right to our worship.) (3) He invites the demons to share in his life. The same words were used in verse 16 when it spoke of "sharing in the blood of Christ" and "sharing in the body of Christ." No wonder the Holy Spirit says, "Abstain from things sacrificed to idols" (Acts 15:29).

10:21 -- *You cannot drink the cup of the Lord and the cup of demons; you cannot partake of the table of the Lord and the table of demons.*

You cannot drink -- This does not mean that they had no physical ability to do this, or that it was a physical impossibility, for they certainly had power to "drink" of both cups. It does mean that a Christian could not consistently do it. It is completely out of character with a Christian profession to insist on eating meats offered to idols in the idol's temple. A Christian just cannot rightly partake of the Lord's Supper and also eat sacrificial meats in the idol's temple. The impossibility is moral, not physical. Whether weak brother or strong, they had no right to sit at demon's tables. They had no right to endorse demon worship, and to invite demons to have an influence over their lives.

The cup of the Lord -- The "cup of the Lord" is the one received during the Lord's Supper.

And the cup of demons -- In the feasts in honor of the gods, wine was both poured out as a libation and drunk by the worshipers. Since demons were behind the idol worship, one was drinking to the demons.[46] The heathens thought their gods were pleased when the

---

[45] This last note addresses an issue that many have seen as a problem in the New Testament, namely, how do you reconcile Acts 15:29 and 1 Corinthians 10? The best way seems to be to understand that Acts 15:29 ("abstain from meats sacrificed to idols") means 'do not go to a feast in the idol's temple!' Acts 15:29 does not require abstaining from sacrificial meat purchased in the market place, or set on the table in a friend's home. In other words, Paul does not contradict the decree of the Jerusalem Conference when he writes 1 Corinthians, but simply helps us see what that prohibition actually covered.

[46] The custom of drinking toasts at feasts and celebrations arose from this practice of pouring out wine, or drinking in honor of the heathen gods. One might say that drinking toasts is still a practice that partakes of the nature of heathenism. (Barnes, *op. cit.*, p.210)

worshipers drank intoxicating beverages. The drinking of such a cup (or the pouring out of such a libation) was usually accompanied with a prayer to the idol-god that he would accept the offering, that he would be propitious, and that he would grant the desire of the worshipper. (Barnes, *op. cit.*, p.210) The original question dealt with idol-meats only and said nothing about the wine served at the idol feasts. But the entire idol feast with any and all food and drink is celebrated in honor of the idol. Hence, it is impossible that a Christian communicant could drink of the wine thus served or partake of anything that is served on the banquet table in the idol's temple.

You cannot partake -- Both infinitives in this verse are durative: you cannot 'be drinking ... be partaking.' A misguided Christian might attend a single idol feast and not immediately lose his Christianity, but he cannot continue this wicked practice without spiritual ruin to himself. If a man accepts the Lord's invitation, he cannot in good conscience also accept the invitation of demons to a "table."

Of the table of the Lord -- This is the first instance in which this expression is used, and it has perhaps originated the name that we many times use. There is an implication from this language that at Corinth, in the place where the congregation assembled on Sunday, there was a table specially used to hold the loaf and the cup. After the prayers of "blessing" were said here, the elements were then distributed. The "table of the Lord" reminds us that the Lord is the host at communion. By parity of reasoning, the "table of demons" indicates that there may be other hosts.

And the table of demons -- The allusion is to the banquet table loaded with food and drink situated in the idol's temple.[47] A Christian who has been at the Lord's Table on Sunday cannot go to the table in the idol's temple and still be consistent in his profession.

10:22 -- *Or do we provoke the Lord to jealousy? We are not stronger than He, are we?*

Or -- "Or" joins verse 22 to verse 21, and offers an alternative. The connection seems to be this: 'You cannot eat of both tables. Or are you brave enough to provoke the Lord to jealousy by the attempt?' Since verse 20 gives the true situation regarding participation in idol feasts, a Christian who refuses to heed Paul's words has only one terrible alternative. He is acting in such a way that will make the Lord angry with him. If some Corinthian Christian continues to insist on his 'rights' to do that which the Lord has prohibited, thus dividing his allegiance between the Lord and demons, he runs the very real risk of provoking the Lord to jealousy.

Do we provoke the Lord to jealousy? -- This expression, "provoke to jealousy," is taken from Deuteronomy 32:21, from the metaphor of a marriage between God and His people, just as the language of verse 20 likely came from Deuteronomy 32. Because Deuteronomy

---

[47] Oxyrhynchus Papyrus 110, an invitation to a banquet in an idol's temple, specifically refers to "the table." The invitation reads, "Chairemon invites you to a meal at *the table of the lord Serapis* in the Serapeum, tomorrow the fifteenth from nine o'clock onwards."

32 refers to Jehovah, some think that God the Father is in view both in Deuteronomy 32 and here in 1 Corinthians 10:22. But here in 1 Corinthians, in verse 21, "Lord" was a reference to Jesus Christ. It is very likely that Paul has Jesus in mind when he writes "Lord" here in verse 22. The Lord is jealous for his bride, the church. Idolatry is spiritual adultery. If the Lord is just, and if the Lord is holy, He must be jealous. He must regard the worship of idols as a direct affront to Himself. Idolatry, more (perhaps) than any other sin, has tended to stir up Jehovah's anger (remember Exodus 20:5, where, after prohibiting the worship of images, God adds, "I, the Lord your God, am a jealous God!"). Jealousy, of course, will incite Him to action in His hatred of sin and mixed allegiances in men. And it is a fearful thing to fall into the hands of the living God.[48]

We are not stronger than He, are we? -- The question expects a negative answer. 'Are we stronger than He? Surely not!' In which areas the Lord's strength is thought of as being exhibited depends in part on how we identified "Lord" in the previous question. Perhaps Paul is asking, 'Are we stronger than Jesus Christ was during his stay on earth? During His incarnation, and especially in the desert, He did not listen to the temptation to worship the devil. It would have been putting God to the test to do so.' Perhaps Paul is asking, 'Does a man think he can defy the Lord's omnipotence, and get away with it? It is safe to arouse the anger only of those who are weaker than we are.' What folly for frail men to insist on their rights, to challenge the Lord by their actions of worshiping demons, thereby daring Him to act.

Paul has now fully answered the question of the Corinthians concerning things sacrificed to idols, as far as going to the idol's temple is concerned.

2. The eating of sacrificial meat purchased at the meat market is permissible. 10:23-26

> *Summary:* The main question about attending idol feasts has been fully answered in the negative. But this still leaves two questions unanswered. Both are matters of Christian liberty (as verse 23 shows). One question concerns meats that were on sale in the markets for consumption by the general public. Does the fact that much of this meat was likely 'left overs' from a banquet in an idol's temple make it taboo for the Christian? The other question concerns accepting an invitation to and eating a meal in a pagan's home where the meat served might originally have been an idol sacrifice. What is a Christian to do in this case? Paul now answers these questions in detail, the first one in verses 23-26 and the second in verses 27-30.

---

[48] To say that God may be aroused to jealousy, vindictive zeal, and wrath is to apply anthropopathic terms to Him. The Scriptures constantly speak about God in this manner, yet without in the least attributing to Him the imperfections and the faults that attach to human jealousy and human anger. Unbelief may latch on to these terms about God's wrath and jealousy, and will always mock at these terms and misuse them for its own purposes until the day of reckoning comes. But that should not cause us to doubt that such qualities actually exist in God. Since heaven's high language exceeds all human speech, God graciously condescends to speak to us in such human terms as we can understand. Yet we well know that they express the divine realities in an inadequate manner.

10:23 -- *All things are lawful, but not all things are profitable. All things are lawful, but not all things edify.*

All things are lawful, but not all things are profitable -- Remember that this was the very language used by Paul (6:12ff) as he enunciated the great principle of Christian liberty. By reminding his readers of the limitations that govern our liberty in Christ, Paul has prepared the way to answer the remaining two questions about meats offered to idols. Going to the idol's temple in order to participate in a feast is a matter that does not fall into the realm of liberty. God had spoken against it. Christians were not, therefore, free to choose to attend such banquets. But God has not specifically legislated on the other two questions, so the Christian applies the guidelines provided to decide matters of liberty as a choice of behavior is made. "Profitable," as it did in chapter 6, means 'spiritually helpful.' One of the things taken into account as a Christian decides how to make use of the liberty he has in Christ is to contemplate what would tend to be to his own spiritual profit.

All things are lawful, but not all things edify -- "Edify" means to "build up" (see notes at 8:1). Perhaps it is the whole body of believers, the church itself, that is in Paul's mind. Perhaps it is each individual Christian's spiritual life that is in Paul's mind. As believers determine how they will behave in areas of Christian liberty, not only do they take into account their own spiritual profit, but they also must take into account how their actions will affect others. If others would be harmed spiritually, then the Christian exercises his liberty not to act. If others will be helped spiritually, the Christian exercises his liberty to act. Paul uses the same limitations in the matter of liberty as he did before when arguing *ad hominem* in chapter 8. This is the way the Christian settles all questions about his or her conduct. The glorious thing is that Christians are free to do that which will be most spiritually beneficial, both to themselves and to their brothers. It is absurd to insist on doing things just because they are lawful when these things do not build up and further the Christian life, but instead damage and destroy it for himself and for others. There are some things that are not wise. They do not build men up in the faith. It is more important to avoid such matters than to assert one's rights.

10:24 -- *Let no one seek his own good, but that of his neighbor.*

Let no one seek his own *good* -- Lest his readers miss the thrust of "edify," Paul spells out exactly what he means. The difficulty is trying to put this into practice, not in understanding the principle itself. The idea is "Let no man, in regard to the question about eating sacrificial meat at home or at a neighbor's house, simply consult his own pleasure, happiness, or selfish convenience, but let him, as the leading rule on the subject, ask what will be for the welfare of others." This same thought occurs at Romans 15:1-3 and Philippians 2:19-21.

But that of his neighbor – The KJV reads "but every man another's *wealth*." The word "wealth" is not found in any manuscript. All the Greek text has at this place is a neuter singular article, "the (something neuter singular)." The English word "wealth" has, in the passing of time, come to bear a limited significance, different from what it used to have.

By "wealth" we now mean temporal possessions or money. It used to mean "good," including moral welfare. Such a word was probably exactly a right choice when the KJV was translated 400 years ago. The other person's moral welfare is what we seek when we determine how to exercise our liberty in Christ. The Greek reads 'Let every man seek the (something neuter singular) ... of the other.' The other person can be a church member or someone outside the church (see verse 32).

In all open questions, it is the well-being of the other persons concerned, and not one's own rights, that should determine one's action. This principle is now applied: first, in the case of things bought (verses 25,26), and second, in the case of what is eaten when visiting in another's home (verses 27-30).

10:25 -- *Eat anything that is sold in the meat market without asking questions for conscience' sake;*

Eat anything that is sold in the meat market -- The ASV reads "the shambles" where the NASB has "the meat market." The Greek word, *makellōn*, found only here in the New Testament, refers to what we could call a butcher shop, such as one still finds in open-air market places in the Third World.[49] These butcher shops stood right next door to the idol's temples, making it more than probable that some of the meat offered for sale in the shop has come from carcasses of animals recently offered as sacrifices in the idol's temple. All the meat left after the worshipers finished their banquet would be taken to the butcher shop, and there offered for sale.

The apostle says it is perfectly permissible to purchase and eat the meat sold in the market, since the mere fact that it had been offered in sacrifice could not change its quality or render it unfit for use. This is an entirely different matter than what the previous paragraph dealt with. They were to avoid attending the feasts made to the idols, and from participating in the sacrificial feasts in the idol's temple. But if the meat was displayed indiscriminately in the market with other meat, Christians were not to be hesitant about purchasing it or eating it. "If a Christian merely bought his meat in the open market, no one could suspect him of meaning thereby to connive at or show favor to idolatry." Paul tells the Corinthian Christians to be altogether unconcerned about the nature of the meat that is sold in the ordinary butcher shops; they may buy and eat and be satisfied.[50]

---

[49] The word *macellum* is thought to be a Roman word taken over into the Greek cities after Rome conquered the world. See H.J. Cadbury, "The Macellum of Corinth," *JBL* 53 (1934), p.134-41. The *macellum* was one of the more prominent shops in the ancient marketplaces, if what archaeologists have found at Pompeii and Corinth are typical. The architecture was eye-catching and the building materials used were expensive. Cadbury describes some of these lavish buildings, and notes that a Latin inscription with the word *macellum* has been found in the marketplace at Corinth. Mare (*op. cit.*, p.253) also has a discussion of the derivation of the word (showing it may be a word of Greek rather than Latin origin), as well as a description of the typical meat market.

[50] Farrar, *op. cit.*, p.325. The rules for Christians are different than the rabbinic rules for the Jews (see the Misnaic tractate *Hullin* which is devoted to regulations for 'animals killed for food'). Such meat was expressly forbidden to Jews; it was not kosher, and besides that, it may have been butchered by pagan priests who served in the idols' temples.

Without asking questions for conscience' sake -- Whose conscience? Some say the conscience of an observer, and appeal is made to verse 29. However, verse 28 indicates a definite break in thought, from one person to another. Therefore, it seems best to understand this of the conscience of the person doing the eating. Verse 26 is a reason for so understanding this verse. The "questions" have to do with the origin of any piece of meat displayed for sale in the butcher shop. Don't trouble your conscience by scruples arising from needless investigation about the source of the meat offered for sale. There is no need to be so scrupulous about your meats. The Christians are not to inquire whether the piece they are about to purchase is a portion from an idol sacrifice or not. Eat the meat without inquiry about whether or not it was an idol offering – so that your conscience won't be bothered or burdened. Buying food for our own table is an entirely different thing from dining at a feast given in honor of some idol.

10:26 -- *FOR THE EARTH IS THE LORD'S, AND EVERYTHING THAT IS IN IT.*

FOR THE EARTH IS THE LORDS', AND EVERYTHING THAT IS IN IT -- This is quoted verbatim from the LXX of Psalm 24:1 (23:1 per the LXX). "For," which ties this verse to verse 25, shows that verse 26 is urged as a reason why it is permissible to eat the meat offered for sale in the market place without any twinge of conscience. It all belongs to the Lord. Everything the earth produces belongs to Him. He causes it to grow, and He has given it for food to man. "For everything created by God is good, and nothing is to be refused, if it be received with gratitude" (1 Timothy 4:4). Meat does not cease to be God's creature and possession because it has been offered in sacrifice; what is His will not pollute any one.

3. It is Permissible for the Christian to eat at an unconverted friend's house (unless his eating gives offense to one sitting at the table). 10:27-30

> *Summary:* Here is Paul's answer to the last of the questions involving meat offered to idols. 'Should I worry about where my host purchased the food he offers to me?' The answer to this question, too, falls into the realm of Christian liberty, so the Christian determines his behavior by the well-known limitations to liberty.

10:27 -- *If one of the unbelievers invites you and you wish to go, eat anything that is set before you without asking questions for conscience' sake.*

If one of the unbelievers invites you -- "Unbelievers" are non-Christians – people who are unconverted. It would not be unheard of for former acquaintances, relatives, and friends, who do not yet share the Christian faith of the church members, to invite their old friends[51] to a meal. Evidently the feast is in the home, not the idol's temple, for eating in an idol's temple has been dealt with and forbidden above.

---

[51] The "you" is plural here in verse 27 and verse 28.

And you wish to go -- Most commentators see in these words a slight hint that remaining away would be a little better than going to the feast. Heathenish customs were everywhere in vogue, and the temptation to deny Christ on the part of those not firmly established in the faith would be stronger at such a feast. They might be better off if they did not go, but Paul does not prohibit their attending the feast. Here, again, Paul is giving different directions to the Christians than Jewish people would have heard from their rabbis in similar situations. Jewish traditional law would have forbade attendance at such meals in a non-Jewish home.

Eat anything that is set before you, without asking questions for conscience' sake -- 'Don't worry about the food set before you, as to whether or not it has been offered to idols.' The same rule of conduct (as given in verse 25) applies in this case. The unbeliever may or may not have bought idol meat for the meal; it makes no difference. Go ahead and eat the meat. Eat without inquiry that the conscience may not be offended. There is no need to make investigation as to the origin of the meat. The case, however, is altered when the attention of the guest has been turned to the sacrificial character of the meat presented.

10:28 -- *But if anyone says to you, "This is meat sacrificed to idols," do not eat it, for the sake of the one who informed you, and for conscience' sake;*

But if anyone should say to you -- This means any other person at the feast. It might be the host, or some scrupulous fellow Christian, or one of the heathen guests. It is not unheard of for the host, or a fellow guest, to deliberately point out something they think is questionable just to see what the Christian will do. Even unconverted people have been known to have a conscience about some of their own behavior. The reference more likely is to some weak brother who also is present, and who is trying to warn his brother in Christ. (The context has been speaking of weak Christian brothers.) This may well be a hypothetical case, and not the general occurrence.

"This is meat sacrificed to idols" -- The word (*hierothuton*) used here (according to the best manuscripts) for "sacrificed to an idol" is different from the condemnatory word (*eidolōthutos*) elsewhere used. Natural courtesy would lead a Christian at the table of a heathen to use an epithet which would not be offensive to his host. (Learn here a lesson in controversy – do not conceal your conscientious convictions, but do not express them in language unnecessarily painful to your opponent.[52]) Farrar has commented, "The mere fact of attention being called to the food as previously being part of a heathen sacrifice is enough to make it your duty to give no overt sanction to idolatry."[53] Kling insists that Farrar has given a forced interpretation. He says that the real issue is the matter of wounding the informer's conscience. Kling, we believe, is on the right track.[54] A 'weak brother' has somehow found out the origin of the meat, and the fact that he feels constrained to 'warn' his Christian brother shows that the weak brother needs loving attention and

---

[52] Shore, *op. cit.*, p.96.

[53] Farrar, *op. cit.*, p.325.

[54] Kling, *op. cit.*, p.218.

help. So the strong Christian must then use his liberty in a truly intelligent and loving way. Liberty (to eat or not to eat) is given us, not in order to hurt ourselves and others, but in order to help ourselves and others. Don't eat – and thus help the weak brother.

Do not eat *it*, for the sake of the one who informed *you* -- Do not offend him; do not behave in such a way as to lead him to be tempted to do something against his conscience; do not pain and wound his feelings. "Informed" is *mēnuō*, 'to disclose what does not appear on the surface.'

And for conscience' sake[55] -- As next verse shows, it is the conscience of the informer that is intended. Out of consideration for the weaker conscience of such a one the strong should abstain from eating.

10:29 -- *I mean not your own conscience, but the other* **man's***; for why is my freedom judged by another's conscience?*

I mean not your own conscience, but the other *man's* -- Verse 29 explains the "for conscience' sake" with which verse 28 concluded. It is the 'informer's' conscience that the Christian is concerned about. Taking verse 29 as an explanation of verse 28 also reconciles the instructions in this case with those given in verses 25 and 27, and also brings the Christian's behavior into line with the limitations on liberty given in verse 23.

For why is my freedom judged by another's conscience? -- Commentators and translators have had much difficulty with this clause. Beginning with "for," it seems to give a reason for something just said, but does it not then become entirely contradictory to what the apostle had been saying? Paul had been urging the Corinthians to have respect for other men's consciences, and in some sense to give up their liberty for the opinions and feelings of the weak brother. As it reads, this clause seems to ask, 'Why is my freedom bound by someone else's scruples?' Two different ways are offered to explain this difficult clause.

(1) One is to put a period at the end of 29a, and to then begin a new thought with 29b and 30. Verses 29b-30 are then considered to be someone's reply to Paul's argument about abstaining. 'Why should my freedom be at the mercy of someone else's conscience? After all, I gave thanks to God for my food. Why should anyone criticize me about food for which I gave thanks?' Then Paul answers the retort in 10:31-11:1, 'Because, whatever you do, eating or drinking, everything should be done to bring glory to God ....' This commentator, however, does not think this phrase is a retort given by some objector to Paul's teaching about being concerned over the conscience of the weaker brother who informed about the meat since there are no introducing words to let us know that verse 29b is a different speaker from 29a.

---

[55] Some English versions again have the words "for the earth is the Lord's and the fullness thereof" at the close of verse 28. The repetition of these words in this verse is an interpolation not found in the best manuscripts and tends to interrupt the thought of verse 28 which is carried on in verse 29.

(2) The better way is to follow the NASB's punctuation, with a semi-colon in the middle of verse 29. This punctuation treats 29b and 30 as a reason why the "conscience" mentioned in verse 28 is not that of the eater, but of the *informer*. The *eater's* conscience is not affected one way or another by what another man says (as far as matters of liberty are concerned). The *eater's* freedom is not subject to the weakness of some other individual's conscience. The *informer* does not have the right to sit in judgment on the *eater's* liberty, and order the *eater* to do what the *informer's* conscience considers right, or forbid the *eater* to do what his conscience considers wrong.

10:30 -- *If I partake with thankfulness, why am I slandered concerning that for which I give thanks?*

If I partake with thankfulness -- Scripture presents God's people giving thanks[56] before eating. Even in a pagan home, the Christian "partakes with thankfulness." My own conscience will not be affected by the food which I eat if I have given thanks for it.

Why am I slandered concerning that for which I give thanks? -- "Slandered" (to criticize, to speak evil of – literally, to blaspheme) is a sharp word denoting the bitter condemnation pronounced upon the eater of the meat, as a man who is false to his principles. Exactly what Paul means by this question is a matter of dispute. Some suppose he is impressing the duty of not giving occasion for others to condemn. Others suppose he is rebuking those who, showing no proper love, judged another person. The best interpretation has Paul asking a question in this fashion: 'If I have given thanks for the food, why should my conscience bother me for eating it? It was the other person's conscience, not my own, that I was talking about in verse 28.'

C. Conclusion of Answers to their Questions About Meats Offered to Idols. 10:31-11:1

10:31 -- *Whether, then, you eat or drink or whatever you do, do all to the glory of God.*

Whether, then -- Beginning with *oun* ('therefore') Paul now draws the final conclusion. Two broad principles underlie all his instructions about meat offered to idols.[57] The first principle has to do with the glory of God. The second has to do with the salvation of men.

You eat or drink or whatever you do -- The two principles about to be highlighted give a Christian the guidelines he needs, not only in the matter of eating meats (whether in the idol's temple or at home), but in other areas of conduct as well. "Drink" reminds us of

---

[56] *Charis*, the word often translated 'grace,' can also express the idea of 'being grateful for,' and at such times is translated 'thanks' or 'thankfulness.'

[57] Some treat verse 31ff as a summary conclusion to only the last two questions about meats offered to idols, especially since verses 23-24 introduced the limitations to Christian liberty by which the answers to the questions are settled. This commentator sees no reason why it cannot be a summary of the answers to all three questions.

verse 21, which spoke of "[drinking] the cup of demons." A man could not do that and bring glory to God. "Whatever you do" means 'doing anything else besides eating and drinking.' These words embrace all of life. "The modern idea of some acts being religious and some secular is neither here nor elsewhere recognized by Paul. No act of life is in itself either religious or secular. The quality of each act depends on the spirit which guides it, and the motive from which it springs."[58]

Do all to the glory of God -- This rule is true of all we do, but especially is it true in the realm of Christian liberty. Acting so as to bring honor to God reminds us of what Paul has already written at 6:20. If we establish this in our hearts (go or stay, keep or give, doing or restraining), that all is to be to the glory of God, then the Kingdom will go forward and the cause of Christ will be advanced. Paul's admonition amounts to this: 'Let your eye be fixed on God. Let the promotion of His glory be your object in all you do. Strive in everything to act in such a way that men may praise the God whom you profess to serve.' The following verse will give not only a second principle, but also a practical test of whether one's course of conduct is "to the glory of God." If one's course of conduct causes any human being to be offended, then it is not to God's glory.

10:32 -- *Give no offense either to Jews or to Greeks or to the church of God;*

Give no offense -- The ASV reads "give no occasion of stumbling." Don't put a stumbling block in another man's path. Don't act in such a way that others are encouraged to sin. The action which to the strong is a simple exercise of *liberty* must not be allowed to become the cause of stumbling to another. Paul is likely addressing not only the Christian who was insisting on his 'rights,' but also the strong brother who was sitting at a feast in a friend's home and is informed about the meat being served (verses 28,29). 1 Corinthians 8:13 spoke about causing a brother to stumble. The theme introduced there is repeated here for emphasis. Care must be taken not to wrench this prohibition out of its context, for in some things the Jews and Gentiles must be offended. This certainly does not mean that Paul was going to cease preaching "Christ crucified, to the Jews a stumbling block, and to the Gentiles foolishness," or that the Corinthian Christians likewise should stop trying to convert their heathen neighbors lest they be offended.

Either to Jews or to Greeks or to the church of God -- These are three separate bodies. The third does not include the other two. "Jews" refers to unconverted Jews. "Greeks" refers to unconverted Greeks. The "church of God" has reference to our brothers and sisters in Christ.[59] In 9:20-22 Paul spoke of how he was careful how he lived (i.e., he vol-

---

[58] Shore, *op. cit.*, p.97.

[59] On the language "church of God" see notes at 1 Corinthians 1:2. Paul adds "of God" lest *ekklēsia* ('assembly, church') be taken to mean the 'city council' at Corinth which also was designated as an *ekklēsia*. Furthermore, reminding them that the church belongs to God supplies a new deterrent from self-indulgence. God's interests, more than the individual Christian's 'rights,' are the things that really matter.

 A topic of theological interest is also raised here. Is "church" a reference to a local congregation, or is it the church universal? Some affirm this text is the first example of Paul's use of the term "church" in a comprehensive sense. Others appeal to 12:28 as being the first example. 10:32 is ambiguous. It could be either the congregation in Corinth, or the church at large. There are unambiguous verses where

untarily waived some of his 'rights' so he might win Jews and Greeks to Christ). He also earlier in the letter has spoken about the edification of his fellow brothers and sisters in Christ. He repeats those emphases again as he gives this summary conclusion. The sphere of his moral obligation includes Jew and Greek and members of the Christian church. All are objects of his Christian care and concern. Christian conduct must be regulated with reference to those outside the church as well as those within. The Christian must beware of putting difficulties in the way of unconverted Jews by ill-considered use of liberty, or of unconverted Greeks by narrow-minded scruples, or of the church of God by unchristian self-seeking. No action of ours should give a Jew or Greek an excuse for not coming to Christ, and no action of ours is to prevent a Christian from remaining with Christ, and from ever drawing nearer to Him.

10:33 -- *just as I also please all men in all things, not seeking my own profit but the* **profit** *of many, that they may be saved.*

Just as I also please all men in all things -- Paul's own personal example played a large part in the argument in chapter 9. Here he again proposes his own example as their guide. It is fitting that he refers to it as he sums up his teaching about meats offered to idols and about waiving 'rights' to benefit others. "All things" are the "things" that are in the realm of Christian liberty, that are within the realm of expediency. Paul was not a man-pleaser. But if it meant the building of the kingdom, he was willing to "please men" by foregoing rights and privileges and pleasures (in the realm of expediency). After all, what is eternally important is that the cause of Christ is furthered. At Corinth, Paul waived asking for living wages. Before he came to Corinth, while he was there, and after he left, he continued to live in such a way that people would not be offended and refuse to give the gospel a hearing. His main object had been to "please all men," that is, not to alarm their prejudices, or needlessly to excite their opposition, while he made known to them the truth, and sought their salvation.

Not seeking my own profit – Paul again asserts that self-seeking is not his chief desire. Freedom in Christ (Christian liberty) does not mean one is free to do whatever one wishes with no regard for others.

But the *profit* of many, that they may be saved -- The conclusion shows what kind of "profit" Paul had in mind. It was spiritual profit. Compare what he wrote at 9:19-22. "Saved" means to have one's sins forgiven, to be redeemed from a life of slavery to sin, and to be on the way to heaven. The word is used here as it was in 9:22. The "many" means 'the whole great mass of men,' and not as the English seems to imply, merely 'a great number.'

"church" is used of the church universal, so that we do not need to press 10:32 into service to show that such an idea is Scriptural.

11:1 -- *Be imitators of me, just as I also am of Christ.*

Be imitators of me -- The first verse of chapter 11 properly belongs with the argument being urged in chapter 10, and the previous chapters. The new chapter should begin with what is now verse 2 of chapter 11. (The original manuscripts did not have chapter and verse breaks. Both kinds of divisions were added by men, and sometimes the men made mistakes concerning where sentences and paragraphs begin and end. The division into chapters has been variously attributed to Cardinal Hugo de St. Cairo, c. AD 1248, or to Stephen Langton, archbishop of Canterbury, AD 1207-1228. Verse markings were first put into the text by Stephanus, c. AD 1550, while crossing France on horseback, riding hurriedly from Paris to Lyons.)

Paul sets a marvelous example, as he is willing to forego rights and privileges that the kingdom might grow. What Paul practices, he urges upon all. Those who imitate Christ have a right to call upon others to imitate them. "Imitator" translates the Greek word from which our English word 'mimic' comes. Of course, no man is sinless perfect, not even Paul, so he does not expect men to copy everything he does. But there is an obligation on the part of a leader to set an example. When we see a man putting into practice the ideals of the Christian system, it makes them easier for us to follow. It would be well for all leaders to be able to say, 'Follow me as I show you how Christ lived.'

Just as I also am of Christ -- We are not to do all that Paul did. There is a limit placed on our following. We are to imitate Paul only in the places he is following Christ. This addition dispels the idea that there is any spirit of arrogance when he asks them to imitate him. Once more he is only asking them to do what he does himself: follow the example of Christ. The point of comparison between Christ and Paul has already been stated: Christ sought not His own advantage but that of others. He came to seek and to save. Let this mind that was in Christ, and then in Paul, be also in us.

With this exhortation, the answer to their questions about food offered to idols that began in 8:1 reaches its natural climax and conclusion.

SECTION SEVEN: CONCERNING PUBLIC WORSHIP DISORDERS IN THE CORINTHIAN CHURCH. 11:2-14:40

A. Disapproval of the Manner of Dress (heads covered or uncovered) When Men and Women Were Praying and Prophesying in the Public Assembly. 11:2-16

> *Summary:*
> 1. The principle stated (i.e., the doctrinal basis of these instructions). 11:3
> 2. The principle applied. 11:4-6
> 3. The principle defended. 11:7-10
> 4. The principle clarified. 11:11,12
> 5. The principle agreed to. 11:13-16

11:2 -- *Now I praise you because you remember me in everything and hold firmly to the traditions, just as I delivered them to you.*

Now I praise you -- Paul always chose to commend Christians when it could be done. It is good psychology. When folk are praised, they will more readily receive words of instruction and direction. Paul has some negative words to say later in the chapter, but he begins on a positive note by praising the church.

The new subject now dealt with for several chapters is that of public worship, or conduct in the public assembly. After prohibiting the Corinthian Christians from becoming involved in pagan worship (chapters 8-10), Paul now turns to ways Christians ought to behave at the assemblies where Jesus is worshiped. The Corinthians had asked Paul about one topic he deals with (see the "now concerning" at 12:1). But whether the topics covered in chapter 11 are ones Paul takes up on his own (the word Paul uses is *de* not *peri*), rather than simply answering a question they have asked, is not easy to decide. Perhaps chapter 11 is Paul's response to their affirmation that they were trying to remember what Paul told them. Perhaps 11:18 indicates Paul has learned about the matters covered in chapter 11 from those who carried the Corinthians' letter to him. 11:2-16 (and indeed chapters 11-14 as a whole) have some notoriously difficult verses to exegete. Some have tried to solve one problem by suggesting Paul did not write 11:2-16.[1] However, the manuscript evidence is that this paragraph enjoys integrity; it was not a later addition. Some have suggested verses 3-7 (or 3-10) – the most objectionable portion for many modern interpreters – are in fact a Corinthian position that Paul goes on to refute in verses 11-16. But this suggested interpretation neglects the fact that verses 13-16 support (rather than refute) the position outlined in 3-10. Doctoral dissertations have been written about the meaning of some absolutely crucial terms, including "head" (verses 3-5), "having some-

---

[1] For example, see W.O. Walker, "1 Corinthians 11:2-16 and Paul's View Regarding Women," *JBL* 94 (1975), p.94-110, and L. Cope, "1 Corinthians 11:2-16: One Step Further," *JBL* 97 (1978), p.435-36.

thing on the head" (verse 4), "uncovered" (verse 5,13), "glory" (verse 7), "authority on her head" (verse 10), "because of the angels" (verse 10), "for a covering" (verse 15), and "no other practice [custom]" (verse 16). Further, extra-biblical literature from the 1st centuries BC and AD is far from providing adequate information concerning prevailing customs in the cultures and in the churches, and concerning the complex question of early Christian worship. Complicating our study even more is the influence in recent decades of the feminist movement, both inside and outside the church. Many recent studies are overt attempts to rewrite the ancient record in such a way as to promote the feminist agenda.[2]

[Brethren] -- This word in the King James Version is an interpolation. It is found in D, E, F, G, K, L. It is omitted by *Aleph*, A, B, C, P.

Because you remember me in everything -- This is probably a quotation from their letter. "You remember me," at first sight, is a surprising statement in light of what has been written earlier in 1 Corinthians, where many were rejecting Paul and were preferring Apollos or Cephas to him. Perhaps the matter of dress while praying and prophesying, as indeed all their behavior at public worship, was something that cut across all the party lines at Corinth, so that in this matter they could indeed say 'we try to remember and do what you taught us.' For Paul to praise them for trying to remember what he taught them, indicates Paul's own self-awareness of the authority behind his teaching. He is aware that if they remember his teaching as they went about their everyday efforts to live in harmony with the will of the Lord, they would be doing the very thing the Lord who sent him to be an apostle wanted done.

And hold firmly to the traditions, just as I delivered them to you -- The word *paradoseis* ("traditions") speaks of 'a handing down,' 'a delivery by word of mouth,' or even 'a delivery in writing.'[3] In the beginning of Christianity, for the first 20 or 25 years, all teaching was by word of mouth. What the apostles and ministers of the word had heard from Jesus, they repeated to audiences all over the Roman Empire. Those memorized and oft-repeated lessons were 'traditions,' 'oral traditions.' There is no significant difference, contentwise, between the oral traditions in those early years and what we now read in the written books that together make up our New Testament Scriptures.[4] The word "traditions" carries an entirely bad connotation today that it did not have in New Testament times. In the New Testament, it was used of both good and bad teachings. In the bad sense, the word is used of the traditions of men (traditions that originated with men) that are to be avoided (Matthew 15:2,3,9; Colossians 2:8; Galatians 1:14). In the good sense,

---

[2] Linda Mercadante, *From Hierarchy to Equality: A Comparison of Past and Present Interpretations of 1 Cor. 11:2-16 in Relation to the Changing Status of Women in Society* (Vancouver: G-M-H Books, 1978) gives a good overview of how exegesis of this passage has been influenced by culture.

[3] The KJV uses "ordinances" here to show what the translators thought was involved in the word "traditions" – i.e., something no less important than a commandment or rule of order from God Himself.

[4] Readers should be aware of the use of this verse by the Roman Catholic Church to justify their "traditions" as being on a par with Scripture. Paul's "traditions" were "Scripture" (the word of God), not some doctrine that grew with added accretions through the years, and which, after centuries passed, eventually became dogma.

the word is used of the traditions that originated with God the Father, or the Lord Jesus Himself (1 Timothy 6:20; 2 Timothy 1:14). "Delivered" (*paradidomi* and its cognate noun) is a technical term in Judaism for the oral transmission of religious instruction.[5] The apostle had *delivered* certain doctrines, or rules, respecting the facts of the gospel and the good order and government of the church; the Corinthian Christians had, in general, observed them. This verb indicates that Paul's teachings did not originate in 'the fertile mind of the teacher.' It does say the "traditions" were not Paul's; for example, he received revelations from Jesus (Galatians 1:12). The teachings had been handed down to him, and he passed them on to his converts. The term stresses the derivative nature of the gospel message Paul preached. For whatever inclination or disposition they had to regard the apostolic authority, and to carefully practice what he had enjoined, Paul commends them. Have differences of opinions or disputes arisen on how much the various regulations Paul taught really included? Have new questions sprung up about which Paul had not given any teaching, and about which even the most loyal of Paul's friends were in doubt?

1. The principle stated (the doctrinal basis of these instructions). 11:3

11:3 -- *But I want you to understand that Christ is the head of every man, and the man is the head of a woman, and God is the head of Christ.*

But I want you to understand -- "I want you to understand" is a formula for introducing something not previously mentioned. The same formula is found at Colossians 2:1 with a similar meaning. Another formula for introducing a new topic of teaching is 'I would not have you ignorant.' Compare with this the words "Do you not know?" (as at 1 Corinthians 3:16) which remind the readers of something they already know. Paul is laying the doctrinal basis on which the practical instructions which follow are grounded. Paul often applies the loftiest principles to the solution of the humblest difficulties. Given a question as to what is right or wrong in a particular instance, he always aims at laying down some great eternal fact to which the duty or decision is ultimately referable, and deduces the required rule from the fact. It is important not only to do certain things, but to do them intelligently, for the right reason. While he was preaching in Corinth when the church was planted, Paul had not specifically taught about the proper decorum of men and women[6] who were participating in the public assembly. He does so now, first laying a theological foundation, and then giving specific applications arising out of those theological truths.

---

[5] See B. Gerhardsson, *Memory and Manuscript* (Lund: G.W.K. Gleerup, 1964). K.E. Bailey, "Middle Eastern Oral Tradition and the Synoptic Gospels," *Expository Times* 106 (Sep 1995), p.363-367, shows that "minister of the word" is the regular title for the *haflat samar* (party of preservation) who made sure the traditions were handed down without variation.

[6] In our outline, the topic of the first paragraph of chapter 11 was given as "Disapproval of the manner of dress (with heads covered or uncovered) when men and women were praying and prophesying in the public assembly." As Paul covers this topic, he instructs both men and women about their dress. It does not seem proper, as some authors do, to treat the paragraph as if the whole emphasis was on the behavior of the women.

That Christ is the head of every man -- The word "head" (*kephalē*) appears 9 times in this paragraph, and each time the commentator must decide whether it is to be taken literally (referring to a part of a human body) or metaphorically[7] (referring to something other than a part of one's anatomy). It is likely that here in verse 3 the word "head" is used metaphorically, but there is no agreement among commentators as to the exact import of the metaphor. (1) Some have argued the word *kephalē* means 'source,' as in 'source of life' (like a progenitor is the 'source of all the descendants' or parents are the 'cause' of their children's living). This view is defended by many modern scholars and is popular with the Women's Rights Movement since the verse would no longer say woman is 'subordinate' to man as the traditional view has argued.[8] (2) The traditional view has been that *kephalē* indicates a relationship of superior authority, so commentators have opted for "master," "ruler," "chief" as words that might convey the idea of superior authority.[9] The word *rosh* (Hebrew) is often thus used in the Old Testament.[10] In the New Testament, the word is used in the sense of Lord, ruler, chief (cf. Ephesians 1:22, 4:15, 5:23; Colossians 2:10). In another passage in which Paul calls a man "head" over a woman, it refers to wives' subordination to their husbands (Ephesians 5:22-24). Here it means that Christ is the ruler, director, or Lord of the Christian man.[11] The context would seem to imply that "every man" means 'every Christian,' rather than 'head of the whole human race.' There is nothing degrading about each Christian recognizing his subordinate position to Christ. In fact, such recognition brings a person his ultimate sense of fulfillment.

---

[7] Verse 3 is metaphorical, and probably also in verses 4,5 (in the phrase "disgraces his/her head"). It is probably to be taken literally in verses 4,5, when it talks about the "head" being uncovered or covered.

[8] While illustrations from Greek literature may be given where *kephalē* might mean 'source' or 'beginning,' one could get into trouble using this meaning in the last clause of 1 Corinthians 11:3, where it says "God is the *kephalē* of Christ." It will not do to use "source" there if one were then to use this verse as a proof text that Jesus is a created being, for that would be an anti-Biblical doctrine. Fee (p.503) in his commentary has a fine summary of the recent scholarly articles on the meaning of *kephalē*. In particular he calls attention to Stephen Bedale's "The Meaning of *kephalē* in the Pauline Epistles," *JTS* 5 (1954), p.211-215, the most widely cited article in support of *kephalē* as "source." (Bedale's own view is consistently misrepresented by feminist writers who omit his conclusions, such as "That is to say, male is *kephalē* in the sense of *archē* [beginning] relative to the female; and, in St. Paul's view, the female in consequence is 'subordinate'.") Fee also calls attention to Wayne Grudem's "Does *Kephalē* Mean 'Source' or 'Authority Over' in Greek Literature?" *Trin.J*, n.s. 6 (1985), p.38-59; and to B. and A. Mickelsen's "What Does *Kephalē* Mean in the New Testament?" in *Women, Authority, and the Bible* (ed. A. Mickelsen: Downers Grove, IL, 1986). These articles defend the proposition that if *kephalē* ever means "head," about the only place it is so is in Paul's writings. Fee then contends that the phrase about "Christ being the source of man" must refer either to the original creation which was done by Jesus, or to the new creation which was also effected by Jesus. Fee must then say that God being the 'source' of Christ has reference to the incarnation (since Jesus is not a created being).

[9] Those who wish to pursue the debate at greater length should consult Wayne Grudem, "The Meaning of *Kephalē* ('head'): A Response to Recent Studies," in *Recovering Biblical Manhood and Womanhood*, ed. John Piper and Wayne Grudem (Wheaton, IL : Crossway, 1991), p.425-468, and the literature there reviewed.

[10] For Scriptures, see Barnes, *op. cit.*, p.201.

[11] Even if we grant that *kephalē* means "source," this verse indicates some kind of subordination of man to Christ, or some kind of dependence upon one who is the provider.

And the man is the head of a woman -- What translation shall we give to *anēr* and *gunē* – "man" and "woman," or "husband" and "wife"? In every other place where these words are paired (including, in this commentator's judgment, 1 Timothy 2:8-15), they refer to husband and wife. It is difficult to see that Paul is claiming that every male has authority over every female (which is the implication if we read 'man and woman'), but it is not difficult to agree with Paul's statement about 'headship' if husbands and wives are meant throughout (cf. verse 5). Even the references to Adam and Eve (verses 8-9) could refer to the first married couple as much as to male and female. The NRSV may well be on the right track with its translation of this clause of verse 3 as "the husband is head of his wife." Paul is teaching the subordination of the wife to the husband, because this is directly connected with higher relations. The subordinate position of wives is also stated in 1 Timothy 2:11,12 and 1 Peter 3:1,5,6. The subordination indicated here in verse 3 is grounded in the creation and fall. Verses 11 and 12 will develop this truth, by alluding to Genesis 2:21ff. Wives are to be subordinate to their husbands, both because man was created first and because the wife was first in the transgression (1 Timothy 2:14). The 'hierarchy' of marriage in Ephesians 5:22-33 is not the authority of extra privilege, but one of extra responsibility. Husbands do not domineer, but love their wives sacrificially. Wives are not commanded to obey, but to voluntarily submit to their husbands. The "subordination" here indicated is not degrading or dishonoring. There is no suggestion that the wife is the husband's toy or slave. As the church is not dishonored by being subject to Christ, so neither is the wife dishonored by being subject to her husband. Numerous have been the egalitarian attempts to make Galatians 3:28 the norm when it comes to the distinction of the sexes and the role of male and female in the church. The significant thing about Galatians 3:28, that is often missed, is that the context is speaking not of roles in the church; rather, Galatians 3:28 deals rather with equal opportunity or eligibility to participate in the salvation (forgiveness of sins) available in Christ. "There is neither male nor female," that is, man and woman are equal before God in reference to salvation. So in one respect, man and woman are equal. But there is still to be the subordination of wife to husband here on earth. Galatians 3:28 does not do away with the divine order of subordination that has been true ever since the creation and fall.

And God is the head of Christ -- We suppose that Paul deliberately wrote as he did (putting this phrase last in the sentence) to call attention to the fact that what he was teaching about "headship" (subordination) of men (to Christ) and wives (to their husbands) did not differ greatly from Christ's relationship to the Father. Jesus Christ, because He volunteered to become incarnate, occupied a subordinate station to the Father (1 Corinthians 15:27,28), both during the time of His incarnation and (apparently) throughout His mediatorial work. When the passage speaks of God as being Christ's head, we are talking of Christ's temporary subordination in function, a subordination for the purpose of becoming mankind's redeemer (see notes at 1 Corinthians 8:6). We are not talking about subordination in being or deity.[12] It was the Father who sent Christ into the world. It

---

[12] 1 Corinthians 11:3 was a favorite Arian text, and they argued that it implied more than inferiority because of Christ's human nature. See Shore (*op. cit.*, p.64,65), and Godet at 1 Corinthians 11:3, who show that Arians argued this verse teaches that eternally Jesus was less deity than the Father.

was the Father who worked through Jesus to reconcile the world to Himself (2 Corinthians 5:19; John 3:16). Jesus emptied himself of the independent exercise of the prerogatives of deity when He became incarnate (Philippians 2:6-8). But He did not become a shriveled up deity, or somehow less deity. He was "God in the flesh" (Immanuel, Isaiah 7:14). Jesus could declare without any sense of contradiction both that "the Father is greater than I" (John 14:28) and "I and the Father are one" (John 10:30).

The mention of the various "headships" here in verse 3 is the theological basis for the remainder of this paragraph. The key to a proper role relationship is to recognize who one's superiors are. *The general thrust of Paul's argument is that none of the subordinates should ever act in such a way as to reflect badly on their "head" (superior).* There is a hierarchy of descending authority – God, Christ, husband (man), wife (woman). As God is the head of Christ, and as Christ is the head of the Church, so the husband is the head of the wife. From the doctrine now established in this verse, Paul first draws an inference for the husband (man) in the matter of his apparel while at church (verse 4), and then applies the facts concerning headship to the problem of the wife's (woman's) dress while at church (verses 5ff).

2. The principle applied. 11:4-6

11:4 -- *Every man who has something on his head while praying or prophesying disgraces his head.*

Every man -- "Man" is *anēr* – man as opposed or contrasted to woman or child. It is also the word for "husband." A man ought to have his head uncovered when he is praying in the public assembly, that is the thrust of this verse. This was something new for Paul the Christian. Jewish men always prayed with their heads covered (as they still do). By contrast, both Greek women and Greek men prayed with heads uncovered. Christians adopted a distinctive practice of their own, a practice that portrays the Biblical idea of subordination.

Who has *something* on his head -- "Head" here is literal, referring to a part of the man's anatomy. "Something" is in italics because the Greek reads *kata kephalēs echōn*, "having down the head." Having *what* down on the head? Long hair,[13] a shawl, a skull cap (yar-

---

[13] The NIV margin reads "every man who prays or prophesies with long hair dishonors his head." The NIV marginal reading continues on in verse 5 to say that a woman "with no covering of hair on her head dishonors her head." Coffman (*op. cit.*, p.169) argues that the thing discussed in this whole paragraph is not veils but hair (i.e., long hair v. short hair). We will admit that in many verses his explanation might make sense. Verse 4 says men ought not have long hair. Verse 5 would say women ought not have short hair, nor should their hair styles be similar to that of the notorious Corinthian prostitutes. Verse 15 would say a woman's hair is given instead of a covering. Rather than having to wear a veil (the only place a word for veil appears in this whole paragraph), the woman's long hair is sufficient covering. But we also note that Coffman has trouble following this train of thought, and is forced to rather quickly skip over verses 7-9. The fact that 7-9 do not seem to fit the scenario Coffman suggests causes us to be hesitant to adopt it. In fact, Fee comments (*op. cit.*, p.499), "How this option made the NIV margin is a great puzzle. It does disservice to the Greek at too many places to be viable."

mulke), their toga? The "something" may be a veil, or turban, or cap, or whatever else is worn on the head. For a man to remove his hat, or turban, or the covering of the head, is a mark of respect for a superior when in his presence. Custom concerning dress while worshiping differed in the ancient world. Jewish men, when praying in public, put over their heads a veil, called the Tallith, to show their reverence before God and their unworthiness to look upon Him.[14] In the Old Testament, a veil was worn only in times of mourning (2 Samuel 15:30; Jeremiah 14:3,7). So customs in the 1st century world had changed from what they were in Old Testament times. The Jew (like Orientals generally) uncovered his feet because the place on which he stood was holy ground; but he covered his head by way of humility, even as the angels veil their faces with their wings. Roman men also worshiped with their head covered, and the Roman covering was called a *pileus*.[15] The Greek men's custom was to worship with the head uncovered.[16]

At first sight, it might seem that, since Corinth was in Greece, Paul simply decided in favor of the Greek custom for the Greek community in Corinth. But in a moment we shall see that Paul does not follow the Greek custom concerning the dress of ladies when worshiping in public. The fact that Paul sometimes follows local custom, and sometimes does not, shows that it is not the custom as a custom that is vital, but *the significance* of the custom. The custom of Greek men had a good significance. It showed submission to one's superior. He bids them therefore to abide by their custom.

> The fact that Paul sees the significance of the Greek custom with a Christian eye as pertaining to the true God and not with a pagan's eye as pertaining to idol gods should cause no confusion. The fact that he would use the Christian's eye if he were dealing with the opposite custom of other nationalities and not the pagan's eye is again beyond question. By so doing Paul is not introducing into these national customs something that is foreign and unjustifiable, but is unveiling to Christians the full and true significance of these customs which non-Christians grasped or felt only partially because the glory of the true God was hidden from them.[17]

All of this has application for us. When missionaries go to a foreign field, how far can they go in endorsing local customs while evangelizing and teaching what Christianity expects of new converts? If Paul were writing to Jews, or to Romans, or to Germans, all of whom covered the head during worship, he would have doubtless told them that a man

---

[14] A caution needs to be heeded about this comment. The Talmud articles, *B.Shab.* and *Abot R. Nat.* which tell of Jewish custom, may not reflect 1st century practices (since some were not written down until the 5th century AD).

[15] Aeneas introduced the custom to Italy, says Servius, *Ad Aen.*, iii.407. Goodenough, *Jewish Symbols in the Greco-Roman Period* (NY: 1964), v.11, fig. 98 and 99 show Roman men at Pompeii, worshiping with their heads covered.

[16] Plato, *Phaedo*, 89 BC. Illustrations on Greek pottery of the period, uncovered by archaeologists, also show the Greek men worshiping with uncovered heads.

[17] Lenski, *op. cit.*, p.435-436.

who violated this custom among them thereby showed lack of reverence and humility. But to write this to Greeks would be incomprehensible to them, for they had an entirely different custom which had an entirely different *significance*. (See also note 34 on page 381, in the commentary associated with verse 7, for further discussion on why the *meaning* and *significance* of the local custom is crucial.)

While praying or prophesying -- In verses 4 and 5, the reference to "praying or prophesying" shows that the context likely is public worship,[18] though it is not until verse 17 that Paul specifically mentions the public assembly.[19] The latter action, "prophesying," in particular required an audience to be effective. So "praying" here likely means 'praying in public.' Although "praying" could be silent prayers offered at the public assembly, because it is linked with "prophesying" (a public function), we take them both as vocal public acts. Praying was something done aloud in the worship service. In chapter 14:3, Paul himself explains what "prophesying" can signify – it signifies to speak unto men to edify them, to exhort them, to console them. It is something that also was done aloud in public. Farrar has said that a good English equivalent is "preaching," expounding the will of God, public teaching.[20] However, Thayer gives this meaning: "1) To prophesy, to be a prophet, to speak forth by divine inspiration, to predict: a) foretelling future events; b) to utter forth, declare a thing which can only be known by divine revelation; c) to break forth under sudden impulse in lofty discourse ...; d) to teach, refute, reprove, admonish, comfort others (see 1 Corinthians 14:1-5); e) to act as a prophet, discharge the prophetic office."[21] So, 'to prophesy' is more than simply 'preaching.' To 'prophesy' is to speak by

---

[18] All through this section about "disorders in public worship," we are using "worship" in our popular sense of the word. We use "worship" to describe what we do at the public assembly of Christians on the Lord's Day. To call that "assembly" a 'worship service' may not quite be true to the slogan, "call Bible things by Bible names," but we use it for lack of a better or more descriptive term for the regular public assembly.

[19] The locus for the activities of praying and prophesying is the public assembly. While it is true that the only explicit reference to the congregational gathering is in 11:18,20,33 and 14:26, the whole context early here in chapter 11 assumes a public worship assembly. 1) Verse 17 ties 11:3-16 with 11:18-34. 2) Prophecy assumes a public audience. It is not something one does in private. 3) The analogies of Greco-Roman and Jewish religious behavior all involve public worship. 4) Chapters 12-14 speak of the exercise of spiritual gifts (including praying and prophecy) in the public assembly. 5) Verse 16 refers to the practice of other "churches" – i.e., assemblies – which favors a reference to the gathered assembly for all of verses 3-16.

[20] Farrar, *op. cit.*, p.361. While it may be true that "preaching" is a good word, extreme care must be taken; we do not agree with the view currently being advocated by some, that "prophecy" and "preaching" (as done by today's preacher) are somehow the very same function. In chapter 13, we shall document that the miraculous spiritual gifts ceased. If "prophecy" was a spiritual gift (and it was), and if the gifts have ceased, then today's "preacher" would not be functioning by the same kind of inspiration as helped apostles and prophets to speak in the early days of the church age. Wayne Grudem (a member of the Vineyard Fellowship group of charismatic churches) has argued (in his *The Gift of Prophecy in the New Testament And Today* [Washington, DC: University Press of America, 1982]) that the gift of prophecy still endures in the modern preacher. Robert Thomas, "Prophecy Rediscovered? A Review of *The Gift of Prophecy in the New Testament and Today*," *Bib. Sac.* 149:593, p.83-96, critiques Grudem's book.

[21] Thayer, *op. cit.*, p.553.

inspiration in the language of the people, no matter the content of the message.[22] Prophecy was the inspired proclamation of a message given by God to a Christian speaker for the benefit of the whole congregation. Of course, as we explain what was happening when men were prophesying at Corinth, we must remember that 1 Corinthians 12:29 indicates that not all Christians are 'prophets.'

Disgraces his head -- There is a great deal of discussion here as authors attempt to identify which "head" Paul has in mind. (1) Some see a reference to Christ as the head of the man (verse 3). "Head," this time, is taken metaphorically. The man worshiping with his head covered dishonors Christ; that is, he does not, in His presence and in His service, observe the usual and proper custom by which a subordinate station is recognized, and which indicates respect for a superior. In the presence of a prince or a noble man, it would be considered as a mark of disrespect should the head be covered. (2) Some take it literally – of the man's own head. And it is true that the immediate context does use the word "head" in a literal sense. On the other hand, unless we take "head" metaphorically in this verse, there is really no reason why Paul should have given the theological statement he did in verse 3. (3) Others take it as a reference to both – they dishonored both their own persons and also Christ. There is no way to know whether or not the men at Corinth had been making this mistake (i.e., worshiping with covered heads) in the congregation. Perhaps converts from Judaism had carried their old habits over into church life. Perhaps the conduct which would be improper for men is mentioned in order to give point to the corrective about to be given to the wives (women). The point Paul is making is that man is to do nothing that would leave the impression that he no longer honors the divine order of subordination to Christ.

11:5 -- *But every woman who has her head uncovered while praying or prophesying disgraces her head, for she is one and the same as the woman whose head is shaved.*

But every woman -- "But" indicates that what is said in this verse about "wives" (women)[23] is a contrast to what was just said about husbands (men). The word order in verse 5 is the same order as was found in verse 4. Whatever was the meaning of the words in verse 4, they have the same meaning in verse 5. Verse 5 is the second inference drawn from the doctrine of "headship" (subordination) established in verse 3.

---

[22] A series of scholarly articles has recently appeared, pro and con, regarding the view that there were two kinds of 'prophecy' or 'gifts of prophecy' in the early church – and though one has ceased, the other still continues. For example, see F. David Farnell, "Does the New Testament Teach Two Prophetic Gifts?" *Bib. Sac.*, 150 (Jan-Mar 1993), p.62-88; Wayne Grudem, "Does God Still Give Revelation Today?" *Charisma* (Sep 1992), p.38-44; Kim Clement, "Prophecy: God Speaks Through Ordinary people," *Charisma* (May 1994), p.30-38. The claim (part of an attempt to prove that the spiritual gifts have not ceased) that 'prophecy' at Corinth was 'personal prophecy,' and was not on a par with Scripture, and that the Corinthian exercise of the gift, like that of all other spiritual gifts, is subject to error and misinterpretation by the prophet himself or herself (cf. esp. Acts 21:4 with 1 Corinthians 14:11,13-14), is a false claim.

[23] *Gunē* is the same word that was used in verse 3, and has the same import here that it did in verse 3.

Who has her head uncovered -- Whatever "*something* on the head" meant in verse 4, "uncovered" (verse 5) is the exact opposite. Commentators have offered one of three basic options to answer the question about "coverings." (1) The traditional view has the woman discarding some kind of external covering. Because of the word *peribolaion* (literally, "a wrap-around," hence, something like a shawl) in verse 15, writers often speak of a 'veil,' which married women wore whenever they were in public, being removed.[24] Just why the removal of the covering would disgrace her husband (her head) will be explained when we come to the phrase that so reads. There was something about being "uncovered" that would give bystanders a wrong impression about the wife's morals. According to the traditional view, "uncovered" is not being properly attired in the public worship service. (2) A second explanation for the "covering" is that Paul has reference to "long hair" (see verses 14-15). The problem at Corinth was that some women were "uncovering their head" by having their hair cut short. However, this explanation has against it the language and grammar of verses 5 and 6. If she already has short hair, the passive "let her cut her hair" must be given a forced explanation. (3) A third explanation, offered recently, is that on the basis of usage in the LXX, the adjective "uncovered" refers to 'loosed hair,' that is, letting the hair down in public. This interpretation, too, has its own set of difficulties. How are we to explain the man's not covering himself (verse 7)? What are we to do with verse 15 which implies long hair, not piled-up hair, serves in place of a shawl? And if 'loosened hair' is the topic in earlier verses, then verses 13-15 must talk about some other topic. Each of these ramifications is hard to accept. Perhaps we should accept the traditional view. In Oriental lands, the veil is the dignity, power, and honor of the woman. She is respected. A man who would dare touch a veiled woman would be in jeopardy of his life. But a woman in public, without her veil, was a thing which anyone could insult; she was in danger of losing her dignity and honor, and was considered immoral and lustful. (See W.M. Ramsey, *The Cities of St. Paul*, London: Houder & Stoughton, 1908, p.204-205.)

While praying or prophesying -- Whatever was meant by "praying or prophesying" in verse 4 (in respect to husbands) is what the words mean here in verse 5 (in respect to wives). The language is therefore to be understood as evidence that at Corinth the women (wives) were participating aloud in the public worship service – both praying and prophesying. It should not seem surprising to find that women (wives) functioned as "prophetesses." Joel predicted that in the church age "daughters" would prophesy (cf. Acts 2:17). In the Old Testament, prophetesses are not infrequently mentioned (e.g., Miriam, Deborah, Huldah, Noadiah). Anna, a prophetess, was functioning when baby Jesus was brought to the temple for His presentation (Luke 2:36). In the New Testament, prophetesses are also mentioned (e.g. Philip's virgin daughters who prophesied, Acts 21:9).

Because in two other places (1 Corinthians 14:34; 1 Timothy 2:12) Paul severely limits what wives may do in the public worship service, it is usually understood that what

---

[24] Ancient paintings from Pompeii show women worshiping Isis. Some have their heads covered by a shawl, and some have no shawl. For some of the "uncovered" women, the only thing uncovered was the woman's head and shoulders. But for some of the "uncovered," they are actually uncovered down to the waist. (Goodenough, *op. cit.*, fig.99)

Paul is doing here in chapter 11 is not touching on the question of whether wives (women) *ought* to be so participating, but rather critiques the improper *manner* ("uncovered") in which the ladies at Corinth were praying and prophesying. If they were properly "covered," was there still a prohibition on wives praying and prophesying? Scholars have struggled as they attempt to harmonize 1 Corinthians 11 with 14:34 and 1 Timothy 2:12.[25] Lurking under the surface of this whole discussion is the emotionally loaded question of whether or not the New Testament church should allow or encourage women to be preachers. Before we can say that 11:5 gives Scriptural precedence for women to teach and preach in the public service and to lead in public prayer, we must answer these questions: (1) What is Paul's argument in this verse (11:5), and how is it harmonized with 1 Corinthians 14:34 and 1 Timothy 2:12? (2) In each of these passages, does *gunē* refer to all women, or just to wives (married women)? (3) What does 1 Timothy 2:12 mean when it prohibits 'teaching and exercising authority over a man'? Does it prohibit any teaching when any man is present, or does it prohibit teaching when the woman's husband is present in the assembly? (4) Just when did the unmarried daughters of Philip prophesy (Acts 21:9)? Was it in the public assembly, or in informal meetings in their home? (5) Are the first 16 verses of 1 Corinthians 11 speaking of an informal home gathering or of a public worship service? (6) If 1 Corinthians 11:2-16 is speaking of informal home gatherings, could 14:34 and 1 Timothy 2:12 indicate that was also a time when it was wrong for the women to teach? (7) Are the prohibitions in 1 Corinthians 14:34 and 1 Timothy 2:12 absolute, or are there modifications and limitations placed upon the prohibitions?

There are various interpretations of 11:5 that do not seem quite satisfactory: (1) Paul is talking about women praying and prophesying in informal gatherings. Some say verse 20 indicates that the first half of the chapter talks of informal meetings, and the last half talks of formal meetings for worship.[26] But verse 20 does not definitely indicate the prophesying done by women (mentioned in verses 1-16) was done elsewhere than in the worship service. If we were able to show that the assembly of the first 16 verses was not the assembly of the church, it might be easier to harmonize this passage with 14:34, but we know of no satisfactory way to interpret all of the first 16 verses as though the praying and prophesying were being done in private gatherings. (2) 1 Corinthians 11:5 permits women to teach as long as they are under the inspiration of the Holy Spirit.[27] The "silence" en-

---

[25] Grayson H. Ensign, typical of many in the Restoration Movement, took both 14:34 and 1 Timothy 2:12 as the norm or rule by which all other passages about 'women speaking' were to be interpreted. The usual approach is to speak of all women (not just wives) as being prohibited from teaching or exercising authority. But the difficulty comes when one tries to harmonize all the passages which deal with women in the public worship service after starting with this "silence" as a given rule.

[26] This is the position advocated by Lenski (*op. cit.*, p.437). Lenski's arguments that public worship services are not under consideration in verses 4-16 have not convinced many others. L. Edsil Dale used to opt for the view that Philip's daughters did not speak in the public worship service, and he was adamant that no churches today are to have women preachers.

[27] Warren Wiersbe, *Be Wise* (Wheaton, IL: Victor Books, 1983), p. 110, opts for this view. He writes that "women who had the gift of prophecy were allowed to exercise it [in the public meetings]. They were also permitted to pray in the public meetings." He also calls attention to the fact that our 'preaching' or 'ex-

joined in 14:34 would not then be in opposition to the Holy Spirit. Women are to be silent except when the Holy Spirit directed them to speak. Women who did not have the gift of prophecy were not to speak at all in the public services. If this interpretation were correct, and miracles have ceased, then no women would be permitted to speak or teach today. (3) Some say 11:5 has reference to women singing a sacred hymn under the influence of the Holy Spirit. This would be difficult to prove, and the interpretation cannot be confined to this. Further, even if the "praying or prophesying" were done through the words of a hymn, would it still not be possible to affirm she might be 'teaching a man' as she sings, and that therefore even this exercise is not permitted by 1 Corinthians 14:34 and 1 Timothy 2:12? (4) Some say Paul grudgingly gives women permission to speak in public (11:5), and then in 14:34 he gives his real opinion. (Or he has changed his mind by the time he comes to 14:34?) This would deny the inspiration of 11:5, or it would imply that God's truth can change as the years pass during the church age, so this view is hard to accept. (5) Another suggestion is that we should see verses 3-7b as a quotation of the Corinthian position, and verses 7c-15 Paul's response. One would need to read verses 13-15 as indicatives rather than questions. However, there are no hints of any kind that Paul is citing the Corinthian's erroneous position. Further, it is difficult to follow the train of thought if we try to make verses 13-15 indicatives. (6) Some contemporary holiness groups explain 11:5 as a reference to praying and prophesying in an ecstatic state, over which the person did not have control. This is very similar to the second idea given above. The only speaking then permitted a woman would be at such a time when she was praying or prophesying in an ecstatic state; otherwise, she was to keep silent. However, this interpretation is also hard to accept because being in an ecstatic state and not having control over the praying or the prophesying is inconsistent with 1 Corinthians 14:32, which clearly teaches that "the spirits of the prophets are subject to the prophets." (7) George Mark Elliott explained that 11:5 is an *ad hominem* argument, whereas 14:34 and 1 Timothy 2:12 give the rule straightforwardly. The idea would be this: Even if the women were permitted to pray and prophesy in the public services, they are not to do it unveiled. Then in 14:34 Paul withdraws any permission to pray or prophesy even if properly veiled. Elliott then harmonized the other passages about women's role in the public service by calling attention to a distinction between the 'office' of teacher and the 'function' of teacher. He would say women could do the latter, but not the former. He built a case for the distinction by several analogies. He noted that apostles sometimes functioned as a 'pastor' (elder), but did not hold the office of elder. He called attention to Daniel's placement among the Holy Writings in the Old Testament canon, and affirmed this was due (according to Jewish belief) to the fact that Daniel held the function of prophet, but not the office. One had to hold the office of prophet for his writings to be included in that portion called "the Prophets." Likewise, Elliott believed there was an office of teacher in the early church. The prohibitions on women teaching prohibit her from holding the office, but not the function.

---

pounding the word' is not quite the same as the person who prophesied. "A person with the gift of prophecy proclaimed God's message as it was given to him *immediately* by the Spirit. The modern preacher studies the Word and prepares his message."

The conclusion this commentator has reached after years of study on this issue is that the passages speak of husbands and wives (rather than men and women in general). Chapter 11 assumes the women are praying and prophesying in the public services, though some in a wrong manner of dress. We shall also observe that chapter 14 presumes that the women were involved in the songs, the teachings, the revelation, just as much as the men. But they still must take care about their dress, and the impressions they leave on others by their decorum.

Disgraces her head -- What is the meaning of "head"? Does it refer to her own head, or to her husband (as verse 3 spoke of the husband being head of the wife)? (1) Her own head, say some commentators. And this idea might be in accordance with what Paul says in the rest of the verse. To go unveiled was as disgraceful as it would be for the woman to have her head shaved, or her hair shorn. (2) Her husband (the man who is the head of the woman), say other commentators. The wife who removes her veil in public shows a lack of proper respect to her husband. The veil is a token of modesty and subordination. A wife appearing abroad so shamelessly and exposing herself to the gaze of other men would bring disgrace upon her husband.

Perhaps both ideas can well be included, but the chief idea again is that the woman is acting in such a way as to show she is disregarding the divine order of subordination. Wherein is the "disgrace," the dishonor? Greek women in pagan worship settings laid aside their veils. By removing their veils, they were offering themselves for sexual relations to any man who came along. The sexual relations were part of the worship of the god.[28] In Greek worship, when women laid aside their veil, it was an indication that for that moment when 'in worship' she belonged to 'the god' and not to the husband. Christian wives were not to embrace any behavior that would say they belonged to God, but not their husbands, while they were worshiping. An unveiled woman in the congregation at Corinth would have been a shocking thing. She would have been considered an immoral woman.[29]

For she is one and the same with her whose had is shaved -- Goodspeed translated it, "It is just as though she had her head shaved." Verse 6 will say that for a woman to have her head "shaved" is disgraceful. Commentators have not been able to agree on just what is denoted by a woman having her hair shaved off. Some have affirmed that 'shaving of

---

[28] For a woman to engage in sex with someone other than her husband (even if it were in honor of the god) certainly broke the union God intended between husband and wife, and whether the pagans recognized it or not, it certainly dishonored the husband. In fact, it dishonored the wife, too.

[29] Wiersbe, *Be Wise*, p.111, has a helpful note, which in part reads, "Eastern society at that time was very jealous over its women. Except for temple prostitutes, the women wore long hair and, in public, wore a covering over their heads. [Wiersbe explains that Paul did not use the word for "veil" [a little cloth covering the lower part of one's face], but is speaking of a shawl that covered head and shoulders, a covering symbolizing her submission and fidelity to her husband.] For the Christian women in the church to appear in public without the shawl, let alone pray or prophesy uncovered, was both daring and blasphemous."

the head' was one of the punishments for an adulteress (Numbers 5:18).[30] Others suggest that a shaven head was the characteristic mark of a disreputable woman. Only the lower class of prostitutes shaved their heads. Others suggest that when people saw a woman whose head was shaved, everyone would know from her appearance that she was a 'tramp.'[31] To be shaven was to be disgraced as a punishment for some scandalous thing.

11:6 -- *For if a woman does not cover her head, let her also have her hair cut off; but if it is disgraceful for a woman to have her hair cut off or her head shaved, let her cover her head.*

For if a woman does not cover her head, let her also have her hair cut off -- "For" seems to connect verse 6 to verse 5 in this fashion: verse 6 gives a reason why "uncovered" in verse 5 was a disgrace. As the marginal note shows, *keirasthō* is middle voice. It would well be translated 'Let her cut off her own hair!' If the lady insists on her right to remove her covering while she prays and prophesies in a public assembly, then let her be consistent by cutting her hair short. One is just as disgraceful as the other.

But if it is disgraceful for a woman to have her hair cut off or her head shaved -- The verbs used in this verse (*keirō* and *xuraō*) mean 'cut short' and 'shaved (with a razor).' For the difference in meaning, see the aphorism from Tiberius, quoted in Dio Cassius' *History of Rome*: "I want my sheep shorn (*keiresthai*) not shaven (*apoxuresthai*)."[32] The shame involved when a female had a "shaved" head has been explained in verse 5. But what made it a "disgrace" to have short hair? It has been pointed out that the "masculine" partners in a lesbian relationship cut their hair as short as a man would.[33] Homosexuality was a shameful relationship, and no decent woman would want to act or dress in such a way that folk looking at her might accuse her of being a lesbian. Why then should the Christian women want to discard the head covering? With a mannish hairstyle, a woman has lost her "glory" (verse 15).

Let her cover her head -- The Greek verb used by Paul is an imperative; it is a command. 'If it is a disgrace for a woman either to cut her hair short (verse 6a) or be shaved (verse 5b) – and it obviously was – then let her be covered!' The verb *katakaluptō* ordinarily im-

---

[30] The LXX reads *apokalupsae ten gunaiken*, and the words are translated "uncover the head" in the KJV, and "let down the hair" in the ASV.

[31] In France, during World War II, when the French underground caught a woman who had collaborated with the Germans, the punishment for the woman was that they would cut all her hair off. Then for months (till her hair grew back) all her neighbors would know that she had betrayed France by bestowing her favors on the hated Germans.

[32] For a New Testament use of *xuraō* see Acts 21:24, and for a New Testament use of *keirō* see Acts 18:18.

[33] See the Loeb Classical Library, the volumes on *Lucian*, V.85 and VII.383.

plies an external covering of some kind, like a shawl or a scarf.[34]

3. The principle defended. 11:7-10

11:7 -- *For a man ought not to have his head covered, since he is the image and glory of God; but the woman is the glory of man.*

For -- "For" indicates that Paul is giving a reason for what was said in verses 4-6 about men's heads being uncovered and women's being covered as they pray and prophesy. Perhaps a preview of the thread of argument in verse 7 and following is needed here. (1) In verses 7-10, Paul gives further proof of the position taken about men's and women's dress while participating in public worship being somehow related to the divine order that pervades the universe (verse 3), which Christ exhibits in His subordination to the Father. He bases what he says about the headship of man on the record of creation, where it is exhibited that man is a direct reflection of God, while woman is derived and auxiliary (verses 7-9). Then he urges that because of the angels (11:10) women are to have "authority" on their heads. (2) In verses 11-12, Paul then adds a statement to prevent his readers from pressing the matter of submission to an extreme.

A man ought not to have his head covered -- Just as before (verses 4 and 5), where Paul stated first what the husband is not to do, and then what the wife is to do, so he does here. See at verse 4 the notes concerning the Jewish men's custom of putting a prayer shawl on their heads. That is the kind of covering a Christian man is not to do. A man ought not have his head covered because on earth there is no visible superior to man; Christ is man's head.

Since he is the image and glory of God -- This is the reason why a man should not have his head covered. "Image" reminds us of Genesis 1:27 – man is made in the image of God. God is both the architect and, within certain limits, the archetype of man. Some would limit "image" to man's intellect, will, and reason. Delitzsch in his *Biblical Psychology*[35] suggests that man's body resembles the body God has (e.g., the Bible speaks

---

[34] This commentator is not convinced that Paul is binding upon all women of all time the rule of wearing a hat (or covering) while participating in a church worship service. First of all (if our conclusions at verse 3 are correct), Paul is discussing wives, not all women. Second, there is a principle behind the specific direction about covering. The dress of both men and women was to be such that their "heads" were not dishonored. Neither is to dress in such a manner that would bring disrepute on the church, or would be misconceived by the world, or would brazenly proclaim that they no longer intend to be submissive to their respective "head." It is very doubtful that the wife's wearing or not wearing a hat in the public assembly would be interpreted in our culture as a sign of respect or disrespect to one's husband. Throughout this section Paul appeals to principles. The wearing of a covering (or the not wearing) may seem to be a small matter. Everything depends on what the wearing (or the not wearing) implies, and what kind of sanction the one practice or the other can claim. Third, Paul does not use *dei* ("it is necessary") about the matter; there is no intrinsic necessity. But he does use both the verb *opheilō* ("ought," verses 7,10) and the phrase *prepon esti* ("it is proper," verse 13). There is both a moral obligation and a natural fitness in the instruction he gives.

[35] Franz Delitzsch, *A System of Biblical Psychology* (Grand Rapids, MI: Baker, 1966 reprint), p.55ff.

of God's eyes, hair, hands, feet, mouth). God created the world, fish, beasts, creeping things. But these were not intelligent, spiritual beings. They did not have the power of making a choice. Then God created a being – a special and moral being – in His own image, and gave him dominion over all else (Genesis 1:28). The dominion invested in man made him superior to all other creatures on earth. When Paul writes that man is the "glory of God," it does not carry the idea that man has such a majesty about him that woman *has* to veil herself before him, like the seraphim do before the majesty of Jehovah. When God created man, man was made just a little lower than the angels (Heb. *Elohim*, Hebrews 2:7). Man, of all the creatures, has an exalted position, next to God. Man is here as part of God's creation to make God look good! Man is to bring to Him glory and honor, thus causing others to praise God. When insisting that a man while worshiping God ought not cover his head, Paul bases his instruction on creation where, being the image and glory of God, man is to be subject to and represent God in authority. He may or may not cover his head for other reasons that have nothing to do with his relation to God and with a proper expression of that relation. But, when the act of covering his head appears in any way to be a denial of his being God's image and glory, it would certainly be improper, even wrong, to cover his head.

But the woman is the glory of man -- This is an exact parallel of the reason given for the husband's being uncovered while worshiping. It has to do with the hierarchy of authority indicated in verse 3: God, Christ, husband, wife. None of the subordinates may behave in such a way as to bring dishonor on their immediate superior. Not the husband (by covering his head while worshiping). Not the wife (by uncovering her head while worshiping). A simple remembrance of woman's original creation (she was created to be the man's help meet) will serve to recall that the woman was intended by God to help and bring honor to the man.[36] She, too, just like the man, has a special place.[37] It would be improper and wrong for the wife to unveil, if that act was a denial of her subordinate position to her husband or would be a denial of the "glory" of her husband. Before Paul adds the obligation that rests upon woman as far as expressing her relation to man is concerned (verse 10), he adds further explanations concerning woman's position (verses 8,9).

11:8 -- *For man does not originate from woman, but woman from man;*

For man does not originate from woman -- Beginning as they do with "for," verses 8 and 9 give a double reason for what was asserted in the last clause of verse 7, namely, that the woman is man's glory. The first reason is that Adam was created first, then Eve. The man was not formed from the woman. Adam was not in any way derived from a woman.

---

[36] Hodge (*op. cit.*, p.210) has this note: "She always assumes his station; becomes a queen if he is a king; and manifests to others the wealth and honor which belong to her husband."

[37] The man stands in a special relationship to God as does nothing else, and so man is called "the glory of God." The wife stands to the husband in such a special relation as does nothing else, and so she is called "the glory of man." This expression ("glory of the man") assures her of a high place in the scheme of things, and also gently implies that it is not precisely the same as man's place.

'Man was created first. He does not owe his origin to woman, but woman owes hers to him' is the sense of the verse.[38]

But woman from man -- This appears to be an allusion to Genesis 2:18,22,23. Woman was taken from man, made after he was, from the rib taken from his side. Man in no way was derived from a woman – but the woman, Eve, was derived from Adam.

11:9 -- *for indeed man was not created for the woman's sake, but woman for the man's sake.*

For indeed man was not created for the woman's sake, but woman for the man's sake -- This is a simple summary statement of what God said as recorded in Genesis 2:18, "It is not good that the man should be alone; I will make him an help meet for him." Woman was made for man's sake, and not he for hers. This is the second reason why Paul said (verse 7) that "woman is the glory of man." Woman was created to be a helper suitable for man (Genesis 2:18) and not the reverse. The fact that the Hebrew word for "helper" is often used for God, as He helps humans out of many difficult circumstances throughout the pages of the Old Testament, proves that the term itself does not inherently imply subordination, but it does not prove that it *cannot* imply subordination. In the context of verses 3-7, it is hard to escape the feeling that Paul intended to speak of a hierarchy in verse 9, too. Barnes (*op. cit.*, p.222) has worded it his way:

> The woman was made for the comfort and happiness of the man.
> Not to be a slave, but a help meet;
> Not to be a minister of his pleasures, but to be his aid and comforter in life;
> Not to be regarded as of inferior nature and rank, but to be his friend,
> To share his sorrows, and to multiply his joys;
> Yet still to be in a station subordinate to Him.

Man is to be the head, the ruler, the leader in the family circle; woman was created to aid him in his duties, to comfort him in his afflictions. Neither the man nor the woman is complete without the other. The two together make a whole, doing together what one could not do alone.

11:10 -- *Therefore the woman ought to have a symbol of authority on her head, because of the angels.*

Therefore -- What follows is a conclusion drawn from what has already been said. On account of the indisputable facts (verses 7-9) that woman is derived and auxiliary and the

---

[38] Some have objected that verse 8 supplies an argument from God's original creation that makes no sense. They insist that the order of creation has no logical connection to any hierarchy of authority; if it did, animals ought to be above people since in Genesis 1 they were created before humanity. But Paul's argument involves more than the idea that chronological order always implies rank. Do not forget that of all the creatures, it is only man who is made in the image of God. Paul's argument based on the order in which men and women were created does imply rank. Further, people in the ancient world, who were familiar with the privileges that firstborn sons retained (of dynastic succession, inheritance, responsibility for the family, etc.), would not have found Paul's argument unusual.

glory of the man (facts which are still true today), all cultural customs that truly symbolize these facts will meet approval on the part of all who bow fully to God, and all cultural customs that contravene and deny this symbolism will meet with disapproval.

The woman ought to have *a symbol of* authority on her head -- There is scarcely a passage in the New Testament which has so taxed the learning and ingenuity of commentators as this. Two problems in particular must be explained: (1) the phrase that reads "ought to have ... authority on her head." Note there is no word for "symbol of" or 'sign of' in the original;[39] and (2) the following phrase that reads "because of the angels."

Under the heading of futile attempts to explain this we may place: (1) All explanations which require an alteration of the Greek text at this place.[40] (2) All explanations which seek to find some other primary meaning for *exousia* besides "authority" or 'right' or 'power.' (3) All explanations which suppose that *exousia* is the name of some jewel-like ornament which married women wore on their heads.

Now let's call attention to a few ideas that may help us give this passage its rightful interpretation. (1) The context seems to require that the word *exousia* ("authority" or 'power') denotes a veil, or a covering for the head. (2) Every other use in the New Testament of this three word construction (*exousian echein epi* ...) is translated "to have authority (or control) over."[41] This suggests a translation along these lines for this place, 'For this reason ... a wife should exercise control over her head [i.e., keep the appropriate covering on it].' (3) Leon Morris highlights the fact that *exousia* is something the woman herself exercises, not something that is forced upon her.[42] By voluntarily covering her head (with a veil or shawl[43]), the 1st century wife secured her own place of dignity and authority. By keeping her head covered, she shows the world she is 'some one.' When in public, the covering or veil protected her. But her authority and dignity vanished along with the head-covering when she discarded it. *Exousia* is the same word translated "right," a word used by the Corinthians when they claimed they had certain 'rights.' Indeed, in

---

[39] Fee (*op. cit.*, p.519) calls attention to the fact that there is no other known evidence that *exousia* ("power, authority") can be translated by adding some word like 'sign of' or 'symbol of.' It is not so translated that way even once in the 103 other instances where this word occurs in the New Testament, nor is it so translated in the LXX, nor in Philo, nor Josephus.

[40] The Greek is *exousia* ("power, authority"). Some have tried a different spelling, e.g., *exiousa* ('when she goes out in public'). Others have even suggested the letters make up two words, e.g., *ex ousias* ('in accordance with her nature'). However, there is not one manuscript to support any other reading than *exousia*.

[41] See Matthew 9:6 (and parallel passages), or Revelation 11:6, 14:8, 16:9, 20:6.

[42] Morris, *op. cit.*, p.153-154. The NASB's addition of "symbol of" could leave readers with a wrong idea, namely, that the veil is a "symbol" or "sign" that there is an authority to which the woman is subject. What the original actually says is that the woman has a "right" or "power" that she herself is exercising.

[43] Those writers who insist that the woman's long hair is the topic through this whole paragraph are delighted to point to several places in ancient literature where *exousia* is a term used for such hair, just as was "glory." Even the Jews could have recollected Samson's history and have found in "power," when applied to hair, a remarkable significance.

the realm of Christian liberty, we do have freedom, we do have certain rights. We have a right to do what is best, not just a right to avoid what is wrong. Christian wives thus have a "right" to show the world how a wife relates to her husband, how a wife brings honor and glory to the man who is her "head." This is exactly how wives should conduct themselves when praying or prophesying in public. (4) In view of the unchangeable facts of creation (i.e., man was created first, woman was created to be his helper), the point Paul is making, we believe, is that established customs which beautifully symbolize these creation facts "ought" not to be changed arbitrarily, but intelligently retained until, without prejudice to these facts, in due course, customs may change of their own accord. Just as Paul used "ought" when he instructed the men how to dress when praying or prophesying (verse 7), so here he uses "ought" (*opheilei*) when instructing wives.

Because of the angels -- "Because" shows this clause is a reason why women should have 'authority on their heads.' But there has been a great difference of opinion regarding the meaning of this clause. A number of suggestions have been offered:

(1) Some have offered a conjectural emendation of the text. Instead of *aggelous* ("angels") it has been suggested that perhaps the original reading was *agelas* ('crowds'), or *agelaious* ('when men crowd in'), or *aggelias* ('message'), or perhaps *ochlous* ('crowds'). Any one of these is thought to picture the crowds of people who are attending the assembly, and there was no need to create unnecessary opposition to or questioning of what was happening as the ladies prayed or prophesied. The problem with such sanctified guesses is that there is no objective evidence for such an emendation of the text. No manuscript reads other than *aggelous*.

(2) Some have proposed that the word be translated 'messengers' and that it is a reference to some human being who is visiting the church, perhaps in an official capacity. Appeal is made to Revelation 2 and 3 where "angels" of the churches are likely some human 'messenger' who would vocally relay the "letter" to the respective congregation. Some have supposed the 'messengers' were the New Testament prophets and/or evangelists. If male visitors are intended, would the rule about 'covering' not be required at those services when there were no official visitors?

(3) Some opt for an explanation of "angels" that results in Paul appealing to a reason that has no Biblical basis of fact behind it. J.A. Fitzmeyer draws attention to passages in the Dead Sea Scrolls in which men with any blemish (crippled, diseased) are excluded from the army or from the assembly because of the presence of angels. No unseemliness must come before them.[44] Schüssler Fiorenza notes that, according to Jewish and Christian apocalyptic literature, angels mediate the "words of prophecy." Paul would be warning the wives they should not offend the angels who are helping them to prophesy.[45]

---

[44] *New Testament Studies*, IV (1957), p.48-58. Jewish beliefs as reflected in the Dead Sea Scrolls may or may not have a Biblical basis behind them.

[45] Elisabeth Schüssler Fiorenza, *In Memory of Her* (New York: Herder & Herder, 1994). Apocalyptic theology was informed by eastern mysticism. What are called "angels" in apocalyptic literature are called "mediums" in Scripture, or 'channelers' in New Age jargon. Such "spirits" are hardly the source of genuine

(4) Some have opted for the translation "angels," the reference being to those supernatural beings who are identified by this name. (a) Some suppose Paul has in mind evil angels. They appeal to Genesis 6:2 as an analogy, interpreting that passage to say that the "sons of God" who had improper relationships with the "daughters of men" were fallen angels. The argument is that, if evil angels can be 'invited' to enter into such an evil relationship by how women behave, women should be careful to protect themselves from demonic attacks. Questions are raised by this suggestion. Do evil angels have the "freedom" to visit the public worship assembly of Christians? If evil angels can have sexual relations with women (a point that is debated), why do women have to watch their dress at public worship? Would the evil angels be tempted only during worship service time? Is it a misinterpretation of Genesis 6:1,2, to say the "sons of God" are evil angels? Could not the "sons of God" be the descendants of Seth? (b) Some have supposed Paul has in mind the good angels,[46] but exactly why women should be concerned about these is not easily explained. Some draw the inference that good angels attend the worship services[47] and not only would expect all things to be done properly, but would also be offended by irreverence and misconduct. Another suggestion is that each Christian has a guardian angel appointed to take care of the Christian, and that these angels could be offended by improper behavior.

This commentator is inclined to the interpretation that good angels are the ones Paul speaks of, and Ephesians 3:10 may help to explain why the ladies should be concerned about what they see and think. Ephesians 3:10, 1 Corinthians 4:9, and 1 Peter 1:12 suggest that the good angels are watching and learning lessons about God's plans and purposes by watching the church. Angels, in the presence of their direct and visible Superior, veil their faces (Isaiah 6:2). A woman, when worshiping in the presence of her direct and visible superior (husband), should do the same. Women praying and prophesying in a wrong manner (uncovered) would give the angels a bad lesson about how to show subjection to the proper authority that God has ordained.

4. The principle clarified. 11:11-12

11:11 -- *However, in the Lord, neither is woman independent of man, nor is man independent of woman.*

However -- Paul has been speaking of the woman being the glory of man. Now, lest the woman suppose she really does not need to demonstrate her submission, and lest the man

---

prophecy. New Testament prophets spoke by the Holy Spirit's inspiration. Paul is hardly to be thought of as countenancing occult 'prophecy' nor would he be warning Christian women to be careful lest they offend these "angels" who were actually servants of the devil.

[46] "Angels" (when no qualifying adjective is used) almost always, in Scripture, has reference to the good angels. A possible exception to this general usage might be 1 Corinthians 6:3.

[47] On the matter of angels being present in public services, passages often appealed to as proof are Luke 15:10; Ephesians 3:10; Hebrews 1:14, 12:1; Ecclesiastes 5:6; and Psalm 138:1 in LXX. However, observe that not many of these passages are specifically limited in scope to public worship assemblies.

look with contempt on the woman, Paul speaks some words of caution. The principle is true (i.e., there is a certain hierarchy – God, Christ, husband, wife), and men and women are to behave so as to exemplify the principle.[48] The wife's behavior at worship may be different than the husband's (i.e., her head is covered to indicate her submission to her husband, his is not covered to indicate his submission to Christ) but that does not mean woman is inferior to the man. Beginning with a strong contrast (*plēn* means "however," "nevertheless"), Paul reminds the Corinthians that as Christians, notwithstanding their order by virtue of creation, husbands and wives (or perhaps men and women more generally) are fundamentally interdependent.

In the Lord -- Since Paul usually uses "in the Lord" to mean 'in the Christian state' or 'in union with Christ through faith and obedience,' it seems proper to interpret this verse giving Paul's words their usual significance. "In the Lord" means 'under the rule of Christ' – where woman's rights are realized as nowhere in heathenism or Judaism.

Neither is woman independent of man -- Woman is not to overvalue herself or her position.[49] Paul is qualifying what he has just said about the woman having "authority on her head" or "exercising control over her head." She so behaves because she is not independent of man.

Nor is man independent of woman -- This is meant to correct any tendency on the part of men to domineer. The matter of submission of wives must not be pressed to the extreme that one finds in the oriental world (certain Jewish and Arab societies) today. The husband is not to assume himself too superior. This verse and the next "are designed to show that man and woman are united in the most tender interests: the one cannot live comfortably without the other, the one is necessary to the happiness of the other" (Barnes, *op. cit.*, p.252). The husband does not use Paul's words about submission as an excuse to treat the woman as though she were merely his slave.

11:12 -- *For as the woman originates from the man, so also the man* **has his birth** *through the woman; and all things originate from God.*

For as the woman originates from the man -- "For" shows that verse 12 is a reason for what was just written in verse 11. In the original creation, she was formed from the man

---

[48] Jos. M. Webb (*Open Letter on Christian Communication*, Vol.4, No. 10, p.2) has used this passage to show that Christian doctrine (verse 11ff) is different from traditional Jewish doctrine (verses 3-10). He wrote, "In two dramatic lines, Paul says that 'in the Lord' [i.e., under the new dispensation] the *traditional* hierarchical order that was taught in the past to exist between man and woman is abolished and replaced with a new order" [i.e., egalitarian, not hierarchical]. Such a use of verse 11 is hardly correct for several reasons. First, the patriarchal rules found in the early chapters of Genesis are God's intention for all time, not just the Old Testament period. Second, it is difficult to show that 'traditions' (verse 2) were pre-Christian Jewish beliefs, as Webb tries to show. Third, it is also difficult (as Webb tries to do) to show that verse 3 (headship, hierarchy) was only true during the Jewish dispensation, but is no longer.

[49] Observe the change in word order here. The Majority Text, with no early support, has reversed the order, so that the verse reads "the man is not independent of the woman, nor is the woman independent of the man." This reversed order can cause commentators to completely alter the comments offered on the two phrases, and speak of woman 'undervaluing herself' because she is expected to be submissive.

(Genesis 2:21ff). Since the creation vividly shows God's original intent, the idea of hierarchy (expressed in verse 3) is still valid. The affirmation made in the first part of verse 11 is thus shown to be God's intent.

So also the man *has his birth* **through the woman** -- This phrase shows that the affirmation made in the second part of verse 11 is likewise still God's intent. Man does not act like he does not need the woman, or that, because of her expected submissive position, she really is of little value to him. Without woman, there soon would be very few men left in the world.

And all things originate from God -- All things were created and arranged by Him. This expression seems designed to suppress any spirit of complaint or dissatisfaction with the arrangement of subordination as we find it; it is designed to help the woman be contented in her subordinate station, and to make the man aware that his responsible position also involves submission to his head. Each owes his or her position to the appointment of God the Creator. All things are through Him and to Him, made by Him, and tending to Him as their end (Romans 11:36). The whole universe owes its origin to God.

5. The principle agreed to.   11:13-16

11:13 -- *Judge for yourselves: is it proper for a woman to pray to God* **with her head** *uncovered?*

Judge for yourselves -- "Judge for yourselves" is an appeal to the Corinthians to recognize that what Paul is saying is true.[50] Paul now returns to the point he made in verses 4-6. In the verses before this, he had appealed to their 'shame' to get them to correct their abuses and then practice aright. Now he appeals to their own judgment and sense of propriety (verse 13) based on "nature" (verses 14,15). Then he will appeal to the universal practice in all the churches (verse 16).

Is it proper -- The question obviously expects a negative answer, though Paul used no interrogative particle at this place to specifically indicate what answer he expected. 'Is it decent? Is it becoming? Is it proper?' The Grecian women were accustomed to appear in public with a veil. Paul alludes to that established and proper habit, and asks whether it does not accord with their own views of propriety that women in Christian assemblies should also wear the same symbol of modesty.

For a woman to pray to God *with her head* **uncovered?** -- Paul does not mean silent participation in public worship, but as in verse 5, taking the lead in audible prayer. When the Corinthians consider the custom of the day, they certainly will not consider it proper for the woman to be unveiled.

---

[50] As at 10:15, the question does not give the Corinthians the option of agreeing or disagreeing with Paul. It is obviously an attempt to get them to agree with him. Rhetorical questions have that built into their very fabric.

11:14 -- *Does not even nature itself teach you that if a man has long hair, it is a dishonor to him,*

Does not even nature itself teach you -- This question expects a "yes" answer, the Greek shows. "Does not nature show you ...?" It certainly does! But what does Paul mean by "nature"? Does this mean 'the laws of nature,' or does it mean simply 'sense of propriety (instinctive feelings)'? A similar appeal to "nature" is found in Romans 1:26, 2:14,27, 11:21,24; Galatians 2:15, 4:8; Ephesians 2:3; James 3:7; 2 Peter 1:4. In many of these verses "nature" means 'without any written revelation' (e.g., Romans 2:14). Fee writes about "nature" being "the given regular order of things," and he calls attention to "natural theology," i.e., the idea that truths about God may be learned from carefully studying His creation – nature, man, the world.[51] Nature, as God has formed it when He created the world, is the idea. Barnes (*op. cit.*, p.207) noted that in almost every place in the world, men have short hair and women long hair – such is the general custom the world over – "and if any reason is asked for the numerous peoples of the world wearing their hair the same (as well as having other habits in common), no better answer can be given than that *nature*, as arranged by God, has ordered it." Robertson & Plummer (*op. cit.*, p.235) paraphrase by asking, 'Even if your own sense of propriety (verse 13) does not so dictate, does not nature show you that man being short-haired is by divine order unveiled? And that woman, being long-haired, is by divine order veiled,' when the veil shows submission to the husband as it did in Greece?

That if a man has long hair, it is a dishonor to him? -- "Only a few have regarded it as comely for a man to wear his hair long."[52] There are a few examples in classical Greek where men had long hair. Among those who wore their hair long were the Spartans, some philosophers, and Homer's warriors. Among the Hebrews, it was regarded as disgraceful to a man to wear his hair long, except if he had a Nazarite vow (Numbers 6:1-5; Judges 13:5, 16:17; 1 Samuel 1:11). But the general habit among men has been to have short hair. All one has to do is consult the ancient coins and the art archaeologists have uncovered and study men's hair lengths to get a feeling for what was common in the ancient world. Men who respect the teaching of the Word and the intent of their Creator as observed in nature, will, every one, be very careful concerning their own personal hair lengths, whatever the current popular fad.

11:15 -- *but if a woman has long hair, it is a glory to her? For her hair is given to her for a covering.*

But if a woman has long hair -- The matter is quite the reverse in the case of the woman. There is no shame if she wears long hair – in fact, it is an honor for her to have long hair. The Bible nowhere specifies the precise length of hair, either for women or men. It simply

---

[51] Fee, *op. cit.*, p.527. Paul let his hair grow for a time when he had a vow (Acts 18:18), but the very nature of the vow indicates the normalcy of shorter hair on men.

[52] Barnes, *op. cit.*, p.254. Among Athenian youth, who cropped their hair at age 18, long hair was a mark of foppery or effeminacy, save except for aristocrats. Absalom's long hair either speaks of his superior attitude about himself, or was permitted because he was an aristocrat.

states that there ought to be a noticeable difference between the length of men's hair (short) and the length of women's hair (long).[53]

It is a glory to her? -- The whole question is, "Does not nature teach you ... that long hair is a glory to her?" This question expects a "yes" answer. Long hair on the woman is an ornament, an adorning. "Glory" seems to be the opposite of 'dishonor' in the previous question. Something about long hair makes females more lovely and attractive.

For her hair is given to her for a covering – The English word "for" appears twice in this clause.
- The first time, it translates the Greek word *hoti* ("because"). This *hoti* clause shows that the final part of verse 15 is tied to the rest of the question in a causal relationship. God is the implied agent who did the 'giving.' God, when He created, gave the man short hair and the woman long hair. The mere fact of one sex being unveiled (i.e., having short hair) and the other being veiled (i.e., having long hair) plainly teaches that man was intended by God to be uncovered, and woman covered. "Covering" translates *peribolaiou*, a 'mantle,' a 'covering thrown around [the head and shoulders],' or as the margin has it, a "veil."[54]
- The second time the word "for" appears, it translates the Greek word *anti*, sometimes translated "against" and sometimes "instead of." It probably has the meaning "instead of" at this place. If so, then the Christian woman's long hair is considered to be a proper substitute for a cloth mantle or veil. God gave long hair to the woman as a sort of natural covering. Before the arts of dress were invented, it served the purposes of a veil, when it was allowed to grow long, and to spread over the shoulders. Wiersbe has explained the teaching here in this way: "In other words, if local custom does not dictate a head covering, her long hair can be that covering. I do not think that Paul meant for all women in every culture to wear a shawl for a head covering; but he did expect them to use their long hair as a covering and as a symbol of their submission to God's order. This is something that every woman can do."[55] The fact that woman's hair grows quite long by nature, much longer than a man's even if he never cuts it, and that thus there is bestowed on woman the gift of a "covering," is nature's own indication that, when it comes to significant customs, she and not man is to have her head covered in the presence of God during worship.

11:16 -- *But if one is inclined to be contentious, we have no other practice, nor have the churches of God.*

---

[53] This language seems to call for a rejection of unisex styles. It seems to imply that it is a departure from the God-created order for a man to look like a woman, or the woman to look like a man.

[54] It has been observed that this is the only place in this whole paragraph that the word for 'head cover' appears. Before we read about "something on the head," and we have had the words "covered" and "uncovered."

[55] Warren Wiersbe, *Be Wise*, p.114. Kenneth T. Wilson, "Should Women Wear Headcoverings?" *Bib.Sac.* 148 (Oct. 1991), p.442-462, has a helpful study of this passage which attempts to apply what Paul writes to the question of whether women today must wear some kind of shawl or headcovering in the public worship.

But if one is inclined to be contentious -- Paul cuts his presentation short, as though impatient of any further discussion of a subject already settled by appeal to the Scriptural principle (verses 3-12), and to personal judgment based on what "nature" shows to be appropriate (verses 13-15). This is one of four times this phrase about being contentious occurs in 1 Corinthians (see also 3:18, 8:2, and 14:37). It is a far weightier argument to appeal to the universal and unbroken practice in the churches all over the brotherhood than simply to personal judgment based on a natural sense of propriety. "Inclined to be contentious" is a polite way of saying 'is contentious.' 'If anyone is so contentious as to dispute this conclusion about hair lengths and the covering or uncovering of the head while worshiping ... if any of you wish to be disputatious and quarrelsome about this matter of dress while leading in public worship, I must content myself with saying that he must remember that no other Christian congregation deems it proper for men to cover their heads while worshiping, or for women to appear uncovered in public.' If after all the above arguments, one is still minded to debate the issue, he must be put down by authority.

We have no other practice -- "We" – when contrasted with "the churches" – equals 'I and the apostles generally,' or 'I and the other leaders of the churches.' The word translated "practice" is *sunētheia*, and could be translated 'custom,' something one is used to, something habitual. What is it that is called a "practice" or 'custom'? (1) Some say Paul means, 'We have no custom of being contentious. Let every man decide for himself.' But surely, it would be very unlikely that after so long a treatment of the propriety of appearing veiled in public, that the apostle should wind up the discussion by saying, 'Do what you want to.' (2) Some say that the wearing of a veil or mantle was a local custom at Corinth, and therefore everyone must decide for himself in the light of local custom. Again, we would emphasize that verse 3 stated a principle – God, Christ, husband (man), wife (woman). That principle is of permanent validity, but the application of it to the contemporary scene need not yield the same result in every place. Any custom that would violate this principle would be disapproved. The manner of dress (or behavior) in the public services was to be such that the principle was demonstrated, and this was true for all the congregations. (3) The meaning rather seems to be this: None of the other churches, whether in Judea or Asia or Europe, has the practice of allowing women to pray in public with their heads uncovered.

Nor have the churches of God – Paul is saying, "If you Corinthians prefer these abnormal practices in spite of Scripture, reason, common sense, and my arguments, you must stand alone in your innovations upon universal Christian practice."[56] Even universal custom is against your "self-opinionated particularism."

We might summarize the topic that began at 11:2 in this fashion:

THE CORINTHIAN ARGUMENT was that "Women do not need to be veiled. They are free in Christ." Was this thinking right? No! The following points show their errors.

---

[56] H.T. Spence, *The Canon of Scripture* (Dunn, NC, Foundations Press, 2010), p.176. This appeal to congregations all over the Roman Empire should cause us to be hesitant to affirm that what Paul was giving was simply a local ruling, and therefore not applicable to our present time and place. It was more than simply a local ruling, especially in light of the Scriptural principle on which the directives are based.

PAUL'S ARGUMENT	CORINTH CUSTOM	UNIVERSAL CUSTOM
Wives ought to be in subjection to their head (husbands). They were first in transgression, second in creation. Therefore they ought to be veiled or covered.	Wives were to be veiled at times when in public. (The only ones who did differently were immoral women.)	In all the other churches of Christ, women are veiled or covered. Therefore, you Corinthians ought to be veiled.

Importantly, this verse tends to confirm our conclusion at verses 2ff – dress at "congregational" meetings was the thing in view, not "Christian attire" away from the assemblies.

> Wiersbe concludes that the important fact is this: "Both men and women must honor the Lord by submitting to their respective roles (11:3) – and by respecting the symbols of this headship – hair and head-covering. Whenever a woman prays or prophesies in the assembly, she must have long hair or wear a head-covering. The man should have short hair and not wear any covering."[57]

B. Correction of Abuses Regarding the Love Feasts and the Partaking of the Lord's Supper. 11:17-34

> *Summary:* The Corinthians were making a mockery of the Lord's Supper because of abuses at the love feast (i.e., the dinner part of their assembly which preceded observance of the Lord's Supper), verses 17-22. To correct these abuses, Paul reminds the Corinthians what he had received from Jesus and taught them concerning the institution and observance of the Lord's Supper, verses 23-26. He then warns about partaking of the Lord's Supper in an unworthy manner, verses 17-31. To help the Corinthians to be ready to partake of the Lord's Supper in a worthy manner, he concludes with directions to correct the love feast abuses, verses 33,34.

11:17 -- *But in giving this instruction, I do not praise you, because you come together not for the better but for the worse.*

But in giving this instruction -- "This instruction" refers to 'this which follows,' i.e., their conduct in regard to the love feast and Lord's Supper.[58] We are still in the long section dealing with disorders at the public assembly. Paul now moves from his consideration of the improper manner of praying and prophesying, and turns to disorders connected with the love feast and Lord's Supper. After giving the reason for his instructions (verses 17-32), Paul finally (verses 33,34) gives the "instruction" he all along had in mind.

---

[57] Wiersbe, *op. cit.*, p.112.

[58] Shore disagrees (*op. cit.*, p.106-107). He thinks that "this" points back to the contentiousness glanced at in verse 16.

To have a right understanding of this section, some things must be observed: (1) It was the primitive custom to celebrate the Lord's Supper in private houses. At first there were no church buildings or separate places of meeting. However, though not having a specially constructed meeting place, there is some evidence that by this time the Corinthian church had a separate place of meeting (cf. verses 20,22). (2) The celebration of the Lord's Supper was usually connected with an ordinary meal (called the love feast – or *Agape*). This meal was made up of contributions brought by the people (i.e., what we call a basket-lunch or pot-luck supper). A loaf and a cup was taken from this common meal, blessed, and used as the elements for the Lord's Supper. (3) Exactly where and how the love feast originated is not known. There are several possibilities. Perhaps it was adopted from something Greeks were already doing. Before Christianity entered the world, the custom of enjoying a social feast existed among the Greeks; they were called *eranoi*, "club feasts." This was the Greek way of handling 'community service.' The poor could come to these club feasts and find food to satisfy their hunger. Or perhaps the love feast was adapted from the Passover meal which preceded the original institution of the Lord's Supper. Or perhaps the love feast originated as a kind of enlarged family meal in the Jerusalem church, as Acts 2:46 indicates was observed. It is even possible that "fellowship" in Acts 2:42 includes such meals where those with means would share with those who had less. Love feasts were not restricted to Corinth (see Jude 12, 2 Peter 2:13). In many towns the love feast was a regular part of the public assembly. (4) "Instruction" ("charge," ASV) translates a participle from the verb *paraggellō*, the verb frequently used of military commands; thus the ASV translates, "in giving you this charge". It also has the meaning of 'passing along directions or orders.'[59] As explained at 11:21ff, the disorder at the public assembly of the church in Corinth was serious, and Paul is not simply offering a few academic comments. With apostolic authority he is commanding that it be set right.

I do not praise you -- There is a deliberate contrast with what Paul had said in verse 2 of this chapter. There, Paul commended the Corinthians in general for their regard of the ordinances which he had appointed when he was with them. But they had certainly departed from his teaching in their present method of observing the love feast and the Lord's Supper. Paul says, "I cannot praise you[60] in this." The Corinthians apparently had written in their letter to him that they were faithfully trying to hold firmly to what he had taught them. But Paul has additional information (verse 18) that horrifies him, and so he "blames" them for their behavior. Paul's spirit is marvelous. He both praises and criticizes, but all is done lovingly, warmly, and sternly. Perhaps the first serious irregularity in their public worship could be attributed to ignorance (verses 3,16). But no such excuse is possible in regard to the disorders he now begins to speak about. Their wrong behavior at the church meetings, their gross selfishness and disregard of others, cannot be attributed to ignorance.

Because you come together -- That is, they were assembling for public worship. "Because" (*hoti*) introduces the content or the ground of the Paul's rebuke.

---

[59] Compare the use of this verb for "command" at 1 Corinthians 7:10; 1 Thessalonians 4:11; 2 Thessalonians 3:6,10,11; 1 Timothy 1:3,18.

[60] Technically there is no "you" in the Greek. What Paul wrote was, 'I do not praise your coming together not for the better, but for the worse.'

Not for the better but for the worse -- Congregational meetings were intended to promote the edification, piety, spirituality, and harmony of the members – in a word, to help them grow and become better citizens of the Kingdom of God. "Not for the better" says the congregational meetings at Corinth did not produce this result. Their gatherings ("for the worse") did more harm than good. Their assembling tended to promote division, alienation, and disorder. Whether the activity was the love feast, or the Lord's Supper, or the exercise of spiritual gifts, their behavior left them worse off spiritually rather than better. Paul's preliminary charge that the Corinthians came together, not for the better, but for the worse, really extends from 11:17 to 14:40, for it pertains to the love feast and Lord's Supper and to the spiritual gifts, each of which Paul takes up, one after the other.

11:18 -- *For, in the first place, when you come together as a church, I hear that divisions exist among you; and in part I believe it.*

For, in the first place -- Paul now proceeds to explain just how it was that their gatherings were for the worse rather than for the better. Where is the 'second of all' – answering to this first particular? (1) Some say the first particular rebuked are the schisms between "haves" and "have-nots" at the love feast, and that the second thing rebuked is the unworthy manner of partaking of the Lord's Supper. (However, the close of chapter 11 does not support this interpretation. Chapter 11 closes by speaking of the love feast; so the whole rest of the chapter is speaking of the abuses of the love feast, and the results of such abuse.) (2) Others indicate the first thing rebuked is the disorder at the love feasts and Lord's Supper, and the second thing rebuked is the abuse of spiritual gifts (12:1ff). This commentator is in agreement with this interpretation. While Paul does not say at 12:1 that this is 'the second point', he does say in 14:40, "Let all things be done properly and in an orderly manner," which thus forms the conclusion to the whole matter of disorders.

When you come together as a church -- Church is *ekklēsia*, "assembly, congregation." The ASV reads "in the church," a translation that leaves some English readers thinking about the building where the Christians meet. However, there is no article ('the') in the Greek. Church buildings were not built until about the 2nd century. "The earliest known church buildings were erected in Edessa, Arbela, and vicinity before the year 200 AD."[61] Arbela was in Assyria, near Nineveh; Edessa was 40 miles north of Haran in Mesopotamia. If we translated, 'as often as you come together in assembly,' we would have the idea of repeated occurrence indicated in the present participle.

I hear that divisions exist among you -- 'I am hearing' suggests continued information from various quarters. 'I hear continually (present tense) that dissensions among you prevail' (*huparchein*, not *einai*); these splits are the rule. With so many reports coming to him, Paul has come to believe at least a part of what he hears. What is signified by "divisions" (*schismata*, 'schisms')? (1) Perhaps the same divisions (*schismata*) alluded to in 1:10 are intended here. It may be that the same factions who were divided about leaders

---

[61] Lars P. Qualben, *A History of the Christian Church* (New York: Thomas Nelson & Sons, 1942), p.113.

(chapter 1) were also eating in their own little groups during the love feasts. Their factious spirit contributed to the problem and abuse at the love feasts. Some doubt this identification of "divisions," since "in part I believe it" (next phrase) is hard to fit with the situation described at 1:10-4:21. (2) Perhaps it is better to speak of divisions between the haves and have-nots (rich and poor) in a given house church. Verse 21 appears to support the idea that it was a "division" between haves and have-nots. The minority of well-to-do believers (1:26) and owners of the homes in which the believers met would have had the leisure time and resources to arrive earlier and bring larger quantities and finer food than the rest of the congregation. Following the practice of hosting festive gatherings in ancient Corinth, they would have quickly filled the small private dining room. Late comers (the majority, who would have to finish work before coming to the meeting place – the first day of the week was not as yet a legalized day off in the Roman empire) would be seated separately in the adjacent atrium or courtyard. Those who could not afford to bring a full meal, or a very good one, did not have the opportunity to share with the rest in the way that Christian unity and brotherhood demanded. (3) Neither the "divisions" nor the 'factions' have yet separated from the congregation; the dissensions are still within the congregation. But while they have not gone so far as to form separate congregations, that tragic thing could happen if the abuses are not corrected.

And in part, I believe it – Apparently, Paul is saying, 'I am unwilling to believe *all* I hear concerning the point, but *some* I cannot help believing.' The evil may have been exaggerated, yet Paul believed there was some basis for what he had been told. 'To some extent I believe it' means "that he really does believe it, but also acknowledges that his informants are scarcely disinterested observers."[62] Shore suggests Paul's hesitant acceptance of what he hears should be an example to us regarding our belief of evil reports, even when reaching us on 'the very best authority.' Our general practice is often to believe a little more than what we are told, whereas Paul believed only a part of what he was told.[63] But although he might discount part of what he heard, Paul felt he had to believe some of it.

11:19 -- *For there must also be factions among you, in order that those who are approved may have become evident among you.*

For there must also be factions among you -- "For" probably is an explanation of exactly what it is that he must "believe in part." The word "factions" here is *haireseis*, the word that is often translated 'heresies.' The word speaks of a party or group or clique one gets involved in by deliberate choice.[64] ("Factions" are a work of the flesh, Galatians 5:19,20, and those involved in such are in danger of forfeiting the Kingdom of Heaven.) Are "factions" synonymous with "divisions" in the previous verse? Some try to distinguish between the words for "divisions" (verse 18) and "factions" (verse 19). They try to make

---

[62] Fee, *op. cit.*, p.537.

[63] Shore, *op. cit.*, p.107.

[64] The word occurs in Acts 5:17, 15:5, 24:5,14, 28:22 where it is used of religious parties or sects, and in Titus 3:10 (*hairetikos*) to denote one who occasions divisions in the church by turning aside from sound doctrine.

"factions" refer to doctrinal differences, and "division" to ecclesiastical differences, i.e., division without separation. Others say "divisions" and "factions" refer to the same thing, and both are defined in the following context.

Dei means "it is necessary, it is expected," but why does Paul say there "must be" divisions? (a) Some writers fall back on God's sovereignty, and insist that He so made us that there have to be such "divisions." Commentaries based on the KJV put this phrase and the following one together, and are likely to understand this passage as though it were *God* who did the recognizing and approving of some (the faithful) as being genuine. And it is not unusual to find reference being made to Matthew 18:7 and 2 Peter 2:1,2 as verses which explain how it works when God does the approving. (b) But the Bible does not teach that sin is God ordained, or that divisions have to be simply because God wills it. If it is "divisions" that are thought of as being necessary, the *necessity* would lie, not with God, but in the moral realm. Human nature being what it was at Corinth, factions were inevitable. (c) This commentator is not convinced the passage means "divisions" are bound to happen. Rather it means the reports of such must be true. Paul is simply saying that the reports "must be true, or I wouldn't be hearing so many sad and disturbing reports."

In order that those who are approved may have become evident among you -- Who does the 'approving'? *Dokimoi*, "approved," is used elsewhere both for approval from God (2 Timothy 2:15) and approval from men (1 Corinthians 16:3). (a) As noted above, some commentaries and versions treat this 'approval' as being something God does. The NIV reads, "No doubt there have to be differences among you to show which of you have God's approval," even though there is no word for "God" in the original text. One defender of this view wrote, "Similarly John (1 John 2:19) speaks of the aberrations of false teachers as destined to prove that they did not belong to the true church." (b) Other commentaries treat the 'approving' as something man does. J.B. Phillips' translation suggests there is reference to the party leaders introduced in chapters 1-4. "For first, when you meet for worship, I hear that you split up into small groups, and I think there must be truth in what I hear. For there must be cliques among you, or your favorite leaders would not be so conspicuous."[65] (c) Others, who suppose there is no connection between the "divisions" of chapters 1-4 and the divisions at the love feasts, offer a different explanation of who does the approving and who is approved. The "haves" approve of other "haves," and prefer their company to the company of the "have-nots." "Those who are approved" speaks of others whom the "haves" prefer to associate with.

One other use of this passage needs comment. Taking the verse out of context, some among churches of Christ and Christian churches have used this passage to justify separations or withdrawals from brethren over matters of interpretation and opinion, as though such "divisions" (choosing of sides) make it plain who is to be approved and who is to be rejected. How sad! In the Greek, the clause begins with *hina*, which can introduce either a purpose clause, or a result clause. Both options have been suggested in the commentaries. Calvinistic writers prefer to call this a purpose clause. They find sup-

---

[65] LeRoy Garrett, writing in the *Restoration Review*, March 1974, p.246ff, defends Phillip's translation as giving the correct idea for the passage.

port here for the idea that it was necessary for God to introduce faction to find the loyal ones. Non-Calvinistic writers insist that, in fact, it was not God who introduced the factions.[66] In this commentator's opinion, it is better to take it as a result clause. One result was that it soon became evident who a man's favorites were. The "haves" favored other "haves." The "have-nots" were shunted aside. The result of the factions is that people showed who they really preferred to be with as they separated and showed favoritism to the other "haves" while excluding the "have-nots."

11:20 -- *Therefore when you meet together, it is not to eat the Lord's Supper,*

Therefore when you meet together -- "Therefore" points to the factions and divisions verses 18 and 19 spoke of. Because of these, it was not possible to properly partake of the Lord's Supper. "Together" translates *epi to auto*, "in the same place."[67] Paul is speaking of the regular assembly of Christians on the Lord's Day. In this verse and the next, Paul intimates that what transpired in their church assemblies rendered the celebration of the Lord's Supper *impossible*. A supper they may eat, but it is not the *Lord's*.

It is not to eat the Lord's Supper -- The ASV translated *ouk estin* as "It is not possible." The impossibility stemmed, not from the lack of bread and wine, but from the lack of requisite disposition in the hearts of those assembled. The Corinthians intended to observe the Lord's Supper, but their unworthy behavior at the love feast nullified their purpose. Paul's language here reminds us of Acts 20:7. The church at Troas met to observe the Lord's Supper. Likewise, the language of this verse implies that the church at Corinth met "to eat the Lord's Supper."[68] Where there are divisions and factions, you can have a communion service but not real communion. There is nothing intrinsic in the cup and the loaf that will absolve you from sins; instead, there must be repentance and a discrimination of the body. Unless there is repentance and the proper spirit, there can be no communion in the true sense. These Corinthians were assembling together as a congregation and eating a bit of loaf and drinking the cup, but they were not having real communion.

The designation of communion as the "Lord's Supper" deserves a brief comment. It

---

[66] To interpret as do the KJV and NIV, we must take verse 19 as irony, for Paul has already condemned partyism (chapters 1-4). It would hardly do now to have Paul saying that some good comes out of partyism (the idea being, supposedly, that divine providence can turn this evil tendency to good account).

[67] See E. Ferguson, "When You Come Together: *epi to auto* in Early Christian Literature," *Restoration Quarterly* 16 (1973), p.202-8, who shows it means "together," not in the sense of Christian unity, but in the sense of being "in an assembly." The same phrase is found in Acts 2:44,47, 2:1, 3:1.

[68] Two points of emphasis should be highlighted. First, in a day when we are witnessing an attack on the idea of a need for assembling as a congregation, it is important to emphasize the fact that the apostles assembled the converts into congregations. Second, in a day when many assemble and do not include the Lord's Supper as a part of the service, it is important to emphasize that the early churches found the observance of the Lord's Supper an indispensable part of the activities at the assembly.

is the "Lord's," for He instituted it to commemorate His death; it is in honor of Him.[69] It is called a "supper" because it was instituted in the evening. It was the very purpose of these meetings to celebrate the Lord's Supper. But if anyone came to the meeting at Corinth and expected this purpose to be carried out, he found himself completely disappointed. The action of the members at the love feast made a celebration of the Lord's Supper impossible. The Lord's Supper reminds of Calvary, and once again Paul compares the Corinthians' behavior with the "word of the cross" (1:18), and by this means their behavior is shown to be faulty and blameworthy.

11:21 -- *for in your eating each one takes his own supper first; and one is hungry and another is drunk.*

For in your eating -- Paul now explains why their "observance" ceased to be "the *Lord's* Supper." The factions spoken about in verses 18 and 19 became obvious when it came time to sit down and eat the basket dinner. Each little "clique" sat together, freezing out all others who were not part of their group.

Each one takes his own supper first -- The ASV reads, "each one taketh before other his own supper." It catches the fact that "takes" is a compound verb, made up of *pro* and *lambanō*. Each was hurrying to eat "before" (*pro*) others had a chance to arrive. Instead of waiting for one another (verse 33), the Corinthians, as they entered the assembly room bringing their provisions for the dinner, sat down at once to consume each his own supply, like private diners at a restaurant. Each one ate by himself (or in cliques) and each ate what he himself had brought, instead of waiting for all to arrive and sharing with one another what they had. (Since the poor might get only one good meal a week – at the love feast at the church meeting – to rob them of this was doubly painful and distressing!) It was a selfish and hasty act of eating, without waiting to put all the food together and divide it for the common good. "Cliques were formed, and relatives, friends, those of one clique sat together, probably at private tables, the rich and prosperous separated from the poor, letting those who could bring little or nothing sit by themselves, and go hungry, and feel excluded" (Lenski, *op. cit.*, p.458-459). Paul's language "his own supper" may reflect the fact that the people who were gathering together had essentially forgotten the real purpose of meeting (i.e., of eating the Lord's Supper). Many of the people were coming, not for the Lord's Supper, but to eat and drink. They forgot about their spiritual needs in favor of the physical food. The present tense verbs picture repetitions; this has come to be the regular practice at Corinth.

And one is hungry and another is drunk -- The poor man, whose small supply of food was insufficient, or who arriving late (for his time was not his own) found the food gone and the table cleared, is the one who was still "hungry" when the love feast was finished. What went on at Jerusalem (James 2:2ff) was being repeated at Corinth. The rich members were gathering in their own little cliques, and the poor were left with little or no

---

[69] The adjective *kuriakon*, translated "the Lord's," is found in the New Testament only here and at Revelation 1:10. Adjectives ending in *-kos* (*-kos, -ka, -kon*) signify 'kind' or 'nature.' It is impossible to eat a supper of the kind the Lord's Supper is supposed to be, is the idea. The disorders have given a different character to the commemorative supper.

food. On the other hand, the rich had more than enough. The literal meaning of the word (*methuō*) is "intoxication." The metaphorical meaning is 'surfeited,' 'gorged.' John 2:10 indicates it need not always be taken literally to denote intoxication.[70] It may mean no more than that the early arrivals have had too much to eat and drink, more than enough to satisfy; they are 'stuffed.' The consequence of their abuse of the love feast was that one man cannot even satisfy his hunger, while another gorged himself to excess. By behaving in this manner, all fellowship was destroyed. The love feast had ceased to be a love feast, and had degenerated into a selfish meal. By their attitudes they had made it impossible to be in the right spirit when it came time to set apart some of the bread and fruit of the vine and use these to observe the Lord's Supper.

11:22 -- *What! Do you not have houses in which to eat and drink? Or do you despise the church of God and shame those who have nothing? What shall I say to you? Shall I praise you? In this I will not praise you.*

What! -- This whole verse is designed to rebuke them for having so grossly perverted the design of the love feast.

Do you not have houses in which to eat and drink? -- The object of the "love feast" was something higher than the mere gratification of appetite.[71] If any one raised the objection, 'we just can't wait to eat,' Paul answered by showing that they should eat something at home before coming to the assembly. What an abuse of fellowship. What a mockery of charity – when in this love feast the poor man is forced to fast though he is starving, while the rich man feasts until he is gorged. Hunger and gluttony face to face! And this in the church of God!

Or do you despise the church of God -- This is the other horn of a dilemma (the first horn, above: "do you not have houses ..."). Even if their voracity could be excused (and it could not, for they did have houses where they could have taken the edge off their hunger before they came to the assembly), then the only possible conclusion one could draw from their actions is that they were *deliberate*. The rich must have intended to pour scorn on the church and to insult their poorer brethren. Their contemptuous treatment of the poorer members of the congregation was a course of conduct which involved a disparagement of the assembly (church[72]) as God intended her to be. Their contempt was expressed by their not sharing with the congregation the portion which they brought. 'Do you think that you need have no reverence or respect for what God wants done in the congregational meeting?' Have you forgotten so completely that this is God's gathering? Have you forgotten the real purpose of the gathering?'

---

[70] Some take the word literally and then see in this a proof that the wine used at the Lord's Supper in the primitive church was fermented and people could get intoxicated by drinking too much. But the word need not be taken literally. Being surfeited from eating too much would suffice in this place.

[71] Paul is not condoning getting intoxicated at home when he speaks about drinking in their homes.

[72] Some understand "church" here to be the *place* or building where the congregation assembled, but this commentator is not at all inclined to this theory.

And shame those who have nothing? -- Have not what? Some say 'have not houses to eat and drink in.' (Many of the Corinthians were slaves, so would not have houses.) Others interpret it, 'have not – in general,' i.e., they are poor. This commentator thinks this latter is the better idea. In fact, the margin has "are poor." 'Do you think that because a man is poor that you may treat him with contempt?' The Corinthians, by their selfish actions, were exposing to public shame those who were not so fortunate. It is bad enough to be poor, but it compounds this issue to be exposed to public shame.

What shall I say to you? Shall I praise you? In this I will not praise you -- See verse 17 and verse 2. 'What am I to say to you? Do you expect me to commend you? In this matter that is impossible.' Paul stands as a person who is nonplussed and shocked, and he asks himself, "What shall I say?" Then he remembers that in 11:2 he praised the Corinthians. With irony he asks now, "Shall I praise you again? Indeed, I cannot!" "I will not praise you" is a strong litotes for "I blame you."

11:23 -- *For I received from the Lord that which I also delivered to you, that the Lord Jesus in the night in which He was betrayed took bread;*

For -- This and the following verses explain why he could not praise them. Their behavior was entirely at variance with the solemn and sacred atmosphere in which the Lord's Supper is to be observed. The love feast was not a divine ordinance. Therefore, Paul lays down the regulations that govern the Lord's Supper; once this is understood aright, there will be no problem getting one's conduct at the love feast into harmony with the need to get into the right spirit to partake of the Lord's Supper. The Corinthians had said they tried to keep the "traditions" which Paul had delivered unto them (verse 2). Since the proper observance of the Lord's Supper was one "tradition" the Corinthians were not keeping, Paul feels compelled to remind them of the account which he had before given them about the proper manner of observance of the Lord's Supper.

I received from the Lord -- Taking this claim at face value, Paul is saying the source of his information about the institution of the Lord's Supper is the Lord Jesus Christ Himself, who made the information known to Paul by direct revelation. The "I" that begins the verse is emphatic in the Greek. This implies that there was a difference between Paul and others. 'I in contrast to others' received the information by direct revelation. There seems no reason why Paul should say "I received from the Lord" if he means 'I learned from other men a tradition that derived ultimately from Jesus.'[73] Nevertheless, it is surprising how many commentators affirm there was nothing supernatural about the source of Paul's knowledge of the institution of the Lord's Supper. Instead of a direct revelation from Jesus Himself, it is claimed that Paul got his information from one of the apostles who had been in the upper room. Such claims are based on several arguments. (1) One argument is based on the fact that the preposition translated "from" is *apo*, where one would expect

---

[73] The New Testament has several references to revelations made directly to Paul (Acts 18:4ff, 22:18, 23:11, 27:23-25; Galatians 1:12, 2:2; 2 Corinthians 12:7). In the Galatians 1:12 passage Paul directly affirms that he did not receive his gospel from men, but directly from Jesus. Why should we read this passage in 1 Corinthians 11:23 as though it meant something entirely different?

para after a verb compounded with *para*.[74] The use of *apo* rather than *para* for "from" does not necessarily indicate an indirect report (though it would be consistent with it), for it refers to direct communication in Colossians 1:7, 3:24, 1 John 1:5. (2) Another argument is based on the fact that the verbs "received" and "delivered" are almost technical terms for receiving and passing on the Christian oral traditions (cf. notes at verse 2). This has led many commentators to feel that Paul should not be taken as meaning that he had a personal revelation from the Lord on this matter. But why not? Jesus told Paul (sometime after his conversion) by word of mouth, and Paul passed on what he had learned by word of mouth. That is exactly what the verbs about oral tradition would require. (3) Another argument is based on the similarity of Paul's words about the Supper to the accounts found in Matthew 26:26-29, Mark 14:22-25, and Luke 22:14-20. Matthew was present. According to early Christian literature, Mark records Peter's preaching. Peter too was personally present at the institution of the Lord's Supper. Luke records Paul's preaching; hence, Luke's account is similar to this passage in 1 Corinthians 11 since Luke traveled with Paul and recorded the facts of the gospel that Paul preached. But instead of the similarity of words being proof that Paul got his information from one of the apostles who were present, it rather shows how the revelation from Jesus was precisely like Matthew and Peter used to tell it. When men are Holy Spirit inspired, their accounts will be alike for they will be telling nothing but the truth.

(Readers will be rewarded by taking all four accounts of the institution of the Lord's Supper and making a critical study. Note the similarities and differences – still there is no contradiction.[75] The details which are common to all four accounts are these: (a) The taking of bread, (b) the giving of thanks, (c) the breaking of bread, (d) the words "This is My body," (e) the cup, and (f) the words "blood" and "covenant.")

Contrary to all arguments for a naturalistic source for Paul's account of the institution of the Lord's Supper, Paul's language points to direct revelation from Christ to Paul. Paul did not hear this from one of the apostles. His message came by revelation and was repeated by inspiration (cp. 1 Corinthians 2:6ff). His source is "from the Lord" (cf. Galatians 1:12 and 2 Corinthians 12:7). If Arabia (Galatians 1:12,17) is not the time and place, we do not know when he received this direct revelation. The similarity between Luke's gospel and Paul's words here indicates *not* that Paul copied Luke but that Luke attached high value to the account Paul received directly from the glorified Christ.

That which I also delivered to you -- Paul founded the church at Corinth, and of course he first taught them to observe the Lord's Supper. That is when this 'delivery' was first made to the Corinthians. The thing he delivered unto them was the account of the institution of the Supper. 1 Corinthians 11:23ff is probably the second earliest written ac-

---

[74] See Lenski, *op. cit.*, p.462, and Findlay, *Expositor's Greek Testament, in loc.*

[75] Source criticism has consumed much paper and ink trying to explain which account (Matthew's, Mark's, Luke's, or Paul's) of the institution of the Lord's Supper is the original one, from which all the others are copied. Much paper and ink have also been expended trying to explain why each writer varied the 'tradition' they received. This is all a dead-end as far as contribution to our knowledge is concerned.

count of the institution of the Lord's Supper. (Matthew's account would be the earliest.[76]) This would be Paul's own reply to the assertion of some today that he, and not Jesus, is the founder of Christianity. He simply delivered exactly what he received – with no additions or alterations or subtractions.

That the Lord Jesus -- Shore has called attention to the fact that

> "It is worthy of note that in the heated controversies which have raged around the Lord's Supper as to its spiritual significance, ITS EVIDENTIAL VALUE HAS FREQUENTLY BEEN LOST SIGHT OF." If the betrayal and crucifixion are not historical facts, how can we account for the existence of the Lord's Supper? Here is an epistle whose authenticity the most searching and ruthless criticism has never disputed. And in this epistle we have evidence of the existence of this communion practice and of its connection with events which occurred only 25 or so years before. If we bear in mind that the apostles were Jews, and yet spoke of that wine which they drank as "blood," and that they were lovingly devoted to the person of Christ, and yet spoke of that bread which they ate as His "flesh" – can the wildest imagination conceive of that practice having originated with themselves? Could anything but the record given in the Gospel narratives possibly account for such a ceremony holding such a place in a group composed of Christianized Jews?[77]

Higher criticism also tries to portray Jesus as nothing more than a Palestinian peasant around whom, as the years passed, legends grew up, until under pagan influence folk started calling him 'Lord,' and eventually turned Him into a deity to be worshiped. Note that Paul here calls Jesus "Lord" – and whether it is a reference to Arabia, or to Paul's own views at the time he writes this letter, there has not been time for a legend to grow up, as is alleged to have happened in Jesus' case. The clear evidence is that Jesus referred to Himself as "Lord" in the upper room (John 13:13) and the early church simply took up the refrain.

In the night in which He was betrayed -- The inclusion of this item shows how detailed and matter-of-fact was the account of the Lord's Supper and Jesus' passion given to Paul's converts. The Greek verb *paredideto* is an imperfect tense, 'was being betrayed.' The imperfect tense stresses that the betraying process was already in motion when Jesus instituted the Lord's Supper. Jesus was breaking bread at the very time when Judas was out of the upper room, getting the soldiers who would eventually arrest Jesus.[78] (For an interesting description of what happened in the upper room, concerning Judas taking Peter's

---

[76] See the author's *New Testament Survey* notes, where evidence is given for the dates for the Gospels. (Matthew was first written about AD 45 or 50; Mark at AD 68; Luke about AD 60.) In the introductory studies we dated the writing of 1 Corinthians at ~AD 57.

[77] Shore, *op. cit.*, p.111.

[78] If we were to read straight through Luke's account of the upper room, it might appear that Judas was present when the Lord's Supper was instituted. However, Paul's language here in Corinthians indicates he was not, and therefore we treat Luke's account as being topical rather than chronological.

usual place at the table, the resulting contention, how Judas is finally pointed out as the traitor, and his departure to get the soldiers, followed by the institution of the Lord's Supper by Jesus, see Edersheim, *Life and Times of Jesus the Messiah*, Vol. II, pages 494-5.) Paul is trying to bring before the minds of the Corinthians the deeply moving circumstances of Christ's death, and thus show them the utter impropriety of celebrating the Lord's Supper in the manner they were. It is almost as though Paul were indicating that the Corinthians, partaking in the manner they were, were also betraying the Christ. Compare the sad solemnity of the upper room, with the irreverent selfishness of the Corinthians, and thus see the impropriety of the Corinthians' conduct.

Took bread -- The word is *artos* ("bread," of any kind, leavened or unleavened). Since it was in connection with a Passover observance that the Lord's Supper was instituted, evidently it was one of the thin loaves (*azumos*, 'unleavened bread') used in the Passover supper that Jesus "took"[79] and used. Since in Scriptural accounts of the observance of the Lord's Supper we find both *artos* and *azumos* used, it becomes evident that no part of the significance of the rite depends on the kind of bread used. There is no specific command on the subject, only precedent. The use of *artos* by the apostles indicates it is evidently a matter of indifference what kind of bread is used.

11:24 -- *and when He had given thanks, He broke it and said, "This is My body, which is for you; do this in remembrance of Me."*

And when He had given thanks -- The Greek word for "thanks" is *eucharistēo*, which transliterated becomes "Eucharist," the name given to the Lord's Supper by many. (This commentator does not like this terminology. It is a misnomer.) Matthew reads "and blessed it" (Matthew 26:26). Luke has the same word as is used here by Paul. Both expressions declare the act of consecration[80] by a grateful acknowledgment of God's mercy, and the invocation of His blessing.

He broke it -- It is this commentator's preference, when observing the Lord's Supper, to have a single loaf from which all can break a piece, and thus partake of one loaf. The breaking of the loaf is one of the significant parts of the service. It is included in the accounts of Matthew, Mark, Luke, and Paul. It is symbolic of the suffering Christ went through.

---

[79] This commentator suggests that Jesus took the broken loaf called *aphikomen* (by modern Jews) and used it for the "bread" part of the Lord's Supper. It is just possible that the verb "took" means more than that He simply picked up a piece of bread. Perhaps Jesus held up the broken loaf for all those at the table to see, and once He had their attention, He then spoke the words explaining the meaning of what He was doing. Perhaps from this action comes the Catholic practice of 'elevating the host.'

[80] "Consecration" is here defined as 'setting it apart for sacred use,' and does not imply anything like the Transubstantiationists mean when they use the word "consecrate." Jesus merely took some common Passover food that was at hand and set it apart for a different purpose.

And said (Take, eat) -- The words "Take, eat," found in the KJV at this place, are omitted by all the best uncials. (Matthew's Gospel has the words, and there they are genuine. Jesus said the words, though not all the writers record them.) There is no great difference in the reports of the words Jesus actually uttered in the institution of the Lord's Supper. There is no contradiction. The accounts supplement one another. The Gospel writers also mention that Jesus passed the bread to the disciples. Paul only implies this fact.

This is My body -- The demonstrative "this" is neuter, whereas "bread" is masculine.

- It is on this basis that the Lutherans argue that "this" cannot refer grammatically to the bread. They say it must mean "this gift," i.e., Christ holds in his hand and passes to the disciples something no longer mere bread out of the oven, but bread which is Christ's body ("body" is neuter in the Greek). The Lutheran doctrine of the Lord's Supper is called impanation – i.e., that Christ's body is represented 'in the bread.'
- Catholics use the neuter "this" to help support their doctrine of transubstantiation; namely that when Jesus consecrated the loaf it changed into the actual body of Christ.
- There are several reasons to reject the ideas of impanation and transubstantiation. (1) "This" is neuter, while "bread" is masculine, so the pronoun does not modify the word "bread." Instead, it must refer to the entire action of blessing, breaking, and distributing the loaf. (2) At 10:4, "is" clearly means something like 'represents.' (In the Aramaic Jesus originally spoke, the actual verb would have been entirely absent from the sentence.) (3) The "cup" is equated with the New Covenant (Luke 22:20), not with the blood directly. Many writers think Jesus' language means 'This is a symbol, a token of my body. This represents my body.[81] This broken bread will serve to recall to your minds My whole incarnate life.'[82] In this commentator's opinion, Jesus' words could not be intended to mean that the bread was *literally* His body. His body was then before them *living*. No one reclining with Jesus in the upper room would have thought He was saying the bread was somehow a literal extension of His flesh.

The language employed by Christ accords with a common mode of speaking among the Jews, and is exactly similar to that used by Moses at the institution of the Passover (Exodus 12:11). Moses said, "It (that is, the lamb) *is* the Lord's Passover." That is, the lamb and the feast represent the Lord's passing over the houses of the Israelites. It serves to remind us of it.

Which is (broken) for you -- If we read as does the KJV, "which is broken for you"[83] then

---

[81] "Is" can denote various kinds of identification, as we see from its use in passages like John 8:12, 10:9, 1 Corinthians 10:4, to name no others.

[82] In chapter 10, we explained the Hebrew idea of "body" as indicative of the whole life – in Christ's case, His whole incarnate life. Again, we get into misunderstanding if we give "body" the modern connotation of the physical flesh and bones which make up the 'house' in which we live. Commentaries based on the KJV, which reads "my body which is broken for you" tend to speak of how the loaf reminds us (not of Christ's whole incarnate life but) of His dying sacrificial sufferings.

[83] The word "broken" as added by many ancient manuscripts, and as found in the KJV, does not enjoy integrity. It is omitted by P[46], *Aleph*, A, B, C.

the loaf is intended to remind participants in communion of the sacrificial nature of the crucifixion (which already, in a sense, was underway since Judas is already on the way to get soldiers to arrest Him). Some have objected to adding the word "broken" because they recall how the Bible specifically says none of Jesus' bones were broken (John 19:36). But Jesus' body was broken in respect to His pierced side, and the lacerations made by the scourge and the punctures by the crown of thorns. The better attested Greek text reads, "This is my body which is for you." The loaf reminds us believers that Christ's whole incarnate life was for our benefit.

Do this in remembrance of Me -- "Do this" is a present imperative. Jesus was giving a command. 'Continue to do this; continue to take bread; continue to give thanks; continue to break it; continue to eat it!' is the idea.[84] Notice! It is because Jesus gave such a command as 'Continue to do this!' that the early church and we, too, observe anything like the Lord's Supper. The Lord's Supper is an ordinance given to the church by Jesus. While these words ("Do this ...!") are not found in Matthew, Mark, or Luke (except in disputed verses), we still have Paul's word that Jesus gave such a command that instituted the continued celebration of the Lord's Supper. We may *not* imply Paul was the one who first taught the church to observe the Lord's Supper, and that he did so by putting words into Jesus' mouth which Jesus never spoke.[85] On the contrary, the celebration of the Lord's Supper was a firmly established practice before Paul even became a Christian (Acts 2:42). That can only be because Jesus actually spoke the command to "Do this!"

What does "in remembrance of Me" mean? (1) Some suppose the "remembrance" is directed Godward, in the sense that as we break the bread God is thereby being petitioned to "remember" Jesus' atoning death and thus show mercy to His people. This is the interpretation favored by Jeremias, and it does have a bit of truth to it. In both the Old and New Testaments, "remembrance" is not just a mental activity. When God remembers, it includes action. When He remembers, he 'visits' or 'forgives' or 'blots out.' (Compare Hebrews 8:12). (2) The more accepted explanation is that the "remembrance" is directed manward. The celebration of the Lord's Supper helps Christians remember Jesus' life and sacrifice on their behalf.[86] Just as the Passover celebration helped Israel to remember their deliverance from Egypt, so Jesus instituted the Lord's Supper as a memorial for the Israel of God, to help us remember our deliverance from sin. This phrase adds force to the idea that the loaf, rather than changing into the body of Christ, is a symbol to help us remember

---

[84] The proposal to give "do this" (*poieite touto*) the meaning of "sacrifice this" must be abandoned. Neither this passage nor Hebrews 1:3 (Vulg., "He makes purification for sins") can be made to support the dogma of the perpetual sacrifice of the Mass, as some large religious bodies teach it.

[85] German critics have called the whole matter of the Lord's Supper being instituted by Jesus into question. Remember, the critics insist that among the Gospel writers, everyone copied Mark, and if Mark does not have it, it is of doubtful authority.

[86] It is doubtful that the language of Jesus means 'Do this *because* you remember Me,' versus how we have explained it, '*in order to* remember Me.' It is true, of course, that if we gather around the Lord's Table out of compulsion or because we think it a duty, rather than gathering because we love our Lord, the Table may be of little profit. We suppose Christians should desire to be at the Lord's Table when it is spread, rather than at any other place under God's heaven.

the sacrifice of Christ in our behalf.[87]   "In remembrance of Me" implies that hereafter He is to be absent from sight.

What was wrong at Corinth was that their behavior at the love feast leading up to the Lord's Supper made it virtually impossible to remember *Him*. Paul insists that they correct their behavior so that they are thinking more of *Him* than themselves personally or their cliques. Christians do not have to look with envious eyes at the people who have beads to finger and wish we had something about our religion that is tangible. We do have that which we can handle and touch. As we break the bread with thanksgiving, and divide it, it helps us realize more vividly the sacrifice which He made for us.

11:25 -- *In the same way* **He** took *the cup also after supper, saying, "This cup is the new covenant in My blood; do this, as often as you drink* **it**, *in remembrance of Me."*

In the same way *He took* **the cup also** -- That is, Jesus took it and gave thanks, just as He did for the bread. There is no verb "took" (compare KJV) in the Greek, though this may give the sense of it. The language is terse and vivid.

After supper -- That is, all this about the cup occurred *after* all the different dishes of food on the Passover table had been eaten. In terms of a chronology of the death and resurrection, it is suggested that Jesus used the third cup of the Passover meal, which followed the eating of the paschal lamb.[88] The language implies that the blessing of the bread took place earlier, during the meal. Thus the passing of the bread, and then the cup, by Jesus, were separated by some moments.

Saying, "This cup is the new covenant in My blood -- Mark's record of Jesus' words reads, "This is My blood of the covenant, which is poured out for many." Luke wrote, "This cup which is poured out for you is the new covenant in My blood." Though the quotes of what Jesus said differ a bit, they all convey the same idea. By metonymy, "cup" stands for its contents. The Greek language has two synonyms translated "covenant." *Suntēkē* speaks of an agreement made between equals, where both parties can suggest or reject terms of the agreement by mutual consent. *Diathēkē* suggests a compact between two unequal partners, where one gives all the provisions and the other has no choice but either to accept or reject the whole compact, nor can he dicker as to the terms included in the compact. (A *suntēkē* between God and man is impossible. When God enters into a contract, He sets all the rules and provisions.)   The word "testament" (as the KJV renders this word) may not be a good translation. "Testament" means 'will' (as in "last will and testament"). The Jews knew nothing of the practice of making wills until they learned it

---

[87] This phraseology teaches us that the dynamic view of the Supper is the proper idea. In the language of the theologians, 'dynamic' is distinguished from 'real.' 'Dynamic' means Christ is present in the bread only in a spiritual or symbolic sense. He is not 'really' present (as impanation and transubstantiation affirm).

[88] C.E.B. Cranfield in "Mark" in *The Cambridge Greek Testament Commentary*, ed. by C.F.D. Moule (Cambridge: Cambridge University Press, 1966), p.436 comes to the same conclusion about Jesus using the third of the Passover cups.

from the Romans. True, *diathēkē* is the usual Greek word for 'last will and testament.' This is practically the only meaning it has in Greek writings generally, and it has it with great frequency. But in the Septuagint, the word is used regularly (227 times, in fact) to translate *berith*, the Hebrew for "covenant." The question in the New Testament is, 'Is *diathēkē* to be understood as in Greek generally, or as in the Greek Old Testament?' Probably, the answer differs from passage to passage, though Barnes (at Galatians 3:15, *Barnes' Notes on the New Testament* on "Galatians," p.339) argues that *diathēkē* always has the meaning "covenant" in the writings we call the "New Testament." Hebrews 9:16 and Galatians 3:15 are the only possible exceptions to Barnes' conclusion, and not even those passages need to be rendered "testament." The main idea in the word *diathēkē* is that of compact, agreement, covenant. The covenant which Jesus' blood ratified is called "new" (*kainē*, 'fresh') as distinct from the former Mosaic covenant which is now (since Christ died) obsolete. The covenant the Lord's Supper reminds us of is a 'renewed' (*kainē*) covenant. It is the Abrahamic covenant that was renewed, as contrasted to the Mosaic which was temporary and obsolete, worn out, and abrogated. Compare Jeremiah 31:31 where the same language "new covenant" occurs. Jesus, as He institutes the Lord's Supper, is referring to the "new covenant" prophesied in Jeremiah 31:31ff. The idea of covenant dominates the Old Testament. The people entered into a covenant with the Lord (as narrated in Exodus 24), and from then on they were God's people. The prophecy of Jeremiah shows that the Mosaic covenant was not permanent, but that the old covenant in due time would be replaced by a new one, based on forgiveness of sins, and with the law of God written in the hearts of the people. See this point clearly made in Hebrews 8-10. Jesus is saying, then, that the shedding of His blood is the means of establishing or ratifying the new covenant. His death provides forgiveness of sins, and opens the way for the activity of the Holy Spirit in the heart of the believer. When Jesus says "the new covenant in my blood," He means the new covenant was established, ratified, put into force, because of Christ's blood. 'My blood is the thing that establishes the new covenant prophesied in Jeremiah.' The language "covenant in My blood" may be an allusion to Exodus 24:8, where blood, designated by this exact term, was sprinkled over the people to ratify the covenant. The 'real' view of the Lord's Supper (see n.87) is hard to support in light of this verse. Jesus certainly did not mean that the cup He was holding and passing to them contained his literal blood. The cup, with the juice it contains, symbolizes the shed blood by which this new covenant is established, namely the blood of Christ. When communicants partake of the contents of the cup, they are to be remembering the blood that makes a covenant relationship with their God possible.

Do this -- Paul alone has these words concerning the cup. In the similar passage in Luke, the words are missing. Christ does not merely give permission: He commands this observance be done in remembrance of Him. "This" equals the *act* and the accompanying *words*. Without these, the "remembrance" is imperfect.

As often as you drink *it* -- See the notes under the next verse concerning the frequency of the Lord's Supper. There is no "it" in the Greek. Literally it says, "as often as you drink." This can scarcely be taken as a command to make all occasions of bodily refreshment virtually a celebration of the Lord's Supper, but must be regarded as referring definitely (as in the following verse) to this particular rite. We therefore agree with the translators in the insertion of "it" as giving the right idea.

In remembrance of Me" -- See notes on this language in the previous verse. Paul repeats this command about 'Doing this in order to remember Me!' precisely because this is where his concern lay. The Corinthians had to change their behavior if they were going to remember the *Lord!*

11:26 -- *For as often as you eat this bread and drink the cup, you proclaim the Lord's death until He comes.*

For -- The words of verse 26 are the words of Paul, not the words of Jesus. Paul is giving an explanation either of the statement "Do this in remembrance of me," or possibly "for" refers to the whole passage (verses 23-25): 'Such being the original institution, it follows that as often as ye eat ....' In the *Apostolic Constitutions*, VIII. 12, 16, these words are put in Jesus' mouth, with the change, "*My* death till I come." But the word "for" introduces Paul's explanation. With this second "for," Paul draws the Corinthians' attention to the real gravity of the Corinthian disorders at the communion service. This is what you must remember you are doing when you assemble to partake of the Lord's Supper.

As often as -- This suggests a certain frequency for the observance of the Lord's Supper, as do other New Testament passages. In Acts 2:42, "steadfastly" (ASV) speaks to the matter of frequency. According to 1 Corinthians 16:2, the Corinthian brethren met on the first day of the week, and when they met (1 Corinthians 11:20) they had a love feast and celebrated the Lord's Supper. According to Acts 20:7, the church at Troas met on the first day of the week for the purpose of breaking bread (i.e., celebrating the Lord's Supper). For the first three centuries, the early church observed the Lord's Supper every Lord's Day (first day of the week). We must admit Paul gives no specific directions as to *how* frequently the Lord's Supper is to be celebrated, but this language implies that it is to be done frequently, in order to keep the remembrance of the Lord fresh in mind. A comparison of 1 Corinthians 16:2 and 1 Corinthians 11:17ff indicates it was weekly observance in Corinth.[89]

You eat this bread and drink the cup -- Paul is still giving instructions about the Lord's Supper; he will return later to the topic of the love feast. Note the word is *bread* – bread still, even after the consecration. Again, the 'real' view of the Supper is hard to maintain here. Before the Savior instituted the ordinance he took *bread*. It was *bread* then, it was bread when he blessed and broke, it was bread when he gave it to them, and now Paul tells us it was bread when they ate it.

---

[89] What about communion on, say, Thursday night before "Easter"? Or on days other than the first day of the week? Or as part of a wedding ceremony? If apostolic precedent is not binding, it would not be proper to affirm that observance of the Lord's Supper on such occasions would be sinning. This commentator might approve, or might disapprove. It depends on the impression left on the general public. One might want to go back to the reason for having it on Thursday night. The danger is in the implications. Are we simply copying the Roman Catholic practice? What was the origin of that practice? If the date of observing the Lord's Supper is in the realm of opinion, then the limitations to liberty which Paul has set forth elsewhere in this letter would come into play. What would be the influence of our example? Is one day to be regarded as more holy than another?

You proclaim the Lord's death -- The word is *kataggellō*, 'proclaim, announce, proclaim down.' It doesn't say, 'sacrifice.'[90] 'You proclaim down through the centuries, as you roll toward the second advent, the Lord's death. You set forth in an impressive manner the fact that Christ was put to death. You exhibit the emblems of his broken body and shed blood, and your belief in the fact that He died for the sins of the world. You preach to the whole world the fact that the Lord suffered a sacrificial death on behalf of His church, and thereby achieved their redemption.' Perhaps as communicants share the loaf and cup, it is a sort of object lesson presentation of the facts of the gospel. (It is an illustration much like the "showing forth" of the deliverance of Israel at the Passover). Or perhaps the presider tells the meaning of the loaf and the cup, and thus 'proclaims' Christ's death.

Until He comes -- The "object lesson" the Lord's Supper presents is to be proclaimed throughout church history until the second coming of Christ. It was designed that the ordinance should be perpetuated and observed to the end of time. In every generation, therefore, and in every place where there are Christians, it is to be observed, until the Son of God shall return. This commentator takes it that the Lord's Supper will not be observed in heaven. It is to be observed only until He comes. The necessity for its observance shall cease when the whole body of the redeemed shall be permitted to see their Lord, and at that time there shall be no need of those emblems to remind us of Him for we shall see Him as He is. What kind of message radiates from the way we partake of the Lord's Supper? Do others see an impressive object lesson about the incarnation, the death of Jesus, and the new covenant He inaugurated? If not, are we any better than the Corinthians who were partaking in an unworthy manner?

11:27 -- *Therefore whoever eats the bread or drinks the cup of the Lord in an unworthy manner, shall be guilty of the body and the blood of the Lord.*

Therefore -- *Hōste* stresses consequence. It follows from what has been said of the origin and intention of the Supper that whoever partakes of it in an improper manner shall be guilty of the body and blood of the Lord. After reminding them about what the Lord's Supper is really to be, Paul draws some grave conclusions and warnings concerning "unworthy" partaking of the Lord's Supper, and then gives some directions to correct their abuses at the love feast, lest they continue to partake in an unworthy manner.

Whoever eats the bread or drinks the cup of the Lord -- Though the KJV has "eat ... *and* drink," the proper rendering should be "eat ... *or* drink." It is possible to partake in a

---

[90] The important word here is that rendered "proclaim" (shew). It has sometimes been made the proof text for positions that assert that we present Christ or his sacrifice to the Father. But we present, and can present, only ourselves. *Kataggellō* means 'announce' or 'proclaim,' it does not mean 'present (something) to.' In the New Testament it is used mostly of preaching the gospel. Always it denotes an activity exercised toward men, and never an activity exercised toward God.

wrong manner either or both of the elements.[91] Even if only one is received "in an unworthy manner," the whole Supper is ruined and profaned. The language used here gives the realists trouble:

> But here it may be asked, "If Christ is really present in the sacrament, of what does the unworthy communicant partake? Does he actually partake of Christ Himself?" Certainly not! He shares only in that which he is capable of sharing in. As Calvin (*op. cit.*, p.251) says, "he receives nothing but the sign." Or as Augustine: "he eats the bread of the Lord, but not the true bread who is the Lord." But how can the unworthiness of the communicant change what has been "blessed and changed"?[92]

In an unworthy manner -- *Anaxiōs* is an adverb that modifies the verbs "eats" and "drinks," not an adjective describing the moral state of the worshiper. In a sense, we are all unworthy to partake of the supper, but that is not the meaning of the word here. "Unworthy" is not an adjective describing the partaker.[93] It is an adverb describing the manner of partaking. No one of us need eat or drink *unworthily*, that is, in a careless, irreverent, impenitent, selfish, or defiant spirit. None of us need to be so interested in the clique we share with, or the food we put on our plate at the love feast, that when it comes time for the Lord's Supper, we cannot but help partake in an unworthy manner. There is no reason why the communicant's heart, mind, and conduct cannot be in harmony with the sacredness of the occasion. Partaking in an unworthy manner is what the entire section is about. It was to be a time of remembering the Lord, but their behavior at the love feast made such a memory almost impossible. At Corinth, if the Corinthians would correct their behavior at the love feasts, they would have gone a long way toward having their hearts in the right frame of mind to observe the Lord's Supper in a worthy manner.

---

[91] In the use of "or" here (and not 'and') is found the basis for the Roman Catholic argument for communion in one kind only, and it is the only one that can be found in Scripture. Various arguments have been raised in the effort to show the Roman Catholic dogma to be in error. (1) It is the eating the bread *and* drinking the cup that proclaims the death of the Lord. *Both* are commanded ("Do this!"). See notes at verse 29, where Sharp's Rule of grammar shows that "eats" and "drinks" are conceived as part of one action. (2) Was there a considerable interval of time between the partaking of the loaf and the partaking of the cup? Per Lenski (*op. cit.*, p.475), Winer and a number of commentators resort to the explanation that the first half of the Lord's Supper preceded the love feast, and the second half followed it. Thus, it is thought, a person might receive the bread in an unworthy manner, and might actually have gotten into the right spirit by the time the cup was given, and thus could take the cup in a worthy manner. (3) Lenski (*ibid.*) also cites A.T. Robertson, who wrote that "or" "does not mean that some partook of one and some of the other, but that, whatever element was taken in this way (unworthily), there was guilt." (In passing, whether or not Robertson's interpretation is right, there is truth in his idea that we may take one in the right spirit, and not the other element – and thus there is guilt.) (4) Lenski (*op. cit.*, p.476) then suggests the grammatical answer is simple. In some cases, "or" presents alternatives, only one of which is accepted, while the other is excluded. But there are also cases where "or" connects alternatives (two or more), both or all of which the writer accepts (Romans 1:21, Matthew 21:23).

[92] An editorial comment added by Philip Schaff, translator of Kling's commentary from German to English, *op. cit.*, p.238.

[93] Many people, mistakenly, have refused to partake of the Lord's Supper because they have been afraid they were *morally* unworthy to partake of it. It is when a person has sinned and needs forgiveness that is the very time to participate in the blood of Christ (1 Corinthians 10:16).

How does one come to the Lord's Table in a worthy manner? Verse 28 will explain: (1) come believing, (2) come discerning the Lord's body, (3) come examining ourselves (all of us are guilty of rationalizing our own sins – till we compare our lives and thoughts against the pureness of Jesus Christ), (4) come repenting, (5) come pledging anew our allegiance to Christ (we do this partially in the breaking of the bread), (6) come recognizing the continuing imperative of an abiding covenant relationship with our God, (7) come realizing that the Lord's Supper is a promise of the *parousia*, the return of our Lord. It is quite certain that selfish and greedy irreverence is incompatible with the intention of Christ when He instituted the Supper. Paul's message is that no one should take the Lord's Supper as a matter of course, as just another thoughtless activity. The Lord's Supper is a solemn thing, instituted by the Lord Himself, charged with deep significance.

For whom is the Lord's Supper intended? This verse begins with "whoever" – i.e., members of the Corinthian congregation.[94] It is not for a disbelieving world. The cup reminds the communicants of the new covenant, so it stands to reason that unless one is a penitent, obedient believer who is in covenant relationship, there is nothing to remember. It is not for a disobedient world. The Lord's Supper is not a substitute for obedience to the gospel. It is not for an impenitent church, or impenitent church members. The man who is not willing to repent should not partake (this is manifest in the whole context). It is for repentant, immersed believers. It is not as easy to come to the Lord's Table as some people think!

Shall be guilty of the body and the blood of the Lord -- Literally, it reads, 'shall be answerable (or held liable) for the body and blood of the Lord.' Back of the emblems is what they signify. Thus, to come in an unworthy manner is to sin against the Lord. It would be crucifying the Son of God afresh and putting Him to an open shame. Dishonor to the symbols is dishonor to that which they represent. Irreverent, thoughtless participation in the Lord's Supper leaves a man liable for the same penalty as those responsible for the death of Christ in the first place. The death of the Lord was brought about by the breaking of His body and shedding of His blood. We proclaim this death in the ordinance by the bread broken and the fruit of the vine poured out, of which we partake. Whoever therefore shall either eat the bread or drink the cup of the Lord in an unworthy manner shall be subject to the penalty that would have been pronounced if Christ had not died! Partaking of the Supper in an unworthy manner makes the death of Christ a murder, not a sacrifice. Such attitudes and behavior as the Corinthians exhibited at the love feast carried over to the Lord's Supper and made it impossible for them to remember the Lord. This left them liable for the very death they were supposed to be proclaiming.

---

[94] The vexing question of "open" or "closed" communion is not settled here. Perhaps Paul was writing to an individual congregation, and the admonition was to members of that congregation alone. Or perhaps several house churches would receive this letter, but whether members of one house church could commune when visiting another congregation, is not touched upon one way or another. This commentator teaches that the table belongs to the Lord. If one is a member of the body of Christ, he is welcome to partake of communion even when visiting another congregation of believers than the one with which he regularly assembles and communes.

11:28 -- *But let a man must examine himself, and so let him eat of the bread and drink of the cup.*

But let a man examine himself -- "But" means 'in order to avoid partaking in an unworthy manner.' "Let a man examine himself."[95] What Paul seems to be asking the Corinthians to do is to make an attitude check – to make sure they are not behaving in the manner that verses 20-22 condemn. This attitude check is to be done solemnly before they partake of the bread and cup of the Lord's Supper. When a person "examines himself" he is carefully ascertaining what his or her present attitude is towards other members of the congregation, and whether or not 'remembrance' of the Lord is uppermost in thoughts and attitude. Before He instituted the Lord's Supper, Jesus gave opportunity for the Twelve to examine themselves in the way He gradually revealed the traitor. When He said, "One of you will betray Me," all of them would have examined themselves personally. Before any of us partake of the Lord's Supper, this injunction requires us to see whether we are in a proper state of mind for commemorating and proclaiming the death of the Lord. Have we ever heard whoever presides at the Lord's Table cautioning the congregation against partaking if they are unwilling to be generous in helping the poor in their midst, or if they remain unreconciled with a fellow Christian over some interpersonal dispute or squabble?

And so let him eat of the bread and drink of the cup -- "So" means 'after the examination.' The case in which the self-examination ends in an unfavorable verdict does not get further consideration, since he has already spoken of how one incurs liability for the body and blood of the Lord, if such is the case. Certainly, where one finds improper attitudes or behavior as the self-examination is made, repentance and making amendment of life will be the first priority, and only then will he or she partake of the loaf and cup. This exhortation to self-examination and partaking in a worthy manner Paul now reinforces by referring to the penalty incurred by unworthy communion.[96]

11:29 -- *For he who eats and drinks, eats and drinks judgment to himself if he does not judge the body rightly.*

For he who eats and drinks -- "For" seems to show that verse 29 is intended to explain further why one should "examine himself" before partaking of the Lord's Supper. Lack of examination can lead to failure to "judge the body rightly," and failure to judge the body rightly leads to "judgment." The exact emphasis of this verse is not sure because of a manuscript variation. In the KJV, the word "unworthily" is added to this clause, and the words "of the Lord" are added to "body" at the end of the verse.[97] (The added words are

---

[95] On this verse is based the so-called Preparatory or Confessional Service that precedes the communion service proper in some religious bodies. Nothing is said here about seeking the help of a minister or priest (as in confession). Rather, the language shows the individual Christian can do this examining (proving) for himself.

[96] In notes at verse 27 we spoke of communion under one or both kinds. In notes at verse 26 we called attention to the fact that it is still "bread" does not harmonize well with theories like transubstantiation.

[97] While one might suppose the addition of the word "unworthily" was simply an accidental repetition of what had already been written in verse 27, it is hard to assign a similar "accidental" reason for adding

not found here in verse 29 in P⁴⁶, *Aleph*, A, B, C, and 33.) Their addition makes verse 29 say the same thing as verse 27. This may be unfortunate, since it thrusts on us the understanding of the copyists who added the words to the text. (While their understanding of what the text was saying may have been right, that is not warrant for adding the words to the text.) The text of the ASV/NASB (omitting the words added in the KJV) emphasizes not the unworthy manner so much as the lack of self-examination. The person who comes to the Lord's Supper without proper mental preparation is a *mere* eater and drinker. He is not 'communing,' or 'remembering,' or 'proclaiming.' He who eats and drinks[98] without examining himself eats and drinks judgment unto himself.

Eats and drinks judgment to himself -- The word *krima* properly denotes a "judgment" or 'a judicial sentence.' It is difficult to choose an English word that gives the reader a good idea of what Paul is speaking about here. The word "damnation" (as *krima* is translated in the KJV) we now apply to the future and final punishment of the wicked in hell. But verse 32 indicates the judgment intended here (where *katakrima*, "condemnation" is used) is not the future damnation in hell. The *krima* is something that happens in this life. Examples of such "judgment" are delineated in the words "sick and sleep" of verse 30. In addition, a continued profane and irreverent manner of observing the Lord's Supper will surely meet with the Lord's displeasure in the eternal world, as well as in this life.

If he does not judge the body rightly -- Anyone who approaches the Lord's Supper without thinking carefully about the "body" (precisely what the Corinthian cliques were guilty of), draws on himself the judgments mentioned in the next verse. The use of the term "body" has proven ambiguous enough to result in several proposed interpretations for this passage. (1) Some use the verse to support certain views of transubstantiation or impanation – that the "bread" is now the "body" of the Lord. In reply, it is not just the "bread" this verse speaks of, for the verse began with both verbs "eat and drink."

> To refer these words directly or indirectly to the question of a physical presence in the Lord's Supper, is to divorce them violently from their surroundings, and to make them allude to some evil for which the explicit and practical remedy commended in verses 33 and 34 would be no remedy at all. Moreover, if the word "body" means the Lord's physical body, would not the words "and the blood" have been added (for the non-recognition of the blood would be just as great an offence).[99]

(2) Some have offered the suggestion that there was a failure to distinguish between the "food" of the Lord's Supper and the common food at their love feast. The Corinthians were treating both as though there was no difference.

"of the Lord" since the last phrase of verse 29 does not repeat exactly the last phrase of verse 27.

[98] The one article in the Greek phrase *ho ... esthiōn kai pinōn* combines the acts of eating and drinking, thus negating the Roman Catholic inference imposed on "or" in verse 27. See notes there.

[99] Shore, *op. cit.*, p.114.

(3) Others speak of a failure to recognize that the loaf and the cup are emblematic of the body and blood of Jesus.[100] This view may be based on the reading supported by the Textus Receptus and represented in the KJV (i.e., the words "unworthily" and "of the Lord" are added in some texts at this place). If a person's mind wanders here and there, and he just goes through the motions, he is not judging rightly; he does not have his mind on the emblems and what they stand for. Behavior that hinders one's meditation upon Calvary carries with it the promise of punishment from God. These Corinthians – with their cliques and divisions, in their spirit of disdain for the poor, in their selfishness and excess (in eating and drinking) – certainly were not discerning the Lord's body. They did not have their minds on what they were doing. To go through the service in such an improper manner (with no self-examination) brings the judgments listed in the following verses.

(4) More and more in the commentaries, one reads how "body" is likely used here in 11:29 just as it was in 10:17 – with reference to the congregation being the "body" of Christ.[101] The treatment of the "have-nots" by the "haves" is directly traced to a failure to understand what is involved in being a part of the "body of Christ." Brethren cannot destroy the "unity" that Christ wants for his church, and at the same time escape "judgment" – both now and hereafter. Shore, who takes "body" here as a reference to the congregation, has this note of explanation of this verse:

> The fault which Paul was condemning was the practice which the Corinthians had fallen into of regarding these gatherings as opportunities for individual indulgence, and not as church assemblies. They did not rightly estimate such gatherings as being corporate meetings; they did not rightly estimate themselves as not now isolated individuals, but as members of the common body. They ought to discern in these meetings of the Church a body; they ought to discern in themselves parts of a body. Not only is this interpretation, I venture to think, the most accurate and literal interpretation of the Greek, but it is the only view which seems to me to make the passage bear intelligibly on the point which Paul is considering, and the real evil which he seeks to counteract.[102]

11:30 -- *For this reason many among you are weak and sick, and a number sleep.*

For this reason -- "Reason" means on account of a lack of self-examination and a failure to judge the body rightly. Paul now applies what he has just been saying directly to the Corinthians. Here is the "judgment" he has been warning about.

---

[100] For this view to be viable, it would have to be recognized that "body" is shorthand for "the body and blood of the Lord."

[101] Shore (*op. cit.*, p.114) has this paragraph of reasons for believing "body" is a reference to the church. "Paul never uses the word 'body' in reference to our Lord's physical body without some clear indication that such is meant (see Romans 7:4, Philippians 3:21, Colossians 1:22). On the other hand, the use of the word 'Body' or 'Body of Christ,' meaning the Church, is frequent (as its use in 1 Corinthians 10:16,17 illustrates). See Romans 12:5, Ephesians 1:22, and 5:23,30."

[102] Shore, *ibid.*

Many among you are weak and sick, and a number sleep -- There is a great difference of opinion on this verse. Is the reference to sickness and death *physical* or *spiritual*?

(1) Most ancient and modern commentators opt for *physical* sickness and death. Barnes is a typical example:

> Evidently referring to prevailing bodily sickness and disease. This is the natural and obvious interpretation of the passage. The sense clearly is that God had sent among them bodily distempers as an expression of the divine displeasure and judgment for their improper mode of celebrating the Lord's Supper ... It may possibly have been the case that the intemperance and gluttony which prevailed on these occasions was the direct cause of no small part of the bodily disease which prevailed, and which in some cases terminated in death.[103]

Support for the view that some physical malady is here alluded to is the fact that God did send visitations of divine wrath including physical death against wrongdoers – as in the case of Ananias and Sapphira, and perhaps also the incestuous man mentioned earlier in this epistle. Perhaps the expression "disciplined by the Lord" (verse 32) indicates that physical is the sense to take this. That is, we are physically disciplined by the Lord in the present in order to avoid being condemned with the world. "Weak" is said to be the chronic case. "Sick" is said to be the acute case. "Sleep" is said to be death.[104]

(2) To take this as *spiritual* sickness and death would run counter to most contemporary commentaries, and is difficult to reconcile with verse 32, yet some attempt to make a case for it. Careless and thoughtless communion certainly can contribute to spiritual malaise and eventually spiritual death. The Scriptures do speak of Christians listening to the devil so much that they die spiritually (Romans 6:23). It is possible for Christians to defect from Jesus, with the result being "it is impossible to renew them again to repentance" (Hebrews 6:6). What was once a thriving congregation at Sardis was spiritually dead when Christ addressed a letter to her (Revelation 3:1ff). Compare also Matthew 13:15 for spiritual blindness. Careless attitudes and actions while participating in the public assembly can indeed leave the worshipers spiritually weak and sickly; if left untreated, the sickness can lead to spiritual death.[105] Improper observance of the Lord's Supper will lead to: (a) the hardening of the heart, (b) increased coldness and dullness in the service of God, (c) the loss of favor with God, (d) spiritual death.

---

[103] Barnes, *op. cit.*, p.221.

[104] There are passages (e.g., John 11:11-14, Acts 7:60) where "sleep" is a euphemistic expression for 'death.' If this explanation is correct, how astounding what we have been told. Though it is not the cause of all sickness and death, we are told here that personal and corporate suffering can be a judgment from God against Christian lovelessness. Perhaps if we saw the link more often between wrong behavior and physical suffering, we would not be so slow to acknowledge it as an option when we see it occur in the church.

[105] Coffman (*op. cit.*, p.188) observes that if spiritual death is here intended, then the condition of those who were once "awake" but who have fallen "asleep" is terminal and irrevocable. This same condition is evident in Mark 3:29; Hebrews 6:6; 1 Timothy 5:6; 2 Peter 2:20; 1 John 5:16; and 1 Thessalonians 5:19.

11:31 -- *But if we judged ourselves rightly, we would not be judged.*

But if we judged ourselves rightly, we should not be judged -- 'If we made a practice (imperfect tense) of rightly judging ourselves.' "Judged rightly" repeats what was written in verse 29. If we would examine ourselves, if we would exercise a strict scrutiny over our hearts and feelings and conduct, and if we would come to the Lord's Table with the proper spirit, we should escape the condemnation to which they are exposed who observe it in an improper manner. The time to do such an examination is before it is time to observe the Lord's Supper, and even before one begins to eat the love feast. Some have supposed that a few moments of time set aside for such self-examination in order to prepare for communion is a useful way to help worshipers make the attitude check and any necessary amendment of life in order to partake of the Lord's Supper in the right way. The second phrase, "we should not be judged," repeats the words about "judgment" written in verse 29. Paul is telling the Corinthians how to avoid the weakness, the sickness, and the death. This is a contrary-to-fact condition in the Greek, expressing something (i.e., judging the body rightly, examining themselves) that the Corinthians are not doing (given their abuses at the love feast, and wrong attitudes at the Lord's Table), but something they could begin doing.

11:32 -- *But when we are judged, we are disciplined by the Lord so that we will not be condemned along with the world.*

But when we are judged, we are disciplined by the Lord -- "When we are judged" (present tense) indicates they were in fact being judged by the Lord at the present time. This verse, since it is not easily explained if the "judgment" of verses 29 and 30 are spiritual, is the strongest indication that the sickness and death spoken of are physical. It is not uncommon in Scripture for God in an extraordinary manner to visit men with calamity, sickness, or death for their sins (cf. Acts 5:1-10, 13:11). Hebrews 12:5-13 teaches that God disciplines those whom He loves to protect them from further damaging themselves or others. Paul is saying, 'These temporal sufferings (verse 30) are indeed punishment for sins. Your behavior at the love feast and Lord's Supper is not just bad manners, it is sin.' If the "judgment" is physical, it is obvious that the purpose of this verse is to console those who had been afflicted on account of their improper manner of observing the Lord's Supper; the chastening was for their own good. This verse would explicitly declare the condemnation following an unworthy partaking was not final condemnation, but temporal suffering to save them from being condemned with the heathen. If the "judgment" is spiritual, there is a daily testing given to us by the Lord that we may more perfectly follow Him (James 1:2ff; 1 Peter 1:7).[106] "Disciplined by the Lord" tells us that the weakness and sickness, yes and the "sleep" of verse 30 were intended by God to be remedial. 'To treat as a child,' i.e., to correct, when necessary, with severity; to discipline with a view to correction, is what *paideuomai* means. Chastening is God's loving way of dealing with his children to encourage them to mend their ways and mature spiritually.

---

[106] To explain how spiritual sickness and sleep would be construed as something that would "chastise" a person, and be hurtful enough to prompt him to repent, so as to end the "judgment," is not easy. It is probably the chief reason most writers speak of physical hurts as being the judgment for improper participation in the Lord's Supper.

In order that we may not be condemned along with the world -- The 'condemnation' (*katakrithomen*) here in view is the future condemnation at the final judgment. "The world" would speak of those who are not Christians. Men who are chastened of the Lord are so treated in order to bring them to repentance. Careless Christians are in danger of being condemned to hell along with the unbelieving world. But God does not let a man go to hell without first giving him ample warning. We should note the verb tenses carefully. 'Being visited with judgment' and 'are being chastened' are present tense. 'May not be finally judged adversely' is aorist tense. The former two speak of something going on regularly now, whereas the latter speaks of the final judgment.[107]

The careful reader will have noted that Paul has listed several serious consequences of partaking of the Lord's Supper without the proper self-examination or judging the body rightly: (1) one is liable to be held guilty of the body and blood of the Lord, verse 27; (2) one is liable to bring temporal judgments and chastening from the Lord on himself, verses 28-30; (3) one is liable to be condemned eternally at the final judgment, verse 32.

11:33 -- *So then, my brethren, when you come together to eat, wait for one another.*

So then, my brethren -- Paul now briefly sums up the practical remedies for the discreditable manner in which the Corinthians were conducting themselves at the love feast and Lord's Supper. To correct the abuses of which he has spoken, and to enable them to escape the judgments which were falling upon them, Paul gives them this practical advice.

When you come together to eat -- He goes back to the point he started from in verse 20, the love feast. This verse, this commentator takes it, does *not* have reference to the Lord's Supper. Paul is not referring to a simultaneous eating of the bread and drinking of the cup of the Lord's Supper (sometimes called 'partaking in unison'). Neither is he making reference to using *one* cup. And neither is Paul discussing the starting of services at the time announced, nor waiting until all get there.

Wait for one another -- This is a reference to their behavior at the love feast. Those who got there first were not to gobble down all the food before all those coming had a chance to arrive. The behavior outlined in verse 21 is to be stopped! This way, none would go hungry. Chrysostom points out the delicacy of the expression. It is the rich who are to wait for the poor; but neither rich nor poor is expressly mentioned. If some were so hungry they could not wait to eat, then they could have eaten at home. The primary reason for the love feast is not the eating, but the association and opportunity to encourage one another. Having charged the Corinthians to understand the body of Christ aright (verse 29), he now insists upon the necessity for the correct external expression of it. The verb is *ekdechomai* – to 'receive, accept, welcome, wait for.' Each time this word occurs, the context must

---

[107] The Roman Catholics use this verse to speak of the dead Corinthians who are in purgatory, and the verse is said to urge that proper observance of the Lord's Supper will lessen the danger of spending time in purgatory, as some (according to the Catholic belief) are already doing. The refutation of the Roman interpretation is that they ignore the verb tenses.

help pick one of the meanings. Perhaps "welcome" or "receive" fits since they were to quit their cliquishness along sociological lines. Let your behavior be such that all feel welcome – especially the have-nots. Perhaps they were to wait and eat together ('wait for all to get to the meeting place before you begin eating'). From this we get the basic principle that 'when they come together, they ought to have regard for one another,' i.e., they should be their brother's brother!

11:34 -- *If anyone is hungry, let him eat at home, so that you will not come together for judgment. The remaining matters I will arrange when I come.*

If anyone is hungry, let him eat at home -- See notes at verse 22. Let no one make of the love feast an ordinary meal, a feast merely for satisfying hunger.

So that you may not come together for judgment -- "For judgment" is a reminder of what has been written in verses 27-32. Eating in an unworthy manner – either at the Lord's Supper or at the love feast – brings judgment.

And the remaining matters I shall arrange when I come -- From "when I come" it is evident that Paul was planning to visit Corinth soon, but the exact time and the circumstances were still uncertain (as the Greek *hōs an elthō* implies). As indicated in the Introductory Studies, this letter was written from Ephesus. His planned trip (while taking up the Jerusalem offering) was preceded by the trip called 'the intermediate trip.' But when he wrote 1 Corinthians, we doubt that Paul had the intermediate trip in mind. It is anybody's guess as to what is referred to in the words "the remaining matters." Perhaps they had asked him other questions as to the time and manner of the celebration of the Lord's Supper. Perhaps some other "traditions" they said they were trying to keep needed further attention. We cannot know for sure. Whatever these matters were, they were not sufficiently urgent for Paul to deal with them here in this letter.[108]

As a concluding note on the topic that Paul began at 11:17, it is evident that

> Great changes occurred in the early church as the years passed. The love-feast did not prove to be a permanent feature of their assemblies. It was first transferred from the evening to the early morning "before it was light" (Pliny, *Epistles*, X. 42.,43, about AD 110; and Tertullian, *De Corona*, 3). Then the love-feast was separated from the Lord's Supper. It was finally abolished altogether. Justin Martyr, about AD 150, describes the Lord's Supper without mention of the love-feast.[109]

---

[108] Recall that in the notes at 11:2 the whole matter of 'tradition as a source of authority for doctrine or practice' as taught by the Roman church was evaluated. Roman Catholic theologians use Paul's statement here in verse 34 as a proof for their idea of apostolic tradition. We might even grant that such unwritten traditions were circulated in the churches. Still, Catholic theologians are unable to state what these traditions were. For instance, here in Corinth, what it was that Paul set in order when he arrived some months later is unknown.

[109] Lenski, *op. cit.*, p.488.

C. Correction of Abuses in the Exercise of Spiritual Gifts. 12:1-14:40

1. Principles by which to guide one's behavior in these matters. 12:1-13:13

a. Principle #1 – Tests by which the Holy Spirit's leading may be discerned. 12:1-3

> *Summary:* Paul's discussion of this subject of spiritual endowments is masterful. He begins by showing that it is the Lordship of Christ that is important. All spiritual gifts must be brought to this touchstone. If their exercise is antithetic to the Lordship of Christ, they are not of God. The chief tokens by which any genuine spiritual utterance may be known are that (1) a Holy Spirit-led person is not 'led away' (he does not surrender his self-control) like 'unholy spirits' led the pagans; (2) The Holy Spirit doesn't lead men to 'curse' Jesus; and (3) The Holy Spirit leads men to confess "Jesus is Lord."

12:1 -- *Now concerning spiritual gifts, brethren, I do not want you to be unaware.*

Now concerning spiritual *gifts*, brethren -- "Now concerning" shows this is something about which the Corinthians had asked Paul in their letter to him (cp. notes at 7:1,25 and 8:1). This may be the second of the points alluded to in 11:18. In any case, at the end of chapter 11, Paul had said there were some things he would take care of when he next visits Corinth. But chapter 12 begins in such a way that it implies that, 'Whatever matters I postpone, I must not delay explaining about the nature and utility of spiritual gifts.'[1] "Spiritual" translates the adjective *pneumatikōn* (note that our translation adds "gifts" in italics), and the word may be either masculine or neuter. If masculine, it refers to the people who possess spiritual gifts.[2] If neuter, then we must supply some neuter noun, such as 'things' or "gifts." There seem to be several compelling reasons for taking the word as neuter. (1) In his introduction to this letter, Paul had mentioned the spiritual gifts that had been bestowed on the Corinthians, 1:4-7. (2) In the following verses in chapter 12, the emphasis is more on the operations of the Spirit who distributes the gifts, rather than on the persons who are endowed. (3) The whole context would support the neuter reading. In 14:1, the same word appears in a form which can only be neuter, so it is likely the word

---

[1] This topic is the second longest (159 lines in the Greek New Testament) in the letter. Only the matter of "division and dissension" in the congregation, chapters 1-4, is longer (being 161 lines in the Greek). If we may judge the seriousness of the matter by the amount of instructions Paul writes, then these two were surely among the most troubling issues in the congregation.

[2] What if we take it as masculine, 'spiritual people'? We might have to go back and rewrite our notes at 3:1, suggesting that 'spiritual people' are those who are not only Christians (i.e., people whose 'spirit' is alive), but also are people in whom the Holy Spirit lives and works (some with *charismata*, some with "ministries," etc.). Comments offered to explain 2:15 and 14:37 might also be affected. *Pneumatikoi* would not be exactly synonymous with *charismata*. *Pneumatikoi* would include people who have "spiritual gifts" as well as those who have different "ministries" and different "workings" assigned to them by Jesus or the Father (see verses 4-6).

should be so interpreted in 12:1. In 12:4, we do have the word "gifts" (*charismatōn*, a neuter word in the Greek) and some think it would be natural to interpret "spiritual" here in verse 1 in the light of the following verses which do speak of "gifts."[3]

Since most of the next three chapters deal with "spiritual gifts" it seems appropriate to recall that the possession of spiritual gifts (*charismata*) in the New Testament times was in harmony with the prophecies of the Old Testament and New Testament. The ancient prophets had clearly predicted that the Messianic period should be attended by a remarkable outpouring of the Holy Spirit, e.g., Joel 2:28ff. The Joel passage started to be fulfilled on Pentecost, according to Peter (Acts 2:17ff). It still has yet to be completely fulfilled. Part of the prophecy was fulfilled on the day of Pentecost, part ten years later ("all flesh" – the Holy Spirit did not fall on the Gentiles until Cornelius), part is yet to be completely fulfilled and won't be until the Second Coming. Our Lord, before His crucifixion, promised to send the Comforter, who is the Holy Spirit, to instruct and guide His apostles (John 14-16), and through them the church. After His resurrection He said to His disciples, "These signs will accompany those who have believed: in My name they will cast out demons, they will speak with new tongues, they will pick up serpents, and if they drink any deadly *poison*, it will not hurt them; they will lay hands on the sick, and they will recover" (Mark 16:17,18). Immediately before His ascension he said to the apostles, "You shall be baptized with the Holy Spirit not many days hence" (Acts 1:5). Accordingly, on the day of Pentecost and after, these promises and prophecies began to be literally fulfilled. There was a general distribution of these spiritual gifts. They were not confined to any one class of people, but extended to all classes – male and female, young and old, slave and free. There was a great diversity of these spiritual gifts.[4]

What was the purpose of spiritual gifts? (1) They gave the church trained leaders. McGarvey said the spiritual gifts aided the evangelists and missionaries to propagate the faith in new fields with greater speed. (2) They confirmed the message of God. McGarvey said the gifts assured weak converts that God, for Whom they had abandoned their former religions, was indeed in the church. (3) They helped edify the saints. McGarvey said the gifts edified the church, and provided that body of perfect revealed truth which has been preserved and made permanent in the New Testament.[5]

In harmony with the prophecies and the needs of the early church, many in the church at Corinth had been given *charismata* (spiritual gifts).[6] But several had greatly abused

---

[3] *Pneumatikos* is not the usual one for the spiritual gifts; *charismata* is the common term. But the term *charisma* (in the plural it is *charismata*) is found in the following verses, which makes it rather apparent in this context that the terms are related somehow, speaking of the same manifestations of the Spirit. Just as was true if we take the word as masculine, we can take *pneumatikos* as neuter ('things' or 'gifts') without making the word exactly synonymous with *charisma* ("gift"). It could still include the 'ministries' and 'workings' of verses 5 and 6.

[4] Cf. 1 Corinthians 12:8-10, 12:28-30, and Romans 12:6-8 where different listings identify 15 or more different kinds of endowments that were given.

[5] McGarvey and Pendleton, *op. cit.*, p.120.

[6] This commentator accepts the view that some of the gifts at Corinth were genuine gifts which were

these endowments. Because a man was Holy Spirit-inspired did not mean that he could not sin (see Moses, Daniel, Peter [Galatians 2:11,12], Paul [1 Corinthians 9:27]). Some might claim to be Holy Spirit-inspired, but they were actually impostors making false claims, trying to take advantage of the church. Some would be dissatisfied with the gift they had received, and envy those whom they regarded as more highly favored. With others, the gifts would become a source of pride; they would make an ostentatious display of their extraordinary powers. And it is true that some of the gifts were more spectacular than others. The Corinthians seemed to love the spectacular! So in the public assemblies, the greatest confusion would arise as each of these persons would be desirous of exercising his or her own gifts at the same time. Paul devotes chapters 12-14 to correcting the evils which had manifested themselves in the church at Corinth. In chapters 12 and 13, he lays down the basic principles that should mold a Christian's thinking and guide his behavior. In chapter 14, he applies these basic principles as he gives specific instruction about the true and right use of the spiritual gifts. Thus Paul set about to correct the abuses of spiritual gifts in the public worship services. Note the affectionate "brethren" introducing a section where there may be much rebuke.

I do not want you to be unaware -- As was learned at 11:3, this is Paul's characteristic formula used to introduce important instructions, instructions that were new to the readers, not having been taught by Paul when he was earlier preaching and teaching among them. Barnes summarized the instructions Paul is about to give (lest they continue to be unaware) as being "in regard to the nature of the spiritual endowments, in regard to the spirit with which they should be received, in regard to the rules to which they who are thus favored should be subjected, and in regard to the feelings and views which should be cherished in all the members of the church in regard to them."[7] In light of what Paul next writes, he may be warning them, 'Do not be misled by your past heathen thinking and experiences.'

12:2 -- *You know that when you were pagans, you were led astray to the dumb idols, however you were led.*

You know that when you were pagans -- As it stands in our current Greek text, this verse in the Greek is ungrammatical. To 'fix' the grammar, two possibilities have been suggested, each with some plausibility. One is Hort's suggestion, that for *hote* we should read

---

being abused. He also holds to the view that there were some counterfeits, not produced by the Holy Spirit, since Paul talks about folk who were 'out of control' as they exercised their "gifts." Paul also contrasts what it is like to be led by the Holy Spirit and to be led by some other spirit, implying some were led by that other spirit. Coffman (*op. cit.*, p.223ff) is "amazed" at how readily commentators on chapters 12-14 have assumed that the gifts at Corinth, especially tongues, were all genuine manifestations of a legitimate gift. He then attempts to explain the whole passage by affirming that *all* the activities at Corinth were counterfeit, and that Paul's instructions were intended to squelch forever the counterfeit, while not prohibiting the exercise of the genuine gift to those who had one. In this commentator's opinion, Coffman's position cannot be defended. As Coffman attempts to explain each verse on the basis of this presupposition that it is counterfeits which are being rebuked, it quickly becomes obvious that the reason there are no comments offered on some verses is because those verses can in no way be made to match his working hypothesis. This would seem to be fatal to Coffman's attempt to explain 1 Corinthians 14.

[7] Barnes, *op. cit.*, p.225.

pote, resulting in a sentence which would read, 'You know that *formerly* you were Gentiles, carried away ....' The other is that we supply another "you were" (*hote*) with the participle *agapomenoi* ("carried away"), which in the Greek stands at the end of the sentence. This would yield the translation as found in the ASV/NASB. Whichever way we choose to smooth the Greek grammar, the resulting meaning of the verse is about the same. "Pagans" translates *ethnē*, the very word also translated "Gentiles" or "nations." Sometimes when this word occurs in the New Testament it speaks of those who are non-Jews. Sometimes the word identifies all those who are not Christian (e.g., 1 Thessalonians 4:5), and this is likely the case here. So our translators have chosen to render the word by "pagans" – a word that carries the idea of being not converted. The design of this verse seems to be to remind the Corinthians of their former miserable condition as idolaters, before their conversions. Many of these Corinthian brethren came from backgrounds of heathenism. In fact, heathenism, too, claimed inspiration. Many of the Gentiles had been deceived by the false claims to inspiration given by the priests of the idols whose temples the Gentiles used to visit for worship and for having their fortunes told.

You were led astray to the dumb idols -- "Led astray" (the imperfect tense of the verb *agō*, 'to lead') is probably not to be understood as meaning the heathen had been seduced from a better religion to idolatry. It likely implies the Corinthians had experienced the effects of evil spirits in their lives in their former pagan worship. True, the passage does not specifically say by whom they were led away. It might have been by the heathen priests and leaders, or by local custom. It might have been by their own passions and desires. But in all those instances, the real leader is Satan, or the demons. Previously, when the Corinthians had been lost, they were under the control of demons (10:20).[8] Idols are often called "dumb" in the Scriptures. Paul places "dumb" in contrast with the Holy Spirit, who not only speaks, but makes men speak what they could never say on their own initiative. The Holy Spirit makes it possible for us to confess Christ as Lord; He even enabled men to speak "the word of wisdom" and "the word of knowledge" (verse 8), and even divine prophecy (14:1). Paul may also be thinking about the gift of tongues, of which he knew the Corinthians were inordinately proud. What had "dumb" idols done in comparison with that gift? Paul merely says that the idols were dumb; that is an understatement, for they were actually lifeless. "Dumb" means they could not speak. What a folly to worship them! Idols could not confer supernatural powers. They could not give their followers the gift of speaking in tongues. *They could not even speak themselves.*

Archaeology has uncovered some of the deceit used to fool worshipers in the pagan temples. We find a good illustration of this in the statue of Isis at Pompeii. The ruined temple shows the secret stair by which the priest mounted to the back of the statue. The head of the statue shows the tube which went from the back of the head to the parted lips. Through the tube, the priest (concealed behind the statue) spoke the answers of Isis. A

---

[8] Some contemporary scholars try to suggest a wholly naturalistic explanation for such 'leading.' T. Paige, "1 Corinthians 12:2: A Pagan *pompe*?" (*JSNT* 44 [1991], p.57-65) suggests that vocal participation in religious parades was in Paul's mind, and he offers this translation "Whenever you were led [in the processions] you were [really] being carried away captive." However, there is something more than merely naturalistic in the Holy Spirit's leading, and in the leading by the evil spirits as well.

similar idol's statue has been found at Corinth. Near the forum is the remains of a round, circular shrine. Columns supported the roof that covered the altar. People would come to the god Apollo's oracle for advice. (E.g., Should I marry? What about this business deal? Should I enter this profession?). They would make their offering, and the 'god,' in a voice issuing from under the altar, would answer them. Archaeologists have found is a tunnel leading from the wall of a near-by shop to a spot underneath the altar. The tunnel is large enough to permit a man to crawl up under the altar, where he would answer the worshiper's questions. The priests not only fooled the people, but collected the offerings made to the oracle.

The dumb idols had no revelation to give, and could not have communicated it if they had. The previous idolatrous life of the Corinthians left them not only ignorant as to the ways of God's Spirit, but also tended to mislead them. Spiritual manifestations were utterly unknown to them. All they knew were dumb idols.

However you were led -- 'As you were led from time to time.' *Apagō* implies *force* rather than charm. The language implies a bondage to power outside themselves. The verb is often used of leading away a prisoner or a condemned person (e.g., Mark 14:44, 15:16). The heathen are pictured, not as men freely following the gods their intellects have fully approved, but as under constraint, as helpless, as being dragged away. There is something pathetic about idol worship. "They were hurried along, like dumb brutes, to pay reverence to dumb idols – objects of worship which, so far from inspiring others to speak, could not speak themselves."[9] Christian worship is different from pagan worship. You lost your self-control during worship in the pagan temples. Instead of receiving anything from these dumb and lifeless idols, they were miserably cheated. They even lost their freedom. Not so in Christian worship. As a Christian, you are responsible for how you act, even when under the Holy Spirit's influence. This phrase serves to underline the plight of the heathen. Far from reaching the dignity of the sons of God, they were continually led about like miserable slaves.

The test given in verse 2 by which the Holy Spirit's leading can be discerned seems to be this: a man does not find himself robbed of his self-control when the Holy Spirit is leading him – very unlike the bondage he found in his old pagan religious activities.

12:3 -- *Therefore I make known to you that no one speaking by the Spirit of God says, "Jesus is accursed"; and no one can say, "Jesus is Lord," except by the Holy Spirit.*

Therefore -- Seeing that in their heathen state they could know nothing about spiritual gifts, or how to discern whether a person is Holy Spirit-inspired or not, Paul must give them a test to apply.

I make known to you -- *Gnōridzō* might mean "I remind you" of what you should already know, but seem to have forgotten. (Compare notes on the same expression at 1 Corinthians 15:1 and Galatians 1:11.) The force of this expression is 'I give you this rule to distin-

---

[9] Robertson and Plummer, *op. cit.*, p.259.

guish' – this rule to help you determine if a man is Holy Spirit-inspired or not. Paul gives this test first negatively, then positively.

That no one speaking by the Spirit of God -- Their old experiences of the spells and ecstasy (altered states of consciousness) of heathenism had not prepared the Corinthians to understand the workings of the Holy Spirit or to ascertain the evidences of His presence. On this subject they had asked Paul for more information (verse 1). They knew how men could be 'carried away' by supernatural influences; they wanted a criterion for distinguishing those which were truly holy. The Holy Spirit can lead a man to speak, and the demons behind the false gods can speak through men. So they needed criteria to judge who it is who was speaking – the Holy Spirit or some other spirit. We suppose Paul has in view some things the pagan worshipers had said when influenced by demons. Whichever spirit (holy or evil) prompted the speaking, the actual mechanics of the "speaking" would be similar, but the content of what was said would be wholly un-Christian if the spirit prompting the speaking were an evil spirit.

Says, "Jesus is accursed" -- "Accursed" (the margin offers another translation, "anathema") means 'that which is devoted to destruction, or to bitterest woes.' It was often used of an animal for which there was no redemption.

> Originally, the word meant "something laid up," i.e., laid up in a sacred place. So it came to mean that which is given to a deity. Since what is thus given is totally lost to the giver, the word came to have the meaning of "that which is destroyed." Particularly was this the case when the destruction itself was a religious act, for example, when Jericho was totally destroyed at the command of the Lord. So the meaning passed gradually over to "accursed," and this is the usual sense of the term in New Testament days.[10]

When applied to Jesus, the word says that Jesus is rejected by God. The expression 'anathema Jesus' may be taken either as a wish ('Let Him be anathema') or as a declaration ('He is anathema'). Note, it is not "Christ" but "Jesus" who is anathematized. The Savior's historic name is used. Any man speaking evil of Jesus of Nazareth is not Holy Spirit-inspired. Whether they be Judaizers, or Gnostics, or heathen priests, or whomever – no man is Holy Spirit-inspired who speaks evil of Jesus of Nazareth.

That someone, under the influence of evil spirits, had called Jesus accursed is the natural inference from these words, but who is that 'someone'? (1) Some believe the cries came from *heretics*, who (similarly to what was done by Cerinthus and the Ophites) separated Jesus from the Christ (cp. 1 John 2:18ff, 4:1-6). Some have even suggested that since Paul elsewhere (Galatians 3:13) says Christ 'was made a curse for us,' that some heretic had distorted that thought into an ecstatic utterance.[11] (2) Some have affirmed that the cries came from *Jews*. 'Anathema' is a Jewish word. The 12th and 18th benedic-

---

[10] Morris, *op. cit.*, p.167,168.

[11] Findlay, *Expositor's Greek Testament*, p.886, says this identification of heretics as the ones who did the crying is foreign to the situation and context and is surely an anachronism.

tions used in the synagogue services, and also spoken three times a day, include a curse (an 'anathema') on all heretics and apostates. (Remember an immersed Jew is viewed as an apostate by other Jews.[12] But this benediction is post-Christian – after AD 85 – when Christians were finally excluded from the synagogues.) Since the Judaizers were very active at the time 1 Corinthians was written, some have supposed they were the ones who were saying "Jesus is accursed." It has even been suggested that Deuteronomy 21:23 ('cursed is everyone who hangs on a tree') was used by the Jews as proof of the correctness of their cries. But in a context that deals with "spiritual gifts," it is difficult to see how anything the false believers (Pharisaic Judaizers) were saying has a relevance. (3) Some have affirmed that the cries came from some worshiper who was *inspired by demonic spirits*. In a context that speaks of spiritual gifts, where 'inspired' people took part in the public assembly, such a view would not be impossible. We suppose that this "speaking" is an example of speaking in tongues. If so, then the verse implies 'tongues' may be prompted both by the Holy Spirit, and by unholy spirits – and careful discernment and judgment must be exercised to determine which is behind any utterance.

Satan can imitate the genuine gift of tongues so cleverly that many people have been and are still being deceived by him. It is evident that speaking in tongues is not always the result of the work of the Holy Spirit. The religions of heathenism furnish many examples of speaking in tongues. In his book, *Primitive Culture*, Dr. Edward B. Taylor describes a scene in the Sandwich Islands when the god Oro was supposed to give his teaching through a priest who "ceased to act or speak as a voluntary agent, but with his limbs convulsed ... would roll on the ground, foaming at the mouth and reveal the will of the god in shrill cries and sounds violent and indistinct, which the attending priest duly interpreted to the people." There is the account in Louis Bauman's book, *The Modern Tongues Movement*, where a missionary home on furlough from China was in a Sunday service where a woman was supposed to be speaking in tongues. The missionary became very agitated and asked the lady if she knew what she had spoken in a Chinese dialect. When she replied that she did not possess the gift of interpretation, the missionary informed her "It was so vile and obscene – what you said – that I dare not repeat it in English." The lady, speaking in tongues, was cursing Jesus in a Chinese dialect. Which raises the question, 'How long had the woman's utterances been taken as unmistakable evidence of the Holy Spirit's power?'

Which brings us to the original question, how does one distinguish whether a person is Holy Spirit-led, or is being 'carried away' by evil spirits? Verses 2 and 3 jointly warn against automatically assuming that all apparently 'spirit-led' behavior is from God – a caution needed in a day when folk first have a moving experience, then try to find Biblical warrant or justification for their experience as having come from God. There are behaviors found in contemporary sects and pagan religions that closely resemble the genuine gifts of the Holy Spirit. There are behaviors that result from altered states of consciousness that folk claim are Spirit-led behaviors. Paul has reminded the Corinthians of one test

---

[12] Compare what some Jewish leaders today tell their people about Jesus, to keep them from embracing Christianity. See Stephen D. Ecstein, *From Sinai to Calvary* (Kansas City, MO: Published by the author, 1967), p.75.

by which men can discern the genuine from counterfeit spiritual utterance. There are other criteria for checking such matters. (1) There is doctrinal orthodoxy, especially concerning the Messiahship of Jesus (1 John 5:1) and His perfect human nature while on earth (1 John 4:2). (2) There is the observing of the "fruit" (Matthew 7:15-20). (3) If a prophecy is inspired of God, it will come true (Deuteronomy 18:22). One thing seems rather obvious from the immediate context – the person who was saying "Jesus is accursed" was being "led astray" by some '*unholy* spirit' rather than being led by the *Holy* Spirit.

And no one can say, "Jesus is Lord" -- The confession that "Jesus is Lord" involves both His deity and His humanity. The *deity* of Christ is involved. The Greek word *kurios* (Lord) is the usual Septuagint word used to translate the Hebrew ineffable name "Jehovah" (see Matthew 16:16; John 4:2, 3,15). To call Jesus "Lord" is tantamount to saying He is one of the three members of the self-existent Godhead – Jesus is "Jehovah" just as much as the Father and Holy Spirit are also "Jehovah." "Lord" also indicates He is in active control of the universe, and thereby of what happens in people's lives. The *humanity* of Christ is involved (cf. 1 John 4:2-4). John is combating Gnosticism, which denied the humanity of Christ. John lays down this test: a man who denies the humanity of Christ is not a true teacher. Likewise, at Corinth, a man who denies the lordship of Jesus is not Holy Spirit-led. "Jesus is Lord" was the fundamental early Christian confession of faith (cf. Romans 10:9,10).

Except by the Holy Spirit -- In this context, where Paul is writing about spiritual gifts, it seems unlikely that an initial confession about Christ that a man makes as he becomes a Christian is the thing Paul is speaking about.[13] Nor should we immediately think of the confession "Jesus is the Christ" which Christians are to make regularly.[14] In this context, it is more likely that some inspired utterance spoken in tongues (one of the spiritual gifts) is in the background behind Paul's reminder of what the Holy Spirit would lead a person to say. This phrase "by the Holy Spirit" is a Hebrew one, used to describe *inspiration*. Inspiration was not something the Holy Spirit did for all Christians. It was limited to God's specially chosen mouthpieces.[15] So, something said "by the Spirit" is, by Scriptural analogy, a reference to a special spiritual gift. Though the physical result of speaking by demonic inspiration or by Holy Spirit inspiration may be similar, the content of what is said is the test by which one can determine which 'spirit' is speaking. One simple test of a person's claims to divine inspiration is his loyalty to the Lordship of Jesus Christ.

---

[13] Although, apparently, a person's initial confession of faith is not the topic of this verse, the Scriptures do teach elsewhere that the Holy Spirit has something to do with a person becoming a Christian in the first place, as through the Word He leads the potential convert to belief in Jesus as the Christ. See comments at 1 Corinthians 12:13.

[14] This verse is quite frequently taken to mean that 'All men who say from the heart "Jesus is Lord" are Holy Spirit-inspired in a supernatural way.' But this verse must be wrested from its context to use it to prove all Christians are inspired in a supernatural way. The faith from which the confession of faith in Jesus comes results from the hearing of the Word of Christ (Romans 10:17). Believers can say "Jesus is Lord" without being Holy Spirit-inspired.

[15] In comments on 1 Corinthians 2:13, "inspiration" was defined as the act of the Holy Spirit helping God-chosen messengers to express in God-chosen words the truths they had learned by revelation.

b. Principle #2 -- The need for a diversity of gifts in the church. 12:4-11

> *Summary:* After having presented the true tests of a genuine utterance by the Spirit, Paul points to the diversity yet essential oneness of the Spirit's operations. Different tasks or functions are given to church members by the Father, Son, and Holy Spirit, verses 4-6. The variety of "gifts" (*charismata*) or "manifestations" of the Spirit are given by the Spirit as He wills, verses 7-11.

12:4 -- *Now there are varieties of gifts, but the same Spirit.*

Now -- Leading men to confess Jesus as "Lord" is one 'work' of the Holy Spirit (verse 3). There are other ways in which the Holy Spirit works (verses 4-6).

There are varieties of gifts -- Some render *diaireseis* by "diversities" or "varieties," others by "distributions." "Diversities" would call attention to different kinds of gifts of the Spirit. "Distributions" would emphasize the idea that different gifts are given to different people. Whichever way you take it, you come out at about the same place. The context might favor the translation "distributions," for see how many times the words "to another" appear. The thing being spoken of is not distinctions within the gifts themselves (as though there were several types of healing, several types of discerning of spirits, etc.), but different kinds of gifts given to different people. The gifts He parceled out, so that one individual has this gift, another has that one. "Gifts" is the Greek word is *charisma*. In 1 Corinthians 7:7 the word is used of a man's natural abilities. Here, however, this commentator believes the word has its technical sense of *supernatural gifts*, just as at 1 Corinthians 1:7. The word denotes miraculous endowments wrought by the Spirit of God (cp. Romans 12:6 and 1 Peter 4:10).[16] The apostle enumerates the different gifts in verses 8-10 and 28-30.

But the same Spirit -- This commentator thinks *pneuma* here is a reference to the "Holy Spirit." So did George Mark Elliott. So it is interpreted by the translators of the NASB who capitalize the word "Spirit."[17] That the Holy Spirit – the third person of the Godhead – is here intended by the word "Spirit" seems to be manifest on the face of the passage.[18] In three connected verses, we see the Spirit, the Son, and the Father (the order is in reverse of what we usually see) all at work in the great redemptive plan of God. The Holy Spirit is the gracious giver of all the *charismata*. Paul's purpose in referring to these various en-

---

[16] See the Special Study on "The Person and Work of the Holy Spirit" in the author's *Acts* commentary, which discusses "spiritual gifts."

[17] Each time we come across the Greek word *pneuma* in the Scriptures, we must decide the meaning from the context, except where *hagios* ('holy') appears in conjunction with it.

[18] In fact, this has been the universal interpretation of the church until recently when some German commentators (the first being Eichhorn) called it into question. To say with Eichhorn that it means "nature," and that these are some natural endowments, though cultivated in various measures by art and education, makes manifest nonsense, and is contrary to the whole structure and scope of the passage.

dowments is evidently to show the Corinthians that since all the gifts are produced by the same Spirit, and all are intended to edify the church, *none are to be despised*, nor is one man authorized to treat another with contempt merely because he has a more showy or spectacular gift. The problem seems to have been that the Corinthians were using their God-given gifts in such a way as to result in division and dissension between brethren, rather than (as they were intended) to help edify the brethren. It looks like they regarded the possession of certain "gifts" as a matter of pride, and praised or disdained one another on the basis of the possession of this or that gift. Paul insists this is the wrong attitude. The gifts were not personal abilities, but were endowments conferred by the *same Spirit*. The Spirit does not fight against Himself. He does not cause brethren to inflate with pride. Neither should the people use the gifts in a way contrary to the Giver's intention.

12:5 -- *And there are varieties of ministries, and the same Lord.*

And there are varieties of ministries -- It appears the word *diakoniōn* ("ministries") is to be taken in the same sense as in Acts 6:1 or 2 Corinthians 8:4. It thus signifies the different services or ministries Christians could perform for one another. Service is the idea of the word. There are different ways of serving.[19] But the differences are not important, for it is the same Lord who assigns the ministry tasks.

And the same Lord -- The term "Lord," when it stands by itself in the New Testament, usually refers to the Lord Jesus (see notes at 1 Corinthians 11:23). Since in the previous and the following sections it is the action of the Spirit or God the Father that produces the variety of gifts and workings in the life of the believer, we should probably understand this verse to say that the Lord Jesus assigns different ministries or calls His people to a variety of ministries where they may serve. Though the ministry differs from person to person, it is the same Lord who called them to the work.

---

[19] In years gone by, because of the context here in 1 Corinthians 12-14, and because *diakonia* appears in Romans 12:6,7 as a *charisma*, this commentator just automatically assumed "gifts" (verse 4) and "ministries" (verse 5) and "varieties of workings" (verse 6) were all synonyms for some kind of *miraculous* spiritual gifts – the kind of "spiritual gifts" one received when apostles laid hands on Christians. This assumption led this commentator into numerous difficulties when trying to explain and harmonize all that the Bible says about spiritual gifts. For example, it was difficult to explain when the gifts were received, how they were received, and whether or not every individual Christian could expect to get some kind of *miraculous* spiritual gift.

The more this commentator has studied this passage, the more it has become evident that "gifts" (*charisma*, verse 4), "ministries" *(diakoniōn*, verse 5), and "effects" *(energēmata*, verse 6) are not all to be thought of as *miraculous* spiritual gifts. "Spiritual people" or "spiritual gifts" (verse 1) come in a variety of forms – some miraculous, some not miraculous. Verses 4,5,6 give us different 'measures' or 'manifestations' of the Holy Spirit – some miraculous, some not. Every Christian at Corinth would have one of these "manifestations" (*phanerōsis*, verse 7), but not all would have *charisma* (miraculous spiritual gifts). Charismata could still well be temporary (as 1 Corinthians 13:8-10 says), received by the laying on of an apostle's hands, but not the other two. Of the three kinds of "manifestations," *charisma* becomes the subject of the next 100-plus verses (see the word used in verses 9 and 31). The "gifts" listed in verses 8ff and in verses 28,29, would be examples of *charismata*. Charismata is the subject Paul is especially dealing with, because they were being abused and were producing divisiveness in the congregation.

12:6 – *And there are varieties of effects, but the same God who works all things in all persons.*

And there are varieties of effects -- The NASB translators chose "effects" to translate *energēmatōn*. The ASV translated it "workings," while the KJV had "operations." Following the lead of the KJV/ASV, commentators spoke of some activity of God. Some take this to refer to the works God performed in creation and providence; but that seems too distant from the topic of the context. Others note the context is speaking of tasks and jobs Christians are given to do as part of the body of Christ. As God formed the human body and assigned each member a job, so God determines what jobs are needed for the church, and He gives different jobs to different members for the good of the whole body.[20] Following the lead of the NASB, commentators talk about the "effects" or "results" produced by the works of God in the lives of those to whom Christians minister. Either way, *energēmatōn* is not simply a synonym for *charismata*. Rather, "workings" is either a distinct category of tasks to be done in the body, tasks which are not all miraculous or temporary, or it speaks of the "effects" produced when those tasks are carried out.

But the same God -- Since the Spirit (verse 4) and the Lord Jesus (verse 5) have already been designated, it is likely that 'God the Father' is intended by this phrase. This is one of the several passages teaching with perfect clearness the pluralistic unity of the Godhead. (See also Ephesians 4:4-6; 2 Corinthians 13:14; Matthew 28:19.) The Father, Son, and Holy Spirit are all at work in the great redemptive plan of God. They worked together in the creation of the world. They worked together at the baptism of Christ. They worked together in the establishment of the church. Now they are pictured as working together in the equipping of the saints for the work of service and ministry so the body can continue to function. Each member of the Godhead had His certain function. The Godhead is involved in the distribution of the "spiritual *things*" which verse 1 introduced. Some of those "spiritual *things*" are *charismata*, some are "ministries," some are "effects (workings)."[21]

Who works all things in all *persons* -- In the phrase "all things in all persons," the first "all" is neuter; the second can be either masculine or neuter. Since the passage talks of the workings of God in men, the masculine is preferred. "All things" refers to the "varieties of gifts," the "varieties of ministries," and the "varieties of workings." "All persons" would be limited to those who are in the church (the body of Christ, verse 27). "Works" translates an articular participle, *ho energōn*. The RSV translates, "who inspires them all in every one." But "inspires" is a poor choice of words to translate *energōn*, for some have supposed it means no more than that God inspired men to do their best. Instead

---

[20] Shore (*op. cit.*, p.114-115), for example, suggests the "gifts" (verse 4) and the "ministries" (verse 5) result in a variety of "workings (operations)."

[21] Note that *energēmata* occurs again in verse 10 ("effecting of miracles") as one of the Spirit's activities, and in verse 11 the Spirit is said to be "working" all these things. In verse 27 all of the believers and their various gifts are said to constitute the body of Christ. Hence, the connection of the Spirit with the *charismata*, of the Lord with the ministrations, and of God with the effects (or energies) is not intended to be exclusive but inclusive. All three persons of the Godhead are involved in all three of the relations.

what Paul seems to be saying is that when God's servants exercised the gifts and ministries they had been given, God Himself operated or worked alongside them, producing "effects" in the people being ministered to.

12:7 -- *But to each one is given the manifestation of the Spirit for the common good.*

But to each one is given -- Paul is speaking of the church members at Corinth when he says "each one." The idea is not that the manifestation of the Spirit was given to *all* men indiscriminately – to pagans, infidels, and scoffers, as well as to Christians. How shall we explain the verb tense "is given" (a present passive)? A present tense indicates continuing action. Does this verb then indicate that the manifestations were not an abiding power, but were given to each as the need arose? Or are we to think of the manifestations as being repeatedly given, not only to the Corinthian Christians as needed, but also given down through the ages, to first one generation and then to another? How shall we explain the whole phrase? Shall we read it with emphasis on "each one" so that the verse says that each individual Christian receives some manifestation of the Spirit?[22] Or shall we read the whole verse so that the emphasis is on the *diversity* of manifestations given, one to this person, another to a second, and still another to a third, and so on?

The manifestation of the Spirit -- We treat "manifestation" as synonymous with the "varieties" of gifts given by the Holy Spirit described in verses 4-6 – gifts, ministries, effects. The word "manifestation" (*phanerōsis*) means properly that which makes visible or known what has been hidden or unknown, to expose to view, to show. The Holy Spirit himself, being spirit, is invisible. But by these manifestations operating through a believer, the presence of the Holy Spirit is made manifest to human senses. The results produced by His actions are within the realm of the senses; they can be seen or heard or felt. "Of the Spirit" can be either a subjective or objective genitive. That is, the Spirit may be manifesting Himself, or the gifts (as they were exercised) were visible and tangible evidence that the Spirit was at work. Either way, the thought is of the spiritual gifts and of the exercise of them as something public and open, which others and their possessors

---

[22] A little reflection on what the Scriptures say elsewhere will cause us to be hesitant to affirm that *every* individual Christian in the early church had a *miraculous* "spiritual gift" (*charisma*). In Acts 8, Elymas was a Christian, but did not have one of the *miraculous* spiritual gifts. Not every individual Christian at Samaria had *miraculous* spiritual gifts. Not every Christian at Corinth, even, had *miraculous* spiritual gifts. At 14:11 and 14:23,24, we will see that there were those who were "ungifted." Even Fee, p. 589, has written, "Whether or not every last person in the church has a 'gift' may depend on how broadly or narrowly one defines the word *charisma*."

To understand that verse 7 affirms that every individual Christian had a *miraculous* "spiritual gift" leads to some naturally-asked, but difficult-to-answer, questions. (1) If all had *miraculous* spiritual gifts in the early church, should we likewise expect all Christians today to receive a *miraculous* spiritual gift? Are the cessationists wrong? (2) If all Christians are expected to have such a gift today, are the charismatics right when they affirm the reason some church members today do not have gifts is because they have fallen away from the faith, or their lives are not right? (3) If every believer is to have a *miraculous* spiritual gift, when and how does he/she receive it? Do some get the gift when they are baptized, while others may receive it later in their Christian life when someone lays hands on them? Do some get their "gifts" when they are born, and the Holy Spirit simply helps them to recognize and develop with what they were born? (Is there any difference between "spiritual gifts" and "talents" with which one is born?) It will be necessary to keep these questions in the back of our minds and look for possible clues as we study the following verses in Corinthians.

can perceive. If it were only for the possessor's own benefit that he had a "gift," it would cease to be a *manifestation*. It is not a "manifestation" if no one else but the possessor is conscious of the Spirit's presence and activity. The gifts at Corinth were such as to be evident to others; that is the point of the word "manifestation".

For the common good (literally, "for the profit of all") -- This truth is repeated so many times in the rest of this discussion about the abuse of spiritual gifts that it obviously is a pivotal point as Paul attempts to correct the Corinthian's behavior. When certain persons were endowed with spiritual gifts, the gift given was clearly intended, not for the special profit or gratification of the one endowed, but for the benefit of the whole congregation (and perhaps the whole world). When, therefore, the gifts of God are perverted as a means of self-exaltation or aggrandizement, it is a sin against their Giver, as well as against those for whose benefit they were intended. In the following, verses 8-11 explain the words "to each one is given," and verses 12ff explains the phrase "for the common good."

12:8 -- *For to one is given the word of wisdom through the Spirit, and to another the word of knowledge according to the same Spirit;*

For -- When a verse begins with "for," it is often an explanation of something just said. We suppose the idea begun in verse 8 is intended to explain what was just said in verse 7. Verse 7 has stated the idea that there is a diversity of manifestations given by the Holy Spirit. In verses 8-10 some of the different manifestations are listed. Once the different manifestations have been highlighted, Paul restates the idea of diversity of manifestations in slightly different words (verse 11).

To one ... to another -- Nine different gifts are specified in verses 8-10. The nine listed here do not exhaust all the possible gifts, as a comparison of 1 Corinthians 12:28ff, Romans 12:6-8, and 1 Peter 4:10,11 shows.[23] Scholars have struggled to classify the gifts into broad categories. No attempt has proven entirely satisfactory.

- Where our English translations have "another" the Greek has two different words, sometimes using *heteros* and sometimes *allos*.[24] Hodge (*op. cit.*, p.246) and Meyer (*op. cit.*, p.280) tried to classify the gifts by using *heteros* for the main divisions, and *allos* to show subordinate divisions.[25] Objection has been raised to this approach when

---

[23] "The various gifts are named in 12:8-10 and 28-30, and also in Ephesians 4:11 and Romans 12:6-8. When you combine the lists, you end up with [at least] 19 different gifts and leadership functions. Since the listing in Romans is not identical with the listings in Corinthians, we may assume that Paul was not attempting to exhaust the subject in either passage." Wiersbe, *Be Wise*, p.124. Some writers have suggested the list of nine gifts in 1 Corinthians (while not inclusive) do itemize the gifts the Corinthians were overly stressing in divisive ways.

[24] Of the two synonyms, *heteros* refers to one of a different kind, while *allos* means another of the same kind.

[25] *Allos* is used in verses 8b, 9b, 10a, 10b, 10d, and 10e. *Heteros* is the Greek word in verses 9a and 10c. Thus verse 8 is one grouping (wisdom and knowledge); verses 9 to 10c are another grouping (faith, healings, miracles, prophecy, distinguishing of spirits); verse 10d-e is a third grouping (tongues and interpretation of tongues).

it is noted that such an arrangement does not always put similar gifts together in the same category.
- Others have noted the different prepositions used (sometimes it is *dia* ["through"], sometimes it is *kata* ["according to"] and sometimes *en* ["by"]) in these verses and have tried to use these to arrange the gifts in meaningful categories.
- Sometimes, we suspect, an attempt to defend certain denominational practices and preferences has dictated the identification of categories.[26]

It may very well be that the apostle had no strict logical arrangement in mind. When we try to indicate what was the precise nature or function of each of the gifts, we also find little agreement. Definitions or explanations of the individual gifts tend to be polarized along party lines.[27] Thus it requires special care as we try to give Biblically compatible definitions and explanations, while consciously trying to avoid those that tend to support our preconceived biases or notions.

Is given ... through the Spirit -- To each is "given" whatever gift he has – a point that was very necessary for the instruction of the Corinthians who liked to boast about their gifts and forgot that they were *given*! On "through the Spirit," see notes on verse 4 and verse 11. This refrain "through the Spirit" is repeated over and over again, lest the Corinthians forget the *origin* of whatever manifestation they might have.

The word of wisdom -- It is not "wisdom of words" (like 1 Corinthians 1:17), but it reads "a word of wisdom." To be very truthful, we just do not know what many of these gifts were, or what distinction there is between, for example, the "word of wisdom" and the "word of knowledge." As long ago as Chrysostom, the same thing was confessed. If we look to Scripture elsewhere for help, we might recall what 1 Corinthians 1:30 and 2:10-13 taught about "wisdom" from God spoken by inspiration. It included such themes as

---

[26] W.R. Jones, "The Nine Gifts of the Holy Spirit," in *Pentecostal Doctrine*, ed. P. S. Brewster, 1976, gives the traditional Pentecostal view of the categories of gifts: 1) illumination (wisdom, knowledge, discernment); 2) action (faith, miracles, healings); 3) communication (prophecy, tongues, interpretation). Fee (*op. cit.*, p.590) uses a three-fold category, also: 1) instruction (wisdom and knowledge); 2) gifts of supernatural power (faith, healings, miracles); 3) gifts of inspired utterance (prophecy, discerning prophecies, tongues, interpretation). Bill Gothard, in his *Basic Youth Conflicts II* series, uses the words of 1 Corinthians 12:4-6 (motivations [*charismata*], ministries [*diakoniōn*], and manifestations [*energma/phanerōsis*]) as his categories. He taught that Romans 12:3-9 and 1 Corinthians 12:31 and 14:1 list the seven motivations (declaring truth, serving, teaching, exhorting, giving, ruling, empathizing). He found ministries at 1 Corinthians 12:27-30, and manifestations at 12:7-11. He then taught, "When we exercise our motivation (Romans 12) through our ministry (1 Corinthians 12:27-30, Ephesians 4:11), the Holy Spirit determines what manifestations (1 Corinthians 12:7-11) will benefit the receiver the most (1 Corinthians 12:7). We are not to seek after manifestations but to concentrate on our motivational gift and the most effective ministry of expressing it."

[27] Scholars of liberal theological persuasion have tended to offer naturalistic explanations. Charismatic writers often tend to give explanations that would harmonize with current practice in the charismatic churches. Jack Deere, *Surprised by the Power of the Spirit* (Grand Rapids: Zondervan, 1993) is a contemporary source of definition that would be satisfactory to many modern charismatic readers. On the other hand, Gordon Fee, "1 Corinthians" in the *New International Commentary on the New Testament* (Grand Rapids: Eerdmans, 1987), is an old-line Pentecostal, and his definitions and explanations of the various gifts tend to be more in harmony with old-line Pentecostal ideas.

"righteousness, sanctification, and redemption."[28] This is what J.W. McGarvey did as he tried to explain what "word of wisdom" might have been. He suggested the "word of wisdom" might have been the ability to reveal divine truth ...."[29] At the time Paul was writing to Corinth, most of the New Testament had not then yet been written, so someone therefore needed to reveal God's will to the people. So a "word of wisdom" might well be a discourse which expounds the mysteries of God's counsels and makes known the means of salvation. Lenski suggested that *logos* indicates the expression of "wisdom" in words or discourse, for the benefit of others.[30] The Spirit gives the power to utter a "word" (*logos*) of wisdom or knowledge, as the case may be.

And to another -- The word here is *allos* (see notes above on *heteros* and *allos*). One gets the impression that each gifted person had one manifestation (one spiritual gift).

The word of knowledge -- As indicated above, we are uncertain exactly what this gift was. Our ignorance of the situation makes our distinctions between the "word of wisdom" and the "word of knowledge" precarious. To the Corinthians, among whom these two gifts were of common occurrence, the difference would be clear enough. In 1 Corinthians 13:2, knowledge is linked with understanding "mysteries," so it may involve an element of explaining what was not clearly revealed in the Old Testament, but now is.[31] This is one of the gifts specifically named as ceasing when the "perfect" comes (1 Corinthians 13:8-10).

According to the same Spirit -- See notes at verses 4 and 11 for commentary.

---

[28] How much better to go to Scripture than to modern religious experience for an explanation. In Pentecostal circles, the "word of wisdom" is the ability to give a special word of insight or advice when a congregation or an individual Christian is going through a time of difficulty or decision. The word of wisdom often silences opponents to current charismatic leaders. See "Wisdom" in *Discipleship Journal* Issue 90 (Nov-Dec. 1995), p.71.

[29] McGarvey and Pendleton, *op. cit.*, p.122.

[30] Lenski, *op. cit.*, p.500.

[31] Macknight suggested that the gift of knowledge helped this class of gifted persons to unravel the 'mysteries' hidden before times eternal, and but partially revealed in the Old Testament – matters such as the call of the Gentiles, the rejection of unbelieving Israel, the salvation of all men through faith and obedience to Christ. Another suggestion is that it is related to receiving Christian insight into the meaning of Old Testament Scriptures, especially the prophecies.

Some commentators who rely on the meaning of the Greek word "knowledge" speak of such a gifted person as knowing what to do in any given situation, or of the ability to seek out and make effective use of a variety of information on a number of diverse subjects. Some have even seen a reference to the secret heretical "knowledge" needed to ensure entrance into heaven as taught by the Gnostics. However, it is anachronistic to suppose Paul is giving such a meaning to the word 'know' as one finds in the pseudepigraphical Gnostic *Gospel According to Thomas*, for that writing is from a century or more later than Paul's letter to Corinth. Charismatics think that someone with this gift of knowledge will get a sense that God is revealing to them detailed information (you will get a new job, or undertake a new mission, you are suffering from this emotional scar, etc.) about some other specific individual or situation. (*Discipleship Journal*, p. 56).

12:9 -- *to another faith by the same Spirit, and to another gifts of healing by the one Spirit,*

To another faith -- There is a "faith" that comes by hearing the word of Christ (Romans 10:17) that is one of the prerequisites for becoming a Christian, but that is hardly the "faith" here spoken of since this passage is speaking about the "gifts" given to people who are already Christians. As noted above in the discussion about how to classify or categorize these gifts, some have supposed that "faith" is the second major category of gifts, not being a gift itself, but rather being a generic heading (after *heteros*) under which healing and miracles and prophecy fall. While there is something attractive about this idea, it would be the only category in this whole list given a title. Another writer suggests that "faith" here should be translated "faithfulness" since it speaks of the deeper expression of faith a Christian needs in order to undergo hardships, martyrdom, etc. If such a "faith" is given by the Spirit, would that not imply that it is the Spirit's fault when someone facing hardship or persecution fails to be faithful till death? Pentecostal writers think "faith" here is a supernatural conviction that God will reveal His power or mercy in a special way in a specific instance. Some speak of a special faith that God can work miracles, or that He can sustain a person when He chooses not to work a miracle. As an illustration, the story of Elijah at Mt. Carmel (1 Kings 18) is often given as an Old Testament example of such a gift in operation. Since we are in a context of "manifestations of the Spirit" or "spiritual gifts," why not identify this gift of "faith" with what we read in 1 Corinthians 13:2 (a "faith so as to remove mountains") and Matthew 17:20 (Jesus' disciples lacked the "faith" needed to be able to heal the demon-possessed boy)? Perhaps this "faith" is the same faith which Peter lacked when he began to sink after walking on the water (Matthew 14:25-31, "O you of little faith").[32]

By the same Spirit See the notes at verses 4 and 11 for commentary.

And to another, gifts of healing -- Both "gifts" (*charismata*) and "healings" are plural in the Greek. It could be translated 'Gifts which result in healings.' "Healings" refer to supernatural cures of physical maladies. The plurals seem to imply that different persons each had a disease or group of diseases that they could cure, and that no one could cure all sicknesses and all maladies. Lenski and Fee explain the plurals in a different way. They suppose the plural "gifts" indicates that the ability to heal was not a permanent "gift" as it were, but that each occurrence is a "gift" in its own right.[33] Lenski worded it this way:

---

[32] Derek Prince, "Faith as a Gift," *New Wine* (June 1977), p.8, also called attention to James 5:15, where we are told the "prayer of faith" will restore to health a man who is sick. Prince reminds his readers that as an example of "the prayer of faith" James refers to Elijah, whose prayer first resulted in rain being withheld for three and one-half years, and then resulted in the rains coming again.

[33] Fee (*op. cit.*, p.594) also calls attention to the Pentecostal doctrine that there is "healing" in the atonement (cf. Matthew's use in 8:17 of Isaiah 53:4).

We are not to think that healings and miracles were wrought at will by the person concerned. In each instance a specific intimation came to them from the Spirit that the act should be performed, and not until that moment did it occur, but then it always took place without fail.

It was thus when Peter and John healed the lame man at the Gate Beautiful, Acts 3:1ff. How many times had they walked past this lame man as he sat daily begging at the gate! But on that morning the Spirit conveyed information to the apostles that they should heal him. For this reason Peter and John looked earnestly upon the beggar and spoke the words that healed him with such assurance.

The case of the damsel crying after Paul in Philippi is equally plain, Acts 16:16ff. On many days she cried, and Paul did nothing. Then Paul suddenly turned and healed her. He must have received the intimation to do so from the Spirit.

A third plain case is that of Peter at Joppa, Acts 9:36. This we may place among the energies of miracles. When the friends of Dorcas brought Peter into the death chamber, he prayed in order to learn the Lord's intention, which in this case was to bring Dorcas back to life. We may conclude that every case of healing from sickness or of working a miracle was similar to these although the Biblical narratives do not always supply us with the details that show the Spirit's intimation. In each instance the gift or the energy is bestowed by a communication from above for that case alone. Lacking such communication, even the apostles made no attempt to perform a miracle.[34]

By the one Spirit -- See this phrase explained at verses 4 and 11. We have had the phrases, "*through* the Spirit," "*according to* the Spirit," and "*by* the Spirit." By the use of this variety of expression, Paul probably means to indicate no more than the variety of methods of operation of the Spirit.[35]

12:10 -- *and to another the effecting of miracles, and to another prophecy, and to another the distinguishing of spirits, to another* **various** *kinds of tongues, and to another the interpretation of tongues.*

And to another the effecting of miracles -- "Effecting" translates the same word (*energēmata*) we had in verse 6.[36] "Miracles" translates *dunameis*, an act of power (cp. Acts 1:8; 1 Corinthians 12:28,29). Mare offers "activities that bring forth miracles" as a translation.[37] Again, both words are plural, "workings of miracles" (ASV). As before,

---

[34] Lenski, *op. cit.*, p.502,503.

[35] Shore, *op. cit.*, p.119.

[36] Lipscomb's note (*op. cit.*, p.183) that "inworkings of miracles" refers to "the bestowing on persons of the ability to impart the power of working miracles to others" appears to be incorrect. It seems that only apostles could pass on the spiritual gifts (of course, if you limit 1 Corinthians 12:10 to the apostles, Lipscomb's note would be satisfactory). He gives Acts 9:17,18 as a proof text, but the "Holy Spirit" in those verses may be only the indwelling gift.

[37] Mare, *op. cit.*, p.224.

the plurals suggest either the gifts came on each occasion they were needed, or that there were different gifts for different needs. Since Paul has already listed "healing" as a separate gift, we must think here of miracles other than healings. Those that come to mind are raising the dead; inflicting judicial punishments (Ananias and Sapphira, Elymas being stricken blind, and perhaps Hymenaeus and Alexander, 1 Timothy 1:20); safe handling of serpents (Mark 16:18, and Paul, Acts 28:1ff); Jesus' miracles of stilling the storm, cursing the fig tree, feeding the multitudes (though there is no record that His followers did such miracles). The casting out of demons is added to this list of non-healing miracles by Barclay.[38]

And to another prophecy -- "Prophecy" was inspired speaking or preaching as the Holy Spirit moved one to speak.[39] Once a revelation had been received from God, "prophecy" was the way it was delivered to the audience for whom it was intended. Fee explains that "prophecy" consisted of spontaneous, Spirit-inspired, intelligible messages, delivered orally in the gathered assembly.[40] Again it is helpful to appeal to Scripture for an understanding of what "prophecy" was. Prophets in Old Testament times received a message from the Lord, which they then delivered to the people. They were inspired as they spoke to the people what they had received directly from God. Their prophecies were not always predictions. Sometimes the prophecies (inspired speaking) dealt with the past, and sometimes they dealt with the present. New Testament prophets (Acts 13:1) were an order of leaders distinct from the apostles, and *next* to apostles in authority and rank (Ephesians 4:11).[41] The ministry of the prophet was to edify, encourage, and comfort (1 Corinthians 14:3). After receiving their revelation from God (1 Corinthians 14:30) the prophets were still in control of themselves, and they could speak or keep silent as they chose.[42] The office or the endowment was (like that of apostle) *temporary* (Ephesians 2:20), designed for the settlement and establishment of the church, and then, like the apo-

---

[38] Barclay, *op. cit.*, p.123.

[39] 1 Corinthians 2:13 has explained how the Holy Spirit helped God-chosen messengers to speak in God-chosen words. Prophecy was inspired speaking in the native language of the people to whom it was addressed, and it was understood by them (1 Corinthians 14:2ff). In the notes at 1 Corinthians 11:4,5, there is a discussion of the modern suggestion that there were two kinds of "prophecy" in the early church, one that might be called "personal prophecy" and one that might be called "public (i.e., equal to Scripture) prophecy." It is hard to see how if one has a revelation from God (14:30), that the content of what he then predicts or forthtells could at times be subject to error or misinterpretation (as certain Charismatic circles claim for "personal prophecy" -- who even appeal to Agabus, Acts 21:4, and to 1 Corinthians 14:13,14 and 14:29, for Scriptural corroboration of "erroneous" prophecies).

[40] Fee, *op. cit.*, p.595. "Prophecy" is *not* the same as the delivery of a previously prepared sermon.

[41] See Don DeWelt, *The Church in the Bible* (Joplin, MO: College Press, 1958), p.82ff. Also see W. Harold Mare, "Prophet and Teacher in the New Testament Period," *JETS* 9:3 (Summer, 1966), p.146-148.

[42] See 1 Corinthians 14:32. There is a profound difference between New Testament prophets and prophecy as found in pagan religions. Heathen 'prophecy' is related to 'ecstasy,' 'frenzy,' or 'mania.' Heathen prophets were out of control when under the influence of the "spirits."

stolic office, having accomplished its purpose, to be disused and to cease.[43] In the New Testament, prophecy might be occasional (Acts 19:6) or a settled office (1 Corinthians 12:28). Morris believes Paul has the second class in mind, though admitting that Paul's expression is broad enough to include both.[44] Paul's point is that the Spirit gives to some the ability to utter inspired words, which convey the message of God to the hearers. The mention of the gift of prophecy anticipates what will be written in 1 Corinthians 14.

And to another the distinguishing of spirits -- In the Greek, both these words are plural, "discernings of spirits" (ASV). Whatever the plurals meant in verses 9 and 10a, the plurals mean here. This apparently refers to a God-given ability to discern immediately whether a teacher was speaking by the power of God or by the power of some other spirit. A man with this spiritual gift would be able to discern between true and false teachers (prophets), without having to apply the criterion as we do (cf. 1 John 4:1).[45] There were such things as "deceitful spirits" who spoke "doctrines of demons" (cf. 1 Timothy 4:1). There were also false apostles (2 Corinthians 11:13, Revelation 2:1,2) and false prophets (Matthew 24:11, and perhaps 1 Corinthians 14:29). It appears (from John's epistles) that pretenders to inspiration were numerous in the apostolic age. The devil's counterfeits were distressingly similar to the real, genuine gifts of prophecy and teaching. Since we do not know precisely what the entire range of "discernings of spirits" was, we find a number of suggestions in the commentaries. (1) Some suppose Peter's immediate perception that Ananias and Sapphira were being untruthful when they pretended to bring all the money they had received for selling a field (Acts 5:1ff) is an example of discerning of spirits. Peter does speak about how Ananias tried to "lie to the Holy Spirit." (Presumably, Peter had an ability given by the Spirit to recognize faulty behavior without having to ask a lot of questions.) (2) Some in the modern Charismatic movement understand "discerning of spirits" to mean the ability to "sense" when they are in the presence of demons, or when someone else is demon possessed. (3) Wayne Grudem has rightly objected to the view advanced by Dautzenberg, who supposed that prophecy in the church needed "explanation" like the "prophecies" one found being spoken by heathen "prophets" (babbling while in an ecstatic frenzy).[46]

To another *various* kinds of tongues -- There is no need for the addition of the word "various." Note also, the apostle puts last the gift the Corinthians evidently desired most. Fisher neatly summarizes the conclusions that this commentator has also reached after long research on the topic of "speaking in tongues:"

---

[43] See Ephesians 2:20 and 1 Corinthians 13:8-10. See also Barnes' *Notes* on "Romans," p.276.

[44] Morris, *op. cit.*, p.172.

[45] Listeners to teachers today can identify true and false teaching by judging what they hear in the light of the teacher's faithfulness to the Word of God.

[46] Wayne Grudem, *The Gift of Prophecy in the New Testament and Today* (West Chester, IL: Crossway Books, 1988), p.263-288.

Tongues was the ability to speak different foreign languages. The gift was given to certain Christians to enable them to proclaim the gospel to the visitors who came through the harbors of Corinth from many lands. Used in its proper place and for its proper function, it was a useful gift. The problem at Corinth was that men brought this gift into the church services for display purposes [rather than evangelistic purposes]. This was not a proper use of the gift.[47]

"Kinds" of tongues would refer to "families of languages."[48] Each person who had a gift of tongues could speak one "family" of languages.[49]

And to another the interpretation of tongues -- This means the power of "translating" foreign languages. *Hermēneia* ("interpretation") is the regular word for 'translation' from one language to another. It puts a message spoken in a foreign language into words which are understood by those listening to the translator. This fact is obvious when one reads such verses as Mark 5:41 and 15:34, where we are accustomed to have foreign words translated for us, and introduced by the words "which being translated means." If our translators had used the word "translation" rather than "interpretation," it would have saved us much time trying to correct certain erroneous beliefs about what the gift of "interpretation of tongues" was.[50] One with this gift could translate what those speaking in tongues said (i.e., translate for that part of the congregation who did not understand the

---

[47] Fisher, *op. cit.*, p.198.

[48] The word translated "kinds" in 1 Corinthians 12:10,28 is *genē*. *Genē* has to do with birth, with families, "class, kind, species." Then, as now, there were families of languages – we can think of the Latin family, the Semitic family, etc. If we know Italian, we can understand a little Spanish, a little French, etc., because they all belong to the Romance family of languages. If we know Hebrew, we can understand a little Arabic, a little Syriac, etc., because these all belong to the Semitic family of languages. See Frank Pack's book *Tongues and Holy Spirit* (Abilene, TX: Biblical Research Press, 1972) for more detailed information showing that the tongues at Corinth in all likelihood were human languages foreign to the speaker.

[49] The theories concerning "speaking in tongues" are catalogued in the Special Study at Acts 2:4 in the author's commentary on *Acts* entitled "Special Study Concerning Glossolalia." The conclusion of that paper is that the "speaking in tongues" in Corinth was no different from what was done on Pentecost, which was foreign languages (Acts 2:6,8). See also in this commentary, Special Study #10, *Do All Speak in Tongues?* Authors who agree that the "tongues" at Pentecost (Acts 2) and the tongues at Corinth (1 Corinthians 12-14) were similar phenomena (i.e., the ability to speak in a human language foreign to the speaker) include Robert Gromacki, *The Modern Tongues Movement* (Philadelphia: Presbyterian and Reformed, 1967), and John MacArthur, *The Charismatics* (Grand Rapids : Zondervan, 1978). MacArthur gives seven reasons or evidences for his conclusion that the "tongues" at Corinth were languages, p.160,161. Robert Gundry came to a similar conclusion in "Ecstatic Utterance (N.E.B.)?," *JTS* 17 (1966), p.299-307.

An author who defends the position that while the tongues at Pentecost were foreign languages, those at Corinth were not, is Watson E. Mills, in his books *A Theological/Exegetical Approach to Glossolalia* (Grand Rapids: Eerdmans, 1986) and *Speaking in Tongues* (Lanham, MD : University Press of America, 1985).

[50] "Interpretation" does not mean to make up out of one's imagination some "message" he supposes the speaker in an unknown tongue has just spoken. In some religious circles the "interpreter" always gives a message about "repentance," no matter what the tongues speaker has supposedly just said. That's not "translation" – that's prevarication.

foreign language being spoken by the tongues' speaker). Should a foreigner come into the worship services, one with the ability to "translate" would have the power to understand what he is saying. This gift belonged either to the person himself who spoke with tongues (compare 14:5,13) or, as one passage intimates, to a distinct class of people.

12:11 -- *But one and the same Spirit works all these things, distributing to each one individually just as He wills.*

But ... all these things -- "All these things" include all the gifts, ministries, effects, and manifestations just mentioned since verse 4. After having given a sampling of the gifts in verses 8-10, Paul binds them all together in verse 11.

One and the same Spirit works -- The Holy Spirit is intended. He is the common source of all the gifts and workings. The emphasis is on the fact that the Spirit is "working." Although the gifts are many and various in their form, the energy back of them and in them is the same – the one and same Spirit. Previously Paul has spoken only of "the same" (verses 4,5,6), but the stronger form here (we might render it 'self-same') underlies the truth that the divergent gifts do not point to divergent divine purposes. It is the one Spirit who is working to produce all these gifts. The inference is that the gifts are not to be set over against one another, with the possessors appearing as rivals. Perhaps Shore is right as he calls attention to the contrast between Paul and the Corinthians.

> The Corinthians estimated these gifts variously, according to their variety in operation. Paul estimates their common value as proceeding from the One Spirit, distributed according to His will. Those who valued men more or less according to what kind of gift they possessed were really, if unconsciously, criticizing the Giver.[51]

The unity of the source from which all the gifts came ought to have excluded the possibility of a boastful comparison of the gifts, and of all depreciation of those gifts which, because they were less dazzling, were deemed inferior.

Distributing to each one individually just as He wills -- "Distributing" translates *diairoun*, the same root word that was translated "varieties" in verse 4. The Spirit is conferring on each one whatever power or energy He pleases. There is *diversity* in the Spirit's gifts. To be as interested in only one gift (tongues), as the Corinthians were, was to be at cross purposes with the Holy Spirit. "To each one individually" says the Holy Spirit deals with each recipient by himself, individually and appropriately. He gives to each man the gift which He sees to be best, and most wise, and proper. He gives in a way that is suitable to the mission God has in mind for that person. In "just as He wills," we have the personality and deity of the Holy Spirit indicated, as was also indicated in verse

---

[51] Shore, *op. cit.*, p.119.

6.[52] Hebrews 2:4 teaches the same thing when it says that God bore witness to the truth being preached through distributions of the Spirit, according to the Spirit's will. The "workings" are distributed just as the Spirit wills. He is the one who decides who gets which ability. "Just as He wills" should remove all complaint on our part, and thus all envy on the one hand, and all boasting on the other. In the variety of His workings, the Holy Spirit acts in the distribution upon His own *choice* and *judgment*, and in this lies the hidden reason for the giving or withholding of each particular gift. Perhaps also implied is the idea that "desire" on the part of the recipient for this or that gift is not the thing which determines which gift is received. Also refuted would be all claims that any one gift is necessary for someone to be a Christian, or to be a mature Christian, or to be in the center of God's activity in some part of the world.

c. Principle #3 -- The need for a unity of purpose as the different gifts are used in the church. 12:12-31a

> *Summary:* The point Paul has just driven home is that the diversity of gifts in the church is just the way the Holy Spirit wills it. One can see a similar diversity in the human body as created by God, each member having the function God desired it to have, and each member needful to the body, verses 12-26. Likewise, one can compare the congregation, made up as it is of individual Christians (each with a different gift), to the human body with its differing members. Think of your gift as the task God has assigned to you in the body of Christ, verses 27-30. If you look on yourself and your gift as part of the body of Christ, you will desire to use the gifts only if they will bring benefit to the body, verse 31a.

12:12 -- *For even as the body is one and yet has many members, and all the members of the body, though they are many, are one body, so also is Christ.*

For even as the body is one and *yet* has many members -- In the closing comments on verse 7, it was observed that both verses 8 and 12 begin with "for." In this commentator's opinion, verse 8ff explains the words of verse 7, "to each is given a manifestation of the Spirit," and verse 12ff explains the words "for the common good" (verse 7). In verse 12 Paul introduces the thesis that he is about to expound. It takes many different members to make up one human body. The members are clearly different, but their differences do not affect the fact that there is a fundamental unity. The "body" in this verse is a human being's physical body. Look at a human body. What do you see? One body made up of a multiplicity of parts (hands, feet, eyes, etc.).

And all the members of the body, though they are many, are one body -- "The members of the body" are the arms, legs, fingers, toes, ears, eyes, etc. Though a human body is made up of many individual parts, the parts all function as a unit, or the body is in trouble

---

[52] The Jehovah's Witness version says "As IT will." "It" cannot be right. Whoever heard of an inanimate force *willing* (desiring, planning) to do something? It would be absurd to say of an *attribute* of God, that it confers favors, and distributes the various endowments of speaking with tongues, and raising the dead.

and so are the members! After emphasizing the fact that all the endowments which were possessed in the church were the work of the same Holy Spirit, Paul now illustrates by a similitude taken from the mutual dependence of the various parts of the human body, that all the gifted people in the church ought to be appropriately cherished and prized, as being all useful and valuable in their places.

So also is Christ -- We might expect this phrase to read, "so also is the church." Instead it reads "Christ." "Christ" stands by metonymy for the congregation united through Him and grounded in Him. This becomes evident as one reads verse 27 ("you are Christ's body") followed by verse 28 ("God has appointed in the church"). The church is one body with many members. Elsewhere, the Bible labors at length to show that Christ is the head, and the only head, of the church (cf. Ephesians 5:23, Colossians 1:18, etc.). But that is not what Paul is discussing here. The whole church (i.e., the whole Christ) includes both head and body. The church is the body of Christ (verse 27). Christ and the church form one body, of which Christ is the head. Christ and the church form one vine, of which Christians are branches (John 15). Christ and the church form one building, of which Christians are the living stones (1 Peter 2:5). Christ and the church combine to form one unit (cf. Galatians 3:28). The fact that the church is one fits the revelation elsewhere, which speaks of one flock, one shepherd, one kingdom, one king (Christ), one head, one body, one church (not one congregation). Both the Old Testament and the New Testament predict and set forth "one church." Paul's favorite thought that the Christian is in Christ (see notes at 1:30) is at the basis of this statement. Since all believers are in Him, they are one body. As with the human body, so with Christ: there is unity in diversity.

12:13 -- *For by one Spirit we were all baptized into one body, whether Jews or Greeks, whether slaves or free, and we were all made to drink of one Spirit.*

For -- Verse 13 seems to be an explanation of how it is that "we all" become part of the one body, and (in the latter part of the verse) how it is that we have gifts that differ.[53]

By one Spirit we were all baptized into one body -- "By one Spirit"[54] evidently means

---

[53] To connect verse 13 to verse 12 seems to be a better option than to suppose verse 13 is parallel to verse 12, which would thus make verse 13 a second elaboration of "for the common good."

[54] The Greek construction is *en* and the dative case. It might be a dative of means, a dative of agent, or a dative of sphere. The usual way of showing "agent" after a passive voice verb (and "baptized" is a passive verb) is by *hupo* and the genitive (or sometimes *dia* and the genitive) to indicate a personal agent, or by *en* and the dative which usually indicates the agent is impersonal (but note well, *en* and the dative is used of a personal agent in Matthew 9:34; 1 Corinthians 6:2, 6:11, 14:21; Acts 17:31). Theologians have argued whether the construction is a dative of sphere (i.e., the "Spirit" is the sphere or substance into which they are baptized), or a dative of agent. Beasley-Murray calls attention to the fact that "in one Spirit" recalls baptism *en hudati* ("in water"), and in 1 Corinthians 10:2 we have the statement "all were baptized ... in the cloud and in the sea" (*en tē nephelē kai en tē thalassē*) suggesting that when Paul uses *en* with the verb "baptize" he has in view the element in which the baptism takes place. Scholars replying to Beasley-Murray's argument point to the whole context here in 1 Corinthians 12 which leads us to think the Spirit is the agent. The whole context has talked about the agency of the Holy Spirit, and different prepositions were used, but in 12:9, we had *en* and the dative (used as an agent).

"under His influence, under His direction, by His agency."[55] Interpreting the Greek construction as being a "dative of agent," 12:13a says that under the influence of the Spirit, we (who are now Christians) were all led to the place where we were baptized (in water for the remission of sins) into the body of Christ. Because of the work of the Holy Spirit[56] in conversion, we are members of the one body – the church.

"We were all baptized" – immersed! If the passage is dealing with how individuals come to be members of the body of Christ in the first place, it seems likely that the "baptism" spoken of is the baptism in water as commanded in the Great Commission. Other explanations of the possible meaning of this verse have been offered.

- Some think all converts experience a "baptism in the Spirit" that precedes and is different from baptism in water.[57] Some, even, have mistakenly suggested that such a "baptism in the Spirit" makes immersion in water unnecessary.[58]
- Some have insisted that "baptism in the Spirit" has reference to a post-conversion 'deeper-life' experience.[59]

Since none of these alternatives is free of difficulties, so as to commend itself to our acceptance, we treat the phrase as affirming the Holy Spirit was active in the conversion of each of the Corinthian Christians, leading each of the converts to faith and obedience in baptism in response to the preached Word.

---

[55] Translators know verse 13a reads just the same in the Greek as "baptized with the Holy Spirit" reads in Greek at Acts 1:5, yet have deliberately treated the construction as a dative of agent at this place. This commentator agrees with the decision made by the NASB and other translators. An issue that needs further careful study is whether or not the phrase "baptized with the Spirit" in John 1:33 and Mark 1:8 should perhaps be treated as a dative of agent, too. If it were, those verses would promise that the Spirit would baptize the apostles (giving them spiritual gifts). This verse in Corinthians with its phrase "into one body" would then show that what the Spirit does for the church member is different from what was promised to the apostles.

[56] We take *pneuma* as being the Holy Spirit here, because of the context.

[57] Even if Scripture did teach a 'first work of grace' as being prerequisite to any person's becoming a believer, it would only create greater confusion to try to identify such a 'first work' with "baptism in the Spirit" in the seven times that expression occurs in Scripture (Matthew 3:11; Mark 1:8; Luke 3:16; John 1:33; Acts 1:5, 11:6; and 1 Corinthians 12.13a).

[58] When instructing a prospect concerning the way of salvation, one should not lessen the importance of immersion in water, or attempt to substitute a "baptism in the Spirit" for the baptism commanded in the Great Commission. After Paul heard the voice of Christ on the road to Damascus, after Cornelius had been baptized in the Spirit and spoke with tongues, water baptism still stood as supremely important in regard to the soul's salvation (Acts 9:1-19, 10:44-48, 22:16). Peter, an apostle of Jesus Christ, *commanded* Cornelius and his household to be immersed in water. If anything, instead of saying one may ignore water baptism if one has been baptized in the Spirit, one should say that "baptism in the Spirit" makes immersion in water mandatory.

[59] This is the interpretation commonly given in classic Pentecostal circles. In Pentecostal theology, such an experience is supposed to produce a holy life ('saved and sanctified'). In response, if this verse in Corinthians does refer to such a post-conversion experience (a second work of grace [?]), it certainly did not bring any spiritual maturity to the lives of the Corinthians, as is clearly evidenced by all the correctives Paul has had to impress on them in this letter.

How shall we take the word "all" in both parts of verse 13? Does it speak of all the members of the church – Paul including himself? If we take "all" in a universal sense (meaning every last Christian) in verse 13a, can we take it any other way except universally in the latter part of the verse? "Into one body" means 'so as to become one body.' That all converts might form "one body" was the goal of the Spirit's activity in their conversions. In 1:13ff Paul has already appealed to the one baptism into Christ as pointing the Corinthians away from their factions and rivalries, and to the essential unity of believers in Christ. That is the point of this verse, too. Jews or Gentiles, bond or free, all alike are baptized into the one body. It likely would not be in error to say that without the one baptism in water (resulting from the Spirit's leading), a person is not part of the one body.

Whether Jews or Greeks -- Here is a distinction by nature. Racial differences were no obstacle to becoming part of the body of Christ.

Whether slaves or free -- Here is a distinction by custom or law. Social differences were no obstacle to becoming part of the body of Christ. Ethnic differences and social differences did not prevent the immersed from forming "one body."[60] We should not let the greatness of the variety (who have been baptized into one body) escape us. Think what the Jew was and then picture the pagan Greek. Then see how these extremes of humanity were drawn into Christ and thus melded and fused together. What was lower than a slave, a human chattel with practically no rights? Picture the free citizens, many of them lordly and likely owning slaves. Now, having been immersed into Christ, they are one (Lenski, *op. cit.*, p.515). In Christ, these old distinctions have been obliterated, not in the sense that there is no longer any such thing as a Jew or a Greek, a slave or free, but in the sense that these distinctions have no longer any significance.

And we were all made to drink of one Spirit -- Did every Christian at Corinth (all those baptized into the one body) have this "drink of one Spirit"? "All" would seem to be as universal as the "all" in the first phrase of this verse. If we recall what Paul wrote in verses 4-6, where two of the verses apparently have in view something other than miraculous *charismata*, and where he specifically says "all persons" (i.e., Christians) have the Spirit at work in them, we can easily assent to the fact that "all were made to drink of one Spirit." "Were made to drink" is an aorist passive verb in the Greek. One would expect the aorist tense to refer to the same time as the aorist tense in the verb "baptized." We may deviate from such an implication if it gets us into contradictions with other passages. If it points to a time other than their baptism, we might say that the aorist tense may simply point to a time in the past (say to the time when the apostles' hands were laid on the Corinthians, subsequent to their baptism). The same verb (*potidzō*) here translated "drink" was translated "watered" when speaking of Apollos' work (1 Corinthians 3:6), but it would be difficult to limit the time when "all were made to drink of the one Spirit" solely to the time when Apollos "watered" them while he was their preacher at Corinth. Whenever the time they all "drank," the verb is sometimes used for irrigating, whence comes the thought of abundant supply.

---

[60] A person who obeys the gospel is not taken out of the classification of slave or Greek or woman. The point being stressed in Galatians 3:28 is that redemption is no more for one class than for another. All are eligible to respond to the call of God offered through the gospel.

Four different views have been proposed to explain what measure or activity of the Spirit is in view when Paul writes "of one Spirit:"

1) The whole verse (13a and 13b) refers to the work of the Holy Spirit in conversion.[61] In its favor are these points: (a) It easily permits the "all" in both phrases to be taken the same way. (b) It would treat the aorist tenses ("baptized" and "made to drink") as pointing to the same time in a person's life. No man ever became a Christian without the work of the Holy Spirit, 13a. When, Paul says, we have drunk of the Holy Spirit, the Holy Spirit has worked on our hearts until we have been converted, 13b.

2) The first phrase ("by one Spirit were we all baptized into one body") refers to baptism, the second ("made to drink of one spirit") to the cup in the Lord's Supper.[62] In its favor are these points: (a) It permits the "all" in both phrases to be equally extensive. (b) The second aorist verb ("drink") would be given the idea of subsequence. (c) The verb drink is the same root as the cup (*poteriōn*) of the Lord's Supper. Objections to the idea that verse 13 refers to baptism and the Lord's Supper: (i) The word "drink" is aorist, which is an action completed in past time. This cannot be regarded as "aorist of custom," since that would not be parallel with "baptized," which is aorist. This drinking of the Spirit was no more habitual than was the baptism. (ii) Nowhere else do we read of the Lord's Supper, and still less of the drinking of the cup, as a means of partaking of the Spirit.

3) The first part (13a) refers to baptism, the second part (13b) to the indwelling Spirit.[63] In its favor are these points: (a) It would satisfy the "all" in both phrases. (b) It would take the aorist "drink" as referring to the same time in the past as their "baptism." (c) Further, when we compare John 7:37-39, where both terms "drinking" and "receiving the Spirit" are used, we can see there a rather similar use of language. (d) This explanation would fit the context here in chapter 12. As Findlay puts it:

> That Jews and Greeks, slaves and freedmen, had received at the outset an identical Spirit [the indwelling gift], shows that they were intended to form a single body, and this body was designed to have a wide variety of members.[64]

4) The first part (13a) refers to baptism, the second part (13b) to the bestowal of spiritual gifts after baptism.[65] In its favor are these points: (a) The context is talking about spiritu-

---

[61] This is the view of George Mark Elliott, Chrysostom, Theophylact, Oecumenius, Meyer, DeWette, Alford, Robertson and Plummer, Mare, and others.

[62] This is the explanation favored by Luther, Calvin, Beza, Estius, Grotius, Kling, Barnes, and others.

[63] This explanation is defended by Findlay in the *Expositor's Greek Testament*, Morris, Scott Robertson (*Seminary Review*, Dec. 1977), S. Lewis Johnson (*Wycliffe Bible Commentary*), Paul Marsh (*New Testament Commentary*, edited by Howley), Holladay, and others.

[64] Findlay, *op. cit.*, p.890.

[65] This is the explanation adopted by Gifford ("Romans" in the *Bible Commentary*, p.335), many Pentecostal interpreters (see documentation in Brunner, *A Theology of the Holy Spirit*, p.60, and Cottle, "All Were Baptized," *JETS* 17 [1974], p.75-80), Evans (*Bible Commentary*), and Dummelow. (The traditional Roman Catholic view is that verse 13b refers to confirmation. See Schnackenberg, *Baptism in the Thought of St. Paul*, English Translation, NY, 1964, p.84.)

al gifts – such gifts as were given by the laying on of hands after conversion. (b) It is possible, if verses elsewhere require it, to take the aorist "made to drink" as being subsequent to the baptism. Objections to the idea that 13b refers to spiritual gifts: (i) It does not seem to do justice to "all," unless we are prepared to affirm that each and every member at Corinth was gifted with some miraculous 'spiritual gift.' And as noted earlier, 14:11,23,24 indicate that not every member was miraculously 'gifted' in the early church. (ii) It does not seem to harmonize well with other passages which show miraculous spiritual gifts were received, not at baptism, but at a subsequent time (i.e., when apostles laid hands on the recipients so they might receive the gifts).

Having weighed the different options, it seems to us that the central idea of the passage is likely different than the four commonly proposed views. What Paul writes is that by the one Spirit we were all baptized into the body of Christ, and by this same Spirit we all were given whatever gift, or ministry, or effect (energy) we have.[66]

12:14 -- *For the body is not one member, but many.*

For -- This is the third verse in a row that begins with "for." We have suggested that, in fact, since verses 8,12,13,14 all begin with "for," all are further explanation of the statement made in verse 7, about each Christian receiving a manifestation of the Spirit for the common good.[67]

The body is not one member, but many -- Our physical bodies are organic wholes composed of many parts, each with its special function. But even though there are many parts, it is still one body. "Many" indicates that each part has its own function to exercise and work to perform. The body cannot get along as well without each function, as it does with them. Applying the figure of the body to the church, we can see that the church, too, is a whole, made up of many parts, each part having its special function.

12:15 -- *If the foot says, "Because I am not a hand, I am not a* **part** *of the body," it is not for this reason any the less a* **part** *of the body.*

If the foot should say, "Because I am not a hand, I am not a *part* **of the body" --** In verses 15 and 16 it is an 'inferior member' which is pictured as feeling unimportant or left out. The needed unity of purpose can be lost when some discouraged or disaffected members begin to feel they are not appreciated or wanted. Note how these verses are treated in the various versions. The ASV/NASB treats them as statements of fact. The implication is that the members who felt inferior were grumbling out of discontent. Paul's rejoinder indicates the members are very much still part of the body and such discontented grumbling is totally out of place. The KJV treats these verses as questions: "Is it there-

---

[66] Verse 13a speaks of how one becomes a Christian, then verse 13b speaks of what happens at baptism (indwelling gift) or after (spiritual gifts, or whatever other measure one may receive, which is the topic of this context).

[67] In the Greek, verses 13 and 14 both begin with *kai gar*, "for indeed" or "for also." Fee thinks these two verses explain what was just said in verse 12. Verse 13 explains *how* the many became one body, and verse 14 picks up the need for "diversity" that the Spirit manifested in the different gifts given.

fore not of the body?" This way of translation implies that the 'inferior' members were feeling unimportant and left out. We believe the KJV translators were right at this point. Morris suggests that the disputes at Corinth had disparaged some of the less spectacularly gifted members of the church. They may have been made to feel that they were not very important nor did they have much of a right to belong to the body, including as it did people who possessed very wonderful and spectacular gifts. Paul gives encouragement to such first of all.[68]

It is not for this reason any the less a *part* of the body -- "For this reason" (*para touto*) refers back to the feeling of unimportance. The foot may very well be disparaged because of its inability to exercise the complicated functions of a hand. But that lack of dexterity does not mean it is no longer a useful part of the body.

12:16 -- *And if the ear says, "Because I am not an eye, I am not a* **part** *of the body," it is not for this reason any the less a* **part** *of the body.*

And if the ear should say, "Because I am not an eye, I am not a *part* of the body" -- As with foot and hand, so with ear and eye. The ear is still part of the body, even though it feels it is less gifted.

It is not for this reason any the less a *part* of the body -- Bodies need feet as well as hands, ears as well as eyes. Chrysostom acutely pointed out that the foot contrasts itself not with the eye, but with the hand. We are prone to envy those who surpass us a little, rather than those who are patently in a different class. This same figure and illustration of the body occurs among non-Christian writers.

> Menenius Agrippa, as related by Livy (ii.32), used it as he attempted to repress a rebellion which had been excited against the nobles and senators as useless and cumbersome to the state. Menenius, in order to show the folly of this, represents the different members of the body as conspiring against the stomach, as being long inactive, and as refusing to labor, and consuming everything. The consequence of the conspiracy which the feet, and hands, and mouth entered into, was a universal wasting away of the whole frame for want of the nutriment which would have been supplied by the stomach. Thus he argued it would be by the conspiracy against the nobles, as being inactive, and as consuming all things. The representation had the desired effect, and quelled the rebellion.[69]

The idea is that no Christian, however humble his endowments, should pretend or think that he is useless because he was not more highly gifted and did not occupy a more elevated rank. Why should my foot grumble that it is not my hand? If I had no feet, I would be worse off than I am now. There is a need for each member, both in my body, and in the church. Each has a place. The hand gains nothing by being puffed up against the foot, or the rest of the body. Neither will the members of Christ gain anything. The members

---

[68] Morris, *op. cit.*, p.174.

[69] Barnes, *op. cit.*, p.234.

of the body must conform to the will of the body. There is no place for discontent or a feeling of unimportance among the members. This illustration would be a strong condemnation of the Corinthian pride. It would be absurd for pride to lead the hand to treat the foot with contempt. It would be absurd for pride to lead the eye to treat the ear with contempt. It would be just as absurd for the Corinthians to allow pride to lead them to treat gifted members (whatever the God-given gift) as though they were unimportant.

12:17 -- *If the whole body were an eye, where would the hearing be? If the whole were hearing, where would the sense of smell be?*

If the whole body were an eye ... If the whole were hearing -- Paul now emphasizes the necessity of having a diversity of members in the human body. Without such a diversity, the body couldn't operate, much less even be a body. Two rhetorical questions show that the very existence of the body depends on a variety of members which function differently. Suppose the wish of the ear were granted, and, since it esteems the eye so highly, suppose that it actually should become an eye. Other members may then have the same opinion about the eye, and the same privilege of becoming an eye. What would be the result? The whole body would become an eye. And then what would you have? One big eye, but no body! Each member has a function which it alone can discharge, and no organ ought to think little of its own function, or covet that of another organ. Each part has its function; each is necessary to the well-being of all. It would be absurd to require or expect that all the members of the church should have the same endowments. If all were apostles, where would the church be? Or if all were deacons? or if all were evangelists? For a congregation to function as God intends it to function, it must have different gifts and offices.

Where would the hearing be? ... where would the sense of smell be? -- Instead of saying "ears" and "nose," Paul uses terms that suggest more than the mere mention of the organ would. For example, when Paul speaks of the "sense of smell" without mention of the nose, our minds are led to think of all the other functions of the body, any one or all of which could be mentioned in this connection.

12:18 -- *But now God has placed the members, each one of them, in the body, just as He desired.*

But now -- The cure for all such wrong and absurd desires is a return to the great divine fact of how God made the body.

God has placed the members, each one of them, in the body, just as He desired -- Paul here teaches the human body had its origin and arrangement as a direct result of God's original creation (Genesis 1). The aorist tenses look back to the time of creation. God ordained the present form of man; to rebel against the form is to rebel against God. In the human body, each member has its part assigned by God. So it is in the church. Every member cannot have the same function; therefore, there must be higher and lower gifts. But pride and discontent are quite out of place, for they are the outcome of selfishness and rebellion against God's will. Do any of us presume to have a right to find fault with the way God did things? The context is speaking about "manifestations of the Spirit" (verse 7). The Holy Spirit bestowed the miraculous gifts. The man who prophesied was not to be jealous of the one speaking in tongues. The one speaking in tongues was not to be pridefully disdainful of any of the other manifestations.

12:19 -- *If they were all one member, where would the body be?*

And if they were all one member -- The incongruity of the exaggerated reverence the Corinthians had for one or another of the gifted members is brought out by a rhetorical question. No matter how important any one member may seem to be, there can be no body formed from it alone.

Where would the body be? -- This is the second absurdity. The first was, 'Where were the other members?' The second here is, "Where would the body be?" The sense seems to be this: if there were nothing but an eye, an ear, or a limb, there would be no body. If there were not a variety of manifestations and endowment in the church, the church itself could not exist. If there were nothing but apostles or prophets, or teachers, if there were none but those who spoke with tongues or could interpret them, the church could not exist.

12:20 -- *But now there are many members, but one body.*

But now there are many members, but one body -- Paul's statement can without difficulty be applied to the spiritual body of Christ. The church is an organic whole.[70] There is unity, but not uniformity since members are differently endowed. Each member of the church has a gift and function. The Spirit has assigned each one to the place which he or she occupies in the great organism. Blessed are those who joyfully accept what the Spirit has done, and therefore rid themselves of all dissatisfaction and pride. God's creative act of producing the human body is one example of God placing the individual bodily parts as He determined, and it lies in the historic past, hence, the aorist tense (verse 18). The whole work of the Spirit who forms the spiritual body of Christ still continues; hence, the durative present tense.

12:21 -- *And the eye cannot say to the hand, "I have no need of you"; or again the head to the feet, "I have no need of you."*

And the eye cannot say to the hand, "I have no need of you"; or again the head to the feet, "I have no need of you" -- In verse 15 and following it was the 'inferior' member who was voicing feelings of uselessness. Beginning with verse 21, it is the 'superior' member who is voicing disdain for the inferior. Again, just as the attitude of the 'inferior member' could destroy any unity of purpose, so the unity of purpose can be destroyed by a superior attitude that says "I can get along without you!" Paul's illustration is a rebuke of

---

[70] The "many members" are individual Christians in the congregation at Corinth. This is not saying that the body of Christ is made up of many denominations. There are two ways to get into error: apply tests of fellowship not found in the Bible, and not apply tests of fellowship found in the Bible. A variety of members that would endorse all sorts of sectarian ideas (one church as good as another, sprinkling or pouring for immersion) would not be under the one head, Christ.

those who, being themselves possessed of what were considered important spiritual gifts, despised the gifts which the Spirit had bestowed on others. Here is a rebuke to the pride of those who thought their own gifts to be exclusively valuable. What would become of the desire of the eyes if there were no hand to grasp it in? There is no such thing as independence either in an organism or in society. The hand in its place is as needful as the eye, and the feet as the hand. The eye and the head could not perform their appropriate functions, or would be in a great measure useless, but for the aid of the hands and the feet. As in the human body, so it is in the church. Those who are most conspicuously talented and endowed with gifts cannot say to those less so, that there is no need of their aid. All are useful in their place. Those who are most conspicuously endowed could very imperfectly perform their duties without the aid and cooperation of those of more humble attainments. Barclay reminds us that we cannot think in terms of relative importance regarding our own services as compared with the services of others (that we might think we can get along without). "Whenever we begin to think about our own importance in the Christian church, the possibility of really Christian work is gone."[71]

12:22 -- *On the contrary, it is much truer that the members of the body which seem to be weaker are necessary;*

On the contrary -- Paul's rebuke of the pride of the members who supposed themselves superior is forceful.

It is much truer that the members of the body which seem to be weaker are necessary -- "Weaker" translates *asthenestera*. The KJV/ASV used "more feeble." Both of these choices are to be preferred to "smaller." Unless the following verses do so, Paul does not specifically identify which members he thought of as being the "weaker" members.[72] Nor are we certain in what sense the members are "weaker." Perhaps Paul was thinking of some members being weaker physically. Perhaps it means less able to bear fatigue. Perhaps it means more easily affected with disease and injury. "Are necessary" says the "weaker" parts are not only indispensable, but are as indispensable as the rest of the parts of the body. One need only have a broken arm, or loss of sight or hearing, to learn how indispensable each member of the body is. We may, with difficulty, get along without an arm or a leg, but it is rather difficult to get along without a heart, or the brain, or the lungs. This is a beautiful thought: those members of the church who are most retiring and feeble apparently, who are concealed from public view – unnoticed and unknown – the humble, the meek, the prayerful, the peaceful – are often more necessary to the true welfare of the church than those who often are in the front of things (Barnes, *op. cit.*, p.235).

12:23 -- *and those members of the body which we deem less honorable, on these we bestow more abundant honor, and our unseemly members come to have more abundant seemliness,*

And those *members* of the body, which we deem less honorable -- The "less honorable"

---

[71] Barclay, *op. cit.*, p.127.

[72] Barnes, *op. cit.*, p.235, suggests Paul has in mind the internal organs, such as heart or lungs as compared with the arm or leg.

(*atimotera*) members seem to be distinguished from the "weaker" members of the previous verse. What do we do with those parts of the body which we consider less honorable? Do we despise them? Do we say we do not need them? Do we wish we were rid of them? Nothing of the sort – upon these we bestow more abundant honor.

On these we bestow more abundant honor -- Clothing bestows honor to the less beautiful parts. Those parts of the body which decency requires us to conceal we not only cover, but we endeavor as far as we can to adorn them. The face, in the meantime, we leave uncovered. In dressing, we give *most* honor to the *least* honorable. It would make quite a difference if we did the same thing in the church. We should not despise or disregard those members of the church who are of lower rank or who are less favored than others. Rather, bestow more honor on the less favored. If we treated the members of the congregation as we treat some parts of the body, we should have an entirely new type of congregation.

And our unseemly *members come to* have more abundant seemliness -- "Unseemly" is an attempt to translate *aschēmona*. The NIV uses "unpresentable," a good choice of words to refer to the genitalia and the excretory tracts.[73] Since Paul used discretion in his choice of words, it is well for the translators and for us to do likewise.

12:24 -- *whereas our seemly* members *have no need* of it. *But God has* so *composed the body, giving more abundant honor to that* member *which lacked,*

Whereas our seemly *members* have no need *of it* -- Notice the punctuation of the NASB. They put a period after "it" and start a new sentence with the next phrase. The division of the verses in the KJV and ASV is most unfortunate. We are nearly caused to miss the meaning. Verses 22-25 in Goodspeed's translation read:

22. On the contrary, the parts of the body that are considered most delicate are indispensable,

23. and the parts of it that we think common, we dress with special care, and our unpresentable parts receive especial attention which our presentable parts do not need.

24. God has so adjusted the body and given such especial distinction to its inferior parts

25. that there is no clash in the body, but its parts all alike care for one another.

There are three different classes (parts of the body) described in these verses: (1) *ta atimotera* – "less honorable" – verse 23a, the parts which are usually clothed and often adorned; (2) *ta aschēmona* – "uncomely parts" – verse 23b, the parts which are always carefully clothed; (3) *ta euschēmona* – "comely parts" – verse 24, the parts which have no

---

[73] In the comments given below for verse 24, the statement that the "less honorable" (verse 23) parts are the ones always covered is fully explained.

need of clothing or adornment, and which are commonly exposed to view.

But God has *so* composed the body -- "Composed" (*sunekerannumi*) pictures God 'mixing together' or 'blending' the members together as He created the body. The word means to 'compound, blend, commingle, unite.' The word is used of the harmonious blending of colors. God has formed one part dependent on another, and necessary to the harmony and proper action of another. He made every part useful and fitted to the harmonious action of the whole. God's arrangement of the members in the body does away with clashing, and blends all into one harmonious whole. Both verbs in this verse ("composed" and "giving") are aorist tense, and indicate contemporaneousness. It is probably a reference to the creation. Thus in this verse we have an assertion of God's workmanship in the structure of the physical organs of the body. It is significant, too, that Paul made such an assertion in an age when many contemporary philosophers affirmed that matter was evil, and denied that a good God could create such matter. Paul neither thought of matter as inherently evil, nor would he doubt that God created everything just as He wanted it to be.

Giving more abundant honor to that *member* which lacked -- God is the one who taught men to "honor" (cover) the unpresentable parts. God made a rib cage and a skull to protect the "weaker" parts, while he left the fingers out in the open. God's actions toward the unpresentable and weaker members should be the model to help men decide how to behave. Rather than being useless, those members are essential to the well-being of the rest of the body, and the whole body would do well to have a positive unity of purpose towards these "weaker" members. All the parts are to mutually respond to each other's needs.

12:25 -- *so that there may be no division in the body, but* **that** *the members may have the same care for one another.*

That there should be no division in the body -- This is one reason God "composed" the body as He did. (It is a *hina* clause – "God composed ... in order that.") God made the body so that it is united, one harmonious whole. There are no separate interests. All the parts are equally necessary, and dependent on each other. No member of the church, however feeble or illiterate or obscure, should be despised or regarded as unnecessary or valueless. The meaning of the word "division" is not so much the idea we give to the word; instead, our word 'dissension' better catches the flavor. See notes at 1:10 where the word has been explained. In His perfect blending of the parts of the human body, it was God's plan to prevent such dissension. So with the church, as the next phrase shows. Far from dissension, God planned that the members should have care one for another. "The existence of differences of gifts in the church had been used by the Corinthians to cause schisms, exalting some gifts and depreciating others, when this very variety in the church ought, as was the intention of variety in the human body, to create a mutual interdependence, which would promote unity" (Shore, *op. cit.*, p.337).

But *that* the members should have the same care for one another -- This is another reason why God made the body as He did. As far as the human body is concerned, a pain in the foot, the hand, or the head excites deep concern for it from the other parts of the body. A disease in any one part tends to diffuse itself through the whole frame. We should have a heartfelt concern for each other in the church. We need each other. (*Merimneō* often has the idea of 'anxiety.' Thus our word 'concern' is better than "care.") God did not ordain that those who obey the gospel should go it alone. Where there are several baptized believers, God ordained that there should be an assembly, a congregation, in order to help, pray, warn, and exhort each other.

12:26 -- *And if one member suffers, all the members suffer with it; if one member is honored, all the members rejoice with it.*

And if one member suffers, all the members suffer with it -- The analogy is easily illustrated and understood. If we get a stone in our shoe, the whole body cooperates together to remove the stone. When your finger is hurt, you do not say, 'My finger is in pain' but 'I have a pain in my finger.' It is difficult for the body to function when there is an attack of appendicitis or a severe toothache. The whole body suffers with the part that is aching. Verse 26 rounds out the idea of the need of unity of purpose between the various members of the body. Paul uses both the ideas of suffering and honor to illustrate the unity of the body. The suffering of any member means that the whole body suffers. It is impossible to think of one part of the body as being in pain, and the remainder of the body as being at peace. This verse completes the statement of the perfect unity of the members in one body and with one another. They are not only physically joined together, but they are so united as to feel together. Making application to the church is obvious. If a member of the congregation suffers, then the whole congregation cooperates to relieve the suffering.[74] "If one is tempted or afflicted, the other members of the church should feel it, and 'bear one another's burdens, and thus fulfill the law of Christ.' If one is poor, the others should aid him and supply his wants. If one is persecuted and opposed for righteousness' sake, the others should sympathize with him and make common cause with him ... No man should regard it as any more a burden and hardship to aid a poor or afflicted brother in the church than it would be deemed a hardship" to get a thorn out of the heel.[75]

If *one* member is honored, all the members rejoice with it -- This phrase is the converse of the first part of the verse. *Doxadzō*, translated "honored," suggests the member is extra healthy and strong, gets special adornment, is treated with special care. In the church, if one of the members should be favored with extraordinary endowments, all the members of the church partake of the benefit. It is for the common good of all. All should rejoice in it. Note that Paul does not speak of sharing in the honor, but sharing in the rejoicing.[76]

---

[74] While the verb "suffer" (in "all the members suffer with it") can be either an indicative or imperative form, we have opted to treat it as a simple statement, rather than as a command. The same will be true of "rejoice" in the next phrase.

[75] Barnes, *op. cit.*, p.237.

[76] The Roman Catholic expositors, with great impropriety, deduce from this expression the doctrine of an overflow of merit from the saints upon the rest of the church. Paul's purpose, however, is to mortify the pride of some of the Corinthians, who were boasting of their more noted gifts, and did not take to heart the welfare or the suffering of the church and its members.

His choice of words emphasizes the impossibility of rivalry within the body. Luther's comment on this verse is:

> See what the whole body does when a foot is trodden on, or a finger is pinched; how the eye looks dour, the nose draws up, the mouth cries out, and all the members are ready to rescue and to help, and none can leave the other, so that it means, not the foot or a finger is trodden on and is pinched, but the entire body. Again, when good is done to one member, that suits all the others, and the entire body rejoices therein. This is how it ought to be also in Christendom since it, too is composed of many members in one body and has one mind and heart – for such unity naturally has the effect that one is concerned in the good and the hurt of the other as in his own.[77]

12:27 -- *Now you are Christ's body, and individually members of it.*

Now -- We have already been making applications of the illustration of the body to the church in our notes. Now Paul does this in his text, doing what we have anticipated.

You are Christ's body -- "You" is plural. It speaks of the individual Christians at Corinth (not denominations). "You" is also emphatic. The Christians and no one else are Christ's spiritual body. There is no "the" (no article) in the Greek. "You are (a) body of Christ." "Paul is writing to the Corinthians and therefore cannot use the article: 'you are *the* body of Christ,' for this might make the impression that they are Christ's entire body. Yet, the absence of the article does not mean that the Corinthians are '*a* body' of Christ [i.e., one of many bodies], for no plurality of bodies of Christ exists. As in so many instances the omission of the article stresses the quality of the noun" (Lenski, *op. cit.*, p.535). "*Body*" is what you are, and a body that belongs to Christ. The figure of the congregation being like a human body is kept up. "All the members of the human body compose one body, having a common head. So it is with the members and parts of any Christian congregation" (Barnes, *op. cit.*, p.237). This figure of the church being like a body occurs frequently in Scripture. See Ephesians 1:23, 2:16, 4:4,12,16, 5:23,30; Colossians 1:18,24, 2:19, 3:15

And individually members of it -- The meaning of *melē ek merous* is not certain: 'members out of part' or 'members of a part' or 'members in particular' (KJV). It seems certain he is not saying (as some translate) 'partial members of the body' – i.e., imperfect church members. This new idea does not seem to fit the context. The expression literally means "in part," which is the way it is translated at 13:9. From this it gets the meaning "individually." Paul's meaning is that each one of them belongs to the body. None can claim to be the whole body, but none is excluded, either.[78] Paul nowhere identifies eye, ear, smelling, hand, foot, head, even by implication, with definite members of the church. In other words, Paul is not in any sense writing an allegory.

---

[77] Quoted by Lenski, *op. cit.*, p.533.

[78] Morris, *op. cit.*, p.178.

12:28 -- *And God has appointed in the church, first apostles, second prophets, third teachers, then miracles, then gifts of healings, helps, administrations,* **various** *kinds of tongues.*

And God has appointed in the church -- Note the progression of thought: Verse 18 – God created the body. Verse 24 – God harmoniously blended together the various members of the body. Verse 28 – Likewise, God has placed or appointed some for His own purpose in the church. "Appointed" is an aorist middle form of *tithēmi*, 'to put, place, set.' The middle voice verb form in the Greek indicates that God placed these functions or gifts in the church for His own benefit, for His own purpose.[79] This verse will go on to list some of the different parts of the body of Christ. Paul here insists that just as it was the Creator's act that made the human body as it is (verses 18-24), so it was God's act and will that made the spiritual body as it is. He is the one who determines which member shall contribute which needed function. Men do not choose to be apostles, prophets, etc.

There is a word in the Greek (*hous*) which was translated in the ASV as "some" but which is not translated in the NASB. (a) Several commentators, relying apparently on the English translation, suggest Paul changed his mind while writing. They suppose he intended to say "Some ..., others ...," but as he dictated he failed to finish the second member of the sentence he had started. It is argued that after he said "Some," he said "first, second, third," and then left the "others ..." out. (b) Another possibility suggested by I.H. Marshall is that we have in this verse an idiomatic expression for which it is not feasible to give a literal rendering in the English. (c) It is best to treat *hous* as exactly what it is, the accusative plural of the relative pronoun *hos*, 'who' or 'which'. The plural pronoun picks up the plural in the word "you" in the previous verse. It is precisely these members that God has placed in the body of Christ.

What seems to be intended in "church" is the church universal, not just the Corinthian congregation. The reason we take it as the church universal is because the "apostles" are mentioned. The apostles were over the whole body. Not even at this early time did each congregation have an apostle to itself, so we do not agree with giving "church" in this place a local sense only. The act of God ("God has appointed in the church") extends far beyond the Corinthian congregation. His act was for the entire church of all times and places. Some of the different parts of the body of Christ are now identified.

First ... second ... third ... then -- We have three groupings, then a listing. Compared to verses 8-10 where we had a list of gifts, this list begins with people who exercised certain gifts or functions in the church. The very gift which the Corinthians desired most, Paul placed last in this listing. Perhaps "first, second, third" is a ranking in order of significance or authority. Perhaps this listing is only the chronological order in which these functions appeared in the church. Either way, the list includes some of the same gifts as in verses 8-10, plus some different gifts.

Apostles -- In the notes at 1 Corinthians 1:1 it was indicated that "apostle" is a term that can

---

[79] Writers whose theology rests on the foundation of the sovereignty of God are wont to comment about that sovereignty here. It is rather common to read comments similar to, "'Appointed' emphasizes the sovereign act of God in determining who will exercise which gifts in His church."

be used with two different meanings. It can be used definitely to speak of 'apostles of Jesus' and indefinitely to refer to 'apostles of churches' (as at Philippians 2:25 and 2 Corinthians 8:23). In this place the reference seems to be to 'apostles of Jesus,' the term being used definitely to refer to the apostolic college – the Eleven plus Matthias, Paul, Barnabas, James, etc. (Acts 2:14ff, 14:14, Galatians 1:19, Romans 16:7). In the church, the apostles were first in rank, first in time, first in dignity (Ephesians 2:20, 4:11). The New Testament nowhere contemplates the making of room for an office for Peter. It is not written here, 'First Peter, second, apostles.' It stands "First, apostles." Peter is not an order by himself. He was the first to use the keys of the kingdom of heaven, but he did not make the keys. There is no room for a person to come between Christ and the apostles – in the order of rank, time, and dignity. The apostles of Jesus had administrative functions in the church, but no local jurisdiction. They belonged to the whole church. The revelation of Christ was complete before the apostolic college had passed away.[80] The apostles constitute the foundation of the church for all time (Ephesians 2:20) – not indeed in their persons, but through the word which they conveyed to the church. Do we have apostles and prophets today? Not in the flesh! But we do have them in the church, in the sense that we have their writings. The office of apostle is permanent, in the sense that their writings are permanent. But the office of apostle is not permanent in the sense that the office of elder and evangelist are permanent. The churches did not select the apostles, Christ (God) did. It was essential that an apostle should have seen the Lord, and especially the risen Lord (1 Corinthians 9:1,2; Luke 24:48; Acts 1:8,21-23). The apostles could lay their hands on men and those men could prophesy. The laying on of hands by an apostle was the means by which other spiritual gifts were conferred. But the laying on of hands would not ever bestow the office or function of an apostle. The apostolic office was not passed from one person to another.

Prophets -- In the notes at 1 Corinthians 11:4,5, and at 12:10, this office of prophet has been explained. Prophets were specially gifted men who as a result of the gift spoke by inspiration as they delivered God's message. As they spoke by inspiration they could utter the deep things of God, they could convict men of sin, they could edify or comfort the church, or they could also predict the future. Along with the apostles of Jesus, the New Testament prophets were characterized as being "the foundation" of the church (cf. Ephesians 2:20). Some explain Ephesians 2:20 to mean that the apostles and prophets form the foundation. Others think it is better to understand Ephesians 2:20 to be a genitive of originating cause. Either way, the designation likely suggests both apostles and prophets were temporary offices in the church, intended to help the church get started in the world. Agabus, Mark, Luke, Silas, and Jude (the Lord's brother) would be examples of New Testament "prophets."

Teachers -- It appears from several passages that "teacher" was a separate, specially gifted office in the early church. Acts 13:1 seems to speak of two leadership functions at Antioch – one called "prophets" and one called "teachers." Of the five people mentioned,

---

[80] Cf. Lightfoot, *Galatians*, p.89-97. Jesus had promised to the apostles that they would be led into all truth (John 14:26, 16:13). Jude 3 indicates it happened, for by the time Jude is written the "faith" has been "once for all delivered to the saints."

some seem to have been prophets and some seem to have been teachers. 1 Corinthians 12:29 indicates that there was a class of teachers to which only some Christians belonged. The context leads readers to classify this "gift" along with the other special abilities given by the Holy Spirit. A teacher is a person who instructs, or communicates knowledge. Teachers in the ancient world limited themselves largely to the communication of a fixed body of information to their students, often solely by rote memory work. In the church, the importance of teachers lies in the fact that it wasn't until 20 years or so after the crucifixion and resurrection of Jesus that we have the first written Gospel. During these years, apostles, prophets, and evangelists were winning converts, but someone had to instruct these converts about 'observing all Jesus had commanded.' During the first several decades of the church, the story of Jesus and the teaching of Jesus had to be handed down by word of mouth. This was the tremendously important task of the teacher. If "teacher" was a supernaturally inspired work in the 1st century (and we think it was, in this context, at least), then we would expect 100% accuracy, or inerrancy, from those with the gift of teaching, just as we do from those with the gift of prophecy, or those who were apostles of Jesus. In the listing of "first, second, third," it is teachers who are "third." We might not have expected that "teachers" would rank so high. The fact that they do indicates the importance attached to teaching in the apostolic age. We must bear in mind that the cost of hand-copied books was high, so high that, according to A.Q. Morton's estimate, "a gospel represents in papyrus alone a year's wages and a New Testament about eight years' pay of a skilled workman." Few believers could look forward to owning a Bible. The function of a teacher in such a church must have been tremendously important.[81] One is led to contemplate whether we know these "teachers" by any other title. Some suppose that Ephesians 4:11, which names 'pastoring teachers' (i.e., the elders[82]) as distinct from apostles, prophets, and evangelists, points the way for us. Others suppose that "teacher" is but another name for "evangelist" in the early church.[83] Perhaps a better explanation is that "teacher" was a temporary office, like apostles and prophets were temporary functions in the early church.[84]

Then miracles -- "Powers," (*dunameis*) is a reference to those who had the power of working miracles (see verse 10). With "then," we have now moved from some people who

---

[81] Morris, *op. cit.*, p.179.

[82] The Greek construction indicates that "pastor and teacher" refer to the same person.

[83] Bible students respond to this suggestion in light of their preconceived notions about church polity. Those who think the elders have the rule over the local churches, not the preacher/evangelist, are rather quick to reject the idea that "teachers" and "evangelists" were two names for the same job. They like to point out that in Ephesians 4:11, the evangelist and the pastor-teacher are separate offices. On the other hand, after they see, in the letters to Timothy and Titus, the leadership an evangelist is expected to exercise at the local church level, many have little problem with the idea that "teachers" who were "third" in the line of authority just might be the evangelists. Furthermore, in the light of 2 Timothy 1:11 and 1 Timothy 2:7, where Paul calls himself an apostle, preacher, and a teacher, we should not suppose that every time Paul lists the name of an office in the church that he is following a stereotyped list. It may well be that the higher office (say apostle) also includes some of the functions of the lower offices (say prophet, or teacher).

[84] George Mark Elliott did not want to make "teacher" refer to one of the permanent offices in the church.

were given certain leadership gifts for the church as a whole, to another listing of gifts one would find in each local congregation.[85]

Then gifts of healings -- See verse 9. It is assisting the sick to become well again.

Helps -- The word *antilempseis* is a *hapax legomena* in the New Testament. It comes from *antilambano*, and means 'aid, assistance, help'; and then 'those who render aid, assistance, or help; helpers.' The word was in common use in the 1st century to express the assistance given to government officials by inferiors. What these "helps" enabled their possessors to do in the church is not known. They might have been those to whom was entrusted the care of the poor and sick, the widows, orphans, strangers, travelers, and what not, i.e., the *diaconate*. The NIV rendering, "those able to help others," causes us to think of persons gifted so as to be able to help the church officers deal with the poor and the sick. It might be a reference to those who attended and waited on the apostles to aid them in their work (cf. Phoebe at Romans 16:2 or John Mark at Acts 13:5). Since this is in a context of spiritual gifts, it is a spiritual gift of some kind. Shore (commenting on the KJV text) has compared the listing of gifts here and the one in verses 9 and 10. He notes that here we have "helps" and "governments," which were not in the earlier verses, and that "tongues" and "discerning of spirits" which were in the earlier list are not here. Then he writes, "Possibly, therefore, the words inserted here are only another designation of the same thing. The 'helps' being the aid required for those who heard tongues in order to understand them., and the 'governments' being the due regulation of the acceptance of certain spiritual powers and rejection of others."[86]

Administrations -- This is the only place this word *kubernēseis* is found in the New Testament. Its classical meaning is that of piloting a ship, i.e., guiding the ship through the rocks and shoals into harbor. From this usage it is suggested that those with the gift of 'administration' had an ability to govern and manage the affairs of the congregation.[87] Several things cannot be determined with any certainty: (1) Whether or not this refers to a permanent office, is one. Since the other spiritual gifts were temporary, perhaps this one also was temporary. (2) Whether or not this gift had anything to do with relatively new Christians being selected to be elders, who then had the responsibility of taking the lead in the congregation, is another. Less than a decade after 1 Corinthians was written, Paul will instruct Timothy that one of the qualifications for elder is that he not be a "new convert" (i.e., a new Christian). Yet, in Acts 14:23, men who had been Christians for only about

---

[85] This author does not think we are to consider the rest of the things as 'fourthly ... fifthly,' etc. The classification according to rank ends with "teachers." The RSV attempts to continue a listing of people by translating "workers of miracles, then healers, helpers, etc.," but this is not a formal equivalent rendering of the Greek.

[86] Shore, *op. cit.*, p.122.

[87] Some commentators, searching for Scriptural justification of their particular group's hierarchical model of church polity, find it in this verse. They would translate it "hierarchies." However, the development of a ruling model in the church similar to the Roman government model appears to be a post-apostolic development. We doubt this verse, in the mid-1st century AD, already reflects such a governmental polity.

two or three years are appointed elders. "Administrations" might have been some special endowment that was temporary. Men who were being made elders in the early church only a year or two after their conversion were perhaps helped in a supernatural way to carry out their responsibilities of leadership and shepherding and guiding.

What is the relationship between the gifts and the offices? Must one be spiritually empowered with the gift of apostle, teacher, or administrator before he may be involved in congregational leadership? If one must be gifted to hold office, how do we explain that the qualifications for elder and deacon (Acts 10:17-20; 1 Timothy 3:1-13; Titus 1:5ff) emphasize spiritual *character and experience*, rather than spiritual *gifts*? Perhaps there is something flawed in the contemporary emphasis on ascertaining what one's own spiritual gift is, in order to know what job to do in the church. We must also be careful whenever someone asserts that, because he or she is gifted, of course he or she should be expected to exercise that gift. It is still important to understand when and how the gifts are received, and to inquire whether there is Scriptural warrant for an individual's claimed experiences.

***Various* kinds of tongues** -- See verse 10. Different "families" of foreign languages are indicated.

12:29 -- *All are not apostles, are they? All are not prophets, are they? All are not teachers, are they? All are not* **workers of** *miracles, are they?*

All are not apostles, are they? -- All the questions in verses 29 and 30 have the Greek word *mē*, which indicates that the implied answer to each question is "No!" So the NASB words the questions so that English readers will supply the implied answer. Verses 29 and 30 reinforce the idea stressed since verse 12 that in order for a body to exist and function there needs to be a variety of members. "God did not give the same gifts to every man. That would have been to make each member a kind of complete body, independent of the other members; and this would have been fatal to the whole. He has made no one member self-sufficient. Each needs much from others and supplies something to them" (Robertson and Plummer, *op. cit.*, p.282).

All are not prophets, are they? -- The implied answer is, 'No, not every one is a prophet.'

All are not teachers, are they? -- Teacher here in verse 29 would be the same temporary office intended in verse 28. The implied answer is, 'No, not every one is a teacher.'

All are not *workers of* miracles, are they? -- The words "workers of" (supplied in the English) have no representation in the Greek. We've already seen the meaning of "miracles" (powers) at 1 Corinthians 12:10. There are two possible ways it can be taken: (1) "Miracles" (*dunameis*) could be *objective*, governed by "have" (*echousin*) in verse 30, in which case it would read, "Have all *dunameis*"? 'Powers' (miracles) would then be emphatic, standing first in the sentence. (2) It could be simply the abstract for the concrete (in the subjective case). For example, we call men of great power the "powers that be." So, here, 'powers' (miracles) stands for workers of miracles. Whichever way we take it, the implied answer to the question is, 'No, not every one is a worker of miracles.'

12:30 -- *All do not have gifts of healings, do they? All do not speak with tongues, do they? All do not interpret, do they?*

All do not have gifts of healings, do they? -- "Gifts of healings" was explained in verse 9. The implied answer to the question is, 'No, all do not have such gifts.' As in the body all is not eye, or all ear, so in the church all have not the same gifts and offices.

All do not speak with tongues, do they? -- This question, like all the others in verses 29 and 30, expects a negative answer. Not everyone in the church then (or today) can be expected to speak with tongues.[88]

All do not interpret, do they? -- See notes at verse 10 concerning "interpretation" being the ability to translate a foreign language. The implied answer to the question is, 'No, not every one is able to translate foreign languages.' The point of the seven questions in verses 29 and 30 rests on the seven-times repeated "all." Let prophet, teacher, healer, and the rest, fulfill each contentedly his 'part' in the body.[89] No member of the body can expect either to be the whole body, or to do away with the other members. The unity of the body is made up by each member of the body being himself, having and exercising his own gift, and not wishing he were some other member.

12:31a -- *But earnestly desire the greater gifts.*

But earnestly desire the greater gifts -- "But" says there is a diversity of gifts, yes, but it is perfectly proper to desire that the "greater gifts" be exercised more frequently than the other gifts. The Greek form *dzēloute* ("desire") can be either indicative or imperative. Those who take it as indicative treat all of verse 31 as an introduction to chapter 13. An example would be the Syriac version which reads, "Because you are zealous of the best gifts, I will show you a more excellent way." The "greater gifts" thus become those by which the most "love" for the other person can be expressed. If it is taken as an imperative, verse 31a concludes the thought about diversity in the body, and a new paragraph begins with verse 31b (as the NASB has it).[90]

---

[88] This verse is telling in regard to the current tongues movement, which demands that every man, at least once, should speak in tongues as evidence of the baptism in the Holy Spirit. See the author's pamphlet, *Do All Speak in Tongues?* for a detailed discussion of the modern tongues movement. It is included in this volume as part of Special Study #10.

[89] Findlay, *op. cit.*, p.895. This directive needs emphasis in the present day. In some groups much is made of attempting to acquire all the gifts for each member. Just as logical would be a human body in which each finger also had eyes, feet, and internal organs! Paul will instruct the Corinthians to "desire the greater gifts," but he nowhere says to desire them all.

[90] So the KJV and ASV treated this verse. Even if we were to take 13:31a as indicative, there is probably no way that 14:1 (which repeats the language) could be taken as indicative. So we likely should attempt to explain both verses in some such way as to take into account what is written about "love" (Exercise your gifts in a loving way!) in chapter 13 (i.e., the verses in between 12:31b and 14:1).

In a context where God or the Spirit decides which gifts a person gets, the imperative "desire" cannot have reference to how one *gets* the gifts in the first place.[91] "Desire" must have reference to how one *uses* the gifts God has given. The command to desire the greater gifts would command the readers to desire to see the more useful ones exercised, the more useful ones being the ones that will benefit the most people. "Desire the greater gifts!" is a rebuke of the Corinthians' wrong attitudes and actions. They desired the showy ones, the self-praise ones, the ones that made them feel good personally. Paul says, 'Change your desires, so that you are motivated by love (chapter 13), not by selfishness. There is a more excellent way of using your gifts than the way you have been using them. Rather than envy and jealousy and spite and boasting, *let love rule your actions*!'

What are the "greater gifts"? Those gifts that benefit the largest number of people, those which are advantageous to the whole body of Christ. For example, in chapter 14, Paul tells them to desire prophecy rather than the gift of tongues, since prophecy will benefit more people. Any gift that helped the whole congregation was a greater gift. The Corinthians had perhaps formed a wrong estimate as to what actually were the greater gifts. Instead of coveting the more *spectacular* gifts, the Corinthians were urged to desire the more *useful* gifts.

d. Principle #4 -- Love must be the motive that controls the use of our gifts. 12:31b-13:13

12:31b -- *And I show you a still more excellent way.*

And I show you a still more excellent way -- That "more excellent way" is the way of love, as unfolded in chapter 13. Verse 31b serves to introduce chapter 13. Paul is not saying to forget the spiritual gifts and seek love alone. Love is not some gift to be desired to the exclusion of the other gifts. Rather, love is to be the dominating force or motive behind a man's use of his gifts. Even after a man has received some gift or another, he is still in control of when and where he may exercise his gift. Instead of just "showing off," it would be much better only to exercise one's gift when he can do it in a loving fashion (i.e., when he can be actively involved in doing what is spiritually best for the other person). The "more excellent way" is to exercise the gifts in such a way that you can demonstrate you love others and desire to help them grow.

---

[91] Thinking the command to "desire the greater gifts" speaks of how one gets the gifts in the first place, rather than how one exercises the gifts God has already given, some have expressed the belief that verse 31a is out of place, for it makes Paul encourage people to desire greater gifts after what he has just written about the members of the body – how no superior is to look down on an inferior, and how no inferior is to feel unwanted and unneeded. Paul certainly did not intend to say anything here in 31a that would contradict all he has written heretofore.

1) The necessity of being motivated by love. 13:1-3

13:1 -- *If I speak with the tongues of men and of angels, but do not have love, I have become a noisy gong or a clanging cymbal.*

If I speak -- We should never forget that chapter 13 comes between chapters 12 and 14. 12:31b and 14:1 read so much alike that it is certain that chapter 13 explains the "more excellent way."[1] This is why we have followed the lead of the NASB and put our paragraph title at the head of 12:31b. "Love" (i.e., doing what is spiritually best for the other person) is the "more excellent way." In fact, all the gifts are nothing if they are not exercised in a loving way. As he gave us the first three principles by which the use of spiritual gifts are to be governed (12:1-31), Paul has carefully and thoroughly set forth all the variety of the Spirit's manifestations that contribute to the common life of the congregation. All are necessary, all are honorable in their proper use, all are of God's ordination. Some gifts may be "greater" than others, but if they are exercised in a selfish spirit, their true purpose and blessing will be missed.

This beautiful love chapter of First Corinthians is often quoted out of context; many Christians do not realize that it was occasioned by the abuses in the Corinthian church with regard to spiritual gifts. In chapters 12 to 14, Paul is dealing with these abuses. In order to provide a Christian basis by which to judge the merits and demerits of the Corinthians' practices, he pens this chapter telling the Corinthians that all such questions must be decided by the requirements of Christian love. This chapter falls into three clearly marked parts: (1) The necessity of being motivated by love, verses 1-3; (2) The characteristics of love, verses 4-7; (3) The permanence of love in contrast to the transitory nature of their prized gifts, verses 8-13.

Two Greek words are used to express "speak" – *laleō* and *legō*. *Laleō* means articulated words (speech) as contrasted with silence, with no reference to the content of the speech. When the dumb man (*alalos*) in Mark 7:37 was restored to human speech, it is said that he "spoke" (*elalēsen*). (See also Matthew 9:33 and Luke 11:14.) The Gospel writers fitly use *laleō* for 'speaking' since they are not concerned with reporting what the man said, but only with the fact that he who before was dumb is now able to employ his organs of speech. *Legō* means "to say, to discourse."[2] *Legō* means to speak thoughtfully, using one's mind. From this word that we derive the English words 'logic' and 'logi-

---

[1] There is no valid reason to suggest, as some have done, that chapter 13 was composed at another time and place, and inserted here later as an afterthought. That misses the fact that the point of chapter 13 (the necessity for love) is like a keystone that holds chapters 12 and 14 together. Without it, the following applications (chapter 14) miss much of their force. We do not think that the exalted nature of the prose, nor any changes of style, prove that this chapter was not composed for the first time as part of Paul's directions to the Corinthians concerning how to correct some of the abuses that had crept into their public worship services. We doubt it had an independent existence before being adapted and inserted here. Even less believable are the allegations of some that Paul is not the author of chapter 13. Exegetes and preachers must be careful lest we unthinkingly detach chapter 13 from its context.

[2] Ammonius (the Greek philosopher, AD 175-250) says of them, "*Laleō*, speaking, and *legō*, differ; on the one hand *legō*, saying, is offering thought in an orderly manner; but *laleō*, speaking, is the articulation of words as they come to you."

cal.' *Laleō* is used at 13:1. In fact, it is always the word *laleō* used in the expression 'speaking with tongues.' Why? Because the Holy Spirit acts upon the believer to speak; it is not the product of his own mind, but the message of God. The believer is merely the agent of transmission. He could not, through his own thought processes, put together words of a language that he did not understand and make sense to his hearers.[3] Paul writes in the first person, "If I speak," rather than in the second person, "If you speak." This is a very powerful way to bring home the point of the argument to the readers. Both Paul and some of the Corinthians did speak in tongues. But if such speaking were motivated by any other motive than love, it was an improper use (yea, an abuse) of the gift.

With the tongues of men and of angels -- Paul first takes up the "gift" last mentioned (12:30), apparently the one most valued at Corinth. Paul begins with tongues because that is where the real abuse at Corinth was found. "Tongues of men" denotes the different languages men use.[4] "If I were able to speak all the languages which are spoken by men," is what Paul is saying. Evidently, a person gifted with tongues could not speak all languages, but only one 'kind' (family?) of languages.[5] (See notes at 12:10 and 12:28.) To speak all languages was beyond what any gifted Corinthian could do. Even if one had such a surpassing ability, but used it only selfishly, it would vitiate and negate the gift's value.

If "tongues of men" are languages men use, then "tongues of angels" are languages angels use. There has been considerable speculation as to what language(s) angels speak. On occasion, angels spoke to men in human language (e.g., Luke 1:13-20, 26-38). The Rabbis were confident the angels always spoke in pure Hebrew. Many contemporary writers affirm that the language(s) spoken by the angels in heaven is different from all the languages men on earth speak.[6] Commentators give two main ideas for the meaning or

---

[3] To be sure, *laleō*, speaking, occurs often in the epistle to the Hebrews, where it is even ascribed to God Himself (e.g., Hebrews 1:1.2). This does not mean God spoke without thought, for God's speech is always purposeful, but stresses the wonder of the fact that God should have spoken to men at all, rather than kept silent. Very interestingly, the word *laleō* is rarely used in Modern Greek. For the most part, the Greeks prefer the word *legō* when referring to speech, perhaps to emphasize their feeling that when we speak we had better have something to say! When Paul calls the Corinthians' actions *lalein glossais*, he indicates they were uttering sounds without themselves thinking about what they were uttering. The Holy Spirit was giving them the words.

[4] That "tongues" means languages has been shown in the notes at 1 Corinthians 12:10, and in the Special Study in the author's commentary on *Acts*, titled, "Speaking in Tongues." This verse has considerable weight when deciding what the "gift of tongues" was at Corinth. It was a language!

[5] There is a question as to whether Paul could speak all the languages, or more than one family of languages. Paul did have this gift of languages to a high degree (1 Corinthians 14:18). Since the measure of the Holy Spirit received by the apostles was not limited to one ability or "power," some believe he could. Others insist this verse is only hypothetical. The apostle is thought to be using himself as an illustration, but intends that his readers understand it as applying to themselves.

[6] To substantiate this view of "tongues of angels," one sometimes reads something like the following: It is possible that Paul may have some allusion here to what he refers to in 2 Corinthians 12:4, where he says that when he was caught up into Paradise, he heard unspeakable words which it was not possible for a man to utter. When angels speak to men, they sometimes did use human language; but Daniel, John in Revelation, and Paul himself when he was caught up to Paradise, heard unutterable things. Perhaps we may say that they actually heard the language of the angels as they speak in heaven, but a language that we humans do not understand or ordinarily speak.

application of this phrase (if we understand that the "tongues of angels" are non-human languages): (a) Some suppose men can use the language of angels, that it is a sort of prayer language for use especially in private devotions.[7] (b) It might be better to affirm that "tongues of angels" are beyond anything the Corinthians could do.[8] Even if they could (which they don't) so speak, without love, it would be nothing. In any case, Paul puts the thought into the superlative, beyond which it is impossible for a creature to go. Paul's supposition is this: If the entire range of languages, including even the languages used in heaven, were given me – if I have not love, even such a supreme gift would be all in vain as far as God's purpose in the bestowal is concerned.

But do not have love -- This is not the first time in Scripture that we are instructed about love. Christians are "taught by God to love one another" (1 Thessalonians 4:9). God the Father taught us to love by sending His Son (1 John 4:19). The Son taught us to love by giving His life (John 15:13), and He commanded his followers to love one another (John 13:34, 35). The Holy Spirit pours out God's love in our hearts (Romans 5:5). We suppose the Corinthians already knew about the need to be loving in their thoughts and actions. "Love" (*agapē*) can be defined as deliberately doing what is spiritually best for the one who is the object of this love.[9] The word is used very often when the Bible is speaking of God's love for mankind.[10]

---

[7] This commentator has a number of objections to the idea that tongues at Corinth were used for private devotional use, and were different than the tongues at Pentecost which had an evangelistic use. (a) Some contemporary churchmen have had an experience and then have gone to the Scriptures looking for proof texts that will prove that their experience was legitimate. For the contemporary exercise of speaking in tongues, they arrive, in their search, at 1 Corinthians 13:1 ("tongues of angels"). But the context here (chapters 12-14) is not private devotions, but abuses of the gifts in the public assembly of the church. (b) The other chief proof-text that "tongues" might be a prayer language (the "language of angels") is Romans 8:26. But this verse actually says there are no words at all (none human, none angelic) when the Spirit intercedes for us. (c) Fee's appeal (*op. cit.*, p.630) to the *Testament of Job* is telling of the lack of canonical evidence for the modern practice of "tongues." Fee says there is evidence from Jewish sources that angels were believed to have their own heavenly language (or dialects) and that by means of the "Spirit" humans could speak these dialects. Thus, in the *Testament of Job* 48-50, Job's three daughters are given "charismatic sashes." When these were put on, they allowed Hemera, for example, to speak "ecstatically in the angelic dialect, sending up a hymn to God with the hymnic style of the angels." And as she spoke ecstatically, she allowed "the Spirit" to be inscribed on her garment. It has always been a suspect method to search in non-canonical books for possible sources for Christian doctrine.

[8] "Tongues of angels" is treated as an abstract conception, intended to express the greatest possible climax. Remember, angels are greater than men. Because of the word order (the Greek reads, "If in tongues of men I speak, and of angels ..."), it seems likely this is hyperbole.

[9] There are several Greek synonyms all translated "love." (1) *Eraō* – our word "passion" describes what this word connotes, or "romance," love between the sexes, a selfish love. (2) *Storgeō* – describes the love of parents for children, or of children for parents (e.g., 2 Timothy 3:3, Romans 12:10). (3) *Phileō* – is love for the lovely, friendship, affection, personal liking and attachment. In the New Testament, it is used of love of father, mother, son, and daughter (Matthew 10:37, John 11:3,36, 20:2). (4) *Agapaō* – is a loving attitude that is willed, even if the object of the love is unlovely; love for someone because in him can be seen an intrinsic worth.

[10] We were down and disfigured by the marks of sinning, as unattractive as a drunken man in the gutter, wallowing in his own vomit. But God saw a worth in each human being, and sent His Son to try to help such sinners.

It is one thing to love those who love you. It is quite another thing to love someone who is absolutely repulsive in appearance or behavior. The following description shows that love to man is intended – a love patterned after God's love (*agapē*). To "have love" means 'to act in a loving fashion' towards other men.[11] Such "love" is a quality that can be developed. The more it is exercised, the more it grows. What Paul wants is *agapē*, an active effort for the other's good because we see an intrinsic value in him as a soul. In the case where it is a fellow Christian who is loved, we love because that man or woman is our brother or sister in Christ! Speech is a God-given ability, as are all our faculties, and must be governed by principle. Sounding off in public, without regard to the edification of our hearers (as the Corinthians were doing with their gift of tongues), is a self-inflationary practice, too often indulged in even by Christians. In whatever language we speak, Paul says, let it always be in the context of love, out of consideration of others.

I have become a noisy gong or a clanging cymbal -- It is interesting to note that Paul does not say "I am an echoing brass or a shrilling cymbal," but "I *have become* an echoing brass ...." In Greek it is *gegona* (a second perfect, active, indicative), which implies three things: (1) It implies, 'This is not the way I was when I first believed. This is the state to which I have degenerated. Carnal love and self have managed to get the upper hand. I have descended to the level of sounding brass or a clanging cymbal.' (2) *Gegona*, "I have become," implies that I am responsible for my degenerate state. God did not cause me to descend to the carnal level. He gives me freedom of action in the Christian life; and if I have degenerated, it is my own doing. If we speak unintelligibly in public worship, using our spiritual gifts in such a way as to edify no one but ourselves, then let us admit our own responsibility for our actions instead of claiming that God is speaking through us. (3) The perfect tense indicates a past act with present continuing results. "I have become" implies that acting this way regularly causes us to become that way, just as a falsehood that at first took effort to say, if repeated often enough, has the effect of convincing the one speaking that it is really true after all. Let us be on our guard lest thoughtless speaking with tongues becomes so much a part of our being that acting in the loving way God expects becomes the exception in our conduct, requiring a great effort.

Exactly what "a noisy gong" (*chalkos ēchōn*, "sounding brass," ASV) was, we are not certain.[12] It apparently was not a musical instrument made out of brass (like a trumpet). Not a few writers are reminded of the huge "gongs" one regularly found in pagan temples. It might be a "sounding board;" a gong; a resonant piece of bronze.[13]

---

[11] Some writers speak of "love" as being a gift from God. To call love a "gift" in the same sense that the *charismata* were gifts is, in this commentator's opinion, a great mistake. "Love" is one of the fruit of the spirit (Galatians 5:22), but that is hardly the same as any of the "spiritual gifts" which were given by the Spirit. To "have love" means to act in a loving fashion, just like to "have prophecy" (verse 2) means 'to speak a prophecy.'

[12] W.W. Klein's suggestion, "Noisy Gong or Acoustic Vase? A Note on 1 Corinthians 13:1" in *NTS* 13:1 (1986), p. 2876-289, and illustrated in Wm. Harris, "'Sounding Brass' and Hellenistic Technology," *BAR* 8:1 (Jan-Feb, 1982), p.38ff, has not received wide acceptance from the scholarly community.

[13] In passing, we might note that the word 'brass' is not technically correct for any object coming down from antiquity. The term 'brass' properly denotes an alloy of copper and zinc, and this the ancients used

"Noisy" or "sounding" we might render "resounding" since the verb is *ēchōn* (from which we derive our word 'echo'). One can't even play a tune on a gong. All one hears is a resounding noise when that gong is struck by the mallet. This language seems to be a metaphor for an empty, hollow sound – exactly what one would hear when tongues were abused (as they were being abused) in the public services. The "clanging cymbal" to which Paul refers here was not like our modern instrument of percussion of indefinite musical pitch. The small cup-shaped cymbal of Paul's day sounded a definite note. The participle denoting the sound produced by the cymbal (*alalazon*) is onomatopoetic; it is often used to describe 'crying out loudly over one who has died, to wail loudly.' It likely indicates a shrill tone or noise.[14] In Paul's day, cymbals and gongs were used in the worship of Dionysius, Cybele, and Corybantes. It is quite possible Paul is here comparing the Corinthians' selfish use of tongues in Christian worship with the din of gongs and cymbals in pagan worship. Without love guiding their exercise of the gift of tongues, the sound made by the selfish exercise of this admired endowment was just so much senseless noise, not much different from the hollow noises one found in the pagan cults. But where love was present, no one would ever speak in tongues just to be heard. The gift would be exercised only when it would benefit the listener (14:6,12-19,27).

13:2 -- *And if I have the gift of prophecy, and know all mysteries and all knowledge; and if I have all faith, so as to remove mountains, but do not have love, I am nothing.*

And if I have *the gift of* **prophecy** -- See notes at 12:10 for an explanation of the gift of prophecy. In 13:1, Paul spoke of the gift the Corinthians valued the most – tongues. Here in verse 2, Paul alludes to the gift he values most (see chapter 14) – prophecy – and shows that the same thing is as true for it as for tongues. If its exercise is not controlled by a loving motive, all is worthless.[15] Implied is the fact that whether one's gift were tongues or prophecy, the gift could be used either in a loving way or in a selfish way. Men were not overwhelmed, or overpowered, by the gifts, so that they no longer had personal self-control as to whether or not they were exercised. Both "speaking with tongues" and "prophecy" were inspired utterances. The difference between the two was that one was inspired preaching in a language other than the local dialect, while the other (prophecy) was inspired preaching in the local dialect.

And know all mysteries -- A "mystery" was something only dimly taught in the Old Testament, but now in the New Testament age is clearly taught. For "mysteries" see notes at 2:7. Mysteries are truths that men could never penetrate for themselves, or discover by

---

but rarely. The correct term for the ancient's metal is 'bronze,' an alloy of copper and tin.

[14] Todd K. Sanders, "A New Approach to 1 Corinthians 13:1," *NTS* 36 (1990), p.614-618, offers the hypothesis that "*kumbalon alalazon*" was a musical sound that 1st century hearers enjoyed hearing. He then offers an alternative suggestion for translating the Greek, resulting in this reading, "If I speak ... but do not have love, I am a dinging piece of bronze *rather than* a joyfully sounding cymbal." He insists this rendering strengthens Paul's argument for the presence of love. Tongues exercised in a loving way are a joyful sound.

[15] Paul has just ranked "prophecy" as second only to the apostolate (12:28), so that he cannot be accused of minimizing its importance. But loveless prophecy must be condemned.

unaided human research. They are truths known only because it has pleased God to reveal them. Some examples of "mysteries" can be studied at Romans 11:25-27 (where the salvation of "all Israel" was dimly predicted in the Old Testament and is now explained by Paul), and perhaps Acts 13:34 (where Isaiah 55:3's "the sure blessings of David" is explained by the apostle to be a prediction of the resurrection of Jesus from the dead). "Know"[16] probably has the sense of "understand" as in the KJV. To understand the "mystery" would involve direct revelation as to the full meaning of obscure language of the Old Testament prophecies, so that their meaning could be infallibly unfolded by the New Testament speaker or writer.

And all knowledge -- Though this word, too, is governed by the same verb "know" as was "all mysteries," we believe it speaks of the spiritual gift of "knowledge" (see notes at 12:8). The question has been raised whether "knowing all mysteries and all knowledge" are parts of the gift of prophecy mentioned first in the verse. Some say "understanding mysteries" and "knowledge" should not be viewed as component parts of the gift of prophecy, since elsewhere Paul distinguishes "prophecy" from "knowledge" (cf. 12:8,10). Others say the fact that "if" is not repeated in the Greek until the next clause supports the view that the gift of prophecy is hypothetically depicted (for the sake of the argument) as including knowing all mysteries and knowledge,[17] something way beyond what any prophet could do. Superlatively depicting the gift of prophecy in this manner would then be parallel to how the gift of tongues was depicted in verse 1 ("of men and angels").

And if I have all faith, so as to remove mountains -- In this context of spiritual gifts, this is wonder-working faith, not saving faith (see 12:9). It is possible that Paul is alluding to our Lord's saying (Mark 11:22, Matthew 17:20, 21:21), "If you have faith as a [grain of] mustard seed, you shall say unto this mountain, 'Move from here to there,' and it shall move ...." The present infinitive suggests 'moving mountain after mountain.'

But do not have love -- See notes on 13:1. The apostle Paul has said that speech without love – whether in human or heavenly languages – was mere noise. Since this statement occurs in connection with the practice of speaking in tongues in the church at Corinth, it was his way of rebuking this practice as senseless and selfish. But not only does he condemn loveless speaking in tongues, he also condemns loveless prophesying. For though Paul considered prophecy a far greater gift than speaking with tongues, he knew that even the best of gifts without love is nothing. The same is true of the gift of knowledge, and the gift of wonder-working faith. Your motive and the use to which you put your gift determine its real value in God's eyes.

---

[16] The Greek verb *eidō* comes from *oida*, the synonym for "know" that speaks of knowledge that comes by instruction, as contrasted with *ginōskō* which denotes a knowledge that comes from experience.

[17] Lenski defends the view that "knowing all mysteries and knowledge" are added by Paul to heighten to the superlative degree the value of prophecy over tongues. Just like "tongues of angels" was hyperbole, so "know all mysteries and all knowledge" is hyperbole. He thinks it carries the supposition beyond the bounds of human possibility (*op. cit.*, p.549-550).

I am nothing -- The abruptness of *outhen eimi* after the prolonged three-clause "if" condition is impressive. Contrary to Corinthian beliefs that the possession and mere exercise of certain gifts would make them important in other people's estimation, Paul says that when love is absent from the exercise, the man is "nothing," he is a 'nobody!' Or, perhaps, "I am nothing" means 'I do not fulfill any of the great purposes which God has designed me to fulfill.' If I have all the spiritual gifts – prophecy, understanding of mysteries, knowledge, and the powers to perform all manner of miracles – and if I have these gifts to a superlative degree, yet do not exercise them as *love* dictates, I am of no value. I am not doing for the body of Christ what God intended these gifts should do. Pride can certainly lead to an over-inflated notion of one's worth in the sight of God and men. In a spirit of love, Paul has been tactfully trying to bring the Corinthians to realize that showing off their spiritual gifts is hardly commensurate with Christian love and selflessness. The Corinthians clearly thought the possessors of certain gifts were extremely important persons. Paul stoutly maintains that if they have even the highest gifts, and that in full amount, but exercise them in a selfish rather than loving manner, not only are they unimportant, but they are actually nothing. The choice of words here is very impressive.

13:3 -- *And if I give all my possessions to feed the poor, and if I deliver my body to be burned, but do not have love, it profits me nothing.*

And if I give all my possessions to feed *the poor* -- The word *psōmisō* ("give" or 'bestow,') means 'to break off, to distribute in small portions, to feed by morsels.' The five words "give to feed the poor" are all used by our translators to render this one Greek word. Paul is speaking of giving one's goods in small amounts to large numbers of people. The verb is in the aorist tense, pointing to a once-for-all action, the action of a man who, in one grand sweeping gesture, sells all that he has and gives it away. The Greek has nothing corresponding to "the poor." The emphasis in the original is on the giver, not on the recipients (Morris, *op. cit.*, p.183). If a man gave all that he had, if he dealt it out in small portions so as to benefit as many as possible, and yet that act was not attended *with true love toward God and toward man*, while it would benefit the recipients, the act of giving would be false, hollow, hypocritical, and of no value or benefit whatever to the giver.[18] In verses 1 and 2, Paul alluded to certain supernatural gifts. The context might require that verse 3 still be an allusion to 'spiritual gifts,' rather than explaining it as though Paul were merely dealing with human acts of kindness or benevolence. 'Giving all of one's possessions' might be synonymous with the gift called "helps" in 12:28. Paul prefaces this third supposition with *ean*, just as he has prefaced his previous suppositions. It should be translated the same way the previous verses were, with "if" rather than "though" (as the KJV). Verses 1,2, and 3 all begin with this same conditional conjunction, a conjunction of supposing rather than fact (which is *ei*).

---

[18] Barnes, *op. cit.*, p.244. It is sobering to reflect that one may be generous to the point of beggary, and yet completely lack the spirit of love. In Acts 5 we have a classic example of wrong motivation for an ostensibly good act. Ananias and Sapphira sold a field and brought part of the money to the apostles for God's work. They deliberately created the impression that they were giving the full price of the field to God. But in their generosity there was a conscious desire to show off. This is what Paul wants to correct in the Corinthian church, doing things for the sake of creating an impression rather than out of love.

And if I deliver my body to be burned -- The original reading of this phrase is extremely uncertain. (1) Some manuscripts read "that I may boast" -- *kauchēsōmai*. P[46], *Aleph*, A, B, 33, and several versions. It is the better attested reading and is adopted in the text of NA[26] and UBS[3]. Such self-glory would fit the context as being the exact opposite of the "love" motive Paul is speaking of as being indispensable. People being martyred by burning was yet about six years in the future from this writing (Nero in AD 64). Therefore some think "boast" is correct.[19] Paul may have deliberately referred to 'boasting' because that was precisely the motive that led to the abuse of spiritual gifts at Corinth. (2) Several manuscripts read "to be burned" – *kauthēsomai*.[20] Exegetes have struggled to explain the verse if we read, "that I may be burned." Some see a reference to the practice of branding slaves with a hot iron. But the usual words for this are *stidzein* and *stigmatadzein*. Some call attention to immolating oneself like the heathen sometimes do. In the city of Athens was the Tomb of the Indian. The epitaph on it reads, "Here lies Zarmanochegas who made his own self immortal." Self-sacrifice without charity is unavailing. For instance, "when a Buddhist ascetic leaps with smiling face on the blazing pyre, immolating his body that he may immortalize his spirit, what does it profit him? Nothing: the fanatic is in love with himself and with no one else; he seeks his own sole happiness whether in the shape of a coming deification or of a present glorification of self" (F.N. Peloubet, *Notes on the International Lessons for 1884*, Boston: W.A. Wilde & Co., p.107). Others suppose this is a picture of a man rushing into a burning building in order to save someone's life, but who perishes in the attempt. Against this view is the word *hina* ('in order that') which itself seems to imply the intention of perishing. The only purpose or motive behind the man's behavior referred to here was selfish – there was no act of love to it.

Just as the suppositions in verses 1 and 2 were depicted as way beyond reality, so we suppose this clause is intended as hyperbole, too.[21] The picture would be this: one is so committed to feeding the poor that he not only parcels out all of his possessions, but in one heroic act even gives his body. A still greater proof of devotion to some person or cause rather than giving all one's goods is the sacrifice of life; yet even that may be without love.

But do not have love -- It is the same "love" motive that verses 1 and 2 have spoken of as lacking.[22] If a man, from the motive of pride rather than love, should speak as the angels,

---

[19] Fee (*op. cit.*, p.634) gives several arguments why "burn" is a suspicious reading, and therefore why "boast" was more likely the original reading. He notes that "deliver my body" is not the usual word for martyrdom. He also believes that a scribal change from "boast" to "burn" can be easier explained, than could a possible change from an original "burn" to "boast."

[20] C, D, F, G, L,, and several versions have *kauthēsomai* (a future indicative form). K, ψ, 614, 1881, and the majority text read *kauthēsōmai* (a future subjunctive passive form).

[21] There is no "gift" in the lists from chapter 12 to which this one might be compared. It seems doubtful, therefore, that "deliver my body" was intended as another example of a *charisma* ('spiritual gift').

[22] The KJV reads "charity", following the example of Wycliffe, who took it from the *charitas* of the Vulgate. Jerome used this rendering because he recognized the unsuitability of the Latin *amor* as a rendering of the Greek *agapē*. How sad, in the light of what is here written, that "deeds of charity" came to be thought of as meritorious. In the middle ages "the alms-giving of certain monasteries, or the courts of the Spanish and Sicilian bishops and archbishops, where immense revenues were syringed away in

have a superlative gift of prophecy, have all faith so as to move mountain after mountain, and be willing to sacrifice all he has while helping another, from the world's standpoint it might look as if that man were really something. Such acclaim from the world might even feed the man's pride. But it gets no acclaim from God, for God looks into a man's heart.

It profits me nothing -- Perhaps the profit is something received in this life, perhaps it is the life to come. Selfish actions do not produce spiritual maturity in this life. And when a man stands at the judgment seat of Christ, where both his motives and actions are taken into account, there will be no reward for loveless actions (see 2 Corinthians 5:10; Matthew 25:31-46). Lenski (*op. cit.*, p.553) indicates the three suppositions in verses 1-3 have a gradation of results because of the absence of love. (1) I produce nothing of value, verse 1. It is just so much noise like a brass gong. (2) I am of no value, verse 2. I have missed my God-given purpose for being here. (3) I gain nothing of value, verse 3. The credit or profit that might come to him from God for his deeds is declared to be nothing. The man who possessed all the gifts mentioned might be useful to the church, but in character he would be worthless. The *gifts* are not valueless, but *he* is. So Paul has taken all conceit out of the possession of these gifts. In the first three verses, Paul has demonstrated the absolute necessity of being motivated by love when one exercises his gifts.

2) The characteristics of love. 13:4-7

13:4 -- *Love is patient, love is kind,* **and** *is not jealous; love does not brag* **and** *is not arrogant,*

Love is patient -- Instead of attempting a definition of "love," Paul gives us a rich description. If love is so important, how can one judge whether or not he is acting from a loving motive? Verses 4-7 list some of the characteristics of love. He shows us what love does and does not do. "This photograph of love is given to us in order that we may hold it alongside of our love to see whether the two are as exactly alike as they ought to be."[23] We have entered the verses where the characteristics of *agapē* ("love") are set forth – not our love towards God, but what everyday love toward our brothers in Christ should look like.[24] The Corinthians had been impatient toward one another in their public meetings (1 Corinthians 11:21,22 and 14:29-32). "There were contentions and strifes among the Corinthians, suspicions and jealousies, unkind judging, the imputation of improper motives, selfishness, envy and pride and boasting, all of which were inconsistent with love. Paul designed this chapter to correct these evils, and to produce a different state of things by showing them what would be produced by the exercise of love."[25] Several

---

farthings to herds of beggars," certainly must be branded as nothing of value (to the giver) by these words of Paul. (Quote from Marvin R. Vincent, *Word Studies in the New Testament*, Vol. II, p.233)

[23] Lenski, *op. cit.*, p.554. Someone has suggested that we could substitute "Jesus" for the word "love," and the passage would become a simple and perfect description of Jesus. Then the same person asked his listeners if they could substitute their own names for "love."

[24] All the verbs in this section are present tense verbs. That implies the actions are continuous, habitual, repeated actions, the kind of actions that are true of genuine love at all times.

[25] Barnes, *op. cit.*, p.245.

authors call attention to the fact that there are 14 characteristics, arranged in seven pairs.

1) One pair – love is patient and is kind – contains both positive statements.
2) Then follow four pairs:
    a) Three pairs are negative:
        Not jealous, does not brag
        Is not arrogant, does not act unbecomingly
        Does not seek its own, is not provoked
    b) Then one pair with both a positive and a negative:
        Does not take into account a wrong suffered, does not rejoice in iniquity
            but rejoices with the truth
3) Finally we have two pairs of positive characteristics or attributes of love:
        bears all things, believes all things
        hopes all things, endures all things

"Patient" (*makrothumei*) in the New Testament always describes *patience with people*, rather than patience with circumstances.[26] Chrysostom said that *makrothumia* is the word used of the man who is wronged and who has it easily in his power to avenge himself, and who yet will not do so. When other people are ungrateful, rude, insulting, and provocative, the person who loves is long-suffering, long-tempered, and bears long with calumniating and injurious behavior. It isn't revengeful, nor does it become resentful, nor attempt to inflict punishment as payback.

Love is kind -- *Chrēsteuetai* means 'good-natured, gentle, tender, affectionate, useful, helpful.' It is the opposite of harsh, sour, morose, ill-natured. It dispenses deeds of gentle kindness. This first pair thus has both a passive and an active side: *passive* – love endures evils; *active* – love actively confers blessings. It does good.

> Paul does not describe love to us in the role of performing great, wonderful and astounding deeds; he prefers to show us how the inner heart of love looks when it is placed among sinful men and weak and needy brethren. He does not picture love in ideal surroundings of friendship and affection where each individual embraces and kisses the other, but in the hard surroundings of a bad world and a faulty church where distressing influences bring out the positive power and value of love.[27]

***And* is not jealous** -- *Zēloi* can be translated both "jealousy" and "envy." (*Zeō* means to boil. Love does not boil with either jealousy or envy.) At 1 Corinthians 3:3 we have learned that envy was one problem a number of people at Corinth had. There is an "envy" that covets the possessions of others; the Corinthians were envying each other's gifts. There is also a "jealousy" that grudges the fact that others have what it does not. It is not

---

[26] Compare the notes of explanation given for "bears all things" in verse 7.

[27] Lenski, *op. cit.*, p.555.

so much that the things are wanted as it is a wish the others did not have them. Men who genuinely love do not envy. Love does not envy others the happiness which they enjoy. Love does not attempt to squelch the praise that another man deserves. "If other men are increased in their endowments, their rank, their reputation, their wealth, their learning – those who are influenced by love rejoice in all this" (Barnes, *op. cit.*, p.246). Love never detracts from the praise that is due another, nor does it try to make him seem less and one's self to seem more by comparison. The practice of the world is the opposite. Love is not displeased when others do well or are successful.

Love does not brag – *Ou perpereuetai* says that love does not call attention to itself through self-centered actions, does not boast, is not ostentatious, does not show off, does not strut around like a peacock, is not given to false pretense or worldly glitter. Love, for instance, does not do "its alms before men, to be seen of them" (Matthew 6:1). "Bragging" likely reflects the desire on the part of some at Corinth to have the more showy gifts. Behind boastful bragging there lies conceit, an overestimation of one's own importance, abilities, or achievements.

And **is not arrogant** – *Ou phusioutai*, as explained earlier, means "to blow, to puff, to pant, to inflate with pride, vanity, and self-esteem." The word is used to describe how a frog swells up just before it lets out a croak. The word came to picture the subjective state of conceit and self-exaltation that a self-centered man can harbor. If the person who loves is not arrogant, that person is free from the characteristic vice of the Corinthian church (4:6, 18,19, 5:2; 8:1). Paul has pictured the order that lovelessness takes – from envy to boasting, from boasting to puffing one's self up. There are many ways of manifesting pride, and love is incompatible with them all. Love is concerned rather to give itself than to assert itself.

13:5 -- *does not act unbecomingly; it does not seek its own, is not provoked, does not take into account a wrong* **suffered,**

Does not act unbecomingly – *Ouk aschēmonei* says the person who loves is not ill-mannered; is not crude; is not discourteous, indecent, repulsive, self-assertive. The word means to behave shamefully or disgracefully. Love is tactful, and does nothing that would raise a blush. Perhaps this word reflects the disorderly conduct at the public assembly where folk so clamored to be up front and seen by others that they would interrupt those who already had the floor (see chapter 14).[28] "This is the next link of the chain. When pride puffs up the heart, unseemly bearing and conduct naturally follow. Tactlessness forgets its own place and fails to accord to others their proper dues of respect, honor, or consideration. Love is forgetful of self, and thoughtful toward others."[29]

It does not seek its own – *Ou zētei ta heautēs* says the person who loves does not seek

---

[28] Some see a particular reference here to the disorderly conduct referred to in 11:2-16, but this commentator is not sure a reference to 11:2-16 was intended.

[29] Lenski, *op. cit.*, p.557.

above all else its own pleasure, advantage, or honor. It was not just in the exercise of gifts that such selfishness was evident at Corinth. Shameless self-seeking has been condemned earlier in the letter (e.g., 10:24 and 10:33). There is perhaps not a more striking or important expression in the New Testament than Matthew 20:20-26, which shows that Jesus' own apostles at an earlier time struggled with this sinful attitude. The plain fact is that Christians who ought not be selfish must work at their attitudes to keep this one at bay. This beautifully sets forth the nature and power of the love which should animate Christians. Instead of seeking first one's own happiness and pleasure, Christians who truly love will seek the happiness of others first.[30] Love will stop the lover from self-promotion and replace it with a desire to promote others.

Is not provoked -- "Is not touchy," says Phillips. *Ou paroxunetai* means 'does not fly into a rage, is not embittered' by injuries inflicted by others. In fact, with this verb the list of characteristics of love begins to speak of how one responds to evil committed by others. The word comes from *oxunō*, 'to sharpen.' It may be applied to the act of sharpening a knife or sword; then it means to sharpen the mind, temper, courage of any one; to excite, impel. Here it means *rouse to anger*, or be irritable.[31] A man who has love may be injured, yet he governs his passions, restrains his temper, subdues his feelings. Love not merely does not fly into a rage, but does not yield to provocation; it is not embittered by injuries, whether real or supposed.

Does not take into account a wrong *suffered* -- The ASV's "takes not account of evil" is better than the KJV's "thinketh no evil."[32] The NIV reads "It keeps no record of wrongs." The word *logizetai* ("take into account") is an accountant's word. It is the word used for entering an item onto the page of a ledger so it will not be forgotten. *Ou logizetai to kakon* describes one who does not record the evil, has no bookkeeping system for recording hurts until they can be paid back.[33] "The wrong" (the Greek has an article) means the baseness

---

[30] Barnes (*op. cit.*, p.249) has a thoughtful application. "When ALL Christians make it their grand object not to seek their own, but the good of others, when true love shall occupy its appropriate place in the heart of every Christian: then the world shall be speedily converted to the Savior; there will be no lack of funds to spread Bibles and tracts, to send missionaries, to establish schools and colleges; there will be no want of men who shall be willing to go to any part of the earth to preach the gospel; there will be no want of prayer to implore the divine mercy on a ruined and perishing world. Oh, may the time soon come when all the selfishness in the human heart will be dissolved; and when the whole world shall be embraced in the love of the Christians; and the time, talents, and wealth of the whole church shall be regarded as consecrated to God and employed and expended under the influence of Christian love."

[31] The word "easily" (found in the KJV) is not in the original Greek text. The KJV translators added this word as a swipe at King James II because he had a quick and hot temper.

[32] The KJV translators interpreted the expression to mean that 'love does not devise evil against someone else,' and was likely based on the fact that the language is very close to the LXX of Zechariah 8:17. In the Corinthian context of how one exercises his gifts, the idea is that no one uses his or her gift if by doing so you make another person look bad.

[33] The ASV/NASB translators took this expression to mean that the one who loves does not keep a record of hurts suffered at the hand of others, so as to get even. In the context of abuse of spiritual gifts, the idea is that Christians are not to be resentful if others wrongfully use their gifts to make you look bad.

or meanness inflicted upon us by others. Another explanation of this phrase gives it a wholly different emphasis. It says that love does not impute evil in others. Love puts the best possible construction upon the motives and conduct of others. Love is not disposed to think that there was any evil intention, even in cases which might tend to irritate or exasperate us.

13:6 -- *does not rejoice in unrighteousness, but rejoices with the truth;*

Does not rejoice in unrighteousness – *Ou chairei epi tē adikia* says a person whose motivation is love does not rejoice or gloat when it sees unrighteousness, whether it is the wrongdoing committed by others, or whether it refers to the disasters others experience. Love isn't happy when other men fall into sin, yet the Corinthians had been boasting when there was sin in the congregation (chapter 5). "Anything that is wrong in God's sight grieves a heart that is full of love, not merely because the wrong hurts the one to whom it is done, but especially because God is displeased with the wrong and must punish the wrongdoer."[34] Love grieves when another person (especially a fellow believer) has done something wrong.

But rejoices with the truth -- The Greek is *sunchairei de tē alētheia*. It is better to translate "rejoices *with* the truth" as does the ASV/NASB, than "rejoiceth *in* truth" as did the KJV. "Truth" has been understood in several ways. (1) Some feel the "truth" is to be taken as the opposite of "unrighteousness" in the previous phrase. Love does not rejoice in the vices, but in the virtues of others. Love is pleased when others do well. "There is a stern moral element throughout the New Testament, and nothing is ever said to obscure this. Love is not to be thought of as indifferent to moral considerations."[35] (2) The better understanding of this phrase is that it refers to the 'fundamental truth of the gospel.' Love rejoices when men obey the gospel of Christ.[36] So explained, the Corinthians are to rejoice when the gifts are used in the spread of the gospel – rather than as they were doing, rejoicing just to be able to exercise them whether they contributed anything to others or not.

13:7 -- *bears all things, believes all things, hopes all things, endures all things.*

Bears all things – *Stegei* properly means to 'cover' (from *stegē*, a roof, covering), and then 'hide, to conceal, not to make known.' Love is disposed to hide or conceal the faults and

---

[34] Lenski, *op. cit.*, p.559.

[35] Morris, *op. cit.*, p.185.

[36] Compare notes at 2 Thessalonians 2:10,12, where "truth" is set over against "unrighteousness" (the same Greek word as in the previous phrase here in Corinthians).

imperfections of others, not telling all you know, keeping to yourself the bad things you know about others. There are exceptions to this, of course. There are times when we should expose evil and false teachers. *Stegei* can also mean to 'endure, bear up under.'[37] If this meaning is accepted, then the verse says that "love never complains that it is made to endure and to suffer too much; its capacity for suffering is very great. Remember all that the Lord's love suffered."[38]

Believes all things – *Panta pisteuei* does not mean that a man under the influence of love is credulous. We do not have to believe $2 + 2 = 5$ in order to love. It does not mean that the Christian believes white is black. 'Not in a hurry to impute false motives,' is the idea. Love withholds judgment until all the evidence is in. "There is a disposition to put the best construction on the conduct of others: to believe that they are actuated by good motives, to believe that they intend no injury."[39] Moffatt's rendering, "always eager to believe the best," is apt.

Hopes all things -- These last three characteristics (believes, hopes, endures) form a climax. "When love has no evidence, it believes the best. When the evidence is adverse, it hopes for the best. And when hopes are repeatedly disappointed, it still courageously waits."[40] The one who loves still hopes what is good of another, even when others have ceased to do so. It hopes that the other person's failure is not final.

Endures all things -- The word here is *hupomenei*. Trench has distinguished between "endurance" (*hupomonē*) in this verse and "patient" (*makrothumia*) of verse 4 in this fashion: *hupomonē* refers to things, and *makrothumia* refers to persons. In the Scriptures "patience (long-suffering)" has to do with injurious persons, and does not let their mean or malicious actions arouse resentment and anger. "Endurance" deals with trials and tribulations which it bears with noble courage.[41] Love bears up under trials, not with passive resignation, but with deliberate fortitude (Barclay, *op. cit.*, p.139). If life is adverse, and full of trials, love does not despair and quit. "If life hands you a lemon, make lemonade!" is a way of explaining this characteristic. Love will take the hard things and turn them into something beautiful for the Lord. "All things" in this context speaks of unloving acts done either deliberately or thoughtlessly by our fellow church members that affect us adversely. This expression is of course to be taken with a degree of allowance. Loving our fellow men does not mean that: (1) We are to approve sin, 2 Corinthians 7:1. (2) We must have precisely the same sentiment toward all men, Mark 2:5; Matthew 23:33;

---

[37] "Jonathan Edwards preferred the translation 'suffers all things,' and he then interpreted the clause as denoting a disposition which makes us willing for Christ's sake to undergo all sufferings to which we may be exposed in the way of duty. But this is hardly consistent with the drift of the passage." Kling, *op. cit.*, p.270.

[38] Lenski, *op. cit.*, p.560.

[39] Barnes, *op. cit.*, p.252.

[40] Robertson and Plummer, *op. cit.*, p.295.

[41] R.C. Trench, *Synonyms of the New Testament* (Grand Rapids, MI: Eerdmans, 1950), p.195ff.

Philippians 2:29; Galatians 5:12. Some we may *phileō* and some we may *agapaō*. (3) We are to love all men the same way we love our loved ones, Ephesians 5:33; John 21:20; Ephesians 6:2; John 11:3,5. (4) We do not have special obligations for certain men, Galatians 6:10. (5) All men are to be treated alike, Matthew 7:6; Acts 18:5,6; Jude 22,23. Loving our fellow men does mean that: (1) We are to regard all men as the off-spring of God, hence, very precious, Acts 17:26ff; Mark 8:36. (2) Any man is to be the object of our good will. We are to rejoice in his well-being, Romans 10:1, 9:1-3; Luke 23:34; Acts 7:60. (3) We will be unselfish in our dealings with our fellow men, Luke 14:13,14; Romans 15:1-3. (4) We must be willing to forgive, Luke 17:4; Matthew 6:12,14,15. (5) It involves the foregoing of hypocritical judging, Matthew 7:1; James 2:1.

3) The permanence of love in contrast to the temporary nature of the gifts the Corinthians prized. 13:8-13

13:8 -- *Love never fails; but if there are gifts of prophecy, they will be done away; if there are tongues, they will cease; if there is knowledge, it will be done away.*

Love never fails -- Paul has not forgotten the reason he is describing how love prompts a man to act. Beginning here in verse 8, Paul is going to show that love is something more permanent than any of the spiritual gifts. If that is true, then the Corinthian Christians should be more intense about developing the quality of love in their lives than they were about simply exercising this or that gift in public. The verb *piptō*[42] has two technical meanings between which it is not easy to decide. It may mean 'is never *hissed off the stage* as a bad actor.' The implication is that some of the Corinthians' behavior as they exercised their gifts was of the kind that made others want to hiss them off the stage. The word may also mean "falls away" like the petals of a withered flower, or stars falling in the heavens; 'to collapse, to suffer ruin.' Love is more permanent[43] than the spiritual gifts are intended to be, is the thrust of the whole verse. It is from this verse that we have drawn the summary title for verses 8-13.

But if *there are gifts of* -- The word translated "if" is *eite*. This conditional particle, 'whether there be,' compared to 'love that never fails,' points to the temporary nature of these miraculous gifts. Whether or not there is any significance in the choice of gifts named in this verse, which "are done away ... will cease," cannot be determined with absolute certainty. Perhaps those writers are correct who insist that only these three are temporary, and all the other spiritual gifts were intended to be available to Christians long

---

[42] The manuscripts vary between "fall," *piptō* (P[46], *Aleph*, A,B,C, 33, etc.) and "fail," *ekpiptō* (Western Text and TR).

[43] Besides using the present tense to write the verb "never fails," Paul will write (verse 13) that faith, hope, and love "abide." From this statement that "love never fails" (continuous action implied) added to the verb "abides" (interpreted to mean it abides even after a man dies physically), has been inferred the doctrine that the saints at rest pray for those on earth. It seems to this commentator that certain denominations were hard pressed to find Biblical support for the doctrine of the intercession of the saints if these two phrases blended together must be appealed to as evidence.

after these three had ceased to be needed.[44] Perhaps those writers are correct who affirm that the significance lies in the fact that the first, "prophecies," was Paul's own preference of the greater gift, whereas the other two were the Corinthians' favorites.

Prophecy ... tongues ... knowledge -- Care must be exercised lest when commenting on these words we ignore the context ("spiritual gifts," chapters 12-14). "Prophecy" is a reference to the exercise of the miraculous gift of prophecy (see 12:10,28,29). The word is plural in the Greek, as the NASB margin shows. The plural indicates that deliverance of inspired messages in the local dialect was customarily a regular part of the public worship assemblies. "Tongues" is a reference to the ability to speak in an unlearned foreign language (see 12:10). "Knowledge" is a reference to the supernatural gift[45] talked about in chapter 12:8-10.[46]

They will be done away ... they will cease ... it will be done away -- The word translated "done away" is *katargeō*,[47] while the word translated "cease" is *pauō*. "Done away" is a passive form. God will cause them to cease. "Cease" is middle voice in the Greek.[48] The verb *pausontai* is exactly suited to the subject of tongues. As a speaker 'pauses' and speaks no more, so tongues (Paul asserts) shall lapse into complete silence. Again, let it be noted that the emphasis in verses 8-13 is on the fact that there will be a need for love much longer than there will be any need to exercise spiritual gifts. Love is going to last longer than the gifts.[49]

---

[44] If the others are permanent, it might mean that apostles, teachers, etc. (12:28-30), are still with us, as indeed could be healings, discerning of spirits, etc. We say "might" because it has yet to be determined (in our study) how much longer (to the end of the church age?) love "abides" than do the gifts.

[45] Some writers, interpreting the word "perfect" (verse 10) to be a reference to the second coming, have supposed that "knowledge" speaks of all human knowledge, and they write about how human knowledge (in general) will pass away. This commentator wonders why it should be thought there is any reference to human knowledge in general. Even if "perfect" is a reference to the second coming of Christ (which we doubt), why (when commenting on "knowledge") would we ignore the context which deals with the abuse of spiritual gifts in the assembly at Corinth?

[46] A few manuscripts (*Aleph*, A, F, G, 33, etc.) make this word plural also, thus making it conform to "prophecies" and "tongues" which also were plural. The plural would make it clear that "utterances of knowledge" were a customary part of the public assemblies, too.

[47] This one word in the Greek was rendered in two different ways by the translators of the ASV, and four different ways in the KJV. If readers were not careful, this needless variety could lead to wrong ideas. We have commented on the word *katargeo* at 1:28.

[48] A.T. Robertson, *Word Pictures*, V.4, p.179, believes the change to middle voice is significant in this verse. He says this means that tongues "shall make themselves cease or automatically cease of themselves." Others see the change in verb and voice as simply rhetorical (e.g., Myron J. Houghton, "A Reexamination of 1 Corinthians 13:8-13," *Bib Sac* 153 [Jul-Sep 1996], p.344-356).

[49] When it is that the gifts will cease, Paul will go on to explain. Suffice it to be said, at this point, that if the time when the gifts were to cease was sometime far distant in the future, Paul's argument to the Corinthians is robbed of its force. If the gifts were going to last till long after the Corinthian Christians had all died, why should they at the present time be more interested in love than they were in simply exercising

13:9 -- *For we know in part, and we prophesy in part;*

For we know in part -- Paul has said the spiritual gifts would cease. With "for" Paul begins his explanation of how and when that cessation would take place. If we let the context be our determining guide, "know" still refers to the spiritual gift called "knowledge." "In part," is the same construction (*ek merous*) already commented upon in 12:27, where we had "individually members of it." Two meanings have been suggested for this phrase. (1) Some suggest our human knowledge is imperfect and obscure. The attempt to make verse 9 refer to human knowledge, when the whole context has been talking of spiritual gifts, has been defended by the following arguments:

> This idea of obscurity and imperfection of our knowledge, as compared to perfection (verse 10), the apostle illustrates: (a) by comparing it with the knowledge a child has, compared with that in more mature years (v. 11); and (b) by the knowledge which we have looking through a glass – an imperfect medium – compared with that which we have in looking closely and directly at an object without any medium (v. 12).[50]

We tend to reject the idea that verse 9 speaks of human knowledge, for such a thought has not been the subject of discussion in the context. The context speaks of spiritual gifts.

(2) A better suggestion is that each person, in his own place and function in the body, exercising his particular spiritual gift, still presented God's word, but "in part" meant that only a part of the whole message was given. So explained, the verse makes a contribution to the argument. One author put it like this:

> Here we have the reason why the gifts of knowledge and prophesy were to cease. As then exercised, they were partial and imperfect, and therefore must pass away when the state of perfection arrived. The most that the most endowed could boast of, were but momentary glimpses, whether they were into the mysteries of the spiritual world around them, or into the future beyond them.[51]

No one person with the gift of knowledge could explain all of God's new covenant will to the listeners. All the gifts together might give a more complete picture, but no one gifted person alone could give the complete revelation. In the early days of the church, men were given the new covenant revelation in bits and pieces. It remained for the apostles and prophets to unfold the "mysteries" and share the "knowledge" – until the complete body of truth had been expounded and inculcated.

---

their gifts? Could they not reason in reply to Paul, 'We'll keep on for the present with our gifts – we'll worry about love when the time comes'? (At the conclusion his study, Thomas R. Edgar, "The Cessation of Sign Gifts," *Bib Sac* 145 [Oct-Dec 1988], p.371-386, writes, "In every attempt to prove that the New Testament gifts exist today, the charismatic movement fails.")

[50] Barnes, *op. cit.*, p.254.

[51] Kling, *op. cit.*, p.271.

And we prophesy in part -- This does not mean that the Corinthians, exercising their spiritual gift of prophesy, gave the truths of Christianity imperfectly. Rather, it says that out of the whole of the truths of God, those spiritually endowed knew and preached only a few of them. Picture several people at work assembling a picture puzzle. Each person has a part or two in his hand. When he adds his part, you still do not have the whole picture as you will be able to see it when all the pieces are in place. In a similar way, only a part of the divine picture was seen, when each person had finished with his inspired message for the day.

13:10 -- *but when the perfect comes, the partial will be done away.*

But when the perfect comes -- The Greek word translated "perfect" is *teleion*, something fully developed, mature, complete.[52] Each time we come to *teleion* we must let the context determine what is "complete" or "perfect" or "mature" as contrasted to what is incomplete/imperfect/immature. What is the thing which is "perfect" in this context? (It is a neuter construction, "the perfect thing" or "the complete thing.")

(1) Many writers answer this question by making "perfect" a reference to heaven or to the second coming of Jesus. The verse then teaches that when the final consummation is reached, then the miraculous gifts will be done away. Implicit in this interpretation is belief that the miraculous gifts will last all through the church age.[53] Defenders of this view give the following arguments to corroborate their conclusion: (a) Appeal is made to verse 12 for support, where it speaks of "knowing face to face." It is very hard to make verse 12 refer to this age, they argue. (b) It is alleged that words related to *teleion*, namely *telos* and *teleō*, are used when speaking of the second coming. Therefore, the related word used here might do likewise. Weighing heavily against this interpretation of "perfect" is: (a) Why would Paul use a neuter form ("the perfect") if he were making reference to Christ's second advent, or to heaven? (b) In the context "perfect" is contrasted with "in part." Making "perfect" a reference to heaven destroys this contrast.[54] (c) "Who can believe Paul was trying to control the outrageous abuses of spiritual gifts in Corinth by assuring them that all these miraculous gifts would disappear when they all got to heaven" (now known to be some 2000 years later)?[55]

---

[52] We have had the word before in 1 Corinthians 2:6, where because of the context it was translated "mature." In a similar way, the word is translated "mature" in Hebrews 5:14.

[53] Gordon Fee, *The First Epistle to the Corinthians*, New International Commentary on the New Testament Series (Grand Rapids: Eerdmans, 1987), an ordained Assemblies of God preacher, represents Pentecostal views very well. So does Wayne Grudem, *The Gift of Prophecy in 1 Corinthians* (Lanham, MD: University Press, 1982), who includes a refutation of Warfield's classical exposition of the cessationist arguments, but who, given his involvement in the Vineyard Ministries, is hardly a disinterested witness.

[54] If these verses (8-13) mean that the spiritual gifts will last 2000+ years after all the Corinthians were dead, what dissuasion would these verses be to the way the Corinthians were using them? Is Paul not saying, in your own lifetimes you will live to see "love" lasting longer than the gifts?

[55] Coffman, *op. cit.*, p.218.

(2) A popular explanation given by cessationists is that "perfect" has reference to the time when the New Testament canon was completed around the end of the 1st century AD.[56] Several things may be said in favor of this view: (a) With this view, the term "prophecies" (verse 8) is taken narrowly as referring to direct, inspired revelatory communication from the Holy Spirit. Just like 400 years of silence after Ezra's time marked the close of the Old Testament canon, so the silence of prophets after the apostle John's time marked the close of the New Testament canon. (b) With this view, 1 Corinthians 13:10 would imply something about the formation of the New Testament canon. This commentator has regularly affirmed the canon was accepted when the books were first received, and that what happened in the 3rd and 4th centuries AD was simply a re-affirmation of what had already been decided in the period of the making and accepting of the books of the New Testament canon. (c) With this view, we would understand that all the special aid given by the Spirit – revelation, inspiration, helps, tongues, the special gift of knowledge to help men know the New Testament revelation – was to cease, Paul here teaches, within about a generation after he wrote 1 Corinthians. (d) With this view could be harmonized what the New Testament says elsewhere about the "faith once for all delivered to the saints" (Jude 3). There is something to commend this view as an argument against the position that the gifts mentioned in verses 8-10 continue all through the church age, especially prophetic revelation. For if such revelation is held to continue, then could it not be argued that the *Koran*, the *Book of Mormon*, and *Science and Health* are also to be considered inspired revelations from God? In spite of all its attractive features, several things have been said against the view that the completed New Testament canon is in view in the word "perfect." For instance, some suppose that the indefinite temporal relative adjective *hotan* with the subjunctive verb, "whenever [the *teleion*] should come" (verse 10), suggests Paul felt an indefiniteness about when the "end" he has in mind would come. (In reply, it may be said that Paul is confident that "faith, hope, and love" will last long after the gifts are gone. That means he is not too undecided about the time when the gifts are going to cease. Also note that Paul shows no such indefiniteness in regard to the written Scriptures, or the soon-ending of the special position of the apostles (9:1,2), whose work would be assumed to be coming to an end shortly as the last of them died.[57])

---

[56] The cessationist view was given its classical exposition by B.B. Warfield in *Miracles Yesterday and Today* [1908 title, "Counterfeit Miracles"] (Grand Rapids, Eerdmans, 1953). This view has been modified in a variety of ways by contemporary Reformed and Dispensationalist theologians. L. Philip Barnes, "Miracles, Charismata and Benjamin B. Warfield," *Evangelical Quarterly* 67:3 (1995), p. 219-243, is a critique of Warfield's conclusion by a non-cessationist defender. On the other side of the issue, see Gary W. Derickson, "The Cessation of Healing Miracles in Paul's Ministry," *Bib Sac.* 155 (July-Sept. 1998), p. 299-315.

[57] Some of the above material is adapted from Mare, *op. cit.*, p.269. This commentator has been hesitant to speak about the "completed canon" when explaining "perfect" because there is little agreement about when the New Testament canon was completed. This commentator teaches that the canon was determined when the New Testament Scriptures were first written and accepted by the people to whom they were originally addressed. That period is dated AD 45-96. However, not a few New Testament scholars argue the canon was not officially agreed upon until the 4th century AD. Were we to speak of a "completed canon" and our listeners attach a 4th century date to it, they might be led to suppose Paul is predicting that spiritual gifts will last for several hundred years. That would hardly suit the dissuasion from abuse of the gifts that the context calls for. Nor would it harmonize well with the prevailing belief as early as AD 200 that the spiritual gifts were only for the apostolic period, and had already passed. See the author's booklet *Do All Speak in Tongues?* for documentation from early Christian literature that the spiritual

(3) Since *teleion* can be translated "mature," some have emphasized maturity as the key for explaining the passage. (a) Some speak about the gifts ceasing when each Christian becomes "mature" in his or her own personal faith. Appeal is made to 1 Corinthians 2:6, where the same word is used to mean mature, a full-grown Christian (versus one who was still a babe in understanding). However, to think the contrast here in chapter 13 is between "maturity" and "immaturity" of personal faith will not do, since the contrast has to do with the *gifts* being partial, not the believers themselves. Even though Paul says "*we* know in part," the emphasis is not on the immaturity of individual Corinthians, but on the relative nature of the gifts. (b) Some speak about the gifts ceasing when the body, the congregation, becomes mature. Some of these writers then suggest that only when the "gifts" give way to the rise of a more regular clergy can a congregation be said to be "mature." Others suggest a congregation becomes "mature" when there are no longer dissensions between Jews and Gentiles, but all together form one harmonious congregation.[58]

(4) A fourth view is that "perfect" means "loving perfectly," loving like the context speaks about, where all the characteristics of love are beautifully demonstrated.[59] If "perfect" is "perfect love," then the person who insists on exercising a spiritual gift all his life is saying he has never grown out of spiritual infancy. In this view, the Corinthian desire for gifts reflects their immaturity. When they have come to the fullness of love, they will put away such childish desires.

Now, we shall present the view this commentator believes is most likely correct.

(5) In the context, the thing spoken about is a 'full-grown revelation,' a knowledge about God's plans that is complete as compared to the "in part" currently available to the church; i.e., the "perfect thing" is the *completed New Testament revelation*. When the entire New Testament revelation is given, then the miraculous gifts will cease. In the context, "perfect" is contrasted with "in part." Miraculous gifts are like tugboats. When their job is complete, they return to the shore. They are like scaffolding that is torn down when the building is complete. The implication is that at the time Paul is writing this letter to Corinth (AD 57), the new covenant revelation (made through the apostles) has not yet been completely preached or unfolded. But there was coming a day, soon, when it would be. Christ promised that the Holy Spirit would guide His apostles into "all truth" (John 16:13) – a complete revelation and knowledge.[60] If His promise was fulfilled, then the revelation

---

gifts had ceased by about AD 180 to 200. It is part of Special Study #10 at the end of this volume.

[58] See J.R. McKay, "*To Teleion* in 1 Cor. 13:10," *Restoration Quarterly* 14 (1971), p.168-183, and R. L. Thomas, "Tongues ... Will Cease," *JETS* 17 (1974), p.81-89.

[59] This is the view of Staton, *Spiritual Gifts for Christians Today*. It is also the view adopted by Findlay, Bruce, Holladay, and others.

[60] John 14:26, John 16:13. New Testament prophets and teachers would, under the guidance of and within the parameters of the apostles' teaching, help to unfold and reinforce the truths shared first and wholly with the apostles. As the apostles were enabled to know and reveal more of the new covenant revelation, so the scope and content of the messages delivered by prophets and teachers would grow.

of this "all truth" was completed before the last apostle died.[61]

The partial will be done away -- "The partial" recalls what was written in verse 9 about knowing "in part" and prophesying "in part." We have already commented on "done away" in the notes at verse 8. Its repetition here indicates that the same topic – the only-for-the present nature of the gifts – is still in view. The gifts of knowledge and prophecy and tongues were useful as lamps in the darkness, but they became useless when the bright daylight of the complete revelation had dawned.

13:11 -- *When I was a child, I used to speak as a child, think as a child, reason as a child; when I became a man, I did away with childish things.*

When I was a child -- Verses 11,12 seem to be an analogy to show that the gifts should be expected to cease, just like childish behavior is expected to cease. 'Childhood' is comparable to "in part;" "a man" is comparable to when the 'mature' or "perfect" comes.[62] Paul himself grew from childhood to manhood. "Child" (*nēpios*) denotes a babe, an infant. It refers to the first periods of existence, before the period which we call youth.

I used to speak as a child -- The verb is in the imperfect tense, implying what was the customary or repeated behavior during childhood. During childhood, one seldom hears complete sentences. Instead, what is heard are "parts" of sentences, one or two words, as the child begins to speak words. Too, as little ones learn to speak, their words are often difficult for others besides their parents to understand. (We wonder if there is an aside here to the way the Corinthians were using their gift of tongues.) We are tempted to apply the condition of childhood, in its contentedness with its own prattle and acts and thought, to illustrate the self-centeredness of the Corinthians in the possession and use of their gifts.

---

[61] In fact, it is affirmed that the revelation was completed even before the last books of the New Testament were written on scrolls. What was put in the writings was no different from what the apostles had already been teaching by word of mouth in lesson and sermon. Jude 3 indicates that by AD 75 (the date we give to the writing of Jude) the faith had already been delivered to the saints. So the revelation was complete before the last books were written, or even before they had all been collected.

(This footnote has been written to clarify this commentator's presentation of the "completed revelation" being the "completed thing." It is specifically written to answer an objection to the view here presented, an objection that has often been voiced by those holding one of the other views of "perfect." Others have taken a different approach to counter the presentation herein offered. They have asked, "What is the great difference between 'completed revelation' [the language you prefer] and 'completed canon' [the language others since Warfield have used]?" The unvoiced accusation behind this question is that this commentator's choice of words is just a subtle way of avoiding the language "completed canon" in order to neutralize certain non-cessationist's arguments. Far from an attempt to avoid anything, this commentator has taken pains to present [albeit in brief outline form] how the New Testament writings were first accepted as inspired from the day they were first received, how the canonical ones were collected, and how the collection was then guarded, precisely to counteract the often-heard claims for the late date for the completion of the New Testament canon.)

[62] Perhaps there is more to the comparison. As the child is in the man when he has fully developed, so the messages delivered by knowledge and prophecy will be included in the "completed revelation."

Think as a child -- *Phronein* denotes 'thinking, feeling, inclination.' Babes fix their attention on objects which in later life seem to be of little value. As this analogy is applied to the abuse of gifts at Corinth, can it mean anything if it is not a suggestion that the Corinthians, as they view and exercise their gifts, should expect to quit being children?[63] In case the point is missed, he will write later, 'Stop being children in your thinking!' (1 Corinthians 14:20).

Reason as a child -- *Logizesthai* can be translated 'reason, judge, to purpose, behave.' A child's thoughts and plans and argumentations are puerile, and are often shortsighted. Sir Isaac Newton, just before his death, made this remark, "I do not know what I may appear to the world: but to myself I seem to have been only a boy playing on the sea-shore, and diverting myself now and then by finding a smoother pebble or a prettier shell than ordinary, while the great ocean lay all undiscovered before me."[64] Were not the Corinthians doing something analogous as they selfishly exercised their gifts in the public services?[65] Were they not missing what was really important?

When I became a man, I did away with childish things -- Paul no longer speaks or thinks or reasons as he did 30 or 40 years before. The heart of the comparison is not between the true and the false. Rather, it is between the relatively unimportant things that occupy the mind and action of children, and the more weighty matters that adults heed and ponder. The thoughts and feelings of a child may be correct as far as they go – sufficient for childhood, but inadequate for manhood. The spiritual gifts were not wrong and sinful, but the Corinthians were acting like little children as they insisted on displaying their gifts with little thought of anyone but themselves and their momentary personal gratification. The gifts like prophecy and knowledge will be "done away" (*katērgēka*) when the complete "revelation" (1 Corinthians 1:7) has come.

13:12 -- *For now we see in a mirror dimly, but then face to face; now I know in part, but then I shall know fully just as I also have been fully known.*

For -- With "for" Paul makes application of verse 11's analogy, while at the same time introducing another analogy, or illustration, to show the 'partial' nature of their knowledge during the age of spiritual gifts.[66]

---

[63] The analogy in verse 11 picks up the themes of "in part" and "the complete," and even picks up the verb "done away" that was found in verse 10.

[64] Quoted in Barnes, *op. cit.*, p.255.

[65] Perhaps there is an allusion in "speak, think, reason" to the three spiritual gifts of tongues, prophecy, and knowledge.

[66] This interpretation hinges on taking verse 9, as we have done, as speaking of spiritual gifts.

Now we see in a mirror dimly -- "Now" (*arti*) equals 'now during the age when spiritual gifts are extant,' i.e., contemporary with Paul and his readers.

There is some question as to the meaning of *di' esoptrou*. Some render it "mirror," while others prefer "glass." Those who prefer "glass" write about the opaque 'windows' made out of mica (or isinglass) or some other translucent or semi-transparent substance.[67] While allowing some light through the thin silicate sheets, the view was far from clear and distinct.[68] Those who prefer "mirror" call attention to the fact the finest bronze mirrors in antiquity were made at Corinth. Ancient mirrors were of polished metal,[69] and Corinthian mirrors were famous. But the best of them would give an imperfect and somewhat distorted reflection;[70] think of the reflection one gets from the bottom of a tin can. To see a friend's face in a polished bronze mirror[71] would be very different from looking at the friend face-to-face.

Instead of "dimly," the marginal note offers "in a riddle" as a translation for *en ainigmati*. This Greek word appears only here in the New Testament. The word does occur in the LXX at Numbers 12:8, where we are told God spoke to Moses "mouth to mouth" and not "in riddles" ["dark speeches," KJV]. God spoke to the other Old Testament prophets through visions or dreams (Numbers 12:6), but the pictures they got of God's truth were not as clear as the direct words to Moses. Weymouth tried to catch the idea in *en ainigmati* when he translated "For the present we see things as if in a mirror, and are puzzled." The point of the comparison here in Corinthians is found in the fact that men could see only an indistinct image, not the real thing, in the years before that which is perfect (verse 10) came. "Enigma" (*en ainigmati*) says some of the things that were heard as the spiritual gifts were exercised were 'puzzling.'[72] The knowledge we get about ourselves looking at ourselves in a bronze mirror is like the knowledge learned from the prophets and gifts of knowledge – it was partial.

---

[67] The ancients did have glass. Many glass vessels have been discovered in the ruins of Pompeii and in ancient shipwrecks. However, there is another Greek word *(hualinos)* for this kind of glass.

[68] To speak of a window made of *lapis specularis* (mica) is inconsistent with the usage of *esoptron*, which always means "mirror," the window of *lapis specularis* being *dioptra*. Alford, *op. cit.*, p.588.

[69] The art of silvering glass to make mirrors was not discovered till the 13th century AD.

[70] In the article "Corinth in Paul's Time" (*BAR* 14/3, p.17) there is a stunning picture of a bronze mirror from the 1st century AD. In an excavated bronze foundry in Corinth, archaeologists discovered an oven for heating the metal, a bench for working it, and channels that once brought water from the spring of Peirene.

[71] The preposition here is *dia*. Translators cannot agree whether to translate it 'by means of' or 'through' (the image appearing to be behind the mirror).

[72] Remember, the Thessalonians got the time of the second coming wrong as they read 1 Thessalonians. Somehow they came up with the idea that the return of Christ was imminent. Paul had to write 2 Thessalonians to correct some of their mistaken conclusions. With the completed revelation, men would not make the same mistake the Thessalonians initially made.

But then -- *Tote* points to when – when that which is perfect is come (verse 9), when the gifts have ceased, when we no longer have to prophesy "in part" because of possession of the completed revelation. "Then" is some time after Paul's day (which he characterizes as "now" earlier in verse 12).

Face to face -- We shall have the full, completed revelation, as when one looks upon an object openly and not through an obscure and dark medium.

Now I know in part -- "Now" is *arti* in the Greek, just as it was earlier in this verse. The word for "know" is the simple verb *ginōskō*. "In part" reminds us of what was written in verse 9.

But then I shall know fully just as I also have been fully known -- "Then" (*tote*) points to the same time in this phrase as it did in the previous one – i.e., some time after Paul's day when the completed revelation had been given. What is Paul writing about when he says "I shall know"? (1) Some, forgetting the context, or having interpreted verse 9 as non-supernatural, say, 'Every man's uninspired knowledge will be made more complete. His present knowledge of the universe, rockets, etc., is nothing compared to what it will be.' But such an interpretation ignores the context which deals with spiritual gifts, including the gift of knowledge. (2) Some say, in harmony with the context, every man's knowledge of God and His ways will be more complete, because of the completed revelation. They will better understand the Old Testament prophecies. They will better understand the various parts of the New Testament revelation when they have it all before them, so it can be compared. The verb translated "fully known" is a compound verb, *epignōskō*. The addition of the preposition *epi* normally would be understood to strengthen or intensify the verb (*ginōskō* in this instance) to which it is affixed. Thus, we agree with the *International Critical Commentary* which states,

> It is difficult to believe that here the compound is not meant to indicate more complete knowledge than the simple verb ... and [we agree with] with Lightfoot, who wrote, "The compound *epignosis* is an advance upon *gnosis*, denoting a larger and more thorough knowledge ... So, too, Paul himself contrasts *ginoskein*, *gnosis*, with *epignoskein*, *epignosis*, as the partial with the complete, in two passages, Romans 1:21,28, and 1 Corinthians 13:12.[73]

The verb is an aorist passive form in the Greek.[74] The implied agent who did the 'knowing' is either God the Father or the Lord Jesus Christ. The aorist tense points to a time in the past. Commentators offer various suggestions as to what time in particular Paul has in mind. The view that there is an oblique reference here to God's electing grace

---

[73] Robertson and Plummer, *op. cit.*, p.299.

[74] The KJV has unwarrantedly treated this aorist tense as a present tense when it reads "as also I AM known." This does not help the reader grasp the import of what Paul actually wrote.

back in eternity before He created, is hardly warranted by the context. Perhaps it speaks of God's knowledge of each of us prior to the time of our conversion. He knew fully and directly exactly what fallen men would need, and He went about to provide it. In God's completed revelation men can see how precisely God's knowledge fit the situation, and precisely how men are to respond to His overtures for our salvation.

13:13 -- *But now abide faith, hope, love, these three; but the greatest of these is love.*

But now -- Earlier, the Greek word translated "now" was *arti*. Here the word is *nuni*. "Now" in verse 13 has been taken in two ways. (1) Some give it a *temporal* significance. Taken this way, the "now" of verse 13 picks up the "nows" (in the age of spiritual gifts) of verse 12. For the present, all three qualities (faith, hope, and love) abide – whereas the "gifts" are temporary. And love is the greater, because it will last longer than the other qualities. (2) Some give it a *logical* significance. "Now, in conclusion ...." The "so" of the RSV catches logical force of *nuni*. This pictures verse 13 as being the conclusion or the summary of the paragraph just ending. "When all the spiritual gifts have been done away with by the advent of that which is perfect, there will remain still these three things that abide long after – faith, hope, and love." Whether we take it as temporal or logical depends on our view of the entire passage. Of course, those who believe "perfect" speaks of heaven are wont to take "now" in a temporal sense. They picture Paul as contrasting life in the here and now with that in the hereafter.[75] Those who think that the "perfect" thing is the completed revelation are obliged to take "now" in a logical sense.

Abide faith, hope, love, these three -- The verb *menei*, "abides," or "remains," is present tense, indicating permanency, as compared with things that are temporary and pass away. Being first in the clause, "abide" is strongly emphatic, as opposed to the previously mentioned things which are 'being done away.' In the Greek, "abide" is singular, and it is not a slip in grammar. What we must do is mentally repeat the verb with each noun – "faith remains," "hope remains," "love remains." "The three graces (virtues) are a triplet distinguished by a durability which the brilliant *charismata*, so coveted by the Corinthians, do not possess."[76] The virtues continue to "abide" or "remain" long after the miraculous spiritual gifts have ceased. We might have expected Paul to write only about "love" in this context. Instead, to "love" (the topic of this chapter) he adds "faith" and "hope."[77] Adding "these three" after listing their names is an effective way of emphasizing the sur-

---

[75] This commentator thinks this is a flawed explanation of verse 13, as the notes will show.

[76] Robertson and Plummer, *op. cit.*, p.300.

[77] What Paul does here reminds us of what Jesus did one day. When trying to correct Pharisees, He spoke about "justice and mercy and faithfulness" as being more important than simply the act of tithing even the tiniest herbs and seeds (Matthew 23:23). Paul's addition of "faith" and "hope" seem to say the Corinthians' abuse of gifts is inimical to these important Christian virtues – both in the one who selfishly exercises the gift, and in the one who was supposed to be benefitted by the gift (when properly exercised).

passing importance of these virtues.[78] "Faith" here likely means 'fidelity to God' or 'fidelity to Christ.' Such faithfulness is one of Paul's dominant themes. Will the Corinthians change their ways so that their participation in the body-life of their congregation (12:12ff) reflects what the Creator intended? "Hope" is "a compound emotion, made up of a *desire* for an object and an *expectation* of obtaining it."[79] It is not difficult to understand why Paul included this virtue as one of his triplets. "In the first centuries, Christianity made a habit of taking people from the depressed classes – slaves, women, outcasts, sinners needing forgiveness – and giving them a living hope. That hope was an anchor for the soul (Hebrews 6:19,20)."[80] Men cannot live without it. So how will the Christian behave towards his brother who needs a reason to hope? Will he display encouraging behavior and loving concern that will fan the flames of hope in the discouraged and struggling? Will the Corinthians begin to use their gifts in such a way that men's hopes soar? "Love" has been explained in notes on verses 1-3 of this chapter as being 'doing what is spiritually best for the other person.'

Against the charismatic interpretation that "perfect" (verse 10) refers to the second coming is the powerful statement of this verse that the graces (faith, hope, love) abide longer than the gifts. There is hardly any way one can say that the graces last into eternity after the Second Coming (which they would have to do, if "perfect" is the second coming). When folk are in heaven, 'walking by faith' gives way to 'walking by sight' (2 Corinthians 5:7). Hope gives way to fruition (Romans 8:24,25). It appears that verse 13 is against the idea that "perfect" of verse 10 is the second coming, and that the miraculous spiritual gifts can be expected to last until Jesus returns.

Also against the charismatic interpretation is the fact that there are passages that make no sense unless the spiritual gifts were temporary, for the infancy of the church, just as cessationists teach. (1) Matthew 10:17-20 as compared with 1 Peter 3:15. In one place Christians are instructed not to plan ahead what they will say when on trial. In the other they are commanded to carefully plan ahead. Why the need to plan, unless the gifts available earlier are passing? (2) Mark 16:17-20. Written about AD 68, Mark tells us in verse 20 that what Jesus had predicted some 38 years earlier (these gifts will follow) had actually occurred. The participle translated "confirming" is a present tense, indicating action contemporaneous with the past tense verb "preached." If the gifts were still continuing, the past tense verb would have been the wrong verb tense to use. (3) Hebrews

---

[78] This is not the only passage in the New Testament where "faith, hope, and love" are emphasized. See Romans 5:2-5; Galatians 5:5-6; Colossians 1:4-5; 1 Thessalonians 1:3, 5:8; Hebrews 6:10-12; and 1 Peter 1:21-22. Just as Jesus highlighted certain important qualities from Micah 6:8 when talking to an Old Testament audience (Matthew 23:23), so the New Testament writers constantly highlight the importance of these three virtues.

[79] Barnes, *op. cit.*, p.257.

[80] Morris, *op. cit.*, p.189. Morris adds, "It is not a gain, but a grievous loss, that so often today Christians are men whose hope is nothing other than the hope that worldly men have."

2:3,4. Hebrews shows the "miracles and distributions of the Spirit" had as their purpose the confirmation of the apostles' message. The aorist tense "confirmed" indicates the actual confirmation was past when Hebrews was written – a statement that is true only if the confirming gifts were temporary and had already passed away. (4) If we still have the miraculous gifts, then we must say Christ's promises about the Spirit leading the apostles into all truth (John 14:26; 16:13) have failed. But Christ's promises have not failed. Peter says so in 2 Peter 1:3. By the time Peter writes, he can say Christ's "divine power [the Holy Spirit?] has granted to us [us apostles?] everything pertaining to life and godliness." The apostles had been led into all truth. The "perfect" must have been something "completed" within the lifetime of the apostles. Therefore we speak of the "completed New Testament revelation." When that revelation is complete, the gifts will be done away (verses 8-10 have said). Verse 13 indicates the graces (faith, hope, and love), too, will last longer ("abide") than the gifts. The graces will last till the return of Christ and the end of the age (but not the "gifts"!).

But the greatest of these is love -- In the Greek, the word "greatest" is comparative ('greater'), not superlative, as the KJV, ASV, and NASB have it.[81] In what way is love greater? We can only guess, for Paul makes no statement. Love is the climax of all the other virtues, and is one of the last ones to be developed in any Christian's walk with Christ (2 Peter 1:5-7). When it is developed, it is the "perfect bond of unity" (Colossians 3:14), the very thing the divided and factious congregation at Corinth needed. The last word in this chapter (in the Greek) fittingly is love. Love occupies the supreme place. In the face of the self-centered regard the Corinthians had for the spectacular, Paul is saying, 'The really important thing is not whether you have this or that spiritual gift, but that you display these three virtues, faith, hope, and love. And there is nothing greater than love. That is why it is desperately urgent that you let love be the motive behind your decisions whether or not to exercise your gifts in the public assembly.'

Paul has now concluded his presentation of the principles that God intends should guide the Christian's behavior when he is in the public assembly. In chapter 14 Paul will make application of these principles to the abuses that were marring the life of the congregation at Corinth.

---

[81] Perhaps in New Testament times the distinction between Greek comparatives and superlatives was beginning to fade from use. See Robertson, *Grammar*, p.668.

2. Applications of the principles to the abuses of spiritual gifts. 14:1-40

a. Application #1 -- Edification. 14:1-5

> *Summary:* In this chapter the subject of the abuse of spiritual gifts in the public assembly is concluded. If one recognizes the diversity of the gifts, the unity of the body, and the absolute necessity of acting in a loving manner, he will exercise his gift only when he is aware it will edify the congregation.[1]

14:1 -- *Pursue love, yet desire earnestly spiritual gifts, but especially that you may prophesy.*

Pursue love -- "Pursue" (*diōkō*) is the word used of a hunter chasing his game, or of men pressing on toward the goal in a race. "Pursue" has the idea of pursuit with persistence; the present tense verb indicates a never-terminating pursuit. The Greek reads "the love." There is an article in the Greek, the article of previous reference. It calls attention to the "love" just identified in chapter 13:1ff. We *pursue* (an old English word that has lost its original meaning) love when we earnestly desire it, strive to possess it, cultivate it in our hearts, set our hearts earnestly to practice love. The result that occurs when a person who genuinely loves exercises his spiritual gifts will be identified in the following verses by the word 'edify' – build up the church.

Yet desire earnestly spiritual *gifts* -- The Greek particle *de* is translated "and" in the KJV, "yet" in the NASB. The KJV translation causes us to think that "love" is in the same class as the "spiritual gifts." This may not be right. The ASV/NASB treat the particle as adversative, and by so doing place "love" in a category different from spiritual gifts. Paul seems to be saying that *after* you have love as the basic motive underpinning your behavior, *then* it is proper to seek to exercise your spiritual gifts, and especially is it proper to exercise the gift of prophecy. The words here at 14:1 are similar to what Paul wrote in 12:31. In 12:31 the word was *charismata*. Here the word Paul used was *pneumatika*, a word explained in comments at 12:1 and following. The word "gifts" added in italics in our versions is correct in light of the use of "gifts" at 12:4. The Greek verb "desire" can be either an indicative form or an imperative. Rather than simply writing 'you are desiring spiritual gifts,' we think the imperative is the intended force of the verb – 'Desire to use the gifts you have in a loving fashion!'[2] As we explained at 12:31, we are of the conviction that these imperatives teach the readers how to *use* the gifts they *already had* from the Lord; they are not instructions on how to get them in the first place. In the age when the

---

[1] Commentators have proposed different outlines for this chapter versus the one we are offering. A different outline suggests that verses 1-19 are the first and main portion of the chapter and are intended to show the superiority of prophecy (inspired preaching) over tongues (as they were being used at Corinth). This superiority is supported by two series of arguments (6-11 and 14-19). These two series of arguments are connected by two exhortations (verses 12,13).

[2] M.C. Tenney may be correct when he observes that the verb "follow" in the first part of verse 1 is a stronger word than "desire." The implication is that the gift is secondary to the attitude (love) with which the gift is used.

gifts were needed and useful, of course it would have been proper to want and use the abilities God made available through the laying on of an apostle's hands.³ The present tense verbs emphasize continuous action. Habitually pursue love! Habitually desire to use your gifts! Habitually emphasize prophecy!

But especially that you may prophesy -- Paul instructs the Corinthians that when it comes time to exercise their gifts in the public assembly, they should prefer the gift of prophecy to the gift of tongues.⁴ As human bodies have a need for all their members, so there is a need for all the spiritual gifts in the church at Corinth. However, some are more to be desired in the public assembly (because they benefit more people, 12:31), and thus are to be given preference. Paul's instructions about 'desiring spiritual gifts' (here and at 12:31), since they bracket the 'love chapter,' seem to be an exhortation to the Corinthians to change their attitudes about how to exercise their spiritual gifts. Be motivated by love! In your congregational meetings, desire to use those spiritual gifts which will benefit the most people. By this criterion, prophecy is the gift more to be desired than tongues.⁵ This is not belittling the gift of tongues; it was a God-given gift. But as a regular thing at the public assembly, a message in the language of the people (prophecy) would benefit more people than a message in a foreign language (tongues).

14:2 -- *For one who speaks in a tongue does not speak to men but to God; for no one understands, but in his spirit he speaks mysteries.*

For -- What Paul now writes makes it reasonably certain that the abuse of tongues was one of the Corinthians' major problems in the exercise of their gifts during the public assembly. Apparently those so gifted were insisting that they 'speak in a tongue' even when there was no need for the gift, and when there were not even any translators functioning. The motives behind their actions were something other than love for their brethren. Thus their behavior was to be faulted and Paul orders it stopped. Verses 2-5 show the superiority of inspired preaching (prophecy) to speaking in tongues during the public assembly. "For" introduces an explanation of what was said in verse 1, "especially that you prophesy." What value is to be attached to the gift of tongues as the Corinthians were exercising them? Very little, in in comparison with prophecy.

---

³ The Corinthian church members already had the gifts and were abusing them in the public assembly. The gifts were given by God (12:11), not received in response to any worshiper's desire. But the gifts could be exercised under the control of the person gifted, and thus we have the instructions in these chapters about exercising the gifts they already had, only in a loving fashion.

⁴ The first word in the Greek is *de*, the same word with which the second clause of this verse began. It should not be translated in a way that leaves the impression that "prophesying" is not one of the spiritual gifts, for that would be completely out of context with the teaching contained in the three chapters now being studied about abuse of spiritual gifts. Nor is it proper to use this repeated particle as proof that there were two different kinds or degrees of "prophecy" in the early church – one of which was available to all Christians, and one of which was not (12:29). See this matter discussed in notes at 11:4-5 and 12:5,10.

⁵ See notes at 1 Corinthians 11:4-5 and 12:10 on what the word "prophesy" means. It is inspired preaching in the language of the people. It was not the delivery of a carefully prepared sermon, but the spontaneous uttering of words directly inspired by God (see 1 Corinthians 14:30).

One who speaks in a tongue -- For the evidence that "speaks in a tongue" (*lalōn glōssē*) means to speak in a human language which was foreign to the speaker, and often foreign to most of the audience in the assembly, see the special study on tongues at the close of chapter 2 in the author's commentary on *Acts*.[6] The KJV reads "*unknown* tongue." The ASV is correct in omitting the word "unknown," since it has been used to prove the "tongues" at Corinth were a 'heavenly language' unknown to any men on earth. There is nothing in the Greek corresponding to the word "unknown" that appears in the KJV at verses 2,4,14,19,27. The KJV translators were somewhat right in their understanding of the passage, for the languages spoken by the Corinthians were unknown to those in the assembly who had to continually listen as the tongues speakers displayed their 'talents.' As already indicated in notes above, this verse, this commentator feels, is designed to show that prophecy (the faculty of speaking intelligibly in the local language, for the edification of the church) is of more value in the public assembly than the gift of speaking a foreign language (the way the Corinthians were using the gift).

Does not speak unto men, but to God -- The tongues speaker "does not speak unto men," that is, he does not speak so that the people present, within hearing, can understand him. The context implies a speaking done in a public assembly, where men and women were present, and heard the sound, but didn't understand what was being spoken. "Speaking unto men" was the proper use for tongues, and was what the Corinthians should have been doing, if there were folk present who were fluent in the language that was being spoken. But at Corinth they were not using the gift properly. As a result, Paul says, they were speaking "to God." God understood what the tongues speaker was saying, because God is fluent in all human languages. Though no man in the audience may have been fluent in the language the speaker was speaking, yet God understood what the words meant.[7] Paul is not undervaluing the power of speaking in foreign languages when foreigners fluent in the language spoken were present in the assembly, or when they went to the docks or the street corners to preach to foreigners (see verse 22). It was only when it was needless, when all present spoke one language, that the gift of tongues (a language foreign to the

---

[6] Because of the difficult nature of the material being discussed in this context, a number of attempts have been made to explain it. Some have said the tongues at Corinth were languages. Some have said it was emotional babbling. One author has tried to take a position halfway between the two. Says he, whenever "tongue" (singular) is used, it speaks of human-inspired gibberish; and whenever "tongues" (plural) is used, it speaks of Holy Spirit-inspired languages. A valiant try, in our opinion, but one has only to read the 14th chapter through, attempting to substitute such meanings for the singulars and the plurals, to see that such a method of explaining Paul's meaning would have Paul changing subjects every half-verse, or so. We do not feel that any such distinction was intended by Paul when he used the singular sometimes, and the plural sometimes.

[7] Charismatics and Pentecostals use this verse in an attempt to show that "tongues" at Corinth were a prayer language, for use when communicating with God. The difficult thing for this at-face-value handling of "speaks unto God" is that some unusual meaning must be found for "mysteries" in the latter part of this verse – "mysteries" being the content of what the person is saying when he speaks in tongues. The usual meaning of "mystery" – God's revelation being made plain in this New Testament age – would hardly be the content of what was being spoken back to God in prayer. Hardly can it mean the person is speaking something that is mysterious even to God. Nor will it do to say that a tongue speaker's 'strange words' are mysterious to bystanders who may hear the prayer. One cannot speak of tongues being for private devotions, and at the same time talk about bystanders overhearing the devotions.

present location) was of little value.[8] The way the Corinthians were using their "tongues" – in a way that was essentially selfish and just showing off – is what Paul is objecting to.

For no one understands -- A verse or phrase that begins with "for" is intended either to be a reason for something just said, or a further explanation of something just said. This "for" explains why, even though the tongues speaker was speaking in a congregational meeting, he was "not speaking unto men, but to God." The reason it was not "speaking unto men" is because none of the people present understood the foreign language the speaker was using. The word translated "understands" is *akouō*, and it can have two meanings: either "hear" or "understand."[9] Here, we think the meaning "understand" is the correct one. The man, speaking in tongues as they were doing it at Corinth, in reality speaks not unto men but only unto God. "For no one understands" makes plain why this is. The people hear the speaking but, not knowing the language, do not comprehend the meaning of what is said. "No one understands" does not mean absolutely no one, as the following verses will show. One who has the gift of interpretation, i.e., who is conversant with the particular foreign language used, would understand. Verses 27,28 indicate the possible presence of an interpreter, while verses 5,13 indicate the speaker himself/herself may be able to act as interpreter. But in this opening statement, these ramifications of the subject are not touched. Paul pictures a scenario where the audience in general does not understand the strange, foreign language. In that case, such a speaker, therefore, spoke to God. Of all the persons present and able to hear the speaker, God alone understands.[10]

But by the Spirit (NASB margin) -- The word *pneumati* here is dative singular. When the word *pneumati* in the New Testament refers to the Holy Spirit, there is usually a qualifying word, like the preposition "in" (*en*) preceding it; or we may find the article "the" preceding the noun. Not so here. So, interpreters are divided, some thinking it should be "spirit" and others thinking it should be "Spirit."

(1) Some would use the lower case "s" – spirit – the man's own human spirit. Note the NASB text, "but in *his* spirit he speaks mysteries." (a) W. Harold Mare has argued that *pneumati* is not to be understood as referring to the Holy Spirit, since He is not mentioned in the context.[11] But Mare forgets that the whole context is dealing with

---

[8] Barnes, *op. cit.*, p.260.

[9] Cf. Acts 9:7 and 22:9, where we learn that the men with Paul (on the Damascus Road) heard the sound, but did not understand what the voice said.

[10] As indicated in comments on chapter 12, this phrase has been used by some to prove the tongues at Corinth were different from the tongues at Pentecost, where all men understood what was being spoken (by the apostles) in tongues. But as verse 16ff will show, the reason they were not understood at Corinth was not because the "tongues" were different, but because no one was present in the services whose mother tongue was like the ones being spoken. There were people present at Pentecost whose mother tongues were being spoken, and therefore at Pentecost there was understanding of what the tongue speakers said.

[11] Mare, *op. cit.*, p.272.

spiritual gifts, powers and manifestations of the Holy Spirit. (b) Zodhiates has argued the tongues at Corinth were not like the tongues at Pentecost. He believes those at Pentecost were Holy Spirit-inspired, but that those at Corinth were human ('spirit') in origin.[12] *Reply*: Not only do we question his explanation of "spirit" in verses 12 and 32, but we would also remind the reader that chapter 14 is not all Paul has to say about the gift of tongues. He also speaks about this gift and others in chapters 12 and 13, where we plainly have references to the Holy Spirit. (c) Staton[13] takes it as small "s." But his definition of "spirit" as being man's self-consciousness is somewhat suspect.

(2) Others would capitalize the "s" – Spirit – the Holy Spirit. (a) The context since chapter 12 is speaking of the miraculous gifts conferred by the Holy Spirit. (b) The expression "to speak *in*" or "speak *by*" the Spirit is an established Scriptural phrase meaning to speak under the guidance of the Holy Spirit. (c) If we were to read "spirit" (small "s"), this phrase "by the spirit" (which is distinct from the "understanding" in verse 2) must then refer to a man's *affections*, which does not suit the passage.

So, this commentator concludes the reference is to the Holy Spirit. Paraphrased, Paul writes, 'The man speaking with tongues is not understood, even though he is guided by the Holy Spirit while he is speaking.' The NEB has, "He no doubt is inspired, but he speaks mysteries." The Good News Bible has, "He speaks ... by the power of the Spirit."

He speaks mysteries -- In Bible terms, a "mystery" was something not clearly revealed in the Old Testament times, but now in the New Testament times it is clearly revealed. This is the usual Scriptural meaning of the word.[14] There is no compelling reason to give the word a different meaning in this place.[15] As the speakers exercised their gift of tongues, speaking as the Spirit gave them utterance, they were unfolding (in foreign languages) the things that had not been clearly revealed in Old Testament times. In other words, explaining the hidden "mysteries" made up the content of what the tongues speakers were saying. Of course, what the speaker was saying might well be those 'truths about God, once hidden, but now revealed' – but as long as there was no interpreter and no one present who understood the speech, there was no revelation, and therefore no advantage to the hearers.

---

[12] Spiros Zodhiates' paragraph (*Tongues? An Exegetical Commentary on 1 Corinthians 12-14* (Chattanooga, TN: AMG Publications, 1974), p.45 reads: "In 1 Corinthians 14:1-33, where Paul discusses the practice of speaking with tongues in the Corinthian church, he makes no reference to the Holy Spirit. True, the word 'spirit' is mentioned seven times, but in each case Paul is referring to the spirit of man and not the Holy Spirit. [See verses 2,12,14,15,15b,16, and 32.] In later studies we shall fully explain these verses and our statement that they refer to man's spirit and not to God's. Could it be that this whole practice of speaking with tongues, as engaged in by the Corinthians, had nothing to do with the Holy Spirit and His work? The manifestations of man's spirit are not necessarily the manifestations of God's Spirit."

[13] Knofel Staton, *Spiritual Gifts for Christians*, p.76.

[14] See notes at 1 Corinthians 2:7, 4:1, 13:2, 15:51.

[15] For example, there is no real need to explain "mysteries" as being an explanation of why "no one understands." Such an explanation presumes that, since the whole clause begins with the weak adversative *de*, the point of the phrase is that what the person was speaking in the foreign language was a mystery (hidden) to the listeners who did not understand the language.

14:3 -- *But one who prophesies speaks to men for edification and exhortation and consolation.*

But one who prophesies -- "But" marks a contrast between tongues (as the Corinthians were using the gift) and prophecy.[16] Unlike untranslated tongues (which benefited only the speaker), prophecy edified the whole congregation. "Prophecy" is used here as it has been throughout 1 Corinthians. It refers to one who speaks under the influence of inspiration in the common language of the hearers. We see these similarities and differences between prophecy and tongues: both were under the influence of the Holy Spirit, both might speak the same truths, and both might occupy a necessary place in the church. But the language of the one – if not intelligible to the assembled worshipers – would not edify the worshipers as would the other, which was spoken in the local language.

Speaks to men -- The prophet speaks and was understood by those who were present. The prophet spoke in the local language of the audience being addressed.

For edification and exhortation and consolation -- This is one of the key verses in the New Testament which indicates what the gift of prophecy was. "Edification" (*oikodomēn*) in this place refers to a building up of the spiritual life – a building up of the Christian faith. When the prophet speaks there is indoctrination and enlightenment, help for the spiritually undeveloped. "Edification" in the Biblical sense of the term is every presentation of divine truth which increases and strengthens faith and spiritual life. *Paraklēsin* has several facets – encouragement, comfort, exhortation (appeal).[17] "Exhor-tation" is a stimulus to move forward. It is a sharp call to show a person what his duty is and urge him to do it. "Consolation" (*paramuthian*) is the quieting, cheering word spoken under the influence of the Spirit to the afflicted and sorrowing.[18] A man needs help in those situations – not a beating. "Consolation intends to lead the Christian to understand the nature of what he must endure, and to enable him to hold out cheerfully and valiantly unto the end."[19] Because Paul used these three words (edification, exhortation, consolation), we learn that "prophecy" means more than simply to predict the future.

14:4 – *One who speaks in a tongue edifies himself; but one who prophesies edifies the church.*

One who speaks in a tongue edifies himself -- Paul is continuing his comparison of the usefulness of tongues (as the Corinthians were exercising them) over and against prophecy.

---

[16] Those who opted for small "s" in "in *his* spirit he speaks mysteries" are likely to comment that "but" here marks a contrast between uninspired speech by the tongues speaker, and the inspired speech of the prophet. This commentator has serious doubts, in this context, that either tongues or prophecy were uninspired actions.

[17] See notes at Acts 4:36 (where this word is used to describe Barnabas), and at John 14:16 where a cognate word, used of the Holy Spirit, is translated "Helper."

[18] Cf. Philippians 2:1 and 1 Thessalonians 2:11 on the meanings of "exhortation" and "comfort."

[19] Lenski, *op. cit.*, p.578.

The comparison simply put is this: If you speak in a foreign language which no one present can understand, then none of the assembled listeners will be edified. But if you prophesy (in the vernacular of everyone), then all the listeners may be built up.[20] "Edifies himself" is contrasted in this verse with "edifies the church." One person is benefitted versus a whole congregation being benefited. In the greater number being benefited is the superiority of prophecy to tongues.

Some have questioned, in light of verse 2 ("no one understands") how a man speaking in tongues could "edify himself." (1) Perhaps "no one understands" means none of the listeners would know, but only the tongues speaker would know what he was saying, and thus would be personally edified. Verse 5 indicates that the one speaking in tongues could sometimes (perhaps often) translate what he himself said. This being the case, he would know the content of the message he had just delivered in a foreign language, even though the hearers (the way the gift was used at Corinth) might not understand the language they heard. Knowing the content of the message that he had received by revelation from God would certainly have an edifying effect on the speaker, unless he is absolutely insensitive to the leading of the Spirit. However, verse 28 indicates that at times the one speaking in tongues could not translate what he himself had said in a foreign language. If verse 28 was the common rule, it would be difficult to see how there would be any real edification of the speaker. But all we can do is question: Was verse 28 the common rule? What percent of those who spoke in tongues could not afterward translate what they said, all or just a few? (2) Others suppose that even though neither the speaker nor the audience understood the foreign language, still the speaker would derive some psychological benefit from the personal awareness that he or she was a tool being used by the Holy Spirit. (Those who doubt the validity of this explanation have asked how a personal psychological benefit alone could be called an "edification" or "building up"? Isn't there more to edification than feeling good or having personal satisfaction?)

But one who prophesies edifies the church -- Herein lies the superiority of prophecy to tongues in the public assembly. All the assembled Christians (the Greek reads "an assembly") understand what the prophet says, and all are helped spiritually by the message. As the prophet exhorts and consoles (verse 3) in a language all understand, the whole congregation is benefitted and strengthened.

14:5 -- *Now I wish that you all spoke in tongues, but **even** more that you would prophesy; and greater is one who prophesies than one who speaks in tongues, unless he interprets, so that the church may receive edifying.*

Now I wish that you all spoke in tongues -- Paul shows that it was not from antipathy or prejudice against tongues that he speaks this way about the gift of tongues. He says, "Now I wish that all of you might speak with tongues, yet I wish still more that you should

---

[20] Some modern Pentecostals and Charismatics use verse 4 as a proof text that tongues at Corinth were for private devotions. Why anyone talks about private devotions in this context – where the topic is abuses of spiritual gifts in the public assembly – is perplexing. One wonders if it is not a case of special pleading – an attempt to find a Scripture to defend an experience already presumed to be valid.

all prophesy ...."[21] The gift of tongues was not to be entirely disregarded because of its inferiority in the public assembly when compared to prophecy. The body still has need of all its parts! Consistently, Paul refuses to speak disparagingly of this gift. He wants it understood that he is not prohibiting all use of tongues. He wants it understood that he recognizes quite fully what the real value of tongues is, and by no means does he desire to rob the Corinthians of this gift. What he wants them to do is quit abusing it, and instead to use it properly in the public assemblies.

But *even* more that you would prophesy -- Paul's emphasis at this place is not that tongues are to be discarded altogether, but that they are not to be overrated and prophecy underrated. That tongues (as the Corinthians were using them) stand on a lower level than prophecy is the point to be remembered. Since more are benefitted when prophets function, Paul would have such benefits abound. He wishes all would speak God's messages to men in languages easily understood by the listeners.

And greater is one who prophesies than one who speaks in tongues -- "Greater" because the congregation is edified; "greater" in usefulness to the most people. The way the Corinthians were speaking in tongues, only the individual speaker was built up (assuming no one translated). In the case of prophecy, the whole church is built up, and this without the aid of another gift. The gift of prophecy is of more value in the public assembly because more people are benefitted, and love always seeks that kind of profit. As we have seen in several places, here again is evidence that the Corinthians exaggerated the importance of speaking in tongues. This exaggeration is what Paul is correcting.

Unless he interprets -- "Unless" denotes an exception to the statement that prophecy is greater than tongues. If the tongues are translated so that all the assembly understands, then the gifts are equal. However important and valuable the truth might be which the tongue speaker had uttered, it would be useless to the church, unless it should be imparted in language which the people could understand.[22] From this verse, it is evident that the man who spoke foreign languages sometimes had the power of translating. From verses 27 and 28, it appears that the office of interpreting (translating) was sometimes performed by others. The possibility that a second person might act as a translator is not mentioned here since, at the moment, Paul is comparing only the person who is prophesying with the person who is speaking with tongues. "Unless he interprets" seems to say that the transla-

---

[21] At 1 Corinthians 12:30 (in a question which expects a negative answer) it was noted that not every Christian had the gift of tongues. Now here in chapter 14 ("I wish that you all spoke in tongues") we have another implicit statement that not every Christian could or did speak in tongues. This fact is hard to reconcile with some current charismatic dogma which insists every Christian should speak in tongues as the initial evidence of having been baptized in the Spirit. We neither believe that every Christian may expect a baptism in the Spirit, nor do we believe the doctrine about tongues being the initial evidence of such a gift. Both these claims are wide of the Scriptural mark.

[22] It has been shown in earlier notes that "interpreting" is *translating* the words of a foreign language into the local language of the people.

tor is the same person who just spoke in tongues.[23] (However, because of verses 27 and 28, some argue that the NRSV is on the right track when it offers "unless *someone* interprets" as the preferable rendering of the Greek at this place.) Paul prefers prophecy (which was spoken in the local language) to tongues (the way the Corinthians were using the gift) in the gathered assembly, since prophecy is understood.

Verse 5 seems to indicate the real issue is not tongues *per se*, but *untranslated tongues*, since a translated tongue could edify, just like prophecy did. Verse 5b demonstrates that all of verses 2-5a must be understood as Paul's criticism of tongues 'when they are not translated' or 'when no one understands the language.' When they are translated, tongues, like prophecy, contain a fundamental instructional and exhortational purpose/component. (Again, it should be observed that this paragraph is hardly speaking about a devotional use of tongues.) Verse 5b provides an important qualification of Paul's disparaging of tongues. He is criticizing the Corinthians' abuse of the gift. But when a translation is given, then tongues plus their translation closely resemble prophecy in function. In a way, by adding the interpretation (i.e., translation) and thus securing the end that some edification results for the listeners, the speaker with tongues rises somewhat to the level of a prophet. (We, of course, must not forget that tongues were for a sign to unbelievers, while prophecy was for believers, verse 22.)

So that the church may receive edifying -- "Church" in this passage is the local congregation. Throughout the New Testament, the church, the local assembly of believers, is indicated as the central collective unity of God's people. And indeed, the building up of the local church of Jesus Christ where each of us worships should be our main concern. This is the Scriptural emphasis, and it should be ours. Let our concern not be how we can show off to our own best advantage in the local assembly. Rather, our concern should be what we can do to edify and build up that assembly. There must be a conscious striving and sense of purpose in this. The Christian ought not to be motivated by what he can get out of his church, even in the matter of admiration for his natural or supernatural abilities, so much as by what he can do for the edification of his church. The reason Paul wished for prophecy more than tongues (the way the Corinthians were using the gift) is because prophecy carries with it understanding and strengthening of the church. Prophecy was greater in usefulness than untranslated tongues.

b. Application #2 -- Understanding. 14:6-25

> *Summary:* Paul continues to make application of the principles given in chapters 12 and 13 in order to correct the abuses of spiritual gifts in the public assembly. One who acts in harmony with those principles will no longer exercise his gift when no one listening can understand what he is saying. Paul now gives several illustrations of the

---

[23] This verse does have some bearing on the statement made earlier that a spiritually gifted person *usually* received but one gift. In some cases the tongues speaker apparently also had the ability to translate – thus he had two gifts. But having two gifts evidently was not the rule (as verses 27,28 seem to show). See also the instruction at verse 13, "pray that he may interpret."

> importance of 'understanding.' By this criterion, prophecy is better than tongues for edifying believers (6-19). And by this criterion, prophecy is better than tongues for convicting unbelievers (verses 20-25).

14:6 -- *But now, brethren, if I come to you speaking in tongues, what shall I profit you unless I speak to you either by way of revelation or of knowledge or of prophecy or of teaching?*

But now, brethren -- This expression denotes a turn in the argument. The emphasis in verses 1-5 was on *edification*. Now, it is on *understanding*, or intelligibility. Eight times in verses 6-25 Paul uses Greek words which in the KJV are translated "understanding." Where there is understanding, there is the possibility of edification (verse 12). As he often did, Paul here softens his rebuke with the affectionate address, "brethren." Paul was in disagreement with these Corinthians over their behavior as they abused their spiritual gifts. Yet, observe how he treated them. He did not call them enemies of the gospel, the lunatic fringe, holy rollers, or any other derogatory name. He called them "brethren." We, too, need to learn from Paul. While differing with and correcting people, he never ceased to be loving and tender. In chapter 14 of this epistle he practices what he preached in chapter 13. He admonishes them, but he still calls them "brethren."

If I come to you speaking in tongues -- As he writes this letter, Paul was planning to make a trip to Corinth again soon (1 Corinthians 16:6-9). What good would he do them, if, after he arrived, all they got from him throughout his whole visit were messages spoken in different foreign languages (something he could do, verse 18), but which they could not understand. To do them good, he must speak in an intelligible language, one they can understand. What he must speak to do them good, he signifies in the last part of the verse.

What shall I profit you -- The implied answer to the question is "nothing!" There would be no profit, no benefit, no edification if the listeners have no idea what the speaker is saying. Even if it is an apostle speaking, the congregation would not be edified unless his speaking were in a language understood by his listeners. The first illustration supporting the need for 'understanding' is thus drawn from Paul's coming visit to Corinth.

Unless I speak to you either by way of revelation or of knowledge or of prophecy or of teaching? -- If when Paul visits Corinth the next time he speaks only in languages with which his listeners are not fluent, there will be no understanding, no profit to his hearers. The principle of the body needing what each part can supply, the principle of acting in a loving fashion, the principle of edification, and the principle of making sure the hearers understand, would lead a person to exercise his gift only if it profits others (i.e., a circumstance wherein none of the principles is violated). Each of the gifts mentioned – revelation, knowledge, prophecy, teaching – is something done in the public assembly in such a way that people can understand what is being said, and thus be profited. The precise differentiation between these four terms is difficult.[24] And the problem hinges on

---

[24] Notes of explanation have already been given for each of these four words. 1) On "revelation," see 2:12. From the standpoint of the hearers, it would be an uncovering of God's will. 2) On "knowledge,"

the question of whether the gifts are being looked at from the speaker's standpoint or from the hearer's standpoint. Some have given comments on the words as though what the *speaker* delivered was the result of divine revelations or the result of inspired knowledge, etc. Some have given comments on the words as though what the *hearer* received was a new revelation, or new knowledge, or a prediction of the future, or some instruction. Perhaps the most common way of handling the four words is to treat two as if from the speaker's standpoint, and two from the hearer's. The speaker has received a revelation or a bit of inspired knowledge. Then when the gifted speaker exercises his gift, the hearer hears a word of prophecy, or receives some instruction.[25] Now we can understand wherein lies the real profit to be derived from Paul's coming visit. Only if he speaks in the vernacular of the people, and only if they receive "revelation" or "knowledge" or "prophecy" or "teaching," will his visit be edifying to the Corinthians. If Paul were to speak in a multitude of different foreign languages during his coming visit to Corinth, his listeners would receive no revelation or knowledge or prophecy or teaching if they could not decipher what Paul was saying. It would be a waste of time for Paul to so speak, and a waste of time for the listeners to listen. It would be a great display of tongues, but there would be no spiritual profit to the listeners from Paul's display. Neither was there any spiritual profit from the way the Corinthians were abusing their gift of tongues.

14:7 -- *Yet* even *lifeless things, either flute or harp, in producing a sound, if they do not produce a distinction in the tones, how will it be known what is played on the flute or on the harp?*

Yet *even* lifeless things ... in producing a sound -- This is the second illustration to demonstrate the absolute necessity for understanding. It is from the analogy of musical instruments. Things without life[26] would be musical instruments, as the following context shows.[27] *Phōnēn* can be translated either "sound" or "voice."[28] This gives two possible meanings for this verse. Taking it as "sound," the verse says that whether the instrument was a harp or flute being played, you could not know which instrument it was unless each gave a distinct sound of its own. Taking it as "voice," the verse says the music must be

---

see notes at 12:8. Knowledge is the understanding of any portion of divine truth, a clear insight into what that truth contains. 3) On "prophesying," see notes at 12:10 and 14:1. 4) On "teaching," *didachē*, see notes at 12:28. This would be instruction or a lesson in the Christian faith, a Spirit-inspired utterance intended to instruct, not the contemporary meaning of the word which implies formal teaching of some kind.

[25] Shore, *op. cit.*, p.130, has taken the last method and modified it a bit. He has noticed the near parallelism between verses 5 and 6. Verse 5 had two parts, one about speaking and another about interpreting. Verse 6 has two parts, one about speaking and another about "revelation, etc." Shore suggests such a parallelism shows that these four words in verse 6 are an expansion of what is involved in "translating tongues." The "revelation" and "knowledge" are the internal gifts that the interpreter himself has, and they are the sources of his power to communicate "prophecy" (i.e., general exhortation, Shore defines it) or "doctrine" (i.e., systematic religious instruction) to his hearers.

[26] The Greek is *apsucha* – 'without soul' (an alpha privative, and *psuchē*, soul or life).

[27] For musical instruments being characterized as "inanimate," see Euripides, *Ion* 881 and Plutarch, *lib. educ.* 9c.

[28] The use of *phōnē* (here rendered "sound") with musical instruments reflects common usage, also.

different if it is to guide people to be joyous or sorrowful or devout. You will not accomplish much unless you work out a system of notes, modulation, etc.[29]

Either flute or harp -- "Flute" ("pipe," KJV) translates *aulos*. This wind instrument was an ancient ancestor to the clarinet. They were made from a bamboo tube, or shank bone, or hollowed out stick, with finger holes for pitch control, and a reed or reeds to produce the sound vibrations. "Harp" translates *kithara*. It was a stringed instrument, usually of ten strings, and was struck with a plectrum (pick). These two instruments were commonly used at banquets, funerals, and religious ceremonies in the Hellenistic world.

If they do not produce a distinction in the tones -- "Tones" translates the plural form of *phthoggos*. The expression "distinction in tones" might refer to pitch, or the interval between notes. It might be a nontechnical term for what we call a melody.[30]

How will it be known what is played on the flute or on the harp -- The sound made by a flute or harp is of little value unless there is enough distinction in tones to form a melody. 'Noise' made by musical instruments means nothing. Paul's argument runs as follows: 'You say that speaking in unknown tongues has some value. But would you enjoy hearing a pipe or harp played by someone who knows no music and produces only noise?' The analogy to tongues is clear, says Fee. He suggests that in modern culture, the analogous figure to what the Corinthians were doing with their tongues would be the cacophony of the symphony orchestra tuning instruments and warming up just before the conductor raises the baton.[31]

14:8 -- *For if the bugle produces an indistinct sound, who will prepare himself for battle?*

For if the bugle produces an indistinct sound, who will prepare himself for battle? -- The Greek literally reads 'trumpet,' but we customarily use the word "bugle" when speaking of soldiers and battle as this verse does. In ancient times, army commanders did not direct the various units of the army by radio or walkie-talkie. The bugler did this by giving a certain series of sounds on the bugle. Then the soldiers in the field knew whether to advance or retreat, etc. Both Jews and Greeks would understand this analogy. In Homer's *Iliad* (18.219) we read about the use of the *salpigx* ("war trumpet"), and the Jews were familiar with the *shophar*, the rams horn (Numbers 10:9; Joshua 6:4,9). A trumpet

---

[29] In passing, Meyer (*op. cit.*, p.317), taking it as "voice," regards this passage as decisive against the opinion that tongues used in the gift in question were distinctly articulated foreign languages. He feels that the utterance – tongues – was a confused jargon of sounds, such as that which would be made through the instruments without observing their proper modulations. We are of the opinion that this is pressing the analogy too far.

[30] Fee, *op. cit.*, p.664. Someone observed that, by analogy, this verse may say something to instrumentalists in the public assembly who are playing a prelude, or who are playing while people are meditating. They should be playing known tunes at such times, so the people will 'understand' what is being played.

[31] Fee, *op. cit.*, p.664.

of war that merely 'makes an indistinct sound,' even though its sound be ever so loud, means nothing to the soldier. The proper notes of the signal must be blown, and blown in such a way that the soldiers understand. Otherwise, the blowing is useless. To get a soldier "to prepare himself for battle," the trumpet sound must be understandable. If the commander wanted the army to march, and the bugle call sounded like "mess call" (i.e., not the right call in the right way), everyone would be confused. Or if the bugle gave forth only an unintelligible blare, its sounds were useless.

14:9 -- *So also you, unless you utter by the tongue speech that is clear, how will it be known what is spoken? For you will be speaking into the air.*

So also you -- Paul proceeds to apply the illustrations given in verses 7 and 8. "You" is emphatic in the Greek. It applies particularly to them. Paul's point is that it is not the mere sound of speaking that is important (think of tongues as the Corinthians were exercising them), but whether the sounds can be understood by the hearers. Of what use is speaking in a foreign language if none of the hearers understands what is being spoken?

Unless you utter by the tongue -- "Tongue" here is singular, and the organ of speech is intended.[32] 'Unless you use your tongue to produce speech that is intelligible to the listeners, how will anyone know what you are saying?'

Speech that is clear -- The ASV translated "speech easy to be understood."[33] Paul is writing about "words which the hearers are accustomed to hear," words in the vernacular of the listeners.[34] The phraseology surely indicates that "tongues" at Corinth were foreign languages – but languages not understood by the majority of the worshipers present.

How will it be known what is spoken? -- As the musical instruments referred to in the illustrations are made for the purpose of producing sounds, so the tongue is to produce speech in the assembly of the church. Unless the tongue utters words that are easily understood, how shall the hearers know what is spoken? We at once see what Paul means: tongues (as the Corinthians were using them) merely made a sound in the hearer's ears; but prophecy conveys a meaning that is easy to understand, because it is spoken in the vernacular of the congregation.

---

[32] This was George Mark Elliott's explanation. It seems to be nearer what Paul is saying than some other contemporary explanations of the use of the singular "tongue" (i.e., that when the word is singular, it is not a known foreign language, but perhaps only gibberish) versus the plural "tongues" (i.e., foreign languages).

[33] The expression "words easy to be understood" comes from *eusēmon logon*. The word *eusēmon* comes from *eu* ("well") and *sēma* ("sign, mark, token"). "Speech" (*logon*) conveys meaning, it is a sign of something.

[34] Origen suggested that this text intimates that the obscure portions of Scripture, such as the account of the sacrifices in Leviticus and of the tabernacle in Exodus, ought not to be read in public worship unless someone explains their meaning.

For you will be speaking into the air -- Our idiom is "you are just talking to the wind." It implies non-reception by the hearers. The speaker's words are just going out "into the air." The Corinthians did not speak these foreign languages in the assembly simply because they could not help it, or because they did not know the mother tongue of their hearers. They kept speaking foreign languages in public because they wanted to speak apparently for no other reason than self-gratification and to demonstrate that they were filled with the Holy Spirit. It was a selfish purpose, and Paul exposes it as such. Paul's directive that words spoken in the public assembly should be in the language of the people strongly suggests public worship services are to be conducted in the language of the people. It may be observed here, that the sometime practice of the Roman Catholic Church accords with what the apostle here condemns – where worship is conducted in a language not understood by the people. It ought not to be so. "Preaching, too, should be plain, simple, perspicuous, and adapted to the capacity of the hearers (Barnes, *op. cit.*, p.182)." Terms that might be unintelligible should be clearly explained. Vocabulary words used should be words that are not above the comprehension of the listeners.

14:10 -- *There are, perhaps, a great many kinds of languages in the world, and no kind is without meaning.*

There are, perhaps -- Here begins the third illustration to demonstrate the absolute necessity for understanding before tongues are used, otherwise it is an abuse of the gift. Paul now makes it plain that he is not absolutely forbidding all use of foreign languages in the public assembly. There are ever so many languages in the world, and all of them have the power of communicating thought. Tongues speakers (as a group) could speak all of them. In the right circumstances (i.e., when thought is conveyed, when the audience would be helped to understand if the speaker spoke in the native tongue of the listeners) he encourages the use of foreign languages. "Perhaps," apparently, is an expression of uncertainty as to the exact number of languages there are in the world.[35]

A great many kinds of languages in the world -- We have a change here in the words used by Paul. "Tongues" has been *glōssa*. Now he is talking about "voices" or "languages" (*phōnē*). In classical Greek, *phōnē* often meant "languages." The use of *phōnē* as though it were a synonym for *glōssa* is significant. It helps us to see that the "tongues" at Corinth were human languages. "Kinds of languages" may refer to "families of languages." Or it could even refer to different dialects one finds in any family group. Goodspeed has translated it, "There are probably ever so many different languages in the world ...."

---

[35] There is some question as to the interpretation of this expression (*ei tuchoi*) translated "perhaps" or "it may be." Some take it with the verb "there are." The phrase then would say, 'for the sake of example.' Others take it with the words "so many kinds" in the phrase which follows in the Greek. Grotius who so interpreted supposed that Paul meant to indicate that there were, perhaps, or might be, as many languages as the Jews supposed – to wit, 70. Beza and others suppose it means that there "may be" as many languages as there are nations of men.

And no *kind* is without meaning -- There is a play on words in the Greek. "Languages" is *phōnē*; "without meaning" is *aphōnon*, 'dumb, unable to speak or communicate.' Paul is affirming that "*every language has the power of communicating thought*" to those who speak them and to those who understand them.[36] The emphasis in this whole paragraph is on understanding.[37] Every language spoken in the world can communicate thought under the proper circumstances, if both speaker and hearer understand the language. When those circumstances do not prevail, when no one present in the public assembly understands the language being spoken, it is useless to insist on an opportunity to speak.

14:11 -- *If then I do not know the meaning of the language, I shall be to the one who speaks a barbarian, and the one who speaks will be a barbarian to me.*

If then I do not know the meaning of the language -- The point of verse 10 is pressed home by means of the inferential conjunction "then" (*oun*). "Meaning" is a translation given to *dunamis*, which ordinarily is translated 'power' or 'force.' Plato often used *dunamis* in the sense of 'signification' or 'meaning.' So it is used here. Think of the 'power' to convey meaning. Language has such power if we recognize the words and know the meaning attached to each word spoken. "Speech is an effective instrument of communication, but speech that is not understood is of no power at all."[38] "All kinds of languages met at commercial Corinth, with its harbors on two seas, and difference of language was a frequent barrier to common action. Moreover, it was well known how exasperating it could be for two intelligent persons to be unintelligible to one another. Yet the Corinthians were introducing these barriers and provocations into Christian worship, and all for the sake of display!"[39] How selfish and how foolish!

---

[36] A language can be broken down into uniform phonetic sounds that have the same consistent meaning each time they are uttered. 'No voice is without signification.' There are phonetic sounds that actually constitute a whole science of linguistics that the expert translators of the Bible societies can recognize. And it is instructive to note that whenever these experts have had the opportunity to hear modern tongue-speakers, they have not been able to break them down into consistent phonetic sounds, which is an indication that they are not the product of intelligent thinking for the purpose of conveying meaning.

[37] Hodge (*op. cit.*, p.284) wrote, "The illustration contained in this verse goes to prove that speaking with tongues was to speak in foreign languages." Blomberg, who thinks tongues at Corinth were simply syllabication, writes the opposite. He insists that Paul's language in verse 10 does not prove that tongues at Corinth were languages, any more than verses 7-8 prove that tongues sounded like flutes, harps or trumpets. It has been interesting and confusing to hear the commentators both affirm and deny that these illustrations help us to determine whether the "tongues" at Corinth were languages or not. We see no reason to deviate from our conclusion that the tongues at Corinth were human languages, and that the thing Paul is insisting upon (lest the gift be abused) is 'understanding' the meaning of the language.

[38] Morris, *op. cit.*, p.193. If you turn on a foreign language radio station, you do not just sit there and absorb sounds that are meaningless to you. You switch to another station, unless for some reason you intend to learn the language. Only someone devoid of thought is content either to listen to, or to engage in speaking a language that the hearers do not understand. Intelligent people are concerned with understanding, not just with the sound.

[39] Robertson and Plummer, *op. cit.*, p.310.

I shall be to the one who speaks a barbarian -- "Barbarian" was the common term used to designate anyone who did not speak Greek, anyone who stood outside the sphere of the Greek language and culture.[40] *Barbaros* ("barbarian") is an example of onomatopoeia. It denotes a man whose language sounds like "bar, bar, bar, bar," i.e., whose language makes no sense. The listeners at the public assembly of the church at Corinth, when they hear the Corinthians all speaking in foreign languages, will be like barbarians. The language they are hearing communicates nothing.[41]

And the one who speaks will be a barbarian to me -- That is, what the speaker is saying is not understandable. Paul is hardly to be thought of as calling the speaker by a derogatory epithet. "Barbarian" in this context does not so much convey an idea of superiority or inferiority as it does the frustration people feel when they cannot communicate with each other because of language barriers.

14:12 -- *So also you, since you are zealous of spiritual gifts, seek to abound for the edification of the church.*

So also you -- Having finished three of the illustrations he uses to emphasize the importance of 'understanding,' Paul pauses here in verses 12 and 13 to make a practical application of these arguments to the Corinthians. "You" is emphatic in the Greek again. Paul pointedly urges it upon the Corinthians to emphasize the use of the gifts that will strengthen the church precisely because they are understandable.

Since you are zealous of spiritual *gifts* -- The Corinthians were zealots for "spiritual things" (spiritual gifts), but their zeal (which was a fine thing) needed some guidelines and boundaries, lest it end up in erroneous behavior and abuse of the spiritual gifts. We think the NASB translators were correct when they supplied "gifts" to help translate the neuter plural *pneumatōn*.[42] In 1 John 4:1, John uses the plural "the spirits" when he commands Christians to "test the spirits whether they be of God" and immediately explains that many false teachers are abroad in the world. Then in 4:2, he speaks of what is produced when the Holy Spirit prompts a man to speak. The juxtaposition of these two ideas shows that

---

[40] Aeschylus, *Persians*, 255; Herodotus 1:58. The Greeks classified all men as either Greeks or barbarians. See Acts 28:4 where the "natives" of Malta are classified as "barbarians" (ASV).

[41] Some have thought there is a tone of rebuke in the use of this word "barbarian." True, people do sometimes use "barbarian" to register the disdain they may feel for one who is beneath them in culture. (When such judgments are made on only one criterion [say language], the judgments are often wrong, for many 1st century "barbarians" were better educated than the people who spoke Greek.) We doubt the apostle Paul was using the term in a derogatory sense. Men were called barbarians (without any idea of contempt), at times, simply because of the unintelligibility of their speech. Paul's use of "barbarian" tends to corroborate the conclusion that in his discussion of tongues he has in mind known foreign languages.

[42] The use of "spirits" (*pneumata*), rather than the words he has used earlier (*pneumatikōn* and *charismata*), has puzzled some. The idea that certain heavenly "spirits" are connected with the *charismata*, just as evil spirits operate in the possessed, is an idea evidently foreign to the Scriptures. It is not the angels (spirits) who inspire a man to speak in tongues. The view that Paul is accommodating himself to a form of expression that was used by the Corinthians (but which he himself did not believe or teach) is also unacceptable. Nor does Paul now (in the plural "spirits") contradict what he wrote in 12:11, etc., that "the one and same Spirit" is the source of all gifts.

"spirits" designate manifestations produced by evil spirits. Paul likewise seems to use "spirits" as synonymous with manifestations produced by the Holy Spirit. It is a gentle reminder that the gifts they were zealous to exercise had their origin in the Holy Spirit (12:4ff).

Seek to abound for the edification of the church -- Paul does not try to cool their zeal for spiritual gifts, but he directs them to have the right motive for exercising them. Their goal should be the building up of others, rather than their own self-gratification. 'Try to excel in using the gifts that help others,' is his charge. Worded another way, 'If there is no understanding there will be no edification. If there is no edification, then there should be no exercise of your gift!' While it is right to desire to use one's spiritual gift, a man should pointedly refrain from exercising his gift unless it will be useful for edification of others.[43] The chapter on love has pointed the way to more than the mere possession of gifts. The gifts must be used in a loving way.

14:13 -- *Therefore let one who speaks in a tongue pray that he may interpret.*

Therefore -- This inferential conjunction (*dio*) shows that verse 13 is one way folk in the church could apply the principle of "edification (building up the church)" with which verse 12 closed.[44] Because of the fact that speaking in tongues was a gift of the Spirit, given for helping the body, Paul does not dictatorially insist that they stop it altogether. Having by three illustrations shown them the unhappy results of their abuse of the gift, he now gives instructions for the proper use of tongues.[45]

Let one who speaks in a tongue pray that he may interpret -- This passage, simple as it seems, has caused no little perplexity among the commentators. One problem involves the question of how we should harmonize what is here said with the rest of Paul's discussion regarding the interpretation of tongues.[46] Another problem is whether the last clause, "that he may interpret" (a *hina* clause in the Greek), is a purpose clause or a result clause. Whichever way we take it, "that he may interpret/translate" is surely intended to be a limitation that would bring an end to the abuses of tongues at Corinth. Remember, the spiritually gifted Corinthians were speaking in tongues when no one present understood the language.

---

[43] Fee (*op. cit.*, p.667) thinks the Pentecostal and Charismatic renewal movement has failed at this verse. He doubts that corporate worship should be turned into a thousand individual experiences of worship; rather, they are to build each other up.

[44] In the light of the close of verse 12 and the "therefore" (*dio*) at the beginning of verse 13, it is right to say that verses 13-19 speak of a worship setting, a congregational meeting, rather than a private setting.

[45] Someone has said that Paul uses sound psychology here. To tell people not to do something is seldom as effective as showing them the unhappy results of their action, thus motivating them to decide for themselves that it is not worthwhile. This is a good principle to remember when seeking to correct someone in the church.

[46] In verse 5, the speaker himself is pictured as doing the translating. In verses 27,28, someone else was the translator.

Several ways of explaining this verse (and the other passages involved) have been proposed. The following notes will of necessity be a bit extended, but it is the only way possible to deal with the whole question.

(1) Some take this verse as an instruction by Paul that the one gifted with tongues, before he speaks any message in a foreign language, should pray for the gift of interpretation.[47] 'Let him pray that he may be granted the ability to translate it for the assembly.'[48]

(a) What are the implications of this interpretation? (i) Reading the verse this way would make it a limitation on their behavior that would honor the expectation that all things be done for the edification of the church. It would be understood that unless a translation was certain, there was no need to speak in tongues. (It also assumes the gift is being used when no one present normally spoke the language being used, in which case a translation would not be necessary.) (ii) Another implication is that those speaking with tongues ordinarily did not know what they were saying. However, remember that in verse 5 we learned that sometimes they did know the meaning of what they said in a foreign language. (iii) It seems that the prayer is not for the initial reception of the gift of interpretation, but rather is a prayer that God would grant permission to exercise a gift already received in the past.[49] (iv) A fourth implication would be that a person might have more than one spiritual gift.[50] (v) The answer to such a prayer as this would involve another revelation being made by God – one revelation was needful before the tongue-speaker could exercise his gift, and another would be needful before a translation could make clear to the audience what had just been said in tongues. Paul's idea is to control the abuse of tongues by the Corinthians by asking, in effect, 'Do you Corinthians not see that to require such repeated revelations is surely unnecessary?'

---

[47] A quick perusal of 20th century translations into English will show that this is the common understanding of this verse by the majority of translators.

[48] The context has led us to speak about 'translating for the sake of the assembly.' Not a few writers (e.g., Calvin, Grosheide, Morris, Mare, etc.) take verse 13 to mean that the speaker "prays for understanding so as to benefit himself." This commentator doubts that verse 13 or the following verses should be so explained.

[49] We find apostles and prophets praying before they healed a sick person, or raised a dead one. So we might suppose it was with those who were spiritually gifted. Power was granted in answer to prayer. We do not see this call for prayer as proof that the gift of interpretation was initially received simply in answer to prayer. Rather each gifted person prayed before exercising his or her gift, so as to discern God's will as to whether or not it was in His interests to grant the exercise of a gift already possessed. So explained, this instruction about praying for interpretation would not be contrary to the usual way such spiritual gifts were initially received, that is, through the laying on of an apostle's hands. (Compare what was said in 14:1 about "desire earnestly spiritual gifts.")

[50] This follows if we take the subject of the verb "interpret/translate" to be the same as the person speaking in tongues. Some have supposed that it is a prayer that someone (not necessarily limited to the tongues speaker) will be granted permission by God to exercise his or her gift of translation. (They even read it "pray that *people* may interpret it.") It seems more likely that the speaker himself is the subject of the verb "interpret/translate." Not only might he have tongues, but he also had the gift of translation, which he was praying for permission to exercise. (That said, how would we harmonize this with 12:7-10, where it seems to say that only one gift was given to each gifted person?)

(b) The chief objection to this interpretation is that verse 13 does not say the person is to pray *for* interpretation before he speaks in tongues. Rather, the verse says that the prayer itself is spoken in a tongue (a foreign language). "Pray" is used the same way in both verses 13 and 14. The prayer itself is what is spoken in a foreign language.[51]

(2) Another way this verse has been taken is that Paul teaches the Corinthians not to pray in tongues unless they can also translate. 'Let him not pray unless he can translate.'

(a) This interpretation also has implications: (i) It harmonizes with the stricture that all things be done for edification of the whole congregation. It would require that the speaker doesn't just speak a language no one present could understand. He is also to translate into the local language, or remain silent. (ii) Another implication is that one of the things a person speaking in tongues could do is offer a public prayer. (iii) A third implication would be that those speaking with tongues sometimes did not know what they were saying as they uttered words in a foreign language. (iv) As Paul corrects the abuses of spiritual gifts, this verse becomes a tough restriction. If the tongues speaker doesn't know what he is saying, he is to keep silent, even if he is just offering a prayer. In the public assembly, Paul implies that the ability to translate an unknown tongue is the factor that makes speaking with tongues tolerable, with the further implication that if you can translate, why should you not speak in an understandable language to begin with? 'I have no objection,' Paul says, 'to your speaking in tongues as long as others somehow have the ability to understand you.'

(b) The chief objection to this interpretation is that it seems to treat the *hina* clause in an unacceptable way. It is taken neither as a purpose or result clause.[52]

(3) A third way this verse has been explained is this: 'Since the church is to be edified by hearing an intelligible message, let the tongues speaker pray in the public assembly (if no foreigners are present) only if he is confident there will be an interpretation.'

(a) Like the other suggested explanations, this one too has certain implications. (i) It assumes the Corinthians were in the habit of just speaking out, whether or not anyone

---

[51] Bleek's objection that we find two different meanings for "giving thanks" in verses 17,18, and therefore there is nothing wrong with finding two different meanings for "pray" in verses 13,14, does not hold. Verses 17 and 18 do not stand in direct logical connection (remember verse 14 begins with "for") as verses 13 and 14 do. On the contrary, verse 18 starts a new thought distinct from the thought in the preceding verse 17. Verse 14 is linked by "for" (*gar*) to verse 13. Therefore verse 14 ("If I pray in a tongue, my spirit prays") repeats and clarifies what verse 13 has said about "letting the one who speaks in a tongue pray ...." The *hina* clause is not the content of the prayer (verse 13); the *hina* clause is not a request for a translation. The *hina* clause is a limitation on speaking/praying. Only if interpretation/translation is available does the tongues speaker offer his or her prayer in the public assembly.

[52] The idea that 'praying' in the public assembly was one of the things a person was able to do when he spoke in tongues has caused some to question this explanation of verse 13. We are not convinced this is a valid objection. The following verses (14,15) show that among other things a person could do in tongues was pray and sing. Tongues are for a sign to the unbeliever (verse 22), and there would be times when prayers with unbelievers and songs sung in their hearing (unbelievers were welcome to visit the public services, verse 23) would be exactly appropriate.

present spoke or understood the language the speaker was using. 'If you must speak when no foreigners are present, at least make sure there will be a translation!' No more are the Corinthians to just make a display of their gift of tongues. (ii) "Pray that he may interpret/translate" is a limitation on their zeal. If there is no possibility of translation, then the tongues speaker is to remain silent. (iii) Another implication is that the one speaking in tongues could ascertain before he spoke whether or not a translator was present. This matches what will be clearly spelled out later in this very chapter (verses 27,28). (iv) This approach, like the second, recognizes that the tongues speaker is praying in the public assembly, exactly as the Greek says. It properly takes the *hina* clause as a 'contemplated result' clause. (v) This might imply that the person who speaks in tongues did (in some cases) understand what he has been saying in the foreign language and could act as his own translator.[53] Thus the verse would harmonize with what we learned in verse 5.

(b) In favor of accepting this third approach are these factors: (i) The illustrations preceding seem to require that this verse somehow harmonizes with the idea that the person who speaks in tongues is to make it a point to do so only if the listener understands. (ii) The train of thought in the following verses then flows on in an uninterrupted fashion. Verses 14-19 all speak of only using tongues in the assembly when others understand. (iii) It matches what we have been saying as we have added the phrase 'as the Corinthians were doing' when we speak of abuses of tongues. They were just speaking out in the foreign languages, whether or not anyone present understood. That is, they were using the tongues in a way other than how God intended tongues to be used.

We conclude that the thrust of verse 13 is this – let the one who proposes to offer a prayer in a foreign language give careful consideration to whether or not there is a very real possibility of translation (either by himself, or by one with the gift of translation, or by listeners who happen to be present and who know the language). If he does not do this, or if there is no possibility of understanding, then the speaker is to remain silent. 'Do not speak in tongues merely because you can. Consider what effect it will have on others, whether or not they understand.' This is the application of the basic principles of 1 Corinthians 12, 13, and 14.

14:14 -- *For if I pray in a tongue, my spirit prays, but my mind is unfruitful.*

For if I pray in a tongue -- If "for" enjoys integrity,[54] then, as noted above, verse 14 is linked to verse 13. Both verses are speaking of the same topic. Verse 13 asked tongues

---

[53] Did the apostles on Pentecost know in their own minds what they were saying as they spoke in foreign languages? We have always supposed they did. If so, couldn't at least some of the tongues speakers at Corinth also know, so as to be able to do their own translation?

[54] "For" is not found in P[46], B, F, G, etc., and Fee doubts it is original (*op. cit.*, p.669). If it is omitted, it is more difficult to follow the flow of thought through the verses in the immediate context. What must be decided is whether or not there is some way verse 14 could begin a whole new thought, and how that thought is connected to the argument as a whole.

speakers to ascertain if translation is likely to occur. Now Paul gives a reason why the translation is needed and vital. "If I pray in a tongue" shows that praying was one form of utterance possible to the person who had the gift of tongues; other forms are indicated in verse 6 and in verse 15. Though Paul speaks in the first person, he means it as a regulation to be observed at Corinth. As at 13:1, the use of the first person ("I") is an effective way to draw the readers into the argument. The examples of prayer and singing (verses 14,15) illustrate the propriety of the general sentiment which he is defending, namely, that if people are to be edified, public worship should be conducted in a language that would be intelligible to the people.[55]

My spirit prays -- We have here the same problem we met in verses 2, 4. Shall we use a capital or lower case "s"? We believe that the lower case is proper here, just as the NASB translators have it.[56] It is not possible to affirm that the speaker had lost all self-control and has been taken over by the "spiritual gift" that was in him (see notes at 12:2-3 and 14:32). Furthermore, it would be a rather strange designation for "spiritual gifts" to call them "the spirit of me" (literally the Greek so reads). Elsewhere in these notes, we have made the distinction between the three constituent elements found in a man – body, soul, and spirit. We understand that it is this "spirit" part that here is pictured as being involved in the offering of the prayer. I know that I am speaking a prayer as the Holy Spirit causes me to utter words in a foreign language.[57] I also am conscious that I am in control enough of my faculties that I may pray or not, even after the Spirit has come upon my tongue ("for the spirits of the prophets are subject to the prophets", 14:32). Further, I am conscious that I am uttering words and thoughts (though because of the language they come out in, I am not aware of the meaning). So it can be said, 'my spirit is praying.' Again, we must insist that "my spirit prays" does not speak of private devotions in this context. It speaks of praying aloud in a tongue in a public meeting or worship service.

But my mind is unfruitful -- The Greek translated "mind" in the NASB is *nous*. Consistent with the definitions for this word given in Thayer, the ASV translates the phrase as "my understanding is unfruitful." Verse 19 also uses the word *nous* with the meaning of "understanding." This phrase has been interpreted in several ways by commentators as they try to make all the verses in this context harmonize. (a) Some understand this phrase to mean, *my own mind does not understand what I am saying*. This option is favored by those who think verse 13 teaches the tongues speaker is to pray for the ability

---

[55] We are in the midst of one of the passages in 1 Corinthians 12-14 where both Pentecostals and non-Pentecostals must "assume" something in the background before they attempt to interpret. What the Pentecostal assumes is that some of the expressions refer to private devotions. "I will pray in the Spirit" is taken to mean private devotions, in contrast with "in church" (verse 19) which is taken to be the first reference to congregational activities. What the non-Pentecostal assumes is that the whole topic in chapters 12-14 is public worship, and that whether one "prays in spirit" or "prays with understanding," it is something that was done in public, not private.

[56] It would be a rather unusual designation for the "Holy Spirit" to call Him "my *pneuma*."

[57] Compare the language of Acts 2:4, "they ... began to speak with other tongues as the Spirit was giving them utterance."

to translate.[58] (b) Others, correctly in this commentator's view, understand it to mean that *no one else understands me.* The verses in this whole paragraph (verses 6-25) all talk of the effect on the *hearers*, i.e., whether or not they understand. When Paul applies this to the Corinthians in verse 16, it is definitely the hearer's understanding in view. So it is argued that this phrase has the same meaning, namely, the effect on the hearers. The prayer my spirit offers (i.e., I know it is a prayer) in a foreign language will produce nothing that will be of advantage to the rest of the congregation. The assembled worshipers cannot understand what I am saying. I am not leading them in prayer. So, of course, they cannot be profited by what I say. The word "unfruitful" ('fruitless') implies the result, or rather, the absence of result, as regards others in attendance at the worship services. The fruit the Christian seeks is found in his hearer making progress, not in his own delight at his performance, or in others' admiration of his gift.

14:15 -- *What is* the outcome *then? I will pray with the spirit and I will pray with the mind also; I will sing with the spirit and I will sing with the mind also.*

What is *the outcome* then? -- This question indicates the conclusion to which the reasoning had conducted Paul. 'What is the proper course for me to pursue? What are the consequences of what was just said in the previous verses? What is the proper behavior when one would speak in tongues in the assembly?'

I shall pray with the spirit and I shall pray with the mind also -- What it means to "pray with the spirit" has been explained in verse 14.[59] The person speaking in tongues is thought of as offering a prayer. His mind and affections are directed toward God. The future tense ("I shall pray") states a determination on Paul's part. Should not the Corinthians also have the same determination? 'When I speak in tongues, I am going to involve *nous* (i.e., mind, understanding, reason, thinking mind),' says Paul. Paul may be talking about using his own mind. If we take *nous* ('mind, understanding') in both verse 14 and verse 15 as being the speaker's *nous*, then Paul is saying, 'When I pray in tongues, I'm going to do so with my mind engaged also. I'm not going to shift my mind into neutral!'[60] On the other hand, since there is no "my" in the Greek, it could be speaking of the

---

[58] This option is also favored by those who think "tongues" at Corinth was syllabication/gibberish. Paul is then supposed to be arguing *ad hominem*. He does not say he actually does this, but the Corinthians were, and Paul supposes himself doing it in order to teach the Corinthians how misguided this practice is, even in prayer.

[59] *Pneuma* has regularly been rendered "spirit" (small "s") in the NASV at verses 1,14,15, and 32. In the Greek, there is no possessive pronoun in either clause, merely the definite article and a noun in the dative case. "I shall pray in (by) the spirit." "I shall pray by (in) the understanding." There is an interesting manuscript variation here. The Textus Receptus uses a future indicative for both verbs – "I shall pray" and "I shall pray." However, several manuscripts (*Aleph*, A, D, E, F, G, etc.) have a subjunctive verb in the first clause, and a future indicative in the second. This makes the first phrase to be a condition. The translation would be, "If I am to pray with spirit, I shall pray also with understanding."

[60] So explained, this verse is a strong correction for the modern neo-Pentecostals who urge the release of all conscious control of speech faculties when they are teaching their converts how to speak in tongues. Beware of any action of the spirit that ignores the God-given faculty of thinking!

'understanding' of the audience.⁶¹ (As said before, when Paul applies this to the Corinthians in verse 16, it is definitely the hearer's understanding in view.) In the public assembly when I pray, the only time I will do so in a foreign language is when I am certain listeners can understand what's being said. When there is a need for it (e.g., someone in the audience speaks the foreign language), I will pray with the spirit in a foreign language. But I will only exercise my gift when someone "understands."

I shall sing with the spirit and I shall sing with the mind also -- From this phrase we understand that not only could people "pray" in a foreign language, they could also "sing" in a tongue/foreign language. The Greek word *psalō*, says Morris, "properly means 'to sing to the accompaniment of a musical instrument'."⁶² "A psalm, strictly speaking, according to contemporary usage, is a song sung to the harp."⁶³ Singing with accompaniment in the public assembly does not violate any preceptory or prohibitory law, and therefore is surely allowable to the Christian.⁶⁴ Singing was a common part of worship in Judaism and was carried over as an integral part of early Christian worship as well (see 1 Corinthians 14:26).⁶⁵ Both the present passage and verse 26 seem to picture the singing in a tongue as being a solo. Since a foreign language was involved, the same rules applied to singing as applied to praying. Paul will limit his singing in a foreign language to those occasions when people are present who understand the words of the language he is singing.⁶⁶ "I shall sing with the mind (understanding)" states a determina-

---

⁶¹ Whether a man's "spirit" and his "mind" are two separate entities, see notes at Ephesians 4:23 and in Delitzsch's *Biblical Psychology*, p.184. Those who conclude "spirit" and "mind" are separate names for the inner man use this conclusion to corroborate the idea that "mind" here in verse 15 must refer to the hearer, not the speaker. They word their argument this way: If *pneuma* in the first part of the verse is translated small "s" (spirit), then *nous* (mind or understanding) in the latter part of the verse could not be the speaker's "mind" -- it would have to be the hearer's 'understanding.'

⁶² Morris, *op. cit.*, p.195.

⁶³ Liddell-Scott, *op. cit.*, p.2018.

⁶⁴ See the author's paper on the "Anti-Instrument Controversy in the Churches of Christ." See also the informative note on synonyms for "sing" (hymns, psalms, songs) in Thayer, *op. cit.*, p.637. The note shows that some are accompanied, some unaccompanied, and some can be either.

⁶⁵ It is from this passage that we learn that "singing" was one of the parts of the worship services in the early church. 14:26 also shows the same thing. Some think Ephesians 5:19 and Colossians 3:16 also speak of a public worship setting, though there is no certainty to this conclusion. If those two Prison Epistle passages refer to corporate worship, then the context says the songs there were to be vehicles of instruction to the gathered community. The following verses here in 1 Corinthians seem to suggest that as these prayers and solos were being voiced, the words uttered expressed praise and thanks to God.

⁶⁶ Paul is supposing himself to be in the place of the Corinthians who were speaking in foreign tongues when no one understood what was being said. He did not actually mean that there were times when he prayed only "in spirit," or sang only "in spirit" without at the same time being concerned about *nous* (understanding). He was placing himself in the position of the Corinthians, as is shown by the fact that in verses 16 and 17 he shifts from the first person to the second person, from "I" to "you."

tion on Paul's part. Should not the Corinthians also have the same determination?

14:16 -- *Otherwise if you bless in the spirit* **only**, *how will the one who fills the place of the ungifted say the "Amen" at your giving of thanks, since he does not know what you are saying?*

Otherwise -- Verses 14 and 15 have called for exercising the gift of tongues in the public assembly only on those occasions when an understanding of what is said results. "Otherwise" indicates what happens if understanding does not accompany the use of tongues.

If you bless in the spirit *only* -- Perhaps Paul begins a fourth illustration here to show the need for understanding.[67] Perhaps what he writes in verses 16-19 is further application of earlier illustrations to curtail the abuse of tongues at Corinth.[68] "Bless" is probably explained in the words "giving of thanks" in the latter part of this verse.[69] Paul is supposing that while the Corinthians are speaking in a foreign language they are praying, giving thanks to God for mercies and favors He has bestowed. "In the spirit only"[70] repeats what was said in verse 14 ("my spirit prays") and verse 15 ("with the spirit"). What is intended is praying or singing in a foreign language that no one present understands or can translate.

How will the one who fills the place of the ungifted -- The precise meaning of both *topos* ('room, place') and *idiōtēs* ('ungifted, unlearned') is uncertain. *Idiōtēs* was sometimes used to designate a person who does not possess the skill or knowledge which is immediately in question – a common man rather than a professional man, a common soldier rather than an officer. a layman rather than a priest, a private citizen rather than those in public life, such as magistrates.[71] 'Illiterate' is sometimes the idea of the word *idiōtēs*; the person is not

---

[67] In verses 14 and 15 Paul has written in the first person, "If I pray," etc. Now in verses 16 and 17 he changes to the second person, "if you bless," etc. This new illustration might be summarized, "Take me, for instance" (verses 14, 15), and then, "Take yourself, for instance" (verses 16,17).

[68] Basically, in verses 16-19, Paul shows that praying and/or singing in an untranslated language violates chapters 12 and 13. Such actions do not meet other worshiper's needs; the other man does not understand and is not edified.

[69] Some writers talk about 'praise to God' (rather than thanksgiving) as being what is denoted by "bless." We would need more than this verse before we could affirm with confidence that one of the things done as folk spoke in tongues was simply to offer praise to God.

[70] The ancient manuscripts differ at this place. The better attested reading is either *pneumati* (P^{46}, A, F, G, 0243, 33 and other minuscules) or *en pneumati* ($Aleph^2$, B, D, P, 82 and other minuscules). The reading in the Textus Receptus (*tō pneumatic*) is perhaps a copyist's addition from 14:2. Translations based on the Textus Receptus often translate "with the Spirit," arguing that the reference is to what the Holy Spirit is doing through the gifted tongues speaker. The NASB has small "s" since the translators thought the better attested reading had reference to the man's own spirit, not the Holy Spirit.

[71] See Moulton and Milligan's book, *The Vocabulary of the Greek Testament*. The same word is used in Acts 4:13 of men without special training, and in 2 Corinthians 11:6 of one who was not a trained orator.

learned enough to understand how to read or write. Because the NASB reads "ungifted," some mistakenly might get the idea it speaks of all those who possess no spiritual gifts at all. It might be understood here as a term for those who are not Christians were it not for the fact that verse 23 seems to distinguish between "ungifted ("unlearned") and "unbelievers."[72] Here it means one who was not leading in the prayer and who at the same time was unacquainted with the foreign language being spoken by him who gave thanks. It is not likely that "place" indicates a special seating arrangement where all the "ungifted" were to sit when the congregation assembled.[73] It more likely speaks of "one who has this nature," one who occupies this place or station in life. In the present connection, the word "ungifted" refers to a Christian who is inexpert in the matter of tongues. By using the phrase "the place of the ungifted," Paul implies to his readers, "Just imagine yourself in his place."

Say the "Amen" -- The Greek says, "The Amen."[74] The article points to a customary use

---

[72] English translations vary greatly at this place. (a) The ASV/NASB speak of a person who is without spiritual gifts. If we accept this translation, then this is one of the passages in the New Testament which intimates that not everyone in the New Testament church had spiritual gifts. However, it would be difficult to say that only those who had no spiritual gifts were the ones who did not understand what the tongue speaker was saying. (b) The RSV reads "outsider." The RSV translators thought the person in mind was one who had not been converted but who was attending the public services, perhaps with the expressed purpose of learning the gospel. (BAGD does give some evidence that *idiōtēs* was a technical term in pagan religious life for non-members who still participated the pagan sacrifices.) But would "outsiders" be pictured as saying "Amen" to a Christian's prayers? (c) The NIV margin reads "inquirer." That choice of words is based on the belief that "ungifted" is a person who stands somewhere between the non-believer and the full-fledged Christian (a common view in German scholarship), i.e., a "catechumen." It does assume (probably rightly so) that the "ungifted" alluded to in both verses 16 and 23 are the same person (or class of persons). (d) This commentator is of the conviction that we should save the definition "unconverted" or "outsider" for the term "unbeliever" of verse 24, and that "ungifted" refers to a separate class of people. It seems best therefore to say the "ungifted" person is a Christian, a church member who does not understand the foreign language being spoken by the tongues speaker.

[73] This passage cannot be used to show that the New Testament makes a distinction between 'clergy' and 'laity.' It is unlikely that at this early period there was a portion of the room (where the church assembled) set apart for the 'unlearned' (the laity), or that these who did not possess the spiritual gifts were seated in a different place than those (the clergy) endowed with spiritual gifts. Likewise, we decline to accept the view that these were 'guests' who occupied special places that were reserved for them in the meetings. If we wanted to speak of a seating arrangement, we would use this expression "place of," but we doubt that that is the intended meaning here. We also decline to accept the interpretation (that Morris takes) that they were catechumens who had not yet been baptized, and that Paul mentions one of these because he is concerned about missionary interests. Morris (*op. cit.*, p.195) notes that Arndt and Gingrich tell us that "unlearned" was used in some religious associations for "non-members who may participate in the sacrifices." This, he thinks, gives us a clue as to the meaning. He goes on to note that Paul speaks of the "room" (place) for these people, which he believes indicates that they had their "place" (a reserved section) in the Christian assembly. They would be "inquirers," people who were interested in Christianity, but who had not yet committed themselves to it, he concluded. He bases his assertion that they were not yet Christians on the fact that (in his view, a view we have rejected) in verse 23 "the unlearned" seem to be distinguished from the church members ("the whole church").

[74] For those who wish the technical information, "Amen" is a transliteration into English of a Greek word that was itself already a transliteration from the Hebrew. The Greek word *amēn* is the participle of the verb 'to confirm' and is the word often translated "Verily" or "Truly" in the Gospels. The Hebrew word "Amen" is an adjective meaning 'true' or 'faithful.' It is roughly equivalent to 'This is most certainly true!' At the end of prayers, "Amen" was spoken in concert by the people assembled in the synagogue to express agreement to what was said by one in the name of all (Nehemiah 5:13, 8:6; 1 Chronicles 16:36; Psalm

of "Amen" in the church at this time as a way for the congregation to give its wholehearted approval and assent to the thanksgiving that was spoken in public prayer. "Amen" assumes the setting of public worship. "Say" indicates it was not just a silent, mental "Amen!" It was expressed out loud. 'Others are listening when you give thanks in your foreign language, and they would respond at the appropriate time if they knew what you were saying.' Paul's question is this, "If you are speaking in a language that can't be understood when you lead in prayer, how can any listener intelligently say 'Amen'?"[75]

At your giving of thanks -- The person speaking in tongues (a foreign language) was actually offering a prayer of thanks to God. God would understand the prayer, of course, but none of the bystanders would, for what was being said was spoken in a language that was foreign to them. "Giving of thanks" translates *eucharistia*, but the reference is hardly to be restricted to the giving of thanks at the Lord's Supper (which some have denominated as "Eucharist"). Prayers of "blessing" or "thanksgiving" in any part of the service are intended.

Since he does not know what you are saying? -- In order to make perfectly plain the reason that this inexpert hearer is unable to add intelligent approval to what he hears, Paul adds, "Since he does not know what you are saying." Here Paul himself defines what he means by "the unlearned." This is the disadvantage connected with speaking in tongues the way the Corinthians were doing it. There often were none present who understood the foreign language. And unless intelligent translation were added, no one knew what was being said, and no one could approve.

14:17 -- *For you are giving thanks well enough, but the other person is not edified.*

For you are giving thanks well enough -- Verse 17 is tied to verse 16 with an explanatory "for." It spells out why the tongues (as the Corinthians were practicing them) were so unacceptable. Paul insists the problem has nothing to do with the content of the prayer

---

106:48). Saying "Amen!" (i.e., 'So be it!' or 'So let it be!') was a way whereby a worshiper could make the words uttered by someone else his own prayer too. To illustrate the importance attached to the "Amen," A.P. Stanley quotes from the Rabbis: "Whoever says 'Amen' to him the gates of paradise open, according to Isaiah 26:2. An 'Amen' if not well considered was an 'Orphan Amen.' Whoever says an 'Orphan Amen,' his children shall be orphans. Whoever says an 'Amen' hastily or shortly, his days shall be shortened; whoever answers 'Amen' distinctly and at length, his days shall be lengthened (*Berashoth*, 47,1). From the synagogue the "Amen" passed into the Christian church. Justin Martyr (*Apol.* 65) says, "When the president has finished the prayers and the thanksgiving, the whole people present give assent, saying, Amen. And in later times, the Amen was only repeated once by the congregation, and always after great thanksgiving, and with a shout like a peal of thunder." (Material in this note adapted from Kling, *op. cit.*, p.289)

[75] Some have wondered about certain practices that have crept into the public assemblies in the late 20th and early 21st centuries. They observe that the text reads "say 'Amen'." It does not say "clap the hands" to show assent.

("you are giving thanks well"[76]). The problem lies with the lack of understanding on the part of those who were being led in prayer. If the other persons assembled and listening cannot understand the words you speak as you lead in prayer, the whole thing results in no edification.

But the other man -- The ungifted one of the previous verse.[77] It is a public meeting, with other worshipers listening to the prayer being offered in public. Your prayers may be heard by God, but the other worshipers (who are ungifted, who do not understand the language being spoken) are not edified.

Is not edified -- See notes on 14:3 on "edified." Public prayer has a by-product. Not only would one give thanks to God, but the listeners would receive edification if the prayer were offered in a language they could understand. The lack of edification (resulting from a lack of understanding), as he has been saying throughout this whole discussion, is the reason for his condemnation of "tongues" at Corinth. The Corinthians were abusing the gift by using it when it was not needed.

14:18 -- *I thank God, I speak in tongues more than you all;*

I thank God -- What Paul has been saying about the use of tongues by the Corinthians is not due to "sour grapes." Paul has no blanket objection to any use of tongues by them. Nor does his objection arise from his own inability to speak in tongues. Paul himself can speak more languages than all the Corinthians. Moreover, this gift is not something he regards with indifference. He thanks God for the ability to so speak.

I speak in tongues more than you all -- There is a difference in manuscript readings here. Some manuscripts and ancient versions (among them, *Aleph*, A, D, E, F, G, 17, Latin, Armenian) read "tongue," singular. Some manuscripts and versions (among them, B, K, L, P, Syriac, Coptic, Aethiopic, Chrysostom, Theodoret, NA^{26}, UBS^2) have "tongues," plural. Textual critics are so confident that the plural reading is correct that modern critical apparatuses do not even call attention to the singular reading. If the plural reading is correct, then this verse is one of the reasons for explaining "tongues" at Corinth to be foreign languages.[78] If the plural is the correct reading, we then have a little known fact

---

[76] There is no reason to treat "well" as being ironical.

[77] Fee wrote (*op. cit.*, p.674), "The 'you' and the 'other person' are the two mentioned in verse 16, the one praising God in tongues and the one who takes the place of the 'unlearned' because he/she does not understand."

[78] Even if we adopt the singular reading here, it is not automatically certain that "tongues" at Corinth were not foreign languages. How might we explain the singular? In chapter 14, when individuals are spoken of as being endowed with this gift, *glōssa* (the singular) is used. Each person endowed with the gift could speak ONE foreign language. In this place, in connection with one individual, Paul could be saying he speaks his one language with greater frequency than any of the folk at Corinth do.

about the life of Paul enunciated. He was a man able to speak more foreign languages than all the people of Corinth put together. If tongues had an evangelistic purpose, "it is reasonable to presume that Paul was able to speak the language of any people to whom God, in His providence and by His Spirit, called him to preach.[79] He had been commissioned to preach to the Gentiles, and it is probable that he was able to speak the languages of all the nations among whom he ever traveled. There is no account of his being under a necessity of employing an interpreter wherever he preached."[80] "I speak" is present tense, and this indicates either that Paul does this kind of speaking regularly in his work, or that he has the ability to do it. He is not deprecating a gift of which he has no experience.

14:19 -- *however, in the church I desire to speak five words with my mind so that I may instruct others also, rather than ten thousand words in a tongue.*

However -- Paul has the ability to speak in tongues more than any of the Corinthian Christians; "however," he will not personally abuse his gift, as the Corinthians were. He will only speak a foreign language when there are people present who will understand the words being spoken.

In the church – Paul refers to 'an assembly' of Christians (there is no "the" in the Greek). The word "church" does not refer to the building in which Christians assembled, but rather to the assembled congregation. It was in their "church" (assembly) where the Corinthians have been abusing their gifts of tongues. To halt that abuse is why these corrections are offered. Somewhere in his work and travels, Paul had occasion and opportunity to speak in more languages (tongues) than all the Corinthian Christians put together could speak. Here he contrasts that with "in an assembly." Does that mean that the place where Paul regularly used his ability to speak foreign languages was on the docks, and in the midst of other groups who spoke different languages, but that it was not something he regularly did when meeting with a group of assembled Christians? It seems so. If we have understood the implied contrast aright, then "tongues" as practiced by Paul (and by implication how they should be practiced at Corinth) was limited to when the gift had an evangelistic purpose (just as in Acts 2). The gift was properly used in order to address a foreign audi-

---

[79] It is difficult to understand how some modern writers suppose the only contrast to the public assembly is private devotions. One Pentecostal writer, defending the idea that tongues at Corinth were for private devotions, has this thoughtful application. "... those who have rediscovered this gift [devotional tongues] as a meaningful expression of their personal lives of devotion need to be especially conscious of the greater concern of this paragraph that the gathered assembly be a time for the building up of others individually and the body as a whole" (Fee, *op. cit.*, p.676).

[80] Barnes, *op. cit.*, p.267. In case someone raises the case at Lystra (on the first missionary journey, Acts 14:11ff) as an objection to the view that Paul could speak numerous languages, remember that the ability to speak a foreign language is different from the ability to understand a foreign language (which is the gift of interpretation).

ence in their own language, a sign for unbelievers (1 Corinthians 14:22).[81]

I desire to speak five words with my mind -- "My mind" is the same expression used in verses 14,15, where it spoke of 'understanding.' Verse 16 especially supports this meaning of *nous* throughout this paragraph, so it likely carries the same meaning here that it did in those earlier verses. "Five" stands figuratively for a 'few.' It is probable that in any given assembly of believers in Corinth, there would be few who spoke and understood foreign languages (that is, there would be few foreign visitors). Paul, therefore, made a resolution (*thelō*, "I desire") not to speak in a foreign language when its only use would be mere display. How different was his resolution from the way the Corinthians were acting. Instead of boasting in the mere ability to speak, should they not make the same resolution Paul lives by?

That I may instruct others also -- The word rendered "instruct" or "teach" (KJV) is the root of our word "catechize." *Katēchēsō* means to instruct thoroughly by word of mouth, to 'sound down into the ear.' This explains what is meant by "speak with my mind (understanding)." Note should also be made from this passage that two of the things that occurred in the public assembly was someone led in prayer and someone led in giving instruction.

Rather than ten thousand words in a tongue -- "In a tongue" means 'in any given instance of speaking a foreign language.' "Ten thousand" was the largest word for numbers in Greek. As an adjective it means 'countless, innumerable, tens of thousands.' Five words in the language of the people that help them learn more of God's will are of far more value than an excessive number of words that convey nothing to the hearers. Paul's practice was to speak in such a way that the hearers would be benefitted. We are still in the paragraph where the application of *understanding* is being emphasized. One might say it is a matter of priorities. While Paul did not oppose the use of tongues under proper circumstances, he did try to put it in a right perspective. The issue was not quantity of words, but quality of communication.

14:20 -- *Brethren, do not be children in your thinking; yet in evil be infants, but in your thinking be mature.*

Brethren -- Calling his readers "brethren" is a further reminder of Paul's affection for them, and it also serves to focus attention on what follows. There is some question whether this is the continuation of the argument of verses 6-19, or the beginning of a new argument and a new paragraph that now reaches to verse 25. We follow the view that the major theme still being developed is the need for the audience to *understand* what is being spoken, otherwise the gifts are being abused. The only difference has to do with *who* it is who needs to understand. In verses 6-19 it is *believers* who need to understand, or the gift is being abused. In verses 20-25 the emphasis is that *unbelievers* who are present in the assembly

---

[81] The contrast to "in the church" is not "in private devotions," as some in the late 20th century have been wont to interpret.

also need to understand. The gift of prophecy is superior to the gift of tongues (the way the Corinthians were using them) for believers and unbelievers alike. In verses 20-25, Paul draws attention to a feature connected with the use of tongues, a feature which the Corinthians, it seems, have not thought of at all. In the case of unbelievers, instead of their being helped toward belief by the Corinthians' use of tongues, the way the Corinthians were doing things would only tend to confirm the unbelievers in their unbelief.

Do not be children in your thinking -- The force of the present imperative is "Stop being children in mind." Stop doing what you are doing! Stop behaving like little children! Earlier in this chapter, when the NASB reads "mind" (verses 14,15,19), the word in the Greek was *nous*. Because some versions read "mind" here in verse 20, the reader might not be aware that the Greek is not the same word as used before. So the NASB translators use "thinking."[82] The term *phren* was used by the Greeks to designate (metaphorically) the ability of the mind to think and judge. "Little children admire and are astonished at what is striking, novel, and what may be of no real utility. They are pleased with anything what will amuse them, and at little things that afford them play and pastime" (Barnes, *op. cit.*, p.280). So, to be like children in mind is to act immaturely, as though one's mental development had been arrested in childhood. Paul's language is a sharp rebuke. It implies that despite all their pride in knowledge and wisdom, the Corinthians are still "children" as far as judging aright concerning the effect of their exercise of tongues. Like children, they delight in the gift as such, and fail to see all that is involved in the inconsiderate use and display they were making of the gift.

Yet in evil be babes -- "Yet" translates the strong adversative *alla*, 'but.' With a quick turn of thought that is suggested by the idea of being children in a certain respect, Paul is reminded of an area in which it would be creditable to the Corinthians to be children, even to be babes.[83] Paul's language reminds us of Matthew 18:3, where the Savior declared that in order to enter into heaven, it was needful that we become as little children. "Evil" (*kakia*) can also mean 'malice.' It is the exact opposite of love. They were to be babes (unskilled) when it comes to practicing evil or showing malice. Be as free from any envy-produced ill-will toward others as infants are. What is clearly implied is that the motive behind the way the Corinthians were desiring to use their "tongues" is nothing less than 'malice,' ill-will toward those who were not so (in their estimation) highly gifted. It was *kakia* to use a gift (here, that of tongues) so that it does not serve its true purpose. To use it with a display of vanity is childish; to ignore its true purpose of edification is wrong. Add to this what Paul is now about to show, that a foolish use of tongues tends to rebuff the unbelievers who might be won to the faith, and we understand exactly what is "evil" about it.

---

[82] Other versions have used "understanding" for *nous* and "mind" for *phren*, so the English readers will grasp the idea that the words in the original are not the same.

[83] A *paidia* (in the previous phrase) is an older child than *nēpios*, which speaks of babies, infants. Infants would be even less experienced than children.

But in your thinking be mature -- "Thinking" again is *phren*, as used earlier in the verse. "Mature" translates *teleioi*, the same word used at 2:6 and 13:10; it means 'perfect, complete, adult, mature.' The verb *ginesthe*, translated "be," is actually 'become,' which here implies continuous growth. They won't become "mature" in their thinking overnight, but they can become progressively more mature as they continually put into practice what Paul here teaches. 'The next time you have an opportunity to speak a foreign language in the assembly, do it only if there is understanding on the part of the hearers. Practice such self-control a few times and it will soon become a habit, and you will have become "mature" in this matter of the use of spiritual gifts.' Parents understandably dread it when someone gives a drum or other noise-making toy to a child. The little ones become so enthralled with the volume of sound they are producing that they are lost to all other considerations. They don't care how much noise they make, as long as they are enjoying themselves. Young children at times exercise no discretion. That is the kind of childish Christians the Corinthians were. As long as their tongues possessed this exciting and enthralling ability to rattle, why not let them do it full force. Instead of being thoughtless like children, Paul appeals to them to become mature in thinking. (See the same imagery in 3:1,2). 'Use your minds in an adult fashion, and produce understandable speech in the assemblies, rather than rattling on in languages no one present can understand.'

14:21 -- *In the Law it is written, "BY MEN OF STRANGE TONGUES AND BY THE LIPS OF STRANGERS WILL I SPEAK TO THIS PEOPLE, AND EVEN SO THEY WILL NOT LISTEN TO ME," says the Lord.*

In the Law it is written -- Paul starts this portion of his corrective to the Corinthians' behavior by appealing to a passage of Scripture. Sometimes "the Law" refers to the five books of Moses (see Romans 3:19; John 10:34, 12:34, 15:25). Other times, "the Law" can refer to the whole Old Testament canon. Here the citation is from Isaiah 28:11ff.[84] "It is written" translates the perfect tense *gegraptai*; it was written long ago and is still there in the Book. Perhaps we have Paul putting into practice the fact that the Old Testament was "written for our instruction upon whom the ends of the ages have come" (1 Corinthians 10:11).

"BY MEN OF STRANGE TONGUES AND BY THE LIPS OF STRANGERS WILL I SPEAK TO THIS PEOPLE -- The passage cited is from Isaiah 28, but it is not a precise

---

[84] The setting of the quotation is this: The original passage is a threat pronounced by Isaiah, in the Hebrew language, upon the children of Israel for their unbelieving and contemptuous treatment of God's messengers. Drunken priests had made fun of God's Word and messenger. They had asked derisively whether it was thought they ought to be treated like little children, in that they were perpetually taught with line upon line and precept upon precept, after the fashion in which little children are instructed. In reply, God threatens that because they had despised this simple teaching, He would hereafter instruct them through persons of a different language and foreign utterance. The foreign persons He meant were the Assyrians, by whom the Israelites were to be treated just as contemptuously as they had treated God's Word. (Kling, *op. cit.*, p.290)

quotation of either the Septuagint or the Hebrew, though it is close to the Hebrew.[85] The connection Paul is making between Isaiah 28 and the situation at Corinth has been debated. (1) Some suppose Isaiah is a direct prophecy of the gift of tongues in the church. The points made in the prophecy would be: (a) as to the essential fact, that in both cases "foreign tongues" were employed, and (b) as to the effect, that in neither instance "would the people hear." This commentator, however, doubts there is any prophetic reference in Isaiah to the events in Corinth. (2) Barclay accuses Paul here, again, of Rabbinic exegesis – finding hidden meanings in the passages that certainly were not originally meant to be there (*op. cit.*, p.146). But such an accusation against Paul is a not-so-subtle denial of inspiration and of truthfulness. It is completely unacceptable. (3) Others, correctly, understand that Paul is using the Old Testament text by way of *accommodation*. The situations in Isaiah's time and in Corinth are similar, so Paul can use the words of Scripture because they express a thought similar to the one he wishes to convey.

AND EVEN SO THEY WILL NOT LISTEN TO ME," says the Lord -- The word "listen" (*eisakousontai*) includes obedience as well as hearing. The reason there was no obedience is that there was no understanding of what was being spoken to them in the foreign language. This Isaiah passage is remarkably suited to the problem in Corinth:

> In both instances unbelievers are involved: the unbelieving people of Judah; and in Corinth, pagans who may attend the services of the church. In both instances an unintelligible language is spoken: in the case of Judah, Assyrian; and in Corinth, "tongues" (i.e., whatever language the one gifted could speak). In both instances the effect is negative: the men of Judah remain unbelieving; the Corinthian unbelievers scoff.[86]

Once more we should note that Paul's parallel between the foreign language of the Assyrians and the tongues spoken in Corinth rests on the fact that "tongues" at Corinth were likewise foreign human languages. In Isaiah's time, the stern lesson God was trying to teach would not be understood or make any difference in their behavior toward God because it was going to be delivered to them by a people of an alien tongue. The power of speaking a foreign language (the way the Corinthians were using it) would not secure the obedience of unbelievers either.

---

[85] Paul does several things with the Isaiah passage: (1) He inverts the order of "stammering lips" and "foreign tongues" in order to put the topic he is interested in ("foreign tongues") in first position. (2) He changes "stammering lips" into "lips of strangers." (3) In keeping with the Masoretic text (and against the LXX), Paul changes "He (the Lord) will speak" to "I will speak," and then Paul concludes with the formula "says the Lord." (4) He skips a considerable portion of the Isaiah passage, picking up at the end of verse 12, where he changes "but they would not listen" to "they will not listen to Me." (5) Paul follows neither the LXX nor the MT, although he is closer to the MT than the LXX. Since there is some similarity between Paul's citation and the later (ca. 100 years) translation of Aquila, it is possible that both Paul and Aquila were dependent on an earlier form of the Greek text no longer available to us. (Fee, *op. cit.*, p.679-680)

[86] Lenski, *op. cit.*, p.600.

14:22 -- *So then tongues are for a sign, not to those who believe but to unbelievers; but prophecy* **is for a sign,** *not to unbelievers but to those who believe.*

So then -- "So then" (*hōste*) introduces two inferences derived from the Isaiah passage just referenced. One is an assertion about when tongues should be used, the other an assertion about when prophecy is appropriate.

Tongues are for a sign -- Tongues used properly serve as a "sign." Used as the Corinthians were using them (the next verse will show), they ceased to be a "sign." "Sign" expresses, not the nature of the gifts, but the effect these gifts are intended to produce. Barnes (*op. cit.*, p.269) notes that a "sign" is an indication, an evidence, or a proof that God has imparted His power, and that He attends the preaching of the gospel with His approval. When used as their Giver intended, tongues were a sign which helped to credential the Divine messenger. The view that "tongues" at Corinth were foreign languages finds its strongest support here. If God meant them for a sign to unbelievers, it must mean they conveyed a message to unbelievers. How could this be? The unbeliever, hearing the gospel in his own dialect, thinks "It must be from God that these 'strangers' to me are able to speak to me in my own language!" (Cp. Acts 2:7,8.)

Not to those who believe -- That is, the proper place to use the gift of tongues is when the audience is made up of non-believers, non-Christians.[87] If the Christians in Corinth are going to live in harmony with this directive, there will be no speaking in (untranslated) "tongues" when the audience is made up of believers.

But to unbelievers -- Here is the audience for whom God intends the gift of tongues to be used. Just as tongues were used on Pentecost (Acts 2), God wants the tongues at Corinth to be used for an evangelistic purpose. "Unbelievers" are people who are outside of Christ. Unbelievers are unconverted Jews or Gentiles who may visit the services (and whose mother-tongue was different from the language spoken to the congregation by those gifted with tongues). Verse 23 so explains it. We see Paul as saying that God intended the "tongues" to be used in situations where *unbelievers* needed directions in order to know the way. God never intended the gift of tongues to be exercised in the assembly of believers like the Corinthians were wont to exercise them. 'Tongues,' he says, 'are not intended to give directions to the Christians, but to give directions (a sign) to the unbelievers.'

But prophecy *is for a sign,* **not to unbelievers, but to those who believe** -- This is the second inference deduced from the Isaiah passage quoted in verse 21. Concerning the meaning of "prophecy," see notes at 12:10 and 14:3. It was inspired preaching in the language of the people. "Is for a sign" is repeated from the first part of the verse in perfect harmony with well-known practice of translating parallel clauses in the Greek. It has the same force here it did earlier in the verse. "Unbelievers" again refers to those who happen

---

[87] The "those who believe" is a present participle denoting a condition that continues; it is a way of designating "Christians." See 1:18 and Galatians 3:22.

to visit the Christian services, as verses 23 and 24 show.[88] Likewise, "believers" are Christians, assembled for worship, instruction, and edification.[89] What Paul affirms is that whereas the proper use of tongues is in an evangelistic situation to help reach and win the unbeliever to Christ, the proper time and place to use the gift of prophecy is in the assembly of believers,[90] to edify, exhort, and console them (14:3). Taking this phrase just as we did the same language in the previous clause of this verse, Paul says, 'Prophecy is the gift God intended to be used regularly in the assembly of the believers – not tongues, like you Corinthians are doing!'

14:23 -- *Therefore if the whole church assembles together and all speak in tongues, and ungifted men or unbelievers enter, will they not say that you are mad?*

If therefore -- "Therefore" shows there is a connection with the assertions made in verse 22 that tongues and prophecy serve as signs. Both verses 23 and 24 begin with *ean* and the subjunctive, a Greek construction which shows Paul is asking his readers to "just suppose." When the idea they are to suppose (i.e., the effect certain behavior has on the audience) has been fully grasped, the readers will see exactly how both tongues and prophecy – when used as God intended the gifts to be used – can function as signs.

The whole church should assemble together -- "Together" is a translation of *epi to auto*, the same phrase that occurs at Acts 2:41,44,47,[91] and 1 Corinthians 11:20. The whole congregation assembled 'in the same place' or 'for the same object' – they assembled for the

---

[88] Several recent writers, thinking there is something not quite right when one compares the original setting of the Isaiah passage (Isaiah's audience were unbelieving Jews) and the inference Paul draws from it (unbelieving visitors to a Christian service), have proposed that "unbelievers" (for whom tongues are intended to serve as a "sign") are Jewish people. Appeal is made to Matthew 12:38,39 ("an adulterous generation craves for a sign"), 1 Corinthians 1:22 ("Jews ask for signs"), Acts 2 and 10 (where tongues served to convince Jews), to demonstrate that tongues are to be used only when you are trying to reach unbelieving Jews; so if no unbelieving Jews were present at Corinth, there would be no need to use the gift of tongues. In response to the idea of limiting "unbelievers" to Jewish unbelievers, it may be said that not every use of the word "sign" or "tongues" is limited to when the audience is only Jewish. For example, see 2 Corinthians 12:12 and Acts 19:6.

Wiersbe interprets similarly. He argues (contrary to what has been affirmed in this commentary) that tongues were not used for evangelistic purposes, even at Pentecost, but were a sign (of approaching judgment, or simply to arouse the listener's interest) for Jews in particular. We see no reason to limit "unbeliever" here in 1 Corinthians 14 to Jews only. So limiting "unbeliever" gives little help in connecting the idea of the quotation of verse 21 to the rest of Paul's argument. Rather, in this commentator's opinion, it obscures the connection.

[89] There is no justification in the extant Greek manuscripts for J.B. Phillip's translation at this place, where he reverses what all the other versions read and makes the verse say that "tongues are for believers" while "prophecy is for unbelievers." Nor is there any need for a conjectural emendation at this place, as though verse 22 contradicts what is said in verses 24 and 25, or as though what is here said about tongues and prophecy being a sign is opposite what is said about the effects of tongues and prophecy on the day of Pentecost (Acts 2).

[90] While prophecy was the gift to be used when the audience is made up primarily of believers, as the next verses show, it would also be profitable to unbelievers who might happen to be visiting that day.

[91] See notes on this phrase in the author's commentary on *Acts*, at Acts 2:47.

purpose of what we call worship. Again, let it be emphasized that the use of this phrase makes it clear that Paul has been speaking of the exercise of spiritual gifts in the assembly, rather than the private use of the gifts.

And all speak in tongues -- In his first "just suppose" example, Paul pictures the congregation assembling together and the only thing that happens during the whole meeting is people talking in tongues. It is difficult to decide if "all" in this phrase is synonymous with the "whole church" of the previous phrase, or whether Paul has in mind "all" the folk who take the lead.[92] Some have understood the "all" in Paul's supposition to mean that the entire congregation was speaking in tongues at the same time – much like one sees everyone "speaking" at once in many modern charismatic congregational meetings. Verse 27 may indicate more than one was speaking at a time. Paul is "supposing" an extreme case for the sake of argument. Against the idea that a kind of bedlam was part of Paul's present hypothesis is the thought that if we understand this verse to say all were speaking in tongues at the same time, then we must also understand the next verse to say that all were prophesying at the same time. That will hardly do.[93] In this commentator's view, the better way to understand Paul's hypothesis is to imagine that "all" refers to every person who took the lead in any given meeting of the whole congregation. The Corinthians loved and admired tongues above the other gifts, so in his first supposition, for the moment, Paul grants their wish. He pictures a time when the whole congregation has assembled, and everyone who leads out in the meeting speaks a foreign language. Every single person who gets up to speak utters something unintelligible to the assembled audience. No other kind of utterance takes place during the whole meeting – everything is done in a language no one understands. Having granted their wish, he now vividly lays out the disastrous results.

And ungifted men or unbelievers enter -- The "ungifted" person is one who does not understand the language being spoken by the person who was speaking in tongues.[94] An "unbeliever," of course, is the person who has not been converted, one does not believe in

---

[92] Obviously not all spoke in tongues – 1 Corinthians 12:29,30. Obviously there was more that happened at the assembly than just the exercise of tongues – see 14:3,19,26. But for the moment Paul ignores these facts as he says "just suppose!"

[93] Pentecostal and Charismatic doctrine currently teaches all Christians are to speak in tongues as evidence they have been baptized in the Holy Spirit. In this commentator's opinion, it is an indication of how little Scriptural evidence there is that *all* Christians should be expected to speak in tongues that this supposition must be taken at face value and then be appealed to as evidence that 'all believers could potentially do so.' Furthermore, in order to justify the claim that 'all Christians speak in tongues,' a peculiar interpretation must be given to 12:29,30. In spite of the illustration about the variety in the different members of the body being absolutely essential to the body, and in spite of the fact that the questions at the end of chapter 12 expect a negative answer, we are told by one Pentecostal writer, "1 Corinthians 12:30 doesn't mean all can't speak in tongues; it is only intended to discourage all from doing so" (Fee, *op. cit.*, p.684).

[94] There is little reason for Mare (*op. cit.*, p.273-274) to suggest that "ungifted" in this passage is different from "ungifted" in verse 16, and here refers to an unbeliever who has begun to show an interest in the gospel – one we might characterize as being an inquirer or seeker.

Jesus Messiah. Some suppose that "or" in this case is not disjunctive (i.e., "ungifted" and "unbelievers" are two different classes of people), but conjunctive, as in Luke 20:2. But in our opinion, it is disjunctive, thus suggesting the "ungifted" is a Christian who is not fluent in the language being spoken, and "unbelievers" are simply non-Christian visitors to the services, he or she, too, being unfamiliar with the language. In apostolic times, the assemblies were directed towards believers and their needs for instruction and edification. Yet this verse suggests that at times there would be non-Christians who visited the meetings.[95]

Will they not say that you are mad? -- The implied answer the question expects is "Yes!" In congregational meetings, the leaders would usually speak the same language as the people who were assembled. Church services were ordinarily conducted in the language of the people who made up the congregation. Suppose visitors came to the services, having in some way been attracted to the assembly. They enter the congregational meeting place, sit down, and listen to the Christians who got up to speak. One after another the Christian speakers uttered words in a foreign language unknown to anyone in the audience; no one said anything that ordinary persons could understand. What conclusion could the visitor reach other than the impression that he had just witnessed an instance of "mania" (Greek) like that which attended inspired speaking in pagan religions.[96] Surely, they would think, 'No intelligent person who was in control of his faculties would act in such a way. You must be "mad"!' The "ungifted" person, instead of getting instruction that leads to growth, is repulsed by what he or she has witnessed, while the "unbeliever" flatly rejects Christianity – all because of the improper use of a spiritual gift by the Christians. Is it beyond the realm of possibility that some at Corinth have actually rejected Christ because of what they saw when they visited the assembly? Paul's implication is this: 'Don't you see what public condemnation you are exposing the gospel to by your practice of speaking non-understandable languages?' Is there any way the Corinthians could miss the plain thrust of what Paul has been writing? His statement that "tongues are not for believers" amounts to a command to abstain from the use of the gift of tongues

---

[95] Verses 21-25 remind us that non-Christian visitors may be expected in the weekly assemblies of believers. Those who plan the music and the lessons, while emphasizing the edification and instruction of the believers, may wish also to reflect on how to be intelligible and understandable to the interested outsiders. This is far from giving an imprimatur to conducting exclusively 'seeker-sensitive services' where the whole emphasis is geared towards the visitors. Surely, Paul's instructions here about prophecy for believers should give us some guidance for our assemblies. Many congregations are increasingly moving away from solid instructional sermons based on Biblical content, in favor of a more entertainment-oriented style of music and message. While the motive may be worthy – i.e., there is a desire to attract the unbeliever or seeker who judges local congregations on the value of the many services provided – believers could go home from such 'seeker-sensitive' meetings spiritually unfed and unedified. Solid guidance in these matters may be gleaned from the following sources: Bruce and Marshall Shelly, *Consumer Church* (Downers Grove, IL: InterVarsity, 1992); Jeffrey Peterson, "How Shall the Seeker say Amen?" *Christian Studies* 13 (1993), p. 22-31; and "Viewpoint: Pro and Con on the Seeker Church Movement," *Christian Research Journal* (Spring 1996), p.54-55.

[96] The word translated "you are mad" is *mainesthe*, cf. John 10:20, Acts 26:24,26. The cognate noun *mania* occurs in various texts reflecting the ecstasies (altered states of consciousness) of the mysteries. (E.g., Pausanias, 2.7.5: "These women they say are sacred to Dionysus and maddened by his inspiration." Cf. also Loeb, I, 285 and Herodotus 4.79.)

in their worship services when such use was needless, or when it would leave visitors with a poor impression of Christianity. For visitors to observe and go away calling Christianity 'madness' is a response totally unworthy of the gospel. The Corinthians must cease their abuse of tongues in the public assembly!

14:24 -- *But if all prophesy, and an unbeliever or an ungifted man enters, he is convicted by all, he is called to account by all;*

But -- In contrast to the Corinthians' admiration of tongues, Paul has insisted that prophecy – where the listeners do understand what was being spoken – was the greater gift in the public assembly (14:5). As in verse 23, Paul again begins, "Just suppose" (*ean* and the subjunctive). Now, he pictures a congregational meeting where the only thing that occurs is prophecy.[97] 'Suppose everyone who speaks in the assembly prophesies. Just see the difference as to the effect when the greater-than-tongues-gift of prophecy is put into action in the same congregational setting.'

If all prophesy -- In this example, each person who took the lead in the public service, in proper order and time, uttered an inspired message in a language intelligible to all.[98] The present subjunctive pictures the act in progress: 'Suppose all are continually engaged in the act of prophesying ....'

And an unbeliever or an ungifted man enters -- This supposition proceeds as did the previous one. It pictures the very same people ("unbeliever or ungifted") visiting the church services. The visitors come in and listen to all of this prophesying, which is, of course, entirely intelligible to them because it is in their own language. What will be the effect? Interestingly, Paul now writes in the singular – "an unbeliever or an ungifted man" – and not the plural as in verse 23. Perhaps the reason is that conversion is a personal and individual matter. The gift of prophecy was really intended for use where the audience was composed of believers (verse 22). Verse 3 has explained what "prophesying" does for believers. But now, in the rest of verse 24 and 25, we learn what effect prophesying

---

[97] Again, not all could prophesy. And again, more occurred at the assembly than an uninterrupted string of prophecies. See what is said in Acts 2:42 for example. See also the Scriptures cited in footnote #92 above.

[98] Chapter 12 has already shown not every person could prophesy. 14:39 may imply that people with the gift of prophecy at Corinth actually were reticent to get up to speak at all. Paul is simply supposing such a case for the sake of argument. Pentecostal interpreters treat Joel's prophecy (Joel 2:28-30; cf. Acts 2:17,18) as evidence that in the Messianic age *all* of God's people will be able to "prophesy." When they then attempt to use verses 23 and 24 in an effort to show that every Christian may be expected to speak in tongues or prophesy, they have missed the point that this is merely supposition (i.e., Paul's sentence begins with *ean* and the subjunctive). Each Bible reader must be careful lest he or she come to this passage seeking to justify some practice already accepted as legitimate in their churches. It will not do to use this passage to prove a devotional use of tongues, or to prove that there are two kinds or degrees of prophecy, one that was authoritative (like the Old Testament prophet), and one that was merely a loose prediction of the future, a prediction that may or may not come to pass. There is no Biblical warrant for accepting such a less-than-Biblical definition for "prophecy."

could have on unbelievers who might happen to be present.[99] Now we see why Paul wishes even more that "all" would prophesy (verse 5) – he knows what will happen.

He is convicted by all -- Prophecy – inspired preaching – can convict a man of his own sin. Unconverted visitors will be just as convicted of their sin by the inspired speakers, whose preaching arouses the conscience, as are the Christians. The word is *elegchetai*, and is translated (NASB) "convict" both here and at John 16:8, where it speaks of the Holy Spirit's work of convicting the world of "sin, and righteousness, and judgment." Here the word indicates the man who hears divine truth being communicated by the prophet would be convicted or convinced of his error and of his sin; he would see that his former opinions and practice had been wrong. This is one of the effects of inspired preaching in the language of the people. Other effects follow. Quite a difference from the effect produced by "tongues", where the hearer went away still an unbeliever, thinking the Christians were mad.

He is called to account by all -- For the meaning of "called to account" or 'investigated or examined to determine guilt' (*anakrinetai*) see notes at 2:14ff.[100] The effect of inspired preaching in language the man understands is to reveal to that man his spiritual state. His whole inner being is searched out. Each person who speaks, one prophet after another, gives a message that strikes home and reveals his sin and his guilt to him.

14:25 -- *the secrets of his heart are disclosed; and so he will fall on his face and worship God, declaring that God is certainly among you.*

The secrets of his heart are disclosed -- Secrets he imagined were locked in his heart are called to his mind. See Hebrews 4:12, "The Word of God is living and active, and sharper than any two-edged sword ... *and is able to judge the thoughts and intentions of the heart*." What is described here in Corinthians as being effected through prophecy is described in Hebrews 4:12,13 as being accomplished through the Word of God. It seems to the listener like the sermon was made for him. Oft-times a preacher will deliver a sermon, and the message will fit a situation in a congregation, without the preacher ever knowing the situation or how well the message fits. A man listening will think the sermon was specially aimed at him, even though the preacher is just preaching a general message. This is the awe-inspiring power of the gospel.

And so he will fall on his face – 'Falling on the face' was performed by sinking down on

---

[99] Instead of saying that there is a seeming discrepancy between verses 22 and 25, it is better to say that in Paul's supposition the gift of prophecy is not nearly as limited in its effect on unbelievers as was the gift of tongues (the way the Corinthians were using them). We still are in the paragraph about 'understanding' being a chief guideline or parameter to govern the exercise of one's gifts.

[100] There are three Greek words that are not always adequately translated in our English versions: *krinein* (which means 'to judge'), *katakrinein* (which means 'to condemn'), and *anakrinesthai*, the verb used here (which is a judicial term meaning 'cross-examination' before a judge in a court of law). As the believers in Corinth give one testimony after another bringing out God's requirements for men's lives, this becomes a detailed examination of the life of the unbeliever, to uncover his guilt. And according to John 16:8. while the preacher is speaking, the Holy Spirit, too, is at work to bring about conviction.

one's knees, and then after extending the hands above the head, the person bends forward from the waist till the palms of his hands and his face touch the ground. (Muslims still assume this position when praying. Some have called attention to the fact that Orientals are often more demonstrative than Occidentals.). This is the usual posture of submission or reverence or deep conviction in the Eastern countries (e.g., Isaiah 45:14 and 1 Samuel 19:24). After describing what takes place inwardly in the sinner's heart as a result of the prophecy, Paul adds the outward, visible, and audible effects of the prophecy.

And worship God -- The word is *proskuneō*; it speaks of 'submission.' If the ungifted believer "worships God," it is a greater level of submission to the will of God than he had before he heard the prophecy.[101] If it is the unbeliever who "worships God," it says 'he will be converted;'[102] the "unbeliever" who came in, departs as a "believer." Both of these results have been accomplished through the gift of prophecy. This is an effect that the gift of tongues, as used by the Corinthians, could not produce. We think it is likely that what Paul here "supposes" (ungifted people's lives changed, unbelievers converted) has actually already happened in Corinth when the audience has been exposed to prophecy.

Declaring that God is certainly among you -- "Declaring" (*apaggellōn*) is a present participle showing that this declaration was an act contemporaneous with his falling on his face and worshiping God. In the Greek text, the word for God, *theos*, is preceded by the definite article (*ho theos*, "the God"), which is most significant in the case of this unbeliever. He confesses that he no longer believes in his pagan gods, but in THE only true God, as a result of the prophesying to which he has listened. "Among you" (*en humin*) might mean 'in your midst' or 'in your hearts.' The NASB translators thought of it as 'in your midst as a congregation.' When Paul spoke about the effect of tongues (as the Corinthians were wanting to use them), he used only one brief statement, namely, the assertion of the unbelievers: "You are mad." When he describes the effect of prophecy, he dwells on it at length and reaches a climax in the declaration of the new convert, "God is certainly among you."[103] Farrar (*op. cit.*, p.459) quotes a poem by Goldsmith:

> Truth from his lips prevailed with double sway,
> And fools, who came to scoff, remained to pray.

Paul has now concluded his presentation of the need for 'understanding.' If the Corinthians will exercise their gifts only after carefully making sure the listeners can understand, they will go a long way toward curbing the abuse of spiritual gifts in the public assemblies.

---

[101] In verse 3 we learned that "prophecy" was something that edified believers. Paul has pictured it doing just that for the ungifted believer. When applied to believers, "edification" refers to their spiritual growth.

[102] It has been said that prophecy can 'build up' an unbeliever. When it does, it speaks of their being added to the body of Christ.

[103] Verses 24 and 25 do not guarantee that all who hear prophecy rather than tongues will be saved. They simply stress that an intelligible proclamation of the gospel stands a far better chance of convicting unsaved people than untranslated tongues do.

c. Application #3 -- Orderliness. 14:26-40

> *Summary:* Paul has shown prophecy is superior to tongues (as the Corinthians used them) when it comes to edification and when it comes to understanding, two absolutely necessary ingredients for acceptable public worship services. There is a third criterion which, if followed, will make public services acceptable to God and helpful to the people who have assembled – it is 'order,' or 'orderliness.' To ensure the Corinthians do not violate this criterion, Paul gives some regulations respecting the orderly use of spiritual gifts and instruction to married women about "silence" for the sake of orderliness. Finally, Paul demands recognition that the things which he has been writing were from the Lord.

14:26 -- *What is the outcome then, brethren? When you assemble, each one has a psalm, has a teaching, has a revelation, has a tongue, has an interpretation. Let all things be done for edification.*

What is *the outcome* then, brethren? -- We have the same phrase here as in verse 15. 'What is the proper course to pursue? What are the consequences of the applications that have been enunciated? How are you, in point of fact, to conduct your worship service?' In answering his own question, Paul insists that all the gifts were to be practiced only when edification of others would result, and even then the gifts were to be practiced under strict regulation. He is going to tell the Corinthians just what to do in their church assemblies so as to employ each person's spiritual gifts in the most beneficial way. The kindly address "brethren" asks the Corinthians to receive these directions in a brotherly spirit.

When you assemble -- Christians regularly assembled for instruction, for prayer, for observing the Lord's Supper (Acts 2:42), for the love feast (1 Corinthians 11), and to encourage one another to love and good works (Hebrews 10:24). We tend to call such meetings "worship services." "When" (or 'whenever,' *hotan*) indicates that the coming together of the saints of God for worship was a matter of frequent occurrence. While it is true that we can worship God individually at home, this cannot and should not take the place of fellowship and participation with other believers in the regular public assembly.

Each one -- Not absolutely every one had gifts[104] nor did every member always have to have an opportunity to take part in each and every church service (unless the congregation was a small house church where time would permit every member to exercise his or her gift). But since all members of the body are needful (1 Corinthians 12:14ff), each gifted person must, over a period of time, be given an opportunity to exercise his or her gift for the benefit of the whole body. What cannot be allowed is several gifted persons exercising their gifts at the same time.

This verse gives us an intimate glimpse of some of the activities that occurred in the public worship services at Corinth. Each individual perhaps had one gift. Each of the

---

[104] On the question of whether every individual Christian was "spiritually gifted" see notes at 1 Corinthians 12:6-13.

worshipers came prepared to participate, to exercise his or her spiritual gift – a hymn, an instruction, a revelation, a tongue, a translation, a prayer. Each came to the assembly ready and anxious to manifest his or her gift. But instead of waiting for an invitation from the presiding officer in the assembly, or speaking in succession and in order, each one (under the influence of the Holy Spirit as they were) regarded himself or herself as having an important message to communicate, or as being called on immediately to celebrate the praises of God. Thus, confusion and disorder would prevail. Many of them, we may suppose, would be speaking at the same time, with the result that not many would be edified, and a most unfavorable impression would be made on the minds of any visitors who should be present. Abbott has written, "Just when ye are assembling for sacred worship, and ought to be thinking of Christ and of Christ's Body, the congregation, each one is perhaps thinking of himself, 'I have a Psalm,' 'I have a doctrine,' 'I have a revelation.' Be done with this! Let all be done to edification."[105] Paraphrased, Paul says, 'Right now, the uppermost thought in your minds as you are assembling for public worship is the individual gift which you possesses. You just must change your attitudes! These gifts are not to be used for your own gratification, but for the good of the listeners. You just must begin to give first consideration to what is best for the other.'

Has a psalm -- "Psalm" has come to mean for us one of the "songs" (chapters) in the Book of Psalms.[106] The word was not so narrowly defined in apostolic times. In apostolic times, it signified a song sung to the accompaniment of an instrument, and often was a poem composed and set to music by the person singing it. Verse 15 shows the words were uttered in the language of the listeners so that they could understand. Perhaps under the guidance of the Holy Spirit, worshipers had written music to which the canonical Psalms were sung. Or it may have been that the worshiper had a song of his own composition (composed by the Spirit's help, just as the canonical Psalms were) to sing for the other worshipers. We do not know whether this involved singing by a congregation, a choir, or simply a solo by the gifted individual alone. We do not have any evidence for hymns that were universally accepted by the early Christian church for public worship. But whatever this psalm was, Paul is concerned that it be given forth in a manner to bring edification to the whole group. Since he mentions the psalm first, it is quite possible this is an indication of how the Christians began their meetings – with singing.

Has a teaching -- At 14:6 the word "teaching" was explained. The word speaks of a 'lesson,' systematic religious instruction, any piece of instruction on some appropriate point of doctrine, an exposition of some particular Christian truth. The Greek word here is *didaschō*, which can refer either to the act or to the content of teaching.

---

[105] Quoted in Robertson and Plummer, *op. cit.*, p.320.

[106] The word *psalmos*, "psalm," was used in the LXX chiefly for *mizmor* ("psalm") from *zamar,* to strike the chords of a musical instrument. Thayer's *Lexicon*, p.637 gives a brief explanation of the synonyms *humnos, psalmos*, and *ode*. "*Ode* is a generic term; *psalmos* and *humnos* are specific, the former designating a song which took its general character from the Old Testament 'Psalms', although not restricted to them (see 1 Corinthians 14:15,26), the latter a song of praise. 'While the leading idea of *psalmos* is musical accompaniment, and that of *humnos* praise to God, *ode* is a general word for a song, whether accompanied or unaccompanied, whether of praise or on any other subject ...." For a detailed study, this commentator has a separately published study on "The Anti-Instrument Controversy."

Has a revelation -- "Revelation" is the act of the Holy Spirit imparting to God-chosen messengers truth they were incapable of discovering by unaided human research. This activity has been explained in notes at 1 Corinthians 2:10-12 and 14:6. This gifted person is pictured coming to the worship service prepared to share some truth which had been particularly revealed to this person.

Has a tongue -- A person with this gift had the power of speaking the truths of God in a foreign language. See the comments at 1 Corinthians 12:10.

Has an interpretation -- As explained at 1 Corinthians 12:10, this gift was the ability to translate what someone else spoke in a foreign language into the language spoken locally.

Here we have another intimation of what the assemblies were like in the early church. Fee[107] suggests this is an *ad hoc* list, not intended to give the 'order of worship,' nor to be an exhaustive list of what "each one has" to offer by way of ministry. The list clearly is not exhaustive; neither "prayer" nor "prophecy" nor "discernment" occur in this list, yet these are regulated in the verses that follow, implying that they, too, were part of the public service. M.C. Tenney had a different explanation of what the early churches services were like. On the basis of this section, Tenney tried to argue that early worship services were like what we know as "testimony meetings," where people shared with each other.[108] The services in Bible times, he thought, were not as preaching-centered as the services we are accustomed to. There is some truth in the idea that the services of the early church included or consisted of a time of mutual sharing. But the items included in the worship at Corinth were the effect of spiritual gifts. There is a fundamental difference between prophecy (Spirit-inspired preaching) and someone giving a personal testimony, however powerful and persuasive. Further, if only some had the gift of prophecy, or the gift of teaching, how could this passage be speaking of everyone getting up and prophesying or teaching like in a testimony meeting? This passage in Corinthians is hardly a biblical example that demonstrates the legitimacy of testimony meetings.

Let all things be done for edification -- 1 Corinthians 14:1-5 have already shown the importance of the principle of edification. Again, Paul insists that all the gifts were to be practiced only when edification of others would result. This is the great principle in the regulation of these gifts – let all be done to promote the edification of the church. This is the golden rule of the worship service.

Paul is determined that anyone who possesses a gift should receive every chance to exercise that gift; but he is equally determined that the services of the congregation should not thereby become a kind of competitive disorder. The Corinthians were eager to mani-

---

[107] Fee, *op. cit.*, p.690. Robertson and Plummer, *op. cit.*, p.320, wonder if prophecy is not included in this list because it was so despised at Corinth that those who possessed the gift did not often come forward.

[108] Dr. Tenney's comments were offered in a class on 1 Corinthians at Wheaton College. There is a difference between Brethren and Methodist class (small group) meetings. The Brethren meetings are Scripture centered. The Methodist meetings are experience centered.

fest their gifts. But, perhaps, Paul intimates that they did not come to their weekly assemblies in quite the right spirit. The object of the gifts is to be edification – not idle self-display or self-ostentation. Let all these gifts be so employed and timed that the whole church shall be built up and perfected thereby.

While in verse 27ff Paul gives rules for the exercise of prophecy and tongues, we suppose the principle behind the rules applies to all the gifts. Having restated the guiding principle, Paul will now give detailed instructions regarding how the Corinthians are to proceed. He gives some strict regulations so that, when any of the gifts is exercised, edification may result.

14:27 -- *If anyone speaks in a tongue,* **it should be** *by two or at the most three, and* **each** *in turn, and one must interpret;*

If any one speaks in a tongue -- Paul has just said, "Let all things be done for edification." Here is how tongues and interpretation are to be regulated so that edification may result. We assume verse 27 pictures a meeting when no foreigner is present, so neither tongues nor a translator are really needed. Both, however, may have a part in the assembly – one speaks, and the other translates – and through the translator the hearers understand and are edified. There is also a limit on the number of tongues speakers or interpreters who may function at any one service. This, too, will aid in edification.

It should be **by two or at the most three** -- The Greek needs no verb, but in English we add 'let it be' or "it should be" in order to obtain a smoothness of translation. That is, two or at most three in one day or in one meeting, are to speak in tongues. It is probable that many were endowed with the gift of tongues, and from the prevalence of unchristian pride in the church, it seems all were disposed to exercise the gift even when it would be of no real advantage. Speakers with tongues are not to take up the entire time of the meeting, and thus leave little or no opportunity for prophecy. Some feel "two or three *sentences*" are intended. (We have to supply the noun, be it *sentences* or *speakers*.) The speaker was to speak two or three sentences in the foreign language, and then wait for the translator to translate – the same as when modern preachers preach through an interpreter. But this commentator thinks the reference is to two or three speakers in any one service.

And *each* **in turn** -- This is the second limitation on those with the gift of tongues or interpretation, as "and" indicates. Each speaker is to exercise his or her gift separately, one after another. These "two or at the most three" speakers should not all speak at the same time, but sequentially. This sounds as though in Corinth these speakers at times failed to restrain themselves and spoke simultaneously and created unseemly confusion. Apparently the Corinthian Christians were so eager to show off their ability to speak in tongues that they interrupted one another, a breach of orderliness that stifles edification within the public assemblies.

And let one interpret -- This is the third limitation or guideline regulating the use of tongues: there must be a translation. Unless the Corinthians carefully observe these limitations, edification will have little chance of resulting. Only one person was needed to translate (12:10). After a translation had been given, there would be no need for another translator to get up and merely repeat the same translation. There is no reason to stress "one" to mean that one person does the translating for all the speakers with tongues. What Paul requires is that no one speak with a tongue unless a prompt translation follows. Whether one person translates for two or for three speakers with tongues will depend on whether the two or three use the same foreign language. In comments earlier, at 12:10 and at 14:6, 13, we noted that sometimes the one who spoke in tongues could also translate. To make this verse harmonize with those, a few have argued that "one" (who translates) is one of the two or three tongue speakers. One of them was to translate.[109] Just as only one person at a time was to speak with a tongue, so one person was to follow the tongue with an interpretation. Earlier in this letter Paul has explained the real purpose of tongues as being for unbelievers. Now we are learning that the use of tongues in the presence of believers is not absolutely ruled out. If a translator is present, who can explain in language the assembled believers would understand (since the tongues would not otherwise be understood), then tongues could be used in an assembly of believers.

14:28 -- *but if there is no interpreter, he must keep silent in the church; and let him speak to himself and to God.*

But if there is no interpreter, let him keep silent in the church -- Though earlier verses have suggested that sometimes the speaker in tongues might do the translation, the inference here is that it would probably be someone else. Paul is anticipating the occasion when no translator would be present. In such an event, no one is to speak with a tongue in the public assembly (church).

This also clearly implies the speaker with a tongue can ascertain in advance whether a translator is present or not. How could he do this? (1) He could *not* do it if tongues are the language of heaven or a mystical syllabication since the interpretation would have to come as a special revelation for each case. Who is ready to assume that interpretation consists in the actual knowledge of the language of heaven or of the meaning of those mystical syllables? No speaker of some non-human language could possibly ascertain in advance whether the Spirit were ready to grant someone the required revelation at that specific time. Thus he could never determine whether he should proceed to speak or not. This requirement concerning the presence of a "translator" indicates the "tongues" at Corinth were foreign languages spoken by men. (2) He could ascertain if a translator were present if "tongues" are foreign human languages.

> Any speaker with a tongue may easily determine in advance whether someone is present in the assembly who understands the particular language which the Spirit communicates to him. Previous tests and experiences will help the speaker to know if there is an interpreter present. Each may speak a different foreign lan-

---

[109] Earlier verses in 1 Corinthians seem to show that sometimes the speaker knew what he was saying, and sometimes the speaker did not. If one did know, then that person could translate what he had just finished speaking in a foreign language. In such a case, one wonders why the person didn't just give the message in the local language in the first place. Only, it seems, if a second person could exercise his or her gift of translation would these instructions allowing all to have a part in the service make sense.

guage (each, that is, of the two or three speakers that Paul allows for any one service). Each will know the name of the particular language which the Spirit grants him to speak. A glance tells him whether an interpreter is present or not. If none is at hand, he remains silent. Such interpreters will have interpreted before and will thus be known for their ability by all.[110]

The word translated "silent" is *sigatō* – the same word that will be used in 14:34 where wives are instructed to be "silent." This silence for the sake or orderliness – silence when no edification would take place – is what is enjoined on the tongues speakers.

And let him speak to himself and to God -- Several interpretations have been offered for this phrase. (1) Some suggest that the thing denoted is to use "tongues" in private devotions at home. (It is affirmed that this cannot mean "under his breath" in a public assembly – for "speak" (*lalein*) throughout the chapter is that of making audible utterance.) (2) Another suggestion is the speaker is to speak quietly, in hushed tones, in the assembly rather than speaking loudly enough that others would hear. If he has to speak, let him do it in almost a whisper. There is to be no exercising it just for the sake of showing off. (3) A third suggestion is the speaker simply speaks softly and quietly to himself; he can move his lips forming the words and syllables, but no sound escapes his mouth. God who reads the hearts will be the only audience. After all, to remember that God is the audience will have greater positive influence on the speaker's behavior than if he thinks his audience is composed of a whole church full of human listeners. Not a few commentators remind their readers that at verse 4, we learned that in such a case the speaker will be edified.

14:29 -- *Let two or three prophets speak, and let the others pass judgment.*

And let two or three prophets speak -- Now follow the regulations for prophets, which are consistent with the principle stated at the close of verse 26 about all being done in such a way as to edify. A "prophet" could be a man or a woman (1 Corinthians 11). The regulations for prophets are similar to that for tongues. Only a limited number – not over three – should speak on the same day, or at the same service. Paul does not in this verse need to repeat "each one in turn"; that is understood. Nothing is said about making a selection, say by the elders, as to who the two or three are to be on any given Sunday, yet we might suppose such a practice was followed.

And let the others pass judgment -- Pass judgment (*diakrinetōsan*) is the same thing introduced as "distinguishing (*diakrisis*) of spirits" in 12:10.[111] Who are these *others*? (1) Some say 'other prophets.'[112] That is, the other prophets were to decide whether what the speaker just said was dictated by the Holy Spirit, and was therefore accurate and ortho-

---

[110] Lenski, *op. cit.*, p.609-610.

[111] Charismatics, it would seem, are in error when they have regularly insisted that the gift of "distinguishing of spirits" (12:10) and "pass(ing) judgment" are not to be identified as being the same thing.

[112] The Greek word "others" (*alloi*) is the word that implies "others of the same kind." So the issue is whether it means "other prophets" or "other gifted people."

dox. The other prophets would be able to tell, to an extent, whether the speakers had spoken in harmony with what had been repeated to them as they sat listening to the speakers. We have regularly affirmed that the higher offices did include the lower gifts. Thus, a prophet might also have the gift of discernment. (2) Some say "members of the congregation." Compare Acts 17:11, where the Bereans were "more noble-minded" because they studied and examined the Scriptures to see if what the preacher said was true. It is right for members of the congregation, as they listen to a speaker, to use the Scriptures to discriminate and test what is being spoken. But, in a context of how spiritual gifts are to be exercised, we doubt that the action here called for is the same as what the Bereans were doing. Furthermore, under this interpretation that church members do the judging, there is an objectionable tendency to read into this verse the idea that the evaluation is needed because the "prophets" could sometimes be wrong.[113] (3) The correct view is that the "others" were those individuals who had the "gift of distinguishing of spirits." There was a need for such discerning of spirits. In the days before Christ's new revelation was complete (i.e., before Hebrews 1:1-3 and Jude 3 were written), new, additional truth would be revealed from time to time. With this progressive revelation went the danger of false doctrine being introduced. There needed to be a check on the teaching of the "prophets" lest evil spirits inject false teaching. The one with the gift of discernment had the task of determining what 'spirit' had prompted the prophet or preacher to speak. The exercise of this gift would preserve the congregation from being misled by one who was not really guided by the Holy Spirit.[114] "Pass judgment!" The utterance of a prophet is not to be given uncritical acceptance but is to be tested by those who were Spirit-equipped.

14:30 -- *But if a revelation is made to another who is seated, the first one must keep silent.*

But if -- It appears that not only tongue speakers but also the prophets were displaying a certain amount of selfishness in their behavior at the public meetings. It looks as though when someone had the floor and was the center of attention, that person was being very hesitant to yield being the center of attention or to permit someone else to be in the spotlight. Paul here indicates that when someone has the floor, he or she is to be ready and willing to yield to another who has a message from God for the audience.

---

[113] In previous discussions of the gift of prophecy, we have already rejected the idea that there were two kinds of prophecy in the early church – one that was authoritative (and had the weight of Scripture), and the other which was not authoritative, but might be accepted or rejected as the listener chose to do. Not only do charismatics find warrant here (and in Acts 21:4,11) to sometimes ignore what a prophet says, but the Reorganized Church of Latter Day Saints 'votes' on the validity of a 'revelation' after it is given. In 1984, for example, after a 'revelation' that women should be ordained to the priesthood, the vote was 95% in favor of accepting the revelation. While listeners in Bible times sometimes outright rejected what the prophet said, whoever heard of listeners to Bible prophets voting on whether or not the message they just heard was valid?

[114] Someone has asked, "Where are the elders?" "Isn't 'passing judgment' their job?" The fact that Paul never mentions local church leaders (elders and deacons) in his letters to Corinth does not mean they are not present at Corinth. Acts 14:23 describes Paul and Barnabas appointing elders in all the congregations they planted. We doubt such actions occurred only on the first missionary journey and never at Corinth. In the light of the letter to the Philippians (written by Paul, no later than AD 63) which speaks of elders and deacons, it is not a proper conclusion to relegate elders to a late, post-Pauline time in church history.

A revelation is made to another who is seated -- As did Jewish worshipers in the synagogue (Luke 4:16 and Acts 13:16), the Christian congregation seems to be pictured as sitting to listen to reading or preaching while the reader or speaker or the one prophesying stood while doing so. This is still talking about the prophets. Before any prophet spoke, he would receive a revelation from the Lord, and then be inspired to speak.[115]

Let the first keep silent -- The prophet (the one who "is seated") who had just received a new revelation would, no doubt, give some kind of signal (perhaps he stood up) to the one speaking ("the first" one) that he had just received a fresh revelation from God. This would signal the one speaking that he or she was to give way, to yield the floor. The apostle does not say, "Let the first (speaker) *at once* be silent." He can finish the thought or sentence he is speaking, and then give the other prophet opportunity to speak. The one to whom the revelation had just been made should keep silent till the one speaking finished. The fact that a revelation was granted to one of the prophets sitting in the audience would show that it was a truth needed then and there. This should be an obvious hint to the first speaker that it was time for him to yield to the newer revelation. But they were to speak one by one. There was not to be any confusion arising as would occur if two persons tried to speak at the same time. Clearly, the first speaker was not ejected by the second in any disorderly manner. If a direct revelation is given to one of the prophets sitting in the audience while one prophet was speaking, then the speaker should in this case give way. He should let the one with the new revelation make it known to the congregation. No one was to occupy the whole time to the exclusion of others, and each ought to rejoice that others possessed this gift as well as himself. The first speaker can quickly finish speaking, and the second can wait his turn, since both are able to control their own behavior even after receiving a message from the Lord (verse 32). Verse 30 parallels verse 27 in its insistence that prophets, like tongue speakers, exercise their gifts in turn.

14:31 -- *For you can all prophesy one by one, so that all may learn and all may be exhorted;*

For you can all prophesy one by one -- "For" indicates Paul is giving a justification for the preceding regulation. There is time enough for all. There is no need for speaking in confusion and disorder or speakers trying to out-yell other speakers who are trying to make themselves heard. All the prophets will get to speak in due time. Two or three can speak in one service. They do not all need to speak in one service. Two prophets do not need to speak at the same time. There were to be other services, and as those meetings came and went, all would get an opportunity to speak. After all, if two or three are speaking at one time, to which one will the audience members listen? Verse 31 parallels verse 5, illustrating Paul's desire that all exercise their gifts in a way that will edify all.

---

[115] Those who urge that the early church knew of two types of prophecy (see notes at 11:4) tend to opt for two kinds of revelation, too. Mare (*op. cit.*, p.276) writes about the kind of revelation that produces Scripture as being distinct from the kind of revelation a prophet might receive during a worship service. How much better to opt for one type of prophecy (inspired preaching), and for one kind of revelation. This way, there is no difference between the inspired preaching (the result of a previous revelation), and inspired Scripture (the result of a previous revelation). We have regularly affirmed that there was no difference between the content of inspired preaching and the content of inspired writing.

So that all may learn -- These last phrases of verse 31 give the reason for such orderliness as the earlier verses demand. "May learn" is *manthanō*, 'to receive instruction.' Both the congregational members who were not endowed with the gift of prophecy (12:29) and other prophets would be included in those who are learning.

> All ... having gifts may prophesy, one at a time, so that all might know what had been revealed to each and all. The same things were not revealed to the different prophets [see "we know in part and prophesy in part," 1 Corinthians 13:9]. This was true of the apostles, also. Some things were revealed to one, other things revealed to another. A conference of all was needful that the full revelation of God might be known (Acts 11). So of these prophets or gifted persons, each should hear what was revealed to the others, so that each would learn all that was revealed to all and be comforted thereby.[116]

And all may be exhorted – *Parakaleō* is to be 'comforted, cheered, exhorted, strengthened,' or 'encouraged to remain faithful to Christ' (see 14:3). These are things "prophecy" did for the listeners.

There may be a sense in which the result expected from modern preaching is much like the result from the spiritual gift of prophecy. It is the preacher's duty to take time to unearth fresh facts and words of encouragement and admonition from the Word of God for the hearts and minds of his people. When we preach, we must teach, so that others may learn something which they did not know before that will further glorify God and be life-transforming.

All three verbs in this verse – prophesy, learn, and exhort – are not in the aorist tense in Greek, which would indicate a once-and-for-all matter. Rather, all are present tense verbs, which imply a continuous process of prophesying, of learning, of admonition. In other words, not all who prophesy can expect to do so at one meeting. Not all the comfort and admonition God has for us can be appropriated at any one meeting. At every occasion of public worship there must be opportunity for these; and the more we experience the more we feel we need. We can never be fully taught, fully comforted, fully admonished.

14:32 -- *and the spirits of prophets are subject to prophets;*

And -- When Paul directs that speakers with tongues are to be silent in the event that no interpreter is present, he intimates that these speakers are able to control themselves. When Paul directs that prophets are to give way to other prophets who receive a new revelation, and that they are to speak one at a time, he intimates that these speakers are able to control the exercise of their gifts. What he intimated in each of these cases, he now states directly in the case of the prophets.

---

[116] Lipscomb, *op. cit.*, p.215.

The spirits of prophets -- On "spirits of prophets," see notes at 14:2,14,15.[117] The Holy Spirit is behind the spiritual gift (see notes at 14:12). Several translations render this phrase, "Prophets can control their own prophetic spirits" (Moffatt, New English Bible).

Are subject to prophets -- "Are subject to" is present tense, pointing to how things regularly are. The revelation from the Holy Spirit, and the speaking by inspiration, were not powers that caused a man of God to lose self-control (cp. 1 Corinthians 12:2). The prophet could control his "spirit" and thus, if he were the one speaking, could be silent when another received a revelation. Likewise, the one sitting in the audience who just received the revelation could wait to deliver it until the first speaker finished. Verse 32 gives a reason for what was said in verses 30 and 31, 'you can all prophesy one by one,' or 'you can speak in tongues one after another.' They were not under an uncontrollable urge to speak, even though they were inspired. They were not 'out of control' when under the Holy Spirit's influence.[118] There was no need of disorder. Each of the prophets, by restraining his impulse to speak, was able to speak one after another. There is a contrast between Christian prophets and the sibyls and pythonesses of the pagan religions. 'Inspiration' in pagan religions did not allow the mouthpieces to control their own speaking. They were compelled, and controlled, and continued speaking until the impulse died. "Mantic inspirations, the violent possession which threw sibyls and priestesses into contortions – the foaming lip and streaming hair and glazed or glaring eye, the unconsciousness of what they said – find no parallel in the self-controlling dignity of Christian inspiration" (Farrar, *op. cit.*, p.460). The inspiration produced by the Holy Spirit never obliterates the self-consciousness or overpowers the reason of the Christian. The Spirit who gave the gifts did not control the prophet (as we control a musical instrument when we play it) and compel him to speak. Hence, a prophet may desire to speak and may have something important to convey which has been given him by the Holy Spirit, and yet for good reasons may refrain from speaking.[119]

14:33 – *for God is not a God of confusion but of peace, as in all the churches of the saints.*

For -- Here is the reason why the prophets and tongues speakers are able to control when

---

[117] This is one of the places where translators must make a difficult decision, whether or not to capitalize "Spirits." Lower case "s" ("spirits") would call attention to the man's spirit. Capital "S" ("Spirits") while an unusual way of speaking of the Holy Spirit, might be similar in meaning to the expression "seven Spirits of God" (Revelation 4:5), a phrase usually explained as having reference to the variety of the Spirit's manifestations.

[118] Verse 32 indicates Christian prophecy, tongues, and interpretation were not 'ecstatic' in the technical sense of that term. In other words, believers in the process of exercising their spiritual gifts are never so 'out of control' as to be unable to stop or regulate their own behavior. One wonders whether this emphasis on self-control (cp. also 12:1-3) is something that needs to be heard when folk accept "slain by the spirit" as a phenomena from God. If a person is genuinely 'out of control,' he or she is not being controlled by the Holy Spirit.

[119] When the Holy Spirit convicts of sin, He may be resisted. It is possible to "quench" the Spirit (1 Thessalonians 5:19). Similarly, the one in whom the Spirit works has some degree of control over His manifestations. Since this is so, Paul can advise the speaker of tongues to refrain from speaking in the absence of an interpreter (14:28), and can urge the prophets to defer to one with a fresh revelation, and neither of these would be considered to be 'quenching the Spirit.'

they speak, and why one inspired speaker can yield to another who can wait till the first speaker finishes. The God who was behind their gifts is not a God of confusion. Verse 33 states the doctrinal basis which underlies this whole set of instructions about orderliness in the public assemblies. The church services should reflect and conform to the character of God Himself.

God is not *a God* of confusion but of peace -- If God were the One who prompted two or three to speak at once, He would be the Creator of chaos, rather than cosmos. His religion does not tend to produce disorder. The word "confusion" is a very strong one in Greek. *Akatastasias* means 'instability, a state of disturbance, anarchy, turbulence, tumult.' God's religion is calm, peaceful, orderly. It is not boisterous. If the prophets had no control over their spirits, gone would be any prospect of an orderly assembly. But Paul sees a guarantee against such disorder in the character of God. Such a God will produce peace, not confusion. Peace equals no conflicts between those wishing to speak or exercise their spiritual gifts.[120] Barnes notes some principles herein stated:

> Where there is disorder, there is little religion. [I do not have the right (by my actions) to rob the one sitting next to me of the right to worship God. If I have made no preparation for the service, and if I did not come to worship, I still do not have the right to throw a barrier in front of my neighbor. The reason men act badly as they do in the worship services is because they have not been taught.] True religion will not lead to tumult, to outcries, or to irregularity. It will not prompt many to speak or pray at once. It will not justify tumultuous and noisy assemblages. Christians should reflect the fact that their God is the author of peace. [They should always in the congregational meeting behave themselves in a reverent manner. They should act in a reverent manner, and with such decorum as becomes men when they are in the presence of a holy and pure God, and engaged in His worship.][121]

"Most of our churches are no longer guilty of confusion and disorder, but they are often guilty of stiffness, formality, and insipidity. This type of service is no more representative of God than was the type of services which Paul sought to correct in Corinth."[122]

As in all the churches of the saints -- With which paragraph should this phrase be connected? (1) With verse 31? Westcott and Hort contended that 33b belongs to 31, and thus 32 and 33a are parenthetical. (2) With verses 26-33a? It was so understood by most of the ancients, Luther, and many of our versions, viz., KJV, NASB. If taken this way, then Paul is saying orderly services characterized the churches by-and-large in the New Testament world. All the congregations acted in such a manner that worshipers would get the idea that God is a God of order and peace – and so should the Corinthians. If Paul notes that orderly reverence is a characteristic of *all* the churches of the saints, the implica-

---

[120] Or if we allow a Jewish definition of peace, it means that which will produce "peace," i.e., win the favor of others.

[121] Barnes, *op. cit.*, p.274. [Notes in brackets are additions and paraphrases by the author.]

[122] Fisher, *op. cit.*, p.230,231.

tion contained in such a note might be that the absence of such orderliness could raise doubts as to whether the church at Corinth is a church of the saints. (3) With verses 34 and 35? It is so construed by most modern exegetes (e.g., Shore, Fisher), as well as several of the modern versions, viz., ASV. Taken this way, Paul is saying that it was the universal practice that women keep silent in the churches. Why should the Corinthians be different? If this phrase is understood as the beginning of a paragraph about women keeping silent, it gives an extra emphasis to the paragraph. Paul is not talking of something applicable to Corinth only. He wants the people in Corinth to do what is done in all the congregations. If verse 33b goes with verses 34-35, then we construe it to mean, 'As (the practice is) in all the assemblies of the saints, let the women keep silence in the assemblies.' Exactly what this practice includes will be made plain in the next verse.

Paul is calling on the Corinthians to conform to accepted Christian practice. "Churches of the saints" speaks of congregations composed of saints, people who belonged to God and are set apart to His service. Though each congregation was free and independent, Paul felt that common practice should prevail in all congregations, and he makes appeal to this universal practice in order to correct what the Corinthians were doing. This is the fourth time Paul has appealed to the 'uniform practice' in all the churches as he tries to correct the Corinthians' behavior (cf. 4:17, 7:17, 11:16).

14:34 -- *The women are to keep silent in the churches; for they are not permitted to speak, but are to subject themselves, just as the Law also says.*

Let the women keep silent in the churches -- Before offering an explanation of verses 34 and 35, the matter of the integrity of these verses must be addressed because of the manuscript variations at this place. Most manuscripts (including P^{46}, A, B, K, ψ, Maj. Text) include these verses after verse 33.[123] But the whole Western text (D, F, G, 88, a, b, d, f, g, etc.) includes these verses after verse 40. Verses 34 and 35 are found in all known manu-scripts, either after verse 33 or after verse 40. Our options are these: (1) Paul wrote verses 34,35 after verse 33, and someone deliberately moved them to a place after verse 40 in the manuscript(s) that became the exemplar for the Western text. (2) Paul wrote the words after verse 40, and some copyist deliberately moved them to a place after verse 33, and that copy became the exemplar for all the other texts since. (3) The verses were not part of the original text, but were a very early marginal gloss that was subsequently placed in the text at two different places. Not a few writers doubt their authenticity.[124] In liberal circles, a popular view is that Paul did not write these words; rather, they were added later by some scribe far more conservative than Paul himself. However, the verses are missing

---

[123] Jerome's Vulgate made the present order (verses 34 and 35 after 33) standard in the Western Church, so the verse order we find in our English translations (based on Eastern and Neutral Texts as well) has been accepted by both eastern and western churches as representative of what Paul originally wrote.

[124] See E.E. Ellis, "The Silenced Wives of Corinth (1 Cor. 14:34,35)," in *New Testament Textual Criticism, Its Significance for Exegesis: Essays in Honor of Bruce M. Metzger* (ed. E.J. Epp, and G.D. Fee), Oxford, 1981, p.213-220. Fee (*op. cit.*, p.701ff) seems to opt for this explanation, objecting to their authenticity on intrinsic grounds: (1) verse 36 follows very nicely what was said in verse 33 [if we leave 34-35 out]; (2) We no longer have the problem that 14:34,35 stands in apparent contradiction to 11:2-16; (3) some of the usages and expressions are quite foreign to Paul. He claims, "One can give good histori-

from no known manuscript, and are found in the majority of witnesses after verse 33. So it is our task to make sense of them in this context.

Among the several attempts to explain these verses – none of which is free of difficulties – are these:

(1) One view is that Paul is quoting someone at Corinth, perhaps in the letter written to Paul, who said, 'Women must be silent!' and then corrects that by stating his own view in verse 36ff.[125] Against this is that there is no hint in verse 34 that Paul suddenly has begun quoting something being said and imposed (without his approval) at Corinth. As best we can determine, the idea that these words are a Corinthian slogan was never proposed in the history of the church until the 20th century.
(2) Another view is that this passage is a prohibition of any form of speaking in public except inspired speech, either tongues or prophecy. Against this view is the fact that the whole chapter deals with abuses of spiritual gifts. What evidence is there that we have suddenly changed topics?
(3) A third view takes note of the context (the use of tongues and prophecy in the public assembly) and prohibits women from being the speakers or translators. Whether or not they have the gift of prophecy or tongues, Paul prohibits any public speaking in the assembly. However, this seems to be a flat contradiction of what has already been written in 1 Corinthians 11:2-16, and it would require that all that is said in verses 26-33 be understood to apply only to the men.
(4) A fourth view is that this is a ban on women being involved in "passing judgment" on the prophecies (verse 29). If their husbands were the prophets, such discernment would put the wives in the unbiblical position of sitting in authority over their own husbands. However, verse 29 is not the near-context or antecedent for verse 34. Nor does this view fit the next verse, "if they desire to learn anything," which involves not "judging" but failing to understand what was going on at all.
(5) A fifth view adopted by many contemporary writers is that the "silence" was a cultural thing for Achaia. Noting that women had a much more public posture in Macedonia, those writers posit that had Paul been writing to Macedonia, he might not have spoken so insistently on the women being "silent" and "not speaking in the public assembly." The argument continues that since woman's position in today's culture is so different from the culture at Corinth, this prohibition would not be applicable today. To adopt this "cultural argument" explanation, verse 33b ("as in all the churches") must refer to verses 26-33a (or, with Westcott-Hort, to verse 31 alone). But if verse 33b belongs

---

cal reasons for both the gloss itself and for its dual position in the text; but one is especially hard pressed to account for either [its location after verse 33or after verse 40] had the other been original." One certainly wonders whether Fee's notes are a case of special pleading in an attempt to ease the rebuke these verses would give to the female tongue speakers and prophecies one finds predominating in Pentecostal/Charismatic circles.

[125] See Neal M. Flanigan, "Did Paul Put Down Women in 1 Cor. 14:34-36?" *Bib. Theol. Bulletin* 11 (1981), p.10-12; or David W. Oddel-Scott, "Let the Women Speak in Church: An Egalitarian Interpretation of 1 Cor. 14:33b-36," *Bib. Theol. Bulletin* 13:3 (July 1983), p.90-93; or Robert W. Allison, "Let Women Be Silent in the Churches (1 Cor. 14:33b-36), *JSNT* 32 (Feb. 1988), p.27-60.

with verses 34 and 35, then the "silence" enjoined on Corinth was as true in Macedonia as in Asia, and this limitation on the women (wives) is something more than a temporary cultural phenomena, such that it may not be safely ignored.

Historically, the passage has been taken as part of a long series of Paul's instructions on "order" in the public assemblies. In some way, the wives (women[126]) were contributing to an atmosphere that made edification of the whole congregation difficult, and this disorder is what Paul corrects with this command to be "silent." Were the sexes segregated in the church assembly as they were in the synagogues? Were the women calling out in loud voices asking disruptive questions? Were they simply chattering so loudly that it had a disruptive effect? Or were they sitting beside their husbands and asking enough questions that nearby worshipers were hindered from hearing what was being preached or taught? Has the new elevation of women in Christianity led to extreme behavior? Where little or no learning was permitted to women before Christianity came, now they are welcome and expected to learn Christian doctrine. Have they abused their efforts to learn (see verse 35) to the extent that 'orderliness' was threatened? "Churches" refers to 'assemblies for worship,' (see verse 26). This rule applied to the weekly assemblies as they come and went, or to all the numerous congregations wherever they met. The 'silence' prescribed for the wives (women) is not total silence.[127] *Sigatōsan* ('let them be silent') is a third person plural present imperative. It is to be a habitual or repeated or customary action. It is the same word used in verses 28 and 30, and is likely to be understood as having the same meaning here in verse 34 that it did earlier. It is a 'silence' necessary for the sake of orderliness that is the topic of this paragraph.

For they are not permitted to speak -- The rest of the verse begins with an explanatory "for," and so gives a reason for the injunction to silence. This order in regard to wives (women) does not emanate from Paul personally; we shall be told in a moment who withholds this permission. The right to speak is 'not turned over to wives (women),' i.e., it is withheld from them. "To speak" is a present tense infinitive. It does not prohibit all speaking. To prohibit any and all speaking, it would have to be an aorist infinitive. While the verb tense permits some speaking, the wives (women) are not permitted to be speaking habitually, customarily, repeatedly, regularly.

But let them subject themselves, just as the Law also says -- What the Law required was that wives submit themselves to their own husbands ('to their own husbands' is implied from the context). It is as though Paul were saying, 'Your own Bible tells you that such submission of wives to their husbands is God's will.'[128] As to the meaning of the verb

---

[126] This commentator is convinced that both in this passage and in 1 Timothy 2:12ff, it is not *women* in general who are addressed, but *wives* in particular. In this passage, verse 35 speaks about the wives asking their husbands at home.

[127] If we take the 'silence' as absolute, then in the public assemblies we may permit no wife (woman) to sing, ever! Even though they have a song or a teaching or a prophecy from the Lord (verse 26), ever! No wife (woman) could ever pray or prophesy in public, ever, 11:2-16 notwithstanding! Let it be noted that it is necessary to wrest this passage from its context to make it teach absolute silence.

[128] This is a much more satisfactory explanation than the one which speaks of women in general, and

used here, "subject themselves," see verse 32. *Hupotassō* means "to place or arrange under, to subordinate, to bring under influence, to be brought under a state or influence, to submit one's self, render obedience, be submissive."[129] The verb form here, *hupotassesthōsan*, is a present imperative middle voice, implying that such submission is something the subject does for her own benefit.[130] "Just as the Law also says" points to the original authority which refuses to turn over to wives (women) the right to speak in public as the Corinthian wives were doing. Where does the Law state what Paul now claims[131] it states? Genesis 3:16 ("Your desire shall be for your husband, and he shall rule over you") and Numbers 30:3-16 are two places. Paul himself expounds this thought in 1 Timothy 2:12-14, where he notes the Law teaches that the wife is to be in subjection to the husband – because, (1) she was created second, and (2) she was first in the transgression – as the first several chapters of Genesis show. Paul informs the Corinthians that what is recorded concerning wives in Genesis is not a temporary arrangement,[132] but a permanent one that endures as such in the church. Any act on the part of the wife which sets aside her subjection to her husband is in violation of "the Law," the will of God, expressed in creation and stated in His Word. Here in 14:34 the prohibition is on speaking which would disrupt the orderliness that should pervade a Christian assembly, a prohibition on speaking which would conflict with the scriptural submission of the wife to her husband, a submission taught as long ago as the time of the Fall.[133]

14:35 -- *If they desire to learn anything, let them ask their own husbands at home; for it is improper for a woman to speak in church.*

And if they desire to learn anything -- If anything has been spoken which they do not un-

---

then goes on to affirm that there is no specific Old Testament passage which tells women to be silent in public worship. But the Old Testament does teach wives to be submissive to their husbands. Compare also the argument in 1 Corinthians 11:8,9 about the wife's behavior being such as to honor her husband.

[129] Harper's *Analytical Greek Lexicon* (New York: Harper & Brothers, nd.), p.419.

[130] If instead of *hupotassesthōsan* (a present, imperative, middle) – as reads Aleph, A, B, 17, etc. – we read *hupotassesthai* (a present, infinitive, middle) – as reads D, F, G, K, L, etc. – then we have a touch of irony. 'Women are not permitted to speak; they are permitted *to keep their proper place*.' Commentaries based on this variant reading will explain that we have here an instance of brachylogy. It is a condensed expression, omitting the word or words not absolutely essential to the Greek construction, but which we must supply to complete the meaning. So the KJV translators supplied "it is commanded."

[131] Some modern theologians have urged that Genesis 3 does *not* say anything like what is here said, and then Paul is accused of Rabbinic exegesis. Hardly! Jesus Himself also taught submission of wives (see Ephesians 5:22).

[132] Some will recall that the Law was temporary, and therefore wonder why appeal can be made to Genesis 3. We remind such thinkers that Genesis 3 is not part of the Mosaic Covenant. Exodus 20-24 is the Old Covenant which was temporary.

[133] The role of women in the church – speaking, teaching, preaching, praying – has been covered in notes at 1 Corinthians 11:2-16 and in notes at 1 Timothy 2:12, plus in Special Study #1 in the author's commentary on *Timothy and Titus*, a study entitled "What Did Wives and Women Do in the New Testament Church Assemblies?"

derstand, or if on any subject they desire more full information, there is a proper time and place for the wives to gain the desired information. It seems that in the early church the custom prevailed to ask questions at the public services, very probably on subjects that were brought up by the prophets. Wives are here directed to ask their questions at home, rather than in the public assembly.

Let them ask their own husbands at home -- *Andras* is the usual word for "husband." If Paul intended "men" in general, the better word for that would be *anthrōpoi*. It is rather obvious Paul is dealing with wives and husbands, rather than women and men in general. Wives were not to habitually ask questions in the public assemblies, at least in such a way as to result in a lack or orderliness in the assembly. At the same time, the wife's interest and quest for knowledge of things spiritual was not to be denied. Paul's solution is for the wife to ask her husband for answers to her spiritual questions, not in the public service but at home.

For it is improper for a woman to speak in church -- *Aischron* is the same strong word translated "disgraceful" used at 11:6. "Improper" may mean 'improper in the judgment of the general public,' since such behavior was inconsistent with the accepted standards of submission. Or, "improper" may mean 'improper" in the light of God's revelation of His will in the Law.' It was "improper" for wives to speak in the way the Corinthians were doing, and destroying the 'orderliness' of the public worship in the process.

14:36 -- *Was it from you that the word of God* **first** *went forth? Or has it come to you only?*

Or -- The word translated "or" in the NASB margin, and "What!" in the ASV, is ἤ, and both questions begin with this word, showing they are tied directly to the immediately preceding sentiments.[134] It seems Paul is ironically asking the Corinthians whether they thought their behavior in regard to tongues, prophecy, and wives' questions really had any warrant or justification. This might even be another glance at the Corinthian pride. He is challenging them not to treat his instructions lightly!

Was it from you that the word of God *first* went forth? – 'Were you the starting point of the gospel (the "Word of God")? Is the Corinthian church the mother church? You are practicing some unusual customs. Have you any right to differ from all the other churches?' "Are you the original church, so that your wisdom is to set the standard of propriety; or are you the only church, so that you are at liberty to stand alone by yourselves and your own conceits?"[135] 'Are you the authors of the Christian system, that you may lay down rules about it? By your actions, you imply that you know better than God how things should be done!'

---

[134] It has been noted that Thayer calls this particle a "disjunctive conjunction." A good summary article of the problems involved in the verses now being studied can be found in Daniel C. Arichea, Jr., "The Silence of Women in the Church: Theology and Translation in 1 Corinthians 14:33b-36," *Bible Translator* 46:1 (Jan 1995), p.101-112.

[135] Kling, *op. cit.*, p.297.

Or has it come to you only? – 'Do you contend that you are the only church and therefore have a right to maintain all these irregularities: women discarding veils in public worship, people thinking only of self at the love feast and Lord's Supper, people speaking in tongues and no one interpreting, several people all speaking (or singing, or praying, or teaching) at once, prophets refusing to give place to one another, wives failing to be submissive to their husbands while at the same time disrupting the orderliness that would honor God.[136] Do you really assert that you have a right to act independently of the other churches who have responded to the gospel?' If every other Christian congregation practiced what Paul taught on this matter, who are they to be the sole exceptions?

14:37 -- *If anyone thinks he is a prophet or spiritual, let him recognize that the things which I write to you are the Lord's commandment.*

If any one thinks he is a prophet -- For a third time in this letter, Paul attacks the Corinthian position head-on with the formula "if any one thinks he is ..." (see 3:18 and 8:2[137]). What is implied again is that someone or several someones at Corinth were rejecting Paul's authority, perhaps those especially whose wrong behavior has been rebuked. Paul here is speaking directly to those who, for whatever reason (even if he thinks he is a prophet), suppose they can deviate from directions given by an apostle of Jesus. The thrust of Paul's language is that his opponents were not what they thought they were if they suppose they can ignore rules given on God's authority.

Or spiritual -- See the same term used at 1 Corinthians 2:15 and 3:1. It seems to have the connotation that the opponent thought of himself as being a leader because of his spiritual attainment.

Let him recognize that the things which I write to you are the Lord's commandment -- "Which I write" is present tense – i.e., the things which I am now writing. The expression at least covers all he has been saying about disorders in public worship (chapters 11-14.) The Greek translated "Let him recognize" (or 'acknowledge') asks for constant recognition. "If anyone thinks he is a prophet or spiritual," let him prove that he is not mistaken in his opinion of himself. 'Let him show his spiritual discernment by recognizing inspiration when he sees it, by acknowledging that what I am writing is the Lord speaking.' Failure to acknowledge the divine character of Paul's written word is proof positive the man is not spiritual as he claims. Paul gives the same test Jesus did in John 8:47, "He who is of God hears the words of God." Compare also 1 John 4:6, where another apostle claimed the same test for the words written or spoken by an apostle: "We are from God; he who knows God listens to us; he who is not from God does not listen to us. By this we know the spirit of truth and the spirit of error." In the phrase, "are the Lord's com-

---

[136] Some of the ideas in this long sentence were suggested by Robertson and Plummer, *op. cit.*, p.326.

[137] It has been observed that each time this formula occurs, it is in one of the major sections of the letter (chaps. 1-4, 8-10, 12-14).

mandment,"[138] the word "Lord" is emphatic. The reference is to Jesus. Paul says his writing carries the authority of Christ. Here Paul makes a direct assertion of his inspiration. Submission to the infallible authority of the apostles (who were speaking as Jesus' mouthpieces) is made a test of a man's claim to a divine mission and even of conversion.

14:38 -- *But if anyone does not recognize* **this**, *he is not recognized.*

But if anyone does recognize *this* -- 'If any one refuses to recognize that Jesus Christ is the source of my rulings in these matters' seems to be the intention. A man's failure to acknowledge the divine source of Paul's instructions does not alter the fact that they are from the Lord.

He is not recognized -- There is some question as to the proper reading and the correct form. There is a manuscript variation here, some having an indicative and some an imperative form. (1) *Indicative* – "He is ignored" (*agnoeitai*) read some manuscripts. Perhaps it means he is ignored by God. He fails to recognize God's apostle; God refuses to recognize him. Perhaps it means, he is ignored by Paul. 'I do not care to dispute with him (argue with him) further.' "The words mean that a person who could not recognize such an evident and simple truth must be of a perverse mind – his opposition would give the apostle no further concern."[139] It is possible the indicative is not present tense, but a future tense, in which case the meaning is as Moffatt reads, "Anyone who disregards this will be himself disregarded." The reference then will be to the Day of Judgment. The NIV follows Moffatt's lead. (2) *Imperative* – "Let him be ignored (*agnoeitō*) read other manuscripts. If a man wants to reject the Lord's teaching, he simply will have to remain ignorant, is one possible interpretation. 'Let him ignore my teaching, Paul says, and let him take the consequences!' Or, it is possible the imperative means, 'Let him be ignored by the rest of the congregation.'[140] The congregation should listen to the claims of Jesus' apostle, and not listen further to the claims of one who is crossways of an apostle of Jesus! Whether we read it as a warning about dire consequences in the final judgment, or as an appeal to the Corinthians to quit following this opponent of Paul's, this is a very forceful claim of apostolic authority and prerogative.

14:39 -- *Therefore, my brethren, desire earnestly to prophesy, and do not forbid to speak in tongues.*

Therefore, my brethren -- We are coming to the concluding verses in this discussion

---

[138] A few manuscripts read "commandments" (plural). Likely some scribe attempted to make this term match the plural "things" written earlier in the verse. The singular is simply a "collective singular" to cover all He has written on this present matter – especially the need for edification, understanding, and order in the assembly.

[139] Shore, *op. cit.*, p.138.

[140] The NEB reads "If he does not recognize this, he himself should not be recognized."

about disorder in the public worship service and abuses of spiritual gifts. The entire matter is now briefly summed up with the same idea as presented in 14:1.

Desire earnestly to prophesy, and do not forbid to speak in tongues -- "Desire earnestly to prophesy" repeats the imperative found in 14:1. As at that place, the command does not deal with how one initially acquired the gifts, but rather with how they were to be used for the life and welfare of the congregation. Prophecy edifies the believer and leads to the conversion of unbelievers, so of the two gifts named in this verse, prophecy is the one that is to get major use week after week in the assembly. "Do not forbid to speak in tongues" may be correcting a possible false conclusion. Paul was not prohibiting all use of the gift of tongues in the congregational meetings, but he is saying it should be exercised less than the gift of prophecy. Both gifts are Spirit-inspired, and there is a need in the body for both. But there is this difference: (1) One gift (preaching by inspiration in the language of the audience) is to be greatly longed for. (2) The other (to speak in tongues) was not to be forbidden so long as the proper conditions were met. The Greek is, "stop forbidding to speak in tongues."[141] In its own place, the gift of tongues was a valuable endowment; on proper occasions it was to be exercised. The gift of speaking in foreign languages was not useless nor to be prohibited altogether. Verse 39 is a summary of the first part of this chapter (verses 1-25).

14:40 -- *But all things must be done properly and in an orderly manner.*

But let all things be done -- This is a general rule, which was intended to guide them. It is a present imperative, 'Let them continue to be done ...!' It is a simple rule and easily applied. It settles many a question about the modes and forms and customs of worship. As far as the practical directions were concerned, these are summed up in this one short sentence.

Properly -- *Euschēmonōs* means 'with decorum, in an appropriate and becoming manner.' It expresses the idea of the beauty and harmony which ought to prevail in church services, as becomes the worship of God. Some have supposed this word has reference to the behavior of the wives, and to the behavior of the cliques at the love feast and Lord's Supper, in particular. This seems to be too limited; we believe it is a general rule that sums up all the corrective directions given by Paul in chapters 11-14.

And in an orderly manner – 'In the right time and in due proportion, regularly, without confusion, discord, tumult, one at a time,' as instructed previously. Some have supposed this word refers to the exercise of the spiritual gifts; but again, we do not think it possible to so limit it. Just as verse 39 summed up the first part of chapter 14, so verse 40 sums up the instructions in verses 26-38, as well as the other directions concerning order in the public services.

---

[141] Has someone at Corinth ever told another church member to "stop speaking in tongues"? All the commands in this letter to 'stop doing (this or that)!' give us an insight into the life of a congregation wracked by squabbles and factions. Some insist on doing their thing with more frequency; their opponents insist they cease altogether.

The object of all church assemblies is to be the building up of the body of Christ, and therefore seemliness and ordered regularity are absolutely necessary to this end. Here again, as in so many other instances in this epistle, while the particular and unique circumstances which called forth the apostolic instructions have for centuries passed away, God's will as revealed, reiterated, and illuminated by the writings of Paul is of permanent and abiding application. Paul's Spirit-inspired instructions are based on the general and eternal principles which God as ordained.

Special Study #6

WORSHIP IN THE NEW TESTAMENT

INTRODUCTION

It is Sunday morning. The saints have gathered in their weekly assembly. I'm sitting with them. The haunting question keeps coming to mind, "WHAT ARE WE DOING HERE?" or "WHAT AM I SUPPOSED TO BE DOING HERE?"

Some Scripture texts may help us: John 4:21-24, Acts 2:42, Hebrews 10:24,25.

A. IT IS A SOLEMN RESPONSIBILITY TO TEACH OR PREACH

>   A blind man was walking towards me in the grocery store. I stopped to let him by. He was tapping with his cane and was about to bump into the end of a row of shelves. I quickly told him to go left – and pointed to my left. Obediently, he moved to his left – and ran right into the rack of groceries. He backed up, went to his right, and gave me the funniest "look" as he passed me. I should have said – "Right!" (for left to me was right to him).
>
>   If we give wrong directions as we teach or preach, we'll see people go off in error.
>
>   *What if I send you in the wrong direction spiritually?*
>
>   If I am teaching, I take a text and unfold it. One must be so very careful on controversial passages, knowing the power the teacher has to rightly mold or wrongly warp people's thinking.
>
>   If I am preaching on a topic like "Worship," when you may well sway people's behavior for the rest of their lifetime, how you "worry" you may be telling them something not quite right.
>
>   Of course, it is not possible to say all that needs to be said on this subject in a single Special Study. Editing and paring is inevitable. I pray that the emphases and points that remain will convey to you what I have found in the New Testament.

B. THIS IS A STUDY ABOUT WHAT WE CALL "WORSHIP" -- What we do when we assemble as a body on the Lord's Day.

>   PREPARATION FOR THIS MESSAGE HAS TAKEN A LONG WHILE:
>
>   >   1955 – A term paper in New Testament theology, "The Worship of God."
>   >   1961 – A sermon prepared for Benton City, MO, "Worship."

Nearly a year's study went into the preparation for an assignment for a sermon to the Central Missouri Christian Evangelizers' Meeting. It involved extensive reading in dozens of articles and books. It included a questionnaire on "Seeker Sensitive Services" to all the faculty of Central Christian College.

Another college teacher related that in graduate school he was told, "What the New Testament says about worship could be put on a 3x5 card, and half of it would be empty!" Happily, that observation is not consistent with what I find when I read my New Testament!

C. TIMELINESS OF THE SUBJECT

I admit that, long ago, some things done at worship turned me off.

> Some songs were sung almost every Sunday: "I Love to Tell the Story," "Years I Spent in Vanity and Pride." (Sometimes the same song was even sung twice, once at the Bible school opening and again at worship.) It took me several years to get turned off.

> It has taken a lot less time to get turned off to singing the same phrase over and over for 5 or more minutes (modern praise choruses repeated 3 or more times).

I have been bothered by how prone we in the Christian Churches are to copy something we find in the denominations, with seemingly little thought as to whether or not it is appropriate, or whether or not it is Scriptural.

> E.g., Special Days emphases – Mother's Day, Father's Day, Grandparents' Day, etc. are made part of our Sunday school exercises.

> And even more recently "baby dedication day." Because we find in the Bible that baptism is the immersion of penitent adults, we may not actually sprinkle water on the infants (tho' some churches substitute rose petals for water). If we must give recognition to little ones, why not call it "parent dedication day"?

I'm bothered by the "rut" our Sunday assemblies seem to be in.

> While in the assembly, does my mind wander more than it should?
> Do I sing the songs without thinking (because they have been used so often?)
> When you look across the congregation during times of worship, do a lot of people seem uninvolved and bored? Not participating?
> Can I confidently predict what will happen next in the service?

I am bothered by the "hard feelings" sometimes prompted by clashes in "music styles" as people try to pump life into the services.

> "Ornery Christian Soldiers" marching off to war over music styles, fill many of our congregations.

> I wonder if the clash over music styles isn't simply symptomatic of a deeper problem – namely, a lack of Scriptural understanding of "worship"?

I am bothered when I go to the parking lot, at the close of the service, sad that nothing really happened this morning at the assembly.

> I've sat through many Sunday services and a lot of chapel services, and frankly, I haven't really been worshiping.
>
> Worship doesn't happen very often. Many Christians have an unfulfilled need for worship, and the mindless boredom fostered on Sunday morning in many of our church buildings leaves them hungry and disappointed.
>
> I, for one, am tired of going home from services feeling that nothing has happened, and wondering what was supposed to happen that I somehow missed.

I am bothered when new converts learn so quickly that you won't miss much if you happen to miss a Sunday service or two.

> In one community, a drunkard was baptized into Christ in the middle of the week. His new life was filled with joy. He came to his first Sunday service. He expected to find all the people assembled exuding the same joy. What a jolt!
>
> "I was 53 years old when I found out there was a God. The shock and wonder of that discovery has never worn off in the more than 20 years since. But I've had another shock in my life, almost as great as the first. In fact, it happened the very next Sunday. It was meeting my first church-goers," he related.
>
> "I'd never been to church in my life, and I remember how eagerly I awaited the first Sunday. I'd just had a glimpse of the Almighty – me, an alcoholic, a drug addict, rich, lonely, and miserable – and already I was beginning to know what joy really was. And now, on Sunday, I was going to meet people who had known Him for years! What ecstatic people, these long-time Christians would embarrass me with their love and enthusiasm."
>
> "Well, Sunday came, and I went to church, and of course you know what I found: bowed heads, long faces, and funeral whispers. Far from alarming me with the warmth of their welcome, nobody spoke to me at all.
>
> "At first, I was sure this was just one isolated experience. But, as time went on, and I attended other churches in various parts of the country, I made a bewildering discovery. These long-faced, listless people were present in every congregation. How could they come together Sunday after Sunday without breathing in the joy that danced in the very air?" (Illustration copied)

D. "DO BIBLE THINGS IN A BIBLE WAY!" is one of the slogans of our movement.

How are our people to "worship" in a Bible way, when *we have had so few lessons from the Bible on worship in our churches?*

With little instruction about "worship," we sit and watch others who have been "in church" longer than we have. We copy what they do, thinking that must be what "worship" is supposed to be.

Timeliness of the subject? It is long past time we gave some serious thought to what we are doing and why, when we assemble on the Lord's Day!

PROPOSITION: It is time we who propose to participate in, or lead, the "Sunday services" make a careful study of what the New Testament says about the weekly assembly of the Christians – so we can hear the Lord's directions for our thinking and practice, so we can know "What I am supposed to be doing here"!

I. A HISTORY BEHIND THE WAY WE DO THINGS ON SUNDAY MORNING

(A brief overview of "worship" in the early church and since the Reformation)

A. SUNDAY MORNINGS (or "worship") IN THE EARLY CHURCH

They met on the first day of the week – for the breaking of bread, for preaching, for singing, for encouragement of one another.

The synagogue pattern was followed – save the Christians substituted "Jesus Christ" in the places where Jews spoke of the Father. Praise, prayer, Scripture reading, instructions, alms for the poor.

As the centuries passed, some of the activities ceased, and others were added, till by the end of the Middle Ages, one could hardly recognize that what happened on Sunday "at church" had any relationship to what one reads in the New Testament.

B. SUNDAY MORNINGS SINCE THE REFORMATION

1. The 16th CENTURY REFORMATION made some changes. The key passage of Scripture that informed their actions was 2 Chronicles 5:12-14.

   The Reformers, as they attempted to correct the religious situation they had inherited, wished to get rid of everything not in the Scriptures.

   REFORMERS – They worked to correct abuses that had come into the church. They tended to return to the way things were done in the 4th century.

   During the 16th century Reformation, in an effort to remove from worship the theological errors and the liturgical excesses of the Middle Ages, evangelical leaders threw out much that was both meaningful and orthodox.

   Zwingli, for instance, eliminated all music from his services, and Calvin tried to do the same. When the Genevan Reformer finally admitted music into worship it was limited to metrical psalms, sung in unison by the congregation. All choir books had been burned and organs put to the ax! Calvin was against "part singing" – he called it a work of the devil.

PURITANS – The English church was strongly influenced by Calvin, and especially during the rebellion that established a commonwealth under Cromwell, Puritans eradicated choral and instrumental music, all written liturgy, and all worship symbolism.

> The English Puritans, even more than the Protestant Reformers before them, were determined to purge worship of all practices not mentioned in Scripture (e.g., holy water, clerical collars, choral and instrumental music). Simplicity was the order of the day.

> To the Puritans, worship was primarily a matter of the mind. Thus, the sermon, not communion, was the focus of the service, and the role of the preacher was central. Congregational participation shrank to a minimum. Even hymns were suspect for a time.

In time, the religious bodies which descended from the Reformation did come up with a theology of worship based on 2 Chronicles 5:12-14.

> The passage describes the dedication of Solomon's temple. Singers, orchestra (the instrumentalists played cymbals, trumpets, stringed instruments, harps), choir directors, ministers, and people all shared in the worship.

> They were as one, making one sound to be heard in praising and thanking the Lord, saying, "For He is good; For His loving kindness is everlasting" (Psalm 106.1). As they were offering these wonderful sounds of praise, "the house of the Lord was filled with a cloud ... for the glory of the Lord filled the house."

> Song services in Protestant worship were based on this passage of Scripture – where the emphasis is on God's acts in history.

> Here was music with a purpose – an attempt to bring to all the people assembled a sense of the presence of God, for we read, "The glory of the Lord filled the house."

> Their idea was that for a few moments we are ushered into the presence of God (as though we were not everywhere and all the time in His presence).

Many denominations still follow customs inherited from the Reformation.
> Some services are structured around the *ACTS* acrostic: Adoration, Confession, Thanksgiving, and Supplication.

Some hymnals are divided into sections to assist with planning a service.

> *Creation* -- "O Worship the King, all glorious above ..."
> *Providence* -- "Through all the changing scenes of life ..."
> *Gratitude* -- "Now thank we all our God ..."
> *Time & Eternity* -- "O God, our Help in Ages past ..."
> *Mystery* -- "God moves in a mysterious way ..."
> *History* -- "Praise, my soul, the King of heaven ..."
> *Sanctification* -- "Love divine, all loves excelling ..."

2. 19th CENTURY REVIVALISTS made changes and additions to "worship" in America.

In the late 1700's and early 1800's, outdoor camp meetings and brush harbor services, with their appeal to the lost to come to Christ, were brought indoors. The "new measures" (i.e., new methods) were intended to "awaken the unconcerned and re-awaken the complacent." The "worship" assembly was intended to serve evangelistic purposes.

Spiritual songs and gospel songs were introduced after the Great Awakening.

> *Spiritual Songs.* Music at the camp meetings had much in common with that of today: simplistic, highly repetitive, often improvised in the fervor of a worship experience, and centering in a refrain like many of today's "praise choruses."

> *Gospel Songs* dominated much of evangelical life for 150 years.

>> The camp meeting movement was part of a long succession of revival phenomena that culminated in the Second Awakening under Charles Finney and the missions of Dwight L. Moody later in the 19th century.

>> The camp meeting "spiritual" became the model for later gospel songs. As expressions of Christian experience, gospel songs were the logical and helpful adjuncts of evangelistic preaching.

The "revival meeting" atmosphere was brought into the church house.

> There was a "song service" to elevate the emotional pitch of the congregation. To this end, "gospel songs" were introduced. (Remember the old blue song-book, *Great Songs of the Church* which was divided between "hymns" and "gospel songs.") An offering was received "for the spread of the gospel." There would be a special number emphasizing conversion or personal holiness. The service reached its climax with an evangelistic sermon and an "invitation" (sometimes called an "altar call" in

denominational churches) to the unconverted and unsanctified.

C. CHANGES IN "WORSHIP" IN THE 20th CENTURY

1. Some models of worship are based on the revivalist format

   BILLY SUNDAY REVIVALS. Homer Rodeheaver led singing and provided special music. Then came the preaching and invitation given by Billy Sunday.

   BILLY GRAHAM CRUSADE MODEL. A rousing song service was led by Cliff Barrows. Next came Scripture reading by Grady Wilson and special music by Bev Shea. Then came Graham's message and the invitation. That's the revivalist model of "worship." What happens on Sunday morning, in many churches today, is based on this revivalist model.

   When this model was first introduced into Sunday morning services, there were tensions over the old and new ways of conducting the Sunday meetings.

   Tensions between the old and the new were solved by having two services each Sunday. The morning service might be more traditional, while the evening service was dedicated to winning the lost.

   Many churches today are simply trying to modify this inherited form of worship.

   Perhaps expository preaching replaces the evangelistic sermon.

   The invitation is enlarged to include a desire for church membership or a life rededication.

   The growth of counseling and the influence of popular culture have also modified our approaches. The preacher may focus on the felt-needs of the worshipers, so the people go home feeling encouraged and affirmed. TV leads us to swing and sway with our microphones, just like the TV stars. Applause regularly punctuates the service, as if each congregation were a studio audience.

   Music styles have also changed. We have had the hymns of Watts and Wesley, followed by the Black soul music of Thomas A. Dorsey's "Peace in the Valley" and "Precious Lord, Take My Hand." Then came Stamps-Baxter with Moise Lister and Albert Brumley. Then came Ralph Carmichael, the Gaithers, and John Peterson. And then came contemporary Christian music.

   But the order of service still essentially reflects the basic revivalist format.

2. Seeker-sensitive services

    As part of a deliberate attempt to apply modern marketing principles and targeting the audience you wish to sell your product to, the revivalist and reformation models of worship have been abandoned.

    Willow Creek Church in suburban Chicago aimed at the tastes of baby boomers and busters, in a deliberate effort to reach the unchurched. The meetings on Saturday night and Sunday are not announced as "worship," only as "events" where seekers may hear the gospel of Jesus Christ.

    > The setting is an auditorium with a stage. The pre-sermon performance is professional quality activity by a stage orchestra, excellent singers, and a dramatic presentation to "set up" the sermon by showing its relationship to real-life situations.

    > Willow Creek Church clearly explains that the Saturday/Sunday services are not for mature believers. For Christians – "The New Community" – significant activities are offered in Wednesday/Thursday evening services, and in the cell groups organized for all those who are members of the church.

    >> How misguided (as many another church has done) to copy the seeker model for the services, and then aim the services (not at seekers, but) at those who are already believers, and involved.

    World Magazine, January 11, 1977, reported on "Culture-Friendly Worship" in Great Britain.

    > Churches whose leaders believe that worship should change to fit the demands of the culture should brace themselves for the next step, which is already taking place in England. In an article in the English newspaper *The Guardian*, David Tomlinson, author of a book titled *The Post-Evangelical*, complains about how traditional evangelicals are too conservative in doctrine and morality.

    > He then describes the approach to worship in his congregation. They hold their services on Tuesday nights in a pub. "These are invariably conducted in a relaxed atmosphere with people sitting around tables rather than in rows," he reports. "Smoking and drinking are permitted, there are no preachers, sermons or hymns, and the group decides what subjects it would like to discuss."

    > To be sure, in our culture, people like to sleep in on Sundays; few people sing anymore; and most folks are not used to sitting still through a speech. With this logic, why not eliminate the Sabbath, hymns, and sermons? Mr. Tomlinson's culture-friendly liturgy is what people have always done in bars. Churches have usually offered something different, such as holiness, salvation, and the Word of God.

    A number of contemporary articles on "Post-Modern Evangelical Worship" decry the blurring of meaningful distinctions between evangelicalism and the contemporary culture. With the sweep of the "Praise & Worship" phenomenon, evangelicals have abandoned Biblical forms of worship in droves. The idea that the whole thrust of the Sunday service is a matter of evangelism and trying to reach the unreached, has led us to adopt the "idiom and style" of the unchurched. As we do, we clearly run the risk of losing much that is distinctively and uniquely Christian.

3. The Charismatic/Pentecostal praise and worship model is a third model being tried in the late 20th and early 21st centuries.

No longer is 2 Chronicles used as the key passage to explain our theology of worship. A different Old Testament verse is appealed to by Charismatics/Pentecostals as they arrive at their theology of worship.

The new key passage is Psalm 100:4 (KJV) – "Enter into his gates with thanksgiving, and into his courts with praise."

Never mind that the context is entering the temple at Jerusalem during Old Testament times, and these are instructions about worship there.

The whole thrust of the Charismatic/Pentecostal song service is to help the people meet the transcendent God, and experience a dramatic encounter that produces both miracles and great enjoyment.

In "Praise & Worship" music, "praise" and "worship" are different things.

In Charismatic theology, "praise" silences the devil, and prepares people to enter God's presence.

Terry Law, one of the leading exponents of this idea, speaks of praise in almost sacramental terms: "Praise silences the devil. Praise is a garment of the Spirit. Praise leads the believer into the triumph of Christ. Praise brings revelation. Praise prepares us for miracles. Praise is the way into God's presence. God inhabits our praises (Psalm 22:3)."

For Charismatics, "worship" occurs only in a transcendent, often glossolalic experience in which a believer enters a spiritual "Holy of Holies" in God's very presence. The approach to this intimate, ecstatic experience is through the "Holy Place": here, during this part of the song service, the would-be worshiper sings only songs of praise, songs that are expressions of God's attributes or of God's biblical names.

It takes an hour or more to go through the different phases of a worship workout.

Some of the Charismatic/Pentecostal musicians and companies – Bill Gaither, Maranatha Music, Hosanna, Manna Music, Integrity Music – have exerted an extraordinary influence on the worship of non-charismatic churches.

> They not only have written many of the tunes modern believers sing, but they have sent worship teams around the world to teach non-charismatic churches how to worship in charismatic style. (Don Moen, through Worship International, has trained 25,000 people and sent them out to teach anyone who will listen. *Charisma*, Dec 1995.)
>
> If you are not Charismatic/Pentecostal, and have tried to adopt their worship and praise format, don't you find it hard to try to go from "praise" to "worship" in only 15 minutes, when the Charismatics take an hour or more to do it? And don't you feel a little let down when there is no "worship" – i.e., no glossolalic experience or other ecstatic moment with God?

Vineyard Churches have five phases to a "worship workout" (see the phases in the illustration on the next page (*Songs that Fit the Flow*).

> Eddie Espinosa and John Wimber have developed a five-phase pattern for their "worship set." Instead of singing songs and choruses in a random order, they have come up with a sequence to be followed. (The congregation stands during first three phases. All 5 phases last a total of 40 minutes or so.)
>
> i. Invitation
>
>> This phase is a call to worship. It accepts people where they are and begins to draw them into God's presence. They say most people need to wake up, warm up, and be energized before they are ready for the spiritually strenuous work of true worship.
>>
>> The usual feeling is celebration, upbeat, praise-oriented. This first phase may be accompanied with hand clapping. The lyrics are directed to the people, not God, telling them what they are about to do.
>>
>> The chorus, "Don't You Know It's Time to Praise the Lord" is an example of an "invitation to worship" song. "We Bring a Sacrifice of Praise" is another. So is "Let's forget about ourselves."
>
> ii. Engagement
>
>> In the engagement phase, people begin to turn their attention directly to God. Often lyrics are addressed specifically to God. "Come thou almighty King, Help us Thy praise to sing."

SONGS THAT FIT THE FLOW

The list below illustrates song possibilities for each of the five worship phases. The assigned categories are not rigid; a song may serve in more than one category. The list below includes both choruses and hymns.

Invitation
We Bring a Sacrifice of Praise
Don't You Know It's Time to Praise the Lord
I Just Came to Praise the Lord
Let's Forget about Ourselves
Spirit Song
Come, Worship the Lord
As We Gather
This Is the Day That the Lord Has Made
Come Christians Join to Sing
Praise the Savior Ye Who Know Him
My Faith Has Found a Resting Place
Let's All Go Up to Zion
Come We That Love the Lord

Engagement
Our God Is an Awesome God
How Majestic
Rejoice in the Lord Always
He Is the King
Great and Mighty Is He
The Celebration Song
I Will Sing of the Mercies of the Lord
I Shall Prepare Him My Heart
O Worship the King
All Creatures of Our God and King
Guide Me O Thou Great Jehovah
Come Thou Almighty King
O for a Thousand Tongues to Sing

Exaltation
All the Earth Shall Worship
Let There Be Glory and Honor and Praises
All Hail King Jesus
We Exalt Thee
Our God Reigns
Thou Art Worthy
Majesty
Crown Him with Many Crowns
Immortal, Invisible
Rejoice, the Lord Is King
How Great Thou Art
All Hail the Power of Jesus' Name

Adoration
We Worship and Adore You
Glorify Your Name
His Name Is Wonderful
I Love You, Lord
Emmanuel
Lord, We Praise You
Father, I Adore You
Praise Song
Fairest Lord Jesus
My Jesus I Love Thee
Be Thou My Vision
Jesus, Priceless Treasure
Majestic Sweetness Sits Enthroned
Of the Father's Love Begotten
How Sweet the Name of Jesus Sounds
He Hideth My Soul

Intimacy
O Lord, You're Beautiful
Turn Your Eyes Upon Jesus
My Delight
Alleluia, Alleluia
As the Deer
Sweet Perfume
Holy Ground
In Moments Like These
Jesus, I Am Resting, Resting
Jesus the Very Thought of Thee
Children of the Heavenly Father
Close to Thee
O to Be Like Thee
Savior, Like a Shepherd
I Need Thee Every Hour
In the Garden

Close-out
We Are One in the Spirit
In My Life, Lord, Be Glorified
Holy, Holy, Holy
Shine, Jesus, Shine
He Is Able, More than Able
Thank You, Lord, for Saving My Soul
Our God Reigns
It Is Well with My Soul
My Tribute
To God Be the Glory
And Can It Be
Our Great Savior
May the Mind
Fairest Lord Jesus
Great Is Thy Faithfulness
Because He Lives

You can arrange your own chorus and hymn repertoire into these phases. Notice I have chosen upbeat choruses in the first three phases. You, however, might fill these cells with an entirely different array of choices and obtain a quite different mood and feel, and yet be guided by the same principles and techniques, namely:

- worship that has a goal and direction
- worship that respects the psychological dimension
- worship that reflects the character of God (both transcendence and intimacy)
- lyrics that point to function (singing "about" and later "to" God)
- mixing of hymns and choruses (richness, variety)
- smooth transitions (linking both pieces and phases)
- avoiding distractions (not "jumping around")
- common tempos
- common words
- common keys
- adequate preparation yet open to the leading of the Spirit.

— *Barry Liesch*

This is a typical Charismatic/Pentecostal "Worship Set." Before we simply copy the five worship phases, we should carefully think through the theological and Biblical implications of what we are doing and singing.

iii. Exaltation

In this phase, people sing to the Lord with power, giving meaningful expression to the lofty words of transcendence – words like great, majesty, worthy, reigns, Lord, and mountains. Musically, this phase generally uses greater pitch spans than in other phases. "All hail the power of Jesus' name." "Majesty." "Our God Reigns."

Praise normally precedes adoration. They say that people need time to get ready to express adoration and intimacy.

iv. Adoration

In the adoration phase, people are usually seated, the dynamics gradually subside, the melody range may reduce to five or six notes, and the key words may be you, Jesus, and terms of personal worship and love, as in the chorus "We Worship and Adore You."

In the exaltation and adoration phases, two sides of God's character receive expression. Exaltation focuses on His transcendence. Adoration focuses on His immanence (His closeness to us).

Here is where the whole audience will begin to pray or sing in tongues, as for a few moments they are personally "experiencing God in their very lives" (as the deliberately induced altered state of consciousness is explained to the participants).

v. Intimacy

This is the last phase of Charismatic/Pentecostal "worship." This is the quietest and most personal expression of worship, with God addressed in terms such as Abba. "Now that He has moved us to glossolalic experience – and thrilled our souls – we will tell God how much He means to us." The choruses "In Moments Like These" or "O Lord You're Beautiful" reflect the tone of this phase.

This is the "kiss" of worship. One meaning for the Greek word for worship, *proskuneo*, is "to turn toward to kiss," as in to kiss the feet, the hands, or the lips. Kissing requires closeness, which comes only if properly prepared for in the preceding phases.

Sometimes it is good to change the wording of familiar songs to make them fit this intimate phase. E.g., "our" can change to "my" in the lyric, "Marvelous grace of *my* loving Lord: grace that exceeds *my* sin and *my* guilt." "Tis so sweet to trust *you* Jesus; just to take *you* at *your* word."

Musically, this phase means a softer mood. Percussion may not suit the intimacy phase.

    vi. Closeout

The worship set ends when the people stand for a close-out chorus or hymn – "My Tribute" for instance – that leads out of intimacy and helps people adjust for the next event in the service, the sermon.

4. NEW AGE THRUST

The New Age desire "to get in touch with our higher spiritual power" is being pandered to in some of our Sunday assemblies. That "higher spiritual power" is not God or Christ, but some inner sense or feeling.

D. With all these "models" to choose from, it seems to me it is time to go to the Word and to the Testimony!

II. "WORSHIP" – WHAT IS IT?

A. The need for a clear definition.

George Barna conducted a survey of evangelicals, asking them to define the meaning of "worship."

    36% gave a reasonable definition.
    25% provided answers that were too generic to evaluate.
    39% offered definitions that were plainly wrong.

Without a clear definition, how will we know what we are supposed to be doing, and how will we be able to teach others what they are supposed to be doing as we assemble? WHAT ARE WE DOING HERE?

B. I searched my library for help with a definition of "What is worship?"

Worship is defined as "Appreciation for God." How do you teach someone how to "appreciate"?

Worship has been defined as "Admiration for the greatness of God." How do you "admire"?

Worship is "Adoration of God." How does one "adore"?

C. Webster's Dictionary is not always a good place to go for a definition (it only gives the modern usage of a word).

For example, we have learned you don't go to Webster to learn what the Bible means when it uses the word "baptize."

So, it might be in error to go to Webster to learn what the Biblical words for "worship" mean. Nevertheless, here is what we find:

"Worship" comes from the old Anglo-Saxon word *woerthscipe,* meaning "to attribute worth to someone or something."

The idea is that, when we worship, we are saying that the thing of supreme worth in my life is God/Christ and how my life can count for Him.

German and French words for "worship" are a little more expressive than the English word.

German -- *Gottesdienst* -- means "God's service (to us) and our service to God."

French -- *le culte* – a life-long engagement ... a relationship of giving and receiving.

"I pledge allegiance to the Lamb ... with all I am and all I have ..." – is "worship"!

We want to love the Lord our God (Jesus Christ) with our whole heart, mind, and physical strength. (Mark 12:30)

We want to take inventory. Carefully plan the changes that need to be made so that our devotion to Jesus is whole-hearted.

"WORSHIP" IS A VERB! It is not something done to us or for us, but by us!

Out of habit, we call what we do on Sunday a "worship service". Is there any service? (Is it not like the "opening exercise" at Sunday school that didn't open anything, and didn't exercise anyone?) If the traditional Sunday morning "worship" is all we do, we very likely have missed a great part of what New Testament worship really is.

D. If we want to know what the Bible explains "worship" to be, we'll have to take a look at the Hebrew and Greek words translated "worship." We find several words in each language so translated.

- The HEBREW words emphasize two ideas -- **submission** and **service**

    The most common Hebrew term for worship was SHACHAH, meaning 'to bow down' or 'to prostrate oneself.' There is an overtone of *submission* to one who is superior.

Another common Hebrew word was ABAD, meaning 'to serve.' It is from the same root that the term 'slave, servant' (*'ebed*) is taken. This is important. The highest designation for a Hebrew in his engagement with the worship of God is this word, 'servant.' He delighted to call himself 'God's servant.' It was a privilege and an honor (not a galling servitude) to be such a servant!

- The GREEK words also emphasize the same two ideas, **submission** and **service**, plus an additional idea, **fear** (lest we break any of His commands)

    The most common Greek word translated worship is PROSKUNEO, a word that means 'to kiss [*kuneō*] toward [*pros*].' It was the word used to describe the custom of kissing the feet or hem of the garment of a superior. People prostrated themselves in the presence of a king, indicating their submission to and dependence upon the king.

    Another common Greek term was LATREUO, meaning 'to serve,' and it regularly has to do with 'service rendered to a deity.' We do such acts of service because we know they will please the God for whom we do them.

    Another set of Greek words – *eusebeo, sebomai, sebazomai* – all have the idea of 'paying honor and respect and reverence to.' There is a healthy fear that keeps us from breaking any of God's commands.

  Do you see the parallel between the terms?

    The Hebrew SHACHAH and the Greek PROSKUNEO both suggest a submission of our selves and wills, an homage that is the token of awe and surrender.

    The other two terms, ABAD and LATREUO, suggest 'a total lifestyle dedicated to the service of the One to whom we submit our lives.'

E. Some key NEW TESTAMENT verses that should help guide our thinking and actions.

  Matthew 4:10 – "You shall worship (*proskuneo*) the Lord your God, and serve (*latreuo*) Him only!" (Jesus spoke of submission and service.)

  John 4:23,24 – "worship" (*proskuneo*) must be "in spirit and [in] truth."

    How well do we function in the realm of the spirit? Are our hearts and minds wholly involved in what we are doing?

    How well do we understand the truth that Jesus came to give us about God? The religious people in Isaiah's day, and in Jesus' day, worshiped in vain, because they taught as doctrines the commandments of men. (Matthew 15:1-9 quotes Isaiah. 29:13.) Unfortunately, few of us ask the obvious and hard questions about "spirit" and "truth". How does one go about worshiping "in spirit" and "in truth"?

> Be sure to notice how Jesus tells us what God wants –
>   God wants something -- worship
>   God wants someone -- US!

Romans 12:1 -- "I urge you therefore, brethren, by the mercies of God, to present your bodies a living and holy sacrifice, acceptable to God, *which is* your spiritual service of worship (*latreuo*)."

F. Now for a preliminary definition which will embrace these ideas in these Biblical words translated "worship." **"WORSHIP" is SUBMISSION and SERVICE!**

III. IN THE NEW TESTAMENT TIMES, TO WHOM WAS THIS WORSHIP (SUBMISSION AND SERVICE) DIRECTED?

A. Some New Testament verses have "worship and service" directed to God the Father.

John 4:24 -- God is spirit, and those who worship Him must worship in spirit and truth. The Father seeks such to worship Him.

1 Peter 2:5 -- Christians are a holy priesthood who offer up spiritual sacrifices, acceptable to God through Jesus Christ.

Acts 24:14 -- "According to the Way, which they call a sect, I do serve (*latreuo*) the God of our fathers."

Matthew 4:10 -- "You shall worship the Lord your God, and serve Him only." (Is "Lord" in this passage the Father, or Jesus?)

Romans 6:13 -- "Present yourselves to God as those alive from the dead, and your members as instruments of righteousness to God."

Romans 12:1 -- "Present your bodies a living and holy sacrifice, acceptable to God which is your spiritual service of worship."

B. But a surprising number have the worship and service directed to Jesus! Christians worship JESUS, too!

Acts 13:2 -- "They were ministering (offering service) to the Lord" – i.e., Jesus.

Acts 2:21, 9:14, 22:16, Romans 10:13ff. -- "Calling on the name of the Lord." Jesus was hailed in worship as the one worthy of adoration and surrender.

1 Corinthians 1:2 -- Addressed to all "who ... call upon the name of our Lord Jesus Christ" -- i.e., all who worship Jesus.

Hebrews 1:6 and Revelation 1:17 show Jesus being worshiped by angels and men.

Isaiah 6 -- Isaiah saw Jesus. He submitted to His will, and went to serve. What a wonderful example of worship from the Gospel Prophet in the Old Testament!

"Honor" the Son -- as they honor the Father.

> John 5:22,23 -- "The Father has given all judgment to the Son, in order that all men may honor the Son, even as they honor the Father. He who does not honor the Son does not honor the Father who sent Him."
>
> 1 Peter 2:4-5. "Keep coming to Jesus and let Him build you up into a spiritual house, a royal priesthood" is an encouragement to continue worshiping Jesus and letting Him do with us what He knows is best.

C. Early Christian literature shows the Christians were worshiping Jesus.

Pliny (the younger) to Trajan.

> Christians admitted their guilt to be only this, that on an appointed day they were accustomed to meet before daybreak, and to sing hymns to Christ, as to a God, and to bind themselves by an oath (sacrament), not for the commission of any crime, but to abstain from theft, robbery, adultery, and breach of faith, and not to deny a deposit when it was claimed. After the conclusion of this ceremony it was their custom to depart and meet again to take food; but it was ordinary and harmless food ....

Justin Martyr, First Apology 67.
> On the day called Sunday there is a gathering together in the same place of all [believers] who live in a given city or rural district. The memoirs of the apostles or the writings of the [New Testament] prophets are read, as long as time permits. Then when the reader ceases, the president in a discourse admonishes and urges the imitation of these good things. Next we all rise together and send up prayers.
>
> When we cease from our prayer, bread is presented and wine and water. The president in the same manner sends up prayers and thanksgivings, according to his ability, and the people sing out their assent, saying the "Amen." A distribution and participation of the elements for which thanks have been given is made to each person, and to those who are not present they are sent by the deacons.
>
> Those who have means and are willing, each according to his own choice, gives what he wills, and what is collected is deposited with the president. He provides for the orphans and widows, those who are in need on account of sickness or some other cause, those who are in bonds, strangers who are sojourning, and in a word he becomes the protector of all who are in need.
>
> We all make our assembly in common on Sunday, since it is the first day, on which

God changed the darkness and matter and made the world, and Jesus Christ our Savior arose from the dead on the same day. For they crucified him on the day before Saturn's day, and on the day after (which is the day of the sun) He appeared to his apostles and disciples and taught these things, which we have offered for your consideration.

D. SUCH WORSHIP OF JESUS IS A FORETASTE OF WHAT HEAVEN WILL BE.

Revelation 4-22 picture the inhabitants of heaven casting their crowns at Jesus' feet, bowing before Him, and spending time in wondrous service for Him.

Revelation 4:10 -- The 24 elders worship Him who lives forever. "Worthy art thou O Lord to receive glory and honor and power ...," they say.

Revelation 5 -- Worthy is the Lamb ... the elders fell down and worshiped (5:14).

Revelation 22:3 - His bondservants shall worship (serve) Him ....

E. NOW, WE ARE READY TO HONE OUR NEW TESTAMENT DEFINITION OF WORSHIP.

"WORSHIP" is SUBMISSION and SERVICE and REVERENCE to Christ – expressed in a number of ways.

This definition will give form and direction to our Sunday assemblies – and the assemblies will, not surprisingly, be similar to what we read in the New Testament.

IV. **SEVERAL VERSES GIVE US SOME IDEA WHAT WAS DONE WHEN EARLY CHRISTIANS ASSEMBLED TOGETHER ON SUNDAY.** These will help us to appreciate the New Testament concept of "worship."

We have done a word study in the Hebrew and Greek of "worship." Another way to learn what to do at the Sunday assembly is to study the New Testament passages that describe what 1st century assemblies were like.

Several verses give us glimpses into what church assemblies were like in Bible times.

A. Acts 2:42 -- Church meetings included "the apostles' doctrine, the fellowship, the breaking of bread, and the prayers." (The preaching and teaching surely emphasized what Jesus had taught, and who He is, and what He expects of His disciples.)

B. Church meetings also included the reading of Scripture.

We know from Colossians 4:16 and 1 Thessalonians 5:27 that Paul intended his letters to be read in the public assemblies. Revelation 1:3 indicates that book was to be read out loud in the churches to which it was addressed.

Whole books were read out loud at the public services! That's how they heard about Jesus – Who He is, what He expects of them, sins to quit, and virtues to practice.

C. Church meetings also included congregational and individual singing.

Remember Pliny's words – "they sang hymns to Jesus as to God" (*Carmen Christo*).

Colossians 3:16 and Ephesians 5:19 -- "Psalms, and hymns, and spiritual songs"

> The singing in these verses is not limited to the Sunday assembly in either passage, but certainly would include what was done at the assembly. After all, other New Testament verses speak of singing in the public assembly.

> Psalms -- "While the leading idea of *psalmos* is a musical accompaniment, and that of *humnos* praise to god, *ode* is a general word for a song, whether accompanied or unaccompanied, whether of praise or on any other subject. Thus it is quite possible for the same song to be at once a psalm, a hymn, and a spiritual song." (Lightfoot, on Colossians 3:16).

> "Psalms" may be a reference to the Davidic Psalms (as in James 5:13). If the word "spiritual" goes with all three words, then 'spiritual psalms' would be Christian compositions rather than the Davidic psalms.

> "Hymns" were *a cappella* songs. "Hymn" is the word used of the Hallel Psalms at Matthew 26:30. There is no way to know the genre of the "hymns" which Paul and Silas sang in the Philippian jail. There is no reason they couldn't have been the Davidic Psalms.

> "Spiritual songs" may well have been Christian lyrics set to popular music. Or they may have been songs inspired right at the moment by the Holy Spirit, and then sung or played by the worshiper. The Holy Spirit can still be in the business of writing words and music for the songs we sing.

It was not long until New Testament Scriptures were sung in the assemblies.

> The Magnificat (Luke 1:46-50), the Benedictus (Luke 1:68-79), the Gloria in Excelcis (Luke 2:14), and the Nunc Dimittis (Luke 2:29-32) are all given the titles these songs were known by in later church services.

> Some scholars find traces of the lyrics of Christian hymns in the majestic Christological passages in the New Testament – Ephesians 5:14, 1 Timothy 3:16, Philippians 2:6-11, Colossians 1:15-20, Hebrews 1:3. All of these were, we presume, composed by Paul.

> With their high Christological content, they would be very suitable in a worship setting where one's thoughts and praise are addressed to Jesus!

D. 1 Corinthians 11-14, 16

1 Corinthians 11-14 tell some of the things that occurred when the church members came together.

There was praying and prophesying – by both men and women.

Individual members contributed to the "service." "When you assemble, each one has a psalm, has a teaching (a word of instruction), has a revelation, has a tongue, has an interpretation" (14:26).

Indeed, visitors who were non-members were present (14:23-25), but the assembly was not structured to their wants and tastes. The assembly was structured to the needs of the church members.

Chapter 13 is in the middle of a paragraph about misuse of spiritual gifts in the public assembly. Its thrust is this: *Use your gifts in a loving way!* Use them to benefit the other person, to help the other person.

1 Corinthians 12:7 - to the profit of all. 12:25 - care for one another. 14:3,4 – edification, exhortation, consolation. 14:12 – seek to excel in edifying the church.

1 Corinthians 14:26 - when you meet for worship ... let all things be done for edification. I.e., the assembly is conducted in such a manner that people are built up. 14:31 -- "so that all may learn and all may be exhorted."

Several verses in this section express the purpose for the assemblies. Edification (14:3,4,5,12,17,26), exhortation (14:3,31), and consolation (14:3).

"Let all things be done for edification." "Seek to edify the church."

1 Corinthians 14:16 -- The people said "the Amen" at the close of prayers of thanks and when blessings were offered, and they were edified thereby.

Worshipers said a 'grand Amen' (full-throated) to enter into a song or message or prayer. (Clapping may or may not be the best way to show approval of a helpful song or message.)

1 Corinthians 14:31 -- prophecy (inspired preaching) was another of the activities at the public meeting. Listeners learned and were edified.

1 Corinthians 16:1-3 -- Other things occurred at the assembly. Offerings were collected. Benevolent concerns were attended to. Stewardship was taught.

E. Romans 14-15 -- public worship is in the background.

   What are worshipers to do? Welcome weak brothers. Help them grow stronger.

   What promotes righteousness (right attitudes and actions towards men), peace, and joy (and this every day, not just only on Sunday) was to be the thing emphasized as they met together -- 14:17. In this way a man "serves" (*douleuo*) Christ.

   Worshipers were to glorify God together (Romans 15:6,9). Jewish and Gentile backgrounds and special interests were to be ignored and forgotten.

F. The letters to Timothy and Titus give instructions to the preacher concerning his leading of public worship.

   1 Timothy 1:1ff -- These verses concern the evangelist and his sound doctrine (i.e., what he preaches in the assembly).

   1 Timothy 2:1ff -- These verses concern prayers to be offered. There are instructions for men and women in public worship. Wives receive instruction, but are not to habitually teach or exercise authority over their husbands.

   1 Timothy 4:13 -- These concern public reading of scripture, exhortation, doctrine.

   Titus 2 and 3 -- These instruct the preacher what to preach in the public assembly.

G. Hebrews

   Hebrews 10:24,25 -- Tells Christians to encourage each other to love and good works (this is the service part of our worship).

   Hebrews 12:28 -- Let us show gratitude, by which we may offer to God an acceptable service (*latreuo* -- public worship) with reverence and awe, for our God is a consuming fire.

H. "Greet one another with a holy kiss." – 1 Peter 5:14

   Orientals won't kiss another on his cheeks if they are at odds with each other. Only when old hurts are forgiven (now that we are both reconciled to God through Jesus Christ) is it possible to greet one another with such a kiss.

   We may greet one another at the assembly – before the service begins, or after the service – but seldom in the middle of the service (in this writer's opinion).

I. We are ready to try our hand, once more, at a New Testament definition of worship.

   We want to acknowledge both ideas found in the Hebrew and Greek words – bow down in submission to, and service.

I want Jesus to be the focus of my honor and submission and service!

> Worship is seeing and acknowledging who Jesus is (He is my God and Savior), and enthusiastically serving Him in whatever way we can (whether the recipient of that service is my brother, or the lost).

> Worship is the honor and homage we pay to Jesus, the submission of our wills to His will, and our service to Jesus, expressed in a number of ways.

V. **HOW CAN WE HELP THE SAME THINGS TO HAPPEN AT OUR SUNDAY ASSEMBLIES** that we read about in the New Testament?

A. Get rid of inherited denominational ideas and forms!

For the assembly of the saints, no longer pick songs that fail to either exalt Jesus, or that fail to call us to service.

There is a place for psalms, hymns, and spiritual songs – and for gospel songs, and for contemporary Christian music – if they fit the Biblical purpose for which we assemble.

Let us no longer go to the Old Testament for rationale for our forms for 'worship'!

[NOTICE, MANY CONTEMPORARY 'WORSHIP SERVICES' ARE BASED ON OLD TESTAMENT VERSES AND PRACTICES? Denominational churches – children of the Reformation – based their theology of worship on 2 Chronicles 5:12-14. Charismatic/Pentecostal worship uses Psalm 100:4 ("Enter into his gates with thanksgiving, and into his courts with praise") to give form to their worship service. But the Old Testament has been nailed to the cross! The New Testament is our rule of faith and practice!]

Many of our songbooks are arranged on denominational form – praise God for who He is, and for what he has done.

We live in God's presence every moment of the day, rather than coming into His presence to experience a few moments of rapture and bliss.

Let us no longer mindlessly copy what the mega-churches are doing.

B. Be aware (and beware!) of potential obstacles to worship.

1. The American emphasis on self-sufficiency is one of our worst obstacles.

Two of the words for worship (one Hebrew and one Greek) mean "to bow down." But Americans have no concept of bowing. We don't do that for anyone – not the president, not a congressman, not a king. Bowing to others is totally un-American. We spend all week holding the notion that we are independent people. Then we come to Sunday morning assembly and we are instantly expected to change our whole orientation. It often just does not happen.

2. Affluence is another obstacle.

Most of us come to the assembly with no pressing felt needs. We have to work at even being truly thankful. (Are we not sort of like Laodicea? "I am rich, and have become wealthy, and have need of nothing." And we can't even hear Jesus saying, "But you do not know that you are wretched and miserable and poor and blind and naked. I advise you to buy of Me ...," Revelation 3:17)

3. American's increasing hunger for entertainment is another obstacle.

Church leaders are aware that many churchgoers now shop around for the most pleasing Sunday morning experiences they can find.

Church has become a spectator sport. We watch football games; we watch baseball games; we watch concerts; and we watch religion on TV. So we come to the church building, and we want to watch it happen there.

4. Our own fuzzy and careless language is another obstacle.

"Sunday Morning Worship Service" and "Evening Evangelistic Service" are misnomers!

The slogan "Enter to Worship! Depart to Serve!" may not express the Biblical concept.

We'll need to be careful about our language, lest we give our people wrong ideas of what we are doing here.

5. We fail to teach our people how to worship.

We teach them how to teach. We teach them how to sing. We teach them how to work with children and youth. We teach them almost everything, but we don't teach them a worship concept. We don't preach about it.

All most of us know about "worship" is what we have learned from watching others.

Most of us don't have a clue about how to worship. There were no classes in Bible College offered on this topic.

It is right at 50 years since this writer preached his first sermon in southern Michigan. It has been his privilege to preach in many States, and in several countries outside the United States. In all these years, and all these places, he cannot recall a single instance of someone asking him for help in learning to worship.

Church leaders regularly will have to explain to the congregation what we are doing so new Christians and visitors can know and grow a New Testament theology of worship.

C. What do we do in preparation for meeting together with the brethren.

Whether we lead, or are simply a participant, there is preparation to be made.

Before we arrive at the place of meeting, we could begin even on Saturday night to plan and think. We can read and study the Scripture that is the text for the day.

We can contemplate about what kind of meeting this is going to be?

> Is there a time for seeker events?
> Is there a time for revivalist formats?
> Is there a time for edification, exhortation, and consolation of the brethren?

In the Sunday assembly for Christians, I am coming to learn about my Lord Jesus, His will for me, and how I can live for him.

D. What is there to do in the assembly?

We deliberately set our focus on Jesus!

> We can learn what we can about Jesus and His will for our lives.
> We can pledge anew our allegiance to Jesus.
> > "I love Him too much to fail Him now ... Too much to break my vow."
> > "I have decided to follow Jesus ... No turning back, no turning back!"

We should check our submission to His will.

> *"What shall I give Thee, Master, Giver of gifts divine. I shall not withhold, time, talents, or gold, but everything shall be Thine. What shall I give Thee, Master? Thou hast given all for me. Not just a part, or half of my heart. I will give all to Thee."*

We should encourage one another to love and good works.

We should plan ahead to contribute something for the benefit of the brethren who have assembled.

> SING!
> Compose a poem of encouragement, exhortation, consolation, and share it!
> Do a drama!
> Enlist someone to help you in your ministry to the brethren!
> Give a generous offering!

We can look for ways to be involved in His service.

> What can I do for Jesus this week? For my brothers? For my unconverted neighbors and friends?
>
> > *"There's a place for every worker in the kingdom of our Lord. ... O may I find it, where my mission I can fill. Be it humble, or exalted, may I hold it with a will. Help to serve my generation with a heart of love and grace. Help me, Lord, from this time onward, find and occupy my place."*

What do you do if the message doesn't meet your needs? Spend the time (the preacher is meeting others' needs) in prayer. "Show me what you want me to do for You this week," is what you ask of the Lord. He will plant thoughts in your mind wherein He suggests areas of service that are fitting and proper for you to do.

We can get some training on how to carry out your chosen area of service.

E. The fine art of going home from church.

Jesus showed us how to do this. He attended the meeting in the synagogue at Capernaum. He then went home and put the sermon into action. He healed Peter's mother-in-law. (Luke 4:38,39)

We hear from the Word of Christ what He expects of us. We leave the assembly with the express intention during the coming week of putting into practice what we have heard.

CONCLUSION

1. What are we doing here? What am I supposed to be doing here?

   We are paying homage to Jesus, and encouraging each other's service to Him Who is our great God and Savior.

   ### *WORSHIP -- HOW IMPORTANT IS IT? IT IS OUR #1 PRIORITY!*

2. Let's work to teach our people a New Testament theology of worship!

   Let us no longer use Old Testament verses as the rationale behind our 'worship service,' and let us no longer be satisfied with simply copying denominational formats (which often omit even such essentials as the Lord's Supper).

   Jesus has been here. He is our Lord and our God. He is the focus of our Lord's Day assembly. His will is our will; His work is our work.

   The people He died for are my brothers, and by His grace I will help my brother to grow in his Christian knowledge and service!

3. Let's make it our aim to lead authentic and Biblical congregational meetings.

   Not every assembly we attend is "worship" – there are chapels, singspirations, praise gatherings, basket dinners – but certainly one of the assemblies on the Lord's Day is intended to be "worship." And in that one, we consciously plan to lead people both in "worship" and in "service."

   Let there be no more purposeless preparation of the music, or the rest of the activities that will be included in our Sunday assembly!

4. Such meetings would have a bite, a thrill to them, an excitement that is contagious.

   When you feel the tug of the fish on the line or the breath-taking thrill when the big deer steps into the clearing about 100 yards away – that's "bite", that's excitement!

   There is no reason our Sunday services should be missing such excitement.

   At Christmas and Easter services, there is emphasis on Jesus and His work. Those are thrilling times of the year. It could happen every Sunday!

5. Remember, God seeks people who will worship Him in spirit and truth. (John 4:24)

   "The Father SEEKS worshipers!" That statement is unparalleled in the entire corpus of Holy Scripture. Nowhere else do we read of God's seeking anything else from one of His children. But He DESIRES worshipers who will worship Him in spirit and truth."

   Let's quit letting God go home from church unfulfilled and unsatisfied!

SECTION EIGHT: CONCERNING THE FINAL RESURRECTION OF DEAD BODIES. 15:1-58

A. Arguments for the Resurrection of the Body. 15:1-34

1. The historical argument. 15:1-11

> *Summary:* There has already been one resurrection. The resurrection of Jesus Christ is an essential article of the gospel. Scripture and eyewitness testimony to the fact that Christ arose from the dead are indisputable. Paul and the other apostles are in perfect agreement on these matters.[1]

15:1 -- *Now I make known to you, brethren, the gospel which I preached to you, which also you received, in which also you stand,*

Now -- This may mean 'now concerning,' and we can picture Paul as answering a question addressed to him in the letter sent to him by the Corinthians (see notes at 7:1, 8:1, etc.). On the other hand, Fisher may be right when he wrote, "Paul dealt with the problem though the church had not asked for his opinion. There is no suggestion that they had raised the question [in their letter to him] at all. On the contrary, he raised it. Perhaps his source of information was the same visitors who had furnished him with the information about the dissensions in [the church at] Corinth."[2] The issue which is addressed in this chapter is clear from 15:12: "How do some among you say that there is no resurrection of the dead?" Someone[3] at Corinth was denying that there would be any future resurrection of the dead. The Corinthians were not denying the resurrection of Jesus Christ from the dead; they were denying the future bodily resurrection of dead men in general. What Paul is insistent upon is that if a man denies the possibility of the resurrection of the body, then he must also deny the fact that Jesus arose. If one does that, he has emptied the Christian message of its truth and the Christian life of its reality.

> The first sentence of this chapter is masterful in every way. It fits the situation exactly. Paul does not begin by naming the subject he intends to treat. Instead

---

[1] Another good summary of these opening verses is this: "The substance of my preaching has been and is the historical fact of the resurrection of Christ, which was predicted in Scripture, and is vouched for by competent witnesses, most of whom are still living. Among these are the other apostles and myself; and, greatly as they differ from me in calling and work, we are absolutely agreed about this."

[2] Fisher, *op. cit.*, p.234.

[3] Little is to be gained from the old attempts to decipher which of the four parties (Peter, Paul, Apollos, or Christ) might have been denying the resurrection. It is pure speculation to say it was the Apollos party which spearheaded the teaching against any future resurrection. To assume Apollos has to be the one who opposed the doctrine of resurrection, simply because we have no details of Apollos' preaching (like we do Peter's or Paul's, who taught the resurrection in so decided a manner) is to argue from ignorance.

he starts with a reminder of the pertinent gospel facts on which the Christian faith rests. Not until he reaches verse 12 are we introduced to the topic that makes this entire chapter necessary. This form of presentation is highly effective for securing the fullest and the most unbiased attention.[4]

Why some were denying the possibility of any future bodily resurrection can only be surmised. (1) Perhaps it was skepticism rooted in Greek philosophy. Epicureans held no belief in life after death. The last phrase of their famous slogan, "Eat, drink, and be merry, for tomorrow we die," expresses their ideas about no life after death. The Stoics looked for the soul to merge with deity when a man dies. To the Stoic there was no individual existence beyond the grave. When a man died, his body simply dissolved into the elements of which it was made, but the divine spark that had animated it returned to the "divine fire" out of which it had sprung and was absorbed in the divinity of which it was a part. Plato believed in the immortality of the soul, but his philosophy had no room for a resurrection of the body. The Greeks had some proverbs about this: "The body is a tomb," and "I am a poor soul, shackled to a corpse." Plato taught that the human body was a prison from which man escaped at the time of death. Were the man to get a resurrection body out in the future, he simply would be back in prison, and that would be a great tragedy. So for the Greek, immortality lay precisely in getting rid of the body. And if there were a resurrection, a man would not be rid of his body. Some Greeks believed in a life beyond (immortality of the soul), but none had any hope for a resurrection of the body. (2) Maybe the "some" at Corinth denied the resurrection because of Jewish theology.[5] We remember that the Sadducees denied there was life after death, as well as denying that there was any future resurrection (Matthew 22:23, Acts 23:8). Even the doctrine about the resurrection held by the Pharisees was not in harmony with what really will occur in the future. They pictured that the resurrection body would be an exact reproduction of the one we live in during this life (Matthew 22:23ff), whereas Scripture anticipates a glorified body. (3) Maybe the "some" were saying the resurrection was already past (as incipient Gnosticism would attempt to teach, cp. 1 Timothy 1:20 and 2 Timothy 2:17,18). This heresy that the resurrection is already past was so serious and dangerous that at the time Paul wrote those letters to Timothy (about 8 or 10 years after he wrote 1 Corinthians), the heretics had been excluded from the fellowship by a "delivery to Satan." Just what those heretics taught when they said "the resurrection is already past" we are not sure. Perhaps they applied all the verses about 'resurrection' to the rising from the deadness in trespasses and sins to walk in newness of life that occurs when a man first becomes a Christian. This effectively would be a denial of the hope of any future bodily resurrection. (4) The fact of the matter is, whether it was Sadducees or incipient Gnostics or pagan Greeks, the denial of any resurrection for the body was rooted in Greek philosophy. It was from Greek philosophy the Sadducees learned their doctrine, and it was from Greek philosophy that the Gnostics learned theirs.

---

[4] Lenski, *op. cit.*, p.625.

[5] While the church at Corinth was mainly made up of Gentile converts, there have been traces of Jewish doctrine in some of the disputes dealt within this epistle.

The points of Paul's argument in chapter 15 are: (a) There is going to be a future resurrection of dead bodies, verses 1-34. The certainty of this doctrine is based on an historical argument (verses 1-11), on a logical argument (verses 12-19), on a theological argument (verses 20-28), and on an *ad hominem* argument (verses 29-34). (b) The nature of the bodies after they are raised is explained, verses 35-50. (c) Then he covers what will become of those who shall be alive at the time of the second advent, verses 51-54. (d) He closes by stating some of the practical consequences of this doctrine, verses 55-58.

I make known to you, brethren -- The verb *gnōridzō* here has the force of "I remind you." Compare Galatians 1:11.[6] This seems to be a gentle rebuke. Paul begins his presentation by reminding the Corinthians of what had been the staple of his gospel preaching, a message they at one time had embraced wholeheartedly. When he talks about resurrection, he is not declaring a new truth to them. He is impressing on them the force of what they already believed. "Brethren" helps to express the kindly tones Paul uses as he addresses these erring folk. Compare notes at 14:20.

The gospel – *Euaggelion* is 'the good news, the glad announcement' about the coming of the Messiah, His life, His sufferings, His death, and especially His resurrection (cf. Isaiah 52:7 and Nahum 1:15). The basic facts Paul enumerates in the next several verses are not all there is to the gospel, but these four facts are the foundation of the gospel. The gospel not only includes facts such as these to be believed, but commands to be obeyed, warnings to be heeded, and promises to be received and enjoyed.[7]

Which I preached to you -- The reference is to the time when Paul first went into Corinth and preached to them, laying the foundation of the Corinthian church (see Acts 18:1ff).

Which also you received -- The repetition of *kai* ("also") makes a climax. When Paul first preached to them, they embraced in their entirety the facts of the gospel, which included the teaching about the resurrection of Jesus from the dead. The word "received" was the regular word for the reception of a 'tradition' handed down by word of mouth from teacher to student. Paul was the teacher, the Corinthians were the students who heard the doctrines of the gospel over and over again as they were being instructed.

In which also you stand -- "In which you stand" speaks of the present time in the spiritual lives of the Corinthians. "Stand" is a perfect tense verb; they took their stand in the gospel in the past, and still stood on it.[8] The gospel facts (about to be enumerated) were and are

---

[6] *Gnōridzō* properly means 'to make known, to declare, to reveal, to tell, to inform, to remind, to impress, to confirm.'

[7] Compare Romans 2:16 and 2 Timothy 2:8 where Paul also alludes to some items in the body of doctrine which he regularly preached as an integral part of the Gospel.

[8] While the Corinthians have not yet denied that Jesus arose from the dead, they will eventually have to if they are going to hold consistently with the doctrine of "some" that there is no such thing as resurrection.

vital and foundational to the Christian faith. Without these facts, Christianity is not a worthwhile religion. The immediate implication is that when they began to deny the idea of resurrection, they were attacking and undermining the very foundation on which their life and hope rested.[9]

15:2 -- *by which also you are saved, if you hold fast the word which I preached to you, unless you believed in vain.*

By which also you are saved -- "You are saved" is a present tense verb. There are verses in the Scriptures where salvation is looked at as a thing that happened in the past.[10] In others, as something that is still future.[11] It is also often depicted, as here, as something that is progressive in the believer's present day-by-day experience.[12] Salvation is not something that is exhausted by a man's experience when he first believes. It is something that goes on from strength to strength and from glory to glory. Our salvation depends on the facts of the gospel about to be highlighted. Because of their reception of and belief in these facts of the gospel, they "are being saved" – they are those who were in the way of salvation. By the use of the present tense (*sōzesthe*), the attainment of salvation is here presented as something that is in the process of being realized. Its complete fulfillment, something that is still future, is conditional on their continuing to believe and embrace these facts, as the conditional clause following emphasizes.

If you hold fast the word -- The idea is that they would continue to be saved by this gospel if they faithfully retained, or held, the doctrine as he delivered it.[13] The duty of 'holding fast' what they had heard is often impressed upon the early converts (e.g., 1 Corinthians 11:2, 1 Thessalonians 5:21, Hebrews 10:23). Specifically what the Corinthians needed to hold fast to was the fact of the bodily resurrection of Jesus. Once this is granted, the argument about the "future resurrection of the dead" has already been settled.

---

[9] Barclay (*op. cit.*, p.159) has offered some devotional thoughts at this place. He calls attention to the function of the gospel here emphasized, that it gives a man stability. In a dangerous and slippery world it keeps a man on his feet. In a tempting and seducing world it gives him power to resist. In a hurting world it gives him power to withstand a broken heart or an agonized body and not to give in. He calls attention to Moffatt's translation of Job 4;4, "Your words have kept men on their feet." That, he comments, is precisely what the gospel does.

[10] See Romans 1:16, 2 Timothy 1:9, Titus 3:5.

[11] See Romans 5:9,10, 1 Thessalonians 5:8ff, 1 Peter 1:5, and 1 Corinthians 5:5.

[12] See 1 Corinthians 1:18, 2 Corinthians 2:15, Philippians 2:12,13, 3:10,20,21, Romans 8:24, and Ephesians 2:8. Refer again to the discussion of "salvation" at 1 Corinthians 1:18.

[13] The advocates of the Calvinistic doctrine of unconditional eternal security have problems with this verse. It says they are saved, "if ...." (It is amazing how many learned articles have been written on the implication of first, second, and third class conditional sentences, in an attempt to make otherwise apparently contradictory verses harmonize with Calvin's doctrine.) We affirm that the security of the convert to Christianity everywhere in the Bible is conditioned on his faithfulness.

The word which I preached to you -- The word order in the Greek poses some problems.[14] But while there is some debate as to how the words should be smoothly translated, there is no doubt as to the point Paul is driving home. Their standing erect in the way of salvation depends on their keeping a firm hold not only on what Paul taught, but on keeping a firm hold on 'the very expression' which he used when he preached to them. Words cannot be redefined, or given a spiritual or esoteric meaning, without eviscerating the gospel and making it powerless and worthless.

Unless you believed in vain -- Here is another place in the Scriptures where "believed" and "received" (verse 1) are used synonymously (cp. John 1:12). The adverb "in vain" (*eikē*) may have either of two possible implications. (1) It might mean "haphazardly, rashly, superficially, unreal." If this meaning is accepted, then Paul would be wondering whether the Corinthians (at the time when he preached to them) gave serious attention to what he taught. Did they grasp the truth of the facts involved? He would be asking them whether or not their faith was superficial. Several previous verses cause us to think this is not the proper meaning for this verse. The people in Corinth wholeheartedly believed the gospel. They had believed, repented, confessed, and been baptized and justified (1 Corinthians 6:11). There was nothing make-believe or superficial about their conversion. (2) It might mean 'to no purpose, useless, empty, without effect.' You will be saved by the gospel, if you adhere to it, unless the gospel in which you believe produces no blessed effects in a man's life. That it does indeed produce blessed effects, Paul goes on to demonstrate.

15:3 -- *For I delivered to you as of first importance what I also received, that Christ died for our sins according to the Scriptures,*

For -- Paul now explains ("for") or restates to the Corinthians the "word" (i.e., the exact expression, the language) which embodies the very heart of the gospel which he had preached to them.

I delivered to you -- This is the technical word used for the transmission of religious instruction (cp. 1 Corinthians 11:23). As was true of his instructions given to them about the Lord's Supper, this language indicates that the essential matters of the gospel go back to the beginning of things. Of crucial importance here is the clear implication that the basic tenets of the gospel – the atoning death of Christ, the fact of his bodily resurrection, etc. – were accepted historical facts before Paul ever began to teach the "tradition" to his listeners.[15] In this context Paul emphasizes four things that he regularly included in his sermons from the first day he taught them – namely, that Christ died, was buried, He arose,

---

[14] The order is "by what word I preached the gospel to you if you hold fast." Most of our translators (KJV, ASV, NASB) treat it as a conditional clause connected with the verb "I preached," with the "if" clause coming late in the sentence, in order to give emphasis to what precedes. Some however connect "with what word I preached the gospel to you" with "I make known" at the beginning of verse 1, thus giving the sense "I remind you ... in what terms I preached the gospel to you." This then requires "if you hold fast" to be attached to the verb "you are being saved" (which is how Goodspeed, RSV treat it).

[15] Catholic scholars use the word "deliver" in support of the legitimacy and authority of "tradition" as well as Scripture. We've discussed "tradition" before in our comments on 1 Corinthians 11:2,11,23.

and He appeared![16]

As of first importance -- It is possible the NASB treats the Greek phrase *en prōtois* correctly, making Christ's death, burial, resurrection, and post-resurrection appearances the primary, cardinal, central, and indispensable facts of the Gospel. These matters, among all the gospel teachings, are the ones that are most important! They are the heart of Christianity. Apart from them, everything – the whole scheme of redemption, the whole Bible message – is gone. It is also possible the ASV was right in translating the Greek "first of all," making it a temporal reference.[17] If so, Paul's point is that he preached these truths in the very beginning of his ministry in Corinth. "Resurrection" was not something he was now introducing to them for the first time. Paul's meaning then is, 'What I now hold up before you, viz., the truth of Christ's resurrection in its bearing on our salvation, is only a repetition of the very expressions I used when I preached to you at the beginning.'

What I also received -- On the basis of Galatians 1 and 2, we affirm Paul received his gospel by divine revelation, not from human teachers. In fact, in this very letter (2:6ff), Paul asserts the source of his message was revelation from God.[18] The source of these

---

[16] Note carefully that the verb "I delivered" is followed by four particulars – each introduced by "that."

[17] Some have affirmed that we would expect Paul to have written *en archē* ("in the beginning") if he really were intending to remind them what he preached at Corinth from day one.

[18] We have already noted (15:1) that "received" is the regular word for a student's learning something from a teacher. Paul's own affirmation is that his teacher in gospel matters was divine, not human. How utterly disappointing and frustrating to find commentators looking for human sources from which Paul allegedly might have learned his message. It will not do to affirm Paul's doctrine of the resurrection is to be traced to certain mediating views of the ancient Jews. We are told by these negative critics that Paul belonged to certain Jewish circles and adopted their teaching concerning a spiritual and ethereal resurrection body which was eventually to be received by the soul. Old beliefs – whether Jewish or pagan – are not the source of Paul's doctrine about the resurrection (or any of the rest of his preaching, for that matter)! Nor will it do to affirm Paul has modified the verses of some ancient Christian confession. Most writers who appeal to an early Christian confession go on to question the validity of what Paul affirms, since the sources of those early creeds are themselves suspect. Hans Conzlemann, "On the Analysis of the Confessional Formula in 1 Corinthians 15:3-5," trans. by Mathias Rissi, *Interpretation* (Jan 1966), p.15-25, puts forth such an idea. He asserts that several factors in the verses indicate they were not an original formulation by Paul: (1) "I delivered ... what I also received"; (2) The parallelism of the four expressions, "died, buried, raised, appeared"; (3) The use of the plural "sins" is another mark of the un-Pauline character of this formula; (4) The use of the Aramaic "Cephas" instead of the Greek "Peter" marks the confession as originating in the Palestinian community before the spread of the gospel to the Greek world. Everything in verses 3-5 except the four expressions are held to have been added by Paul. Other commentators have taken up the debate about how far the "Early Christian Creed" extends – through verse 5, or through verse 4, or through verse 7? See J. Kloppenborg, "An Analysis of the Pre-Pauline Formula in 1 Corinthians 15:3b-5 in Light of Some Recent Literature," *CBQ* 40 (1978), p.351-67. Form and redaction critics have sought to "divine" the original language and geographical area where the "creed" originated. Was it written in Palestine (hence originally in Aramaic), or was it written in Hellenistic circles (therefore originally in Greek)? Naturally enough, such dissection of the passage has also resulted in a number of scholarly articles defending the "unity of the creed" while others have rejected the "unity" of this paragraph. When Conzlemann and Fisher and the others finish, we are left with serious doubts about the objective fact of Jesus' bodily resurrection, and even about the value of Paul's witness to the resurrection. In light of what follows in verse 12, about the resurrection being the heart of the gospel, what Conzlemann and Fisher do to this section is not very comforting. Nor would it have served in any way to correct the Corinthians' arguments against the certainty of a bodily resurrection.

gospel "facts" is to be found in the historical events themselves, not in some early Christian's fertile imagination! In the case of Paul's initial reception, the source was Jesus Himself, not men (if we allow Paul's own testimony in Galatians 1:11,12 to guide us). This statement in 1 Corinthians 15 of Paul's gospel message is very important. It is a very early summary. And Paul is not giving us his *interpretation* of what he had been told. He is giving us *exactly* what he had been told. This takes us back to the gospel as originally preached, the *kerygma*, to use an expression currently popular. The point is, Paul did not invent what he communicated to them. They received what he received, and Paul's teacher was divine!

That Christ died -- In verses 3 and 4 we have a bare-bones summary of the gospel that saves. Item one is that "Messiah died to take away our sins (cf. 1:23, 2:2)." Paul says that Messiah (Christ) *died* (i.e., His soul separated from His body). It is an historical fact that Christ died on the cross! However, not all modern scholars agree. Some modern scholars say Dr. Luke administered a drug to help Christ through the pain of the cross. Thus, it is supposed, Jesus slipped into a cataleptic state (a sudden suspension of consciousness, with muscular rigidity) which the bystanders mistakenly interpreted as death. Others (e.g., Christian Science) suppose Jesus did not actually die. Somehow, it is said, He hid within the midst of the tomb and finally grew stronger and then somehow got out. Several telling points can be made in refutation of these theories: (1) John 19:34-35. (2) Christ was crucified by His enemies, not His friends; His enemies would make sure of His death. (3) Pilate, the Centurion, the guards, Joseph of Arimathea, Nicodemus, Matthew, Luke, Mary, John, his friends – *all thought He was dead*. They had no doubt about it. (4) If Christ was not dead, and therefore not really raised from the dead, then how do we account for what happened fifty days later on Pentecost and all the following events? (5) Roman historians record Christ's death.

It might seem that we are giving too much emphasis to these theories of the negative critics, for here is Paul saying, "Christ died." But some do not credit Paul. However, there is no reason to doubt Paul's word. None of the theories (the drug theory, the Christian Science theory, etc.) meets the requirements of the record. Jesus was beaten and emaciated, and impaled for several hours on the cross. How could a man in such a condition as that, three days later, having been without food or nourishment, come forth and make the impression on the disciples that Christ did?

For our sins -- The fact that Christ died is not the whole story. Christ died was "*for our sins*," i.e., to take away our sins. The Christian cannot be content merely with the fact that Christ died. The Bible goes beyond that and so must the Christian. Other passages teach Christ died *in behalf of others*, as their *substitute*, to atone for their sins (Isaiah 53; Romans 3:21-26, 8:1-3, 31-34; Acts 20:28; Matthew 20:28; Titus 2:14; 1 Peter 2:24; 1 John 2:2; 1 Corinthians 6:20). That Christ could die "for our sins" implies He was sinless. Implied, too, is the idea of alienation between God and man because of human rebellion and sin, which can only be removed by the death of the sinless Son of God.

The fact that Christ died "for our sins" as a vicarious substitute destroys certain false theories concerning the atonement. (1) It does away with the *moral influence theory*. This theory denies that Christ died to satisfy any principle of divine justice, and holds that His death was designed primarily to impress men with a sense of God's love, and thus soften their hearts and lead them to repentance. According to this view, Christ died as a martyr for the cause He thought to be right, and the crucifixion was a dramatic exhibition of suffering intended to produce a moral impression in the awe-stricken spectators. The atonement is conceived of as directed *not* toward God, with the purpose of maintaining His justice, but toward men, with the purpose of persuading us to right action. While we do not deny that there was moral influence in the cross (e.g., Christ showed us how to live, and He showed us how to die. 1 Peter 2:21 tells us "to follow in His steps"), there is more to the death of Christ than merely a moral influence. Why God could not forgive without sending His own son as a sacrifice, we cannot answer. We are plunged into the depths of the plan of atonement, and no man can fully comprehend this. The moral influence theory furnishes no proper explanation of the suffering and death of Christ, but rather makes absurd His voluntary acceptance of such suffering and death in the very prime of His life. Furthermore, if He died simply as a martyr instead of the sinbearer for His people, it is impossible to explain why in His deepest suffering He was utterly forsaken by the Father.

(2) "That Christ died for our sins" also does away with the *governmental theory*. This theory holds that because of His absolute sovereignty, God is able to relax at will the demands of His Law, and to forgive men freely without any expiation or sacrifice for sin. In order to preserve a fair degree of discipline and respect for His laws, it is said, God had to give some exhibition of the high estimate which He Himself set upon His laws. Man was not to be encouraged to believe he could commit sin with impunity. According to this view, the suffering of Christ was not to satisfy an eternal principle of divine justice, but to secure man's reformation by inducing in him a horror for sin through the awful spectacle of Christ on the cross. Having given this exhibition of His displeasure with sin, God is now able to offer salvation on much easier terms than those originally announced. Instead of demanding perfect obedience, He now demands only faith and a reasonable amount of good works. There is an element of truth in this theory, too. God will not allow sin to go unpunished. Orderly government of the universe can continue only as men have respect for God's laws. But the governmental theory is not all there is to the atonement. It makes no provision for, and in fact denies, the possibility of the imputation of the sinner's guilt to Christ, or of Christ's righteousness to us. It makes God unjust in that He punishes an innocent Person merely for the sake of the impression it will make on others. The view of sin under this theory is too shallow and casual. The stroke that was intended for us was received by Jesus Christ so that our sins might be forgiven. There would be no hope if it were not for the death of Christ for our sins (Galatians 3:13). The Law demanded consistency in the keeping of the statutes of God, but men living under the Law were not consistent in their living (Hebrews 9:15). So the Law was broken, but the Law itself provided no perfect sacrifice for the atonement of sins. Christ is the perfect sacrifice for sins.

(3) We should be cautious about accepting "theories of atonement" that propose the purpose of Christ's death was to get God to love man. These theories are based on ideas found in heathen idolatry and religion – i.e., that Christ died to appease an angry God, to cause God to look favorably upon us. There is nothing of this sort of theory in the Bible

(see John 3:16). God loved us long before Christ died.

Instead of trying to explain away the Biblical account of the meaning of Christ's death, we should hear in the words "Christ died for our sins" the clear statement of the Biblical emphasis that His death was a vicarious, substitutionary atonement.

According to the Scriptures -- The fact that Jesus' death was an atoning sacrifice was not something evolved by the apostle's own consciousness, but something that was long beforehand clearly taught in the Scriptures. "Scriptures" is a reference to the Old Testament.[19] 1 Peter 1:10-12 contains a summary of the Old Testament prophecies about the coming Messiah. See also Luke 24:26,27 and 24:44ff. The Old Testament expected One who would make atonement for sins.[20]

15:4 -- *and that He was buried, and that He was raised on the third day according to the Scriptures,*

And that He was buried -- This is the second item in Paul's bare-bones summary of the gospel. The inclusion of this detail in so brief a statement of the facts is remarkable. The burial was carefully recorded in all four Gospels, and that record is important. It is His body that was buried. The burial is evidence of the reality of Christ's death.[21] The burial was evidence of a bodily resurrection. The body was laid in the tomb and the tomb was afterwards found to be empty.[22] The phrase "according to the Scriptures" is not repeated for this second item, but many commentators think it is implied, and look to Isaiah 53:9 as one passage where the Old Testament predicted the burial.

And that He was raised -- With this third item in his list, Paul comes to his present concern – the matter of resurrection. It has happened once, to Jesus. It cannot therefore be denied that such a thing is possible. We have a change of verb tenses. "Died" and "buried" were aorist tense verbs, indicating what took place once and for all. "Raised" is a perfect tense verb in the Greek, indicating something that took place in past time, whose result still re-

---

[19] Throughout much of the New Testament we find an emphasis on the unity of the facts of Christ's life and the predictive utterances of the Old Testament prophets. See Acts 17:2,3, 17:11, 18:5, Acts 9:11.

[20] References in the Old Testament to the vicarious death of the Messiah include Isaiah 53; Psalm 22; Daniel 9:26; Zechariah 12:10, the paschal lamb, the ram substitute at the sacrifice of Isaac, etc.

[21] It seems that the "burial" is emphasized in the gospel, not only to prove the reality of the death and resurrection, but also to answer some who were saying Jesus had not really died after all. The account of the piercing of Jesus' side also was designed to contradict such stories, John 19:34,35.

[22] The reality of the empty tomb is thus verified. See R. Stein, "Was the Tomb Really Empty?" *JETS* 20 (1977), p.20-27; W.L. Craig, "The Historicity of the Empty Tomb of Jesus," *NTS* 31 (1985), p.39-42; J. Manek, "The Apostle Paul and the Empty Tomb," *Nov.Test.* 2 (1957), p.276-280.

mains. HE REMAINS ALIVE, and He always will be alive.[23] It is not said that Christ arose, but that He was raised. The passive voice verb points to the activity of another. Christ's resurrection is the work of God (Ephesians 1:20), and is the divine seal upon the work of Christ.[24] The delightful article in the *International Standard Bible Encyclopedia* on the proofs of the resurrection of Jesus Christ (Vol. 4, pp.2565-69, 1929 edition, edited by James Orr), includes these points:

(1) The life of Jesus

> A perfect life characterized by divine claims ends in its prime in a cruel and shameful death. Is that a fitting close? Surely death could not end everything after such a noble career. The Gospels give the resurrection as the completion of the picture of Jesus Christ. Christ anticipated his own resurrection. He said, "Destroy this temple and in three days I will rebuild it." John 2:19-21. Also, "The son of man must be raised the third day." See Matthew 12:38-40, 16:21, 17:9,23, 20:19,27-63, Mark 8:31, 9:9,31, 10:34, 14:58; Luke 9:22, 18:33. His veracity is at stake if He did not rise. If after a perfect life there should be a shameful death, then we are faced with an insoluble mystery – the permanent triumph of wrong over right.

(2) The empty grave

> On the third morning, the body was gone. There are two solutions to this: the body was removed by human power, or the body was removed by superhuman power. If removed by human power, then either by his friends or his foes. If by his friends, could they have done this against the stone, the seal, and the guards? If by his foes, what was their purpose? Why did not they produce His body when the disciples began to preach that Jesus had risen? They could have stopped Christianity cold by producing the body. The body could not have been stolen. They could not have stolen the body naked, because of the delay in stripping it of the burial clothes and the spices that had been administered on Friday afternoon. The position of the grave clothes proves the impossibility of the theft of the body. So the fact of the empty tomb must still be faced. The vision-theory is fallacious. The survival of the soul is not resurrection. It is impossible to be "agnostic" about the facts that are writ so large on the face of the records. The empty tomb points to a bodily resurrection.

(3) The transformation of the disciples

> The disciples had seen their Master die; and through that death, they lost all hope. Yet hope returned three days after. What can account for the astonishing change of these men in so short a time? Not the mere removal of the body from the grave. Three days are not enough time for a legend to spring up. There is nothing more striking in the history of Primitive Christianity than the marvelous change wrought in the disciples by a belief in the resurrection of their Master.

---

[23] The perfect tense verb is repeated throughout this chapter when referring to Christ (verses 12,13,14,16,17,20).

[24] Paul will shortly make the point that just as God raised Jesus, God will raise others from the dead. God can do that in spite of what man's philosophy and man's reasoning might lead him to believe.

(4) The existence of the primitive church

There is no doubt that the church of the apostles believed in the resurrection of their Lord. When we consider the commencement of the church as recorded in the book of Acts, we see two simple and uncontrovertible facts: the Christian society was gathered together by preaching, and the substance of that preaching was the resurrection of Jesus Christ. In answering the mythological theory concerning Christianity, "As the church is too holy for a foundation of rottenness, she is too real for a foundation of myth."

(5) The witness of Paul

Paul wrote 1 Thessalonians (AD 51) just 20 or 21 years after the resurrection. It states that Jesus was killed (2:15, 4:14) and was raised from the dead (4:14). Paul wrote 1 Corinthians a few years later, and see chapter 15, where Paul is concerned to prove (not Christ's resurrection, but) the resurrection of Christians. He naturally adduces Christ's resurrection as his greatest evidence. If, therefore, Paul's 25 years of suffering and service for Christ were a reality, then his conversion was true, for everything he did began with that sudden change. And if his conversion was true, Jesus Christ rose from the dead, for every thing Paul was and did, he attributed to the sight of the risen Christ.

(6) The gospel record

No one can read the story of the walk to Emmaus (Luke 24) or of the visit of Peter and John to the tomb (John 20), without observing the striking marks of reality and personal testimony in the accounts. (In answer to those disclaiming the credibility of Luke – Luke was either a greater poet, or more creative genius than Shakespeare, or, he did not create the record.) The fact that Christ appeared in both Jerusalem and Galilee is really an argument in favor of the credibility of the record of the appearances.

Conclusion

That the apostles really believed in a miraculous, true, physical resurrection, is beyond all question. (Yet very much of the present day refuses to believe in the miracle. We are told (1) not allowed to believe, or (2) no need to believe, in the reanimation of the body.[25]) The only proper explanation to Christianity today is the resurrection of Christ. The resurrection is the best-attested fact in human history.

The eternal significance of the resurrection results from its objective reality. Many negative critics have tried to deny the *fact* of the resurrection by using 1 Corinthians 15. (a) It is denied that Christ's body came out of the tomb. Rather, it is taught that each of His followers, reflecting back over the past years' events, came to realize the value of Jesus' teaching. Subjectively, the One who had been crucified appeared, as it were, in a vision (in their mind's eye), and they better saw the vitality of His teaching. So it is, the negative

---

[25] See the Special Study #7 entitled "He is Alive! You Had Better Believe It!" at the close of this chapter.

critics say, that Christ arose from the grave.[26]   But immortality of the soul or a recollection of some teachings is not resurrection in the sense that Paul here speaks of resurrection. (2) Another way to word this subtle denial is to make a distinction between *historie* and *geschichte* – between the objective events and the interpretation of those events. It is an effort to mold Christianity to a currently popular philosophy. Negative critics have been trying to interpret the Bible through the glasses of the currently popular philosophy for centuries, so it is not surprising to find such an attempt here. However, Acts 17 shows that the resurrection of Jesus Christ creates a world view, yea, a world view that destroyed the prevailing philosophies of Stoicism and Epicureanism. Acts 17 teaches us not to start with the currently prevailing human philosophy, but instead to start with what God has said and done in history! The resurrection is an objective fact.

The resurrection is the central, pivotal point, the heart of the whole scheme of redemption. It is absolutely impossible to prove Biblical ethics without the fact of the resurrection. The resurrection is essential to general theology. The resurrection is a fine starting point for an apologetics course. Without the resurrection the Bible would not be a book with the last chapter missing; it just would not be a book! The God of the Bible is the God who raised Christ from the dead (Romans 4:24, 8:11; 1 Peter 1:21). Jehovahism is a better word for Old Testament theology than monotheism. Old Testament theism points to Theanthropism (the incarnation is the completion of the Old Testament). Biblical theism (belief in God) is resurrection theism. Apart from the resurrection, one cannot have Biblical theism.

On the third day -- How long was Christ's body in the tomb? What is the date of the crucifixion? There is a special study titled "Chronology of the Death and Resurrection of Christ," in the author's Gospel's III notes. The conclusion of that paper is that there is no contradiction between John and the Synoptic Gospels as to the date of the crucifixion. Since John can be harmonized with the idea of a Friday (Nisan 15) crucifixion, and the Synoptic Gospels (especially Luke 23:54-24:1) cannot be harmonized with anything but a Friday (Nisan 15) crucifixion, we therefore conclude that Christ was crucified on Friday, Nisan 15. The implication of the text, too, is that He arose about sunrise ("early" on the first day of the week, Mark 16:9), Sunday morning, Nisan 17.[27]

---

[26] See Howard E. Short, *Christian Evangelist* 3-14-1951, p.260, "No doubt the body of Jesus went the way of all flesh."

[27] The Bible uses various expressions to describe the length of the stay in the tomb. Sometimes when Jesus spoke of His coming resurrection, he spoke of it being "after three days." At other times He said it would be "on the third day" after his death. On one occasion he spoke of "three days and three nights" in the heart of the earth." Now these expressions do not seem to us to be equivalent, but they evidently were. It is a mistake to attempt to get exactly 72 hours in the tomb. What we must realize is that we have a Jewish reckoning of time, which would include parts of Friday afternoon, all of Saturday, and a portion of Sunday morning. Compare the parts of two Sundays implied in "after eight days" (John 20:26).

According to the Scriptures -- What was it that Paul affirms was "according to the Scriptures," i.e., predicted in the Old Testament Messianic prophecies? Was it that Messiah would "rise from the dead," or that He would rise "on the third day"? That Messiah would be raised from the dead was foretold in the Old Testament Scriptures. There are particularly definite predictions in Psalm 16:10; Isaiah 53:8-10; Hosea 6:2; Jonah 2:10 (cp. Acts 2:31, 13:34; Matthew 12:40, 16:4). According to Luke 24:46, Christ is said to have included the resurrection "on the third day" as one of the predictions contained in the Old Testament.[28] Paul does likewise here.[29] One of the lines of evidence Paul appeals to in order to demonstrate the truth of the resurrection of Jesus is the Old Testament Scriptures. In a moment he will appeal to a second line of evidence, namely, the eyewitnesses who saw Jesus alive after his death and burial.

15:5 -- *and that He appeared to Cephas, then to the twelve.*

And that He appeared -- This is the fourth item (the fourth in a series of phrases that begin with "that") in the bare-bones presentation of Paul's gospel preaching. The verb form translated "appeared" is in the passive voice in the Greek. The passive ('he was made to be seen') suggests Jesus Himself initiated these appearances. It was not just a subjective 'seeing' because the people were wishing so hard for such a thing. There is a difference between a vision (like Peter's on the housetop, Acts 10) and an actual objective appearance of Christ. "Appeared" means He was very visible to the physical eyes of those who saw Him. The post-resurrection appearances were more in the nature of revelations than discoveries. The appearances were objective, actual happenings – something done by an outside agent, rather than something that only occurred subjectively in the mind's eye of the beholder.

Some would argue that whether the appearances were objective or subjective, it makes no difference. But if, for example, what happened to Paul on the way to Damascus *was only in his mind*, then all of his appeals to the eyewitnesses (note how the word "appeared" is repeated) are invalidated. And if there is no objective evidence of Jesus' resurrection, then the basis of Paul's argument that all the dead will be raised is likewise relegated to the realm of wishful thinking rather than objective concrete fact. Paul's presentation of the historical facts of the gospel is emphatic and compelling. The post-resurrection appearances of Jesus are as historically real as His death and burial. The res-

---

[28] Appeal has been made to Hosea 6:2, Jonah 1:17, and 2 Kings 20:5, as being passages where the Old Testament Scriptures referred to the coming resurrection of Jesus "on the third day."

[29] Because Old Testament references to "the third day" are not easy to find, some current form critics think Paul has reference to New Testament writings, in particular the "Passion Stories" which were already circulating in written form when Paul wrote 1 Corinthians. We reject the whole concept of form criticism as a valid tool for New Testament study. But even if we did accept it, we would hardly equate such "Passion Stories" with the 'short written accounts' Luke 1:1-4 speaks of, nor would we classify these short written accounts as Scripture since Luke seems to say those accounts were not inspired (since their writers were neither "eyewitnesses or ministers of the Word"). At the time Paul writes to the Corinthians, when he appeals to "Scripture," we will have to agree that he has the Old Testament Scriptures in view since very few of the New Testament Scriptures (inspired writings) have yet been penned. (As documented in the author's *New Testament Survey Notes*, only Matthew's Gospel and the letters to the Thessalonians antedate 1 Corinthians.)

urrection of Jesus from the dead was not just something akin to His memory living on in the minds of His followers. Just as He was truly dead and truly buried, so He was truly raised from the dead bodily, and truly seen by a large number of witnesses on a variety of occasions in a variety of places.

The resurrection of Christ was a fact to be proved, like all other facts, by competent and credible witnesses. First, Paul appealed to the Scriptures which predicted the resurrection of the Messiah. Now, Paul appeals to the witnesses who had attested, or who yet lived to attest, to the historical fact of the bodily resurrection of the Lord Jesus. The point of his argument is this – so many witnesses as these is abundant testimony to the fact that bodily resurrection has occurred in at least one instance. What follows is a list of certain of the eyewitnesses of the resurrection of Jesus. Having presented the prophecies of Scripture as proof, he now introduces as witnesses those to whom Jesus appeared after His resurrection. Paul's testimony here has important bearing on the negative critic's theories concerning the post-resurrection appearances as recorded in the four Gospels. Paul mentions six appearances (Cephas, the 12, the 500, James, the apostles, Paul). In the New Testament there are at least 11 post-resurrection appearances listed:

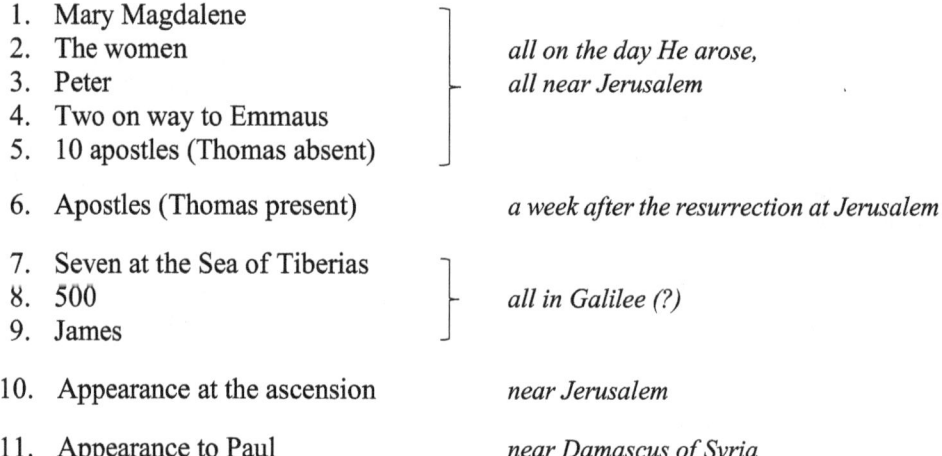

1. Mary Magdalene
2. The women
3. Peter
4. Two on way to Emmaus
5. 10 apostles (Thomas absent)

    all on the day He arose, all near Jerusalem

6. Apostles (Thomas present)   *a week after the resurrection at Jerusalem*

7. Seven at the Sea of Tiberias
8. 500
9. James

    all in Galilee (?)

10. Appearance at the ascension   *near Jerusalem*

11. Appearance to Paul   *near Damascus of Syria*

Paul does not mention 1,2,4,6,7, which are mentioned elsewhere. He does mention 3,9 (and 11) which are not mentioned elsewhere. Does the Bible seem to indicate that these are all the appearances Jesus made, or just a fraction of them?

(a) Just a fraction, seems to be the correct answer to this question. See Acts 1:3. Note that no one writer mentions all the appearances. One writer mentions the Judean appearances, another the Galilean appearances.

(b) Some say Paul gives a full list. But there is no legitimate ground for such a statement. Paul, in the main, mentions what might comprise an "official list," all of whom (being officials) would preach the story of the resurrection. The witnesses Paul cites were persons well-known to the Corinthians as church leaders: Peter, the apostles, James, himself – a large company who could be easily found and questioned. The evidence would not have been strengthened by listing persons with whom the Corinthians were not acquainted. The appearances Paul does list seem to be arranged chronologically.[30]

To Cephas -- Peter was the first apostle to whom Jesus appeared after His resurrection (see Luke 24:34). It occurred on the same day as He arose from the dead. Roman Catholic commentators use this verse to support the primacy of Peter – the Lord appeared to Peter first because he was the *first of* the apostles. But rather than supporting the primacy of Peter, Paul is giving a chronological listing of official witnesses of the resurrection. (The appearances to the women are omitted, perhaps, as being evidential to the apostles rather than to the world.) Peter's denial of Jesus at the trials and his consequent dejection made an appearance to him necessary. He needed to be encouraged (cp. Luke 22:32, 24:34).

Then to the twelve -- After the mention of the appearance to Peter, the Western Text substitutes "and after these things" (*kai meta tauta*) for Paul's "then" (either *eita* or *epeita*). One wonders if this addition by later copyists was part of a theological tendency to heighten the role of Peter.[31] "The twelve" is a technical term for the whole body of the apostles. This title was the official designation for the group. (This figure of speech is common to all languages, where any body of persons who act as colleagues are called by the number of which the body is properly composed, though on any given occasion the number present may not be the total number of which the body is composed.[32]) At the appearance here alluded to, only 10 were present, it seems. The appearance to the apostles the night of the very day Jesus arose from the dead seems to be the one in Paul's mind (Luke 24:36-43; John 20:19,24). On this occasion, there were only ten of the apostles present; Thomas was absent, as was Judas Iscariot.[33]

---

[30] For the sake of thoroughly covering the material, a brief survey of two theories concerning the post-resurrection appearances as advanced by the negative critics is needed: (1) Some say that evidently there are two traditions incorporated by the Bible writers. The *Galilean Tradition*, which is the older of the two, formed the basis for the *Judean Tradition*, they say. Because most of the appearances recorded by the Gospel writers were in Judea, it is not necessary to believe these Galilean appearances actually happened. The writers, we are told, just got mixed up in their copying. By contrast, Paul is viewed as an A-1 historian. Many of the negative critics who believe the Gospel writers were confused will credit Paul with reliability. Therefore, Paul gives a full list, some say. (Of course, in their thinking, all the appearances were subjective.) Note that Paul mentions appearances that occurred both in Judea and Galilee. (2) Some say Paul had a subjective vision, and that he is not arguing in 1 Corinthians 15 for the actual resurrection of the body of Christ. But the Acts record of the conversion of Paul indicates that the vision was not subjective but objective. Note in 1 Corinthians 15:8 that Paul claims for himself the same kind of 'appearance' the other post-resurrection 'appearances' were. Recall what was explained above about the passive voice verb translated "appeared."

[31] The conjecture that the reading of the Western Text shows that the 'tradition' which Paul is repeating ended with the appearance to Peter satisfies neither the requirements of the divine source of Paul's 'tradition' nor the needs of the present argument, which is to list the primitive evidences of the resurrection.

[32] Examples of the name of a whole body applied to just a portion include the Decemviri (a body of 10 magistrates in ancient Rome, c. 450 BC), and the Hebdomadal Council.

[33] The Western Text reads "to the Eleven." If this reading were accepted, then the appearance in Paul's mind would be the one made a week after Jesus arose (John 20:26-29), this time when Thomas was present, and of the original twelve, only Judas would have been missing. Too, if this reading be accepted, we do not need to explain why "twelve" was used when "twelve" were not present. "Eleven" was used because that is how many of the apostles were present.

15:6 -- *After that He appeared to more than five hundred brethren at one time, most of whom remain until now, but some have fallen asleep;*

After that He appeared to more than five hundred brethren at one time -- "After that" translates *epeita*.[34] Some time elapsed between the appearance to the twelve, and the appearance to the 500.[35] We cannot be certain whether this memorable appearance took place in Jerusalem or Galilee, or when it occurred. It is probably to be identified with Matthew 28:16, the giving of the Great Commission.[36]

> There is a slight circumstance hinted at in Matthew 28:10 which may throw some light on this passage. After His resurrection, Jesus said to the women who were at the tomb, "Go tell my brethren to depart into Galilee, and there they shall see me." In verse 16, it is said, "The 11 disciples went away into Galilee, into a mountain where Jesus had appointed them." Jesus had spent most of His public ministry in Galilee. He had made most of His disciples there. It was proper, therefore, that those disciples, who would of course hear of His death, should have some public confirmation of the fact that He had risen. It is very probable that the 11, who went to Galilee upon the command of Jesus, would tell those there what had been said to them, that Jesus would meet them on a certain mountain. It is morally certain that they who had followed Him in so great numbers in Galilee would be drawn together by the report that the Lord Jesus, who had been put to death, was about to be seen alive again. In Matthew 28:17 the presence of others than the apostles is implied in the words "some doubted."[37]

"At one time" translates *ephapex*, "once for all." Some commentators treat *ephapex* as though it meant "simultaneously" (at once). While this is true, we think more is intended by the use of this word. *Ephapax* shows this post-resurrection appearance was the culminating manifestation of the risen Christ, made at a general gathering to which His brethren as a group had been invited by Him, as is related in Matthew 28:7,10, Mark 16:7. This note by Paul is extremely valuable. If Christ appeared to only one at a time, then people could argue about subjective appearances. But 500 would not have hallucinations all at the same time.

---

[34] *Epeita* indicates a longer interval of time than *eita*. Both words can be translated "then," though here in chapter 15 (see verses 23 and 24) our translation consistently uses "after that" for *epeita* and "then" for *eita*.

[35] It is not proper to press *epeita* so that it implies that the remaining four post-resurrection appearances which Paul cites were not part of his original gospel preaching to the Corinthians, nor is it proper to use the term as evidence that Paul is making use of a different source of information here than he used before.

[36] Having indicated our conviction as to the identification of this appearance to the 500 with the commissioning of the disciples recorded in Matthew 28:16-20, we also note that other commentators place the appearance to the 500 at the time of the ascension.

[37] Barnes, *op. cit.*, p.284.

Most of whom remain until now -- Paul wrote 1 Corinthians about 27 years after the resurrection. Of these 500 witnesses to whom Jesus appeared, the greater part were still alive and could be questioned. Paul is saying, "If you don't believe me when I tell you Jesus arose from the dead, ask those of the 500 (who saw Him) who are still living!" What more conclusive proof for the fact of Jesus' resurrection could there be than 500 persons who had seen Him giving their eyewitness testimony? If the testimony of 500 could not prove His resurrection, no number of witnesses could. If 500 men could be thus deceived, any number could; it would then be impossible to substantiate *any* simple matter of fact by the testimony of eyewitnesses (Barnes, *op. cit.*, p.284). Here we have the most striking proof of the fact before us. Had the resurrection of Christ been only a fiction, "so many false hearts and tongues could never have acted in concert; nor could they all have kept a secret, which remorse, interest, and perhaps often torture, might urge them to divulge – especially as there had been one traitor among the 12; on account of which had they been conscious of a fraud, a general suspicion of each other's secrecy must have arisen" (Doddridge, cited by Kling, *op. cit.*, p.311).

But some have fallen asleep -- This is the usual expression in the Scripture to describe the death of the saints (see Acts 7:60; 2 Peter 3:4; 1 Corinthians 7:39, 15:18). Some of the 500 have died between the time of Jesus' post-resurrection appearance to them and the time Paul writes this letter. We wonder if Paul chose "asleep" with the idea in the background that sleeping people can be awakened, and so dead bodies can arise, too?

15:7 -- *then He appeared to James, then to all the apostles;*

Then He appeared to James -- Of the four people named "James" in the New Testament,[38] it is generally accepted that *James, the brother of the Lord*, is the man referred to here in 1 Corinthians 15:7. This James (the Lord's brother) was not the same as "the son of Alphaeus." This James would have been leader of the Jerusalem church at the time 1 Corinthians was written.[39] Our Lord's physical brothers had refused to believe on Him during His ministry (John 7:5). However, they are found among the believers after the ascension (Acts 1:14). What made the difference? 1 Corinthians 15:7 would give the answer. The appearance of the risen Lord to the eldest of them would have done so. Paul had gone up to Jerusalem (cf. Galatians) after his conversion, and talked with both Peter and James. It is natural to suppose they compared notes about the appearance of the Christ to each of them.[40] There is no mention of the appearance of Jesus to James in the Gospels. But the *Gospel of the Hebrews* (an apocryphal book of no authority) contains a curious legend that James made a vow neither to eat nor drink till he had seen Jesus risen from the

---

[38] Two are James, the son of Zebedee, and James, the Son of Alphaeus, both of whom were numbered among the twelve apostles. The other two are James, the father of one of the apostles, and James, the brother of the Lord.

[39] Witnessing one of Jesus' post-resurrection appearances was a qualification for being an apostle of Jesus (Acts 1:21ff). This appearance of Jesus to James explains why he is subsequently a leader of the Jerusalem church and also called an apostle (Galatians 1:18,19), though he was not one of the Twelve.

[40] For further information, see the "Introduction to James" in the author's commentary on *James & 1,2,3 John*.

dead, and that Jesus appeared to him, said, "My brother, eat thy bread, for the Son of Man is risen from the dead." Commentators are divided as to whether this appearance took place in Judea or Galilee. This commentator suggests it was in Galilee, where Jesus' mother and brothers lived. We do not know, either, when this appearance took place. Assuming Paul's list is chronological, it would have been between the appearance to the 500 and His appearance at the time of His ascension.

Then to all the apostles -- There is some question as to the occasion referred to by Paul. (1) Some say the reference is to Jesus' appearance to the 11, eight days after the resurrection (Thomas being present). Because Paul says "*all* the apostles," it is argued that Paul was aware of the absence of Thomas on the occasion of the appearance spoken of in verse 5, and of his consequent skepticism (John 20:24,25). Because Thomas was present a week later, Paul distinctly says "all" witnessed this latter appearance. But this does not seem to fit since Paul seems to be giving a chronological list of the appearances. (2) Some say the occasion at the Sea of Galilee (John 21) is the event in Paul's mind. But there were only 7 disciples present at this time (John 21:2). This says, "all the apostles." (3) It is possible Jesus frequently met the apostles assembled together, and that Paul here means to say that during the 40 days after His resurrection, He was often seen by them. (4) It is most likely a reference to the time of the Ascension (cp. Acts 1:3; Luke 24:50). As Paul at once passes on to the appearance to himself, he evidently means this manifestation to the whole body of the Apostles as the final one, at the time of the ascension. Note that Paul mentions appearances that occurred both in Judea and Galilee.[41]

We pause to re-examine the evidence for the resurrection of Christ. According to Acts 1:3, Jesus showed Himself alive after His passion "by many convincing proofs." What were these proofs, so conclusive, so compelling, that every New Testament Christian was convinced? (1) First of all, **Jesus actually appeared alive, to the sight of multitudes** They saw Him face to face. Read 1 Corinthians 15:4-8 again. There is no hallucination here, no 'vision.' Too many honest, hardheaded, sensible people saw Jesus Christ personally after His resurrection for it to be doubted. (2) Not only did the disciples see Jesus after His resurrection, but **they put their hands upon Him; they felt of His body**; they saw Him eat and drink before them. In Luke 24:37-43 we have an account of how Jesus convinced the unbelieving disciples that it was really He, risen in the flesh. It was not a ghost, a spirit that appeared to the disciples. They saw His hands where the nails had torn them, and His feet, and felt the bones underneath. "A spirit does not have flesh and bones as you see that I have," He said. Then further to prove that He was there, physically, literally before them, He called for food "and they gave Him a piece of broiled fish." How fascinated and delighted they were to see Him pick the bones out of the broiled fish and eat it. It was really Jesus, their own Savior, the One they had seen and heard so often. He was *really* risen bodily from the dead! And they were convinced. Doubting Thomas was not with the other disciples the day Jesus rose from the dead, and he declared that he would not believe – "unless I shall see in His hands the imprint of the nails, and put my finger into the place of the nails, and put my hand into His side, I will not believe," John 20:25. When Jesus appeared to the disciples, He offered the proof that Thomas wanted. Then said He to Thomas, "Reach here your finger, and see My hands; and reach here your hand, and put it into My side; and be not unbelieving, but believing." Thomas answered and said to

---

[41] This section is extracted from the Special Study on "The Post-resurrection Appearances of Jesus" in the author's course syllabus titled "The Climax of Jesus' Earthly Ministry."

Him, "My Lord and my God," John 20:27-28. The women, on the way back to Bethany from the empty tomb, held Him by the feet, Matthew 28:9. Every honest inquirer, everyone who found it difficult to believe that Jesus had risen from the dead, had the proof presented to him. (3) Acts 1:3 adds "**appearing to them over a period of forty days**, and speaking of the things concerning the kingdom of God." Forty days this went on – Jesus appearing to His disciples, answering their questions, teaching them, giving them the Great Commission. Forty days it went on, and the doubting and fearing were convinced beyond any shadow of a doubt. This was their Savior, risen from the dead. Literally hundreds of Christians saw Jesus alive after His resurrection. Peter could well say, "We did not follow cleverly devised tales," 2 Peter 1:16. (4) In our land **only 12 men are required to agree on the jury** to settle any important case. In the case of the resurrection, literally hundreds of eyewitnesses agreed that Jesus rose from the dead. Not one person ever appeared to say they had seen His dead body after the third day, or to contradict the evidence that He had risen. The testimony of the witnesses – eyewitnesses – witnesses who had handled the Savior, touched Him, felt the prints of the nails in His hands and feet, saw Him eat, communed with him 40 days; that testimony was stronger than any case required before the Supreme Court of the United States, or before any other court in the world. (5) The **arguments against the resurrection of Christ are unbelievable**. (a) For over 1900 years, enemies of Christ and of the Bible and of Christianity, have been trying with intense zeal to disprove the resurrection of Jesus Christ. An examination of the arguments of those who deny the resurrection of Christ is one of the strongest proofs that Jesus really did rise from the dead. (b) Consider who makes these arguments. The Jewish religious leaders who hated Jesus Christ and murdered Him were the first to deny the resurrection. Liars and murders they were. What honest person would believe their testimony, their unsupported word that Jesus did not rise from the dead? Down through the ages that is the kind of people who deny the resurrection. Who would risk their judgment? (c) The denials of Christ's resurrection have never been based on evidence, but most always on prejudice. The bribed soldiers who guarded the tomb of Jesus said, "His disciples came by night, and stole Him away while we were asleep." Well, if they were sleeping, they could not tell who got His body. That testimony would not be received in any court as valid evidence. No man is a good witness to what takes place while he is asleep. Not a single person was ever found who declared that he had seen the body of Jesus after His third day in Joseph's tomb. Not a single Christian was ever found to confess that the apostles and other converts had conspired to pretend that Jesus had risen from the dead. Were these hundreds of people who said they saw Jesus alive all liars and deceivers? And would they go to their death for the lie? Many an expedition has tried to find Joseph's tomb, and then to prove by chemical analysis that the body there decayed. (Even that would not prove that the body of Jesus was the one that decayed there.) There has never been found any evidence to substantiate any denial of the bodily resurrection. (d) These suppositions invented by infidels who try to account for the apparent resurrection of Christ are so unconvincing that unbelievers themselves can never agree. They are always trying to find some new and, they hope, more convincing and plausible answer to the evidence that Christ indeed arose from the dead. (It seems as if every unbeliever has his own theory, and that the theory of one never satisfies even another unbeliever.) (i) "His disciples came by night, and stole Him away while we were asleep," said the soldiers. Then why did not the Jews mount an intensive search to find His body? They hated the Christians so much; and the Christian movement was doing them so much harm that surely they did everything in their power to find the body of Jesus, if they really thought that theft of the body was a live possibility. That would have stopped Christianity at its source. But they never found any such body, never claimed to, never even mounted a search. In fact, the leading Jews themselves did not believe that Christ's body had been stolen away. Many of the chief priests themselves were converted later (Acts 6:7) because they were convinced of the truth of the resurrection. (ii) Another theory says Jesus did not really die on the cross, but only swooned; and after some time in the grave, He revived and came forth and appeared to the disciples. (See verse 3 above where this theory was refuted.) (iii) Another theory of the unbelievers is that the disciples had hallucinations and visions and simply thought they saw Jesus. But how strange that hundreds of people could have the same vision. And it is particularly improbable that the disciples should have hallucinations and think they saw Jesus alive when none of them expected Him to rise from the dead. All of them had to be convinced against their former convictions that He was really alive front the dead. Hallucinations do not reappear again and again, day after day, to hundreds of people, for 40 days, and always remain the same. Hallucinations do not eat and drink in the presence of people, as Jesus did. (iv) Other people say that the disciples agreed, all of them, to lie about it and say that they saw Jesus. But consider that those disciples were not liars. They gave up home and comforts and friends. They spared not their own lives, but gave them up in order to witness that Jesus rose from the dead. To believe that it was only a lie, and that every single one of them stayed with the lie until his death, is unbelievable. (6) The **witnesses are competent and honest**. The men whose testimony is set out in the Gospels and in the Acts had perfect opportunity to know the fact to which they testified. They accompanied Jesus all the time, from the baptism of John to the Ascension. There was a variety of circumstances many people, many places, many times of the day and night, many sorts of conditions, many mental attitudes on the part of those appeared to. Still, some will say that no one saw Him come out of the tomb. But this does not deny the resurrection. George comes home from college without telling his family. None of them see him leave the college or make the trip. He surprises them. Yet father, mother, brothers, and sisters all say, "Yes, that is George!" They are positive in their identification. Would someone question their identification, saying that they could not possibly know it was George, since they did not see him leave college or did not actually see him make the trip? The problem here is the identification of a person. Was this person whom they saw the same person with whom they had been associated for three years? He died just the other day. Today He comes claiming to be the one who died. Could you tell if He was the same one with whom you had associated intimately for so long a period of time? The witnesses of Jesus' resurrection were not superstitious and credulous men. The records show how full of doubts they were, and how their Master reproved them for their slowness of heart to believe (cp. Luke 24:45 and John 20:24-29). They were not men of bad character, whose vices discredited them. They were men against whose moral life no impeachment was ever brought. The apostles were honest. They had no motive to deceive. They could gain nothing by preaching that Jesus had risen if what they said was false. On the contrary, they lost everything, some losing life itself for declaring the fact of the resurrection. They did not suffer and die for a subjective appearance. These men knew whether or not Christ came out of the grave. There is not a man living who ever has been able to concoct an adequate motive to explain why these men gave their lives if they knew the facts were not true. The witnesses were not deceived. It is not conceivable that such a large number of witnesses could have been deceived for so long a period of time. (7) The **earmarks of the credibility of the resurrection testimony**. The fact that the apparent discrepancies are on the surface, but underneath there is a unique harmony, is a mark of credibility. Testimony is not credible where the witnesses have been coached. Coached testimony will have no discrepancies on the surface, but there will be underlying disharmony. If these were fabricated stories, the fabrication would be either independent or in collusion. If independent, why the unique harmony? If in collusion, why the seeming contradictions on the surface? The simplicity and the freedom and the naturalness of the narrative is another mark of the credibility of the testimony. So also is the sobriety and restraint. How could these men, after witnessing such a fact, write so little about it? And there is unintentional evidence as to the credibility. If it were a fabricated story, would the following be true: the fact that Christ was not always recognized? That the appearances were in the main to the disciples who disbelieved? That the appearances are occasional, rather than following a set pattern? That the account is so incomplete; each record gives almost a different list of appearances. (Note, the accounts may each be incomplete, but they are not incorrect.) If the accounts are false, how do you account for the monumental institutions that originated right at that time – the Lord's Day, the Lord's Supper, and Christian Baptism? If there never had been a revolutionary war, would there be a July 4 celebration? If there never was a resurrection, then why have these institutions?

15:8 -- *and last of all, as it were to one untimely born, He appeared to me also.*

And last of all -- At the time when Paul was writing, Jesus' appearance to Paul was the last of the post-resurrection appearances that had been made.[42] If one must have seen the risen Lord to be qualified to be an apostle (Acts 1:21ff), then Paul here makes a definite, unambiguous, and theological claim to be the final apostle of Jesus. The post-resurrection appearance of Jesus to him was the "last."

As it were to one untimely born -- The word here ("untimely," *ektrōmati*) speaks of 'one born prematurely,' or an 'abortion.' It is found nowhere else in the New Testament. Some interpretations given to this passage seem to us to be incorrect: (1) Some have supposed there is a reference to the suddenness and violence of Paul's conversion. The other followers were won over a period of time, through teaching. Paul was different, the theory goes. The problem with this is that it views what happened on the Damascus Road as being Paul's conversion, whereas what happened on the road was his call to apostleship (Acts 26:16). His conversion took place later in Damascus as Ananias came and taught him. (2) Some see a reference to Paul's supposed diminutive stature. The theory says that Paul's deprecators called him a "dwarf" or a "freak" (a twist on the word translated "abortion"), or a "runt." Arndt-Gingrich speak of *ektrōma* as sometimes being a term of insult or abuse.[43] Some writers suggest Paul's enemies have hurled this insult at him, and that Paul here simply repeats the slur, as if to say, "My enemies, whatever they call me, have not witnessed a post-resurrection appearance of Jesus as I have!" (3) A more likely interpretation, in this commentator's opinion, follows these lines: Paul is referring either to his call to apostleship, or to the mode of his training as an apostle. Paul had not trained at the feet of Jesus for over three years, as did the others. Instead of a normal time for training and for discipleship to bloom, perhaps Paul refers to the fact that he was torn suddenly from opposition to Jesus to become an ambassador for Jesus. Instead of being trained at Jesus' feet during Jesus' earthly ministry, Paul's training involved receiving revelations about Jesus while Paul spent three years in Arabia immediately after his call and conversion. Or perhaps Paul refers to how unusual it was for an appearance of the risen Lord to occur as happened in Paul's case. To have seen the risen Lord later than the other apostles was an exceptional case, Paul realizes. (If this explanation has merit, then

---

[42] Later, of course, the apostle John (exiled to the island of Patmos) will see a vision of the glorified Christ. But this was not the "post-resurrection" appearance that first qualified him to be an apostle. Nor was that vision exactly like the "appearances" to the eyewitnesses that Paul has been listing here in 1 Corinthians 15.

[43] Arndt and Gingrich, *op. cit.*, p.276.

we should not hope to also have a vision as Paul did, in order to be qualified to be an apostle.) It is important to notice that two of the witnesses cited in this list, James and Paul himself, had previously been unbelievers. Paul had been a persecutor. Afterwards, the intensity of his conviction that he 'had seen the Lord' became the determining factor in Paul's theology.

He appeared to me also -- The reference is to the events that occurred on the Damascus Road, (Acts 9:3-6,17, 22:14, 26:16). "Appeared to" (*ōphthē*) is the same word used of the appearances of Jesus to the others listed by Paul. Paul saw the risen Lord as really as they did.[44] Note that *ōphthē* is passive voice – someone else caused it to happen!

15:9 -- *For I am the least of the apostles, who am not fit to be called an apostle, because I persecuted the church of God.*

For -- Paul is here giving his own explanation of why he called himself an "abortion." He is going to indicate that though there was a difference in their lifestyles before Jesus called them, and perhaps even in the jobs the various apostles did, they were all in perfect agreement in regard to the resurrection of Christ.

I am the least of the apostles -- He does not call himself "least" on account of any defect in his commission, or because of any lack of qualification to bear witness to what he saw. It does not refer to any gradation within the apostolate, for elsewhere Paul claims to be an equal with the twelve. This phrase is more fully explained in the next clause.

Who am not fit to be called an apostle -- "Fit" (*hikanos*) means 'worthy, fit, suitable.' Paul did not think of himself as "fit" to be selected as an apostle by Jesus because of his pre-conversion lifestyle. Paul never forgot the blot on his past life, though he knew he had been forgiven (Galatians 1:13; 1 Timothy 1:12-14; Acts 26:9). It tended to ever keep him humble. Such should be, and such will be, the effect of the remembrance of a life of sin on those who become converted to the gospel.

Because I persecuted the church of God -- This is the reason he did not feel worthy to be called an apostle (cf. 1 Timothy 1:13, Acts 9:2,13 and 26:10). It may very well be that the persecution was more deadly than has been usually supposed, involving not only torture but actual bloodshed – and in more cases than that of Stephen. Paul deeply felt his unworthiness and unfitness to be called an apostle. But he had no doubt that he had seen the Lord Jesus risen from the dead. Amidst all the expressions of his deep sense of unfitness for his office, he never once intimates the slightest doubt that he had seen the Savior.

Note, this is one of the verses in the New Testament where church ("church of God")

---

[44] One commentator, who all along has subtly undermined the value of the post-resurrection appearances, wrote, "Paul believed that Christ's appearance to him was of the same nature as the appearances to the others." (I.e., it did not really happen. Paul just "believed" it.) This is a sad attempt to continue to promote the Enlightenment's false dichotomy between faith and reason; it is an attempt to say that much of Christianity is simply an attempt to promote faith biased by emotion, rather than facts backed by hard, tangible evidence.

is used in a universal sense, rather than being a reference to simply a local congregation (cp. notes at 1 Corinthians 1:2, 10:32 and 12:28).

15:10 -- *But by the grace of God I am what I am, and His grace toward me did not prove vain; but I labored even more than all of them, yet not I, but the grace of God with me.*

But by the grace of God I am what I am -- Starting with "but," it is possible that verse 10 is a typical Pauline digression. The thought of the radical change in his life from persecutor to preacher led him to express how that change came about. It was because of the grace of God that all that he was had changed into what he now is. "I am what I am" in this context (see verse 9) certainly is a reference to his being an apostle of Jesus Christ. "Grace" in this passage speaks of his call to the apostleship as being out of the unmerited love and favor of God. Paul was now an apostle whose message was "Jesus and the resurrection" (Acts 17:18).

And His grace toward me did not prove vain -- "Toward me" is emphatic. In some people's cases, the bestowed grace accomplished nothing. Not so in Paul's case. Though unqualified by background to be an apostle, he was not inferior when it came to labors as an apostle. Perhaps Paul did not have all the advantages the other apostles had, especially companionship with Jesus during His ministry. He was overwhelmed with the recollection that he had been a persecutor. But God had called him to be an apostle. That call had not proven empty or fruitless or without result.[45] Paul's apostleship was not simply a titular office. Paul has worked at the task of being an apostle with quite extraordinary energy.

But I labored even more than all of them -- "Labored" (*kopiaō*) means to 'be weary, or become weary, then, to exhaust one's self by working, to strain one's self.' It calls attention to the exertion involved, the painful and exhausting toil. "More than all" could have either of two possible meanings: Paul labored more than any one of them, or he labored more than all the other apostles put together. Paul does not say he accomplished more, but that he has worked harder than others. He was more diligent in preaching; he encountered more perils; he exerted himself more. Perhaps by his missionary labors he extended the kingdom of Christ over a region wider than all the twelve had traversed up to this date.

Yet not I, but the grace of God with me -- Paul may have exerted himself, but he was not alone in his labors. The "grace of God" was working right along beside him. God and Paul were co-laborers.[46] This is not a statement of boastful pride; it is a statement intended to corroborate the truth of Paul's preaching. If Paul were working without God's help and blessing, his detractors might say "What Paul has been doing and preaching is just his own human effort and opinion." They could thus deny there was any truth to his message when

---

[45] The word translated "vain" (*kenē*) means "void of reality, empty of content" (rather than "void of result or purpose" as *mataia*, the synonym for "vain," would imply).

[46] Compare 1 Corinthians 3:7ff, 12:6; Philippians 2:12ff; Ephesians 3:20; Colossians 1:29.

he preached "resurrection." But such is not the case, for God was working with Paul. Perhaps "grace of God" is a reference to the miracles that credentialed his message (cp. 2 Corinthians 12:12).

15:11 -- *Whether then* it was *I or they, so we preach and so you believed.*

Whether then *it was* I or they -- "They" refers to the other apostles. Whether it was Paul or the other apostles who labored more abundantly is something that might be questioned. But what could not be questioned was that there was no variation in their message about the resurrection of Jesus from the dead – or on any of the other facts of the gospel, for that matter. In verses 5-10 we have had a list of eye-witnesses who testified about the bodily resurrection of Jesus. Paul introduces himself as one of those witnesses. In verse 11 the testimony of these witnesses is summarized. All agreed that Jesus rose from the dead. Resurrection is something that can happen. In fact, it already has happened once.

So we preach -- "So" refers to the essential facts of the gospel given in verses 1-5.[47] "We" refers to the list of witnesses mentioned in verses 5-8. There are two words for "preach" in the New Testament: *euaggelidzō* (which means 'preach the gospel, the good news') and *kerussō* (which means 'proclaim, herald,' with some other word being necessary, either stated or in the context, to explain the subject matter of the proclamation). *Kerussō* is the word used here, and it is a present tense verb, implying continuous action. Paul is indicating what he and the other apostles habitually preach. This is authentic gospel! It is what they preached at the beginning, and what they still are heralding. "There is not the least variation in the authoritative testimony: Peter, James, Paul – Jerusalem, Antioch, Corinth – are in one accord, preaching, believing, with one mind and one mouth, that the crucified Jesus rose from the dead" (Findlay, *op. cit.*, p.922).

And so you believed -- "So you believed" reminds the Corinthians that "death, burial, resurrection, and post-resurrection appearances" was the content of their faith when they

---

[47] Notice carefully what we have in the first eleven verses of chapter 15. First, there are historical facts. We must begin with this. The eyewitnesses were not believing an illusion. Those items (verses 1-8) actually happened. Second is the theological significance of the historical facts. "For our sins" is why Jesus died, and the resurrection is the ground of our forgiveness and the basis of our hope. Third, there was the "grace of God" working along with such messengers as Paul so they got the message right when they proclaimed it.

This passage in 1 Corinthians 15 is a wonderful basis on which to show the error of the modern dichotomy between *historie* (the event that actually happened) and *geschichte* (the writer's subjective idea and presentation of what happened). Modern philosophic critics classify the resurrection of Jesus not as *historie* but merely as *geschichte*. An illustration may help: Suppose you have been away from home on a trip, only to come home and find that a burglar has been through the house. Silver, the coin collection, jewelry and other valuables are missing, and the house is in disarray. You would interpret the facts thus: (1) There has been a loss suffered by the home owner. (2) There was malice on the burglar's part. We could arrive at these interpretations even though we didn't actually see the burglar at work. But there could be no interpretation without the historical fact of the burglar being there. So there can be no resurrection faith without there first being some historical facts on which to base that faith. Those historical facts are precisely the basis of the Christian faith. That Jesus arose is not just someone's personal opinion, with no historic fact behind the opinion.

first became Christians. It was this message, and not another, that they had wholeheartedly embraced when they became Christians. What Paul implies is this – 'If you Corinthians now believe otherwise, if you are listening to the voices in Corinth that deny the idea of resurrection, you do not believe the gospel the apostles preach! The apostles still preach resurrection! Their message has not changed.' With this doctrinal basis (i.e., the common preaching and common faith) laid, Paul now begins a direct confrontation with the Corinthians concerning the denial of the future resurrection of dead bodies.

2. The logical argument. 15:12-19

Summary: There is an essential connection between Christ's resurrection and the future resurrection of all the dead. How is it that, in the face of the apostolic proclamation, some people go about and declare that a resurrection of dead bodies is impossible? This makes apostolic preaching to be a lie, faith to be a delusion, the condition of dead Christians to be quite hopeless, and the condition of living Christians to be pitiable in the extreme.

15:12 -- *Now if Christ is preached, that He has been raised from the dead, how do some among you say that there is no resurrection of the dead?*

Now -- In this verse, Paul introduces the topic for which he has been laying the doctrinal foundations in verses 1-11. Paul's argument is that, if there is no resurrection of the dead (as some at Corinth were affirming), then Jesus cannot have been raised, and if He has not risen from the dead, that would have monstrous consequences to living and dead believers alike.

If Christ is preached, that He has been raised from the dead -- The apostles and others had preached this for more than 25 years. They still are preaching it (*kerussetai* is a present tense verb[48]). This is not a hypothetical condition, but an actual condition. We might translate, "Since Christ is continually preached ...." Paul assumes beyond fear of contradiction that Christ is so preached. "Has been raised" is a passive voice verb, implying God as the agent who raised Christ (see notes on this point at verse 15). "From the dead" in the Greek is 'from among dead (something plural).' There is no Greek article ("the"). Christ came out from among dead bodies, or dead people. He was victorious over death itself. Christ has not been raised from death itself, but from among those who have died. There has been one resurrection! There is no way people can say there is no such thing as a resurrection from among dead bodies.

---

[48] From *kerussō* we get the theological term "kerygma." It has become popular in certain theological circles to "demythologize" the gospel narratives. They claim to attempt to separate the *kerygma* (i.e., the kernel of truth contained in the apostolic proclamation) from the *didache* (i.e., the embellished form which we supposedly have in our present New Testament books). Here in verse 11, and again in verse 14, etc., Paul tells us part of the content (or kernel) of the *kerygma* he preached: it includes no less than the bodily resurrection of Jesus from the dead. This was not a later embellishment, it was *kerygma,* part of the primitive preaching of the historic facts.

How -- 'How is it possible to say this? How can it be maintained?' is the idea contained in the interrogative pronoun.

Do some among you say that there is no resurrection -- Here in verse 12 is stated for the first time the reason for the whole of chapter 15. Some people (it was more than one) in Corinth were teaching that there is no future resurrection of dead bodies to be looked forward to.[49] Paul has shown how full and unanimous is the testimony to the historical fact of the bodily resurrection of Jesus Christ. On the one hand, the apostles (each and every one) and other eyewitnesses continue to preach (*kerussetai*) that Christ has been raised and abides ever as the risen Lord. On the other hand, the skeptics, without any evidence, continue to assert (*legousin*) that resurrection just does not happen. Who will the Corinthians, who long ago accepted apostolic preaching, now believe? If resurrection is impossible, how do you account for the large volume of testimony from official and unofficial witnesses, who are still alive to be questioned, that one resurrection has already taken place? If it is certain that any one man has arisen, then the position that resurrection is impossible is untenable. Paul's logic is unassailable. If one fact to the contrary exists (Christ has risen!), you cannot have a universal negative (dead bodies don't rise). As we follow Paul's presentation, we can see the essentiality of the future resurrection, especially when we see what follows from a denial of it.

Of the dead? -- All through this whole chapter, Paul is talking of the resurrection of the *body*. As earlier in this verse, "dead" (in this phrase in the Greek) is an adjective, and it is plural; all through this context, the adjective "dead" is plural in the Greek. Paul gives us the adjective; we must supply the noun to go along with the adjective. 'Bodies' is a good noun to supply. Notice also, until verse 29 there is no "the" in the Greek before the adjective "dead." In the first part of the verse, the Greek is *ek nekrōn* (translated, "from the dead"), while in the last part of the verse, there is no preposition. In the last part of the verse, the Greek is simply *nekrōn* (in the genitive case, hence the translation "of the dead").

Certain premillennialist interpreters speak of two resurrections – one at the beginning (the resurrection of the righteous) and another (the resurrection of the wicked) at the end of the millennium. To support this teaching they take *ek nekrōn* to mean, 'from among,' or 'out from among the dead.' This phrase is then used to prove there will be a resurrection of the righteous which leaves the wicked behind. The second expression (*nekrōn*) is then said to speak of the resurrection of all the rest of the dead at the end of the millennium. In their literature on this subject, they print the Greek and point to the Greek preposition, which aims to impress those who know little or no Greek. Instead, the whole matter of whether or not one should take the "thousand years" of Revelation 20 as literal or figurative language must be decided from a study of the pertinent prophetic passages in both Old and

---

[49] Who were these who denied the resurrection? In our notes at verse 1 we have indicated that the specific identification of the "some" is not possible. (Were they church members or outsiders to whom the Corinthians were listening?) But the reasons why some might deny the possibility of the future resurrection might be any one of various embodiments of the Greek philosophical notion of metaphysical dualism (that spirit is good and matter is evil). No matter which philosophy a man held, or which one of the many offshoot philosophies is held by skeptics today, Paul meets any and each with one master stroke.

New Testaments.[50] Whether or not the Bible teaches one general resurrection of all the dead (righteous and wicked), or whether it has a resurrection of the righteous at a different time than the resurrection of the wicked, will have to be decided on grounds other than the presence or absence of the preposition *ek* here in 1 Corinthians. Here in 1 Corinthians 15, *ek nekrōn* and *nekrōn* seem to be used interchangeably. Furthermore, how can the premillennialists argue that a "resurrection from the dead" (*ek nekrōn*) means that some are raised (the righteous) and some are left dead (the wicked only), when at the time of Christ's resurrection (*ek nekrōn*) from the dead, the expression cannot mean that *only* the wicked remained behind? Actually the terms are interchangeable, and the use of the one (with the preposition) or the other (without the preposition) determines nothing regarding the time of the resurrection.

Leaving such technical niceties behind, let us return to the point of this verse. Paul sees at once what others at first apparently failed to see: the resurrection in general cannot be denied without ultimately advancing to a denial also of Christ's resurrection. Both stand or fall together. The logical basis of Paul's reply is absolutely unassailable. A universal negative cannot be established if one fact to the contrary exists. Thus the single fact of Christ's bodily resurrection once for all invalidates the assumption that denies the bodily resurrection in general.

15:13 -- *But if there is no resurrection of the dead, not even Christ has been raised;*

But if there is no resurrection of the dead -- For the sake of argument, let's suppose the doctrine that some were teaching is correct, and there is no resurrection of dead bodies. What are the logical consequences of such a position? In verses 13-15, Paul lists four consequences if there is no resurrection: (1) Christ did not rise (verse 13); (2) apostolic preaching is without any objective basis (verse 14a); (3) the faith of the Corinthians is baseless (verse 14b); and (4) apostolic testimony is false witness (verse 15).

Not even Christ has been raised – If the dead do not rise, then not even Christ can have risen.[51] It is not possible to say that something different happened in Christ's case than happens in the rest of mankind's. He died as other men die. When He died, His body was buried. His body lay in the grave three days. His soul had left the body. His frame became cold and stiff. The blood ceased to circulate and the lungs to breathe. There would be the same difficulty in raising Him up as would be encountered in the raising of any other man. If no man can rise, then Christ is not risen. "Resurrection" deals with the body. Christ's body was given into death on the cross and then, like any dead human body, was placed in the tomb. Paul's argument assumes a real incarnation in a body just like other men's bodies (Hebrews 2:14), and it assumes Christ's resurrection was also bodily. It

---

[50] See the author's *Let's Study Prophecy* (Moberly, MO: Scripture Exposition Books, 1970).

[51] The verb is *egēgertai*, a perfect tense form, emphasizing past completed action with present continuing results. There is a present reality resulting from a past historic fact (cp. Galatians 2:20). The same verb form is used seven times in this chapter with reference to Christ (verses 4,12,13,14,16,17,20).

cannot be argued He was a different and higher being and therefore He was exempt from the dictum of the Corinthians that the dead are not raised.

15:14 -- *and if Christ has not been raised, then our preaching is vain, your faith also is vain.*

And if Christ has not been raised -- We have here a second consequence which follows if it is held there is no resurrection. The consequences of such a belief are linked together by Paul. First, Christ must not have been raised. Second, the gospel preaching is vain.

Then our preaching is vain -- Twice in recent verses (verses 11,12) we have been told what is the continuing content of apostolic preaching (*kerygma*, see notes at 1:21 and 15:11,12). "Then" (*ara*) is an inferential particle. It implies that what follows is a logical consequence of the preceding. "Vain" is a translation of *kenos*. The word *kenos* (and *kenē* in the next phrase) means 'empty, hollow, devoid of reality, worthless, useless, idle, false, without basis, meaningless.' It is the same word we had in verse 10. If Christ were not raised, if Christ were dead forever, both the proclamation of the resurrection and a faith in the resurrection would be empty and hollow, like a nut without a kernel. All gospel preaching, every assertion and every promise which are a part of the gospel, would be a mere sound of words without reality back of them. All the preaching of Christ and Him crucified, raised, and glorified (the telling of the old, old story of Jesus and His love) is null and void; it is vain if Christ has not risen.

Your faith also is vain -- This is the third consequence that logically follows if dead bodies are not raised (including even Jesus'). The resurrection of Jesus is the chief evidence that He indeed is the long-promised Messiah. Take away His resurrection, and there is little or no reason to continue to believe in Him. Such faith would be without basis ("vain" here is *kenē*), void of content. If Christ was not raised, He was an imposter, since He repeatedly declared that He would rise. Their faith would be in a crucified man, not in the risen Messiah. All of Christianity stands or falls with the resurrection. If Christ be not risen, their faith in God, the church, and in eternity was all an empty shell. In plain language, the preaching would be a lie, and the believing would be trusting a lie.

15:15 -- Moreover we are even found **to be** *false witnesses of God, because we witnessed against God that He raised Christ, whom He did not raise, if in fact the dead are not raised.*

Moreover we are even found *to be* **false witnesses of God** -- If resurrection doesn't happen (and, of course, if Jesus has not been raised), there is a fourth consequence. The apostles are not just mistaken witnesses, they were false witnesses and liars, and all their testimony is nothing but a lie. For a man to be a liar is reprehensible when the testimony deals with ordinary matters of this life. But it is infinitely worse when the testimony deals with God himself and with the acts of God (Lenski, *op. cit.*, p.652). Either Jesus arose from the dead, or the apostles lied when they affirmed He did. The dilemma admits no escape. "We are found" draws an analogy from the courtroom, as though the apostles were on trial before men. What is the verdict? 'We are now (present time) exposed, discovered to be, just plain lying witnesses. We were lying under oath, for we testified that God did something He has not done (if dead bodies are not raised).' The apostles have perjured themselves every time they preached that God raised Jesus, if indeed dead bodies – Christ's or anybody else's – are not raised at all. If there is no resurrection, the apostles are liars.

The same thing would be true of those who deny the resurrection in our own day. They make the apostles liars.

> This is the plain proposition which all of those must accept who today deny the reality of the bodily resurrection of Christ. They can maintain their denial only by making all of the witnesses who beheld the risen Savior (like Peter downward to Paul) liars. Besides, they make also the ancient prophets liars, who bore a witness that God himself had told them that he would raise up the Messiah (whom He never intended to raise if the dead are not raised). Yet this blasphemous denial is today made from many pulpits which claim the Christian name. They may tone down their statement by saying that the prophets were subjective liars who did not know that they were lying; but a well-intentioned liar is often much worse than a conscious liar.[52]

Either the men today are false in their denial of the resurrection or else all the apostles and prophets were false. This is the alternative choice given to us, and to the Corinthians.

Because we witnessed against God that He raised Christ -- In typical Pauline fashion, he repeats the substance of the apostolic testimony that has all along been giving – that Christ has been raised from the dead – because this is the key point in the argument against those who deny any resurrection of the body at all. For *kata tou theou*, "against God" is one possible translation; 'concerning God' is another possible translation. "We witnessed ... He raised Christ." Apostles have been testifying that God raised Jesus. Think of Peter's presentation: whom you crucified, but "whom God raised from the dead" (Acts 3:15, 2:23,24); or "this Jesus God raised up again, to which we all are witnesses" (Acts 2:32). Actually, the Scriptures make several other statements concerning who raised Jesus: (1) God raised Christ (Romans 6:4, 8:11; Matthew 16:21, 17:23, 26:32; Acts 13:30); (2) Christ Himself arose (Mark 9:31; Luke 18:33; Acts 2:32, 4:33). Jesus had power to lay down his life and to take it back again (John 10:18). (3) The Holy Spirit raised Jesus (Romans 8:11).

Whom He did not raise, if in fact the dead are not raised -- Someone in Corinth was affirming the fact that dead bodies do not rise from the dead. Paul says if this were true, then Jesus has not been raised, and he had been lying when he told the Corinthians that God raised Him. By repeating their position (there is no resurrection), Paul seems to be implying it is they who are the false witnesses, not the apostles of Jesus! The wording in verses 15 and 16 is even stronger than what was written in verses 5-8 concerning the objective verifiable reality of the resurrection of Jesus. Paul is discussing the resurrection of dead bodies, and arguing that such a resurrection is precisely what happened in the case of Jesus. This leaves no room for modern existential double talk which attempts to affirm "resurrection language" as being meaningful, while at the same time denying that anything

---

[52] Lenski, *op. cit.*, p.652.

actually happened as an event in history. If nothing happened to Jesus in history, then (if we may reverse Paul's argument) nothing will happen to dead bodies either, and the "some" at Corinth who denied any resurrection of dead bodies are proven to be right.

15:16 -- *For if the dead are not raised, not even Christ has been raised;*

For if the dead are not raised, not even Christ has been raised -- This is a repetition of verse 13, and Paul repeats this key fact to stress the point. Some at Corinth were saying, "Dead bodies are never raised." To be consistent, they would have to insist Christ was never raised. If one does that, then everything positive one might receive from Jesus' life and death is lost. Paul bases everything on the resurrection. If Christ did not come out of the grave, then everything about Christianity is gone. In verses 17-19 Paul will list some additional consequences that result if those folk at Corinth are right who affirm there is no resurrection. Among the fateful consequences hidden in the claim there is no resurrection (Christ included) are these: (1) Faith in Christ has no benefits (verse 17a); (2) Believers' sins have not been forgiven (verse 17b);   (3) Christians who have died are lost (verse 18);   (4) People whose lives are based on hope in Christ are to be pitied (verse 19).

15:17 -- *and if Christ has not been raised, your faith is worthless; you are still in your sins.*

And if Christ has not been raised, your faith is worthless -- This is a slightly different consequence than the one already mentioned in verse 14. The difference lies in the words translated "vain" and "worthless." In verse 14 Paul says, 'your faith is *kenē*, empty of any content, without an objective basis on which to rest.' Here he says, 'your faith is *mataia*, useless, idle, it gets you nothing, it produces nothing, it is fruitless.' Some of our versions use "vain" to translate both Greek synonyms, and this obscures the important difference, and even leads some commentators to say verse 17 is merely a repetition of verse 14. That is not correct. "Faith" (the Christian religion) is intended to benefit us and bring us something, namely the greatest of all treasures, the forgiveness of sins. Unless Christ arose from the dead, it brings us nothing, it is 'useless' or "worthless."

You are still in your sins -- A permanently dead Redeemer is no redeemer at all! If He is no redeemer, then it is no longer possible to say "such were some of you, but you were washed ... sanctified ... justified" (6:11). The resurrection of Jesus from the dead is evidence that His sacrifice for the sins of the world has been accepted by God (Romans 5:1; Hebrews 9:6-15). If He has not been raised, His death would amount to nothing. There would have been no offering of His blood in the greater and more perfect tabernacle (Hebrews 9:11-13). There would be no cleansing of the conscience from dead works so men could serve the living God (Hebrews 9:14). There would be no new covenant with its blessings (Hebrews 9:15ff). Without resurrection, Jesus would be a dead man who could not even save Himself. How could He be the Savior of others? How could He secure for others a life beyond the grave which He Himself does not possess (if it is true that the dead do not rise)? If He did not arise from the dead, no atoning sacrifice for sins has yet ever been offered to God.   That means God cannot be in the business of justifying men by faith. To be "still in your sins" is the exact opposite of Romans 5:1. Even though you are a follower of Christ, an obedient believer, your sins have not been forgiven. God still reckons your sins against you. This is a monstrous consequence of denying the resurrection of the body. Lenski (*op. cit.*, p.655-656) explained it very well:

> To be in our sins equals – in their deadly sphere where all of our sins surround us and accuse us before God as so many deadly wolves about to tear us to pieces. Make the Savior what you please, if he failed to rise from the dead he is useless, for he cannot save us from our sin, the one thing for which we need a Savior. If there is no resurrection, there is also no redemption, no reconciliation with God, no justification, no life and no salvation. If Christ is still dead, then every believer is still dead in trespasses and sins. As long as Christ, our surety, is not released, it is certain that our debt is not paid; we are still liable, no matter how much we may trust in some supposed payment. Christ's resurrection is the positive proof that his sacrifice was, indeed, sufficient and fully accepted by God.

15:18 -- *Then those also who have fallen asleep in Christ have perished.*

Then those also who have fallen asleep in Christ -- If they were still in their sins (verse 17), "then" something else must also be true. When Paul wrote this letter in AD 57, some of the Corinthian Christians had already died. 'To fall asleep in Christ' (see notes at 15:6) is the beautiful Scriptural expression to designate what physical death is for the Christian; his body sinks into peaceful slumber, presently to be awakened by the risen Lord to a new and a glorious life in His presence. To speak of death as 'sleep' is a quiet denial of the Corinthian dogma about death being final. It is a clear testimony to the heavenly hope of the resurrection of the dead at the last day just as Jesus promised (John 6:40).

Have perished -- 'Perish' (*apōlonto* from *apōllumi*) is a term regularly used for the fate of the wicked. The verb form is an aorist tense – it pictures something quite final. 'Perishing,' according to the Scripture, is not annihilation, but the state of damnation, being consigned to Gehenna. 2 Peter 3:6 shows that *apōllumi* does not mean annihilation, whether the "world" that perished in Noah's flood is thought to be the globe or the people. The wicked do not cease to exist upon their death (cp. Isaiah 14:4ff, Luke 16:19ff, Revelation 20:10). The souls of the wicked that went to Hades when physical death occurred, will find themselves cast into the lake of fire at the time of the final judgment. In sacred language *apōllumi* means perishing by losing salvation in contradistinction to *sōzō*, being saved by obtaining salvation. He who perishes is forever separated from God, heaven, and a blessed eternal life. His destiny is to share the fate of Satan in the eternal torment of hell. In the word "perished" is involved all that would follow if a man had no salvation, no atonement for sins. They will miss heaven; they are doomed, lost, damned. What an amazing result! Elsewhere we read that it is those who are *not* in Christ who perish when they die. Here (if the dead are not raised), those who died in Christ are the ones who perish. Notice how the denial of the resurrection of the dead throws everything into confusion. If Christ did not rise and therefore no basis for justification exists, then those whose death seemed but a blessed sleep to be followed shortly by a happy awakening in fellowship with their living and glorified Redeemer, so far from having been received into eternal life, were doomed to abide under the wretched condition of the lost dead. The dead are beyond the possibility of restoration: their sins are not atoned for, they do not rise – and it is certain there is no second chance after death.

> In this crushing way, Paul brings home to his readers what the denial of the resurrection really involves. He who persists in this denial writes over every believer's tomb: "Lost!" or, what amounts to the same: "Damned!" Nothing more heart-rending could be said. It would leave the entire hereafter shrouded in the blackest mystery. This blackness has swallowed up those who have passed beyond, and waits to swallow up those whose life is now swiftly passing away. And this some foolish Corinthians, whether they realize it or not, were putting in place of the light and the hope that shine beyond the grave for every believer.[53]

15:19 -- *If we have hoped in Christ in this life only, we are of all men most to be pitied.*

If we have hoped in Christ in this life only -- "Hoped" is a perfect tense verb in the Greek, implying that 'we fixed our hope in the past and still continue to hope.' Who is meant by the "we"? (1) Based on verse 15, some say this refers to the apostles only. (Compare also Paul's use of "you" rather than "we" in verse 17.) The idea is that, if there was no resurrection, the apostles, of all men, were to be most pitied. After all, they had exposed themselves to a variety of dangers and trials, they suffered more from persecutions, poverty, and perils than other men. If, after all, they were to be deprived of all their hopes, and be disappointed in their expectation of the resurrection, their condition was certainly one to be pitied. (2) Others say it refers to all Christians. Christians often were persecuted and harassed by their unconverted neighbors. If it were all for nothing (there being no life hereafter), they were to be pitied. Christians lived a God-fearing lifestyle based on the hope of a future resurrection. How sad, if there were no such thing, to have missed the "merry" things this life has to offer. The word order in the Greek allows for some variation in the English translation, but the thrust seems to be this, 'If our hopes in Christ are confined to this life ....' Assuming the perdition of the dead in Christ (previous verse), then the present state of Christians seems to be the emphasis of this verse.[54] 'Hope in Christ' (see Hebrews 6:18-20) is the anchor of the soul. There is no such anchor if Christ has not risen and ascended. If our hopes will never come true, if there is no possibility of life with Him hereafter, what could be more pathetic?

We are of all men most to be pitied -- This, of course, implies that all who are without faith and hope in Christ, all non-Christians, are certainly also to be pitied. They live and die without God and hope in this world. But Lenski (*op. cit.*, p.658) writes that the Christian is more deserving of pity because "it is far more tragic to have a great hope in the heart throughout life, to shape the whole life according to that hope, to crucify the flesh, to war against temptation, to bear the cross, to suffer reproach and many other ills for the sake

---

[53] Lenski, *op. cit.*, p.657.

[54] Another way of reading the verse is "If in this life we have hoped only in Christ, we are ...." The meaning would be, 'If Christ has not risen, what value is hope in a crucified, dead leader?'

of this hope, and then in then end to have that hope turn out to be an iridescent bubble, a vacuous dream." And that is exactly what would happen – all their hopes and expectations would be disappointed if it is true that dead bodies are not raised.[55]

Paul has concluded what we have called the logical argument. He has listed a total of 8 intolerable consequences that logically must also be embraced if the dictum of some at Corinth ('dead bodies do not rise again') is true. Paul's answer has been, 'If you take that position, it means Jesus Christ has not risen, and if that is so, then the whole Christian system is invalidated.'[56]

3. The theological argument. 15:20-28

> *Summary:* Just as there were consequences of denying resurrection (verses 12-19), so there are consequences resulting from the fact of Christ's resurrection (verses 20-28). Among these results is a guarantee of our final resurrection from the dead, the victorious reign of Christ preceding that resurrection, and of the consummation of God's plan of the ages following His reign.

15:20 -- *But now Christ has been raised from the dead, the first fruits of those who are asleep.*

But now -- "But" is adversative. Christian hope and doctrine based on His resurrection is not a false hope nor a baseless belief. "Now" is logical. "Now," as things are. Verses 12-19 detailed the logical results that follow if Christ has not been raised, the consequences if what some say ("no resurrection") is true. Now, in verses 20-28, Paul will argue the other side of the coin: Christ *has* been raised, and there are blessed consequences!

Christ has been raised from the dead – As Barnes says (*op. cit.*, p.292), the apostle, as it were, has become impatient with the slow process of arguing. Weary of meeting objections and of stating consequences, he ceases to argue. He simply states the truth he knew to be a fact. He had seen Jesus after He had risen (15:8). There was no more doubt about this fact than he could have of any other fact which he had witnessed with his own eyes and validated by Scripture (15:4). Paul once more uses the perfect tense of the verb "raised" (see notes at verse 4). It is a past completed action with present continuing results. Christ continues to be the risen Lord! George Mark Elliott suggested several lines of thought prompted by what Paul has just written:

---

[55] The word *eleeinoteroi* is a comparative adjective in the Greek. The KJV need not have tried to treat it as a superlative ("most miserable"). Care must be taken here as we offer comments on what Paul has written. In this statement, Paul is by no means stooping to the level of common eudemonism (i.e., he is not basing his argument on a belief that happiness is the ultimate end in living). Nor does this mean there is no peace and joy in the Christian way of living (in this life, regardless of the final destiny). Nor is Paul stating that, if there were no life hereafter, a man living in sin would be happier than a man living the Christian life.

[56] Modern scholars who try to explain away the verses about the resurrection of Jesus from the dead should hear carefully what Paul here says. There is no way evade Paul's argument, that to deny Christ's resurrection is tantamount to repudiation and rejection of everything Christianity teaches.

The resurrection is one of the proofs that Jesus Christ was the only begotten Son of God. The resurrection is one of the proofs of the deity of Christ. The resurrection is one of the proofs of the validity of His sayings. The resurrection is one of the proofs of the credibility of the New Testament records. The resurrection is one of the proofs that the God of the Bible exists. (If a man denies the resurrection, there is no other way under heaven to prove the existence of the God of the Bible. The God of the Bible raised Christ. If Christ is not risen, then He is a false prophet. And if what He said is false, then where is the God of the Bible? The negative critic who denounces the literal resurrection also invariably denounces some of the truths about God which the Bible reveals.)

The resurrection of Christ is essential to His person and work. (1) To His person, Luke 13:32; Hebrews 2:10, 5:9, 7:28. In the incarnation God became man. He became a man, but He could not continue through eternity in a flesh and blood body (since flesh and blood cannot inherit the kingdom). Therefore the resurrection and the ascension were necessary to the person of Christ. (2) To His work. To be prophet, priest, and king, He had to be adapted to the wants and needs of man. Thus also it was needful for Him to go to the cross to make atonement for our sins. The atonement was not complete when He died on the cross. When the Old Testament sin-offering animal was slain, there was no redemption until the blood was taken into the Holy of Holies and sprinkled on the ark of the covenant. Likewise, according to Hebrews 9, Christ entered into the antitype of the Holy of Holies – Heaven – and there offered, as it were, His blood on the altar. This entrance occurred at the ascension. Without the resurrection this entrance could not have taken place.

On the basis of the fact of the resurrection, many false systems of philosophy and religion are invalidated. Atheism. Materialism. Agnosticism. Positivism (ignores final causes, but it is evident there is some phenomena behind all the acts of Jesus). Pantheism. Deism. Arianism. Monarchianism (only one person in the Godhead). Unitarianism (denies the deity of Christ). Modernism. Humanism. Theistic naturalism (God is just one aspect of the natural world). [Neo-orthodoxy (no belief in the historical fact of the resurrection; you just believe in the resurrection because a change has taken place in your life as you have had an "encounter" with God – see Brunner, Tillich). Neo-liberalism (resurrection is *geschichte*, not *historie* – see Bultmann). Heilsgeschichte.][57]

That Christ has been raised "from the dead" indicates a bodily resurrection, for Christ could not be thought of as being among the spiritually dead. This is the final specific mention of Christ's resurrection in this argument. Now, the presentation deals with what is predicated on the fact that Christ arose – especially the future resurrection of the dead as part of the plan of God.

The first fruits of those who are asleep -- 'Sleep' has been explained in notes at 1 Corinthians 15:6 and 18 as a euphemism for physical death. Whether Paul here has in mind just the Christian dead, or all the dead, will depend on how "all" in verse 22 is interpreted.

---

[57] Notes in brackets have been added by the author. The rest of Elliott's "lines of thought" were shared in a class on 1 Corinthians at The Cincinnati Bible Seminary in the early 1950s.

sion in verses 13-17, is concluded in verse 18). In Romans 5:12-18, the effects of the 'fall of Adam' and the 'justifying act of Christ' are compared and contrasted. Adam's sin, by the decree of God, brought physical death into the world.[64] In diametric contrast to this, Christ's death and resurrection brings "justification of life" (i.e., resurrection) to all who were condemned to physical death in Adam (Romans 5:18). The physical life we lost in Adam through no act of our own, we have regained in Christ (in the resurrection) through no act of our own, and much more. While the 'condemnation to death' and the 'resurrection' are unconditional, the 'much more' (forgiveness of personal sins) is conditional (Romans 5:17). Whether or not a man believes in Jesus, he will be raised from the dead on the resurrection day, to appear at the judgment seat of God. The "much more" (than the resurrection of the body) is conditional. Whether or not a man's own sins are forgiven depends on whether or not he has been faithful to the revelation he has had from God; justification is based on the condition of faithfulness. We affirm what the Scriptures teach elsewhere about a universal resurrection; this is also the thrust of 1 Corinthians 15:21,22. The argument of the apostle requires the universal reference. His object is to show that the effect of the sin of Adam (physical death) will be counteracted by Christ raising up *all* who die. On this rests his argument to the Corinthians that "some" were in error when they affirmed there was no resurrection. If it is only *a part* of those who die in consequence of Adam's sin who are to be raised, his argument against the denial of resurrection is greatly weakened. In summary: The whole human race (with the few exceptions of Enoch, Elijah, and those alive at the second advent) will die physically because Adam sinned. Even the exceptions would have died, save for the intervention of God. Because Jesus is risen, the whole human race will be raised from the dead. This is the teaching of 1 Corinthians 15:22.[65]

15:23 -- *But each in his own order: Christ the first fruits, after that those who are Christ's at His coming,*

But -- Perhaps there is a suppressed thought here. With his "but" Paul answers a possible objection he hears "some" (verse 12) at Corinth raising. Perhaps he anticipates some Corinthians are thinking, 'We've seen many people die physically, so we'll grant that part of your argument about the race's relation to Adam. But we have not seen anyone raised like Christ. Perhaps they are still right who say there is no such thing as resurrection.'

Each in his own order -- The word *tagmati* means "rank, place, time, order." Think of

---

[64] That it is physical death, and not hereditary total depravity (an inherited sinful nature), is documented in the author's commentary on Romans, *in loc*. We die physically, not because *we* sin, but because *Adam* sinned. While it is true that Adam did not die the moment he sinned, (he was 930 years old when he died), he entered into a mortal state, and the dying process began. God had said "Dying, you shall die!" The same process of dying is now experienced by all of Adam's descendants. The reason we shall die physically is because *Adam* sinned. Even if we lived a sinless life, we would die *physically*. Many who never sin (babes, for example) die. Physical death is not the result of our sins; it is the result of Adam's sin.

[65] After this verse, the wicked drop out of the picture, and Paul deals specifically with the resurrected believers. Believers are the object of God's grand plan for the ages, to which the future resurrection furnishes the grand finale. Paul will show that without such a resurrection, God's plan would never be consummated.

a band marching in a parade. First comes the drum major, then the majorettes, then the flag carriers, then the woodwinds, then the drums, then the brass, etc. Each group has its proper place in the line of march. Or think of an army, with its advance guard going first, then the body of troops following. Here it means there was a proper order to be observed in the resurrection of the dead. Just like a body of troops would come marching by in proper position and order, just so are there 'sections' of the resurrection of the dead. Paul's design is still to counteract the idea of some (verse 12) that no future resurrection was to be expected. Paul is saying there *would* be a future resurrection. In fact, in a sense, it had already started. Like a band parade, the drum major (Christ) has already been raised. It is certain that others are to follow. How many of these "orders" are there? (1) Two are clearly indicated in this passage. First is Christ – who has already reached the goal of the resurrection. Second are those who belong to Christ – who will reach it when He comes again. "Each in his own order" seems to indicate two, not three. "First fruits" is followed by the harvest. (There wasn't any 'second harvest.') (2) Some argue Paul indicates three "orders" – Christ, then the righteous dead, and third, the wicked dead. If there is a third "order," and if there is an interval between the resurrection of the just and the resurrection of the wicked, the length of that interval is not mentioned here. As we read on, we shall have to pause on the expression in verse 24, "then comes the end," before we can decide confidently how many "orders" Paul has in mind.

Christ the first fruits -- "First fruits" has already been explained at verse 20. The resurrection of others depends on Christ's resurrection. It is appropriate that the commander-in-chief should have the first place in the soldiers' line of march, and it is proper that Christ should be first in the resurrection.

After that -- The word is *epeita*, and likely implies a longer interval of time than *eita* with which verse 24 begins. (See comments on *epeita* at 1 Corinthians 15:6). It has now been nearly 2000 years since the first of the procession in the resurrection has gone by. How much longer will elapse, no man knows, only the Father (Matthew 24:36).

Those who are Christ's -- The phrase likely denotes Christians (see footnote #61 above). Those who are Christians form the second "order," or 'section,' in the resurrection.

At His coming -- Literally, "in His coming," i.e., as forming part of, involved in, His appearing. The word translated "coming" is *parousia*, a word also used at 1 Thessalonians 2:19 and 4:15. *Parousia* is regularly used for the visit of a king to one of the lands or cities in his realm.[66] It was an exciting time, a time of celebration, a time that brought with it a feeling of honor that the king had come to visit. Sometimes coins were struck to commemorate the occasion, and a new era was dated from such a coming. Jesus, the King of kings, is going to visit this planet again. He will come on the clouds of heaven, accompanied by the holy angels and the souls of the redeemed. What a happy time for the redeemed!

---

[66] See examples cited in Adolf Deissmann, *Light From the Ancient East*, p.368-373.

Three different Greek words, *epiphany, apocalypse,* and *parousia,* are all used to describe the return of Christ.[67] There is no reason to believe these words describe (as some eschatological systems insist) three different returns of Christ. Compare 1 Thessalonians 4:15-17. "We who are alive, and remain until the coming (*parousia*) of the Lord, shall not precede those who have fallen asleep. For the Lord Himself will descend from heaven (accompanied by the souls of the righteous dead, verse 14) ... and the dead in Christ shall rise first. Then we who are alive and remain shall be caught up together with them in the clouds, to meet the Lord in the air, and thus we shall always be with the Lord."

15:24 -- *then* comes *the end, when He delivers up the kingdom to the God and Father, when He has abolished all rule and all authority and power.*

Then *comes* the end -- It is evident that there is an interval of time between the first and second "order," verse 23. Is there also to be an interval between His coming and the end? Or does Paul mean that the coming is the end – that the two are simultaneous? As far as this passage is concerned, it is impossible to solve this question. *Eita* ("then") may introduce either what is subsequent (i.e., after) or what is immediately consequent (i.e., then, next in sequence).[68] Some commentators understand that there is a period of time between the resurrection of the righteous, the resurrection of the wicked, and the end. Others teach that there is to be one general resurrection,[69] with the righteous and wicked being raised at the same time, and that the judgment and the consummation ("the end") follow in almost immediate juxtaposition. The time when "the end" comes is defined by two "when" clauses that follow in this verse. It will be "the end" (1) when Jesus yields up the kingdom to His God and Father, and (2) when He has abolished every rule and authority and power, including the last enemy, death. The word translated "end" is *telos*, and it could also be translated 'goal.'[70] If we opt for 'goal,' then the implication is that God has a goal toward which He is moving history. Without resurrection, this goal can never be reached or accomplished. If we opt for "end," then the subject is the consummation (the winding up, the grand finale) of the affairs of the mediatorial reign of Christ. It will be the end of human affairs, the end of the kingdoms of this world, the end of the mediatorial kingdom of the Redeemer, the end of the scheme of redemption.

When He delivers up the kingdom to the God and Father -- This is the first of the two "when" clauses defining the "then" (in "then comes the end") with which this verse begins.

---

[67] On *epiphaneia*, which means to become visible to human eyes, see notes at 2 Thessalonians 2:8 and 1 Timothy 6:14. On *apokalupsis*, translated "revelation," see notes at 1 Corinthians 1:7. Consult Trench, *Synonyms*, #xciv.

[68] For a detailed discussion of *eita*, see G. Vos, *The Pauline Eschatology* (Grand Rapids: Eerdmans, 1953), p.243 or F. Hamilton, *The Basis of the Millennial Faith* (Grand Rapids: Eerdmans, 1955), p.95,96, who argues that *eita* implies something that follows almost at once.

[69] Appeal is made to "one harvest" in Matthew 13, and to John 5:28,29 and Daniel 12:1,2, to show that the idea of one general resurrection is quite in harmony with the picture everywhere given in Scripture.

[70] Some give the word "end" a metaphorical twist, and make it mean "last," i.e., the last of the dead to be raised, or the "end" of the resurrection (as though the wicked were raised some time after those who belong to Christ are raised). This seems to be a forced and improbable interpretation of *telos*.

What exactly is meant by "delivers up the kingdom" is probably beyond our complete comprehension, even though verses 25-28 are Paul's explanation of this phrase.

- One of the things that happens when the "end" comes is that Jesus is going to hand over the kingdom of God to "the God and Father." "He" is Christ, the One who is the subject of this whole sentence.
- "Deliver" translates *paradidōmi*, a word that means 'to give to any one, to give over, to deliver up.' It is used of the act of delivering up persons to judges for a trial (Matthew 5:25; Mark 15:1; Luke 20:20). The verb is a present tense subjunctive, and likely indicates that the handing over of the kingdom is a process, rather than a single act.
- To what does "kingdom" refer? (1) Some Bible students, whenever they hear the word "kingdom," immediately think of the Millennial Kingdom, which they suppose is of 1000 years duration, and which, they believe, follows Christ's *parousia* advent.[71] Accordingly, this verse would mean the Millennial Kingdom would be handed over to "the God and Father." Such a handling of 1 Corinthians 15 is hard to harmonize with 15:25, which indicates the reign (kingdom) of Christ is now, before the resurrection, not in the future after the resurrection. (2) According to Acts 2:34-36, the reign of Christ (the "kingdom," the rule or sway of the king) on David's throne is something that already had begun by the time Peter preached his Pentecost sermon. (3) Most probably the word "kingdom" speaks of all the redeemed (all the Old Testament saints, as well as the New Testament saints).[72] It seems this verse speaks of all the redeemed being handed over to "the God and Father."
- How shall we explain "the God and Father"? Sharp's rule of grammar is important here. It states that "When two nouns in the same case are connected by the Greek word 'and,' and the first noun is preceded by the article 'the' and the second noun is not preceded by the article, the second noun refers to the same person or thing to which the first noun refers, and is a further description of it." This is exactly the Greek construction here. "God" and "Father" are both dative case, they are connected by "and," there is a "the" in the Greek before "God," but there is no article "the" before "Father." The word "Father" as applied to God is used in two senses in Scripture: (1) to designate the Father, the first person of the Godhead, as distinguished from the Son, and (2) to designate God as a Father to His creatures, as the Father of all, without any distinction as to the individual members of the Godhead. It seems to be in this second sense that the word "Father" is used here. This verse, then, does not say the second person of the Godhead is to surrender all power into the hands of the first, or that the second is to cease to exercise dominion and control. This verse teaches that at the close of the work of redemption, the *particular* arrangement that we know (Christ being all authoritative) is to cease. God, as the universal Father and Ruler of all, the three in one, will exercise the government of the kingdom which is delivered over to Him.

---

[71] For more detailed information, see the author's *Let's Study Prophecy* (Moberly, MO: Scripture Exposition Books, 1970).

[72] The term "kingdom" is often used in the New Testament of the church, but the Biblical use of the term "kingdom" includes more than just the church. See this matter discussed in the author's *New Testament History: Acts* (Moberly, MO: Scripture Exposition Books, 2002), at Acts 1:4 and 14:22, and in his syllabus on *The Beginning of the Earthly Ministry of Jesus* (Moberly, MO: Scripture Exposition Books, 1998), at Mark 1:15 (and parallel passages).

When He has abolished all rule and all authority and power -- This is the second of the two "when" clauses defining the "then" (in "then comes the end") with which this verse begins. The word *katargeō* was translated "abolished" at 1 Corinthians 1:28. Its basic meaning is 'to make inoperative, to render null and void, to bring to nought.' As the verb tense shows, this abolishing takes place before Jesus hands over the kingdom to the God and Father. Paul will go on to explain (verses 25 and 26) that the last rule or power to be rendered inoperative is death. Death is overcome when men are raised from the dead. "Rule, authority, power" are all the mighty powers opposed to God and who resist His reign; all evil influences, human and superhuman, are included. The devil and all his host of demonic powers, the powers of darkness, the spiritual dominions that oppose God are all included.[73] Death and the grave are included (see next verse). The point of verse 24 is this: Christ will hand over the kingdom to the Godhead when He has utterly abolished all opposition. There shall be the "end" – and the resurrection of the dead is vitally connected with this future consummation ("end").

What we read in this paragraph certainly affects the shape of our theology: (1) The Lord Jesus has been entrusted with an important office – *mediator*. He is exercising the sovereignty of God over all the creation ("He sat down at the right hand of the Majesty on high", Hebrews 1:3). Christ is vice-regent, but this is not a permanent arrangement. (2) At present, during the church age, He is executing that office. According to Matthew 28:18-20, during this age *all authority* is given unto Christ. Jesus is the supreme Monarch of the world, He is Lord. He fought Satan, and came off the battlefield victorious. He nailed the Law to the cross. He made atonement for sin. He triumphed over the powers of darkness through the cross. Jesus is temporarily subordinate in function to the Father. When He emptied Himself to come to earth, while He did not give up Who He was (one of the members of the Godhead), He temporarily gave up the independent exercises of the prerogatives of deity. At the same time, the Holy Spirit became subordinate to both the Father and the Son. (3) At the "end" (the consummation, or the end of the mediatorial reign – see above) Christ is going to render back to the Godhead that office or authority which He now has. The mediatorial reign is for the purpose of redeeming mankind. When the kingdom has been recovered from sin and brought to glory, there will be no further need of the present order of things. (4) The kingdom of Christ, in its beginning, its furtherance, and its completion, has one great end – the glorification of the Father. Christ's reign will endure (not like that of earthly kings, *when* He shall have put all enemies under His feet, but) only *until* He shall have put all enemies under His feet (verse 25). It is proper that the government of God should be administered as it was before the work of redemption was begun. (5) This handing over of the kingdom to the God and Father does not mean Christ will surrender *all* power, or *cease* to exercise government. Even though He delivers the kingdom up to the Father, He will continue to reign. He will reign, not as the mediator He is now, but as a co-equal member of the Godhead. Christ will have the glory which He ever had before the world was (John 17:5). "The kingdom of the world has become *the kingdom* of our Lord, and of His Christ ..." (Revelation 11:15). The throne of God and the Lamb are in the New Jerusalem (see also Revelation 22:1,3). (6) The sec-

---

[73] Christ is exalted "far above all rule and authority and power and dominion" (Ephesians 1:21). He is triumphing over God's opposition because of the cross (Colossians 1:16; Romans 8:38).

ond coming will not be the beginning of the reign of Christ, but the end of it (verse 25ff). Millennial expectations predicated upon the supposition that Christ will solitarily reign upon the earth with His saints after the second advent cannot be harmonized with what we read here in 1 Corinthians 15.

15:25 -- *For He must reign until He has put all His enemies under His feet.*

For -- With "for" Paul explains why Christ does not transfer the kingdom until after He has put down all hostile powers. It is because that is the way God has so planned it, and His plan was made known in prophecy (Psalm 110:1).

He must reign -- Jesus must reign in His mediatorial kingdom. In fulfillment of the Old Testament prophecy, Christ is not full prophet and priest and *king* unless He reigns. (He might be prophet and priest, but unless He reigns, He is not king.) "Must" (*dei*) means "It is necessary" that the great mediatorial kingdom should continue until this great work is accomplished, necessary because God so planned it. There is compelling divine necessity suggested by Paul's "must." Paul is speaking about what God – back in eternity when He made His eternal plan – has determined, and therefore there is no uncertainty about it. The Bible presents Christ as reigning now, in His mediatorial kingdom.[74] The Old Testament predicted Christ would reign on David's throne (2 Samuel 7:12-17; 1 Kings 1:35,37, 47; 1 Kings 2:12; 1 Chronicles 29:23).[75] This Old Testament prediction of the reign of Christ is fulfilled in His mediatorial reign over the church and over the world. The New Testament writers thought so (e.g., Peter's affirmation to this effect, Acts 2:33). Hebrews, with its presentation of what the risen Christ is doing in heaven now that He has ascended, gives an argument in favor of this. Further lines of thought may also be helpful. At Sinai, God set up a theocracy. The theocratic king was a type of Messiah (2 Samuel 7:12-17). The Old Testament expected Christ to reign. The Old Testament expected the setting up of a new order in which both Jew and Gentile could be 'citizens of the kingdom.' (Paul, in Romans, referencing Hosea, shows that Jews and Gentiles are invited into the church, just as the Old Testament prophets predicted. Those "not my people," become "my people," Romans 9:25.)

In the prophecies of the Old Testament, many times *we have Messianic prophecy in Mosaic terminology.* Malachi 1:11 is one example.[76] A summary of the Old Testament expectations concerning Messiah and His kingdom includes these emphases: (1) a perfect

---

[74] The infinitive "to reign" (the Greek reads, "it is necessary for Him to reign") is in the present tense, indicating continuous action in the present. He reigns now, and will reign before death is conquered by the final resurrection.

[75] These references speak of David's throne and Solomon's throne. Both were "God's throne," though they did not both sit on the same particular chair. Nor do we teach David's actual chair will be discovered and used by Messiah. We take the language figuratively.

[76] Roman Catholic commentators claim this is a prophecy of the universality of the Eucharist. That is hardly right. Nor are those correct who use this passage to show that there will be a reinstitution of animal sacrifice out in the future. Rather, this is a Messianic prophecy in Mosaic terminology.

sacrifice for sin; (2) a way to appropriate that sacrifice unto ourselves; (3) the society that results; (4) the ultimate consummation. The New Testament indicates the fulfillment of these Old Testament expectations. (1) Christ became the perfect sacrifice for sin. (2) Concerning the method of appropriation of His sacrifice: (a) Christ is the seed of Abraham (so spoke Nathan), 2 Samuel 7:12-17. (b) They that are Christ's are also part of the seed[77] of Abraham, Galatians 3:29. (c) Paul shows the Jews, when they rejected Christ, were cut off, Romans 11:20. (d) And the Gentile who apostatizes, or rejects Christ, will be cut off, Mark 16:15,16, Romans 11:22. (3) Concerning the resulting society, the New Testament writers say the fulfillment of the Old Testament expectation was ushered in with the formation of the New Testament church. The only way to refute this idea is to say that the "new covenant" predicted in Jeremiah 31:31-34 has not yet been established. Such an argument (the "new covenant" has not yet begun) contradicts Hebrews 8-10 where Paul quotes Jeremiah 31 as being fulfilled. (4) 1 Corinthians 15:20-28 deals with the ultimate consummation.

Until He has put all His enemies under His feet -- 'Putting an enemy underfoot' is a classic picture of complete subjugation. When an ancient king conquered another king, he made that defeated king lie on the floor, and the victor, while sitting on his throne, used the defeated king's body for a footstool. We are reminded of Psalm 110:1, where the Father says to the Messiah, "Sit at My right hand until I make Thine enemies a footstool for Thy feet." As indicated above, Christ reigns until the last enemy is vanquished. When all enemies are put under Christ's feet, then He will deliver up the kingdom to the God and Father. When death is conquered, that will be the end of the mediatorial reign. Death will not be completely conquered until the resurrection of all the dead. Paul here in Corinthians is in perfect harmony with the book of Revelation. In eternity, Christ will not be a silent partner, while God is on the throne. Christ will reign with God, as the order that was before redemption was begun is restored.

15:26 -- *The last enemy that will be abolished is death.*

The last enemy that will be abolished is death -- Now we know why the resurrection must precede the final consummation. Death (an enemy) has not been rendered inoperative as long as men die physically. Only the resurrection will abolish this enemy. All the other foes of God will be subdued *before* the final resurrection, the time when death shall be finally annulled. When death ("the last enemy") is finally abolished, there shall be no more enemies on the scene. Then, according to God's eternal plan, it will be time for the consummation, time for Messiah to hand over the kingdom to the God and Father. Death is here personified, as in Revelation 20:14. "Abolished"[78] is present tense in the original. Because Christ has come out of the tomb, the destruction of death is regarded as

---

[77] "Seed" is not plural, in the sense of more than one kind of seed. The word "seed" (a collective noun) can include one or a million of the same kind. The word "seeds" (plural) means several types of seed.

[78] The verb is *katergeō* again. See comments at verse 24. Death is going to be robbed of all its power; it is going to be 'put out of working order.'

already begun. The dogma of some at Corinth that denied any future resurrection is thus refuted by a third argument: Resurrection was a part of gospel preaching (*kerygma*) from the very first. A world with no resurrection would be a hopeless place. God's plan of redemption, in its purpose and scope, needs resurrection to complete it.

15:27 -- *For HE HAS PUT ALL THINGS IN SUBJECTION UNDER HIS FEET. But when He says, "All things are put in subjection," it is evident that He is excepted who put all things in subjection to Him.*

For -- Verse 27 may be further explanation of why Christ must reign until all things, including death, are subjected to Him. Or, verse 27 may be an explanation of the 'subjecting of enemies' and the 'abolishing of death' alluded to in verses 25 and 26. Whichever way we read them, verses 27 and 28 reaffirm, in words of Old Testament Scripture, the unlimited dominion assigned to Christ (verses 25-27a), in order to reassert more impressively the truth that only through His absolute victory (death included) can the kingdom of God be consummated (verses 24a,28a).

HE HAS PUT ALL THINGS IN SUBJECTION UNDER HIS FEET -- Not until the next phrase does Paul use words which indicate he is quoting the Old Testament. The words quoted come from Psalm 8:6. Psalm 8 is the psalmist's reflection on what he read in Genesis 2, about dominion over creation being promised to man at the time man was first created. Compared to all that God had created, David notes how special man was. A careful reading of Hebrews 2:6-18 shows us just how Psalm 8 has Messianic implications.[79] At the time Hebrews was written, the writer can say "we do not see all things subject to man," i.e., something has happened to man's dominion. What happened is that Adam had sinned, and the entrance of sin and death into the world impinged on man's dominion. Then the Hebrew writer calls attention to Jesus Messiah, who during His incarnation was a little lower than the angels. "We see Him crowned with glory and honor!" (Hebrews 2:9) The glorified Christ is in the process of winning back man's lost dominion. When death is conquered, man will have his dominion back. As Paul uses the language of Psalm 8 here in 1 Corinthians, he simply words it that God has put all things under Christ's feet. "All things" is emphatic. Death is included. God has made all things subject to Christ. He has appointed Christ to be head over all things.[80]

---

[79] Many Bible students have suggested Psalm 8 has two "layers" of meaning. First the Psalmist speaks of "man" – referring to human beings in general. Then he speaks of the "son of man." Because "Son of man" was a Messianic title (cf. Daniel 7:13, and Jesus' own use of this title), Bible students think the reference is to Jesus especially. We think this interpretation misses the way Hebrew poetry, with its parallelism, works. For a detailed discussion of this matter, see the author's *New Testament Epistles: Hebrews* (Moberly, MO: Scripture Exposition Books, 1992), p.22ff. While we are not convinced that "son of man" in this Psalm is a reference to Messiah, it is obvious that Paul here in 1 Corinthians applies the language of the Psalm to Jesus, just as the Hebrew writer applied it to Jesus' perfect humanity.

[80] Just before He ascended, Christ claimed "all authority in heaven and on earth" had been given to Him (Matthew 28:18). Jesus had that authority during His ministry (Mark 2:10; John 3;35, 5:27). Since Scriptures picture Him as a "Lamb slain from the foundation of the world" we suppose the "authority" was granted to Him back in eternity before the work of creation was even begun. If it came to the place the creation ever needed a Savior, Jesus volunteered to be the one to be the Savior. That is why "all authority" was given to Him.

But when He says, "All things are put in subjection" -- In order to guard against any possible misunderstanding, Paul now explains the limitation one must remember when he thinks of Christ's dominion and authority. "He" is God. In the line quoted from the Psalm, God the Father is the subject of the sentence (in the Hebrew), and the speaker of the words here quoted. That God "says" these words is an indication that the previous words in this verse are a citation of an Old Testament passage.

It is evident that He is excepted who put all things in subjection to Him -- While the Son is reigning and abolishing enemies, God the Father is not subject to God the Son, even though the Son is reigning in all authority.[81] This remark may have been made for several reasons: (1) To avoid the possibility of misunderstanding the "all," as if it meant that God the Father were included as also being subordinate to Christ.[82] (2) The expression may also be regarded as intensive or emphatic, denoting in the most absolute sense that there was *nothing* in the universe, except God the Father, which was not subject to Christ.

15:28 -- *And when all things are subjected to Him, then the Son Himself also will be subjected to the One who subjected all things to Him, that God may be all in all.*

And -- When we put the nouns in the place of the pronouns, the verse reads thus: "And when all things shall be subdued under Christ, then shall the Son also subject Himself unto the Father who did subject all things unto the Son, that God-Father may be all in all." The resurrection of the dead – the last enemy to be subjected to Christ – forms a climax to God's grand eternal plan. When that grand moment arrives, the Son shall do what Paul now says – He shall hand over to the God and Father.

When all things are subjected to Him -- At the time of the resurrection (death having been subjected also), when the eternal home of the blessed will be entered by the redeemed (the kingdom) – that's "when." It is therefore evident that the time has not yet arrived, and also that Christ's dominion is *now* exercised, and that He is carrying forward His plans for the subjugation of all things to God.

Then the Son Himself also will be subjected to the One who subjected all things to Him -- "Then" is *tote*, which means "at that time." It indicates the two events are contemporaneous, rather than one following the other. The "One who subjected all things to [Jesus]" is none other than God the Father. "Will be subjected" (*hupotagēsetai*) is middle

---

[81] The ASV carries a footnote that offers an alternate translation. That translation pictures a scene at the end of time, when Christ makes, as it were, His final report to the Father, and states that the work of subjecting all things, even death, is completed. Substituting nouns for the pronouns that appear in the Greek of the ASV's alternate reading, we would have, "But when Christ shall have said (to God at the last day), 'All things are put in subjection!', it is evident that God Himself is excepted." The alternate translation requires Paul to have written a broken sentence, and requires a change of speakers from God to Christ (without any warning of such a change). These and other objections (including the fact that some of the words in the verse must be given an unusual meaning before the alternative reading could be arrived at) have caused the NASB translators not even to offer the alternative reading in the margin.

[82] In heathen mythology, we have Jupiter fabled to have expelled his father Saturn from his throne and from heaven. Paul is not reworking heathen mythology at this point.

voice.⁸³ Christ will subject Himself unto the Father, and do it for His own benefit. Care must be exercised here. The 'subjection' of Jesus to the Father does not seem to imply that Jesus will continue a subordinate position to the Father all through eternity after the consummation. Nor is the passage a proof that Christ is, in some way, not full deity.⁸⁴ These words hardly indicate an eternally subordinate position for Jesus. Rather, they imply the eternal equality of the Father, Son, and Holy Spirit. When Christ turns His kingdom over to the Father, this does not mean the Son will then be deprived of this kingdom and His rule, with the Father taking the Son's place. Rather, passages like Revelation 22:3 indicate the Triune God will rule in the unity of the three persons. The "benefit" that accrues to Christ is that He is no longer subordinate in function to the Father. Father, Son, and Holy Spirit are again, each one, free to exercise the independent prerogatives of deity.⁸⁵ By a free act, in harmony with the whole divine plan that sent Him to earth, and gave Him "all authority" over all things, Christ subjects Himself back to the Godhead. Things will be as they were before the creation – with the Godhead supreme.

That God may be all in all -- In the phrase "the God and Father", we have indicated that "God" refers to the Godhead – all three personalities. "May be all" (*panta*, all things) means "that God may be Supreme." "In all" (*en pasin*) may be either masculine or neuter. If we take it as masculine, it says 'God is supreme over all believers.' If we take it as neuter, it says 'God is supreme over all created existences.' In the destruction of the wicked (who are part of the creation), God's glory will be conspicuous. The redeemed basking in the glory of Heaven show the majesty and glory of God. God is the sovereign of the universe –and after the consummation all will see this.

McGarvey (*op. cit.*, p.152) has written, "The chain of Paul's logic in this just-completed paragraph is long, but it runs thus:

> No glorification until the mediatorial kingdom is turned over to God;
> No turning over of this kingdom until its work is complete;
> No completion of its work until all its enemies are destroyed;
> No destruction of all these enemies while death, the chief one, survives;
> No destruction of death, save by the resurrection.
> Therefore there can be no full glorification of God without a resurrection."

---

⁸³ Our versions treat it as a future passive, but it is a future middle verb form, so a middle voice meaning should be used.

⁸⁴ The middle voice verb (with its assertion of submission) has been used by both Arians (Christ was a created being, and therefore subordinate to the Father) and Sabellians (the one Person who was God assumed various roles in His dealings with man) as they try to give Scriptural proof for their views. The temporary subordination of Jesus to the Father for the purpose of redemption is a difficult concept to master or explain, but it involves no other subjection of the Son than was involved in His emptying Himself as He became incarnate. There was no inferiority of nature (Jesus was "God," John 1:1), there was no lack of an eternal existence (remember the implications of Jesus being called "Jehovah"), nor is there any lack of "glory" experienced by Jesus (John 17:5) while He awaits the consummation.

⁸⁵ Says Barnes, *op. cit.*, p.302, "The interpretation which affirms that the Son shall then be subject to the Father *in the sense of laying down His delegated authority, and ceasing to exercise His mediatorial reign*, has been the common interpretation of all times." [Emphasis mine, GLR.] Recall the discussion of Christ's temporary subordination to the Father in notes at 3:22,23 and 11:3.

4. *Ad Hominem* arguments in favor of resurrection. 15:29-34

> *Summary:*   Paul shows the absurdity of their present way of life, and his, if those folk are right who insist there is no future resurrection.   Among the points he makes in this, his fourth argument for resurrection, are these: (1) Why be immersed, if there is no resurrection?   (2) What motivates the apostles to risk their lives daily? (3) What motivates the Corinthians to self-control and self-denial instead of an Epicurean lifestyle?   (4) A man whose doctrine is wrong is more likely to sin!

15:29 -- *Otherwise, what will those do who are baptized for the dead? If the dead are not raised at all, why then are they baptized for them?*

Otherwise -- "Otherwise" equals (as the last half of the verse shows), "If the dead are not raised up at all."   Once more there is a very abrupt change of tone.   Some explain it by suggesting Paul paused in his dictation, perhaps overnight.[86]   A simpler suggestion is that Paul groups his material perfectly.   In the previous paragraph, he spoke of the relation of the general resurrection to the work of Christ, and has carried that work to its final end – the consummation. He has thus shown that the final resurrection is absolutely essential to the completion of the work of Christ, and one therefore could not deny the reality of the resurrection.   In the paragraph which begins with this verse, Paul presents our resurrection as being vital to the entire Christian life from the moment of its beginning in baptism onward to its close in temporal death.   To word it another way, Paul has been emphasizing what *God* has been doing.   Now he will argue for resurrection from what *men* are doing.

What will those do -- 'What will they gain?   What will be their position?   What will they accomplish?   What do they hope to achieve?'   The question, using a future tense verb, is intended to get the Corinthians to think.   When we characterize this paragraph as an *ad hominem* argument, care must be exercised so the term is not misunderstood.

- Some interpreters call this an *ad hominem* argument, and go on to say, 'By use of the third person Paul indirectly separates himself from those who were participating in this action of baptism for the dead.'   It is then inferred that Paul does not approve of their action (usually explained as being vicarious baptism[87]).   It is inferred that, even though Paul does not approve, he still uses it as an argument to show the absurdity of the Corinthian belief in the doctrine of "no resurrection of the body."   The argument would be, 'Why be baptized for the dead, if the dead do not benefit by being raised?'
- There is a better explanation of what "baptized for the dead" is than to call it vicarious baptism, and it requires no peculiar definition to be given to the term *ad hominem*.   All that is implied in the term *ad hominem* is that Paul is arguing "to the man" when he points out that there is no consistency between their claims and their actions.

---

[86] See Shore, *op. cit.*, p.147, for example.

[87] There are numerous interpretations offered for this difficult verse.   See several briefly presented, along with arguments pro and con, in Special Study #8 at the close of comments on chapter 15.

Who are baptized for the dead? -- *Baptidzomenoi* is a present passive participle, not a past tense. It indicates continuing action – 'those who are being baptized for the dead' – going on at the present time. This verb tense has been turned into one very strong argument that the proper interpretation of this difficult passage is not a reference to Christian baptism, but to some other form of baptism (i.e., vicarious baptism, or the baptism of suffering) which an individual might experience on repeated occasions. But there are other very satisfactory explanations of this present tense. "The present timeless participle describes those who are baptized at any time, whether in the past, present, or future" (Lenski, *op. cit.*, p.689). New converts, one after another, continue to be immersed at the very time this letter was being written.

In "for the dead", the preposition translated "for" (*huper*) can have either of two meanings, and each has been incorporated into one or more of the various interpretations offered for this disputed passage. (1) When used of place, it can mean 'above' or 'over.' (2) Used of persons or things, it means 'instead of,' 'on behalf of,' or 'for the benefit of.'

As noted previously, "dead" is a plural adjective; the noun must be supplied. The point at issue among the skeptics at Corinth was the *resurrection of the **body** from the grave* (verse 12). Greeks always believed in the immortality of the soul, but could never accept the doctrine of the resurrection of the body. This Greek philosophy had infiltrated the thinking of some church members at Corinth, leading them to deny any future resurrection.

It is exceedingly important to the proper understanding of the verse to note that the *definite article* ("the") is in the Greek text at this place. In verses 12-19, the adjective "dead" is anarthrous. But here in verse 29 the article is used. The presence of the Greek definite article implies either of two things. (1) It points back to some earlier reference in the same context. It is called "the article of previous reference." (2) It points to some well-known, generally recognized person or thing. (The absence of the article implies *nature* or *quality*. The presence of the article points out a specific something in the context.) It is most likely that in this place it is an article of previous reference. Paul is talking about the same dead bodies he has been talking about in all of chapter 15. In verses 12-19, Paul shows what is involved in giving up the doctrine of the resurrection of dead bodies. After reading verses 12-19, let the reader skip verses 20-28 and read verse 29, noting the presence of the definite article in verse 29. The definite article here (after its absence earlier) indicates that Paul has in mind (and wants his readers to know that in verse 29 he has in mind) the same dead bodies that were discussed in verses 12-19 – that is, our own dead bodies, Christian believers' dead bodies.

Baptism – immersion – pictures "death, burial, and *resurrection*" (Romans 6:1ff). How inconsistent to submit to an ordinance like baptism that pictures "resurrection" if you do not believe in resurrection of the body! My baptism is a picture of the open attestation that I believe, first, that Jesus died for me, was buried, and was raised again; second, that I am going to die, be buried, and *be raised again*; third, because of this I am to consider myself dead to sin, buried, and raised in newness of life with Christ. Christ died to benefit men's bodies as well as their souls. My baptism pictures my belief in my participation in the final resurrection of all dead bodies. Baptism is the act of committal by which I testify to the world that I believe there will be a resurrection of dead bodies. Paul clinches his argument to Greek Christians, who were skeptical on the point, with an argument from their own baptism. 'Why were you baptized if there is no resurrection? Why did you show to the world through this beautiful pictorial act that you believed Christ died and rose again? Why did you show the world you believe you will die and be raised again? *Your baptism becomes a meaningless mockery if there is no resurrection.* If dead bodies are not to be raised at all, then why be baptized on behalf of your own dead bodies?'

If the dead are not raised at all -- This phrase repeats the assertion of some at Corinth (see verse 12). In this second question, the condition (which is compressed into "otherwise" in the first question) is fully written out. We suppose the idea introduced in the first part of verse 29 is repeated, lest the readers miss the point. "Dead" in this case is masculine plural, *nekroi*. There is no article in the Greek, so that we render it, "if dead ones (or dead bodies) are not raised at all ...."

Why then are they baptized for them? -- Whatever "baptism for the dead" means, the Corinthians are being inconsistent in their practice when compared with their assertion of "no resurrection." This second question seems to explain the first, and in our opinion limits the interpretation of "baptized for the dead" to the immersion commanded in the Great Commission. Note the difference in punctuation in the KJV and NASB. The NASB is surely the proper punctuation. The KJV reads, "Else what shall they do which are baptized for the dead, if the dead rise not at all? Why are they then baptized for the dead?" The NASB reads, "Otherwise what will those do who are baptized for the dead? If the dead are not raised at all, why then are they baptized for them?" The present tense *baptidzontai* has the same meaning as the participle in the first question: it includes all baptisms at any time. The KJV reads, "for the dead." But according to the best manuscript evidence (*Aleph*, A, B, D, E, F, G, K, P, etc.) the reading should be "for them." "Them" points back to their own dead (bodies). These persons are thinking about the future of their own bodies when they are baptized. Part of the reason they are immersed is that they are looking forward to their own resurrection.

15:30 -- *Why are we also in danger every hour?*

Why are we also in danger -- In this commentator's opinion, verse 30 (with its emphasis on suffering) is a different argument from verse 29.[88] If Christ was not raised, and if the dead are not to be raised, what motivates the apostles to risk their lives? Just as being immersed would be devoid of all meaning if there is no such hope as the resurrection of dead bodies, so also the risks incurred by men like Paul would be senseless and foolish. The emphatic "we" cannot include all of the Corinthians or all of the baptized, for they do

---

[88] It is because of an apparent change of argument that we have hesitated to treat 15:29 as the "baptism of suffering."

not always stand in jeopardy. But this *is* true regarding Paul and his fellow workers.[89] The apostles, who devote all their energies to preaching the resurrection, go joyfully from one danger into another. What would be the sense of such a course of conduct if no resurrection awaited them at the end? What is the "danger?" Not of losing their souls. This does not fit. In danger of losing their lives, mortal danger, does fit. This becomes another link in the grand argument for the case of the resurrection. Stated hypothetically: 'If there is no resurrection, Christ hasn't been raised. If Christ hasn't been raised, we are false witnesses. If we are false witnesses, why do we stand in jeopardy every hour?' Stated categorically: 'We are suffering every hour. Because we suffer we are true witnesses. If we are true witnesses, then Christ was raised. And if Christ has been raised, then there is a resurrection of the dead (in general)'.

Every hour -- Constantly, is the idea. From the record in Acts, what Paul here says about danger and peril was certainly true his whole life, almost from the day of his conversion. So numerous were the dangers that they might be said to occupy every hour. The constant danger caused him to daily hover on the brink of death (Romans 8:36). Paul's point, of course, is that he and the other apostles are foolish to put their lives in constant danger for the sake of others, if neither he nor they have any hope of resurrection.

15:31 -- *I protest, brethren, by the boasting in you, which I have in Christ Jesus our Lord, I die daily.*

I protest, brethren -- No longer does he speak of dangers he faced in common with all the apostles (verse 30). Now he alludes to dangers he faced personally. This is the only place in the New Testament where "I protest" (*nē*) occurs, but we meet it frequently in the Septuagint. It is a particle used to introduce a solemn affirmation when a man is under oath. Our expression "I solemnly swear ..." would be similar to its meaning in New Testament times.[90] Paul takes an oath to seal his assertion about the daily danger he and the other apostles encounter as they testify about resurrection. This oath is intended to cause the Corinthians to listen more carefully to what he is saying.[91] It is interesting to see this expression of Paul's own feelings toward the Corinthian converts (he calls them "brothers") despite the many things for which he has had to rebuke them.

By the boasting in you -- The possessive pronoun may be either subjective ('your boasting in me') or objective ('my boasting in you'), and the context must determine. Here it is the

---

[89] This is one of the rare instances of the personal pronoun in the nominative case being used. It is a construction that puts emphasis on the pronoun – "we" as contrasted to others. "We" in verse 11 denoted all the apostles. So it is likely to refer to apostles here.

[90] In later years it came to mean 'I affirm against' (cf. the KJV and ASV, "I protest"), but that is not the meaning here in verse 31. If it were, then there is an imaginary objector, who has denied Paul and the apostles are in any daily danger, whom Paul is testifying against.

[91] In light of Jesus' command to "Swear not at all!" (Matthew 5:37), some have been surprised by Paul's taking of an oath. What is obvious is that Jesus' prohibition was never intended to be absolute. He Himself took an oath while on trial (Matthew 26:63,64). On several occasions Paul takes an oath (2 Corinthians 1:23, 2:17, 11:11, 12:19).

latter. Rather than saying, "I swear by God," he said "I swear by the fact that I am proud of you." To swear by something means that one is willing to forfeit that something, if his word is not true (Fisher, *op. cit.*, p.249). Paul was proud, in a Godly sense, of the church in Corinth which he had planted. Their very existence as Christians was something he had regularly put his life in danger to accomplish. Implied also is this thought, 'How can I still continue to be proud of you if you so wretchedly act as to disbelieve the resurrection?' There were many occasions when Paul presented the great facts of the faith in calm, deliberate, objective fashion. There are also times, as in this verse, when he is not so calm. His feelings and emotions boil to the surface as he presents the facts. The resurrection is absolutely vital. When the apostle thinks of his past work and of his daily experience in facing death, the resurrection is vital. Take away the resurrection, and everything related to Paul, all his work and all his trying ordeals, would be nothing but folly.

Which I have in Christ Jesus our Lord -- This boasting over the Corinthians (over their submission to the faith, and his success in establishing a church so renowned and gifted) is not self-praise. Paul is giving Christ the glory and honor. It was actually Christ working through him that had accomplished such remarkable work.

I die daily -- His life was constantly in danger (cp. Romans 8:36 and 2 Corinthians 4:10-12). On one occasion in Asia, the peril was so ominous that Paul "despaired of his life" (2 Corinthians 1:8-11). "Daily I die" comes first in the Greek for emphasis. The deadly dangers Paul faces are so constant that he writes, 'from day to day I die.' He never knows at what moment some blow of persecution may strike him down. Findlay writes (*op. cit.*, p.931), "He was never out of peril. There was not a day, nor an hour of the day, when they were free of an expectation of being seized and led out to execution." In his own mind, Paul forfeited his life every time he went out to preach.[92]

15:32 -- *If from human motives I fought with wild beasts at Ephesus, what does it profit me? If the dead are not raised, LET US EAT AND DRINK, FOR TOMORROW WE DIE.*

If from human motives -- "Human motives" would be money, applause or position, and would have to leave out any eternal considerations if the dictum of some at Corinth ("there is no resurrection") were true. From the general danger that stalks an apostle "every hour" (verse 30), Paul moved on to the threats of death that come to him personally one after another, day after day (verse 31). Now he closes this argument with a particular instance that must have occurred in Ephesus at about the time he was writing this letter.

I fought with wild beasts at Ephesus -- Is this literal or metaphorical? Did Paul actually fight with wild beasts in the arena, or is the expression figurative to designate a battle with vicious human enemies?

(1) If taken literally, Paul has had an actual fight with wild beasts in the Ephesian circus

---

[92] Care must be taken lest this verse be lifted out of context and made to mean that Paul died to himself and to sin every day, so that he could live a more holy life for God. That may be true, but this is not the verse to prove it.

and lived to tell about it. Arguments for this *interpretation:* (a) The words Paul uses are the regular words used of a gladiator in the arena who had to fight with the lions. (b) At the martyrdom of Polycarp, the Asiarchs (who are mentioned in Acts 19:31, as restraining the tumult of Demetrius) had the charge of the wild beasts. (c) There was a stadium at Ephesus, located between the theater and the temple of Artemis. (d) Some young men of Ephesus were famous for their bull fights (Artimedor 1.9), so fights with animals were not something foreign to the stadium at Ephesus. (e) There are later legends that Paul did actually so fight, and that he was wondrously preserved because the beasts would not attack him. *Arguments against this interpretation:* (a) If he fought a literal battle with wild beasts, why not list this in 2 Corinthians 11? (b) Paul was a Roman citizen, and Roman citizens had certain rights: they could not be crucified, nor could they be placed in the arena to fight with wild animals.[93]

(2) If taken metaphorically, then it means encounters with men. He means he was near being torn to pieces by infuriated men. In the classic writers (e.g., Heraclitus) the Ephesians were called "wild beasts." See also Titus 1:12, where the Cretans are called "evil beasts." 2 Timothy 4:16,17 probably does not refer to literal lions. Ignatius (*Epis. ad Rom.* 5.1) speaks of "fighting with beasts by land and sea," and having been bound to "ten leopards," that is, a band of soldiers. Both Hebrew and Greek literature would have made such a form of expression familiar to the apostle and his readers.[94] Paul's allusion to fighting with wild beasts at Ephesus is not a reference to the riot of Demetrius since this letter to Corinth was written before that riot occurred. Acts 20:19 does speaks of "trials which came upon me through the plots of the Jews." One of these could be what Paul here makes reference to.

What does it profit me? – 'What benefit shall I have? Why go through all this suffering and persecution and opposition if there is no hope of resurrection?'[95] His conflict was an aimless, useless risking of life if there is no resurrection. Only on the supposition that Christ arose, and that therefore we too shall rise, is Paul not foolish for facing the danger of death in the pursuit of his great calling.

If the dead are not raised, LET US EAT AND DRINK, FOR TOMORROW WE DIE -- This the sixth time the foolish statement of some ("dead bodies are not raised!") is quoted. When Paul says there would be 'no profit' for him, does he overlook the thought that the souls of the dead might live in glory with Christ, even if their bodies are not raised from the grave? Cannot the Corinthians answer all of Paul's arguments by this single reply? They cannot! If there is no resurrection, then Christ is not risen, and salvation for

---

[93] The privileges Roman citizens enjoyed should not be pressed, for even Roman aristocrats, on occasion, were forced to appear in the arena. For example, Acilius Glabrio, an eminent Roman, was compelled by Domitian to fight wild beasts.

[94] A helpful summary of the arguments pro and con on literal or metaphorical beasts is written by Ronald E. Osborne, "Paul and the Wild Beasts," *JBL* 85 (1966), p.225-230.

[95] The punctuation of the ASV/NASB is better than the KJV. The KJV has a comma here, the ASV/NASB a question mark. The next conditional clause belongs to the next sentence.

the soul as well as for the body disappears. There won't be any intermediate state of glory. If the dead are not raised (as some in Corinth claim), then the Christian gains little for his devotion to Christ. He gets sick, suffers ills, and dies. What did his devotion to Christ gain him? Nothing, unless you view it from the Christian rather than the human viewpoint. When eternity and the resurrection are brought into the picture, the devotion of the Christian is seen to be well worth the risks taken and the losses suffered.

The NASB puts the phrase "Let us eat and drink, for tomorrow we die" in small caps, supposing this is a quotation of Isaiah 22:13 (in the LXX), rather than a quotation of an Epicurean maxim. In their original setting, the words in Isaiah are words the Jews said when they were besieged by Sennacherib and the Assyrian army. Isaiah rebukes the Jews because instead of weeping and fasting and humiliation, as would have been fitting under such circumstances, they had given themselves up to feasting and revelry. They felt they were going to die. There was no use in offering resistance, or in calling on God. They might as well enjoy life as long as it lasts. The language of the hopeless Jews appropriately expresses the idea Paul is making. If there is no resurrection of the dead, and no future state, if there is no happy result to the toils and sufferings of this life, it is vain and foolish to subject ourselves to them. If death ends all, life has little to offer except the creaturely comforts of eating and drinking. "Tomorrow," that is, very soon, "we die." The idea is that 'We must die, without the prospect of living again.' Unless the doctrine of the resurrection is true, if death ends all, life has little more to offer than eating or drinking and gratifying one's appetites – and we should best make the most of these comforts.

15:33 -- *Do not be deceived: "Bad company corrupts good morals."*

Do not be deceived -- 'Stop being deceived!' or 'Stop wandering off!' the Greek says.[96] The Corinthians were already being led away from the Christian truth. They were to stop what they were doing. Paul closes his presentation about the reality of the resurrection of the body with a pointed admonition and rebuke. Some false teacher or false philosophy has been leading them astray. They are to quit following this dead end.

"Bad company corrupts good morals" -- Paul notes two sources for the error taught at Corinth about the resurrection: association with evil companions (verse 33) and ignorance of God (verse 34). "Company" translates *homiliai*. It refers to something more than casual acquaintances. It denotes 'association' or 'conversation.'[97] "Morals" is *ēthē*, a mode of action, character, disposition, moral quality. "Good" translates *chrēsta*, 'serviceable, full of worth, promoting good.' The whole phrase may be a quotation of a popular proverb (as the quotes in the NASB suggest).[98] The message Paul is sending is

---

[96] See an explanation of the Greek construction at 1 Corinthians 6:9.

[97] The word often denotes "communications" people make with each other, especially "speeches" (see our word "homily" which comes from the Greek word). Morris, *op. cit.*, p.221.

[98] Some affirm this is a quotation of Menander, *Thais*. On other occasions, Paul shows familiarity with non-Christian poets, as he also quotes Aratus at Acts 17:28 and Epimenides in Titus 1:12.

this: Christians don't keep company with folk who deny the resurrection! Association with folk who are full of skeptical ideas about resurrection is bound to have a negative effect on the good ways (*ēthē*) of the Christian life. If divine truth doesn't mold a man's thinking, then false and insidious ideas learned from their associates will surely mislead them. Already the harmful effects of unbelief in the future resurrection are painfully apparent in the relaxed moral tone of a certain part of the Corinthian church. Regular and intimate association with wrong companions is dangerous to Christian doctrine and life. Jesus did go to the publicans and sinners, but not like a man who picks for his companions those who are of a low morality, and not because He did not feel at home with the God-like people. He went to save the sinner. We too must go to them, in an attempt to save them. The church is the society (companionship) of the redeemed. In Jesus' parable, some seed fell by the wayside, and there was the constant tramp, tramp, tramp until it was quenched. On billboards, in newspapers, and on the radio and TV, we have the tramp, tramp, tramp of the world. The world is not where the Christian looks for companionship or close associates. God has given us good companionship, in order that we may have rest from the constant tramp, tramp, tramp, and may be able to take root and grow. There is a danger in choosing the wrong companions because of the unconscious effect they have on us. One of the most difficult things to counteract is the atmosphere. Not merely the teaching, or the words of the evil companions, but the very atmosphere in which they move. He who rejects the resurrection cannot live and act like one who truly believes this divine reality. This is, of course, a sharp edge which is turned against those who were the authors of the skepticism about the future resurrection.

15:34 -- *Become sober-minded as you ought, and stop sinning; for some have no knowledge of God. I speak* **this** *to your shame.*

Become sober minded as you ought -- Verse 34 is a call to the Corinthians to get their thinking right, to stop denying the resurrection – a denial that has been leading to loose living. The ASV translates it "awake to soberness righteously." In their willingness even to listen to those who say there is no resurrection, the Corinthians are pictured as having been in a drunken sleep, and Paul commands them to 'sober up!' The intimation is, 'You have been wandering around in a foolish belief, reeling like a drunken person.' "Righteously" (ASV) is an adverb (*dikaiōs*), "in a righteous manner." Perhaps the NASB translators have caught the idea when they rendered it "as you ought." This is the right thing to do. "He is rightly sober who sees and believes the divine realities as God reveals them, and who does all his thinking so every thought accords with these realities."[99] The aorist imperative "become sober minded" speaks of a single act. 'Do it and do it at once!'

And stop sinning -- This imperative is a present tense. It prohibits the continuance of an action already going on. It is implied that some at Corinth were already living carelessly, missing the mark (*hamartanō*) that God had set out for their thinking and their actions. Their denial of the resurrection would reflect itself even more in their lives. 'You cannot believe crooked and live straight. When you strike at the root (doctrine), you strike at the

---

[99] Lenski, *op. cit.*, p.700.

fruitage (love and Christian virtues). Do not err any longer, do not continue to depart from the truth and holiness. No longer embrace a doctrine which tends to lead into sin. No longer associate with bad company.'[100] These first two admonitions in verse 34 are directed to those in the church who are in danger of being led away by those denying the resurrection.

For some have no knowledge of God -- "For" shows there is a connection between "no knowledge of God" and the Corinthians' failure to think soberly and their failure to live rightly. The original Greek is stronger: "For utter ignorance of God is what some have." "Some" here might very well be a reference to the "some" (verse 12) who were denying the doctrine of resurrection. Or it might be saying that those who have listened to this denial were the ones who had no knowledge of God. If this is the idea, then a second source of their error about the resurrection is directly due to their ignorance of God. Verse 33 identified the first source – bad company. "No knowledge of God" is perhaps similar to what Jesus one day said to the Sadducees, who also denied the possibility of any future resurrection. "You are greatly mistaken, because you do not know the Scriptures, or the power of God," He charged them. Perhaps Paul is saying that, like the Sadducees, those at Corinth who deny the possibility of resurrection don't know the power of God to give a body (to make a body) for each one's resurrection. Perhaps there is a glance back at verses 20-28, where God, by raising Jesus, set in motion a whole series of events that lead ultimately to the consummation. Denial of resurrection *is* ignorance of what God is doing in His world! This would be quite a blow to the Corinthian pride. They prided themselves on their intelligence. Now to be told they knew as little about God as the heathen know! It would be quite a blow!

I speak *this* to your shame -- Compare what Paul wrote at 6:5. 'To your shame as a church' is the idea. They had had abundant opportunities to know the truth. It was a shame that to Christians the apostle should have to vindicate one of the very fundamental truths of the faith. It was a great disgrace that there were those in the church who denied the doctrine of the resurrection, and that there were those who listened to such a denial, and not only listened but also lived carelessly (sinfully). The Corinthians prided themselves on their knowledge (chapter 1, 3, etc.). "No knowledge" is what some have, Paul insists. He wanted them to feel ashamed of themselves for being so gullible that they allowed themselves to be swayed by men who did not really know God at all.

B. Consideration of Objections to Bodily Resurrection. 15:35-49

> *Summary:* From arguments that there will be a resurrection (verses 1-34), Paul now turns his attention to the nature of the resurrection body. In verse 35 he introduces two objections raised to the doctrine of resurrection, and answers each in turn: (1) How can the body be raised? (36-38); (2) What kind of body will it be? (39-49)

---

[100] Modern readers of this letter are likewise encouraged to become sober minded, to never condone or excuse erroneous teaching by telling ourselves that it has little effect on right living.

15:35 -- *But someone will say, "How are the dead raised? And with what kind of body do they come?"*

But someone will say -- "Someone" (*tis*) is likely to be identified as one of the "some" (*tines*) of verses 12 and 34. The strong adversative "but" (*alla*) seems to indicate Paul knows his presentation of arguments for the resurrection is only partly done. Before his readers will be completely convinced, he must answer the plausible objections he knows are being used against his position, as "some" insist there will be no resurrection of dead bodies (verse 12). Paul uses the very questions they asked ("How are the dead raised?" and "With what kind of body do they come?") to introduce his answers. In answering the objections raised by "some" at Corinth, Paul uses analogies. We must be careful not to press the analogies too far.

"How are the dead raised? -- When one contemplates all the things that can happen to a dead body, the general thrust of this question becomes more obvious. Some bodies simply disintegrate after physical death occurs.

> The bodies return to their native dust. They become entirely disorganized. Their dust may be scattered – how shall it be recollected? They may be burned at the stake or in a fire, and how shall the particles which composed their bodies be collected and reorganized? They may be devoured by the beasts of the field, the fowls of the heaven, or the fish of the sea. Their flesh may have served to constitute the food of other animals, and to form *their* bodies. How can it be recollected and reorganized? Or it may have served as fertilizer for other plants, flowers, and trees, as the roots of those drew nourishment from the decaying flesh. How can it be remolded into a human frame?[101]

When one thinks about how the particles that made up the human body can be scattered, at first it seems the question "How can the dead be raised?" (a question that asks about the mechanics of the process) has some convincing weight. Paul answers this first objection in verses 36-38.

And with what kind of body do they come?" -- "Body" – a word occurring ten times in the verses following – is the topic of this paragraph. "What kind" is a translation of *poiōs*. 'What will be the form, the shape, the size, the make-up of the new body?'[102] "Come" seems to picture the dead as coming out of the graves. How else can one picture resurrection to the imagination? Compare Jesus' use of a similar figure (John 5:29). Since the dead body quickly decomposes, skeptics might ridicule the whole idea of resur-

---

[101] Barnes, *op. cit.*, p.309-310, slightly edited and adapted by this commentator.

[102] Gordon Fee has called attention to what Bultmannian scholars tried to do with this passage. "One of the curiosities of a preceding generation of New Testament scholarship was its readiness to adopt so wholeheartedly the view of Bultmann that by *sōma* Paul meant the essential person. ("Man does not HAVE a *sōma;* he IS *sōma*." *Theology* I, p.194.) Yet that proved so difficult for Bultmann to maintain in the light of this passage that he accused Paul of betraying himself – never allowing that it may have been his own reconstruction of Paul that was at fault." See Ron Sider, "The Pauline Conception of the Resurrection Body in 1 Corinthians 15:35-54," *New Testament Studies* 21 (1974/75), p.428-439.

rection by asking, 'What kind of body would arise from a heap of decomposed rubbish?' If parts of the dead body were scattered, or became digested into some scavenger's body, what would be the shape of the new body? Will it be missing some of its parts? Are we to suppose *all* the matter which at any time entered into the composition of the body here is to be recollected, and to constitute a colossal frame? Are we to suppose it will be the same as it is here, with the same organization, the same necessities, the same wants? Will those who died in old age be raised in aged bodies? Will those who died young or in infancy be raised in the same state, and remain such forever? Paul answers this second question or objection in verses 39-49.[103]

1. First objection: *How can the body be raised?* 15:36-38

15:36 -- *You fool! That which you sow does not come to life unless it dies;*

You fool! -- The English translation is too strong, and so seems to run contrary to the distinct censure of such language by Christ (Matthew 5:22).[104] The word here is *aphrōn*, 'unreasonable, unwise, irrational, senseless, unthinking.' It is a blunt way of saying 'You aren't thinking! Your objections are worthless!' Perhaps there is a further thought in Paul's use of "fool!" He may be using "fool" in its Old Testament sense, of one who has failed to take God into account. (At Psalm 14:1, 53:1, and 92:6, it is the same word *aphrōn* that is used to describe such people.) Based on a preconceived notion that a resurrected body must be just like our present earthly bodies, has the objector tried to make a joke of the idea of a resurrected body? Has he tried to make his point by drawing a hilarious picture of a dead body being "patched together again from the dust, once more to begin its round of life in eating and drinking, digesting and eliminating, sleeping and working, begetting and keeping house?" (Lenski, *op. cit.*, p.703) 'How senseless to think of the resurrection in so pitiful and limited a way!' replies Paul.

That which you sow -- "You" is emphatic in the Greek, and with it Paul points a finger at the objector. The thrust of Paul's reply is, 'Every time *you* sow some seed, *you* supply the answer to your own objection. Your own experience of planting seeds and watching them grow would teach you if you had the sense to comprehend its significance.' Paul goes on to show by an analogy from nature how a resurrection of a body is possible. (In due time, he will use an analogy from the resurrection of Christ to show what kind of body the resur-

---

[103] The resurrection of Christ dominates Paul's analogy as he answers this question. Since Christ was raised bodily (He was *buried*, raised, and *seen*), there must be something analogous to that in man's future resurrection body. The analogy should not be pressed to prove that because Jesus' body was about 35 years old when it was raised from the dead, we all will have 35-year old bodies when we arise.

[104] The word "fool" (*mōros*) forbidden by Christ (Matthew 5:22) has quite a different meaning and implies quite a different tone than the word *aphrōn* which Paul uses here. *Mōros* involves moral depravity or obstinacy. Jesus Himself used the word (*mōros*) when denouncing the Pharisees (Matthew 23:17,19). There is a feeling of bitterness and hatred when men utter this word.

rection body will be.) Shore has warned us to be careful lest we press the details of the analogy too far.

> The apostle does not here *prove* anything. Analogy cannot ever be regarded as logically conclusive as an argument. The object of analogy is to show how a difficulty is not insuperable. The doctrine of the resurrection has been logically established (verses 1-34). A difficulty is suggested as to how resurrection is possible. Analogy shows that the same difficulty exists in theory in other directions where we actually see it surmounted in fact. The fact of a buried seed rising into flower does not and cannot prove that man will rise; but it does show that the objection suggested in the question, "How are the dead raised up?" is not a practical difficulty.[105]

Does not come to life unless it dies -- Jesus used the same illustration to correct some Greeks' misunderstanding of death (John 12:24). We may suppose Paul learned from the Master how to answer Greek philosophical objections to Christian truth. Death doesn't preclude the possibility of resurrection. The NASB translation "does not come to life" hides the fact that the Greek verb is passive. The seed does not come to life of itself,[106] but God gives it life.[107] More will be said about God's activity in the resurrection in the verses following. "Unless it dies" leads to the emphasis that God's purposes are not thwarted by physical death. Seeds that are planted in the ground decompose, yet out of them comes new life. Dead bodies buried in the ground decompose, too, and return to dust, but dissolution is no argument against resurrection. Paul's answer to "How are the dead raised?" based on the analogy of the seed is that in death and resurrection *there is dissolution but continuity*.

15:37 -- *and that which you sow, you do not sow the body which is to be, but a bare grain, perhaps of wheat or of something else.*

And that which you sow -- "And" shows that verse 37 is intended to explain precisely the point Paul had in mind when he introduced the seed analogy in verse 36. Verse 37 does not offer a second or new point of the analogy; rather, it aids us in understanding the true

---

[105] Shore, *op. cit.*, p.150,151.

[106] Here is one place where pushing the details of the analogy has gotten commentators and theologians in trouble. Seeds have a germ of life in them which, though the body decays, continues to live. There is nothing in the old dead body of a man (laid in the grave) which would produce new life. As far as humans are concerned, when the 'germ of life' departs completely from the body at death, there is nothing left hidden within the body from which new life springs. Moreover, plant seeds decay and remain in the ground. That is not how it will be when the dead are raised; it is pushing the details of the analogy too far. Lenski also calls unwarranted the dogma of some that the Lord's Supper is intended, during this life, to preserve in our bodies this resurrection "germ" which then slumbers in the grave until the resurrection morn (*op. cit.*, p.704).

[107] *Zōopoieō* is substituted here for *egeirō* in the question submitted by the doubter, when he asked "How are the dead raised?" See notes at verse 22 on the meaning of *zōopoieō*, used there of the activity "in Christ" of bringing the dead to life.

point which has already been stated. Far from the decomposition of the body presenting an obstacle to the idea of resurrection, the analogy of planting a seed prepares us for the thought that the body which is to be raised is much more wonderful than the body that was buried.

You do not sow the body which is to be -- When you sow a seed, you do not expect the same seed to come up out of the ground. You do not expect the plant to be simply a reproduction of the seed. Of course, the plant will eventually reproduce the same kind of body (seed) that was sown, but this part of the analogy is not used by Paul. It is implied here that the body which will be raised will not be the same in the sense that the same particles of matter shall compose it. It is the same in the sense that it will have sprung from the one buried. "As the same particles of matter (in the plant world) which are sown do not enter into that which shall be the harvest, so the analogy teaches that the same particles of matter which constitute the body when it dies do not constitute the new body at the resurrection."[108] The identity of the earthly body and the resurrection body is not in the particles that compose them, nor yet in the sameness of structure.[109] Not even Ezekiel's picture of the valley of dry bones may be used to teach this. All conceptions of the resurrection that picture the bodies of the dead returning to their former mundane existence are eliminated by Paul's analogy. Paul's first answer to the question 'How can the body be raised?' is that there will be dissolution but continuity.

But a bare grain -- "Bare" means a mere kernel, without any husk, leaf, blade, or covering of any kind. If a bare kernel is sown, and from that kernel there appears a leaf, stalk, flower, and a whole head of grain, who is to say that when the body is sown that it will not be raised in a more glorious form? There may well be many ornaments and appendages on the resurrection body which were not there when the body died.[110]

Perhaps of wheat or of something else -- Paul is just using wheat for an example. Wheat was the chief food crop in the ancient world, but other types of grain and vegetables also were grown from seeds. The illustration is one with which everyone would be familiar.

---

[108] Barnes, *op. cit.*, p.311. The Greek construction here, *to genēsomenon*, "which is to be," is a rare future participle.

[109] Why should we think the resurrection body must be made of the same particles? Our present physical bodies are not even made up of the same particles during the days of our earthly lives. "As to the matter of the composition of our physical bodies, we are no more the same in two successive moments than is the river that we call by the same name and yet is ever passing" (Kling, *op. cit.*, p.336). Certainly no one can argue there is no "continuity" if our resurrection body is incomparably more glorious than the body that was buried.

[110] Barnes, *ibid*. Caution must be given again about pressing the details of the analogy. Some have attempted to press this verse into duty to prove that souls in the *intermediate state* have bodies. (Appeal is also made to 2 Corinthians 5.) The "body which is to be" (being spoken of here) is the body given at *the time of the resurrection*. The resurrection body is the thrust of Paul's argument against the objector; he is not speaking of a body (allegedly) given in the intermediate state.

15:38 -- *But God gives it a body just as He wished, and to each of the seeds a body of its own.*

But God gives it a body just as He wished -- This point is important. Plants don't just rise of their own volition, and neither do dead bodies. Nor do they do it by chance. God has a hand in it. "The word 'body' here, as applied to grain, seems to mean the whole system of roots, stalks, leaves, flowers, and kernels that grow out of the seed that is sown."[111] There is an interesting change of verb tenses in this verse. "Gives" is present tense, indicating something God does habitually. God is always giving to seeds a body in this way. "Just as He wished" is past tense, pointing back to what seemed good and proper to Him before He created.[112] God doesn't deal with each plant separately on a moment by moment basis, but according to fixed laws which were part of His plan when He formed His eternal purpose. The thrust of the analogy is this: God will raise the dead at the proper time, and give them the proper bodies, just as He causes the seed to grow.

And to each of the seeds a body of its own -- God has fixed proper laws, and He takes care that they shall be observed. "Great oaks from little acorns grow," and not great elms or beeches, nor little currant nor raspberry bushes.[113] So it will be in the resurrection. "How are the dead raised?" you ask. Paul's answer is this: God can give a body exactly suited to man's redeemed nature, a body exactly suited for the heavenly world in which it will live. This is the way God works in the natural realm. We can expect the same working in the spiritual realm.

2. Second objection: *What kind or manner of body is raised?* 15:39-49

15:39 -- *All flesh is not the same flesh, but there is one* flesh *of men, and another flesh of beasts, and another flesh of birds, and another of fish.*

All flesh is not the same flesh -- In case someone doubts whether or not there can be such a great variety of bodies as the last clause of verse 38 implies, Paul simply says 'Look around at your world and see the variety of bodies already in existence.' From here through verse 49 we have Paul's answer to the second question posed in verse 35, "With what kind of body do they come?" While Paul may use the word "flesh", he is talking about "bodies." There are many kinds of bodies, yet they are all bodies. They have different qualities, forms, and properties – yet they are still bodies. The point of the new analogy is that it is not necessary to suppose the body that shall be raised will be precisely like that which we have here. It is certainly possible that there may be as great a differ-

---

[111] Barnes, *op. cit.*, p.311.

[112] Romans 8:28 speaks about God's eternal purpose, i.e., the plan He made back in eternity before He ever began to create. 1 Corinthians 12:18 has spoken of how God placed the members in the body just as it pleased Him. Genesis 1:11,12 says God ordered that bodies be "after its own kind" since the beginning. According to the New Testament, what we call "natural law" is only God providentially ruling the earth in an orderly manner, just as He has since He willed it and created it.

[113] Lenski, *op. cit.*, p.707.

ence between that future body and our present body as there is between the human frame and a reptile, or between a seed and the plant that springs from it. *There will be diversity, but identity* is the point made as to the kind or manner in which the body is raised. It probably will be very different from the body we now have. Yet our resurrection body will be in some way identified with the body we now have. Not only is it not the same seed that comes up for the harvest, but what comes up at the harvest is usually more beautiful than what was planted. Consider tulips. Few things are as ugly as a tulip bulb, yet it produces a beautiful flower. If, at the resurrection, all God did was put us back together again, there would be no improvement. "Flesh and blood cannot inherit the kingdom," Paul will affirm in verse 50. That implies there will be improvement, or adaptability to that new world. Though there will be diversity, still there will be identity. We will still be in the realm of humanity. We will not be exactly like the angels, or other creatures. Our omnipotent and omniscient God has an infinite number of options from which to choose when it comes to body styles. He is not limited in His power and wisdom so that he must make all bodies alike.

But there is *one flesh* of men, and another flesh of beasts, and another flesh of birds, and another of fish -- "Men" (human beings), "fish" and "birds" are clear enough. "Beasts" (*ktēnōn*) is a word usually used of domesticated animals, such as sheep, oxen, and horses. However, in the contrast in this verse, it seems to denote quadrupeds in general. The word *allos* (translated "another") is the Greek word that indicates a comparison of things of like kind. Yet body shapes are different, and so is the texture of the "flesh." We are all acquainted with the idea that "chicken" and "fish" and "beef" (and human flesh?) are different textured meats. Paul is preparing the way for the thought that there can be a difference between the kind or texture of the body we have before the resurrection and the kind or texture we shall have after the resurrection. God is not limited to one kind of body; He can make the kind of body needed by the resurrected ones.[114] In creation God was not restricted to one kind of flesh; four are here enumerated, and are probably intended to stand for all the different kinds of flesh. How can He then be restricted in the resurrection?

15:40 -- *There are also heavenly bodies and earthly bodies, but the glory of the heavenly is one, and the glory of the earthly is another.*

There are also heavenly bodies -- The four varieties of bodies named in verse 39 are all suitable for existence here on earth. There are also bodies of a different kind that are suitable for existence in heaven. Several interpretations have been given to this verse: (1) Angels have bodies, and those bodies differ from men's and animals' bodies. "It is held by many that this is a distinct illustration from that which occurs in the next verse, and that the 'celestial bodies' here spoken of are the bodies of angels, whose appearances on earth are accompanied (Matthew 28:3; Acts 12:7) by a blaze of light."[115] (2) Some see a

---

[114] Shore, *op. cit.*, p.151, has explained, "If we had only seen flesh in the form of one animal, and we were told that 'flesh' could live in the ocean, we might have equally argued, 'How? With what kind of body?' But seeing that there are a variety of bodies in our world, we feel no such difficulty."

[115] Shore, *op. cit.*, p.152.

reference to glorified saints in the intermediate state. On the basis of this verse it is then thought that in the intermediate state the redeemed have bodies. (3) Others believe "heavenly bodies" is explained by verse 41 – i.e., the reference is to the heavenly bodies, such as sun, moon, and stars. Perhaps the KJV reading "celestial bodies" shows this was the view of the translators of that version. While the first option is intriguing, this third one is probably correct. Paul is not speaking about bodies, one class of which we cannot see. He is speaking about bodies, all of which we can see – and we thus can get some idea that the doctrine of the resurrection of the body really has no insuperable objections against it. If this referred to some bodies that men have never seen, say the bodies of angels or of men in the intermediate state, it would have little bearing on the argument being made.[116]

And earthly bodies -- The KJV has "terrestrial bodies." Paul refers to the bodies of men, beasts, birds, fish, as enumerated in verse 39. These bodies were created for this earth, and they are suitable for living on this earth. Bodies that will inhabit heaven are different. See how God can make a body exactly suited to the place where it will dwell. Fish have bodies suited to their water environment. Birds have bodies suited to their air environment. Man's physical body is suited to this atmosphere environment. (One needs space equipment to leave this environment.) So it will be with the resurrection body. God can make it so it will be exactly suited to that eternal dwelling place.

But the glory of the heavenly is one -- Paul has made the point that earthly bodies differ from heavenly bodies. Now he is making the point that when one limits himself to one sphere (whether heavenly bodies, or earthly), he finds even more startling variation. He finds diversity! "Glory" talks about splendor, beauty, dignity, magnificence. If he is comparing the bodies of angels, they are not all alike (some angels have six wings, some four, some two); there are archangels, cherubim, and seraphim. If he is comparing the sun, moon, and stars, they do not appear to us to all be alike.[117]

And the glory of the earthly is another -- "Another" represents *heteros*, the Greek word which indicates a comparison of things of a different kind. We might translate it "different." Earthly organisms have a different way of manifesting themselves than the heavenly. Can it be thought strange if there should be a difference between our earthly bodies and our heavenly bodies (after the resurrection)? God who has wrought all the wonders of heaven and earth is most certainly able to perform what has been promised with

---

[116] "Heavenly bodies" has even been used to show that there is life on other planets. Whether or not there is such life, it is undoubtedly pressing this verse too far to draw such a conclusion from it.

[117] Lenski, *op. cit.*, p.709, calls attention to the fact that "Paul is not addressing a group of chemists regarding the molecular or atomic structure of heavenly and earthly bodies. He is writing to plain, ordinary people regarding a matter that all of them constantly see. The fact that the material of which all of these bodies in our universe are composed is quite the same (so the present scientific theory suggests) really helps Paul's thought; it certainly causes no interference with it. Although their structure is the same, their appearance is vastly different. Although the substance of our human bodies is the same whether they are lying in the grave, or are glorified in the resurrection, their appearance in these two states is vastly different."

regard to the resurrection.

15:41 -- *There is one glory of the sun, and another glory of the moon, and another glory of the stars; for star differs from star in glory.*

There is one glory of the sun, and another glory of the moon, and another glory of the stars -- It seems best to understand this verse as a continuation of the discussion begun in the previous verse. The "heavenly bodies" there spoken of are here identified. "Another" translates *allos*, 'another of the same kind.' There is a "glory" of the same kind among the different heavenly bodies. It is not only that the heavenly bodies differ from earthly, but when it comes to "glory" they differ from each other, sun from moon, moon from stars.[118] To put it another way, there is a diversity between the heavenly bodies (like the sun, moon, and stars) and yet there is identity (in that they are all heavenly bodies).

For star differs from star in glory -- To the observer on earth, the stars differ from one another in size and luster. Some are bright, some dim; some steady, some pulsating or twinkling.[119] The point of the analogy is that with all these known and obvious differences between "bodies" in our universe, why should it be thought impossible for God to make a resurrection body that differs greatly from our present human body. Cannot our God work out diversity and identity at the same time?

15:42 -- *So also is the resurrection of the dead. It is sown a perishable* **body,** *it is raised an imperishable* **body;**

So also is the resurrection of the dead -- With "so,"[120] Paul begins to make direct application to the subject at hand ("With what kind of body do they come?") of all the analogies he has given (i.e., different kinds of bodies and different degrees of glory). The Greek reads "the dead" – an article of previous reference.[121] He is talking about the same "dead (bodies)" that has been the topic since 15:1. Just as certainly as there are different bodies on earth and in heaven, the same is true when it comes to comparing our earthly bodies with our heavenly bodies: there shall be dissolution but continuity, and there shall be diversity but identity. To emphasize the diversity, four statements are now made, and each statement forms a pair. Each phrase describes the condition of the body – first, when it is buried; secondly, when it is raised.

---

[118] As before, we suppose the differences between sun, moon, stars, describe them as they appear to us, looking at them from the earth.

[119] Daniel 12:3 tells us the righteous shall shine "like the brightness of the expanse of heaven and ... like the stars forever and ever." Since the analogy has something to do with the resurrection body (verse 42), is it appropriate to say 'star differing from star in glory' is further evidence of degrees of honor and glory after the resurrection? Or is that pushing the details too far?

[120] *Houtōs kai* is the expression we are used to when Paul wants to apply an analogy. See 2:11, 12:12, 14:9,12; Galatians 4:3; Romans 6:11.

[121] See notes at 15:29 on the article of previous reference.

It is sown a perishable *body* -- "It" is the body, not the soul. Thus, "it is sown" is to be understood figuratively: like a seed being "sown" in the ground, the dead body is buried in the grave.[122] "Perishable" reminds us of "You are dust, and to dust you shall return"

---

[122] Some Bible students have wondered whether the proper way to dispose of a dead body is by burial or cremation. When Paul says "it is sown," he certainly pictures the body being treated like a seed that is planted. It assumes the Corinthian Christians were burying their dead.

(1) There was no uniform way to dispose of dead bodies in the ancient world. In Egypt bodies were mummified, because they believed preservation of the body was essential for the next life. Cremation (the disposal of the dead body by reducing it to ashes) was common in the ancient world. Celts, Norsemen, Aztecs and American Indians all burned dead bodies. Hindus believe the corpse must be completely consumed to allow the spirit to depart to a new body (reincarnation). With the spread of Buddhism, cremation also spread to the Far East. Japanese and Burmese practiced cremation. Cremation was common in Greece, and then in the Roman Empire. Some in the ancient world buried their dead. China, Tibet, (in more modern times, the Baha'is), and Orthodox Jews have always buried, though many did not believe in the resurrection of the body. In the *Talmud* cremation is condemned as a heathen practice.

(2) What follows is a short study of the disposal of dead bodies in Scripture. There are some examples of bodies being burned in Old Testament times. The bodies of King Saul and his sons were burned by the men of Jabesh-Gilead (1 Samuel 31:11-13) to prevent further desecration of the dead bodies by the Philistines; later, their bones were buried. Amos 2:1-3 is a specific instance of God's condemnation of the Moabites because they had burned "to lime" the bones of the king of Edom. Was the burning of the bones a way to dishonor the king who previously had been an ally of Judah? In the time of the Prophets, and among the Hebrews, cremation was held in detestation because it was something their enemies did to the bodies of dead Israelis. No greater insult, no more horrible evidence of brutality, was possible. (Here, the burning was not just disposing of the dead body by loved ones. It was an act of an enemy to show spite.) God's people sometimes burned the bodies of God's enemies. It was an act of desecration because of their sins against God. Moses and his people burned Achan and his household, after they had stoned them to death, as an expression of God's wrath against them (Joshua 7:25). Josiah defiled (polluted) the idolatrous altar at Bethel and the bones of the opponents of God by burning the bones upon the cursed altar (1 Kings 13:2). By taking the bones to burn, Josiah dishonored the bones of the dead. There are examples of burial being practiced among the family of God. Abraham purchased a cave for Sarah's burial (Genesis 23:1-4, 50:13). Later Abraham, Isaac and Rebekah, Jacob and Leah were buried (Genesis 49:29-32). The bones of Joseph were brought from Egypt in the Exodus and buried (Joshua 24:32; cf. Genesis 50:25; Exodus 13:19). When God wanted to dispose of Moses' body, we are told God "buried" him (Deuteronomy 34:5-6).

(3) Christianity got its practice of "burial" from several sources: (a) From Jewish practices, "as the practice of the Jews is to bury" (John 19:40). (b) From what was done with the body of Jesus ("He was buried ...," 1 Corinthians 15:4). (c) From something Jesus said one day ("Let the dead bury the dead ...," John 8:22, which acknowledges the common practice in His day). (d) From the burials recorded in the book of Acts. E.g., the bodies of Ananias and Sapphira were buried by Christian young men (Acts 5), and Stephen was buried by devout men (Acts 7). No specific verse teaches the "Christian" way dead bodies must be treated. (We have examples and apostolic precedent, but no express commands.)

(4) A short history of the practice of cremation in the Western world will help us understand our present situation. As a result of the spread of Christianity, cremation gave way to burial from the 2nd century AD and later. Cremation ceased in Western Europe by the 5th century AD because of the influence of Christianity. Charlemagne (AD 789) made it a capital offense to cremate a pagan body according to the pagan rite. Cremation was done in rare emergencies – e.g., to stop a plague, or to dispose of massive numbers of bodies resulting from the plague. Martyrs were burned at stake. Late in the 19th century, the practice of cremation began to be revived in Europe. Laws were passed recognizing it as an acceptable funeral custom. Proponents appealed to public hygiene and conservation of the land. The Catholic Church continued to forbid Catholics to cremate as they had done since the decretal by Boniface VIII in AD 1300. Freethinkers practiced cremation to ridicule Christian belief in the resurrection of the body. The Catholic Church prohibited cremation for its members from 1886 to 1963. The ban began to be relaxed in America as the 20th century came to a close. Late in the 1900s, some U.S. Catholics began to encourage cremation as a protest to lavish funerals that put an overemphasis on the importance of the body.

(Genesis 3:19; Ecclesiastes 12:7). When the body is put in the grave, it decays, becomes disorganized, and finally become dust. "Perishable" reminds us that the body begins to die as soon as it is born (and this has been the rule ever since "death" became the penalty to the race when Adam sinned). Part of our body dies every day.[123] A layer of dead skin cells is washed off, and new ones take its place. All the cells of the body change every 7 years. But the time comes when the "dying" takes precedence over the replacement. 100,000 nerve cells die every day when we get older, which explains why we have trouble remembering, and why it is harder to learn. When physical death occurs, there is no longer any replacement at all, only decay and disintegration.

It is raised an imperishable *body* -- "Imperishable" (*aphtharsia*) means the resurrection body will not be liable to decay, sickness, disorganization and return to dust. Peter spoke of the future as "an inheritance which is imperishable and undefiled, and will not fade away" (1 Peter 1:4). Not only will the dwelling place be imperishable, so will the bodies of those who live there. The subject of this second phrase is identical with that of the first phrase. The identical body that is first buried is afterward raised. We still have the point being made concerning the relationship of the resurrection body to the present body – that there is diversity but identity. Here we have a direct answer to those who deny the actual bodily resurrection, and believe only in a spiritual resurrection. Paul's presentation here is that of life in a new body, not just some immortality of the soul living on in some shadowy, ghostly existence. "The chief objection the typical Greek had to any doctrine of resurrection was that the body was essentially perishable (corruptible). The Greek looked, accordingly, for a future when the soul would be untrammelled and unlimited by such a frail, sickly, dying body."[124] Paul replies that one does not have to think of always having a perishable body. It is possible for God to change the body so that it is no longer "dying" as it has been for all humans since Adam sinned.

---

(5) Some guidelines for our thinking: (a) It has been argued that cremation was practiced in the ancient world precisely among those peoples who did not have a Biblical respect for the body. (b) The act of body disposal by cremation does not make it harder for a resurrection body to be available. (What about bodies buried at sea, or carrion eaten by scavenger birds? What about the bodies that have become fertilizer for trees and plants? Does cremation provide any more of a problem for God when it comes time to raise those bodies?) (c) The resurrection body is not made up of collected and assembled particles of the dead physical body, so we don't have to worry about them being "collected", as though cremation and scattering ashes would make that harder for God to do. (d) Some argue cremation only speeds the natural process of the body returning to dust. (e) Christians should have a respect for the body. Dispose of it in a way that reflects that respect. (f) Cremation is becoming more popular in U.S., simply because the cost of cremation is much lower than the cost of interring a dead body in the ground. Some would argue cremation is good stewardship. (g) Burial is the pattern found in Scripture, and has historically been followed by the church. Some argue that burial is an important symbol in Scripture, whereas cremation is a poor symbol of Scriptural truth.

[123] See the feature, "I am Joe's Skin" *Reader's Digest*, 1972.

[124] Morris, *op. cit.*, p.226.

15:43 -- *it is sown in dishonor, it is raised in glory; it is sown in weakness, it is raised in power;*

It is sown in dishonor -- "Dishonor" translates *atimia*, a word sometimes used of loss of citizenship. A corpse has no rights, except, perhaps for a decent burial. Sometimes men do try to honor the body of the deceased (e.g., fine clothes, fine caskets, elaborate services), but we do not want to keep the dead body around very long. It is hurried away from the sight of friends because it soon becomes an offensive mass turning to decay. Paul continues to pick out those features of this earthly life which seemed to the Greeks to demonstrate the folly of the idea of resurrection, and he continues to show that they have no relevance to the resurrection body God is going to give.

It is raised in glory -- "In honor, in beauty. Honored by God, and in a form and manner that shall be glorious."[125] This does not mean that the honor and glory are merely heaped upon it from the outside, but the body itself is made glorious. Perhaps it is like Christ's body at the time of the Transfiguration, radiant and shining (Mark 8:28). It certainly is like the glorified body Jesus now has. Paul is still talking only of the resurrection of the righteous, when he says the body is to be raised in honor and dignity. That new body will be the exact opposite of that which people are reluctant to keep around very long.

It is sown in weakness -- There are few things weaker than a dead body. When the spirit leaves the body, it is miserably weak. A corpse is perfectly powerless, incapable of even resisting corruption. "All of its strength is gone. Not enough strength is left to draw one breath."[126]

It is raised in power -- We do not know all that is involved in the "power, glory, imperishable" mentioned by Paul. But the resurrection body will be filled with the ability to do all that the new state requires. Concerning "power", this is not power as we know it now in our living bodies, but transcendent power, beyond all that our minds can now conceive. We shall have the fresh and eternal energy of the new body free from disease and pain. We shall be free from the limitations of the earthly body. We will still be humanity, but it will be an improved model. Our resurrection body will be like the glorified body Jesus now has (cf. Philippians 3:20,21; 1 John 3:2). Since in His glorified body Jesus was no longer subject to time and space limitations, perhaps we too will not be dependent on modes of transportation; when we want to go from one place to another, likely there will be no waiting on a bus or a plane. After His resurrection, Jesus' body was such that when people saw Him, they recognized Him as the Son of Man (Revelation 1:9ff). Yet it could also appear in a different form (Mark 16:12). And it seems that the marks of the nails are still visible in His glorified body, but they are no handicap. Perhaps 1 Peter 5:10 indicates that parts of the body that were amputated or lost by accident or persecution in this life will be replaced in the next. God made our present physical bodies suitable for

---

[125] Barnes, *op. cit.*, p.314.

[126] Lenski, *op. cit.*, p.712.

this world, and He will fashion the resurrection body anew, suitable for the heavenly. A man sows seed, expecting a harvest. Something greater than what he sowed is what he gets at harvest time. So the body is sown, expecting a greater harvest.

15:44 -- *it is sown a natural body, it is raised a spiritual body. If there is a natural body, there is also a spiritual* body.

It is sown a natural body -- See notes at 2:14 on "natural" (*psuchikos*). The translation in some of our older versions, "physical," gives the wrong connotation now, though it didn't used to. "Physical" now means 'that which is composed of or has to do with matter.' Paul is not describing the components that make up the body. He is speaking of what animates the body. A "natural body" (*sōma psuchikon*) is a body that is animated by a soul.[127] It is the type of body perfectly suited to a being who is 'soulical.' It is able to respond to the directions of the soul. It is the type of body in which we exist in this world.

It is raised a spiritual body -- After the general resurrection, the righteous will have spiritual bodies. The new body is not going to be exactly like the one we have now. There will be identity, yes, but diversity. In the resurrection, our bodies (which are now natural bodies) will be changed so that they are "spiritual bodies." The distinction in verse 44 is not between material versus immaterial.[128] The new body may be material, but it will have different properties than the body we now possess. It will be a body dominated and animated by our "spirit" (*pneuma*) rather than by the animal (*psuchē*) impulses. Shore has used a beautiful analogy to explain:

> The body which a plant has when it is a "seed" is perfectly suited to its condition as a seed. The "body" which it has as a grown up plant is perfectly suited to the changed condition in which the plant now exists. This adaptability in plants is not accidental, but a purposeful variety. The same thing can be said about adaptability of our bodies to the realm where we are living. The body which we have here on earth is suited with a marvelous detail of adaptability to the life, physical and intellectual, amid which we are placed, and of which we form a part.

---

[127] This commentator teaches that man is made up of body, soul, and spirit. God intended that the spirit should give directions to the soul, which in turn animates the body. That is the way things work until a man commits his first sin. But once he commits that first sin, his spirit fails to function as originally intended; the Bible says the man has died 'spiritually,' and the man has become what the Bible calls "fleshly" (i.e., dominated by his body), or "natural" (dominated by the soul). Both these parts are subject to temptation and eventually to slavery to the devil. The new birth restores the spirit part of man back to life ("that which is born of Spirit is spirit," John 3:6), and under the direction of the indwelling Holy Spirit, the man's spirit is able to direct the man in Godly paths. What Paul tells us here in 1 Corinthians about a natural body indicates that our present body is naturally attuned to and suited to getting directions from the soul. The resurrection body, being a spiritual body, will be naturally attuned to getting directions directly from our spirits.

[128] That by "spiritual" here in verse 44 and 46 Paul means completely immaterial is incompatible with the whole context, which discusses the differing organizations of material substance. To say the resurrection body is going to be a "spiritual body" does not mean that the body will be constituted entirely and only of 'spirit,' anymore than "natural (*psuchikon*) bodies" means that our present body is composed only of soul (*psuchē*).

This physical body can be a hindrance to the spiritual man in each of us (see 2 Corinthians 5 and Romans 7). There will come a time (the time when we have been raised in our glorified "spiritual bodies") for each man when the body will become as perfectly adapted to the spiritual man in each of us as the human body here is to the natural man – no longer its hindrance, but its help. That glorified body will answer to the needs of the "willing spirit," and will not ever hamper or hinder the spirit from expressing itself.[129]

If there is a natural body, there is also a spiritual *body* -- Paul wants to make sure his readers understand what he means by "natural body" and "spiritual body" so he uses an analogy between Adam and Christ to explain. The ASV/NASB rightly makes the first phrase a condition and the second the conclusion, "*If* there is a natural body, *then* (just as certainly) there is also a spiritual body." According to the manuscript authority evidence, the word "body" does not occur in the Greek in this last phrase. The Greek simply reads "spiritual" (an adjective), and we very naturally supply the noun ("body") from the first clause in the verse. No one can deny that the natural body exists, a body related to the *psuchē* ("soul"). Well, if man also has a "spirit," is it unreasonable to affirm that there can be a body related to this? The emphatic assertion that there are two "bodies"[130] for man – one that is physical and one that is spiritual, as truly as seed and a blossom are two bodies yet the same plant – is introductory to the further thought expanded in the following verse.

15:45 -- *So also it is written, "The first MAN, Adam, BECAME A LIVING SOUL." The last Adam* **became** *a life-giving spirit.*

So also it is written -- Characteristically, Paul appeals to Scripture and what happened to Christ to clench his argument. His appeal to Scripture is intended to make sure "natural body" is an understandable term. "It is written" introduces a quotation from Scripture, Genesis 2:7.[131] Paul intends to say that, when he speaks about a "natural body," he is speaking of the same kind of body which Adam had, made of the dust of the ground, and animated by a soul. When God finished His creative work on man, we read "man ... a living soul" (KJV). If the first Adam was a living *psuchē*, he must have had a *psuchikon* body.

The first MAN, Adam, BECAME A LIVING SOUL -- This is quoted from the LXX, except that the apostle has added the words "first" and "Adam" (see how parts of the quota-

---

[129] Shore, *op. cit.*, p.153. [A few omissions and additions have been made by this commentator.]

[130] Paul's presentation here is in marked contrast with that of Judaism in general. The rabbis supposed that any body that might be raised would be identical with the body that died. The writer of the *Apocalypse of Baruch* (a pseudepigraphical work) asked whether there will be any change when men rise, and the answer is, "the earth shall then assuredly restore the dead. ... It shall make no change in their form, but as it has received, so shall it restore them" (xlix.2,3; l.2,2). Neither Paul (see verses 42ff. and 52) nor Jesus (Matthew 22:23-33) will have anything to do with this view.

[131] The Greek here is not the usual formula of citation, *kathōs gegraptai*, but *houtōs kai gegraptai*, "So it is written." Paul is saying his use of "natural man" is just like ("so") what the Scripture says.

tion are in small caps in the NASB).[132]   Both the Hebrew and the LXX read, "Man became a living soul." Genesis 2:7 is proof that mankind, descended from Adam, now lives in a natural (a soulical) body. "Soul" comes from the same word group as the word translated "natural" in verse 44. When Paul writes about a "natural body," it is the very thing Genesis 2:7 talks about when Adam is called a "living soul."[133]

The last Adam -- Paul's quotation from Genesis 2:7 ended with the statement concerning Adam becoming a living soul. Paul appeals to Christ to make sure "spiritual body" is a clearly understood term. Earlier in this chapter (verses 21,22), Paul has already employed an Adam-Christ analogy. His language in this verse presupposes his readers will remember its use earlier.[134] In essence, Paul's point now is that there is more to the analogy "as in Adam all die, so also in Christ all shall be made alive" than the simple fact of resurrection. Involved, too, is what kind of body the resurrection body will be. We get our natural body from the first Adam; we get our spiritual body from the last Adam, Christ. Paul could show from Scripture the truth of a natural body. He appeals to the resurrection of Jesus – an event he has amply shown to be an historical fact – as the proof of our coming "spiritual bodies."

---

[132] Lenski, *op. cit.*, p.717, calls attention to what Bible critics say at this place. Paul is taken to task by some modern Bible critics for reproducing this passage in the fuller form, "*The first* man *Adam* became a living soul." Paul is charged with a rabbinical and targumistic practice which adds all manner of remarks to a Scripture text as though they belonged to the original. The specific charge is that Paul put into the quotation the very thought which he intended to draw out of it and thus deliberately altered the Scripture quotation in his own interest. But when Paul adds the word "first" and the name "Adam," he in no wise changes the sense of the original. These additions are intended only to aid Paul's readers in understanding the original sense of the Old Testament passage. It was simpler to do it this way, than to add several phrases of exegetical explanation, and then take up his argument again.

[133] "Living soul" is *nephesh hayyah* in the Hebrew. Our use of "soul" gives the word a bit different connotation than the Biblical usage. We usually apply the word "soul" to the intelligent and the immortal part of man; that which reasons, thinks, remembers, is conscious. The Greek and Hebrew words (*psuchē*, Greek; *nephesh*, Hebrew) more properly denote that which is alive, which is animated, which breathes. The animals are also called *nephesh hayyah* in Genesis 1:20,21,24, and 2:19. How then does man differ from the animals? (1) One not quite satisfactory answer sometimes given to this question is that the superiority ascribed to man in the history of creation is found in the fact that "God breathed into his nostrils the breath of life" (plural in the Hebrew – breath of "lives"). In this it is intimated that, in the act of becoming a living soul, man at the same time was endowed with higher capacities, which brought him into relationship with God, and made him capable of communing with Him, and so of rising to spiritual existence. God – by a special act – gave life to man. Before the creation, there were spiritual beings (angels). Before man's creation, there were brute animals that lived. But when God created man, this was a new being. There was nothing like this. He was a new being clothed with a flesh and blood body. If this new creature could have partaken of the tree of life, he would have lived forever. (2) There is a better answer to the question about man's superiority to animals. Man is superior to animals because only of man is it said he is "created in the image of God" (Genesis 1:27).

[134] Instead of appealing to verses 21,22 for the connection Paul here makes between Adam and Christ, some have affirmed that Genesis 2:7 *implies* what Paul here asserts. The Hebrew for "man" is '*adam*, a collective noun. Adam was the first man; so we might expect a "second" one, or a "last" one. And Genesis speaks both of "breath of lives" (spirit) as well as "living soul" (natural, physical).

***Became* a life-giving spirit**[135] -- Adam was merely a "living soul." Christ is a "life-giving spirit."[136] When it comes to the "natural body," Adam was the recipient; when it comes to the "spiritual body," Christ is the Giver! John 5:21 tells us that "just as the Father raises the dead and gives them life, even so the Son also gives life to whom He wishes."[137] Not only is Christ's glorified body the prototype of men's resurrection bodies, but He is the source of the life that results in resurrection bodies and the glories of heaven for the redeemed. Christ, by His redemptive work, was qualified to be the life-giving spirit (Romans 5:19). He died for all, and came out of the grave. He is the resurrection and the life. One day He will come to earth again; He will speak and the dead will rise (John 5:28,29). Those new, resurrection bodies are the "spiritual bodies" Paul has been describing. When Paul writes that He became a life-giving "spirit," he does not mean Christ discarded His body and that He now exists in heaven only as a spirit. Elsewhere Paul says that because Christ was "obedient to the point of death, even death on a cross," God has "super highly exalted" Him (Philippians 2:8,9). Jesus has something now – a glorified human body – that He didn't have before He became incarnate. Instead of discarding a body, He has a glorified body.

15:46 -- *However, the spiritual is not first, but the natural; then the spiritual.*

However, the spiritual is not first, but the natural; then the spiritual -- Commentators have puzzled over why this whole verse is introduced here. It begins with *alla*, the strong adversative.[138] "However" seems to indicate that this verse is aimed at the Corinthians (at least the "some" from verse 12 who were insisting there is no resurrection) to correct their views and arguments.

---

[135] This phrase has no verb in the original, so the NASB has supplied "became," which tends to cause readers to raise the question, "When did Christ become this life-giving spirit?" Answers to the question vary from commentary to commentary. (1) Some say at the creation (or even before the creation). Then we are told that God created both Adams, the one with a natural, the other with a spiritual body; the one only living, the other life-giving. And then a search is made to find the source from which Paul copied his ideas (with hopes of finding it in some pagan Hellenistic or Jewish source). This whole view is only a modern revival of ancient Gnosticism, and we reject it as being anti-Scriptural. (2) Some say at the incarnation. Then we are told Christ did not have a human nature, since at His birth He became a "spirit." This flatly contradicts numerous passages. (3) Some say Christ became a life-giving spirit at the time the Holy Spirit came upon Him at His baptism. This view is akin to docetism, and we reject it. (4) The proper answer to the question: at His resurrection and glorification Christ literally and historically "became the last Adam ..., a life-giving spirit." The whole context here in 1 Corinthians 15 emphasizes Christ's resurrection from the grave; it is the hinge of Paul's whole argument.

[136] See notes at 15:22 on *zōopoieō* ("made alive").

[137] Some speak of the rising to walk in "newness of life" (Romans 6:4) as also being included in Christ's work as "life-giving spirit." Lenski for example (*op. cit.*, p.722) says, "This giving of life to us begins in our regeneration ... The consummation of this work is the resurrection and glorification of our bodies ... 'who will transform the body of our humble state into conformity with the body of His glory, by the exertion of the power that He has even to subject all things to Himself' (Philippians 3:21)."

[138] The adversative is left untranslated in the NIV.

In Greek, the negative adverb is placed immediately before the word it negates. In this case the word order shows it is not the verb, but the word "first" that is negated. But why would Paul tell the Corinthians that the "spiritual is *not* first"? (1) Perhaps he is refuting an argument given by the "some" who say there is no resurrection. Did the opponents of resurrection hold a Greek philosophical view similar to the views held by Philo (d. AD 50), who taught that the "spiritual" Adam predated the "natural" Adam?[139] If this is the background for Paul's statement, Paul is saying that whole philosophical view is flatly wrong. The "spiritual was *not* first!" (2) Perhaps Paul is alluding to the fact that some at Corinth thought themselves already to be "spiritual" (see 3:1). They didn't have to wait until the second coming to be spiritual, they may have been thinking. 'Well,' says Paul, 'they have things backwards!' "Then" in "then the spiritual" points to the second coming when dead bodies are raised in glorious form. The natural body is first, in this life. The spiritual body is next, afterwards, in the next life. A man becomes like the first Adam at birth. He becomes like the last Adam when he experiences resurrection. This assertion that the natural body precedes the spiritual body is developed in the following verses.

15:47 -- *The first man is from the earth, earthy; the second man is from heaven.*

The first man is from the earth -- Paul is not done with his Adam-Christ analogy, nor with his use of Genesis 2:7 and the resurrection of Jesus. When he is finished, and we have thought his thoughts after him, we will have a fuller answer to the question "with what kind of body do they come?" "From the earth" probably should be taken as qualitative ("of the earth," ASV), rather than speaking of origin. Adam's "natural body" was exactly suited for life here on earth.

Earthy -- This is the reason his body was suited for an earthly existence. It was "made of earth," or, as the NASB margin reads, "made of dust." The first Adam was a mass of animated clay, and could be appropriately called "dust" (Genesis 3:17). The word *choikos* (from *choō*, 'to pour') means the "soil" was loosened and heaped up, rather than just particles of dust.

The second man is from heaven -- The point of this phrase is the difference between "of the earth" and "from heaven." We treat them both as qualitative.[140] Just as Adam's body

---

[139] Philo propounded the idea of two "Adams" based on the duplicate narrative of Genesis 1 and Genesis 2 – the ideal "man after the image of God" (chapter 1) and the actual "man of the dust of the earth" (chapter 2). Those source critics who say Paul got his idea for a "first and last Adam" and an "earthly and heavenly Adam" from Philo (or from the same prevalent theology that Philo himself copied) ignore the following: (1) Philo's first is Paul's last Adam. (2) Both of Paul's Adams are equally concrete men. (3) The resurrection of Christ distinguishes their respective periods, a crisis the conception of which is foreign to Philo's theology of natural development. (4) Moreover, Genesis 1:26 (referred to in 1 Corinthians 11:7,8) speaks of the historical, not the ideal, first man. Fee (*op. cit.*, p.791) documents that Gnostics eventually held the same views that Philo did, namely that the spiritual man was first.

[140] Those who treat "of earth" and "of heaven" (KJV) as referring to the "origin" of Adam and Christ have assigned different meanings to "of heaven." (1) Some think it speaks of Christ's incarnation. This passage was used by the early Gnostics to sustain their doctrine that our Lord was not really born of the

was exactly suited for life here on earth, Christ's glorified body is exactly suited for life in heaven. Paul wrote the term "earthy" in the first statement about Adam to describe him. It is a textual question whether Paul wrote a term to match "earthy" in his statement about the second Adam.[141] "Perhaps Paul left the place for a correlative term in this clause about Christ blank. We suggest he did this because human language affords no term which may describe the substance of Christ's glorified body without the fear of misunderstanding."[142] Now we have a better understanding of Paul's term "spiritual body." Perhaps one further word will help.

15:48 -- *As is the earthy, so also are those who are earthy; and as is the heavenly, so also are those who are heavenly.*

As is the earthy, so also are those who are earthy -- In verses 48 and 49 we have two pairs of balanced sentences in which Paul further explains what "natural" (soulical) and "spiritual" mean. The *psuchikon* body belongs only to the present earthly existence. Our bodies now are just like Adam's body – animated by a "soul" (*psuchē*). All of us humans are by physical descent the children of Adam who was "earthy" (see verse 47). As such, our distinguishing mark is the fact that we are earthy just like the first Adam. All Adam's descendants have the same basic characteristics, i.e., earthy. He ate, breathed, lived, died – just as we all shall. Men bear his likeness in at least two respects. We are living souls, and our bodies are subject to corruption and decay. The expressions we had in verses 42-44 (corruption, dishonor, weakness, natural) explain what the 'likeness' of Adam is.

And as is the heavenly, so also are those who are heavenly -- "As is the heavenly" says that Christ now still has His glorified body. Our resurrection bodies, our glorified bodies,

---

Virgin Mary, but was clothed with a body derived from heaven. (2) F.C. Baur has spoken of the "heavenly Christ" as being the pre-existent Christ, and writes much of *Urmensch* – a prototype of humanity, existing thus, either in fact or simply in God's mind – a copy of which man was eventually a "working model." But to make "heavenly Christ" a reference to Christ's pre-existence misses what was just said in verse 46, which has the natural man first. To make the "heavenly Christ" a reference to pre-existence, misses the point of the whole context which speaks of Resurrection. (3) Since the whole chapter has emphasized Christ's resurrection, not a few writers find another reference to His resurrection body; it was a "heavenly" body, a glorified body. In Christ's case, after He wore the natural body, He wore the heavenly body. (4) Some have supposed "from heaven" looks forward to Christ's second advent, the time when men who once wore a natural body will be clothed upon with their heavenly body. Paul is telling his readers when the dead can expect to get their "spiritual body." It is when Christ comes back "from heaven." All of this discussion is irrelevant if Paul is emphasizing *quality* rather than *origin*.

[141] "Some manuscripts read "the Lord," and this is supposed by some to be the matching descriptor. The KJV follows these manuscripts. We should probably omit "the Lord" since the term is not found in *Aleph*, A, B, C, D, F, G. (Some "KJV only" advocates will pounce on this verse and insist the neutral text waters down the deity of Jesus since it omits "Lord." However, there are numerous places, such as John 1:18, where the neutral text is stronger on the deity of Jesus than the text followed by the KJV.) P[46] has *pneumatikos* ("spiritual") in this second phrase, and this then contrasts to "earthy" that was said of the first Adam. Some Latin manuscripts add "heavenly."

[142] Lenski, *op. cit.*, p.725.

will be the same kind of body that the resurrected and glorified Christ now has.[143]

15:49 -- *And just as we have borne the image of the earthy, we shall also bear the image of the heavenly.*

And just as we have borne the image of the earthy -- There was no question in the minds of either Paul or of the Corinthian converts that all men at present are earthy, that we now have a body like Adam's. "Actually, both verb tenses in this verse view the situation from the moment of the resurrection at the last day. At that moment, we can say, 'We did bear (aorist)' the earthly body; and we can say 'We shall bear forever (future tense)' the heavenly body."[144]

We shall also bear the image of the heavenly -- Here is Paul's simple summary of his answer to the question, "With what kind of bodies do they come?" "We shall bear" translates *ephoresamen*, 'to wear like a garment.'[145] The future tense points to the time of Christ's appearing, and from that time onward we shall 'wear' the same kind of glorified, resurrected body that Christ now wears. The word "image" which Paul uses is very expressive. *Eikon* is used of man who is made in the "image" of God (Genesis 1:26). The word always "supposes a prototype, that which it not merely resembles, but from which it is drawn – as a monarch's head on a coin, the sun's reflection in the water, a statue in stone or metal ...."[146] The shape and makeup of our natural bodies, indeed, is derived from the earthly one, Adam. The shape and makeup of our spiritual bodies is derived from the Heavenly One, Christ. It is an "image" that corresponds to and reproduces the original. Now we, too, know the answer to the question, "with what kind of bodies do they come?" We have a good mental image drawn from the body of the risen Christ.

---

[143] See this astounding but Scriptural truth documented above in notes under "raised in power."

[144] Lenski, *op. cit.*, p.729.

[145] There is a variation in the manuscripts at this place, some having future indicative (*phoresomen*) and some an aorist subjunctive (*phoresōmen*). B, 17, 46 are the authority for this future tense. P[46], Aleph, A, C, D, E, F, G, K, L, P support this subjunctive, and this reading is reflected in the ASV/NASB marginal note.
If we adopt the subjunctive reading, this phrase becomes an exhortation based on the idea that our attaining unto a glorified body depends upon our own faithfulness to Christ. "Let us try to be like the man from Heaven" is how Goodspeed translated it. If we take it as subjunctive, then the exhortation is expressive of the idea that the resurrection life is begun in us even in this life. "If by any means I can attain to the resurrection of the dead" (Philippians 3:11 ASV). It might even be implied that only faithful Christians get to keep their resurrection bodies. Those who are consigned to the "second death" would be thought of as losing their resurrection bodies. Fee (*op. cit.*, p.795) regards the subjunctive as the original reading, and thinks Paul intentionally used it "as a way of calling his readers to prepare now for the future that is to be."
Since the manuscript evidence is about equally divided, textual scholars have advanced reasons why the indicative was likely the original reading. New copies of the Scriptures were written by scribes as a reader read from another roll. You can spell a Greek word correctly if you hear it pronounced correctly. The scribes could easily mistake the one reading for the other as they were listening and writing, especially if the reader were not careful in his pronunciation. There was a universal tendency by later copyists to substitute hortative for direct forms, with a view to edification.

[146] Lenski, *op. cit.*, p.730.

C. Explanation of What Becomes of Those Who are Still Alive on Earth When Jesus Returns to Raise the Dead. 15:50-58

> *Summary:* Perhaps someone at Corinth had a further argument against resurrection. It was, "What about the living? Are they going to inhabit heaven in their present bodies?" In verses 50-57, Paul argues for the absolute necessity of transformation in order for believers to enter their heavenly existence. Transformation must take place, whether believers are dead or alive, if they are to be in bodies suitable for the future kingdom of God.

15:50 -- *Now I say this, brethren, that flesh and blood cannot inherit the kingdom of God; nor does the perishable inherit the imperishable.*

Now I say this, brethren -- "Now this I say" is the phrase with which Paul was accustomed to introduce a statement of profound significance (cf. 1:12, 7:29). We choose to treat verse 50 as the beginning of a new paragraph, rather than as the conclusion of the previous one.[147] If it were a summary we would expect the opening word to be *gar* or *oun*, not *de*. No longer is Paul's argument based on analogies. This is his own authoritative declaration (*phēmi*) that allows no concession to any who might tend to disagree. In the preceding paragraph, two objections to the resurrection were answered. (1) How is resurrection possible after the body has been dissolved in the grave? Answer: The difficulty is the other way. Resurrection would be impossible without such dissolution. (2) What kind of body do the risen have, if the present body is not restored? Answer: A body similar to that of the risen Lord, i.e., a body as suitable to the spiritual condition of the new life as the material body is suited to the present physical life. (3) But a further question may be raised. What will happen to those believers who are alive when the Lord returns at His Second Coming? Answer: They will be transformed from physical to spiritual (resurrection) bodies. God will make the victory over death complete in all cases.

That flesh and blood -- This language is a not uncommon way to describe life here and now in the human body (or what he earlier called the "natural body").[148] Flesh and blood are two important constituent elements of our natural (physical) bodies, and the two elements not only are constantly changing while we live, they are the ones which most quickly decay when the body dies.[149] That the two words refer to a single thing is shown

---

[147] Calvin (*op. cit.*, p.341) argued verse 50 concluded the previous paragraph. A few editors who have produced copies of the Greek text have followed his lead, so have a few commentators, and even the translators of the RSV.

[148] See Matthew 16:17; Galatians 1:16; Ephesians 6:12; Hebrews 2:14. When Jesus showed His resurrection body to His disciples, He did not say, "A spirit does not have flesh and *blood* as you see Me have," but He worded it, "A spirit does not have flesh and *bones*, as you see Me have." The blood of Christ is never spoken of as existing after His resurrection (the better manuscripts read "flesh and bones" as does the KJV at Ephesians 5:30, the one place where some have insisted that the glorified body of Christ is spoken of as still having blood). From this fact some have deduced that one characteristic of the glorified resurrection body is that it shall be bloodless.

[149] This is no reference to any alleged evil propensities such as those who insist the Bible teaches

by the fact that the verb following is singular rather than plural. The expression refers to those who are still living on earth when the Lord comes, and the point would be that they cannot enter heaven until first a transformation of their bodies takes place.

Cannot inherit the kingdom of God -- "Kingdom of God," as it was in 6:9,10, is a reference to heaven.[150] The context speaks about that future day when we shall bear the image of the heavenly, the day following the last trumpet. Heaven is appropriately called God's kingdom, because He shall reign there in undivided and perfect glory forever. "Inherit" implies that enjoyment of the kingdom is a *right* belonging to those who are "children of God" (Romans 8:17, Matthew 25:34), but a heritage unrealized during the present "slavery to corruption" (see Romans 8:21ff). "We do not reduce the significant verb 'to inherit' to the meaning 'to have.' To be sure, the inheritance is given to us – but it is given to us by the Testator as heirs, and we receive it and have it only as heirs, only according to the provisions of the testament [New Testament, Hebrews 9:15-17]. What makes believers heirs according to the testament is not their natural flesh and blood, but their adoption as children and as God's sons. This adoption includes the bodies [Romans 8:23] as well as the souls."[151] The reason the sons cannot inherit is because these flesh and blood bodies are not adapted or suited to life in the heavenly kingdom.[152]

Nor does the perishable inherit the imperishable -- Does "perishable" refer to a different group than "flesh and blood" did, or does this phrase unfold in more detail what has already been said in the first part of this verse?

(1) Some understand "perishable" to refer to those who are dead when Christ comes. So, in the first part of the verse we have a reference to the living. In the latter part, we have a reference to those who have died physically before the day of the Second Coming dawns.[153]

(2) Others understand this as a repetition of what was said in the first part of the verse, in

---

total hereditary depravity tend to find here. For a detailed study of the doctrine of hereditary total depravity, consult the Special Study #4 in the author's commentary on Romans.

[150] The "kingdom of God" (sometimes also called "kingdom of heaven" and sometimes simply "the kingdom") has two dimensions or manifestations in the New Testament. Sometimes the language refers to the present-time spiritual rule of God over the hearts of men (cp. 1 Corinthians 15:24). Christ reigns in this kingdom until He delivers it up to the God and Father. Sometimes the language refers to His rule and dominion after the Second Coming and consummation (e.g. Acts 14:22). One must completely ignore the context here in 1 Corinthians 15:50ff, and Paul's own explanation that follows, to use this verse (as some are wont to do) to show that the "kingdom" has not yet begun, even though 2000 years ago Jesus said it was "at hand."

[151] Lenski, *op. cit.*, p.732.

[152] We wonder what impact this announcement of the need for transformation had on the Corinthians. Did it help some see that they were not yet "spiritual"?

[153] Is "perishable" (*phthora*) limited just to bodies that are already dead? This is precisely what J. Jeremias ("Flesh and Blood Cannot Inherit the Kingdom of God," *NTS* 2 [1955/56] p.155ff) has argued.

order to make the idea perfectly clear.[154] The idea is that something has to happen to the bodies of the living before they can enter heaven. The previous phrase spoke of the "kingdom of heaven;" this one reads "imperishable."[155] When you consider the real nature of "flesh and blood" – that ever since Adam sinned it has been "perishable" or "corruptible" – it is easy to see how incompatible that would be with heaven, a place where nothing dies or perishes or rusts or decays. That's why the bodies of the living must be changed before they can enter heaven.

In light of verse 53, and in the light of the subject now being discussed (i.e., What happens to the living when Christ returns?), the second way of explaining this passage appears to be the correct view. Paul insists that our natural bodies, as they are, are not presently adapted to life in heaven. Instead, God is going to make the necessary provision for those who are living when Christ returns by changing their present earthly bodies into glorified bodies that will be exactly suited to the new life in the future kingdom of God.

15:51 -- *Behold, I tell you a mystery; we shall not all sleep, but we shall all be changed,*

Behold, I tell you a mystery -- "Behold" draws special attention to what he is about to say. He is going to explain a "mystery" so they can understand it. A "mystery," as we have learned, is something not clearly revealed in the Old Testament, but now is.[156] Evidently the topic at hand, namely, the whole process of transformation from natural bodies to spiritual bodies, from perishing bodies to imperishable bodies, is the thing that was a mystery.[157] Where do we find this "mystery" dimly taught in the Old Testament? Paul will shortly quote some words from Isaiah 25:8 and from Hosea 13:14. Those passages[158] evidently are the places where the Old Testament already presented the truth of the transformation of the living and the dead at the return of Christ. How did Paul know what was previously hidden? Has a special revelation (cp. 13:2) just been granted to him as he writes, or is this part of what was revealed to him in Arabia (Galatians 1:12ff), namely, the great mystery of God's plan of salvation in Christ for all, of which this transformation was the final event?

---

[154] Hans Conzlemann (*1 Corinthians* in the Hermeneia series [Philadelphia: Fortress Press, 1975] p.289) is one of many writers who see the last part of verse 50 as being synonymously parallel with the first part of the verse. However, he is certainly mistaken when he suggests the first part of the verse is a piece of traditional material simply included by Paul at this place, while the last part is Paul's explanation of it.

[155] For the meaning of "perishable" and "imperishable" see verse 42.

[156] Concerning the meaning of "mystery" see notes at 2:7, Romans 11:25, Ephesians 3:3-5.

[157] We find the content of the mystery in the words that follow, rather than (as some have done) in what Paul has written prior to verse 51.

[158] It is better to look for Old Testament verses where the "mystery" was but dimly revealed, rather than thinking of something hidden in the heavenly existence of Christ in his "spiritual body."

We shall not all sleep -- "Sleep" (or "fallen asleep") is a reference to physical death.[159] The "we" (first person plural) should not be pressed to imply that Paul felt confident of living until the second coming. (If we were to press such language, then the same process of reasoning at 6:14 would have Paul among the dead at the second coming.) (1) There is no evidence that Paul was mixed up concerning the time of the second coming.[160] In 1 Thessalonians 4:15 he used similar language, "We who are alive, and remain unto the coming of the Lord," and was mistakenly interpreted by the Thessalonians as teaching that the world would soon come to an end. Paul, therefore, took special pains in 2 Thessalonians 2 to show he did not mean any such thing as a soon-coming of Christ. He there indicates that the end of the world was *not* near. He indicates that certain important events had to occur before the return of Christ. Further, in 2 Corinthians 4:14, written just a few months after his first letter to Corinth, Paul includes himself to be among the dead at the time of the resurrection. Paul uses "we" in this clause, not because he expected the return of Christ to occur in his lifetime, but because a second or third person pronoun would make no sense in this context. (2) Nor is it proper to use such language to prove Paul was not inspired. The doctrine of inspiration does not suffer, even if we admit the apostles were ignorant of the exact time when the world would end, for their writings do not reflect the subjective views of the writers. The "we" refers to Christians – all Christians – no matter in what age they might live. Paul was a part of the church, and when Christ comes, some of the church will still be living on the earth.

There is considerable difference here in the way the manuscripts read, the various readings probably arising from an attempt to keep Paul from appearing to be a false prophet. (a) Some[161] have "We shall all sleep, but we shall not all be changed." (b) Some[162] have "We shall all rise, but we shall not all be changed." (c) Some manuscripts[163] read "we shall not all sleep, and we shall not all be changed." (d) Another reading[164] is "we shall all sleep and we shall all be changed." (e) The KJV, ASV, NASB ("We shall not all sleep, but we shall all be changed") reflect the reading found in Codices B, E, T, L, P, the Syriac, Coptic, Ethopic, and Gothic versions, the Majority text, and Chrysostom

---

[159] See 1 Corinthians 11:30 and 1 Corinthians 15:18 where Paul uses this same word.

[160] Refer also to comments on 1 Corinthians 1:7. "The simple fact is that Paul did not know when Christ would return. He was in exactly the same position in which we are. All that he knew, all that we know, is that He may come any time. So Paul spoke in his time exactly as we still speak in ours, namely in two ways: Christ may come immediately; or He may delay a long while." Lenski, *op. cit.*, p.737.

[161] *Aleph*, C, F, G, 17.

[162] D*, Marcion. Jerome says all the Latin manuscripts had this reading, and so does the Vulgate. Since this reading found its way into the Vulgate, it has become the way the Roman Catholics have usually understood the verse. In Knox's translation, this verse reads 'we shall all rise again, but not all of us will undergo the change I speak of' (the second clause referring to the unsaved, who, though raised, will not undergo the glorious transformation)." (Morris, *op. cit.*, p.233). Knox concedes in a footnote that this is probably not the right reading. This interpretation seems to contradict what is written in Romans 5:12ff.

[163] P46 and A^c.

[164] A*.

among the church fathers. It is generally agreed that this reading is the correct reading, especially since it agrees so well with the statement about to be made in verse 52.

But we shall all be changed -- Whether or not the fact that some Christians would be living on earth when Christ comes again was part of the "mystery," we may affirm that "we shall be changed" was included in the content of the mystery. "Changed" translates *allagēsometha* from *allēssō*, a verb which means 'to exchange one thing for another, to transform.' "Changed" is interpreted by "put on (like clothing)" (verse 53) and "fashion anew" (Philippians 3:21 ASV). For those who have died before Christ returns, the change into a new, glorified, spiritual body will come by the process called resurrection. This is not how the change will occur to the bodies of those who are still living on earth when Jesus returns. For those, the change into a spiritual body will come suddenly, in a 'split second.' When the change (transformation) is complete, all will have the same kind of spiritual bodies Jesus now has. (This, of course, does not automatically imply that all will "inherit the kingdom of God." There is still a judgment following the resurrection and transformation, and for the wicked there is a "second death.")

15:52 -- *in a moment, in the twinkling of an eye, at the last trumpet; for the trumpet will sound, and the dead will be raised imperishable, and we shall be changed.*

In a moment -- Both the living and the dead are going to get new bodies. It will happen at the *parousia* (verse 23) and the transformation signals the final defeat of death, the last enemy (verses 54-55). The marvelous change from death to life – from a mortal body to an immortal one, from a perishable body to an imperishable one – will not be a long-drawn-out process, but will be instantaneous. Paul uses two different expressions to indicate the instantaneous nature of this change of body styles. The Greek word translated "moment" (*atomōs*) is derived from an alpha-privative and the verb *timnō*, which means "to cut." It means something which cannot be cut or divided into something smaller. The change occurs in an 'indivisible point of time,' or we might say 'in a flash!'

In the twinkling of an eye -- This is the second expression Paul uses to indicate how quickly the change will be made from perishable to an imperishable body. "Twinkling" is *hripē* (from *hriptō*, 'to throw, to cast [as of a stone],' then to 'a jerk' of the eye, as when one quickly casts a glance in a different direction). Modern idiom probably talks about the 'blink of an eye' to indicate the speed with which something can happen. The change will occur in the least conceivable duration of time, instantaneously.

At the last trumpet -- Now Paul tells us when the change takes place. It is at the *parousia*, the Second Coming of Christ. This language gives the same detail concerning timing as we read in 1 Thessalonians 4:13ff.[165] The dead in Christ rise first, then the living are transformed, and both occur at the *parousia*. In the next clause, Paul will explain about the trumpet sound concerning which he writes. But he does not explain the word "last," so various meanings have been proposed by the commentators.

---

[165] Paul's theology has not changed since he wrote 1 Thessalonians, about 5 years before he wrote 1 Corinthians. Gerd Luedemann ("The Hope of the Early Paul: From the Foundation-preaching at Thes-

(1) Some suppose that Paul includes an old Jewish tradition about seven trumpets, according to which the Rabbis were wont to exhibit the seven stages of the resurrection. When the last one blew, it announced the instant the dead were to stand on their feet. It is doubtful Paul's use of "last" in any way implies that he is simply making use of an old Jewish legend.
(2) Some think we should see some reference to the 'seventh trumpet' of Revelation 11:15.[166] The timing seems to be right, for the resurrection of the dead and the transformation of the living do take place at the time of the second advent of Christ (the *parousia*, 1 Corinthians 15:23).
(3) Shore supposes that this trumpet that signals the resurrection of the dead and the transformation of the living is called "last" because "it is the one which concludes a series [of trumpet blasts] which have already been sounding at intervals in notes of warning to the nations (Psalm 47:5; Jeremiah 51:27)."[167] Trumpet blasts accompanied theophanies (Exodus 19:16; Isaiah 27:13; Zechariah 9:14). The last trumpet announces the last great theophany, or Christophany, by which all the revelations of God in this dispensation will be brought to a close.[168]
(4) Others see "last" as a reference to the finality of the transformation, or a reference to the end of all things as they are presently on earth. These interpreters insist the word "last" does not imply that any trumpet shall have been *before* sounded, but is a word denoting that this is the consummation or close of things. Contemporary Judaism, Morris tells us (*op. cit.*, p.233), associated a trumpet blast with the events of the end time.
(5) Still others think the language is drawn from ancient methods of warfare. The army is on bivouac. Early in the morning, when it is time to be up and moving, a bugler blows reveille. Those on guard duty come in and begin to prepare to move, and those asleep get up and prepare to move camp. So at the Second Coming. The Lord shouts a command. The archangel shouts. The trumpet sounds, calling the sleeping ones (dead) to rise and the living ones to "move.", and to get into column for marching.
(6) Others make reference to the use of a trumpet blast in order to call the people of God to assemble (Exodus 20:18; Psalm 81:3; Isaiah 18:3, 27:13). Here, the trumpet blast is supposed to be the signal for the great act of the all-victorious King, who will call His people out from among the living and the dead into the glory of the heavenly life, and so shall gather them about Himself.

---

salonika to 1 Corinthians 15:51-57" [*PRS* 7 {1980}], p.195-210) asserted he saw considerable differences between the accounts in Thessalonians and Corinthians. When we put the passages side by side, we see the same events in the same order.

[166] The series of seven trumpets (Revelation 8:6ff) do give us a panorama of the whole period of church history (see Hendriksen's *More Than Conquerors* for details of this interpretation of Revelation). The "mystery of God" is finished in the days before the seventh trumpet blows (Revelation 10:7), and when the seventh angel sounds his trumpet, earth's history is already finished, and we are looking back on the consummation when "the kingdom of the world has become the kingdom of our Lord, and of His Christ" (Revelation 11:15).

[167] Shore, *op. cit.*, p.155.

[168] Kling, *op. cit.*, p.346.

For the trumpet will sound -- With an explanatory "for," Paul tells us what will happen when the time comes. The trumpet that heralds the appearance of Christ sounds. What Paul affirms will happen is the same as what Jesus Himself said (Matthew 24:31), "And the Son of Man will send forth His angels with a great trumpet and they will gather together His elect from the four winds, from one end of the sky to the other." A number of other Scriptures speak about the trumpet sound, including 1 Thessalonians 4:16; Zechariah 9:14; Revelation 8:2, and 11:15. Bible students are not in agreement as to whether this use of "trumpet" is literal or figurative language. Some suppose it is a figurative expression, analogous to "Well, the coach blew the whistle on that practice!" I.e., the coach stopped the practice. In a similar way, if this language about a trumpet is figurative, it means that the day is coming when God will blow the trumpet on this world and its activities, and summon all men to stand before Him in judgment. Others think God[169] (or an angel acting for Him[170]) will use a literal trumpet to blow a blast heard around the world. We do not need to suppose that the trumpet sounds are to awaken the dead and summon them from the grave. God does that. "The trumpet likely sounds in order to call the attention of the living to the coming Christ."[171]

And the dead will be raised imperishable -- Since "perishable" flesh and blood cannot inherit the kingdom (15:50), the need of the dead for an "imperishable" body is taken care of by resurrection in their glorified bodies. "The dead (bodies) will be raised" is a promise of what the future holds, just as the whole of chapter 15 has demonstrated. 1 Thessalonians 4:14 tells us that God will bring with Him those who have fallen asleep in Christ Jesus. The disembodied spirits of the redeemed will accompany Christ and receive their resurrection bodies. What Paul writes here is similar to what he wrote in 1 Thessalonians 4:16, "the dead in Christ shall rise first," and that, too, in a state of incorruption (cp. 1 Corinthians 15:42).

And we shall be changed -- "We" means 'the ones still living on earth.' When the dead bodies have been raised, then the living will be instantaneously changed (see notes at verse 51 on "changed") into the same kind of glorified bodies. Those who are living at the return of Christ do not drop dead at the sound of the trumpet, at once to be raised again with the other dead. They will rather be changed "in a moment, in the twinkling of an eye," even as they continue to live. Both of the last two verbs in this verse are passive, and the unnamed agent evidently is God Himself.

15:53 -- *For this perishable must put on the imperishable, and this mortal must put on immortality.*

For this perishable ... and this mortal -- "For" seems to show this verse gives a reason why the dead are raised imperishable and the living are changed. "Perishable" and "mor-

---

[169] 1 Thessalonians 4:16 speaks of the trumpet of God, and Zechariah 9:14 speaks of God blowing the trumpet.

[170] Revelation 8:2 and 11:15 have an angel blowing the trumpet.

[171] Fisher, *op. cit.*, p.259.

tal" are adjectives; we must supply the noun. Consistent with the whole presentation of chapter 15, "body" is the best word to supply. Both of these adjectives relate to the human body in its present state.

Other interpretations have been given which are not quite as satisfactory: (1) Some understand the former as referring to the dead, and the latter to the living, at the time when Christ comes. (2) Some indicate that the word "this perishable" refers to Paul's own body. (3) "Mortal" has been used by annihilationists to prove that the soul is mortal. "Mortal" means that which is subject to death. "Immortality" is that which is not subject to death. Annihilationists often appeal to some argument along the following lines:

> In Greek thought, mortality was identified with the life of men; immortality with the life of the gods. In later thought among the Greeks, immortality was thought to be a property of the soul of man which dwelt within a mortal body. Modern thought has taken this up, and it is characteristic of Christian language today. However, we need to remember that the immortality of the soul is a Greek philosophical teaching, not a biblical doctrine. The thought of the New Testament teaching is not that man is inherently immortal, but that he is mortal. Immortality is received at the resurrection when man enters the new heavenly life. It is not inherent in the nature of man (as the Greeks thought) but a miraculous gift from God.[172]

Annihilationists also appeal to the fact that "immortal" appears only in one other passage in the New Testament (1 Timothy 6:16), which says Christ "alone possesses immortality."

Instead of speaking of the soul as being mortal, it is more likely (in this chapter dealing with resurrection of the body, and transformation of the body of the living) that verse 53 speaks of the *body* as being mortal – and being swallowed up in immortality, instead of undergoing death before getting the resurrection body. Indeed, verse 50, which introduced this whole paragraph, shows that these physical mortal bodies are not able to inherit the kingdom of God.

Must -- 'It is necessary' (*dei*) points back to the truth asserted in verse 50, which declared the absolute necessity for a change or transformation from this earthly body to the resurrection body if we are to enter the kingdom of God. Likely the reason it "must" be this way is that this is how God so planned it! Not only must the resurrection body be suited to the conditions found in the kingdom of heaven, it must also be suited to the duration of life in that place. As a spiritual body, it will be well adapted to the heavenly world. As an immortal and imperishable body, it will be adapted to a life which is everlasting.

Put on -- *Endunō* (the construction is the accusative and an infinitive after *dei*) literally means 'to envelop, to go in.' The word is used figuratively for putting on clothing. It is an aorist infinitive. The incorruptible immortal body is put on in one instantaneous act.

---

[172] Fisher, *op. cit.*, p.260. More detailed discussion of this whole matter, including a refutation of some of Fisher's statements, may be found in the author's article that appeared in the *Sentinel,* published by Central Christian College of the Bible, entitled "Is Man Immortal?" It is included in Special Study #9 following these notes on chapter 15.

What was earlier called a "change" is now represented as an investiture (put on) with incorruption and immortality.[173]

> [Paul's use of the verb "put on"] does not, of course, mean that corruption and mortality shall merely be covered up and hidden from view by having a mantle of incorruptibility and immortality cast over them in order to merely hide what is underneath. This figure, like all others that are employed in connection with this subject, can convey only a part of the great reality. All of them understate even when they are made as strong as possible. The figure of putting on a garment stresses appearances, the visible exterior that meets the eye of others. Paul leaves it to the two nouns incorruptibility and immortality to take care of the total inward change that transforms our bodies, and uses this verb to intimate how we shall then appear to all who behold us in our resurrection bodies.[174]

Our present earthly body is but the garb of the real man. In the life to come, the real man will put on another 'suit,' so to speak. Paul is dealing with the essence of the question. He says nothing here of those who will arise to the judgment of condemnation, or of any intermediate condition.

The imperishable ... immortality -- These two words bring out something of the nature of the change that will take place in the bodies of the living at the time Jesus returns. Corruption and mortality are completely incompatible with the life hereafter. The dying process that all humanity was subjected to when Adam sinned is stopped and reversed. No longer have we to look forward to decline and death. Jesus has brought "life and immortality (*aphtharsia*, 'incorruption') to light through the gospel" (2 Timothy 1:10).

15:54 -- *But when this perishable will have put on the imperishable, and this mortal will have put on immortality, then will come about the saying that is written, "DEATH IS SWALLOWED UP in victory.*

But when this perishable will have put on the imperishable -- With a grand repetition of what he has just written, Paul tries to catch the attention and imagination of his readers. He wants to make sure his readers get the message about this wondrous and glorious change. In his use of the word "when," Paul transports himself in thought to the time when Christ has returned and there has been an actual accomplishment of the needed change into a body suitable for living in the kingdom of heaven to follow.

And this mortal will have put on immortality – In this language, Paul gathers up and repeats all that has been written since verse 50 regarding what happens to the bodies of the

---

[173] The same two ideas are spoken again in 2 Corinthians 5:4, where it is conceived that the living Christians will be "clothed" in the new, spiritual body, "over" (*ependusasthai*) this earthly frame, which will then be "swallowed up" or "absorbed" (*katapothe*) by it.

[174] Lenski, *op. cit.*, p.742,743.

living when Jesus returns.[175] The repetition is rather like the chords of a song being repeated over and over. After the song is finished, they have become so impressed on the mind that they keep returning to our conscious thoughts. That is exactly what Paul wants to happen in the thinking of the Corinthians.

Then will come about the saying that is written -- Verse 51 introduced a "mystery" Paul was going to unfold. It is very likely he now calls attention to those Old Testament passages where this truth was 'hidden.' "The saying that is written" has reference to the verses about to be quoted from Isaiah 25:8 and Hosea 13:14. "The saying" (singular) shows that the two passages belong together, that the same topic is involved in both. The key words "death" and "victory" tie them together.[176] "Come about" means 'fully accomplished, completely fulfilled.' Certainly, the verses had an earlier fulfillment, but they would not be fully accomplished until Christ returns and death (the last enemy) is destroyed. This verse is an example of two Old Testament prophecies that are as yet unfulfilled. (Some Old Testament prophecies referred to the first advent of Christ, some looked forward to His second advent.[177]) When we have arrived at the time and place when the saints all immortal and fair are clothed in their new robes (the dead raised and the living changed), then the farthest-reaching Old Testament prophecies will have become fulfilled and accomplished.

"DEATH IS SWALLOWED UP in victory" -- This quotation comes from Isaiah 25:8. The Hebrew reads, "He (Jehovah) will destroy death forever." The LXX reads, "death has prevailed and swallowed men up." Paul perhaps has made his own translation, leaving God the agent, using the verb "swallowed," which the LXX used, and adding the word "victory" which does not appear in the LXX, though there is a word in the Hebrew text that sometimes is translated "victory."[178] In the Isaiah passage, it is said that "He (God) will swallow up death" (the death which came by the hand of the Assyrian) and that "God would wipe tears away from all faces," a passage quoted in Revelation 21:4 to describe the conditions of heaven after the second coming. Paul must not be accused of giving the Isaiah passage a meaning it never had as he applies it to the events of the end times. Even Jewish interpreters understood Isaiah to proclaim that on the great day of salvation God would

---

[175] There are some manuscripts (Aleph*, C*, M, Vulg, Copt, etc.) which omit this second phrase in verse 54. The omission probably arose through an accidental oversight in copying, especially since these words appeared before in verse 53.

[176] It is not unusual for New Testament writers to tie Old Testament passages together by key words. See Hebrews 4, for example, where "rest" is the word that ties several passages together. See also Romans 11:8 where passages from Isaiah and Deuteronomy are tied together.

[177] Recall the four-point summary of Old Testament prophecies included in the notes at 1 Corinthians 15:25.

[178] The Hebrew word *lanetsach* (from *natsah*, 'to overcome, to prevail over') in the various Greek versions is sometimes translated "to the uttermost" (*eis telos*), sometimes "forever" (*eis tōn aiōna*), and sometimes "into victory" (*eis nikos*).

vation God would swallow up death.[179] "Death" that is swallowed up is physical death, the thing being discussed in the context. "Swallowed up" is placed forward for emphasis. *Katapono* means "to drink down, to swallow down, to absorb, to overwhelm, to drown, to destroy, to remove." The idea in the word is synonymous with "abolished" in 15:26. The power and dominion of death shall be entirely destroyed and brought to an end forever. Victory is gained, and the enemy is overcome. The doom pronounced upon Adam (Genesis 3:19) and his race (1 Corinthians 15:22) is removed.

> Death is not merely destroyed so that it cannot do further harm, while all the harm which it has wrought on God's children remains. The tornado is not merely checked so that no additional homes are wrecked while those that were wrecked still lie in ruin. The destruction of death is far more intense; death and all of its apparent victories are undone for God's children. What looks like a victory for death and like a defeat for us when our bodies die and decay, shall be utterly reversed so that death dies in absolute defeat, and our bodies live again in absolute victory.[180]

15:55 -- *"O DEATH, WHERE IS YOUR VICTORY? O DEATH, WHERE IS YOUR STING?"*

"O death, where is your victory?" -- In light of death being swallowed up, Paul proceeds to taunt death in the words of Hosea, a somewhat free adaptation of Hosea 13:14.[181] This triumphant cry bursts forth from the soul as it contemplates the fact that the work of the second Adam has repaired the ruins of the first. Man is redeemed, both soul and body. If he has died physically, his body will be raised. If he is alive at the time of Christ's return, his body will be transformed into one that is immortal and imperishable. Even though the taunt has to do with the future, Paul uses present tense verbs because Christ has already guaranteed the victory.

Many interpreters understand Hosea 13:14 as though God were challenging death and Sheol to ply all their forces in an attempt to exterminate Israel. However, the implication of the challenge God issues is that they won't conquer. In a very similar sense, death will not ultimately conquer either, now that the risen Christ is exercising His authority. Other interpreters understand that Jehovah's language announces nothing less than the utter abolition of death. If so, the words are very appropriate for Paul's purposes, as he points to the abolition of death in the resurrection of the dead and the transformation

---

[179] Fee, *op. cit.*, footnote #35 on p.803.

[180] Lenski, *op. cit.*, p.744,745.

[181] There are several possible variants found when one compares the LXX with the Hebrew of Hosea 13:14. One difference has the clause about the sting of death first, and the clause about victory second (a reading reflected in the KJV of 1 Corinthians 15:55). Others have the word order as it occurs in the NASB, with the clause about victory first, and sting second. Some manuscripts have "death" in both clauses, while some have two different words, "death" in one, and "hades/sheol" in the other. The LXX uses *dikē* ("judgment") where the Hebrew has "plagues," and Paul substitutes *nikē* ("victory") for the word he found in the LXX. Paul ties this passage to the one from Isaiah by the words "death" and "victory."

of the living at the last day. "Death" is here personified,[182] and then addressed as though it were a person.

> No commentary can add to the beauty and force of the language of this verse. The best way to see its beauty, and to enjoy it is --
>
> To sit down and think of death ...
> Of what death has been, and has done
> Of the millions and millions that have died
> Of the earth strewn with the dead
> Of our own death
> The certainty that we must die, and our parents, and brothers, and sisters, and friends – that all must die.
> And then allow the truth in its full-orbed splendor to rise upon us that the time will come when DEATH SHALL BE AT AN END.[183]

The meaning of "victory" is this: if all the dead are to be raised and no one ever dies after that, where is any victory over men that can be claimed by death? The power of death is vanquished, and Christ is triumphant.

"O DEATH, WHERE IS YOUR STING?" -- The LXX and the Hebrew of Hosea do not use the word "death," but have "Sheol" or "Hades" instead.[184] The Greek manuscripts of 1 Corinthians have a variant at this place. Some carry "Hades" to make the passage conform to the reading found in Hosea.[185] The better attested reading is "death" (*thanate*).[186] Assuming Paul himself wrote *thanate*, what he is doing is freely adapting the

---

[182] Personification of abstract ideas is very common in Paul's writings. Compare Romans 7:7-25.

[183] Barnes, *op. cit.*, p.322.

[184] Readers who are familiar with the KJV should note two things. The KJV translators (in passages other than 1 Corinthians 15) often used the English word "hell" to translate the Greek word *hades*. That makes it very difficult for KJV readers to grasp what the Bible really says about the intermediate state as well as about the final state of the wicked. Further, there is serious doubt that *hades* ever means the "grave" (though the KJV here has "O grave, where is your sting?"). In two instances *sheol* (hades) is clearly distinguished from the grave in the Old Testament (Genesis 37:35 and Isaiah 14:15,19). And as far as the New Testament is concerned, the word "Hades" appears eleven times, and none of them refers to a literal grave. (The regular Greek word for grave is *mnēma*, not *hades*.) For further information on "Hades," see *Lange's Commentary* on Revelation, p.365ff, for an excellent article by E. R.Craven titled "Excursus on Hades." The KJV use of "grave" at this place could only be defended if, instead of thinking of a literal grave, the word is used figuratively for "death." (The KJV translators did at times deliberately introduce synonyms into the English text simply for the sake of improving how the passage sounded to the ears.)

[185] The manuscripts that carry this reading include K, L, M, P, Syr., Arm., Goth., Aeth. It can be easily explained as being the result of some scribe's introducing *hades* into the Greek text of 1 Corinthians in an effort to make it conform with the Hebrew or LXX of Hosea with which he was familiar. He may even have supposed he was correcting an earlier mistake that had crept into the text.

[186] The text as translated by the NASB is the reading found in P^{46}, Aleph, B, C, D, E, F., G, 088, 1739*.

text from Hosea to his discussion about "death" being conquered when men receive their glorified bodies. He can do that because "death" sent men's souls to Hades. The terms "Hades" or "Sheol" refer to the intermediate place of the dead (the abode where the soul is, after physical death has occurred, until the great resurrection morning).[187] *Kentron* is something 'sharp, pointed.' The word elsewhere is translated "goad" (at Acts 26:14; Proverbs 26:3 LXX), and "sting" (at Revelation 9:10). In this context "sting" is probably the right idea, the fatal "sting" of a scorpion, or venomous snake. Death is personified as a monster armed with a fatal sting. By resurrection, that beast is rendered harmless, deprived of its stinger, and its venom is counteracted. The implied answer to the question "Where?" is 'Nowhere!' Paul has seen the risen Lord, and with a clear vision of what is to be (i.e., we'll have bodies just like the glorified Christ's body), he mocks the enemy death whose doom has been sealed by Christ's own death and resurrection.

15:56 -- *The sting of death is sin, and the power of sin is the law;*

The sting of death is sin -- Anyone who has read chapter 15 out loud in public is aware that it is hard to follow the line of thought from verse 55 to verse 56.[188] How is verse 56 to be connected with the triumphant questions just asked? Earlier, Paul stopped to explain how he was using the terms "natural" and "spiritual" to describe the body. Perhaps the easiest way to connect this verse to the context is to think that Paul now explains just how he was using the words "sting" and "death."[189] There are no connecting verbs within the Greek phrases. They simply read "The sting of death – sin. The power of sin – law."

---

[187] Concerning the fact that, before Jesus' resurrection, Hades had two compartments, one for the righteous and one for the wicked, but that after His resurrection, Hades includes only the wicked, since the souls of the righteous have been led captive to be with Jesus in heaven, see Special Study #7 in the author's commentary on *Acts* entitled, "Hades and the Intermediate Place of the Dead."

[188] There is no manuscript evidence for the conjecture of some higher critics that verses 56 and 57 were once a marginal note added to the text by some early Paulinist. The critics make this conjecture on two bases: one, that the verses are out of harmony with the lyrical strain of the rest of the passage; and two, that the thrust of these two verses is out of harmony with the absence of any anti-Judaizing polemic from the whole 1 Corinthian epistle.

Such claims miss the whole grand comprehensive worldview Paul taught. His epistles that are contemporary with 1 Corinthians – i.e., 2 Corinthians, Romans, and Galatians – are full of the blessed effects of God's way of saving men (through the cross of Christ and the empty tomb). There are triumphant expressions about the deleterious effects of sin being overcome, both in Romans 8:31-39 and 2 Corinthians 5:13-21, so why should there not also be here? Verses 56 and 57 are simply Paul showing that his teaching about resurrection and the transformation of the living is in perfect harmony with "the word of the cross" (1:18), and that any other view of things would make the cross and empty tomb of none effect.

[189] It will hardly do to suppose Paul is here justifying his "adaptation" of the passages from Isaiah and Hosea, as though he knew he was pushing the envelope (for, after all, those verses in their original setting spoke of something quite different from the topic to which Paul applies them). Such an interpretation ignores Paul's own statement about "complete fulfillment." Meyer (*op. cit.*, p.390) and Bengel (*op. cit.*, p.341) long ago had a better suggestion. Paul here lays down a firm doctrinal basis for the certainty of the victory over death. That victory is guaranteed by the gospel system of redemption. Their suggestion might have gained wider acceptance if we didn't have to read some of it into this text, for Paul does not here specifically state all they have enclosed in their explanation.

What he says in these two verses (verses 56,57) is a succinct summary of the teaching of Romans and Galatians on the topic of physical death. The "sting" that causes physical death to the whole race is "sin," not ours, but Adam's sin (see Romans 5:12ff; 1 Corinthians 15:22). There apparently would be no physical death in the world if Adam had not sinned; we die physically because Adam sinned. It is a penalty God pronounced on the whole race when Adam sinned. The ideas highlighted in this verse were part of Paul's theological construct long before he enunciated them in Corinthians and Romans.

And the power of sin is the law -- Romans 7:9-13 is a good commentary on this phrase.[190] The devil has no way to tempt men until men are first aware of God's law. Once they know that God has said, "You shall not eat of the tree!" then the devil can come along and stir up all the desires of their bodies in an attempt to get men to violate God's prohibition. The presence of an awareness of God's laws gives sin (the devil) the necessary leverage; it affords him the thing needed to "kill" the man as the man submits to the act to which he had been tempted. And in particular, the Law of Moses, far from giving any help to man in overcoming his sin problem, rather gave the devil another tool to be used in his efforts to tempt and slay men. The point of this verse is then that sin (the devil) exerts its power to bring about death when and where there is an awareness of God's laws. Thus it has always been as the devil goes about his schemes which are in opposition to God. But in the Kingdom of God after the Second Coming and the resurrection, the devil won't be around to use "law" to tempt folk to sin. If death is abolished, then so are the things that brought it about.

15:57 -- *but thanks be to God, who gives us the victory through our Lord Jesus Christ.*

But thanks be to God -- With "but" there is a sudden transition to thanksgiving.[191] Don't read verse 56 without also reading verse 57, which is the glorious opposite of that doleful picture. This is a triumphant note that one feels after comprehending all that chapter 15 has said. God is the ultimate source of the victory over death. He formed the plan of redemption and He executed it in the sending of His Son. That is why the thanksgiving is addressed to Him.

Who gives us the victory -- Paul here repeats the substance of the passages he has quoted from Isaiah and Hosea (verses 54,55). "Us" is 'us Christians.' "The victory" (the article of previous reference) is the "victory" alluded to in the passages from Isaiah and Hosea. It consists in the defeat of death by the resurrection, and the defeat of dying by being clothed with an imperishable body. "Gives" is a present participle, expressing continuous action, 'who is giving us the victory.' Commentators offer different ways of accounting

---

[190] See also Romans 4:15, 5:20, 6:14 and Galatians 2:16, 3:1ff, 4:21-5:4.

[191] Compare 2 Corinthians 2:14; Romans 7:25; 1 Timothy 1:17 for similar sudden transitions. In Romans, after explaining that the Law gave no help with man's sin problem, Paul asked (verse 24), "Who will set me free from the body of this death?" The answer given there is the same thanksgiving we have here, "Thanks be to God through our Lord Jesus Christ!"

for the present tense. One author has explained it this way: The victory is a process which is continually going on, as men receive what has been won for them by Christ.[192] Another author explains the present tense this way: Christ has already won the victory over death, and so the victory has already begun and is so certain of being concluded in the general resurrection, that Paul speaks of it as now taking place. His resurrection is the pledge of our resurrection.

Through our Lord Jesus Christ -- The full title "Lord Jesus Christ" heightens the sense of the majesty of His person and what He has done. The reason Paul can be certain of future victory is because Jesus Messiah is now the risen and reigning Lord. By His death, He destroyed him who had the power of death, that is, the devil (Hebrews 2:14,15). Because of His death, limits have been put on the devil. No longer do men need to fear lifelong slavery to sin. There is, for those in Christ, no longer any condemnation to such slavery (Romans 8:1ff). By Jesus' resurrection, He has introduced "justification of life" (Romans 4:25, 5:18). It is those who own Him as "Lord" who will taste the victory!

With this enthusiastic expression of praise to God, Paul concludes his presentation concerning the resurrection of the dead and the transformation of the living. As he drives home the doctrine of resurrection, Paul has led his readers through arguments historical, moral, and philosophical, through explanations from the analogy of nature, and through an exegesis of Old Testament Scriptures. In closing, he projects his mind and the thoughts of his readers to that grand future time when all the ransomed and raised humanity – after death has been vanquished and the grave has been spoiled – together join in the triumphant cry declaring that death has been conquered!

15:58 -- *Therefore, my beloved brethren, be steadfast, immovable, always abounding in the work of the Lord, knowing that your toil is not in vain in the Lord.*

Therefore -- *Hōste* reaches back to the foregoing argument[193] as the reason why the exhortation he is about to give should be obeyed. Paul always bases practice on doctrine. True doctrine should result in godly living. Because there is a life hereafter, it behooves us to live this life here in harmony with that great truth.

My beloved brethren -- Seldom does Paul use these two terms together. The only other place the two terms are found together is in Philippians 4:1. He has been stern and severe in this letter, and he has been stern and severe in this chapter. Yet he wants the Christians

---

[192] Robertson and Plummer, *op. cit.*, p.379.

[193] Whether it is the whole of chapter 15, or what was written specifically in verse 57, we cannot tell. Barnes *(op. cit.*, p.324) believes the whole chapter is in view, when he wrote, "In view of the great and glorious truths which have been revealed to us respecting the nature of the resurrection body, and the instantaneous transformation of the living into their glorified bodies when Jesus returns, Paul closes the whole of this important discussion with an exhortation to firmness in the faith."

at Corinth to understand that he wrote these words in love.[194] His triumphant cry aroused a flood of affection in Paul for the Corinthians, whom he desires to share in that victory.

Be steadfast -- The word "be" translates *ginesthe*, a present tense imperative. It apparently does not mean 'continue to be.' Rather, it means 'become (something you are not at the present).'[195] 'Become steadfast' apparently says they have a long way to go before they reach this state. "Steadfast" translates *hedraioi*, from *hedra*, which means 'seated, fixed, solid, standing one's ground (a figure used of wrestling).'[196] It speaks of a fixed and stable purpose that is not easily disturbed or shaken because the man's whole heart is set upon it. Likely, the thought is primarily that of doctrinal stability.[197] 'Become solid in your conviction about the resurrection! You can do this because (in the light of chapter 15) there are incontrovertible evidences on which your faith may rest. Don't let false teaching or philosophical skepticism move you from your moorings!'

> Take away correct doctrine with its substance of divine facts, and the life drifts and is blown about by every wind of (false) doctrine, Ephesians 4:14, which ignores or denies the facts. With the facts in our possession we have something to live for; when these facts are absent from our hearts, what have we to live for?[198]

Immovable -- *Ametakinētai* is from *kinein*, to set in motion.[199] The alpha-privative says 'don't let others set you into motion,' or 'be not led away by others.' The Corinthians were to become firm and unshaken in their Christian hopes, and in their faith in the power of the gospel. They must be static. "The Corinthians were prone to fickleness, shifting without good reason from one position to another. Let that all be a thing of the past! Let them get a firm grip on the truth of the resurrection, of God's final plan for all men and all things, and they will not be so easily shaken."[200] "Foes are always ready to assail our faith. Some strike at it with open denial, some with subtle error that leads us to compromise our faith and our confession, and some come with immoral temptation. They seek to turn us into slaves of sin. Paul bids us to stand unmovable against all of them. Com-

---

[194] In spite of theological errors and behavioral errors (including some who preferred other preachers to him) among the Corinthians, from Paul's point of view they are still his dear brothers in Christ.

[195] In disagreement with most other writers, Lenski says that the Greek of the period no longer has the idea of "becoming" when the word *ginomai* is used (*op. cit.*, p.752).

[196] The same word was used at 7:37 of the father who "stands firm in his heart."

[197] Plummer (*op. cit.*, p.379) observes that the Corinthians were not yet stable either in belief or behavior (verses 2,33).

[198] Lenski, *ibid*.

[199] From the Greek verb we get our word "cinema" – continual moving.

[200] Morris, *op. cit.*, p.236.

pare Hebrews 13:9."²⁰¹   If a Christian becomes "immovable," nothing will move him from the hope of the gospel which he has heard (Colossians 1:23).

Always abounding in the work of the Lord -- Becoming firm and settled in one's convictions is the one response to divine truth.   While doing that, the Christian is to be abounding in the work of the Lord.²⁰² The "work of the Lord"²⁰³ is "the work" which "the Lord" (Jesus Christ) prescribes. The plural form shows Paul expects every believer to be excelling in activity for the cause of Christ. It is not possible to identify specifically the kind of activity Paul had in mind by the phrase "the work of the Lord," but perhaps he has in mind the kind of activities in which believers engage as they carry out the Great Commission, activities that are specifically in the interest of the spread of the gospel (including the truth of the resurrection and all that that entails).   "Paul significantly calls this the work 'of the Lord.' Christ has instituted this work, and all of it belongs to Him personally ... This significant genitive 'of the Lord' should correct the so-called 'church work' of many who busy themselves with worldly tasks in the churches, with mere humanitarian 'social service' and a hundred other things with which the Lord and the Gospel are not [primarily] concerned." (Lenski, *op. cit.*, p.754) "Always" (*pantote*, see 1:4) is another emphasis.   "In youth and in age; in pleasant as well as in somber days; when many work with us, and the work is a joy; and when we plod on along with heavy hearts; when we have already done much; and when others have scarcely done anything – *always*" keep working!"²⁰⁴   What a rebuke the word "abounding" is for the thousands of church members who work, pray, give, and suffer as little as possible!²⁰⁵

Knowing that your toil is not *in* vain in the Lord -- "Knowing" (*eidotes*, a perfect active form) is a circumstantial participle.   *Oida* ('know') is a verb that has no present tense forms but uses perfect tense forms as though they were present. We would tend to use the same helping word to translate this participle that we used to translate "abounding." A perfect tense participle ordinarily indicates action that is simultaneous with the main verb, but which results from action prior to it. We cannot tell if "knowing" is dependent on the participle "abounding" or on the main verb "be steadfast." Perhaps Paul means to say that before folk ever 'abound in the work of the Lord' they have known that such labor is not in

---

²⁰¹ Lenski, *op. cit.*, p.753.

²⁰² "Abounding" is a present circumstantial participle in the Greek. "While" is a useful helper to use when translating. "Be steadfast ... while abounding" is the idea. It is also possible to use the helper "by" so that the verse says one becomes steadfast "*by* abounding in the work of the Lord." One has to learn before he can teach others.

²⁰³ See 1 Corinthians 3:13-15, 9:1; Colossians 3:23,24; Matthew 21:28; Mark 13:34.

²⁰⁴ Lenski, *op. cit.*, p.754.

²⁰⁵ George Mark Elliott called attention to the words in Luke 10:35 (ASV), "whatsoever more." He then spoke of "The Whatsoever More" of Christianity. No half-heartedness. No following the lines of least resistance. No drifting toward heaven. None of the 'How worldly can I be, and still get to heaven?' attitude.

vain. Such knowledge becomes an encouragement to labor on. Perhaps Paul means to say that while folk were 'becoming stable' they have known that God rewards the faithful. Such knowledge was an encouragement to become steadfast and unmovable. What was the source of the Corinthians' knowledge? If we may learn from what Paul has written in chapter 15, some of the knowledge comes from Christ's person and work, and some comes from the Scriptures.

"Toil" here translates *kopos*, whereas the word for "work" earlier in the verse was *ergon*, the ordinary, usual word for work. *Kopos* is the synonym that implies that the work leaves the worker tired and weary. "Vain" translates *kenos* (a word explained at 1 Corinthians 15:14), 'empty of results.' "Not vain" is a litotes, a negative form to express a positive idea, namely, 'wonderfully productive' of everlasting results. "In the Lord" goes with "not in vain (empty)." Deissmann sees in the words "your toil (labor) is not in vain" "a trembling echo of the discouragement resulting from a piece of work being rejected for alleged bad finish and therefore not paid for."[206] The Christian has no basis for any such discouragement. Christ has risen! "In the Lord" there is a resurrection and a glorified body! There is a heaven that will be inhabited by souls in these immortal bodies. You have God's Word on it that work done for Christ will be richly repaid![207]

---

[206] Deissmann, *Light From the Ancient East*, p.314.

[207] The exhortation of verse 58 is a wonderful passage to memorize and then to put into practice. Lenski (*op. cit.*, p.755) calls attention to the fact that the results of many earthly tasks are easily measured. Bricklayers lay so many bricks in so many hours and receive so much pay. A merchant sells so much in his store and makes so much profit. But visible and tangible results in the work of the Lord are not always so visible. As a result, workers become discouraged and cease strong exertion, or quit altogether. The apostolic promise that "toil" (while doing the work of the Lord) will be rewarded should sustain our spirit to continue becoming more stable and to continue working.

Special Study #7

HE IS ALIVE!   YOU HAD BETTER BELIEVE IT!

The importance of our study. Both friends and enemies of the Christian faith have recognized that the bodily resurrection of Jesus from the dead is the foundation stone of the Christian faith. To people at Corinth who were starting to listen to some who said there is no such thing as a resurrection of dead bodies, Paul wrote, "If Christ has not been raised, then our preaching is vain, and your faith is also vain." Paul rested his whole case on the bodily resurrection of Jesus the Messiah.

If Jesus *did* rise from the dead, it is the most sensational event in all of history, and we have conclusive answers to the profound questions of our existence: Where have we come from? Why are we here? Where are we going? If Jesus arose, we know with certainty that God exists, what He is like, and how we may know Him in personal experience. The universe takes on meaning and purpose, and it is possible to experience the living God in contemporary life. These and many other wonderful things are true if Jesus of Nazareth rose from the dead.

The resurrection is the foundation for Christianity's exclusive claim that there is no other name under heaven given among men whereby we must be saved (Acts 4:10-12).

The enemies of Christianity concentrate their attack on the resurrection. Why? Because they have correctly seen that this event is the crux of the matter. With the truthfulness of the resurrection Christianity stands or falls. So, it behooves us to know why we believe in the bodily resurrection[1] of Jesus from the dead!

A few years ago, a questionnaire was sent to 521 leaders in the field of science in America, asking if they believed in the bodily resurrection of Christ.[2] As with all questionnaires, not all were returned. But of those returned, only 36 wrote back to affirm their faith in the resurrection of Jesus Christ. 142 wrote back to state definitely that they do not believe in the resurrection. What does that mean? Does this mean that anyone who believes in the resurrection is unscientific? Does it mean that if we believe in the resurrection, there is no actual evidence that can be used as an assurance to our faith? Not at all! Scientists can be wrong, the same as anyone else. (New editions of science books must be printed continually, in order to correct some of the mistakes of the old ones and to

---

[1] The modern theory that "resurrection" means no more than that people had good memories of Jesus after He died, or that there was a revival of Jesus' spiritual influence on the disciples which was temporarily interrupted when He was arrested and killed, has no relationship at all to what the Scriptures mean when they speak of resurrection. The Scriptures indicate that something happened so that His body was gone from the tomb. When we speak of "resurrection" (a word that means "to stand up again"), we mean that the body which had died was able to "stand up" again. We mean that He reanimated His physical body, save that that physical body was now a glorified body as well.

[2] Lewis A. Foster, "Evidences of the Resurrection," *Straight* magazine, 1957.

fill in some of the spaces of ignorance.) Science is primarily interested in the things it can see and feel, that it can bring into the laboratory and test, that can be subjected to the steps of the scientific method: observation, hypothesis, experimentation, and verification. All that science can conclude from observation and experiments is that today, *man* is not able to raise the dead.

The power of God. Belief in the resurrection of Jesus is connected with our faith in God. If a person believes God was able to create us in the beginning, that He was able to give life to His creation, then certainly it is no problem to believe that His power is sufficient to give life again to a dead person if He so chooses. The man who refuses to believe God could raise a person from the dead is the same person who must deny God's power to put us here in the first place. That person is left with no explanation of how we began or where we are going. The reply, "We just happened" is both incredible and unscientific. Room must be left for the power of God. There is no other explanation.

God has provided many incontrovertible proofs verifying Christ's triumph over death. What are these proofs?

Old Testament Scripture

Old Testament Scripture anticipated Messiah's resurrection one thousand years in advance. "All things which are written about Me in the Law of Moses and the Prophets and the Psalms must be fulfilled," Jesus told His disciples. "Thus it is written, that the Christ should suffer and rise again from the dead the third day," He said (Luke 24:44,46). He certainly had Psalm 16:10 in mind, "For thou wilt not abandon my soul to Hades; neither wilt Thou allow Thy Holy One to see the pit." Peter (Acts 2:25-28) and Paul (Acts 13:35) both preached Christ's resurrection from this Psalm. Some of the most powerful evidence given by God for the resurrection is found in the predictions made by the Old Testament prophets, hundreds of years before the event.

The Historical Records

The books of the New Testament are valid evidence. Even if we were to admit (which we do not!) that they are not inspired, they are old books,[3] some of them written by

---

[3] All four Gospels were written between AD 45 and 80. Thousands were still living who could testify to the historicity and veracity of what is contained in the Gospel accounts. A work written within 30 years of the event is written too soon for anyone to claim that enough time has elapsed since the event for a "myth" to have grown up. Peter, writing before AD 68, says "we did not followed cleverly devised tales ("myths" in the Greek) when we made known to you the power and coming of our Lord Jesus Christ, but we were eyewitnesses of His majesty" (2 Peter 1:16). In some scholarly circles in recent years, it has become fashionable to attempt to account for the "resurrection" by appealing to Babylonian or other Eastern religious sources, to say that Christian doctrine is merely warmed-over pagan mythology. Perhaps, it is claimed, the most used 'source' for the Biblical doctrine of 'resurrection' is the myth of Isis and Osiris. But there is literally no link of connection between those pagan stories and the Jewish and

people who were eyewitnesses. Not only do we have the canonical records (good, primary evidence), we also have extra-biblical records concerning Jesus (secondary evidence).

Some deny the Biblical record because they have a preconceived notion that there can be no supernatural. After leaving office, President Thomas Jefferson set out to rewrite the Bible. He had always been enthusiastic about the moral teaching of Jesus, but he was troubled by the records of supernatural events in the New Testament. So with a scissors and a New Testament, Jefferson attempted to separate the "real" message of Jesus from all the "unnecessary." He omitted every supernatural incident – including the resurrection. And the closing words of his new version of the Bible read, "There laid they Jesus, and rolled a great stone to the door of the sepulchre and departed." But how reliable are editors who deliberately rewrite and change the records, rather than letting the records stand on their own merits?

Some may try to say the historical records are unreliable. Are they? The records were written, some by eyewitnesses, some by those who investigated and received facts from eyewitnesses. These eyewitnesses were willing to die for the truth of their testimony.[4] Who will die for what he knows to be wrong?

Each of the four Gospels records the resurrection of Jesus and some of His post-resurrection appearances. The resurrection is also attested in the epistles of the New Testament. When John ran with Peter to the tomb and entered, seeing the tomb empty and the grave clothes lying in their place, the Scripture says simply, "He saw and believed" (John 20:8). The disciples were to receive still more direct knowledge of the resurrection. Jesus appeared to them: they ate with Him, talked with Him, touched Him, examined Him, investigated Him. They ascertained beyond doubt that this was the same Jesus they had known before His death, and that indeed He was real and alive again!

The epistles found in the New Testament are excellent primary sources to discern the history of the 1st century. There is unimpeachable evidence of the contemporary letters of Paul. These epistles constitute historical evidence of the highest kind. The letters addressed to the Galatians, the Corinthians, and the Romans, about the authenticity and date of which there is very little dispute, may be dated in the period AD 55-58. That is within twenty-five years of the event. In each of the letters from this period, Paul is clear that Jesus has risen from the dead. "Note that when the disciples of Jesus proclaimed the

---

Christian beliefs in the resurrection. J. Gresham Machen, *The Origin of Paul's Religion*, has long ago shown how arbitrary and baseless is the attempt to show Christianity's sources are to be found in paganism. The real reason any attempt is made to find a source in paganism is a prejudicial attitude against the supernatural.

[4] "The apostles ... spent the rest of their lives proclaiming the message of the resurrection ... They were willing to face arrest, imprisonment, beating, and horrible deaths, and not one of them ever denied the Lord and recanted of his belief that Christ had risen." James Rosscup, cited in Josh McDowell, *Evidence that Demands a Verdict*, p.245.

resurrection, they did so as eyewitnesses and they did so while people were still alive who had had contact with the events they spoke of. In AD 57 Paul wrote that over 500 people had seen the risen Jesus and that most of them were still alive (1 Corinthians 15:6ff). It passes the bounds of credibility that the early Christians could have manufactured such a tale and then preached it among those who might easily have refuted it simply by producing the body of Jesus."[5]

Not only do we have the Scriptural records, we also have extra-biblical records of Jesus and the resurrection. Clement of Rome (fl. AD 82-96),[6] Polycarp (c. AD 70-c. AD 155),[7] Ignatius (ca. AD 50-115),[8] Josephus (AD 37-c.95),[9] and Justin Martyr (c. AD 100-c. AD 165)[10] are among the extra-biblical writers who document the resurrection of Jesus.

Before one can prove there was no resurrection, he must show that all the historical records telling about Jesus' resurrection are false.[11] That is an impossible task.

Jesus Christ's Own Testimony

The four Gospel writers each included the Lord's own predictions that He not only would die, but that He would rise again.[12] "From that time, Jesus Christ began to show His disciples that He must go to Jerusalem, and suffer many things ... and be killed, and be raised up on the third day" (Matthew 16:21, Mark 9:9, Luke 9:22, John 2:19). Jesus never predicted His own coming death without adding that He would rise.

---

[5] John W. Montgomery, *History and Christianity* (Downers Grove, IL: InterVarsity Press, 1964), p.78.

[6] 1 Clement ch.24. (*ANF*, V.1, p. 11,12).

[7] To the Philippians, ch.1. (*ANF*, V.1, p. 33).

[8] To the Trallians, ch.9. (*ANF*, V.1, p.70).

[9] *Antiquities*, 18.3.3. Attempts have been made to insist that Josephus did not write this paragraph that is now in his collected works, but it was in the text of Josephus used by Eusebius (about 325 AD), and is included in the most recent Loeb edition of Josephus' works.

[10] Justin Martyr's treatise on the resurrection "... deals with distinctively Christian doctrine. Contemporary opposition to the faith asserted that the resurrection was impossible; undesirable, since the flesh is the cause of sins; inconceivable, since there can be no meaning in the survival of existing organs. They further maintained that the resurrection of Christ was only in physical appearance and not in physical reality. To these objections and difficulties Justin made reply" (*ANF*, V.1, p.294-299).

[11] Beware of "revisionist" histories. In recent years, influenced by the currently popular philosophy called existentialism, all ancient histories are being treated as hopelessly in error, and in need of being revised so as to be politically correct, and free from ancient bias. Indeed!

[12] Matthew 12:38-40, 16:21, 17:9,22,23, 20:18,19, 26:32, 27:63; Mark 8:31-9:1, 9:10,31, 10:32-34, 14:28,58; Luke 9:22-27; John 2:18-22, 12:34, chapters 14-16.

Even His enemies testified before Pilate, "Sir, we remember that when He was still alive that deceiver said, 'After three days I *am* to rise again'" (Matthew 27:63).

Not only did David prophesy the resurrection of the Messiah in Psalm, 16, but Jesus (the Messiah) unmistakably announced His own resurrection. No one has ever been able to show anything other than that Jesus was always perfectly truthful in word and deed. "If our Lord said, frequently, with great definiteness and detail, that after He went up to Jerusalem He would be put to death, but on the third day He would rise again from the grave, and this prediction came to pass, then it has always seemed to me that everything else that our Lord ever said must also be true."[13] If Jesus did not arise, after He often announced that He would, then Jesus was a flagrant liar, and hardly an example of morals or ethics for a world to imitate.[14]

The Empty Tomb

The record is very clear that Jesus' dead body was buried. "We know more about the burial of Jesus than we know of the burial of any single character in all of ancient history – whether he be an Old Testament character, the king of Babylon, a Pharaoh in Egypt, a philosopher in Greece, or a triumphant Caesar. We know who took His body from the cross; we know something of the wrapping of the body in spices, and burial clothes; we know the very tomb in which this body was placed, the name of the man who owned it, Joseph, of a town known as Arimathaea. We know even where the tomb was located, in a garden nigh to the place where He was crucified, outside the city walls. We have records of the burial of Jesus, all of them in amazing agreement – records from Matthew, Mark, Luke, John, and Peter."[15]

The power of God is such that He *can* raise Jesus from the dead, and the empty tomb is testimony that God *did* raise Jesus from the dead. "In different parts of the world, tombs have been unearthed which have contained magnificent treasures buried with kings or nobles of wealth. Yet no treasure of this world can compare with the value of the testimony which comes from Christ's empty tomb: 'He is not here, He is risen!'"[16]

---

[13] Wilbur M. Smith, *Therefore Stand: Christian Apologetics* (Grand Rapids, MI: Baker Book House, 1965), p.419.

[14] "If you or I should say to any group of friends that we expected to die, either by violence or naturally, at a certain time, but that, three days after death, we would rise again, we would be quietly taken away by friends, and confined to an institution, until our minds became clear and sound again. This would be right, for only a foolish man would go around talking about rising from the dead on the third day, only a foolish man, unless he knew that this was going to take place, and no one in the world has ever known that about himself except One, Jesus Christ the Son of God" (Smith, *op. cit.*, p.364).

[15] Smith, *op. cit.*, p.370,371.

[16] Foster, *ibid.*

> The mausoleum of Red Square in Moscow displays Lenin's embalmed body. The pyramids of Egypt protected the mummified bodies of ancient Egyptian kings. Mohammed's tomb is noted for the bones it contains. Westminster Abbey of London houses the bodies of English heroes. And Arlington Cemetery in Washington, DC, is the honored resting place of many great Americans. All of those places are famous, attracting tourists because of the bodies they contain. There is all the difference in the world, however, between those monuments and the tomb of Jesus. Although pilgrims still travel to Jerusalem, the traditional site of Jesus' tomb is famous because it is empty! Jesus' bones are not there. Why? He is risen from the dead![17]

What do Buddha, Confucius, Mohammed, Joseph Smith, and Karl Marx all have in common? If signs marked gravesites, theirs would read "Occupied." Only Christ's grave rates a "Vacant!" sign. He arose on the third day, just as He said (Matthew 28:6, Mark 16:6, Luke 24:6, John 20:6-7).

Even Christ's enemies (Matthew 28:11-15) admitted the tomb was empty. The religious officials' explanation of the empty tomb – that the disciples had stolen they body while the guard slept – was an admission that the tomb was indeed vacant! "It should be noticed first of all that the Jewish authorities never questioned the report of the guards. They did not themselves go out to see if the tomb was empty, because they knew it was empty. The guards would never have come back with such a story as this on their lips, unless they were reporting actual, indisputable occurrences, as far as they were able to apprehend them. The story which the Jewish authorities told the soldiers to repeat was a story to explain how the tomb became *empty*."[18] The empty tomb authenticates the resurrection.

Modern "explanations" of the Empty Tomb are Unbelievable

"Maybe Christ was not actually dead when they put Him in the tomb," some might say.[19] What then of the exhausting hours of trial in the night before His crucifixion, what of the scourging, the beatings, the crucifixion and the nails, the spear thrust into His side after He was pronounced dead, the blood and water coming from His open wound, the hours He lay in the cold, dark tomb? Could anyone believe that this man in a thoroughly natural way, with no miracle, discovered He was not dead at all, removed the yards and yards of grave clothes wound tightly about him, pushed away the enormous stone used to seal the tomb, evaded the Roman guard, and appeared to His disciples, and walked miles (it was seven miles to Emmaus) on feet (or ankles) that had been pierced with spikes, with

---

[17] George F. Sweeting, "Dead or Alive?" *Moody* (April 1987), p.30.

[18] Smith, *op. cit.*, p.375,376.

[19] This objection is often called "the swoon theory." It is a modern attempt to explain the 'resurrection' on naturalistic grounds, and first appeared at the end of the 18th century. It is significant that not a suggestion of this kind has come down from antiquity among all the various attacks which have been made on Christianity. All the earliest records are emphatic about Jesus' *death*.

no period of recovery intervening? This is harder to believe, more impossible to maintain than to accept the miracle itself.[20] Jesus actually died. Both the Biblical and extra-Biblical records are one in this affirmation.[21] If He didn't die on the cross, when did He die and under what circumstances?

"Perhaps the tomb was empty because someone stole the body," another might say. Certainly the Romans or the Jews would not commit this theft. Why would they? Having put guards at the tomb, what would be their reason for moving the body? If they did take the body, they would have produced the remains afterwards to prove the story of the resurrection was false.[22] But they could not produce the body of Christ. Well, what of the friends of Jesus? Might they have committed this theft? There was a Roman guard at the tomb and a Roman seal upon the grave. Yards of grave clothes and pounds of embalming spices wrapped within the folds still lay on the floor of the tomb just as they had been left; but the body of Jesus was gone. "How could His friends have stolen the body from the tomb under such circumstances? Furthermore, stealing the body of Jesus was something totally foreign to the character of the disciples and all that is known about them."[23]

"Maybe the distraught women, overcome with grief, in the dimness of the morning, went to the wrong tomb," is another suggestion. And then when they found no one in the

---

[20] Even the German critic, David Strauss, who by no means believed in the resurrection, rejected the "swoon theory" as incredible. He said, "It is impossible that one who had just come forth from the grave, half dead, who crept about weak and ill, who stood in need of medical treatment, of bandaging, strengthening, and tender care, and who at last succumbed to suffering, could ever have given the disciples the impression that He was a conqueror over death and the grave; that He was the Prince of Life. This lay at the bottom of their future ministry. Such a resuscitation could only have weakened the impression which He had made upon them in life and in death – or at the most, could have given it an elegiac voice – but could by no possibility have changed their sorrow into enthusiasm or elevated their reverence into worship." (*The Life of Jesus*, London, 1879, V.1, p.412.)

[21] Jesus died at the ninth hour, or about 3 PM (Luke 23:44). Joseph of Arimathea came to Pilate requesting permission to claim the body for burial. When Pilate had ascertained from the centurion in charge of the crucifixion that Jesus was indeed dead, he granted Joseph's request (Mark 15:42-45). The people who took the body down from the cross are embalming it in preparation for burial – not giving Him first-aid in a desperate effort to revive Him (Luke 23:55,56). Perhaps we could ask a physician to explain the "resurrections" of modern medicine. There are numerous cases where clinical death has been experienced; i.e., the patient's heart has stopped beating, and after 20 or 30 minutes of frantic effort, he is revived. There is a world of difference between such instances and the resurrection of Jesus from the dead!

[22] The enemies did everything in their power to stop the spread of this message about Jesus and the resurrection (Acts 4). They arrested Peter and John, beating and threatening them, in an attempt to close their mouths. How much easier to produce the dead body, if they had it, than the only methods left open to them?

[23] Paul Little, "Did Christ Rise from the Dead?" *Know Why You Believe* (Downers Grove, IL: InterVarsity Press, 1970), p.25.

wrong tomb, they *imagined* that Jesus had arisen.[24] This theory fails because of the same facts that destroy the previous one. If the women went to the wrong tomb, why did the high priests and other enemies of the faith not go to the right tomb and produce the body? Are we to think that Peter and John succumbed to the same mistake? Did Joseph of Arimathea, owner of the tomb, not know where the tomb was, and could he not have solved the problem? In addition, it must be remembered this was a private burial ground, not a public cemetery. What makes us think there were other tombs nearby that would have allowed the women to make this kind of mistake?

The Bible indicates the tomb was empty because Jesus came out of the grave by superhuman power, not by human hands.

The Broken Roman Seal

Here is another evidence that Jesus arose. The seal put on the entrance of the tomb by the soldiers at the order of the governor stood for the power and authority of the Roman Empire. The consequences of breaking it were severe. The authorities of the Roman Empire would have been called into action to find the man or men responsible. When they were apprehended, it meant automatic execution by crucifixion upside down.

Who Moved the Stone?[25]

All the Gospel writers mentioned the removal of the large stone, which would have weighed about two tons (Mark 16:4 describes the stone as "extremely large"). The women coming to the tomb early Sunday morning doubted they could move it. Ordinarily it took

---

[24] This theory is based on a creative rewriting of the Gospel accounts. The women were comparative strangers to Jerusalem (the theory goes), and coming in the uncertain light of early morning, they lost their way. A young man nearby realized their purpose and said, "You seek Jesus ... He is not here. Behold (pointing to another tomb) the place where they laid Him." The women were terrified and ran away. Afterward they came to believe the young man was an angel with an announcement that Jesus had risen from the dead. This sounds all well and good, until it is pointed out that it arbitrarily omits "He is risen!" right from the middle of the words the young man spoke. (See J.N.D. Anderson, *The Evidence for the Resurrection* [Downers Grove, IL: InterVarsity Press, 1971], p.13,14.)

[25] In the 1930s, Albert Henry Ross, a young British lawyer, was convinced the resurrection was simply of fable and fantasy. Sensing that it was the foundation of the Christian faith, he decided to do the world a favor by once-and-for-all exposing this fraud and superstition. As a lawyer, he felt he had the critical faculties rigidly to sift evidence and to admit nothing as evidence which did not meet the stiff criteria for admission into a law court today. However, while he was doing his research, a remarkable thing happened. The case was not nearly as easy as he had supposed it would be. In the first chapter of his book, *Who Moved the Stone*? he explains how he became persuaded of the fact of the bodily resurrection, even though he started out to prove the exact opposite. (Ross' book was originally published under the pseudonym "Frank Morison.")

several men to move such a stone.[26]

> In Matthew 27:60, it is said that a large stone was "rolled" against the entrance of the tomb. The Greek word used, *kulio*, means "to roll." Mark used the same root word in Mark 16:4, but added a preposition to explain the position of the stone after the resurrection. (In Greek, as in English, to change the direction of a verb or to intensify it, you add a preposition.) Mark added the preposition *ana*, which means "up or upward." So *anakulio* can mean "to roll something up a slope or an incline, or up a hill." For Mark to have used that verb, there would have had to be a slope or an incline coming down to the front of the tomb.
>
> In fact, the stone was so far "up a slope" that Luke used the same root word *kulio*, but added a different preposition, *apo* (Luke 24:2). *Apo* can mean, according to Greek dictionaries, "a separation from," in the sense of "a distance from." *Apokulio* means to roll an object some distance away. Someone rolled that huge stone not only away from the entrance to the tomb, but some distance up the nearby slope.
>
> In fact, the stone was in such a position up the slope, away from the tomb, that John had to use a different Greek verb, *airo*, which (according to Arndt and Gingrich Lexicon) means "to pick something up and carry it away" (John 20:1). If the disciples had wanted to tiptoe around the sleeping guards, roll the stone over and steal the body, why would they have moved a two-ton stone up a slope away from the entire tomb, to such a position that it looked like someone had picked it up and carried it away? The soldiers would have to have been deaf not to have heard the stone being moved.[27]

Roman Guard Goes AWOL

The Roman guard[28] fled. They left their place of responsibility. That has to be explained because the military discipline of the Romans was exceptionally good. Many offenses, including falling asleep on duty, required the penalty of death. If it was not apparent which soldier had failed, then lots were drawn to see who would be punished with death for the guard unit's failure.[29]

---

[26] Codex Beza (a Western text) has an astounding addition at Mark 16:4 that the Neutral and Eastern texts of the Gospels do not carry. It reads, "And when He was laid there, he [Joseph of Arimathea] put against the tomb a stone which twenty men could not roll away." See Gilbert West, *Observations on the History and Evidences of the Resurrection of Jesus Christ*, p.37,38.

[27] Josh McDowell, "The Resurrection Factor: Proof Positive," *Moody* (April, 1983), p.12.

[28] That the guard was made up of Roman, rather than Jewish soldiers, is evident from the fact that Pilate gave the orders for the guard to be stationed.

[29] George Currie (*The Military Discipline of the Romans from the Founding of the City to the Close of the Republic*, a thesis prepared at Indiana University, 1928) calls attention to a statement in Dion. Hal. Antiq. Rom. VIII.79 where "the punishment for quitting a post was death." He also quotes the famous discourse on the strictness of Roman camp discipline from Polybius VI.37-38.

One way a guard was put to death was by being stripped of his clothing and then burned alive in a fire started with the garments. The entire unit certainly would not have fallen asleep with that threat hanging over their heads. The history of Roman discipline and security testifies to the fact that if the tomb had not been empty the soldiers never would have left their position, nor would they have gone to the high priest. The fear of the wrath of their superiors and the possibility of the death penalty meant they paid close attention to the minute details on their job.

Why was the guard never punished? Why did the Jewish authorities agree to bribe the soldiers to tell a lie, and also promise to keep the governor from punishing them (likely with another large bribe)? If the stone were simply rolled to one side of the tomb's opening, as would be necessary to enter it, then they might be justified in accusing the men of sleeping at their posts, in which case the guards would have been punished severely. If the men protested that the earthquake broke the seal and that the stone was dislodged by the shifting and cracking of the earth, they would still be liable to punishment for the behavior of leaving their post to go report. But these possibilities do not meet the case. There was some undeniable evidence which made it impossible for the chief priests to bring any credible charge against the guards. No twist of human ingenuity could provide an adequate answer or a scapegoat, so they were forced to bribe the guards and seek to hush things up.

Graveclothes Tell a Tale

As far back as Chrysostom's time (Homily 85), attention has been called to the fact that myrrh was an ointment which adheres so closely to the body that the graveclothes would not easily be removed. Merrill Tenney explained the graveclothes as follows:

> In preparing a body for burial according to Jewish custom, it was usually washed and straightened, and then bandaged tightly from the armpits to the ankles in strips of linen about a foot wide. Aromatic spices, often of a gummy consistency, were placed between the wrappings or folds. They served partially as a preservative and partially as a cement to glue the cloth wrappings into a solid covering ... John's term 'bound' (Gr. *edesan*) is in perfect accord with the language of Luke 23:53, where the writer says the body was *wrapped* ... in linen ....[30]

In a literal sense, the tomb was not empty. After coming into sight of the tomb, and seeing the stone rolled away, Mary Magdalene went and told the disciples. Peter and John then took off running. John outran Peter, but upon arriving at the tomb first, he did not immediately enter. Instead, he leaned over, looked in, and saw something startling. There were graveclothes, in the form of a the body, slightly caved in and empty – like the empty chrysalis of the caterpillar's cocoon. That was enough to make a believer of him.

---

[30] Merrill C. Tenney, *The Reality of the Resurrection* (Chicago: Moody Press, 1963), p.117.

The Bible tells us that John "beheld the linen wrappings lying there, and the face-cloth, which had been on His head, not lying with the linen wrappings, but rolled up in a place by itself" (John 20:6,7). Do you see the picture? A gap would have appeared between the cloths that had wrapped the body from the armpits down, and the face-cloth, a gap where Jesus' face and neck had been. The napkin did not have the crisscross pattern of the linen wrappings. The word "wrapped" could be translated 'twirled.' The people preparing the body for burial had "twirled" the towel into a sort of rope shape, and then tied it around Jesus chin and the top of his head, to keep the mouth shut in death. The face-cloth was still twirled and tied, but there was no head in it! When the apostles reached the tomb, here was what greeted them: the stone slab rolled up the hill; the collapsed graveclothes; the twirled face-cloth; the gap between the two. No wonder John saw and believed!

Christ's Appearances After His Resurrection

With the exception of John, it was not the empty tomb by itself that made believers out of people. It was Christ's post-resurrection appearances which assured them He had actually risen from the dead.

When studying an event in history, it is important to investigate whether enough people who were participants or eyewitnesses were alive when the facts about the event were published. If the number is substantial, the event can be fairly well established. We dare not overlook the large number of witnesses to whom the risen Christ made a post-resurrection appearance.

The Lord Jesus appeared on at least ten separate occasions before a multitude of witnesses after he arose.[31] He showed Himself alive to Mary Magdalene (Mark 16:9), other women (Matthew 28:8-10), Peter (Luke 24:34), two on the Emmaus road (Luke 24:13-35), ten disciples (John 20:19-23), eleven disciples (John 20:26-29), seven disciples in Galilee (John 21:1-23), five hundred at one time (1 Corinthians 15:6),[32] James (1 Corin-

---

[31] One modern attempt to explain away the appearances of Jesus calls them "hallucinations." Modern medicine has observed certain laws that apply to such psychological phenomena, and these make it impossible to accept the "hallucination" theory. (1) Hallucinations occur generally in people who tend to be vividly imaginative and of a nervous makeup. Perhaps one might argue that women are emotional, but there were also hard-headed people, like Peter the fisherman, James, and others, who saw Him. (2) Hallucinations are extremely subjective and individual. For this reason, no two people have the same experience. But in the case of the resurrection, Jesus appeared not just to individuals, but to *groups,* including one of more than 500 people. (3) Hallucinations usually occur only at particular times and places, and are associated with the events fancied. But Jesus' post-resurrection appearances occurred both indoors and outdoors, in the morning, afternoon, and evening. (4) But perhaps the most conclusive indication of the fallacy of the hallucinations theory is a fact often overlooked. In order to have an experience like this, one must so intensely *want* to believe that he projects something that really isn't there and attaches reality to his imagination. In fact, the opposite took place with Jesus' appearances. People were persuaded *against* their wills that Jesus had risen from the dead! Men do not imagine what they do not believe, and the women's intention to finish the embalming of Jesus corpse shows that they did not expect His resurrection.

[32] When Paul wrote affirming that the bodily resurrection of Jesus was a verifiable fact, he reminded his readers that the risen Jesus had been seen by more than 500 people on one occasion, and he reminded

thians 15:7), the eleven at the ascension (Acts 1:3-11), and to Paul (1 Corinthians 9:1). Masses of people affirmed His resurrection to be a fact.

Tom Anderson, former president of the California Trial Lawyers Association, says, "Let's assume that Christ did not rise from the dead. Let's assume that the written accounts of His appearances to hundreds of people are false. I want to pose a question. With a 'false' event so well publicized, don't you think that it is reasonable that one historian, one eyewitness, one antagonist, would record for all time that he had seen Christ's body: 'Listen, I saw that tomb – it was not empty! I was there; Christ did not rise from the dead. As a matter of fact, I saw His body.'"[33] That not one person ever came forward to make such a claim speaks volumes about the fact of the bodily resurrection of Jesus!

The Variety of Locations and People Involved in these Post-resurrection Appearances.

Merrill C. Tenney wrote: "It is noteworthy that these appearances are not stereotyped. No two of them are exactly alike. The appearance to Mary Magdalene occurred in early morning; that to the travelers to Emmaus in the afternoon; and that to the apostles in the evening, probably after dark. He appeared to Mary in the open air. Mary was alone when she saw Him; so were Peter and James. The disciples were together as a group in an upper room when they saw Him. The reactions also were varied. Mary was overwhelmed with emotion; the disciples were frightened; Thomas was obstinately incredulous when told of the Lord's resurrection, but worshiped Him when He manifested Himself to Thomas. Each occasion had its own peculiar atmosphere and characteristics, and revealed some different quality of the risen Lord."[34]

The Witness of the Women

Another authenticating feature of the resurrection narrative is that the first appearances of the risen Christ were not to His male disciples, but rather to women. According to Jewish principles of legal evidence, women were not valid witnesses. They did not

---

his readers that the majority of these people were still alive and could be questioned if the readers still had any doubts about the resurrection. Paul says in effect, "If you don't believe me, you can ask them!" Such a statement in an admittedly genuine letter written within 30 years of the event is almost as strong evidence as we today could hope to get for something which happened nearly 2000 years ago.

Let's take the more than 500 witnesses who saw Jesus alive after His death and burial and place them in a courtroom. If each of these 500 people were to testify only six minutes each, including cross-examination, we would have an amazing 50 hours of firsthand eyewitness testimony. Add to this the testimony of other eyewitnesses and we could well have the largest and most lopsided trial in history!

[33] McDowell, *op. cit.*, p.10.

[34] Quoted by McDowell, *op. cit.*, p.14.

have a right to give testimony in a court of law. For the moment, not considering the astounding nature of the women's report that they had seen the risen Christ, since the testimony of a woman was deemed unreliable, the initial reaction of the eleven was understandably one of suspicion and disbelief. Again, if the resurrection accounts had been manufactured, women would *never* have been included in the story, at least, not as the first witnesses.

Thomas the Doubter is Convinced

Thomas was not present on the Resurrection Sunday evening when Jesus appeared to the group of disciples for the first time (John 20:19-25). They told him about it, but he expressed his doubt, and stated the evidence it would take to convince him (the same evidence, by the way, that had convinced the ten apostles who were present at Jesus' first appearance to the group). He was saying, in effect, "I'll believe when I have personally examined the evidence. I'm an empiricist. Unless I can put my finger into the nail wounds in his hands and my hand into his side, I will not believe." *He* wasn't about to have a hallucination!

John gives us the exciting story (John 20:26-29) of Jesus' appearance to the disciples eight days later. He graciously invited Thomas to examine the evidence of His hands and side. Thomas looked at Him and fell down in worship: "My Lord and my God!" he exclaimed in reverent awe. An appearance of the risen Lord was what convinced Thomas that Jesus had risen from the dead.

The Existence of the Church

It is now admitted on all hands that Christ's church came into existence as a result of a belief in the resurrection of Jesus. A.H. Strong's first volume on *Systematic Theology* rightly says, "The empty tomb has been the cradle of the church." Unless Jesus actually arose from the grave, it is impossible to account for the existence of the primitive church!

When we consider its beginning, as recorded in the history book known to us as "Acts," we see two simple and incontrovertible facts: (1) the Christian society was gathered together by preaching; (2) the substance of that preaching was the resurrection of Jesus the Messiah from the dead. Jesus was put to death on a cross, and would therefore be rejected by Jews as accursed of God (Deuteronomy 21:23). Yet multitudes of Jews were led to worship Him (Acts 2:41), and a great company of priests to obey Him (Acts 6:7). The only explanation of these facts is God's action which raised Jesus from the dead (Acts 2:32). Nothing short of a resurrection could have led to the Jewish acceptance of Jesus as their Messiah.

The apostolic church is thus a result of a belief in the resurrection of Jesus. God's Spirit could only come if Christ arose and ascended to heaven (John 16:7, Acts 1:8, 2:4), and Jesus instructed the apostles to wait for power from on high (Acts 1:4-5). The birthday of the church on Pentecost (Acts 2) would have been impossible if the Lord had not risen earlier.[35] Christ's church annually celebrated His resurrection for centuries, and continues to do so.

The Christian Church has now become world-wide in scope. Its history can be traced back to Palestine about AD 30. Did it just happen, or was there a cause for it? These people who were first called Christians at Antioch turned the world of their time upside down. They constantly referred to the resurrection as the basis of their teaching, preaching, living, and – significantly – dying.[36]

The Transformation and Testimony of the Apostles

The disciples didn't immediately scurry off to Athens or Rome to preach Christ raised from the dead: they went right back to the city of Jerusalem where, if what they were teaching were false, their message would have been disproved.

What was it that changed this band of frightened disciples (who fled when Jesus was arrested, and who went into seclusion behind locked doors for fear of the Jews) into men of courage and conviction? What can account for this astonishing transformation in only three days' time?[37] What was it that changed Peter from one who, the night before the crucifixion, was apparently so afraid for his own life and safety that he denied three times even knowing Jesus, into a courageous proclaimer of this same Jesus? Only the reality of the bodily resurrection of Jesus could have produced a change like this in the disciples.

Historian Paul Maier says, "What happened in Jerusalem seven weeks after the first Easter (at Pentecost) could have taken place only if Jesus' body were somehow missing

---

[35] Peter's sermon on the day of Pentecost is "wholly and entirely founded on the resurrection. Not merely is the resurrection its principal theme, but if that doctrine were removed there would be no doctrine left. For the resurrection is propounded as being, (1) the explanation of Jesus' death; (2) prophetically anticipated as the Messianic experience; (3) apostolically witnessed; (4) the cause of the outpouring of the Spirit, and thus accounting for religious phenomena otherwise inexplicable; and (5) certifying the Messianic and Kingly position of Jesus of Nazareth. Thus the whole series of arguments and conclusions depends for its stability entirely upon the resurrection" (Smith, *op. cit.*, p.365).

[36] It is impossible to allege that the early church did not know its own history, that myths and legends quickly grew up and were eagerly received, and that the writers of the Gospels and Acts had no conscience for principle, but manipulated their material at will. Any modern church (let alone one of the 1st century) could easily give an account of its history for the past 50 years or more. It is absurd to think that the early church had no such capability.

[37] Their discouragement and loss of hope when Jesus was arrested and crucified was changed just three days later. Three days are not enough time for a legend or myth to spring up which could so affect them. Time is needed for a process of legendary growth. There is nothing more striking in the history of primitive Christianity than the marvelous change wrought in the disciples, as they were "begotten again to a living hope by the resurrection of Jesus from the dead" (1 Peter 1:3).

from Joseph's tomb, for otherwise, the Temple establishment, in its imbroglio with the Apostles, would simply have aborted the movement by making a brief trip over to the sepulcher of Joseph of Arimathea and unveiling Exhibit A."[38] The Jewish religious authorities and the Roman governmental authorities did not do this because they could not. The tomb was empty. Jesus had arisen!

The major theme of the apostles' preaching was Christ's resurrection. They must have sounded to some like a broken record. Resurrection preaching dominates the entire book of Acts. Peter proclaimed it (2:32, 3:15, 5:30, 10:40), and so did Paul (13:30, 17:18,31, 28:31). All the apostles continually preached that Jesus rose from the dead (1 Corinthians 15:11). Paul argued that, without the resurrection, his preaching and the Corinthians' faith would be in vain (1 Corinthians 15:14). He would even consider himself a false witness, the Corinthians would still be in their sins, and deceased loved ones would have perished without hope (verses 15-18). If Christ had not risen from the dead, Christians, of all people, should be pitied (verse 19). The apostles, honorable and trustworthy men, unanimously acclaimed the resurrection.

A New Day for Worship

When all the known world of the 1st century worshiped on Saturday, how did Sunday come to be the day of worship for the Christians? Such a shift in the calendar was monumental, and something cataclysmic must have happened to change the day of worship from the Sabbath to Sunday. Christians said the shift came because of their desire to celebrate the resurrection of Jesus from the dead. This shift is all the more remarkable when we remember that the first Christians were Jews.

The early church worshiped on the first day of the week for three reasons: (1) Sunday is the day on which Jesus rose from the dead; (2) Sunday is the day on which Jesus' first post-resurrection appearances were made; (3) Sunday is the day on which the church began.

> On that day, Christ met His disciples in a new intimacy of fellowship (John 20:19), and gave them instruction (Luke 24:36-49). Jesus ascended into heaven as the "firstfruits" or wave sheaf (John 20:17, 1 Corinthians 15:20,23, Leviticus 23:10-12), and breathed the Spirit on them for a special commission (John 20:22). On the first day of the week the Spirit descended from heaven (Acts 2:1-4). The apostle Paul preached then (Acts 20:6-7). Believers came together to break bread on the first day and to give as God prospered them (1 Corinthians 16:2). Christian worship was changed from the seventh day to the first to celebrate Christ's resurrection. The day He arose (Matthew 28:1) reminds Christians weekly of the Lord's victory over death.[39]

---

[38] McDowell, *ibid*.

[39] Richard L. Mayhue, "The Resurrection: Our Faith depends On It," *Moody* (April 1982), p.20,21.

New Testament Scripture

The New Testament speaks more than one hundred times of our Lord's resurrection. Most convincing are His post-ascension appearances. Stephen saw Christ standing at the Father's right hand (Acts 7:56). The Lord stood at Paul's side in Jerusalem (Acts 23:11). The beloved disciple John turned to see Him in the midst of seven golden lampstands (Revelation 1:12-16). The resurrection of Jesus is a truth incontestably supported by the entire New Testament.

Paul's Conversion

A factor crucial to the evidential value of Jesus' post-resurrection appearances is that He also appeared to those who were at first hostile or unconvinced. Over and over again some doubters have commented that Jesus was seen alive after His death and burial only by His friends and followers. Using this argument, they attempt to water down the overwhelming impact of the eyewitness accounts. "Of course, you'd expect His friends to speak well of Him." But this line of argument is wholly incorrect.

No author or informed individual would regard Saul of Tarsus, who was busy killing Christians after he guarded the garments of those who killed the Christian Stephen, to have been a friend or follower of Christ. The facts show the opposite. He despised Christ and persecuted His followers. For Paul, it was a completely life-altering experience when the risen Jesus appeared to him on the Damascus Road. Although he was not at the time a disciple, he later became one of the greatest witnesses for the truth of the resurrection.

> During the nineteenth century, Lord Lyttleton and his friend Gilbert West both left Oxford University at the close of one academic year, each determined to give attention respectively during the long vacation to the conversion of Paul and the resurrection of Christ, in order to prove the baselessness of both. They intended to try to discredit Christianity by disproving Paul's conversion and Christ's resurrection. They met again in the autumn and compared experiences. After examining the evidence, Lord Lyttleton had become convinced of the truth of Paul's conversion, and Gilbert West of the resurrection of Jesus. Both these outstanding leaders confessed Him as Savior and Lord. Lyttleton realized that the Church's most ardent persecutor really did have a personal confrontation with the resurrected Lord (Acts 9:1-22; 22:6-21; 26:4-23).[40]

Not only do we have the record in Acts, but examine Paul's earliest extant writing (1 Thessalonians). What did he know about Jesus? These points stand out: that Jesus Christ was killed (2:15, 4:14), and that he was raised from the dead (4:14). This letter is usually dated c. AD 51, only about 21 years after those events happened. That's a powerful testimony to the historicity of the death and resurrection of Jesus.

---

[40] Michael Green, *Man Alive!* (Downers Grove, IL: InterVarsity Press, 1968), p.55,56.

Only a few years later, Paul wrote 1 Corinthians, and in chapter 15 he adduces the fact of Jesus' resurrection to prove that all Christians can look forward to a resurrection body, too. He even gives a list of Jesus' post-resurrection appearances, ending with Jesus' appearance to Paul himself (1 Corinthians 15:8).[41]

The Conversion of James

Consider James, the half-brother of Jesus. The Gospel record indicates His brothers were anything but believers (e.g., John 7:5). Yet this man James later became a follower of the Lord and joined the band of persecuted Christians. He even became a recognized leader in the church. What made the difference? What caused such a change in his attitude? The historical explanation is that the risen Jesus appeared to James (1 Corinthians 15:7).

Christ's Silent Enemies

Jesus' enemies never built a credible case against His resurrection. If reasonable doubt existed, they would have seized the opportunity. In the early days of the church, the Pharisees only forbade the apostles from preaching the resurrection (Acts 4:17-18, 5:28). They never produced any facts to prove such preaching was in error.

Acts 25 has another revealing instance of official silence. Paul has been imprisoned in Caesarea. Festus, the governor, sat down on the judgment seat and ordered Paul to be brought. The "trial" started with the Jews, who had come from Jerusalem, standing around and bringing many and serious charges against Paul which they could not prove. Just what was it about Paul's preaching that irritated them so? What point did they totally avoid as they made their accusations? Festus, explaining the case to King Agrippa, describes the central issue as concerning "a certain dead man, Jesus, whom Paul asserted to be alive" (Acts 25:19). The Jews would not explain the empty tomb. They could make all kinds of personal attacks on Paul, but as far as the record is concerned, they avoided giving any concrete evidence that Paul's resurrection claims for Jesus were false. They were silent because the grave was empty and they knew it!

Symbolic Ordinances

Baptism by immersion pictures the death, burial, and resurrection, not only of Jesus, but of the person who follows Christ (Romans 6:3-5, Colossians 2:12). Christ's resurrection provides the imagery. If there is no resurrection, why go through a ceremony that pictures such a thing?

---

[41] If the appearance of Jesus to Paul is His appearance when Paul was on his way to Damascus to persecute Christians, the date is c. AD 34. Thus, within 4 years of the time when Jesus rose from the dead, Paul is testifying that He has indeed risen and appeared. Again, this is too little time for a legend or myth to grow up. Within a very few years of the time of the crucifixion of Jesus, the evidence for the resurrection of Jesus was, to the mind of at least one man of education, absolutely irrefutable.

Before He died and arose, Jesus instituted the Lord's Supper, and told his followers to continue to "do this in remembrance" of Him (Luke 22:19). Some years after Jesus arose from the dead, Paul also personally received instructions about the Lord's Supper from the resurrected Christ (1 Corinthians 11:23-27). The bread and the cup regularly remind believers of the Lord's death until He comes (1 Corinthians 11:26). Only the resurrection allows Him to ascend to the Father, then later to appear to Paul, and even still later, to return to judge the world.

Salvation Message

Claiming to be a Christian while denying the resurrection is a contradiction of God's message to the church. "If you confess with your mouth Jesus as Lord, and believe in your heart that God raised Him from the dead, you shall be saved" (Romans 10:9). The resurrection of Jesus Christ cannot be divorced from believing and receiving His free gift of eternal life. Paul inseparably linked the resurrection to salvation.

The Church's Confession

A denial of the resurrection puts one in direct opposition to what has been the historic confession made by Christians across the years. Clement of Rome wrote in AD 96, "Let us understand, dearly beloved, how the Lord continually proves to us that there shall be a future resurrection, of which he has rendered the Lord Jesus Christ the first-fruits by raising Him from the dead."[42] Centuries later, the Westminster Confession (1647) reads, "On the third day He arose from the dead, with the same body in which He suffered; with which also He ascended into heaven, and there sitteth at the right hand of His Father."

One may confidently make the same confession today. Time is the friend of truth. As the centuries progress, skeptics have questioned the resurrection of Jesus. Yet the passing of time has not brought to light new factors which disprove the original testimony of Christ's disciples. Rather, each passing generation lends its testimony to the power of God in the resurrection of Jesus. God, who created life, gave life back again to His Son who died for us. For Christians, the abiding faith in the power of the resurrection has transformed lives through the ages, and this in itself lends testimony to the truth of the resurrection. "Now Christ has been raised from the dead, the first fruits of those who are asleep" (1 Corinthians 15:20).

Can We Be Sure that Jesus Rose From the Dead?

Given the facts, it is more difficult to believe that He did *not* rise from the dead! Something happened almost 2000 years ago that changed the course of history. And it changed the lives of a dozen men so completely that all but one died a martyr's death.

---

[42] 1 Clement xxiv.

Did the resurrection of Jesus actually happen? All the lines of evidence we have advanced shout "Yes!" Taking the various lines of evidence singly, they must be admitted to be strong; taken altogether, the argument is cumulative and sufficient. Every effect must have its adequate cause, and the only proper explanation of Christianity today is the bodily resurrection of Jesus Christ.

We can agree with B.F. Westcott (one of the triumvirate of Bible scholars – Westcott, Lightfoot, and Hort) who said, "Indeed, taking all the evidence together, it is not too much to say that there is no historic incident better or more variously supported than the resurrection of Christ. Nothing but the antecedent assumption that it must be false could have suggested the idea of deficiency in the proof of it."[43]

"The evidence for our Lord's life, death, and resurrection has been satisfactory; it is good according to the common rules for distinguishing good evidence from bad," historian Thomas Arnold said. "I know of no one fact in history which is proved by better and fuller evidence than that Christ died and rose again from the dead."[44]

A student at the University of Paraguay asked Josh McDowell, "Professor, why can't you intellectually reject Christianity?" "For a very simple reason," he answered. "I am not able to explain away an event in history – the resurrection of Jesus Christ."[45]

POSTSCRIPT

In the periodical *Bible Review* (August 1989, p.14ff), Malcom L. Peel, in his article "The Resurrection in Recent Scholarly Research," presents both the historical-critical and redaction-critical handling of the resurrection accounts in the Bible. How sad the conclusions[46] reached by current scholars!

More helpful and satisfactory sources include: "Did Christ Rise from the Dead?"

---

[43] *The Gospel of the Resurrection*, London, 1879, p.4-6.

[44] Thomas Arnold, *Christian Life, Its Hopes, Its Fears, and Its Close*, 6th ed. (London: T. Fellowes, 1859), p.14-16.

[45] Josh McDowell, *The New Evidence that Demands a Verdict* (Nashville: Thomas Nelson, 1999), p.203,204.

[46] Typical of some of the statements are these: "The narratives in Matthew 28, Mark 16, Luke 24, and John 20-21 contain differences that cannot be harmonized, and which display traces of apologetic and Christological reflection that point to later development." "Those subscribing to this principle of historiography must automatically rule out the supernatural as a causative agent." "Q is silent on the issues of Jesus' death and resurrection, and there is no agreement on how to explain this omission in Q." "The predictions of the passion are prophecies made up after the event." "The Gospels cast no direct light on the historicity of the event itself." "The post-resurrection 'appearances' were received in visions by a mind in a state transcending normal consciousness. They were not perceived by bodily senses in the empirical sense of 'seeing'." "The bones of Jesus could yet be lying around Palestine and the resurrection still be true."

by Paul Little in *Know Why You Believe* (Downers Grove, IL: InterVarsity Press, 1970); J.N.D. Anderson, *The Evidence for the Resurrection* (Downers Grove, IL: InterVarsity Press, 1966); Chester E. Tulga, *The Case for the Resurrection of Jesus Christ* (Chicago, IL: Conservative Baptist fellowship, 1951); Josh McDowell, *The Resurrection Factor* (San Bernardino, CA: Here's Life Publishers, 1981); and Wilbur Smith, "The Resurrection of Christ from the Dead: The Apologetic for an Age Demanding Historical Certitude," in *Therefore Stand* (Boston, MA: W.A. Wilde Co., 1945), p.359-437.

Two other more recent books merit attention. They are Norman L. Geisler, *The Battle for the Resurrection* (Nashville, TN: Thomas Nelson, 1989), and Murray J. Harris, *From Grave to Glory* (Grand Rapids, MI: Zondervan, 1990). Geisler has accused Harris of teaching heretical doctrine concerning the resurrection of Jesus. Geisler makes this claim because Harris will not answer affirmatively Geisler's poorly worded question, "Do you believe Christ rose from the dead with the same material body of flesh and bones in which He died?" The kind of body Jesus had after His resurrection is an ancient debate (2nd to the 4th centuries). The Western (Latin) view stressed the identity of the body which was buried with the body that was raised. "As it was in Jesus' case so it will be at the final resurrection. The material particles that composed the earthly body at the time of death will be reassembled by God's power to form the glorified flesh of the resurrection body." This view was formulated in opposition to the pagans who disparaged the body, and the Gnostics who despised anything material. This view was reflected in the creedal statement, "I believe in the resurrection of the *flesh* ...." Tertullian was a strong advocate of this view. The Eastern (Greek) view emphasized the complete transformation that occurs when the body is raised. At the resurrection, the whole person, soul and body, is radically changed so as to form what Paul calls a "spiritual" body, a body responsive to the spirit and suited to heaven. This view opposed the Docetists, who denied the reality of the resurrection, and the Latin school, with its materialistic view of the resurrection. This view was reflected in the creedal statement, "I believe in the resurrection of the *body*" or "I believe in the resurrection of the *dead*." Origen was the principal exponent of this view.

We have said Geisler's statement by which he tests "orthodoxy" is poorly worded, because Jesus' body that died and was buried was gone from the tomb, but Christ's resurrection body was different in some respects from the body He had before He died. His resurrection body was immortal (1 Corinthians 15:53) whereas before it had been mortal; it was capable of appearing and disappearing in a moment; He could eat food but did not need food (Luke 24:41-43); it was imperishable (versus His perishable pre-resurrection body, 1 Corinthians 15:42); the resurrection body was heavenly, not the earthly one He had before His death (15:40); it sometimes was in a "different form" (Mark 16:12); it had flesh and bones (Luke 24:39); it had "wounds" visible (John 20:27, Revelation 5:6); it could be touched and handled (Matthew 28:9, 1 John 1:1-5, Luke 24:39); and like the resurrection body Christians will get, the resurrection body was diverse yet also somehow identical to the body that was buried (1 Corinthians 15:34-44). Geisler's question about the resurrection of Jesus should be so worded that people could give an affirmative answer yet at the same time embracing all these truths about Jesus' glorified resurrection body.

Special Study #8

BAPTIZED FOR THE DEAD

The number of interpretations given to 1 Corinthians 15:29 keeps growing. In the 1950's, the number of interpretations was over 50.[1] Recently, in his commentary on 1 Corinthians, Fisher (*op. cit.*, p.247) wrote, "Over 300 interpretations have been given to this difficult saying." Fee has suggested that most interpreters attempt to find an alternative meaning for one of three words – either "baptize" or "for" or "the dead."[2]

How have interpreters understood these words "baptized for the dead"? The interpretations suggested can be set forth, or classified, under three groups:

I. **Baptism in the proper sense** (dip, submerge, drench, wash in water, or immerse), but not the baptism that is an ordinance of Christ. Many possibilities are suggested:

   A. The washing of dead bodies. (Beza)

   The word "baptized" in this interpretation is taken in the sense of washing or purifying, as in Mark 7:4, Hebrews 6:2 and 9:10. The claim is that dead bodies were carefully washed and purified just before burial, because they hoped for a resurrection.

   REFUTATION: (1) *Baptidzo* does not mean ablution or washing; *baptidzo* is used with no other connotation than full submersion. (2) The participle "baptized" in 1 Corinthians 15:29 is in the middle or passive voice, indicating something the subject does for himself or for his own benefit. We are not to give it an active meaning like Beza did.

   B. The wetting of those who wash the dead. (Beza)

   Based on this interpretation, the supposed meaning is, Why get wet as you prepare the bodies of the dead for burial if there is to be no resurrection?

   REFUTATION: Same as above. Further, if this were the true interpretation, "dead" in 1 Corinthians 15:29 would have to be in the accusative case rather than genitive case.

---

[1] Bernard M. Foschini, *"Those Who are Baptized for the Dead" 1 Cor. 15:29: An Exegetical Historical Dissertation* (Worcester, MA: Heffernan Press, 1951). Foschini's study originally appeared as a series of articles in the *Catholic Biblical Quarterly* beginning with Vol.12 (July 1950), p.260ff, and continuing on in volume 13 (1951).

[2] Fee, *op. cit.*, p.765.

C. The ritual ablution used by the Jews before they offered their sacrifices for the dead. (Cornelius)

REFUTATION: The chief defect in this explanation is that the argument is based on the presupposition of frequent sacrifices for the dead offered by Jewish people, a practice about which we know little or nothing. Paul is not basing his argument to the Corinthians on *Jewish* practices that may not even have existed in Corinth or anywhere else.

D. The washing of purification required when there has been contact with a dead body. (Vasquez)

This idea refers back to the Old Testament Law. See Leviticus 11:8-43.

REFUTATION: What connection *Jewish* ceremonial purification has with the topic of the resurrection of the dead in 1 Corinthians 15 is hard to see.

E. Vicarious purification for those who died in impurity. (Turrianus)

REFUTATION: Turrianus' opinion assumes a *Jewish* practice of vicarious purification or baptism for those who died tainted with legal impurity. Such a practice is nowhere mentioned, and is still to be proved historically.

F. The immersion of divers trying to rescue bodies of shipwrecked sailors. (Flaccius)

REFUTATION: The fishing for the bodies of those drowned at sea has nothing in common with the doctrine of the resurrection. Further, if Greeks denied any future resurrection, who would ever think that attempts to recover the bodies of the drowned was so that they one day might get a resurrection body?

G. A reference to some sort of ceremony or ritual performed in connection with baptism. (Ceulemans, Fouard, Bover)

REFUTATION: Such ceremonies associated with the act of baptism are found only after Paul's time. The book of Acts indicates that, in the 1st century, the act of baptism, i.e., its administration, was very simple.

II. Baptism in a metaphorical (figurative) sense.

A. Baptism (doing the works of penance) for the relief of the dead. (Bellarmane, the Roman Catholic interpretation)

How "relief for the dead" is thought to be an argument for or against resurrection is hard to see.

REFUTATION: This commentator cannot agree to the idea that giving alms, fasting, and praying on the part of relatives of the deceased will bring relief to the deceased (who is supposedly in Purgatory). Philippians 2:12 (KJV) states that each person is to "Work out your own salvation with fear and trembling." No one except each person himself is able to meet any of the conditions prerequisite to personal salvation, and that only while he is living in this world.

B. Baptism for the dead means sadness over the dead. (Brochmann)

That is, people mourned (and shed many tears) because of the death of a loved one, and are thus "baptized for the dead."

REFUTATION: Mourning for the dead in no way indicates a belief in the resurrection. Rather, it might be argued that the more the mourners "cried," that is, "are baptized," the less faith they would be showing in the resurrection.

C. Baptism as the persecutions endured to hasten the Parousia. (Hoekstra)

It is said the faithful undergo persecutions and calamities with the special intention of allowing the cup of iniquity to be filled, so that second coming is hastened, and thus the dead are helped by bringing about their resurrection sooner.

REFUTATION: There is no proof of any such practice, especially that those persecuted were consoled in their tribulations by thinking of the aid they were giving to those already dead. Rather, those persecuted were thinking of the crown that awaited them in heaven. This interpretation is hardly an argument for or against the idea of future resurrection.

D. The baptism of suffering or martyrdom. (Maldanatus)

This seems to be the most popularly accepted interpretation during the 20th century.[3] It is said the word "baptized" is used here as it is in Mark 10:39 and Luke 12:50, in the sense of being 'overwhelmed' with calamities, trials, and sufferings. It is understood as meaning that the apostles and others were subjected to great trials on account of the dead, i.e., in hope of the resurrection or with the expectation that the dead would rise.

This interpretation would agree with the general tenor of the argument. (1) It agrees with the context, verses 30ff. (2) A denial of the resurrection would indicate their sufferings had all been for nought. (3) The tense of *baptidzomai* (see IA on p.684) can be made to harmonize with this view. (4) Grubbs indicated that

---

[3] It is the position presented by Lightfoot, Rosenmuller, Pearce, Homberg, Krause, Robinson, Godet, MacKnight, Grubbs, and G.M. Elliott. The baptism of suffering was defended by Grayson H. Ensign in "Baptism for the Dead" in *Christian Standard* 86 (August 26, 1951), p.540.

a reference to suffering or martyrdom is a necessary, vital, and logical link in the apostle's argument for the resurrection. (a) Verse 13 - If there is no resurrection of the dead, neither has Christ been raised. (b) Verse 15 - If Christ has not been raised, the apostles are false witnesses. (c) Verse 29 - If they were false witnesses, why stood they in jeopardy every hour?

OBJECTIONS to the view that the baptism of suffering is the baptism intended: (1) It is not the usual and natural meaning of the word "baptize." Paul elsewhere uses the word to denote the baptism commanded in the Great Commission.[4] *Oi baptidzomenoi* – "those being baptized" – "unless otherwise defined, can only mean the recipients of Christian baptism."[5] (2) A metaphorical use of a word should not be resorted to unless necessary. (3) This interpretation does not relieve us from any of the difficulties in regard to the phrase "for the dead."

III. Baptism as an ordinance of Christ -- the baptism of penitent believers in Christ

A. Baptism for the benefit of another (usually understood to be someone already dead). There are a number of variations on this theme:

1. Vicarious baptism, baptized on behalf of someone who is dead. (Ambrosiaster, Shore, Anselm, Grotius, Meyer, Alford, the RSV, and the Mormons)[6]

   Vicarious baptism is the baptizing of living proxies in place of those who had died unbaptized.[7]

   a. Arguments for this interpretation: (1) Many strange opinions and practices existed at Corinth. (2) It is affirmed Paul is arguing *ad hominem*.

---

[4] See Romans 6:3ff; 1 Corinthians 1:14,16ff, 10:2, 12:3; Galatians 3:27; Colossians 2:12.

[5] Findlay, *Expositor's Greek Testament.*, V.2, p.930.

[6] Fee (*op. cit.*, p.764) affirms that a fair reading of the Greek is that some were being baptized, vicariously, in behalf of other people who have already died. A. Oepke [in Kittel, *TDNT*, Vol.1, p.542, n.83] wrote that "all interpretations which seek to evade vicarious baptism for the dead ... are misleading." Beasley-Murray [*Baptism in the New Testament*, p.185-192] agrees. A.B. Oliver also advocated this view in "Why are They Baptized for the Dead? A Study of 1 Cor. 15:29," in *Review and Expositor* 34 (1937), p.48-53.

[7] Chrysostom [Hom. 40 on 1 Cor. 1] derisively tells of the practice among the Marcionites that if a person who intended to become a member of the church, and was actually under instruction (a catechumen) died before being immersed, sometimes someone else underwent baptism on behalf of the person who had died unimmersed. The practice sprang from the idea that unless a person is baptized, he was excluded from the bliss of the faithful in heaven. It was to safeguard against this exclusion that sometimes people volunteered to be immersed on behalf of those who had died. While the thrust of his scholarly article is the need to punctuate verse 29 differently from how our KJV version does, K.C. Thompson, "1 Corinthians 15:29 and Baptism for the Dead" in *Studia Evangelica* II (1964), p.647ff, agrees with Chrysostom's view that "baptism for the dead" was vicarious baptism.

Paul would be saying, "What good is this practice of vicarious baptism, if the dead are not raised?" Most commentators who take the verse to refer to vicarious baptism suggest it was practiced at Corinth, but affirm Paul did not approve of the practice.[8]

    b. OBJECTIONS: (1) There is no evidence that such a custom prevailed *during* the time of Paul. (That this custom prevailed in the church *after* the time of Paul has been abundantly proved. Especially was such a practice found among the heretics; see Cerinthus, c. AD 100 and following;[9] the Marcionites, 2nd century through the 6th century.) The practice of vicarious baptism may well have arisen from a perversion of this text. (2) See Philippians 2:12. Man is responsible for his own salvation. Salvation is not by proxy. (3) In a context which talks about "resurrection of dead (bodies)," what would be the point of bringing up such a practice as vicarious baptism. A person's soul could be in bliss or not, and no resurrection is needed in such an argument. (4) To answer the Mormons is difficult, not because of the strength of their arguments, but because they are not on common ground with us. To refute their ideas, we must first refute their "new revelation."[10]

2. Vicarious eschatological baptism. (Preisker)

According to this theory, when the definite, predetermined number of the elect is filled, Christ will return. This baptism (vicariously) helps fill up the number and thus helps hasten the Parousia.

REFUTATION: Both the 'vicarious' and the 'eschatological' ideas are false as far as the Scripture teaches.

3. Baptism of a dead body sought vicariously. (Julian)

The idea is that a relative of the deceased sought a baptism of the corpse, as though it would help ensure salvation.

---

[8] Other evidence is marshaled to defend the idea that Paul disapproved of the practice. For example, attention is called to the fact that Paul uses the third person "they" when he writes ("what will those do ...?") – the suggestion being that the third person indicates that whatever "baptism for the dead" is, it is not something the whole church is doing.

[9] Epiphanius relates that the followers of Cerinthus practiced vicarious baptism. *Haer.* xxviii.6

[10] See Luke P. Wilson, "The Mormon Doctrine of Salvation for the Dead: An Examination of its Claimed Biblical Texts," *Christian Research Journal*, Nov-Dec 1997, p.22ff. According to Mormon teaching, Jesus went to the spirit world during the time between His death and resurrection, where He appointed missionaries from among the righteous to preach to those who had died without the gospel. Because baptism is essential to eternal life, Christ also instituted proxy baptism for the dead as an ordinance for the church so that those who accepted the gospel in the spirit world could have the rite performed on their behalf to seal their salvation.

REFUTATION: See Philippians 2:12.

4. Baptism in defense of the faith in the resurrection on the part of those who died. (Muller)

   It is asserted that baptism was received by those who denied the resurrection with the special intention of defending the Christians who have died in the faith of the resurrection.

   REFUTATION: There is no foundation in this text, or in reason, for this opinion.

B. Baptism for the benefit of the one being baptized.

   1. Baptism of those who have already received the Holy Spirit. (Montanus)

      Montanus referred to Cornelius and his family (Acts 10). He says, "Since Cornelius and his family were already washed of their sins [when they were baptized of the Holy Spirit], the act of baptism bore witness not to the resurrection in newness of life, but to the death of the body and the future resurrection of the body." (*Elucidations*)

      REFUTATION: Montanus, it seems, is right in his conclusion, but wrong in his hypothesis. The Holy Spirit descending upon a man would not save, apart from baptism in water in obedience to Christ. Three times we are told in Acts the Baptism of the Holy Spirit was to convince Peter that the Gentiles were eligible to obey the gospel (Acts 10:47, 11:15-17, 15:8).

   2. Baptism that includes the mortification of the passions. (Julian)

      It is true that we die to sin in baptism, and rise to walk in newness of life.

      REFUTATION: To thus interpret this passage, we must understand the word "dead" in two different senses in the same verse, and there is no warrant for this (Luke 9:60 notwithstanding).

   3. Baptism of those who are on their death bed. (Epiphanius)

      These would be baptized "for the dead," because (having no hope of gaining anything more in this life) they hoped to gain what all righteous dead will gain – the resurrection to life eternal.

REFUTATION: The Scriptures do not encourage waiting to repent until one is on one's death bed.

4. Baptism by which we take the place of the Christians who have died. (Le Clerc, Hammond)

    REFUTATION: This makes verse 29 irrelevant to the argument because, the place of the dead being supplied by their successors, it would be no matter to them whether the dead themselves rose or not.

5. Baptism, at which the names of the dead Christians are received. (Hensius)

    Hensius wrote, "Baptism succeeds circumcision and retains certain of its rites; among which is the giving of a name." Thus, to those to be baptized, and especially infants, the Christians were accustomed to give the names of the dead "apostles, martyrs, holy fathers, deceased relatives ... in order that these might still exist and live ...."

    REFUTATION: How many of the apostles, "holy fathers," and relatives had died by the time of the writing of 1 Corinthians? And the utter folly of his idea that the early Christians baptized infants!

6. Baptism over the sepulchres of the martyrs. (Luther)

    REFUTATION: There is no indication of martyrdom at Corinth at this time.

7. Baptism for the dead means baptism for the sake of Christ who died. (Spanhemius, and see also the article in *Christian Standard*, October 10, 1931)

    REFUTATION: "The dead" (*toi nekroi*) is plural, and cannot be a reference to the death of Christ.

8. Baptized after having been exhorted by a friend or relative now dead. (Robertson and Plummer, so in substance Lenski, G.G. Findlay, and Jeremias)

    The idea is that some are baptized out of respect for folk who have since died. Persons, previously inclined to Christianity, sometimes ended up being baptized out of affection or respect for the dead, i.e., because some Christian relation or friend had died, earnestly desiring and praying for their conversion.

    REFUTATION: How does this add any weight or argument to show the resurrection of the dead? (Jeremias tries to avoid this point by writing "with a view to becoming united with the Christian dead in the resurrection.")

9. Baptism received for fanciful reasons. (Krausins)

'What shall they do who receive baptism because they are urged to, being beguiled and deceived by idle dreams, and thoughts of the dead?'

REFUTATION: What value is this for proving either immortality or the resurrection?

10. Baptism for their own dead bodies.

The baptism Paul alludes to is the baptism commanded in the Great Commission, the baptism administered to all believers, an act that pictures death, burial, and resurrection (cp. Romans 6:3-5). Paul is basing his refutation of their denial of resurrection on the need for them to be consistent. How can they at one time submit to immersion (a vivid picture of resurrection), and then in the next breath insist they do not believe in resurrection?

This is the view advocated by Chrysostom, by the Greek Fathers Theophylact and Theodoret, by Erasmus, Evans, Cornelius A. Lapide, Wordsworth, and Lenski. See this view presented ably by Owen L. Crouch, "Baptism for the Dead" in *Christian Standard* 86 (July 22, 1950), p.461.

This is the view advocated in this commentary.

Conclusions:

Vicarious baptism cannot be accepted as a possible explanation. The phrase cannot mean that the baptism of certain living persons conveys benefit to other persons who are already dead. The presence of the article, "*the* dead," and the close connection of "of the dead" to the participle "baptized" prevent this interpretation from being given.

Two viable interpretations then are left – namely, the baptism of suffering (or martyrdom), and the baptism that puts one into the body of Christ (believer's baptism, it is called). The latter part of this verse (1 Corinthians 15:29) will suggest that the baptism of the Great Commission, the baptism that puts one into the body of Christ, is the one intended.

If there is to be no resurrection of dead bodies, why go through a ceremony (i.e., the baptism in water commanded in the Great Commission) that pictures death, burial and resurrection?

Special Study #9

IS MAN IMMORTAL?

Is man immortal, or is he not? Opinions differ. One of the doctrines currently making the rounds is that the Bible does not teach that the soul is immortal; therefore, eternal punishment of the wicked is unthinkable since before eternal punishment could be inflicted, God would have to deliberately keep the soul alive. Well, then, is man immortal or not?

Definition of Terms

One important term is "soul" (Hebrew, *nephesh*, Greek, *psuchē*). Lexicons give three literal meanings for the word: (1) *Life* on the earth in its external, physical aspects; used in this sense of animals and men; when it leaves the body, death occurs. (2) The *soul*, by which is intended man's desires, feelings, emotions. (3) The *soul* or *immaterial part* of man – which can receive salvation or can be lost, which men cannot injure but which God can hand over to destruction, and which is distinct from the body so far as the body is made up of flesh.[1] It is primarily this third usage with which we are concerned.

It is important to remember that there are two Greek words translated "immortal" in the New Testament. One is *athanasia* (1 Corinthians 15:53,54; 1 Timothy 5:16), which speaks of "deathlessness." The other is *aphtharsia* (1 Corinthians 15:42ff; Romans 2:7; 2 Timothy 1:10) and its cognate *aphthartos* (1 Timothy 1:17; Romans 1:23; 1 Corinthians 9:25; 1 Peter 1:4,24), which mean "uncorruptible, imperishable."

With these brief definitions in mind, let us again consider the question, "Is man immortal?" Is the soul "deathless" and "imperishable"?

Three Modern Attitudes Toward Immortality

Oscar Cullman argues that the idea that the New Testament teaches the soul's immortality is a misunderstanding. He alleges that the immortality of the soul is a Greek doctrine, not a Christian doctrine. The Christian doctrine is that of resurrection, not that of immortality.[2]

Hoeksema, while agreeing with the position that soul-immortality is a non-Christian idea, will permit the term immortality to be applied to man, provided the term is defined. His position, in substance, is that only those who are in Christ are immortal.[3]

---

[1] See the lexicons by Arndt and Gingrich, Thayer, Liddel and Scott, and others.

[2] Oscar Cullmann, "Immortality or Resurrection" an article in *Christianity Today,* July 21, 1958, p.3-6.

[3] H. Hoeksema, *In the Midst of Death,* p.98,99.

The third of the modern attitudes is the opinion that in a sense the souls of all men are immortal (i.e., all have an endless existence), but that the term "immortality" is used in the Bible only of the redeemed, since the heavenly life with its blessings is the only life that meets the real sense of the term.[4]

Which of these three is nearest the truth of the Scriptures?

Old Testament Idea of Immortality

The Bible nowhere explicitly mentions the immortality of the soul, and never attempts to prove it in a formal way. Everywhere it assumes man's immortality as an undisputed postulate, in much the way it assumes the existence of God.

The Old Testament teaches immortality, but not with the clarity of the New Testament, chiefly because God's revelation in Scripture is progressive and gradually increases in clearness. Several Old Testament texts imply the immortality of the soul. The translation of Enoch (Genesis 5:22,24). The phrases "to go to his fathers" (Genesis 15:15) or "to be gathered to his people" (Genesis 25:8, 35:29; Numbers 20:24) speak not of burial in a family cemetery, but of a place where the dead dwell connected together in a society.[5] From Genesis 47:9 (and similar passages where life is called a "journey") Paul argues that the patriarchs expected a life after death.[6] And consider Exodus 3:6 in light of Matthew 22:23. According to Jesus' words, Abraham, Isaac, and Jacob were definitely alive even though their bodies were in the grave. None of them had 'gone out of existence.' All of them were souls that had survived death. Consider further that the dead in the Old Testament descended into Sheol (Greek, *Hades*), and in Sheol they were in a state of conscious existence.[7] A belief in the immortality of the soul is also evidenced by Old Testament Jews from their practice of necromancy, or consulting the dead – against which God gives frequent warnings.[8] Further, the passages that speak of the future resurrection of the dead imply immortality.[9]

Some have attempted to show from the Old Testament that the soul is not immortal. Ecclesiastes 3:19,20 and 9:2-10 are appealed to for proof. There it is stated that the same

---

[4] L. Berkhof, *Systematic Theology,* p.672-78.

[5] Lange's Commentary on Revelation, p.368; McClintock and Strong, *Cyclopedia of Biblical Literature,* V. 4, p.516.

[6] Hebrews 11:13-16.

[7] Genesis 37:35; Isaiah 14:9ff.

[8] Leviticus 19:31, 20-27; Deuteronomy 18:11; Isaiah 8:19, 29:4.

[9] Job 19:23-27; Psalms 16:9-10, 17:15, 49:15, 73:24; Isaiah 26:19; Daniel 12:2; Hosea 13:14.

thing happens to both men and beasts, in that they all die, and the dead know nothing. Surely, it is alleged, such language speaks of non-existence.

How does Ecclesiastes answer the question, "Is man immortal?" Ecclesiastes 12:11 tells us that the book is made up of "goads" and "nails." It may be that the "goads" are *problems* raised to stimulate earnest reflection, and the "nails" are the *solutions* to the problems. The goad would be that which perplexes the man who looks at things from the standpoint of the earth ("under the sun"). Thus, the goad problem – Is it not true that men and beasts all die, and that ends things for them? And the nail solution – viewed from the region above the sun, is that man's spirit does not go out of existence. On the contrary, "Then the dust shall return to the earth as it was, and the spirit will return to God who gave it" (Ecclesiastes 12:7). In fact, in Ecclesiastes 3:11 we are told that man's soul reaches out for the life after this life.[10]

When Ezekiel 18:4,20 says, "The soul that sinneth, it shall die" (ASV), this is not necessarily proof that the soul is mortal. It might mean that sin will *separate* man from God. That is one thing that death is. It is separation.

Certainly, the Old Testament implies the immortality of the soul.

Greek Philosophers on Immortality

It has already been noted that some are of the opinion that immortality of the soul is not a Christian idea, but a Greek idea. Just what did the Greek philosophers teach on the subject of immortality? At death "the soul departs ... to a divine, immortal ... place ... It lives the rest of the time with the gods."[11] In another place is this note,

> ... the soul is an entirely different thing from the body. In actual life, that which makes each of us what he is, is the soul. ... [T]he immortal soul (when we are dead) passes on to other gods to give account of itself, so tradition tells us – an encouraging thought for the good man, but very alarming for the wicked.[12]

The ideas the philosophers taught plainly had come, they said, from "sacred sayings of old" or "tradition." Instead of the Christians getting their beliefs from the philosophers, the Greek philosophers got their teachings from that ancient knowledge which men deliberate-

---

[10] Some interpret Ecclesiastes 3:11 to mean that man is different from the beast in that man is a reflecting, meditating soul, while the beast is not. At least, the "nail" says that "man is not in every respect like the beast."

[11] Adam Fox, *Plato and the Christians*, p.75.

[12] *Op. cit.*, p.86. See similar ideas expressed on pages 88-90.

ly allowed to get away as time passed.[13]

It will further help to see whether immortality is a Greek or Biblical idea by examining the doctrine of immortality in the New Testament.

New Testament Teaching of Immortality

The doctrine of immortality is found everywhere assumed in the New Testament. A future state for both righteous and wicked is clearly taught. The continued existence of believers appears in such passages as Matthew 10:28; Luke 23:43; John 11:25ff; 2 Corinthians 5:1. The survival after death of the wicked is made clear in Matthew 11:21-24, 12:41; Romans 2:5-11; 2 Corinthians 5:10. That even the wicked survive death, and are in a state of conscious existence, is clearly suggested by the narrative of the rich man and Lazarus in Luke 16:19ff. Immortality is implied in all those passages in which the body is represented as a garment which is to be laid aside, or as a tabernacle or house in which the soul dwells.[14] When Jesus Christ appeared in this world, the views about immortality that prevailed were those of the Jews and the Greeks. It was left for Him to advance the revelation of the future state of soul, and this He did. Paul says, "Christ Jesus ... abolished death, and brought life and immortality to light through the gospel."[15] By means of the gospel, men have had disclosed to them the life of the future world, and the incorruptibility (*aphtharsia*) of both body and soul.[16] Paul has pointed out that the wicked survive death, and have wrath, indignation, tribulation, and anguish awaiting them.[17] He also taught that one of the things included in the redemptive act of Christ was the redemption of the body. Christ died for the body as well as for the soul. This is why He can speak of the uncorruptible body which awaits the redeemed at the second coming of Christ.[18]

The statement of 1 Timothy 6:16, that "only God possesses immortality," is often used to refute the conclusion to which this paper is tending. On the basis of that passage, it is alleged by some that no soul is immortal. Is this a true inference to draw from 1 Timothy? No reputable commentary so understands it. To quote just a few:

---

[13] Romans 1:20ff.

[14] 2 Corinthians 12:1-4, 5:1; 2 Peter 1:14; Philippians 1:23,24.

[15] 2 Timothy 1:10.

[16] See *Barnes' Notes* at 2 Timothy 1:10. See also Hendriksen, *1-2 Timothy and Titus*, p.233,234.

[17] Romans 2:6ff.

[18] 1 Corinthians 15; 1 Thessalonians 4:16ff, etc.

Justin Martyr says,

> God is said only to have immortality, because He has it not by the will of another, as the rest who possess it, but of His own proper essence.[19]

Barnes' note is this,

> It seems to mean that God, in his own nature, enjoys a perfect and certain exemption from death. Creatures have immortality only as they derive it from Him, and of course are dependent on Him for it. He has it by his nature, and it is in His case underived.[20]

Only those who disbelieve the overwhelming evidence for the survival of the soul after death try to use 1 Timothy 6:16 as proof that man is mortal.

One other New Testament doctrine needs to be considered. Briefly, it is this: The word "immortality" is used specifically only with reference to the redeemed, when speaking of men. This seems to imply that the Bible writers put an exalted definition on the term, speaking of the blessedness of heaven. There is a sense in which only the saved have "immortality" since the continued existence of the wicked cannot be called "eternal *life*" in the full sense of the word "life."

Conclusion

The reality of a conscious life beyond the grave is uniformly assumed and taught by the inspired Bible writers. To this future life they assign no terminus or end. Cullman's assertion that the idea of immortality was a Greek doctrine has been shown to be false. The wicked have been shown to be immortal in the sense that they have continued existence after death. Those who wish to deny the future punishment of the wicked will have to go elsewhere for arguments.

To the question "Is Man Immortal?" a good answer would be, "Yes, but only in the sense that his existence never ends. The Bible uses the word 'immortal' only for the redeemed. The soul has been endowed with immortality by the God who alone possesses immortality!"

---

[19] Quoted by Henry Alford, *Greek Testament,* V.3, p.362,363.

[20] *Barnes' Notes* on 1 Timothy, p.202. Compare Hendriksen, *op. cit.,* p.208.

SECTION NINE: CONCERNING THE COLLECTION FOR THE POOR SAINTS IN JERUSALEM. 16:1-11

A. Directions Respecting the Collecting and Transmission of Alms for the Poor Saints at Jerusalem. 16:1-4

16:1 -- *Now concerning the collection for the saints, as I directed the churches of Galatia, so do you also.*

Now concerning the collection -- "Now concerning" is the formula used to introduce topics mentioned in the letter sent to Paul by the Corinthians (see notes at 1 Corinthians 7:1). Perhaps they asked for instructions on how to carry out their part in the "collection." "Collection" here translates *logeias*, a word in common use, more especially to denote a collection for religious purposes. This offering meant much to Paul, and this is the first mention of it in his epistles.[1] He made a widespread and intensive effort to encourage the Christians of several countries to participate in the offering.

Studying the different words used in connection with the offering in 1 and 2 Corinthians and Acts helps us appreciate what was involved in the benevolent project.

(1) "Collection" (*logeias*, 1 Corinthians 16:1). Barclay tells us that a *logeia* was something which was the opposite of a tax which a man had to pay; it was an extra piece of giving for religious purposes.[2] In this word there is some precedent for special appeals or for special offerings over and above a person's regular giving.

(2) "Grace" (*charis*, 2 Corinthians 8:4 ASV). The root meaning of *charis* is a free gift freely given. The offering was a tangible response to benefits received from God. Barclay writes, "The really lovely thing is not something which is extracted from a man, however large it may be, but something which is given in the overflowing love of a man's heart, however small it may be."[3] The offering was to be an expression of love by the church members who contributed it for the Jewish Christians at Jerusalem. *Charis* indicates the givers felt delight to have opportunity to participate in the offering.

(3) "Fellowship" (*koinōnia*, 2 Corinthians 8:4 ASV; see 2 Corinthians 9:13 and Romans 15:26). *Koinōnia* indicates participation in a common cause, a sharing. Barclay's comment is, "Christian fellowship is based on the spirit which cannot hug to itself that which it has, but which regards all its possessions as things to be shared with others."[4] The attitude of the good Samaritan is the right one: 'What is mine is yours, and I'll

---

[1] See also Romans 15:26, 2 Corinthians 8,9, and Galatians 6:6-10.

[2] Barclay, *op. cit.*, p.182.

[3] *ibid*.

[4] *ibid*. All the quotes from Barclay on these words used for the offering come from pages 182-184.

give it to you if you need.' Paul's basic hope was this offering would cement relationships between Christians of different ethnic (Jewish, Gentile) backgrounds (Romans 15:25-31).

(4) "Ministering, service, relief" (*diakonia*, 2 Corinthians 8:4, see 2 Corinthians 9:1,12,13). The root word in *diakonia* means 'ministry' or 'practical service.' Barclay (*op. cit.*, p.182-183) explains, "It may sometimes happen that the limitations of life prevent us from rendering personal service, and it may often happen that our money can go where we cannot go."

(5) "Bounty, abundance," "generous gift" (*hadrotēs*, 2 Corinthians 8:20). The emphasis of this word is abundance. This special offering was looked on by Paul as being a special responsibility. When the people had sacrificed and given over and above their regular giving, that fact required special care lest people think Paul was keeping any of the money for himself.

(6) "Praise, adulation," "bountiful gift" (*eulogia*, 2 Corinthians 9:5). There is an idea of "thanksgiving to God" implied in the word. Perhaps the giver is joyfully thankful for the opportunity. There is a giving that is done out of a feeling of necessity, "a bleak and unavoidable duty" (Barclay, *op. cit.*, p.183). In true giving that pleases God, there is a delight that accompanies the opportunity to share. Perhaps Paul has in mind the blessing to the recipients, or perhaps he has in mind the blessing (i.e., thanksgiving) that will go up to God after the gift is received (2 Corinthians 9:12-14).

(7) "Service, public gift, charitable administration" (*leitourgia*, 2 Corinthians 9:12). Barclay (*ibid.*) tells us, "In classical Greek this is a word with a noble history. In the great days of Athens there were generous citizens who volunteered out of their own pockets to shoulder the expenses of some enterprise on which the city was engaged. It might be to defray the expenses of training the chorus for some new drama or some team to compete for the honor of the city in the games; it might be to pay for the outfitting and manning of a trireme or man-of-war in the time of the city's peril." Thus the word came to have the connotation of a voluntary offering, a large gift. This word looks at the offering as an 'act of service to God.'

(8) "Alms, mercy, pity" (*eleēmosunē*, Acts 24:17). This is the regular Greek word for alms. "So central was almsgiving to the Jewish idea of religion that the Jew used the same word for 'almsgiving' and 'righteousness' ... The Jew would have said, 'How can a man show that he is a good man except by being generous?'" (Barclay, *ibid.*).

(9) "Offering, sacrifice" (*prosphorē*, Acts 24:17). This word denotes a sacrifice or an offering made to God. There is a very real sense that when an offering is given to a man who is in need, that offering is given to the Lord. Remember Jesus' words about 'doing it to the least of these My brethren, you do it unto Me.'

In 2 Corinthians 8-9, other important truths about this special offering for the poor are given. The giving is grounded in love. The giving is rooted in the cross. 2 Corinthians speaks of 'first giving of one's self to the Lord.' The whole spiritual empire is to be financed. There is to be the winning of the world. All this is to be brought about by the free-will, systematic giving of the Christian. Giving is an individual matter.

The entire form of the introduction of this subject, as well as the use of the article *tēs* with *logeias* ("*the* collection"), indicates the Corinthians had prior knowledge of this offering. There is some difference of opinion as to where they acquired this knowledge. Some say Paul, when he stayed at Corinth after the founding of the church, urged them to take up this offering. Lenski, who believed in a "previous letter" (see 1 Corinthians 5:9), held that instructions concerning the offering were included in it.[5] Others say Titus was the one who organized the collection at Corinth, and that the Corinthians first heard of the need for this offering from him (see 2 Corinthians 8:6). The "year" of 2 Corinthians 9:2 places this giving of instructions about the offering before the writing of 1 Corinthians. The Christians at Corinth were aware of the need before they wrote their question to Paul. Further, it seems they had expressed the utmost readiness to make this collection. Paul commends their readiness when he was urging the same subject in Macedonia (see 2 Corinthians 9). It is evident, however, that for some cause (perhaps owing to the divisions and contentions in the church) this collection had not yet been made. The thrust of Paul's answer to their question (verses 2,3) deals with the mechanics of collecting and transporting the offering.

For the saints -- These "saints" (*eis tous hagious*) were the poor Christians in Jerusalem. Nothing is said in this verse about the identity of these "saints," but verse 3 makes it clear they were Christians living at Jerusalem. See also Romans 15:26, and compare Acts 24:17 for evidence of the identity of these "saints." The use of the word "saint" (*hagios*) does not mean the Christians at Jerusalem were 'holy' in some special sense. Paul is here indicating *why* the Corinthians ought to give. Those in need are their fellow Christians.

Why did the saints at Jerusalem at this time (c. AD 56,57) need help? We can suggest a number of possible reasons, though perhaps we cannot put our finger on the *one* reason. (1) A famine had occurred in the land of Israel a few years earlier. Perhaps its effects were still being felt. In that famine of AD 44 (Acts 11:27-30), "Queen Helena of Adiabene had kept the paupers of Jerusalem alive by importing cargoes of dried grapes and figs. The Jews often made collections for impoverished Jews" (Farrar, *op. cit.*, p.549). "Jerusalem had a pauperized population, dependent on the periodic influx of visitors. The Jewish world, from Cicero's time at least, supported the poor of Jerusalem by occasional subvention" (Robertson & Plummer, *op. cit.*, p.382). When a man became a Christian, he would lose any possibility of sharing in the Jewish doles. So, if Jews made collections for impoverished Jews, Christians ought to do as much for Christians. (2) Some say the need was because of the 'utter failure of the communistic enterprise,' but this reasoning is invalid. There was no community-wide distribution at Acts 4:32-35, nor was it a requirement that all members of the church participate in a community of goods. *Some* (not all) of the brethren did sell their possessions and the money was given to the leaders of the church, to be used as needed; but the church at Jerusalem never was a commune type of colony. Further, by AD 57, when 1 Corinthians was written, the original Jerusalem congregation that had given so generously had been scattered (Acts 8:1-4), and a whole new congregation had been assembled, to whom this offering was being sent. (3) Persecution was another possible cause for the people's needing help. (4) James 2:1-9 notes a clash between the rich and the poor at Jerusalem, and the marked distinction between rich and poor was probably handed down to the Jews from the earlier periods of their history. (See

---

[5] Lenski, *op. cit.*, p.756.

the denunciations of the rich by Isaiah, Jeremiah, and Nehemiah.) Did the majority of new Christians come from a poorer sociological and economic strata (cp. James 2:5), so that when times became hard, the poor became poorer and their needs were compounded? They might also be subject to persecutions and difficulties because of their Christianity, making it harder for a Christian to get a job than for a non-Christian.

Putting all these together (at least those that are believable), the conclusion is this: The need for financial help at Jerusalem was a chronic condition, rather than an acute emergency that had just recently occurred. The Gentile churches are taking nearly a year to collect the offering, rather than rushing to get relief measures to Jerusalem as quickly as possible. We do not know why this church was so poor, evidently poorer by far than other churches. But Jerusalem as a whole was not rich, being largely dependent on the generosity of Jews from outside Palestine. Christians would not receive such Jewish aid. On the contrary, they would be the objects of special hostility and persecution (1 Thessalonians 2:14ff), and might well be in special straits. In a letter written to Rome just a few months later, Paul asked for prayers concerning the offering to Jerusalem. "Pray that my service for Jerusalem may prove acceptable to the saints" (Romans 15:31). Paul was concerned as to whether or not the Christians in Jerusalem would accept an offering from Gentiles. If the Christians at Jerusalem should accept the gift, it could go a long way toward cementing the bond between the churches. There was a great question in Paul's mind, 'Will the Christians at Jerusalem accept the offering? Will they thus show that they have a grace for receiving, i.e., not be too proud to receive?' Because the gift of salvation came to the Gentiles from the Jews, Paul believed the Gentiles ought to minister to the Jerusalem Christians in physical things (Romans 15:27). Those who gave, those who received, and the cause of Christ – all these would benefit by this collection.

As I directed the churches of Galatia -- *Dietaxa* means "to arrange, to command, to direct, to enjoin." The compound verb indicates that *detailed* directions had been given. There is a tone of authority in the verb "directed" – this is an apostle speaking! He certainly had authority to tell all the churches how to go about collecting the offering. The directions related solely to the *manner* of making the collection, not to the amount. It does not mean Paul had assumed the authority to tax them, or that he had commanded them to make a collection. The collection was voluntary and cheerful in all the churches (Romans 15:26,27; 2 Corinthians 9:2). This is not the pope telling each diocese how much they have to give, nor is this a proof text for pledges being required from the people. Paul did not have to legislate how much was to be given. The early Christians were known for their self-denial and liberality. Paul recommended the same 'order' or 'directions' to all the churches, including the "churches of Macedonia" (2 Corinthians 8:1) and the "churches of Galatia." Galatia was a province in Asia Minor. According to Acts 20:4, the churches of southern Galatia are the ones involved, for the representatives carrying the gift from those churches are Gaius of Derbe and Timothy of Lystra. When and how had these directions been given by Paul to Galatia? This order may have been issued during Paul's residence among the Galatians earlier on this very same missionary tour (Acts 18:23). Or, it may have emanated from him at Ephesus (the third missionary journey), before the writing of 1 Corinthians. Paul's 'order' to the Galatians is not found in the epistle to the Galatians. Allusion to it therein is only incidental (2:10). While 6:6-10 does deal with the offering, there is not the detail in that passage implied in the word 'directions'. If the orders came from Paul's stay at Ephesus, we must presume the 'order' was conveyed either personally by a messenger, or by a letter not preserved.

So do you also -- "So also" indicates that as far as method is concerned, Paul has suggested one good method. All the churches are to use it. The aorist tense imperative gives the exhortation a sense of urgency. 'If you are going to participate in the offering, get to it at once!' Paul uses the Galatians as an example for the purpose of stimulating the Corinthians. "To the Corinthians he proposes the example of the Galatians; to the Macedonians, the example of the Corinthians; to the Romans, that of the Corinthians and Macedonians (2 Corinthians 9:2 and Romans 15:26). Great is the power of example."[6] Verses 2 and 3 will give some of these detailed arrangements similar to what had been given to the churches of Galatia.

16:2 -- *On the first day of every week let each one of you put aside and save, as he may prosper, that no collections be made when I come.*

On the first day of every week -- Paul here repeats the very directions given to the churches of Galatia. The Corinthians are to adopt the same method. Literally rendered, *kata mian sabbatou* says 'upon one of the Sabbath.' If we take "Sabbath" to refer to the day we call Saturday (the seventh day of the week), then the genitive *sabbatou* likely means the first day *from* (i.e., after) the Sabbath.[7] The Jews, however, used the word "Sabbath" to denote the week (see Luke 18:12 and Mark 16:9), as well as the seventh day of the week. Either way the phrase is explained, it is universally agreed this expression here denotes the day we now call Sunday, the first day of the week – the Lord's Day. Apparently the name 'Lord's Day' was not yet widely used to designate the day we call Sunday. Likely the expression 'Lord's Day' as a reference to Sunday occurs first in Scripture at Revelation 1:10. The first day of the week is never called "the Sabbath" in Scripture. Paul says the offering is to be received "every week." As *kata polis* signifies every city, and *kata mona*, every month, and *kata ekklēsian* (Acts 14:23), in every church, so *kata mian sabbatou* signifies the first day of every week.[8] "Sunday by Sunday let each one of you lay by ...."[9]

Chronologically, this language in 1 Corinthians 16 is the first suggestion that Christians were using the first day of the week as their time of meeting.[10] As we consider the day of worship, the strong implication is that the churches of Galatia and Corinth were

---

[6] J.A. Bengel, *Gnomon of the New Testament* (Edinburgh: T&T Clark, 1860), Vol.3, p.343.

[7] The expression here is explained by some as being a Hebraism (see Matthew 28:1, Mark 16:2, Luke 24:1, John 20:1,19, or compare Leviticus 23:15). It is equivalent to 'the day next after the Sabbath.'

[8] James Macknight, *Apostolical Epistles and Commentary* (Grand Rapids, MI: Baker, 1969), p.291.

[9] Lenski, *op. cit.*, p.759.

[10] 1 Corinthians was written in AD 57. Acts 20:7, written in AD 63, represents an event happening in the spring of AD 58. Revelation 1:10 was written in AD 96.

meeting on Sunday for worship. It is very likely that the churches met on this day because they had been so taught by the apostles who evangelized those places and planted the churches. Already the day of the week on which Christ had risen had become noted as a suitable day for distinctively Christian work and Christian worship. It was fitting that the early church should so commemorate the resurrection of Christ. The Jewish Sabbath commemorated the redemption from Egypt; in a similar way the Christian day of worship and service commemorated the redemption from sin.[11] The time the Corinthians will have to gather the offering covers a year (Passover time, AD 57, when Paul writes this letter, to Passover time, AD 58, when the offering bearers begin their journey to Jerusalem, Acts 20:6). The Galatians had even longer to accumulate their portion of the offering.

Let each one of you -- Paul's words encourage each and every individual person to participate in the offering for the poor at Jerusalem. 'Let each one embrace this opportunity and privilege to give.' The poor, as well as the rich, were expected to contribute according to their ability. The slave, as well as the master, was expected to give. *Each* person in each congregation is encouraged to become involved in sharing in this collection. If it was right to do good on the Jewish Sabbath (Matthew 12:19, Mark 3:4), how much more is it right to do good on the Lord's Day?

Put aside – In *par' heautō tithetō*, the word *heautō* can either be masculine or neuter. If neuter, the NASB translation "aside," or 'by itself,' is correct. Each church member was to set the offering aside, to designate a certain portion of his income or possessions for the offering. If treated as masculine, the KJV "lay by him" is correct. When he is alone or by himself, the giver is to decide the amount to be given. "Let him do it not under the influence of pathetic appeals, nor for the sake of display when he is with others."[12]

A difficult question to answer is whether this refers to an offering being taken up at home or an offering taken up in a church assembly. (1) The majority of commentators indicate that this offering was to be "put aside" *at home*. For example: He says nothing of laying by "in a church assembly" (Kling, *op. cit.*, p.355). "This cannot mean, 'let him assign a certain sum as he is disposed, and put it in the church treasury'" (Robertson and Plummer, *op. cit.*, p.384). "Let him lay up at home, treasuring up as he has been prospered" (Barnes, *op. cit.*, p.327). "The Greek phrase implies the laying up was done 'at home'" (Farrar, *op. cit.*, p.549). "Let each one of you lay up at home ..." (Alford, *op. cit.*, p.621, and Lenski, *op. cit.*, p.759). *Par' heautō* is an idiomatic expression meaning "at home" (Kling, *ibid.*). In fact, many commentators from Chrysostom down have maintained that this speaks of "setting aside" the money at home. If the offerings were collected each week at the public assembly, what was the method by which the collected monies were kept safe? In Bible times, would it not be easier to keep individual amounts

---

[11] Other passages which imply the assembly for corporate worship for the church regularly took place on the first day of the week are Acts 20:7, Revelation 1:10, John 20:19,26, and 1 Corinthians 16 as compared with 1 Corinthians 11 (which dealt with abuses at the public assembly). See D.A. Carson, *From Sabbath Day to Lord's Day: A Biblical, Historical and Theological Investigation* (Grand Rapids, MI: Zondervan, 1982).

[12] Barnes, *op. cit.*, p.327.

safe at home than to keep the funds safe after they were collected at the public assembly? (2) In spite of such difficulties, there are several things in this paragraph which cause this commentator to believe that this refers to an offering taken *in an assembly* of the church. (a) If this "putting aside" was something done at home, then why direct it be done on the "first day of every week"? The reason for designating the "first day of every week" here is doubtless that they met for worship on the first day of the week because the resurrection of Christ had occurred on that day. "Fellowship" (participation in a common cause, like this offering for the poor) has been part of the worshipers' involvement in the public assembly on the first day of the week since the church began (Acts 2:42). (b) "That no collections be made when I come" (the end of verse 2) is easier explained if the offerings have already been brought to a single collection point each first day of the week as the weeks passed before Paul's arrival. Paul desires that when he comes, there will be no need of gathering the offering, for it will already have been done. So, even if the amount were set aside at home (before the worshiper arrived at the assembly place), the money was to be brought to the assembly and handed over to the elders *before* Paul arrived.

Whether collected at home or at the public assembly, there is a solid reason behind these instructions about weekly setting aside of some funds for the offering for Jerusalem. Much more will be in the mission offering if it is brought each first day of the week. Systematic, week-by-week giving will be more in total than what might be given if the offering is let go for several weeks, and is then taken up as a single event.

And save -- Literally, *thēsauridzōn* means 'treasuring up,' 'continuing to save,' i.e., the sum increases each week. The older English versions read "in store."[13] The phrase may mean that each one was to put the part which he had designated (by himself) into the common treasury. This interpretation seems to be demanded by the latter part of the verse. They were to lay it by, and to put it into the common treasury, that there might be no trouble of collecting when Paul arrived. On the other hand, as far as the word *thēsauridzōn* itself is concerned, the 'storing up' or 'saving' is something that could have been done at home as the weeks passed until Paul himself arrived to make final arrangements for the money to be sent to Jerusalem.

As he may prosper -- How much each member gives is his own decision. The word translated "prosper" is in the passive voice in the original. The KJV translators supplied "God" as the implied agent (the KJV reads, "as God hath prospered him"). While the verb is passive, the tense may be either present or perfect. The forms are the same, the only difference being in the accent; since there are no accent marks in the older manuscripts, only the context tells us which it is. Either gives a good sense, and both yield the thought of a continuing state. "In any case, the meaning is that the amount set aside is to be fixed by the giver in proportion to his weekly gains; and there is no dictation as to the right proportion, whether a tenth, or more, or less. A tenth might be too little for some, impossible for others, in this special offering. But week by week, each would see how

---

[13] On the basis of the KJV reading, a sermon on "storehouse tithing" was first preached in a Methodist church in Cincinnati, Ohio, in 1895. The church was the "storehouse" into which the tithe was to be brought weekly, was the thrust of the message.

much or how little he had prospered and would act accordingly."[14] This offering for Jerusalem seems to be a special offering – over and above their weekly giving – so Paul says, 'When you see how you've been blessed, then give accordingly.'

That no collections be made when I come -- Paul is not indicating that no offerings were to be taken after he came to Corinth. "Fellowship" (Acts 2:42) seems to show regular offerings were one way the early Christians "participated" in the work of Christ. Giving is basic to worship. Such giving would hardly cease after this offering for the poor at Jerusalem. But the collection of a special offering like this one can be concluded. Paul is saying that by the time he comes to Corinth, this special offering is to have already been "put aside." 'Set aside your offerings on a weekly basis, and have all the money collected before I get there.' That would be much better than hurriedly collecting what might be available while Paul is already present with them. In the Greek, the emphasis is on "then" – 'In order that when I come, *then* there may be no collections for the saints in Jerusalem needing to be made.' Incidentally, Paul uses the indefinite *hotan* for "when." The time of his coming visit to Corinth is uncertain.

16:3 -- *And when I arrive, whomever you may approve, I shall send them with letters to carry your gift to Jerusalem;*

And when I arrive -- Paul now mentions further arrangements respecting the collection, namely, how the funds are to be transmitted to Jerusalem. Just as he did not dictate to individuals how much they are to give (for it is a special offering), he does not dictate who the messengers are to be who will actually carry the offering to Jerusalem. He personally will not touch the money at any time. He arranges for the churches to send men whom they themselves approve, thus avoiding all suspicion of misappropriation of the money (cp. 2 Corinthians 8:16-21). Paul expected to come to Corinth soon (verse 5). The offering was not to be sent off until after the apostle arrived at Corinth.

Whomever you may approve, I shall send them with letters -- "Approve" (*dokimidzō*) means to approve after examination. "You approve (them)" indicates that Paul himself wants no part in the selection of the ones who will bear the money. He is planning ahead, how things will look, intentionally guarding against any possibility that someone may try to use Paul's own actions as evidence that Paul wanted to get his hands on the money for personal use. There has been great variety of opinion in regard to the proper construction of this verse, and thus who it is who is pictured as writing the letters. (1) Westcott and Hort place a comma after "letters", just as does the KJV. According to this punctuation, the letters referred to were not letters written by the apostle, but letters signed and sent by the church at Corinth, *letters of commendation from the church*. Barnes, writing a century ago, indicates this was the usual punctuation of the printed Greek texts of his time (*op. cit.*, p.329). (2) Nestle and Alford (*ibid.*) place the comma after "approve", as does the ASV/NASB. The verse then reads, 'Whomever you shall approve, them will I send with letters to carry your bounty unto Jerusalem.' According to this punctuation, the letters re-

---

[14] Robertson and Plummer, *op. cit.*, p.385.

ferred to were not letters written by the church, but letters signed and sent by Paul, *letters of commendation from Paul.* Verse 4 is said to indicate Paul was willing to go, but was not certain he would go to Jerusalem. And if he did not go, what was more natural than that he should send letters of greeting and commendation to his brethren in Judea? Such letters of introduction or commendation were a regular part of business dealings in the first century. They may have been addressed to the Jerusalem brethren explaining the source and reasons for the offering. They may have been addressed to Paul's friends along the way, and would have secured for the money-bearers safe lodging and assistance on their way. There would be a plurality of bearers. The whole offering would have been in coin form (carried in money belts), there would be more safety in numbers from attempts at robbery by highwaymen, and a plurality of bearers would help insure the basic integrity of the overall enterprise.

To carry your gift to Jerusalem -- "Gift" translates *charis*, 'our donation, your alms, your freely given gift.' The Greek word ("gift") usually signifies grace, or favor. Here it means an act of grace or favor; kindness; a favor conferred; benefaction. The money was a token of their voluntary affection. The Christian saints at Jerusalem were to be the recipients of this special benevolent offering. We may suppose when the bearers arrived at Jerusalem, they could personally represent the congregation which had sent them. When they completed the delivery of the funds, they would return to their home churches. We can see them reporting in detail regarding the conditions prevalent in Jerusalem and the joy the recipients expressed. A positive report from the messengers would do much to involve the home churches in future mission projects.

16:4 -- *and if it is fitting for me to go also, they will go with me.*

And if it is fitting for me to go also -- "Fitting" translates *axios*, 'worthy.' Paul does not put in words what might make a trip for him to Jerusalem fitting or not. Perhaps the requirements of his missionary activities in the Aegean world would preclude any time for a trip to Jerusalem. Perhaps, as at other times, Paul is conscious of the providence of God in his life, and that God might have other plans for him than a trip to Jerusalem. Perhaps the size of the offering has something to do with Paul's travel plans. Unless the collection were a substantial proof of the generosity of the Gentile churches, it would hardly be worthwhile for Paul to go. This last idea by no means conflicts with real humility. Paul might say this from a just sense of his dignity as an apostle. If the offering were small, indicating a small interest in the recipient's welfare, the apostle could not take the lead in so unworthy a mission. At any rate, Paul says that if he should go to Jerusalem, he and their approved messengers could travel together.

They will go with me -- According to Acts 20, when the time came for the trip, Paul did make the journey to Jerusalem. Paul twice went to Jerusalem with money for the poor. Acts 11:29,30 tells of one such trip, before any of his missionary journeys. Acts 20:1-6 compared with 24:17 tells of a second such trip, which came at the end of Paul's third missionary journey. Note in Acts 20:1-6, no Corinthian delegates are mentioned. Delegates who likely carried offerings are named from Berea, Thessalonica, Derbe, and Asia. Does this indicate the Corinthians' part in the offering was only a small contribution? Did the Corinthians ask Paul to carry their portion of the offering? Some have suggested the Corinthians were so distracted and occupied by their dissensions and factionalism that they never got around to taking part in the offering for Jerusalem.[15] Or perhaps Titus was the one who carried the Corinthians' gift. Titus is not mentioned by name in Acts (which Ramsay believed reflected the fact that Titus and Luke were brothers). That Paul did make the trip to Jerusalem seems to indicate the collection from all the churches he had helped found was quite sizable, whatever was the portion of the offering given by the Corinthians. We wonder if these trips to Jerusalem with money formed a background for Felix's thinking he might be bribed (Acts 24:26).

B. The Travel Plans of Paul and his Helpers are Somewhat Related to the Offering. 16:5-11

16:5 -- *But I shall come to you after I go through Macedonia, for I am going through Macedonia;*

But I shall come to you -- In verse 3 Paul indicated he was coming to Corinth to visit them, though the exact timing of the visit was tentative. Here in verse 5, as he writes from Ephesus (cp. verse 8), Paul announces to the Corinthians a change in his travel plans.[16] From 2 Corinthians 1:16 we learn Paul's original plans were to go from Ephesus to Corinth by sea, then visit Macedonia, and return again to Corinth, at which time he would decide on his future travel plans (e.g., to Jerusalem, or elsewhere). Now, instead, for the reason stated in 2 Corinthians 1:23,[17] he is planning to go overland from Ephesus to Macedonia, and then down through Greece to Corinth. He will come to Corinth in time, but he must postpone his visit for the present. The postponement will be compensated by the increased length of his visit when he does come. Further, they will be able to help him on his next journey. He cannot, however, leave Ephesus just yet, for there is a great opportunity for good work, and his presence there is necessary. The delay in his coming will give them time for laying aside and treasuring up the money for the Jerusalem poor.

After I go through Macedonia -- Literally, "*whenever* I have passed through Macedonia,"

---

[15] This suggestion, though not unknown in real life, is probably not true of Corinth, for we remember (16:1) that the Corinthians asked about the offering even while they were being factious (chapters 1-4). That seems to imply they were going to take part in the offering in spite of their bickering and dissensions.

[16] Commentators offer numerous guesses concerning how the Corinthians knew of Paul's original travel plans. Some think he announced his plans in the alleged 'previous letter.' Some think messengers traveling between Paul and the church had carried the news.

[17] According to 2 Corinthians 1:23, he changed his plan because, in the present disgraceful state into which the church had fallen, he felt he could not visit them without being compelled to exercise a severity which he hoped this letter would make unnecessary.

i.e., after I have passed through Macedonia, I will come to Corinth.[18] "After" ('when') is the indefinite *hotan* once more. Paul does not know for certain when this trip is to be. Paul did execute the new travel plan here announced, with a small modification. The planned journey through Macedonia fits the record of Paul's travel in Acts 19:21 and 20:1,2. The small modification was this: he made an unplanned 'intermediate trip' to Corinth, returning to Ephesus.[19] This trip was a hasty visit, and it did not turn out well for Paul. Following this 'sorrowful trip,' Titus was sent to Corinth to attempt to straighten out some of the difficulties in the congregation. While Titus is away at Corinth, Paul eventually did leave Ephesus, traveling north to Troas and Macedonia, and from thence to Corinth. While he was at Troas, and then while he was in Macedonia, Paul kept looking for Titus to return and report on how the church at Corinth was doing. Though it took longer than at first expected, Titus, with a firm hand, solved some of the difficulties. He then left Corinth, journeyed north, in order to report to Paul. They met in Macedonia. The news Titus brought from Corinth was such that it refreshed Paul's spirit. It undoubtedly concerned the subsiding of the factions, and that the impenitent sinner had been excommunicated, and that the church was once again functioning properly. Upon hearing this good news, Paul wrote 2 Corinthians. Shortly after writing 2 Corinthians, distressing news from Galatia led him to write Galatians. When he finally did come to Corinth, he stayed there three months. During this stay, he wrote the letter to Rome. He then went to Jerusalem with the offering. When Paul changed his plans, certain people charged him with levity and fickleness of purpose ('He's not a man of his word! Cp. 2 Corinthians 3:1, 10:10). Mistaking the kindness of his purpose, someone at Corinth accused him of inconsistency. He defends himself from this charge throughout the epistle of 2 Corinthians.

For I am going through Macedonia -- The verb is present tense, 'I am passing through Macedonia' (*dierchomai*). The subscription, as in the KJV, "Written from Philippi," probably was based on a misunderstanding of this verse. It was misunderstood to mean, "I am *at the present time* passing through Macedonia." The word probably should not be interpreted to mean that at the time of writing Paul was already passing through Macedonia (see verse 8). The present tense ("I am going through") must be compared with the verb in the next clause ("I shall stay with you"). The idea is 'It is my *present intention* to go right through Macedonia, without spending much time there. It is my intention to remain with you for awhile.' The use of the present tense, when speaking of future plans, is not uncommon. It lends an air of greater definiteness to the plan. In Acts[20] *dierchomai* seems to be almost a technical term for a missionary tour, or an evangelistic journey.

---

[18] In 1 Corinthians 4:19, Paul has foreshadowed a visit to Corinth, and has intimated that there were some at Corinth who thought he would not come (see notes at 4:18,19). So now the apostle says with certainty that he will come to them. He puts the time of the visit as being "after I have passed through Macedonia" (Morris, *op. cit.*, p.239,240).

[19] See this 'intermediate trip' explained in the Introductory Studies.

[20] Acts 13:6, 14:24, 15:3,41, 18:23, 19:1,21, 20:2.

16:6 -- *and perhaps I shall stay with you, or even spend the winter, that you may send me on my way wherever I may go.*

And perhaps I shall stay with you -- *Pros* ("with"), which is a stronger preposition than *meta* or *sun*, implies that Paul wanted an active communion with them. "You" is emphatic. It contrasts the Corinthians with the Macedonians. On this trip, it is the Corinthians with whom Paul wishes to abide. "Perhaps" translates *tuchon*, 'perchance,' 'it may happen.' Paul is taking into account the fact that there may be circumstances which might prevent him from doing exactly as he desired.

Or even spend the winter -- Acts 20:3 tells us Paul did spend three months at Corinth, which would have been the winter (January-March) of AD 58. Winter travel in the Mediterranean world was difficult. Navigation on the Mediterranean Sea during winter was perilous and most of the time impossible. After September 14, navigation was considered dangerous; after November 11, it ceased until March 5.[21] As he writes 1 Corinthians, Paul planned to stay in Ephesus until Pentecost (see verse 8). If he did not get to Corinth until a time when he must winter with them, then almost a year's time would be involved, during which the Corinthians could be systematically, week-by-week, laying by in store, before it would be time for all the messengers to head for Jerusalem with the money.

That you may send me on my way -- "You" again is emphatic. Paul would rather that it be the Corinthian church (rather than any other) who would have the opportunity of 'sending him forward on his journey,' i.e., providing such things as he had need of for the trip, or "pay my expenses to my next destination."[22] It was also customary to accompany a departing guest for a short distance (see Romans 15:24, Acts 15:3, 17:15). Provision of food, money, and travel companions were key components of 1st century hospitality.

Wherever I may go -- Paul had said (verses 3,4) he would go to Jerusalem only if it were "fitting." Paul was not certain where he would go from Corinth. Perhaps Jerusalem, perhaps elsewhere.

16:7 -- *For I do not wish to see you now* **just** *in passing; for I hope to remain with you for some time, if the Lord permits.*

For I do not wish to see you now *just* in passing -- Both clauses of verse 7 begin with "for" as he explains further the reason for his change in travel plans. This first "for" says if he hadn't changed plans, his visit at Corinth would be too short. "Now just in passing" means 'I do not wish to make only a flying visit now.' A visit of short duration would be unsatisfying. Paul wished to stay more than a short while, likely because there was much to be set in order at Corinth (11:34). Paul apparently feels no tension between himself and

---

[21] See Wm. Ramsay, *St. Paul the Traveller and Roman Citizen* (Grand Rapids, MI: Baker, 1960 reprint), p.332.

[22] For Paul to ask for money for fresh supplies and travel funds to another mission field does not contradict his stated habit of not asking his converts for support while working in their midst, cf. 1 Corinthians 9:7-12.

them at this juncture. Perhaps he presumes this letter will straighten out any potential problem areas.

Nothing in "now" (*arti*) warrants the inference sometimes offered that the 'intermediate trip' was made before 1 Corinthians was written. Some commentators believe that after Paul received the first news of the trouble at Corinth, he made a quick trip there to see if he could settle it, but that he had a very painful experience. Returning to Ephesus, the theory goes, Paul wrote 1 Corinthians. These commentators interpret this phrase to mean, 'I do not wish so quickly to have more difficulty like I just had there, so I'm not going to come right now.' That there was an 'intermediate trip,' we do not doubt; Paul says at 2 Corinthians 12:14 and 13:1 the coming mentioned there is his *third* trip to Corinth. Acts records only two trips to Corinth, the first and the third. This commentator has concluded from his studies that the second trip to Corinth was made after the writing of 1 Corinthians and before the riot at Ephesus.[23] The "now" need be nothing more than another reference to his changed intentions. *Before* he had planned to have only a brief visit to the church at Corinth, *but now* the arrangement he contemplates would permit a longer stay.[24]

For I hope to remain with you for some time -- This clause explains why, after his arrival there (having passed through Macedonia, see verse 5), he was wishing for more than a hasty visit.[25] *Elpidzō* means "I am hoping to tarry ...." "Some time" (*chronon tina*) is in comparison to the amount of time he could spend with them if he followed his original travel plans. Note that Paul does not say "to stay *at Corinth*." He says "with you." It is the people, not the place, which Paul cares about. Two possible reasons have been proposed why Paul wished to tarry with the church at Corinth. First, 11:34 says Paul wished to set in order the things lacking, to see that the people are correctly disciplined and

---

[23] If Paul did make his intermediate trip soon after writing "I do not wish to make a quick visit", we can explain his change of plans on the changed circumstances. Timothy brought news of the grave problems still continuing at Corinth even after they had received Paul's first epistle (the one he is now writing).

[24] Not a few scholars call attention here to the matters of inspiration and inerrancy. We have noted that Paul's declared travel plans were changed at least twice.
- Our definition of inspiration, at least in Mosaic times, must allow for progressive revelation. When inspired men spoke a revelation they had received, what they said was true, even though they may not have understood all they were saying.
- Our definition of inerrancy must also allow room for a change in travel plans, since Paul's future journeys were subject to "God's willing."
- Our definition of inspiration must include room for the kind of changes in travel plans Paul speaks of here. When writing, inspired men were allowed to go until they were about to make an error, and then they were helped to write the right thing (see this matter discussed at 1 Corinthians 2). Similarly, on a missionary journey, they were allowed to travel until about to make an error, then they were limited (e.g., not permitted by the Spirit to go to Asia, or Bithynia, on the second missionary journey). Paul planned a trip to Rome at the end of this third missionary journey, and wrote about it. He eventually got to Rome, but not as he had personally envisioned, but only after he appealed his case to Caesar.
- Our definition of inspiration will also have to include the correct statement of personal opinions ("you will not see my face again," he told the Ephesian elders, Acts 20:25), even when the opinions were in error. (Paul did visit Ephesus again, 1 Timothy 1:3.) We must recognize that the contents of what was spoken by inspiration were not always revelations directly from God.

[25] "But I trust" – *elpidzō de* is only in K and L. "For I hope" – *elpidzō gar* is found in Aleph, A, B, C, D, E, F, G, I, M, P.

that love and not jealousy once more reigned in the church. Second, Paul has a love for the work which he has started in a virgin territory.

If the Lord permits -- 'If the Lord allows me to do this' is *ean ho kurios epitrepsē*. 'If it shall so turn out in the Lord's direction of my work, that I shall find my way open to do so.' Paul's plans were always subject to the will of the Lord. It is very likely that "Lord" here is a reference to Jesus Christ. Jesus has been designated as "Lord" (see Acts 2:36). Paul was an apostle of Jesus. His plans for the future were completely in the hands of his "commander."[26] "He is the Lord's servant. Therefore all his plans must be subject to the proviso (expressed or not) that the Lord may intervene and send him elsewhere."[27] The Christians made a rule of using words like these to indicate their dependence on Jesus. Compare James 4:15, "You ought to say, 'If the Lord wills, we shall live, and also do this or that.'"[28] With human beings, who are finite creatures, no resolution can be absolute. Every act is conditioned on Him who is the sole absolute Sovereign.

16:8 -- *But I shall remain in Ephesus until Pentecost;*

But I shall remain in Ephesus -- Paul is anxious to spend some time in Corinth with his friends, but his visit must be deferred for a time, at least till Pentecost. This language ("I shall remain in Ephesus") indicates this first letter to Corinth was written while Paul was in Ephesus. It is possible that Paul's stated intention of staying till Pentecost was frustrated by the riot stirred up by the silversmiths (Acts 19:23-41). On the other hand, there is no verse that says Paul left Ephesus before Pentecost. Indeed, there is reason to believe the riot started during a feast in honor of Diana, which would have been held about the same time as Pentecost. In any case, the riot occurred when Paul was already preparing to leave (Acts 19:21,22), and he had already sent on two of his helpers (Timothy and Erastus) on a mission trip when that tumult occurred (1 Corinthians 16:10).

Until Pentecost -- Pentecost (a Jewish festival held in late May or early June) is probably no more than a rough indication of time, i.e., about two months after he writes 1 Corinthians. He does not mean that he must observe the Feast of Pentecost according to Jewish rules at Ephesus. He does not imply that the Christian church was observing this Jewish feast, or that such observance is part of the pattern to be observed by Christians of following generations. Paul's plans for this present year are to stay at Ephesus until well into the spring, then travel on to Macedonia during the summer and fall, and finally spend the winter in Corinth. The following spring, by Pentecost time, he will have gone to Jerusalem with the offering (see Acts 20:6 and 20:16).

---

[26] Does this language bear on the idea that Paul's day-by-day moves were all divinely directed? Was every move Paul made subject to the Spirit's control? It would seem that such was hardly the case, though Paul was Spirit-directed on many of his journeys. The very next verse (1 Corinthians 16:8) seems to imply Paul's own judgment also had something to do with his day-by-day activities, and even the length of his stay in certain places.

[27] Morris, *op. cit.*, p.241.

[28] See the same expression at 1 Corinthians 4:19, Acts 18:21, Hebrews 6:3.

16:9 -- *for a wide door for effective* service *has opened to me, and there are many adversaries.*

For a wide door for effective *service* **has opened to me** -- Two reasons are given why he must remain longer in Ephesus. "For" shows that this clause states one reason why he intended to stay a while longer at Ephesus. "Wide door" is a metaphor indicating abundant opportunity.[29] A similar metaphor in our language might be called a 'window of opportunity.' "Has opened" is a perfect tense verb; the door has been open for some time, and continues to stand open. Now is the opportune time. "Effective" (*energēs*) speaks of 'work' or 'much activity' or 'full employment' or 'productive of good results.' It is not quite clear what Paul means, or in what sense a door can be called "effective." Several suggestions have been offered: (1) There is great interest in the gospel message. People are paying attention to what is spoken when the gospel is preached. (2) There is opportunity now which calls for much work to be done by Paul in sharing the gospel, opportunity that for some reason or another heretofore was not available. (3) There are opportunities for far-reaching effects. There is new success in preaching the gospel.[30]

And there are many adversaries -- This is the second reason why he must stay longer in Ephesus. There are many opposed, many who resist the gospel. Paul felt that, because of the opposition, he was needed there all the more. We are not told just who the opponents of the gospel were at this time at Ephesus. The riot of Demetrius has not yet occurred, so it is doubtful the silversmiths are the adversaries Paul refers to. But merely because there was great opposition to his work from outsiders was no reason why Paul should leave Ephesus; rather, it was a reason why he should remain there. The success of the apostle in winning converts provoked strong opposition against him. If the devil has stirred up great opposition to the truth, then the devil must be worried about the great results for God being accomplished. Well, Paul would just stay and see more done for God. After all, is it not exciting to see the devil defeated? The statement about adversaries is unexpected. "Paul's abrupt reference to them reminds us the Christian is not usually left to pursue his task unmolested. It is part of the conditions under which we serve God that when we have great opportunities of service, there are also great difficulties in our way."[31]

16:10 -- *Now if Timothy comes, see that he is with you without cause to be afraid; for he is doing the Lord's work, as I also am.*

Now if Timothy comes -- The NASB has a paragraph break beginning here at verse 10. Instead of a new topic beginning at verse 10, we think rather that Paul is still sharing information about the "collection for the saints" at Jerusalem (the topic begun at 16:1) and the travels of those men involved in administering it. Before Paul wrote this first letter,

---

[29] Compare Acts 14:27, 2 Corinthians 2:12, Colossians 4:3, Revelation 3:8.

[30] Richard B. Cunningham, "Wide Open Doors and Many Adversaries," *Review and Expositor* 89:1 (Winter 1990), p.89-97, has suggested some creative missionary ideas and methods for today based on the words of 1 Corinthians 16:9.

[31] Morris, *op. cit.*, p.241.

Timothy (accompanied by Erastus, city treasurer of Corinth, Romans 16:23) had been sent to visit a number of churches, Corinth being one of them.[32] He will be traveling overland, visiting a number of churches, while this letter will be sent directly from Ephesus to Corinth by way of the Mediterranean Sea. The letter will get to Corinth before Timothy does. At the time Timothy was dispatched, the full knowledge of the state of affairs at Corinth had not reached Paul. Now that he knows how very bad the condition in the church is, he is anxious to protect and shield Timothy from some of the fall-out that such a condition is sure to spew on those who preach the gospel, and especially on those who attempt to help men correct the sin in their lives. This phrase ("if Timothy comes") can be interpreted two different ways. (1) It could be as if Paul had written, "*when* he comes ...." This would merely signify the time of his arrival. When he arrived, he was to be well treated. (2) It may be understood literally, "*if* he comes ...." In this case it would show some doubt that Timothy would get to Corinth. As we indicated at 4:17, Paul may have countermanded Timothy's instructions (but was not sure Timothy had received the order) due to the uncertainties of travel. Did Timothy ever get to Corinth? In 2 Corinthians we will read a good deal about the visit of Titus to Corinth, but nothing is said of Timothy's visit. And while Paul defends his own changes of plan about visiting Corinth, he says nothing about Timothy's having failed to visit them. On the other hand, 2 Corinthians 7:12 has been pressed into service to try to answer this question. If Timothy is the one "that suffered wrong," he may have reached Corinth and have been grossly insulted by someone. However, it is far from certain that Timothy is the "one" about whom Paul writes in 2 Corinthians 7:12. Whichever way we interpret this phrase about Timothy's travels, we do know that Timothy was in Macedonia when 2 Corinthians was written (see 2 Corinthians 1:1). Some think he had never gotten closer to Corinth than Macedonia, where Paul catches up with him. Others suppose Timothy has been to Corinth, reported to Paul in Ephesus, and traveled with Paul from Ephesus to Macedonia.[33]

See that he is with you without cause to be afraid -- There must have been some special reason for this caution respecting Timothy. (1) Some suggest Timothy was of a timid disposition. Scriptures such as 1 Timothy 5:21-23, 2 Timothy 1:6-8, 2:1,3,15, 4:1,2 are said to agree with such a supposition, although they do not necessarily imply it. (2) Some suggest this warning is aimed at the proud partisan leaders at Corinth. It is suggested that Timothy would naturally be depreciated as only a subordinate of Paul, whom so many of them opposed, being in rival factions to the Pauline. (3) Some suggest Timothy's youth as a reason for this admonition. Eight years after this (1 Timothy 4:12) Paul still speaks of him as a 'young' man. Jewish men were considered 'young' (*neotēs*) until they were age 40 or older.

---

[32] Both Acts 19:22 and 1 Corinthians 4:17 indicate Timothy was already on his way. It was noted earlier that to treat 1 Corinthians 4:17 as an epistolary aorist, and then to suppose that Timothy was actually carrying this letter to Corinth which Paul is now writing, is hard to square with what he writes here in 16:10. Philippians 2:19-24 indicates the character of Timothy. There is no other preacher like Timothy. Timothy was highly recommended by Paul. See also the brief summary of information about Timothy included in the comments at 1 Corinthians 4:17.

[33] See the Introductory Studies on 2 Corinthians, where this problem is further discussed.

For he is doing the Lord's work -- This is a reason why the Corinthians are not to do anything to cause Timothy to be full of fear. If they hindered what Timothy was doing, they would in reality be hindering the work of the Lord Jesus Christ in which Timothy was engaged. 'He is engaged in the service of the Lord, and he is worthy of your confidence.' The work of the Lord is either that work in which the Lord Himself is engaged, or that which He has commanded.

As I also am -- This phrase expresses the idea that Timothy's work was of the same nature as Paul's. It may also be that this indicates that Timothy evidenced the same zeal and fidelity to the cause of Christ as did Paul.

16:11 -- *Let no one therefore despise him. But send him on his way in peace, so that he may come to me; for I expect him with the brethren.*

Let no one therefore despise him -- Kling (*op. cit.*, p.358) has written, "Whether it be on account of his youth, or on account of his natural modesty, or on account of party zeal because he came from Paul", let no one despise him. "Despise" means to "set him at nought," "treat him as of no account."

But send him on his way in peace – "Send him on his way" means 'Take care of his expenses' (see 16:6). When Timothy's work was finished in Corinth, the Corinthians were to see he had all his needs supplied, including funds he might need for travel expenses. "In peace" may be connected either with what precedes or with what follows. (1) If with the following, "That in peace ... he may come to me" means 'in safety, in good condition,' he may come to Paul. No feelings of discouragement or lingering temptations to quit the ministry. No bad memories of his time at Corinth. (2) If with the preceding, as the KJV reads, "in peace" means 'with good understanding and kindly affection.' 'When he departs, let him see that he has your good will, and that he leaves with no bad feelings in any of you toward him. Send him on his way with your blessing.' The second is the preferred interpretation.

So that he may come to me -- The fact that Paul looks for Timothy to return to him shows Paul had sent him for specific tasks. Timothy was not on a roving commission.

For I expect him -- This would be a caution to the Corinthians to treat Timothy well. This was to let them know that whatever treatment Timothy received at their hands would be reported to Paul. This would also cause the Corinthians to better respect Timothy. If Paul, the apostle, thought so much of him and praised him so highly, surely they must treat him with civility and respect.

With the brethren -- Who the brethren were, we do not know. Since Acts 19:22 indicates Erastus accompanied Timothy to Macedonia, "the brethren" may have included Erastus. This phrase, and a similar one in the next verse (16:12), might indicate others were in this evangelistic party headed by Timothy. Or it might mean Paul expects certain brethren from Corinth to accompany Timothy as he returns to be with Paul. Or it is possible Paul means that he, and the brethren with him, are looking for Timothy's return.

SECTION TEN: CONCERNING APOLLOS. 16:12

16:12 -- *But concerning Apollos our brother, I encouraged him greatly to come to you with the brethren; and it was not at all* **his** *desire to come now, but he will come when he has opportunity.*

But concerning Apollos our brother -- From the way Paul brings up the matter of Apollos (cp. 7:1, 8:1, 12:1, 16:1[34]), it seems the Corinthians, in their letter to Paul, had requested that Apollos be encouraged to return to Corinth. We don't know when or why Apollos left Corinth after his ministry there (Acts 18:27,28). Paul here is giving the reason why Apollos is not coming. It was not because Paul was jealous of Apollos, and had not said anything to him about the request, as some in Corinth might suggest. On the contrary, Paul had spoken to Apollos, and Apollos himself had refused to come at this particular time, although he did plan to come later, if the opportunity presented itself.[35] Paul calls Apollos "our brother," a designation that identifies Apollos as a co-worker under God (cp. 3:4-9), and implied in this designation is Paul's recognition that Apollos was not responsible for encouraging the party that went by his name (1:12).

I encouraged him greatly to come to you -- Paul had been most urgent (*polla parekalesa*[36]) in his appeals to get Apollos to go to Corinth. It may have been in hope that he could contribute something toward the settling of the difficulties there. Clearly, Paul and Apollos were in no sense the rivals that some at Corinth made them out to be. Apollos must have been ministering at this time in or around Ephesus. This passage has some bearing on the matter of church polity. Even when apostles were living and present, they did not order or assign preachers to the churches. Paul did not have the authority to place men against their will in a certain ministry, nor today is it very satisfactory to have men assigned by the synod, or bishop, or conference. Such things just do not have Scriptural example behind them.

With the brethren -- There is no way to identify these "brethren" with any certainty. (1) Some have supposed "the brethren" here mentioned are the same "brethren" just mentioned in verse 11, who are now traveling with Timothy. If the "brethren" with Timothy (verse 11) do not include Erastus, then it might be possible for the "brethren" of verse 12 to be the same as the brethren of verse 11. This verse would indicate these "brethren" had been sent to Corinth where they would join Timothy when he arrived, and then all were to proceed together on the journey back to Paul in Ephesus. If the "brethren" with Timothy (verse 11) included Erastus (Acts 19:22), then the brethren with whom Paul urged Apollos to travel cannot be Timothy and Erastus. We remember that those two had been sent to Corinth *before* news came from Corinth (by letter, etc.) of the situation there. (2) In light

---

[34] This is the last occurrence of the formula "now concerning," which introduces topics mentioned in the letter from Corinth. The Western text (D*, F, G) and Aleph* add "I make known to you." If Paul wrote this he is protesting his innocence in Apollos' refusal to return.

[35] For further information concerning Apollos, see the notes at 1:12.

[36] See comments on this verb at 1:10 and 4:13,16.

of all this, perhaps the "brethren" with whom Apollos was urged to travel are the three "brethren" who will be named in verse 17, the "brethren" who will carry to Corinth this very letter Paul is now writing. (3) Or it may suggest that when Timothy arrives at Ephesus after his visit to Corinth, a group of brethren will be going to Corinth, and Paul had tried to persuade Apollos to be one of their number on that future trip.

And it was not at all *his* desire to come now -- Some have suggested that it is "God's will" that is intended here (note there is no word for "his" in the Greek). Because this interpretation does not well fit the context, this commentator agrees with the NASB translators, that it is the will (or desire) of Apollos himself that is intended. "Not now," 'not at this time,' softens the refusal. Apollos has not made up his mind never to visit Corinth again. It merely says that he cannot be induced to come now.

But he will come when he has opportunity -- Perhaps the reason the present time was not a suitable time may well be because of the divisions hinted at the beginning of the epistle. Apollos may have anticipated that the party bearing his name would have stirred up real animosity and trouble if its 'claimed' leader were in the midst. It may have depended on the Corinthians (i.e., their changing their ways) whether or not Apollos would come to visit them and work among them. It is possible Apollos had made up his mind that he would not go to Corinth as long as there were parties there opposed to Paul and to each other and to the work of the church. Or, perhaps, the present time was not suitable because of other circumstances and engagements which were holding him back (i.e., a revival in Hierapolis). The KJV uses "convenient" where the ASV has "opportunity." In the thought of Paul and Apollos, "convenient" meant the good of Christ's church, and not the ease or comfort of any individual man. Whether Apollos ever revisited Corinth or not, we do not know. "The Latin Fathers say Apollos did return to Corinth, after the religious differences had been settled."[37]

SECTION ELEVEN: CONCLUSION OF THE EPISTLE WITH VARIOUS EXHORTATIONS AND SALUTATIONS. 16:13-24

A. Summary Exhortations. 16:13-14

> *Summary:* The Corinthians had shown a distressing immaturity in some things, and the apostle in a series of compelling imperatives points them to a better way. The imperatives in these two verses sum up the instructions contained in the earlier sections of the letter. If they are heeded by the Corinthians, the errors in life and doctrine will be corrected.

---

[37] Barnes, *op. cit.*, p.332. Origen speaks of Apollos as being "bishop" of Corinth, a term that likely was synonymous with "evangelist" in Origen's time.

16:13 -- *Be on the alert, stand firm in the faith, act like men, be strong.*

Be on the alert -- The verbs in verses 13 and 14 are all present tense imperatives. These are not just momentary attitudes Paul commands; rather, they are to be the continuing lifestyle of the Christians. In five crisp, clear charges, he gathers together the duties which he has been teaching in this whole epistle. The first four concern their personal response to the gospel with special reference to spiritual foes and perils. The fifth one deals with their relationship with each other. In light of all he has written in earlier chapters, these imperatives likely urge loyalty to the gospel as they have received it from the divinely-sent church planters and waterers. If the Corinthians heed these commands, the problems in their lives and in the congregation will melt and vanish.

Grēgoreite means 'Be continually on guard!', or 'Continue to be alert, be vigilant!' It is the opposite of carelessness, or indifference, or allowing oneself to be deceived. Commentators have offered multiple suggestions as they have attempted to specify exactly what the Corinthians were to "watch" for, or "be alert" for. (1) Some suppose there is a connection between the first four admonitions and the topic of a possible trip by Apollos to Corinth. Paul would be saying, instead of relying on this or that possible preacher, however competent, to settle your problems, you must take a personal responsibility for your conduct. (2) Since Paul elsewhere uses this verb of watchfulness for Christ's second coming,[38] some suppose that is in Paul's mind here. (3) Barnes offers a different explanation. "The sense here is that they were to watch, or be vigilant, against the evils of which he had admonished them: the evil of dissension; the evil of erroneous doctrine; the evil of disorders; the evil of false teachers (like those who denied the resurrection). They were to watch lest their souls should be ruined, and their salvation endangered."[39] The word may be a military metaphor derived from the duty of those who are stationed at guard duty, or as observers of the motions of the enemy. When enemies or hostile influences are observed, the watcher raises the alarm against the danger.

Stand firm in the faith -- "The faith" here likely is objective, not subjective (as the RSV has it, "stand fast in your faith"). The "faith" is the gospel of Jesus Christ, which includes the atonement won by Christ in His death on the cross (chapter 1), and the life guaranteed by His resurrection (chapter 15). What Paul is asking them to do is not to depart from the truths of Christianity.[40] "Stand firm" says there was to be no desertion, no wavering, no uncertainty, no doubt. They were not to yield to any foe who might try to deceive or mis-

---

[38] See 1 Thessalonians 5:6.

[39] Barnes, *op. cit.*, p.332.

[40] Compare 15:1,58, and 10:12. That "the faith" refers to a "body of doctrine" is noteworthy. Modern Bible critics, for example, assert that the objective meaning for "faith" found in the letters to Timothy and Titus is internal evidence that Paul could not have written those letters, for "he always uses 'faith' in its subjective sense of personal belief or conviction." Such critics are judging everything else in the light of Paul's four "generally accepted letters" (1 & 2 Corinthians, Galatians, and Romans), and are ignoring not only this verse, but also Galatians 1:23 and Romans 12:6. (See this matter discussed in the introductory studies of the author's *New Testament Epistles: Timothy and Titus* [Moberly, MO: Scripture Exposition Books, 1999].)

lead them. Instead of falling away from the faith or forsaking the right way, they were to maintain the truth of the gospel.

Act like men -- *Andridzesthe* is a dramatic verb which occurs nowhere else in the New Testament. (1) Perhaps there is an emphasis on courage. The NIV translation has "be men of courage," and Mare calls attention to the fact that women too can show such courage (*op. cit.*, p.295). "Be people of courage" is how Fee translates it.[41] "Have the courage to stand up for what is right even when it is unpopular."[42] (2) Perhaps there is a glance at their immature behavior as shown by some of the things the Corinthians had been doing. Is there a glance at their "childish" display of tongues? They must be like responsible adults, Paul urges (cp. 13:11). Is there a glance back at the discussion about the strong and weak brother? This meaning is very possible when we recall that the weak brother was the one who was doctrinally right. "This carries the weight of 'Stop acting like spiritual infants, quarreling, boasting and indulging yourselves without discipline!' Many church problems are due to pure infantilism on the part of members who did not grow up spiritually."[43]

Be strong -- *Krataiousthe* means 'be firm, fixed, steadfast.' It is the opposite of being weak and easily defeated. If the previous word was not a call to courage, this one is. The verb may be passive, 'be made strong.' The strength of the Christian is not something native or inherent; he derives it from God. The same verb is used in Ephesians 6:10, "Be strong in the Lord, and in the strength of His might." Constantly show your strength in every situation that calls for this quality. "Be not only manly, but mighty!"[44]

16:14 -- *Let all that you do be done in love.*

Let all that you do be done in love -- First, they are to get their personal response to the gospel right (verse 13), then they are to get their relationships with each other right. The metaphor is changed. While the terms in verse 13 may picture the Christian as a "soldier" in battle with those who threaten from the outside, now the Christian is pictured as a comrade and a lover in his relationships to those within the church.[45] In "all you do," instead of being governed by a selfish partisanship, make sure to govern yourselves by a love which looks to the well-being of the brethren. "He is glancing back at the party-divisions, at the selfish disorder at the Lord's Supper, and at their jealousy in the possession

---

[41] Fee, *op. cit.*, p.826.

[42] Fisher, *op. cit.*, p.265.

[43] Coffmann, *op. cit.*, p.281.

[44] Robertson and Plummer, *op. cit.*, p.394.

[45] The verb changes to a third person present imperative in this verse, whereas the verbs in verse 13 were second person imperatives.

of special gifts (*charismata*) and is recalling chapter 13."⁴⁶ "'All things' would include the quarrels in the name of leaders in chapters 1-3; their attitude toward him in chapters 4 and 9; the lawsuits in 6:1-11; husband-wife relationships in chapter 7; the abuse of the weak by those with 'knowledge' in 8:1-10:22; the abuse of the 'have-nots' at the love feast in 11:20-22; the failure to edify the church in worship in chapters 12-14."⁴⁷ The verb "be" (*ginesthe*) suggests they are not yet at this goal, but they are to become "lovers" in their motives and actions. "Love," as we learned in chapter 13, is doing what is spiritually best for the other person. When Paul writes "in love," "the significance of 'in' rather than 'with' (KJV) should not be overlooked. Love is more than an accompaniment of Christian actions. It is the very atmosphere in which the Christian lives and moves."⁴⁸ Recall what 1 Corinthians 13 has said about love being the motive driving the Christian's behavior.

B. Special Entreaty Concerning Stephanas and Others. 16:15-18

> *Summary:* Paul recommends the family of Stephanas to their honorable regard; and by occasion, expresses of his own joy at the presence of Stephanas and his companions. He then reminds the Corinthians that the devotion of teachers, and all who serve in the gospel ministry, ought to be rewarded with a return of sympathy and devotion on the part of those whom they serve.

16:15 -- *Now I urge you, brethren (you know the household of Stephanas, that they were the first fruits of Achaia, and that they have devoted themselves for ministry to the saints),*

Now I urge you, brethren -- "I urge you" is *parekalō*, as in verse 12. Paul has written about workers who possibly will visit Corinth. Now he must speak a word of appeal concerning some of their number who at present are visiting with him in Ephesus. The particular point of this appeal is introduced by *hina* in verse 16, i.e., "I urge you ... *that* you submit yourselves ...."⁴⁹ The Greek sentence is a bit rough grammatically, and the ASV/NASB have tried to make it as smooth as they can by the use of a parenthesis. What is said in the parenthesis forms a reason for the Corinthians to comply with this appeal.

(you know the household of Stephanas -- This appeal seems to have been written to stop the Corinthians from showing disrespect to the house of Stephanas and to Fortunatus and Achaicus. What will happen to Paul – both when the Corinthians received this letter and when they rejected Paul's leadership on his upcoming 'intermediate trip' – shows full well that the Corinthians were capable of disrespect. Just why they might be angry with Steph-

---

⁴⁶ Robertson and Plummer, *ibid*.

⁴⁷ Fee, *op. cit.*, p.828.

⁴⁸ Morris, *op. cit.*, p.244.

⁴⁹ There is a similar appeal in 1 Thessalonians 5:12-14.

anas' household, we can only surmise. Perhaps they were the ones who carried to Paul the report of the unchristian practices at Corinth, about which Paul wrote in this letter, before he took up the specific answers to the questions they asked in their letter to him. People sometimes mistreat those whom they think "squealed." Perhaps the trio has been loyal to Paul during all the present tensions and troubles in the congregation. Instead of using actions of this trio as an excuse for greater party bickering, the congregation has the opportunity to demonstrate it is finished with hostile suspicions and party loyalties.

That they were the first fruits of Achaia -- See 1 Corinthians 1:16, where Paul says he baptized this family.[50] Some commentaries pause to show there is no contradiction between what is here said about the household of Stephanas being "first fruits" and what is written elsewhere in the New Testament. In Romans 16:5, in the KJV, we are told Epaenetus is the first fruits of Achaia, a reading that makes Romans contradict Corinthians. This apparent contradiction is the result of a manuscript variation. The correct reading at Romans 16:5 (as the ASV indicates) is "in Asia," and this clears up any difficulties. Others have supposed there is a conflict with what is written at Acts 17:34, where we are told the first converts in Achaia were Dionysius, Damaris, and "others" at Athens. Perhaps Stephanas was one of the "others," as was suggested in the notes at 1:16. Perhaps Paul uses "Achaia" only of the Peloponnese; since Athens was in another area of Greece, 1 Corinthians 16:15 does not contradict what is said at Acts 17:34, for the converts at Athens would have been won before Paul moved on to Corinth in "Achaia." Another suggests Acts 17:34 speaks only of individuals, whereas 16:15 speaks of a whole "household." Stephanas' household was the first whole household (including family members and slaves) to be won in Achaia.

And that they have devoted themselves for ministry to the saints) – Moffatt speaks of this verb ("they have devoted themselves") as being "a 'trade metaphor' used, for example, by Plato of certain people who 'set themselves to the business of serving the public' by retailing farm produce."[51] Stephanas and his family have taken on some responsibilities in the congregation as their means of ministry. The verb "they have devoted themselves" does not suggest that they pushed their way into leadership. Rather, whenever they saw a need, they went to work to meet it without being asked. "Devoted themselves" indicates that their service was voluntary.

Before we can conjecture about the nature of their "ministry," we must first consider the identity of the "saints." The identical phrase "for the saints" is used to refer to the poor Christians at Jerusalem (16:1; 2 Corinthians 8:4, 9:1). If this is the meaning in Paul's mind, then "ministry" says that Stephanas and his household had taken the lead in trying to get the Corinthians to participate in the offering for Jerusalem. "Saints" was also used

---

[50] Just who made up the "household" has often been a matter of contention, especially since 'household baptisms' have been used as Scriptural warrant for 'infant baptisms.' We doubt that Stephanas' "household," that is to be respected and submitted to, includes the infants and children (if any) in the family, since we are specifically told concerning the household members "*they* have devoted themselves for ministry."

[51] Morris, *op. cit.*, p.244.

to designate the church members at Corinth (1:2). If this is the meaning in Paul's mind, perhaps the "ministry" was in some official capacity.

Diakonian is sometimes used of deacons (1 Timothy 3:8) and sometimes used of evangelists (Colossians 4:17; 2 Timothy 4:5).[52] That the Corinthians are to be "submissive" (16:16) may indicate formal leadership responsibilities, such as ministry of the Word. Or, instead of an official ministry, perhaps Stephanas' ministry was as a volunteer amongst the believers in general – the sick and needy, hospitality to travelers, offering their home for meetings of the congregation, and such. While it is possible Stephanas was an elder or deacon in the church at Corinth, the language "devoted themselves" seems to imply a voluntary, spontaneous entry into this "ministry" – not the way elders and deacons (who were 'appointed') usually got the position. And it was not just Stephanas who ministered. The plural subject of the verb ("*they* devoted themselves") indicates the whole household had this ministry. It is probable that the word "ministry" says Stephanas and his household appointed themselves to a place of lowly service, wherever they were needed, in the congregation at Corinth.

16:16 -- *that you also be in subjection to such men and to everyone who helps in the work and labors.*

That you also be in subjection to such men -- The subordinate clause "that you also be in subjection" functions as the object of the verb "I urge" with which verse 15 began. The word "subjection" sometimes denotes obedience to those in authority (as in Titus 3:1, Romans 13:1-6, 1 Peter 5:5), and sometimes is used where mutual submission is the topic (as in Ephesians 5:21). Mutual submission is not so much based on authority as it is on respect and appreciation for the ministry in which brothers in Christ are engaged. 'Stephanas' household has taken the lead in volunteering to do good works; follow their example.' "To such" (*toioutois*) means 'to persons of like excellence as these' or 'such excellent Christians.' In a moment Stephanas, Fortunatus, and Achaicus are specifically named. Paul does not want the Christians in Corinth to like this trio simply because he does. Rather, they are to observe the devotion to ministry to the saints and submit to them for that reason. In the Greek, there is a play on words that is difficult to render adequately in the English: "You know the house of Stephanas, that they have *ordered themselves* to the ministry of the saints, now I exhort you, *order yourselves* to be subject to them."[53] These are hard workers, the very active members in the congregation, and there was to be subjection on the part of the other members to them. Some would-be leaders at Corinth were not involved in the work of the Lord. 'Quit following them,' is the implication.

And to everyone who helps in the work and labors -- 'Follow the lead of everyone who lends a helping hand in the work of the Lord!' Does "everyone" include Fortunatus and

---

[52] Clement of Rome, speaking of the apostles, says, "So preaching everywhere in country and town, they appointed their firstfruits, when they had proved them by the Spirit, to be bishops and deacons unto them that should believe" (*1 Clement* 42).

[53] Shore, *op. cit.*, p.162.

Achaicus?[54] It is debated to what the *sun-* ("with") in *sunergounti* ("helps with") is to be referred. (1) Some say it means 'work with God.' But there is nothing in the context to justify this interpretation. (2) Some refer it to 'working with Paul.' Thus, the KJV, which reads "helpeth with us." (3) Some refer it to 'working with Stephanas, *and other co-workers of such quality*.' Thus the ASV/NASB with their translation, "helps in the work." 'Co-operation' or 'working together' for the Lord is the idea emphasized, rather than the atmosphere which prevailed among many at Corinth of working for this or that party or clique. The participle "labors" (*kopiōnti*) implies that this 'co-operation' ("helps in ...") was an earnest and laborious effort. The Greek word for "work" is the one which implies 'laboring to the point of weariness.' Folk who work hard for the Lord in our congregations should be supported and encouraged by a positive response and a quick involvement in the work by those who formerly were on the sidelines just watching.

16:17 -- *And I rejoice over the coming of Stephanas and Fortunatus and Achaicus; because they have supplied what was lacking on your part.*

And I rejoice over the coming of Stephanas and Fortunatus and Achaicus -- What Paul says here, including his exhortation to give them recognition when they return to Corinth, helps put verses 15 and 16 into perspective. "Coming" is *parousia* (see 15:23), and it is possible that the visit of these three men was an official visit on behalf of the church at Corinth. It could also be translated 'at the presence of.' These three were with Paul in Ephesus. The men had come from Corinth, probably carrying the letter from Corinth to Paul (cf. 7:1). 'It is a joy for me to have them here,' says Paul. We cannot be certain this is the same "Stephanas" whose household was just mentioned above, but we are probably correct in making such an identification. "Fortunatus," meaning 'lucky,' was a common Latin name for slaves and freedmen. Clement of Rome (AD 96) mentions a "Fortunatus" in his first epistle to the Corinthians. The Fortunatus of Clement's time is the messenger of the church at Corinth to that at Rome, and carried back to Corinth the first epistle Clement sent to them.[55] Whether or not the Fortunatus here and the one in Clement are the same person is conjectural. If so, he was a young man in the AD 50's when he visited Paul. (Per the *Hastings Bible Dictionary* entry on "Fortunatus," Lightfoot felt there was no improbability in identifying these as the same person. However, Robertson and Plummer, *op. cit.*, p.396, indicate such an identification is precarious given the common use of the name "Fortunatus," which is comparable to our "Richard.") Fortunatus is nowhere else referred to in the New Testament. "Achaicus," also a slave name meaning 'one from Achaia,' is nowhere else referred to in the New Testament. In the Introductory Studies and at 1 Corinthians 1:11, we discussed the identity of "Chloe's people." Perhaps Fortunatus and Achaicus were some of Chloe's household slaves. Since the "household of Stephanus" (verse 15) is named, most have doubted that he too could be included among Chloe's slaves. But the other two could have been Chloe's people.

---

[54] "If this includes Fortunatus and Achaicus in the next verse, and the plural 'to such as these' makes that a possibility if not a probability (in verse 18 it clearly refers to the three of them), then in the Christian church a whole new order has been established in which believers lovingly submit themselves to one another out of love and respect for their labors. This could include slaves as well." Fee, *op. cit.*, p.830.

[55] Cf. Clement of Rome, *ANF*, Vol.1, p.21.

Because they have supplied what was lacking on your part -- Does this mean 'my lack of you,' or 'your lack of me'? Both are possible, and each makes good sense. If we take it the former way, Paul is saying, 'I am deprived of you; I miss you; but they have helped somewhat to satisfy my wish to be with you.' This would then be another expression of his Christian affection for the Corinthians, and his joy at having some of them with him. If we take the latter way, Paul is saying, 'You cannot all come to me, but these excellent delegates have shown that some of you, at least, still have a place in your hearts for me.' This is the probable meaning. What was lacking, that these delegates supplied? Some suppose Paul is rebuking the Corinthians for failing to provide food or money for him, but such an interpretation is against the spirit of the whole paragraph. Some suppose the defect was failure to inform him completely about the problems of the church in their letter to him. Some suppose the defect was 'lack of friendly communion between the Corinthian Christians and himself.' Verse 18 might tend to make this the proper interpretation. This trio can answer Paul's questions about the whole congregation.

16:18 -- *For they have refreshed my spirit and yours. Therefore acknowledge such men.*

For they have refreshed my spirit -- "For" seems to explain the "lacking" and how the three men supplied what was missing. "Refreshed" (*anepausein*) means 'to cause to rest, to relieve from care or troubles, to refresh.'[56] These delegates by their presence and conversations refreshed Paul's spirit by telling him all about the church – sad though much of the news was.[57] It was a great comfort to Paul to learn from these delegates how anxious some were for his direction and advice. We could know better how Paul felt if we too had the experience of going into a virgin territory, founding a church, and then after some time leaving that place. As you were separated and the months passed into years, you would wonder about the Christians there, whether or not they were still faithful. And then news comes – some of your first converts come to you, bringing news of the rest of the brethren.

And yours -- The idea is, 'and they have refreshed your spirits.' This can look either forward or backwards. If forward, then it refers to the time when the delegation would return to Corinth, perhaps bearing Paul's letter to the church there. This commentator rather prefers this meaning. 'You owe to them whatever in my letter and their word-of-mouth report serves to refresh you,' is the idea. The Corinthians will be refreshed when the three men return and tell of their visit with Paul. If the phrase looks backwards, then it refers to the satisfaction that came when the delegation was sent.[58] Not only was it good

---

[56] It is the same word used for "rest" in Jesus' memorable promise, "Come to Me all who are weary and heavy-laden, and I will give you rest" (Matthew 11:28). Paul elsewhere uses the same verb in the sense of "refresh" (see 2 Corinthians 7:13, Philemon 7,20).

[57] "This sentence scarcely needs comment for any who have ever been thus visited by longtime friends in the faith, especially those with whom one has worked. Such visits are always 'seasons of refreshing' in the Lord, both because of the personal relationships involved and the news of other believers." Fee, *op. cit.*, p.832.

[58] So the passage was explained by George Mark Elliott.

for Paul to receive news from Corinth, it was also good for the Corinthians to send the messages to Paul that they had done through these three men. The Corinthians might think these men had told Paul much of the evil state of Corinth; and he, therefore, carefully commends them to their consideration as having refreshed, not only his spirit, but 'theirs also.' They had come on behalf of the whole church – not enemies to bear tales, but well-wishing friends to obtain apostolic help and counsel for all.

Therefore acknowledge such men -- "Therefore" refers to the mutual refreshment which these men's travels resulted in. "Such men" has reference to all persons like Stephanus, Fortunatus, and Achaicus, who voluntarily minister to their brethren. The compound verb "acknowledge" (*epiginōskein*, literally 'to know through and through') sometimes carried the meaning 'to acknowledge' or to 'give recognition to.' That seems likely the case here. It is an imperative in the Greek. It means 'to rightly recognize,' i.e., to recognize or acknowledge their true worth. The RSV translates "give recognition to such men."[59] Their service and personal sacrifice should be rewarded by some adequate recognition. Such services as theirs ought to meet with a generous recognition. 'They have undertaken a long and perilous journey on your behalf, and they have brought great relief and refreshment to me as well as to you. Cherish them; treat them kindly.' As indicated in the summary paragraph Shore has written, "Paul here reminds the Corinthians that the devotion of teachers, and all who serve in the Gospel ministry, ought to be rewarded with a return of sympathy and devotion on the part of those whom they serve."[60]

C. Concluding Salutations. 16:19-21

> *Summary:* The letter closes with four salutations: one from the churches of Asia; one from Aquila and Prisca (and the church in their house); one from the church at Ephesus (Ephesian Christians); and one from Paul himself.

16:19 -- *The churches of Asia greet you. Aquila and Prisca greet you heartily in the Lord, with the church that is in their house.*

The churches of Asia greet you -- Papyri show that such salutations as ".... greet you" at the close of a letter were a common feature in ordinary correspondence, and "greet" (the word can also be translated, 'salute' or 'embrace') is commonly the verb used. The salutations or greetings from the various Christians who were with Paul would indicate to the Corinthians that others knew of this letter Paul was just now writing, and they knew of the need for the Corinthians to make some changes. These greetings would also convey to the Corinthians that these brethren were interested in them and were wishing for the Corinthians to comply quickly with these spiritual directives. Such greetings would help

---

[59] The NIV's "Such men deserve recognition" misses too much of what Paul wrote, because it omits the imperative mood, and also the inferential conjunction "therefore."

[60] Shore, *op. cit.*, p.162.

keep the Corinthians aware of their relationship to each other.[61] 'You are a part of a large family of believers' is the connotation.

The word "Asia" in the New Testament usually denotes the Roman province of Asia. Roughly, it is the western part of the country we now call Turkey.[62] Paul regularly used the Roman Provincial titles of geographical areas, and so we understand the word "Asia" here. "Churches of Asia" indicates Paul's church planting work while he was located at Ephesus had an influence on the whole province (Acts 19:10, 26). Perhaps "churches of Asia" refers to the existence of more than one congregation of Christians at Ephesus. More likely, since the "churches of Asia" are distinguished from "the brethren" (verse 20), there is reference to congregations outside of Ephesus. Later, we come to know of congregations at Colossae, Laodicea, Hierapolis (Colossians 4:13-16), and the congregations named in Revelation 2 and 3.

Aquila and Prisca greet you heartily in the Lord -- These greetings are sent from a husband and wife team who formerly were members at Corinth. "Priscilla" (the woman's name we are more familiar with from Acts) is the diminutive form of "Prisca." In fact, the KJV reads "Priscilla" at this place in Corinthians, but P[46] and most of the Uncials have the shorter form, "Prisca." It is unusual here that Aquila's name comes first. Usually, when this couple is named, Priscilla's name comes first, and her husband's name second.[63] Plainly, she was an outstanding person in her own right, and very likely (from the order they are mentioned) she often took the lead in the couple's Christian services. Wherever this couple went, they were active in the work of the Lord. They had lived in Rome, and came to Corinth as refugees (Acts 18:2). They then moved from Corinth to Ephesus (Acts 18:18ff). As this verse will show, by the time 1 Corinthians was written, a congregation of Christians regularly met in their home. Later, they will move back to Rome, and by the time Romans was written, their home in that city had become a meeting place for a congregation (Romans 16:3,5). In due time they will move back to Ephesus (2 Timothy 4:19).[64] "Many" (*polla*) is used here as an adverb to intensify the verb "greet." We would say "greet warmly." It was natural for this couple to send their warm greetings to Corinth, for they had been of much help in the founding of the church at Corinth (Acts 18:2). When you have worked

---

[61] It is well to recall what Paul wrote in the opening verses. There, too, was an emphasis on 'community' to a people who were doing about all people could to divide the community. See 1:2, 4:17, 11:16, 14:33,36, 16:1.

[62] "Asia" is sometimes used in a more limited sense to denote the region immediately around Ephesus, of which Ephesus was the center and capital. "Asia" in Hellenistic times was a much smaller area of land than the "Asia" after 25 BC, when the whole area become Roman provinces. A brief history of the area, including the changes of territorial boundaries, is given in the author's *Acts* commentary, at Acts 16:6.

[63] See Romans 16:3 and 2 Timothy 4:19. Of the seven times this couple is mentioned, Prisca's name comes first five times.

[64] "How many couples today would move as often as did Priscilla and Aquila, just to be able to serve the Lord better? And wherever they moved, they had the need to move their business as well. People with this kind of devotion and sacrifice are not easy to find, but they are great assets to the local church." Wiersbe, *Be Wise*, p.172.

hard to help plant a congregation, you have a life-long special interest in that church. How desperately you want them to do well for the Lord! "In the Lord" would remind the readers at Corinth of Aquila and Priscilla's labors for Christ while they had lived in Corinth. It would also serve to call the readers to behave as fellow Christians (who are also "in the Lord") ought. Implied is the tacit appeal, 'Please don't break the relationship we have to each other as believers in the Lord.'

With the church that is in their house -- The time when large, common buildings were built as meeting places for public worship had not yet arrived (in spite of the fact that in chapter 11 some case could be made for a rather large congregation meeting in one place in Corinth). Hence, when the Christian community numbered more than could meet in one place, the congregational assemblies met in separate homes. The home of Aquila and Priscilla was always a center of Christian activity. We suppose it was this house church that Paul regularly was a part of on the Lord's Day.[65]

16:20 -- *All the brethren greet you. Greet one another with a holy kiss.*

All the brethren greet you -- It is not clear who "all the brethren" are. This may be a reference to other house churches in Ephesus besides the one with which Paul is involved, so that all the Christians in Ephesus are sending their greetings. If these "brethren" are other Christians besides those meeting in the home of Aquila and Priscilla, then we learn that the church at Ephesus is made up of more than one congregation of believers. Other commentators identify these "brethren" as being members of Paul's missionary team, perhaps including Sosthenes and Titus. Still other commentators suppose the reference is to the young men apprenticing for the ministry under Paul at Ephesus.[66]

Greet one another with a holy kiss -- Others warmly greet you. Now you need to warmly greet each other! The tense of the Greek verb ("greet," "salute" ASV) here in Corinthians is present tense. (In Romans 16:16 the verb is an aorist tense, indicating that the apostle is giving the Romans directions, not for a normal and, as it were, liturgical practice, but for a single act.) The present tense here suggests they are to continue warmly greeting one another until all the cliquishness and partyism in Corinth is a thing of the past. The kiss on the cheek was the ordinary form of greeting in the East. It expressed friendly accord, affection, and honor. The directions here assume this letter will be read out loud at the public assembly. When the reading was finished, the men who listened should embrace each other and kiss each other's cheeks, in token that all offenses were forgotten and forgiven, and that there was nothing but peace and goodwill between them. The women were to likewise embrace the other women and show their affection to their sisters

---

[65] The Western Text at this place reads "with whom I am lodging." Aquila and Prisca opened their home to Paul during the early days of the church planting venture at Corinth (Acts 18:2,3), so it would be possible that they again have opened their home to Paul while he is living in Ephesus.

[66] Compare 2 Timothy 4:10-12 which reflects a later date than Paul's present Ephesian ministry. See the author's commentary on *Timothy and Titus*, p.198, for further information about the "school of the evangelists."

in Christ. The warm acceptance of brothers and sisters in Christ which was to be expressed in a holy kiss was to continue long after the letter was read. The early church took a prevailing 1st century custom and poured new meaning into it. To withhold this greeting would be paralleled in our culture by refusing to shake hands because of harsh feelings toward the one we are meeting.[67]

16:21 -- *The greeting is in my own hand – Paul.*

The greeting is in my own hand – Paul -- Paul usually dictated his letters to an amanuensis (secretary) who did the actual writing. When the dictation was complete, Paul would take the pen in his own hand and add several words in his own handwriting. This gave sanction and authority to what was written, and would serve as proof that it came from Paul. Paul always added a word of salutation to his epistles. In 2 Thessalonians 3:17, he says that this is "a distinguishing mark in every letter: this is the way I write," i,e., it is his usual custom to authenticate his letters in this way.[68] Again, this was a common practice in the 1st century for the writer to add a word in his own handwriting at the close of the letter.[69] Deissmann has drawn attention to a letter in which the body is in one hand, the final greeting and date in another, clearly that of the author.[70] This letter that Deissmann cites is dated AD 50, and affords contemporary evidence of Paul's practice. In notes at 1:1 we have noted the suggestion that Sosthenes was the amanuensis for this letter.

D. Final Warning, Prayer, and Blessing. 16:22-24

16:22 -- *If anyone does not love the Lord, let him be accursed. Maranatha.*

If any one does not love the Lord – As Paul continues to write these few final sentences

---

[67] Consult the author's notes at Romans 16:16 where the question of whether or not the "holy kiss" was intended to be an ordinance to the church is discussed. "There are references to such a 'holy kiss' in Romans 16:16, 2 Corinthians 13:12, 1 Thessalonians 5:26, and to a 'kiss of love' in 1 Peter 5:14. These early passages refer to a greeting, and not to the liturgical 'kiss of peace' (a kiss exchanged during the worship service), though doubtless passages like the present one in due time led to the later practice" (Morris, *op. cit.*, p.246,247). It later came to be the way penitents were received back into fellowship (Genesis 33:4 may have influenced this usage). It also expressed mutual forgiveness when it came to be practiced by members of the congregation before the elements of the Lord's Supper were received.

[68] It is possible someone once forged a letter in Paul's name (2 Thessalonians 2:2), and this caused him to adopt such a procedure so recipients of letters could know which were his authentic letters. Compare Galatians 6:11, Colossians 4:18, Romans 16:22. (See also 1 Peter 5:12, which implies a similar practice by Peter.)

[69] One can see an example of the scribe's professional penmanship, and the author's own appended note in an early papyrus letter in *The Good News: The New Testament with over 500 Illustrations and Maps* (NY: American Bible Society, 1955), page G24, in a picture accompanying the letter to Philemon.

[70] Deissmann, *Light from the Ancient East*, p.170ff.

with his own hand, his emotions burst out into words. He reacts with passion to all the errors he has had to correct, and to what he has written about the glorious future which the return of Christ will usher in. First, in what is surprisingly vehement language, he expresses his wish for what will happen to those who do not love the Lord. The person or persons Paul has in mind are professing members of the church at Corinth.[71] The word translated love here is *phileō*. The word generally used for "love of God" is *agapaō*. *Phileō* would signify "personal devotion" in this context. The "Lord" is a reference to Jesus Christ. (Some manuscripts at this place actually read "Lord Jesus Christ.") Barnes writes (*op. cit.*, p.335), "This is a most solemn and [pointed] close to the whole epistle. It was designed to direct them to the great and essential matter of the Christian religion, love for the Lord Jesus Christ. [Instead of exercising their minds on] the disputes and dissensions which had rent the church into factions," the Corinthians are admonished to place their affections in Christ. If they would love Jesus supremely, all the problems addressed in this letter would take care of themselves, for the readers would act correctly toward their fellow men also. "It is implied that there was danger, in their disputes and strifes about minor matters, of neglecting the love of the Lord Jesus, or of substituting attachment to a party in the place of that love to the Savior which alone could be connected with eternal life." Anyone who once loved the Lord, and then continues to behave like the Corinthians were, was in danger of eternal wrath from the presence of God.[72]

Let him be accursed -- The Greek word is *anathema* and means "accursed" or "devoted to destruction."[73] The idea is that the man who did not believe in the Lord Jesus, and love Him, would be, and ought to be, devoted to destruction, or accursed of God.

> The clue to its meaning lies in two places: (1) Paul's own usage of a similar "curse" in Galatians 1:8-9, where it is pronounced on those who deviate from the gospel that Paul preached. There is no good reason to think it means otherwise here, especially in light of the frequent warnings of this letter, some of which take even stronger expression than this (cf. 3:17; 5:4-5; 6:9-10; 11:29; 14:38). (2) The similar warning that moves toward exclusion in 2 Thessalonians 3:14-15, where the warning is precisely for those who "do not obey our instructions in this letter."[74]

It does not mean simply, "Let him be excluded from the Lord's Table," or "Let him be ex-

---

[71] Fisher (*op. cit.*, p.267) is likely correct when he observes that "such a malediction would be unnecessary for pagans in general since they were already under the curse of God."

[72] Defenders of unconditional eternal security will argue that the person who is devoted to destruction never really loved the Lord in the first place, or that the word used here for love (*phileō*, rather than *agapaō*) is the loophole by which one can allege it wasn't true love for the Lord in the first place. Neither of these attempts will bear careful scrutiny.

[73] See the notes at 12:3. The NASB marginal note indicates the Greek word behind "accursed" is *anathema* (which, when transliterated is "anathema").

[74] Fee, *op. cit.*, p.837.

pelled from the church!"[75] It means, "Let him be devoted to God's wrath and judgment." This strong expression is indicative of the depth of Paul's feelings on the importance of a right attitude toward the Lord. He is calling down a solemn curse on anyone who does not love the Lord. Paul's native tongue was Aramaic and perhaps these words (*Anathema, Marana tha*) just readily came to mind as expressing his thoughts.

Marana tha -- Perhaps the most curious mistake in the KJV is that which attaches the two words "anathema" and "maranatha" as if they both formed part of the same imprecation or malediction.[76] The ASV/NASB are exactly correct here. These versions place a period after "anathema." "*Marana tha*" then becomes a complete sentence in itself.

Scholars, however, are not agreed as to the exact meaning of the Greek words. In fact, the Greek is a transliteration of an Aramaic expression, and the Aramaic could have been either "Marana tha" or "Maran atha." The precise translation is difficult. The first part is the word *Mar*, which means "Lord." "Our" is denoted in Aramaic by the addition of the suffix *an* or *ana*. So, *Maran* means "Our Lord." The last letters in the Aramaic represent some form of the verb "to come." (1) If we read *atha*, the verb means "has come," in which case the reference would be to Jesus' incarnation. Chrysostom so understood it, and interpreted it of the incarnation, as if the idea were, "The Lord and ruler of all condescended to come down so low as to die on the cross – and you remain unchanged and persist in sinning. You ought to be accursed!" (2) Some suppose the verb form is present tense and means "comes," and that it refers to the truth also taught in Matthew 18:20. This, too, would be seen as a deterrent to further abuses at the public worship services. (3) Still others think the verb might be taken as a future tense, "Our Lord will come," thus being a reference to the second coming. It would thus be a warning, "The Lord is coming to judge." The man who does not love Christ will be accursed at the judgment. (4) Or, if we divide the words differently, *Marana tha* would then be an imperative form, "Our Lord, come!" It would thus be a prayer similar to Revelation 22:20, "Come, Lord Jesus!" This would suggest the eager longing felt by the Christians for the speedy return of the Lord.

Since the first part of verse 22 was a malediction, perhaps we should understand the

---

[75] We must be careful lest we read back into 1 Corinthians what came to be a later practice in the church. As time passed, the holy kiss became part of the preparation for the observance of the Lord's Supper (Justin Martyr, *Apology*, ch.65). In time, the word "Maranatha" came to be a word spoken by worshipers at the close of the prayer of thanks at the Lord's Supper, or at the end of the celebration (*Didache* 10:6). One further element was added when non-Christians were dismissed from the assembly before the Lord's Supper was observed. It is difficult to see "Anathema" as being the word spoken to dismiss those who "didn't love the Lord" from participation in Communion.

[76] The idea expressed in print by the KJV developed much earlier than that translation. Robertson and Plummer (*op. cit.*, p.400) document that Coverdale's Bible read "be Anathema Maharan Matha" based on the supposition it was an execration similar to the Jewish form of excommunication, "Shammatha." Luther's Bible read "Maharam Motha." The Genevan version has "Let him be had in execration, *yea excommunicate* to death." The idea that Maranatha was part of an imprecation can be traced back to the 5th century, and down to the 17th century was accepted as the correct explanation by many scholars. "Our Lord has come!" is how they might be translated, and this is a reason why the ones who don't love Him should be accursed.

latter part of the verse as a prayer, "O Lord, come!" Paul's emotional prayer ("Our Lord, come!") soon came to be used as a greeting in the early church because it was a watchword and a password that summed up the vital hope of the church.[77] Christians repeated it to each other, identified each other by it, in a language which the heathen would not readily understand. (In passing, various Hebrew and Aramaic words are used in other languages. For example, there are "Amen," "Hallelujah," and "Hosanna.")

16:23 -- *The grace of the Lord Jesus be with you.*

The grace of the Lord Jesus be with you -- Paul's emotions have been expressed. Now it is time to bring the letter to a close. He does so in the words of a prayer.[78] 'Christ's grace to you,' rather than anathema – this is Paul's prayer for the Corinthians. Grace, as we have learned at 1:3, is all that God does to save a man. This is what Paul prays God will continue to do for the Corinthians.

16:24 -- *My love be with you all in Christ Jesus. Amen.*

My love be with you all in Christ Jesus -- This epistle has included some very severe things, but Paul shows his love for them as he closes. Notice the "all." Paul had some tough opponents at Corinth, but he sends his love to them all. Paul loved them all, even the partisans who cried up other preachers (1:12). Barnes writes (*op. cit.*, p.336), "He loved them intensely, and was ever ready to express his affectionate regard for them *all,* and his earnest desire was for their salvation." Every one of those in Christ (Christians), even though many were far off from the straight and narrow path, Paul loves.

After studying 1 Corinthians, we can see the difference between the Old Testament and the New Testament in the matter of *progressive revelation.* In the Old Testament, the prophets delivered oracles to the people. In the New, the apostles wrote letters to the brethren. This constitutes an advancement in the types of revelation. This is not at all speaking disparagingly of the prophets. This commentator merely is saying that he knows of no oracle or prophet that closes with words like these. Many of the oracles closed magnificently, but none are like these.

---

[77] We do not know whether the use of the word in the church started with Paul's use here in 1 Corinthians, or whether Paul was repeating a word used in the Palestinian churches even before he became a follower of Christ. If the use of the expression is pre-Pauline, the significance of the ascription of this title to Jesus in the early days of the Palestinian Church should not be overlooked. The Aramaic-speaking Christians would have been referring to Jesus by a title that in Old Testament times referred to Jehovah. Modern claims that it was not till the close of the 1st century AD that Christ's followers began referring to Him as "Lord" (God) would be largely refuted if *Marana tha* reflects the practice of the early Palestinian churches.

[78] The standard way of saying "good bye" in ancient letters was *errosthe*, "Farewell!" (see Acts 15:29). Paul has adopted his own way of saying "fare well!" "Sometimes he expands it, as in the well-known formula of 2 Corinthians 13:14, while the shortest form is that in Colossians 4:18, 'Grace be with you.' But a prayer for grace is always there" (Morris, *op. cit.*, p.248).

Amen -- "Amen" is absent from the best manuscripts and should be omitted. It is the kind of scribal addition that naturally tends to creep into a text. Paul's last word to the Corinthians is "Jesus."

SUBSCRIPTION

The subscription can be read at the close of chapter 16 in the KJV. It reads, "The first epistle to the Corinthians was written from Philippi by Stephanas, and Fortunatus, and Achaicus, and Timotheus." In these subscriptions, the phrase "by ..." indicates who carried the letter to its recipients, not who wrote it. As already pointed out in notes at 16:5, the note in K, L, and some Latin texts stating that the letter was written from Philippi is based on a misapprehension of what Paul was saying in verse 5. P and some other texts say correctly that it was written "from Ephesus" or "from Asia." The oldest manuscripts (*Aleph*, B, C, D, F, 17) have no such subscription at all, which indicates they were not written by Paul's hand, but were added a considerable time after the epistles were written. The subscriptions found in the manuscripts are conclusions drawn by a copyist from clues within the letters themselves. See further notes of discussion about the subscription in the Introductory Studies.

MY LOVE BE WITH YOU ALL IN CHRIST JESUS.

Special Study #10

DO ALL SPEAK IN TONGUES?
and
THE JOY OF THE HOLY SPIRIT

(The author has been invited to churches and conventions to share an explanation of what church members can see on television and read in books and magazines. The two pamphlets here reproduced were originally prepared for such occasions. They have been included in this commentary on 1 Corinthians by special request.)

Preface (2nd Edition) -- Preface to the Third Edition

DO ALL SPEAK IN TONGUES?
  Historical Background of the Charismatic Movement
  Charismatic Ideas and Practices Explained and Evaluated
      How it Grows
      How Do They Promote it?
      Claims Made Today
      How To Do It
      Acts 2:1-11
      1 Corinthians 12-14
      1 Corinthians 13:8-13
      Tongues in History
      Why Speak With Tongues?
      What About Instructions?
      A Sign for Unbelievers!
      Tongues Among the Pagans
      By Whose Authority?
      A Negative Answer Implied
      Be Filled With the Spirit!
  Conclusions

THE JOY OF THE HOLY SPIRIT
  The Fact of the Indwelling of the Spirit
  What Does the Indwelling Do for the Christian?
      He Leads Us
      He Helps Mortify the Deeds of the Flesh
      He Illuminates the Word
      He Helps the Christian's Prayers
      He Is a Down Payment on a New Body
      He Helps the Christian to Grow
      He Helps us Become Like Christ
      He Bears Witness to Our Salvation
  Conclusion

PREFACE

Now that it has come time for the fourth printing of these two booklets about the Holy Spirit, it has seemed best to include both under one cover. The advisability of this course can be seen with but a little reflection. "Do All Speak In Tongues?" was the first of the two to be published. It has been much more widely read and used than the author ever dreamed it would be. However it gives only one side of the story – the main thrust being some things we need *not* expect the Spirit to produce in our time.

When that first booklet was originally published, the author realized that only part of the story had been told. But a choice was deliberately made to omit the study that subsequently appeared in "The Joy of the Holy Spirit" in order to keep the first booklet brief enough that the average reader would take time to read it.

With the passing of the years, and the continuing interest in the Spirit and His activity, it now seems best to publish the two booklets together, so that the Christian may become more aware of what his Holy Guest *does* do, beyond simply being informed concerning what He does *not* do!

We are convinced that the Christian will no longer be susceptible to the neo-Pentecostal winds of doctrine which claim that there is something more to be experienced before the convert's new life is complete and satisfying, when the Christian begins to realize the joy the indwelling Spirit produces!

PREFACE TO THE THIRD EDITION

Since Plato, the dominant stream of Western thought has been "right reason can grasp the truth." Serious searchers for truth have rightly criticized the old Greek approach to truth because it rejects any idea that propositional revelation from God could be (and is) a source and criteria for judging what is true.

In the last quarter of the 20th century, many men are again giving serious attention to the idea that there is a way to truth other than by revelation from God – namely, through personal experience – and that when truth is known it is unverifiable by the world of facts or reason. We think this is a wrong approach!

It is also an age of "instant everything" – instant coffee, tea, potatoes, and even instant awareness of news from the other side of the world. In such an atmosphere, people can become lazy of mind. We no longer like or want to take time to think for ourselves. We are happy to let others do our thinking and reasoning for us. This too is wrong.

This study about the work of the Holy Spirit calls for thinking and reasoning about what God has revealed in His Word. It also calls for the application of the standard test for truth – systematic consistency. The only way to come to truth in religion is to have the Bible as the ultimate standard of right and wrong, and to have all passages on a given subject of study agree. If any passage contradicts a conclusion we've drawn, we have not come to the truth, for we do not have systematic consistency.

One new thing has been added to this third edition. That new thing is the brief outline study of the historical background of the Charismatic movement. It has often helpful to know the history of any given subject, and especially on this topic.

Moberly, Mo. September 22, 1982

HISTORICAL BACKGROUND OF THE CHARISMATIC MOVEMENT

Wesley and Methodism – 1780's

In Wesley's teaching there was an emphasis on an experience that follows conversion. This experience was thought needful because Wesley found most church members living careless lives, and he sought some method to correct this deficiency. "Sanctification begins at conversion and continues till the Christian reaches an instantaneous completion through an act of the Holy Spirit." Popularly, this idea is expressed in the motto, "Saved and sanctified!" One of the verses in the song *Rock of Ages* expressed the doctrine well – "Be of sin the *double* cure; save from sin and make me pure." The "make me pure" was the experience that Wesley taught followed conversion.

American Revivalism – early 1800's

One of the distinctive features of those frontier revivals were camp meetings and brush-arbor meetings as a method of spreading the gospel. Preachers placed an emphasis on individual commitment and on a *personal experience* of salvation.

Charles G. Finney – 1792-1876

Finney was a renowned evangelist of a previous era (much as Billy Graham is well-known today). His contribution to revivalism is that he brought it inside the church buildings. He institutionalized it. He also insisted on an experience following conversion. He was the first to say that the "experience that follows conversion" is synonymous with "the baptism of the Spirit" one reads about in the New Testament. He also introduced an emotional method of bringing converts to that spiritual crisis; it is sometimes called "using tear-jerking illustrations".

Holiness Movement – 1860's

Methodism had begun to ignore the "second work." In the songbooks, the words of *Rock of Ages* were changed to "be of sin the PROMISED cure ...." The Holiness (sanctification) movement re-iterated the emphasis on the forgotten second experience. Preachers often stated that evidence of holiness could be seen in one's lifestyle – modest dress, absence of lipstick, jewelry – but the preachers could not always agree on the details of the "evidence of holiness" in the absence of specific Biblical words on the subject.

R.A. Torrey – 1904

Torrey was a nationally popular preacher, and his popularity helped to make his re-affirmation of Finney's "baptism of the Holy Spirit is the Second Work of Grace" an accepted doctrine in large segments of the church world. He attempted to give the Pentecostal doctrine of the Holy Spirit a more Biblical and doctrinally correct emphasis.

published works on the Holy Spirit are still used for textbooks in many Pentecostal and Charismatic circles.

Pentecostalism

Richard G. Spurling, in 1896, held a revival in North Carolina, during which there was an extensive outburst of ecstatic "speaking in tongues." In this case, the "tongues" were not something sought by the worshipers. This revival is pointed to as the beginning of the Church of God (Cleveland, Tennessee.).

Charles Parham, in 1901, was president of Bethany Bible College in Topeka, Kansas. During a study of the book of Acts, he found it necessary to be absent from class on a fund-raising tour. He left the students with an assignment to see if they could find any "evidence" that was always spoken of in the Bible as proof that people had received the baptism of the Holy Spirit. The students arrived at the decision that "speaking in tongues" was always the initial evidence. The students even began to pray for the baptism of the Holy Spirit, and for the "tongues" as evidence they had so been baptized. Upon Parham's return from the fund-raising trip, he observed that the student's failure to receive the baptism of the Spirit was because no one had laid hands on them. He did so, and one of the students (Agnes Ozman) began to "speak in tongues." "Agnes Ozman was the first person in modern times to have such an experience as a result of specifically seeking it."[1]

Parham moved his school to Houston, Texas, where W.J. Seymour, a holiness preacher, enrolled. After a year or so, Seymour moved to Los Angeles, and started the Azuza Street Mission in 1906. People came from all over the world to the revival being held at Azuza Street, and from there Pentecostalism spread over the world – to Europe, Brazil, etc.

In more recent times, Aimee Semple McPherson came from Canada. Her evangelistic work resulted in the denomination known as the International Church of the Foursquare Gospel.[2]

Pentecostals often refer to their message as being the "full gospel," emphasizing that they do not leave out the miraculous workings of the Holy Spirit when they present the gospel. Those preachers who do not include the miraculous are not preaching the "full gospel," i.e., are not preaching the whole truth.

---

[1] Klaude Kendrick, *The Promise Fulfilled: A History of the Modern Pentecostal Movement* (Springfield, MO: Gospel Publishing House, 1961), p.53.

[2] Pat Boone, after growing up in the Church of Christ, became involved in the Charismatic movement. After writing *A New Song* to influence other Restoration Movement people to join the Charismatics, Boone has become a member of this International Church of the Foursquare Gospel in Van Nuys, CA. See this documented in *Christianity Today* 17/13 (March 30, 1973), p.695.

The Charismatic Movement – 1960's

A deliberate effort was made to change the image of Pentecostalism, to make it more acceptable to the people in the major denominations. (Many castigated Pentecostals as being "holy rollers" because of their actions while under the influence, they affirmed, of the Spirit.)

Traditional Pentecostalism emphasized (1) the Word of God above experience, (2) "tongues" as normative, the initial evidence of baptism in the Holy Spirit, (3) "tongues" do not prove "unity of the Spirit," (4) emphasis on holiness in lifestyle, and (5) involvement in church (congregational) life.

One can see the change of emphasis in neo-Pentecostalism by noting the new emphases: (1) experience is placed above the Word, (2) "tongues" are not viewed as normative, (3) the "tongues experience" is the basis of unity, no matter what else is believed, (4) less emphasis on lifestyle, and (5) involvement in "renewal communities" more than in congregational life.[3]

Some of the personalities in the forefront of this effort to involve the mainline denominations in neo-Pentecostalism were Harald Bredesen, John Sherrill (whose book *They Speak with Other Tongues* instructed new converts to the movement to keep their involvement in it secret as long as you can as they tried to enlist folk in the churches into the movement),[4] George Otis, Dennis Bennett, and Katheryn Kuhlman.

Jesus People – 1967

Toward the end of the 1960's, the neo-Pentecostal movement made another stride. It entered the new youth culture and became known as the Jesus Movement. It began in Haight-Ashbury in San Francisco and Sunset Strip in Los Angeles. Youth who had fled there by the thousands began looking for a better way than drugs, free sex, occultism, and eastern religions. Many from the drug culture learned you can become "high" on Jesus (the feeling of exhilaration while speaking in tongues) instead of on drugs.

Catholic Pentecostalism – 1967

Neo-Pentecostalism entered the Catholic Church in February, 1967. There were influences in this direction before Duquesne. Many Catholics were frustrated over years of spiritual stagnation. Vatican II called for renewal of the church, i.e., repentance in individual lives. The Cursillo Movement, with its weekend retreats, made use of group dynamics to change the lives of its members. Late in 1966, at Duquesne University, the

---

[3] Ray H. Hughes, "A Traditional Pentecostal Looks at the New Pentecostals," *Christianity Today* 18/18 (June 7, 1974), p.1036-40.

[4] John Sherrill, *They Speak With Other Tongues* (Westwood, NJ: Revell, 1964), p.134-35.

Cursillo Movement was studying Acts, the book *The Cross and the Switchblade*, and *They Speak With Other Tongues*. In February 1967, Dennis Bennett and a Charismatic unit in Pittsburgh helped the Cursillos to get the "baptism in the Spirit." This came at a weekend retreat. Then in March the Duquesne experience was repeated among the Cursillo people at Notre Dame when a Full Gospel Businessmen's Fellowship leader helped them get the "baptism in the Spirit." In April, the event was repeated at Michigan State University. Since then, Catholics, like Edward O'Connor and Cardinal Suenens, themselves involved in the Charismatic movement, have been molding the thinking of the neo-Pentecostals, both Protestant and Catholic. Annual charismatic conferences are held at Notre Dame, with attendance in recent years passing 40,000.

Ecumenical Phase of Pentecostalism – 1970's

The 1970's brought us to a great ecumenical phase of the Charismatic movement. Since Roman Catholics are now receiving the identical Pentecostal experience as Protestants, the old-line Pentecostals are having to re-evaluate their attitude toward Catholicism. Although Pentecostalism was introduced to the Catholic Church initially by Protestant Pentecostals, it is meeting even less resistance in Catholic circles than in Protestant circles. In fact, as many Catholic authors are pointing out, Pentecostalism is more at home in the Catholic Church. It is more at home there because the overwhelming Pentecostal emphasis on the subjective experience is in essential harmony with the tradition of the Roman Church, which since the Middle Ages has had a mystical bent.

In May, 1972, the magazine *New Covenant*, a Catholic charismatic publication, featured Catholics and Protestants uniting in a great charismatic fellowship. It proclaimed that the Charismatic movement holds the hope of "healing the wound" of the 16th century Reformation. This union is not based on objective truth, but on subjective experience. The Charismatic song, *We are One in the Spirit*, proclaims that all doctrinal distinctions are ignored by the ecumenical Charismatics (even when the doctrines are Biblically right!).

Meetings such as the one held in Arrowhead Stadium, Kansas City, in 1978, are visible evidences of growth of the ecumenical emphases of the Charismatic movement.

Fuller Theological Seminary – 1981-82

An "experimental course on the subject of signs, wonders, and church growth" (MC 510 is the course number) is offered. Third World students (whose native evangelists pray for the sick, healings resulted, and conversions followed) insisted that there were things happening in their countries that led to enormous church growth, which Western theologians and missiologists were ignoring. Dr. John Wimber and Dr. Peter Wagner led the course to investigate whether what the Third World people were saying is viable for today. Their conclusion was in favor of the validity of the Charismatic movement.[5]

---

[5] See the October, 1982, issue of *Moody Monthly*. The whole issue is given to a report of MC 510.

From this beginning came what is called "The Signs and Wonders Movement." One emphasis of that movement which has attracted followers is the concept of "Power Evangelism." A "power encounter", according to Wimber, is "a visible, practical demonstration [miracle worked in the name of Jesus] that Jesus Christ is more powerful than the false gods and spirits worshiped or feared by people groups." "Strategic Spiritual Warfare" is another emphasis that has come out of the Signs and Wonders Movement. The presupposition behind such warfare is the idea that there are evil "territorial spirits" who control national, ethnic, religious, and even generational groups. Before one can evangelize these groups, the evil spirit must be identified and expelled. "Prayer walks" around oppressed and unevangelized areas target the evil spirits in those areas and bind them so that the gospel will produce results when it eventually is presented.

The Toronto Blessing – 1994[6]

Rodney Howard-Browne has come from South Africa to Canada and America. He styles himself the "Holy Ghost bartender" who is serving up the "new wine" of "holy laughter." When hands are laid on worshipers, they break out into uncontrollable laughter. When the altered state of consciousness is past, the worshipers are told they have experienced the "joy of the Lord." Holy laughter has been called one of the "signs" of the "revival" that is going on in the land.

The "Glory" of the Lord Came Down – 1999

Flakes and specks of gold dust appeared on the foreheads, in the hair, and on the clothing of several Charismatic evangelists as they preached and ministered. Silver amalgams and dental crowns have turned to gold or platinum or even white enamel, as one of the evidences the Holy Spirit is present in the meeting. Worshipers are told the gold is the "Glory" of the Lord.

Summary

History shows that the belief that there is a one-time experience that follows conversion, and that the idea that this experience is the same as the Biblical "baptism of (in) the Holy Spirit," and that the initial evidence one has had this experience is speaking in tongues, are all relatively recent developments in the theological world. The ideas are not at all as old as the New Testament.

---

[6] This point and the next have been added in order to bring up to date the 1982 edition of the pamphlet here being reproduced.

DO ALL SPEAK IN TONGUES?

Within a week's time, news came to us at the Bible College of two more preachers of the Restoration Movement who have been won to the current charismatic revival, and have claimed to be filled with the Holy Spirit, to speak in tongues, and to be able to work miracles of healing. One of the letters addressed to this writer had this sentence: "Will you explain to me about this Pentecostalism that has split our church?" The purpose of this pamphlet is to examine in the light of the New Testament this tongues movement that is disturbing the churches.

HOW IT GROWS

In 1947, the Pentecostalist Carl Brumback, writer of the book *What Meaneth This?*, lamented, "We might as well face the facts: speaking in tongues is not acceptable anywhere except in the Pentecostal Movement."[7] Some twenty years later, speaking in tongues has become acceptable in a number of different groups, including some among the Christian Churches. What has caused the change?

Many of the cases of tongue-speaking among the people of the Christian Church, which have come to this writer's attention, can be traced to the activity of the Full Gospel Business Men's Fellowship International (FGBMFI), headquartered in Los Angeles. It is an organization of businessmen who are committed to what they call the full gospel message – an emphasis upon the spiritual gifts and the phenomenon of speaking in tongues as evidence of having received the baptism of the Holy Spirit. The organization was founded by Demos Shakarian, a Pentecostal businessman, after being encouraged in the idea by Oral Roberts. The purpose of this organization was stated in one of their regular publications, *Full Gospel Business Men's Voice*, in these words: "I believe one of the specific purposes for FGBMFI is to bridge the gap that has kept the Pentecostal message from the traditional churches."[8] They are accomplishing their purpose.

HOW DO THEY PROMOTE IT?

One way they have worked is by sponsoring banquets to which preachers from all denominations are invited. While the preachers are eating, there are Pentecostal speakers who explain about their reception of the baptism of the Holy Spirit accompanied by the evidence of tongue-speaking. At each of these banquets, held in hotel and convention centers, there are some of the guests who want to hear more, and who soon come to embrace the Pentecostal message, and then go back to the church to which they preach, and in meetings in the homes of influential members, spread the message. Some whole churches are won to the Pentecostal position, while others have divided over it.

---

[7] Carl Brumback, *What Meaneth This?* (Springfield, MO: The Gospel Publishing House, 1947), p.99.

[8] Ralph Mahoney, "Pentecost in Perspective," *Full Gospel Business Men's Voice*, XIII (May, 1965) p.4.

We shall deal with the question later in this study as to why the Pentecostal message appeals to some church members who have grown dissatisfied with their own personal experiences (in some cases, there have been no personal experiences), and with the meager evangelistic program of the congregation with which they worship.

This writer has a brother-in-law who is an elder in the Florissant (MO) Christian Church. That congregation was recently torn over the question of speaking in tongues after the man who was preaching for them at the time attended one of these banquets. My brother-in-law has made a chart showing how the tongue-speaking movement is surely not as spontaneous as its adherents often claim. Time and again, where folk have begun to speak in tongues, he has shown that in the background is either the FGBMFI or one of the Christian Church missionaries who serves in Mexico. (From the same missionary whose influences were in the vanguard of tongue-speaking in the St. Louis area came the influences that led to the tongue-speaking recently among some northeastern Indiana churches, among some missionary recruits in that area, as well as among preachers in southern Missouri.) All this merely shows that Russell Hitt was right when he wrote in *Eternity* magazine, "The most polished of public relations techniques have been enrolled to advance the movement. While there is certainly nothing wrong with using modern techniques, the neo-Pentecostalism cannot claim complete spontaneity."[9]

A second method of promoting the "full gospel" message is by what might be called the "home prayer meeting" method. In area meetings sponsored by the FGBMFI, one person who has received (as they call it) the Holy Spirit will receive a "vision" instructing him to move to a certain town. The vision may even instruct him about what kind of business to open. Once located in the new community, he will invite to his home any one he finds who is interested in Bible study and a more satisfying spiritual life. It is not long before he has met and influenced some folk who are already attending church in the community, and who for one reason or another are dissatisfied with their church. Through these folk other dissatisfied people in the congregation are invited to the Bible studies. These home study meetings are characterized by testimonies concerning how the Spirit has changed the lives of those who have received Him. Instructions are given to those interested (and most are, since they already are tired of the way they have been living) on how to receive the Spirit, and how to speak in tongues as evidence of being filled with the Spirit. It has been this writer's experience that the people who are thus reached in these home meetings are people facing some crisis in their lives – a physical one, like some sickness that will not respond to medical treatment; or a personal crisis, like whether or not to accept a new job that entails a major disruption of the present pattern of everyday life; or an emotional crisis, such as would be involved in a decision like whether or not to get out of church, or get deeply involved in church with one's whole life. And not long after a number of folk in these home study groups have "received the Spirit," a new vision will come to one or more instructing him to go to another town, in order to begin the cycle all over again.

---

[9] Russell T. Hitt, "The New Pentecostalism: An Appraisal," *Eternity*, XIV (July, 1963), p.16.

A third method of promoting the "full gospel" message has been through print media. There are three publications printed by the FGBMFI. Their most popular magazine is the monthly *Full Gospel Business Men's Voice*, which contains testimonies of those who have been "baptized in the Holy Spirit." *Vision* is a magazine with a special appeal to youth. *View* is a quarterly journal that deals with the Charismatic renewal.

Another magazine, which seems to be aimed at the college-age youth, is *Christian Life*, edited by Robert Walker. It actively promotes the Charismatic revival. And, of course, the Pentecostal publications (like *Abundant Life*, The *Voice of Healing*, and others) are openly promoting the movement.

Another group having a part in the growth of this tongue-speaking movement is the Blessed Trinity Society, which sponsors Christian Advance meetings. One of the names associated with this group is David J. du Plessis, a Pentecostal from South Africa, who is trying to take the Pentecostal message to the leaders of the ecumenical movement.

Our churches would do well to keep these names and organizations in mind, for no congregation will be the same after some of their number have "spoken in tongues," and then cast aspersions on the quality of the Christianity in the lives of those members of the congregation who have not "spoken in tongues" as evidence of being filled with the Spirit.

CLAIMS MADE TODAY

To understand the nature of the tongues movement in order to evaluate it, one needs to know what is being claimed by those who have spoken in tongues. The claims could be put under the following headings:

1) **The "baptism of the Holy Spirit" is for all believers.** Thomas Zimmerman, in his article, "Pleas for Pentecostalists," wrote, "while some divergence of doctrine exists, one basic position unites Pentecostals – their common belief that 'the baptism of the Holy Spirit' is a distinct experience which all believers may and should have following conversion."[10] The tongue-speakers of the Restoration Movement make similar statements.[11]

2) **"Speaking in tongues" is evidence that one has been baptized of the Holy Spirit.** In fact, it is claimed that speaking in tongues is the initial physical evidence that such a baptism has taken place. Gene Birney, in *The Spiritual Witness*, has written, "Tongues is the sign of the initial in-filling of the Spirit."[12] Frank Farrell, writing in *Christianity*

---

[10] Thomas F. Zimmerman, "Plea for the Pentecostalists," *Christianity Today*, VII (January 4, 1963), p.319.

[11] Gene Birney, "Studies from the Word of God," *The Spiritual Witness*, I (Summer 1962), p.6. See also May. 1962, p.2.

[12] Birney, *op. cit.*, p.8.

Today, makes this note, "Tongues as initial evidence is distinguished from the gift of tongues (1 Corinthians 12:12), which was not granted to all."[13] Harold Horton makes the same point, "Everybody speaks in tongues at least once at his baptism in the Spirit (Acts 2:4, 10:45), but apparently all do not retain this power to speak in tongues (1 Corinthians 14:5,23). The only Scriptural distinction between the sign of tongues and the gift of tongues is that when tongues are first employed by an individual, the utterance is the *sign* of the baptism in the Spirit; every subsequent use of the supernatural tongue by this same individual is the *gift* of tongues in operation."[14]

3) **Some tongues are alleged to be foreign languages, but most are admittedly not intelligible languages.** McCandlish Phillips, writing for *The Saturday Evening Post*, states that at times those speaking in tongues speak in foreign languages they have never studied.[15] Birney has written, "In answer to the question are these tongues languages that are known or unknown, they can be both. The tongues on the day of Pentecost were unknown to the apostles (Acts 2:7), but were known by many that heard (Acts 2:8). This is sometimes the case today. It is not unknown for a tongue to be understood by someone in the audience who happens to know the language being spoken by the Spirit ... The Spirit chooses the language, and while *most* seem to be the languages of men, i.e., languages that have been or are spoken by men, it can also be a heavenly or angelic language (1 Corinthians 13:1)."[16]

4) **Those who have spoken in tongues have testified to the fact that they now have changed lives.** Mistaken beliefs have been corrected. There is a new interest in church attendance, tithing, counseling, and witnessing for Christ. There is a new desire to read and study the Bible. There is a new power claimed by the preachers for their preaching.[17]

HOW TO DO IT

How does one come to speak in tongues? Does he suddenly speak without having had previous knowledge of or desire for the phenomenon? Or, does he receive assistance in the form of instructions? The latter tends to be truer of the modern tongues movement.

---

[13] Frank Farrell, "Outburst of Tongues: The New Penetration," *Christianity Today* VII (September 13, 1963), p.1163.

[14] Harold Horton, *The Gifts of the Spirit* (Bedfordshire, England: Redemption Tidings Bookroom, 1946), p.155.

[15] McCandlish Phillips, "And There Appeared Unto Them Tongues of Fire," *The Saturday Evening Post*, May 16, 1964, p.32ff. See also Farrell, *op. cit.*, p.1166.

[16] Gene Birney, *The Spiritual Witness*, I (May 1962), p.8.

[17] Gareth L. Reese, "Glossolalia," *New Testament History: Acts* (Moberly, MO: published by the author, 1966, p.88,89. (Pages 118ff in 1976 and later reprints.)

One set of instructions is as follows: "In order to speak in tongues, you have to quit praying in English ... You simply lapse into silence and resolve to speak not a syllable of any language you have ever learned. Your thoughts are focused on Christ, and then you simply lift up your voice and speak out confidently, in the faith that the Lord will take the sound you give Him, and shape it into a language. You take no thought of what you are saying; as far as you are concerned, it is just a series of sounds. The first sounds will sound strange and unnatural to your ear, and they may be halting and inarticulate (have you ever heard a baby learning to talk?)."[18]

Bredesen gave these instructions to tongue seekers at Yale: "(1) to think visually and concretely, rather than abstractedly: for example, to try to visualize Jesus as a person; (2) consciously to yield their voices and organs of speech to the Holy Spirit; (3) to repeat certain elementary sounds which he told them, such as 'bah--bah--bah,' or something similar. He then laid his hands on the head of each seeker, and prayed for him, and the seeker did actually speak in tongues."[19]

One of our students here at the Bible College, who in days past had an ear temporarily healed of deafness, reports that he was instructed to repeat as rapidly as he could, "Thank you, Lord! Thank you, Lord! Thank you, Lord!" He, too, tells how he was in an extremely tight emotional situation because of physical, personal, and emotional crises in his life. He tells of speaking in tongues, of having visions (albeit conflicting visions) giving him instructions, and of becoming disillusioned about the whole thing (and we'll list the causes of his disillusionment before we conclude this study). He tells how he was warned on the very night he received the Spirit – warned by the leader of the home prayer and study session who was a member of FGBMFI – that in two or three weeks he would be tempted to believe all that had happened was purely emotional and not at all the work of the Holy Spirit. "Sure enough," he says, "the thought came to mind one day as I was recalling the things that had happened."

In this first part of this study we have examined how the "speaking in tongues" controversy is growing, the means by which it spreads, the claims made by those who have experienced what they call the "filling" of the Holy Spirit, and we have given some examples of the instructions given to the person who would like to learn to speak in tongues. We now have enough information to be able to evaluate this movement in light of the New Testament. What does the New Testament teach about "speaking in tongues"?

According to modern tongues-speakers, the following passages speak about this Spirit-produced activity: Mark 16:17, Acts 2:1-11, Acts 8:14-19, Acts 10:44-48, Acts 19:1-6, and 1 Corinthians 12-14. From these let us examine in detail the two that give the most concrete information on the subject.

---

[18] Cited by John Miles, "Tongues," *Voice*, XLIV (February, 1965), p.6. (This is the IFCA publication, not the FGBMFI publication.)

[19] Cited by Stanley D. Walters, "Speaking in Tongues," *Youth in Action* (May, 1964), p.11.

ACTS 2:1-11

These verses tell us that in this instance the 'filling of the Spirit' and the 'baptism of the Spirit' are synonymous terms. We are also told that it was the *apostles* (see the nearest antecedent of "they" in Acts 1:26, and the statement that those speaking were "all Galileans," verse 7) who in this case received the filling, and the filling was accompanied by speaking in tongues. Verses 6 and 8 plainly show that the "speaking in tongues" was the utterance of a *foreign language* by the apostles, and the verses plainly show the miracle was done to the tongues of the apostles, and not to the ears of the hearers. Further, there is no evidence that these men, before the day of Pentecost, had been praying for the coming of the Holy Spirit, or that they were desiring the "sign" of His coming.

One other thing needs to be given attention concerning this Acts 2 passage. Verse 13 is often used to prove that the apostles, while speaking in tongues, were in a highly emotional state, and that they must have been staggering and jerking around, thus suggesting to some that they were drunken. Two lines of thought may be suggested in response to this assertion. One, we are not told who made the accusation. Could it have been the Jewish religious leaders? Had not those men on numerous occasions tried to put Jesus in a bad light by saying He acted by the power of the devil? Surely they have not had a change of heart. Are they the ones who are now making similar, slanderous remarks about the apostles in an attempt to discredit them? Second, it should be remembered that even in the Old Testament, when the Spirit came upon the prophets to inspire them to speak, at times the psychological condition of the prophet was one of intense excitement.[20] Such excitement is surely not to be compared to extreme emotionalism that results in jerks, a final collapse on the floor, and a temporary state of semi-consciousness or unconsciousness. The prophets were in complete control of their faculties, ready to deliver the message, the moment the Spirit came upon them. So indeed, the apostles, like the Old Testament prophets, may have been excited as a result of the filling of the Spirit, but the record is plain that they were not ecstatic.[21]

1 CORINTHIANS 12-14

Though most scholars agree that Acts 2 speaks of foreign languages when it records an occasion of 'speaking in tongues,' a number of present-day scholars favor the idea that "speaking in tongues" in 1 Corinthians was *not* a case of languages being spoken, but rather

---

[20] C. von Orelli, "Prophecy, Prophets," *International Standard Bible Encyclopedia* (Grand Rapids, MI: Eerdmans, 1929), V.4, p.2460.

[21] Webster's unabridged dictionary gives this definition for "ecstatic": "state of being beside oneself, state of being beyond all reason and self-control as when given over to an extreme and engrossing emotion; obsession by powerful emotion." A more common term is 'altered state of consciousness.'

of ecstatic babbling or unintelligible utterances. **This writer sees no reason for making this distinction.**[22]

Comparing the accounts in Acts and Corinthians, we see some points that are identical. In both cases, an extraordinary influence and gift of the Spirit was responsible for the speaking. In both, the people were speaking as the Spirit led them to speak. And the intention of the speaking in tongues in both cases was to bring praise and honor to God, and to edify the hearers.

Further, when one examines the verses in Corinthians that are alleged to show the "tongues" in Corinth were different from the "languages" of Pentecost, if we instead proceed under the hypothesis that the "tongues at Corinth were actual foreign languages," the verses make marvelous sense!

For example, it is said that the speaking of the apostles (Acts 2) was understood by the hearers without assistance from others, whereas the Corinthian speaking was not understood without the aid of an interpreter (1 Corinthians 14:2,13,16,27,28). From this it is alleged that the Corinthian "tongues" were babbling and not languages. Yet a better interpretation of 1 Corinthians 14 has Paul asking, 'Why desire the gift of tongues when there may be only a few folk present in the services who can understand the language you are speaking? Why desire a gift that requires an interpreter to make clear to most of the congregation what you have said? Why not desire one of the other spiritual gifts, one that would be more useful in the public assembly?'

Nor can 1 Corinthians 14:23 be used to show that what was happening at Corinth was ecstatic syllabication. The point being made is not that there was a bedlam of babbling that the visitor to the service would frown upon; rather, Paul is assuming an extreme case for the sake of argument. He pictures a case where everyone present in the worship service had the gift of tongues, and that one after another they get up and speak a foreign language. Now suppose a visitor comes to the service. The Christians, one after another, get up and instead of speaking the language of the locale, uttered a speech in a foreign language that the visitor did not understand (he was "unlearned"). On his way home, after hearing a whole service of nothing but words in languages he did not understand, the visitor would conclude that the Christians were crazy.

1 Corinthians 14:27,28 gives the instruction that if there is no interpreter present, the one speaking in tongues is to "keep silent" or "speak to himself." Rather than being evidence that "tongues" at Corinth was ecstatic speaking, these verses point in the other direction, that "tongues" at Corinth were languages. The supposition is that, at Corinth, there might be days when no visitor would come to the services whose native language was the same as the language of the one who had the "gift of tongues." (Each person who had the spiritual gift of tongues evidently was able to speak but one foreign language, 1 Corin-

---

[22] For a more detailed study concerning "tongues" at Corinth, see Gromacki, *The Modern Tongues Movement* (Philadelphia: Presbyterian and Reformed Publishing Co., 1967), p.56ff. Gromacki also documents the idea that tongues at Corinth was a language, just as at Pentecost.

thians 14:18.) Since his gift was really not needed that day, there would be no "edifying" of those present unless someone could interpret what he had said (that someone having another of the spiritual gifts, the gift of interpretation of tongues).

1 Corinthians 14:2 need not be so interpreted as to prove that "tongues" at Corinth was unintelligible babbling. In the context, this verse is designed as an explanation of why men ought to desire the gift of prophecy rather than the gift of tongues. Men who were prophesying (i.e., speaking by inspiration, in the vernacular of the people) would edify the church, whereas men speaking in a language that none of the church members understood (unless an interpreter were present, verse 5) would leave the hearers "in the dark" as to what was said. This would be true, even when the speaker was guided by the Spirit as he explained the mysteries of God.[23]

We have examined the chief passages that explain what "speaking in tongues" was in Bible times. There is no reason to believe that Biblical "tongues" were anything but foreign languages, languages never learned or studied by the speaker whom the Spirit led to speak. This being true, those modern tongue-speakers, who admit what they do is not a foreign language, can find no Biblical precedent for their practices.

Having shown that "speaking in tongues" in Bible times was speaking an unstudied and unlearned foreign language, the passages can be examined for other pertinent points that will help us to evaluate the current tongues-speaking movement.

1 CORINTHIANS 13:8-13

In the midst of Paul's discussion concerning the spiritual gifts, he asserts that prophecy, tongues, and the other spiritual gifts would cease "when that which is perfect is come." If it can be shown that the spiritual gifts one reads about in the New Testament have ceased, then he would have a basis from which to argue that what one sees today is not like what he reads about in the Word. To do this it will be necessary to study first the Word, then history.

1 Corinthians 13:8 makes a contrast between love which "never fails" and the spiritual gifts which "will cease." Someone has defined "love" as doing that which is spiritually best for the other person. It would be the opposite of what the Corinthians were doing, exercising their gifts when it would contribute most to their own selfish interests. Love, not self-exaltation, is the point Paul is trying to teach to the Corinthians. In this age, there will always be a place for love, he says. It never fails, he writes. But there will not always be a place for the spiritual gifts; they shall cease, he says.

---

[23] "Mystery" in the Bible is something not clearly revealed in the Old Testament, but which is clearly revealed in the New. See Ephesians 1:9, 3:3; Romans 16:25,26. "Mystery" has nothing to do with the kind of language used by the speaker, as though it were something puzzling and unintelligible.

Tongues shall cease, he says, and *pausontai* is exactly suited to the subject of tongues. A speaker 'pauses' and speaks no more; so tongues shall lapse into complete silence, he predicts. The gifts of prophecy, speaking in tongues, and the word of knowledge – all the spiritual gifts – will come to an end, Paul tells us. As to when, see verse 10.

Draw for yourself a mental picture. There is a jigsaw picture puzzle to be put together. Each person holds in his hand one piece, which has been given to him by the host of the party. When each one has contributed to the picture that which he has been given, the complete picture emerges.

So it was in the early days of the church, Paul says in verse 9, concerning the matter of God's New Testament revelation. It was as though each of the spiritually gifted members held a part of the revelation ("we know *in part*, and we prophesy *in part*"), and when he contributed what had been revealed to him, the picture was not complete. All the others who were spiritually gifted also had to contribute what had been revealed to them, before anyone would have the complete picture of God's New Testament will. "We know in part, and we prophesy in part" means that each person, in his own place and function in the body, exercising his particular gift, still gave God's will only in part.

Verse 10 gives the reason why the gifts of knowledge and prophecy and tongues would cease. As exercised by the spiritually gifted, they gave but partial and imperfect and momentary glimpses into the mysteries of divine revelation (see also verse 11a). Something better, something "perfect" (Greek, *teleion*), something 'fully developed' (so the Greek word implies) was coming. Verse 11 goes on to carry out the figure ('full grown') suggested by *teleion*, by comparing the age of spiritual gifts with the infancy of a man, and the age when the gifts have passed with his manhood. Those, then, who claim to have the spiritual gifts that 1 Corinthians 12-14 tell about would be forced by this verse to admit that their Christianity is still in its infantile state, and has not at all reached "manhood." They have not yet put away childish things, even though God's revelation has been completed and recorded in the New Testament Scriptures, i.e., that which is perfect (the completed revelation) has come to replace that which was in part.[24]

In verse 12, Paul makes use of another illustration to show the imperfection of the age of spiritual gifts. Twice he uses the word "then" meaning when the infancy is past, when manhood is reached, when "that which is perfect" is come. *Now*, he says, the spiritual gifts give only a partial picture of God's will for man, but *then* every man's knowledge of God and His ways will be more complete. God knew my needs and provided for them, and in the written New Testament I can read His will, His complete will for me, and see my needs and respond to His gracious provision.

---

[24] Some would question the idea of identifying "that which is perfect" with the completed revelation (which came to be recorded in permanent form in the New Testament Scriptures) as we have done. They believe verse 10 speaks of Christ and His second coming. In reply, we point out that "perfect" is neuter in gender in the Greek, and if it referred to Christ, we would expect it to be in the masculine gender. Further, the argument from history tends to confirm our interpretation of this prophecy.

In verse 13, Paul caps this part of his argument by saying that faith, hope, and love will remain in this world long after the gifts of tongues, prophecy, and knowledge have ceased. His point? The readers should regulate their actions by *love*, not self-exaltation (as they were doing in their displays of the gifts they had received).

TONGUES IN HISTORY

Have we been right in our interpretation of 1 Corinthians 13, that tongues were for the infancy of the church? Or are they something one finds all through the pages of church history? Frank Farrell has written, "Perhaps the most common view relates the gifts of the Spirit to the founding of the Church, their cessation during the 2nd century taking place after it was well established under the authority of the completed New Testament Canon. Presbyterian theologian B.B. Warfield believed the *charismata* (spiritual gifts) to be given for authentication of the apostles as God's messengers, a sign of apostleship being possession of the gifts and the ability to transmit them. Gradual cessation of the gifts thus came with the death of those who had received the gifts through the apostles."[25]

Advocates of glossolalia (speaking in tongues) today reply that Warfield's theory flies in the face of history, and they assert that all through history there have been examples of tongue-speaking. So let us look at history.

About AD 150, Justin Martyr made an effort to win the Jew Trypho to the Christian faith. In his *Dialogue with Trypho*, he wrote, "For the prophetical gifts remain with us, even to the present time. And hence you ought to understand that (the gifts) formerly among your nation have been transferred to us."[26] A page or two later, he identifies the gifts, and though he does not specify tongues, it would be hard to exclude this gift from Justin's language. Certainly it would appear that the spiritual gifts were still to be found in Justin's day.

Irenaeus, born about AD 130, wrote five books against heresies about AD 185. In one he comments on 1 Corinthians 2:6 as follows, "... terming those persons 'perfect' who have received the Spirit of God, and who through the Spirit of God do speak in all languages, as he (i.e., Paul) used himself to speak. In like manner we do also hear many brethren in the church who possess prophetic gifts, and who through the Spirit speak all kinds of languages."[27]

Irenaeus' quote is often cited as evidence of the existence of tongues as late as AD 185. The translator, however, footnotes the words "do also hear," and points out that the verb here is actually in the perfect tense and thus shows that the action has been completed in the past. The interval is indefinite. But if Irenaeus were aware of his Latin, he was

---

[25] Farrell, *op. cit.*, p.1164.

[26] *The Ante-Nicene Fathers*, edited by Roberts and Donaldson (Grand Rapids, MI: Eerdmans, 1950), Vol. I, p.240-243.

[27] *Op. cit.*, p.531.

saying that he used to hear this, but does not necessarily hear it now.

Next, the case of Montanus, AD 126-180, should be noted. He spoke in tongues and prophesied, at least so Eusebius tells us. But Eusebius also tells us that Montanus' prophesying and tongue-speaking were contrary to the known procedures of the day. "And he became beside himself, and being suddenly in a sort of frenzy and ecstasy, he raved, and began to babble and utter strange things, prophesying in a manner contrary to the constant custom of the church handed down by tradition from the beginning."[28] Let it be noted well – what the Montanists were doing was different from what was done in the early church!

Tertullian, AD 160-220, labored as a Montanist in Carthage, North Africa. Seeing what the Montanists were doing, he asserted his belief in the continued existence of spiritual gifts.[29] Epiphanius, however, a 4th century bishop, comments that the tongues-speech of the Montanists was quite different from that described in Corinthians.[30]

Origen, AD 185-254, wrote about the continuance of some New Testament signs: "... the Holy Spirit gave signs of His presence at the beginning of Christ's ministry, and after His ascension He gave still more, but since that time these signs have diminished, although there are still traces of His presence in the few who have had their souls purified by the Gospel."[31] The "signs" of which he speaks may or may not include tongues. Perhaps it does. It would not be outside the realm of possibility that near AD 100, the last of the apostles laid hands on a young person, who would still be surviving and manifesting his spiritual gifts at the time Origen wrote. In any case, let it be noted that the infancy of the church is passing, and the gifts are ceasing, just as Paul taught they would.

As early as the 4th century, Chrysostom, AD 354-407, expressed puzzlement at Paul's account of the Corinthian situation. "The whole passage is exceedingly obscure and the obscurity is occasioned by our ignorance of the facts and the cessation of the happenings which were common in those days, but unexampled in our own."[32] A similar testimony from Augustine, AD 354-430, can be cited to show that tongues have "passed away."[33]

---

[28] *The Nicene and Post-Nicene Fathers*, edited by Schaff and Wace (Grand Rapids, MI: Eerdmans, 1952), Vol. 1, p.231.

[29] *The Ante-Nicene Fathers*, Vol. III, p.188 & 477.

[30] Cited by G.B. Cutten, *Speaking with Tongues* (New Haven: Yale University Press, 1927), p.34,35.

[31] *The Ante-Nicene Fathers*, Vol. IV, p.614.

[32] *The Nicene and Post-Nicene Fathers*, edited by Schaff (New York: The Christian Literature Company, 1889), Vol. XII, Hom.29.1.

[33] Augustine, "Ten Homilies on 1 John," trans. H. Browne, Vol. VII of *The Nicene and Post-Nicene Fathers*, ed. Philip Schaff, (New York: The Christian Literature Company, 1888), Vol.VI, p.10.

Two things can be seen from this study of history. Biblical speaking in tongues and the other spiritual gifts passed away, just as Paul taught they would, and this within 100 years of the death of the last apostle. Second, something called "speaking in tongues" sprang up among the Montanists, but it was not like the languages spoken as the Spirit gave utterance, concerning which one reads in the New Testament. Now, if Biblical tongue-speaking ceased, and something else called "tongues" sprang up in its place, under which category would we place what today is labeled as "speaking in tongues"? Is it not to be placed in the latter? And if so, it begins to appear that it is not proper to expect all Christians today to speak in tongues!

We would ask those who would speak in tongues today, why seek only a *piece* of God's revelation, when we have the *whole picture* in the New Testament? (In this question, of course, we are arguing *ad hominem*, and not at all granting that revelations are being made today, even in bits and pieces.)

So far in our study of the modern tongues movement, we have set down the claims made by those who believe they have received a special "filling of the Spirit," and we have begun to give a series of tests by which we can "test the spirits"[34] to see whether or not what they claim is true and Biblical. Two tests have been given. (1) Is it a language? If not, we have suggested, it is not Biblical speaking in tongues. (2) Both Scripture and history testify to the fact that the speaking in tongues about which one reads in the Bible has ceased. If so, how can today's activities be Biblical? Let us now set forth several more tests.

WHY SPEAK WITH TONGUES?

Paul begins 1 Corinthians 14 with the instruction that love must be the thing that motivates our activities. He then shows that the spiritual gift of prophecy is of greater value than the gift of tongues, because it was more useful to the greater number of people (verses 1-4). Prophecy is preaching by inspiration in the language of the people. Tongues, as has been shown, was the speaking by inspiration in a language other than that of a majority of the people.

A builder knows what he is doing, and others see that his efforts make sense. He does not throw bricks and mortar together haphazardly, hoping that something worthwhile will result. He systematically lays the bricks one on top of another according to the recognized principles of construction. So it is with the one who prophesies, says Paul. He "edifies the church." The man who speaks in tongues when no one understands what he is saying does not edify at all. So, why speak in tongues, when they are not needed, is Paul's implication.

---

[34] 1 John 4:1.

The point of verse 5 is this – our speech must be helpful to others, and if what we say (even if it is in a language as led by the Spirit) cannot be understood, then it is not very valuable. Paul keeps pounding the idea 'that he may edify.' The contrast appears to be between edification (which would be the exercise of the spiritual gift in love) and showing off (which would be a selfish, unlovely use of the gift). Our concern should not be how we can show off to best advantage in the public assembly. Instead it should be what we can do to edify and build up that assembly. There must be a conscious striving and sense of purpose in this. The Christian ought not to be motivated by what he can get out of his church or his gift, even in the matter of admiration for his natural or supernatural abilities. Instead, he should be concerned about what he can do for the edification of his church.

In verses 6-20, Paul gives five or six illustrations of the idea that useful speech (prophesying) is of greater value in the public assembly than the gift of tongues. What value would his coming visit to Corinth be if, when he arrived, he spoke only in languages which no one present could understand (verse 6)? After the analogy from musical instruments, he drives home the point (verse 9) that speech, if it is to be useful, must be understandable to the listener. Would you walk into an empty room, and begin to speak? That is speaking into the air. But the results are the same as speaking in an empty room if you deliberately use a language that no one present understands. What the Corinthians were doing was for no other reason than self-gratification and to show off the fact that they were filled with the Holy Spirit. It was a selfish purpose. Paul exposes it as such and rebukes it.

Paul further insists that when one speaks in tongues there must be understanding involved (verses 14-16). Whose understanding? Perhaps it is the understanding of the one doing the speaking. Perhaps it is the understanding of the ones who hear the sound of the one speaking in tongues. In either case, Paul's language is a rebuke of the use of tongues when there is no understanding.

He closes the paragraph with some pointed words (verse 20) about being mature in thought and speech. Parents understandably dread it when someone gives a drum or other noisemaking toy to a child. The little ones become so enthralled with the volume of sound they are producing that they are lost to all other considerations. Bang, bang, bang, they go all day long, whether quiet is necessary or not. They do not care how much noise they make, as long as they are enjoying it themselves. Young children can exercise no discretion. That's the kind of childish Christians the Corinthians were. As long as their tongues possessed this exciting and enthralling ability to rattle, why not do it in full force? Grow up, Paul pleads.

These verses have given us several more tests which we may apply to the modern situation. We have examined one – why speak in tongues when they are not needed (and the context shows they are needed and useful only when there are unbelievers present in the public assemblies who do not understand the local dialect)? Paul's instructions amount to this – keep quiet in the church assembly, unless what you speak is in a language understood locally and is helpful toward edification.[35]

WHAT ABOUT INSTRUCTIONS?

The fourth in our series of tests also comes from these verses in chapter 14. On a previous page we have quoted the instructions regularly given to those who are seeking to speak in tongues. Those instructions include words to this effect, that the seeker is to take no thought about what he was going to say. Just let the words roll out, no matter how strange and funny they might sound.

Surely, such instructions are contrary to verses 13-15, where Paul speaks of using his "understanding" (Greek, *nous*, mind). The Lord gave me my mind in order to use it at all times; if I do not use it, it is deprived of its intended function of producing distinct thoughts that will benefit others. Whether praying, singing, or preaching (prophesying), Paul is determined to use his God-given faculties, including his mind.

Beware, then, of those who would instruct you to ignore your God-given faculty of thinking as they would show you how to do what they call "speaking in tongues."

TONGUES ARE FOR A SIGN TO *UNBELIEVERS!*

Every modern tongue speaker that this writer is acquainted with emphasizes what his "gift" does for him, rather than what he can do with it for others. Is this not the very selfish attitude that Paul was condemning in the church at Corinth?

In 1 Corinthians 14:22 Paul writes, "tongues are for a sign ... to unbelievers: but prophecy is for a sign ... to those who believe." The ability to speak in foreign languages you have never learned is a miracle, says Paul. But it is not a purposeless miracle; it has a goal, and that goal is the salvation of unbelievers. For the believers in the audience, it is not speaking with tongues, but the gift of prophecy (inspired preaching in the vernacular of the people) that is of value. Prophecy is the sign to the believers, not tongues. In light of this passage, can it not be said that those who assert the need of the gift of tongues for their own benefit have it wrong? If one needs his own confidence bolstered, it should be through the exercise of prophecy, for prophecy is for a sign for the believers. That bolstering comes when, in response to prophecy (inspired preaching in the language of the people), men become obedient to the Christ. Such obedience is the result of the work of the Holy Spirit, as He brings about conviction of sin, and revelation of the sinner's innermost secrets. And the Spirit so works through the Word, when believers prophesy (preach in the language of the people).

---

[35] Of course, tongues could be used in church assemblies for edifying and convicting if there was a need (i.e., if there were unbelievers present who did not understand the local dialect), or if there were an interpreter present (1 Corinthians 14:5, 27).

Before someone appeals to 1 Corinthians 14:4, "one who speaks in a tongue edifies himself," as proof that tongues had a devotional purpose in the life of the believer (and then argue that tongues today may also have a similar devotional purpose), he should consider the context. Surely the context is not speaking of private devotions but about how one exercises his "gift" in the public worship service. We do not deny that the man who spoke in tongues (even when no one else present understood) received a certain sense of satisfaction and encouragement because of a personal awareness of the Spirit's presence and activity within. But in a context that speaks of the more excellent way of love – the more excellent way of looking first to the other person's interests – it can be little short of wresting the Scripture to take this verse and make it a proof text defending the present-day claim that tongues are chiefly for personal benefit and assurance.

We have been instructed to "test the spirits, whether they are from God" (1 John 4:1). In this study, thus far, we have proposed five tests with which we may test those who claim a latter-day filling of the Spirit. So far, the present-day claimants have passed none. Two or three tests remain, and our evaluation of the current tongues movement will be complete.

TONGUES AMONG THE PAGANS

Gibberish while in a self-induced trance is common among the heathen tribal dancers, and especially is it used by the witchdoctors.[36] Now, if what some modern people are doing in the churches and call "speaking in tongues" is similar to what is found among the pagans and non-Christians quite regularly, what are we to think? Can we attribute what the pagans are doing to the work of the Holy Spirit? Hardly! If what the Pentecostalists are doing is the same thing the pagans are doing, how can the modern speaker in tongues claim that it is the Holy Spirit who is causing him to do as he does?

BY WHOSE AUTHORITY?

Every one of the modern tongue speakers with which this author has had contact places the value of personal experience above the authority of the Word of God. Some people in northern Indiana, when shown that what they were doing was in many points at variance with the New Testament, replied, "But we've experienced it. How are you going to explain our experience?" A preacher in the St. Louis area said in reply to those who pointed out the places his practice differed from God's Word, "I know that what I am doing is different than what one reads about in the New Testament, but I've experienced it, and I'm going to keep on doing it." At times, one of the things that marks the tongues movement is the way they alter and overemphasize certain points while others are almost ignored. One could almost say this goes as far as to put the person of the Holy Spirit above God Himself. The whole terminology – full gospel, second blessing, baptism (filling) of

---

[36] Several sources will show the similarity between heathen activities and the present-day tongues movement. Kurt Koch, *The Strife of Tongues*, p.47. P. Worsley, *The Trumpet Shall Sound: A Study of 'Cargo' Cults in Melanesia*. Festinger, Riecken, and Shecter, *When Prophecy Fails*. Nilsson, *Greek Popular Religion*, p.121ff., and *A History of Greek Religion*, p.205ff. See also the author's book, *New Testament History: Acts*, p.98-101 (pages 121ff in the 1976 and later editions).

the Holy Spirit, gifts of the Spirit, speaking in tongues, latter rain – shows that for this movement the thing that matters is the extraordinary and the personal experience.

These people appear to be putting their own experience above the authority of the Bible – and when a person does this, this writer can only say that he cannot accept that person's teaching. I must take the Bible, over any person's experience. If a man repudiates the Bible, how can his teaching be anything but false? We cannot take any one person's experiences as the ultimate standard of authority. No two people's experiences are the same. If we repudiate the authority of the Word, whose experience shall we use as the norm by which to test our own? Such a practice would leave us without any objective standard of authority. Clearly, this is not acceptable; we must be driven to the authority of the Word of God for our criteria of judgment. Testing our experiences in its infallible light, we can know that any experience that in any way does not square to the Word is not of God nor of the Holy Spirit!

A NEGATIVE ANSWER IMPLIED

The people among us who claim to be filled with the Spirit also have claimed that speaking in tongues is the initial sign of having been filled with the Spirit. These people also insist that what they have is for everyone who follows Christ. Those same people with whom this writer discussed this matter in northern Indiana have visited almost every church within a fifty to seventy-five mile radius of their own home in an attempt to spread the "full gospel." Let us be careful lest we miss the point. If everyone is to be filled with the Spirit, as they claim a person can be filled (and their actions and words indicate this is exactly what they believe), then clearly they think that everyone is expected to speak in tongues at least once, for by their own argument such speaking is the initial evidence that they have been filled.

Is every Christian to speak in tongues? It is precisely at this point that the modern tongue speakers have failed another Biblical test. "Do all speak in tongues?" Paul asks at 1 Corinthians 12:30 (ASV), and the Greek reads in such a way that the question expects a negative answer. *No, all do not speak in tongues*! Even an examination of the context, where Paul shows that there is more to the body than the eye, or the foot, or the ear, would show that the question "Do all speak in tongues?" must expect an answer of *no*! Everyone speaking in tongues would be like a body that was all mouth (or should we say *tongue*?). Since those who demand that all speak in tongues are again found to be in opposition to the Word of God, this writer must reject their teaching![37]

---

[37] Some Pentecostalists have attempted to avoid the force of this verse by agreeing that the passage does expect a negative answer, but then saying that it applies only to speaking in tongues in a church service. They assert that it says nothing about speaking in tongues as a part of private devotions. In private devotions, they claim, all are expected to speak in tongues as a sign of having been filled with the Spirit. We would ask, Where does one find any information in the Bible about "tongues" as a part of private devotions? The Corinthian chapters cannot be alleged to show such a practice, for they deal with disorders at the public worship service, and the regulation of conduct at the public service. There is not a word in them about private devotions.

There are a number of observations about the new tongues movement that would lead us to call it a dangerous heresy. The most frightening thing is the way it splits churches. The tongues movement is all for making proselytes. Those who are already Christ's must be won over to the 'tongues wonder.' And when some are won, and others are not, then there is trouble in the church. Without any exaggeration, ministers, missionaries, and evangelists all over the world lament the divisions this movement has caused in their congregations. What has taken decades of hard work to build up is torn down by this flood. The Holy Spirit does not split churches, but He does punish sin, stir the conscience, break pride, and show us Jesus. He also gives assurance of salvation. The Holy Spirit unites the church. He does not pull it apart.

This is the age of the Spirit, and the man who becomes a Christian receives the Spirit as an indwelling guest. From the foregoing discussion, it is evident that the Holy Spirit does not, and is not expected to, help those believers in whom He dwells to speak in tongues as evidence of His presence. But what does He do for the believer? Is there anything the believer can experience as a result of the Spirit's indwelling presence?

BE FILLED WITH THE SPIRIT!

Let us consider one more point, and out of it draw an exhortation. The point is this: The modern tongues speaker claims to have received an infilling of the Spirit subsequent to his conversion. He makes a distinction between the indwelling "gift" of the Spirit which everyone receives at conversion,[38] and the filling (or baptism) of the Spirit which (he claims) people who seek it may receive at some time after their conversion. It is thus often called a 'second blessing.' He will even argue after this fashion: (1) If all Christians have been filled with the Spirit at the time of their conversion, why do the majority appear not to have been? They do not give evidence of being led by the Spirit! (2) Some Christians claim to have received a further and distinct experience of the Holy Spirit, and their claim appears to be true, because they are doing things now they never did before.[39] What can be said in reply to all of this, and is there any word of exhortation in it for us?

It has become increasingly clear during this writer's discussions with those who believe in a special filling of the Spirit, that those people have ignored what the indwelling gift of the Spirit does for the believer. Furthermore, they have confounded the "filling of the Spirit" with another of the Spirit's gifts – either the baptism of the Spirit which made a man an apostle, or the spiritual gifts which were useful in the infancy of the church and then ceased – rather than looking on the "filling" of the Spirit as being part of the Spirit's continuous work as He indwells the believer.

---

[38] Acts 2:38, Romans 8:9-11, 1 Corinthians 6:19,20, Galatians 3:2 and 4:6.

[39] Objection two has been answered in the course of this study where it has been shown that Biblically, "speaking in tongues" is not evidence of the filling of the Spirit, even were we to grant that such a 'second blessing' had taken place.

It is very possible, as we reply to objection (1) above, to receive the indwelling of the Spirit, and then to live as though He had not been received. Is this not exactly the case we find at Corinth? The believers there had all been baptized into Christ,[40] and all had received the indwelling gift of the Holy Spirit.[41] Yet Paul must speak to them as unspiritual people, that is, as not being Spirit-filled. He could not address them, he writes as *pneumatikoi*, "spiritual" Christians, but had to address them as *sarkinoi* or *sarkikoi*, "carnal" Christians.[42] Paul's distinction, it will be noted, is between "spiritual" Christians and "carnal" Christians, that is, between Christians who are led and filled with the Spirit, and Christians who were dominated by the flesh. Is not the condition of the Corinthian Christians the condition of many of us today? We have believed, repented, and been baptized, and received the seal of the Holy Spirit. But are we filled with the Spirit? That is the question!

Many people would be unable to answer this question. They know neither whether they are filled with the Spirit nor how it is possible to tell; and when they then come across Pentecostal teaching that "speaking in tongues" is the indispensable sign of having received the Spirit, they conclude they have never received Him, or at least have not received His fullness. The Bible does contain the well-known command to all Christian people to be filled (that is, 'to go on being filled' – a continuous, present-tense imperative) with the Spirit.[43] It has been shown in this study that it cannot be maintained from Scripture that tongues always follow the filling of the Spirit. Is there, then, some evidence that such a filling has taken place? What is the evidence of the Spirit's indwelling and fullness?

Consider the passage in Ephesians 5:18-21 carefully. "And do not get drunk with wine, for that is dissipation; but be filled with the Spirit, speaking to one another in psalms and hymns and spiritual songs, singing and making melody with all your heart to the Lord, always giving thanks for all things in the name of our Lord Jesus Christ to God, even the Father; and be subject to one another in the fear of Christ." In the Greek text this paragraph consists of two verbs in the imperative mood ("do not get drunk with wine ... but be filled with the Spirit"), on which depend five present tense participles (literally, "speaking," "singing and making melody," "giving thanks," and "being subject"). That is, the single command to "be filled" is followed by five descriptive consequences of the Spirit's fullness. In short, the evidence of the fullness of the Spirit consists of certain habitual kinds of behavior, not the gifts (*charismata*) of the Spirit.

Now for the exhortation. Let's come back to the command to "be filled with the Spirit." Notice these three points. First, it is a plural verb. Both imperatives in Ephesians 5:18 – the prohibition and the command – are universal in their application. We

---

[40] 1 Corinthians 6:11.

[41] 1 Corinthians 6:19.

[42] 1 Corinthians 3:1-4.

[43] Ephesians 5:18.

are none of us to get drunk; rather, we are all of us to be Spirit-filled. The fullness of the Spirit is emphatically not a privilege reserved for the few, but a duty resting upon all. It is obligatory, not optional.

Secondly, it is a passive verb, "be filled." That is, "let the Holy Spirit fill you" (NEB). An important condition of enjoying this fullness, of being "spiritual Christians," is to yield to the Spirit without reserve. Still, it must not be imagined that we are purely passive agents in receiving the Spirit's fullness, any more than in getting drunk. A man gets drunk by drinking, and we become filled with the Spirit by drinking too, as can be discerned from our Lord's teaching in John 7:37.

Thirdly, the verb is in the present tense. It is well-known that in the Greek language, if an imperative verb is in the aorist tense, it refers to a single action, while if it is in the present tense, the action is continuous. Thus, when at the wedding in Cana Jesus said, "fill the water pots with water" (John 2:7), the aorist imperative shows that he meant for them to do it only once. The present imperative "be filled with the Spirit" (Ephesians 5:18), on the other hand, indicates not some dramatic or decisive experience which will settle the issue for good, but a continuous appropriation. 'Continually allow the Holy Spirit to fill you.' This is further enforced in the Ephesian letter by the contrast between the "sealing" (indwelling gift) and the "filling" of the Spirit. Twice the apostle writes that his readers have been "sealed" with the Holy Spirit,[44] and in both cases the verb is in the aorist tense. Every penitent believer has been accepted by God and has been given the Holy Spirit as a seal to authenticate him, to mark him, and to secure him as God's own. But although all believers are sealed, not all believers remain filled, for the sealing is past and finished (aorist tense) while the filling is (or should be) present and continuous. There are such things as stages or plateaus of spiritual progress, and Paul urges in prayer that the sealed Ephesian believers may progress upward through these stages,[45] continually being filled with the indwelling Spirit, and continually evidencing in their lives the marks of such a filling, namely, the fruit of the Spirit.

CONCLUSIONS

We must admit that the Full Gospel movement does meet some Scriptural tests that could be applied to it. But we reject the idea that the movement is from God because it fails to meet all the tests. A counterfeit twenty dollar bill would look like the real thing in many respects, but if it failed to meet the tests of authenticity in only one or two areas, we would be "stung" were we to accept one as the real thing. Similarly, we are likely to be the loser if we accept the modern tongues movement as the real thing, because, as we have shown, it fails to pass a number of Biblical tests of authenticity.

In fact, countless folk have accepted it, only to become disillusioned after a while.

---

[44] Ephesians 1:13, 4:30.

[45] Ephesians 1:17-19.

Like the student in college here, who for a while had joy so great he felt "like he were on cloud nine." But when the healings prove to be but temporary, as most do; and when a personal study of Scripture shows the FGBMFI teachers to be less than careful in their hermeneutics; and when an honest post-evaluation of the 'experience' leads one to believe that it was all self-induced while in an emotional crisis; and when the experience loses its "kick," and you must continually keep searching for a bigger and better experience; and when the emphasis in one's life is changed from being interested in the evangelism of others to Christ, to searching for a personal experience; and when the neophyte in the tongues movement is told that it is OK if the new revelation given by tongues contradicts the New Testament; it is little wonder he soon becomes disillusioned!

Read again the information on how the movement spreads, and be on the watch for such meetings among people in our local congregations. Be aware that folk with crises in their lives – either personal, physical, or emotional – are especially vulnerable to the "full gospel" teachers, and give those folk special attention while they need it, in order to protect them from accepting something that may ruin them. This writer has found it helpful to make a list of those people among us who are involved in the "full gospel" movement, not only to pray for them, but to keep watch for and prevent the spread of this dangerous heresy.

Out of the movement that is distressing many congregations should come an exhortation to all who are teachers and preachers among us. No longer can we act as if there is no Holy Spirit. We must teach the believers what the indwelling of the Spirit can be expected to do for them. Babes in Christ must be told about the Spirit's leading,[46] about His prompting of prayers,[47] how He helps the believer overcome the desires of the flesh,[48] how He helps in witnessing,[49] how He assures the child of God of his salvation,[50] how to experience the joy and peace in believing and abound in hope by the power of the Holy Spirit,[51] and how to cultivate the fruit of the Spirit.[52] When the believers are walking in the light, then the darkness of error and false teaching will be unable to make headway among those believers. As in Acts 9:31, the churches will again "enjoy peace and be edified, and they will increase while walking in the fear of the Lord and in the comfort of the Holy Spirit."

---

[46] Galatians 5:16-18.

[47] Romans 8:26,27.

[48] Romans 8:23, 1 John 3:9.

[49] 2 Timothy 1:7,8.

[50] 1 John 4:13, Romans 8:15-17.

[51] Romans 15:13.

[52] Galatians 5:22-24. Because of a desire to keep this pamphlet brief, it has seemed best to include the details about what the indwelling Spirit does for the believer in a second pamphlet, titled "The Joy of the Holy Spirit." It is included in the following pages of this Special Study.

THE JOY OF THE HOLY SPIRIT

Two thousand years have passed since the apostle Paul was teaching about twelve men in Ephesus (Acts 19:1-7). One of their statements was, "We have not even heard there is a Holy Spirit."

A perusal of books written by members of the Christian Churches, and a careful hearing of the sermons preached through the year by the evangelists in the Christian Churches, would leave the average person ready to say the same thing as those twelve whom Paul was teaching. With the exception of a mention of the Spirit as Acts 2:38 is quoted, little is said about what the Spirit does for the Christian in whom He dwells.

"The Kingdom of God is not eating and drinking but righteousness, peace, and joy, inspired by the Holy Spirit."[1] "You remember how, although accepting the Gospel meant bitter persecution, yet you experienced the joy of the Holy Spirit."[2] So it was that Paul wrote to his converts.

Taught in the Bible are concepts to which you and I are mostly strangers. And there are few ideas presented in the Bible that are as strange to us as the doctrine of *how the Holy Spirit can help the Christian*. (1) The Holy Spirit is called "another comforter" – He is called a Paraclete – and yet have I ever received any comfort from Him? And would I recognize it if I did receive it? (2) I have read in my Bible that I am to be "led by the Spirit." The Bible also teaches that I am to "walk by the Spirit." How do I do that? (3) In Romans 8:13,14, Paul teaches me that the Holy Spirit helps me when I am tempted. But if He has helped me in temptation, I do not know it. Why is that? (4) A few verses later in Romans 8:26, we are taught that the Holy Spirit helps us in prayer. How is that? What does He do? (5) The Bible tells me that when a man becomes a Christian, he receives the Holy Spirit.[3] It also says that the Christians can have a knowledge (a knowledge that comes by experience)[4] that we are saved – and that knowledge comes by experiencing the Holy Spirit in our lives.[5] Truthfully now, are we 20th century Christians sure that we have ever been aware of the Spirit's presence? Is this the reason many of today's church members are not sure of their salvation? Likewise, the Bible talks of Him

---

[1] Romans 14:17 (NEB).

[2] 1 Thessalonians 1:6 (Phillips).

[3] The fact of the indwelling of the Spirit in those who become Christians will be shown in detail in Part One of this pamphlet.

[4] The Greek word translated "know" in 1 John 3:24 is *ginōskō*, a word that implies a knowledge gained by personal experience.

[5] 1 John 3:24b reads, "And by this we know that He abides in us, by the Spirit which he has given us."

being a "pledge of our inheritance."[6] But we are not sure we have the Holy Spirit, and therefore we doubt that we have an inheritance awaiting us!

There are a number of New Testament verses about the Holy Spirit and the Christian that sound strangely unfamiliar to us. And if we are honest, would we not include the two passages quoted above that spoke of *the joy of the Holy Spirit*? The word "joy" means a lively emotion of happiness, gladness, pleasantness, being delighted. And these passages talk about the joy that the Spirit produces in the Christian. And about now, most of us are thinking, "Well, I don't know that He produces joy like that in me." We are almost tempted to relegate such passages about the Spirit to the 1st century, and say that He used to so inspire, but He doesn't any more.

Who is there who hasn't wished that someone would include them in a will? It would not have to be much – a million dollars or so, would be sufficient! It is exciting to contemplate what we would do with a million dollars, is it not? Romans 8:16,17 tell us that the Holy Spirit makes us aware that we have been named in a will, and we inherit the same thing Christ got when He went back to heaven after His thirty-some years here. Now that is more than a million! And it ought to be exciting! But how many of *us* have bubbled over with enthusiasm about it lately?

Well, that is what this pamphlet is all about. The joy that the Holy Spirit produces in the Christian is one of the most precious messages in God's Word. The Christian needs to be able to recognize his divine guest, and to be aware when He is at work. Then will come the joy that the Romans and the Thessalonians and the early Christians all had.

THE FACT OF THE INDWELLING OF THE SPIRIT

The New Testament is full of passages that show that the Holy Spirit lives in the bodies of Christians.

John 7:37-39. "Now on the last day, the great day of the feast, Jesus stood and cried, out, saying, "If any man is thirsty, let him come to Me and drink. He who believes in Me, as the Scripture said, 'From his inmost being shall flow rivers of living water'." And John goes on in the following verse to explain what Jesus was talking about. "This He spoke of the Spirit, whom those who believed in Him were to receive; for the Spirit was not yet given, because Jesus was not yet glorified." We could almost add this passage to the ones commented on in the introduction. It speaks of a restlessness, a thirst, a longing deep down that cries to be satisfied – and only the Holy Spirit can satisfy it. Twentieth century man roams here and there, seeking some "kick" or some "trip" or some pleasure that will satisfy and quiet that longing. But he is disappointed, for satisfaction is not found in pleasure, or in "kicks" or in "trips." That satisfaction is found only in the Spirit's activity

---

[6] Ephesians 1:13,14. "Pledge" means 'down-payment, a promise of more to come.'

within us. Be sure to see in these verses that Jesus is predicting the giving of the Spirit to those who believe on Him.

Acts 2:38. "Peter said unto them, 'Repent, and let each one of you be baptized in the name of Jesus Christ unto the forgiveness of your sins; and you shall receive the gift of the Holy Spirit.'" There are some who would say there is no such thing as the Holy Spirit dwelling in a man. They say He only dwells there as the Bible, the Spirit-produced Word of God, is allowed to dwell in the man. But note that Peter did not say they were to repent and be baptized in the name of Jesus unto the remission of sins, and they would receive the Word of God! According to the verses that follow verse 38, the people received the Word *before* they were baptized. Receiving the Word which they did before they were baptized is not equal to receiving the gift of the Spirit after (at) baptism. Furthermore, there are just too many passages that speak about the indwelling of the Spirit to deny the doctrine that He does actually dwell in the Christian. And in the light of these numerous passages, we see no reason to think that the "gift" (Acts 2:38) is something (salvation, for example) the Spirit gives. Rather, *the Spirit Himself is the gift* the baptized penitent receives.

Romans 5:1-5. "Since then it is by faith that we are justified, let us grasp the fact that we have confidently entered into this new relationship of grace, and here we take our stand, in happy certainty of the glorious things He has for us in the future. This does not mean, of course, that we have only a hope of future joys – we can be full of joy here and now even in our trials and troubles. Taken in the right spirit these very things will give us patient endurance; this in turn will develop a mature character, and a character of this sort produces a steady hope, a hope that will never disappoint us. Already we have some experience of the love God has for us flooding through our hearts by the Holy Spirit which He has given us" (Phillips). Not only did the passage speak of happy certainty, and joy, and God's love for us. It also speaks of the *Holy Spirit* which God has given to us!

Romans 8:9-11. "However, you are not in the flesh but in the Spirit, if indeed the Spirit of God dwells in you. But if any one does not have the Spirit of Christ, he does not belong to Him. And if Christ is in you, though the body is dead because of sin, yet the spirit is alive because of righteousness. But if the Spirit of Him who raised Jesus from the dead dwells in you, He who raised up Christ Jesus from the dead will also give life to your mortal bodies through His Spirit who dwells in you." Three times in these three verses we read that the Spirit *dwells in you*. Here would be a good place to ask those folks who say there is no indwelling Holy Spirit – but only an indwelling Word of God – how to explain these verses. Just try reading verse 11 substituting the "Bible" for Spirit, and see where you come out! "And if the Bible that raised up Jesus from the dead dwells in you, He that raised up Christ from the dead shall give life to you through the Bible that dwells in you." Indeed! Was it the Bible, or was it the Holy Spirit who dwelt in Jesus? Not only does this passage speak of a personal indwelling by the Holy Spirit, it also speaks of that indwelling as being a settled sort of thing. The Greek word translated "dwell" does not imply a temporary stopping place; it speaks of a continuation of residence. The Holy Spirit is not an overnight guest. Instead, *He makes His abode in us*.

Galatians 3:2. "I shall ask you one simple question. Did you receive the Spirit by trying to keep the Law, or by believing the message of the Gospel?" (Phillips). The people who say that all the Christian gets is the Word – that Christians don't get any indwelling Spirit – have trouble with this verse, too. Be careful to see that it does not say, 'How did you get the Word?' It says, *'How did you receive the Spirit?'*

Galatians 4:4-6. "But when the fullness of time came, God sent forth His Son, born of a woman, born under the Law, in order that He might redeem those who were under the Law, that we might receive the adoption of sons. And because you are sons, God has sent forth the Spirit of His Son into our hearts, crying, 'Abba, Father'." *His Spirit – sent into our hearts!* Here we have another passage that is inexplicable unless we believe the Bible doctrine of the indwelling of the Holy Spirit.

1 Corinthians 6:19. "Or do you not know that your body is a temple of the Holy Spirit who is in you?" The Holy Spirit is said to be in each one of the Corinthian Christians.

John 14:17. "... the Spirit of truth ... abides with you, and will be in you." Some have thought that it is impossible for the Holy Spirit to dwell in any person. But He did dwell in the apostles, for He was to be *with* them and *in* them. John 14:17 would prove two things: (1) It proves that the Holy Spirit can be in more than two persons at the same time. (2) It proves that there is nothing unreasonable, impossible, or unscriptural about the Holy Spirit dwelling in a human body.

Hebrews 6:4 speaks about Christians as being "partakers of the Holy Spirit." This passage, too, is difficult to explain, unless one keeps in mind the doctrine of the indwelling of the Holy Spirit.

1 John 2:20,27, and 4:13. "But you have an anointing from the Holy One, and you know all things" (NASB margin). "And as for you, the anointing which you received from Him abides in you, and you have no need for anyone to teach you; but as His anointing teaches you about all things, and is true, and is no lie, and just as it taught you, abide in it." The Greek word translated "anointing" speaks of the result of the Holy Spirit's anointing, likely on the apostles. "By this we know that we abide in Him, and He in us, because He has given us of His Spirit." Most writers concur that 4:13 speaks of the indwelling Spirit.

There are other passages to which we could turn to show the fact of the indwelling of the Holy Spirit.[7] Why should anyone doubt that the Holy Spirit dwells, literally dwells, in Christians? It surely cannot be on the ground that it is not clearly enough asserted in the New Testament!

---

[7] Among the passages are 1 Timothy 4:8 and Ephesians 3:16. "Power" (Grk. *dunamis*) in the latter passage probably refers to the Holy Spirit.

WHAT DOES THE INDWELLING SPIRIT DO FOR THE CHRISTIAN?

The Christian has a blessing that the common man in Old Testament times did not have. He has received the Holy Spirit! Is there anything the Christian can experience as a result of the indwelling Spirit? What does the Spirit do for the Christian?

He Leads Us. "For all who are being led by the Spirit of God, these are sons of God."[8] See it! *"Led by the Spirit!"* Before any explanation of what the Christian might experience as the Spirit leads, it is imperative that we understand what the Spirit does NOT do as He leads us. (1) We must rid the air of all ideas of mysticism. If we were required to define mysticism, we should call it the setting up of personal thoughts and feelings as the standard of truth, or as the rule of action. When we say the Spirit leads, it must not be thought that *every* feeling and *every* impulse one has is a result of the Spirit's leading. Christians are well aware that there is another spirit, the devil, who also has the ability to plant thoughts in men's minds,[9] and stir up the desires of their bodies.[10] Consequently when Paul says the Spirit leads, he cannot mean that every inward feeling, every urge, is the result of the action of the Holy Spirit. (2) Again, any thought or feeling contrary to the Word of God cannot be the leading of the Spirit. The apostle Paul said, "If you are led by the Spirit, you are not under the Law (of Moses)."[11] It follows therefore that if any would lead us under the Law, they are not guided by the Spirit of God. This is but one illustration of the fact that anything which leads us contrary to the Word of God cannot be the leading of the Spirit. The Spirit leads only in harmony with the revealed Word. (3) Another thing the Spirit does not do as He leads, He does not reveal any new or additional truth to us. Jesus promised that the apostles would be led by the Spirit into *all* truth.[12] It follows then that all of God's revelation for this age was revealed and taught before the death of the last of the apostles. And if they were led into *all* truth, it follows that there is no extra or additional truth to be given to us today.

How, then, does the Spirit lead? Bible students will agree that *in conversion* – as the Spirit works to bring about conviction of sin and righteousness and judgment – as the seed of the new birth is being planted – the Holy Spirit works *only* through the Word.[13] In conversion, He does not work apart from the reading or preaching of the New Testament.

---

[8] Romans 8:14.

[9] Acts 5:3. "Filled your heart" is the Hebrew's way of saying "plant thoughts in the mind."

[10] Romans 7:5,8.

[11] Galatians 5:18.

[12] John 16:13.

[13] Passages that speak of how the Holy Spirit works through the Word in conversion are those in Acts that show there was *preaching* in every case of conversion. See also Romans 10:13-15. In addition, the passages that speak of the "begetting by the Spirit" (like John 3:8) should be compared with those that speak of "being begotten through the Gospel" (like 1 Corinthians 4:15).

But *after conversion*, when a man has become a Christian and received the gift of the indwelling Holy Spirit, *the Bible shows that the Spirit works both through and apart from the Word.* That He works through the Word is seen from Revelation 2:1 as compared with Revelation 2:7. 2:1 says, "To the ... church in Ephesus write ...," and 2:7 concludes the letter to Ephesus by saying, "Hear what the Spirit says to the churches." In these verses the Spirit was leading not only the Ephesians but also the "churches" ("churches" is plural!). That the indwelling Spirit also works apart from the Word is seen from passages like Ephesians 4:23, which speaks of being renewed (the verb is passive, and the implied agent who does the renewing is the Spirit) in the spirit of our minds. That is, the Holy Spirit plants ideas in our minds.

Right here is where you can have some joy! You can experience this leading – leading in harmony with the Word. What others have experienced of the Spirit's leading, you can experience. Glen Mitchell, one of Central Christian College's graduates, tells of his new convictions about what was right and wrong – convictions not previously held, but which came immediately after being immersed into Christ. Without any previous teaching from the Bible to influence the formation of his new convictions of right and wrong, he immediately knew certain things to be right and certain ones to be wrong. It was not until some time later, as he was studying his way through the Bible that he came upon the verses that taught what he had been aware of all along since his conversion. Glen will tell you that he is convinced that his new convictions from the day of his immersion were the result of the leading of the Holy Spirit. And he rejoices in this leading of the Spirit. Preachers and Bible teachers have long been aware of the way the Spirit leads while they are preaching and teaching. Even after hours of reading and studying in preparation for the day's message, while they are speaking, suddenly an idea or illustration will come to mind that is just the thing needed to get the lesson across. What else is it but the leading of the Spirit that causes such ideas to come to mind? Roy Weece has the custom of seeking the Spirit's leading when it comes to choosing a seat on the bus, or in the restaurant. He prays for wisdom in making the choice with the desire of being able to sit near one who will be ready to hear the message about the Savior. And he testifies that the Spirit leads him regularly to men and women who are eager to hear. It is a joy to be conscious of such leading by the Spirit! And that joy can be yours!

One thing that the Spirit does for the Christian: He leads him, both through and apart from the Word.

He Helps Us Mortify the Deeds of the Flesh. "If you are living according to the flesh, you must die; but if by the Spirit you are putting to death the deeds of the body, you will live."[14] What does it mean to "live according to the flesh"? Simply this. The devil comes along and excites the desires of the body. And if we do what our devil-prompted body suggests, we are "living according to the flesh." The verse goes on to explain that the eternal penalty for such living is death. But then Paul explains that it is possible to put

---

[14] Romans 8:13.

to death the deeds of the body by the help of the indwelling Spirit. Before a man becomes a Christian, he is what the Bible calls "a slave of sin" and cannot put down the desires that the devil has excited. As Paul says in Romans 7:18, in the flesh dwells no good thing, nothing to help the unconverted man control the desires stirred by the devil. But for the Christian all this has been changed! In his body there now dwells some good thing – none other than God's Spirit! And when the Christian avails himself of the God-appointed way of resisting the devil, the Holy Spirit aids in squelching the evil desires that the devil has prompted. And the verse closes with the promise to the man who continually puts to death the deeds of the body that he has eternal life continually abiding in him.

Other passages in the New Testament teach the same thing. Ephesians 3:16-19 speaks of "being strengthened in the inner man." In a regenerated man, the inner man ("spirit" with a small "s") is alive because of righteousness,[15] and the inner man – as prompted by the indwelling Holy Spirit – gives directions to the rest of the man, and so controls the rest of the man. Ephesians 3:16 also makes it clear that it is the indwelling Spirit who does the strengthening of the inner man. 1 John 4:4 teaches a similar truth, "Greater is He (the Holy Spirit) who is in you, than he (the devil) who is in the world." The indwelling Spirit helps the inner man control the body, so that the desires stirred up in the body by the devil are suppressed and squelched.

Here comes the joy that the Spirit inspires. What pleasantness, what a delight it is, to see those old temptations squelched, to see the devil flee from us in disarray and defeat! That's living! As 1 John 3:9 says, the only way you can continually overcome the Devil is by the aid of the Holy Spirit. And when you see temptation after temptation come and go – conquered, rather than succumbed to – that results in *Joy! Joy inspired by the Spirit*!

He Illuminates the Word. "But the natural man does not accept the things of the Spirit of God: for they are foolishness to him; and he cannot understand them, because they are spiritually appraised," wrote Paul in 1 Corinthians 2:14. This is one of the passages on which the doctrine of illumination is based. A Christian reads a passage in the Bible that he has read time and again, and suddenly its meaning becomes plain. That sudden understanding is the work of the indwelling Spirit, helping him to understand the Word. 1 John 2:20,27, which speak of an anointing of the Spirit, teach the same doctrine, as does Ephesians 1:17,18.

Here is joy all the more! As the Spirit opens up passage after passage, the more the Christian is eager to return to his Bible and study it. He can hardly wait until the night is over and he can get back to the study of the Word. And the words of Jesus, about a restlessness and a longing and a thirst that are only satisfied by the Spirit, come to be understandable as the Christian experiences their meaning. The child of God begins to bubble with delight and eagerness, and he is grateful to God for the gift of His Spirit who brings such joys!

---

[15] Romans 8:10 (NASB).

We have found three answers to the question, What does the indwelling Spirit do for the Christian? He leads. He helps squelch temptation. And He helps the Christian understand the Word. There are several more things that the Spirit does that bring *joy* to the Christian.

He Helps the Christian's Prayers. "And in the same way the Spirit also helps our weakness: for we do not know how to pray as we should; but the Spirit Himself intercedes for us with groanings too deep for words; and He who searches the hearts knows what the mind of the Spirit is, because He intercedes for the saints according to the will of God."[16] The "weakness" referred to is the Christian's inability to analyze situations and pray intelligently about them. It is not an ignorance of the right manner of prayer, it is an ignorance respecting the proper content. When sufferings come, for *what* should one pray? It is at this point of destitution on our part that the Holy Spirit comes to our help. We do not know for what we should pray in such circumstances, but the Spirit knows.

Extenuating situations come to all the children of God, and in the midst of those circumstances, we do not know what is the proper thing for which to pray. At this extremity, the Holy Spirit has His opportunity. *He prompts us to "yearn"* – to heave a sigh from the heart – *even though we cannot put it into words* (they are "groanings" which cannot be put into words). Yet God, who knows our hearts and can search them for hidden meanings and wishes, knows what the yearnings that are prompted by the Spirit mean. God answers and complies with the wishes that the Spirit put there, because the Holy Spirit acts in harmony with God's will.

Maybe several illustrations will help us to see what the Scriptures mean when they tell us of this activity of the Spirit. In these verses in Romans, the Spirit is called an "intercessor." The word used here is used nowhere else in all of God's Word,[17] but it speaks of one who is an advocate, a lawyer, present in the court of justice to aid His client. Now there are two things which an advocate does or may do for his client – he speaks for him, and he tells him what to say. There are stages in the course of the trial when the voice of the advocate is not enough, and when the client must speak for himself. The advocate's function, then, is to instruct his client to speak in the way that will be best for his interests. Where there is but one advocate, both functions must devolve upon him – but where there are two, the functions may be divided. *Now the Bible teaches that the Christian has two intercessors!* Up in Heaven, Christ speaks on our behalf, representing our interests to the Father. Down here on earth, the Spirit, at times, prompts us what to say.

These verses might be explained in another way that we might see what the Spirit does for the child of God. The Holy Spirit acts to his people somewhat like a prompter acts for someone who is reciting. A man has to deliver a piece which he has learned, but his

---

[16] Romans 8:26,27.

[17] The form of the word at Romans 8:26 is a compound, *huperentungchanō*. *Entungchanō*, without the preposition *huper*, is found at Romans 8:34 and Hebrews 7:25. These latter passages speak of Christ's intercessory work.

memory is treacherous, and therefore somewhere out of the sight of the audience there is a *prompter,* so that when the speaker is at a loss and might use a wrong word, or cannot think of the words, a whisper is heard, which suggests the right one. When the speaker has almost lost the thread of his discourse, he turns his ear, and the prompter gives him the catch-word to aid his memory. So the Holy Spirit does for our prayer life. In prayer, we, because of infirmities, often come to a dead stand still, but the Spirit incites, suggests, inspires, or prompts, and so we go forward, heaving up sighs from our hearts, and the Father sees and responds to the sighs prompted by the Spirit. *And here comes the joy again*! When you feel within your heart a longing to pray, and you cannot put your thoughts into words – you just do not know what to say – know that your Advocate is at work, prompting you to "sigh." And you go away from that prayer time, filled with joy, in the assurance that the Holy Spirit is present and at work in your life.

He is a Down Payment on a New Body. Another thing the indwelling Spirit is – He is a pledge from God to us that we have a resurrection body coming. Paul put it this way: "Now he who establishes us with you in Christ and anointed us is God, who also sealed us and gave us the Spirit in our hearts as a pledge."[18] 2 Corinthians 5:1-11 also speaks of the coming resurrection body. In verse five, Paul writes, "Now he who prepared us for this very purpose is God, who gave to us the Spirit as a pledge." Again Paul writes, "... having also believed, you were sealed ... with the Holy Spirit of promise, who is given as a pledge of our inheritance ...."[19]

The word "pledge" means what we mean when we use the word 'down payment' or 'first installment.' In the papyri it often refers to earnest money in the purchase of an animal or even a wife.[20] From these passages we learn that when God deposited the Spirit in the hearts of His children, He obligated Himself to bestow upon them subsequently the full remainder of all the blessings of salvation merited for them by the atoning sacrifice of Christ. The first installment is, accordingly, a pledge or guarantee of glory to come. The same thing is spoken of in Romans 8:23, where Paul speaks of Christians having the "first fruits of the Spirit." First fruits are a promise of more to come!

In this thought, the Christian *again finds joy*. He finds himself in a joyous predicament. As a child of God, he already possesses eternal life, but, as a human being, he does not have a suitable body for the heavenly kind of life. He joyously looks forward to the time when he will possess his resurrection body, and thus be able to enjoy his salvation to its fullest extent. He knows he is going to get a resurrection body, because God has made the first installment, and in that pledge of the Spirit, He has obligated himself to pro-

---

[18] 2 Corinthians 1:21,22.

[19] Ephesians 1:13,14.

[20] Moulton, James Hope, and Milligan, George, *The Vocabulary of the Greek Testament* (London: Hodder & Stoughton, 1963), p.79, under *arrabon*.

vide the rest. And the Christian experiences joy produced by the Spirit, in the knowledge that he has more coming.

Indeed, serene in the knowledge that he has a new body coming, the Christian is very careful about the upkeep on his present temple of the Holy Spirit. He certainly does not want to do anything with his body that would cause the Spirit to leave. For only if the Spirit dwells within, will the Christian be assured of inheriting the promise of Romans 8:11, of being raised by the Spirit, of having his mortal body quickened. In this light, it is a joy for the Christian to keep his body pure, and to abstain from using it for sinful actions.

The Spirit Helps the Christian to Grow. "The fruit of the Spirit is love, joy, peace, patience, kindness, goodness, faithfulness, gentleness, self-control," Paul wrote to the Galatians.[21] Really, there is no difference between bearing the fruit of the Spirit and being led by the Spirit. There is no difference between bearing the fruit of the Spirit and putting to death the old man of sin and putting on the new man of righteousness (Colossians 3:1-14). When a man allows the Spirit to lead, that man's heart becomes a garden that is congenial to the growth of the best that is in man.

> Fruit, regarded in the light of an orchard, a garden, or a vineyard, is the most perfect form of development to which a tree or plant can come. Fruit is the thing for which all the enginery of roots and branches and leaves was appointed. All these are servants. They toil and wait. The fruit only, sits regent; it is the final result – the perfect thing. The tree can never go a step further than its fruit. It can stop, and go back and begin again, but it goes only to that limit. And when it has reached that, it has reached perfection. The fruit is the measure of the tree's possibility. So, when we speak of man as a tree, or a vine, and when we speak of the fruit of that tree or vine, we refer to that divine summer which quickens man and renders him productive, and brings forth in him the highest results of which he is capable. When a man comes to that which is called "the fruit of the Spirit," he reaches his full limit as a creature of time. When the fruit of the Spirit in man is spoken of, that which is meant is the fairest, the noblest, the best thing that he can be brought to by the brooding of the divine Spirit. (Henry Ward Beecher)

There is joy in this activity of the Spirit, for when you look at your life and see the attitudes and feelings that the Spirit helps promote and produce – and see them more and more becoming your dominant personality traits – you rejoice that Christ lives, and that you live, and that the Spirit is alive and at work in your life.

There are two other things the Spirit does for the Christian, among the many we could name.

He Helps us Become Like Christ. 2 Corinthians 3:18 speaks of Christians being

---

[21] Galatians 5:22,23.

transformed into the image of the Lord as the Spirit works in them. And Paul told the Galatians that he was anxious for them "until Christ is formed in you."[22] According to Romans 8:29, God intends for the Christian to be conformed to the image of His Son.

Recently there was an art show in our city. One of the attractions was an artist who drew pencil portraits of the visitors to the art show. It was instructive to watch. First he made an outline. In that outline you could only barely recognize the features of the person being portrayed. Then he took his pencil, and, as he gazed upon the countenance he wished to express, he applied the pencil, and by degrees, by touch after touch, the likeness came out, until at last he stood back and said, "It's finished." It was perfected so far as it could be perfected. And the spectators would exclaim, "What a perfect likeness! It looks just like the one you were copying."

So the Holy Spirit has been sitting in our hearts. Out there is Jesus, the great example. The rude outlines have been already formed, for I have been adopted into the family. I bear a family likeness. I can be recognized as something like the blessed Savior, be it ever so little. Then the divine Artist, the Holy Spirit, goes to work, changing, transforming, touching this part and that, making me a little more loving, a little more meek, more self-denying, more active, until by and by I shall be brought into Christ's likeness. One day, it shall be said, "It is finished," and then, released from mortality, I shall mount up as on wings of eagles, and I shall see Him in Glory!

To contemplate this work of the divine Artist, the Holy Spirit, is perfectly delightful! It is one of the joys of the Holy Spirit!

He Bears Witness to Our Salvation. Paul tells us about this joyous result of the Spirit's work as he writes, "The Spirit Himself bears witness with our spirit, that we are children of God."[23] John expresses this idea twice. "And we know by this that He abides in us, by the Spirit which He has given us."[24] "By this we know that we abide in Him, and He in us, because He has given us of His Spirit."[25] In addition, there are the passages quoted earlier which speak of the Christian as being "sealed." Just as we signify ownership by writing our name on some possession, so the ancients would seal official documents with a signet ring pressed into a wax coating, and thus signify *ownership*. These passages tell us that the presence of the Holy Spirit in the heart of the believer is God's way of stamping His ownership upon His children.

---

[22] Galatians 4:19.

[23] Romans 8:10.

[24] 1 John 3:24.

[25] 1 John 4:13.

What a joy it is, when you see the Holy Spirit at work in your life, in all the ways we have indicated, to know that you are saved and are counted as one of God's precious possessions! To know that you are saved, and one of God's dear children is a delight that will fill and change your days and nights. This is what it is to know the joy of the Holy Spirit!

CONCLUSION

We have studied about the fact of the indwelling of the Holy Spirit. We have reflected on some of the things the Holy Spirit does for the Christian in whom He dwells. He leads. He helps mortify the flesh. He illuminates the Word. He helps our prayers. He is a pledge of a resurrection body. He helps us grow. He helps us become more like Christ. He bears witness to our salvation.

When we see the Spirit doing all these things in our lives, it fills us with a sense of gladness and delight. In short, we have what the Bible speaks of when it talks of the *joy inspired by the Spirit.*

An indwelling presence of the Spirit is something that was not experienced in the Old Testament age.[26] The hymn writer Frank Bottome has caught the feeling of delight at the presence of the Spirit in our age.

> O spread the tidings 'round, wherever man is found,
> > Wherever human hearts and human woes abound;
> Let ev'ry Christian tongue proclaim the joyful sound:
> > The Comforter has come!
>
> The long, long night is past, the morning breaks at last,
> > and hushed the dreadful wail and fury of the blast,
> As o'er the golden hills the day advances fast!
> > The Comforter has come!
>
> Lo, the great King of kings, with healing in His wings,
> > To every captive soul a full deliverance brings;
> And thro' the vacant cells the song of triumph rings;
> > The Comforter has come!
>
> O boundless love divine! How shall this tongue of mine
> > to wondering mortals tell the matchless grace divine –
> That I, a child of hell, should in His image shine!
> > The Comforter has come!

---

[26] Galatians 3:1-5.

> The Comforter has come! The Comforter has come!
>   The Holy Ghost from Heav'n, the Father's promise giv'n;
> O spread the tidings 'round, wherever man is found –
>   The Comforter has come!

2 Corinthians 3 is one of the great chapters in the Bible. In verse 3, Paul calls the Corinthians a "letter of Christ ... written with the Spirit of the living God." In fact, in the midst of such a heathen city, with its debauchery and debasement, the man whose life showed the fruit of the Spirit, rather than the works of the flesh, would stand out like a huge signboard in the middle of the road. Paul goes on in the chapter to explain what the Spirit was doing for the Christians. He tells how the New Testament age is much superior to the Old Testament age because of the ministry of the Spirit. And he asserts that there is nothing fading or passing about the New Testament, like there was in the glow that shone from Moses' face after he had been in the presence of the Lord. Instead of the New Testament glow fading and gradually becoming extinguished, it keeps on transforming us, until we bear the image of Christ (verse 18).

Living by the Spirit of Christ, we become 'living epistles,' whom other men can read and by whom they can be influenced. As James M. Campbell observed, "What has been written by the Spirit in the heart becomes visible in the life. The inward handwriting strikes out to the surface. It becomes legible to others, like a letter written in invisible ink when it has been subjected to fire."

Barnabas, evidently, had no trouble reading those epistles of Christ which he found in Antioch, for the Book says, "When he had come and had *witnessed* the grace of God, he rejoiced."[27]

> What do people learn when they read my life and your life?
>
> Do they learn about Christ, and what He is doing in and with human lives?

---

[27] Acts 11:23.

1 CORINTHIANS

SELECTED BIBLIOGRAPHY

Adams, Edward, and David G. Horrell, eds., *Christianity at Corinth. The Quest for the Pauline Church.* Louisville: John Knox Press, 2004.
> A one-volume overview of what scholarship has been saying about the character and disputes of the first Corinthian Christians. Includes eighteen previously published essays and four previously unpublished methodological reflections. Part one, "Extracts from the History of Scholarship on Christianity at Corinth," begins with the view of F.C. Baur (1792-1860) that the "groups at Corinth ... were essentially divided along a single fault line, ... between Peter and Paul, with the Apollos group on Paul's side and the Christ group on Peter's" (p.51). A century later J. Munck contested Baur's views and denied the Peter v. Paul factions, stating that the problem was simply one of "bickerings in the congregation" (p.61). Next is L.W. Schmithal's view that Gnosticism was a "pre-Christian phenomenon" and is the key to understanding the Corinthian conflict. C.K. Barrett's perspective is that there were four "distinct theological emphases and ideas competing with each other (those of Paul, Peter, Apollos and Christ)" (p.79). Part one concludes with several articles that deal with the last thirty years of Corinthian scholarship, beginning with Gerd Theissen's argument "that the Corinthian church was marked by internal social stratification: a few (prominent) members from the upper stratum, the majority from the lower strata" (p.97). Anthony Thistleton's essay on "Realized Eschatology at Corinth" suggests the "Corinthians held to an over-realized eschatology, stressing the 'already' of salvation to the detriment of the 'not yet'" (p.107). Jerome Murphy O'Connor, having observed the remains of "sumptuous villas" in Corinth, suggests these villas were the meeting places of small house churches. The choice of meeting places led to the divisions he suggests. Based on social strata, some believers, he argues, were allowed inside while others had to remain outside. The four final chapters begin with J.J. Meggit's appeal for believers to study popular culture more. Bengt Holmberg stresses historical information over sociological theory. M.Y. MacDonald's comments deal with the importance of women's issues in understanding the Corinthian correspondence. James D.G. Dunn summarizes the various views and states that "the various re-constructions of Corinthian Christianity do not help us get to *the* meaning of the letter [but] they do ... help us to overhear more clearly the dialogue [and] enter into the dialogue for ourselves" (p.309, italics his).

Alford, Henry, "1 Corinthians," in *Alford's Greek Testament*, Vol.2. London: Rivingtons, 1871. Revised and reprinted by Moody Press, Chicago.
> Probably still the best commentary on the complete Greek Testament by a single author. Has a critically revised text, a digest of various readings, marginal references, introductory studies, and a critical and exegetical commentary.

Applebury, T.R., *Studies in First Corinthians*. Joplin, MO: College Press, 1963. (Currently out-of-print, but available for download from College Press.)
> Part of the Bible Study Textbook series. An analysis of each chapter, comments on difficult passages, plus a summary of each chapter, followed by questions and answers to aid the study of the book.

Baird, William, *The Corinthian Church -- A Biblical Approach to Urban Culture.* Nashville: Abingdon Press, 1964.
> Shows how 1 Corinthians is relevant to the problems of the contemporary church, such as dissension and division, morality, secularism, worship, and death. The chapters were first given at the M.T. Burt Lectures at the Cotner School of Religion in 1962, then enlarged for publication.

Barclay, William, *The Letters to the Corinthians*. Philadelphia: Westminster Press, 1956.
> Author is neo-liberal in theology, so the reader must be careful. The Daily Study Bible Series is of value for the light cast on the historical background of the Corinthian church, and for getting the feel of the milieu of the Grecian world of the 1st century AD.

Barnes, Albert, "1 Corinthians," in *Notes on the New Testament*. Grand Rapids: Baker Book House, 1953.

Verse-by-verse coverage of the text, with practical applications of the chapters given at the close of each. Barnes (1798-1870) was an American Presbyterian minister. In the division between strict Calvinists and New School Presbyterians, he sided with the latter. He preached total abstinence from alcohol, the abolition of slavery, and unlimited atonement. He advocated a faith-only doctrine at times, held to unconditional election, and the Calvinistic doctrines of a sinful nature and the perseverance of the saints.

Barrett, Charles Kingsley, *A Commentary on the First Epistle to the Corinthians*. New York: Harper and Row, 1968.
One of the Harper New Testament Commentary Series, it includes some fine insights. The author does not believe in the divine inspiration of the Scriptures, which detracts from the work. He disparages the historical evidence for Christ's resurrection, stamping Paul's eschatological picture of the end times as "mythological."

Barth, Karl, *The Resurrection of the Dead*. Translated by H.J. Steuning. London: Hodder and Stoughton, 1933.
By a neo-orthodox theologian, the work concentrates on 1 Corinthians 15, with brief notes on the rest of the epistle.

Beet, Joseph Agar, *A Commentary on St. Paul's Epistles to the Corinthians*. London: Hodder and Stoughton, 1895.
This study, based on the Greek text, at times tends to be liberal in its theology. The writer is Wesleyan or Arminian in his leanings.

Berding, Kenneth, *What are Spiritual Gifts? Rethinking the Conventional View*. Grand Rapids: Kregel, 2006.
Berding argues the thesis that the Holy Spirit does not give special abilities that need to be discovered (the conventional, charismatic view) so that we may know where to minister. Instead, the Holy Spirit places Christians into various ministries that build up the church. One weakness that has been pointed out is that in his zeal to stress ministry involvement, he tends to downplay any enablement that might come from God to help the believer do the work of ministry.

Blomberg, Craig, *1 Corinthians* in the NIV Application Commentary Series. Grand Rapids: Zondervan, 1994.
After an eleven-page general introduction to 1 Corinthians, an outline, and an annotated bibliography of commentaries, this volume presents for each pericope the NIV text and a three-step exposition. original meaning, bridging contexts (between the world of the Bible and the world of today), and contemporary significance. Blomberg's outline follows the usual two-major-point outline for 1 Corinthians – Paul's response to oral reports about the Corinthian church, and Paul's response to the letter he received from Corinth. 13:10 is interpreted to mean that the spiritual gifts will last until the second coming. 7:36ff refers to engaged couples, not to fathers controlling their daughter's marriage fortunes. He treats 5:9 as a previous letter, and is friendly to charismatic views.

Boyer, James L., *For A World Like Ours: Studies in 1 Corinthians*. Winona Lake, IN: BMH Books, 1971. (Later issued by Baker Book House.)
Intended as an adult study guide on the epistle, each lesson is followed by a series of thought- and discussion-provoking questions. The author is well versed in Greek literature and language, and the comments often reflect this. Archaeological information and a lengthy time spent in Bible lands are also reflected. The comments on spiritual gifts (chapters 12-14) are challenging. Includes maps and some photographs of scenes of historical significance in connection with Corinth.

Braxton, Brad R., *The Tyranny of Resolution: 1 Corinthians 7:17-24*. Atlanta, GA: Society of Biblical Literature, 2000.
Scott Bartchy, 27 years earlier, also produced a work attempting to explain this passage. Braxton's proposal differs from Bartchy's. Braxton, attempting to inflict social-science criticism on the passage,

argues Paul was not condemning the notion of change in social status after one became a Christian, but is condemning the idea that a change must be made as a precondition of the call to become a Christian. Part of the interest in this passage stems from the use or non-use made of it by abolitionist and pro-slavery advocates, which Braxton documents in detail.

Broneer, Oscar, "Corinth," *Biblical Archaeologist* 14:4 (1951), p.80ff.
Provides an idea of the buildings and layout of Corinth and the surrounding area in New Testament times.

Broneer, Oscar, "The Apostle Paul and the Isthmian Games," *Biblical Archaeologist* 25 (Feb. 1962), p.2-31.
Suggests that the reason Paul chose to establish a work in Corinth and spend a great deal of time there rather than at Athens was because of the games held at nearby Isthmia. Describes the archaeological remains and reconstructs a possible history of Paul's visit to the games in AD 50-51. Suggests how Paul could have used the festive occasion with a great number of visitors to establish his work and send messages to the extents of the empire. Paul's subsequent vocabulary shows an abundance of illustrations drawn from the games.

Brown, John, *The Resurrection Life: An Exposition of First Corinthians 15*. Edinburgh: William Oliphant and Sons, 1852. Reprinted by Klock and Klock.
A rich, full expository treatment which includes a lengthy essay on Jesus' resurrection.

Brown, Raymond Bryan, "1 Corinthians," *The Broadman Bible Commentary*, Vol. 10. Nashville: Broadman Press, 1970.
This Southern Baptist series of commentaries began in controversy over the volume on Genesis, which was full of neo-liberalism, was withdrawn, then re-written, but without removing all the objectionable materials. This tendency continues through all the commentaries in the set, which includes a combination of exegesis and exposition of the Revised Standard Version text.

Bruce, Frederick Fyvie, "1 and 2 Corinthians," in *The New Century Bible*. London: Oliphants Ltd., 1971.
A brief, perceptive study, always related to the Greek. Bruce is interesting reading, being one of the new evangelical scholars in England. Valuable discussion of modern views on the "Corinthian Correspondence." Frequent references in the discussion to further literature.

Butler, Paul T., *Studies in First Corinthians*. Joplin, MO: College Press, 1985.
A volume in the Bible Study Textbook Series, replacing Applebury's earlier book. Included are several special studies of lasting interest, such as "Gifts, Miracles," "Is the Church an Organization or an Organism?" and, "The Existential/Neo-Orthodox Philosophy of History." He organizes his comments on the chapters under the titles of "The problem of ..." – such as "The problem of schism," "... of ministry," "...of church discipline," "... of disorderly worship," "... of aiding Christian brethren," etc.

Calvin, John, *The First Epistle of Paul the Apostle to the Corinthians*. Grand Rapids: Wm. B. Eerdmans Publishing Co., 1960. (Torrance Edition)
Calvin, who published commentaries on all of Paul's epistles, wrote this one in 1546. He was the greatest of the Reformation commentators, if one uses the influence of the man's writings as the standard by which to judge. Includes a special note on "Adultery in Roman Law," p.146.

Candlish, Robert Smith, *Life in a Risen Savior*. Minneapolis: Klock and Klock, 1977.
A reprint of a work originally published in 1863, this treatment of 1 Corinthians is helpful for its careful exposition of the text and its application of biblical truth to the life of the believer.

Carson, D.A., *The Cross and Christian Ministry: An Exposition of Passages from I Corinthians*. Grand Rapids: Baker, 1993.
Vintage exegesis and application of 1 Corinthians 1-4 and 9.

Bibliography

Carson, D.A., *Showing the Spirit: A Theological Exposition of 1 Corinthians 12-14.* Grand Rapids: Baker, 1984.
> Exegesis and application. Carson attempts to handle the vexed questions of spiritual gifts in this volume.

Chaffin, Kenneth L., *1, 2 Corinthians* in the Communicator's Commentary. Waco, TX: Word, 1985.
> Very helpful applications. Little exegesis. Some excellent sermon illustrations.

Cheung, Alex T., *Idol Food in Corinth: Jewish Background and Pauline Legacy.* Sheffield: Sheffield Academic Press, 1999.
> Social-science critics focus on ethical passages in Scripture, and chapters 8 to 10 in 1 Corinthians form one of the longest sustained ethical arguments found in Scripture. Cheung's thesis, which goes against the grain of almost all scholarly interpretation of this passage, is that Paul consistently and unequivocally opposes any eating of food that has been offered to idols. Cheung grew up in a house that worshiped idols. When he became a Christian, he had to face the very question raised in 1 Cor 8-10. He is acutely aware that there is a real presence of demons associated with food offered to idols in worship settings.

Chrysostom, "Homilies on the Epistles of Paul to the Corinthians," in *The Nicene and Post-Nicene Fathers of the Christian Church*, Series One, Vol. 12. Grand Rapids: Wm. B. Eerdmans Publishing Co., 1956.
> The oldest complete commentary on 1 Corinthians still extant. Consulted by many commentators through the years.

Coffman, James Burton, *Commentary on 1 and 2 Corinthians.* Austin, TX: Firm Foundation Publishing House, 1977.
> One of a new set called Firm Foundation Series of Commentaries on the New Testament, produced by the Churches of Christ. Coffman regularly gleans the more succinct comments from the old masters and weaves them together for his commentary. Sets are being sent free to Church of Christ missionaries for their use, being purchased by various large congregations for their living-link missionaries.

Conzlemann, Hans, *1 Corinthians: A Commentary on the First Epistle to Corinthians*, translated by James W. Leitch. Philadelphia: Fortress Press, 1975.
> One of the Hermeneia series, it tends to follow the current liberal interpretation of 1 Corinthians. It is an English translation of the current German critical standard commentary. The introductory studies are from a negative critical standpoint. The author fails consistently to avoid both mystical and gnostic interpretations, and draws attention to what is called the biblical writer's "exaltation theology," "exaltation Christology," or "fanaticist eschatology." While filled with a wealth of historical detail not readily accessible elsewhere, the author's consistently idiosyncratic interpretations make its value very uneven.

Craig, Clarence Tucker, "First Corinthians," in *The Interpreter's Bible*, edited by Geo. Buttrick, Vol. 10. Nashville: Abingdon Press, 1953.
> The articles in *The Interpreter's Bible* generally tend to be liberal in theological viewpoint.

Dahl, M.E., *The Resurrection of the Body.* Naperville, IL: Allenson, 1962.
> A thorough study of the interpretation of 1 Corinthians 15.

DeHoff, George W., *Sermons on First Corinthians.* Murfreesboro, TN: The Christian Press, 1947.
> Suggestive outlines that one who would preach from the book of 1 Corinthians could consult with profit.

Deming, Will, *Paul on Marriage and Celibacy. The Hellenistic Background of 1 Corinthians 7.* Society for New Testament Studies Monograph Series 83. New York: Cambridge University Press, 1995.

This revised version of a 1991 doctoral dissertation argues that Paul drew his basic concepts of marriage and its alternatives from a centuries-old debate in which Stoics and Cynics took opposing positions on various issues. After reviewing scholarly opinions about the motivation for celibacy in 1 Corinthians 7, it charts the course of the Stoic-Cynic debate, points out Stoic and Cynic elements in 1 Corinthians 7, and offers a non-ascetic interpretation of Paul's positions. Deming concludes Paul condoned and promoted celibacy at Corinth to keep this congregation during a period of severe tribulation as free as possible from the distractions associated with married life in the ancient world, and that his theological justification depends almost entirely on Stoic and apocalyptic traditions, neither of which denigrate human sexuality or espouse the renunciation of sexual relations as the goal of celibacy.

Edwards, Thomas Charles, *A Commentary on the First Epistle to the Corinthians*. London: Hodder and Stoughton, 1903.
    One of the best older commentaries. Especially valuable for word studies and citations of ancient writers.

Elliott, J. K., "Paul's Teaching on Marriage in 1 Corinthians: Some Problems Considered," *New Testament Studies* 19 (1973:2), p.219-225.
    Elliott believes the unity of 1 Cor 7:25-38 lies in the fact that the whole passage concerns engaged couples, and the argument deals with both the engaged woman and the engaged man. Elliott avers *parthenos* throughout the passage means "betrothed woman." V.27 should be translated: "Are you engaged to a woman? Do not seek a release (i.e., do not break the engagement). Are you free from a woman (i.e., single)? Then do not seek a woman (as wife)." Thus the scheme of the chapter is: marriage and divorce (v.1-24), engagement (v.25-38), and remarriage (v.39,40). Other chapter 7 problems are also discussed.

Evans, T., "1 Corinthians," in *The Bible Commentary*, edited by F.C. Cook. New York: Charles Scribner's Sons, 1886. (Reprinted 1984 by Eerdmans.)
    This whole set is excellent and should be in every preacher's library! Notes by Anglican scholars on the Greek text, additional notes where helpful to enlarge on topics introduced in the comments. It is a bit weak in its treatment of the spiritual gifts in chapters 12-14.

Farrar, F.W., "1 Corinthians," in *Pulpit Commentary*, edited by H.D.M. Spence and Joseph S. Excell. Grand Rapids: Wm. B. Eerdmans Publishing Co., 1962.
    The verse-by-verse comments in *Pulpit Commentary* are one of the first sources this teacher regularly checks, whenever beginning a study of any Biblical book. The set makes a good backbone for any preacher's library, since it is well indexed.

Fee, Gordon D., *The First Epistle to the Corinthians*, in the New International Commentary on the New Testament. Grand Rapids: Eerdmans, 1987.
    This volume is intended as a replacement for the earlier volume (1953) in this series by Grosheide. It is offered because study of 1 Corinthians has been energetically pursued in the years intervening, and new problems have emerged and new questions have been asked. Fee is abreast of and gives help on these issues as he interacts with the scholarly literature. He treats the letter as an occasional, *ad hoc* response to the situation that had developed in Corinth, which, Fee thinks, was one of conflict between the church and its founder (rather than simply a church torn by internal strife and dissension). Paul's problem, in Fee's view, was how to reassert his authority over the congregation, and virtually the whole letter is directed toward this end. Fee tries to treat each verse in its historical, cultural, contextual, and social setting. He holds there was a "previous letter" written before our 1 Corinthians. Since the commentary is intended to aid preachers preparing expository sermons, it deliberately does not regularly deal with standard critical matters – religionsgeschichtliche parallels, or Paul's use of Hellenistic rhetorical conventions, etc. Being both an evangelical and a Pentecostal, Fee aims his commentary primarily for preachers, teachers, and students, giving insights from both these traditions. Among Pentecostals and its offshoots, 1 Corinthians functions as a kind of charter, much the way that Romans functions among Lutherans. At times the author's background in Pentecostalism affects the comments offered on the passage at hand. Fee also works from the assumption that 1 and 2 Thessalonians and 1 Corinthians were written before Galatians (which is probably correct), and then affirms that Paul's opponents should not be

classified as "Judaizers" since (in his opinion) they are not like the Judaizers of Galatia. Fee holds that 14:34-35 is a non-Pauline gloss, and is therefore not binding on the present-day church.

Findlay, G.G., "St. Paul's First Epistle to the Corinthians," in *The Expositor's Greek Testament*, edited by W. Robertson Nicoll, Vol. 2. Grand Rapids: Wm. B. Eerdmans, 1967.
>A commentary by a Methodist writer based on the Greek text, including information for making decisions where the various manuscripts differ in their readings. A student who wishes to keep his Greek fresh would find that working through this book would be a great help, while at the same time throwing fresh insight into his study of Corinthians.

Fisher, Fred, *Commentary on 1 and 2 Corinthians*. Waco, TX: Word Books, 1975.
>A verse-by-verse study is prefaced by a concise and helpful introduction which provides insight into the life and culture of the people to whom Paul was writing. The author is weak on his doctrine of inspiration, suggesting that only what has to do with salvation is inspired.

Friskney, Thomas W., *Solving Church Problems: A Commentary on Paul's First Corinthian Letter*. Cincinnati: Published by the author, 1987.
>Friskney taught Corinthians at Cincinnati Bible College for over two decades. His comments reflect much learned from that master teacher, George Mark Elliott. His thesis is that many of the same problems that troubled the church at Corinth still trouble the church in the 20th century, and that we can learn to solve such problems by seeing the principles and methods Paul used, and then faithfully administering these abiding principles. A church's problems (and all churches have them) can be thus turned from burdens into blessings, to the glory of God. Friskney's comments are based on the ASV (1901). His conclusions on difficult passages (previous letter, women in leadership positions, how to harmonize chapters 11 and 14 which seem to give contradictory conclusions, spiritual gifts, etc.) usually follow the classic, conservative position, and are worded in a sweetly reasonable way. Holds that "baptism for the dead" is a reference to the baptism of suffering.

Furnish, Victor Paul, "Corinth in Paul's Time – What Can Archaeology Tell Us?" *Biblical Archaeology Review* 14:3 (1988), p.14-27.
>Gives a brief survey of an ancient history of Corinth. Corinth is the most exhaustively excavated site of the ancient Greco-Roman world, and demonstrates the manner in which the archaeological data, both inscriptional and artifactual, illuminate many references in the Corinthian letters. Paul has made many allusions to matters social, political, economic, and religious which were a part of the knowledge and common experience of the Corinthians.

Garland, D.E., *1 Corinthians* in the Baker Exegetical Commentary on the New Testament series. Grand Rapids: Baker, 2003.
>The BECNT series seeks "to provide, within the framework of informed evangelical thought, commentaries that blend scholarly depth with readability, exegetical detail and sensitivity to the whole, and attention to critical problems with theological awareness" (p.11). In his introduction Garland discusses Roman Corinth, social relations there, religious influences, misinterpretation of the Christian faith, Paul's response, Paul's ministry in Corinth, the nature of 1 Corinthians, its occasion and context. He provides a literary analysis, exegesis, and exposition of the text following an outline common to the book. Each section of his comments begins with a summary to introduce the reader to the next section within the outline. Within these summaries, Garland often refers to the chiastic structure of the unit. Honor and shame sociological ideas are highlighted.

Gardner, Paul D., *The Gifts of God and the Authentication of a Christian. An Exegetical Study of 1 Corinthians 8-11:1*. Lanham, MD: University Press of America, 1994.
>The title at first is surprising because it is not a topic one usually associates with these chapters, but "boundary markers" are a special interest of social-science critics. Gardner suggests that *gnosis* in 8:1-7 refers to a particular gift of the spirit (mentioned again at 12:8) which the "strong" at Corinth regarded as "authenticating" their standing as members of the community of God's people. Their behavior (eating at

the idol's temple, etc.) reflected their confidence of their standing as Christians. Gardner affirms these chapters are marked by a coherence, and views them as a connected and integrated argument. His work therefore adds further weight to the growing consensus that the chapters should not be divided up and assigned to different letters, as was suggested by Schmithals and Hering, among others.

Gill, D.W.J., "The Importance of Roman Portraiture for Head-Coverings in 1 Corinthians 11:2-16," *Tyndale Bulletin* 41 (1990), p.245-260.

Glen, J. Stanley, *Pastoral Problems in First Corinthians*. Philadelphia, PA: Westminster Press, 1964.
>The author, having learned that 1 Corinthians is very relevant to the life and work of the contemporary modern church, as a result of having to teach courses in both pastoral theology and New Testament over a period of time, and encouraged by missionaries on furlough who indicated the relevance of the letter to their own experience, has produced this small volume which in certain instances cuts across accepted and conventional views of what the letter is saying.

Godet, Frederic Louis, *Commentary on the First Epistle of St. Paul to the Corinthians*. Grand Rapids: Zondervan Publishing House, 1957. (Reprinted from the 1886 edition.)
>Many scholars class this as one of the outstanding treatments of all time. A French theologian with German training, his notes often refute the liberal's handling of the Bible books. Weak and out of date on matters of textual criticism.

Gooch, Peter D., *Dangerous Food: 1 Corinthians 8-10 in Its Context*. Studies in Christianity and Judaism 5. Waterloo, ONT: Wilfrid Laurier University Press, 1993.
>In an approach he describes as "social-historical," Gooch brings to bear an analysis of dining practices at two archaeological sites (the Demeter sanctuary and the Asclepius sanctuary) in Corinth where dining rooms have been found, as well as providing a useful survey of Greek and Roman literary data regarding meals of various types and their possible religious components. He concludes there were meals in "temple restaurants" (1 Corinthians 8:10) and "tables of demons" (1 Corinthians 10:25), the latter of which were to be avoided because they had cultic significance. Gooch thinks the problem with idol food did not originate with the Corinthian Christians, but with Paul (his old Jewish background is rearing its head!). Gooch thinks that Paul changes the position on idol food which he first advocated in a "previous letter" because it was not well received, and is now offering a revised directive on the topic. Gooch rejects the idea that Paul here argues from principle as a theologian (the traditional view), and he also rejects the view that there was an internal conflict at Corinth between strong and weak brothers. He views the position of the weak as "purely hypothetical."

Gromacki, Robert G., *Called to be Saints: An Exposition of 1 Corinthians*. Grand Rapids: Baker Book House, 1977.
>A readable commentary with non-technical vocabulary, based on the King James Version (with careful attention to the Greek text). Questions are placed at the end of each chapter to stimulate personal study. Gromacki's handling of the question of "speaking in tongues" is satisfactory. Black and white photographs are interspersed throughout the presentation

Grosheide, Frederick Willem, *Commentary on the First Epistle to the Corinthians*. Grand Rapids: Wm. B. Eerdmans Publishing Co., 1953.
>Part of the New International Commentary on the New Testament, this one does not measure up to the quality of the other volumes in the series. A Dutch scholar in the Reformed tradition, Grosheide holds that the main thrust of the epistle is against the spiritually proud who insist on their own rights.

Grudem, Wayne, *The Gift of Prophecy in the New Testament and Today*. Westchester, IL: Crossway Books, 1988.
>The same author also has a book on prophecy that is more focused just on 1 Corinthians, entitled *The Gift of Prophecy in 1 Corinthians*.

Grudem, Wayne, "Why Christians Can Still Prophesy," *Christianity Today* (Sep. 16, 1988), p.29ff.
> Defines "prophecy" as "telling something that God has spontaneously brought to mind." NT prophets had "less authority than the OT prophets (who were God's canonical mouthpieces)." Explains that "testing the prophecies," as taught in the NT, means the church can accept or reject what the NT prophet says. He tries to explain "perfect" (1 Corinthians 13:10) as a reference to the end of the age, so that he can have "prophecy" as he defines it continue all through the church age.

Habermas, Gary, and Michael Licona, *The Case for the Resurrection of Jesus*. Grand Rapids: Kregel, 2004.
> A user-friendly apologetic tool for informed and interested evangelical lay persons. The authors use a "minimal facts" approach to argue for the historicity of Jesus' resurrection. They "consider only those data that are so strongly attested historically that even the majority of unbelieving scholars accept them as facts" (p.75). In their view such an approach is more effective than the use of the Bible alone, since this evidence is effective even for those skeptics who disbelieve Scripture. Begins with a brief and simple introduction to historiography, arguing that the principle of multiple independent attestation, by enemies and eyewitnesses and from early sources, provides strong testimony. Then presents five "minimal facts" of the resurrection: Jesus died by crucifixion, His disciples believed in His resurrection and appearances, Paul's life was changed from persecutor to apostle, the skeptic James was converted, and the tomb is empty. Includes a chapter of excellent advice for those engaged in communicating with unbelievers and skeptics. Final chapter summarizes the gospel and provides a "Roman Road" approach to its presentation.

Hall, David R., *The Unity of the Corinthian Correspondence* (JSNT sup. series, 251). London: T&T Clark, 2003.
> A well-researched, well-presented, careful argument for the unity of the Corinthians letters. Hall concludes 1 Corinthians is the sorrowful letter of 2 Corinthians 2:4, and the opponents addressed in 1 Corinthians are those also addressed in 2 Corinthians 10-13. Identifying the problem concerning the exercise of spiritual gifts, Hall writes that in Corinth "exercise of spiritual gifts was individualistic and competitive rather than seeking the good of the whole church" (p.74). He rejects Gerd Theissen's claims that "the strong" at Corinth were the socially privileged folk in the church. Arguments for the unity of 2 Corinthians are well-presented and forceful. Addresses the well-known claim that the tone of chapters 1-9 differs markedly from 10-13, and the change from first-plural to first-singular verbs, showing that neither necessitates a partition theory. Interacts with Betz who argued for the independence of 2 Corinthians 8 and 9.

Hannah, Darrell D., *The Text of 1 Corinthians in the Writings of Origen*. Atlanta, GA: Scholars Press, 1997
> This is one of the series "The New Testament in the Greek Fathers," a series attempting to show the history of the textual transmission through analysis of the quotations from and allusions to the New Testament in the writings of important church fathers. Origen is recognized as the greatest biblical scholar in the ancient church, so the Greek text he had and used is an important witness to the transmission of the text.

Hay, David, *Pauline Theology*, Vol. 2, "1 & 2 Corinthians." Minneapolis: Fortress, 1993.
> The Pauline Theology Group of the Society of Biblical Literature has been trying to produce a definitive volume on Paul's theology. Before an overall view can be delineated, it is necessary for the "group" to determine the "theology" of his individual letters. As this volume shows, it has proven difficult for redaction critics to decide what fundamental conviction Paul is operating from when he writes to the Corinthians. Was it election, or the confirming power of the Spirit, or Paul's personal beliefs, or eschatology, or the resurrection of the dead, or what? While one comes away from this volume still hungry, it does underline the fact that the usual two-point Pauline outline (doctrine and practice) is not found in this letter.

Hays, Richard B., *First Corinthians*. Louisville, KY: John Knox, 1997.
> Last volume in the Interpretation series. Intended to help those engaged in communicating the message of Biblical books. The series' objectives prevent technical discussions of issues and problems in the text, though "reflections for teachers and preachers" at the close of each paragraph of text make for thought-provoking application of the text to issues the contemporary church faces. He considers 14:34-36 to be a

non-Pauline interpolation, and treats "head" in 11:3 as teaching a hierarchical ordering. Treats 7:12 through the rest of chapter 7 as reflecting Paul's uninspired opinion on the subjects covered. Believes chapter 7 (wrongly) teaches an imminent *parousia*, and comments like this leave readers wondering about the authoritative character of a book of Scripture. Embraces the gender-inclusive approach of the NRSV, and at times this inflexible ideology can obscure the meaning of the text (p.95).

Heading, John, *First Epistle to the Corinthians*. Kilmarnock, Scotland: John Ritchie, 1965.
A verse-by-verse conservative exposition with emphasis on the structural organization of the epistle. Holds that Paul's speaking in tongues meant his use of Greek. Premillennial in its eschatology. Refreshingly independent, the work of a British Plymouth Brethren preacher.

Hemphill, K.S., *Spiritual Gifts: Empowering the New Testament Church*. Nashville: Broadman, 1988.
For each of the Pauline texts dealing with "spiritual gifts," Hemphill describes the historical situation, the literary context, and then comments on the theological significance. In 1 Corinthians 12-14, he does four things: he tries to identify the spiritual people, to define the spiritual gifts, to identify who is a spiritual person, and then discusses the spiritual person seeking spiritual gifts. He treats Ephesians 4:1-16 as gifted leaders equipping gifted members.

Henry, Matthew, "1 Corinthians," in *Commentary on the Whole Bible*, Vol. 6. Westwood, NJ: Fleming H. Revell. Printed many times.
First published in 1708-1710, these comments are based on his own outlines of each paragraph of Biblical text. Henry was skilled in applying the truths of Scripture to the needs of those to whom he preached, and his outlines and practical applications are useful today to one who would preach through the books of the New Testament. An abridged edition has been published by Zondervan.

Hodge, Charles, *An Exposition of the First Epistle to the Corinthians*. Grand Rapids, MI: Baker Book House, 1980 reprint. (Reprinted many times. First published in 1857.)
Theological topics introduced in the text of 1 Corinthians are specially emphasized. Strongly Calvinistic.

Holladay, Carl, *The First Letter of Paul to the Corinthians*, in the Living Word Commentary Series, edited by Everett Ferguson. Austin, TX: Sweet Publishing, 1979.
This is one of a series of commentaries based on the text of the Revised Standard Version, produced by Church of Christ writers, who tend at times to reflect modern critical views on Scripture.

Horsley, Richard A., "Gnosis in Corinth: 1 Corinthians 8:1-6," in *NTStud* 27:1 (1980), p.32-51.
The teachers creating the trouble in the Corinthian church that led to portions of what Paul wrote in 1 Corinthians are displaying Hellenistic-Jewish *gnosis* in their slogans. (This is a different approach than simply identifying Paul's opponents as being "Judaizers." See also article below by R. McL. Wilson.)

Horsley, Richard A., *1 Corinthians*. Nashville, TN: Abingdon, 1998.
In line with the Abingdon New Testament Commentary series, this volume provides a concise analysis of the literary, socio-historical, theological and ethical dimensions of 1 Corinthians. The text is analyzed according to the literary-rhetorical macro-units resulting in long, but well-organized and easy-to-read, sections of commentary. What the reader of the comments ends up with is not so much an understanding of 1 Corinthians, as with the results of what happens to a text when subjected to modern attempts to make an ancient work match current popular philosophy.

Hort, Fenton John Anthony, *The Christian Ecclesia*. London: Macmillan & Co., 1914. (Reprinted as one of the Evangelical Reprint Library series by College Press, 1972.)
Valuable for a study of what the early church was like, not only at Corinth, but throughout the Roman Empire. James Strauss added two studies at the close of the reprint volume which help update the work.

House, H. Wayne, "Should a Woman Prophesy or Preach Before Men?" *Bibliotheca Sacra* 145 (Apr. 1988), p.141-161.
> Deals with the meaning of *kephale* (11:3) as indicating some kind of authority/subordination (as over against the idea that it means "source"), and with the difference between prophecy and preaching (urging that because a woman prophesied in the early church, does not mean she can preach today).

Hurley, James B., "Did Paul Require Veils or the Silence of Women? A Consideration of 1 Corinthians 11:2-16 and 1 Corinthians 14:33b-36," *Westminster Theological Journal* 35:2 (Winter 1973), p.190-220.
> In 1 Corinthians 11:2-16 the primary issue was the authority of husbands in relation to their wives as focused in the hair-style of wives at the worship service. Paul did not intend to silence women but rather to regulate their relation to their husbands as they charismatically prayed and prophesied. 1 Corinthians 14:33b-35 should be understood as part of the discussion of prophecy begun at v.29, forbidding women to join in the judging of the prophets. So understood, there is no conflict with ch.11, which (he believes) clearly grants women the right to exercise the charismatic gifts of prayer and prophecy within the assembly. Paul did not require that women wear veils, nor did he require that they always be silent in the assemblies. He insisted instead that the divinely ordained authority structures must not be set aside.

Ironside, Henry ("Harry") Allan, *Addresses on the First Epistle to the Corinthians*. New York: Loizeaux Brothers, 1941.
> Expository messages preached in the Moody Memorial Church, Chicago. Informative and stimulating. Illustrations are pertinent and timely. Dispensational/premillennial in eschatology.

Jeremias, Joachim, *The Eucharistic Words of Jesus*. New York: Charles Scribner's Sons, 1966. (First translated into English by Arnold Ehrhardt, in 1955)
> Marred by adherence to form-criticism, still it is a recognized forceful presentation of the Lord's Supper, with a discussion of the chronological and textual problems involved.

Johnson, A.F., *1 Corinthians* in IVP New Testament Commentary 7. Downers Grove, IL: InterVarsity, 2004.
> A seventeen page introduction explains the socio-cultural and historical background, literary features and theology of 1 Corinthians. Offers some thought provoking titles for some of the major sections of 1 Corinthians, such as the problem of factions – putting clergy and congregation in their place (1:10-4:21); eating idol food and the priority of love over "rights" (8:1 - 11:1); and the dispute over proper head attire for men and women in worship (11:2-16).

Keener, Craig, *1-2 Corinthians*, in New Cambridge Bible Commentary. New York: Cambridge University Press, 2005.
> The New Cambridge Bible Commentary is aimed to help "intellectually curious individuals" to understand the Hebrew and Christian Scriptures better. One section of the book explores 1 Corinthians, the other 2 Corinthians. Each section begins with a brief introduction. The introduction to 1 Corinthians contains an exploration of the rhetorical features of the letter, the nature of ancient letters, the history of the city of Corinth, and the situation of 1 Corinthians. The introduction to 2 Corinthians looks at the genre of the epistle, the situation of the epistle, the opponents, and whether it is a unified whole or not. After each introduction there is a chapter which gives an annotated list of suggested reading. This points the reader beyond the commentary to other up-to-date commentaries, monographs and studies. The comments themselves are based on the text of the NRSV. Keener provides a wealth of material from the ancient world as a background for understanding the specific context of the Corinthian church. Occasional brief excurses under the headings "A Closer Look" include "Paul's use of rhetoric," "*Arsenokoites* and *malakos*," "Idol food," "ancient views on resurrection," and the like. Boxes titled "Bridging the Horizons" deal with parallels between Paul's and current readers' situations.

Kistemaker, Simon, *Exposition of the First Epistle to the Corinthians*, in the New Testament Commentary Series. Grand Rapids: Baker, 1993.

Detailed study of the text, with special sections on key interpretive issues, Greek words, and practical considerations. Breaks little new ground and tends to read in Reformed theology.

Kling, Friedrich Christian, "Commentary on the Epistles to the Corinthians," in *Lange's Commentary*. Translated from the German, with additional notes, by Philip Schaff. Grand Rapids: Zondervan Publishing House, nd.
> Dr. Kling's work was first published in 1860, after years of teaching the epistles to theological students. Exegetical, doctrinal, and homiletical notes afford the student a comprehensive and practical view of the verses under consideration. It is a thorough commentary, from a Lutheran viewpoint, and the student needs to know Hebrew, Greek, and/or Latin to handle this commentary.

Kovacs, J.L., *1 Corinthians. Interpreted by Early Christian Commentators* in the Church's Bible Series. Grand Rapids: Eerdmans, 2005.
> Part of a new series designed to present the Holy Scriptures as understood and interpreted during the first millennium of Christian history. (Postmodernism is not interested in what the text says, but rather in how people were affected by the text: hence, such a series of commentaries.) Kovacs offers fairly lengthy excerpts from patristic commentaries and from series of sermons on 1 Corinthians. The ancient writers whose works are cited most frequently are Origen, Chrysostom, Cyril of Alexandria, Theodoret, Gregory of Nyssa, and Augustine.

Lenski, Richard Charles Henry, *The Interpretation of St. Paul's First and Second Epistles to the Corinthians*. Minneapolis: Augsburg Publishing House, 1937.
> A conservative Lutheran exposition based on the Greek text. Wordy at times, but those who take time to read it will grow in an understanding of Corinthians. Offers many significant word studies. Strongly defends the unity of 2 Corinthians. Combines critical exegetical excellence with popular application.

Lightfoot, Joseph Barber, "1 Corinthians," in *Notes on the Epistles of St. Paul*. Grand Rapids: Zondervan Publishing House, 1957.
> Notes first posthumously published in 1895. Based on the Greek text, his comments on 1 Corinthians are written with ripe knowledge, balanced judgment, and make a satisfactory contribution to the project that he and Westcott and Hort undertook -- a commentary on the whole New Testament, portions of which still endure and are classics. Lightfoot's and Westcott's works should be in every Greek student's library.

Lightfoot, Neil R., "The Role of Women in Religious Services," *Restoration Quarterly* (1976:3), p.129-136.
> Tackles the problem of harmonizing 1 Corinthians 14 with 1 Corinthians 11. Concludes that women may teach and pray in men's presence in home situations, but not in public services.

Lipscomb, David, and Shepherd, J.W., *A Commentary on the New Testament Epistles*, Vol. 2, 1 Corinthians. Nashville, TN: Gospel Advocate Co., 1935.
> Part of a series of commentaries on the whole New Testament by Church of Christ scholars, intended for the Sunday School teacher or Bible student. On passages where several possible interpretations have been known for years, only one conclusion is given, with no reasons given for choosing that one. While often agreeing with the choice, we would be happier if given the reason on which the choice was based.

Lockwood, G.J., *1 Corinthians*. St. Louis, MO: Concordia, 2000.
> Top priority is given to listening to the text, but Lockwood also points out its implications for the church's theology and practice. The "word of the cross" is the basis for the church's unity, holiness, freedom, worship, and hope.

MacArthur, John, *Charismatic Chaos*. Grand Rapids: Zondervan, 1992.
> This volume is a revised and updated version of the author's earlier book, *The Charismatics: A Doctrinal Perspective*. The thrust of the work remains largely unchanged as the California preacher argues for the closing of the canon and the cessation of the sign gifts, but the chapters have been expanded to include

MacArthur, John F., *1 Corinthians*. Chicago: Moody Press, 1984.
> Printed sermons by one of America's well-known preachers. His dispensationalism at times overwhelms sane exegesis.

McGarvey, J.W., and Pendleton, Philip Y., "Corinthians," in the *Standard Bible Commentary*. Cincinnati: Standard Publishing Co., 1916.
> This is one of a series of commentaries written for Christian Church Sunday School workers, and so uses many simple words where other commentaries use a single technical word. McGarvey taught a number of years at the College of the Bible at Lexington, Ky.

Mare, W. Harold, "1 Corinthians" in *Expositor's Bible Commentary*. Grand Rapids: Zondervan Publishing House, 1976.
> Intended to present an evangelical treatment, this commentary is based on the NIV. Mare opts for "a previous letter," 1 Corinthians, a "sorrowful letter" following a "painful visit," and 2 Corinthians. Included are two fine maps of Corinth and its vicinity. At times, Mare, a well-known Biblical archaeologist, refers to what archaeology has taught us about Corinth and the 1st century world. He also offers some choice comments based on the nuances of Greek grammar and Greek word studies. On the negative side, there are times Mare follows Reformed theology's party line as he introduces comments like "covenant children" and "effectual call," "household baptism," and "God saves you," in places where Corinthians seems to contradict Reformed theology. He also inserts a premillennial agenda into comments on chapter 15 when there is no need to do this for clarity or perspicuity. He treats the sin of chapter 5 as though the man has "married" his father's wife. He treats 7:36 as referring to engaged couples getting married, rather than a father giving his daughter in marriage. He gives several reasons for rejecting J. Oswald Sander's views that tongues at Corinth were different from the languages spoken at Pentecost (Acts 2). He rejects the notion that "perfect" (13:10) refers to the completed canon, and then insists "it is better to argue for the cessation of the gifts of prophecy, tongues, and the special gift of knowledge on the basis of the larger context of Paul's writings and on the basis of the grammar of vv. 9,13 ...." On 1 Corinthians 14:34, he writes "for the sake of decorum in the churches, women were not to speak in public worship." He attempts to harmonize the seeming contradiction between 11:5 and 14:34 by following Warfield's view that in chapter 11 the women were not speaking in public worship.

Mare, W. Harold, "Prophet and Teacher in the New Testament Period," *JETS* 9:3 (Summer 1966), p.146-148, etc.
> Mare seems to allow that "prophet" in Corinth includes the ability to give insights into, and to convey the deeper meanings of, God's redemptive program in His Word. Distinguishable from the inspiration of the Holy Spirit (2 Tim. 3:16) given to the apostles and their associates to prophesy in setting forth God's truth.

Meyer, H.A.W., "Critical and Exegetical Commentary on 1 Corinthians," in Meyer's *Critical and Exegetical Commentary on the New Testament*, revised by Heinrici. Edinburgh: T&T. Clark, 1896.
> Meyer and DeWette were the founders of the modern style of commenting, at once both scientific and popular; scientific, through its application of grammatical and philological laws; popular because it presented a terse sifting of learning and research. For the student who can read Greek.

Mills, Watson E., *1 Corinthians* in the series "Bibliographies for Biblical Research." Lewiston, NY: Mellen Biblical Press, 1996.
> This bibliography on 1 Corinthians provides an index to journal articles, essays in collected works, books and monographs, dissertations, commentaries, and encyclopedia and dictionary articles published in the 20th century through 1995.

Moffatt, James, *Commentary on 1 Corinthians*. New York: Harper and Brothers, 1938.
> A volume in the Moffatt New Testament Commentary series, it is liberal in its theology. Moffatt was a British scholar whose work is sometimes helpful in a study of problems arising from the text itself.

Morgan, George Campbell, *The Corinthian Letters of Paul*. Westwood, NJ: Fleming H. Revell Co., 1956.
> A well-regarded preacher addresses himself to the problems which plague the church. Reflects a fervent devotional approach in dealing with those problems.

Morris, Leon, *The First Epistle of Paul to the Corinthians*, in the Tyndale New Testament Commentary Series. Grand Rapids: Wm. B. Eerdmans Publishing Co., revised 1985.
> Each of the Tyndale commentaries is a compact, succinct commentary, and Morris is always readable. Based on the King James Version, but attention is paid to alternate readings. The revised edition is a considerable improvement on the earlier edition. Scholarly opinions are collected by Morris.

Murphy-O'Connor, B.J., *1 Corinthians*. New York: Doubleday, 1998
> Part of the Doubleday Bible Commentary series. The author had a similar-sized commentary in the New Testament Message Series (Collegeville, MN: Liturgical Press, 1979). This volume incorporates some more recent conclusions the author has reached, and advances the positions taken in the former commentary, which in turn was based on numerous detailed studies previously published by the author. The author is one of this generation's foremost negative critical scholars. Castigating Paul is much in fashion today among scholars, so the disdain for Paul encountered in comments on chapters 1-7 is not wholly unexpected. Murphy-O'Connor is Roman Catholic; at times, this theology intrudes into his comments.

Murphy-O'Connor, B.J., *St. Paul's Corinth, Texts and Archaeology*. Wilmington, DE: Michael Glazier, 1983. (3rd Revised edition, Collegeville, MN: Liturgical Press, 2002.)
> This volume is a publishing first. At long last we have a book containing all that vital information on Corinth, its history, society and culture, which is generally unavailable to the layperson or buried in unfamiliar ancient texts, archaeological reports, or obscure exegetical footnotes. As the bibliography shows, there are many informative, secondary studies of ancient Corinth. But until this text there has been no comprehensive collection of the primary source material available to the reader in English translation. Here is included evidence from 33 Greek and Latin authors (Pausanias, Antipater of Sidon, Polystratus, Cicero, Crinagoras, Didorus Siculus, Strabo), 95 quotations arranged chronologically from the 1st century BC to the 2nd century AD, the latest in pertinent archaeological data (Corinthian bronze, the Delphi inscription concerning the proconsul Gallio), as well as the edict of Claudius.

Naylor, Peter, *A Study Commentary on 1 Corinthians*. Webster, NY: Evangelical Press, 2004.
> Treats 1 Corinthians as both disciplinary (to rebuke problems of divisions, impurity, immorality) and didactical (wisdom from the Lord, Christian liberty, proper use of spiritual gifts, resurrection). The heart of 1 Corinthians is a call for the church to unite in doctrine and in selfless love lest Christ's work continue to be hindered by pride and selfishness. Regarding 5:5, delivery of the immoral man to Satan would subject him to "some form of physical suffering preceding repentance and restoration" (p.128). On 10:23-11:1, Naylor says Paul accommodated his lifestyle to "weak brothers," but did not compromise his Christian morality. The accommodation was for the sake of winning others to Christ. Naylor argues "the perfect [thing]" of 13:10 can be "recognized as our New Testament, a collection of books supplementing the Old Testament and concluding the whole body of sacred Scripture. [It is not] unreasonable to believe that Paul was aware of such a development" (p.348). Recognizing his stance is not the popular view, he asks the following questions rhetorically: "Does Paul affirm in 13:10 that Christ will return as 'the perfect thing' at the end of this world, and that a species of perfection (cf. 13:12) will then supervene? No. Had he wished to indicate this he might have written 'the perfect *man*' ... instead of 'the perfect *thing*' ... which our Lord is not" (p.354, italics added). Includes his own translation of the Greek text.

Newton, Derek, *Deity and Diet. The Dilemma of Sacrificial Food at Corinth*. Sheffield: Sheffield Academic Press, 1998.

Scholars have long accused Paul of writing inconsistent arguments in 1 Corinthians 8-10. Newton pictures Corinth as being like modern churches which encounter the ambiguities of idol worship in Eastern societies – i.e., a multiplicity of individual stances which were competing and contradictory. (That is what Newton found when he interviewed Christians in Indonesia, for whom the issue of idol foods continues to be problematic.) He argues that it is precisely because boundary lines are often blurred that these problems surface and create conflicts within the Christian community.

Orr, W.F., and Walther, J.A., *1 Corinthians. A New Translation, Introduction with a Study of the Life of Paul, Notes, and Commentary*. The Anchor Bible Series, No. 32. Garden City: Doubleday, 1976.
> 136 introductory pages cover Paul's conversion, missionary activities, and the significance of the apostle. Commentary follows the usual pattern adopted in this series: English translation, notes on matters of detail, and general comments. Both writers are connected with Pittsburgh Theological Seminary.

Oster, Richard E., *1 Corinthians* in The College Press NIV Commentary Series. Joplin, MO: College Press, 1995.
> "This commentary is intended for use by studious lay people, Bible teachers, and seminary students," the foreword informs us. Oster teaches at Harding University School of Graduate Study and uses what he calls a "historical-exegetical" approach in this commentary, while at the same time acknowledging the fact that he generally follows the conclusions found in Carson, Moo, Morris and Kummel. He holds that 1 Corinthians 5:9 refers to a "previous letter," and dates 1 Corinthians at AD 55. He rejects many of the rhetorical, sociological, and anthropological reconstructions of the Christian community(ies) at Corinth, yet suggests these methodologies do provide some useful insights. He has Paul making the Law of Moses binding on Christians in the case of incest (ch. 5). In comments on chapter 7, he objects to the "eschatological woman" concept widely disseminated recently through the writings of Gordon S. Fee. He also opts for divorce being permitted if the non-Christian mate wants out of the marriage with his/her Christian spouse. He treats 7:36 as though it speaks about male believers who are engaged to be married. Oster spends more time with feminist arguments/questions at chapter 11 than he does on any other problem/issue currently found in Corinthian studies. He needlessly uses the word "liturgy" as a term for the public worship service, thus introducing a concept foreign to the New Testament. Oster accepts the view that "perfect" in 13:10 refers to the second coming, but insists that this is not tantamount to abdication to the Pentecostal/Charismatic view of the present validity of "spiritual gifts." Oster neatly words his comments on "singing" (chapter 14) so one cannot tell if he holds the non-instrument view on music. Oster does not take 14:34's prohibition of women speaking to be normative in all church activities.

Oster, Richard E., "Use, Misuse and Neglect of Archaeological Evidence in Some Modern Works on 1 Corinthians." *Zeitschrift fur die Neutestamentliche Wissenschaft* 83 (1992), p.52-73.
> Oster's first example concerns the "Synagogue of the Hebrews" inscription (a late date inscription, and not found *in situ*, so is of little value in answering questions about a Jewish presence in Julio-Claudian Corinth). The presence of no less than 5 temples supports epigraphic witness to a flourishing of Egyptian cults (Isis, etc.) in Corinth. Does 1 Corinthians 7:1-5 reflect the fact that these cults involved both male and female sacral celibacy? With regard to Christians eating in idol's temples (1 Cor 8-10), an abundance of architectural and epigraphic evidence shows that dining rooms were part of temple precincts (one temple had dozens of dining rooms) and were social gathering places. Oster criticizes commentators for suggesting Paul's mention of liturgical head coverings was hypothetical (1 Cor 11: 4). Considerable evidence points to a pattern of men using head coverings in Roman religions, and it was surely the case at Corinth. The final passage, 1 Cor 12:14-16, recalls the votive body parts excavated in the temple of Asclepius, associated either with prayers for healing or thanksgiving for healing. Oster cautions against using these artifacts to illustrate Paul's message since they are dated four centuries before his epistle.

Parry, R. St. John, *The First Epistle of Paul the Apostle to the Corinthians*. Cambridge: At the University Press, 1916.
> An excellent commentary based on the Greek text. Part of the Cambridge Testament for Schools and Colleges series.

Bibliography

Peterson, Brian K., *Eloquence and the Proclamation of the Gospel in Corinth*. Atlanta: Scholars Press, 1998.
> Applying the methods of rhetorical criticism, Peterson investigates the seeming tension between the positions Paul takes in 1 Cor 1-4 and 2 Cor 10-13 regarding the relationship of the Corinthian congregation to their spiritual leaders, particularly himself, and the possibility of their evaluating apostolic ministry. Peterson argues that the key to explaining Paul's apparent contradictory statements is *Stasis* (the point on which the whole matter turns; the point the orator sees as the most important to make).

Prior, David, *The Message of 1 Corinthians* in The Bible Speaks Today Series. Downers Grove, IL: InterVarsity, 1985.
> Helpful for preachers and teachers looking for contemporary applications of what is written in 1 Corinthians. Prior reflects both international and cross-cultural insights.

Redpath, Allan, *The Royal Route to Heaven: Studies in 1 Corinthians*. London: Pickering and Inglis, 1960.
> Sermons, delivered at the Moody Memorial Church, Chicago, rebuke shallowness and ineffectiveness in the church, expose the tragedy of living in sinfulness and worldliness, and vigorously apply the message of this epistle to the lives of Christians today.

Robertson, Archibald, and Plummer, Alfred, *A Critical and Exegetical Commentary on the First Epistle of St. Paul to the Corinthians*. 2nd edition. Edinburgh: T&T Clark, 1914.
> Though many of the volumes in the International Critical Commentary series are written from a liberal theological viewpoint, this one is not, and has come to be recognized as a monumental work, which should be consulted by any serious student of 1 Corinthians.

Robertson, A.T., *Word Pictures in the New Testament*, Vol. IV, "The Epistles of Paul." New York: Harper and Bros., 1931.
> Not a complete commentary, but strong in its treatment of word meanings and grammatical constructions.

Schmithals, Walter, *Gnosticism in Corinth: An Investigation of the Letters to the Corinthians*. Translated by John E. Steely. Nashville: Abingdon Press, 1971.
> A liberal theologian's treatment of the supposed influence of Gnosticism on the beliefs of Christians in Corinth.

Schrage, Wolfgang, *Der Erste Brief an die Korinther (1 Kor 11:17-14:40)*. Zurich: Benziger Verlag, 1999.
> This is Vol. 3 of what will be, when finished, a four volume commentary. This one covers the proper celebration of the Lord's Supper (11:17-34), and the charismatic community in 12:1-14:40. Schrage uses socio-historical tools wherever possible. He treats 14:34-35 as an insertion by a later interpolator, whose position on the role of women in the public assembly is in clear opposition to that of Paul himself.

Shetler, Sanford G., "Paul's Letter to the Corinthians 55 AD," *Compact Commentary Series*. Harrisonburg, VA: Christian Light Publications, 1971.
> Uses the King James Version. A brief exposition from a firm conservative viewpoint. The concise treatment is especially suited to the beginning student. A Mennonite writer, the author devotes 1/6 of the whole book to the topic of the veiling of women (1 Corinthians 11:1-16) which is presented as a universal teaching for all the church for all time.

Shore, T. Teignmouth, *The First Epistle to the Corinthians*, in The Layman's Handy Commentary series. Grand Rapids: Zondervan Publishing House, 1957.
> Shore writes the commentary on Corinthians for this series edited by Charles John Ellicott. Most students familiar with the Greek will appreciate the comments based on the nuances of the Greek language, and some say no better book can be placed in the hands of the working Greek student.

Snyder, Graydon F., *First Corinthians: A Faith Community Commentary*. Macon, GA: Mercer, 1992.
> A new work by a Mennonite with helpful sections on Biblical theology and historical significance in addition to original meaning.

Soards, Marion L., *1 Corinthians* in the New International Biblical Commentary. Peabody, MA: Hendrickson, 1999.
> The NIBC series is aimed at serious readers who lack theological training. Technical materials are included in fifty-four "additional notes." Soards makes use of modern sociological and rhetorical studies of the Corinthian letters while stressing that Paul taught from an apocalyptic-eschatological point of view. Soards attempts to offer an outline of study units that would be helpful for the teacher or preacher. Soards, noting the use of six plurals in the text, asserts that it is the congregation at Corinth that is the temple of the Holy Spirit in chapter 6, not the individual. He offers the opinion (7:25-38) that the "young woman" is a slave woman and the slave owner is the one who does or does not give the young woman to be married. Aware of issues involved in "head" (11:3) as "ruler" or "source," Soards gives a good bibliography on the debate because discussions of the role of women in public worship are involved. Soards sees 1 Corinthians 13 as an earlier piece written by Paul and used here. Concerning 14:33b-36, Soards cites four major views with critiques of each, accepting that they are Paul's words – not an interpolation – dealing with a local, specific problem, thus not universally applicable today.

Spittler, Russell P., *The Corinthian Correspondence*. Springfield, MO: Gospel Publishing House, 1976.
> Author aims to sketch the literary content and modern relevance of the letters of Paul addressed to a 5-year old charismatic congregation. Explanations of key charismatic proof texts from a charismatic viewpoint.

Stanley, Arthur Penrhyn, *The Epistles of St. Paul to the Corinthians*. 2nd ed. London: John Murray, 1876.
> A scholarly, critical study which illumines the historical and picturesque aspects of the epistle. Numerous digressions on the theme of the epistle, and dissertations on thoughts which have arisen in the writer's mind as a result of this study.

Staton, Knofel, *First Corinthians* in Unlocking the Scriptures Series. Cincinnati: Standard, 1987.
> A workbook to accompany this volume, written by Jonathan Underwood, is also available. Staton's theme is that 1 Corinthians reflects how a church is affected by the kinds of problems that go on within the geographical location in which that church is located. Thus it is important for leaders to understand their own cultures, which will help keep them alert to the kinds of problems that will occur within 20th century congregations. Staton suggests the reader of 1 Corinthians first make a list of the fruit of the Spirit (Galatians 5:22), and then as he studies 1 Corinthians, to list the specific aspect of the fruit of the Spirit that would have solved the specific problem being mentioned. Also, since immaturity marked the church at Corinth and raised its head in many areas of life, and since the Holy Spirit inspired Paul to write 1 Corinthians for our church and our needs (as well as for Corinth in the 1st century), the student will be significantly helped to see where immaturity is raising its head in his own life.

Talbert, Charles H., *Reading Corinthians*. London: SPCK, 1990.
> This writer fills his short book with emphases on literary forms: the types of ancient letters, rhetoric, the use of quotations, the techniques of *inclusio* and *chiasmus*. Talbert thinks that parts of three letters are preserved in our 1 and 2 Corinthians: 1 Corinthians in reply to a letter from the Corinthians and the report from Chloe's people; 2 Corinthians 10-13, part of the "severe" letter; and 2 Corinthians 1-9 making up Paul's third letter. He regards 2 Corinthians 6:14-7:1 as a "digression," a recognized form in the ancient world, and not a fragment of Paul's lost first letter or a non-Pauline piece.

Thiessen, Gerd, *The Social Setting of Pauline Christianity: Essays on Corinth*. Philadelphia: ET, 1982.

Thiessen affirms that the causes of the tension in the church at Corinth, both between the members (some rich, most poor – a socio-economic disjunction) themselves and between the members and Paul, are best explained along sociological lines.

Thiselton, Anthony C., *1 Corinthians: A Shorter Exegetical and Pastoral Commentary*. Grand Rapids: Eerdmans, 2006.
In many ways Thiselton's nearly 1,500 page NIGNTC commentary on 1 Corinthians has become the standard scholarly English language commentary. This work is not a condensed version of his earlier book. The author explains he did not have his earlier commentary or any other open on his desk as he wrote this one. A lifetime of research on 1 Corinthians allowed him to "think" as he wrote (p.xiv). The first volume was aimed at an academic readership. This volume's intended audience is a general, non-scholarly church audience who possess only the most basic background in both Scripture and classical history. Thiselton's concern for hermeneutics comes across in this new book. There are sections entitled "suggestions for possible reflection" at the end of every major block of text. In 1 Corinthians 11:1-16, Thiselton recognizes the role of women as leaders in the Corinthian church (p.169-79), yet he accepts the authenticity of 14:33b-36 (p.250-51). He explains that the latter passage does not contradict the former, since in 14:33-36 Paul is addressing the specific area of prophecy. This explanation, however, is inadequate, since in 11:4 the issue is women prophesying with uncovered heads.

Thiselton, Anthony C., *The First Epistle to the Corinthians: A Commentary on the Greek Text*, in the New International Greek Testament Commentary Series. Grand Rapids, MI: Eerdmans, 2000.
A volume in the New International Greek Testament Commentary series, it interacts with social-science critical interests as attempts are made to explain the text of 1 Corinthians. The author believes that a flood of recent research, mainly in the 1990s, on the social world of Corinth in the era of Paul and on rhetoric, has substantially changed the perceptions of this epistle and its theological importance. Paragraph after paragraph are written explaining this or that modern theory, and attempting to show how it affects our understanding. As these paragraphs are read, one almost spends more time trying to comprehend modern socio-rhetorical theory (with its loyalty-groupings and status-groupings, speech-act theory, etc.), than he spends on trying to grasp what Paul actually wrote. Thiselton opts for the "take freedom" option for 7:21; that the prohibition on speaking in 14:34 is specifically "the activity of sifting or weighing the words of prophets, especially by asking probing questions about the prophet's theology;" 15:29 is a baptism that is submitted to by living persons who decide to be baptized in order to be united, at the resurrection of the dead, with their believing relatives who have already died.

Thrall, Margaret Eleanor, *The First and Second Letters of Paul to the Corinthians*. Cambridge: At the University Press, 1965.
One of the volumes in the Cambridge Bible Commentary series, it consists of brief notes based on the text of the New English Bible.

Vine, W.E., *1 Corinthians*. Grand Rapids: Zondervan Publishing Co., 1951.
A brief commentary that gives the student an overall picture of the book. Based on the English Revised Version. A Plymouth Brethren scholar, he relates his comments to the Greek text. Does not deal with introductory problems.

Vines, Jerry, *God Speaks Today: A Study of 1 Corinthians*. Grand Rapids: Zondervan Publishing House, 1979.
A series of sermons by a Baptist preacher.

Wagner, C. Peter, *A Turned-on Church in an Uptight World*. Grand Rapids: Zondervan Publishing House, 1971.
A study guide on 1 Corinthians with questions for discussion groups. It applies the lessons of the epistle to the current scene, as the author detects in the errors of the Corinthians various pitfalls facing the modern church.

Wagner, C. Peter, *Effective Body Building*. San Bernardino, CA: Here's Life Publishers, 1982.
> Subtitled "Biblical Steps to Spiritual Growth," this is a work intended for a small group study of 1 Corinthians. It includes discussion questions at the end of each chapter. Potential users should beware that Wagner has become Charismatic, and his chapters are likely to so influence those who use his books.

Walker, William O., "1 Corinthians 11:2-16 and Paul's Views Regarding Women," *Journal of Biblical Literature* 94:1 (1975), p.94-110.
> Agrees that the passages advocating male supremacy should be rejected as non-Pauline. Argues that 1 Corinthians 11:2-16 is an interpolation – revised at the hands of one or more editors. Secondly, he argues that the passage actually consists of three originally separate and distinct pericopae, each dealing with a somewhat different though related subject. Thirdly, he insists that none of the three pericopae is authentically Pauline. In his view, it was not Paul, but later generation Christians, who inserted the subordination passages into the New Testament corpus.

Wilson, Geoffrey B., *1 Corinthians: A Digest of Reformed Comment*. London: Banner of Truth Trust, 1971.
> A brief treatment, which is very much abreast of the latest literature on 1 Corinthians by a Baptist preacher.

Wilson, R. McL., "How Gnostic Were the Corinthians?" *NTStud* 19:1 (1972), p.65-74.
> The answer to the question about Gnosticism at Corinth depends on defining one's terms. Wilson makes a distinction between *gnosis* and "Gnosticism," the latter primarily being used of the developed 2nd century systems. While Wilson talks of *gnosis*, he thinks we should avoid as much as possible the ambiguous adjectival form "gnostic" as we make comment on 1 Corinthians. A look at the use of *gnosis* and *sophia*, among other themes in 1 Corinthians, suggests that at Corinth we find at most only the first tentative beginnings of what was later to develop into full-scale Gnosticism.

Witherington, Ben III, *Conflict and Community in Corinth: A Socio-Rhetorical Commentary on I and II Corinthians*. Grand Rapids: Eerdmans, 1995.
> A contemporary and thoroughly modern treatment with a trove of historical background information for each part of 1 and 2 Corinthians, with particular sensitivity to sociological and literary structure.

Wright, N.T., *Paul for Everyone: 1 Corinthians*. Louisville, KY: Westminster John Knox, 2004.
> Writing from a background of the New Perspective on Paul, this popular writer describes 1 Corinthians as full of wisdom and challenge, since the young church at Corinth was as lively as the town itself. The young church was full of questions and problems, and as much joy and excitement as any growing church today. A two-page introduction is followed by an exposition of each pericope. A sixteen page glossary is included. The format makes it appropriate also for daily study (similar to the way one could use Barclay's *Daily Study Bible* series).

Zodhiates, Spiros, *A Richer Life for You in Christ*. Ridgefield, NJ: AMG Press, 1972.
> An exposition of 1 Corinthians 1, based on the original Greek text. The author explains the word pictures in the Greek. Originally these articles were written for daily devotions, and are here assembled under one cover.

-----, *To Love is to Live*. Grand Rapids: Wm. B. Eerdmans Publishing Co., 1967.
> An exposition of 1 Corinthians 13, based on the Greek text.

-----, *Conquering the Fear of Death*. Grand Rapids: Wm. B. Eerdmans, 1970.
> An exposition of 1 Corinthians 15, based on the Greek text.

INDEX

Page numbers in italics indicate information is in Introductory Studies. References by chapter and verse indicate information is in the commentary section of this book.

Abide faith, hope, and love, 13:13
Abounding in the work of the Lord, always, 15:58
Absent in body, but present in spirit, 5:3
According to the Scriptures, 15:3
Accursed: see, Anathema
Achaia, the church in, 1:2
    first fruits in, 16:15
Achaicus, 16:17
Act like men, 16:13
Ad hominem argument, *18*, 8:4,13, 11:5, 15:29ff
Adam,
    in ... all die, 15:22
    Christ compared, 15:22,45,47
    fall of, evils consequent on the, 1:24
    first man, 15:45
    is from the earth, earthy, 15:47
Adiaphora, 6:12
Administrations, 12:28
Admonish, 4:14
Adulterers, 6:9
Adultery, the difference between, and fornication, 6:9
Advent, second: see, Second advent
Adversaries, many at Ephesus, 16:9
Aesclepius: see under, Temples
Age of accountability, 7:14
Ages, 9:17
    before the, 2:7
    Christian, is the last, 10:11
    the ends of the, 10:11
    Patriarchal, Mosaic, Christian, 2:7
Alcoholism, a disease? 6:10
Alert, be on the, 16:13
All men equal? 12:17
All things,
    bears, believes, hopes, love 13:7
    become, to all men, 9:22
    do not edify, 10:23
    lawful? 6:12, 10:23
    not expedient (profitable), 6:12, 10:23
    originate from God, 11:12
Allegory, Alexandrian, 1:12

Altar,
    those who eat the sacrifice offered, share in, 10:18
Amanuensis, 1:1, 16:21
Amen,
    said in worship, 14:16
    final Amen, 16:24
Analogy,
    of Israel, 10:2,4,19
    of Scripture, 2:13
    of seed sown, 15:36ff
    of an army, 15:52, 16:13
Anathema
    no man speaking in the Spirit can say, 12:3
    if any man love not the Lord, let him be, 16:22
Angel of Jehovah, 10:4,9
Angels,
    spectators of what happens on earth, 4:9, 11:10
    because of, 11:10
    judging, 6:2
    tongues of, 13:1
Annihilation of the wicked (?), 15:18,53
Anxiety, free from, 7:32
Aorist tense,
    epistolary aorist, *19*, 5:9, 9:15, 16:10
    historical aorist, *19*, 4:17, 5:9
Aphrodite, worship of, *13*, 6:19
Apollos, 1:12, 3:6,8, 16:12
    colleague of Paul's, 3:8
    instructor of the Corinthian church, *5*, 1:12, 3:6
    urged to go to Corinth, *2*, 16:12
    watered, 3:6
    will come to Corinth when he has opportunity, 16:12
Apollos-party, 1:12
Apostasy, warning against, 10:12
Apostasy, possibility of, 9:27
Apostles and prophets, 12:28
Apostles due support, ch. 9

Index

Apostles,
- foundation of the church, 12:28
- qualifications of, 1:1
- signs of an, 1:6, 2:4
- Jesus appeared to, 15:8
- revelation of the Holy Spirit to, 2:10,12
- sufferings of, 4:9-13, 15:30
- rights of an apostle, 9:4ff
- two kinds of apostles, 1:1
- most were married men, 9:5
- God appointed them in the church, 12:28
- doomed (condemned) to death, 4:9
- roughly treated, homeless, 4:11
- spectacle to angels and men, 4:9
- stand in danger every hour, 15:30
- temporary office, 4:9, 12:28
- the twelve, 15:5

Apostolic decree, 8:1,8, 10:20
Appearances of Christ, 15:5
Aquila and Prisc(ill)a, 16:19
- the church in their house, *3*, 16:19
- travels of, *3,4*, 16:19
- instructor of Apollos, *5*
- a tentmaker, *4*

Argument on support of preachers, 9:6-14
Arian text, favorite, 8:6, 11:3
Arrogant: see, Pride.
Article, the definite,
- absence of the, 15:29
- article of previous reference, 15:29

Ascension: see Christ, ascension
Asceticism, 5:10, 6:13, 7:8,29
Asleep: see, Sleep
Asia, Roman province, *3*, 16:19
- salutations from churches of, *3*, 16:19

Assembly: see, Public worship
Association with immoral people, forbidden, 5:9
Atonement, 15:3,20
- metaphors used to describe, 1:30
- healing in the (?), 12:9

Authority,
- hierarchy of, 11:3,8
- Paul's apostolic, 1:1, 7:25, 11:17
- over the husband's body, 7:4
- over the wife's body, 7:4
- symbol of, a woman ought to have a, on her head, 11:10
- rule, and power, abolished by Christ, 15:24

Babes,
- in Christ, the Corinthians, 3:1
- in evil, be, 14:20

Banquets in idol's temple,
- to be avoided, 10:18ff
- Petronius' description of, 8:1
- *see also*, Meats sacrificed to idols

Baptism
- and circumcision not parallel, 7:14
- did Paul depreciate? 1:14,17
- for the dead, 15:29
- immersion, 10:2, 15:29
- in the name of, 1:13
- in (by) one Spirit, 12:13
- into Moses, 10:2
- into one body, 12:13
- not a figure, 10:2
- not a sign, 10:2
- of infants (?), 1:16, 7:14
- pictures death, burial, and resurrection, 15:29
- required of all, 6:11
- of suffering, 15:30
- vicarious (?), 15:29
- *see also*, Special Study #7

Baptismal formula, 1:13
Baptismal regeneration, 1:17
Barbarian, 14:11
Barnabas, refrained from working, 9:6
Battle, who will prepare for, 14:8
Believed, and "received" used synonymously, 15:2
Believers must hold fast, 15:2
Benedictions,
- in synagogue services, 12:3

Beyond, not to go, 4:6
Bless, blessing,
- used for giving thanks, 10:16, 11:24, 14:16
- when we are reviled, we, 4:12

Blood of Christ, 10:16
Boasting, not good, 5:6
- no flesh should, 1:29
- in men, prohibited, 3:21
- Paul's, about preaching *gratis*, 9:16

Body, bodies
- Christians are members of Christ's, 12:27
- Hebrew idea of, 10:16, 11:24

Index

Body, bodies, *continued*
    of Christ, 10:16
    of Christ, how to become members of, 10:17
    deliver my, to be burned, 13:3
    flesh and blood, described as, 15:50
    God composed the, 12:18,24
    God gives it (sown seed) a body, 15:38
    heavenly, earthly, 15:40
    judge the, rightly, 11:29
    metaphor for the church, 10:16, 11:29, 12:12ff
    mortal, 15:53
    natural, 15:44,46
    Paul buffeted his, 9:27
    one, many members, 12:12,17
    one bread, one, 10:17
    perishable, 15:42,50,53
    glorify God in your, 6:20
    members of Christ, 6:15
    "my, broken for you," 11:24
    temple of Holy Spirit, 6:19
    the members of the human, 12:12,14,17,20
    members of, concerned for one another, 12:25
    the One, 12:12,13
    the spiritual body, 15:44,46
    change from mortal to immortal, 15:53
    is for the Lord, 6:13
    sins committed outside the body, 6:18
    sins committed against the body, 6:18
    some members of, deemed less honorable, 12:23
    "this is my body," 11:24
    resurrection body: see, Resurrection body
    weaker members of, necessary, 12:22
    which is to be, 15:37
Boxing, 9:26
Brag, 13:4
Bread first, then cup, 10:16, 11:26
Bread, unleavened, 11:23
    the breaking of, 10:16, 11:24
    one, one body, 10:17
    we all partake of one, 10:17
Brother, sin against, 8:12
    strong and weak: see, "Strong and Weak Brothers"
Brothers of the Lord: see, Jesus' brothers

Bugle, used as an illustration, 14:8
Building,
    God's, 3:9
    metaphor of, 3:10
    materials used, 3:12
Burn, better to marry than, 7:9

Caesar, *11*
Call, on the name of the Lord, 1:2
    to become a Christian, 1:2
Called, let each remain in the condition, 7:20,24
Called by God, 1:9, 7:17
    to peace, 7:15
Calvin, Calvinism, Reformed theology
    commentary on 1 Corinthians, *25*
    doctrines of, based on 1 Corinthians, *25*, 1:8
    divine sovereignty, 12:28
    effectual call, 1:1,24
    eternal security, 3:12-15, 5:5, 6:10, 8:11, 9:27, 10:12, 15:2, 16:22
    federal theology, 7:14
    predestination, 1:18
    value of theistic arguments, view of, 1:21
    man is wholly passive in salvation, 1:30, 3:8
    hereditary total depravity, 1:30, 15:22,50
    first work of grace, 2:14
    presuppositionalism, 2:15
    sinful nature, 5:5, 9:27
    salvation is monergistic, 3:8
    second work of grace, 12:13
    sola gratia, 10:16
    sovereignty of God, 12:28
Canon, New Testament, 13:10
Carnality, 3:2,3
Catechumens, instruction of, 3:6
Celibacy, 7:1,7
Cephas: see, Peter
Cessation of spiritual gifts: see, Spiritual Gifts, to cease
Changed, we shall all be, 15:51
Channelers, mediums, spirits, 11:10
Chapters, bad division of, 11:1
Charismatic counterfeit, 13:10
Charismatic movement, 12:3,8,10, 14:2,5,11,12,15
    see also, Special Study #6

Index

Charity: see, Love.
Child, children,
    do not be, in thinking, 14:20
    unclean, offspring of mixed marriage not, 7:14
    when I was a, I thought as a, 13:11
    think, reason, as a, 13:11
Chloe's household, 1:11
Christ, active in OT times, 10:4
    all made alive in, 15:22
    ate with publicans and sinners, 15:33
    authority of, 15:27
    baptized into, 1:31
    became a life-giving spirit, 15:45
    belongs to God, 3:22
    betrayed, 11:23
    burial of, 15:4
    crucified, 2:2; 1:23
    death, 15:3
    death of, for others, 8:11
    deity of, 1:3,31, 8:6, 10:22
        see also, Special Study #5
    firstborn, 15:20
    first fruits, 15:23
    foundation of church, 3:10,11
    head of man, 11:3
    head of the church, 12:12
    higher criticism's portrayal of, 11:23
    incarnation, 10:22, 11:24, 15:20, 16:22
    instituted Lord's Supper, 11:23
    judges men, 4:4
    last Adam, 15:45
    liberty in, 6:12
    Lord, 1:2,3, 2:8, 8:6, 10:22, 12:3, 15:58, 16:7
    one Lord, 8:6
    ordained that those who preach the gospel live of the gospel, 9:14
    party at Corinth, 1:12
    post-resurrection appearances, 15:5ff
    pre-existence of, 10:4, 15:47
    reign till enemies, 15:26
    rose from the dead, 15:4,19,20
    second man, 15:47
    temporary subordination, 1:3, 3:22, 8:6, 11:3, 15:24,27
    the last Adam, 15:45
    the spiritual rock, 10:4
    the title of, 1:1,23
    to deliver up kingdom, 15:24

Christ, *continued*
    transfiguration, 15:44
    virgin birth, 15:47
    will subject himself to God, 15:28
Christian ethics: see Special Study #3.
Christian liberty, *18*, 8:9, 10:23ff
    defined, 10:28
    liberty in Christ, 6:12
    can become a stumbling-block to others, 8:9
    in areas of opinion, 1:10
    law and liberty, 6:12
    rights may be voluntarily waived, 8:13, 9:6ff, 10:32
    limitations on our liberty, 6:12ff, 8:9, 10:23ff
    why is my freedom judged by another's conscience, 10:29
Christians, 7:39
    belong to Christ, 3:23
    bought with a price, 6:20, 7:23
    humble rank of the early, 1:26ff
    members of the body of Christ, 12:27
    spoken of as "the called," 1:2
    tested by divisions, 11:19
    competent to judge their differences, 6:2
Christ's resurrection, 15:14ff
    a proof ours, 15:12
    an historical fact, 15:4
    God raised Jesus, 6:14
    see also, Special Study #7
Church, congregation, assembly, 11:18, 14:5, 12,19,23,33,34, 16:2
    as God's temple, 3:10,16
    at Corinth, *14,15*, 1:2
    buildings unknown, 16:19
    church discipline, 5:5
    local vs. universal, 1:2, 3:16, 10:32, 12:28, 15:9
    of God, give no offense to, 10:32
    of God, Paul persecuted, 15:9
    of the saints, 14:33
    parties at Corinth, 1:12, 15:1
    sanctity of, 1:3
    thankfulness for, 1:4
    body of Christ, *16*, 12:27
    pattern for, 4:17, 7:17, 11:16, 14:33, 16:8
    Scriptural names for, 1:2, 10:32
    Christ has one, 12:12

Index

Church discipline, 32
    reasons to practice it, 5:2
    proper procedure, 5:4ff
    penitents, restored to fellowship, 5:5
    see also, Special Study #2
Church polity, 20, 12:28, 14:29, 16:12,15
Circumcision,
    not parallel to baptism, 7:14
    unimportant, 7:18ff
Citizenship, Roman, privileges of, 15:32
Claudius, a famine in the time of, 7:26
Clergy and laity, 4:15
Cleverness of speech, 1:17
Cloud, pillar of, 10:1
    sometimes called "glory," 10:1
    see also, Shekinah
Collection for the poor at Jerusalem, *1,5*, 16:1
    Corinthians' previous knowledge of, 16:1
    churches of Galatia involved in, 16:1
    reasons for, 16:1
    put aside on the first day of the week, 16:2
    different words used for, 16:1
Colwell's rule of grammar, 3:16, 4:4
Commandments of God, keeping of, 7:19
Communication between Paul and Corinth
    from Corinth to Paul, *17*
    from Paul to Corinth, *18*, 5:9ff
    how many letters?, *18*
Communion: see, Lord's Supper.
Company, bad, corrupts good morals, 15:33
Condemned, along with the world, 11:32
Confession, 12:3
Conference at Jerusalem: see, Jerusalem
Conscience, 4:4
    defiled, 8:7
    weak, 8:7, 10:28
    emboldened by other's examples, 8:10
    eat, without asking questions for, 10:25,27
    do not eat for conscience sake, 10:28
    the informer's, 10:28
    wounded, 8:12
Consolation, prophecy speaks to men, for, 14:3
Consummation, 15:24
Contentious, if anyone is inclined to be, 11:16
Contextualization, 9:22
Continence, gift of, 7:7,9
Conversion, 14:25
Convicted, unbeliever is, by prophecy, 14:24

Corinth, 1:2
    Acrocorinth, *10,13,14*
    agora, *13*
    description of, *10*
    Diolkos, *10*
    harbors, *10,12*
    history, *10,11*
    location of, *10*
    destroyed by Mummius, *11*, 3:13
    rebuilt by Julius Caesar, *11*
    religions, *13*, 8:5
    morals, *13,14*, 5:1
Corinthian,
    brass, *12*, 13:12
    words, 2:4,13
Corinthianize, to, *13,15*
Corinthians, First epistle to, introduction
    authorship and attestation, *6*
    authenticity, 11:23
    date of writing, *6,23*
    genuineness, *6*
    integrity, *8*, 11:2, 13:1, 14:34
    occasion of writing, *22*
    outline of, *28ff*, 7:1,2
    place of writing, *23*, 16:8
    text, *9*, 2:2, 7:5,34, 10:9, 11:10,11,24, 15:5,46,49,51,56
    purpose, *22*
    history and influence of the letter, *24*
Corinthians, Second epistle to, introduction
    date and place of writing, *6*, 16:5
Corinthians,
    gross sinners, 6:10
    Paul converted, 4:15
    seal of Paul's apostleship, 9:2
    Paul expected the, to send him on his way, 16:6
Council at Jerusalem: see, Jerusalem
Council of Nicea, 9:5
Courts, Lower and Higher, 4:4
    cases started by Disciples of Christ, 6:7
Covenant,
    the old: see, Old Testament
    the new, 11:25
    or "testament," 11:25
    two Greek words translated, 11:25
Covetousness, 5:10, 6:10
Craftiness, 3:19
Creation, of man and woman, 11:8,9
    woman originates from man, 11:12

Index

Cremation, 15:43
Crispus, 1:14
    ruler of the synagogue, *4*, 1:14
    baptized by Paul, *1*, 1:14
Cross a stumbling block, 1:29
    foolishness, 1:23
    glory of, 1:19
    power of, 1:19
    power of God, 1:24
    wisdom of God, 1:24
Crown, incorruptible, 9:25
Cup,
    eat the bread, or drink the, 11:27
    of blessing: see, Lord's Supper
    of demons, 10:21
    of the Lord, 10:21
    this, is the new covenant in my blood, 11:25
Customs,
    concerning dress while worshiping, 11:4
    local, 11:15
    significance of, important, 11:4
    universal, in the churches, 11:16
Cymbal, 13:1

Darkness,
    hidden things of, brought to light, 4:5
Daughters, to be given in marriage? 7:25-38
Day of judgment, 1:8, 3:13
Day of our Lord Jesus Christ, 1:8, 5:5
Dead,
    baptism for: See under, Baptism, for the dead
    how raised up, 15:35,36
    raised imperishable, 15:52
Death, 3:22
    of Christ: see, Christ, death
    since by man came, 15:21,22
    sting of, 15:55,56
    the last enemy, 15:36
    swallowed up in victory, 15:54,55
Death angel, 5:7
Debater of this age, 1:20
Debts not canceled, 7:17
Deceived, do not be, 6:9, 15:33
Defense, Paul's, 9:3
Deity of Christ: see Christ, deity.
Delivery to Satan, 5:5
Demetrius and the silversmiths, *5*, 15:32, 16:9

Demons, 2:6, 11:10
    led astray by, 12:2
    reality of, 10:20
    and idol worship, 10:20
    sacrifices to, 10:20
    participation in, prohibited, 10:20
    someone under influence of, curses Jesus, 12:3
Denominations, body of Christ not made up of, 12:20
Desire, 10:6
Destroy, destroyed,
    by serpents, Israel was, 10:9
    the temple of God, 3:17
    exclude from salvation, 3:17
    weak brothers may be, 8:11
Destroyer, destroyed by the, 10:10
Destruction of Jerusalem (AD 70), 3:13, 7:26
Devil: see Satan
Directed, churches of Galatia, concerning offering, 16:1
Discern not body, 11:29
Discerning of spirits, 12:10, 14:29
Discipline, church: see, Church Discipline
Disciplined, by the Lord, 11:32
Discrepancies in Scripture, alleged,
    between 1 Corinthians 8 & 1 Corinthians 10, 8:4
    how many perished in wilderness, 10:8
    between Acts 15:29 and 1 Corinthians 10, 10:20
    in accounts of Lord's Supper, 11:23
    between 14:22 and 14:25, 14:24
    between 11:2-16 and 14:34, 14:34
    between Rom. 16:5 and 1 Corinthians 16:15, 16:15
Dispensationalism, 9:17, 10:18
Dispensations: see, Ages
Dissensions
    in church at Corinth, *15-17*, 1:10ff, 11:18
    fatal temptation of partyism, 1:2
    God wants no, in the body, 12:25
Disunity condemned, 1:10
Divine initiative, 1:30
Divisions, factions
    four in number at Corinth (?), *17*, 1:12
    sinful, 1:10, 3:17, 12:21
    actual leaders claimed, not named (?), 4:6
    adversely affect public worship, 11:18

Index

Divisions, factions, *continued*
    help make party leaders who are approved evident, 11:19
    no division in the body, 12:25
Divorce, 7:27
    attempts to harmonize NT verses on, difficult, 7:10
    ends a marriage, 7:8
    "exception clause," 7:10
    Christians not permitted to, 7:10,11,14
    Christ's teaching on, 7:10
    Jewish doctrine concerning, 7:10,11
    Roman law concerning, 7:11
    Scriptural grounds for, 7:15
    willful desertion by an unbeliever results in, 7:15
Door, metaphor of a, 16:9
Dress,
    customs concerning, while worshiping, 11:4
    must women wear a head-covering? 11:6
Drink
    all drank the same spiritual, 10:4
    of one Spirit, 12:13
    whether you eat or, do all to glory of God, 10:31
    all made to drink of one, 12:13
    let us eat and, 15:32
Drunkards, 5:11, 6:10
Dualism, 6:13

Earth, is the Lord's, 10:26
Easter, 5:8
Eat, eating,
    as fellowship, 10:18
    "at church," 11:22
    let us, and drink, 15:32
Ebionites, 1:12
Ecstasy, 12:10, 13:1, 14:32
Edify, edification, 8:1, 14:1,26
    not all things, 10:23
    love edifies, 8:1
    seek to abound for the, of the church, 14:12
Effects, variety of, 12:5,6
Effeminate, 6:9
Egalitarian emphases, 11:3,11
End, then comes the, 15:24

Enemies,
    all Christ's, put under his feet, 15:25
    last, destroyed is death, 15:25
Enemy of the Lord, 10:22
Envy: see Jealousy
Ephesus,
    Paul fought beasts at, 15:32
    Apollos at Ephesus, 16:12
    Aquila and Priscilla at, 16:19
    I shall remain in, until Pentecost 16:8
    open door at, 16:9
Epicureanism condemned, 15:32
Epispasm, 7:18
Epistolary aorist: see, Aorist tense
Erastus, 5, 16:10,12
Escape, the way of, 10:13
Eschatology, 6:14
Esoteric doctrine, 2:7,13
Essenes, 1:12
Ethics, Christian: see Special Study #3.
Evil (wrong suffered), 13:5
Examine,
    himself, Paul does not, 4:3
    himself, let a man, 11:28
    Lord, the one who, Paul, 4:4
    results of lack of, 11:30
Examples, 10:6,11
Excommunication, 5:2
    see also, Church discipline
    three parties active in the work of, 5:4
    of impenitent wicked, commanded, 5:13
Exhorted, exhortation,
    prophecy speaks to men, for, 14:3
    to be steadfast, 15:58
    all may be, 14:31
Extortioners: see, Swindlers

Factions: see, Divisions, factions
Faith,
    a "body of doctrine," 2:5, 16:13
    comes by hearing the Word of God, 4:15, 12:9
    without love, 13:2
    a spiritual gift called, 12:9, 13:2
    A lasting virtue, 13:13
    stand firm in the, 16:13
    is vain, if no resurrection, 15:14,17
Faith only, 6:11
Faithfulness, a condition of salvation, 1:21

Index

Fall,
- lest he, let a man take heed, 10:12
- on his face, 14:25

False doctrine, 3:12

Fasting, 7:5

Father, fathers
- spiritual, 4:15
- Israelites called our, 10:1

Feast, celebrate the, 5:8

Fellowship,
- with Christ, 1:9
- a word for offering, 16:1,2

Fellow-workers, God's, 3:9

Feminist movement, 11:2

Field, God's, 3:9

Financial support, ch.9, 16:11
- Paul's right to, 9:4
- arguments that ministers should receive, 9:7ff
- he who sows spiritual things reaps material things, 9:11
- Lord has ordained, for those who preach the gospel, 9:14

Fire, man's work tested by, 3:13
- figurative use of, 3:13
- saved as through, 3:15

First day of the week, 11:18, 16:2

First fruits, 15:20,23
- of Achaia, 16:15

Five hundred, Jesus appeared to, 15:6

Flee,
- fornication, 6:18
- idolatry, 10:14

Flesh, 2:14,
- men of, 3:1
- the variety of, 15:39
- destruction of the, 5:5
- sinful nature (?), 5:5
- *see also* under Calvinism, hereditary total depravity

Flesh and blood cannot inherit, 15:50

Flock, one who tends, entitled to milk, 9:7

Flute, used as an illustration, 14:7

Food,
- for the stomach, 6:13
- will not commend us to God, 8:8
- not eat, if it causes a brother to stumble, 8:13
- spiritual, all ate the same, 10:3

Foolish, 3:18
- things, chosen of God, 1:27

Foolish, *continued*
- wisdom of this world is, 1:20, 3:19

Foolishness, 1:18
- crucified Messiah, thought, 1:23
- of God, 1:25
- of the message preached, 1:21

Fools for Christ's sake, 4:10

Fornication, 5:1, 6:9, 6:12
- body not for, 6:13
- flee, command to, 6:18

Fornicators, 23,000 fell, 10:8
- keep no company with, 6:9

Fortunatus, 16:15,17

Foundation,
- Christ, the only, 3:11
- Paul laid the, of the church at Corinth, 3:10
- others to be careful how they build upon the, 3:12

Freedman, freedmen, *11*
- as distinct from a free man, 7:22
- Corinth populated with, *11*

Freedom in Christ: see Christian liberty

Gaius, *1*, 1:14
- baptism of, 1:14

Galatia, churches of, 16:1

Gallio, proconsul of Achaia, *4*

Games, regarding the, 9:24
- Isthmian, *11,12*, 9:24
- Olympian, *11*, 9:24

Gentiles,
- Corinthians were, 12:2, 15:1
- Jewish attitudes toward, 1:28
- Paul became "without law," to win, 9:21

Gentleness, spirit of, 4:21

Gifts, Spiritual: see, Spiritual Gifts

Giving, nine words for, 16:2
- as each has been prospered, 16:2

Glorify God, 6:20

Glory, 2:7
- of God, do all to, 10:31
- of heavenly and earthly bodies, 15:40
- *see also* under, Shekinah

Glorying: see, Boasting

Gnostics, gnosticism, *16,25*, 1:5,17, 2:6, 12:8, 15:1

Gold and silver, 3:12

Index

God,
- all in all, 15:28
- all things are of, 11:12
- causes growth, 3:6
- deep things of, 2:10
- faithfulness of, 1:9, 10:13
- father, 8:6, 15:24
- foolishness of, 1:20, 1:25
- from whom are all things, 8:6
- gives us the victory, 15:57
- has put all things in subjection under His feet, 15:27
- placed the members in the body, 12:18
- no knowledge of, 15:34
- power of, 1:18,24, 2:5
- what is it to know, 1:21
- weakness of, 1:25
- the only God, 8:4,6
- is head of Christ, 11:3
- is not a God of confusion, but of peace, 14:33
- is among you, declaring that, 14:25
- wisdom of, 1:21

Godhead, 8:4,6, 12:6
God's building, 3:9
God's husbandry, 3:9
Gods, many so-called, 8:6
- Greek idea of a "god," 1:23

Gong, noisy, 13:1
Gospel,
- by which you are saved, 15:2
- preached by Paul, 15:1
- defined, 15:3
- not dependent on human cleverness, 1:26ff
- preached *gratis*, 9:18
- received by the Corinthians, 15:1
- *see also*, Word of the cross.

Governmental theory, 15:3
Grace, 1:3
- of God, 1:4, 3:10, 15:10
- saying, at mealtime, 10:30
- Grace and peace, 1:3
- of the Lord be with you, 16:23
- second work of (?), 12:13

Grain, bare, sown, 15:37
Greeks, give no offense to, 10:32
Growth, God was causing the, 3:6,7
Grumble, Israel did, 10:10
Guilty of the body and blood of the Lord, 11:27

Habit, not to become slaves of, 6:12
Hades, 15:55
Hair,
- given to women, as a covering, 11:15
- long and short, 11:4
- long hair a disgrace to men, 11:4
- long hair a glory for women, 11:15
- long hair a dishonor to men, 11:14
- long hair "instead of" veil, 11:15
- short hair, a disgrace to women, 11:6

Harlot, members with, 6:15
Harp, used as an illustration, 14:7
Hay, 3:12
Head,
- disgraces his, 11:4
- of man is Christ, 11:3
- of woman is the man, 11:3
- of Christ is God, 11:3

Head covering,
- hair, not veil (?), 11:6
- of women, 11:5
- of men, 11:4,7

Healings, gifts of, 12:9,28
Heart,
- secrets of, disclosed, 14:25
- of man, 2:9

Heaven, 2:7,9, 3:14, 4:8, 9:25, 10:1, 15:18,50
- so-called gods in, 8:5
- Lord's Supper not observed in, 11:26

Hell, Hades, no distinction in KJV, 15:55
- fires of, 3:13
- "perish" refers to, 15:18

Helps, a spiritual gift, 12:28
Higher criticism, 3:18
- portrayal of Christ, 11:23
- *see also*, Special Study #5
- debate on who instituted the Lord's Supper, 11:24

Historical allusions, *1*
Historie vs. *Geschichte*, 15:4,11,20
Holiness: see, Sanctification.
Helps, 12:28
Holy,
- children of mixed marriages are, 7:14
- in body and spirit, unmarried may be, 7:34
- temple of God is, 3:17

Holy kiss,
- greet one another with a, 16:20
- why no more? 16:20
- an ordinance? 16:20

Index

Holy Spirit
- baptism in, 12:13, 14:5
- different measures or activities of, 12:13
- demonstrated the truth of Paul's preaching, 2:4
- and Paul's plans, 16:9
- deity of, implied, 2:11
- denial of his personality by Jehovah's Witnesses, 12:11
- drink of, 12:13
- dwells in the temple (church), 3:16
- gave words, 2:13
- his work in conversion, 12:3,13, 14:24
- indwelling gift of, 6:19, 12:13
- joy of, see Special Study #10
- not source of some "speaking," 12:3
- body is temple of, 6:19
- manifestation of, for profit of all, 12:7
- no one speaking by, curses Jesus, 12:3
- personality of, 12:6,11
- quenching of, 14:32
- searches all things, 2:10
- tests by which his leading may be discerned, 12:1ff
- washed, sanctified, justified, in the, 6:11

Homosexuality, 6:9, 11:6

Hope,
- a lasting virtue, 13:13
- if we have, in Christ, only in this life, 15:19

Household, 1:16, 16:15

Human wisdom, no merit in, 2:6

Hungry, some left, at love feasts, 11:21

Husband
- each woman, has her own, 7:2
- of unbelievers, 7:12
- wives learn from, at home, 14:35
- must fulfill his duty to his wife, 7:3
- if dead, widow is free to remarry, 7:39
- who is an unbeliever, 7:12

"I am of Christ," Paul's words, 1:12, 3:21,22

Idol,
- accustomed to an, some men are, 8:7
- dumb, 12:2
- is nothing, 8:4, 10:19
- sacrifices, 8:1,4

Idol feasts, not permitted, 10:1,14,18
- sitting at, 8:10,

Idolaters, 5:10, 10:7

Idolatry forbidden, 10:14

Idols, eating of meat offered to: see, Meat, sacrificed to idols

Ill-mannered, 13:5

Image, of earthly and heavenly, 15:49

Imitators of Paul, be, 4:16, 11:1

Immoral, immorality, 5:1
- Corinth a cesspool of, *13*
- a kind of, not approved by Gentiles, 5:1
- sin against the body, 6:18
- body not for, 6:13
- do not act immorally, 10:8
- worship of idols, conducive to, 10:8

Immortal, immortality
- see Special Study #9: after chapter 15 notes
- must be put on, 15:53

Immovable, be, 15:58

Impanation, 11:24

In Christ, 1:2
- all blessings, 1:31
- the final word, 16:24

Incest, the case of, 5:1

Increase: see, Growth, God was causing the

Inerrancy of Scripture, 4:19, 16:7

Infant baptism (?), 1:16, 7:14

Ingratitude, 4:7

Inherit, the kingdom, 15:50

Inquisition, 4:21, 5:5

Inspiration, *10*, 1:16, 2:13, 4:17, 7:12,25,40, 10:8, 12:3, 16:7
- verbal, 2:13
- demonic, 12:3

Inspired writings lost (?), *20,21*

Instruction, 11:17, 14:31

Intercourse,
- only within the bounds of marriage, 6:16, 7:9
- good, not to touch a woman, 7:1
- abstinence from, for devotional purposes, a concession, 7:5

Intermediate state, disembodied spirits in (?), 15:37,40

Intermediate trip to Corinth: see under, Paul

Interpreter of tongues required, 14:26

Interpretation of tongues,
- gift of, 12:10,30, 14:5,13
- pray that he may, 14:13

Isaiah, reference to, 1:18, 2:16, 14:21, 15:54

Index

Isis and Osiris,
    priests of, deceived worshipers, 12:2
Israel, Israelites
    example to Christians, 10:6
    wanderings of, 10:1
    God not well pleased with, 10:5
    ate sacrifices, shared in the altar, 10:18
    laid low in the wilderness, 10:5
Israel's history no myth, 10:11
Isthmian Games: see, Games

James, Lord's brother, 15:7
    Jesus appeared to, 15:7
    people named, in New Testament, 15:7
Jealousy, 3:3, 13:4
    do we provoke the Lord to, 10:22
Jehovahism, 15:4
Jerusalem,
    conference at (Acts 15), *4,15*, 8:1,8, 10:20
    Corinthians and Acts 15 harmonized, 10:20
    destruction of (AD 70): see, Destruction of Jerusalem
    offering for poor at: see, Collection
Jesus' brothers, 9:6
    their names, 9:6
Jesus ordained support of preachers, 9:14
Jew, Jews
    Paul became a, to win Jews, 9:20
    give no offense to, 10:32
Job, quoted by Paul, 3:19
Judaism,
    classic, distinct from diaspora, 9:20
Judaizers, 1:12, 12:3
Judas Iscariot
    betrayed Jesus, 11:23
    present (?) at institution of Lord's Supper, 11:23
Judge, judging,
    angels, 6:3
    "appraised," an Athenian law term, 2:14, 4:3,4
    for yourselves, 10:15, 11:13
    outsiders, 5:12
    church members, 5:12
    wise men are to, 10:15
    the body rightly, 11:29

Judge, judging, *continued*
    if we, ourselves, we would not be, 11:31
    three Greek words translated, 6:2, 14:24
    unrighteous, 6:1
Judgment, 4:4
    appeal to the Corinthians to be united in the same, 1:10
    Corinthians to stop passing, 4:5
    daily, by the Lord, 4:4
    man's ability, 2:14
    final, 3:13, 4:5, 6:2, 11:32
    eats and drinks, to himself, 11:28
    let others pass, 14:29
Justification, 1:30, 6:11, 15:22

Kerygma
    see under Neo-liberalism
Kindness, 13:4
Kings, you have become, without us, 4:8
Kingdom of God, 6:10
    flesh and blood cannot inherit, 15:50
    does not consist in words, 4:20
    unrighteous shall not inherit, 6:9
    Christ will deliver up the, to God, 15:24
    two manifestations of, in New Testament, 15:50
    term, rarely used outside of Gospels, 4:20
    a millennial (?), 15:12,24
Kiss, Holy: see, Holy kiss
Knowledge,
    ignorance without love, 8:1
    compared to an image in a mirror, 13:12
    done away, 13:8
    spiritual gift called, 1:5, 12:8, 13:2,8, 14:6
    mystical, 1:5
    of God, some have no, 15:34
    can make arrogant, 8:1
    we all have, 8:1
    word of, 12:8
    we know in part, 13:9,12
"Know ye not" key to ch. 6, 6:2
Korah, Dathan, and Abiram, 10:10
Kosher food, 10:25

Index

Labor,
- different words for, 3:8, 4:12, 15:10,58, 16:16
- is not in vain in the Lord, 15:58

Laborer, has a right to a living wage, 9:7,8

Language, languages
- many kinds of, in the world, 12:10, 14:10
- tongues at Corinth, were, 12:10, 14:2,9,10,11,21
- no kind is without meaning, 14:10
- barbarian, one who doesn't know the meaning of, 14:11

Last days, meaning of, 10:11

Last trump, 15:52

Law of Christ, 9:21

Law of Moses, 14:21
- forbad intermarriage with pagans, 7:14
- Paul was not under the, 9:21
- teaches that ministers to be supported, 9:8ff
- abrogated by the new covenant, 9:8, 11:25, 14:34
- under the, Paul became, to win others, 9:20
- teaches wives to be submissive, 14:34
- the power of sin is the, 15:56

Lawful, all things are, 6:12

Lawsuits at Corinth, 6:1,7

Leaders, proper estimate of, 3:4ff, 4:1ff

Leaven,
- old, to be purged, 5:7
- little, leavens whole lump, 5:6

Legalism, 9:22

Lent, 7:5

Letters of commendation, *21*, 16:3

Letters of Paul,
- group two, *1*
- follow first-century format, 1:1
- lost letters? 5:9
- "a previous letter"? see: Previous letter
- "a severe letter"? see: Severe letter

Libertinism, 6:13, 9:21

Life, 3:22

Lifeless things, 14:7

Litigation, *18*, 6:1

Litotes, 7:40, 10:5, 11:22, 15:58

Living soul, 15:45

Local autonomy, 5:4

Lord: see under, Christ

Lord's Day, 11:20,26, 16:2

Lord's Supper,
- bread, leavened or unleavened, 11:23
- cup of blessing, 10:17
- cup of the Lord, 10:21
- disorders at, 11:18
- dynamic view, vs. real view, 11:24
- early use of, 11:20
- eating and drinking in an unworthy manner, 11:27
- examination, self, in preparation for, 11:28
- fermented wine used (?), 11:21
- for whom intended, 11:27
- frequency of observance, 11:25,26
- indispensable part of public worship, 11:20
- instituted by Jesus, 11:23ff
- Lutheran doctrine of, 11:24
- names for, 11:24
- nature of, 11:34
- open or closed communion, 11:27
- partaking in unison (?), 11:33
- prayers of thanks at, 11:24
- result of partaking in an unworthy manner, 11:30
- table of the Lord, 10:21
- when observed, 11:18,20,26
- "do this in remembrance of Me," 11:24,25
- typified in Old Testament (?), 10:4
- "you proclaim the Lord's death," 11:26

Loss, if a man's work is burned up, he shall suffer, 3:15

Love,
- "charity" in KJV, 13:3
- characteristics of, 13:4-7
- the more excellent way, 12:31
- the motive that controls the use of gifts, 13:1ff
- demands not its rights, 13:7
- a lasting virtue, 13:13
- edifies, 8:1
- if any one does not, the Lord, 16:22
- my, be with you all, 16:24
- pursue after, 14:1
- necessity of, 13:1-3

Index

Love, *continued*
    permanence of, 13:8-13
    love ranked above faith, 13:13
    the greatest thing, 13:13
    four Greek words for, 13:1, 16:22
    let all you do be done in, 16:14
    Love feasts, instructions for proper behavior at, 11:33ff
    purpose of, 11:17
    abused, 11:20,21
    description of, 11:17
    abuses growing out of, 11:20,21
    some are drunk, 11:21
    history of its observance, 11:34
Lower and Higher Courts, 4:4
Luther's,
    conjecture concerning Paul's marriage, 7:8
    comment on bodily member's care for others, 12:26
    low view of epistle of James, 3:12

Macedonia, 16:5
    Paul's travels through, *2*, 16:5
Mad, will they not say you are, 14:23
Malice, 5:8
Man,
    carnal, 3:1,3
    created in image of God, 15:45
    is head of woman, 11:3
    image and glory of God, 11:7
    man saves others, how, 9:22
    natural, 2:14
    not independent of woman, 11:11
    body, soul, and spirit, 2:14
    spiritual, 2:15, 3:1, 12:1
Manna, 10:3
Manumission, 6:20
Maran atha or Marana tha (?), *3*, 16:22
Marble, 3:12
Marriage and marriages, *18*
    alleged low view of, held by Paul, 7:1
    broken by desertion, 7:15
    not disparaged, 7:1
    questions in reference to: ch. 7
    Jesus' teaching on marriage, 7:10ff
    to pagans, 7:12-16
    Paul's advice about in times of distress, 7:26

Marriage, marriages, *continued*
    Paul's teaching about, did not change, 7:1
    Paul's teaching about mixed marriages, 7:12ff
    the children of mixed marriages, 7:14
    rights and obligations, 7:1ff
    second marriages, 7:28,39
    temporary abstinence from marital relations, 7:5
    only in the Lord, 7:39
    better to marry, than burn, 7:9
    married, concerned about things of the world, 7:33
Masterbuilder, 3:10
Meat,
    buying in a market, ch. 10
    clean and unclean, 8:1, 10:25
    eating of, if purchased in market, 10:23
    eating of, in friend's home, 10:27ff
    eating of, in idol's temple, forbidden, 10:14ff
    sacrificed to idols, *22*, 8:1ff, 10:14ff
Meat market, 8:1, 10:23ff
Mediatorial kingdom, 15:24,25,28
Membership, transfer of, 1:2
    voting on church, 5:12
Men, ordinary, not inspired, 2:4
    women mutually dependent, 11:12
    in your thinking, be, 14:20
Messianic,
    prophecy in Mosaic terminology, 15:25
    Psalm 8, is it a messianic psalm? 15:27
Methods, leaders to be careful about, 3:12
Milk and meat (solid food), 3:2
Mind,
    be of the same, 1:10
    become sober, 15:34
    of Christ, 2:16
    reading a man's, 2:11
    my, is unfruitful, 14:14
Ministers of Christ, 3:5, 4:1
    due support, 9:7
Ministry, to the saints, 16:15
    mutual, 3:5
Ministries, variety of, 12:5
Miracles, 12:28
    signs of an apostle, 9:1
    effecting of, 12:10
Mirrors, 13:12

Index

Mixed marriages, 7:12ff
Moment, we shall be changed in a, 15:52
Monism, 8:4
Moral influence theory, 15:3
Morals, bad company corrupts good, 15:33
Mortal: see, Body, mortal
Morality, the new, in Christ, 5:1
Morality, the old, at Corinth, 5:1
Mormonism, 15:29
Moses,
    apocalypse of, 7:19
    baptized into, 10:2
    law of: see Law of Moses
    rock struck by, 10:4
Motives,
    of men's hearts revealed, 4:5
    human, 15:32
Mountains, moving of, 13:2
Mourning, 5:2
Mummius, fire at Corinth in time of, *11,14*, 3:13
Murmuring, 10:10
Mystery, mysteries, 2:1, 13:2, 15:51
    of redemption, 2:7
    of the gospel, 2:7
    of bodily transformation of the living, 15:51
    of God, stewards of the, 4:1
    by the Spirit, he speaks, 14:2
Mystery religions, *13*, 2:1,7

Name,
    of the Lord, in the, 5:4, 6:11
    of the church: see under, Church
Natural man, 2:14
Nature, teaches about long hair, 11:14,15
Neighbor, seek the good of the, 10:24
Neo-liberalism
    Bultmann on Paul's theology, 4:16
    Bultmannian scholars on resurrection, 15:35
    kerygma vs. *didache*, 2:6, 15:12
    demythologization, 15:12
New birth, 4:15
New covenant, 11:25
New Testament canon, 13:10
Nine words for giving, 16:2
Noble, not many called, 1:26
Not to eat with, 5:11

Oath, solemn affirmation under, 15:31
Offense, give no, 10:32
Offering for the poor at Jerusalem: See, Collection
Old Testament,
    use of in the New, 1:18, 14:21
    see also, Quotations often free
    written for our sakes, 9:10
    examples, written for our instruction, 10:11
    summary of expectations concerning Messiah and His kingdom, 15:25
    used by way of accommodation, 14:21
Open door, at Ephesus, 16:9
Opinion,
    judgment, 7:25
    matters of, 9:22
Oral traditions: see, Traditions
Ox, not muzzle, while threshing, 9:9

Pagans,
    when you were, 12:2
    were led astray to dumb idols, 12:2
Paragraphing, questions of, 3:18, 4:21, 15:50
Parousia, 15:23
Part,
    know in, prophesy in, 13:9
    that which is in, shall be done away, 13:10
Participation,
    in the blood of Christ, 10:16
    in demons, 10:20
    those who eat, in the altar, 10:18
Passover,
    Christ our, 5:7
    a church observance (?), 5:8
Patience, 13:4
Pattern for the church: see under, Church, pattern for
Paul,
    a called apostle, 1:1
    a free man, 9:1
    a great scholar, 2:1
    a true apostle, 9:1,3
    absent in body, present in spirit, 5:3
    and Apollos, 3:5, 4:6
    his apostleship rejected by some at Corinth, *15*, 1:1, 9:1,2

Index

Paul, *continued*
- anxious, lest he be disqualified, 9:27
- at Ephesus till Pentecost, 16:9
- authenticated this epistle, 16:21
- a wise masterbuilder, 3:10
- baptized converts, 1:17
- became their father through the gospel, 4:15
- called to be an apostle, 1:1
- calendar of his travels, *6,7*
- caught up to paradise, 13:1
- conscious of nothing against himself, 4:4
- converted the Corinthians, 4:15
- did not deny inspiration, 7:12, 25
- did not hold a low view of marriage, 7:1
- dies daily, 15:31
- empowered like the other apostles, 3:10
- father in the faith to the Corinthians, 4:15
- fear and trembling as he came to Corinth, 2:3
- fought wild beasts at Ephesus, 15:32
- gave up his right to financial support, 9:12,15
- grace of God given to, 3:10
- inspiration of, *2,10*, 7:1,12,25,40, 14:37
- intermediate trip to Corinth, *5,22*, 4:19, 16:5,7
- Jesus appeared to, 15:8
- labored more than all, 15:10
- least of all the apostles, 15:9
- Luke's gospel reflects Paul's preaching, 2:2
- men's opinion of, thought little, 4:3
- method of preaching, 2:1ff, 3:1ff
- not mixed up concerning time of second advent, 15:51
- other apostles preached same gospel, 15:11
- persecuted the church, 15:9
- physical condition of (?),weakness, 2:3
- planted, 3:8
- promised to go to Corinth, 4:21
- refrained from working, 9:6
- refused to speak "tongues," 14:6
- renounced sophistry, 2:4
- revelations given to, by Christ, 7:10, 11:2,23, 15:3

Paul, *continued*
- said, "Be imitators of me," 4:16, 11:1
- saw the risen Lord, 9:1
- seal of his apostleship, 9:2
- sent Timothy, 4:17
- spoke in tongues, at times, 13:1, 14:18
- stewardship entrusted to him, 9:17
- success, not a failure in Athens, 2:2
- taught virgin birth, 15:49
- travel plans, 4:19, 11:34, 16:3ff
- twice took offerings to Jerusalem, 16:4
- under compulsion to preach, 9:16
- unmarried, when he writes 1 Corinthians, 7:7,8
- untimely born, 15:8
- wanted to be fellow-partaker of the gospel, 9:23
- was friend of Apollos, 16:12
- was he (ever) married? 7:8
- visits to Corinth, *2,22*, 2:1, 14:6, 16:5ff
- warning about abuse of liberty, 8:9
- plans made like ours, 16:7,9
- wise precaution, 16:3
- witness that Christ rose from the dead, 15:4
- writes to admonish, not shame, 4:14

Peace, 1:3
- God has called us to, 7:15

Pentecost, 2, 16:8

Pentecostal movement, 12:8,9,13, 14:2,3,12, 14,24

Perfect,
- that which is, 13:10
- in your thinking, be, 14:20

Perish, perishing,
- weak brothers caused to, 8:11
- those who have fallen asleep in Jesus, have, 15:18

Permits, if the Lord, 16:7

Persecution, 7:26

Pesher style of interpretation, 1:19

Peter,
- a married man, 9:5
- his "party" at Corinth, 1:12
- his ministry at Corinth (?), 1:12, 9:5
- post-resurrection appearance of Jesus to, 15:5

Philosophy,
- Greek, at root of problems at Corinth, *16*, 6:13, 7:1, 9:4, 15:1

Index

Philosophy, *continued*
    Greek, alleged source of Paul's ideas, 15:46
    false systems invalidated by Jesus' resurrection, 15:20

Place of writing of this epistle, 16:5,8

Play, sat down to eat and drink, and stood up to, 10:7

Plowman, ought to plow in hope, 9:10

Polygamy, 7:2

Poor, 11:22, 13:3, 16:1

Power, 4:20
    apostolic, 4:20
    body is raised in, 15:43
    of God, 1:18,24, 2:5
    of party leaders, 4:20
    of our Lord Jesus, 5:4
    rule, authority, and, abolished by Christ, 15:24

Praise,
    each man shall have, from God, 4:5
    I praise you, because you remember me in everything, 11:2
    I do not praise you, in this instruction, 11:17,22

Pray, 11:4
    with understanding, 14:14
    impossible to join in, when prayer is in unknown tongue, 14:16
    in a tongue, my spirit, 14:14
    with the spirit, and with the mind, 14:15
    that my ministration for Jerusalem be acceptable, 16:1

Prayer, 7:5
    public, 11:4

Preach, preaching,
    nature of true Christian, 1:18ff
    if Christ is not raised, our, is vain, 15:14
    work of the apostles, 1:17, 15:11
    a "simplicity" in Paul's (?), 1:12, 2:2
    by women, 11:5, 14:34
    not synonymous with "prophesying," 11:4
    so we, and so you believed, 15:11

Precious stones, 3:12

Predestination, 1:18

Pre-existence of Christ: see Christ, Pre-existence.

Present distress, 7:26

Previous letter (?), *19ff*, 5:9, 10:1, 16:1

Price, Christians bought with a, 6:20

Pride, 4:6,18, 5:21, 12:21, 13:4

Priesthood, Jewish, 9:13
    perquisites, 9:13

Principles,
    grand guiding, behind Paul's instructions, 7:17ff, 8:1ff, 10:1ff, 10:31, 11:2ff, 12:1ff

Priscilla: see Aquila and Prisc(ill)a

Prize, one receives, in a race, 9:24

Progressive revelation, 16:24

Prohibitions, in Greek, 3:18, 7:23

Prophecy,
    all may learn from, 14:31
    greater gift than tongues, 14:2,5
    inspired speaking in native language, 12:10
    without love, 13:2
    spiritual gift of, 11:4, 12:10,29, 13:2, 14:1
    under-estimated by the Corinthians, 14:2
    sign for believers, 14:22
    in part, 13:9
    speaks to men, 14:3
    to be desired, 14:1
    done away, 13:8
    rules regarding use of this gift, 14:29ff
    this gift edifies the church, 14:3ff
    this gift convicts unbelievers, 14:24
    two kinds of, in early church (?), 11:4, 12:10, 14:24,29

Prophesying, 11:4, 14:39

Prophetesses, 11:5

Prophets,
    God appointed, in the church, 12:28
    foundation of the church, 12:28
    rules for, 14:29ff
    spirits of, subject to the prophets, 14:32

Propitiation: see, Atonement.

Prosper, put aside and save as he may, 16:2

Prostitution, 5:1, 6:15
    see also, Harlot.

Providence, 1:14, 4:19, 7:17, 15:38, 16:4

Provoked, 13:5

Psalm, each one has a, 14:26

Public opinion, court of, 4:3

Public worship, *18*, 14:26
    assembly, 5:4, 11:18, 14:23,26
    call on the name of the Lord, 1:2

Index

Public worship, *continued*
    for the better, 11:17
    Christ is the object of worship, 1:2, 11:2
    divisions adversely affect, 11:18
    edification at, emphasized, 14:1ff
    rebuke of disorder at, *18*, 11:2ff
    individual participation in, 14:26ff
    instructions concerning, 14:26ff
    let all things be done properly, 14:40
    singing in, 14:15,26
    praying in, 11:4,5, 14:15,26
    prophesying in, 11:4,5,6
    teaching given, 14:6,26
    instruction given, 14:19
    offerings received at, 16:2
    orderliness is important, 14:26ff
    revelations given, 14:6,26
    tongues and interpretation, 14:26
    in the language of the people, 14:19
    let all be done to edification, 14:26
    visitors at, 14:23,24
    understanding what is being spoken is important, 14:6ff
    ungifted at, 14:16,23
    women participating in, 11:5
    see also, Special Study #6: Worship in the New Testament
Punctuation,
    marks, none in original manuscripts 1:13
    questions of, 1:22, 6:7, 9:3,18, 10:29, 12:14,24, 15:29,32
    chapter and verse breaks, 11:1
Purgatory, 3:12,13, 11:32

Quartodeciman controversy, 5:7
Questions,
    expecting a negative answer, 1:13, 9:4, 10:19,22, 12:29
    expecting a positive answer, 10:16,18, 11:14
Quotations often free, 1:31, 3:20, 14:21
    of Old Testament, how introduced, 1:18, 3:19, 4:6

Rabbinical teaching, 5:1, 8:1, 9:20, 10:1,4,25, 14:16,34, 15:45
Race, analogy of, 9:24
Ranks in God's church, 12:28
Redaction criticism, 1:19, 7:10, 15:3
Red Sea, 10:1
Redemption in Christ, 1:31
Refreshed, my spirit and yours, 16:18
Reign,
    you have come to, without us, 4:8
    Christ must, 15:25
    with Christ, 4:8
Remain in the condition when called, 7:20, 24,26
Remarriage, 7:27,28
Renovation of the universe, 7:31
Repentance, 5:5
Restoration Movement, 1:17, 4:15, 7:12, 10:16, 11:5
Resurrection, Christ's: see, Christ's resurrection
Resurrection,
    arguments for the doctrine of, 15:1ff
    arguments against the, of Jesus, unbelievable, 15:7
    God will raise the body, 6:14
    someone at Corinth says there is no, 15:1,12
    vital truth, 15:1,13ff,19
    illustrated by analogy of wheat, 15:37
    order of, 15:12,23
    proofs of the, of Jesus, 15:4
    righteous and wicked all raised, 15:22
Resurrection body,
    described, 15:44
    dissolution but continuity, 15:36
    how raised, 15:36ff
    nature of, 15:39ff
    diversity but identity, 15:39
    imperishable, spiritual, 15:42ff,50
    objections to, considered, 15:35ff
    whence? 15:38
Revelation (God's), 1:7, 2:10, 14:6
    completed, 13:10
    of Jesus Christ, 1:7
    if a, is made, let the first keep silent, 14:30
    progressive, OT was, 16:24
Reverend, please don't call me, 4:15
Reward, degrees of, 3:8,14
Rhetoric, admired by Greeks, 1:17
Rhetorical criticism, 2:1
Righteousness in Christ, 1:31

Index

Rights,
- claimed by Paul, 9:4ff, 9:18
- Corinthian assertion of, 10:1
- voluntarily waived: see under, Christian liberty

Rock, spiritual, 10:3

Rod, figurative use of, 4:21

Roman Catholic doctrines
- confession, before communion, 11:28
- confirmation, 12:13
- elevating the host, 11:23
- hierarchy settles doubtful questions, 2:15
- purgatory, 3:12,13, 11:32
- inquisition, justification for, 5:5
- justification and sanctification, synonymous terms, 6:11
- infused righteousness, 6:11
- marriage, a moral matter, 7:1
- clerical and monastic celibacy, 7:1
- sexual intercourse, only to procreate, 7:3
- sexual abstinence, during times of prayer and fasting, 7:5
- separation of bed and board, but no divorce, 7:11
- counsels of perfection vs. precepts, 7:25
- works of supererogation, 9:17
- flagellation, 9:27
- sacraments considered miraculous, 10:16
- traditions on a par with Scripture, 11:2,34, 15:3
- transubstantiation, 10:16,24
- perpetual sacrifice of the mass, 11:24
- primacy of Peter, 15:5
- communion under one kind, 11:27
- overflow of merit, 12:26
- intercession of the saints, 13:8
- universality of the eucharist, 15:25

Rule and authority abolished, 15:24

Rulers of this age, 2:6,8

Run, not without aim, 9:26

Sacrament, 4:1

Sacrifices,
- Jewish, 10:18
- pagan, 8:1,4, 10:19
- to demons, 10:20

Sadducees, 15:1

Saints,
- at Corinth, 16:15
- poor, at Jerusalem, 16:1
- use of the word by Paul, 1:2, 16:1
- by calling, 1:2
- churches of the, 14:33
- will judge the world, 6:2
- shall judge angels, 6:3

Salvation,
- conditioned on faithfulness, 15:2
- unmerited, 1:29
- how know if you will save your husband? 7:16
- Paul wanted by all means to save some, 9:22

Sanctified, sanctification, 1:30, 6:11
- in Christ Jesus, 1:2
- unbelieving husband is, by the wife, 7:14

Satan,
- delivered to, 5:5
- tempts, because of lack of self-control, 7:5
- the destroyer (?), 10:10
- existence of, denied by modern men, 10:20

Save, Saved,
- though as through fire, 3:15
- man's spirit, by proper discipline, 5:5
- Christians may win their unbelieving mates, 7:16
- Paul became all things to all men, to save some, 9:22, 10:33
- the gospel, by which you are, 15:2

School of the evangelists, 16:20

Scribe, where is, 1:19

Scripture,
- New Testament books considered to be, 4:6
- according to the, 15:3,4

Scum of the world, 4:13

Second Adam: see, Adam

Second advent, 1:7, 4:5, 6:14, 11:26, 13:10, 15:23
- not expected at once, 1:7, 4:5, 7:30, 10:11, 15:51
- Second advent and Maran atha, 16:23

Second marriages: see under, Marriage

Secrets, of heart, disclosed, 14:25

Security, eternal: see under Calvin, Calvinism

Index

Seeker-sensitive services, 14:23
Self-control, 6:12, 7:5,9, 9:23ff
    lost, when worshiping idols, 12:2
Self-denial, meaning of, 10:6
Self-examination, 11:28
Self-sacrifice, 13:3
Selfish, 13:5
Send (one) on his way,
    Paul, 16:6
    Timothy, 16:11
Separation, in marriage, 7:10,11
Serpents, perished by the, 10:9
Servants, preachers as, 3:5, 4:1
Severe letter (?), *20*
Sex,
    not denied when married, 7:1-7
    only within the bounds of marriage, 6:16, 7:9
    abstinence from, for devotional purposes, a concession, 7:6
    as an act of pagan worship, 11:5
Sexual immorality: see, Fornication, Adultery, Prostitution
Shambles: see, Meat market
Shame, 1:27, 4:14, 6:5, 11:22, 15:34
Sharp's rule of grammar, 11:27, 15:24
Shaved head,
    disgraceful, on women, 11:5
    characteristic mark of a disreputable woman, 11:5
Shekinah, 2:8, 10:1
Shema, 8:4
Ships, ancient, *10*, 4:1
Short-cut to spirituality, no, 12:3
Short hair, dishonor, 10:5
Sickness, 11:30
Sign, signs,
    Jews ask for, 1:22
    tongues are for a, to unbelievers, 14:22
    prophecy is for a, to believers, 14:22
Silent, silence,
    if no interpreter, let him keep, in church, 14:28
    if a revelation is made to another, let him keep, 14:30
    let the women keep silent in, 14:34
    required of women, a cultural thing (?), 14:34
    command to, not absolute, 14:34
Silver, 3:12

Sin, sinning
    every, that a man does is without the body, 6:18
    against the body, 6:18
    against the brethren, 8:12
    against Christ, 8:12
    to cause another to, is a sin against Christ, 8:12
    Christ died for our, 15:3
    power of, is the Law, 15:56
    sting of, is death, 15:55,56
    stop, 15:34
    you are still in your, if Christ is not raised, 15:17
Sincerity,
    the unleavened bread of, 5:8
Sing,
    with the spirit and with the mind, 14:14
Singles, should marry? 7:8,9
Sinless perfection, 4:4
Sinners cleansed in Christ, 6:11
Slavery in the Roman world, 7:21
    condition of slaves, 7:21
Slaves,
    of Christ, 7:22
    to seek liberty? 7:21
    do not become, of men, 7:23
Sleep,
    euphemism for physical death, 11:30, 15:6,20
    figurative use of, 15:20
    result of failure to examine oneself, 11:30
    we shall not all, 15:51
Social status of early Christians, 1:26,27,28
Soldier, no, serves at his own expense, 9:7
Sorrowful visit: see, Paul, intermediate trip to Corinth
Sosthenes, 1:1
    ruler of the synagogue, *4*
    amanuensis to Paul, *2*, 1:1, 16:21
Soul, 2:14
    living, 15:45
    see also under, Trichotomy
Source criticism, 2:1,7,13, 11:23, 15:3,46
Speaking in tongues, 1:5, 12:10, 13:1, 14:1
    a symbol of defeat, 14:21
    abuse of at Corinth, a major problem, 14:2
    brought scorn, 14:23
    to cease, 13:8

Index

Speaking in tongues, *continued*
    did not edify the church, 14:4
    Do All Speak in Tongues? See Special Study #10
    do not forbid, 14:40
    examples of, in heathen religion, 12:3
    foreign languages, tongues at Corinth were, 1:5, 12:10, 14:2,9,10,11,21
    genuine gift of, ch. 14
    have revealed nothing, 14:26
    I wish you all, 14:5
    interpretation of: see under, Interpretation
    kid stuff, 14:20
    rules regarding use of this gift, 14:27ff
    no sign of God's blessing, 14:22
    no one understands, 14:2
    not every Christian spoke, 12:30, 14:5
    of no value, 14:19
    one speaking in, edifies himself, 14:4
    various kinds of, 12:10
    over-estimated by Corinthians, 14:5
    Paul's use of tongues, 14:18
    private, devotional use of (?), 13:1, 14:2,4,5,14,18
    sign to unbelievers, 14:19,22
    to the air, 14:9
    at Pentecost, were foreign languages, 12:10
    tongues of angels, 13:1
    uninterpreted, forbidden, 14:8,27,28
    without love, worthless, 13:1
    see also, Special Study #10
Speech (ability to speak in tongues), 1:5
    cleverness of, 1:17
Special Studies (at close of notes on Chap. [])
    The Message of the Cross, Chap.1
    Church Discipline at Corinth and Elsewhere, Chap.5
    Here I Stand, So Help Me God! (Ethics), Chap.6
    Who are the "Virgins"? Chap.7
    "Whom Do You Say I Am," The Deity of Jesus, Chap.8
    Worship in the New Testament, Chap.12
    He is Alive! You Had Better Believe It!, Chap.15
    Baptized for the Dead, Chap.15
    Is Man Immortal?, Chap.15
    Do All Speak in Tongues?, Chap.16
    Joy of the Holy Spirit, Chap.16
Spirit, life-giving, 15:45

Spirit, man's, 2:14,15
    may be saved, 5:5
    my, prays, 14:14
    of prophets, subject to prophets, 14:32
    refreshed, 16:18
Spirits,
    deceitful, 12:10
    discerning of, 12:10
    heathen prophets, out of control when under influence of, 12:10
Spiritual body, 15:44
Spiritual food and drink, 10:3,4
Spiritual gifts,
    abuses in the exercise of, 12:1ff
    bestowed after baptism, 12:13
    charisma, 1:7, 7:7, 12:4
    called "grace" (?), 1:4
    confirmed the gospel message, 1:6
    desire earnestly, 12:31, 14:1
    distributed as the Spirit wills, 12:11
    each gifted person usually received one, 14:5
    given for the good of all, 12:7
    genuine gifts at Corinth, not counterfeit, 12:1
    not lacking at Corinth, 1:7
    not given to every Christian, 12:7,11, 14:16
    listed, 12:8ff
    love, the motive to control our use of, 13:1ff
    diversity of, need for, 12:4
    how imparted, 1:4, 12:7,28, 14:1
    had a purpose, 1:6, 12:1,9
    to cease, 1:7, 12:7, 13:8,10,13
    prophesied in the Old Testament, 12:1
    tests by which the Spirit's leading may be discerned, 12:1ff
    "these signs shall accompany those who believe," 12:1
    traditional Pentecostal categories, 12:8
    unity of purpose needed, in their exercise, 12:12ff
Spiritual marriages: see Special Study #4
Spiritual men: see under, Man, spiritual

Index

Spiritual resurrection (?), 15:42
Spirituality, tongues and, 12:3
Spirituality, true test of, 12:3
Stand,
    firm in the faith, 16:13
    let him who thinks he, take heed, 10:12
    the gospel, in which you also, 15:1
Stars, differ in glory, 15:41
Steadfast, be, 15:58
Stephanas, *3*, 1:11,16, 16:15
    first-fruits of Achaia, *3*, 1:16, 16:15
    household of, 16:15
    household of, baptized by Paul, 1:16
    Paul rejoices at the coming of, 16:17
Stewards, 4:1
Stewardship, not tithing, 9:14
Storehouse tithing, 16:2
Straw, 3:12
Strife, 3:3
Strong and weak brothers, 8:7ff
    Paul became weak, to win the weak, 9:22
Stumbling, do not cause, 8:9,12, 10:32
Stumbling-block, the cross a, 1:23
Subjection, be in, to such men, 16:16
Submission, wives to husbands, 14:34
Subscription, *2*, 16:5,24
Summary exhortation, 16:14
Sunday worship taught, 16:2
Superscription, 1:1
Supersessionism, 10:18
Support: see, Financial support
Swindlers, 5:10,11, 6:10
Synecdoche, 2:2

Table,
    of the Lord, 10:21
    of demons, 10:21
Teachers,
    God appointed, in the church, 12:28
    right attitude re: 4:1
    standards by which to judge, 4:1ff
    temporary office in early church (?), 12:28
Temple,
    different words for, 3:15
    of Aesclepius, *14*, 8:1
    of Aphrodite, *13*, 6:19
    of Apollo, *11*

Temple, *continued*
    of God, church is, *16*, 3:16
    of idols, 8:1ff
    Christian's body is, of Holy Spirit, 6:19
Temptation,
    all have same, 10:13
    God limits, 10:13
    the way of escape, 10:13
    no, overtakes you, 10:13
Tent-making form of ministry, 9:12
Testimonies (florilegium), 1:19
Testimony,
    concerning Christ confirmed, 1:6
    of God, Paul's proclamation of, 2:1
Thanks, thanksgiving, *1*, 14:16
    for God's work at Corinth, 1:4-9
    Jesus gave, 11:24
    for food, 10:30
    to God, who gives the victory, 15:57
The one body, 12:11
Thieves, 6:10
Things, present, 3:22
    to come, 3:22
    offered to idols: see, Meats, sacrificed to idols
    should not crave evil, 10:6
    the, I write, are the Lord's commandment, 14:37
Thinking, 14:20
Third day, on the, 15:4
Threshing, 9:9
Time, is shortened, 7:29
Timothy,
    a "young man," 4:17, 16:10
    Paul's child in the faith, 4:17
    sent by Paul, to Corinth, *2*, 4:17
    journey with Erastus, *5*, 4:17, 16:10
    not to be despised, 16:11
    Corinthians not to cause him fear, 16:10
    to be sent on his way in peace, 16:11
Tithing, 9:14
Titus, *5*, 4:19, 16:1,4,5,10
Titus Justus, *4*, 1:14
Tongue speaking: see, Speaking in tongues
Traditions, 11:11
    two kinds of, 11:2
    delivered by Paul, 11:2,23, 15:3
    oral, 11:2
Tribunals,
    Christian, 6:1
    Heathen, *18*, 6:1

Index

Trichotomy, 2:14, 5:5, 15:44
Trinity, 8:6, 12:4,6
Trumpet,
    the last, 15:52
    seven, 15:52
Truth,
    the unleavened bread of, 5:8
    rejoices with the, 13:6
Trying the Lord, 10:9
Tutor, 4:15
Twelve, Jesus appeared to, 15:5
Types and shadows, 5:8, 10:2, 15:25
    paschal lamb, a type of Christ, 5:7
    Israel, an "example," 10:6

Unbeliever, 6:6, 7:12,13
    invites you to a feast, 10:27
    visiting public worship, 10:23
    convicted, called to account, by prophecy, 14:24
Unbelieving wife,
    the Christian does not leave his, 7:12
    sanctified by the believing husband, 7:14
Uncircumcision, 7:18
Understand, understanding,
    church is to receive, 14:6ff
    illustrations of the importance of, 14:6ff
    I want you to, 11:3
Unfruitful, my mind is, 14:14
Ungifted,
    one fills the place of, 14:16
    doesn't know what you are saying, 14:16
    is not edified, 14:17
    convicted, called to account, by prophecy, 14:24
Union with Christ, 1:2,30, 15:21
Unisex styles, 11:15
Unity,
    duty of, 1:10
    of the church, stirring appeal for, 4:6ff
Universalism, 15:22
Unmarried, 7:8
    inspired advice respecting the, 7:25ff
    concerned about the things of the Lord, 7:32
    holy in body and spirit, 7:34

Unrighteous, not inherit the kingdom, 6:9
Unrighteousness, not rejoiced in, 13:6
Unworthy manner: see under, Lord's Supper

Vain,
    faith is, if Christ was not raised, 15:14,17
    preaching is, if Christ is not raised, 15:14
    unless you believed in, 15:2
    your work in the Lord is not in, 15:58
    two different words for, 15:16
"Veil" a mistranslation (?), 11:15
Veiling of women,
    a shawl rather than face covering, 11:5
    a binding rule for all time? 11:6
Verses, bad division of (?), 12:31, 14:33
Vicarious baptism: see Special Study #7
Vicarious suffering: see Special Study #7
Vices and virtues, 3:3, 5:10,11, 6:9,10
Victory, 15:54ff
Vineyard, one who plants, entitled to eat fruit, 9:7
Virgin birth taught: See, Christ, virgin birth
Virgins,
    who are the, 7:25. *see also*, Special Study #4
    men and women, 7:25ff
    the marriage of, 7:36ff
    full age, 7:36
Visitors at the public assemblies, 14:23,24
Voting on church membership, 5:12

Walk, metaphor for life style, 7:17
Washed, you were, 6:11
Watered, Apollos, 3:6
Weak brothers: see Strong and weak brothers
Weakness,
    Paul's condition while at Corinth, 2:3
    of God, 1:25
    result of failure to examine oneself, 11:30
Wheat, 15:37
Wickedness, 5:8
Widows,
    advice to, 7:8
    as to remarriage, 7:39

Index

Wife,
- bound to, 7:27
- each man has his own, 7:2
- to fulfill her duty to her husband, 7:3
- released from, 7:27
- who is an unbeliever, 7:12

Wild beasts: see, Paul, fought with wild beasts
Wilderness wanderings, Israel's, 10:1
Will of the Lord, 4:19, 16:7
Winter, Paul expected to, at Corinth, 16:6

Wise,
- man, where is, 1:19
- not many called, 1:26
- God knows the reasonings of the, are vain, 3:20
- in this age, 3:18
- reasonings of, useless, 3:20

Wisdom,
- Christ became to us, from God, 1:30
- of the world, made foolish by God, 1:20
- of this age, 2:6, 3:18
- Greeks search for, 1:22
- of God, above men, 2:6,7
- false wisdom, 1:22
- word of, 12:8
- worldly, infected church at Corinth, 16

Woe is me if I preach not, 9:16
Women and tongue speaking, 14:34
- and prophesying, 11:1ff

Women,
- Christianity raised status of, 7:2, 14:34
- is the glory of man, 11:7
- help meet for man, 11:8
- not to speak in church, 14:34

Women, *continued*
- ought to have a symbol of authority on her head, 11:10
- not independent of the man, 11:11
- silence enjoined in church, 11:5, 14:34,35
- submissive to their husbands, 14:34
- if they desire to learn, ask their husbands, 14:35
- the veiling of, ch. 11
- as preachers (?), 11:5

Word formation, Greek
- words ending in -*ma* and -*sis*, 5:6
- words ending in -*kos*, 11:22
- words ending in -*inos* and -*ikos*, 3:1
- verbs ending in -*izo*, 7:38

Word,
- of the cross, power of God, 1:18
- by which you are saved, if you hold fast the, 15:2
- of wisdom: see, Wisdom, word of

Work,
- different words for, 3:8
- of the Lord, 15:58, 16:10

World,
- belongs to the Christian, 3:22
- not using the, to the full, 7:31
- form of this, is passing away, 7:31

Worship: see, Public worship
Wreath, perishable and imperishable, 9:25

Zarmanochegas, epitaph of, 13:3
Zeitgeist, 2:6,12

OTHER BOOKS BY GARETH L. REESE

New Testament History: *Acts* (097-176-5235)

New Testament Epistles: *Romans* (097-176-5200)

New Testament Epistles: *2 Corinthians and Galatians* (097-176-5278)

New Testament Epistles: *Paul's Prison Epistles* (099-845-1800)

New Testament Epistles: *1 & 2 Thessalonians* (099-845-186X)

New Testament Epistles: *1 & 2 Timothy and Titus* (097-176-5227)

New Testament Epistles: *Hebrews* (097-176-5219)

New Testament Epistles: *1 & 2 Peter and Jude* (097-176-5243)

New Testament Epistles: *James & 1,2,3 John* (097-176-526X)

Order from:
Scripture Exposition Books
803 McKinsey Place
Moberly, MO, 65270
www.glreese@cccb.edu

www.ingramcontent.com/pod-product-compliance
Lightning Source LLC
Chambersburg PA
CBHW081414160426
42811CB00097B/963